# Making Connections Using the Framework for Managerial Accounting

Managerial accounting concepts form the basis of how information should be created and reported to internal users for completing the tasks of planning, directing/motivating, and feedback/control. These managerial accounting concepts work together to form the framework for decision making. As the diagram shows, the decisions managers make are central to achieving the strategic and operational needs of the company.



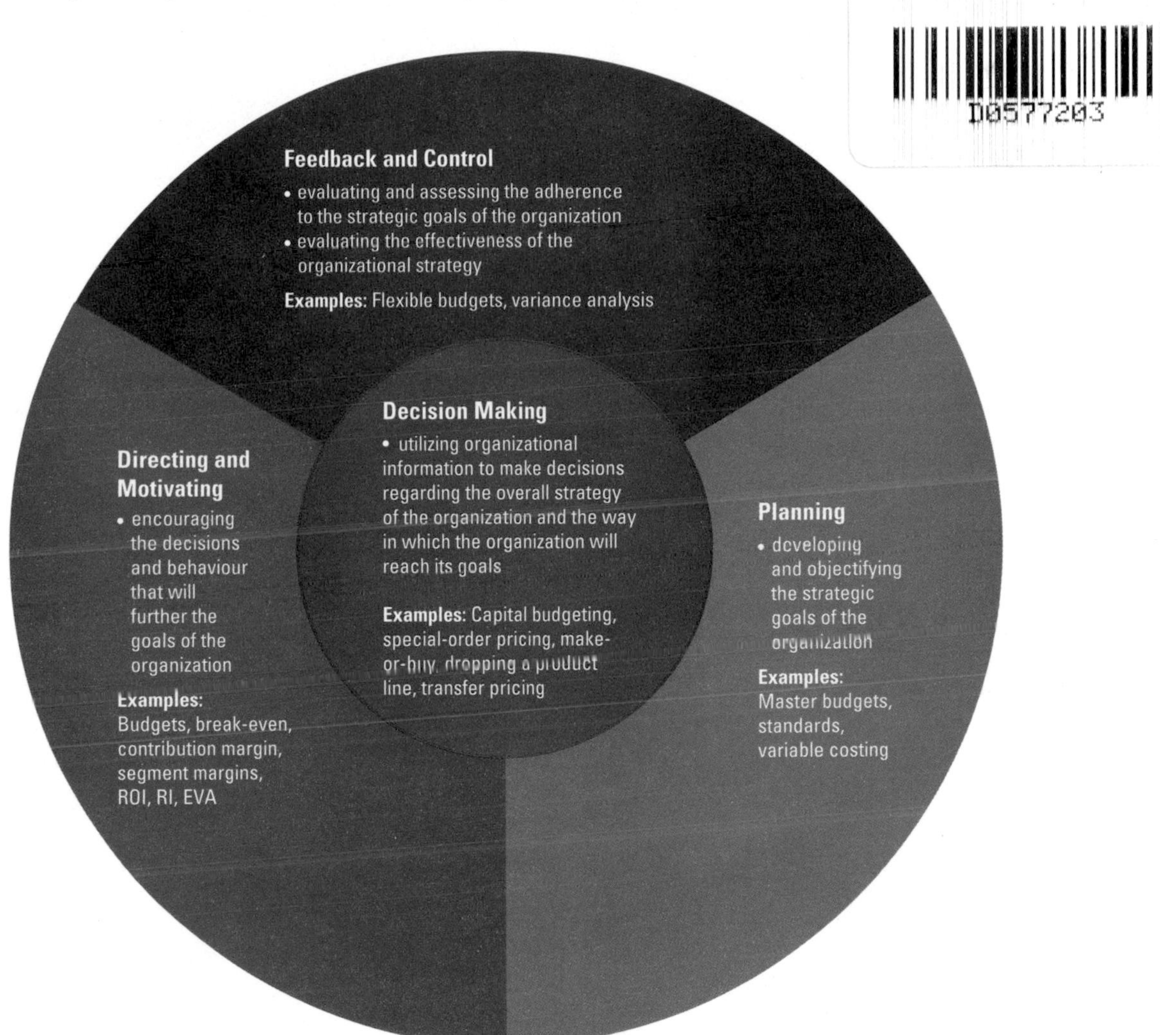


# Acronyms Used in *Managerial Accounting*

| | | | |
|---|---|---|---|
| DM | Direct Materials | VC | Variable Costs |
| DL | Direct Labour | FC | Fixed Costs |
| MOH | Manufacturing Overhead | ROI | Return on Investment |
| COGS | Cost of Goods Sold | RI | Residual Income |
| COGM | Cost of Goods Manufactured | EVA | Economic Value Added |
| OI | Operating Income | CM | Contribution Margin |
| BE | Break-Even | CMA | Certified Management Accountant |
| CGA | Certified General Accountant | CA | Chartered Accountant |
| CPA | Chartered Public Accountant | BI | Beginning Inventory |
| WIP | Work In Process or Work in Progress | FG | Finished Goods Inventory |
| TP | Transfer Price | SM | Segment Margin |

# Brief Contents

# Contents

# Visual Walk-Through

**NEW!** Integration of CPA Competencies. We have increased the focus on covering the competencies outlined in the CPA Competency Map and Knowledge Supplement in the third edition. Each chapter now opens with a list of Professional Competencies, related Knowledge Items, and levels covered in that chapter; also a master list of all Competencies and Knowledge Items is available on the front inside cover. These features will allow students and faculty interested in CPA designation to become familiar with the Competency Map and the material covered in the book.

**Learning objectives** are the important concepts in each chapter. Expressed in everyday language, these LOs are mapped throughout the chapter, end-of-chapter assessment, and MyAccountingLab; this allows students to accurately track their understanding of each learning objective.

A **chapter-opening vignette** shows why the topics in the chapter are important to companies and businesspeople.

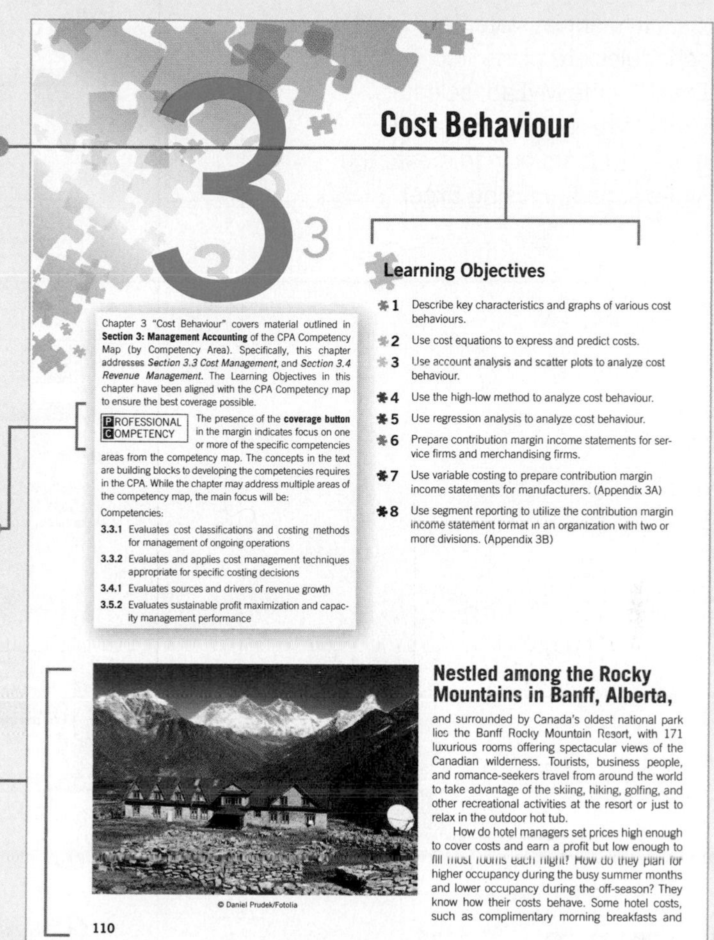

3

## Cost Behaviour

Chapter 3 "Cost Behaviour" covers material outlined in **Section 3: Management Accounting** of the CPA Competency Map (by Competency Area). Specifically, this chapter addresses *Section 3.3 Cost Management*, and *Section 3.4 Revenue Management*. The Learning Objectives in this chapter have been aligned with the CPA Competency map to ensure the best coverage possible.

PROFESSIONAL COMPETENCY The presence of the **coverage button** in the margin indicates focus on one or more of the specific competencies areas from the competency map. The concepts in the text are building blocks to developing the competencies requires in the CPA. While the chapter may address multiple areas of the competency map, the main focus will be:

Competencies:

**3.3.1** Evaluates cost classifications and costing methods for management of ongoing operations

**3.3.2** Evaluates and applies cost management techniques appropriate for specific costing decisions

**3.4.1** Evaluates sources and drivers of revenue growth

**3.5.2** Evaluates sustainable profit maximization and capacity management performance

### Learning Objectives

1 Describe key characteristics and graphs of various cost behaviours.

2 Use cost equations to express and predict costs.

3 Use account analysis and scatter plots to analyze cost behaviour.

4 Use the high-low method to analyze cost behaviour.

5 Use regression analysis to analyze cost behaviour.

6 Prepare contribution margin income statements for service firms and merchandising firms.

7 Use variable costing to prepare contribution margin income statements for manufacturers. (Appendix 3A)

8 Use segment reporting to utilize the contribution margin income statement format in an organization with two or more divisions. (Appendix 3B)

© Daniel Prudek/Fotolia

**Nestled among the Rocky Mountains in Banff, Alberta,** and surrounded by Canada's oldest national park lies the Banff Rocky Mountain Resort, with 171 luxurious rooms offering spectacular views of the Canadian wilderness. Tourists, business people, and romance-seekers travel from around the world to take advantage of the skiing, hiking, golfing, and other recreational activities at the resort or just to relax in the outdoor hot tub.

How do hotel managers set prices high enough to cover costs and earn a profit but low enough to fill most rooms each night? How do they plan for higher occupancy during the busy summer months and lower occupancy during the off-season? They know how their costs behave. Some hotel costs, such as complimentary morning breakfasts and

110

**Try It!**

**NEW!** Found throughout the chapter, Try It! interactive questions give students the opportunity to apply the concept they just learned. Video Solutions, found in the MyAccountingLab, feature the author walking through select Try It! problems on a white board. Designed to give students detailed help when they need it.

Cost Behaviour 121

**TRY IT!**

Assume the local fitness club charges a membership fee of $30 per month for unlimited use of the exercise equipment, plus an additional fee of $5 for every instructor-led exercise class you attend.

1. Express the monthly cost of belonging to the fitness club as a cost equation.
2. What is your expected cost for a month in which you attend five instructor-led classes?
3. If your attendance doubles to 10 classes per month, will your total cost for the month double? Explain.

Please see page 181 for solutions.

Step costs resemble stair steps: they are fixed over a small range of activity and then jump up to a new fixed level with moderate changes in volume. Hotels, restaurants, hospitals, and educational institutions typically experience step costs. For example, regulated day-care centres are required to limit the caregiver-to-child ratio depending on the age of the child. New Brunswick sets a ratio of 1:8 for children between the ages of three and four years. As shown in Exhibit 3-10, a day-care centre that takes on a ninth child must incur the cost of employing another caregiver. The new caregiver can watch the ninth through sixteenth children enrolled at the day-care centre. If the day-care centre takes on a seventeenth child, management will once again need to hire another caregiver, costing another $28,000 in salary. The same step cost patterns occur with hotels (maid-to-room ratio), restaurants (server-to-table ratio), hospitals (nurse-to-bed ratio), and schools (teacher-to-student ratio).

**EXHIBIT 3-10** Step Costs

aregivers' salaries (y)
$112,000
$84,000
$56,000

## Excel Exhibits

**NEW!** To give students a glimpse into the real world presentation of managerial accounting topics, all financial statements and schedules are presented in Excel. In the MyLab, selected exhibits have a video that will teach students how to create the same schedule using Excel.

2. Take a contribution margin approach to determining whether the special order is profitable:

| | A | B | C |
|---|---|---|---|
| 1 | Incremental Analysis for Special Order Decision | Per Unit | Total Order (40,000 units) |
| 2 | Revenue from special order | $ 19.00 | $ 760,000 |
| 3 | Less: Variable expenses associated with the order (DM, DL, Variable MOH) | 15.00 | 600,000 |
| 4 | Contribution margin | $ 4.00 | $ 160,000 |
| 5 | Less: Additional fixed expenses associated with the order | | 5,000 |
| 6 | Increase in operating income from the special order | | $ 155,000 |
| 7 | | | |

**page 472:**

1. Analyze the revenues and costs that would be lost if the salad bar operation is discontinued:

| | A | B | C |
|---|---|---|---|
| 1 | Incremental Analysis for Discontinuation Decision | Total | |
| 2 | Sales revenue from salad bars | $ 750,000 | |
| 3 | Less: Variable expenses related to salad bars | 600,000 | |
| 4 | Contribution margin lost if salad bars are discontinued | $ 150,000 | |
| 5 | Less: Fixed cost savings if salad bars are discontinued | 20,000 | |
| 6 | Operating income lost if salad bars are discontinued | $ 130,000 | |
| 7 | | | |
| 8 | | | |
| 9 | If Salad Bars Are Replaced with Olive Bars | Total | |
| 10 | Contribution margin provided by olive bar | $ 200,000 | |
| 11 | Less: Operating income lost if salad bars are discontinued | 130,000 | |
| 12 | Increase in operating income from replacing salad bars with olive bars | $ 70,000 | |
| 13 | | | |

**page 479:**

1. As shown below, the total cost of outsourcing the ski poles and leaving the freed capacity idle is $325,000 greater than the cost to produce the poles in-house. Rossignol should not outsource production because its operating income would decline by $325,000.
2. However, Rossignol's income would increase by $175,000 if it outsources production and uses the freed capacity to make ski boots.

| | A | B | C | D |
|---|---|---|---|---|
| 1 | Incremental Analysis Outsourcing Decision | Make Ski Poles | Outsource Ski Poles | Difference |
| 2 | Variable Costs: | | | |
| 3 | If make: $13.50 × 100,000 units<br>If outsource: $18.00 × 100,000 units | $ 1,350,000 | $ 1,800,000 | $ 450,000 |
| 4 | Plus: Fixed costs | 650,000 | 525,000 | (125,000) |
| 5 | Total cost of producing 100,000 units | $ 2,000,000 | $ 2,325,000 | $ 325,000 |
| 6 | Less: Income from ski boots if outsource | 0 | 500,000 | 500,000 |
| 7 | Net cost | $ 2,000,000 | $ 1,825,000 | $ (175,000) |
| 8 | | | | |

## Sustainability

Sustainability boxes are integrated into the body of each chapter, providing students with insight on how sustainability applies to accounting concepts. Related questions are included in the end-of-chapter assessment.

462 CHAPTER 8

### Sustainability and Short-Term Business Decisions

See Exercises E8-18A and E8-33B

For companies that embrace sustainability and the triple bottom line, almost every decision will be viewed through the lens of its impact on people and the planet, as well as profitability. For example, let's look at Timberland, a company with $1.4 billion in annual revenue that specializes in outdoor shoes and clothing. Timberland is intentionally "focusing the resources, energy, and profits of a publicly traded…company to combat social ills, help the environment, and improve conditions of laborers around the globe."[1]

In the words of Jeffrey Swartz, President and CEO, "Timberland believes, and has always believed, that we have a responsibility to help effect change in the communities where we work and live." The company is committed to "doing well and doing good." But how does the company work toward such lofty goals? Here are a few examples of the company's many initiatives:[2]

- Employees are given up to 40 hours of paid leave each year to perform community service work.
- The company's strict Code of Conduct ensures that domestic and overseas workers are employed at fair wage rates, work reasonable shifts, and work in safe factories.
- The company is committed to being environmentally conscious in the production of its products. The company labels its footwear with a Green Index rating system. The index educates consumers about the product's climate impact, chemicals used, and materials (percentage of organic, recycled, or renewable materials) used.
- The company uses solar panels on its California distribution centre to provide 60% of its energy. This $3.5 million investment was made, even though cost models showed it might take 20 years for the investment to earn a return.
- By the end of 2013, Timberland met its 2015 goal to reduce GHG emissions by 50% by 2015, based on 2006 baseline.

In 2013 alone, the brand reported a 22% reduction in GHG emissions as compared to 2012. A second goal related to climate change, to source 30% of energy from clean, renewable sources by 2015, based on 2006 baseline, is also on track. By the end of 2013, Timberland derived 26% of its energy from renewable sources, exceeding its 2013 target of 23%, and just one percent shy of its 27% goal for 2014. In 2013 alone, the brand increased its use of renewable energy by 28% versus 2012.

[1] Reingold, Jennifer, "Walking the Walk," *Fast Company*, November, 2005. http://www.fastcompany.com/magazine/100/timberland.html?page=0%2C0
[2] www.timberland.com

### How Do Managers Make Special Business Decisions?

A *Segment* is an independent or semi-independent unit within an organization. A segment could

In this part of the chapter we'll consider five more special business decisions:

- Accept a special order

**STOP & THINK**

What would Kay's operating income be if she sold 501 posters? What would it be if she sold 600 posters?

**Answer:** Every poster sold provides $14 of contribution margin, which contributes first toward covering fixed costs, then to profit. Once Kay reaches her break-even point (500 posters), she has covered all fixed costs. Therefore, each additional poster sold after the break-even point contributes $14 *directly to profit*. If Kay sells 501 posters, she has sold one more poster than break-even. Her operating income is $14. If she sells 600 posters, she has sold 100 more posters than break-even. Her operating income is $1,400 ($14 per poster × 100 posters). We can verify this as follows:

| | |
|---|---|
| Contribution margin (600 posters × $14 per poster) | $ 8,400 |
| Less: Fixed expenses | (7,000) |
| Operating income | $ 1,400 |

*Once a company achieves break-even, each additional unit sold contributes its unique unit contribution margin directly to profit.*

Stop & Think, a question-and-answer section, encourages students to think critically about the application of key concepts.

## The Shortcut Approach Using the Contribution Margin Ratio

It is easy to compute the break-even point in *units* for a simple business like Kay's that has only one product. It is more difficult for companies that have more than one product or service such as Bombardier and Black Fly Beverage Company. Multiproduct companies usually compute break-even in terms of sales dollars (revenue).

To calculate break-even in terms of dollars, fixed expenses plus operating income are divided by the contribution margin *ratio* (not by contribution margin *per unit*) to yield sales in *dollars* (not *units*):

$$\text{Sales in dollars} = \frac{\text{Fixed expenses} + \text{Operating income}}{\text{Contribution margin ratio}}$$

Recall that Kay's contribution margin ratio is 40%. At the break-even point, operating income is $0, so Kay's break-even point in sales revenue is as follows:

$$\text{Sales in dollars} = \frac{\$7,000 + \$0}{0.40} = \$17,500$$

This is the same break-even sales revenue calculated earlier (500 posters × $35 sales price = $17,500). Each dollar of Kay's sales contributes $0.40 to fixed expenses and profit. To break even, she must generate enough contribution margin at the rate of $0.40 per sales dollar to cover the $7,000 fixed expenses ($7,000 ÷ 0.40 = $17,500).



2 Use cost equations to express and predict costs.

Managers do not need to rely on graphs to predict total variable costs at different volumes of activity. They can use a <u>cost equation</u>, a mathematical equation for a straight line, to express how a cost behaves. On cost graphs like those pictured in Exhibit 3-1, the vertical (y-axis) always shows total costs, while the horizontal axis (x-axis) shows volume of activity. Therefore, any variable cost line can be mathematically expressed as follows:

PROFESSIONAL COMPETENCY

Total variable cost ($y$) = Variable cost per unit of activity ($v$) × Volume of activity ($x$)

Or simply:

$$y = vx$$

The hotel's total toiletry cost is as follows:

$$y = \$3x$$

wherein

$y$ = total toiletry cost
$3 = variable cost per guest
$x$ = number of guests

**Why is this important?**
Cost **equations** help managers foresee what their **total costs** will be at **different** operating **volumes** so that they can **better** plan for the future.

Why Is This Important? highlights the connection of accounting to the business environment so students can better understand the business significance of managerial accounting.

We can confirm the observations made in Exhibit 3-1(A) using the cost equation. If the hotel has no guests ($x = 0$), total toiletry costs are zero, as shown in the graph. If the hotel has 2,000 guests, total toiletry costs will be

$$y = \$3 \text{ per guest} \times 2,000 \text{ guests} = \$6,000$$

If the hotel has 4,000 guests, managers will expect total toiletry costs to be

$$y = \$3 \text{ per guest} \times 4,000 \text{ guests} = \$12,000$$

**STOP & THINK**

If the hotel serves 3,467 guests next week, how much will it spend on complimentary toiletries?

**Answer:** You would have a hard time answering this question by simply looking at the graph in Exhibit 3-1(A), but cost equations can be used for any volume. We "plug in" the expected volume to our variable cost equation as follows:

$$y = \$3 \text{ per guest} \times 3,467 \text{ guests} = \$10,401$$

Management expects complimentary toiletries next week to cost about $10,401.

Introduction to Managerial Accounting 29

**Requirement 2**

Because the company has warranty returns and is involved in product liability litigation, it is very possible that the company suffers from a reputation for poor-quality products. If so, it is losing profits because it is losing sales. Unsatisfied customers will probably avoid buying from the company in the future. Worse yet, customers may tell their friends and family not to buy from the company. This report does not include an estimate of the lost profits arising from the company's reputation for poor-quality products.

**Requirement 3**

The Cost of Quality Report shows that very little is being spent on prevention and maintenance, which is probably why the internal and external failure costs are so high. The CEO should use this information to develop quality initiatives in the areas of prevention and appraisal. Such initiatives should reduce future internal and external failure costs.

**Decision Guidelines** summarize key terms, concepts, and formulas in the context of specific business decisions so that students can see how accounting is used to make good business decisions.

## DECISION GUIDELINES

### The Changing Regulatory and Business Environment

Successful companies respond to changes in the regulatory and business environment. Here are some of the decisions managers need to consider.

| Decision | Guidelines |
|---|---|
| I'm a Canadian corporation. Do I need to worry about SOX? | Publicly traded Canadian companies that are listed on the U.S. stock market must comply with SOX. However, Canadian regulations, similar in nature to SOX, have been implemented for the domestic market. These regulations have been designed and recommended by the Canadian Securities Administrators and implemented by the securities organizations for each province and territory. |
| I'm a Canadian company, but I have operations in other countries as well. How will IFRS help me? | Companies that operate in more than one country will no longer be required to prepare multiple financial statements using different standards for each country. Rather, they will prepare one set of financial statements in accordance with International Financial Reporting Standards (IFRS). |
| In the past, I have been able to find information about companies on the internet, but it took a long time to organize it. Can XBRL reduce the time it would take to do so? | XBRL will allow managers to more easily obtain and analyze publicly available financial data from their competitors, from companies they may wish to purchase, or from companies in which they may want to invest. |
| I would like to take my Canadian company into the global market. What might help me compete? | The use of advanced information systems, e-commerce, supply-chain management, lean production, and TQM will help a company to compete more effectively. Also, consider becoming ISO 9001:2008 certified. |
| How do I know if new initiatives such as international expansion, ERP, lean production, and TQM will be worth it in the long run? | By using cost-benefit analysis—comparing the estimated benefits of the initiative with the estimated costs—you will see whether or not the benefits of the project exceed its costs. You can then determine the best alternative for your situation. |

**Summary Problems** allow students to practise the skills outlined in the decision guidelines.

## SUMMARY PROBLEM 3

EZ-Rider Motorcycles is thinking about expanding into Germany. If gas prices increase, the company expects more interest in fuel-efficient transportation, such as motorcycles. As a result, the company is considering setting up a motorcycle assembly plant on the outskirts of Berlin.

EZ-Rider Motorcycles estimates it will cost $850,000 to convert an existing building to motorcycle production. Workers will need training, at a total cost of $65,000. The additional costs to organize the business and to establish relationships are estimated to be $150,000.

## END OF CHAPTER

### LEARNING OBJECTIVES

1 Describe key characteristics and graphs of various cost behaviours.

2 Use cost equations to express and predict costs.

3 Use account analysis and scatter plots to analyze cost behaviour.

4 Use the high-low method to analyze cost behaviour.

5 Use regression analysis to analyze cost behaviour.

6 Prepare contribution margin income statements for service firms and merchandising firms.

7 Use variable costing to prepare contribution margin income statements for manufacturers. (Appendix 3A)

8 Use segment reporting to utilize the contribution margin income statement format in an organization with two or more divisions. (Appendix 3B)

CHAPTER 3

### ACCOUNTING VOCABULARY

**Accounting Vocabulary** lists all the bolded terms in the chapter, with definitions and page references. There is also a complete glossary at the end of the book.

**Absorption Costing (p. 138)** The costing method in which products "absorb" both fixed and variable manufacturing costs.

**Account Analysis (p. 125)** A method for determining cost behaviour that is based on a manager's judgment in classifying each general ledger account as a variable, fixed, or mixed cost.

**Committed Fixed Costs (p. 115)** Fixed costs that are locked in because of previous management decisions; management has little or no control over these costs in the short run.

**Consolidated Financial Statement (p. 146)** A financial statement that incorporates all of the divisions of a company in one report.

**Contribution Margin (p. 134)** Sales revenues minus variable expenses.

**Contribution Margin Income Statement (p. 133)** Income statement that organizes costs by behaviour (variable costs or fixed costs) rather than by function.

**Cost Behaviour (p. 111)** Describes how costs change as volume changes.

**Cost Equation (p. 113)** A mathematical equation for a straight line that expresses how a cost behaves.

**Curvilinear Costs (p. 121)** A cost behaviour that is not linear (not a straight line).

**Discretionary Fixed Costs (p. 115)** Fixed costs that are a result of annual management decisions; fixed costs that are controllable in the short run.

**Fixed Costs (p. 111)** Costs that do not change in total despite wide changes in volume.

**High-Low Method (p. 127)** A method for determining cost behaviour that is based on two historical data points: the highest and lowest volume of activity.

**Mixed Costs (p. 111)** Costs that change but not in direct proportion to changes in volume. Mixed costs have both variable cost and fixed cost components.

**Outliers (p. 127)** Abnormal data points; data points that do not fall in the same general pattern as the other data points.

**Regression Analysis (p. 127)** A statistical procedure for determining the line that best fits the data by using all of the historical data points, not just the high and low data points.

**Relevant Range (p. 114)** The range of operations within which the total fixed costs and the variable cost per unit remain constant.

**Segment Margin (p. 147)** The excess of sales over variable costs and traceable fixed costs for a segment of the organization.

**Segmented Statement (p. 146)** A financial statement that shows the detail of different divisions in separate columns, utilizing the contribution margin income statement format.

**Step Costs (p. 121)** A cost behaviour that is fixed over a small range of activity and then jumps to a different fixed level with moderate changes in volume.

**Variable Costs (p. 111)** Costs that change in total in direct proportion to changes in volume.

**Variable Costing (p. 138)** The costing method that assigns only variable manufacturing costs to products.

**Quick Check** section is a series of questions designed to test student recall of key concepts. Answers are provided in the text.

Most of the questions in the book appear on MyAccountingLab, along with additional interactive resources such as videos, animations, and resources to help students master managerial accounting concepts. This provides students with the ability to re-test assigned questions or attempt alternative versions of the same or similar questions to reinforce learning.

> **MyAccountingLab**
> Exercises marked with # can be found on MyAccountingLab.

We have included **Group A** and **Group B Exercises** in the textbook so that instructors can work through the exercises in one of these groups in class and assign the other group as individual work, giving students more practice on these key concepts.

**Case Assignments** appear in Chapters 3 through 12. They are designed to test the students' understanding of the concepts in realistic, complex scenarios.

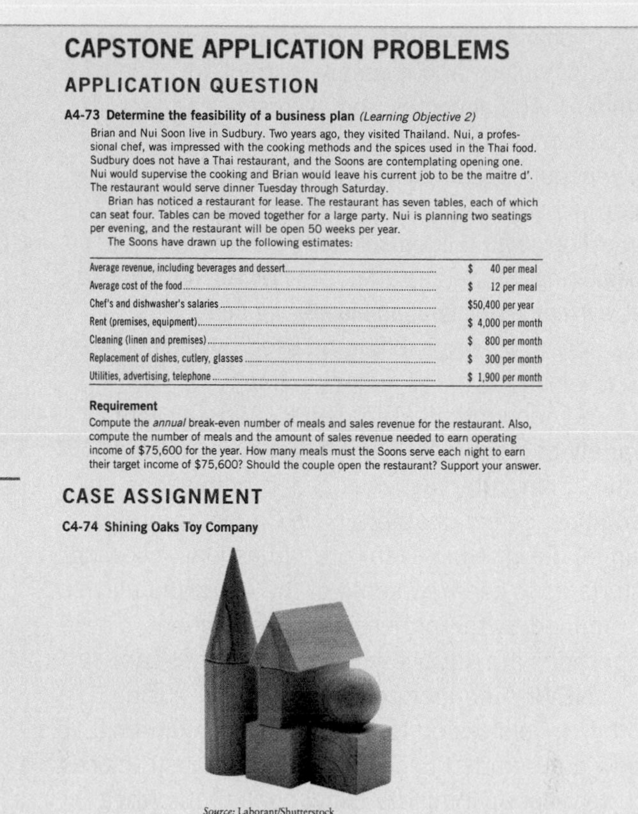

## CAPSTONE APPLICATION PROBLEMS

### APPLICATION QUESTION

**A4-73 Determine the feasibility of a business plan** *(Learning Objective 2)*

Brian and Nui Soon live in Sudbury. Two years ago, they visited Thailand. Nui, a professional chef, was impressed with the cooking methods and the spices used in the Thai food. Sudbury does not have a Thai restaurant, and the Soons are contemplating opening one. Nui would supervise the cooking and Brian would leave his current job to be the maitre d'. The restaurant would serve dinner Tuesday through Saturday.

Brian has noticed a restaurant for lease. The restaurant has seven tables, each of which can seat four. Tables can be moved together for a large party. Nui is planning two seatings per evening, and the restaurant will be open 50 weeks per year.

The Soons have drawn up the following estimates:

| | |
|---|---|
| Average revenue, including beverages and dessert | $ 40 per meal |
| Average cost of the food | $ 12 per meal |
| Chef's and dishwasher's salaries | $50,400 per year |
| Rent (premises, equipment) | $ 4,000 per month |
| Cleaning (linen and premises) | $ 800 per month |
| Replacement of dishes, cutlery, glasses | $ 300 per month |
| Utilities, advertising, telephone | $ 1,900 per month |

**Requirement**

Compute the *annual* break-even number of meals and sales revenue for the restaurant. Also, compute the number of meals and the amount of sales revenue needed to earn operating income of $75,600 for the year. How many meals must the Soons serve each night to earn their target income of $75,600? Should the couple open the restaurant? Support your answer.

### CASE ASSIGNMENT

**C4-74 Shining Oaks Toy Company**

*Source:* Laborant/Shutterstock

**CVP analysis**

Alvarez Garcia grew up always working with his father in a woodshop in their back yard. It was no surprise to the family when Alvarez decided to pursue carpentry as a career. When he was in school, he found that he much preferred the fine detail work of small objects rather than building large cabinets and furniture. Alvarez and two other students in the

**NEW! Accounting in the Headlines** One of the biggest challenges for accounting instructors is that students often feel disengaged from the course material, which can seem abstract and unrelated to their personal experiences. But by incorporating real-life examples, instructors can spark student interest and engagement especially when teaching accounting at the introductory level.

Accounting in the Headlines, an award-winning blog by renowned author Wendy Tietz, does just that, with stories about real companies and events that can be used in the accounting classroom to illustrate introductory financial accounting concepts.

Concise, tailorable, and updated on a weekly basis, these articles easily fit into the typical introductory accounting curriculum, whether the course is delivered in-person or online: http://accountingintheheadlines.com

Accounting in the Headlines multiple-choice questions are available for instructors to assign in MyAccountingLab's Assignment Manager.

**Demo Doc Problems and Solutions** appear in Chapters 4, 5, 6, and 9. These provide walk-through problems for demonstration and comprehension of the concepts.

**Case Appendix** (MyAccountingLab) This innovative tool will provide students with direction on case analysis. Associated with the case appendix and found in the MAL are three **Multi-Chapter Cases**. These situational cases test the students' ability to apply multiple managerial accounting concepts to resolving the scenario. Each scenario is a stand-alone case, allowing instructors to assign only those cases that are applicable to their course.

## MyAccountingLab

MyAccountingLab delivers *proven results* in helping individual students succeed.

It provides *engaging experiences* that personalize, stimulate, and measure learning for each student. And, it comes from a *trusted partner* with educational expertise and an eye on the future. MyAccountingLab is the portal to an array of learning tools for all learning styles—practice questions with guided solutions are only the beginning. Students can access MyAccountingLab at **www.pearsonmylabandmastering.com**.

MyAccountingLab can be used by itself or linked to any learning management system.

MyAccountingLab provides students with a variety of resources, including a personalized study plan, tutorials, videos, and animations. In addition, select chapters have Canadian professional designation exam prep questions, allowing students to see how some of the concepts may be examined by the professional designations. These questions are supplied on MyAccountingLab.

**NEW!** Auto-graded Excel projects—using proven, field-tested technology, MyAccountingLab's new auto-graded Excel projects allow instructors to seamlessly integrate Excel content into their course without having to manually grade spreadsheets. Students have the opportunity to practise important accounting skills in Microsoft Excel, helping them to master key concepts and gain proficiency in Excel. Students simply download a spreadsheet, work live on an accounting problem in Excel, and then upload that file back into MyAccountingLab, where they receive reports on their work that provide personalized, detailed feedback to pinpoint where they went wrong on any step of the problem.

To learn more about how MyAccountingLab combines proven learning applications with powerful assessment, instructors can visit www.pearsonmylabandmastering.com.

## New to this Edition

The third Canadian edition of *Managerial Accounting* brings several important changes. We have updated and refreshed examples from industry and added focus to the elements of sustainability accounting included in previous chapters. We have also developed new Try It! features to give more opportunities for practice alongside closer integration to practical modelling examples (i.e., Excel) and MyAccountingLab. For those students interested in pursuing accounting as a career, all chapters now include CPA competency buttons that help highlight content tied to the key CPA competencies.

Some of the most significant changes include the reorganization of chapter content (as detailed below) to provide a comprehensive discussion of management accounting, outlined in a sequence that fits the modern classroom best!

Thank you for choosing the text!

**Chapter 1:** Introduction to Managerial Accounting

- Streamlined content (e.g. SOX and Production System made more concise).
- Updates for currency of examples, topics, or Canadianizations.
- Further expansion of the strategic aspects and the link between theory and application in management accounting (both for majors and general business students).
- Updates to ethics section—not all illegal behaviour is unethical.

**Chapter 2:** Building Blocks of Managerial Accounting

- Updates for currency of examples, topics, or Canadianizations.
- Further expansion of the strategic aspects and the link between theory and application in management accounting (both for majors and general business students).

**Chapter 3:** Cost Behaviour (formerly Chapter 6)

- New chapter placement—this was formerly Chapter 6.
- Updates for currency of examples, topics, or Canadianizations.
- Includes a more applied discussion of the link between theory and the relevant tasks of running a business.
- Further linkage between theory and practice that keeps the text relevant to majors and non-majors alike.
- Simplified language.

**Chapter 4:** Cost-Volume-Profit Analysis (formerly Chapter 7)

- New chapter placement—this was formerly Chapter 7.
- Updates for currency of examples, topics, or Canadianizations.
- Revised organization to enhance readability and pedagogical value.
- Further linkage between theory and practice that keeps the text relevant to majors and non-majors alike.
- Improved clarity by providing definitions (e.g. relevant range).

**Chapter 5:** Job Costing (formerly Chapter 3)

- New chapter placement—this was formerly Chapter 3.

- Updates for currency of examples, topics, or Canadianizations.
- Further expansion of the strategic aspects and the link between theory and application in management accounting (both for majors and general business students).
- Revised placement of over/under allocated OH.
- Inclusion of further examples to clarify that hybrid costing is not only applicable in manufacturing.

**Chapter 6:** Process Costing (formerly Chapter 5)

- Updates for currency of examples, topics, or Canadianizations.
- Further expansion of the strategic aspects and the link between theory and application in management accounting (both for majors and general business students).
- Reorganized so that the mechanics of process costing comes before sustainability.
- More reference to service companies.
- Section on weighted average versus FIFO methods included as an Appendix.

**Chapter 7:** Activity Based Costing (formerly Chapter 4)

- Updates for currency of examples, topics, or Canadianizations.
- Further expansion of the strategic aspects and the link between theory and application in management accounting (both for majors and general business students).
- Included content on high cost of ABC.
- Mentions individuals who collect the data in the ABC system.
- Revised definition of value-added activity.
- More examples integrated, including an example of ABC in a service industry and an example of under costing/over costing.
- Clarified and provided more detail in the sections on ABC versus ABM.

**Chapter 8:** Short-Term Business Decisions

- Improved organization to enhance readability and pedagogical value.
- Improved linkage between theory and practice to keep the text relevant to majors and non-majors alike. The writing in this chapter can also be simplified.
- Maintaining currency of any examples, topics, and Canadianizations.
- Added content on throughput costing.
- Separated out pricing from the discussion of special order decisions.
- Target costing/pricing identified as a separate learning objective.

**Chapter 9:** The Master Budget and Responsibility Accounting

- Content and language streamlined to make accessible to non-majors.
- Further integration through examples and decision guidelines between Chapters 9 and 10 so that students can make links between concepts.
- Tying relevancy and research to practice.
- Writing simplified.
- Maintaining currency of any examples, topics, and Canadianizations.

**Chapter 10:** Flexible Budgets and Standard Costs

- Content and language streamlined to make accessible to non-majors.
- Further integration through examples and decision guidelines between Chapters 9 and 10 so that students can make links between concepts.
- Tying relevancy and research to practice.
- Writing simplified.
- Maintaining currency of any examples, topics, and Canadianizations.

**Chapter 11:** Performance Evaluation and the Balanced Scorecard

- Writing simplified.
- Maintaining currency of any examples, topics, and Canadianizations.
- Discussion of different strategies; for instance "planned" versus "emergent" strategies, and internally focused strategies (e.g., core competencies of the firm [Prahalad and Hamel, 1991]) and externally focused strategies (e.g., The Five-Forces Model [Porter, 1990]).

**Chapter 12:** Capital Investment Decisions and the Time Value of Money

- Maintaining currency of any examples, topics, and Canadianizations.

## Pearson eText

The Pearson eText gives students access to their textbook anytime, anywhere. In addition to note taking, highlighting, and bookmarking, the Pearson eText offers interactive and sharing features. Instructors can share their comments or highlights, and students can add their own, creating a tight community of learners within the class.

## Instructor's Resources

These instructor supplements are available for download from a password-protected section of Pearson Canada's online catalogue (www.pearsoncanada.ca/highered). Navigate to your book's catalogue page to view a list of those supplements that are available. Speak to your local Pearson sales representative for details and access.

- Instructor's Solutions Manual: This manual contains full solutions for all end of-chapter material.
- Instructor's Resource Manual: Provided in PDF format, this manual includes chapter overviews, chapter outlines, detailed outlines with teaching tips tied to learning objectives, chapter student summary handouts, chapter assignment grids, and chapter quizes with answer key.
- Computerized Test Bank. Pearson's computerized test banks allow instructors to filter and select questions to create quizzes, tests, or homework. Instructors can revise questions or add their own, and may be able to choose print or online options. These questions are also available in Microsoft Word format.
- PowerPoint Presentation for instructors and students is a highly visual and comprehensive set of PowerPoint files with 40 to 60 slides per chapter.

## Learning Solutions Managers

Pearson's Learning Solutions Managers work with faculty and campus course designers to ensure that Pearson technology products, assessment tools, and online course materials are tailored to meet your specific needs. This highly qualified team is dedicated to helping schools take full advantage of a wide range of educational resources, by assisting in the integration of a variety of instructional materials and media formats. Your local Pearson Canada sales representative can provide you with more details on this service program.

We hope you enjoy *Managerial Accounting*!

# About the Authors

**Karen Wilken Braun** is currently a faculty member of the Weatherhead School of Management at Case Western Reserve University. From 1996 to 2004, Professor Braun was on the faculty of the J.M. Tull School of Accounting at the University of Georgia, where she received the Outstanding Accounting Teacher of the Year award from the UGA chapter of Alpha Kappa Psi.

Professor Braun is a certified public accountant and a member of the American Accounting Association (AAA). She is also a member of the AAA's Management Accounting Section and the Teaching, Learning, and Curriculum Section.

Dr. Braun received her Ph.D. from the University of Connecticut, where she was an AICPA Doctoral Fellow, a Deloitte & Touche Doctoral Fellow, and an AAA Doctoral Consortium Fellow. She received her B.A., summa cum laude, from Luther College, where she was a member of Phi Beta Kappa and received the Outstanding Accounting Student award from the Iowa Society of Certified Public Accountants.

She gained public accounting experience while working at Arthur Andersen & Co. and accumulated additional business and management accounting experience as corporate controller for Gemini Aviation Inc.

Professor Braun and her husband, Cory, have two daughters, Rachel and Hannah. In her free time she enjoys playing tennis, gardening, skiing, hiking, and music.

**Wendy M. Tietz** is currently a faculty member in the Department of Accounting in the College of Business Administration at Kent State University, where she has taught since 2000. Prior to teaching at Kent State University, she was on the faculty at the University of Akron. She teaches in a variety of formats, including large sections, small sections, and Web-based sections. She has received numerous college and university teaching awards while at Kent State University.

Professor Tietz is a certified public accountant, a certified management accountant, and a certified information systems auditor. She is a member of the American Accounting Association, the Institute of Management Accountants, the American Institute of Certified Public Accountants, and ISACA®. She is also a member of the AAA's Management Accounting Section and the Teaching, Learning, and Curriculum Section. She has published in *Issues in Accounting Education* and Accounting *Education: An International Journal* and regularly presents at AAA regional and national meetings.

Professor Tietz received her Ph.D. from Kent State University. She received both her M.B.A. and B.S.A from the University of Akron. She worked in industry for several years, both as a controller for a financial institution and as the operations manager and controller for a recycled plastics manufacturer.

Professor Tietz and her husband, Russ, have two sons, who are both in college. In her spare time she enjoys playing tennis, bike riding, reading, and learning about new technology.

**Louis Beaubien** is currently an Associate Professor in the Rowe School of Business in the Faculty of Management, and in the Department of Community Health and Epidemiology in the Department of Medicine at Dalhousie University. From 2008 to 2012, Professor Beaubien was on the faculty of the Sobey School of Business at Saint Mary's University, where he received the University Charter Teacher of the Year award.

Professor Beaubien is a chartered professional accountant and a member of the Canadian Academic Accounting Association (CAAA) and the American Accounting Association (AAA). Dr. Beaubien received his Ph.D. from the Richard Ivey School of Business at the University of Western Ontario. Prior to graduate school he gained professional experience in the financial services and consulting industry. Dr. Beaubien's research has covered areas including accounting in financial services, the co-operative sector, and healthcare.

# Acknowledgments

*Managerial Accounting*, Third Canadian Edition, is the product of a rigorous research and review process to ensure the revision meets the needs of Canadian students and faculty. The feedback helped structure this edition in both content and assignment material. A huge debt is owed to those who provided their time, support, and feedback throughout this process:

Lynn Carty, *University of Guelph*
Tammy Crowell, *Dalhousie University*
Carol Fearon, *Seneca College*
Arsineh Garabedian, *Simon Fraser University*
Rob Harvey, *Algonquin College*
Donna Losell, *University of Toronto (Rotman School of Management)*
Debbie Musil, *Kwantlen Polytechnic University*
Geoffrey Prince, *Centennial College*
Pamela Quon, *Athabasca University*
Rand Rowlands, George Brown College
Victor Waese, *British Columbia Institute of Technology*
Judith Watson, *Capilano University*
Patricia Zima, *Mohawk College*

I would also like to thank the people at Pearson Canada for their hard work and dedication, including Megan Farrell, who put together a wonderful editorial team, including Keriann McGoogan, and Cat Haggert, who took charge of this project, found the resources where none seemed to exist, and guided the project to a fantastic conclusion. Their good spirits, loyalty, and dedication made the long work of completing this project easier and more worthwhile.

Appreciation also goes to the Chartered Professional Accountants of Canada, the Canadian Institute of Chartered Accountants, the Certified General Accountants Association of Canada, the Society of Management Accountants of Canada, and many other publishers and companies for their generous permission to quote from their publications.

# Introduction to Managerial Accounting

1

## Learning Objectives

1 Identify managers' four primary responsibilities.

2 Distinguish financial accounting from managerial accounting.

3 Describe organizational structure and the roles and skills required of management accountants within the organization.

4 Describe the role of CPA Canada, and apply its guidelines for ethical behaviour.

5 Discuss and analyze the implications of regulatory and business trends.

6 Describe a lean production system.

7 Describe and use the costs of quality framework.

Chapter 1, "Introduction to Managerial Accounting," covers material outlined in **Section 5, Part 3: Management Accounting** of the CPA Competency Map (by Competency Area). This chapter offers a general introduction to Management Accounting.

The presence of the **coverage button** in the margin indicates focus on one or more of the specific competency areas from the competency map. The concepts in the text are building blocks to developing the competencies required in the CPA. While the chapter may address multiple areas of the competency map, the main focus will be:

Competencies:

**3.1.1** Evaluates management information requirements*

**3.1.2** Evaluates the types of information systems used and the role they play in an organization*

**3.1.4** Identifies ethical and privacy issues related to information technology*

## The founders of Prime Restaurants Inc. (Prime)

created a niche in the casual dining market in 1980 when they opened their first Casey's restaurant in Sudbury, Ontario. The focus was to provide good food at the right price so that restaurant-goers could still afford to go out for dinner in economic downturns, thereby buffering the restaurant from the effects of a changing economy. Since the first restaurant opened, the company has grown to include the well-known brands of Casey's, Pat & Mario's, East Side Mario's, Finn MacCool's, D'Arcy McGee's, Paddy Flaherty's, Bier Markt, and Tir nan Óg. With significant growth in the past decade, the Prime group of restaurants included about 150 locations in 2014. Some of these restaurants are corporate owned, but the growth is due mostly to franchising. Prime has received many awards and honours for its work, including being named one of Canada's 50 Best Managed Companies for many consecutive years, the Pinnacle Award for Restaurant Company of the Year, the Ontario Restaurant News Restaurant of the Year award, as well as others.

© Richard Buchan/The Canadian Press

*Reprinted from *The Chartered Professional Accountant Competency Map - Understanding the competencies a candidate must demonstrate to become a CPA*, © 2012, with permission Chartered Professional Accountants of Canada, Toronto, Canada. Any changes to the original material are the sole responsibility of the author (and/or publisher) and have not been reviewed or endorsed by the Chartered Professional Accountants of Canada.

A company doesn't grow this quickly, or this well, without having the right information available at the right time. Managerial accounting is a tool to help managers sort through mountains of data, decide what data are necessary, and make the best decisions possible using the data. This text will introduce you to many of the concepts used by those who make managerial accounting decisions.

Managers use accounting information for much more than preparing annual financial statements. Managerial accounting (or management accounting) uses information in short-term decision making and long-term strategy formulation. In this chapter, we will introduce managerial accounting and discuss how managers use it to fulfill their duties. We will also explore how managerial accounting differs from financial accounting. Finally, we will discuss the regulatory and business environment in which today's managers and management accountants operate.

# What Is Managerial Accounting?

As you will see throughout the book, managerial accounting is different from financial accounting. Financial accounting focuses on providing stockholders and creditors with the information they need to make investment and lending decisions. This information takes the form of financial statements: the balance sheet, income statement, statement of shareholders' equity, and statement of cash flows.

1 Identify managers' four primary responsibilities.

Managerial accounting focuses on providing internal management with the information it needs to run an organization efficiently and effectively. This information takes many forms, depending on management's needs.

To understand the kind of information managers need, let us first look at their primary responsibilities.

## Managers' Four Primary Responsibilities

Managerial accounting helps managers fulfill their four primary responsibilities, as shown in Exhibit 1-1: **planning**, **directing**, **controlling**, and **decision making**.

**EXHIBIT 1-1** Managers' Four Primary Responsibilities

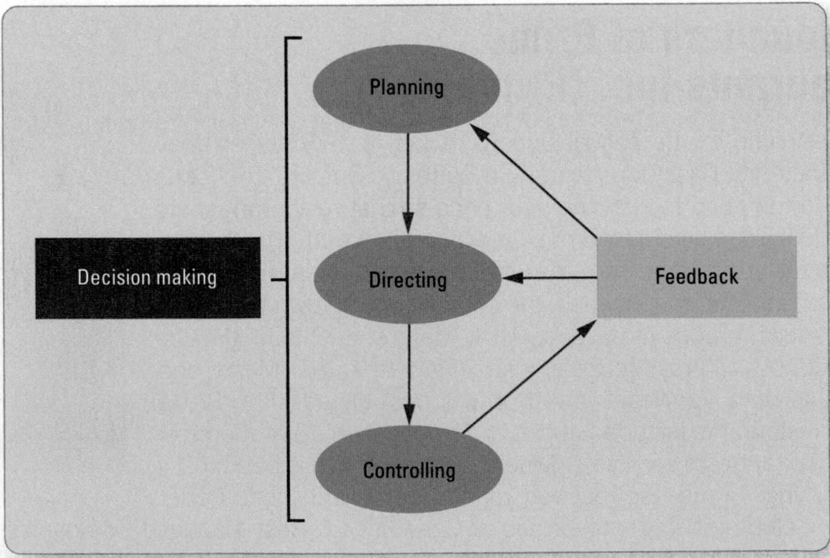


- Planning involves setting goals and objectives for the company and determining how to achieve them. For example, one of Prime's goals is to always use quality products and ingredients to keep customers coming back. One strategy for Prime to achieve this goal would be to establish good relationships with its suppliers. Prime's management team could incorporate new technology to improve communication between the restaurants and their suppliers. Managerial accounting translates plans such as these into budgets—the quantitative expression of a plan. Management analyzes the budgets before proceeding to determine if its integration plans make financial sense.

- Directing means overseeing the company's day-to-day operations. Management uses product cost reports, product sales information, and other managerial accounting reports to run daily business operations. Prime uses product sales data to determine which menu items are generating the most sales and then uses that information to adjust menus and marketing strategies.
- Controlling means evaluating the results of business operations against the plan and making adjustments to keep the company pressing toward its goals. Prime uses performance reports to compare each restaurant's actual performance against the **budget**, and then it uses that *feedback* to take corrective actions if needed. If actual costs are higher or lower than planned, management may revise its plans or adjust operations. Perhaps the newly opened restaurants are not generating as much income as budgeted. As a result, management may decide to increase local advertising to increase sales.
- Management engages in decision making while it plans, directs, and controls operations. Prime must decide where to open new restaurants, which restaurants to refurnish, what prices to set for meals, what entrées to offer, and so forth. Because Prime is in business to generate profits for its owners and operators, management must consider the financial impact of each of these decisions. Managerial accounting gathers, summarizes, and reports cost and revenue data relevant to each of these decisions.

## A Road Map: How Managerial Accounting Fits In

This book will show you how managerial accounting information helps managers fulfill their responsibilities. The rest of the text is organized around the following themes:

1. **Managerial Accounting Building Blocks** Chapter 1 helps you understand more about the management accounting profession and today's business environment. Chapter 2 teaches you some of the language that is commonly used in managerial accounting. Just as musicians must know the notes of the musical scale, management accountants *and* managers must understand managerial accounting terms to effectively use managerial accounting information to run the business. With the building blocks presented and new terminology introduced, it is time to provide the tools for case study analysis. The Case Analysis Appendix is designed to guide you through the process of taking complex, integrated information, determining the critical problems in real-life scenarios, and solving these problems effectively. This appendix can be used throughout the rest of the textbook as you attempt to solve the cases presented with the chapters.
2. **Understanding Cost and Profit Patterns** Before Prime opened any restaurants, management determined how many meals each would have to serve just to break even—that is, just to cover costs. Management had to understand how costs behave before it could calculate a *break-even* point. Chapters 3 and 4 discuss how costs behave and how managers use cost behaviour knowledge to make good decisions and accurate forecasts.
3. **Determining Unit Cost** It is crucial for organizations like Prime to understand how much it costs to make its product or deliver its service in order to effectively set prices. Prime must calculate the cost of each item on the menu to set prices high enough to cover costs and generate a profit. This is tougher than it sounds. Prime's cost to prepare each meal includes more than just the cost of the ingredients. Prime's cost also includes the chefs' and servers' wages and benefits, restaurant lease payments, property taxes, utilities, business licenses, and so forth. Chapters 5, 6, and 7 discuss how businesses determine their product costs. Once management knows its product costs, it uses that information for decision making, planning, directing, and controlling. Then, Chapter 8 addresses common business decisions around costing and pricing, such as *outsourcing*. For example, should Prime outsource its fruit smoothies—that is, have another company make them? Many restaurants do.
4. **Planning and Control** Budgets are management's primary tool for expressing its plans. Chapter 9 discusses the components of the *master budget* and the way a large company like Prime uses the budgeting process to implement its business goals and strategies. As part of this process management uses *budget variances*—the differences

between actual costs and the budget—to control operations. Chapter 10 shows how management uses variance analysis to determine how and where to adjust operations.

5. **Measurement and Evaluation.** It is important for organizations to have effective approaches to managing past and current performance, and to evaluate future decisions. For example, Prime must be able to examine how well the organization is doing in terms of internal operations and business processes; or if future investments are likely to bring positive returns to the company. Chapter 11 discusses other tools that management can use to determine whether individual segments of the company are reaching the company's goals. Chapter 12 shows you how managers decide whether to invest in new equipment, new locations, and new projects.

## Differences Between Managerial Accounting and Financial Accounting

**2** Distinguish financial accounting from managerial accounting.

Prime's financial accounting system is geared toward producing annual and quarterly consolidated financial statements that will be used by potential franchisees and creditors to make investment and lending decisions. The financial statements objectively summarize the transactions that occurred between Prime and external parties during the previous year. However, managerial accounting information differs from financial accounting information in many respects. Exhibit 1-2 summarizes these differences.

Publicly accountable enterprises[1] must, as of January 1, 2011, use **International Financial Reporting Standards (IFRS)**, while private enterprises have an option. Prime is a privately held company; therefore, management can voluntarily select IFRS guidelines or **Accounting Standards for Private Enterprises (ASPE)**.[2] Prime's financial statements are useful to its potential franchisees and creditors, but they do not provide management with enough information to run the company effectively.

Prime's managerial accounting system is designed to provide its managers with the accounting information they need to plan, direct, control, and make decisions. No ASPE- or IFRS-type standards or audits are required for managerial accounting since this information will only be used internally. Prime's managers tailor the company's managerial accounting system to provide the information they need to help them make better decisions. Prime must weigh the benefits of the system (information that helps managers make decisions that increase profits) against the costs to develop and run the system. The costs and benefits of any particular managerial accounting system differ from one company to another. Different companies create different systems, so Prime's system will differ from Bombardier Inc.'s system.

[1]The following definitions have been adopted for the purposes of determining which Part of the CPA *Handbook* applies to a reporting entity:

a. A **publicly accountable enterprise** is an entity, other than a not-for-profit organization or a government or other entity in the public sector, that:
   i. has issued, or is in the process of issuing, debt or equity instruments that are, or will be, outstanding and traded in a public market (a domestic or foreign stock exchange, or an over-the-counter market, including local and regional markets); or
   ii. holds assets in a fiduciary capacity for a broad group of outsiders as one of its primary businesses. Banks, credit unions, insurance companies, securities brokers/dealers, mutual funds, and investment banks typically meet the second criterion above. Other entities may also hold assets in a fiduciary capacity for a broad group of outsiders because they hold and manage financial resources entrusted to them by clients, customers, or members not involved in the management of the entity. However, if they do so for reasons incidental to a primary business (as, for example, may be the case for travel or real estate agents, cooperative enterprises requiring a nominal membership deposit, or sellers that receive payment in advance of delivery of the goods or services, such as utility companies), that does not make them publicly accountable.
b. A private enterprise is a profit-oriented entity that is neither a publicly accountable enterprise nor an entity in the public sector.
c. A not-for-profit organization is an entity, normally without transferable ownership interests, organized and operated exclusively for social, educational, professional, religious, health, charitable, or any other not-for-profit purpose. A not-for-profit organization's members, contributors and other resource providers do not, in such capacity, receive any financial return directly from the organization.
d. A pension plan is any arrangement (contractual or otherwise) by which a program is established to provide retirement income to employees.

*Source:* Based on info from IFRS (http://ifrsincanada.com/PAEdefinition.html)

[2]ASPE guidelines were previously known as Canadian Generally Accepted Accounting Principles (GAAP).

**EXHIBIT 1-2** Managerial Accounting versus Financial Accounting

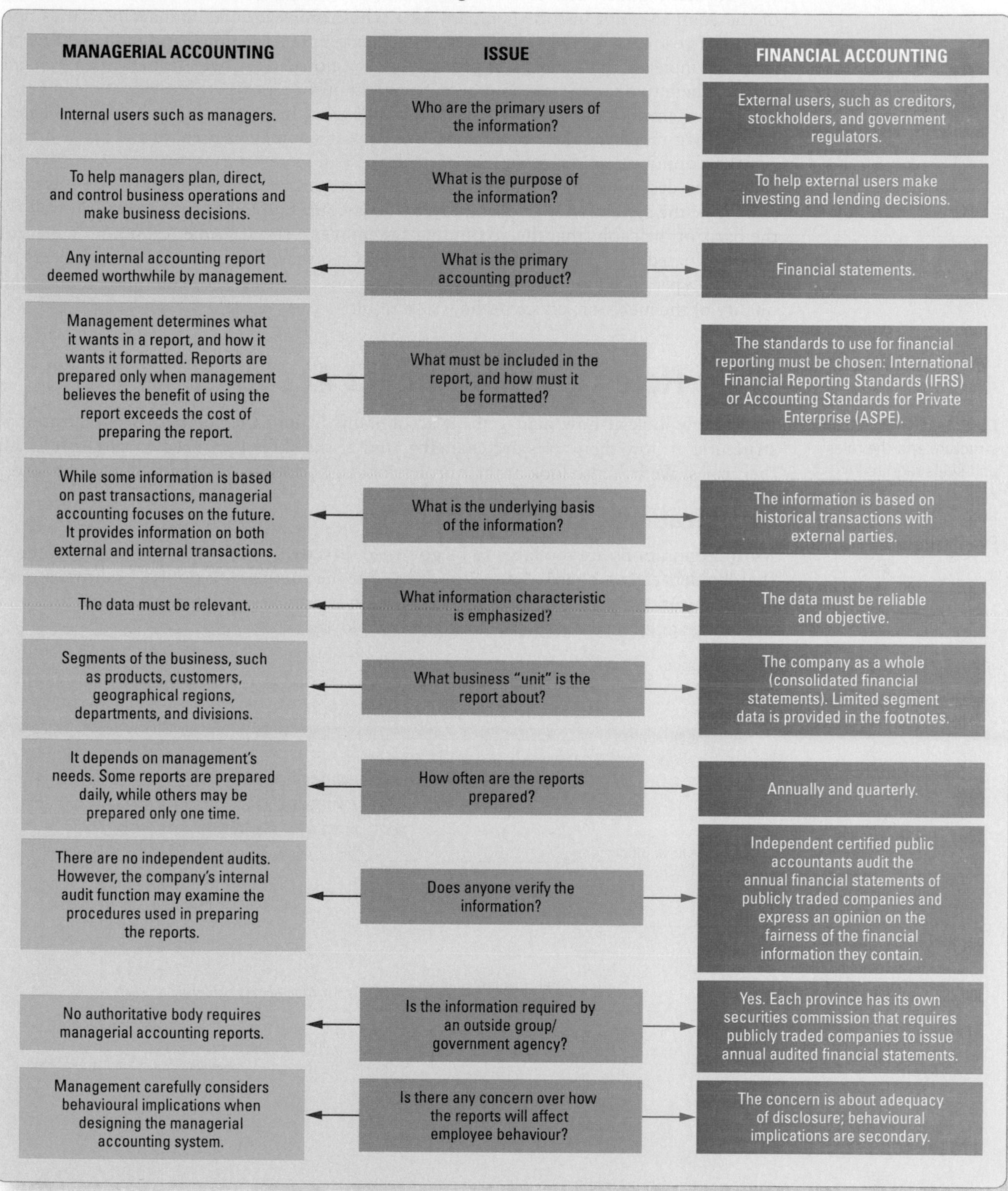

| MANAGERIAL ACCOUNTING | ISSUE | FINANCIAL ACCOUNTING |
|---|---|---|
| Internal users such as managers. | Who are the primary users of the information? | External users, such as creditors, stockholders, and government regulators. |
| To help managers plan, direct, and control business operations and make business decisions. | What is the purpose of the information? | To help external users make investing and lending decisions. |
| Any internal accounting report deemed worthwhile by management. | What is the primary accounting product? | Financial statements. |
| Management determines what it wants in a report, and how it wants it formatted. Reports are prepared only when management believes the benefit of using the report exceeds the cost of preparing the report. | What must be included in the report, and how must it be formatted? | The standards to use for financial reporting must be chosen: International Financial Reporting Standards (IFRS) or Accounting Standards for Private Enterprise (ASPE). |
| While some information is based on past transactions, managerial accounting focuses on the future. It provides information on both external and internal transactions. | What is the underlying basis of the information? | The information is based on historical transactions with external parties. |
| The data must be relevant. | What information characteristic is emphasized? | The data must be reliable and objective. |
| Segments of the business, such as products, customers, geographical regions, departments, and divisions. | What business "unit" is the report about? | The company as a whole (consolidated financial statements). Limited segment data is provided in the footnotes. |
| It depends on management's needs. Some reports are prepared daily, while others may be prepared only one time. | How often are the reports prepared? | Annually and quarterly. |
| There are no independent audits. However, the company's internal audit function may examine the procedures used in preparing the reports. | Does anyone verify the information? | Independent certified public accountants audit the annual financial statements of publicly traded companies and express an opinion on the fairness of the financial information they contain. |
| No authoritative body requires managerial accounting reports. | Is the information required by an outside group/ government agency? | Yes. Each province has its own securities commission that requires publicly traded companies to issue annual audited financial statements. |
| Management carefully considers behavioural implications when designing the managerial accounting system. | Is there any concern over how the reports will affect employee behaviour? | The concern is about adequacy of disclosure; behavioural implications are secondary. |

In contrast to financial statements, most managerial accounting reports focus on the *future*, providing *relevant* information that helps managers make profitable business decisions. For example, before putting their plans into action, Prime's managers determine if their plans make sense by quantitatively expressing them in the form of budgets. Prime's managerial accounting reports may also plan for and reflect *internal* transactions, such as the daily movement of beverages and dry ingredients from central warehouses to individual restaurant locations.

To make good decisions, Prime's managers need information about smaller units of the company, not just the company as a whole. For example, management uses revenue and cost data on individual restaurants, geographical regions, and individual menu items to increase the company's profitability. Regional data help Prime's management decide where to open more restaurants. Sales and profit reports on individual menu items help management choose menu items and decide what items to offer on a seasonal basis. Rather than preparing these reports just once a year, companies prepare and revise managerial accounting reports as often as needed.

When designing the managerial accounting system, management must carefully consider how the system will affect employees' behaviour. Employees try to perform well on the parts of their jobs that the accounting system measures. If Prime restaurant managers were evaluated only on their ability to control costs, they may use cheaper ingredients or hire less experienced servers. Although these actions cut costs, they can hurt profits if the quality of the meals or service declines as a result.

## What Role Do Management Accountants Play?

3 Describe organizational structure and the roles and skills required of management accountants within the organization.

Let us now look at how management accountants fit into the company's organizational structure, at how their roles are changing, and at the skills they need to successfully fill their roles. We will also look at their professional associations and their ethical standards.

### Organizational Structure

Most corporations are too large to be governed directly by their shareholders. Therefore, shareholders elect a **board of directors** to oversee the company. Exhibit 1-3 shows a typical organizational structure with the green boxes representing employees of the firm and the orange and blue boxes representing nonemployees.

**EXHIBIT 1-3** Typical Organizational Structure

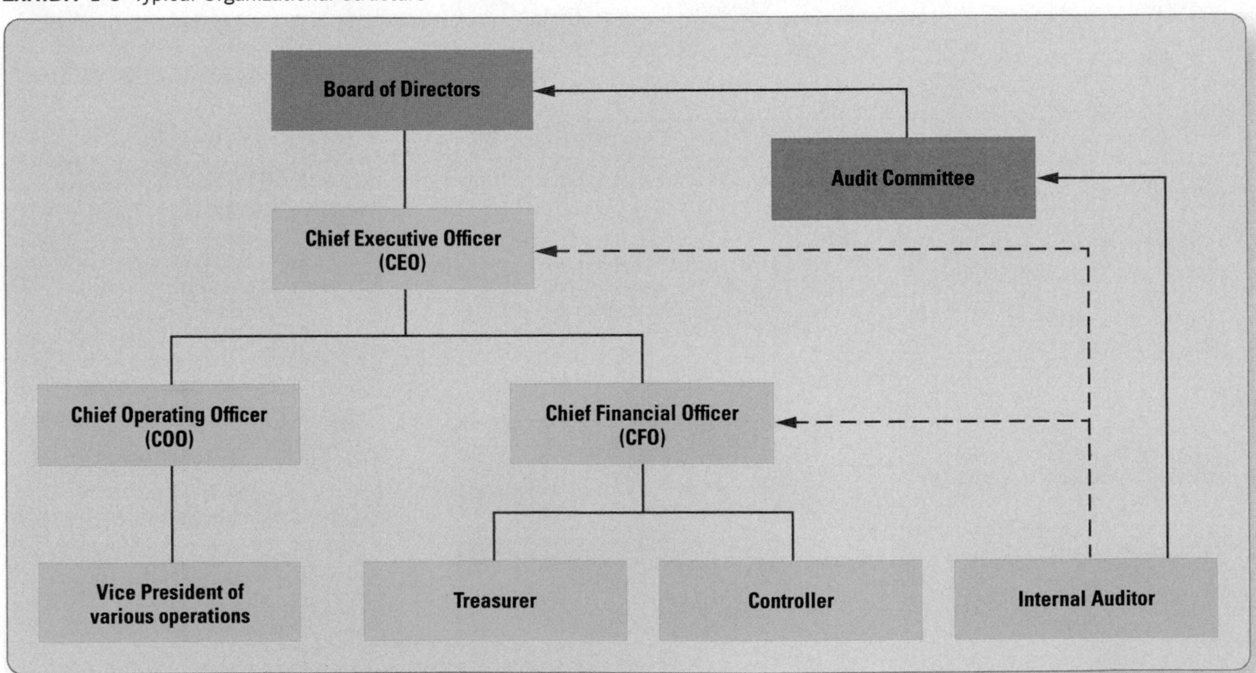


Normally, an organization's board only meets periodically, so it hires a **chief executive officer (CEO)** to manage the company on a daily basis. The CEO hires other executives to run various aspects of the organization, including the **chief operating officer (COO)** and the **chief financial officer (CFO)**. The COO is responsible for the company's operations, such as research and development (R&D), production, and distribution. The CFO is responsible for all of the company's financial concerns. The **treasurer** and the **controller** report directly to the CFO. The treasurer is primarily responsible for raising capital (through issuing stocks and bonds) and investing funds. The controller is usually responsible for general financial accounting, managerial accounting, and tax reporting.

The Toronto Stock Exchange (TSE/TSX) requires that the members of a board of directors for a listed company have sufficient experience in the industry and in governing public companies. It also requires that at least two board members are independent of the firm. However, for those organizations looking to go public in the United States, the New York Stock Exchange (NYSE) requires that listed companies have not only an external auditor but also an **internal audit function**. The role of the internal audit function is to ensure that the company's internal controls and risk management policies are functioning properly. The internal audit department reports directly to the **audit committee**, a subcommittee of the board of directors. The audit committee oversees the internal audit function as well as the annual audit of the financial statements by independent auditors. Both the internal audit department and the independent auditors report directly to the audit committee for one very important reason: to ensure that management will not intimidate them or bias their work. However, since the audit committee meets only periodically, it is not practical for the audit committee to manage the internal audit function on a day-to-day basis. Therefore, the internal audit function also reports to a senior executive, such as the CFO or CEO, for administrative matters.

When you look at the organizational chart pictured in Exhibit 1-3, where do you think management accountants work? It depends on the company. Management accountants have competencies in finance and accounting, strategic thinking, decision-making, and communication that make them valuable in managerial positions throughout the company. These same competencies also make managerial accountants valuable on **cross-functional teams**. Cross-functional teams consist of employees representing various functions of the company, such as R&D, design, production, marketing, distribution, and customer service. Cross-functional teams are effective because each member can address business decisions from a different viewpoint. These teams often report to various vice presidents of operations. Management accountants often take the leadership role in the teams. Lillie Cruikshank, the vice president of the Business Technology Centre at Sobeys Inc., describes her career as a management accountant as providing her with[3]

> the business management skills that help me connect the dots between strategy and action. We're in a highly competitive environment. We have to control costs while providing our customer with the best food offering.

## The Changing Roles of Management Accountants

Technology has changed the roles of management accountants. Management accountants no longer perform routine mechanical accounting tasks; computer programs perform those tasks. Yet management accountants are in more demand than ever. Company managers used to view management accountants as "scorekeepers" or "bean counters" because they spent most of their time recording historical transactions. Now, they view management accountants as internal consultants or business advisors.

> **Why is this important?**
> Management **accountants** act as internal business advisors. They provide the **financial** information and in-depth **analysis** that managers need to make good business **decisions**.

Management accountants must still ensure that the company's financial records adequately capture economic events. They do this by helping design the information systems that capture and record transactions, and they make sure that the information system generates accurate data. Management accountants still need to know what transactions to record and how to record them, but they let technology do most of the routine work and use professional judgment to address non-routine transactions.

Freed from the routine mechanical work, management accountants spend more of their time planning, analyzing, and interpreting accounting data and providing decision support. Because their role is changing, management accountants rarely bear the job title "management accountant" anymore; they may be referred to as business management

[3]Excerpt from Certified Management Accountant (CMA). www.creativeaccountants.org

support, financial advisors, business partners, analysts, or simply managers. Here is what two management accountants have said about their jobs:[4]

> We are looked upon more as business advisors than just accountants, which has a lot to do with the additional analysis and forward-looking goals that we are setting. We spend more of our time analyzing and understanding our margins, our prices, and the markets in which we do business. People have a sense of purpose; they have a real sense of "I'm adding value to the company." (Caterpillar, Inc.)
>
> Accounting is changing. You are no longer sitting behind a desk just working on a computer, just crunching the numbers. You are actually getting to be a part of the day-to-day functions of the business. (Abbott Laboratories)

## The Skills Required of Management Accountants

Because computers now do the routine "number crunching," do management accountants need to know as much as they did 20 years ago? The fact is, management accountants now need to know *more*! They have to understand what information management needs and how to generate that information accurately. Therefore, management accountants must be able to communicate with the computer/IT system programmers to create an effective information system. Once the information system generates the data, management accountants interpret and analyze the raw data and turn them into *useful* information management can use.[5]

> Twenty years ago we would say, "Here are the costs and you guys need to figure out what you want to do with them." Now we are expected to say, "Here are the costs and this is why the costs are what they are, and this is how they compare to other things, and here are some suggestions where we could possibly improve." (Caterpillar, Inc.)

Today's management accountants need the following skills:[6]

- Solid knowledge of both financial and managerial accounting
- Problem-solving and decision-making skills
- Knowledge of how a business functions
- Ability to lead and to work on a team
- Professionalism and ethical standards
- Oral *and* written communication skills

The skills shown in Exhibit 1-4 are crucial to these management accountants:[7]

> We're making more presentations that are seen across the division. So you have to summarize the numbers...you have to have people in sales understand what those numbers mean. If you can't communicate information to the individuals, then the information is never out there; it's lost. So, your communication skills are very important. (Abbott Laboratories)
>
> Usually when a nonfinancial person comes to you with financial questions, they don't really ask the right things so that you can give them the correct answer. If they ask you for cost, well, you have to work with them and say, "Well, do you want total plant cost, a variable cost, or an accountable cost?" Then, "What is the reason for those costs?" Whatever they're using this cost for determines what type of cost you will provide them with. (Caterpillar, Inc.)

Chapter 2 explains these cost terms. The point here is that management accountants need to have a solid understanding of managerial accounting, including how different types of costs are relevant to different situations. Additionally, they must be able to communicate that information to employees from different business functions.

[4]IMA (Institute of Management Accountants, www.imanet.org). Adapted with permission. Adapted *From Counting More, Counting Less: The 1999 Practice Analysis of Management Accounting,* published by Institute of Management Accountants, © 1999.

[5]Institute of Management Accountants, *Counting More, Counting Less: The 1999 Practice Analysis of Management Accounting* © 1999.

[6]Gary Siegel and James Sorenson, *What Corporate America Wants in Entry-Level Accountants*, Institute of Management Accountants, Montvale, NJ, 1994.

[7]Institute of Management Accountants, *Counting More, Counting Less: The 1999 Practice Analysis of Management Accounting.*

**EXHIBIT 1-4** The Skills Required for Management Accountants

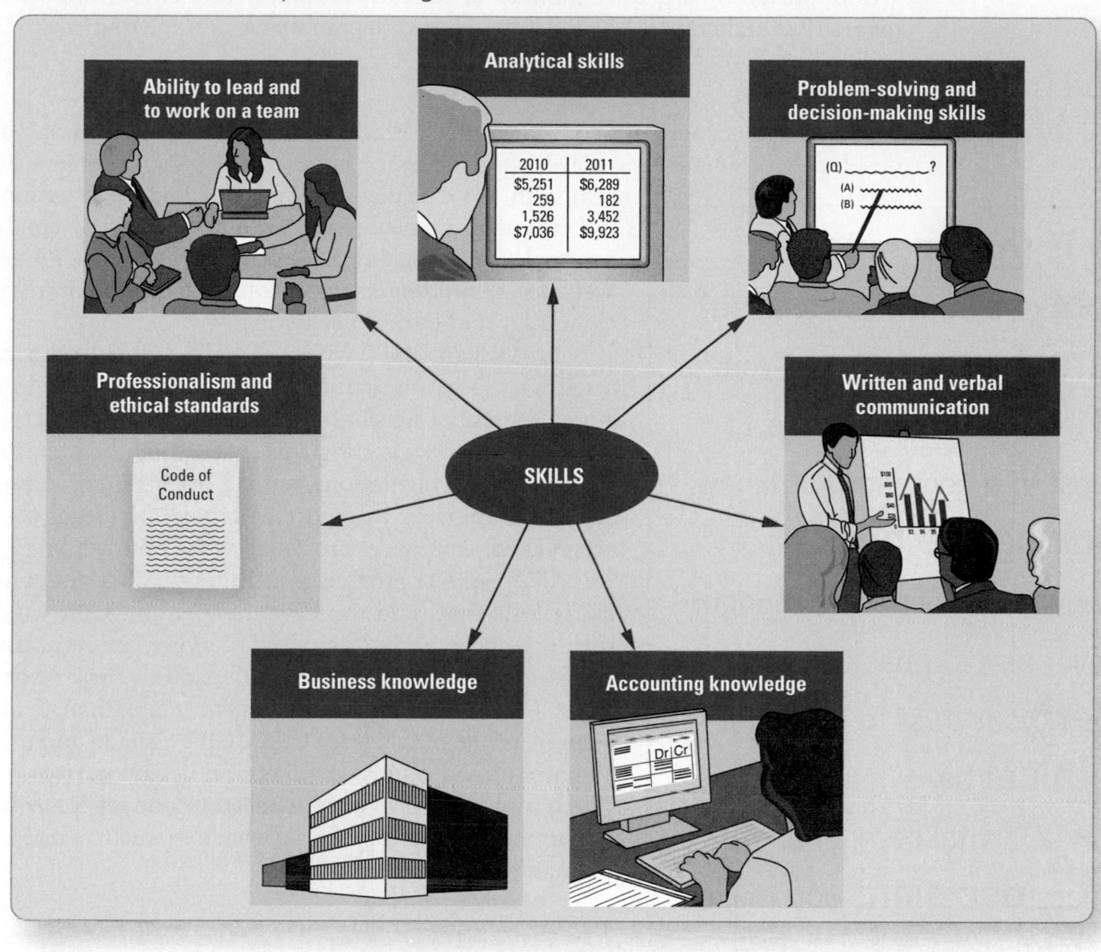


## The Profession of Accounting in Canada

4 Describe the role of CPA Canada, and apply its guidelines for ethical behaviour.

Professional accountants in Canada are represented by the Chartered Professional Accountants of Canada (CPA Canada) in addition to provincial accounting associations (e.g., CPA Ontario). Prior to a multi-year unification process, which began in 2013, there were three professional accounting designations in Canada. The three legacy accounting bodies in Canada were:

- The Society of Management Accountants of Canada, which governed Certified Management Accountants (CMAs);
- The Canadian Institute of Chartered Accountants, which regulated Chartered Accountants (CAs); and
- The Certified General Accountants Association of Canada, which awarded members the Certified General Accountant (CGA) designation.

The **Chartered Professional Accountant** (CPA) designation (in French, comptable professionnel agréé) is the designation by which all new accountants will be known following the unification process and the completion of legislation in each of the provinces and territories of Canada. Individuals that held any of the legacy designations will retain their previous credential and also join the new designation (i.e., Bill Smith, CA, will become Bill Smith, CPA, CA).

One of the reasons the accounting profession in Canada pursued unification was to bring together the strength of training, knowledge, and practice into one accounting body to provide the greatest benefit to the public, to the profession, and to businesses in Canada. For management accountants, this means the diverse set of skills required (see Figure 1-4) are supported by a greater number of educational and peer mentor supports. There are over 190,000 members of CPA Canada, and the numbers continue to grow.

## Ethics

Management accountants continually face ethical challenges. Our accounting bodies have developed principles, standards, and codes of ethics to help management accountants deal with these challenges. You will find information regarding the ethical principles, standards, and codes of conduct on the national CPA association's and each provincial CPA association's Websites, reminding us that professional accountants exhibit the highest level of ethical behaviour.

> **Why is this important?**
>
> At the **root** of all business relationships is **trust**. Would you put your **money** in a bank that you didn't trust, invest in a company you knew was "**cooking the books**," or lend money to someone you thought would never pay you back? As a **manager**, your trust in the other party's **ethical** behaviour, and vice versa, will be a vital component of the business **decisions** you make.

In Canada, Bill 198C was passed in 2002 in response to a series of large international corporate scandals. In the United States, a parallel legislation (the Sarbanes-Oxley Act) was passed in 2002. Similar legislation was enacted in other countries around the world. The regulations, among other things, delineate a process for employees to report violations or illegal and unethical acts. (These employees are called whistleblowers.)

CPA Canada provides guidelines for codes of conduct for all individuals that hold the CPA designation. CPA Canada works with provincial accounting bodies, which are responsible for the regulation of the accounting profession in their respective provinces. This includes the development, maintenance, and enforcement of a code of ethics for CPAs. CPA Canada and the provincial affiliates provide guidance on ethical behaviour (see Exhibit 1-5), which alongside provincial codes of conduct is meant to foster important qualities of ethical behaviour such as integrity, leadership, and trust.

**EXHIBIT 1-5** CPA Guidelines for Ethical Behaviour

| Guideline | Evidence | Example |
|---|---|---|
| Adherence to Rules of Professional Conduct | Compilation of allowed and disallowed behaviours | No ownership interest in an audit client |
| Enabling Competencies | Adherence to laws and professional standards for knowledge and behaviour | Having the requisite knowledge to perform certain tasks |
| Assessing the Situation | Recognition of ethical issues that may arise in work to be performed | Planning and identifying possible conflicts of interest |
| Integrative Analysis | Anticipation of issues and identification of possible alternatives | Scrutinizing ethical constraints to determine the best way forward |
| Conclude/Advise and Communicate | A clear and transparent decision based on the ethical analysis | |

*Source:* Karen W. Braun, Wendy M Tietz and Louis Beaubien, Managerial Accounting, 3rd Ed., © 2018, Pearson Education, Inc., New York, NY.

To resolve ethical dilemmas, management accountants should first follow their company's established policies for reporting unethical behaviour. If the conflict is not resolved through the company's procedures, the management accountant should consider the following steps:

- Discuss the unethical situation with the immediate supervisor unless the supervisor is involved in the unethical situation. If so, notify the supervisor at the next higher managerial level. If the immediate supervisor involved is the CEO, notify the audit committee or board of directors.

- Discuss the unethical situation with an objective advisor.
- Consult an attorney regarding legal obligations and rights.

## Examples of Ethical Dilemmas

Unfortunately, the ethical path is not always clear. You may want to act ethically and do the right thing, but the consequences can make it difficult to decide what to do. Let us consider several ethical dilemmas:

### Dilemma #1

> Ileana Spilca is examining the expense reports of her staff who counted inventory at Canadian Car Parts' distribution centre in Brampton, Ontario. She discovers that Mike Flinders has claimed but not included hotel receipts for over $1,000 of accommodation expenses. Other staff, who also claimed $1,000, did attach hotel receipts. When asked about the receipts, Mike admits that he stayed with an old friend, not in the hotel, but he believes that he deserves the money he saved. After all, the company would have paid his hotel bill.

By asking to be reimbursed for hotel expenses he did not incur, Flinders violates the basic tents of adherence to rules of professional conduct. Because Spilca discovered the inflated expense report, she would not be fulfilling her ethical responsibilities of integrity and credibility if she allowed the reimbursement.

### Dilemma #2

> As the accountant of Entrée Computer, you are aware of your company's weak financial condition. Entrée is close to signing a lucrative contract that should ensure its future. To do so, the controller states that the company must report a profit this year (ending December 31). He suggests, "Two customers have placed orders that are really not supposed to be shipped until early January. Ask production to fill and ship those orders on December 31 so we can record them in this year's sales."

The resolution of this dilemma is less clear-cut. Many people believe that following the controller's suggestion to manipulate the company's income would violate the standards of competence, integrity, and credibility. Others would argue that because Entrée Computer already has the customer orders, shipping the goods and recording the sale in December is still ethical behaviour. You might discuss the available alternatives with the next managerial level in order to determine what course of action would be warranted.

### Dilemma #3

> As a new accounting staff member at the YMCA, your supervisor has asked you to prepare the yearly GST/HST Report, which the government uses to determine its reimbursement to the charity for allowable GST/HST expenditures. The report requires specialized knowledge that you do not believe you possess. The supervisor is busy planning for the coming year and cannot offer much guidance while you prepare the report.

This situation is not as rare as you might think. You may be asked to perform tasks that you do not feel qualified to perform. The competence standard requires you to perform professional duties in accordance with laws, regulations, and technical standards; but laws and regulations are always changing. For this reason, the competence standard also requires you to continually develop knowledge and skills. Accounting professionals are required to complete annual continuing professional education to fulfill this responsibility. However, even continuing professional education courses will not cover every situation you may encounter.

In this case, advise your supervisor that you currently lack the knowledge required to complete the GST/HST Report. By doing so, you are complying with the competence standard that requires you to recognize and communicate any limitations that would preclude you from fulfilling an activity. You should ask for training on the report preparation and supervision by someone experienced in preparing the report. If the supervisor denies your requests, you should ask him or her to reassign the GST/HST Report to a qualified staff member.

### Dilemma #4

Your company is negotiating a large multiyear sales contract that, if won, would substantially increase the company's future earnings. At a dinner party over the weekend, your friends ask you how you like your job and the company you work for. In your enthusiasm, you tell them not only about your responsibilities at work but also about the contract negotiations. As soon as the words pop out of your mouth, you worry that you have said too much.

This situation is difficult to avoid. You may be so excited about your job and the company you work for that it is difficult to keep information from unintentionally slipping out during casual conversation with friends and family. The confidentiality standard requires you to refrain from disclosing information or using confidential information for unethical or illegal advantage. Was the contract negotiation confidential? If so, would your friends invest in company stock in hopes that the negotiations increase stock prices? Or were the negotiations public knowledge in the financial community? If so, your friends would gain no illegal advantage from the information. Cases such as those involving Martha Stewart remind us that insider trading (use of inside knowledge for illegal gain) has serious consequences. Even seemingly mundane information about company operations could give competitors an advantage. Therefore, it is best to disclose only information that is meant for public consumption.

## DECISION GUIDELINES

Prime made the following considerations in designing its managerial accounting system to provide managers with the information they need to run operations efficiently and effectively.*

| Decision | Guidelines |
|---|---|
| I need information that will help me make decisions and determine the future of the organization. The information provided by the financial accounting system doesn't seem to provide what I really need. Is there something else that I can use? | Managerial accounting provides information that helps managers plan, direct, and control operations and make better decisions. The information has a<br>• *future* orientation<br>• focus on relevance to business decisions |
| I've been told that I don't need to follow ASPE or IFRS guidelines when I create my managerial accounting system. What do I use as guidelines for how to establish a managerial accounting system? | Managers design the managerial accounting system so that the benefits (from helping managers make wiser decisions) outweigh the costs of the system. |
| Where should management accountants be placed within the organizational structure? | In the past, most management accountants worked in isolated departments. Now, management accountants are deployed throughout the company. Accountants are trained in strategic leadership and planning, which may be the reason why many are employed as managers or senior analysts and often rise to the position of president or vice president. |
| I'm considering hiring a management accountant for my organization. What skills should I be looking for in this individual? | Because of their expanding role within the organization, most management accountants need financial and managerial accounting knowledge, problem-solving and decision-making skills, knowledge of how a business functions, the ability to lead and to work on teams, knowledge of professional and ethical standards, and written and oral communication skills. |

*Certified Management Accountants of Ontario.

*continued*

| Decision | Guidelines | |
|---|---|---|
| I have encountered an ethical dilemma. Are there some guidelines or principles that I can use to help me make an appropriate decision? | CPA Canada Principles of Ethical Conduct | |
| | Professional Behaviour | *conduct which maintains the good reputation of the profession* |
| | Integrity and Due Care | *practise diligently, in accordance with applicable technical and professional standards* |
| | Professional Competence | *maintaining of professional skill and competence knowledge and compliance, of and with, professional standards and pertinent legislation* |
| | Confidentiality | *information acquired as a function of professional activity will not be disclosed to any third party, without proper cause and specific authority* |
| | Objectivity | *judgment will not be compromised by bias, conflict of interest, or undue influence* |

# SUMMARY PROBLEM 1

**Requirements**

**1.** Each of the following statements describes a responsibility of management. Match each statement to the management responsibility being fulfilled.

| Statement | Management Responsibility |
|---|---|
| 1. Identifying alternative courses of action and choosing among them | a. Planning |
| 2. Running the company on a day-to-day basis | b. Decision making |
| 3. Determining whether the company's units are operating according to plan | c. Directing |
| 4. Setting goals and objectives for the company and determining strategies to achieve them | d. Controlling |

**2.** Are the following statements more descriptive of managerial accounting or financial accounting information?

a. Describes historical transactions with external parties
b. Is not required by any authoritative body, such as the provincial Securities Commissions
c. Reports on the company's subunits, such as products, geographical areas, and departments
d. Is intended to be used by creditors and investors
e. Is formatted in accordance with ASPE or IFRS

**3.** Each of the following statements paraphrases an ethical responsibility. Match each statement to the standard of ethical professional practice being fulfilled. Each standard may be used more than once or not at all.

| Responsibility | Standard of Ethical Professional Practice |
|---|---|
| 1. Do not disclose company information unless authorized to do so. | a. Professional Competence |
| 2. Continue to develop skills and knowledge. | b. Confidentiality |
| 3. Do not bias the information and reports presented to management. | c. Integrity and Due Care |
| 4. If you do not have the skills to complete a task correctly, do not pretend you do. | d. Professional Behaviour |
| 5. Do not base decisions for the organization on what might serve your own personal interests best. | e. Objectivity |
| 6. Avoid actual *and* apparent conflicts of interest. | |

## ▪ SOLUTIONS

**Requirement 1**

1. (b) Decision making
2. (c) Directing
3. (d) Controlling
4. (a) Planning

**Requirement 2**

a. Financial accounting
b. Managerial accounting
c. Managerial accounting
d. Financial accounting
e. Financial accounting

**Requirement 3**

1. (b) Confidentiality
2. (a) Professional Competence
3. (d) Professional Behaviour
4. (a) Professional Competence
5. (c) Integrity and Due Care
6. (e) Objectivity

# What Regulatory and Business Issues Affect Today's Management Accountants?

5 Discuss and analyze the implications of regulatory and business trends.

The business world is continually changing. Let us look at some of the current regulatory and business issues that affect managers and the managerial accounting systems that support them. These issues include the Sarbanes-Oxley Act (SOX), International Financial Reporting Standards (IFRS), Extensible Business Reporting Language (XBRL), and the shifting economy. After considering these issues, we will look at some of the tools companies use to compete in the global marketplace.

**Why is this important?**
**SOX** puts more pressure on companies, their **managers**, and their auditors to ensure that **investors** get financial information that **fairly reflects** the company's **operations**.

## Sarbanes-Oxley Act of 2002

As a result of corporate accounting scandals, such as those at Enron and WorldCom, the U.S. Congress enacted the Sarbanes-Oxley Act of 2002 (SOX). The purpose of SOX is to restore trust in publicly traded corporations, their management, their financial statements, and their auditors. SOX enhances internal control and financial reporting requirements and establishes new regulatory requirements for publicly traded companies and their independent auditors. Publicly traded companies have spent millions of dollars upgrading their internal controls and accounting systems to comply with SOX regulations. Although this legislation originated in the United States, it has had a major impact on Canadian financial reporting practices. Our standards have incorporated many similar features with respect to auditor independence and internal controls. Some of the impacts on the Canadian market are shown in Exhibit 1-6.

## International Financial Reporting Standards (IFRS)

As a result of globalization, the need for consistent reporting standards for all companies in the world has grown. In response, the securities commissions of many countries have recently moved to adopt International Financial Reporting Standards (IFRS) for all publicly traded companies within the next few years. In Canada, this adoption took place in 2011. Currently, a company operating in several different countries often must prepare several sets of financial statements using different accounting standards. These companies will need to prepare only one set of financial statements if all the countries have adopted IFRS. While the transition to IFRS may be time consuming and expensive, in the long run

**EXHIBIT 1-6** Some Important Results of SOX

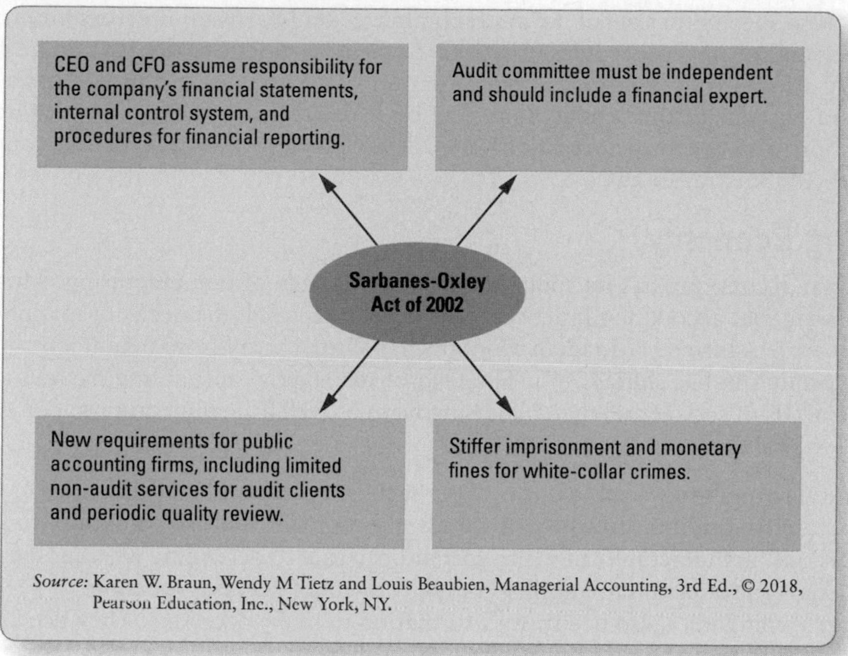


*Source:* Karen W. Braun, Wendy M Tietz and Louis Beaubien, Managerial Accounting, 3rd Ed., © 2018, Pearson Education, Inc., New York, NY.

it should actually save companies money and make the markets more efficient. You can keep abreast of current IFRS developments and implications for accounting information at www.IFRS.org.

## Extensible Business Reporting Language (XBRL)

Wouldn't it be nice if managers, analysts, investors, and regulators could easily access public company information over the internet without having to *manually* read PDF documents and extract the data they need for decision making? Extensible Business Reporting Language (XBRL) enables companies to release financial and business information in a format that can be quickly, efficiently, and cost-effectively accessed, sorted, and analyzed over the internet. XBRL uses a standardized coding system to "tag" each piece of reported financial and business data so that it can be read by computer programs rather than human eyes. For example, *Sales Revenue* would be tagged with the same code by all companies so that a computer program could extract *Sales Revenue* information from an individual company or a selected group of companies.

XBRL has several advantages:

- It decreases the need for laborious, manual searches though corporate reports for specific pieces of information.
- It decreases the time companies spend converting their financial information into various government-prescribed formats.
- It allows managers to easily compare their results to those of other companies and to industry averages.
- Investors and managers can "slice and dice" financial information however they want to suit their decision-making needs.
- It should promote the more consistent use of financial terminology, since all data must be tagged using a preset, yet extensible, classification system.

Canadian organizations began filing their annual financial statements using XBRL codifications on a voluntary basis in May 2007. The financial statements are filed in both XBRL format and PDF format on the online database for Canadian public companies, SEDAR.com. The Canadian Securities Administrators (CSA) published rules regarding the need for the CEO and the CFO to sign, and authorize the accuracy of, annual reports. These CSA rules, implemented over a span of about four years starting in 2003, also specify the role of the audit committee on boards of directors, internal controls, and a number of other rules. These CSA rules are similar to the SOX requirements. The CSA also actively encourages participation of companies in the voluntary implementation because of the benefits that may be realized through the improved access to information. You can keep abreast of XBRL developments at www.XBRL.org and www.securities-administrators.ca/.

### Shifting Economy

Managerial accounting has its roots in the industrial age of manufacturing. Most traditional managerial accounting practices were developed to fill the needs of manufacturing firms. However, since the Canadian economy has shifted away from manufacturing, managerial accounting has shifted, too. The field of managerial accounting has *expanded* to meet the needs of service and merchandising firms as well as manufacturers. For example, consider the following.

1. Manufacturers still need to know how much each unit of their product costs to manufacture. In addition to using this information for inventory valuation and pricing decisions, manufacturers now use cost information to determine whether they should outsource production to another company or to an overseas location.
2. Service companies also need cost information to make decisions. They need to know the cost of providing a service rather than manufacturing a product. For example, banks must include the cost of servicing chequing and savings accounts in the fees they charge customers. And hospitals need to know the cost of performing appendectomies to justify reimbursement from insurance companies and government.
3. Retailers need to consider importing costs when determining the cost of their merchandise. Because many goods are now produced overseas rather than domestically, determining the cost of a product is often more difficult than it was in the past. Management accountants need to consider foreign currency exchange, shipping costs, and import tariffs when determining the cost of imported products.

## How Do Companies Compete in Today's Global Marketplace?

The barriers to international trade have fallen over the past decades, allowing foreign companies to compete with domestic firms. Firms that are not highly efficient, innovative, and responsive to business trends will vanish from the global market. However, global markets also provide highly competitive domestic companies with great opportunities for growth.

Globalization has several implications for managerial accounting:

- Stiffer competition means managers need more accurate and timely information to make wise business decisions. Companies can no longer afford to make decisions by the "seat of their pants." Detailed, accurate, and real-time cost information has become a necessity for survival.
- Companies must decide whether to expand sales and/or production into foreign countries. To do so, managers need comprehensive estimates of the costs of running international operations and the benefits that can be reaped.
- Companies can learn new management techniques by observing their international competitors. For example, the management philosophy of **lean production**, first developed in Japan by Toyota, is now being used by many North American companies to cut costs, improve quality, and speed production.

In the following sections we briefly describe several tools that companies use to compete in the global marketplace. How do managers decide which of these initiatives to undertake? They use **cost–benefit analysis**, which weighs the expected costs of taking an action against the expected benefits of the action.

## Sustainability, Social Responsibility, and the Triple Bottom Line

In recent years, there has been an increasing awareness and growing interest in **sustainability** and social responsibility by both consumers and corporations. Sustainability is most often defined as the ability to meet the needs of the present without compromising the ability of future generations to meet their own needs.[8] Others define it as an expansion on the golden rule: "Do unto others (including future generations) as you would have them do unto you."[9] The first definition focuses more on environmental responsibility, while the second definition recognizes the additional component of social responsibility. As a result, many companies are beginning to adhere to the notion of a **triple bottom line**. The triple bottom line recognizes that a company's performance should not only be viewed in terms of its ability to generate economic profits for its owners, as has traditionally been the case, but also by its impact on people and the planet. Thus, sustainability can be viewed in terms of three interrelated factors that influence a company's ability to survive and thrive in the long-run: profit, people, and planet.

To move toward environmental sustainability, companies are introducing "green initiatives"—ways of doing business that have fewer negative consequences for the earth's resources. They've also recognized the need to be socially responsible—carefully considering how their business affects employees, consumers, citizens, and entire communities. Many companies have introduced means of giving back to their local communities, by monetarily supporting local schools and charities. Businesses are now viewing sustainability and social responsibility as opportunities for innovation and business development. These initiatives not only allow a company to "do the right thing," but they also can lead to economic profits by increasing demand for a company's products and services.

In every chapter of this text, you will see a special section illustrating how management accounting can help companies pursue environmentally sustainable and socially responsible business practices. These sections will be marked with a green recycle symbol and will also point you to corresponding homework problems.

## Tools for Time-Based Competition

The internet, electronic commerce (e-commerce), and other new technologies speed the pace of business. Think about your last trip to the grocery store or hardware store. Did you use the self-scanning checkout? Retailers install expensive self-scanning technology to cut labour costs and give shoppers an alternative to standing in checkout lines. Some studies have shown that, on average, the self-scanning checkout process is really not faster. However, shoppers *perceive* the checkout time to be faster because they are actively engaged rather than passively standing in line. Businesses are doing whatever they can to shorten the time customers have to wait for their orders. Why? Because *time* is the latest competitive weapon in business.

### Advanced Information Systems

Many small businesses use QuickBooks or Sage Simply Accounting software to track their costs, prepare reports, and present information needed to run the business. But large companies are turning to enterprise resource planning (ERP) systems that can integrate all of a company's worldwide functions, departments, and data. ERP systems such as SAP, Oracle, and PeopleSoft gather company data into a centralized data warehouse. The system feeds the data into software for all of the company's business activities, from budgeting and purchasing to production and customer service.

[8]1987 World Commission on Environment and Development, www.un.org/documents/ga/res/42/ares42-187.htm

[9]Gary Langenwalter, *Business Sustainability: Keeping Lean but with More Green for the Company's Long Haul*, 2010, AICPA, Lewisville, Texas.

Advantages of ERP systems include the following:

- Companies streamline their operations before mapping them into ERP software. Streamlining operations saves money.
- ERP helps companies respond quickly to changes. A change in sales instantly ripples through the ERP's purchases, production, shipping, and accounting systems.
- An ERP system can replace hundreds of separate software systems, such as different software in different regions, or different payroll, shipping, and production software systems.

However, ERP systems are expensive and require a large commitment of time and people. For example, major installations at Fujitsu and Allstate cost each of these companies approximately $40 to $60 million. However, the expected benefits from the system are greater, with Allstate reporting to have saved $100 million in processing costs within 18 months.[10]

### E-commerce

To survive in a competitive, globally wired economy, companies use the internet in everyday operations such as budgeting, planning, selling, and customer service. Companies use business-to-business e-commerce to complete transactions with each other. Electronic purchases between businesses are often untouched by human hands, generate little if any paper, and avoid the time and cost of processing paperwork.

E-commerce is also an important means of **supply-chain management**, where companies exchange information with suppliers to reduce costs, improve quality, and speed delivery of goods and services from suppliers to the company itself. For example, companies that supply component parts to Dell use the internet to access Dell's daily inventory levels and current demand for parts. Access to real-time information lets suppliers automate the size of the next day's shipment, which in turn helps Dell cut order-to-delivery times and control costs.

### STOP & THINK

Electronically billing customers has become popular. Analysts estimate the following:

1. Companies save $7 per invoice by billing customers electronically.
2. The average large company issues 800,000 invoices a year.
3. The average cost of installing an e-billing system is $500,000. Should companies that issue 800,000 invoices a year consider e-billing?

**Answer:** Yes, these companies should consider e-billing. Comparing expected benefits to costs reveals significant expected net benefits from e-billing:

| | |
|---|---|
| *Expected benefits:* | |
| 800,000 invoices × $7 savings per invoice .............. | $5,600,000 |
| *Expected costs:* | |
| Installation of e-billing system .............................. | (500,000) |
| Net expected benefits ............................................ | $5,100,000 |

## Traditional Production Systems

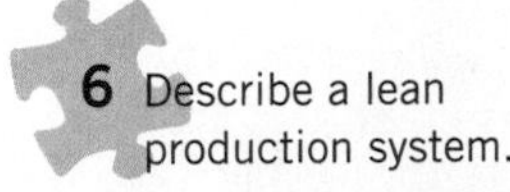
6 Describe a lean production system.

Traditional production systems are often described as "push" systems. Once the production schedule for the period has been determined, products are "pushed" through the manufacturing process and then stored in finished goods inventory until sold. Traditional

[10]R. Banham, "Better Budgets: Replacing a whim and a prayer with relevant data," *Journal of Accountancy*, February 2000, www.journalofaccountancy.com/Issues/2000/Feb/BetterBudgets.htm

systems often keep large inventories of raw materials, work in process, and finished goods on hand. Why?

> **Why is this important?**
> To survive in the **global marketplace**, businesses must quickly respond to customer **demand**, providing high-quality products and **services** at a reasonable price.

1. Companies often buy more raw materials than they need because the materials may be of poor quality. As a result, the materials may not be usable or may break during production and require replacement.
2. Companies often make products in large batches to spread set-up costs over many units. As a result, companies often buy large quantities of raw materials and then have large quantities of finished units.
3. Companies often keep extra work in process inventory *between* departments so that each department will have something to continue working on in the event production stops or slows in an earlier department. For example, in Exhibit 1-7, we see the series of production steps required to produce drill bits from bar stock (the raw materials). If the company keeps some work in process inventory *between* the grinding and smoothing operations, the smoothing operation can continue even if the shaping or grinding operations slow or come to a halt as a result of machine breakdown, absence due to sick workers, or other production problems.

**EXHIBIT 1-7** Sequence of Operations for Drill-Bit Production

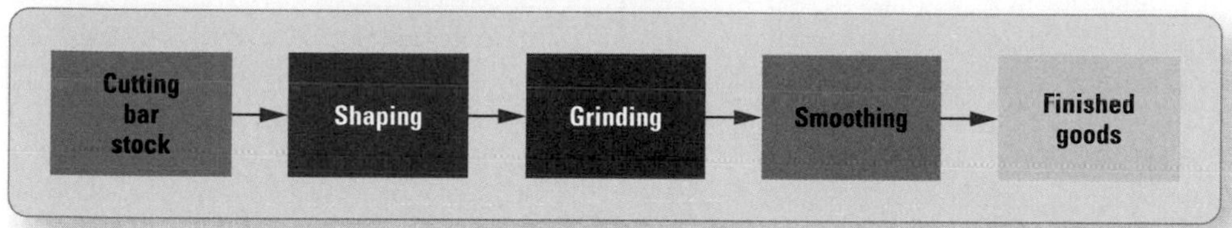


Companies often keep large inventories to protect themselves from uncertainty. Large raw material inventories protect against delayed deliveries from suppliers. Large finished goods inventories protect against lost sales if customer demand is higher than expected. These are all valid reasons for keeping large inventories. However, large inventories can be a problem:

1. Inventories use cash. Companies incur interest expense or forgo interest revenue on that cash. If a company has to borrow money to pay for inventory, it incurs interest expense on the loan. Even if a company uses its own cash to fund the inventory, it misses the opportunity to earn interest on that cash. In other words, if the cash were not used to purchase excessive inventory, the company could invest it and earn a return.
2. Large inventories often hide quality problems, production bottlenecks, and obsolescence. Inventory may spoil, be broken or stolen, or become obsolete as it sits in storage and waits to be used or sold. Companies in the high-tech and fashion industries are particularly susceptible to inventory obsolescence. What would a computer manufacturer do with computer chips purchased six months earlier? The chips are obsolete and unusable.
3. The activities of storing and taking items out of storage are very expensive. Inventory management software such as Activity Based Costing (ABC) and Activity Based Management (ABM) have helped uncover the cost of these non-value-added activities.

Because of the problems associated with large inventories, many companies are now striving to use lean production systems that keep inventories to a minimum.

## Lean Production Systems

Lean production is both a philosophy and a business strategy of manufacturing without waste. One primary goal of a lean production system is to eliminate the waste of time and money that accompanies large inventories. Therefore, lean companies adopt a **just-in-time (JIT)** inventory philosophy. As the name suggests, JIT inventory focuses on purchasing

**EXHIBIT 1-8** Traditional System versus JIT System

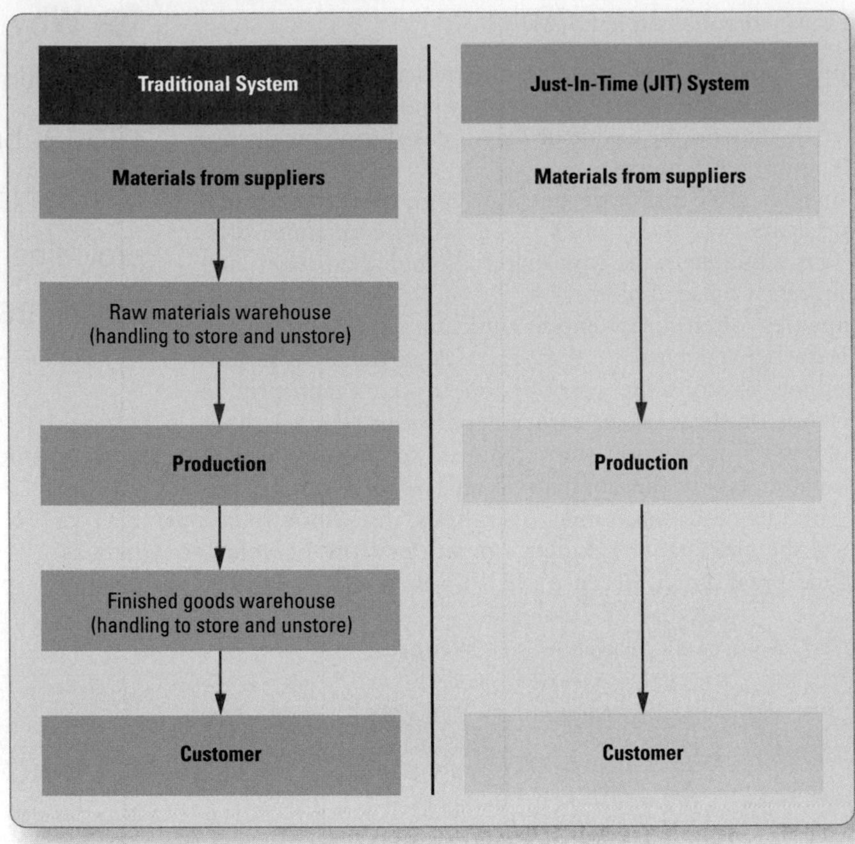


raw materials *just in time* for production and then completing finished goods *just in time* for delivery to customers. By doing so, companies eliminate the waste of storing and unstoring raw materials and finished goods, as pictured in Exhibit 1-8.

For example, Dell workers receive orders via a monitor and assemble a desktop computer every three to five minutes. Most days, workers finish more than 25,000 computers, which ship directly to customers. However, the plant rarely holds more than two *hours* of inventory![11] How do they do it?

Most companies that adopt lean production have several common characteristics that help minimize the amount of inventory that is kept on hand yet enable the company to quickly satisfy customer demand. These characteristics are described next.

### Production Occurs in Self-Contained Cells

A traditional drill-bit manufacturer would group all cutting machines in one area, all shaping machines in another area, all grinding machines in a third area, and all smoothing machines in a fourth area, as illustrated in Panel A of Exhibit 1-9. After switching to lean production, the company would group the machines in self-contained production cells, or production lines, as in Panel B of Exhibit 1-9. The goal is continuous production without interruptions or work-in-process inventories. These self-contained production cells minimize the time and cost involved with physically moving parts across the factory to other departments.

### Broad Employee Roles

Employees working in production cells do more than operate a single machine. They also conduct maintenance, perform set-ups, inspect their own work, and operate other machines. For example, look at Panel B of Exhibit 1-9. A worker in Drill Bit Production Line 1 would be cross-trained to operate all of the machines (cutting, shaping, grinding,

[11]Kathryn Jones, "The Dell Way," *Business 2.0*, February 2003, www.business2.com

**EXHIBIT 1-9** Equipment Arrangement in Traditional and Lean Production Systems

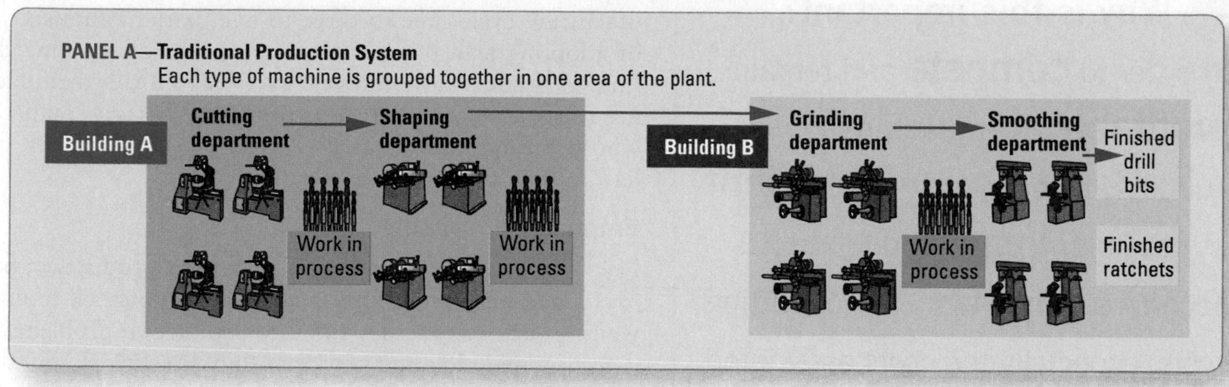


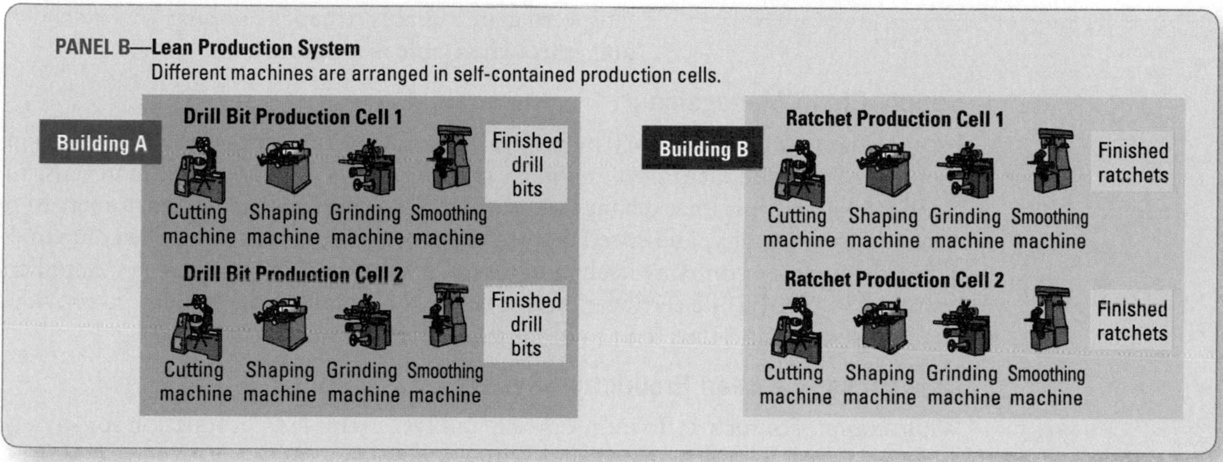


and smoothing) in that cell. This cross-training boosts morale and lowers costs. Employees who perform a number of duties rather than one repetitive duty tend to have higher job satisfaction.

### Small Batches Produced Just in Time

Lean companies schedule production in small batches *just in time* to satisfy customer needs. As a result, they do not need to carry extra finished goods inventory. In this "demand-pull system," the customer order—the "demand"—triggers the start of the production process and "pulls" the batch through production. Each order, even if very small, is usually its own batch. Even raw materials are usually not purchased until a customer order is received. The demand-pull system extends back to suppliers of materials, who end up making frequent, small deliveries of defect-free raw materials just in time for production. The lean "pull" system replaces the traditional "push" system in which large quantities of raw materials are "pushed" through the production process to be stored in finished goods inventory until sold.

### Shortened Set-up Times

Since the product is not started until a customer order is received, lean companies must focus on reducing the time it takes to set up the machines used for more than one product. Employee training and technology helped Toyota cut set-up times from several hours to a few minutes. This increases flexibility in scheduling production to meet customer orders, which, in turn, increases customer satisfaction and company profits.

### Shortened Manufacturing Cycle Times

Lean companies must also produce their products very quickly. Dell's manufacturing cycle time is three to five minutes. GED Integrated Solutions, a window manufacturer, used to

**Why is this important?**

In order to **compete** and remain **profitable**, manufacturers must cut costs by becoming as **efficient** as possible. **Lean** production has become an important tool for cutting costs, especially the costs associated with carrying inventory.

require three weeks to complete an order. GED has cut manufacturing cycle time to three to five days. Within six years of adopting lean production, Harley-Davidson reduced the time to produce a motorcycle by 77%. Shorter manufacturing times also protect companies from foreign competitors whose cheaper products take longer to ship. Delivery speed has become a competitive weapon.

#### Emphasis on Quality

Lean companies focus on producing their products right the *first* time, *every* time. They have no backup stock to give to waiting customers if they run into production problems, and defects in materials and workmanship can slow or shut down production (there is no time to rework faulty products). So lean companies emphasize "building in" quality rather than "inspecting in" quality (that is, hoping to catch defective units through sample inspections).

#### Supply-Chain Management

Because there are no inventory buffers, lean production requires close coordination with suppliers. These suppliers must guarantee *on-time delivery* of *defect-free* materials. Supply-chain management is the exchange of information with suppliers and customers to reduce costs, improve quality, and speed delivery of goods and services from the company's suppliers, through the company itself, and on to the company's end customers. Suppliers that bear the ISO 9001:2008 certification (see below) have proven their ability to provide high-quality products and thus tend to be suppliers for lean manufacturers.

#### Drawbacks to a Lean Production System

While companies such as Toyota, Carrier, and Dell credit lean production for saving them millions of dollars, the system is not without problems. With no inventory buffers, lean producers are vulnerable when problems strike suppliers or distributors. For example, Ford cut production of its SUVs in response to the tire shortage resulting from Firestone's tire recall. It also had to shut down five of its U.S. plants when engine deliveries from Canadian suppliers were late due to security-related transportation delays in the wake of the World Trade Center attacks.

## Total Quality Management

All companies, not just lean producers, must deliver high-quality goods and services in order to remain competitive. <u>Total quality management (TQM)</u> is one key to succeeding in the global economy. The goal of TQM is to delight customers by providing them with superior products and services. As part of TQM, each business function examines its own activities and works to improve performance by *continually* setting higher goals.

### ISO 9001:2008

Many firms want to demonstrate their commitment to continuous quality improvement. The International Organization for Standardization (ISO), made up of 157 member countries, has developed international quality management standards and guidelines. Firms may become <u>ISO 9001:2008</u> certified by complying with the quality management standards and undergoing extensive audits of their quality management processes. The prestigious certification gives firms a competitive advantage in the global marketplace since many companies will conduct business only with certified firms.

The certification does not only apply to manufacturing firms. Service firms account for over 32% of all certificates issued. The Standards Council of Canada actively encourages Canadian participation in national and international standards such as the ISO through its mandate from the Standards Council of Canada Act. This act was established in 1985 and enables the Council to complete a variety of programs and services, including accrediting organizations that meet specific Canadian standards of quality and assisting Canadians and Canadian organizations, both financially and administratively, that wish to seek voluntary standardizations in and outside Canada. For more information regarding the Standards Council of Canada and its programs and services, please refer to its Website: www.scc.ca.

# How Do Managers Improve Quality?

7 Describe and use the costs of quality framework.

As discussed previously, lean companies strive for high-quality production. Poor-quality materials or defective manufacturing processes can slow or even shut down production. Since a lean production system only produces what is currently needed, it is essential that production consistently generates high-quality products.

To meet this challenge, many companies adopt total quality management (TQM). The goal of TQM is to provide customers with superior products and services. Each business function in the value chain continually examines its own activities to improve quality and eliminate defects and waste. Those companies that have already adopted ABC have a head start. They have already identified their primary activities, so now they can concentrate on making those activities more efficient or finding ways to eliminate any non-value-added activities.

Most companies find that if they invest more in the front end of the value chain (R&D and design), they can generate savings in the back end of the value chain (production, marketing, distribution, and customer service). Why? Because carefully designed products and manufacturing processes reduce manufacturing time, inspections, rework, and warranty claims. When world-class companies such as Bombardier adopt TQM, they *design* and *build* quality into their products rather than having to *inspect* and *repair* later, as many traditional manufacturers do.

## Costs of Quality

As part of TQM, many companies prepare **Cost of Quality Reports**. Cost of Quality Reports categorize and list the costs incurred by the company related to quality. Once managers know the extent of their costs of quality, they can start to identify ways for the company to improve quality, while at the same time controlling costs.

Quality-related costs generally fall into four different categories: **prevention costs**, **appraisal costs**, **internal failure costs**, and **external failure costs**. These categories form the framework for a Cost of Quality Report. The following provides a brief description of each.

1. Prevention costs are costs incurred to *avoid* producing poor-quality goods or services. Often, poor quality is caused by the variability of the production process or the complexity of the product design. To reduce the variability of the production process, companies often automate as much of the process as possible. Employee training can help decrease variability in nonautomated processes. In addition, reducing the complexity of the product design or manufacturing process can prevent the potential for error: The fewer parts or processes, the fewer things that can go wrong. Frequently, companies need to literally "go back to the drawing board" (the R&D and design stages of the value chain) to make a significant difference in preventing production problems. For example, Dell reengineered its assembly process to cut in half the number of times humans touch the hard-drive. As a result, the hard-drive failure rate dropped 40%. Likewise, Hewlett-Packard was able to reduce its defect rate by significantly reducing the number of parts that went into a desktop printer.
2. Appraisal costs are costs incurred to *detect* poor-quality goods or services. Intel incurs appraisal costs when it tests its products. One procedure, called burn-in, heats circuits to a high temperature. A circuit that fails the burn-in test is also likely to fail in customer use. Nissan tests 100% of the vehicles that roll off its assembly lines. Each vehicle is put through the paces on Nissan's all-terrain test track. Any problems are identified before the vehicle leaves the plant.
3. Internal failure costs are costs incurred on defective units *before* delivery to customers. For example, if Nissan does identify a problem, the vehicle is reworked to eliminate the defect before it is allowed to leave the plant. In the worst-case scenario, a product may be so defective that it cannot be reworked and must be completely scrapped. In this case, the entire cost of manufacturing the defective unit, plus any disposal cost, is an internal failure cost.

4. External failure costs are costs incurred because the defective goods or services are not detected until *after* delivery is made to customers. For example, Toyota recalled almost 4,000,000 vehicles in 2009 and 2,300,000 vehicles in 2010 because of a problem with the accelerator pedal, which had the potential to cause the cars to accelerate uncontrollably and cause crashes. Along with incurring substantial cost for repairing or replacing the recalled pedals and other parts, the publicity of this defect could cause significant damage to the company's reputation. Damage to a company's reputation from selling defective units to end customers can considerably harm the company's future sales. Unsatisfied customers will avoid buying from the company in the future. Even worse, unsatisfied customers tend to tell their neighbours, families, and friends about any poor experiences with products or services. As a result, a company's reputation for poor quality can increase at an exponential rate. To capture the extent of this problem, external failure costs should include an estimate of how much profit the company is losing due to having a reputation for poor quality.

Exhibit 1-10 lists some common examples of the four different costs of quality. Most prevention costs occur in the R&D and design stages of the value chain. In contrast, most appraisal and internal failure costs occur in the production element of the value chain. External failure costs occur in the customer service stage. Managers make trade-offs among these costs. Many prevention costs are incurred only periodically, while internal and external failure costs are ongoing. One expert estimates that $0.08 spent on prevention saves most manufacturers $1.00 in failure costs.

**EXHIBIT 1-10** Four Types of Quality Costs

| Prevention Costs | Appraisal Costs |
|---|---|
| Training personnel | Inspection of incoming materials |
| Evaluating potential suppliers | Inspection at various stages of production |
| Using better materials | Inspection of final products or services |
| Preventive maintenance | Product testing |
| Improved equipment | Cost of inspection equipment |
| Redesigning product or process | |

| Internal Failure Costs | External Failure Costs |
|---|---|
| Production loss caused by downtime | Lost profits from lost customers |
| Rework | Warranty costs |
| Abnormal quantities of scrap | Service costs at customer sites |
| Rejected product units | Sales returns and allowances due to quality problems |
| Disposal of rejected units | Product liability claims |
| Machine breakdowns | Cost of recalls |

Prevention and appraisal costs are sometimes referred to as "conformance costs" since they are the costs incurred to make sure the product or service conforms to its intended design. In other words, these are the costs incurred to make sure the product is *not* defective. On the other hand, internal and external failure costs are sometimes referred to as "nonconformance costs." These are the costs incurred because the product or service *is* defective.

The costs of quality are not limited to manufacturers. Service firms and merchandising companies also incur costs of quality. For example, public accounting firms spend a lot of money providing ongoing professional training to their staff. They also develop standardized audit checklists to minimize the variability of the audit procedures performed for each client.

These measures help to *prevent* audit failures. Both audit managers and partners review audit work papers to *appraise* whether the audit procedures performed and evidence gathered are sufficient on each audit engagement. If audit procedures or evidence are deemed to be lacking (*internal failure*), the audit manager or partner will instruct the audit team to perform additional procedures before the firm will issue an audit opinion on the client's financial statements. This parallels the "rework" a manufacturer might perform on a product that is not up to par. Finally, recent audit failures, such as those at Enron and WorldCom, illustrate just how expensive and devastating *external failure* can be to a public accounting firm. The once prestigious international firm Arthur Andersen & Co. actually went out of business because of the reputation damage caused by its audit failure at Enron.

Now that we have examined the four costs of quality, let us see how they can be presented to management in the form of a Cost of Quality Report. Let us assume Candent Dental Laboratory, a manufacturer of dental appliances and products, is having difficulty competing with Shaw Group because it does not have the reputation for high quality that Shaw Group enjoys. To examine this issue, management has prepared the Cost of Quality Report shown in Exhibit 1-11.

**Why is this important?**

Businesses compete with each other on the basis of price and quality. Cost of Quality reports help managers determine how they should spend money to ensure that consumers get the best quality product for the price.

**EXHIBIT 1-11** Candent's Cost of Quality Report

| | Costs Incurred | Total Costs of Quality | Percentage of Total Costs of Quality (rounded) |
|---|---|---|---|
| **Prevention Costs:** | | | |
| Employee training | $ 125,000 | | |
| Total prevention costs | | $ 125,000 | 6.1%* |
| **Appraisal Costs:** | | | |
| Testing | $ 175,000 | | |
| Total appraisal costs | | $ 175,000 | 8.5% |
| **Internal Failure Costs:** | | | |
| Rework | $ 300,000 | | |
| Cost of rejected units | 50,000 | | |
| Total internal failure costs | | $ 350,000 | 17.0% |
| **External Failure Costs:** | | | |
| Lost profits from lost sales due to impaired reputation | $1,000,000 | | |
| Sales return processing | 175,000 | | |
| Warranty costs | 235,000 | | |
| Total external failure costs | | $1,410,000 | 68.4% |
| Total costs of quality | | $2,050,000 | 100% |

*The percentage of total is computed as the total cost of the category divided by the total costs of quality. For example: 6.1% = $125,000 ÷ $2,050,000.

Notice how Candent identifies, categorizes, and quantifies all of the costs it incurs relating to quality. Candent also calculates the percentage of total costs of quality that are incurred in each cost category. This helps company managers see just how *little* they are spending on conformance costs (prevention and appraisal). Most of their costs are internal and external failure costs. The best way to reduce these failure costs is to invest more in prevention and appraisal. Candent managers can now begin to focus on how they might be able to prevent these failures from occurring.

## Using the Costs of Quality Framework to Aid Decisions

After analyzing the Cost of Quality Report, the CEO is considering spending the following amounts on a new quality program:

| | |
|---|---|
| Inspect raw materials | $100,000 |
| Reengineer the production process to improve product quality | 750,000 |
| Screen and certify suppliers | 25,000 |
| Conduct preventive maintenance on plant equipment | 75,000 |
| Total costs of implementing quality programs | $950,000 |

Although these measures will not completely eliminate internal and external failure costs, Candent expects this quality program to *reduce* costs by the following amounts:

| | |
|---|---|
| Reduction in lost profits from lost sales due to impaired reputation | $ 800,000 |
| Fewer sales returns to be processed | 150,000 |
| Reduction in rework costs | 250,000 |
| Reduction in warranty costs | 225,000 |
| Total cost savings | $1,425,000 |

According to these projections, Candent's quality initiative will cost $950,000 but result in total savings of $1,425,000—for a net benefit of $475,000. When performing a cost–benefit analysis, some companies simply compare all of the projected costs ($950,000) with all of the projected benefits ($1,425,000) as shown previously. Other

**EXHIBIT 1-12** Cost-Benefit Analysis of Candent Proposed Quality Program

| | Additional (Costs) and Cost Savings | Total New (Costs) or Cost Savings |
|---|---|---|
| **Prevention Costs:** | | |
| Reengineer the production process | $(750,000) | |
| Supplier screening and certification | (25,000) | |
| Preventive maintenance on equipment | (75,000) | |
| Total additional prevention costs | | $ (850,000) |
| **Appraisal Costs:** | | |
| Inspect raw materials | $(100,000) | (100,000) |
| Total additional appraisal costs | | |
| **Internal Failure Costs:** | | |
| Reduction of rework costs | $ 250,000 | |
| Total internal failure cost savings | | 250,000 |
| **External Failure Costs:** | | |
| Reduction of lost profits from lost sales | $ 800,000 | |
| Reduction of sales returns | 150,000 | |
| Reduction of warranty costs | 225,000 | |
| Total external failure cost savings | | 1,175,000 |
| Total savings (costs) from quality program | | $ 475,000 |

companies prefer to organize their cost–benefit analysis by cost category so that managers have a better idea of how the quality initiative will affect each cost category.

Exhibit 1-12 shows that by increasing prevention costs (by $850,000) and appraisal costs (by $100,000), Candent will be able to save $250,000 in internal failure costs and $1,175,000 in external failure costs. In total, Candent expects a net benefit of $475,000 if it undertakes the quality initiative. By spending more on conformance costs (prevention and appraisal costs), Candent saves even more on nonconformance costs (internal and external failure costs).

The analysis shown in Exhibit 1-12 appears very straightforward. However, quality costs can be hard to measure. For example, design engineers may spend only part of their time on quality. Allocating their salaries to various activities is subjective. It is especially difficult to measure external failure costs. The largest external failure cost—profits lost because of the company's reputation for poor quality—does not even appear in the accounting records. This cost must be estimated based on the experiences and judgments of the Sales Department. Because these estimates may be subjective, TQM programs also emphasize nonfinancial measures such as defect rates, number of customer complaints, and number of warranty repairs that can be objectively measured.

## DECISION GUIDELINES

### Lean Production and the Costs of Quality

Dell, a worldwide leader in PC sales, Is famous for its complete commitment to both the lean production and TQM philosophies. The following are several decisions Dell's managers made when adopting these two modern management techniques.

| Decision | Guidelines | |
|---|---|---|
| | **Traditional** | **Lean Production** |
| If we want to change from a traditional production system to a lean production system, what factors do we need to consider in our decision? | Like machines grouped together | Production cells |
| | Longer set-up times | Shorter set-up times |
| | Larger batches | Smaller batches |
| | Higher inventories | Lower inventories |
| | Individuals do fewer tasks | Individuals do a wider range of tasks |
| | Longer manufacturing cycle times | Shorter manufacturing cycle times |
| | Emphasis on using sample inspections to limit the number of defective products sold | Emphasis on building in quality |
| | Many suppliers | Fewer, but well-coordinated, suppliers |

## SUMMARY PROBLEM 1

We know that we would like to improve our costs of quality but are not sure how to start. How can we divide the costs in order to better understand them and determine where best to spend funds on improvement strategies? The total costs of quality can be divided into the following:

1. Prevention costs
2. Appraisal costs
3. Internal failure costs
4. External failure costs

By separating the costs into these categories, decisions can be made about what measures might have the most impact.

How do we decide on which costs of quality to focus? Investment in prevention costs and appraisal costs reduces internal and external failure costs and has the greatest long-term effect.

# SUMMARY PROBLEM 2

The CEO of Edmonton Auto Parts (EAP) is concerned with the quality of its products and the amount of resources currently spent on customer returns. The CEO would like to analyze the costs incurred in conjunction with the quality of the product.

The following cost information was collected from various departments within the company:

| | |
|---|---|
| Warranty returns | $120,000 |
| Training personnel | 10,000 |
| Litigation on product liability claims | 175,000 |
| Inspecting 10% of final products | 5,000 |
| Rework | 10,000 |
| Production loss due to machine breakdown | 45,000 |
| Inspection of raw materials | $ 5,000 |

### Requirements

1. Prepare a Cost of Quality Report. In addition to listing the costs by category, determine the percentage of the total cost of quality incurred in each cost category.
2. Do any additional subjective costs appear to be missing from the report?
3. What can be learned from the report?

## SOLUTIONS

### Requirement 1

| | Costs Incurred | Total Costs of Quality | Percentage of Total Costs of Quality (rounded) |
|---|---|---|---|
| **Prevention Costs:** | | | |
| Personnel training | $ 10,000 | | |
| Total prevention costs | | $ 10,000 | 2.7%* |
| **Appraisal Costs:** | | | |
| Inspecting raw materials | $ 5,000 | | |
| Inspecting 10% of final products | 5,000 | | |
| Total appraisal costs | | $ 10,000 | 2.7% |
| **Internal Failure Costs:** | | | |
| Rework | $ 10,000 | | |
| Production loss due to machine breakdown | 45,000 | $ 55,000 | 14.9% |
| Total internal failure costs | | | |
| **External Failure Costs:** | | | |
| Litigation costs from product liability claims | $175,000 | | |
| Warranty return costs | 120,000 | | |
| Total external failure costs | | $295,000 | 79.7% |
| Total costs of quality | | $370,000 | 100% |

*The percentage of total is computed as the total cost of the category divided by the total costs of quality. For example: 2.7% = $10,000 ÷ $370,000.

**Requirement 2**

Because the company has warranty returns and is involved in product liability litigation, it is very possible that the company suffers from a reputation for poor-quality products. If so, it is losing profits because it is losing sales. Unsatisfied customers will probably avoid buying from the company in the future. Worse yet, customers may tell their friends and family not to buy from the company. This report does not include an estimate of the lost profits arising from the company's reputation for poor-quality products.

**Requirement 3**

The Cost of Quality Report shows that very little is being spent on prevention and maintenance, which is probably why the internal and external failure costs are so high. The CEO should use this information to develop quality initiatives in the areas of prevention and appraisal. Such initiatives should reduce future internal and external failure costs.

# DECISION GUIDELINES

## The Changing Regulatory and Business Environment

Successful companies respond to changes in the regulatory and business environment. Here are some of the decisions managers need to consider.

| Decision | Guidelines |
|---|---|
| I'm a Canadian corporation. Do I need to worry about SOX? | Publicly traded Canadian companies that are listed on the U.S. stock market must comply with SOX. However, Canadian regulations, similar in nature to SOX, have been implemented for the domestic market. These regulations have been designed and recommended by the Canadian Securities Administrators and implemented by the securities organizations for each province and territory. |
| I'm a Canadian company, but I have operations in other countries as well. How will IFRS help me? | Companies that operate in more than one country will no longer be required to prepare multiple financial statements using different standards for each country. Rather, they will prepare one set of financial statements in accordance with International Financial Reporting Standards (IFRS). |
| In the past, I have been able to find information about companies on the internet, but it took a long time to organize it. Can XBRL reduce the time it would take to do so? | XBRL will allow managers to more easily obtain and analyze publicly available financial data from their competitors, from companies they may wish to purchase, or from companies in which they may want to invest. |
| I would like to take my Canadian company into the global market. What might help me compete? | The use of advanced information systems, e-commerce, supply-chain management, lean production, and TQM will help a company to compete more effectively. Also, consider becoming ISO 9001:2008 certified. |
| How do I know if new initiatives such as international expansion, ERP, lean production, and TQM will be worth it in the long run? | By using cost-benefit analysis—comparing the estimated benefits of the initiative with the estimated costs—you will see whether or not the benefits of the project exceed its costs. You can then determine the best alternative for your situation. |

# SUMMARY PROBLEM 3

EZ-Rider Motorcycles is thinking about expanding into Germany. If gas prices increase, the company expects more interest in fuel-efficient transportation, such as motorcycles. As a result, the company is considering setting up a motorcycle assembly plant on the outskirts of Berlin.

EZ-Rider Motorcycles estimates it will cost $850,000 to convert an existing building to motorcycle production. Workers will need training, at a total cost of $65,000. The additional costs to organize the business and to establish relationships are estimated to be $150,000.

The CEO believes the company can earn sales profits from this expansion (before considering the costs in the preceding paragraph) of $1,624,000.

**Requirement**

Use cost-benefit analysis to determine whether EZ-Rider should expand into Germany.

## ■ SOLUTIONS

The following cost-benefit analysis indicates that the company should expand into Germany:

| | | |
|---|---|---|
| *Expected Benefits:* | | |
| Expected profits from expansion sales | | $ 1,624,000 |
| *Expected Costs:* | | |
| Conversion of building to manufacturing plant | $850,000 | |
| Workforce training | 65,000 | |
| Organizing business and establishing relationships | 150,000 | |
| Total expected costs | | (1,065,000) |
| Net expected benefits | | $ 559,000 |

# END OF CHAPTER

## LEARNING OBJECTIVES

1 Identify managers' four primary responsibilities.

2 Distinguish financial accounting from managerial accounting.

3 Describe organizational structure and the roles and skills required of management accountants within the organization.

4 Describe the role of CPA Canada, and apply its guidelines for ethical behaviour.

5 Discuss and analyze the implications of regulatory and business trends.

6 Describe a lean production system.

7 Describe and use the costs of quality framework.

## ACCOUNTING VOCABULARY

**Accounting Standards for Private Enterprises (ASPE) (p. 4)** Reporting guidelines appropriate for organizations that do not fit the definition of publicly accountable. These guidelines replace the Generally Accepted Accounting Principles (GAAP) and have been available for early adoption since 2009.

**Appraisal Costs (p. 23)** Costs incurred to *detect* poor-quality goods or services.

**Audit Committee (p. 7)** A subcommittee of the board of directors that is responsible for overseeing both the internal audit function and the annual financial statement audit by independent public accountants.

**Board of Directors (p. 6)** The body elected by shareholders to oversee the company.

**Budget (p. 3)** Quantitative expression of a plan that helps managers coordinate and implement the plan.

**Canadian Securities Administrators (CSA) (p. 15)** The CSA is an organization made up of securities regulators from each province and territory. The goal of the CSA is to provide guidance in making securities regulations more consistent across the country.

**Certified General Accountant (CGA) (p. 9)** The CGA designation is one of three legacy accounting designations in Canada. The CGA was a professional certification issued by the Certified General Accountants Association of Canada to designate expertise in the areas of financial management in industry, commerce, finance, government, and public practice.

**Certified Management Accountant (CMA) (p. 9)** The CMA designation is one of three legacy accounting designations in Canada. The CMA was a professional certification issued by the Society of Management Accountants to designate expertise in the areas of managerial accounting; economics; and business finance, leadership, and strategy.

**Chartered Accountant (CA) (p. 9)** The CA is one of three legacy accounting designations in Canada. The CA was a professional certification issued by the Canadian Institute of Chartered Accountants to designate expertise in the areas of public accounting, senior management, audit, and tax.

**Chartered Professional Accountant (CPA) (p. 9)** A designation, signifying a professional association of accountants, issued by the Chartered Professional Accountants Canada to indicate expertise in the areas of public accounting, senior management, audit, and tax, managerial accounting; economics; and business finance and strategy. The CPA designation and CPA Canada came into being as a result of the unification of the three legacy accounting designations in Canada.

**Chief Executive Officer (CEO) (p. 6)** The position hired by the board of directors to oversee the company on a daily basis.

**Chief Financial Officer (CFO) (p. 6)** The position responsible for all of the company's financial concerns.

**Chief Operating Officer (COO) (p. 6)** The position responsible for overseeing the company's operations.

**Controller (p. 6)** The position responsible for general financial accounting, managerial accounting, and tax reporting.

**Controlling (p. 2)** One of management's primary responsibilities: evaluating the results of business operations against the plan and making adjustments to keep the company pressing toward its goals.

**Cost–Benefit Analysis (p. 16)** Weighing costs against benefits to help make decisions.

**Cost of Quality Report (p. 23)** A report that lists the costs incurred by the company related to quality. The costs are categorized as prevention costs, appraisal costs, internal failure costs, and external failure costs.

**Cross-Functional Teams (p. 7)** Corporate teams whose members represent various functions of the organization, such as R&D, design, production, marketing, distribution, and customer service.

**Decision Making (p. 2)** One of management's primary responsibilities: identifying possible courses of action and choosing among them.

**Directing (p. 2)** One of management's primary responsibilities: running the company on a day-to-day basis.

**Extensible Business Reporting Language (XBRL) (p. 14)** A data-tagging system that enables companies to release financial and business information in a format that can be quickly, efficiently, and cost-effectively accessed, sorted, and analyzed over the internet.

**External Failure Costs (p. 23)** Costs incurred when the company does not detect poor-quality goods or services until *after* delivery is made to customers.

**Internal Failure Costs (p. 23)** Costs incurred when the company detects and corrects poor-quality goods or services *before* making delivery to customers.

**International Financial Reporting Standards (IFRS) (p. 4)** The provincial securities commissions have moved to adopt IFRS for all publicly traded companies within the next few years. In many instances, IFRS vary from ASPE.

**Internal Audit Function (p. 7)** The corporate function charged with assessing the effectiveness of the company's internal controls and risk management policies.

**ISO 9001:2008 (p. 22)** A quality-related certification issued by the International Organization for Standardization (ISO). Firms may become ISO 9001:2008 certified by complying with the quality management standards set forth by the ISO and undergoing extensive audits of their quality management processes.

**Just-In-Time (JIT) (p. 19)** An inventory philosophy first pioneered by Toyota in which a product is manufactured *just in time* to fill customer orders. Companies adopting JIT are able to substantially reduce the quantity of raw materials and finished product kept on hand.

**Lean Production (p. 16)** A philosophy and business strategy of manufacturing without waste.

**Planning (p. 2)** One of management's primary responsibilities: setting goals and objectives for the company and determining how to achieve them.

**Prevention Costs (p. 23)** Costs incurred to *avoid* poor-quality goods or services.

**Publicly Accountable Enterprise (p. 4)** An organization that fits the definition of "publicly accountable" for the purposes of determining the reporting standards that must be followed.

**Sarbanes-Oxley Act (SOX) (p. 14)** A congressional act in the United States that enhances internal control and financial reporting requirements and establishes new regulatory requirements for publicly traded companies and their independent auditors.

**Supply-Chain Management (p. 18)** Exchange of information with suppliers to reduce costs, improve quality, and speed delivery of goods and services from suppliers to the company itself and on to customers.

**Sustainability (p. 17)** The ability to meet the needs of the present without compromising the ability of future generations to meet their own needs.

**Treasurer (p. 6)** The position responsible for raising the firm's capital and investing funds.

**Total Quality Management (TQM) (p. 22)** A management philosophy of delighting customers with superior products and services by continually setting higher goals and improving the performance of every business function.

**Triple Bottom Line (p. 17)** Evaluating a company's performance not only by its ability to generate economic profits, but also by its impact on people and the planet.



# QUICK CHECK

1. (Learning Objective 1) Which of the following is *not* one of the four primary responsibilities of management?
   a. Controlling
   b. Costing
   c. Directing
   d. Planning
2. (Learning Objective 2) Which of the following about managerial accounting is *true*?
   a. IFRS and ASPE require managerial accounting.
   b. Internal decision makers use managerial accounting.
   c. Public accountants audit managerial accounting reports.
   d. Managerial accounting reports are usually prepared on an annual basis.
3. (Learning Objective 2) Which of the following is *not* a characteristic of managerial accounting information?
   a. Emphasizes relevance
   b. Focuses on the future more than the past
   c. Provides detailed information about parts of the company, not just the company as a whole
   d. Emphasizes reliability
4. (Learning Objective 3) What company position is in charge of raising the firm's capital?
   a. Director of internal audit
   b. Controller
   c. COO
   d. Treasurer

5. (Learning Objective 3) Which of the following statements is *true*?
   a. The COO reports to the CFO.
   b. The treasurer reports to the CEO.
   c. The internal audit department reports to the audit committee.
   d. The controller reports to the internal auditor.
6. (Learning Objective 3) In addition to accounting knowledge, management accountants must possess all of the following skills *except*
   a. written communication skills.
   b. knowledge of how a business functions.
   c. computer programming skills.
   d. analytical skills.
7. (Learning Objective 4) A management accountant who refuses an expensive gift from a software salesperson meets the ethical standard of
   a. professional behaviour.
   b. confidentiality.
   c. integrity and due care.
   d. professional competence.
8. (Learning Objective 6) All of the following tools help companies compete in today's market *except*
   a. JIT.
   b. KJD.
   c. ERP.
   d. TQM.

**Quick Check Answers**

1. *b*, 2. *b*, 3. *d*, 4. *d*, 5. *c*, 6. *c*, 7. *c*, 8. *b*

# SHORT EXERCISES

## S1-1 Roles of managers *(Learning Objective 1)*

Describe the four primary responsibilities of managers and the way they relate to one another.

## S1-2 Contrast managerial and financial accounting *(Learning Objective 2)*

Managerial accounting differs from financial accounting in several areas. Specify whether each of the following characteristics relates to managerial accounting or financial accounting.

**a.** Reports tend to be prepared for the parts of the organization rather than the whole organization.
**b.** Primary users are internal (for example, company managers).
**c.** It is governed by Accounting Standards for Private Enterprises (ASPE) or International Financial Reporting Standards (IFRS).
**d.** Two main characteristics of data are reliability and objectivity.
**e.** Reports are prepared as needed.
**f.** It is not governed by legal requirements.
**g.** Primary users are external (i.e., creditors, investors).
**h.** It is focused on the future.
**i.** Reporting is based mainly on the company as a whole.
**j.** Reports are prepared usually quarterly and annually.
**k.** Information is verified by external auditors.
**l.** It is focused on the past.
**m.** A main characteristic of data is relevance.

## S1-3 Accounting roles in the organization *(Learning Objective 3)*

The following is a list of job duties or descriptions. For each item, specify whether it would most likely describe the duties or responsibilities of someone working for the treasurer, for the controller, or in the internal auditing department.

**a.** Perform cash counts at branch offices.
**b.** Prepare journal entries for month-end closing.
**c.** Issue company stock.
**d.** Ensure that the company's internal controls are functioning properly.
**e.** Create an analysis about whether to lease or buy a delivery truck.
**f.** Calculate the cost of a product.

g. Issue company bonds.

h. Ensure that company risk management procedures are being followed.

i. Work with various departments in preparing operating budgets for the upcoming year.

j. Oversee accounts payable activities.

k. Invest company funds.

l. Report to the audit committee of the board of directors *and* to a senior executive, such as the CFO or CEO.

m. Prepare company tax returns.

**S1-4 Role of internal audit function** *(Learning Objective 3)*

The following table lists several characteristics. Place a check mark next to those items that pertain directly to the internal audit function and its role within the organization.

| Characteristics | Check (✓) if related to internal auditing |
|---|---|
| a. Helps to ensure the company's internal controls are functioning properly | ❑ |
| b. Reports to treasurer or controller | ❑ |
| c. Required by the Toronto Stock Exchange if company stock is publicly traded on the TSE | ❑ |
| d. Reports directly to the audit committee | ❑ |
| e. Ensures that the company achieves its profit goals | ❑ |
| f. Is part of the Accounting Department | ❑ |
| g. Usually reports to the senior executive (CFO) or (CEO) for administrative matters | ❑ |
| h. Performs the same functions as independent certified public accountants | ❑ |
| i. External audits can be performed by the internal auditing department | ❑ |

**S1-5 Importance of ethical standards** *(Learning Objective 4)*

Explain the importance of having guidelines for ethical behaviour.

**S1-6 Violations of ethical standards** *(Learning Objective 4)*

Consider the following situations. Comment on the ethical and behavioural implications of each.

a. You tell your brother that your company will report earnings significantly above financial analysts' estimates.

b. You see that other employees take home office supplies for personal use. As an intern, you do the same thing, assuming that this is a "perk."

c. At a conference on e-commerce, you skip the afternoon session and go sightseeing.

d. You fail to read the detailed specifications of a new general ledger package that you asked your company to purchase. After it is installed, you are surprised that it is incompatible with some of your company's older accounting software.

e. You do not provide top management with the detailed job descriptions they requested because you fear they may use this information to cut a position from your department.

**S1-7 Identify current competitive tools** *(Learning Objective 5)*

Companies are facing a great amount of change in every facet of their operations today. To remain competitive, companies must keep abreast of current developments in several areas. You recently got together with a group of friends who work for different companies. Your friends share information about their current challenges in adopting new tools or complying with new regulations. Excerpts from the conversation are presented in the following section. Tell whether each excerpt describes XBRL, ISO 9001:2008, e-commerce, the Sarbanes-Oxley Act (SOX), or enterprise resource planning (ERP) systems.

a. Suzanne: My company is working to demonstrate its commitment to continuous quality improvement. We are currently undergoing an extensive audit of our quality management processes. We hope to gain a competitive advantage through this process.

b. Ying: We have just installed a system at our company that integrates all of our company's data across all systems. We have one central data warehouse that contains information about our suppliers, our customers, our employees, and our financial information. The software retrieves information from this single data warehouse and all systems are integrated. The process of implementing this system has been very expensive and time-consuming, but we are reaping the benefits of being more streamlined, of being able to respond more quickly to changes in the market, and of not having several different software systems operating independently.

**c.** Steve: I just started a new job in the Auditing Department. My new duties include assisting in the development of testing procedures and methods for determining the effectiveness of internal controls. I also oversee the testing for assurance of compliance with corporate policies. I am coordinating the review of securities filings for the Yukon Superintendent of Securities with our external auditors. I also am responsible for preparing periodic compliance status reports for management, the audit committee, and the external auditors.

**d.** Keisha: We have been working on a system to tag all of the financial information in our quarterly and annual reports so that our financial information can be shared easily. We will be able to attach a tag to each piece of financial information. For example, we can tag "net profits" wherever it appears in the financial reports. Any user accessing the financial reports would then be able to download the numbers for "net profits." Our shareholders and the analysts will be able to retrieve the information they need quickly, efficiently, and cost effectively.

**e.** Roland: My company has been shifting much of its purchasing system to the internet. We are able now able to complete many of our business-to-business transactions via the Web, which generates little or no paperwork, lessens the chance of error, and decreases the costs of each transaction.

### S1-8 Understand key terms *(Learning Objectives 6 & 7)*

Listed below are several terms. Complete the following statements with one of these terms. You may use a term more than once, and some terms may not be used at all.

| Internal failure costs | Appraisal costs | External failure costs | Lean production | Prevention costs |
|---|---|---|---|---|

a. ______________ are incurred to avoid producing poor-quality goods or services.

b. The philosophy and business strategy of manufacturing without waste is called ______________.

c. ______________ are costs incurred to detect poor-quality goods or services.

d. ______________ are costs that arise from product defects that are discovered before the product is shipped to the customer.

e. The costs of providing warranty service are ______________.

### S1-9 Identify lean production characteristics *(Learning Objective 6)*

Indicate whether each of the following is characteristic of a lean production system or a traditional production system.

**a.** Management works with suppliers to ensure defect-free raw materials.

**b.** Products are produced in large batches.

**c.** Large stocks of finished goods protect against lost sales if customer demand is higher than expected.

**d.** Suppliers make frequent deliveries of small quantities of raw materials.

**e.** Set-up times are long.

**f.** Employees do a variety of jobs, including maintenance and set ups, as well as operating machines.

**g.** Machines are grouped into self-contained production cells or production lines.

**h.** Machines are grouped according to function. For example, all cutting machines are located in one area.

**i.** Suppliers can access the company's intranet.

**j.** The final operation in the production sequence "pulls" parts from the preceding operation.

**k.** Each employee is responsible for inspecting his or her own work.
**l.** There is an emphasis on building in quality.
**m.** The manufacturing cycle times are longer.

### S1-10 Classifying costs of quality *(Learning Objective 7)*

Classify each of the following quality-related costs as prevention costs, appraisal costs, internal failure costs, or external failure costs.

1. Reworking defective units
2. Litigation costs from product liability claims
3. Inspecting incoming raw materials
4. Training employees
5. Warranty repairs
6. Redesigning the production process
7. Lost productivity due to machine breakdown
8. Inspecting products that are halfway through the production process
9. Incremental cost of using a higher-grade raw material
10. Cost incurred in producing and disposing of defective units

### S1-11 Quality initiative decision *(Learning Objective 7)*

Wharfedale manufactures high-quality audio speakers. Suppose Wharfedale is considering spending the following amounts on a new quality program:

| | |
|---|---|
| Additional 20 minutes of testing for each speaker | $ 500,000 |
| Negotiating with, and training, suppliers to obtain higher-quality materials and on-time delivery | 300,000 |
| Redesigning the speakers to make them easier to manufacture | 1,400,000 |

Wharfedale expects this quality program to save costs as follows:

| | |
|---|---|
| Reduce warranty repair costs | $200,000 |
| Eliminate inspection of raw materials | 400,000 |
| Reduce rework (fewer defective units) | 650,000 |

It also expects this program to avoid lost profits from the following:

| | |
|---|---|
| Lost sales due to disappointed customers | $850,000 |
| Lost production time due to rework | 300,000 |

1. Classify each of these costs into one of the four categories of quality costs (prevention, appraisal, internal failure, external failure).
2. Should Wharfedale implement the quality program? Give your reasons.

### S1-12 Categorize different costs of quality *(Learning Objective 7)*

Fierenze Inc. makes electronic components. Michelle Millan, the president, recently instructed Vice President Pablo Tapia to develop a total quality control program: "If we don't at least match the quality improvements our competitors are making," she told Tapia, "we'll soon be out of business." Tapia began by listing various costs of quality; the first six items that came to mind are listed below. Classify each item as a prevention cost, an appraisal cost, an internal failure cost, or an external failure cost.

1. Costs of electronic components returned by customers
2. Costs incurred by customer representatives travelling to customer sites to repair defective products
3. Lost profits from lost sales due to reputation for less-than-perfect products
4. Costs of inspecting components in Fierenze's production processes
5. Salaries of engineers who are designing components to withstand electrical overloads
6. Costs of reworking defective components after discovery by company inspectors

## EXERCISES Group A

**E1-13A Managers' responsibilities** *(Learning Objective 1)*

Categorize each of the following activities according to which management responsibility it fulfills: planning, directing, controlling, or decision making. Some activities may fulfill more than one responsibility.

a. Management conducts variance analysis by comparing budget to actual.
b. Management reviews hourly sales reports to determine the level of staffing needed to service customers.
c. Management decides to increase sales by 10% next year.
d. Management uses information on product costs to determine sales prices.
e. To lower product costs, management moves production to Mexico.

**E1-14A Define key terms** *(Learning Objectives 1 & 2)*

Complete the following statements with one of the terms listed here. You may use a term more than once, and some terms may not be used at all.

| | | | |
|---|---|---|---|
| Budget | Creditors | Managerial accounting | Planning |
| Controlling | Financial accounting | Managers | Shareholders |

a. Companies must follow IFRS or ASPE in their ______ systems.
b. Financial accounting develops reports for external parties such as ______ and ______.
c. When managers evaluate the company's performance compared to the plan, they are performing the ______ responsibility of management.
d. ______ are decision makers inside a company.
e. ______ provides information on a company's past performance to external parties.
f. ______ systems are not restricted by IFRS or ASPE but are chosen by comparing the costs and the benefits of the system.
g. Choosing goals and the means to achieve them is the ______ function of management.
h. ______ systems report on various segments or business units of the company.
i. ______ statements of public companies are audited annually by public accountants.

**E1-15A Identify users of accounting information** *(Learning Objective 3)*

For each of the following users of financial accounting information and managerial accounting information, specify whether the user would primarily use financial accounting information, managerial accounting information, or both.

1. Potential shareholders
2. Loan officer at the company's bank
3. Manager of the Sales Department
4. Bookkeeping Department
5. Managers at regional offices
6. Canada Revenue Agency agent
7. Current shareholders
8. Toronto Stock Exchange analyst
9. News reporter
10. Company controller
11. Board of directors
12. Nova Scotia Securities Commission employee
13. External auditor (public accounting firm)
14. Internal auditor

**E1-16A Classify roles within the organization** *(Learning Objective 3)*

Complete the following statements with one of the terms listed here. You may use a term more than once, and some terms may not be used at all.

| | | | |
|---|---|---|---|
| Audit committee | Board of directors | CEO | CFO |
| Treasurer | Controller | Cross-functional teams | COO |

a. The _______ and the _______ report to the CEO.
b. The internal audit function reports to the CFO or _______ and the _______.
c. The _______ is directly responsible for financial accounting, managerial accounting, and tax reporting.
d. The CEO is hired by the _______.
e. The _______ is directly responsible for raising capital and investing funds.
f. The _______ is directly responsible for the company's operations.
g. Management accountants often work with _______.
h. A subcommittee of the board of directors is called the _______.

**E1-17A Professional organizations and certification** *(Learning Objective 4)*

Describe areas of focus in contemporary managerial accounting.

**E1-18A Ethical dilemma** *(Learning Objective 4)*

Mary Gonzales is the controller at CarTown, a car dealership. She recently hired Anik Cousineau as a bookkeeper. Cousineau wanted to attend a class on Excel spreadsheets, so Gonzales temporarily took over Cousineau's duties, including overseeing a fund for topping off a car's gas tank before a test drive. Gonzales found a shortage in this fund and confronted Cousineau when she returned to work. Cousineau admitted that she occasionally uses this fund to pay for her own gas. Gonzales estimated that the amount involved is close to $300.

**Requirements**

1. What should Gonzales do?
2. Would you change your answer to the previous question if Gonzales was the one recently hired as controller and Cousineau was a well-liked, long-time employee who indicated that she always eventually repaid the fund?

**E1-19A Classify ethical responsibilities** *(Learning Objective 4)*

Comment on each of the following responsibilities to which a professional accountant should adhere. How do they relate to ethical practice?

1. Refrain from using confidential information for unethical or illegal advantage.
2. Maintain an appropriate level of professional expertise by continually developing knowledge and skills.
3. Communicate information fairly and objectively.
4. Recognize and communicate professional limitations that would preclude responsible judgment or successful performance of an activity.
5. Mitigate actual conflicts of interest. Regularly communicate with business associates to avoid apparent conflicts of interest. Advise all parties of any potential conflicts.
6. Provide decision support information and recommendations that are accurate, clear, concise, and timely.
7. Abstain from engaging in or supporting any activity that might discredit the profession.
8. Disclose all relevant information that could reasonably be expected to influence an intended user's understanding of the reports, analyses, or recommendations.
9. Inform all relevant parties regarding the appropriate use of confidential information. Monitor subordinates' activities to ensure compliance.
10. Perform professional duties in accordance with relevant laws, regulations, and technical standards.
11. Refrain from engaging in any conduct that would make it difficult to carry out duties ethically.
12. Keep information confidential except when disclosure is authorized or legally required.
13. Disclose delays or deficiencies in information, timeliness, processing, or internal controls in conformance with organization policy and/or applicable law.

**E1-20A Define key terms** *(Learning Objective 5)*

Complete the following statements with one of the terms listed here. You may use a term more than once, and some terms may not be used at all.

| E-commerce | Shift to service economy | Future |
|---|---|---|
| Sarbanes-Oxley Act of 2002 | Just in time | ISO 9001:2008 |
| Present | Lean production | Supply-chain management |
| IFRS | ERP | Cross-functional teams |
| Total quality management | XBRL | |

**a.** _______________ is a language that uses a standardized coding system companies use to tag each piece of financial and business information in a format that can be quickly and efficiently accessed over the internet.

**b.** _______________ involves the exchange of information with suppliers to reduce costs, improve quality, and speed delivery of goods and services from suppliers to the company and its customers.

**c.** The _______________ was enacted to restore trust in publicly traded corporations, their management, their financial statements, and their auditors.

**d.** The goal of _______ is to meet customers' expectations by providing them with superior products and services by eliminating defects and waste throughout the value chain.

**e.** Most of the costs of adopting ERP, expanding into a foreign market, or improving quality are incurred in the _______; but most of the benefits occur in the _______.

**f.** _______ serves the information needs of people in accounting as well as people in marketing and in the warehouse.

**g.** Firms adopt _______ to conduct business on the internet.

**h.** Firms acquire the _______ certification to demonstrate their commitment to quality.

**i.** ____________ is a philosophy that embraces the concept that the lower the company's waste, the lower the company's costs.

**j.** ____________ is a data-tagging system that enables companies to release financial and business information in a format that can be quickly, efficiently, and cost-effectively accessed, sorted, and analyzed over the internet.

**k.** Canadian companies were expected to adopt _____________ for all publicly traded companies by 2011, which differs from the ASPE that companies are currently required to use.

**l.** Toyota first pioneered an inventory philosophy in which a product is manufactured ____________ to fill customer orders; companies are able to substantially reduce the quantity of raw materials and finished goods inventories.

**m.** _______________ is a management philosophy of delighting customers with superior products and services by continually setting higher goals and improving the performance of every business function.

### E1-21A Summarize the Sarbanes-Oxley Act *(Learning Objective 5)*

You just obtained an entry-level job as a management accountant at an international firm based in Winnipeg. Other newly hired accountants have heard of the Sarbanes-Oxley Act of 2002 (SOX) but do not know much about it. (They attended a different university.) Write a short memo to your colleagues discussing the reason for SOX, some of the specific requirements of SOX that will affect your company, and why this is applicable to the Canadian firm that you work for.

### E1-22A Lean production cost-benefit analysis *(Learning Objective 6)*

Check sum: Total costs of lean production are $60,000.

Wild Rides manufactures snowboards. Mohammad Al-Zoubi, the CEO, is trying to decide whether to adopt a lean production model. He expects that adopting lean production would save $97,000 in warehousing expenses and $46,000 in spoilage costs. However, adopting lean production will require several one-time up-front expenditures: (1) $15,000 for an employee training program, (2) $37,000 to streamline the plant's production process, and (3) $8,000 to identify suppliers that will guarantee zero defects and on-time delivery.

**Requirements**

1. What are the total costs of adopting lean production?
2. What are the total benefits of adopting lean production?
3. Should Wild Rides adopt lean production? Why or why not?

### E1-23A Differentiate between traditional and lean production *(Learning Objective 6)*

Briefly describe how lean production systems differ from traditional production systems using each of the following dimensions:

1. Inventory levels
2. Batch sizes
3. Set-up times
4. Physical layout of plant
5. Roles of plant employees
6. Manufacturing cycle times
7. Quality

### E1-24A Prepare a Cost of Quality Report *(Learning Objective 7)*

The CEO of Salty Snackfoods is concerned about the amount of resources currently spent on customer warranty claims. Each box of snacks is printed with the guarantee "Satisfaction guaranteed or your money back." Since the claims are so high, she would like to evaluate what costs are being incurred to ensure the quality of the product. The following information was collected from various departments within the company:

Check sum: Total appriasal costs are $60,000.

| | |
|---|---:|
| Warranty claims | $400,000 |
| Cost of defective products found at the inspection point | 94,000 |
| Training factory personnel | 26,000 |
| Recall of Batch #59374 | 175,000 |
| Inspecting products halfway through the production process | 55,000 |
| Cost of disposing of rejected products | 12,000 |
| Preventive maintenance on factory equipment | 7,000 |
| Production loss due to machine breakdowns | 15,000 |
| Inspection of raw materials | 5,000 |

**Requirements**

1. Prepare a Cost of Quality Report. In addition to listing the costs by category, determine the percentage of the total costs of quality incurred in each cost category.
2. Do any additional subjective costs appear to be missing from the report?
3. What can be learned from the report?

### E1-25A Classify costs and make a quality-initiative decision *(Learning Objective 7)*

Chihooli manufactures radiation-shielding glass panels. Suppose Chihooli is considering spending the following amounts on a new TQM program:

| | |
|---|---:|
| Strength-testing one item from each batch of panels | $65,000 |
| Training employees in TQM | 30,000 |
| Training suppliers in TQM | 40,000 |
| Identifying preferred suppliers who commit to on-time delivery of perfect quality materials | 60,000 |

Chihooli expects the new program to save costs through the following:

| | |
|---|---:|
| Avoid lost profits from lost sales due to disappointed customers | $90,000 |
| Avoid rework and spoilage | 55,000 |
| Avoid inspection of raw materials | 45,000 |
| Avoid warranty costs | 15,000 |

**Requirements**

1. Classify each item as a prevention cost, an appraisal cost, an internal failure cost, or an external failure cost.
2. Should Chihooli implement the new quality program? Give your reason.

# EXERCISES Group B

## E1-26B Managers' responsibilities *(Learning Objective 1)*

Categorize each of the following activities according to which management responsibility it fulfills: planning, directing, controlling, or decision making. Some activities may fulfill more than one responsibility.

a. The store manager posts the employee time schedule for the next week so that employees know when they are working.
b. The manager of the Service Department investigates why the actual hours spent on a recent repair job exceeded the standard for that type of repair by more than 20%.
c. Management creates a sales budget for the upcoming quarter.
d. Top management selects a location for a new store.
e. Management is designing a new sales incentive program for the upcoming year.

## E1-27B Define key terms *(Learning Objectives 1 & 2)*

Complete the following statements with one of the terms listed here. You may use a term more than once, and some terms may not be used at all.

| | | | |
|---|---|---|---|
| Budget | Creditors | Managerial accounting | Planning |
| Controlling | Financial accounting | Managers | Shareholders |

a. _______ systems are chosen by comparing the costs versus the benefits of the system and are not restricted by IFRS or ASPE.
b. Public accountants audit the _______ statements of public companies.
c. Financial accounting develops reports for external parties such as _______ and _______.
d. Companies must follow IFRS or ASPE in their _______ systems.
e. Decision makers inside a company are the _______.
f. Choosing goals and the means to achieve them is the _______ function of management.
g. _______ systems report on various segments or business units of the company.
h. When managers evaluate the company's performance compared to the plan, they are performing the _______ responsibility of management.
i. Information on a company's past performance is provided to external parties by _______________.

## E1-28B Identify users of accounting information *(Learning Objective 3)*

For each of the following users of financial accounting information and managerial accounting information, specify whether the user would primarily use financial accounting information, managerial accounting information, or both.

1. Reporter from the *Globe and Mail*
2. Regional division managers
3. Manitoba Securities Commission examiner
4. Bookkeeping Department
5. Division controller
6. External auditor (public accounting firm)
7. Loan officer at the company's bank
8. Provincial tax agency auditor
9. Board of directors
10. Manager of the Service Department
11. Toronto Stock Exchange analyst
12. Internal auditor
13. Potential investors
14. Current shareholders

## E1-29B Classify roles within the organization *(Learning Objective 3)*

Complete the following statements with one of the terms listed here. You may use a term more than once, and some terms may not be used at all.

| Audit committee | Board of directors | CEO | CFO |
|---|---|---|---|
| Treasurer | Controller | Cross-functional teams | COO |

a. Management accountants often work with _______.
b. The _______ and the _______ report to the CEO.
c. A subcommittee of the board of directors is called the _______.
d. Raising capital and investing funds are the direct responsibilities of the __________.
e. Financial accounting, managerial accounting, and tax reporting are the direct responsibilities of the _________________.
f. The internal audit function reports to the CFO or _______ and the _______.
g. The CEO is hired by the _______.
h. The company's operations are the direct responsibility of the ____________.

## E1-30B Professional organization and certification *(Learning Objective 4)*

Complete the following sentences:

a. The _______ is the professional association for accountants.
b. Prior to the formation of the CPA the three professional accounting designations in Canada were __________________, _________________, and ___________________.

## E1-31B Ethical dilemma *(Learning Objective 4)*

Claudia Chan is the controller at Sangood Kitchens, a large food and kitchen store. She recently hired Helen Smith as a bookkeeper. Smith wanted to attend a class on information systems, so Chan temporarily took over Smith's duties, including overseeing a fund for giving in-store cooking and product demonstrations. Chan discovered a shortage in this fund and confronted Smith about it. Smith admitted that she occasionally uses the fund to pay for her own store purchases. Chan estimated that the amount involved is close to $500.

### Requirements

1. What should Chan do?
2. Would you change your answer to the previous question if Chan was the one recently hired as controller and Smith was a well-liked, long-time employee who indicated that she always eventually repaid the fund?

## E1-32B Classify ethical responsibilities *(Learning Objective 4)*

Comment on each of the following responsibilities to which a professional accountant should adhere. How do they relate to ethical practice?

1. Keep information confidential except when disclosure is authorized or legally required.
2. Communicate information fairly and objectively.
3. Refrain from using confidential information for unethical or illegal advantage.
4. Inform all relevant parties regarding the appropriate use of confidential information. Monitor subordinates' activities to ensure compliance.
5. Mitigate actual conflicts of interest. Regularly communicate with business associates to avoid apparent conflicts of interest. Advise all parties of any potential conflicts.
6. Maintain an appropriate level of professional expertise by continually developing knowledge and skills.
7. Recognize and communicate professional limitations that would preclude responsible judgment or successful performance of an activity.
8. Disclose all relevant information that could reasonably be expected to influence an intended user's understanding of the reports, analyses, or recommendations.
9. Disclose delays or deficiencies in information, timeliness, processing, or internal controls in conformance with organization policy and/or applicable law.
10. Perform professional duties in accordance with relevant laws, regulations, and technical standards.
11. Abstain from engaging in or supporting any activity that might discredit the profession.
12. Refrain from engaging in any conduct that would prejudice carrying out duties ethically.
13. Provide decision support information and recommendations that are accurate, clear, concise, and timely.

## E1-33B Define key terms *(Learning Objective 5)*

Complete the following statements with one of the terms listed here. You may use a term more than once, and some terms may not be used at all.

| | | |
|---|---|---|
| E-commerce | Shift to service economy | XBRL |
| IFRS | ERP | Future |
| Present | Just in time | ISO 9001:2008 |
| Cross-functional teams | Lean production | Supply-chain management |
| Sarbanes-Oxley Act of 2002 | Total quality management | |

**a.** _______________ is a language that utilizes a standardized coding system companies use to tag each piece of financial and business information in a format that can be quickly and efficiently accessed over the internet.

**b.** _______________ involves the exchange of information with suppliers to reduce costs, improve quality, and speed delivery of goods and services from suppliers to the company and its customers.

**c.** Toyota first pioneered an inventory philosophy in which a product is manufactured ___________ to fill customer orders; companies are able to substantially reduce the quantity of raw materials and finished goods inventories.

**d.** The _______________ was enacted to restore trust in publicly traded corporations, their management, their financial statements, and their auditors.

**e.** _______________ is a management philosophy of delighting customers with superior products and services by continually setting higher goals and improving the performance of every business function.

**f.** The goal of _______ is to meet customers' expectations by providing them with superior products and services by eliminating defects and waste throughout the value chain.

**g.** Most of the costs of adopting ERP, expanding into a foreign market, or improving quality are incurred in the _______, but most of the benefits occur in the _______.

**h.** _______ serves the information needs of people in accounting as well as people in marketing and in the warehouse.

**i.** Firms adopt _______ to conduct business on the internet.

**j.** Firms acquire the _______ certification to demonstrate their commitment to quality.

**k.** ___________ is a philosophy that embraces the concept that the lower the company's waste, the lower the company's costs.

**l.** ___________ is a data-tagging system that enables companies to release financial and business information in a format that can be quickly, efficiently, and cost-effectively accessed, sorted, and analyzed over the internet.

**m.** Canadian companies were required to adopt _____________ for all publicly traded companies by 2011, which differs from the ASPE that private companies are currently required to use.

## E1-34B Summarize the Sarbanes-Oxley Act *(Learning Objective 5)*

At a family gathering, your grandmother comes to you and asks you, since you have taken many business classes, to explain the Sarbanes-Oxley Act of 2002 (SOX). She has heard about SOX on television and the internet but does not really understand it. Explain to your grandmother the reason for SOX, some of the specific requirements of SOX, and why it is important in Canada.

## E1-35B Lean production cost-benefit analysis *(Learning Objective 6)*

Snow Wonderful manufactures snowboards. John Gallagher, the CEO, is trying to decide whether to adopt a lean production model. He expects that in present-value terms, adopting lean production would save $95,000 in warehousing expenses and $48,500 in spoilage costs. However, adopting lean production will require several one-time up-front expenditures: (1) $12,500 for an employee training program, (2) $36,000 to streamline the plant's production process, and (3) $8,750 to identify suppliers that will guarantee zero defects and on-time delivery.

### Requirements

1. What are the total costs of adopting lean production?
2. What are the total benefits of adopting lean production?
3. Should Snow Wonderful adopt lean production? Why or why not?

Check sum: Benefits of adopting lean production: $143,500

### E1-36B Differentiate between traditional and lean production *(Learning Objective 6)*

Categorize each of the following characteristics as being more representative of either traditional manufacturing or lean production.

1. Quality tends to be "inspected-in" rather than "built-in."
2. Manufacturing plants tend to be organized with self-contained production cells.
3. The company maintains greater quantities of raw materials, work in process, and finished goods inventories.
4. Set-up times are longer.
5. High quality is stressed in every aspect of production.
6. Products are made in smaller batches.
7. Emphasis is placed on shortening manufacturing cycle times.
8. Manufacturing plants tend to group like machines together in different parts of the plant.
9. Set-up times are shorter.
10. Units are produced in larger batches.
11. The company strives to maintain low inventory levels.
12. Cycle time tends to be longer.

### E1-37B Prepare a Cost of Quality Report *(Learning Objective 7)*

The CEO of Sweet Snackfoods is concerned with the amount of resources currently spent on customer warranty claims. Each box of snacks is printed with the guarantee "Satisfaction guaranteed or your money back." Since the claims are so high, she would like to evaluate what costs are being incurred to ensure the quality of the product. The following information was collected from various departments within the company:

Check sum: Total appraisal costs are $56,000

| | |
|---|---:|
| Warranty claims | $436,000 |
| Cost of defective products found at the inspection point | 91,000 |
| Training factory personnel | 25,000 |
| Recall of Batch #59374 | 175,000 |
| Inspecting products when halfway through the production process | 52,000 |
| Cost of disposing of rejected products | 11,000 |
| Preventive maintenance on factory equipment | 8,000 |
| Production loss due to machine breakdowns | 16,000 |
| Inspection of raw materials | 4,000 |

**Requirements**

1. Prepare a Cost of Quality Report. In addition to listing the costs by category, determine the percentage of the total costs of quality incurred in each cost category.
2. Do any additional subjective costs appear to be missing from the report?
3. What can be learned from the report?

### E1-38B Classify costs and make a quality-initiative decision *(Learning Objective 7)*

Clegg manufactures radiation-shielding glass panels. Suppose Clegg is considering spending the following amounts on a new TQM program:

| | |
|---|---:|
| Strength-testing one item from each batch of panels | $68,000 |
| Training employees in TQM | 30,000 |
| Training suppliers in TQM | 32,000 |
| Identifying preferred suppliers who commit to on-time delivery of perfect-quality materials | 60,000 |

Clegg expects the new program would save costs through the following:

| | |
|---|---:|
| Avoid lost profits from lost sales due to disappointed customers | $95,000 |
| Avoid rework and spoilage | 67,000 |
| Avoid inspection of raw materials | 57,000 |
| Avoid warranty costs | 16,000 |

**Requirements**

1. Classify each item as a prevention cost, an appraisal cost, an internal failure cost, or an external failure cost.
2. Should Clegg implement the new quality program? Give your reason.

# PROBLEMS Group A

**P1-39A Management processes and accounting information**
*(Learning Objectives 1 & 2)*

Allison Hopkins has her own chain of music stores, Hopkins' Music. Her stores sell musical instruments, sheet music, and other related items. Music lessons and instrument repair are also offered through the stores. Hopkins' Music also has a Website that sells music merchandise. Hopkins' Music has a staff of 80 people working in 6 departments: Sales, Repairs, Lessons, Web Development, Accounting, and Human Resources. Each department has its own manager.

**Requirements**

1. For each of the six departments, describe at least one decision/action for each of the four stages of management (planning, directing, controlling, and decision making). Prepare a table similar to the following for your answer:

| | Planning | Directing | Controlling | Decision Making |
|---|---|---|---|---|
| Sales | | | | |
| Repairs | | | | |
| Lessons | | | | |
| Web Development | | | | |
| Accounting | | | | |
| Human Resources | | | | |

2. For each of the decisions/actions you described in Part 1, identify what information is needed for that decision/action. Specify whether that information would be generated by the financial accounting system or the managerial accounting system at Hopkins' Music.

**P1-40A Ethical dilemmas** *(Learning Objective 4)*

Kate Royer is the new controller for ED Software, which develops and sells educational software. Shortly before the December 31 fiscal year-end, Justin Torabi, the company president, asks Royer how things look for the year-end numbers. He is not happy to learn that earnings growth may be below 15% for the first time in the company's five-year history. Torabi explains that financial analysts have again predicted a 15% earnings growth for the company and that he does not intend to disappoint them. He suggests that Royer talk to the assistant controller, who can explain how the previous controller dealt with this situation. The assistant controller suggests the following strategies:

a. Persuade suppliers to postpone billing until January 1.
b. Record as sales certain software that is being held in a public warehouse awaiting sale.
c. Delay the year-end closing a few days into January of the next year so that some of next year's sales are included as this year's sales.
d. Reduce the allowance for bad debts (and bad debts expense).
e. Postpone routine monthly maintenance expenditures from December to January.

**Requirement**

Which of these suggested strategies are inconsistent with the ethical standards of a professional accountant? What should Royer do if Torabi insists that she follow all of these suggestions?

**P1-41A ERP cost-benefit analysis** *(Learning Objective 5)*

As CEO of SeaSpray Marine, Bianca Saikaley knows it is important to control costs and to respond quickly to changes in the highly competitive boat-building industry. When

IDG Consulting proposes that SeaSpray Marine invest in an ERP system, she forms a team to evaluate the proposal: the plant engineer, the plant foreman, the systems specialist, the human resources director, the marketing director, and the management accountant.

A month later, management accountant Mike Cobalt reports that the team and IDG estimate that if SeaSpray Marine implements the ERP system, it will incur the following costs:

a. $350,000 in software costs
b. $80,000 to customize the ERP software and load SeaSpray's data into the new ERP system
c. $125,000 for employee training

The team estimates that the ERP system should provide several benefits:

a. More efficient order processing should lead to savings of $185,000.
b. Streamlining the manufacturing process so that it maps into the ERP system will create savings of $275,000.
c. Integrating purchasing, production, marketing, and distribution into a single system will allow SeaSpray Marine to reduce inventories, saving $220,000.
d. Higher customer satisfaction should increase sales, which, in turn, should increase profits by $150,000.

### Requirements

1. If the ERP installation succeeds, what is the dollar amount of the benefits?
2. Should SeaSpray Marine install the ERP system? Why or why not? Show your calculations.
3. Why did Saikaley create a team to evaluate IDG's proposal? Consider each piece of cost-benefit information that management accountant Cobalt reported. Which person on the team is most likely to have contributed each item? (*Hint:* Which team member is likely to have the most information about each cost or benefit?)

## P1-42A E-commerce cost-benefit analysis *(Learning Objective 5)*

Sun Gas wants to move its sales order system to the Web. Under the proposed system, gas stations and other merchants will use a Web browser and, after typing in a password for the Sun Gas Website, will be able to check the availability and current price of various products and place an order. Currently, customer service representatives take dealers' orders over the phone; they record the information on a paper form, and then manually enter it into the firm's computer system.

CFO Carrie Smith believes that dealers will not adopt the new Web system unless Sun Gas provides financial assistance to help them purchase or upgrade their PCs. Smith estimates this one-time cost at $750,000. Sun Gas will also have to invest $150,000 in upgrading its own computer hardware. The cost of the software and the consulting fee for installing the system will be $230,000. The Web system will enable Sun Gas to eliminate 25 clerical positions. Smith estimates that the new system's lower labour costs will save the company $1,357,000.

### Requirement

Use a cost-benefit analysis to recommend to Smith whether Sun Gas should proceed with the Web-based ordering system. Give your reasons, showing supporting calculations.

## P1-43A Continuation of P1-42A: Revised estimates *(Learning Objective 5)*

Consider the Sun Gas proposed entry into ecommerce in P1-42A. Smith revises her estimates of the benefits from the new system's lower labour costs. She now thinks the savings will be only $933,000.

### Requirements

1. What are the expected benefits of the Web-based ordering system?
2. Would you recommend that Sun Gas accept the proposal?
3. Before Smith makes a final decision, what other factors should she consider?

# PROBLEMS Group B

## P1-44B Management processes and accounting information
*(Learning Objectives 1 & 2)*

Dale Ohh has his own electronics retail chain, Circuit Pro. His stores sell computer parts, audio-visual equipment, consumer electronics, and related items. Custom computer building and electronics repair are also offered. In addition, Circuit Pro has a Website to sell its merchandise. Circuit Pro has a staff of 90 people working in 6 departments: Sales, Customization, Repairs, Web Development, Accounting, and Human Resources. Each department has its own manager.

### Requirements

1. For each of the six departments, describe at least one decision/action for each of the four stages of management (planning, directing, controlling, and decision making). Prepare a table similar to the following for your answer:

| | Planning | Directing | Controlling | Decision Making |
|---|---|---|---|---|
| Sales | | | | |
| Customization | | | | |
| Repairs | | | | |
| Web Development | | | | |
| Accounting | | | | |
| Human Resources | | | | |

2. For each of the decisions/actions you described in Part 1, identify what information is needed for that decision/action. Specify whether that information would be generated by the financial accounting system or the managerial accounting system at Circuit Pro.

## P1-45B Ethical dilemmas *(Learning Objective 4)*

Kourtney Lystiuk is the new controller for Colours, a company that designs and manufactures sportswear. Shortly before the December 31 fiscal year-end, Lashea Lucas (the company president) asks Lystiuk how things look for the year-end numbers. Lucas is not happy to learn that earnings growth may be below 10% for the first time in the company's five-year history. Lucas explains that financial analysts have again predicted a 12% earnings growth for the company and that she does not intend to disappoint them. She suggests that Lystiuk talk to the assistant controller, who can explain how the previous controller dealt with this situation. The assistant controller suggests the following strategies:

a. Postpone planned advertising expenditures from December to January.
b. Do not record sales returns and allowances on the basis that they are individually immaterial.
c. Persuade retail customers to accelerate January orders to December.
d. Reduce the allowance for bad debts (and bad debts expense).
e. Ship finished goods to public warehouses across the country for temporary storage until Colours receives firm orders from customers. As Colours receives orders, it directs the warehouse to ship the goods to nearby customers. The assistant controller suggests recording goods sent to the public warehouses as sales.

### Requirement

Which of these suggested strategies are inconsistent with the responsibilities to which a professional accountant should adhere? What should Lystiuk do if Lucas insists that she follow all of these suggestions?

## P1-46B ERP cost-benefit analysis *(Learning Objective 5)*

As CEO of AquaBoat Marine, Rick Wilson knows it's important to control costs and to respond quickly to changes in the highly competitive boat-building industry. When IDG Consulting proposes that AquaBoat Marine invests in an ERP system, he forms a team to evaluate the proposal: the plant engineer, the plant foreman, the systems specialist, the human resources director, the marketing director, and the management accountant. A month later, management accountant Matt Cook reports that the team and IDG estimate that if AquaBoat Marine implements the ERP system, it will incur the following costs:

a. $360,000 in software costs
b. $95,000 to customize the ERP software and load AquaBoat's data into the new ERP system
c. $115,000 for employee training

The team estimates that the ERP system should provide several benefits:

a. More efficient order processing should lead to savings of $185,000.
b. Streamlining the manufacturing process so that it maps into the ERP system will create savings of $270,000.
c. Integrating purchasing, production, marketing, and distribution into a single system will allow AquaBoat Marine to reduce inventories, saving $230,000.
d. Higher customer satisfaction should increase sales, which, in turn, should increase the present value of profits by $155,000.

The team knows that because of complexity, some ERP installations are not successful. If AquaBoat Marine's system fails, there will be no cost saving and no additional sales. The team predicts that there is an 80% chance that the ERP installation will succeed and a 20% chance that it will fail.

### Requirements

1. If the ERP installation succeeds, what is the dollar amount of the benefits?
2. Should AquaBoat Marine install the ERP system? Why or why not? Show your calculations.
3. Why did Wilson create a team to evaluate IDG's proposal? Consider each piece of cost–benefit information that management accountant Cook reported. Which person on the team is most likely to have contributed each item? (*Hint:* Which team member is likely to have the most information about each cost or benefit?)

## P1-47B E-commerce cost–benefit analysis *(Learning Objective 5)*

West Coast Gas wants to move its sales order system to the Web. Under the proposed system, gas stations and other merchants will use a Web browser and, after typing in a password for the West Coast Gas website, will be able to check the availability and current price of various products and place an order. Currently, customer service representatives take dealers' orders over the phone; they record the information on a paper form, and then manually enter it into the firm's computer system.

CFO Yun Ma believes that dealers will not adopt the new Web system unless West Coast Gas provides financial assistance to help them purchase or upgrade their PCs. Ma estimates this one-time cost at $760,000. West Coast Gas will also have to invest $155,000 in upgrading its own computer hardware. The cost of the software and the consulting fee for installing the system will be $225,000.

The Web system will enable West Coast Gas to eliminate 25 clerical positions. Ma estimates that the benefits of the new system's lower labour costs will have a present value of $1,370,000.

### Requirement

Use a cost-benefit analysis to recommend to Ma whether West Coast Gas should proceed with the Web-based ordering system. Give your reasons, showing supporting calculations.

## P1-48B Continuation of P1-47B: Revised estimates *(Learning Objective 5)*

Consider the West Coast Gas proposed entry into e-commerce in P1-47B. Ma revises her estimates of the benefits from the new system's lower labour costs. Ma now thinks the saving will be only $925,000.

### Requirements

1. What are the expected benefits of the Web-based ordering system?
2. Would you recommend that West Coast Gas accept the proposal?
3. Before Ma makes a final decision, what other factors should be considered?

# CAPSTONE APPLICATION PROBLEMS

## APPLICATION QUESTION

*Source:* Alexander Chaikin/Shutterstock

### A1-49 Ethical standards *(Learning Objective 4)*

Professional ethical standards can seem abstract. However, they are also relevant to post-secondary students in very tangible ways. Explain at least one situation that shows how each CMA standard is relevant to your experiences as a student. For example, the ethical standard of competence would suggest that you do not cut classes.

## ETHICAL ISSUE

### I1-50 Ethical dilemma *(Learning Objective 4)*

Ricardo Valencia recently resigned his position as controller for Tom White Automotive, a small, struggling car dealer in Edmunston, New Brunswick, that sells automobiles made by a foreign manufacturer. Valencia has just started a new job as controller for Mueller Imports, a much larger dealer for the same car manufacturer. Demand for this particular make of car is exploding, and the manufacturer cannot produce enough cars to satisfy demand. The manufacturer's regional sales managers are assigned a certain number of cars. Each regional sales manager then decides how to divide the cars among the independently owned dealerships in the region. Because most dealerships can sell every car they receive, each dealer's objective to is receive a large number of cars from the regional sales manager.

Valencia's former employer, White Automotive, receives about 25 cars a month, and the dealership is not very profitable.

Valencia is surprised to learn that his new employer, Mueller Imports, receives over 200 cars a month. Valencia soon gets another surprise. Every couple of months, a local jeweller bills the dealer $5,000 for "miscellaneous services." Franz Mueller, the owner of the dealership, personally approves the payment of these invoices, noting that each invoice is a "selling expense." From casual conversations with a salesperson, Valencia learns that Mueller frequently gives Rolex watches to the manufacturer's regional sales manager and other sales executives. Before talking to anyone about this, Valencia decides to work through his ethical dilemma by answering the following questions:

1. What is the ethical issue?
2. What are my options?

3. What are the possible consequences?
4. What should I do?

# TEAM PROJECT

## T1-51 Interviewing a local company about ecommerce *(Learning Objective 5)*

Search the internet for a nearby company that also has a Website. Arrange an interview with a management accountant, a controller, or another accounting/finance officer of the company. Before you conduct the interview, answer the following questions:

1. What is the company's primary product or service?
2. Is the primary purpose of the company's Website to provide information about the company and its products, to sell online, or to provide financial information for investors?
3. Are parts of the company's Website restricted so that you need password authorization to enter? What appears to be the purpose of limiting access?
4. Does the Website provide an e-mail link for contacting the company?

At the interview, begin by clarifying your answers to questions 1–4, and then ask the following additional questions:

5. If the company sells over the Web, what benefits has the company derived? Did the company perform a cost-benefit analysis before deciding to begin Web sales? Or, if the company does not sell over the Web, why not? Has the company performed a cost–benefit analysis and decided not to sell over the Web?
6. What is the biggest cost of operating the Website?
7. Does the company make any purchases over the internet? What percentage?
8. How has e-commerce affected the company's managerial accounting system? Have the management accountant's responsibilities become more or less complex? More or less interesting?
9. Does the company use Web-based accounting applications such as accounts receivable or accounts payable?
10. Does the company use an ERP system? If so, does it view the system as a success? What have been the benefits? The costs?

Prepare a report describing the results of your interview.

# DISCUSSION & ANALYSIS

1. What are the four main areas of management's responsibility? How are these four areas interrelated? How does managerial accounting support each of the responsibility areas of managers?
2. What is the Sarbanes-Oxley Act of 2002 (SOX)? How does SOX affect financial accounting? How does SOX impact managerial accounting? Is there any overlap between financial and managerial accounting in terms of SOX impact? If so, what are the areas of overlap?
3. Why is managerial accounting more suitable for internal reporting than financial accounting?
4. A company currently has all of its managerial accountants reporting to the controller. What might be inefficient about this organizational structure? How might the company restructure? What benefits would be offered by the restructuring?
5. What skills are required of a management accountant? In what university courses are these skills taught or developed? What skills would be further developed in the workplace?
6. How has technology changed the work of management accountants? What other business trends are influencing managerial accounting today? How do these other trends impact management accountants' roles in the organization?
7. What significant regulatory trends are affecting accounting in general today? How do these regulatory trends affect the field of managerial accounting?
8. Compare a traditional production system with a lean production system. Discuss the similarities and differences.

9. It has been said that external failure costs can be catastrophic and much higher than the costs of other categories. What are some examples of external failure costs? Why is it often difficult to arrive at the cost of external failures?

10. What are the four categories of quality-related costs? Name a cost in each of the four categories for each of the following types of organizations:

    a. Restaurant
    b. Hospital
    c. Law firm
    d. Bank
    e. Tire manufacturer
    f. University

# APPLICATION & ANALYSIS

## 1-1 Accountants and Their Jobs

### Discussion Questions *(Learning Objective 1, 2, and 3)*

1. When you think of an accountant, who do you picture? Do you personally know anyone (family member, friend, relative) whose chosen career is accounting? If so, do they fit your description of an accountant or not?
2. Before reading Chapter 1, what did you picture accountants doing, day in and day out, at their jobs? From where did this mental picture come (e.g., movies, first accounting class, speaking with accountants, etc.)?
3. What skills are highly valued by employers? What does that tell you about what accountants do at their companies?
4. Chapter 1 includes quotes from accountants at Sobey's, Abbott Laboratories, and Caterpillar. After reading these quotes and from what you know about accountants, how would you describe the role/job responsibilities of accountants?
5. Many, if not most, accounting majors start their careers in public accounting. Do you think most of them stay in public accounting? Discuss what you consider to be a typical career track for accounting majors.

### Classroom Applications

**Web**: Post the discussion questions on an electronic discussion board. Have small groups of students choose two or three of the questions to discuss.

**Classroom:** Form groups of three or four students. Assign each group a question and give the students 5–10 minutes to prepare a short presentation of their group's response to the question. Have the group present to the class.

**Independent:** Students research answers to each of the questions, and then turn in a two- or three-page typed paper (12 point font, double-spaced with 2.5 cm margins), including references.

## 1-2 Ethics at Enron

Watch the movie *Enron: The Smartest Guys in the Room* (Magnolia Home Entertainment, 2005, Los Angeles, California).

### Discussion Questions *(Learning Objective 4 and 5)*

1. Do you think such behaviour is common at other companies, or do you think this was a fairly isolated event?
2. How important is the "tone at the top" (the tone set by company leadership)?
3. Do you think you could be tempted to follow if the leadership at your company had the same mentality as the leadership at Enron, or do you think you would have the courage to "just say no" or even be a whistle-blower?
4. Why do you think some people can so easily justify (at least to themselves) their unethical behaviour?
5. In general, do you think people stop to think about how their actions will affect other people (e.g., the elderly in California who suffered due to electricity blackouts) or do they just "do their jobs"?

6. What was your reaction to the psychology experiment shown in the movie? Studies have shown that, unlike the traders at Enron (who received large bonuses), most employees really have very little to gain from following a superior's directive to act unethically. Why, then, do some people do it?
7. Do you think people weigh the potential costs of acting unethically with the potential benefits?
8. You are a business student who will someday work for a company or own a business. How will watching this movie affect the way you intend to conduct yourself as an employee or owner?
9. The reporter from *Fortune* magazine asked, "How does Enron make its money?" Why should every employee and manager (at every company) know the answer to this question?
10. In light of the "mark-to-market" accounting that enabled Enron to basically record any profit it wished, can you understand why some of the cornerstones of financial accounting are "conservatism" and "recording transactions at historical cost"?
11. How did employees of Enron (and employees of the utilities company in Oregon) end up losing billions in retirement funds?

## Classroom Applications

**Web:** Post the discussion questions on an electronic discussion board. Have small groups of students choose three to five of the questions to discuss among their group.

**Classroom:** Watch the movie before class. Once in class, form groups of three or four students. Assign each group a question and give the students 5–10 minutes to prepare a short presentation of their group's response to the question, which the group then presents to the class.

**Independent:** Students watch the movie and take notes. Students turn in a copy of their notes for full credit (without the notes students are only eligible for 1/2 credit). Leave notes handwritten. Students also turn in a two- to four-page typed paper describing their gut reactions to the movie. *Each paper should not be a summary of the movie; it should be the student's reaction to the movie.* Papers should try to address *most* of the questions.

# Building Blocks of Managerial Accounting

2

## Learning Objectives

1 Distinguish among service, merchandising, and manufacturing companies.

2 Describe the value chain and its elements.

3 Distinguish between direct and indirect costs.

4 Identify the inventoriable product costs and period costs of merchandising and manufacturing firms.

5 Prepare financial statements for service, merchandising, and manufacturing companies.

6 Describe costs that are relevant and irrelevant to decision making.

7 Classify costs as fixed or variable, and calculate total and average costs at different volumes.

Chapter 2, "Building Blocks of Managerial Accounting," covers material outlined in **Section 5, Part 3: Management Accounting** of the CPA Competency Map (by Competency Area). Content examined in this section includes discussions of cost classifications and cost behaviours, particularly as they apply to decision making.

PROFESSIONAL COMPETENCY — The presence of the **coverage button** in the margin indicates focus on one or more of the specific competency areas from the competency map. The concepts in the text are building blocks to developing the competencies required in the CPA. While the chapter may address multiple areas of the competency map, the main focus will be:

Competencies:

**3.3.1** Evaluates cost classifications and costing methods for management of ongoing operations*

**3.3.2** Evaluates and applies cost management techniques appropriate for specific costing decisions*

The first quarter results posted for Bombardier Inc. in May 2015 show revenues of $4.4 billion (up 1% from the previous year) and Earnings Before Interest and Taxes of $237 million (up 5.4% from the previous year).† Bombardier executives claim that Bombardier has weathered the economic turbulence of the past several years well and has over $65 billion in back-ordered planes, down $3.3 billion from December 2013. Executives argue that this demonstrates that Bombardier is able to execute its production model effectively and continues to meet the demands of its customers.

In terms of looking ahead to the future, Bombardier executives argue that its $6 billion of liquid assets make the company well positioned to advance development programs and to continue to be innovative. The company literature points to new advances in the Bombardier fleet including the first Challenger 650 aircraft and the new model 7000/8000 fleet currently in development. The company sees weakening demand and has already adjusted production schedules to meet this market change.

© Joe Sohm/Visions of America, LLC/Alamy

*Reprinted from *The Chartered Professional Accountant Competency Map - Understanding the competencies a candidate must demonstrate to become a CPA*, © 2012, with permission Chartered Professional Accountants of Canada, Toronto, Canada. Any changes to the original material are the sole responsibility of the author (and/or publisher) and have not been reviewed or endorsed by the Chartered Professional Accountants of Canada.

†Karen W. Braun, Wendy M Tietz and Louis Beaubien, *Managerial Accounting*, 3rd Ed., © 2018, Pearson Education, Inc., New York, NY.

The dual focus on research and development on meeting customer needs raises several questions about Bombardier: How much should be spent on research and development of new products when orders for current models are being cancelled? Is the current manufacturing design working efficiently? Are there cost-cutting measures that can be implemented during times of reduced cash inflow? In this chapter, we talk about many costs: costs that both managers and management accountants must understand to successfully run a business.

So far, we have seen how managerial accounting provides information that managers use to run their businesses more efficiently. Managers must understand basic managerial accounting terms and concepts before they can use the information to make good decisions. This terminology provides the common basis on which managers and accountants communicate. Without a common understanding of these concepts, managers may ask for (and accountants may provide) the wrong information for making decisions. As you will see, different types of costs are useful for different purposes. Both managers and accountants must have a clear understanding of the situation and the types of costs that are relevant to the decision at hand.

# What Are the Most Common Business Sectors and Their Activities?

Before we talk about specific types of costs, let's consider the three most common types of organization, and the business activities in which they incur costs: service, merchandising, and manufacturing.

## Service Companies

1 Distinguish among service, merchandising, and manufacturing companies.

Service companies are in business to sell intangible services—such as health care, insurance, banking, and consulting—rather than tangible products. Recall from Chapter 1 that service firms now make up the largest sector of the Canadian economy. Because these types of companies sell services, they generally do not have inventory.[1] Some service providers carry a minimal amount of supplies inventory; however, this inventory is generally used for internal operations—not sold for profit. Service companies incur costs to provide services, develop new services, advertise, and provide customer service. For many service providers, salaries and benefits make up over 70% of their costs.

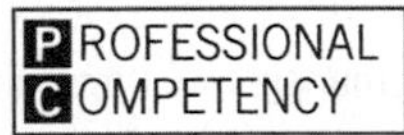

## Merchandising Companies

Merchandising companies such as Lowe's and Le Château resell tangible products they buy from suppliers. For example, Lowe's buys tools, electrical and plumbing fixtures, and gardening supplies and resells them to customers at higher prices. Merchandising companies include **retailers** (such as Lowe's) and **wholesalers**. Retailers sell to consumers such as you and me. Wholesalers buy products in bulk from manufacturers, mark up the prices, and then sell those products to retailers.

Because merchandising companies sell tangible products, they have inventory. The cost of inventory includes the cost merchandisers pay for the goods *plus* all costs necessary to get the merchandise in place and ready to sell, such as freight-in costs and any import duties or tariffs. A merchandiser's balance sheet reports just one inventory account called Inventory or Merchandise Inventory. Besides incurring inventory-related costs, merchandisers also incur costs to operate their retail stores and Websites, advertise, research new products and new store locations, and provide customer service.

## Manufacturing Companies

Manufacturing companies use labour, plant(s), and equipment to convert raw materials into new finished products. For example, Bombardier's production workers use the company's factories (production plant and equipment) to transform raw materials, such

[1]It should be noted that there are many organizations that have both services and products for sale. The service portion of the organization usually does not have an inventory account. For example, a hairstylist is really selling his or her time. If there are no customers for the afternoon, the hairstylist's time cannot be "inventoried" for another day—the time is simply lost. However, some organizations create work in process inventory accounts to accumulate the costs of long-term service projects. For example, a software developer may put the costs of developing a new software program into an inventory account if the job is going to take an extended period of time.

**EXHIBIT 2-1** Manufacturers' Three Types of Inventory

as steel, into high-performance trains and airplanes. Manufacturers typically sell their products to retailers or wholesalers at a price that is high enough to cover their costs and generate a profit; however, many also sell directly to their customers.

Because of their broader range of activities, manufacturers have three types of inventory (see Exhibit 2-1):

1. **Raw materials inventory:** all the raw materials used in manufacturing. Bombardier's raw materials include steel, glass, tires, upholstery fabric, engines, and other train and airplane components. It also includes other physical materials used in the plant, such as machine lubricants and janitorial supplies.
2. **Work in process inventory**: goods that are partway through the manufacturing process but not yet complete. At Bombardier, the work in process inventory consists of partially completed vehicles.
3. **Finished goods inventory**: completed goods that have not yet been sold. Once the vehicles Bombardier creates are completed, they are no longer considered work in process, but rather they become part of the finished goods inventory. Manufacturers sell units from the finished goods inventory to merchandisers or directly to consumers.

Exhibit 2-2 summarizes the differences among service, merchandising, and manufacturing companies.

**EXHIBIT 2-2** Service, Merchandising, and Manufacturing Companies

| | Service Companies | Merchandising Companies | Manufacturing Companies |
|---|---|---|---|
| Examples | Advertising agencies<br>Banks<br>Law firms<br>Insurance companies | eBay.ca<br>Walmart<br>La Senza<br>Wholesalers | Bombardier Inc.<br>Clodhoppers<br>McCain Foods Ltd.<br>Rocky Mountain Bicycles |
| Primary Output | Intangible services | Tangible products purchased from suppliers | New tangible products made as workers and equipment convert raw materials into new finished products |
| Type(s) of Inventory | None | Inventory (or Merchandise Inventory) | Raw materials inventory<br>Work in process inventory<br>Finished goods inventory |

## STOP & THINK

What type of company is Prime Restaurants Inc.?

**Answer:** Some companies do not fit nicely into one of the service, merchandising, or manufacturing categories. Restaurants are usually considered to be in the service sector. However, Prime has some elements of a **service company** (it serves hungry patrons), some elements of a **manufacturing company** (its chefs convert raw ingredients into finished meals), and some elements of a **merchandising company** (it sells ready-to-serve bottles of juice).

**Why is this important?**

All employees should have an **understanding** of their company's basic business model. The **Enron scandal** was finally brought to light as a **result** of someone seriously asking, "How does this company actually **make money**?" If the business model does not make **logical sense**, something fishy may be going on.

As the Stop & Think shows, not all companies are strictly service, merchandising, or manufacturing firms. Recall from Chapter 1 that the Canadian economy is shifting more toward service. Many traditional manufacturers, such as Bombardier, have developed profitable service divisions that provide much of their companies' profits. Even merchandising firms are getting into the service game by selling extended warranty contracts on merchandise sold. Retailers offer extended warranties on products ranging from furniture and major appliances to sporting equipment and consumer electronics. While the merchandiser recognizes a liability for these warranties, the price charged to customers for the warranties exceeds the company's cost of fulfilling its warranty obligations.

## Which Business Activities Make Up the Value Chain?

Many people describe Bombardier, McCain, and Dell as manufacturing companies. But it would be more accurate to say that these are companies that *do* manufacturing. Why? Because companies that do manufacturing also do many other things. Bombardier also conducts research to determine what type of new technology to incorporate into the next models, such as the new Learjet 85. Bombardier designs the new models based on its research and then produces, markets, distributes, and services the planes. These activities form Bombardier's __value chain__—the activities that add value to the company's products and services. The value chain is pictured in Exhibit 2-3.

2 Describe the value chain and its elements.

**EXHIBIT 2-3** The Value Chain

Value chain activities also cost money. To set competitive yet profitable selling prices, Bombardier must consider all of the costs incurred along the value chain, not just the costs incurred in manufacturing airplanes. Let us briefly consider some of the costs incurred in each element of the value chain.

__Research and Development (R&D):__ *Researching and developing new or improved products or services or the processes for producing them.* Bombardier continually engages in researching and developing new technologies to incorporate in its airplanes in order to lower the environmental impact of airplanes. For example, reducing emissions, fuel burn, and creating more aerodynamic designs will reduce weight, drag, and noise. Changes that positively affect environmental impact also occur in its manufacturing plants. Increased efficiency and innovation in its manufacturing environment is one of Bombardier's goals for corporate responsibility, which include implementing lean production methods and quality control initiatives. Bombardier spent $2.2 billion on research and development in 2013,[2] showing that considerable resources are being invested in finding new technologies and processes.

[2]www.bombardier.com/en/sustainability/sustainability-news/details.bombardier-inc-20141112bombardiertopscanadianrdspendersforsecond.sustainability.sustainability.html

Design

**Design**: *Detailed engineering of products and services and the processes for producing them.* Bombardier is a world leader in aerospace and rail transportation products and services. Since Bombardier also provides services such as fleet operations and maintenance, vehicle modernization, comprehensive training, and technical support, the products need to be designed in such a way that the services are integrated with the many different products that are offered.

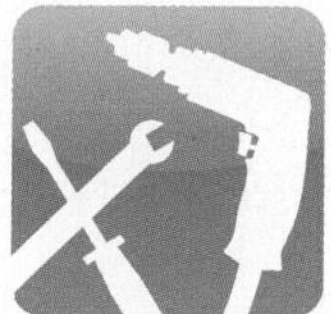
Production or purchases

**Production or Purchases**: *Resources used to produce a product or service, or to purchase finished merchandise intended for resale.* For Bombardier, the production activity includes all costs incurred to *make* planes and trains. Costs include raw materials (such as fabrics for plane and train interiors), plant labour (such as machine operators' wages and benefits), and manufacturing overhead (such as factory utilities and depreciation on the factory). As you can imagine, factories are very expensive to build and operate. In 2000 and 2001, Bombardier invested over US$170 million just to build and equip a manufacturing plant at the Montreal airport to build its new 90-seat CRJ900 jet aircraft.

For a merchandiser such as Le Château, this value chain activity includes the cost of purchasing the inventory that the company plans to sell to customers. It also includes all costs associated with getting the inventory to the store, including freight-in costs and any import duties and tariffs that might be incurred if the merchandise was purchased from overseas.

Marketing

**Marketing**: *Promotion and advertising of products or services.* The goal of marketing is to create consumer demand for products and services. Bombardier uses an integrated approach to marketing the aircraft division. The products are separated into three divisions: Learjet, Challenger, and Global. Each product division is differentiated by colour in print advertising, on the company's Website, in videos, and in other marketing elements such as trade show and headquarters designs. Some companies use sponsorship of star athletes and sporting events to market their products. Each method of advertising costs money but adds value by reaching different target customers.

Distribution

**Distribution**: *Delivery of products or services to customers.* Bombardier sells most of its trains and airplanes through a bidding process. The company must put together a proposal for supplying aircraft and compete with other companies in order to win the bid. It anticipates delivering 12,500 new airplanes over the next 20 years; 5,600 units are incremental sales due to increasing air travel, while 6,900 units are expected to replace aircraft as they are retired. Bombardier's distribution costs include the costs of shipping the vehicles to customers. Other industries use different distribution mechanisms. For example, Tupperware primarily sells its products through home-based parties, while Amazon.ca sells only through the Internet. Sears was quite well known for its catalogue, which was provided to consumers across Canada, and especially the "Wish Book" that was first distributed in 1933 so that people could order goods in time for Christmas.

Customer service

**Customer Service**: *Support provided for customers after the sale.* Bombardier offers a diverse range of services to support its products. These services include providing parts and service for aircraft maintenance. There are two main storage warehouses for parts: one in Chicago, Illinois, and another in Frankfurt, Germany. There are also six parts depots around the world. For a full understanding of the types of services available to customers of Bombardier's aerospace division, you can refer to its Website.[3]

**Why is this important?**

All activities in the **value chain** are important, yet each costs **money** to perform. Managers must understand how **decisions** made in one area of the value chain will **affect the costs** incurred in other areas of the value chain.

## Coordinating Activities Across the Value Chain

Many value chain activities occur in the order discussed here. However, Bombardier managers cannot simply work on R&D and not think about customer service. Rather, cross-functional teams need to work simultaneously on R&D, design, production, marketing, distribution, and customer service. As the teams develop new model features, they also plan how to produce, market, and distribute the redesigned airplanes and trains. They also consider

[3]www.bombardier.com

how the new design will affect warranty costs. Cross-functional teams such as these help organizations integrate their activities throughout the value chain, even at the highest level of global operations.

The value chain in Exhibit 2-3 also reminds managers to control costs over the value chain as a whole. For example, it is likely that Bombardier spends more in R&D and product design to increase the quality of its transportation products, which, in turn, reduces customer service costs. Even though R&D and design costs are higher, the total cost of the vehicle—as measured throughout the entire value chain—is lower as a result of this trade-off. Enhancing its reputation for high-quality products has also enabled Bombardier to become a world leader in aerospace and transportation products.

The value chain applies to service and merchandising firms as well as manufacturing firms. For example, an advertising agency such as MediaFlame in Vancouver incurs the following:

- *Design* costs to develop each client's ad campaign
- *Marketing* costs to obtain new clients
- *Distribution* costs to get the ads to the media
- *Customer service* costs to address each client's concerns

## Sustainability and the Value Chain

Progressive companies will incorporate environmental sustainability throughout every function of the value chain. However, experts estimate that 90% of sustainability is designed in. At the design stage, companies determine how the product will be used by customers, how easily the product can be repaired and eventually recycled, and the types of raw materials and manufacturing processes necessary to produce the product. Thus, good design is essential to the creation of environmentally friendly and safe products that enhance people's lives. Companies can integrate sustainability throughout the value chain by:

See Exercises E2-18A and E2-35B

- ***Researching and developing environmentally safe packaging.*** Frito-Lay has developed a compostable bag for its original Sun Chips product. The bag is made out of vegetables rather than plastic.
- ***Designing the product using lifecycle assessment and biomimicry practices.*** Life cycle assessment means the company analyzes the environmental impact of a product, from cradle to grave, in an attempt to minimize negative environmental consequences throughout the entire life span of the product. Biomimicry means that a company tries to mimic, or copy, the natural biological process in which dead organisms (plants and animals) become the input for another organism or process. Ricoh's copiers were designed so that, at the end of a copier's useful life, Ricoh can collect and dismantle the product for usable parts, shred the metal casing, and use the parts and shredded material to build new copiers. The entire copier was designed so that nothing is wasted or thrown out except the dust from the shredding process. PepsiCo recently announced the development of a plastic bottle that is made entirely out of nonedible plant materials such as corn husks, pine bark, and switch grass. These byproducts are the result of manufacturing its other food products (for Frito-Lay, Quaker Oats, and Tropicana).
- ***Adopting sustainable purchasing practices.*** Companies can purchase raw materials from suppliers that are geographically proximate, or from suppliers that embrace sustainability. For example, Walmart has recently mandated that all of its suppliers conform to certain sustainability requirements. As the leading retailer in the world, Walmart's own purchasing policies are forcing other companies to adopt sustainable practices.
- ***Marketing with integrity.*** Consumers are driving much of the sustainability movement by demanding that companies produce environmentally friendly products and limit or eliminate operational practices that have a negative impact on the environment. Thus, many companies are successfully spotlighting their

sustainability initiatives in order to increase market share and attract potential investors and employees. Honesty and integrity in marketing are imperative, however, as "greenwashing," the unfortunate practice of *overstating* a company's commitment to sustainability, can ultimately backfire when investors and consumers learn the truth about company operations.

- ***Distributing and using fossil-fuel alternatives and carbon offsets.*** While the biofuel industry is still in its infancy, the production and use of biofuels, especially those generated from nonfood waste, are expected to grow exponentially in the near future. Companies whose business is heavily reliant upon fossil fuels, such as oil companies (Petro-Canada), airlines (Air Canada), and distribution companies (Canada Post), are especially interested in the development of biofuel alternatives. Continental Airlines in the United States offers a carbon-offset program that allows companies (and consumers) to calculate the carbon emissions resulting from their business travel and air-freighting activities. The customer has the option to purchase carbon offsets (reforestation projects, renewable energy projects, etc.) to mitigate the emissions resulting from shipping and travel.
- ***Providing customer service past the warranty date.*** Currently, the average life of many home appliances such as dishwashers and refrigerators is less than 10 years. However, the original manufacturer could provide valuable customer service and prevent appliances from ending up in landfills, while at the same time creating a new revenue stream, by offering reasonably priced repair services for products that have exceeded the warranty date. For those products that are not repairable, the company could institute a policy such as Ricoh's, in which the company takes back the old product and recycles it into new products.

# How Do Companies Define Cost?

How do companies such as Scotiabank determine how much it costs to serve a customer? How do companies such as Bombardier determine the cost to produce a high-speed train? Before we can answer this question, let us first consider some of the specialized language that we use when referring to costs.

**3** Distinguish between direct and indirect costs.

## Cost Objects, Direct Costs, and Indirect Costs

A <u>cost object</u> is anything for which managers want a separate measurement of cost. Bombardier's cost objects may include the following:

- Individual units (a specific, custom-ordered high-speed train)
- Different models (Learjet 45, Learjet 85, Q400, etc.)
- Product divisions (aerospace or transportation)
- Geographic segments of the business (North America, Europe, Africa)
- Departments (human resources, R&D, legal)

Costs are classified as either direct or indirect with respect to the cost object. A <u>direct cost</u> is a cost that can be easily traced to the cost object. For example, let's say the cost object is one Learjet 85. Bombardier can easily <u>trace</u> the cost of seats to a specific Learjet 85; therefore, the seats are a direct cost of the airplane.

It should be noted that not all costs that can be traced to a cost object are classed as direct costs. If the cost isn't easily traced to the cost object, it may not warrant the effort required, and therefore it will be classed as an <u>indirect cost</u>. An indirect cost is a cost that relates to the cost object but cannot easily be traced to it. For example, Bombardier incurs substantial costs to run a manufacturing plant, including utilities, property taxes, and

**Why is this important?**

As a manager **making decisions**, you'll need different types of **cost information** for different types of decisions. To get the **information** you really want, you must be able to **communicate** with the accountants using precise **definitions** of cost.

depreciation. Bombardier cannot build a Learjet 85 without incurring these costs, so the costs are related to the Learjet 85. However, it is impossible, or too difficult and costly, to trace a specific amount of these costs to one Learjet. Therefore, these costs are considered indirect costs of a single Learjet 85.

Whether a cost is direct or indirect depends on the specified cost object. As shown in Exhibit 2-4, the same costs can be indirect with respect to one cost object but direct with respect to another cost object. For example, plant depreciation, property taxes, and utilities are indirect costs of a single Learjet 85. However, if management wants to know how much it costs to run the Learjet 85 manufacturing plant in Montreal, the plant becomes the cost object, so the same depreciation, tax, and utility costs are direct costs of the manufacturing facility. In most cases, we will be talking about a unit of product (such as one Learjet 85) as the cost object.

**EXHIBIT 2-4** The Same Cost Can Be Direct or Indirect, Depending on the Cost Object

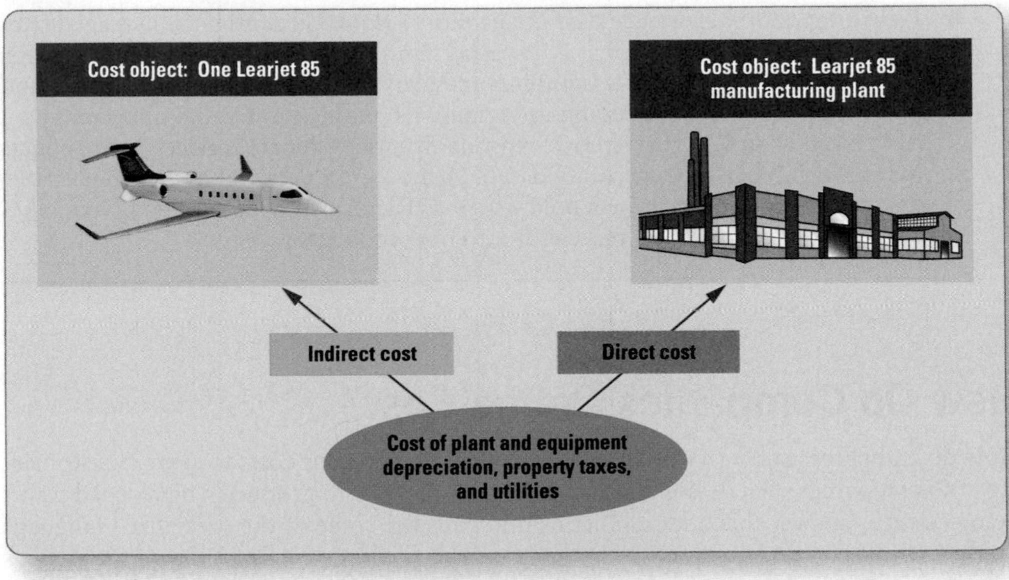

If a company wants to know the *total* cost attributable to a cost object, it must **assign** all direct *and* indirect costs to the cost object. Assigning a cost simply means that you are "attaching" a cost to the cost object. Why? Because the cost object caused the company to incur that cost. In determining the cost of a Learjet 85, Bombardier assigns both the cost of the seats *and* the cost of running the manufacturing plant to the Learjet 85s built at the plant.

Bombardier assigns direct costs to each Learjet 85 by tracing those costs to specific airplanes. This results in a very precise cost figure, giving managers great confidence in the cost's accuracy. However, because Bombardier cannot trace indirect costs to specific airplanes, it must **allocate** these costs among all of the planes produced at the plant. The allocation process results in a less precise cost figure being assigned to the cost object (one plane). We will discuss the allocation process in more detail in the following two chapters; but for now, think of allocation as dividing up the total indirect costs between all of the units produced, just as you might divide a pizza among friends. Exhibit 2-5 illustrates these concepts.

**EXHIBIT 2-5** Assigning Direct and Indirect Costs to Cost Objects

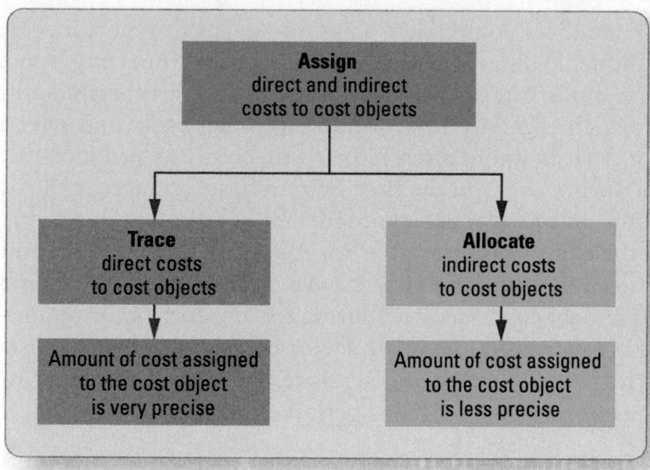


## TRY IT!

Assume a grocery store manager wants to know the cost of running the Produce Department. Thus, the Produce Department is the cost object. Which of the following would be considered direct costs of the Produce Department?

1. Wages of checkout clerks
2. Wages for workers in the Produce Department
3. Depreciation on refrigerated produce display cases
4. Cost of weekly advertisements in local newspaper
5. Cost of bananas, lettuce, and other produce
6. Baggies and twist ties available for shoppers in the Produce Department
7. Monthly lease payment for grocery store retail location
8. Cost of scales hanging in the Produce Department

Please see page 109 for solutions.

## Costs for Internal Decision Making and External Reporting

4 Identify the inventoriable product costs and period costs of merchandising and manufacturing firms.

Let us look more carefully at how companies determine the costs of one of the most common cost objects: products. As a manager, you will want to focus on the products that are most profitable. But which products are these? To determine a product's profitability, you subtract the cost of the product from its selling price. But how do you calculate the cost of the product? Most companies use two different definitions of cost: (1) **total costs** for internal decision making; and (2) **inventoriable product costs** for external reporting. Let us see what they are and how managers use each type of cost.

### Total Costs for Internal Decision Making

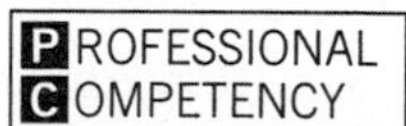


Total costs include the costs of *all resources used throughout the value chain*. For Bombardier, the total cost of a particular model, such as the Learjet 85, is the total cost to research, design, manufacture, market, distribute, and service that model. Before launching a new model, managers predict the total costs of the model in order to set a selling price that will cover *all costs* plus return a profit. Bombardier also compares each model's sale revenue to its total cost to determine which models are most profitable. Perhaps the Learjet 85 is more profitable than the Q400. Marketing can then focus on advertising and promoting the most profitable models. We will talk more about total costs in Chapter 8, where we discuss many common business decisions. For the next few chapters, we will concentrate primarily on inventoriable product costs.

### Inventoriable Product Costs for External Reporting

IFRS and ASPE do not allow companies to use total costs to report inventory balances or cost of goods sold in the financial statements. For external reporting, reporting standards allow only a *portion* of the total cost to be treated as an inventoriable product cost. IFRS and ASPE specify which costs are inventoriable product costs and which costs are not. Inventoriable product costs (quite often referred to simply as product costs) include *only* the costs incurred during the "production or purchase" stages of the value chain (see Exhibit 2-6). Inventoriable product costs are treated as an asset (inventory) until the product is sold. Hence, the name "inventoriable" product cost. When the product is sold, these costs are removed from inventory and expensed as cost of goods sold. Since inventoriable product costs include only costs incurred during the production or purchases stage of the value chain, all costs incurred in the other stages of the value chain must be expensed in the period in which they are incurred. Therefore, we refer to R&D, design, marketing, distribution, and customer service costs as **period costs**.

Period costs are often called "operating expenses" or "selling, general, and administrative expenses" (SG&A) on the company's income statement. Period costs are *always* expensed in the period in which they are incurred and *never* become part of an inventory account.

**EXHIBIT 2-6** Total Costs, Inventoriable Product Costs, and Period Costs

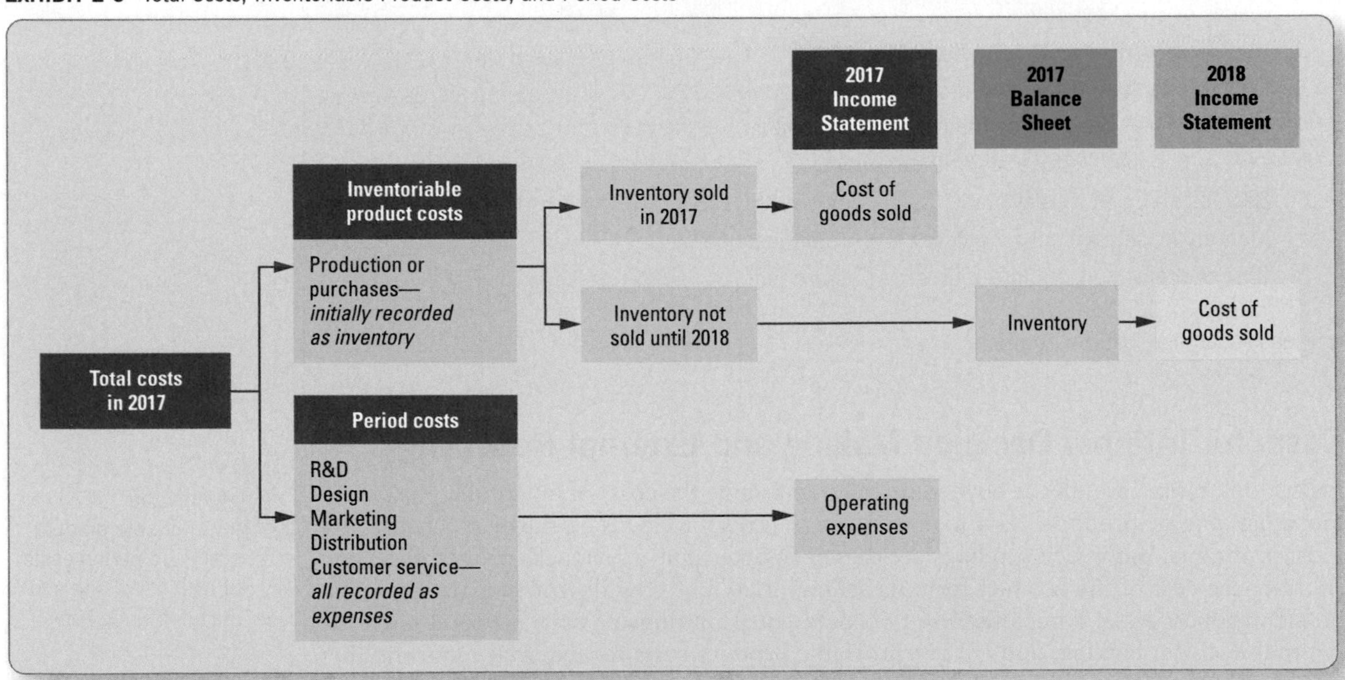


Exhibit 2-6 shows that a company's total cost has two components: inventoriable product costs (those costs treated as part of inventory until the product is sold) and period costs (those costs expensed in the current period regardless of when inventory is sold). IFRS and ASPE require this distinction for external financial reporting. Study the exhibit carefully to make sure you understand how the two cost components affect the income statement and balance sheet.

Now that you understand the difference between inventoriable product costs and period costs, let us take a closer look at the specific costs that are inventoriable in merchandising and manufacturing companies.

## TRY IT!

Pepsi Corporation uses trucks to transport bottles from the warehouse to different retail outlets. This problem focuses on the cost of operating a truck. Gasoline costs are $0.15 per km driven. Insurance costs are $6,000 per year. Calculate the total costs and the cost per mile for gasoline and insurance if the truck is driven:

(a) 20,000 km per year or

(b) 30,000 km per year

Please see page 109 for solutions.

## Merchandising Companies' Inventoriable Product Costs

Merchandising companies' inventoriable product costs include *only* the cost of purchasing the inventory from suppliers plus any costs incurred to get the merchandise to the merchandiser's place of business and ready for sale. Typically, these additional costs include freight-in costs and import duties or tariffs if the products were purchased from outside Canada. Why does the cost of the inventory include freight-in charges? Think of the last time you purchased a book from an online store such as Chapters. The Website may have shown the book's price as $20, but by the time you paid the shipping and handling charges, the book really cost you around $25. Likewise, merchandising companies pay freight-in charges to get the goods to their place of business (plus import duties if the goods were manufactured out of the country). These charges become part of the cost of their inventory.

For instance, Lowe's inventoriable product costs include what the company paid for its store merchandise plus freight-in and import duties. Lowe's records these costs in an asset account—Inventory—until it sells the merchandise. Once the merchandise sells, it belongs to the customer, not Lowe's. Therefore, Lowe's takes the cost out of its inventory account and records it as an expense—the cost of goods sold.

Lowe's expenses costs incurred in other elements of the value chain as period costs. For example, Lowe's period costs include store operating expenses (such as salaries, utilities, and depreciation) and advertising expenses.

Some companies, such as Pier 1 Imports, refer to their cost of goods sold as "cost of sales." However, we use the more specific term *cost of goods sold* throughout the text because it more aptly describes the actual cost being expensed in the account—the inventoriable product cost of the goods themselves.

## STOP & THINK

What are the inventoriable product costs for a service firm such as H&R Block?

**Answer:** Service firms such as H&R Block have no inventory of products for sale. Services cannot be produced today and stored up to sell later. Because service firms have no inventory, they have no inventoriable product costs. Instead, they have only period costs that are expensed as they are incurred.

## Manufacturing Companies' Inventoriable Product Costs

Manufacturing companies' inventoriable product costs include *only* those costs incurred during the production element of the value chain. As shown in Exhibit 2-7, manufacturers such as Bombardier incur three types of manufacturing costs when making a plane: **direct materials**, **direct labour**, and **manufacturing overhead**.

**EXHIBIT 2-7** Summary of the Three Types of Manufacturing Costs

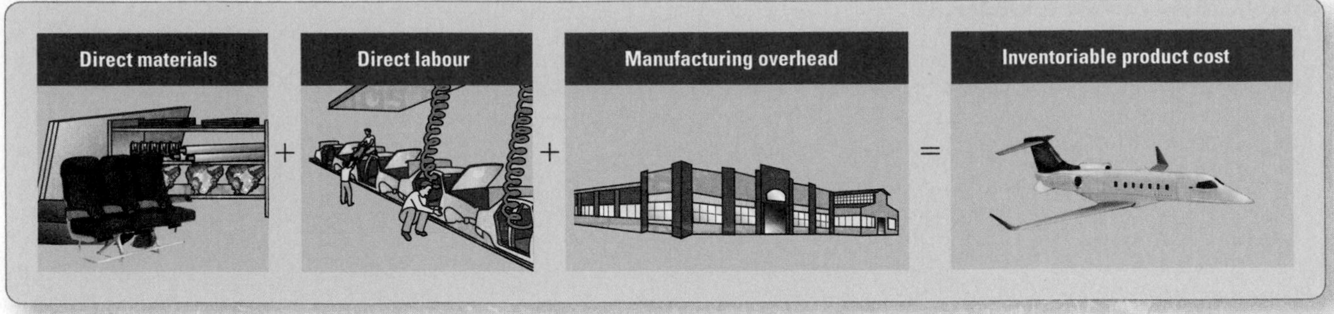


## Direct Materials (DM)

Manufacturers convert raw materials into finished products. Direct materials are the primary raw materials that become a physical part of the finished product. The Learjet's direct materials include aluminum, tires, seats, engines, plastic components, carpet, cockpit instruments, and so forth. Bombardier can trace the cost of these materials (including freight-in and import duties) to specific units or batches of planes; thus, they are considered direct costs of the planes.

## Direct Labour (DL)

Although many manufacturing facilities are highly automated, most still require some direct labour to convert raw materials into a finished product. Direct labour is the cost of compensating employees who physically convert raw materials into the company's products. At Bombardier, direct labour includes the wages and benefits of machine operators and technicians who assemble the parts and wire the electronics to build the completed planes. These costs are direct with respect to the cost object (the plane) because Bombardier can trace the time each of these employees spends working on specific units or batches of planes.

## Manufacturing Overhead (MOH)

The third production cost is manufacturing overhead. Manufacturing overhead includes all manufacturing costs other than direct materials and direct labour. In other words, manufacturing overhead includes all indirect manufacturing costs. Manufacturing overhead is also referred to as factory overhead, because all of these costs relate to the factory. As shown in Exhibit 2-8, manufacturing overhead has three components: **indirect materials**, **indirect labour**, and **other indirect manufacturing costs**.

**EXHIBIT 2-8** Components of Manufacturing Overhead

Indirect materials $

Indirect labour $

Other indirect manufacturing costs $

Manufacturing overhead $$$

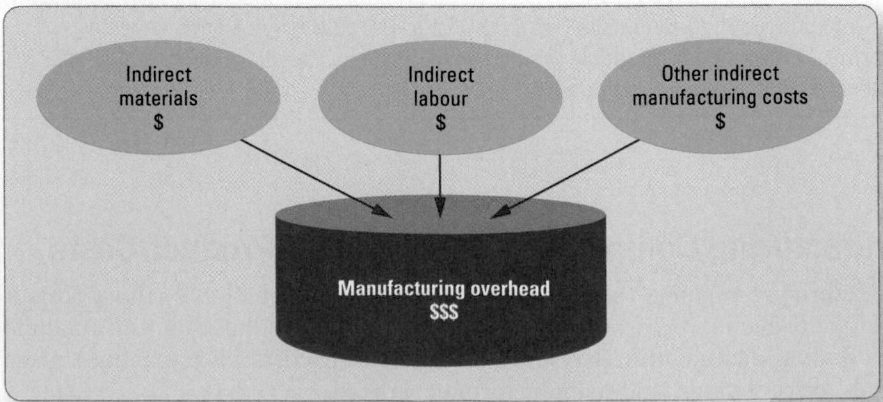

- Indirect materials include materials used in the plant that are not easily traced to the cost object. For example, indirect materials often include oil and lubricants for the machines and any physical components of the finished product that are very inexpensive. For example, Bombardier might treat the solder used to attach different components as an indirect material rather than a direct material. Even though the cost of the solder *could* be traced to the plane, it would not make much sense to do so. Why? Because the cost of tracing the solder to the plane outweighs the benefit management receives from the increased accuracy of the information. Therefore, Bombardier likely treats the cost of the solder as an indirect material, which becomes part of manufacturing overhead.
- Indirect labour includes the cost of all employees in the plant, other than those employees directly converting the raw materials into the finished product. For example, at Bombardier indirect labour includes the salaries, wages, and benefits of plant forklift operators, plant security officers, plant janitors, and plant supervisors.
- Other indirect manufacturing costs include such plant-related costs as insurance and depreciation on the plant and plant equipment, plant property taxes, plant repairs and maintenance, and plant utilities. Indirect manufacturing costs have grown in recent years as manufacturers automate their plants with the latest technology.

In summary, manufacturing overhead includes all manufacturing costs other than direct materials and direct labour.

## Review: Inventoriable Product Costs or Period Costs?

Exhibit 2-9 summarizes the differences between inventoriable product costs and period costs for service, merchandising, and manufacturing companies. Study this exhibit carefully. When are such costs as depreciation, insurance, utilities, and property taxes inventoriable product costs? *Only* when those costs are related to the manufacturing plant. When those costs are related to nonmanufacturing activities such as R&D or marketing, they are treated as period costs. Service companies and merchandisers do no manufacturing, so they always treat depreciation, insurance, utilities, and property taxes as period costs.

**EXHIBIT 2-9** Inventoriable Product Costs and Period Costs for Service, Merchandising, and Manufacturing Companies

| | Inventoriable Product Costs | Period Costs |
|---|---|---|
| Accounting Treatment | • Initially recorded as inventory<br>• Expensed as *cost of goods sold* only when inventory is sold | • Always recorded as an expense<br>• Never considered part of inventory |
| Type of Company: | | |
| Service company | • None | • All costs along the value chain<br>• For example, salaries, depreciation expense, utilities, insurance, property taxes, and advertising |
| Merchandising company | • Purchases of merchandise<br>• Freight-in; customs and duties | • All costs along the value chain *except* for the purchases element<br>• For example, salaries, depreciation expense, utilities, insurance, property taxes, advertising, and freight-out |
| Manufacturing company | • Direct materials<br>• Direct labour<br>• Manufacturing overhead (including indirect materials, indirect labour, and other indirect manufacturing costs) | • All costs along the value chain *except* for the production element<br>• For example, R&D; freight-out; all expenses for executive headquarters (separate from plant), including depreciation, utilities, insurance, and property taxes; advertising; and CEO's salary |

When you studied financial accounting, you probably studied nonmanufacturing firms for the majority of examples. Therefore, salaries, depreciation, insurance, and taxes were usually expensed.

## Prime and Conversion Costs

Managers and accountants sometimes talk about certain combinations of manufacturing costs. As shown in Exhibit 2-10, **prime costs** refer to the combination of direct materials and direct labour. Prime costs used to be the primary costs of production. However, as companies have automated production with expensive machinery, manufacturing overhead has become a greater cost of production. **Conversion costs** refer to the combination of direct labour and manufacturing overhead. These are the costs of *converting* direct materials into finished goods.

**EXHIBIT 2-10** Prime and Conversion Costs

| | | | | |
|---|---|---|---|---|
| Prime costs | = | Direct materials | + | Direct labour |
| Conversion costs | = | Manufacturing overhead | + | Direct labour |

## Additional Labour Compensation Costs

In all areas of the value chain, the cost of labour includes more than the salaries and wages paid to employees. The cost also includes company-paid benefits such as health insurance, retirement plan contributions, payroll taxes, and paid vacations. These costs are very expensive.

Health insurance premiums for dental and extended health care (the largest cost of this being the prescription medication coverage) often amount to $300 per month for each employee electing family coverage. This does not include coverage for life insurance or accidental death and dismemberment, both of which are dependent upon the salary of the individual for the cost of the premium.

Many companies also contribute an amount up to 9% of their employees' salaries to company-sponsored retirement (RRSP) plans or company pension plans. Larger employers must pay workplace health and safety premiums and provincial health taxes. In addition, most companies offer paid vacation and other benefits. Together, these benefits usually cost the company an additional 35% beyond gross salaries and wages. Thus, an assembly-line worker who makes a $40,000 salary costs Bombardier approximately $14,000 more (= $40,000 × 35%) in benefits. Throughout the remainder of this book, any references to wages or salaries also include the cost of benefits.

# DECISION GUIDELINES

## Building Blocks of Managerial Accounting

Dell engages in *manufacturing* when it assembles its computers, *merchandising* when it sells them on its Website, and support *services* such as start-up and implementation services. When Dell first began operating, the managers probably had to make the following types of decisions as the company developed its accounting systems.

| Decision | Guidelines |
|---|---|
| I'm setting up a new accounting system and the system designer asked me what type of organization this is. Why would this make a difference? | The type of organization affects how the financial statements are produced.<br>*Service companies:*<br>• Provide customers with intangible services<br>• Have no inventories on the balance sheet<br>*Merchandising companies:*<br>• Resell tangible products purchased ready-made from suppliers<br>• Have only one category of inventory<br>*Manufacturing companies:*<br>• Use labour, plant, and equipment to transform raw materials into new finished products<br>• Have three categories of inventory:<br>**1.** Raw materials inventory<br>**2.** Work in process inventory<br>**3.** Finished goods inventory |
| I would like to analyze what activities the company does that add value. How can I divide the activities I analyze? | The organization's activities can be divided into the activities of the value chain, including the following:<br>• R&D<br>• Design<br>• Production or Purchases<br>• Marketing<br>• Distribution<br>• Customer Service |
| I'm trying to determine the cost of my products. What costs should be assigned to cost objects such as products, departments, and geographic segments? | Both direct and indirect costs are assigned to cost objects. Direct costs are *traced* to cost objects, whereas indirect costs are *allocated* to cost objects. |
| Is the cost that I calculate the same for internal use as it is for external reporting? | Managers use *total costs* for internal decision making. However, reporting standards require companies to use only *inventoriable product costs* for external financial reporting. |
| How does the type of organization affect what I report as the cost of my product according to the applicable reporting standards (IFRS or ASPE)? | • *Service companies:* No inventoriable product costs<br>• *Merchandising companies:* The cost of merchandise purchased for resale plus all of the costs of getting the merchandise to the company's place of business (for example, freight-in and import duties)<br>• *Manufacturing companies:* Direct materials, direct labour, and manufacturing overhead |
| How will the treatment of the costs affect the financial statements? | Inventoriable product costs are initially treated as assets (Inventory) on the balance sheet. These costs are expensed (as cost of goods sold) on the income statements when the products are sold. |

# SUMMARY PROBLEM 1

**Requirements**

1. Classify each of the following business costs into one of the six value chain elements:
   a. Costs of warranties and recalls for a manufacturer
   b. Cost of shipping finished goods to overseas customers
   c. Costs of developing new drugs for a pharmaceutical company
   d. Cost of a 30-second commercial during the Stanley Cup playoffs
   e. Cost of making a new product prototype
   f. Cost of assembly labour used in the plant
2. For a manufacturing company, identify the following as either an inventoriable product cost or a period cost. If it is an inventoriable product cost, classify it as direct materials, direct labour, or manufacturing overhead.
   a. Depreciation on plant equipment
   b. Depreciation on salespeople's automobiles
   c. Insurance on plant building
   d. Marketing manager's salary
   e. Cost of major components of the finished product
   f. Assembly-line workers' wages
   g. Costs of shipping finished products to customers
   h. Forklift operator's salary

## ▪ SOLUTIONS

**Requirement 1**

a. Customer service
b. Distribution
c. Research and Development
d. Marketing
e. Design
f. Production

**Requirement 2**

a. Inventoriable product cost; manufacturing overhead
b. Period cost
c. Inventoriable product cost; manufacturing overhead
d. Period cost
e. Inventoriable product cost; direct materials
f. Inventoriable product cost; direct labour
g. Period cost
h. Inventoriable product cost; manufacturing overhead

## How are Inventoriable Product Costs and Period Costs Shown in the Financial Statements?

5 Prepare financial statements for service, merchandising, and manufacturing companies.

The difference between inventoriable product costs and period costs is important because these costs are treated differently in the financial statements. All costs incurred in the production or purchases area of the value chain are inventoriable product costs that remain in inventory accounts until the merchandise is sold—then, these costs become the cost of goods sold. However, costs incurred in all other areas of the value chain (R&D, design, marketing, distribution, and customer service) are period costs, which are expensed on the income statement in the period in which they are incurred. Keep these differences in mind as we review the income statements of service firms (which have no inventory), merchandising companies (which purchase their inventory), and manufacturers (which make their inventory). We will finish the section by comparing the balance sheets of these three different types of companies.

## Service Companies

Service companies have the simplest income statement. Exhibit 2-11 shows the income statement of eNow!, a group of e-commerce consultants. The firm has no inventory and thus, no inventoriable product costs, so eNow!'s income statement has no cost of goods sold. Rather, all of the company's costs are period costs, so they are expensed in the current period as operating expenses.

**EXHIBIT 2-11** Service Company Income Statement

**eNOW!**
**Income Statement**
**Year Ended December 31, 2017**

| | | |
|---|---|---|
| Revenues | | $ 160,000 |
| Operating expenses: | | |
| Salary expense | $106,000 | |
| Office rent expense | 18,000 | |
| Depreciation expense—furniture and equipment | 3,500 | |
| Marketing expense | 2,500 | |
| Total operating expenses | | (130,000) |
| Operating income | | $ 30,000 |

In this textbook, we always use *operating income* rather than *net income* as the bottom line on the income statement since internal managers are particularly concerned with the income generated through operations. To determine net income, we would have to deduct interest expense and income taxes from operating income and add back interest income. In general, operating income is simply the company's income before interest and income taxes.

## Merchandising Companies

In contrast with service companies, merchandisers' income statements feature cost of goods sold as the major expense. Consider Apex Showrooms, a merchandiser of lighting fixtures. Apex's *only* inventoriable product costs are the costs of the chandeliers and track lights that it purchases from suppliers, plus freight-in. Merchandisers such as Apex compute the cost of goods sold as follows:[4]

| | | |
|---|---|---|
| Beginning inventory | $ 9,500 | What Apex had at the beginning of the period |
| + Purchases, freight-in and import duties | 110,000 | What Apex bought during the period |
| = Cost of goods available for sale | 119,500 | Total available for sale during the period |
| − Ending inventory | (13,000) | What Apex had left at the end of the period |
| = Cost of goods sold | $106,500 | What Apex sold during the period |

[4]Even companies that use perpetual inventory systems during the year recalculate cost of goods sold in this manner before preparing their annual financial statements.

Exhibit 2-12 shows Apex's complete income statement, in which we have highlighted the cost of goods sold computation. Many companies do not show the computation of cost of goods sold directly on the face of the income statement, preferring to show only the cost of goods sold figure that was obtained through the calculation performed above ($106,500). However, either presentation is acceptable. Cost of goods sold is then deducted from Sales Revenue to determine the company's gross profit. Finally, all operating expenses (period costs) are deducted from gross profit to arrive at the company's operating income.

**EXHIBIT 2-12** Merchandiser's Income Statement

| APEX SHOWROOMS<br>Income Statement<br>Year Ended December 31, 2017 | | |
|---|---|---|
| Sales revenues | | $ 150,000 |
| Cost of goods sold: | | |
| Beginning inventory | $ 9,500 | |
| Purchases, freight-in, and import duties | 110,000 | |
| Cost of goods available for sale | 119,500 | |
| Ending inventory | (13,000) | |
| Cost of goods sold | | 106,500 |
| Gross profit | | 43,500 |
| Operating expenses: | | |
| Showroom rent expense | 5,000 | |
| Sales salary expense | 4,000 | 9,000 |
| Operating income | | $ 34,500 |

## TRY IT!

Compute cost of goods sold for Ralph's Sporting Goods, a merchandising company, given the following information:

| | |
|---|---|
| Advertising expense | $, 25,000 |
| Purchase of merchandise | 400,000 |
| Salaries expense | 80,000 |
| Freight-in and import duties | 20,000 |
| Lease of store | 75,000 |
| Beginning inventory | 35,000 |
| Ending inventory | 38,000 |

Please see page 109 for solutions.

## Manufacturing Companies

Exhibit 2-13 shows the income statement of Top-Flite, a manufacturer of golf clubs. Compare its income statement with the merchandiser's income statement in Exhibit 2-12. The only difference is that the merchandiser (Apex) uses purchases and freight-in to compute cost of goods sold, whereas the manufacturer (Top-Flite) uses the **cost of goods manufactured** (we have highlighted both in blue). Notice that the term *cost of goods manufactured* is in the past tense. It was the cost of manufacturing the goods that Top-Flite finished making during 2017. This is the manufacturer's cost to obtain new, finished goods that are ready to sell. Thus, it is the counterpart of the merchandiser's purchases. Next, we will show you how to calculate the cost of goods manufactured.

**EXHIBIT 2-13** Manufacturer's Income Statement

| TOP-FLITE<br>Income Statement<br>Year Ended December 31, 2017 | | |
|---|---|---|
| Sales revenue | | $65,000 |
| Cost of goods sold: | | |
| Beginning finished goods inventory | $ 6,000 | |
| Cost of goods manufactured* | 42,000 | |
| Cost of goods available for sale | 48,000 | |
| Ending finished goods inventory | (8,000) | |
| Cost of goods sold | | 40,000 |
| Gross profit | | 25,000 |
| Operating expenses: | | |
| Sales salary expense | 3,000 | |
| Delivery expense | 7,000 | |
| Operating income | | 10,000 |
| | | $15,000 |

*From the Schedule of Cost of Goods Manufactured in Exhibit 2-15.

## Calculating the Cost of Goods Manufactured

The cost of goods manufactured summarizes the cost of activities that take place in a manufacturing plant over the period. Let us begin by reviewing these activities, pictured in Exhibit 2-14. The manufacturer starts by buying direct materials, which are stored in raw materials inventory until they are needed for production. Only those direct materials

**EXHIBIT 2-14** Flow of Costs through a Manufacturer's Financial Statements

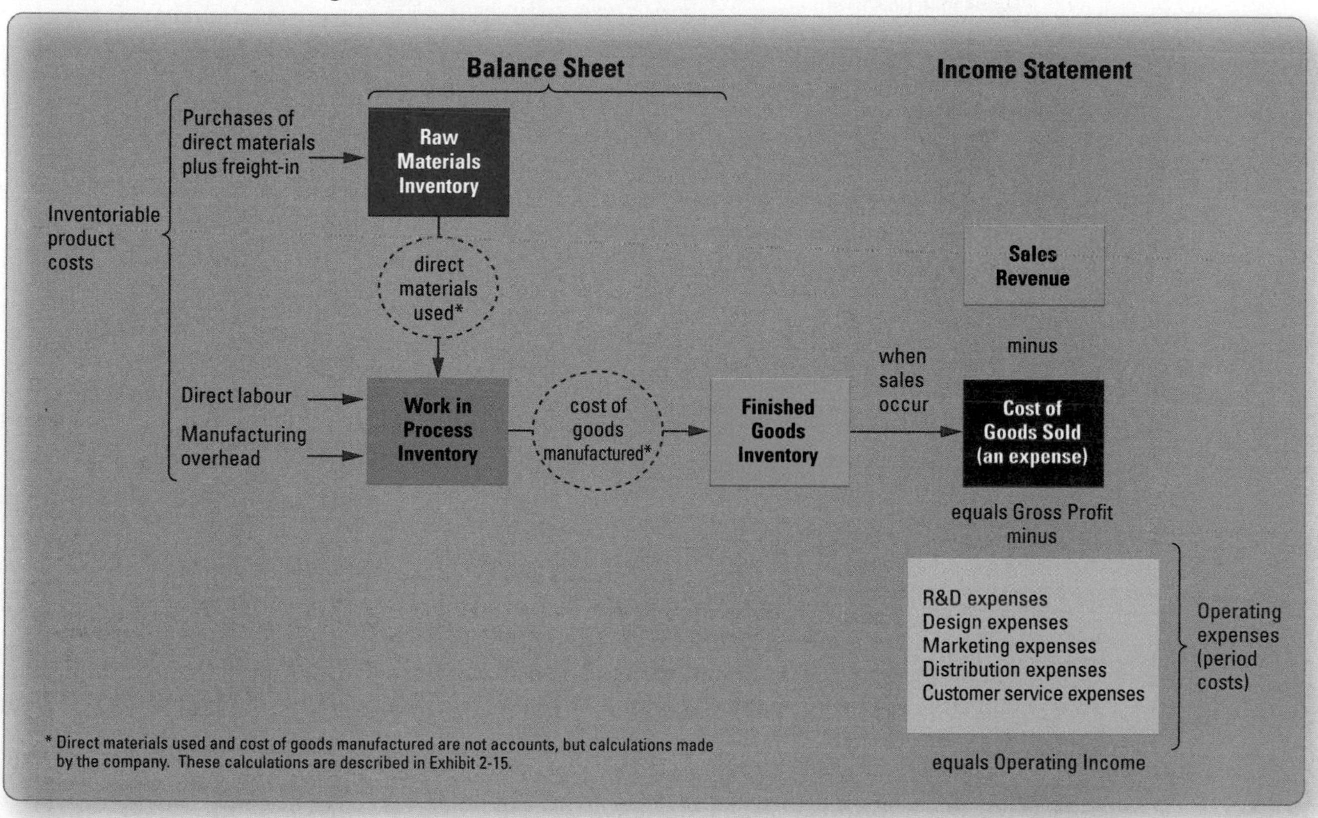

used in production are transferred out of raw materials inventory and into work in process inventory. During production, the company uses direct labour and manufacturing overhead to convert these direct materials into a finished product. All units currently being manufactured are in work in process inventory. When the units are completed, they are moved out of work in process inventory into finished goods inventory. The amount transferred into finished goods inventory during the year is the cost of goods manufactured.

The finished units remain in finished goods inventory until they are sold. When the manufacturer sells finished units, the cost of those units becomes the cost of goods sold on the income statement. Costs incurred in nonmanufacturing elements of the value chain are expensed in the period incurred as operating expenses. Exhibit 2-14 shows that these operating expenses are deducted from gross profit to obtain operating income.

With this overview in mind, let us walk through Exhibit 2-15, which shows how Top-Flite computes its cost of goods manufactured—the cost of the goods the plant *finished* during 2017. For simplicity, we will assume that Top-Flite's raw materials inventory contains only direct materials.

Exhibit 2-15 shows that Top-Flite began 2017 with $2,000 of partially completed golf clubs that remained on the plant floor at the close of business on December 31, 2016.

**EXHIBIT 2-15** Schedule of Cost of Goods Manufactured

**TOP-FLITE**
**Schedule of Cost of Goods Manufactured**
**Year Ended December 31, 2017**

| | | | |
|---|---|---|---|
| **Beginning work in progress inventory** | | | $ 2,000 |
| Add: Direct materials used | | | |
| Beginning raw materials inventory* | $ 9,000 | | |
| Purchases of direct materials including freight-in and any import duties | 27,000 | | |
| Available for use | 36,000 | | |
| Ending raw materials inventory | (22,000) | | |
| **Direct materials used** | | $14,000 | |
| **Direct labour** | | 19,000 | |
| **Manufacturing overhead:** | | | |
| Indirect materials | $ 1,500 | | |
| Indirect labour | 3,500 | | |
| Depreciation—plant and equipment | 3,000 | | |
| Plant utilities, insurance, and property taxes | 4,000 | | |
| Manufacturing overhead | | 12,000 | |
| **Total manufacturing costs incurred during year** | | | 45,000 |
| **Total manufacturing costs to account for** | | | 47,000 |
| **Less: Ending work in process inventory** | | | (5,000) |
| **Costs of goods manufactured** | | | $42,000 |

*For simplicity, we assume that Top-Flite's Raw Materials Inventory account contains only direct materials because the company uses indirect materials as soon as they are purchased.

During 2017, Top-Flite's production plant used $14,000 of direct materials, $19,000 of direct labour, and $12,000 of manufacturing overhead. The sum of these three costs ($45,000) represents the total manufacturing costs incurred during the year. Adding the total manufacturing costs incurred during the year ($45,000) to the beginning work in process inventory balance ($2,000) gives the total manufacturing costs to account for ($47,000). This figure represents the total manufacturing cost assigned to *all* goods the plant worked on during the year.

The plant finished most of these goods and sent them to finished goods inventory, but some were not finished. By the close of business on December 31, 2017, Top-Flite had spent $5,000 on partially completed golf clubs that were still in work in process inventory.

By subtracting the cost of the units still in work in process inventory ($5,000)[5] from the total costs to account for ($47,000), Top-Flite is able to calculate the cost of goods manufactured during 2017. This figure is then used in Exhibit 2-13 to complete the cost of goods sold calculation.

## Flow of Costs Through Inventory Accounts

Exhibit 2-16 diagrams the flow of costs through Top-Flite's three inventory accounts. Notice how the final amount at each stage flows into the next stage. The format is the same for all three inventory accounts:

- Each inventory account starts with a beginning inventory balance.
- Top-Flite adds costs to each inventory account. (It adds direct materials purchased to raw materials inventory; it adds direct materials used, direct labour, and manufacturing overhead to work in process inventory; and it adds the cost of goods manufactured to finished goods inventory.)
- Top-Flite subtracts the ending inventory balance to find out how much inventory passed through the account during the period and on to the next stage. At all stages, the flow of costs follows the flow of physical goods.

**EXHIBIT 2-16** Flow of Costs through Top-Flite's Inventory Accounts

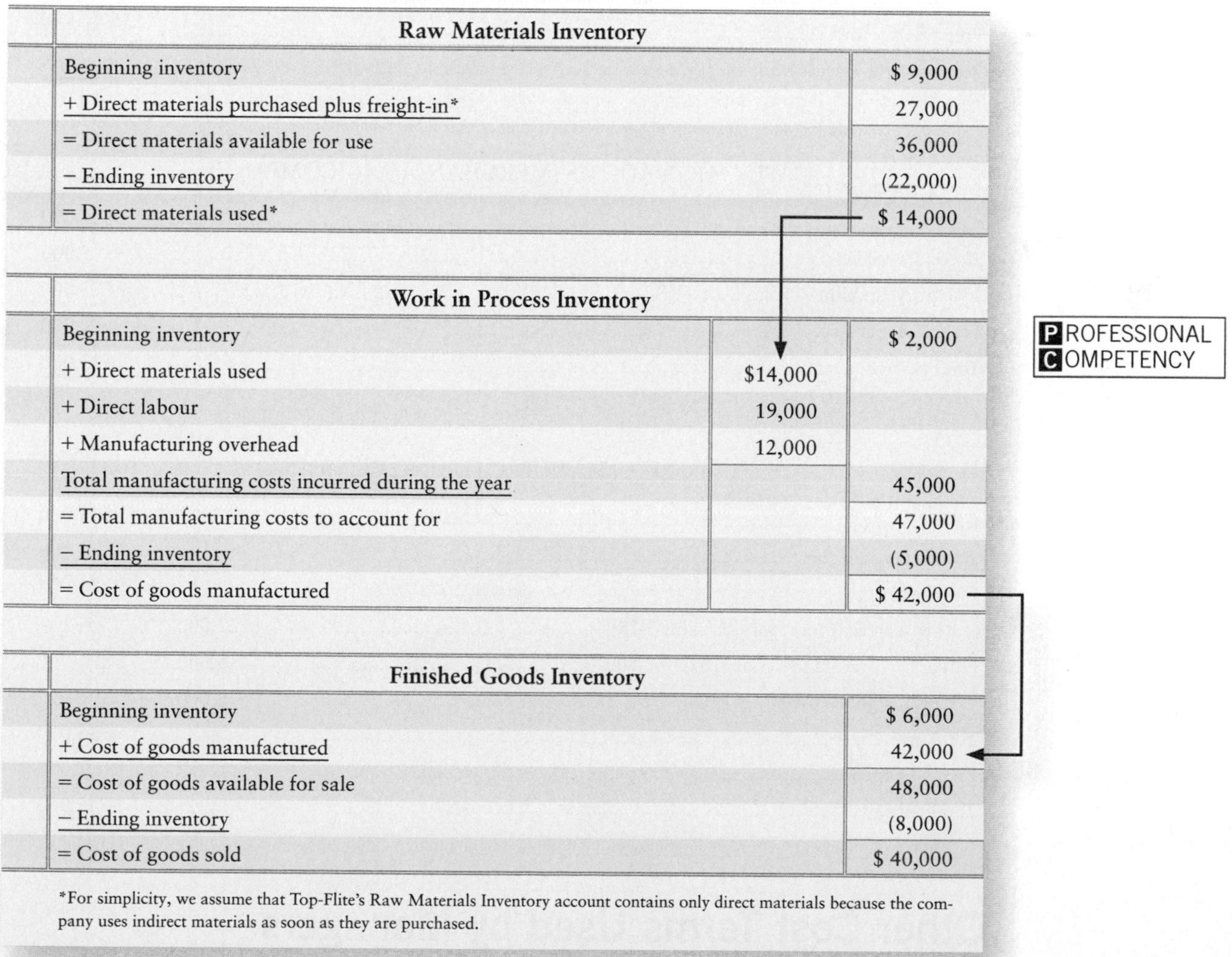

| Raw Materials Inventory | |
|---|---|
| Beginning inventory | $ 9,000 |
| + Direct materials purchased plus freight-in* | 27,000 |
| = Direct materials available for use | 36,000 |
| − Ending inventory | (22,000) |
| = Direct materials used* | $ 14,000 |

| Work in Process Inventory | | |
|---|---|---|
| Beginning inventory | | $ 2,000 |
| + Direct materials used | $14,000 | |
| + Direct labour | 19,000 | |
| + Manufacturing overhead | 12,000 | |
| Total manufacturing costs incurred during the year | | 45,000 |
| = Total manufacturing costs to account for | | 47,000 |
| − Ending inventory | | (5,000) |
| = Cost of goods manufactured | | $ 42,000 |

| Finished Goods Inventory | |
|---|---|
| Beginning inventory | $ 6,000 |
| + Cost of goods manufactured | 42,000 |
| = Cost of goods available for sale | 48,000 |
| − Ending inventory | (8,000) |
| = Cost of goods sold | $ 40,000 |

*For simplicity, we assume that Top-Flite's Raw Materials Inventory account contains only direct materials because the company uses indirect materials as soon as they are purchased.

PROFESSIONAL COMPETENCY

[5]We will discuss how managers calculate the cost of work in process inventory in later chapters.

Take time to see how the Schedule of Cost of Goods Manufactured (Exhibit 2-15) captures the flow of costs through the raw materials and work in process inventory accounts. The Income Statement (Exhibit 2-13) captures the flow of costs through the finished goods inventory account. Some manufacturers combine the flow of costs through all three inventory accounts into one combined Schedule of Cost of Goods Manufactured and Cost of Goods Sold, and then show only the resulting cost of goods sold figure ($40,000) on the income statement.

## Comparing Balance Sheets

Now that we have looked at the income statement for each type of company, let's turn our attention to the balance sheet. The only difference in the balance sheets of service, merchandising, and manufacturing companies relates to inventories. Exhibit 2-17 shows how the current asset sections of eNOW! (service company), Apex Showrooms (merchandising company), and Top-Flite (manufacturing company) might differ at the end of 2017. eNOW! has no inventory at all; Apex Showrooms has a single category of inventory; and Top-Flite has three categories of inventory.

**EXHIBIT 2-17** Current Asset Sections of Balance Sheets

| eNOW! (SERVICE COMPANY) | |
|---|---|
| Cash | $ 4,000 |
| Accounts receivable | 1,000 |
| Prepaid expenses | 1,000 |
| Total current assets | $10,000 |

| APEX SHOWROOMS (MERCHANDISING COMPANY) | |
|---|---|
| Cash | $ 4,000 |
| Accounts receivable | 5,000 |
| Inventory (Exhibit 2-12) | 13,000 |
| Prepaid expenses | 1,000 |
| Total current assets | $23,000 |

| TOP-FLITE (MANUFACTURING COMPANY) | | |
|---|---|---|
| Cash | | $ 4,000 |
| Accounts receivable | | 5,000 |
| Inventories: | | |
| Raw materials inventory (Exhibit 2-15) | 22,000 | |
| Work in process inventory (Exhibit 2-15) | 5,000 | |
| Finished goods inventory (Exhibit 2-13) | 8,000 | |
| Total inventories | | 35,000 |
| Prepaid expenses | | 1,000 |
| Total current assets | | $45,000 |

# Other Cost Terms Used by Managers

So far in this chapter, we have discussed direct versus indirect costs and inventoriable product costs versus period costs. Other cost terms that managers and accountants use when planning and making decisions can address many aspects of operations.

## Controllable versus Uncontrollable Costs

6 Describe costs that are relevant and irrelevant to decision making.

When deciding to make business changes, management needs to distinguish **controllable costs** from **uncontrollable costs**. In the long run, most costs are controllable, meaning management is able to influence or change them. However, in the short run, companies are often "locked in" to certain costs arising from previous decisions. These are called uncontrollable costs.

For example, Bombardier has little or no control over the property tax and insurance costs of its existing plants. These costs were locked in when Bombardier built its plants. Bombardier could replace existing production facilities with different-sized plants in different areas of the world that might cost less to operate, but that would take time. To see *immediate* benefits, management must change those costs that are controllable in the present. For example, management can control costs of R&D, design, and advertising. Sometimes Bombardier's management may choose to *increase* rather than decrease these costs in order to successfully gain market share. However, Bombardier may also able to *decrease* other controllable costs, such as the price paid for raw materials, by working with its suppliers.

## Relevant and Irrelevant Costs

Decision making involves identifying various courses of action and then choosing among them. When managers make decisions, they focus on those costs and revenues that are relevant to the decision. For example, Bombardier built a new state-of-the-art production facility just outside Montreal for the new CSeries aircraft. After considering alternative locations, management decided on Mirabel, Quebec. The decision was based on relevant information such as the **differential cost** of building and operating the facility in Quebec versus building and operating the facility in other potential locations. Differential cost refers to the difference in cost between two alternatives.

Suppose you want to buy a new car. You narrow your decision to two choices: the Nissan Sentra or the Toyota Corolla. As shown in Exhibit 2-18, the Sentra you like costs $14,480, whereas the Corolla costs $15,345. Because sales tax is based on the sales price, the Corolla's sales tax is higher. However, your insurance agent quotes you a higher price to insure the Sentra ($365 per month versus $319 per month for the Corolla). All of these costs are relevant to your decision because they differ between the two cars.

**EXHIBIT 2-18** Comparison of Relevant Information

| | Sentra | Corolla | Differential Cost |
|---|---|---|---|
| Car's price | $14,480 | $15,345 | $ (865) |
| Sales tax (8%) (rounded to the nearest dollar) | 1,158 | 1,228 | (70) |
| Insurance* | 21,900 | 19,140 | 2,760 |
| Total relevant costs | $37,538 | $35,713 | $1,825 |

*Over the five years (60 months) you plan to keep the car.

Other costs are not relevant to your decision. For example, both cars run on regular unleaded gasoline and have the same fuel economy ratings, so the cost of operating the vehicles is about the same. Likewise, you do not expect cost differences in servicing the vehicles because they both carry the same warranty and have received excellent quality ratings in *Consumer Reports*. Because you project operating and maintenance costs to be the same for both cars, these costs are irrelevant to your decision. In other words, they will not influence your decision either way.

Based on your analysis, the differential cost is $1,825 in favour of the Corolla. Does this mean that you will choose the Corolla? Not necessarily. The Sentra may have some characteristics you like better, such as a particular paint colour, more comfortable seating, or more trunk space. When making decisions, management must also consider qualitative factors (such as effect on employee morale) in addition to differential costs.

Another cost that is irrelevant to your decision is the cost you paid for the vehicle you currently own. If you just bought a Ford F-150 pickup truck two months ago, but you have decided you need a small sedan rather than a pickup truck, the cost of the truck is a **sunk cost**. Sunk costs are costs that have already been incurred. Nothing you do now can change the fact that you bought the truck. Thus, the cost of the truck is not relevant when you decide whether to buy the Sentra or the Corolla. The only thing you can do now is (1) keep your truck or (2) sell it for the best price you can get.

Management often has trouble ignoring sunk costs when making decisions, even though it should. Perhaps it invested in a factory or a computer system that no longer serves the company's needs. Many times, new technology makes management's past investments in older technology look like bad decisions, even though they were not at the time. Management should ignore sunk costs because its decisions about the future cannot alter decisions made in the past.

## Fixed and Variable Costs

7 Classify costs as fixed or variable, and calculate total and average costs at different volumes.

Managers cannot make good plans and decisions without first knowing how their costs behave. Costs generally behave as **fixed costs** or **variable costs**. We will spend all of Chapter 3 discussing cost behaviour. For now, let's look just at the basics. Fixed costs stay constant in total over a wide range of activity levels. For example, let's say you decide to buy the Corolla, so your insurance cost for the year is $3,828 ($319 per month for 12 months). As shown in Exhibit 2-19, your total insurance cost stays fixed whether you drive your car 0 km, 1,000 km, or 10,000 km during the year.

**EXHIBIT 2-19** Fixed Cost Behaviour

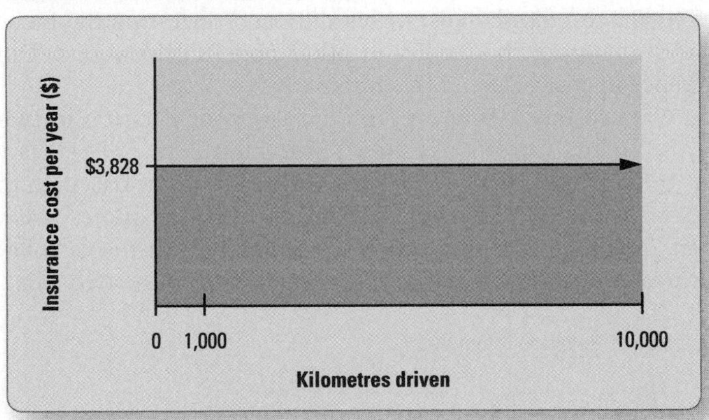


However, the total cost of gasoline to operate your car varies, depending on whether you drive 0 km, 1,000 km, or 10,000 km. The more kilometres you drive, the higher your total gasoline cost for the year. If you do not drive your car at all, you will not incur any costs for gasoline. Your gasoline costs are variable costs, as shown in Exhibit 2-20.

**EXHIBIT 2-20** Variable Cost Behaviour

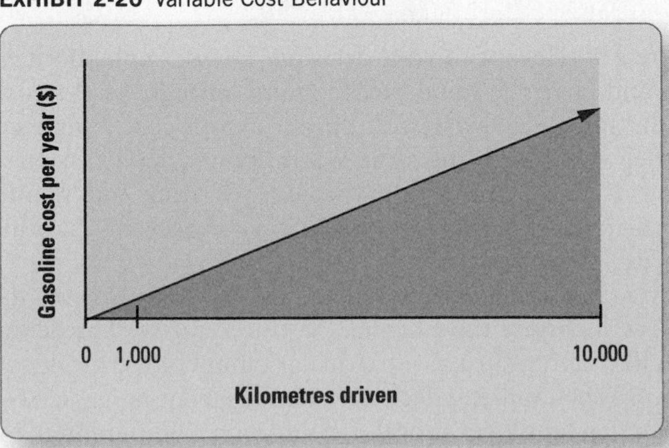

In total, variable costs change in direct proportion to changes in volume. To accurately forecast the total cost of operating your Corolla during the year, you need to know which operating costs are fixed and which are variable.

> **Why is this important?**
> Most **business decisions** depend on how costs are **expected** to change at different volumes of **activity**. Managers can't make good decisions without first **understanding** how their costs **behave**.

## Manufacturing Costs

Most companies have both fixed and variable costs. Manufacturing companies know that their direct materials are variable costs. The more planes Bombardier makes, the higher its total cost for tires, steel, and parts. The behaviour of direct labour is harder to characterize. Salaried employees are paid a fixed amount per year. Hourly wage earners are paid only when they work. The more hours they work, the more they are paid. Nonetheless, direct labour is generally treated as a variable cost because the more planes Bombardier produces, the more assembly-line workers and machine operators it must employ. Manufacturing overhead includes both variable and fixed costs. For example, the cost of indirect materials is variable, while the cost of property tax, insurance, and straight-line depreciation on the plant and equipment is fixed. The cost of utilities is partially fixed and partially variable. Factories incur a certain level of utility costs just to keep the lights on. However, when more planes are produced, more electricity is used to run the production equipment. Exhibit 2-21 summarizes the behaviour of manufacturing costs.

**EXHIBIT 2-21** The Behaviour of Manufacturing Costs

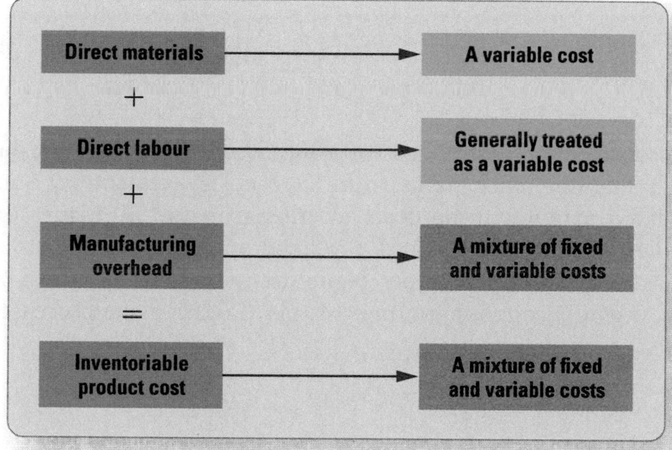


## Calculating Total and Average Costs

Why is cost behaviour important? Managers need to understand how costs behave to predict total costs and calculate average costs. In our example, we will predict Bombardier's total and average manufacturing costs for the new plant in Quebec.[6] Although we will be using only manufacturing costs in the example, the same principles apply to nonmanufacturing costs.

Let's say Bombardier wants to estimate the total cost of manufacturing 50 CSeries planes next year. To do so, Bombardier must know (1) its total fixed manufacturing costs and (2) the variable cost of manufacturing each plane. Let's say total fixed manufacturing costs for the year at the CSeries plant are $20,000,000 and the variable cost of

[6]All references to Bombardier in this hypothetical example were created by the author solely for academic purposes and are not intended in any way to represent the actual business practices of, or costs incurred by, Bombardier Inc.

manufacturing each CSeries plane is $250,000. How much total manufacturing cost should Bombardier budget for the year? Bombardier calculates it as follows:

| Total fixed cost + | (Variable cost per unit × | Number of units) = | Total cost |
|---|---|---|---|
| $20,000,000 + | ( $250,000 per plane × | 50 planes ) = | $32,500,000 |

What is the average cost of manufacturing each CSeries plane next year? It is the total cost divided by the number of units:

$$\frac{\text{Total cost}}{\text{Number of units}} = \text{Average cost per unit}$$

$$\frac{\$32{,}500{,}000}{50 \text{ planes}} = \$650{,}000 \text{ per plane}$$

If Bombardier's managers decide they need to produce 75 CSeries planes instead, can they simply predict total costs as follows?

| Average cost per unit × | Number of units = | Total cost |
|---|---|---|
| 650,000 × | 75 = | $48,750,000 |

No! They cannot! Why? Because the average cost per unit is *not* appropriate for predicting total costs at different levels of output. Bombardier's managers should forecast total cost based on cost behaviour:

| Total fixed cost + | (Variable cost per unit × | Number of units) = | Total cost |
|---|---|---|---|
| $20,000,000 + | ( $250,000 per plane × | 75 planes ) = | $38,750,000 |

Why is the correct forecasted cost of $38,750,000 less than the faulty prediction of $48,750,000? The difference stems from fixed costs. Remember, Bombardier incurs $20 million of fixed manufacturing costs whether it makes 50 planes or 75 planes. As Bombardier makes more CSeries planes, the fixed manufacturing costs are spread over more airplanes, so the average cost per plane declines. If Bombardier ends up making 75 planes, the new average manufacturing cost per CSeries plane decreases as follows:

$$\frac{\text{Total cost}}{\text{Number of units}} = \text{Average cost per unit}$$

$$\frac{\$38{,}750{,}000}{75 \text{ planes}} = \$516{,}667 \text{ per plane (rounded)}$$

The average cost per unit is lower when Bombardier produces more planes because it is using the fixed manufacturing costs more efficiently—taking the same $20 million of resources and making more planes with it.

*The moral of the story: The average cost per unit is valid only at ONE level of output—the level used to compute the average cost per unit. Thus, NEVER use average costs to forecast costs at different output levels.*

Finally, a **marginal cost** is the cost of making one more unit. Fixed costs will not change when Bombardier makes one more CSeries plane unless the plant is operating at 100% capacity and simply cannot make one more unit. (If that is the case, Bombardier will need to incur additional costs to expand the plant.) So, the marginal cost of a unit is simply its variable cost.

As you have seen, management accountants and managers use specialized terms for discussing costs. They use different costs for different purposes. Without a solid understanding of these terms, managers are likely to make serious judgment errors.

# DECISION GUIDELINES

## Building Blocks of Managerial Accounting

As a manufacturer, Dell needs to know how to calculate its inventoriable product costs for external reporting. Dell also needs to know many characteristics about its costs (that is, which are controllable, which are relevant to different decisions, which are fixed, and so forth) in order to plan and make decisions.

| Decision | Guidelines |
|---|---|
| The company has service, merchandising, and manufacturing divisions. How will this impact the calculation for cost of goods sold? | • *Service divisions:* No cost of goods sold because they do not sell tangible goods<br>• *Merchandising divisions:*<br>Beginning inventory<br>+ Purchases plus freight-in and import duties, if any<br>= Cost of goods available for sale<br>− Ending inventory<br>= Cost of goods sold<br>• *Manufacturing divisions:*<br>Beginning finished goods inventory<br>+ Cost of goods manufactured<br>= Cost of goods available for sale<br>− Ending finished goods inventory<br>= Cost of goods sold |
| When working with inventories, you typically take the beginning inventory and add the costs of what has been added to the inventory over the period. For a manufacturing environment, what costs are added in? | The cost of goods manufactured must be calculated and added to the beginning work in process inventory as follows:<br>Beginning work in process inventory<br>+ Total manufacturing costs incurred during year<br>(direct materials used + direct labour + manufacturing overhead)<br>= Total manufacturing costs to account for<br>− Ending work in process inventory<br>= Cost of goods manufactured |
| How do you decide which costs are relevant to decisions? | Costs are relevant to a decision when they differ between alternatives and affect the future. Thus, differential costs are relevant, whereas sunk costs and costs that do not differ are not relevant. |
| The production volumes fluctuate over time, making it difficult to estimate total costs. What is the best way to forecast total costs? | To forecast total costs, managers should compute the following:<br>Total cost = Total fixed costs + (Variable cost per unit × Number of units)<br>Managers should *not* use a product's *average cost* to forecast total costs because it will change as production volume changes. As production increases, the average cost per unit declines (because fixed costs are spread over more units). |

# SUMMARY PROBLEM 2

### Requirements

1. Show how to compute cost of goods manufactured. Use the following amounts: direct materials used ($24,000), direct labour ($9,000), manufacturing overhead ($17,000), beginning work in process inventory ($5,000), and ending work in process inventory ($4,000).
2. Auto-Canada spent $300 million in total to produce 50,000 cars this year. The $300 million breaks down as follows: The company spent $50 million on fixed costs to run its manufacturing plants and $5,000 of variable costs to produce each car. Next year, it plans to produce 60,000 cars using the existing production facilities.
   a. What is the current *average cost* per car this year?
   b. Assuming there is no change in fixed costs or variable costs per unit, what is the *total forecasted cost* to produce 60,000 cars next year?
   c. What is the *forecasted average cost* per car next year?
   d. Why does the average cost per car vary between years?

## SOLUTIONS

### Requirement 1

Cost of goods manufactured:

| | | |
|---|---|---|
| Beginning work in process inventory | | $ 5,000 |
| Add: Direct materials used | 24,000 | |
| Direct labour | 9,000 | |
| Manufacturing overhead | 17,000 | |
| Total manufacturing costs incurred during the period | | 50,000 |
| Total manufacturing costs to account for | | 55,000 |
| Less: Ending work in process inventory | | (4,000) |
| Cost of goods manufactured | | $51,000 |

### Requirement 2

a.

| Total cost | ÷ | Number of units | = | Current average cost |
|---|---|---|---|---|
| $300 million | ÷ | 50,000 cars | = | $6,000 per car |

b.

| Total fixed costs | + | Total variable costs | = | Total projected costs |
|---|---|---|---|---|
| $50 million | + | (60,000 cars × $5,000 per car) | = | $350 million |

c.

| Total cost | ÷ | Number of units | = | Projected average cost |
|---|---|---|---|---|
| $350 million | ÷ | 60,000 cars | = | $5,833 per car |

d. The average cost per car decreases because Auto-Canada will use the same fixed costs ($50 million) to produce more cars next year. Auto-Canada will be using its resources more efficiently, so the average cost per unit will decrease.

# END OF CHAPTER

## LEARNING OBJECTIVES

1 Distinguish among service, merchandising, and manufacturing companies.

2 Describe the value chain and its elements.

3 Distinguish between direct and indirect costs.

4 Identify the inventoriable product costs and period costs of merchandising and manufacturing firms.

5 Prepare financial statements for service, merchandising, and manufacturing companies.

6 Describe costs that are relevant and irrelevant to decision making.

7 Classify costs as fixed or variable, and calculate total and average costs at different volumes.



## ACCOUNTING VOCABULARY

**Allocate (p. 60)** To assign a portion of an indirect cost to a cost object or cost objects.

**Assign (p. 60)** To attach a cost to a cost object.

**Average Cost (p. 77)** The total cost divided by the number of units.

**Controllable Costs (p. 75)** Costs that can be influenced or changed by management.

**Conversion Costs (p. 66)** The combination of direct labour and manufacturing overhead costs.

**Cost Object (p. 59)** Anything for which managers want a separate measurement of costs.

**Cost of Goods Manufactured (p. 70)** The cost of manufacturing the goods that were finished during the period.

**Cost of Goods Sold (p. 73)** The inventoriable product cost of goods.

**Customer Service (p. 57)** Support provided for customers after the sale.

**Design (p. 57)** Detailed engineering of products and services and the processes for producing them.

**Differential Cost (p. 75)** The difference in cost between two alternative courses of action.

**Direct Cost (p. 59)** A cost that can be traced to a cost object and is worthwhile to do so after a cost/benefit analysis has assessed the cost of tracing the cost and compared it with the benefit received from the additional accuracy.

**Direct Labour (p. 63)** The cost of compensating employees who physically convert raw materials into the company's products; labour costs that are directly traceable to the cost object.

**Direct Materials (p. 63)** Primary raw materials that become a physical part of a finished product and whose costs are traceable to the cost object.

**Distribution (p. 57)** Delivery of products or services to customers.

**Finished Goods Inventory (p. 55)** Completed goods that have not yet been sold.

**Fixed Costs (p. 76)** Costs that stay constant in total despite changes in volume.

**Indirect Cost (p. 59)** A cost that relates to the cost object but cannot be easily traced to it.

**Indirect Labour (p. 64)** Labour costs that are difficult to trace to specific cost objects.

**Indirect Materials (p. 64)** Materials whose costs are difficult to trace to specific cost objects.

**Inventoriable Product Costs (p. 61)** All costs of a product that IFRS or ASPE require companies to treat as an asset (inventory) for external financial reporting. These costs are not expensed until the product is sold.

**Manufacturing Company (p. 55)** A company that uses labour, plant, and equipment to convert raw materials into new finished products.

**Manufacturing Overhead (p. 63)** All manufacturing costs other than direct materials and direct labour; also called factory overhead or indirect manufacturing cost.

**Marginal Cost (p. 78)** The cost of producing one more unit.

**Marketing (p. 57)** Promotion and advertising of products or services.

**Merchandising Company (p. 55)** A company that resells tangible products previously bought from suppliers.

**Other Indirect Manufacturing Costs (p. 64)** All manufacturing overhead costs aside from indirect materials and indirect labour.

**Period Costs (p. 62)** Cost that are expensed in the period in which they are incurred; often called Operating Expenses, or Selling, General, and Administrative expenses.

**Prime Costs (p. 66)** The combination of direct material and direct labour costs.

**Production or Purchases (p. 57)** The portion of the value chain where resources are used to produce a product or service, or to purchase finished merchandise intended for resale.

**Raw Materials Inventory (p. 55)** All raw materials (direct materials and indirect materials) not yet used in manufacturing.

**Research and Development (R&D) (p. 56)** Researching and developing new or improved products or services or the processes for producing them.

**Retailer (p. 54)** Merchandising company that sells to consumers.

**Service Company (p. 55)** A company that sells intangible services rather than tangible products.

**Sunk Cost (p. 76)** A cost that has already been incurred.

**Total Costs (p. 61)** The costs of all resources used throughout the value chain.

**Trace (p. 59)** To assign a direct cost to a cost object.

**Uncontrollable Costs (p. 75)** Costs that cannot be changed or influenced in the short run by management.

**Value Chain (p. 56)** The activities that add value to a firm's products and services; includes R&D, design, production or purchases, marketing, distribution, and customer service.

**Variable Costs (p. 76)** Costs that change in total in direct proportion to changes in volume.

**Wholesalers (p. 54)** Merchandising companies that buy in bulk from manufacturers, mark up the prices, and then sell those products to retailers.

**Work in Process Inventory (p. 55)** Goods that are partway through the manufacturing process but not yet complete.



# QUICK CHECK

1. (Learning Objective 1) Sears Canada is a
   a. service company.
   b. retailer.
   c. wholesaler.
   d. manufacturer.
2. (Learning Objective 2) The cost of oranges to a fruit juice manufacturer is an example of a cost from which element in the value chain?
   a. Design
   b. Production
   c. Marketing
   d. Distribution
3. (Learning Objective 2) Which is not an element of a car manufacturer's value chain?
   a. Administrative costs
   b. Cost of shipping cars to dealers
   c. Salaries of engineers who update car design
   d. Cost of print ads and television commercials
4. (Learning Objective 3) For Bombardier, which is a direct cost with respect to the Learjet 85?
   a. Depreciation on plant and equipment
   b. Cost of vehicle engine
   c. Salary of engineer who rearranges plant layout
   d. Cost of customer hotline
5. (Learning Objective 3) Which one of the following costs would be considered a direct cost of serving a particular customer at a McDonald's restaurant?
   a. The salary of the restaurant manager
   b. The depreciation on the restaurant building
   c. The cost of the hamburger patty in the sandwich the customer ordered
   d. The cost of heating the restaurant
6. (Learning Objective 4) Which of the following is not part of Bombardier's manufacturing overhead?
   a. Insurance on plant and equipment
   b. Depreciation on its North American corporate headquarters
   c. Plant property taxes
   d. Plant utilities
7. (Learning Objective 4) The three basic components of inventoriable product costs are direct materials, direct labour, and
   a. cost of goods manufactured.
   b. manufacturing overhead.
   c. cost of goods sold.
   d. work in process.
8. (Learning Objective 5) In computing cost of goods sold, which of the following is the manufacturer's counterpart to the merchandiser's purchases?
   a. Direct materials used
   b. Total manufacturing costs incurred during the period
   c. Total manufacturing costs to account for
   d. Cost of goods manufactured
9. (Learning Objective 6) Which of the following is irrelevant to business decisions?
   a. Differential costs
   b. Sunk costs
   c. Variable costs
   d. Qualitative factors

10. (Learning Objective 7) Which of the following is true?
    a. Total fixed costs increase as production volume increases.
    b. Total fixed costs decrease as production volume decreases.
    c. Total variable costs increase as production volume increases.
    d. Total variable costs stay constant as production volume increases.

**Quick Check Answers**

1. b 2. b 3. a 4. b 5. c 6. b 7. b 8. d 9. b 10. c



# SHORT EXERCISES

## S2-1 Identify type of company from balance sheets *(Learning Objective 1)*

The current asset sections of the balance sheets of three companies follow. Which company is a service company? Which is a merchandiser? Which is a manufacturer? How can you tell?

| X-Treme | | Y-Not? | | Zesto | |
|---|---|---|---|---|---|
| Cash | $ 2,500 | Cash | $3,000 | Cash | $ 2,000 |
| Accounts receivable | 5,500 | Accounts receivable | 6,000 | Accounts receivable | 5,000 |
| Inventory | 8,000 | Prepaid expenses | 500 | Raw material inventory | 1,000 |
| Prepaid expenses | 300 | Total | $9,500 | Work in process inventory | 800 |
| Total | $16,300 | | | Finished goods inventory | 4,000 |
| | | | | Total | $12,800 |

## S2-2 Identify types of companies and inventories *(Learning Objective 1)*

Fill in the blanks with one of the following terms.

| | | | |
|---|---|---|---|
| Manufacturing | Service | Merchandising | Retailer(s) |
| Wholesaler(s) | Raw materials inventor | Merchandise inventory | Work in process inventory |
| Finished goods inventory | Freight-in | The cost of merchandise | |

a. _______ companies generally have no inventory.
b. Bombardier is a _______ company.
c. A merchandiser's inventory consists of _______ and ______.
d. _______ companies carry three types of inventories: ______, ______, and ______.
e. TD Insurance is a _______ company.
f. Two types of _______ companies include _______ and ______.
g. Direct materials are stored in ______.
h. Le Château is a _______ company.
i. Manufacturers sell from their stock of ______.
j. Labour costs usually account for the highest percentage of _______ companies' costs.
k. Partially completed units are kept in the ______.

## S2-3 Label value chain functions *(Learning Objective 2)*

List the correct value chain element for each of the six business functions described below.

a. Delivery of products and services
b. Detailed engineering of products and services and the processes for producing them
c. Promotion and advertising of products or services
d. Investigating new or improved products or services and the processes for producing them
e. Support provided to customers after the sale
f. Resources used to make a product or obtain finished merchandise

**S2-4 Classify costs by value chain function** *(Learning Objective 2)*

Classify each of BlackBerry Ltd's. costs as one of the six business functions in the value chain.

a. Depreciation on Waterloo plant
b. Costs of a customer support centre Website
c. Transportation costs to deliver BlackBerrys to retailers
d. Depreciation on research lab
e. Cost of a prime-time TV ad featuring a new BlackBerry logo
f. Salary of scientists at BlackBerry laboratories who are developing new cellular technologies
g. Purchase of plastic used in handheld casings
h. Salaries of engineers who are redesigning the BlackBerry's interactive screen
i. Depreciation on delivery vehicles
j. Plant manager's salary

**S2-5 Classify costs as direct or indirect** *(Learning Objective 3)*

Classify the following as direct or indirect costs with respect to a local Lowe's store (the store is the cost object). In addition, state whether Lowe's would trace or allocate these costs to the store.

a. Store utilities
b. The CEO's salary
c. The cost of lumber
d. The cost of national advertising
e. The wages of store employees
f. The cost of operating the corporate Payroll Department
g. The cost of ceiling fans, light switches, and lamps
h. The cost of shopping bags sold at the store

**S2-6 Classify inventoriable product costs and period costs** *(Learning Objective 4)*

Classify each of the following costs as either inventoriable product costs or period costs. The company is a manufacturer of stud lumber, veneer, specialty panels, oriented strand board, and wood chips.

a. Depreciation on the veneer plant
b. Purchase of lumber to be cut into boards
c. Life insurance on CEO
d. Salaries of scientists studying ways to speed forest growth
e. Cost of new software to track inventory during production
f. Cost of electricity at a paper mills
g. Salaries of a top executives
h. Cost of chemical applied to lumber to inhibit mould
i. Cost of TV ads promoting environmental awareness

**S2-7 Classify a manufacturer's costs** *(Learning Objective 4)*

Classify each of the following costs as a period cost or an inventoriable product cost. If you classify the cost as an inventoriable product cost, further classify it as direct material (DM), direct labour (DL), or manufacturing overhead (MOH).

a. Depreciation on automated production equipment
b. Telephone bills relating to customer service call centre
c. Wages and benefits paid to assembly-line workers in the manufacturing plant
d. Repairs and maintenance on factory equipment
e. Lease payment on administrative headquarters
f. Salaries paid to quality control inspectors in the plant
g. Property insurance—40% of building is used for sales and administration; 60% of building is used for manufacturing
h. Standard packaging materials used to package individual units of product for sale (for example, cereal boxes in which cereal is packaged)

**S2-8 Classify costs incurred by a dairy processing company** *(Learning Objective 4)*

Each of the following costs pertains to MilkIt, a dairy processing company. Classify each of the company's costs as a period cost or an inventoriable product cost. Further classify inventoriable product costs as direct material (DM), direct labour (DL), or manufacturing overhead (MOH).

| Cost | Period Cost or Inventoriable Product Cost? | DM, DL, or MOH? |
|---|---|---|
| 1. Cost of milk purchased from local dairy farmers | | |
| 2. Lubricants used in running bottling machines | | |
| 3. Depreciation on refrigerated trucks used to collect raw milk from local dairy farmers | | |
| 4. Property tax on dairy processing plant | | |
| 5. Television advertisements for MilkIt's products | | |
| 6. Gasoline used to operate refrigerated trucks delivering finished dairy products to grocery stores | | |
| 7. Company president's annual bonus | | |
| 8. Plastic 4 litre containers in which milk is packaged | | |
| 9. Depreciation on marketing department's computers | | |
| 10. Wages and salaries paid to machine operators at dairy processing plant | | |
| 11. Research and development on improving milk pasteurization process | | |



**S2-9 Determine total manufacturing overhead** *(Learning Objective 4)*

Snap's manufactures disposable cameras. Suppose the company's March records include the items described below. What is Snap's total manufacturing overhead cost in March?

| | |
|---|---|
| Glue for camera frames | $ 250 |
| Depreciation expense on company cars used by sales force | 3,000 |
| Plant depreciation expense | 10,000 |
| Interest expense | 2,000 |
| Company president's salary | 25,000 |
| Plant supervisor's salary | 4,000 |
| Plant janitor's salary | 2,000 |
| Oil for manufacturing equipment | 25 |
| Flashbulbs | 51,000 |

**S2-10 Compute cost of goods sold for a merchandiser** *(Learning Objective 5)*

Given the following information for Circuits Plus, an electronics e-tailer, compute the cost of goods sold.

| | |
|---|---|
| Website maintenance | $ 7,000 |
| Delivery expense | 1,000 |
| Freight-in | 3,000 |
| Import duties | 1,000 |
| Purchases | 40,000 |
| Ending inventory | 5,500 |
| Revenues | 60,000 |
| Marketing expenses | 10,000 |
| Beginning inventory | 3,500 |

**S2-11 Prepare a retailer's income statement** *(Learning Objective 5)*

Salon Secrets is a retail chain specializing in salon-quality hair care products. During the year, Salon Secrets had sales of $38,230,000. The company began the year with $3,270,000 of merchandise inventory and ended the year with $3,920,000 of inventory. During the year, Salon Secrets purchased $23,450,000 of merchandise inventory. The company's selling, general, and administrative expenses totalled $6,115,000 for the year. Prepare Salon Secrets's income statement for the year.



**S2-12 Calculate direct materials used** *(Learning Objective 5)*

You are a new accounting intern at Sunny's Bikes. Your boss gives you the following information and asks you to compute the cost of direct materials used (assume that the company's raw materials inventory contains only direct materials).

| | |
|---|---|
| Purchases of direct materials | $16,000 |
| Import duties | 1,000 |
| Freight-in | 500 |
| Freight-out | 1,000 |
| Ending raw materials inventory | 1,500 |
| Beginning raw materials inventory | 4,000 |

**S2-13 Compute cost of goods manufactured** *(Learning Objective 5)*

Smith Manufacturing found the following information in its accounting records: $524,000 of direct materials used, $223,000 of direct labour, and $742,000 of manufacturing overhead. The work in process inventory account had a beginning balance of $76,000 and an ending balance of $85,000. Compute the company's cost of goods manufactured.

**S2-14 Consider relevant information** *(Learning Objective 6)*

You have been offered an entry-level marketing position at two highly respectable firms: one in St. John's, Newfoundland, and one in Vancouver, British Columbia. What quantitative and qualitative information might be relevant to your decision? What characteristics about this information make it relevant?

**S2-15 Classify costs as fixed or variable** *(Learning Objective 7)*

Classify each of the following personal expenses as either fixed or variable. In some cases, your answer may depend on specific circumstances. If so, briefly explain your answer.

a. Apartment rental
b. Television cable service
c. Cost of groceries
d. Water and sewer bill
e. Cell phone bill
f. Health club dues
g. Bus fare

# EXERCISES Group A

**E2-16A Identify types of companies and their inventories** *(Learning Objective 1)*

Complete the following statements with one of the terms listed here. You may use a term more than once, and some terms may not be used at all.

| | | |
|---|---|---|
| Finished goods inventory | Inventory (merchandise) | Service companies |
| Manufacturing companies | Merchandising companies | Work in process inventory |
| Raw materials inventory | Wholesalers | |

a. ______ produce their own inventory.
b. ______ typically have a single category of inventory.

c. ______ do not have tangible products intended for sale.

d. ______ resell products they previously purchased ready-made from suppliers.

e. ______ use their workforce and equipment to transform raw materials into new finished products.

f. ______ sell to consumers.

g. Pelter Furniture, a company based in Saskatchewan, makes furniture. Partially completed sofas are ______. Completed sofas that remain unsold in the warehouse are ______. Fabric and wood are ______.

h. For McCain's, potatoes, cardboard boxes, and waxed paper liners are classified as ______.

i. ______buy in bulk from manufacturers and sell to retailers.



## E2-17A Classify costs along the value chain for a retailer *(Learning Objective 2)*

Suppose Rogers Plus incurred the following costs at its Ottawa, Ontario, store:

| | | | |
|---|---|---|---|
| Research on whether store should sell satellite radio service | $ 400 | Payment to consultant for advice on location of new store | $2,500 |
| Purchases of merchandise | 30,000 | Freight-in | 3,000 |
| Rearranging store layout | 750 | Salespeople's salaries | 4,000 |
| Newspaper advertisements | 5,000 | Customer complaint department | 800 |
| Depreciation expense on delivery trucks | 1,000 | | |

### Requirements

1. Use the following format to classify each cost according to its place in the value chain.

| R&D | Design | Purchases | Marketing | Distribution | Customer Service |
|---|---|---|---|---|---|

2. Compute the total costs for each value chain category.
3. How much are the total inventoriable product costs?

## E2-18A Value chain and sustainability efforts *(Learning Objective 2)*

Each of the scenarios to follow describes some cost item for organizations in the recycled carpet industry. For each scenario, identify which function of the value chain that cost would represent (R&D, Design, Purchasing/Producing, Marketing, Distributing, or Customer Service). *Note:* The companies and products used in this exercise are real companies with a strong sustainable practices commitment.

- Fibre[B]lock® Flooring is manufactured using the waste generated from the manufacture of commercial nylon carpet. The cost of the research into how to create Fibre[B]lock® Flooring would fall into which function in the value chain?
- Ford Motor Company purchases cylinder-head covers made from a nylon resin containing 100% recycled carpet in its 2011 Mustangs. The cost of the cylinder-head covers would fall into which function in the value chain?
- Los Angeles Fiber Company (LAFC) received the EPA/CARE award to recognize Los Angeles Fiber Company's sustainability efforts. Since 2000, LAFC has recycled more than 464 million pounds of post-consumer carpet. Its carpet brand, Reliance Carpet, is made entirely from post-consumer carpet fibre. The cost of promoting the company's products and its sustainability efforts would fall into which function in the value chain?
- Axminster Carpets offsets the carbon emissions from its carpet distribution process by investing in renewable energy projects such as wind power and hydro power plants. This carbon offset is verified independently by the Verified Carbon Standard. The cost of these carbon offsets would fall into which function in the value chain?
- Flor®, a company that produces residential carpet tiles made from recycled carpet, has an R&R (return and recycle) program. Homeowners can arrange to have old tiles picked up and shipped back to the plant for recycling. The cost of operating this R&R program would fall into which function in the value chain?

- Shaw Industries is a flooring manufacturer. It has created Cradle to Cradle Silver Certified carpet, which is carpet that can be recycled back into new carpet again and again at the end of its useful life, or it can be composted. The costs to develop the production process for the Cradle to Cradle Silver Certified carpet would fall into which function in the value chain?



## E2-19A Classify costs along the value chain for a manufacturer

*(Learning Objectives 2 & 3)*

Suppose the cell phone manufacturer Samsung Electronics provides the following information for its costs last month (in hundreds of thousands):

| | | | |
|---|---|---|---|
| Salaries of telephone salespeople | $ 5 | Transmitters | $61 |
| Depreciation on plant and equipment | 65 | Rearrange production process to accommodate new robot | 2 |
| Exterior case for phone | 6 | Assembly-line workers' wages | 20 |
| Salaries of scientists who developed new model | 12 | Technical customer support hotline | 3 |
| Delivery expense to customers via Canada Post | 7 | 1-800 (toll-free) line for customer orders | 1 |

### Requirements

1. Use the following format to classify each cost according to its place in the value chain. (*Hint:* You should have at least one cost in each value chain function.)

| | | Production | | | | | |
|---|---|---|---|---|---|---|---|
| R&D | Design of Products or Processes | Direct Materials | Direct Labour | Manufacturing Overhead | Marketing | Distribution | Customer Service |

2. Compute the total costs for each value chain category.
3. How much are the total inventoriable product costs?
4. How much are the total prime costs?
5. How much are the total conversion costs?

## E2-20A Classify costs as direct or indirect *(Learning Objective 3)*

Classify each of the following costs as a *direct cost* or an *indirect cost* assuming the cost object is the Produce Department (fruit and vegetable department) of a local grocery store.

a. Produce manager's salary
b. Cost of the produce
c. Store utilities
d. Bags and twist ties provided to customers in the Produce Department for packaging fruits and vegetables
e. Depreciation expense on refrigerated produce display shelves
f. Cost of shopping carts and baskets
g. Wages of checkout clerks
h. Cost of grocery store's advertisement flyer placed in the weekly newspaper
i. Store manager's salary
j. Cost of equipment used to peel and core pineapples at the store
k. Free grocery delivery service provided to senior citizens
l. Depreciation on self-checkout machines

## E2-21A Define cost terms *(Learning Objectives 3 & 4)*

Complete the following statements with one of the terms listed here. You may use a term more than once, and some terms may not be used at all.

| | | |
|---|---|---|
| Prime costs | Cost objects | Inventoriable product costs |
| Assigned | Direct costs | Fringe benefits |
| Period costs | Assets | Cost of goods sold |
| Indirect costs | Conversion costs | Total costs |

**a.** ______ can be traced to cost objects.
**b.** ______ are expensed when incurred.
**c.** ______ are the combination of direct materials and direct labour.
**d.** Compensation includes wages, salaries, and ______.
**e.** ______ are treated as ______until sold.
**f.** ______ include costs from only the production or purchases element of the value chain.
**g.** ______ are allocated to cost objects.
**h.** Both direct and indirect costs are ______to ______.
**i.** ______ include costs from every element of the value chain.
**j.** ______ are the combination of direct labour and manufacturing overhead.
**k.** ______ are expensed as ______when sold.
**l.** Manufacturing overhead includes all ______ of production.

## E2-22A Classify and calculate a manufacturer's costs *(Learning Objectives 3 & 4)*

Check sum: Total manufacturing overhead costs are $315.

An aircraft manufacturer incurred the following costs last month (in thousands of dollars):

| | |
|---|---|
| a. Airplane seats | $ 250 |
| b. Depreciation on administrative offices | 60 |
| c. Assembly workers' wages | 600 |
| d. Plant utilities | 120 |
| e. Production supervisors' salaries | 100 |
| f. Jet engines | 1,000 |
| g. Machine lubricants | 15 |
| h. Depreciation on forklifts | 50 |
| i. Property tax on corporate marketing office | 25 |
| j. Cost of warranty repairs | 225 |
| k. Factory janitors' wages | 30 |
| l. Cost of designing new plant layout | 175 |
| m. Machine operators' health insurance | 40 |
| Total | $2,690 |

### Requirements

1. If the cost object is an airplane, classify each cost as one of the following: direct material (DM), direct labour (DL), indirect labour (IL), indirect materials (IM), other manufacturing overhead (other MOH), or period cost. (*Hint:* Set up a column for each type of cost.) What is the total for each type of cost?
2. Calculate total manufacturing overhead costs.
3. Calculate total inventoriable product costs.
4. Calculate total prime costs.
5. Calculate total conversion costs.
6. Calculate total period costs.

**E2-23A Prepare the current assets section of the balance sheet** *(Learning Objective 5)*

Consider the following selected amounts and account balances of Lords:

| | | | |
|---|---|---|---|
| Cost of goods sold | $104,000 | Prepaid expenses | $ 8,000 |
| Direct labour | 47,000 | Marketing expense | 30,000 |
| Direct materials used | 20,000 | Work in process inventory | 40,000 |
| Accounts receivable | 80,000 | Manufacturing overhead | 26,000 |
| Cash | 15,000 | Finished goods inventory | 63,000 |
| Cost of goods manufactured | 94,000 | Raw materials inventory | 10,000 |

Show how this company reports current assets on the balance sheet. Not all the data are used. Is Lords a service company, a merchandiser, or a manufacturer? How do you know?

Check sum: Operating income is $219,000.

**E2-24A Prepare a retailer's income statement** *(Learning Objective 5)*

Amanda Boyd is the sole proprietor of Precious Pets, an e-tail business specializing in the sale of high-end pet gifts and accessories. Precious Pets's sales totalled $987,000 during the most recent year. During the year, the company spent $56,000 on expenses relating to Website maintenance; $22,000 on marketing; and $25,000 on wrapping, boxing, and shipping the goods to customers. Precious Pets also spent $642,000 on inventory purchases and an additional $21,000 on freight-in charges. The company started the year with $17,000 of inventory on hand and ended the year with $15,000 of inventory. Prepare Precious Pets' income statement for the most recent year.

Check sum: Direct materials used is $54,000.

**E2-25A Compute direct materials used and cost of goods manufactured** *(Learning Objective 5)*

Beasann's Die-Cuts is preparing its cost of goods manufactured schedule at year-end. Beasann's accounting records show the following: The raw materials inventory account had a beginning balance of $13,000 and an ending balance of $17,000. During the year, Beasann purchased $58,000 of direct materials. Direct labour for the year totalled $123,000, while manufacturing overhead amounted to $152,000. The work in process inventory account had a beginning balance of $21,000 and an ending balance of $15,000. Compute the cost of goods manufactured for the year. (*Hint:* The first step is to calculate the direct materials used during the year. Model your answer after Exhibit 2-15.)

Check sum: Cost of goods manufactured is $213,000.

**E2-26A Compute cost of goods manufactured and cost of goods sold** *(Learning Objective 5)*

Compute the cost of goods manufactured and cost of goods sold for Strike Marine Company for the most recent year using the amounts described below. Assume that raw materials inventory contains only direct materials.

| | Beginning of Year | End of Year | | End of Year |
|---|---|---|---|---|
| Raw material inventory | $25,000 | $28,000 | Insurance on plant | $ 9,000 |
| Work in process inventory | 50,000 | 35,000 | Depreciation—plant building and equipment | 13,000 |
| Finished goods inventory | 18,000 | 25,000 | Repairs and maintenance—plant | 4,000 |
| Purchases of direct materials | | 78,000 | Marketing expenses | 77,000 |
| Direct labour | | 82,000 | General and administrative expenses | 29,000 |
| Indirect labour | | 15,000 | | |

Check sum: Operating income is $72,000.

**E2-27A Continues E2-26A: prepare income statement** *(Learning Objective 5)*

Prepare the income statement for Strike Marine in E2-26A for the most recent year. Assume that the company sold 32,000 units of its product at a price of $12 each during the year.

**E2-28A Work backward to find missing amounts** *(Learning Objective 5)*

Smooth Sounds manufactures and sells a new line of MP3 players. Unfortunately, Smooth Sounds suffered serious fire damage at its home office. As a result, the accounting records for October were partially destroyed—and completely jumbled. Smooth Sounds has hired you to help figure out the missing pieces of the accounting puzzle. Assume that Smooth Sounds' raw materials inventory contains only direct materials.

| | |
|---|---|
| Work in process inventory, October 31 | $ 1,500 |
| Finished goods inventory, October 1 | 4,300 |
| Direct labour in October | 3,000 |
| Purchases of direct materials in October | 9,000 |
| Work in process inventory, October 1 | 0 |
| Revenues in October | 27,000 |
| Gross profit in October | 12,000 |
| Direct materials used in October | 8,000 |
| Raw materials inventory, October 31 | 3,000 |
| Manufacturing overhead in October | 6,300 |

**Requirement**

Find the following amounts:

a. Cost of goods sold in October

b. Beginning raw materials inventory

c. Ending finished goods inventory
(*Hint:* You may find Exhibits 2-15 and 2-16 helpful.)

**E2-29A Determine whether information is relevant** *(Learning Objective 6)*

Classify each of the following costs as relevant or irrelevant to the decision at hand, and briefly explain your reason.

a. The cost of operating automated production machinery versus the cost of direct labour when deciding whether to automate production

b. The cost of computers purchased six months ago when deciding whether to upgrade to computers with a faster processing speed

c. The cost of purchasing packaging materials from an outside vendor when deciding whether to continue manufacturing the packaging materials in-house

d. The property tax rates in different locales when deciding where to locate the company's headquarters

e. The type of gas (regular or premium) used by delivery vans when deciding which make and model of van to purchase for the company's delivery van fleet

f. The depreciation expense on old manufacturing equipment when deciding whether to replace it with newer equipment

g. The fair market value of old manufacturing equipment when deciding whether to replace it with new equipment

h. The interest rate paid on invested funds when deciding how much inventory to keep on hand

i. The cost of land purchased three years ago when deciding whether to build on the land now or wait two more years

j. The total amount of a restaurant's fixed costs when deciding whether to add additional items to the menu

**E2-30A Describe other cost terms** *(Learning Objectives 6 & 7)*

Complete the following statements with one of the terms listed here. You may use a term more than once, and some terms may not be used at all.

| | | |
|---|---|---|
| Differential costs | Irrelevant costs | Controllable costs |
| Marginal costs | Fixed costs | Average cost |
| Uncontrollable costs | Sunk costs | Variable costs |

a. Managers cannot influence ______ in the short run.
b. Total ______ decrease when production volume decreases.
c. For decision-making purposes, costs that do not differ between alternatives are ______.
d. Costs that have already been incurred are called ______.
e. Total ______ stay constant over a wide range of production volumes.
f. The ______ is the difference in cost between two alternative courses of action.
g. The product's ______ is the cost of making one more unit.
h. A product's ______ and ______, not the product's ______, should be used to forecast total costs at different production volumes.

**E2-31A Classify costs as fixed or variable** *(Learning Objective 7)*

Classify each of the following costs as fixed or variable:

a. Thread used by a garment manufacturer
b. Property tax on a manufacturing facility
c. Yearly salaries paid to sales staff
d. Gasoline used to operate delivery vans
e. Annual contract for pest (insect) control
f. Boxes used to package breakfast cereal at Kellogg's
g. Straight-line depreciation on production equipment
h. Cell phone bills for sales staff—contract billed at $.03 per minute
i. Wages paid to hourly assembly-line workers in the manufacturing plant
j. Monthly lease payment on administrative headquarters
k. Commissions paid to the sales staff—5% of sales revenue
l. Credit card transaction fee paid by retailer—$0.20 per transaction plus 2% of the sales amount
m. Annual business license fee from city
n. Cost of ice cream sold at Cow's Dairy in PEI
o. Cost of shampoo used at a hair salon

**E2-32A Compute total and average costs** *(Learning Objective 7)*

Fizzy-Cola spends $1 on direct materials, direct labour, and variable manufacturing overhead for every unit (12-pack of soda) it produces. Fixed manufacturing overhead costs $5 million per year. The plant, which is currently operating at only 75% of capacity, produced 20 million units this year. Management plans to operate closer to full capacity next year, producing 25 million units. Management does not anticipate any changes in the prices it pays for materials, labour, and manufacturing overhead.

### Requirements

a. What is the current total product cost (for the 20 million units), including fixed and variable costs?
b. What is the current average product cost per unit?
c. What is the current fixed cost per unit?
d. What is the forecasted total product cost next year (for the 25 million units)?
e. What is the forecasted average product cost next year?
f. What is the forecasted fixed cost per unit?
g. Why does the average product cost decrease as production increases?

# EXERCISES Group B

## E2-33B Identify types of companies and their inventories *(Learning Objective 1)*

Complete the following statements with one of the terms listed here. You may use a term more than once, and some terms may not be used at all.

| | | |
|---|---|---|
| Wholesalers | Work in process inventory | Service companies |
| Manufacturing companies | Raw materials inventory | Merchandising companies |
| Finished goods inventory | Inventory (merchandise) | |

a. ______ do not sell tangible products.

b. ______ buy in bulk from manufacturers and sell to retailers.

c. ______ produce their own inventory.

d. ______ typically have only one category of inventory.

e. Keller Inc. builds bicycles. Partially completed bikes are ______. Completed bikes that remain unsold in the warehouse are _______. Aluminum and plastic are ______.

f. ______ sell merchandise to consumers.

g. ______ transform raw materials into new finished products using their workforce and equipment.

h. ______ resell products they previously purchased ready-made from suppliers.

i. For Sony, blank compact discs, CD cases, and unprinted case liners are classified as ______.

## E2-34B Classify costs along the value chain for a retailer *(Learning Objective 2)*

Suppose Accessory Shack incurred the following costs at its Thunder Bay store.

| | |
|---|---|
| Research on whether store should sell satellite radio service | $ 500 |
| Purchases of merchandise | 35,000 |
| Rearranging store layout | 800 |
| Newspaper advertisements | 5,800 |
| Depreciation expense on delivery trucks | 1,900 |
| Payment to consultant for advice on location of new store | 2,200 |
| Freight-in | 3,600 |
| Salespeople's salaries | 4,500 |
| Customer complaint department | 900 |

### Requirements

1. Classify each cost according to its place in the value chain.

| R&D | Design | Purchases | Marketing | Distribution | Customer Service |
|---|---|---|---|---|---|

2. Compute the total costs for each value-chain category.
3. How much are the total inventoriable product costs?

## E2-35B Value chain and sustainability efforts *(Learning Objective 2)*

Each of the following scenarios describes some cost item for organizations in recent years. For each scenario, identify which function of the value chain that cost would represent (R&D, Design, Purchasing/Producing, Marketing, Distributing, or Customer Service.) *Note:* The companies and products used in this exercise are real companies with a strong sustainable practices commitment.

- ShipGreen is a service that American companies can use to purchase carbon offsets for the carbon generated by shipments to customers. Any shipments made with UPS, FedEx, or the post office can be tracked. The GreenShipping™ calculator uses weight, distance travelled, and mode of transport to calculate the carbon generated by that shipment. A carbon offset is then purchased so that the shipment becomes carbon neutral. The carbon offset helps to fund the development of renewable energy sources. The cost of these carbon offsets to the company making the shipment to its customer would fall into which function in the value chain?

- The Red Wing Shoe Company manufactures work boots. The company has a philosophy that products should be repaired, not thrown away. After the 12 month warranty has expired on Red Wing boots, the company offers free oiling, free laces, low-cost replacement insoles, and low-cost hardware repairs. The cost of operating this shoe repair service would fall into which function in the value chain?
- Ford Motor Company's Rouge Center in Dearborn, Michigan, has a "living roof" on the Dearborn Truck Plant final assembly building. It is the largest living roof in the world, encompassing 10.4 acres. The living roof is made from living grass, and its primary purpose is to collect and filter rainfall as part of a natural storm water management system. It also provides cooler surroundings and offers a longer roof life than a traditional roof. The cost of promoting the company's products and its sustainability efforts would fall into which function in the value chain?
- Nike Products, an athletic apparel and shoe manufacturer, developed the Environmental Apparel Design Tool over a period of seven years. The Environmental Apparel Design Tool helps apparel and shoe designers to make real-time choices that decrease the environmental impact of their work. With the tool, the designers can see the potential waste resulting from their design and the amount of environmentally preferred materials used by their design. When designers make changes to the preliminary product design, they can see instantly the effect of those changes on waste and input usage. The $6 million investment used to develop the Environmental Apparel Design Tool would fall into which function in the value chain?
- Nyloboard® produces decking materials made from recycled carpet. The cost of the research into how to create Nyloboard® from recycled carpet would fall into which function in the value chain?
- Late in 2010, the U.S. National Park Service approved the use of an erosion control system from GeoHay® for a roadway construction project in the Great Smoky Mountains National Park. GeoHay® erosion and sediment control products are produced from recycled carpet fibres. The cost of these erosion and sediment control products would fall into which function in the value chain?

## E2-36B Classify costs along the value chain for a manufacturer

*(Learning Objectives 2 & 3)*

Suppose the cell phone manufacturer Plum Electronics provides the following information for its costs last month (in hundreds of thousands):

| | | | |
|---|---|---|---|
| Salaries of telephone salespeople | $ 4 | Transmitters | $58 |
| Depreciation on plant and equipment | 55 | Rearrange production process to accommodate new robot | 1 |
| Exterior case for phone | 8 | Assembly-line workers' wages | 9 |
| Salaries of scientists who developed new model | 11 | Technical customer-support hotline | 3 |
| Delivery expense to customers via Canada Post | 5 | 1-800 (toll-free) line for customer orders | 2 |

### Requirements

1. Classify each of these costs according to its place in the value chain. (*Hint:* You should have at least one cost in each value chain function.)

| | | Production | | | | | |
|---|---|---|---|---|---|---|---|
| R&D | Design of Products or Processes | Direct Materials | Direct Labour | Manufacturing Overhead | Marketing | Distribution | Customer Service |

2. Compute the total costs for each value chain category.
3. How much are the total inventoriable product costs?
4. How much are the total prime costs?
5. How much are the total conversion costs?

### E2-37B Classify costs as direct or indirect *(Learning Objective 3)*

Classify each of the following costs as a direct cost or an indirect cost, assuming the cost object is the Garden Department of a local hardware store.

a. Garden manager's salary
b. Cost of shopping carts and baskets
c. Wages of checkout clerks
d. Cost of the merchandise
e. Depreciation expense on demonstration water feature
f. Cost of hardware store's advertisement flyer placed in the weekly newspaper
g. Depreciation on self-checkout machines
h. Bags provided to garden customers for packaging small items
i. Store manager's salary
j. Free garden delivery service provided to senior citizens
k. Cost of equipment used to plant and water plants at the store
l. Store utilities



### E2-38B Define cost terms *(Learning Objectives 3 & 4)*

Complete the following statements with one of the terms listed here. You may use a term more than once, and some terms may not be used at all.

| | | |
|---|---|---|
| Assigned | Indirect costs | Cost objects |
| Assets | Fringe benefits | Total costs |
| Cost of goods sold | Direct costs | Prime costs |
| Period costs | Inventoriable product costs | Conversion costs |

a. ______ include costs from only the production or purchases element of the value chain.
b. ______ are allocated to cost objects.
c. The combination of direct materials and direct labour is ______.
d. The combination of direct labour and manufacturing overhead is ______.
e. Both direct and indirect costs are ______to ______.
f. All ______ of production are included in manufacturing overhead.
g. ______ are expensed when incurred.
h. Wages, salaries, and ______ are considered compensation.
i. ______ include costs from every element of the value chain.
j. ______ can be traced to cost objects.
k. Until sold, ______ are treated as ______.
l. ______ are expensed as ______ when sold.

### E2-39B Classify and calculate a manufacturer's costs *(Learning Objectives 3 & 4)*

An airline manufacturer incurred the following costs last month (in thousands of dollars).

Check sum: Total manufacturing overhead costs are $455.

| | |
|---|---|
| a. Airplane seats | $ 270 |
| b. Depreciation on administrative offices | 70 |
| c. Assembly workers' wages | 690 |
| d. Plant utilities | 140 |
| e. Production supervisors' salaries | 150 |
| f. Jet engines | 1,200 |
| g. Machine lubricants | 35 |
| h. Depreciation on forklifts | 90 |
| i. Property tax on corporate marketing office | 15 |
| j. Cost of warranty repairs | 215 |
| k. Factory janitors' wages | 40 |
| l. Cost of designing new plant layout | 180 |
| m. Machine operators' health insurance | 60 |
| Total | $3,155 |

**Requirements**

1. If the cost object is an airplane, classify each cost as one of the following: direct material (DM), direct labour (DL), indirect labour (IL), indirect materials (IM), other manufacturing overhead (other MOH), or period cost. What is the total for each type of cost?
2. Calculate total manufacturing overhead costs.
3. Calculate total inventoriable product costs.
4. Calculate total prime costs.
5. Calculate total conversion costs.
6. Calculate total period costs.

### E2-40B Prepare the current assets section of the balance sheet *(Learning Objective 5)*

Check sum: Total Current Assets are $210,900.

Consider the following selected amounts and account balances of Esquires:

| | | | |
|---|---|---|---|
| Cost of goods sold | $107,000 | Prepaid expenses | $5,600 |
| Direct labour | 45,000 | Marketing expense | 28,000 |
| Direct materials used | 20,100 | Work in process inventory | 38,000 |
| Accounts receivable | 79,000 | Manufacturing overhead | 22,000 |
| Cash | 14,900 | Finished goods inventory | 63,000 |
| Cost of goods manufactured | 92,000 | Raw materials inventory | 10,400 |

Show how this company reports current assets on the balance sheet. Not all data are used. Is Esquires a service company, a merchandiser, or a manufacturer? How do you know?

### E2-41B Prepare a retailer's income statement *(Learning Objective 5)*

Check sum: Operating income is $279,300.

Estephan Rouhana is the sole proprietor of DigiPet, an e-tail business specializing in the sale of high-end pet gifts and accessories. Prestigious Pets' sales totalled $1,060,000 during the most recent year. During the year, the company spent $53,000 on expenses relating to Website maintenance, $33,000 on marketing, and $28,500 on wrapping, boxing, and shipping the goods to customers. Prestigious Pets also spent $643,000 on inventory purchases and an additional $20,500 on freight-in charges. The company started the year with $15,500 of inventory on hand and ended the year with $12,800 of inventory. Prepare Prestigious Pets' income statement for the most recent year.

### E2-42B Compute direct materials used and cost of goods manufactured *(Learning Objective 5)*

Check sum: Direct materials used is $70,000.

Lawrence's Die-Cuts is preparing its cost of goods manufactured schedule at year end. Lawrence's accounting records show the following: The raw materials inventory account had a beginning balance of $18,000 and an ending balance of $14,000. During the year, Lawrence purchased $66,000 of direct materials. Direct labour for the year totalled $135,000 while manufacturing overhead amounted to $155,000. The work in process inventory account had a beginning balance of $27,000 and an ending balance of $21,000. Compute the cost of goods manufactured for the year. (*Hint:* The first step is to calculate the direct materials used during the year.)

### E2-43B Compute cost of goods manufactured and cost of goods sold *(Learning Objective 5)*

Check sum: Total manufacturing costs incurred during the year are $224,200.

Compute the cost of goods manufactured and cost of goods sold for South Marine Company for the most recent year using the amounts described below. Assume that raw materials inventory contains only direct materials.

| | Beginning of Year | End of Year | | End of Year |
|---|---|---|---|---|
| Raw materials inventory | $28,000 | $30,000 | Insurance on plant | $ 10,500 |
| Work in process | 54,000 | 37,000 | Depreciation—plant building and equipment | 13,400 |
| Finished goods inventory | 13,000 | 29,000 | Repairs and maintenance—plant | 4,300 |
| Purchases of direct materials | | 76,000 | Marketing expenses | 78,500 |
| Direct labour | | 81,000 | General and administrative expenses | 26,500 |
| Indirect labour | | 41,000 | | |

### E2-44B Continues E2-43B: prepare income statement *(Learning Objective 5)*

Check sum: Operating income is $188,300.

Prepare the income statement for South Marine Company for the most recent year, using the information in E2-43B. Assume that the company sold 37,000 units of its product at a price of $14 each during the year.

### E2-45B Work backward to find missing amounts *(Learning Objective 5)*

Great Sounds manufactures and sells a new line of radios. Unfortunately, Great Sounds suffered serious fire damage at its home office. As a result, the accounting records for October were partially destroyed and completely jumbled. Great Sounds has hired you to help figure out the missing pieces of the accounting puzzle. Assume that Great Sounds' raw materials inventory contains only direct materials.

| | |
|---|---:|
| Work in process inventory, October 31 | $ 1,800 |
| Finished goods inventory, October 1 | 4,700 |
| Direct labour in October | 3,900 |
| Purchases of direct materials in October | 9,100 |
| Work in process inventory, October 1 | 0 |
| Revenues in October | 27,200 |
| Gross profit in October | 12,100 |
| Direct materials used in October | 8,500 |
| Raw materials inventory, October 31 | 3,600 |
| Manufacturing overhead in October | 6,000 |

**Requirement**

Find the following amounts:

a. Cost of goods sold in October
b. Beginning raw materials inventory
c. Ending finished goods inventory

### E2-46B Determine whether information is relevant *(Learning Objective 6)*

Classify each of the following costs as relevant or irrelevant to the decision at hand, and briefly explain your reason.

a. Cost of barcode scanners purchased six months ago when deciding whether to upgrade to scanners that are faster and easier to use
b. The fair market value of an ice cream truck when deciding whether to replace it with a newer ice cream truck
c. Cost of operating automated production machinery versus the cost of direct labour when deciding whether to automate production
d. Cost of purchasing packaging materials from an outside vendor when deciding whether to continue manufacturing the packaging materials in-house
e. The cost of an expansion site purchased two years ago when deciding whether to sell the site or to expand business to it now
f. The property tax rates in different locales when deciding where to locate the company's headquarters
g. The interest rate on invested funds when deciding how much inventory to keep on hand
h. The gas mileage of delivery vans when deciding which make and model of van to purchase for the company's delivery van fleet
i. Depreciation expense on old manufacturing equipment when deciding whether to replace it with newer equipment
j. The total amount of a coffee shop's fixed costs when deciding whether or not to introduce a new drink line

## E2-47B Describe other cost terms *(Learning Objectives 6 & 7)*

Complete the following statements with one of the terms listed here. You may use a term more than once, and some terms may not be used at all.

| | | |
|---|---|---|
| Variable costs | Sunk costs | Differential costs |
| Marginal costs | Uncontrollable costs | Average costs |
| Fixed costs | Irrelevant costs | Controllable costs |

a. In the short run, managers cannot influence ______.
b. Costs that do not differ between alternatives are ______, for decision-making purposes.
c. Total ______decrease when production volume decreases.
d. A product's _____ and ______, not the product's ______, should be used to forecast total costs at different production volumes.
e. Total ______stay constant over a wide range of production volumes.
f. ______ are costs that have already been incurred and cannot be recovered.
g. The cost of making one more unit is the product's ______.
h. The difference in cost between two alternative courses of action is the ______.

## E2-48B Classify costs as fixed or variable *(Learning Objective 7)*

Classify each of the following costs as fixed or variable:

a. Credit card transaction fee paid by retailer—$0.20 per transaction plus 2% of the sales amount
b. Yearly salaries paid to marketing staff
c. Gasoline used to drive company shuttle
d. Syrup used by an ice cream parlour
e. Property tax on an electronics factory
f. Annual contract for company landscaping
g. Boxes used to package computer components at Dell
h. Wages paid to hourly retail staff at the company store
i. Annual Web hosting fee for company Website
j. Cost of coffee sold at Starbucks
k. Monthly lease payment on branch office
l. Straight-line depreciation on production equipment
m. Rental car fees for company business travelers—contract billed at $0.25 per kilometre
n. Commissions paid to the sales staff—7% of sales revenue
o. Cost of paint used at an auto body shop

## E2-49B Compute total and average costs *(Learning Objective 7)*

Grand-Cola spends $1 on direct materials, direct labour, and variable manufacturing overhead for every unit (12-pack of soda) it produces. Fixed manufacturing overhead costs $6 million per year. The plant, which is currently operating at only 70% of capacity, produced 15 million units this year. Management plans to operate closer to full capacity next year, producing 20 million units. Management does not anticipate any changes in the prices it pays for materials, labour, or manufacturing overhead.

### Requirements

a. What is the current total product cost (for the 15 million units), including fixed and variable costs?
b. What is the current average product cost per unit?
c. What is the current fixed cost per unit?
d. What is the forecasted total product cost next year (for the 20 million units)?
e. What is the forecasted average product cost next year?
f. What is the forecasted fixed cost per unit?
g. Why does the average product cost decrease as production increases?

# PROBLEMS Group A

**P2-50A Classify costs along the value chain** *(Learning Objectives 2 & 4)*

ShaZam Cola produces a lemon-lime soda. The production process starts with workers mixing the lemon syrup and lime flavouring in a secret recipe. The company enhances the combined syrup with caffeine. Finally, ShaZam dilutes the mixture with carbonated water. ShaZam Cola incurs the following costs (in thousands):

| | |
|---|---:|
| Plant utilities | $ 750 |
| Depreciation on plant and equipment | 3,000 |
| Payment for new recipe | 1,000 |
| Salt | 25 |
| Replace products with expired dates upon customer complaint | 50 |
| Rearranging plant layout | 1,100 |
| Lemon syrup | 18,000 |
| Lime flavouring | 1,000 |
| Production costs of "cents-off" store coupons for customers | 600 |
| Delivery truck drivers' wages | 250 |
| Bottles | 1,300 |
| Sales commissions | 400 |
| Plant janitors' wages | 1,000 |
| Wages of workers who mix syrup | 8,000 |
| Customer hotline | 200 |
| Depreciation on delivery trucks | 150 |
| Freight-in | 1,500 |
| Total | $38,325 |

### Requirements

1. Use the following format to classify each of these costs according to its place in the value chain. (*Hint:* You should have at least one cost in each value-chain function.)

| | | Production | | | | | |
|---|---|---|---|---|---|---|---|
| R&D | Design of Products or Processes | Direct Materials | Direct Labour | Manufacturing Overhead | Marketing | Distribution | Customer Service |

2. Compute the total costs for each value-chain category.
3. How much are the total inventoriable product costs?
4. Suppose the managers of the R&D and design functions receive year-end bonuses based on meeting their unit's target cost reductions. What are they likely to do? How might this affect costs incurred in other elements of the value chain?

CHAPTER 2

### P2-51A Prepare income statements *(Learning Objective 5)*

*Part One:* In 2016, Hannah Summit opened Hannah's Pets, a small retail shop selling pet supplies. On December 31, 2016, her accounting records show the following:

| | |
|---|---|
| Inventory on December 31, 2016 | $10,250 |
| Inventory on January 1, 2016 | 15,000 |
| Sales revenue | 54,000 |
| Utilities for shop | 2,450 |
| Rent for shop | 4,000 |
| Sales commissions | 2,300 |
| Purchases of merchandise | 27,000 |

**Requirement**

Prepare an income statement for Hannah's Pets, a merchandiser, for the year ended December 31, 2016.

*Part Two:* Hannah's Pets was so successful that Hannah decided to manufacture her own brand of pet toys—Best Friends Manufacturing. At the end of December 2017, her accounting records show the following:

| | |
|---|---|
| Work in process inventory, December 31, 2017 | $ 720 |
| Finished goods inventory, December 31, 2016 | 0 |
| Finished goods inventory, December 31, 2017 | 5,700 |
| Sales revenue | 105,000 |
| Customer service hotline expense | 1,000 |
| Utilities for plant | 4,600 |
| Delivery expense | 1,500 |
| Sales salaries expense | 5,000 |
| Plant janitorial services | 1,250 |
| Direct labour | 18,300 |
| Direct material purchases | 31,000 |
| Rent on manufacturing plant | 9,000 |
| Raw materials inventory, December 31, 2016 | 13,500 |
| Raw materials inventory, December 31, 2017 | 9,275 |
| Work in process inventory, December 31, 2016 | 0 |

**Requirements**

1. Prepare a schedule of cost of goods manufactured for Best Friends Manufacturing for the year ended December 31, 2017.
2. Prepare an income statement for Best Friends Manufacturing for the year ended December 31, 2017.
3. How does the format of the income statement for Best Friends Manufacturing differ from the income statement of Hannah's Pets?

*Part Three:* Show the ending inventories that would appear on these balance sheets:

1. Hannah's Pets at December 31, 2016
2. Best Friends Manufacturing at December 31, 2017

### P2-52A Fill in missing amounts *(Learning Objective 5)*

Certain item descriptions and amounts are missing from the monthly schedule of cost of goods manufactured below and the income statement of Tretinik Manufacturing. Fill in the missing items.

| Tretinik Manufacturing Company | | | |
|---|---|---|---|
| ________________ | | | |
| ______ June 30 | | | |
| Beginning ________ | | | $ 21,000 |
| Add: Direct ________: | | | |
| Beginning raw materials inventory | $ X | | |
| Purchases of direct materials | 51,000 | | |
| ________ | 78,000 | | |
| Ending raw materials inventory | (23,000) | | |
| Direct ________ | | $ X | |
| Direct ________ | | X | |
| Manufacturing overhead | | 40,000 | |
| Total ________ costs ________ | | | 166,000 |
| Total ________ costs ________ | | | X |
| Less: Ending ________ | | | (25,000) |
| ________ | | | $ X |

| Tretinik Manufacturing Company | | |
|---|---|---|
| ________________ | | |
| ______ June 30 | | |
| Sales revenue | | $ X |
| Cost of goods sold: | | |
| Beginning ________ | $115,000 | |
| ________ | X | |
| Cost of goods ________ | X | |
| Ending ________ | X | |
| Cost of goods sold | | 209,000 |
| Gross profit | | 254,000 |
| ________ expenses: | | |
| Marketing expense | 99,000 | |
| Administrative expense | X | 154,000 |
| ________ income | | $ X |

**P2-53A Identify relevant information** *(Learning Objective 6)*

You receive two job offers in the same big city. The first job is close to your parents' house, and they have offered to let you live at home for a year so you will not have to incur expenses for housing, food, or internet service. This job pays $30,000 per year. The second job is far enough from your parents' house that you will have to rent an apartment with parking ($6,000 per year), buy your own food ($2,400 per year), and pay for your own internet ($600 per year). This job pays $35,000 per year. You still plan to do laundry at your parents' house once a week if you live in the city, and you plan to go into the city once a week to visit with friends if you live at home. Thus, the cost of operating your car will be about the same either way. In addition, your parents refuse to pay for your cell phone service ($720 per year), and you cannot function without it.

### Requirements

a. Based on this information alone, what is the net difference between the two alternatives (salary, net of relevant costs)?

b. What information is irrelevant? Why?

c. What qualitative information is relevant to your decision?

d. Assume that you really want to take Job #2, but you also want to live at home to cut costs. What new quantitative and qualitative information will you need to incorporate into your decision?

## P2-54A Calculate the total and average costs *(Learning Objective 7)*

The owner of Pizza-House Restaurant is disappointed because the restaurant has been averaging 3,000 pizza sales per month, but the restaurant and waitstaff can make and serve 5,000 pizzas per month. The variable cost (for example, ingredients) of each pizza is $2.00. Monthly fixed costs (for example, depreciation, property taxes, business licence, and manager's salary) are $6,000 per month. The owner wants cost information about different volumes so that he can make some operating decisions.

### Requirements

1. Fill in the following chart to provide the owner with the cost information he wants. Then use the completed chart to help you answer the remaining questions.

| Monthly pizza volume | 2,500 | 3,000 | 5,000 |
|---|---|---|---|
| | | | |
| Total fixed costs | $ | $ | $ |
| Total variable costs | ____ | ____ | ____ |
| Total costs | ____ | ____ | ____ |
| | | | |
| Fixed cost per pizza | $ | $ | $ |
| Variable cost per pizza | ____ | ____ | ____ |
| Average cost per pizza | ____ | ____ | ____ |
| | | | |
| Sales price per pizza | $10.00 | $10.00 | $10.00 |
| Average profit per pizza | ____ | ____ | ____ |

2. From a cost standpoint, why do companies such as Pizza-House Restaurant want to operate near or at full capacity?

3. The owner has been considering ways to increase the sales volume. He believes he could sell 5,000 pizzas a month by cutting the price from $10 a pizza to $9.50. How much extra profit (above the current level) would he generate if he decreased the sales price? (*Hint:* Find the restaurant's current monthly profit and compare it to the restaurant's projected monthly profit at the new sales price and volume.)

# PROBLEMS Group B

## P2-55B Classify costs along the value chain *(Learning Objectives 2 & 4)*

Best Value Cola produces a lemon-lime soda. The production process starts with workers mixing the lemon syrup and lime flavouring in a secret recipe. The company enhances the combined syrup with caffeine. Finally, Best Value dilutes the mixture with carbonated water. Best Value Cola incurs the following costs (in thousands):

| | |
|---|---|
| Plant utilities | $ 750 |
| Depreciation on plant and equipment | 2,800 |
| Payment for new recipe | 1,040 |
| Salt | 25 |
| Replace products with expired dates upon customer complaint | 45 |
| Rearranging plant layout | 1,400 |
| Lemon syrup | 17,000 |
| Lime flavouring | 1,120 |
| Production costs of "cents-off" store coupons for customers | 470 |
| Delivery truck drivers' wages | 285 |
| Bottles | 1,310 |
| Sales commissions | 400 |
| Plant janitors' wages | 1,050 |
| Wages of workers who mix syrup | 8,000 |
| Customer hotline | 190 |
| Depreciation on delivery trucks | 200 |
| Freight-in | 1,300 |
| Total | $37,385 |

CHAPTER 2

### Requirements

1. Classify each of these costs according to its place in the value chain. (*Hint:* You should have at least one cost in each value-chain function.)

| | | Production | | | | | |
|---|---|---|---|---|---|---|---|
| R&D | Design of Products or Processes | Direct Materials | Direct Labour | Manufacturing Overhead | Marketing | Distribution | Customer Service |

2. Compute the total costs for each value-chain category.
3. How much are the total inventoriable product costs?
4. Suppose the managers of the R&D and design functions receive year-end bonuses based on meeting their unit's target cost reductions. What are they likely to do? How might this affect costs incurred in other elements of the value chain?

## P2-56B Prepare income statements *(Learning Objective 5)*

*Part One:* In 2016, Lindsey Tapia opened Lindsey's Pets, a small retail shop selling pet supplies. On December 31, 2016, her accounting records show the following:

| | |
|---|---|
| Inventory on December 31, 2016 | $ 9,400 |
| Inventory on January 1, 2016 | 12,200 |
| Sales revenue | 55,000 |
| Utilities for shop | 1,500 |
| Rent for shop | 3,400 |
| Sales commissions | 4,100 |
| Purchases of merchandise | 34,500 |

### Requirement

Prepare an income statement for Lindsey's Pets, a merchandiser, for the year ended December 31, 2016.

*Part Two:* Lindsey's Pets succeeded so well that Lindsey decided to manufacture her own brand of pet toys—Best Friends Manufacturing. At the end of December 2017, her accounting records show the following:

| | |
|---|---|
| Work in process inventory, December 31, 2017 | $ 4000 |
| Finished goods inventory, December 31, 2016 | 0 |
| Finished goods inventory, December 31, 2017 | 3,000 |
| Sales revenue | 103,000 |
| Customer service hotline expense | 1,400 |
| Utilities for plant | 4,500 |
| Delivery expense | 2,500 |
| Sales salaries expense | 4,200 |
| Plant janitorial services | 1,150 |
| Direct labour | 20,000 |
| Direct material purchases | 39,000 |
| Rent on manufacturing plant | 8,400 |
| Raw materials inventory, December 31, 2016 | 10,000 |
| Raw materials inventory, December 31, 2017 | 8,000 |
| Work in process inventory, December 31, 2016 | 0 |

### Requirements

1. Prepare a schedule of cost of goods manufactured for Best Friends Manufacturing for the year ended December 31, 2017.
2. Prepare an income statement for Best Friends Manufacturing for the year ended December 31, 2017.
3. How does the format of the income statement for Best Friends Manufacturing differ from the income statement of Lindsey's Pets?

*Part Three:* Show the ending inventories that would appear on these balance sheets:

1. Lindsey's Pets at December 31, 2016.
2. Best Friends Manufacturing at December 31, 2017.

## P2-57B Fill in missing amounts *(Learning Objective 5)*

Certain item descriptions and amounts are missing from the monthly schedule of cost of goods manufactured and income statement of Chili Manufacturing Company. Fill in the missing items.

Chili Manufacturing Company

______________________

______ June 30

| | | | |
|---|---|---|---|
| Beginning ________ | | | $ 27,000 |
| Add: Direct ________: | | | |
| Beginning raw materials inventory | $ X | | |
| Purchases of direct materials | 56,000 | | |
| ________ | 80,000 | | |
| Ending raw materials inventory | (28,000) | | |
| Direct ________ . | | $ X | |
| Direct ________ | | X | |
| Manufacturing overhead | | 43,000 | |
| Total ________ costs ________ | | | $174,000 |
| Total ________ costs ________ | | | X |
| Less: Ending ________ | | | (21,000) |
| ________ | | | $ X |

Chili Manufacturing Company

______________________

______ June 30

| | | |
|---|---|---|
| Sales revenue | | $ X |
| Cost of goods sold: | | |
| Beginning ________ | $114,000 | |
| ________ | X | |
| Cost of goods ________ | X | |
| Ending ________ | X | |
| Cost of goods sold | | 228,000 |
| Gross profit | | 242,000 |
| ________ expenses: | | |
| Marketing expense | 98,000 | |
| Administrative expense | X | 166,000 |
| ________ income | | $ X |

**P2-58B Identify relevant information** *(Learning Objective 6)*

You receive two job offers in the same big city. The first job is close to your parents' house, and they have offered to let you live at home for a year so you will not have to incur expenses for housing, food, or internet service. This job pays $49,000 per year. The second job is far enough away from your parents' house that you will have to rent an apartment with parking ($9,000 per year), buy your own food ($3,500 per year), and pay for your own internet ($550 per year). This job pays $54,000 per year. You still plan to do laundry at your parents' house once a week if you live in the city and plan to go into the city once a week to visit with friends if you live at home. Thus, the cost of operating your car will be about the same either way. Additionally, your parents refuse to pay for your cell phone service ($690 per year), and you cannot function without it.

**Requirements**

a. Based on this information alone, what is the net difference between the two alternatives (salary, net of relevant costs)?
b. What information is irrelevant? Why?
c. What qualitative information is relevant to your decision?
d. Assume you really want to take Job #2, but you also want to live at home to cut costs. What new quantitative and qualitative information will you need to incorporate in your decision?



## P2-59B Calculate the total and average costs *(Learning Objective 7)*

The owner of Dartmouth Restaurant is disappointed because the restaurant has been averaging 5,000 pizza sales per month but the restaurant and waitstaff can make and serve 10,000 pizzas per month. The variable cost (for example, ingredients) of each pizza is $1.20. Monthly fixed costs (for example, depreciation, property taxes, business licence, manager's salary) are $5,000 per month. The owner wants cost information about different volumes so that he can make some operating decisions.

**Requirements**

1. Fill in the chart to provide the owner with the cost information he wants. Then use the completed chart to help you answer the remaining questions.

| Monthly pizza volume | 2,500 | 5,000 | 10,000 |
|---|---|---|---|
| | | | |
| Total fixed costs | $ | $ | $ |
| Total variable costs | ____ | ____ | ____ |
| Total costs | ____ | ____ | ____ |
| | | | |
| Fixed cost per pizza | $ | $ | $ |
| Variable cost per pizza | ____ | ____ | ____ |
| Average cost per pizza | ____ | ____ | ____ |
| | | | |
| Sales price per pizza | $ 5.50 | $ 5.50 | $ 5.50 |
| Average profit per pizza | ____ | ____ | ____ |

2. From a cost standpoint, why do companies such as Dartmouth Restaurant want to operate near or at full capacity?
3. The owner has been considering ways to increase the sales volume. He believes he could sell 10,000 pizzas a month by cutting the sales price from $5.50 a pizza to $5.00. How much extra profit (above the current level) would he generate if he decreased the sales price? (*Hint:* Find the restaurant's current monthly profit and compare it to the restaurant's projected monthly profit at the new sales price and volume.)

# CAPSTONE APPLICATION PROBLEMS

## APPLICATION QUESTION

*Source:* asharkyu/Shutterstock

**A2-60 Determine ending inventory balances** *(Learning Objective 5)*

PowerBox designs and manufactures switches used in telecommunications. Serious flooding throughout Alberta affected PowerBox's facilities. Inventory was completely ruined, and the company's computer system, including all accounting records, was destroyed.

Before the disaster-recovery specialists clean the buildings, Annette Plum, the company controller, is anxious to salvage whatever records she can to support an insurance claim for the destroyed inventory. She is standing in what is left of the Accounting Department with Paul Lopez, the cost accountant.

"I didn't know mud could smell so bad," Paul says. "What should I be looking for?"

"Don't worry about beginning inventory numbers," responds Annette. "We'll get them from last year's annual report. We need first-quarter cost data."

"I was working on the first-quarter results just before the storm hit," Paul says. "Look, my report's still in my desk drawer. But all I can make out is that for the first quarter, material purchases were \$476,000 and that direct labour, manufacturing overhead (other than indirect materials), and total manufacturing costs to account for were \$505,000, \$245,000, and \$1,425,000, respectively. Oh, and cost of goods available for sale was \$1,340,000."

"Great," says Annette. "I remember that sales for the period were approximately \$1.7 million. Given our gross profit of 30%, that's all you should need."

Paul is not sure about that, but decides to see what he can do with this information. The beginning inventory numbers are as follows:

- Raw materials, \$113,000
- Work in process, \$229,000
- Finished goods, \$154,000

He remembers a schedule he learned in school that may help him get started.

### Requirements

1. Exhibit 2-16 resembles the schedule Paul has in mind. Use it to determine the ending inventories of raw materials, work in process, and finished goods.
2. Draft an insurance claim letter for the controller, seeking reimbursement for the flood damage to inventory. PowerBox's insurance representative is Bassil Boulos, at Industrial Insurance, 1122 Main Street, Sudbury, Ontario, P2B 4K9. The policy number is #3454340-23. PowerBox's address is 5 Research Triangle Way, Red Deer, Alberta, T2A 3H7.

# DISCUSSION & ANALYSIS

1. Briefly describe a service company, a merchandising company, and a manufacturing company. Give an example of each type of company, but do not use the same examples as given in the chapter.
2. How do service, merchandising, and manufacturing companies differ from each other? How are service, merchandising, and manufacturing companies similar to each other? List as many similarities and differences as you can identify.
3. What is the value chain? What are the six types of business activities found in the value chain? Which type(s) of business activities in the value chain generate costs that go directly to the income statement once incurred? What type(s) of business activities in the value chain generate costs that flow into inventory on the balance sheet?
4. Compare direct costs to indirect costs. Give an example of a cost at a company that could be a direct cost at one level of the organization but would be considered an indirect cost at a different level of that organization. Explain why this same cost could be both direct and indirect (at different levels).
5. What is meant by the term "inventoriable product costs"? What is meant by the term "period costs"? Why does it matter whether a cost is an inventoriable product cost or a period cost?
6. Compare inventoriable product costs to period costs. Using a product of your choice, give examples of inventoriable product costs and period costs. Explain why you categorized your costs as you did.
7. Describe how the income statement of a merchandising company differs from the income statement of a manufacturing company. Also comment on how the income statement from a merchandising company is similar to the income statement of a manufacturing company.
8. How are the cost of goods manufactured, the cost of goods sold, the income statement, and the balance sheet related for a manufacturing company? What specific items flow from one statement or schedule to the next? Describe the flow of costs between the cost of goods manufactured, the cost of goods sold, the income statement, and the balance sheet for a manufacturing company.
9. What makes a cost relevant or irrelevant when making a decision? Suppose a company is evaluating whether to use its warehouse for storage of its own inventory or to rent it out to a local theatre group for housing props. Describe what information might be relevant when making that decision.
10. Explain why "differential cost" and "variable cost" do *not* have the same meaning. Give an example of a situation in which there is a cost that is a differential cost but that cost is *not* a variable cost.

# APPLICATION & ANALYSIS

## 2-1 Costs in the Value Chain at a Real Company and Cost Objects

Choose a company with which you are familiar that manufactures a product. In this activity, you will be making reasonable assumptions about the activities involved in the value chain for this product; companies do not typically publish information about their value chain.

### Discussion Questions

1. Describe the product that is being produced and the company that produces it.
2. Describe the six value chain business activities that this product would pass through from its inception to its ultimate delivery to the customer.
3. List at least three costs that would be incurred in each of the six business activities in the value chain.
4. Classify each cost you identified in the value chain as either being an inventoriable product cost or a period cost. Explain your justification.

5. A cost object can be anything for which managers want a separate measurement of cost. List three different potential cost objects *other* than the product itself for the company you have selected.
6. List a direct cost and an indirect cost for each of the three different cost objects in #5. Explain why each cost would be direct or indirect.

## Classroom Applications

**Web:** Post the discussion questions on an electronic discussion board. Have small groups of students choose a company that manufactures a product.

**Classroom:** Form groups of three or four students. Each group should choose a company that manufactures a product and prepare a five-minute presentation about its company and product that addresses the listed questions.

**Independent:** Have students research answers to each of the questions and then write and turn in a two- to three-page typed paper (12-point font, double-spaced with 2.54 cm margins).

# TRY IT SOLUTIONS

**page 61:**

Only those costs that can be traces directly to the Produce Department would be considered direct costs: 2, 3, 5, 6 and 8. All other costs (1, 4, and 7) would be considered indirect costs because they are part of the cost of selling produce at the store, yet cannot be traced directly to the Produce Department.

**page 63:**

The only costs that become inventoriable costs of the produce are numbers 3, 5 and 8. All other costs are classified as period costs, which are shown as "operating expenses" on the income statement.

**page 70:**

| | |
|---|---:|
| Beginning inventory | $ 35,000 |
| Plus: Purchase of merchandise | 400,000 |
|     Freight-in and import duties | 20,000 |
| Cost of goods available for sale | 455,000 |
| Less: Ending inventory | 38,000 |
| Cost of goods sold | $417,000 |

# 3 Cost Behaviour

Chapter 3 "Cost Behaviour" covers material outlined in **Section 3: Management Accounting** of the CPA Competency Map (by Competency Area). Specifically, this chapter addresses *Section 3.3 Cost Management*, and *Section 3.4 Revenue Management.* The Learning Objectives in this chapter have been aligned with the CPA Competency map to ensure the best coverage possible.

PROFESSIONAL COMPETENCY — The presence of the **coverage button** in the margin indicates focus on one or more of the specific competency areas from the competency map. The concepts in the text are building blocks to developing the competencies required in the CPA. While the chapter may address multiple areas of the competency map, the main focus will be:

Competencies:

**3.3.1** Evaluates cost classifications and costing methods for management of ongoing operations*

**3.3.2** Evaluates and applies cost management techniques appropriate for specific costing decisions*

**3.4.1** Evaluates sources and drivers of revenue growth*

**3.5.2** Evaluates sustainable profit maximization and capacity management performance*

## Learning Objectives

1. Describe key characteristics and graphs of various cost behaviours.
2. Use cost equations to express and predict costs.
3. Use account analysis and scatter plots to analyze cost behaviour.
4. Use the high-low method to analyze cost behaviour.
5. Use regression analysis to analyze cost behaviour.
6. Prepare contribution margin income statements for service firms and merchandising firms.
7. Use variable costing to prepare contribution margin income statements for manufacturers. (Appendix 3A)
8. Use segment reporting to utilize the contribution margin income statement format in an organization with two or more divisions. (Appendix 3B)

© Daniel Prudek/Fotolia

## Nestled among the Rocky Mountains in Banff, Alberta,

and surrounded by Canada's oldest national park, lies the Banff Rocky Mountain Resort, with 171 luxurious rooms offering spectacular views of the Canadian wilderness. Tourists, business people, and romance-seekers travel from around the world to take advantage of the skiing, hiking, golfing, and other recreational activities at the resort or just to relax in the outdoor hot tub.[†]

How do hotel managers set prices high enough to cover costs and earn a profit but low enough to fill most rooms each night? How do they plan for higher occupancy during the busy summer months and lower occupancy during the off-season? They know

*Reprinted from *The Chartered Professional Accountant Competency Map - Understanding the competencies a candidate must demonstrate to become a CPA*, © 2012, with permission Chartered Professional Accountants of Canada, Toronto, Canada. Any changes to the original material are the sole responsibility of the author (and/or publisher) and have not been reviewed or endorsed by the Chartered Professional Accountants of Canada.

[†]Karen W. Braun, Wendy M Tietz and Louis Beaubien, Managerial Accounting, 3rd Ed., © 2018, Pearson Education, Inc., New York, NY.

how their costs behave. Some hotel costs, such as complimentary morning breakfasts and concierge services, vary with the number of guests staying each night. These *variable* costs rise and fall with the number of guests. But most hotel costs, such as depreciation on the building and furniture, stay the same whether 50 or 2,000 guests stay each night. These costs are *fixed*. Most hotel costs are fixed, so the extra costs to serve each additional guest are low. Once these costs are covered, the revenue from extra guests goes toward profits.

To make good decisions and accurate projections, managers must understand **cost behaviour**—that is, how costs change as volume changes. In this chapter, we discuss typical cost behaviours and explain the methods managers use to determine how their costs behave. The Appendices discuss alternative product costing systems based on cost behaviour that manufacturers can use for internal decision making. This chapter will discuss how understanding cost behaviour techniques will help develop effective tools for planning and decision making.

## Cost Behaviour: How Do Changes in Volume Affect Costs?

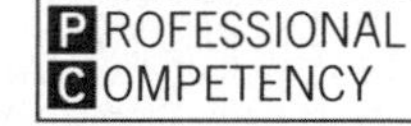


1 Describe key characteristics and graphs of various cost behaviours.

The Banff Rocky Mountain Resort has 171 guest suites that can accommodate between 171 and 684 people (four to a room) per night. If every hotel room is booked (100% occupancy rate), the hotel can accommodate between 1,197 and 4,788 guests per week. How do managers plan for such a wide range of volume? They use historic occupancy patterns to determine the most likely range of volume. The room occupancy rate (percentage of rooms booked) varies depending on the season and day of the week. In addition to understanding occupancy patterns, managers must know how changes in volume (number of guests) can affect their costs. We first consider three of the most common cost behaviours:

1. Variable costs are costs that change in total in direct proportion to changes in volume. For Banff Rocky Mountain Resort, any complimentary refreshments and in-room toiletries (soap, shampoo, and lotion) are variable costs because these costs increase in total with the number of guests.
2. Fixed costs are costs that do not change in total despite wide changes in volume. For Banff Rocky Mountain Resort, property taxes, insurance, and depreciation on the hotel building and furnishings are fixed costs that will be the same regardless of the number of hotel guests.
3. Mixed costs are costs that change in total but *not* in direct proportion to changes in volume. Mixed costs have both variable and fixed components. For Banff Rocky Mountain Resort, utilities (electricity, gas, water) are mixed costs. Some utility costs will be incurred no matter how many guests stay the night. However, utility costs will also rise as the number of guests rises, because they turn up the heat or air conditioning, take showers, and use freshly laundered linens.

### Variable Costs

Let's assume that every guest at Banff Rocky Mountain Resort is entitled to a complimentary morning breakfast and afternoon refreshment hour (drinks and snacks). In addition, guests receive complimentary toiletries, including shampoo, soap, lotion, and mouthwash, which they typically use or take with them. Let's also assume that these toiletries cost the hotel $3 per guest and that the breakfast and refreshment hour cost the hotel $10 per guest. Exhibit 3-1 graphs these costs for the Banff Rocky Mountain Resort. The vertical axis (y-axis) shows total variable costs, while the horizontal axis (x-axis) shows total volume of activity (thousands of guests, in this case).[1]

**Why is this important?**

Cost behaviour is a **key** component of most **planning** and operating decisions. Without a thorough understanding of **cost behaviour**, managers are apt to make less **profitable** decisions.

[1]The data presented here are hypothetical, for teaching purposes only.

**EXHIBIT 3-1** Variable Costs

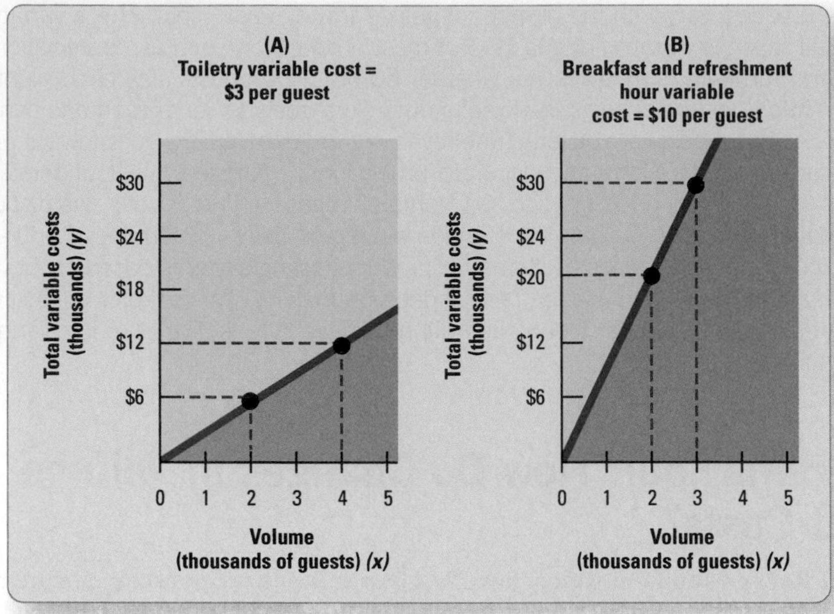


Look at the total variable toiletry costs in Exhibit 3-1(A). If there are no guests, Banff Rocky Mountain Resort does not incur any costs for the toiletries, so the total variable cost line begins at the bottom left corner, called the *origin*, representing zero volume and zero cost. Total variable cost graphs always begin at the origin. The *slope* of the total variable cost line is the *variable cost per unit of activity*. In Exhibit 3-1(A), the slope of the toiletry variable cost line is $3 because the hotel spends an additional $3 on toiletries for each additional guest. If the hotel serves 2,000 guests, it will spend a total of $6,000 on complimentary toiletries. Doubling the number of guests to 4,000 likewise doubles the total variable cost to $12,000. This example illustrates several important points about variable costs—total variable costs change in direct proportion to changes in volume. If volume of activity doubles, total variable costs double. If volume triples, total variable costs triple.

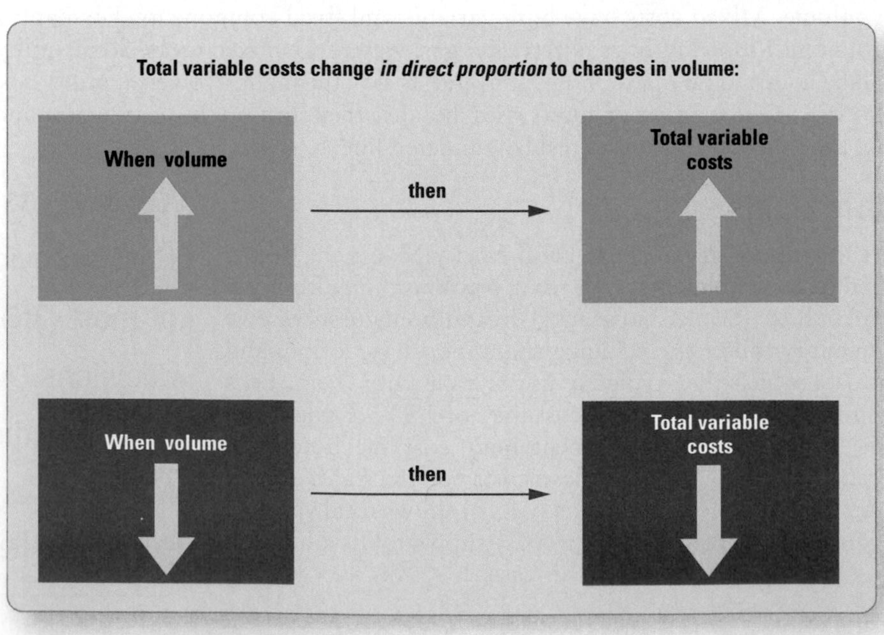

Managers do not need to rely on graphs to predict total variable costs at different volumes of activity. They can use a <u>cost equation</u>, a mathematical equation for a straight line, to express how a cost behaves. On cost graphs like those pictured in Exhibit 3-1, the vertical (y-axis) always shows total costs, while the horizontal axis (x-axis) shows volume of activity. Therefore, any variable cost line can be mathematically expressed as follows:

**2** Use cost equations to express and predict costs.

PROFESSIONAL COMPETENCY

Total variable cost ($y$) = Variable cost per unit of activity ($v$) × Volume of activity ($x$)

Or simply:

$$y = vx$$

**Why is this important?**

Cost **equations** help managers foresee what their **total costs** will be at **different** operating **volumes** so that they can **better** plan for the future.

The hotel's total toiletry cost is as follows:

$$y = \$3x$$

wherein

$$y = \text{total toiletry cost}$$
$$\$3 = \text{variable cost per guest}$$
$$x = \text{number of guests}$$

We can confirm the observations made in Exhibit 3-1(A) using the cost equation. If the hotel has no guests ($x = 0$), total toiletry costs are zero, as shown in the graph. If the hotel has 2,000 guests, total toiletry costs will be

$$y = \$3 \text{ per guest} \times 2{,}000 \text{ guests}$$
$$= \$6{,}000$$

If the hotel has 4,000 guests, managers will expect total toiletry costs to be

$$y = \$3 \text{ per guest} \times 4{,}000 \text{ guests}$$
$$= \$12{,}000$$

## STOP & THINK

If the hotel serves 3,467 guests next week, how much will it spend on complimentary toiletries?

**Answer:** You would have a hard time answering this question by simply looking at the graph in Exhibit 3-1(A), but cost equations can be used for any volume. We "plug in" the expected volume to our variable cost equation as follows:

$$y = \$3 \text{ per guest} \times 3{,}467 \text{ guests}$$
$$= \$10{,}401$$

Management expects complimentary toiletries next week to cost about $10,401.

Now, look at Exhibit 3-1(B), the total variable costs for the complimentary breakfast and refreshment hour. The slope of the line is $10, representing the cost of providing each guest with the complimentary breakfast and refreshments. We can express the total breakfast and refreshment hour cost as follows:

$$y = \$10x$$

wherein

$$y = \text{total breakfast and refreshment hour cost}$$
$$\$10 = \text{variable cost per guest}$$
$$x = \text{number of guests}$$

The total cost of the breakfast and refreshment hour for 2,000 guests is

$$y = \$10 \text{ per guest} \times 2{,}000 \text{ guests}$$
$$= \$20{,}000$$

This is much higher than the $6,000 toiletry cost for 2,000 guests, so the slope of the line is much steeper than it was for the toiletries. *The higher the variable cost per unit of activity (v), the steeper the slope of the total variable cost line.*

Both graphs in Exhibit 3-1 show how total variable costs vary with the number of guests. But note that the variable cost per guest *(v)* remains constant in each of the graphs. That is, Banff Rocky Mountain Resort incurs $3 in toiletry costs and $10 in breakfast and refreshment hour costs for each guest no matter how many guests the hotel serves. Some key points to remember about variable costs are shown in Exhibit 3-2.

**EXHIBIT 3-2** Key Characteristics of Variable Costs

- *Total* variable costs change in *direct proportion* to changes in volume.
- The *variable cost per unit of activity (v)* remains constant and is the slope of the variable cost line.
- Total variable cost graphs always begin at the origin. (If volume is zero, total variable costs are zero.)
- Total variable costs can be expressed as follows:

  $y = vx$

  where

  $y$ = total variable cost
  $v$ = variable cost per unit of activity
  $x$ = volume of activity

## Relevant Range

The **relevant range** is important to understand before we begin our discussion of variable and fixed costs below. It is the range of operations within which the total fixed costs and the variable cost per unit remain constant. Most commonly this is an issue of organizational capacity, and changes in the relevant range are often (but not always) the result of a management decision to increase or decrease the capacity of the organization, which results in a change in the cost structure of the organization. For instance, an automotive manufacturing company may choose to add (or eliminate) a factory to change production volumes, or a law firm may open a new regional office in a different city to better serve its clients (and expand its market). In either case, the operational change affects the fixed costs (the rent, utilities, depreciation, etc.) of the new facilities, and may impact the variable costs in terms of how efficiently operations can be conducted. A change in cost behaviour means a change to a different relevant range.

**EXHIBIT 3-3** Fixed Costs

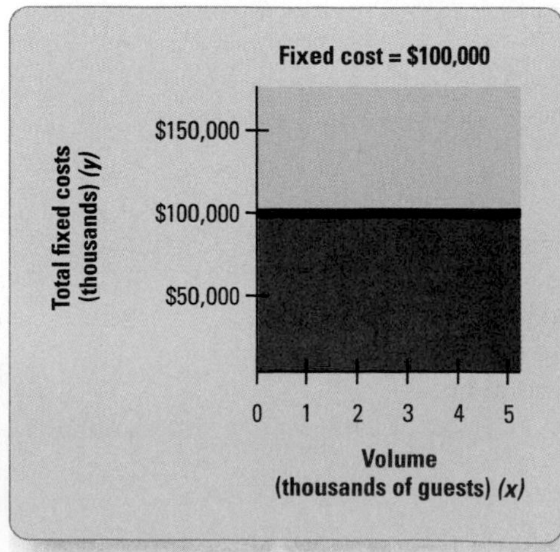


As shown in Exhibit 3-3, Banff Rocky Mountain Resort's fixed costs are $100,000 per week. Managers might make a strategic and operational decision to expand the dining facilities, in order to accommodate increasing occupancy rates and the larger number of people wanting to dine at the hotel. In addition, management may also add a 30-passenger elevator bank. These decisions would change the fixed costs.

## Fixed Costs

In contrast to total variable costs, total fixed costs do *not* change with fluctuations in volume within the relevant range. Many of Banff Rocky Mountain Resort's costs are fixed because the hotel continues daily operations regardless of the number of guests. Some of the hotel's fixed costs include the following:

- Property taxes and insurance
- Depreciation and maintenance on parking ramp, hotel, and room furnishings
- Pool, fitness room, and spa upkeep
- Cable TV and wireless internet access for all rooms
- Salaries of hotel department managers (housekeeping, food service, special events, etc.)

Most of these costs are **committed fixed costs**, meaning that the hotel is locked in to these costs because of previous management decisions. For example, as soon as the hotel was built, management became locked in to a certain level of property taxes and depreciation, simply because of the location and size of the hotel and management's choice of furnishings and amenities (pool, fitness room, restaurant, and so forth). Management has little or no control over these committed fixed costs in the short run.

However, the hotel also incurs **discretionary fixed costs**, such as advertising expenses, that are a result of annual management decisions. Companies have more control over discretionary fixed costs because the companies can adjust the costs as necessary in the short run.

Suppose Banff Rocky Mountain Resort incurs $100,000 of fixed costs each week. In Exhibit 3-3, the y-axis shows total fixed costs, while volume of activity (thousands of guests) is plotted on the x-axis. The graph shows total fixed costs as a flat line that intersects the y-axis at $100,000 (known as the y-intercept) because the hotel will incur the same $100,000 of fixed costs regardless of the number of guests who stay during the week.

The cost equation for a fixed cost is

$$\text{Total fixed cost } (y) = \text{Fixed amount over a period of time } (f)$$

Or simply

$$y = f$$

Banff Rocky Mountain Resort's weekly fixed cost equation is

$$y = \$100{,}000$$

wherein

$$y = \text{total fixed cost per week}$$

In contrast to the total fixed costs shown in Exhibit 3-3, the fixed cost per guest depends on the number of guests. If the hotel serves 2,000 guests during the week, the fixed cost per guest is

$$\$100{,}000 \div 2{,}000 \text{ guests} = \$50/\text{guest}$$

If the number of guests doubles to 4,000, the fixed cost per guest is halved:

$$\$100{,}000 \div 4{,}000 \text{ guests} = \$25/\text{guest}$$

The fixed cost per guest is inversely proportional to the number of guests. When volume increases, the fixed cost per guest decreases. When volume decreases, the fixed cost per guest increases.

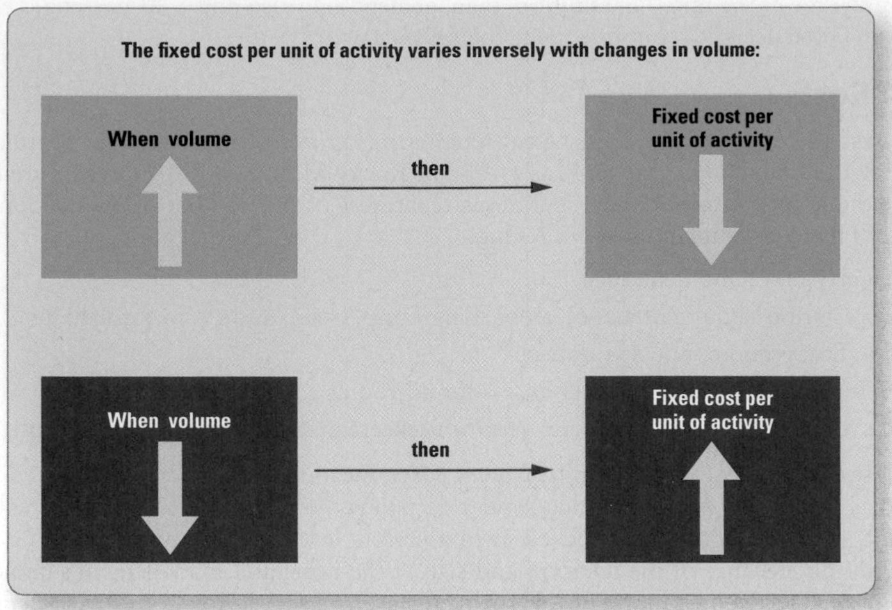


Key points to remember about fixed costs appear in Exhibit 3-4.

**EXHIBIT 3-4** Key Characteristics of Fixed Costs

- *Total* fixed costs stay *constant* within a *relevant range.*
- Fixed costs *per unit of activity* vary *inversely* with changes in volume:
    - Fixed cost per unit of activity *increases* when volume *decreases.*
    - Fixed cost per unit of activity *decreases* when volume *increases.*
- Total fixed cost graphs are always flat lines with no slope that intersect the *y*-axis at a level equal to total fixed costs.
- Total fixed costs can be expressed as $y = f$ where

  $y$ = total fixed cost

  $f$ = fixed cost over a given period of time

## STOP & THINK

Compute the (1) total fixed cost and (2) fixed cost per guest if the hotel reaches full occupancy of 4,788 guests next week (171 rooms booked with four people per room). Compare the fixed cost per guest at full occupancy to the fixed cost per guest when only 2,000 guests stay during the week. Explain why hotels and other businesses like to operate near 100% capacity.

**Answers:**

1. Total fixed costs do not react to wide changes in volume; therefore, total fixed costs will still be $100,000.
2. Fixed costs per unit decrease as volume increases. At full occupancy, the fixed cost per guest is as follows:

$100,000 ÷ 4,788 guests = $20.89 (rounded) per guest

When only 2,000 guests stay, the fixed cost per guest is much higher ($50 = $100,000 ÷ 2,000 guests). Businesses like to operate near full capacity because it lowers their fixed cost per unit. A lower cost per unit gives businesses the flexibility to lower their prices to compete more effectively.

## TRY IT!

Compute the (a) total fixed cost and (b) fixed cost per guest if the hotel has 16,000 guests next month. Compare the fixed cost per guest at the higher occupancy rate to the fixed cost per guest when only 2,000 guests stay during the month.

Please see page 181 for solutions.

## Mixed Costs

Mixed costs contain both variable and fixed cost components. Banff Rocky Mountain Resort's utilities are mixed costs because the hotel requires a certain amount of utilities just to operate. However, the more guests at the hotel, the more water, electricity, and gas are required. Exhibit 3-5 illustrates mixed costs.

For example, let's assume that if the hotel were completely empty, the utilities would cost \$2,000 per week. These costs increase by \$8 per guest as each cools or heats his or her room, takes showers, turns on the TV and lights, and uses freshly laundered sheets and towels.

Notice the two components—variable and fixed—of the mixed cost in Exhibit 3-5. Similar to a variable cost, the total mixed cost line increases as the volume of activity increases. However, the line does *not* begin at the origin. Rather, it intersects the y-axis at a level equal to the fixed cost component. Even if no guests stay this week, the hotel still incurs \$2,000 of utilities cost.

**EXHIBIT 3-5** Mixed Costs

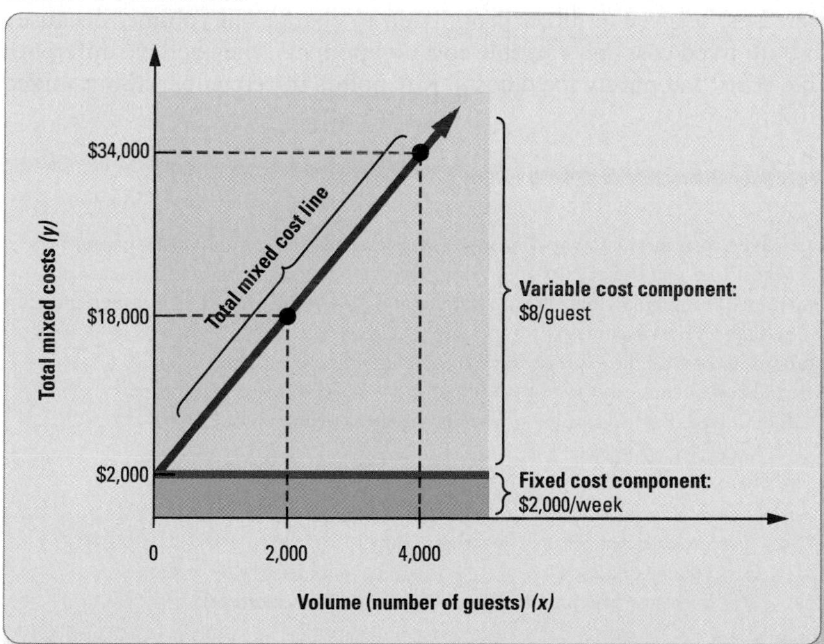


Managers can once again use a cost equation to express the mixed cost line so that they can predict total mixed costs at different volumes. The mixed cost equation simply combines the variable cost and fixed cost equations:

| Total mixed costs | = | Variable cost component | + | Fixed cost component |
|---|---|---|---|---|
| $y$ | = | $vx$ | + | $f$ |

Banff Rocky Mountain Resort's weekly utilities cost equation is

$$y = \$8x + \$2,000$$

wherein

$y$ = total utilities cost per week
$x$ = number of guests

If the hotel serves 2,000 guests this week, it expects utilities to cost

$$y = (8 \text{ per guest} \times 2{,}000 \text{ guests}) + \$2{,}000$$
$$= \$18{,}000$$

If the hotel serves 4,000 guests this week, it expects utilities to cost

$$y = (8 \text{ per guest} \times 4{,}000 \text{ guests}) + \$2{,}000$$
$$= \$34{,}000$$

Total mixed costs increase as volume increases, but not in direct proportion to changes in volume. The total mixed costs do *not* double when volume doubles because of the influence of the fixed cost component. Additionally, consider the mixed cost per guest:

If the hotel serves 2,000 guests: \$18,000 total cost ÷ 2,000 guests = \$9.00 per guest
If the hotel serves 4,000 guests: \$34,000 total cost ÷ 4,000 guests = \$8.50 per guest

The mixed cost per guest does *not* decrease by 50% when the hotel serves twice as many guests, because of the variable cost component. Mixed costs per unit decrease as volume increases, but *not* in direct proportion to changes in volume. Because mixed costs contain both fixed cost and variable cost components, they behave differently than purely variable costs and purely fixed costs. Key points to remember about mixed costs appear in Exhibit 3-6.

**EXHIBIT 3-6** Key Characteristics of Mixed Costs

- *Total* mixed costs increase as volume increases because of the variable cost component.
- Mixed costs *per unit* decrease as volume increases because of the fixed cost component.
- Total mixed cost graphs slope upward but do *not* begin at the origin—they intersect the y-axis at the level of fixed costs.
- Total mixed costs can be expressed as a *combination* of the variable and fixed cost equations:

  Total mixed costs = variable cost component + fixed cost component

  $$y = vx + f$$

  where

  $y$ = total mixed cost
  $v$ = variable cost per unit of activity (slope)
  $x$ = volume of activity
  $f$ = fixed cost over a given period of time (vertical intercept)

## STOP & THINK

If your cell phone plan charges \$10 per month plus \$0.15 for each minute you talk, how could you express the monthly cell phone bill as a cost equation? How much will your cell phone bill be if you (1) talk 100 minutes this month or (2) talk 200 minutes this month? If you double your talk time from 100 to 200 minutes, does your total cell phone bill double? Explain.

**Answer:** The cost equation for the monthly cell phone bill is as follows:

$$y = \$0.15x + \$10$$

wherein

$y$ = total cell phone bill for the month
$x$ = number of minutes used

1. At 100 minutes, the total cost is \$25 [= (\$0.15 per minute × 100 minutes) + \$10]
2. At 200 minutes, the total cost is \$40 [= (\$0.15 per minute × 200 minutes) + \$10]

The cell phone bill does not double when talk time doubles. The variable portion of the bill doubles from \$15 (\$0.15 × 100 minutes) to \$30 (\$0.15 × 200 minutes), but the fixed portion of the bill stays constant (\$10).

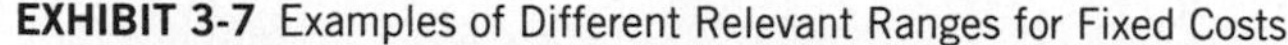

## Changing Costs in the Relevant Range

The hotel expansion, if carried out, will increase the hotel's fixed costs to a new level. Exhibit 3-7 illustrates the hotel's current relevant range and future potential relevant range for fixed costs.

**EXHIBIT 3-7** Examples of Different Relevant Ranges for Fixed Costs

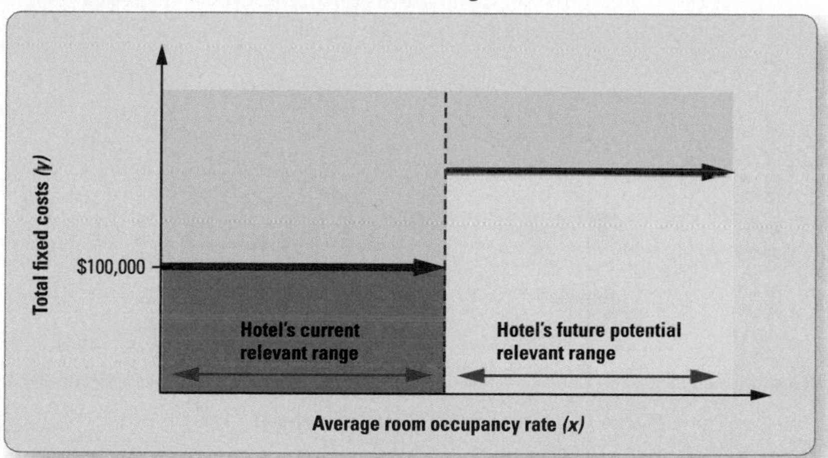


The change in operations also impacts the variable costs. For example, the hotel's current variable cost for toiletries is \$3 per guest. However, as room occupancy rates continue to grow, management hopes to negotiate greater volume discounts on the toiletries from its suppliers. These volume discounts will decrease the variable toiletries cost per guest (for example, down to \$2.75 per guest). Exhibit 3-8 illustrates the hotel's current relevant range and future potential relevant range for variable toiletries costs.

**EXHIBIT 3-8** Examples of Different Relevant Ranges for Variable Costs

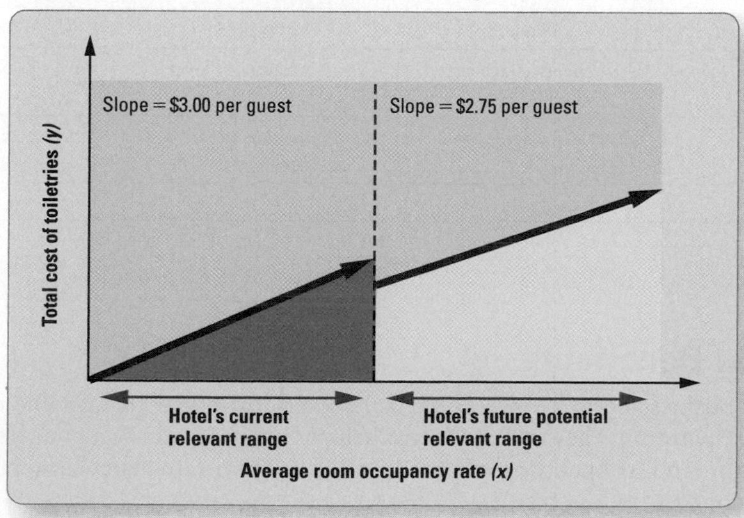

Managers can predict costs accurately only if they use cost information for the appropriate relevant range. For example, many cell phone plans offer a large block of "free" minutes for a set fee each month. If the user exceeds the allotted minutes, the cell phone company charges an additional per-minute fee. Exhibit 3-9 shows a cell phone plan in which the first 1,000 minutes of call time each month cost \$50. After the 1,000 minutes are used, the user must pay an additional \$0.30 per minute for every minute of call time. This cell phone plan has two relevant ranges. The first relevant range extends from 0 to 1,000 minutes. In this range, the \$50 fee behaves strictly as a fixed cost. You could use 0, 100, or 975 minutes and you would still pay a flat \$50 fee that month. The second relevant range starts at 1,001 minutes and extends indefinitely. In this relevant range, the cost is mixed: \$50 plus \$0.30 per minute. To forecast your cell phone bill each month, you need to know in which relevant range you plan to operate. The same holds true for businesses: To accurately predict costs, they need to know the relevant range in which they plan to operate.

**EXHIBIT 3-9** Examples of Relevant Ranges

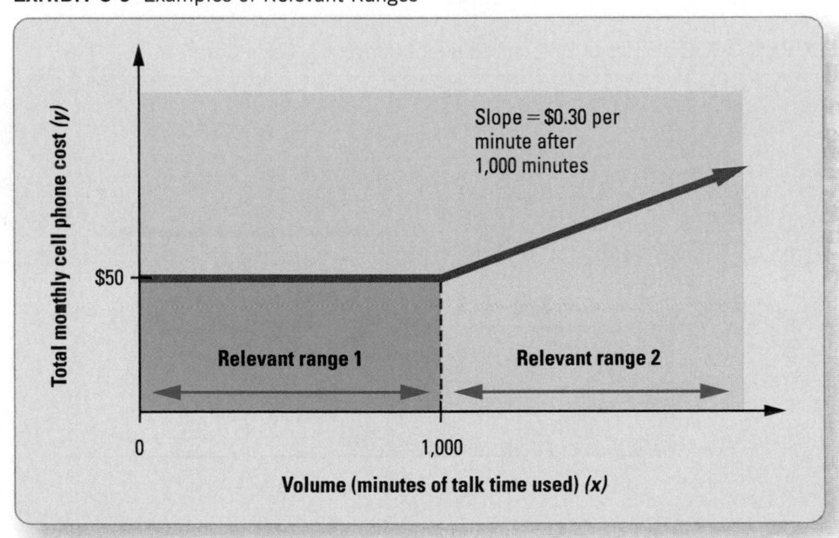


The following chart summarizes the three different cost behaviours for the impact on total cost and unit cost with respect to changes in activity levels and provides the formula for each.

**Comparison of Types of Costs**

| Measurement | Fixed | Variable | Mixed |
|---|---|---|---|
| Total Cost | Unchanged as activity level changes | Varies as activity level changes | Varies as activity level changes |
| Unit Cost | Varies as activity level changes | Unchanged as activity level changes | Varies as activity level changes |
| Equation | $y = f$ | $y = vx$ | $y = vx + f$ |

## Other Cost Behaviours

While many business costs behave as variable, fixed, or mixed costs, some costs do not neatly fit these patterns. These alternate cost behaviours impact how managers understand an organization and its operations. In many cases, they will influence how pricing strategies are developed.

Assume the local fitness club charges a membership fee of $30 per month for unlimited use of the exercise equipment, plus an additional fee of $5 for every instructor-led exercise class you attend.

1. Express the monthly cost of belonging to the fitness club as a cost equation.
2. What is your expected cost for a month in which you attend five instructor-led classes?
3. If your attendance doubles to 10 classes per month, will your total cost for the month double? Explain.

Please see page 181 for solutions.

**Step costs** resemble stair steps: They are fixed over a small range of activity and then jump up to a new fixed level with moderate changes in volume. Hotels, restaurants, hospitals, and educational institutions typically experience step costs. For example, regulated day-care centres are required to limit the caregiver-to-child ratio depending on the age of the child. New Brunswick sets a ratio of 1:8 for children between the ages of three and four years. As shown in Exhibit 3-10, a day-care centre that takes on a ninth child must incur the cost of employing another caregiver. The new caregiver can watch the ninth through sixteenth children enrolled at the day-care centre. If the day-care centre takes on a seventeenth child, management will once again need to hire another caregiver, costing another $28,000 in salary. The same step cost patterns occur with hotels (maid-to-room ratio), restaurants (server-to-table ratio), hospitals (nurse-to-bed ratio), and schools (teacher-to-student ratio).

**EXHIBIT 3-10** Step Costs

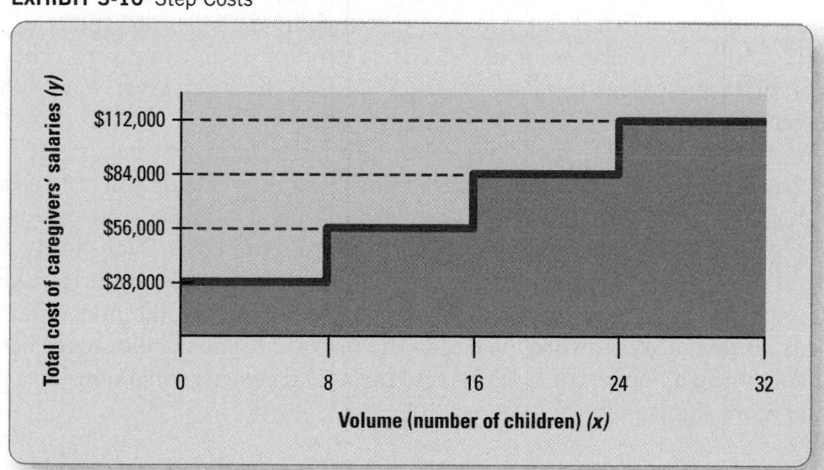

Step costs can be variable or fixed. A variable cost such as hourly wages for cleaning staff at Banff Rocky Mountain Resort is likely to increase in increments. If the cleaning staff is able to clean 100 rooms, it is unlikely that cleaning labour costs would increase if one additional room is rented; however, if ten additional rooms are rented, this would cause a small increase in the total variable cleaning costs. A fixed cost, such as depreciation, is only fixed for a relevant range. A hotel expansion would not be limited to only a few additional rooms, therefore expansions will create large incremental changes in the total fixed costs. The difference between step variable and step fixed costs is that fixed costs hold constant over much larger ranges of volume.

As shown by the red lines in Exhibit 3-11, **curvilinear costs** are not linear (not a straight line) and, therefore, do not fit into any neat pattern. Most linear costs are

**EXHIBIT 3-11** Curvilinear Costs and Straight-Line Approximations

actually curvilinear in nature. For example, the purchase of shampoos and soaps has been described as a linear cost. However, if the hotel bought only a few bottles, the cost per bottle would likely be a little higher than if they bought a few thousand bottles. On the other hand, if the hotel bought 100,000 bottles, the supplier would probably offer a discount and the price per bottle would be less than if they bought a few thousand bottles. This would create a curvilinear cost.

As shown by the straight green arrows in Exhibit 3-11, businesses usually *approximate* these types of costs as mixed costs. Sometimes managers also approximate step costs the same way: They simply draw a straight mixed cost line through the steps. If managers need more accurate predictions, they can simply break these types of costs into smaller relevant ranges and make their predictions based on the particular relevant range. For example, the day-care centre may want to predict total caregiver salaries if it enrolls 26 children. The manager knows this enrollment falls into the relevant range of 25 to 32 children, where he or she needs to employ four caregivers. The manager can then predict total caregiver salaries to be $112,000 (four caregivers × $28,000 salary per caregiver).

It is important to note that the assumption of linearity in cost behaviour is adopted because it has many advantages, including simplicity, ease of calculation, and ease of communication. However, as noted above, costs are not always linear, and this assumption can lead to errors when using a linear function to estimate costs. Non-linear behaviour can result in "accelerating" changes in costs, for example a moderate price reduction at 100 units (e.g., 5%) and a disproportionately large reduction at 500 units (e.g., 30%). In other words, as one moves toward the end of the relevant range the difference between the predicted cost using a linear cost function and the actual cost seen in a non-linear relationship will be more significant.

## Sustainability and Cost Behaviour

Many companies adopting sustainable business practices experience changes in the way their costs behave. For example, many banks, credit card companies, and utilities offer e-banking and e-billing services as an alternative to sending traditional paper statements and bills through the mail. E-banking and e-billing drive down a company's variable costs.

See Exercises E3-28A and E3-52B

The environmental consequences of this action are tremendous if you consider the entire production and delivery cycle of the bills and statements, all the way from the logging of the trees in the forest to the delivery of the bill at the customer's doorstep. Not only are fewer trees cut down, but also less energy is consumed in the transportation of the timber, the processing of the paper, the distribution of the paper,

*continued*

the delivery of the statements via Canada Post, and the final disposal of the paper at landfills or recycling centers. In addition, less wastewater is generated and fewer toxic air emissions are produced.

From the customer's perspective, adoption of e-billing and e-banking services provides one means for households to embrace a greener lifestyle. It is estimated that, on an annual basis, the average household that receives e-bills and pays bills online reduces paper consumption by 3 kg, saves 17 litres of gasoline, saves 238.5 litres of water, and cuts greenhouse gas emissions equal to the amount that would be emitted by driving 283 km.

From the company's perspective, this practice also reduces the total variable costs associated with processing, printing, and mailing statements (and cancelled cheques) to each customer. In place of these variable costs, the company must incur additional fixed costs to develop secure online banking and billing Websites. However, the variable cost savings generated must be substantial and cost effective.

We have just described the most typical cost behaviours. In the next part of the chapter, we will discuss methods that managers use to determine how their costs behave.

# DECISION GUIDELINES

## Cost Behaviour

Suppose you manage a local fitness club. To be an effective manager, you need to know how the club's costs behave. Here are some decisions you will need to make.

| Decision | Guidelines |
|---|---|
| It is time to begin planning for the next year for the fitness club, and you need to predict how costs behave. How can you tell if a total cost is variable, fixed, or mixed? | ■ Total variable costs rise in direct *proportion* to increases in volume.<br>■ Total fixed costs stay constant over a wide range of volumes.<br>■ Total mixed costs rise but not in direct proportion to increases in volume. |
| How can you tell if a per-unit cost is variable, fixed, or mixed? | ■ On a per-unit basis, variable costs stay constant.<br>■ On a per-unit basis, fixed costs decrease in proportion to increases in volume (that is to say they are inversely proportional).<br>■ On a per-unit basis, mixed costs decrease with increases in volume, but not in direct proportion. |
| How can you tell by looking at a graph if a cost is variable, fixed, or mixed? | ■ Variable cost lines slope upward and begin at the origin.<br>■ Fixed cost lines are flat (no slope) and intersect the y-axis at a level equal to total fixed costs (this is known as the y-intercept).<br>■ Mixed cost lines slope upward but do not begin at the origin. They intersect the y-axis at a level equal to their fixed cost component. |
| How can you mathematically express different cost behaviours? | ■ Cost equations mathematically express cost behaviour using the equation for a straight line:<br>$y = vx + f$<br>Wherein<br>$y$ = total cost<br>$v$ = variable cost per unit of activity (slope)<br>$x$ = volume of activity<br>$f$ = fixed cost (the vertical intercept) |

*continued*

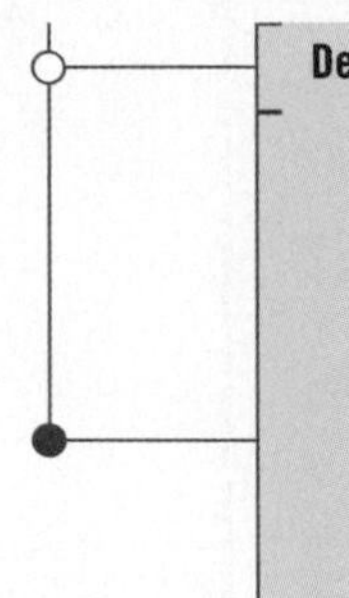

| Decision | Guidelines |
|---|---|
| | ■ For a variable cost, $f$ is zero, leaving the following: $y = vx$<br>■ For a fixed cost, $v$ is zero, leaving the following: $y = f$<br>■ Because a mixed cost has both a fixed cost component and a variable cost component, its cost equation is $y = vx + f$ |

# SUMMARY PROBLEM 1

The previous manager of Fitness-for-Life started the following schedule but left before completing it. The manager was not sure but thought the club's fixed operating costs were $10,000 per month and the variable operating costs were $1 per member per month. The club's existing facilities could serve up to 750 members per month.

### Requirements

1. Complete the following schedule for different levels of monthly membership assuming the previous manager's cost behaviour estimates are accurate.

| Monthly Operating Costs | 100 Members | 500 Members | 750 Members |
|---|---|---|---|
| Total variable costs | | | |
| Total fixed costs | | | |
| Total operating costs | | | |
| Variable cost per member | | | |
| Fixed cost per member | | | |
| Average cost per member | | | |

2. As the manager of the fitness club, why should you not use the average cost per member to predict total costs at different levels of membership?

## ■ SOLUTION

### Requirement 1

As volume increases, fixed costs stay constant in total but decrease on a per-unit basis. As volume increases, variable costs stay constant on a per-unit basis but increase in total in direct proportion to increases in volume.

| | 100 Members | 500 Members | 750 Members |
|---|---|---|---|
| Total variable costs | $ 100 | $ 500 | $ 750 |
| Total fixed costs | 10,000 | 10,000 | 10,000 |
| Total operating costs | $10,100 | $10,500 | $10,750 |
| Variable cost per member | $ 1.00 | $ 1.00 | $ 1.00 |
| Fixed cost per member | 100.00 | 20.00 | 13.33 |
| Average cost per member | $101.00 | $ 21.00 | $ 14.33 |

**Requirement 2**

The average cost per member should not be used to predict total costs at different volumes of membership because it changes as volume changes. The average cost per member decreases as volume increases due to the fixed component of the club's operating costs. Managers should base cost predictions on cost behaviour patterns, not on the average cost per member.

# Determining Cost Behaviour

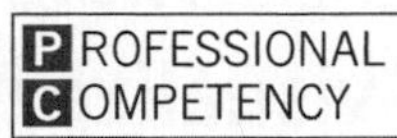


**3** Use account analysis and scatter plots to analyze cost behaviour.

In real life, managers need to figure out how their costs behave before they can make predictions and good business decisions. In this section, we discuss the most common ways of determining cost behaviour.

## Account Analysis

When performing **account analysis**, managers use their judgment to classify each general ledger account as a variable, fixed, or mixed cost. For example, by looking at invoices from the supplier, the hotel manager knows that every guest packet of toiletries costs $3. Because guests use or take these toiletries, the total toiletries cost rises in direct proportion to the number of guests. These facts allow the manager to classify the complimentary toiletries expense account as a variable cost.

Likewise, the hotel manager uses account analysis to determine how the depreciation expense accounts behave. Because the hotel uses straight-line depreciation on the parking ramp, building, and furnishings, the manager classifies the depreciation expense accounts as fixed costs. Thus, the manager can use this knowledge of cost behaviour and his or her judgment to classify many accounts as variable or fixed.

## Scatter Plots

Hotel managers also know that many of the hotel's costs, such as utilities, are mixed. But how does the manager figure out the portion of the mixed cost that is fixed and the portion that is variable? In other words, how does the manager know from looking at the monthly utility bills that the hotel's utilities cost about $2,000 per week plus $8 more for every guest? One way of figuring this out is by collecting and analyzing historical data about costs and volume.

For example, let's assume that a large city hotel has collected the information shown in Exhibit 3-12 about last year's guest volume and utility costs.

**EXHIBIT 3-12** Historical Information on Guest Volume and Utility Costs

| Month | Guest Volume ($x$) | Utility Costs ($y$) |
|---|---|---|
| January | 13,250 | $114,000 |
| February | 15,200 | 136,000 |
| March | 17,600 | 135,000 |
| April | 18,300 | 157,000 |
| May | 22,900 | 195,400 |
| June | 24,600 | 207,800 |
| July | 25,200 | 209,600 |
| August | 24,900 | 208,300 |
| September | 22,600 | 196,000 |
| October | 20,800 | 176,400 |
| November | 18,300 | 173,600 |
| December | 15,420 | 142,000 |

As you can see, the hotel's business is seasonal: More people visit in the summer. However, special events such as holiday shopping, business conferences, and a nearby casino attract people to the hotel throughout the year.

Once the data have been collected, the manager creates a scatter plot of the data. A scatter plot, which graphs the historical cost data on the y-axis and volume data on the x-axis, helps managers visualize the relationship between the cost and the volume of activity (number of guests, in our example). If a fairly strong relationship exists between the cost and volume, the data points fall in a linear pattern, meaning they resemble something close to a straight line. However, if little or no relationship exists between the cost and volume, the data points appear almost random. Scatter plots can be prepared by hand, but they are simpler to create using spreadsheet software. (See the Technology Makes It Simple feature for instructions on creating a scatter plot using Microsoft Excel.)

**Why is this important?**
Scatter plots **help managers** easily **visualize** the **relationship** between cost and volume.

Exhibit 3-13 shows a scatter plot of the data in Exhibit 3-12. Notice how the data points fall in a pattern that resembles something *close* to a straight line. This shows us that there is a strong relationship between the number of guests and the hotel's utility costs. In other words, the number of guests could be considered a driver of the hotel's utilities costs (a cost driver is an activity that causes costs to be incurred and will be discussed in Chapter 7). On the other hand, if the relationship between the number of guests and the utility costs was weaker, the data points would not fall in such a tight pattern. They would be more loosely scattered but still in a semilinear pattern. If *no* relationship existed between the number of guests and the utility costs, the data points would appear almost random.

**EXHIBIT 3-13** Scatter Plot of Monthly Data

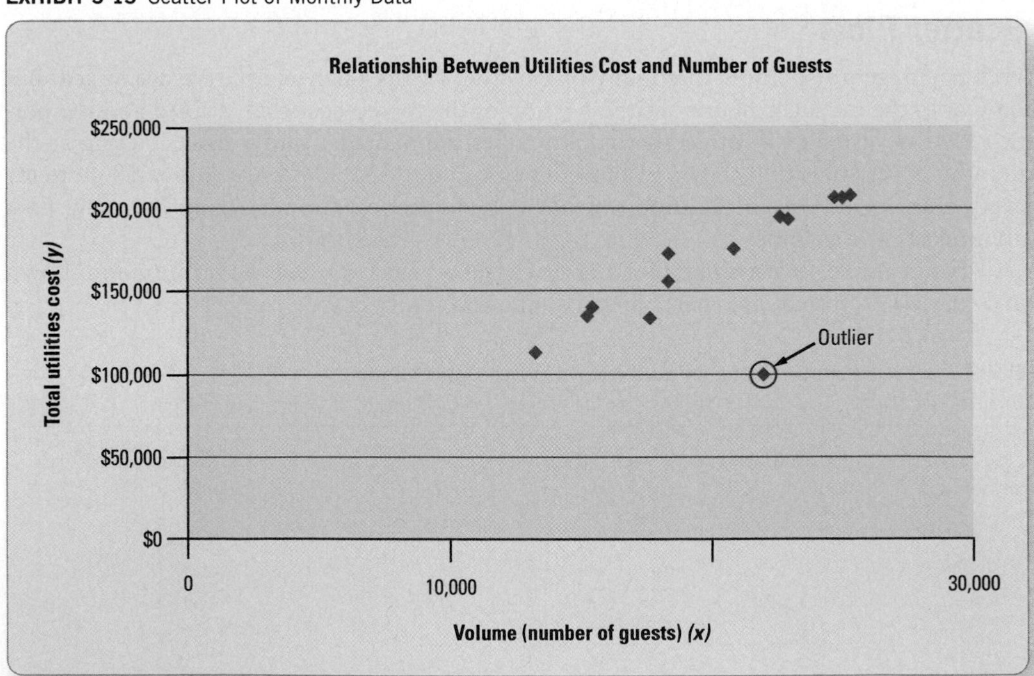


Why is this important? If the data points suggest a fairly weak relationship between the cost and the volume of the chosen activity, any cost equation based on that data will not be very useful for predicting future costs. If this is the case, the manager should consider using a different activity for modelling cost behaviour. For example, many hotels use *occupancy rate* (the percentage of rooms rented) rather than number of guests as a basis for explaining and predicting variable and mixed costs.

Scatter plots are also very useful because they allow managers to identify **outliers**, or abnormal data points. Outliers are data points that do not fall in the same general pattern as the other data points. If a manager sees a potential outlier in the data, he or she should first determine whether the data are correct. Perhaps a clerical error was made when gathering or inputting the data. However, if the data are correct, the manager may need to consider whether to delete that data from any further analysis.

Once the scatter plot has been prepared and examined for outliers, the next step is to determine the cost behaviour that best describes the historical data points pictured in the scatter plot. Take a moment and pencil in the cost-behaviour line that you think best represents the data points in Exhibit 3-13. Where does your line intersect the y-axis? At the origin or above it? In other words, does the utilities cost appear to be a purely variable cost or a mixed cost? If it is a mixed cost, what portion of it is fixed?

Instead of guessing, managers can use one of the following methods to estimate the cost equation that describes the data in the scatter plot:

- High-low method
- Regression analysis

The biggest difference between these methods is that the **high-low method** uses only *two* of the historical data points for this estimate, whereas **regression analysis** uses *all* of the historical data points. Therefore, regression analysis is theoretically the better of the two methods.

We will describe both of these methods in the next sections.

**TECHNOLOGY** *makes it simple* **Excel 2007**

### Scatter Plots

1. In an Excel 2007 spreadsheet, type in your data as pictured in Exhibit 3-12. Put the volume data in one column and the associated cost data in the next column.
2. Highlight all of the volume and cost data with your cursor.
3. Click on the Insert tab on the menu bar and then choose Scatter as the chart type. Next, click the plain scatter plot (without any lines). You will see the scatter plot on your screen. Make sure the volume data are on the x-axis and the cost data are on the y-axis.
4. To add labels for the scatter plot and titles for each axis, choose Layout 1 from the Chart Layout menu tab. Customize the titles and labels to reflect your data set.
5. If you want to change the way your graph looks, right-click on the graph to check out customizing options. For example, if your data consist of large numbers, the graph may not automatically start at the origin. If you want to see the origin on the graph, right-click on either axis (where the number values are) and choose Format Axis. Then, fix the minimum value at zero.

## High-Low Method

**4** Use the high-low method to analyze cost behaviour.

The high-low method is an easy way to estimate the variable and fixed cost components of a mixed cost. The high-low method basically fits a mixed cost line through the highest and lowest volume data points, as shown in Exhibit 3-14, hence the name *high-low*. The high-low method produces the cost equation describing this mixed cost line.

To use the high-low method, we must first identify the months with the highest and lowest volume of activity. From Exhibit 3-12 we see that the hotel served the *most* guests in July and the *fewest* guests in January. Therefore, we use the data from only these two months in our analysis. We ignore data from all other months. Even if a month other than July had the highest utility cost, we still use July. Why? Because we choose the "high" data point based on the month with the highest volume of activity (number of guests)—not the highest cost. We choose the "low" data point in a similar fashion.

**EXHIBIT 3-14** Mixed Cost Line Using the High-Low Method

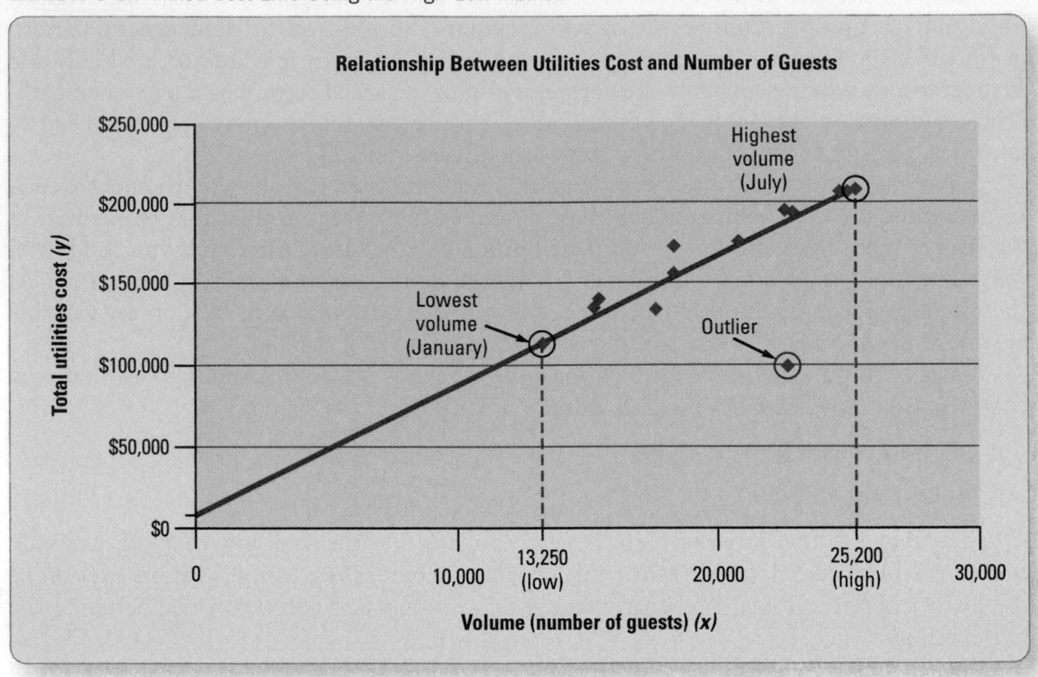


**STEP 1: The first step is to find *the slope of the mixed cost line* that connects the January and July data points. The slope is the variable cost per unit of activity. We can determine the slope of a line as "rise over run." The rise is simply the difference in cost between the high and low data points (July and January in our case), while the run is the difference in volume between the high and low data points:**

$$\text{Slope} = \text{Variable cost per unit of activity } (v) = \frac{\text{Rise}}{\text{Run}} = \frac{\text{Change in cost}}{\text{Change in volume}} = \frac{y\text{ (high)} - y\text{ (low)}}{x\text{ (high)} - x\text{ (low)}}$$

Using the data from July (as our high) and January (as our low), we calculate the slope as follows:

$$\frac{(\$209{,}600 - \$114{,}000)}{(25{,}200\text{ guests} - 13{,}250\text{ guests})} = \$8\text{ per guest}$$

The slope of the mixed cost line, or the variable cost per unit of activity, is $8 per guest.

**STEP 2: The second step is to find the y-intercept—the place where the line connecting the January and July data points intersects the y-axis. This is the fixed cost component of the mixed cost. We insert the slope found in Step 1 ($8 per guest) and the volume and cost data from *either* the high or low month into a mixed cost equation:**

$$\begin{aligned}\text{Total mixed costs} &= \text{Variable cost component} + \text{Fixed cost component}\\ y &= vx + f\end{aligned}$$

For example, we can insert July's cost and volume data as follows:

$$\$209{,}600 = (\$8\text{ per guest} \times 25{,}200\text{ guests}) + f$$

And then solve for *f*:

$$f = \$8{,}000$$

Or we can use January's data to reach the same conclusion:

$$\begin{array}{ccccc} y & = & vx & & + f \\ \$114{,}000 & = & (\$8 \text{ per guest} \times 13{,}250 \text{ guests}) & & + f \end{array}$$

And then solve for *f*:

$$f = \$8{,}000$$

Thus, the fixed cost component is $8,000 per month regardless of whether we use July's or January's data.

**STEP 3: Using the variable cost per unit of activity found in Step 1 ($8 per guest) and the fixed cost component found in Step 2 ($8,000), write the equation representing the costs' behaviour. This is the equation for the line connecting the January and July data points on our graph.**

$$y = \$8x + \$8{,}000$$

wherein

$$\begin{aligned} y &= \text{total } \textit{monthly} \text{ utilities cost} \\ x &= \text{number of guests} \end{aligned}$$

Recall that this equation was based on *monthly* utility bills and *monthly* guest volume. In our discussion of the hotel's mixed costs in the first half of the chapter, we said that the mixed utilities cost was $8 per guest plus $2,000 per *week*. The manager had used the high-low method, but because there are about four weeks in a month, the hotel manager approximated the fixed costs to be about $2,000 per week ($8,000 per month).

One major drawback of the high-low method is that it uses only two data points, in this example, January and July. Because we ignored every other month, the line might not be representative of those months. In this case, the high-low line is representative of the other data points, but in other situations, it may not be. Despite this drawback, the high-low method is quick and easy to use.

## Regression Analysis

5 Use regression analysis to analyze cost behaviour.

Regression analysis is a statistical procedure for determining the line and cost equation that best fits the data by using all of the data points, not just the high-volume and low-volume data points. In fact, some refer to regression analysis as "the line of best fit." Therefore, it is usually more accurate than the high-low method. A statistic (called the R-square) generated by regression analysis also tells us *how well* the line fits the data points. Regression analysis is tedious to complete by hand but simple to do using technology. (See the Technology Makes It Simple feature on page 131 for instructions on how to use Microsoft Excel for regression analysis.) Many graphing calculators also perform regression analysis.

Regression analysis using Microsoft Excel gives us the output shown in Exhibit 3-15.

It looks complicated, but for our purposes, we need to consider only three highlighted pieces of information from the output:

1. Intercept coefficient (this refers to the y-intercept) = 14,538.05
2. X Variable 1 coefficient (this refers to the slope) = 7.85 (rounded)
3. The R-square value (the "goodness-of-fit" statistic) = 0.94726

**EXHIBIT 3-15** Output of Microsoft Excel Regression Analysis

| Regression Statistics | |
|---|---|
| Multiple R | 0.973273 |
| R Square | 0.94726 |
| Adjusted R Square | 0.941986 |
| Standard Error | 8053.744 |
| Observations | 12 |

ANOVA

| | *df* | *SS* | *MS* | *F* | *Significance F* |
|---|---|---|---|---|---|
| Regression | 1 | 11650074512 | 1.17E + 10 | 179.6110363 | 1.02696E-07 |
| Residual | 10 | 648627988.2 | 64862799 | | |
| Total | 11 | 12298702500 | | | |

| | *Coefficients* | *Standard Error* | *t Stat* | *P-value* | *Lower 95%* | *Upper 95%* | *Lower 95.0%* | *Upper 95.0%* |
|---|---|---|---|---|---|---|---|---|
| Intercept | 14538.05 | 11898.3624 | 1.221853 | 0.249783701 | −11973.15763 | 41049.25 | −11973.16 | 41049.25 |
| X Variable 1 | 7.849766 | 0.585720166 | 13.4019 | 1.02696E-07 | 6.5446997 | 9.154831 | 6.5447 | 9.154831 |

### Why is this important?

Regression analysis is **fast** and **easy** to perform using Excel. **Regression analysis** usually gives managers the most **representative** cost equations, allowing them to make the most **accurate** cost projections.

Let's look at each piece of information, starting with the highlighted information at the bottom of the output.

1. The *intercept coefficient* is the y-intercept of the mixed cost line. It is the fixed cost component of the mixed cost. Regression analysis tells us that the fixed component of the monthly utility bill is $14,538 (rounded). Why is this different from the $8,000 fixed component we found using the high-low method? It is because regression analysis considers *every* data point, not just the high- and low-volume data points, when forming the best fitting line.
2. The *X variable 1 coefficient* is the line's slope, or our variable cost per guest. Regression analysis tells us that the hotel spends an extra $7.85 on utilities for every guest it serves. This is slightly lower than the $8 per guest amount we found using the high-low method.

Using the regression output, we can write the utilities *monthly* cost equation as follows:

$$y = \$7.85x + \$14{,}538$$

wherein

$y$ = total *monthly* utilities cost
$x$ = number of guests

3. Now, let's look at the R-square statistic highlighted near the top of Exhibit 3-15. The R-square statistic is often referred to as a goodness-of-fit statistic because it

tells us how well the regression line fits the data points. The R-square can range in value from zero to one, as shown in Exhibit 3-16. If no relationship existed between the number of guests and the hotel's utility costs, the data points would be scattered randomly (rather than being in a linear pattern) and the R-square would be close to zero. If a perfect relationship existed, a perfectly straight line would run through every data point and the R-square would be 1.00. In our case, the R-square of 0.947 means that the regression line fits the data quite well (it is very close to 1.00). In other words, the data points almost fall in a straight line (as you saw in Exhibit 3-13).

**EXHIBIT 3-16** Range of R-square Values

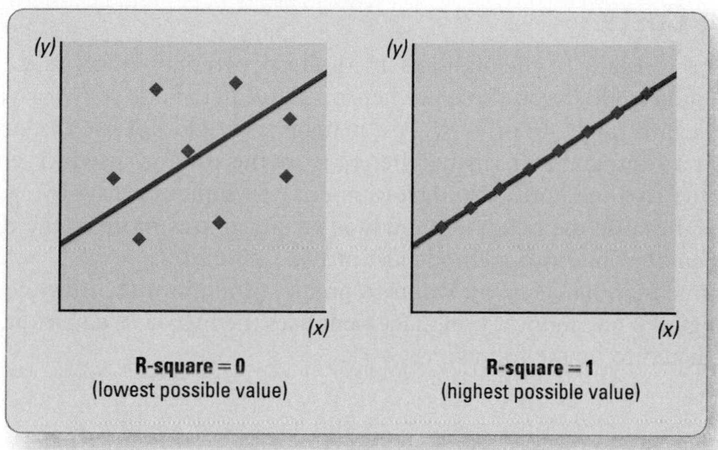


The R-square provides managers with very helpful information. The higher the R-square, the stronger the relationship between cost and volume. The stronger the relationship, the more confidence the manager would have in using the cost equation to predict costs at different volumes within the same relevant range. As a rule of thumb, an R-square over 0.80 generally indicates that the cost equation is very reliable for predicting costs at other volumes within the relevant range. An R-square between 0.50 and 0.80 means that the manager should use the cost equation with caution. However, if the R-square is fairly low (for example, less than 0.50), the manager should try using a different activity base (for example, room occupancy rate) for cost analysis because the current measure of volume is only weakly related to the costs.

**TECHNOLOGY** *makes it simple* **Excel 2007**

## Regression Analysis

1. Create a scatter plot as outlined in the Technology Makes It Simple feature on page 127.
2. Click on the Data tab on the menu bar.
3. Next, click on Data Analysis. If you do not see it on your menu bar, follow the directions for add-ins given next before continuing.
4. From the list of data analysis tools, select Regression, then OK.
5. Follow the two instructions on the screen:
   i. Highlight (or type in) the y-axis data range (this is your cost data).
   ii. Highlight (or type in) the x-axis data range (this is your volume data).
   iii. Click OK.
6. That is all. Excel gives you the output shown in Exhibit 3-15.

DIRECTIONS FOR ADD-INs: It is easy and free to add the Data Analysis Toolpak if it is not already on your menu bar. You will need to add it only once, and then it will always be on your menu bar. Simply follow these instructions:

1. While in Excel, click the Microsoft Office button (the colourful button in the upper-left corner) and then click on the Excel Options box shown at the bottom.
2. Click Add-Ins.
3. In the Manage box at the bottom of the screen, select Excel Add-ins and click GO.
4. In the Add-Ins available box, select the Analysis Toolpak check box and then click OK.
5. If asked, click Yes to install.

## Predicting Costs

Managers use the results of the high-low method or regression analysis to plan for costs at different volumes. However, these predictions should be made only for volumes falling in the same relevant range. In other words, managers should not use the cost equation to predict costs at a volume that is vastly different from the volumes used to generate the cost equation. Of the two methods, the regression analysis equation usually gives better predictions. Why? Because the regression analysis equation uses more of the historical data. However, remember that both methods just provide *estimates*.

Let's assume that management wants to predict total monthly utility costs if the hotel serves 23,000 guests one month. If management uses the high-low equation, the total utility cost is predicted to be the following:

$$y = (8 \text{ per guest} \times 23{,}000 \text{ guests}) + \$8{,}000$$
$$y = \$192{,}000$$

But if management uses the regression equation, the total utility cost is predicted to be the following:

$$y = (\$7.85 \text{ per guest} \times 23{,}000 \text{ guests}) + \$14{,}538$$
$$y = \$195{,}088$$

The predictions are similar in this situation. However, that will not always be the case, especially if the high- and low-volume data points are not representative of the other data points.

## Data Concerns

Cost equations are only as good as the data on which they are based. For example, if the hotel's utility bills are seasonal, management may want to develop separate cost equations for each season. It might develop a winter utility bill cost equation using historical data from only the winter months and do likewise for each other season. Inflation can also affect predictions. If inflation is running rampant, managers should adjust projected costs by the inflation rate. Even if the economy has generally low inflation, certain industries may be experiencing large price changes. For example, a drought in the Prairies could result in above-average increases in food costs.

Another cause for concern is outliers, or abnormal data points. Outliers can distort the results of the high-low method and regression analysis. Recall that the high-low method uses only two data points—the data points associated with the highest and lowest volumes of activity. If either of these points is an outlier, the resulting line and cost equation will be skewed. Because regression analysis uses all data points, any outlier in the data will affect the resulting line and cost equation, but to a lesser extent. To find outliers, management should first plot the data as we did in Exhibit 3-13. The graph suggests there is a likely outlier, or abnormal data point (as labelled in the graphic), though the majority of data points fall in the same general pattern. With a data point that is atypical with respect to the others, we would investigate it to see if it was accurate. Based on this assessment, it may be excluded from further analysis.

# The Contribution Margin Income Statement

6 Prepare contribution margin income statements for service firms and merchandising firms.

Almost all businesses, including Banff Rocky Mountain Resort, have some fixed costs, some variable costs, and some mixed costs. Companies use account analysis, the high-low method, or regression analysis (or a combination of these methods) to determine how their costs behave. They may analyze cost behaviour on an account-by-account basis, as we did in the previous examples. (They prepare separate cost equations for toiletry costs, complimentary breakfast and refreshment costs, utilities costs, and so forth.) Or if they do not need so much detail, companies may develop one mixed cost equation for all operating costs lumped together. Once they have cost behaviour information, how do companies communicate it to their managers so that the managers can use it for planning and decision making? Let's look at some potential options.

## Traditional Income Statements Are Organized by Cost Function

Traditional income statements are organized by *function* (such as operating expenses, administrative expenses, and selling expenses), not by cost behaviour. Costs related to the production or purchases function of the value chain appear as cost of goods sold, *above* the gross profit line, when the manufactured products or merchandise are sold. All other costs (related to all other value-chain functions—R&D, for example) appear as operating expenses, *below* the gross profit line.

Exhibit 3-17 illustrates this functional separation of costs for a retailer specializing in fitness equipment. Notice how the traditional format does not provide managers with much information on cost behaviour. The cost of goods sold is a variable cost for a retailer, but contains a mixture of variable and fixed production costs for manufacturers. Recall from Chapter 2 that manufacturers usually classify direct materials and direct labour as variable costs, but treat manufacturing overhead as a mixed cost. In addition, traditional income statements do not distinguish fixed operating costs from variable operating costs. While external users, such as investors and creditors, find traditional income statements useful, these statements are not very useful for internal managers, who need cost behaviour information for planning and decision making.

**EXHIBIT 3-17** Traditional Income Statement of a Retailer

| AAA FITNESS EQUIPMENT<br>**Income Statement**<br>Month Ended July 31 | |
|---|---|
| Sales revenue | $ 52,500 |
| Less: Cost of goods sold | (27,300) |
| Gross profit | 25,200 |
| Less: Operating expenses | (14,600) |
| Operating income | $ 10,600 |

## Contribution Margin Income Statements Are Organized by Cost Behaviour

<u>Contribution margin income statements</u> organize costs by *behaviour* rather than by *function*. Therefore, managers find contribution margin income statements more helpful than traditional income statements for planning and decision making. Contribution margin income statements can be used only internally. Financial reporting standards do not allow companies to use the contribution margin format for external reporting purposes.

**Why is this important?**
The **contribution margin** income statement allows **managers** to **quickly** see which costs will **change** with **volume** and which will remain **fixed**.

The contribution margin income statement (shown in Exhibit 3-18) presents all variable costs—whether relating to the merchandise sold or selling and administrative activities—above the contribution margin line, and all fixed costs—whether relating to the merchandise sold or selling and administrative activities—below the contribution margin line.

The **contribution margin** is equal to sales revenue minus variable expenses. Mixed costs present a small challenge in that a mixed cost needs to be separated into its variable and fixed portions. Once separated, the variable portion is included with the other variable costs above the contribution margin line, and the fixed portion is included below the contribution margin line.

**EXHIBIT 3-18** Contribution Margin Income Statement

| AAA FITNESS EQUIPMENT<br>**Contribution Margin Income Statement**<br>Month Ended July 31 | |
|---|---|
| Sales revenue | $ 52,500 |
| Less: Variable expenses | (30,900) |
| Contribution margin | 21,600 |
| Less: Fixed expenses | (11,000) |
| Operating income | $ 10,600 |

Managers can use contribution margin income statements to predict how changes in volume will affect operating income. Changes in volume will affect total sales revenue and total variable costs (and, therefore, the contribution margin). However, changes in volume will not affect fixed costs within the same relevant range. Therefore, the contribution margin income statement distinguishes the financial figures that *will* change from those that *will not* change in response to fluctuations in volume. Traditional income statements do not make this distinction.

Appendix 3A discusses variable costing, an optional product costing system that manufacturers can use for internal purposes. Variable costing results in contribution margin income statements for manufacturers.

## TRY IT!

Sony makes DVD players and uses both absorption and variable costing. Assume Sony incurred the following manufacturing costs in producing 10,000 DVD players last month:

| Manufacturing Costs | Total Cost | Per Unit Cost |
|---|---|---|
| Direct material | $ 70,000 | $ 7.00 |
| Direct labour | 40,000 | 4.00 |
| Variable MOH | 90,000 | 9.00 |
| Fixed MOH | 120,000 | 12.00 |
| Total | $320,000 | $32.00 |

1. What is the inventoriable product cost per unit, using absorption costing?
2. How will fixed MOH be expensed if absorption costing is used?
3. What is the inventoriable cost per unit, using variable costing?
4. How will fixed MOH be expensed if variable costing is used?

Please see page 181 for solutions.

# DECISION GUIDELINES

## Cost Behaviour

As the manager of a local fitness club, Fitness-for-Life, you want to plan for operating costs at various levels of membership. Before you can make forecasts, you need to make some of the following decisions.

| Decision | Guidelines |
|---|---|
| How can I sort out the fixed and the variable components of mixed costs? | ■ The high-low method is fast and easy but uses only two data points to form the cost equation and, therefore, may not be very indicative of the costs' true behaviour.<br>■ Regression analysis uses every data point provided to determine the cost equation that best fits the data. |
| I have used the high-low method to formulate a cost equation. Can I tell how well the cost equation fits the data? | The only way to determine how well the high-low cost equation fits the data is by (1) plotting the data, (2) drawing a line through the data points associated with the highest and lowest volume, and (3) "visually inspecting" the resulting graph to see if the line is representative of the other plotted data points. |
| I have used regression analysis to formulate a cost equation. Can I tell how well the cost equation fits the data? | The R-square is a goodness-of-fit statistic that tells how well the regression analysis cost equation fits the data. The R-square ranges from zero to 1, with 1 being a perfect fit. When the R-square is high, the cost equation should render fairly accurate predictions. |
| Do I need to be concerned about anything before using the high-low method or regression analysis? | Cost equations are only as good as the data on which they are based. Managers should plot the historical data to see if a relationship between cost and volume exists. In addition, scatter plots help managers identify outliers. Managers should remove outliers before further analysis. Managers should also adjust cost equations for seasonal data, inflation, and price changes. |
| Can I present financial statements in a manner that will help with planning and decision making? | Contribution margin income statements organize costs by *behaviour* (fixed versus variable) rather than by *function* (product versus period). |

# SUMMARY PROBLEM 2

As the new manager of a local fitness club, Fitness-for-Life, you have been studying the club's financial data. You would like to determine how the club's costs behave in order to make accurate predictions for next year. Here is information from the past six months:

| Month | Club Membership (number of members) | Total Operating Costs | Average Operating Costs per Member |
|---|---|---|---|
| July | 450 | $ 8,900 | $19.78 |
| August | 480 | $ 9,800 | $20.42 |
| September | 500 | $10,100 | $20.20 |
| October | 550 | $10,150 | $18.45 |
| November | 560 | $10,500 | $18.75 |
| December | 525 | $10,200 | $19.43 |

### Requirements

1. By looking at the Total Operating Costs and the Average Operating Costs per Member, can you tell whether the club's operating costs are variable, fixed, or mixed? Explain your answer.
2. Use the high-low method to determine the club's monthly operating cost equation.

3. Using your answer from Requirement 2, predict total monthly operating costs if the club has 600 members.
4. Can you predict total monthly operating costs if the club has 3,000 members? Explain your answer.
5. Prepare the club's traditional income statement and its contribution margin income statement for the month of July. Assume that your cost equation from Requirement 2 accurately describes the club's cost behaviour. The club charges members $30 per month for unlimited access to its facilities.
6. *Optional*: Perform regression analysis using Microsoft Excel. What is the monthly operating cost equation? What is the R-square? Why is the cost equation different from that in Requirement 2?

## SOLUTION

### Requirement 1

By looking at Total Operating Costs, we can see that the club's operating costs are not purely fixed; otherwise, total costs would remain constant. Operating costs appear to be either variable or mixed because they increase in total as the number of members increases. By looking at the Average Operating Costs per Member, we can see that the operating costs are not purely variable; otherwise, the per-member cost would remain constant. Therefore, the club's operating costs are mixed.

### Requirement 2

Use the high-low method to determine the club's operating cost equation:

**STEP 1: The highest volume month is November and the lowest volume month is July. Therefore, we use only these two months to determine the cost equation. The first step is to find the variable cost per unit of activity, which is the slope of the line connecting the November and July data points:**

$$\frac{\text{Rise}}{\text{Run}} = \frac{\text{Change in } y}{\text{Change in } x} = \frac{y\text{ (high)} - y\text{ (low)}}{x\text{ (high)} - x\text{ (low)}} = \frac{(\$10{,}500 - \$8{,}900)}{(560 - 450\text{ members})} = \$14.55\text{ per member (rounded)}$$

**STEP 2: The second step is to find the fixed cost component (y-intercept) by plugging in the slope and either July or November data to a mixed cost equation:**

$$y = vx + f$$

Using November data:

$$\$10{,}500 = (\$14.55/\text{member} \times 560\text{ guests}) + f$$

Solving for *f*:

$$f = \$2{,}352$$

Or we can use July data to reach the same conclusion:

$$\$8{,}900 = (\$14.55/\text{member} \times 450\text{ guests}) + f$$

Solving for *f*:

$$f = \$2{,}352\text{ (rounded)}$$

**STEP 3: Write the monthly operating cost equation:**

$$y = \$14.55x + \$2{,}352$$

wherein

$$x = \text{number of members}$$
$$y = \text{total monthly operating cost}$$

**Requirement 3**

Predict total monthly operating costs when volume reaches 600 members:

$$y = (\$14.55 \times 600) + \$2{,}352$$
$$y = \$11{,}082$$

**Requirement 4**

Our current data and cost equation are based on 450 to 560 members. If membership reaches 3,000, operating costs could behave much differently. That volume falls outside our current relevant range.

**Requirement 5**

The club had 450 members in July and total operating costs of $8,900. Thus, its traditional income statement is as follows:

**FITNESS-FOR-LIFE**
**Income Statement**
Month Ended July 31

| | |
|---|---|
| Club membership revenue (450 × $30) | $13,500 |
| Less: Operating expenses (given) | (8,900) |
| Operating income | $ 4,600 |

To prepare the club's contribution margin income statement, we need to know how much of the total $8,900 operating costs is fixed and how much is variable. If the cost equation from Requirement 2 accurately reflects the club's cost behaviour, fixed costs will be $2,352 and variable costs will be $6,548 (= $14.55 × 450). The contribution margin income statement would look like this:

**FITNESS-FOR-LIFE**
**Contribution Margin Income Statement**
Month Ended July 31

| | |
|---|---|
| Club membership revenue (450 × $30) | $13,500 |
| Less: Variable expenses (450 × $14.55) | (6,548) |
| Contribution margin | 6,952 |
| Less: Fixed expenses | (2,352) |
| Operating income | $ 4,600 |

**Requirement 6**

Regression analysis using Microsoft Excel results in the following cost equation and R-square:

$$y = \$11.80x + \$3{,}912$$

wherein

$$x = \text{number of members}$$
$$y = \text{total monthly operating costs}$$

R-square = 0.8007

The regression analysis cost equation uses all of the data points, not just the data from November and July. Therefore, it better represents all of the data. The high R-square means that the regression line fits the data well and predictions based on this cost equation should be quite accurate.

# APPENDIX 3A

## How Does Variable Costing Differ from Absorption Costing?

PROFESSIONAL COMPETENCY

7 Use variable costing to prepare contribution margin income statements for manufacturers. (Appendix 3A)

Variable costing is an alternative technique to absorption costing that assigns only variable costs (direct materials, direct labour, and variable overhead) to products or services. Variable costing can be used to prepare the contribution margin income statement; however, both variable costing and the contributions margin income statement can be used for internal management decisions only. For external reporting, financial reporting standards *require* managers to use absorption costing, which results in traditional income statements. Under absorption costing, products "absorb" fixed manufacturing costs as well as variable manufacturing costs. In other words, both fixed and variable manufacturing costs are treated as inventoriable product costs. Supporters of absorption costing argue that companies cannot produce products without fixed manufacturing costs, so these costs are an important part of the inventoriable product costs. In all preceding chapters, we have treated fixed manufacturing costs as an inventoriable product cost; therefore, we have been using absorption costing.

Variable costing assigns only variable manufacturing costs to products. Variable costing treats fixed manufacturing costs as period costs (so they are expensed in the period in which they are incurred). Supporters of variable costing argue that fixed manufacturing costs (such as depreciation on the plant) provide the capacity to produce during a period. Because the company incurs these fixed expenses whether or not it produces any products, they are period costs, not product costs.

All other costs are treated the same way under both absorption and variable costing:

- Variable manufacturing costs are inventoriable products costs.
- All nonmanufacturing costs are period costs.

Exhibit 3-19 summarizes the differences between variable and absorption costing.

**EXHIBIT 3-19** Differences Between Absorption Costing and Variable Costing

| | Absorption Costing | Variable Costing |
|---|---|---|
| **Product Costs** (Capitalized as Inventory until expensed as Cost of Goods Sold) | Direct materials<br>Direct labour<br>Variable manufacturing overhead<br>Fixed manufacturing overhead | Direct materials<br>Direct labour<br>Variable manufacturing overhead |
| **Period Costs** (Expensed in periods incurred) | Variable nonmanufacturing costs<br>Fixed nonmanufacturing costs | Fixed manufacturing overhead<br>Variable nonmanufacturing costs<br>Fixed nonmanufacturing costs |
| **Focus** | External reporting—required by IFRS/ASPE | Internal reporting only |
| **Income Statement Format** | Conventional income statement | Contribution margin statement |

## Variable versus Absorption Costing

To see how absorption costing and variable costing differ, let us consider the following example. Sportade incurred the following costs for its powdered sports beverage mix in March:

| | |
|---|---|
| Direct materials cost per case | $ 6.00 |
| Direct labour cost per case | 3.00 |
| Variable manufacturing overhead cost per case | 2.00 |
| Sales commission per case | 2.50 |
| Total fixed manufacturing overhead expenses | 50,000 |
| Total fixed marketing and administrative expenses | $25,000 |

Sportade produced 10,000 cases of powdered mix as planned but sold only 8,000 cases at a price of $30 per case. There were no beginning inventories, so Sportade has 2,000 cases of powdered mix in ending finished goods inventory (10,000 cases produced − 8,000 cases sold).

What is Sportade's inventoriable product cost per case under absorption costing and under variable costing?

| | Absorption Costing | Variable Costing |
|---|---|---|
| Direct materials | $ 6.00 | $ 6.00 |
| Direct labour | 3.00 | 3.00 |
| Variable manufacturing overhead | 2.00 | 2.00 |
| **Fixed manufacturing overhead** | 5.00* | |
| **Total cost per case** | $16.00 | $11.00 |

$$^*\frac{50{,}000 \text{ fixed manufacturing overhead}}{10{,}000 \text{ cases}} = \$5 \text{ per case}$$

The only difference between absorption and variable costing is that fixed manufacturing overhead is a product cost under absorption costing but a period cost under variable costing. That is why the cost per case is $5 higher under absorption costing (total cost of $16) than under variable costing ($11).

Exhibit 3-20 shows that absorption costing results in a traditional income statement.

**EXHIBIT 3-20** Absorption Costing Income Statement

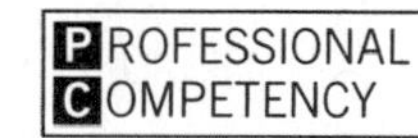


SPORTADE
**Income Statement (Absorption Costing)**
Month Ended March 31

| | | |
|---|---|---|
| Sales revenue (8,000 × $30) | | $ 240,000 |
| Deduct: Cost of goods sold: | | |
| Beginning finished goods inventory | $ 0 | |
| Cost of goods manufactured (10,000 × $16) | 160,000 | |
| Cost of goods available for sale | 160,000 | |
| Ending finished goods inventory (2,000 × $16) | (32,000) | |
| Cost of goods sold | | (128,000) |
| Gross profit | | 112,000 |
| Deduct: Operating expenses [(8,000 × $2.50) + $25,000] | | (45,000) |
| Operating income | | $ 67,000 |

Notice the following:

- The absorption costing income statement in Exhibit 3-20 groups costs by *function*: manufacturing costs versus nonmanufacturing costs. We subtract manufacturing costs of goods sold *before* gross profit, whereas we subtract all nonmanufacturing costs (operating expenses) *after* gross profit.

**Why is this important?**

Variable costing **helps** manufacturers **identify** the **variable cost** of making each unit of a product. This information is **critical** to making many business **decisions**, such as whether or not to outsource the product.

- Total cost of goods manufactured is the number of cases *produced* multiplied by the $16 total manufacturing cost per case. In contrast, total variable marketing expense (for sales commissions) equals the number of cases *sold* times the sales commission per case.
- Absorption costing holds back as an asset (ending inventory) $32,000 of the manufacturing cost that Sportade incurred this period (2,000 cases × $16 total manufacturing cost per case). This $32,000 is not expensed in the month when Sportade incurred these manufacturing costs. Instead, these manufacturing costs are held back as the asset *Inventory* until the related 2,000 cases are sold.
- The absorption costing income statement does not distinguish between variable and fixed costs. This limits the statement's usefulness for managerial decisions. If the CEO of Sportade wants to predict how a 10% increase in sales will affect operating income, the absorption costing income statement is of little help: It does not separate variable costs (which increase with sales) from fixed costs (which do not change).

The limitations of absorption costing-based income statements lead many manufacturing managers to prefer variable costing and contribution margin income statements *for internal reporting and decision making*. Exhibit 3-21 recasts the Sportade information using variable costing and a contribution margin income statement that groups costs by behaviour—variable versus fixed.

**EXHIBIT 3-21** Variable Costing Contribution Margin Income Statement

| SPORTADE<br>Contribution Margin Income Statement (Variable Costing)<br>Month Ended March 31 | | |
|---|---|---|
| Sales revenue (8,000 × $30) | | $ 240,000 |
| Deduct: Variable expenses: | | |
| Variable cost of goods sold: | | |
| Beginning finished goods inventory | $ 0 | |
| Variable cost of goods manufactured (10,000 × $11) | 110,000 | |
| Variable cost of goods available for sale | 110,000 | |
| Ending finished goods inventory (2,000 × $11) | (22,000) | |
| Variable cost of goods sold | 88,000 | |
| Sales commission expense (8,000 × $2.50) | 20,000 | (108,000) |
| Contribution margin | | 132,000 |
| Deduct: Fixed expenses: | | |
| Fixed manufacturing overhead | 50,000 | |
| Fixed marketing and administrative expenses | 25,000 | (75,000) |
| Operating income | | $ 57,000 |

Compare the general format of the absorption costing income statement in Exhibit 3-20 with the variable costing contribution margin income statement in Exhibit 3-21. The conventional absorption costing income statement subtracts cost of goods sold (including both variable and fixed manufacturing costs) from sales to obtain *gross profit*. In contrast, the contribution margin income statement subtracts all variable costs (both manufacturing and nonmanufacturing) to obtain the *contribution margin*. The following chart highlights the differences between gross profit and contribution margin:

| Conventional Income Statement | Contribution Margin Income Statement |
|---|---|
| Sales revenue | Sales revenue |
| Deduct Cost of Goods Sold: | Deduct Variable Expenses: |
| Variable manufacturing cost of goods sold | Variable manufacturing cost of goods sold |
| Fixed manufacturing cost of goods sold | Variable nonmanufacturing expenses |
| = Gross profit | = Contribution margin |

The two major differences are as follows:

1. Fixed manufacturing cost of goods sold is subtracted from sales to compute gross profit, but not to compute contribution margin.
2. Variable nonmanufacturing expenses are subtracted from sales to calculate contribution margin, but not to compute gross profit.

Now, let us look more closely at the variable costing contribution margin income statement in Exhibit 3-21. First, notice that the details of the (variable) cost of goods sold computation parallel those in the absorption costing income statement (Exhibit 3-20), except that we use the \$11 variable costing product cost per case rather than the \$16 absorption cost per case. Second, variable costing holds back as an asset (ending inventory) only \$22,000 (2,000 cases × \$11 variable manufacturing cost per case). Third, the variable costing contribution margin income statement subtracts all of the variable costs (both the \$88,000 manufacturing variable cost of goods sold *and* the \$20,000 variable sales commission expense) from sales to get contribution margin. Finally, we subtract fixed costs (both the \$50,000 fixed MOH and the \$25,000 fixed marketing and administrative costs) from contribution margin to get operating income. To summarize, the variable costing contribution margin income statement subtracts all variable costs *before* contribution margin and all fixed costs *after* contribution margin. Separating variable and fixed costs, the variable costing contribution margin income statement (Exhibit 3-21) allows managers to estimate how changes in sales, costs, or volume will affect profits.

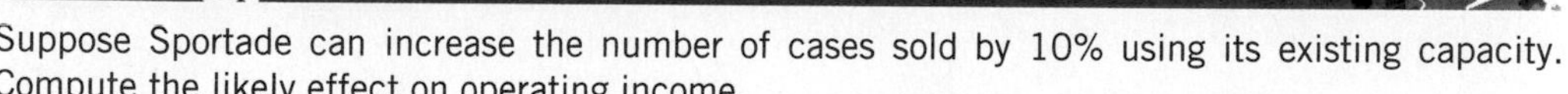


Suppose Sportade can increase the number of cases sold by 10% using its existing capacity. Compute the likely effect on operating income.

**Answer:** Because Sportade can accommodate the increased production using existing capacity, fixed costs will be unaffected. Thus, the entire increase in contribution margin flows through to operating income. A 10% increase in sales is an extra 800 cases (10% × 8,000).

| | |
|---|---|
| Increase in sales revenue (800 cases × \$30/case) | \$ 24,000 |
| Increase in variable costs (800 cases × \$13.50/case*) | (10,800) |
| Increase in contribution margin | \$ 13,200 |
| Increase in fixed costs | 0 |
| Increase in operating income | \$ 13,200 |

*Total variable costs per case = \$6.00 direct materials + \$3.00 direct labour + \$2.00 variable manufacturing overhead + \$2.50 sales commission. (All variable costs, including the sales commission as well as variable manufacturing costs, must be considered to estimate how the sales increase will affect contribution margin and operating profit.)

## Reconciling the Difference in Income

Exhibit 3-20 shows that Sportade's absorption costing operating income is \$67,000. Exhibit 3-21 shows that variable costing yields only \$57,000 of operating income. Why? To answer this question, we need to understand what happened to the \$160,000 (\$110,000 variable + \$50,000 fixed) total manufacturing costs under each costing method.

Manufacturing costs incurred in March are either

- expensed in March, or
- held back in inventory (an asset).

Exhibit 3-22 shows that of the \$160,000 total manufacturing costs incurred during March, absorption costing holds back \$32,000 (2,000 × \$16) as inventory. This \$32,000 assigned to inventory is not expensed until next month, when the units are sold. Thus, only \$128,000 (\$160,000 − \$32,000) of the manufacturing costs are expensed as cost of goods sold during March.

**EXHIBIT 3-22** Inventory versus Expenses Under Absorption and Variable Costing

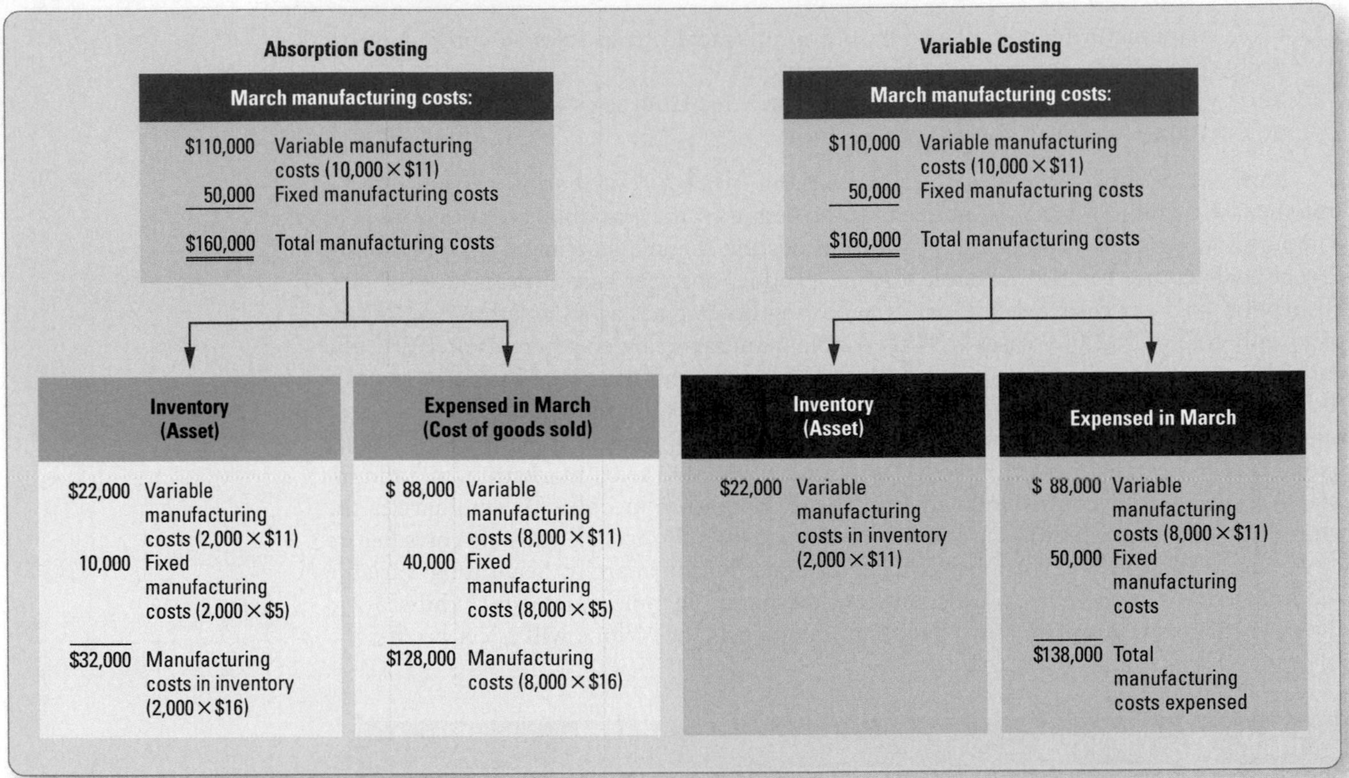


Variable costing holds back in ending inventory only \$22,000 (2,000 × \$11) of the total manufacturing costs. This is \$10,000 (\$32,000 − \$22,000) *less* than absorption costing holds back. The difference arises because absorption costing assigns the \$5 per case fixed MOH costs to the 2,000 cases in ending inventory. In contrast, variable costing does not—it expenses all of the fixed MOH in the current month.

Costs that are not held back in inventory are expensed in the current period, so variable costing expenses are \$138,000 (\$160,000 − \$22,000) of manufacturing costs in March. (This \$138,000 also equals the \$88,000 variable cost of goods sold plus the \$50,000 fixed MOH.) This is \$10,000 *more* than the \$128,000 absorption costing manufacturing expenses during March. *Variable costing has \$10,000 more expenses in March, so its income is \$10,000 lower than absorption costing income.*

## STOP & THINK

Suppose Sportade has no inventory at the end of the next month, April. Will absorption costing report higher or lower operating income than variable costing for the month of April?

**Answer:** Absorption costing will report lower income than variable costing during April. Ending inventory in March becomes the beginning inventory of April. Absorption costing assigns a higher value to beginning inventory in April. When that beginning inventory is sold, the higher beginning inventory costs increase cost of goods sold for April, which, in turn, reduces income.

## Operating Income with Decreasing Inventory

Let's see how absorption and variable costing income statements are created when we assume all the same costs as in March but in April Sportade manufactures 10,000 units and sells 12,000 units.

| SPORTADE<br>Income Statement (Absorption Costing)<br>Month Ended April 30 | | |
|---|---|---|
| Sales revenue (12,000 × $30) | | $360,000 |
| Deduct: Cost of goods sold: | | |
| Beginning finished goods inventory | $ 32,000* | |
| Cost of goods manufactured (10,000 × $16) | 160,000† | |
| Cost of goods available for sale | 192,000 | |
| Ending finished goods inventory | (0) | |
| Cost of goods sold | | 192,000 |
| Gross profit | | 168,000 |
| Deduct: Operating expenses [(12,000 × $2.50) + $25,000] | | (55,000) |
| Operating income | | $113,000 |

*Ending inventory from March 31 (Exhibit 3-20).
†Absorption costing cost per case = $6 + $3 + $2 + $5.

We can compare this to the Operating Income created when using variable costing.

| SPORTADE<br>Contribution Margin Income Statement (Variable Costing)<br>Month Ended April 30 | | |
|---|---|---|
| Sales revenue (12,000 × $30) | | $360,000 |
| Deduct: Variable expenses: | | |
| Variable cost of goods sold: | | |
| Beginning finished goods inventory | $ 22,000* | |
| Variable cost of goods manufactured (10,000 × $11) | 110,000† | |
| Variable cost of goods available for sale | 132,000 | |
| Ending finished goods inventory | (0) | |
| Variable cost of goods sold | 132,000 | |
| Sales commission expense (12,000 × $2.50) | 30,000 | (162,000) |
| Contribution margin | | 198,000 |
| Deduct: Fixed expenses: | | |
| Fixed manufacturing overhead | 50,000 | |
| Fixed marketing and administrative expenses | 25,000 | (75,000) |
| Operating income | | $123,000 |

*Ending inventory from March 31 (Exhibit 3-21).
†Variable costing cost per case = $6 + $3 + $2.

When you compare the two income statements for April, the operating income from the variable costing statement is higher by $10,000. Why? In the absorption costing statement, the beginning finished goods inventory value is $10,000 higher due to the fixed manufacturing costs that are included in the inventory at the end of March. Since all of the excess inventory is being sold in April, all of the fixed manufacturing costs that had been set aside in the inventory account are now released and therefore expensed on the absorption costing income statement. This means that there are higher costs associated with the absorption costing income statement of $10,000, explaining why the income from the absorption costing statement is $10,000 lower than the income from the variable costing income statement.

## Comparing Operating Income: Variable versus Absorption Costing

For manufacturers, operating income will not always be the same between the two costing systems. In fact, it will be the same only if the manufacturer sells *exactly* what it produced during the period. This scenario is typical of a lean producer. However, traditional manufacturers in a growing economy often produce extra safety stock, increasing their inventory levels to ensure against unexpected demand. On the other hand, in periods of economic recession (such as in the years 2008–2009) companies often *reduce* their inventory levels to decrease costs, build cash reserves, and adjust for lower sales demand.

We will discuss how inventory levels impact operating income, for both absorption and variable costing, under three possible scenarios (Exhibits 3-23, 3-24, and 3-25):

1. Inventory levels remain constant
2. Inventory levels increase
3. Inventory levels decrease

### Scenario 1: Inventory levels remain constant

When inventory levels remain constant, both absorption costing and variable costing result in the same operating income. This scenario usually occurs at lean manufacturers since they produce only enough inventory to fill existing customer orders.

**EXHIBIT 3-23** Inventory Levels Remain Constant

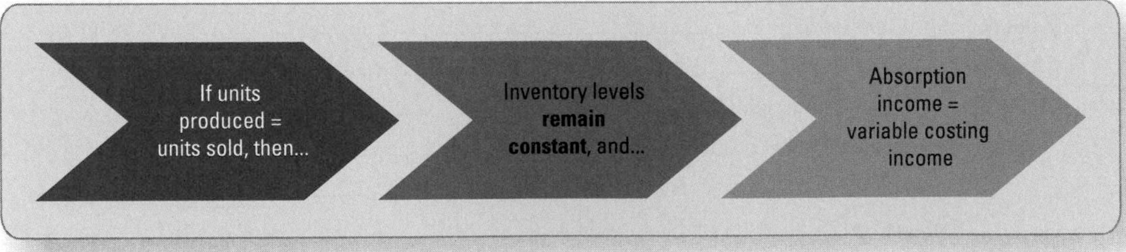


In this situation, *all* fixed MOH incurred during the period is expensed under both costing systems. Under variable costing, it is expensed as a period cost. Under absorption costing, it is first absorbed into the product's cost and then expensed as cost of goods sold when the product is sold.

**EXHIBIT 3-24** Inventory Levels Increase

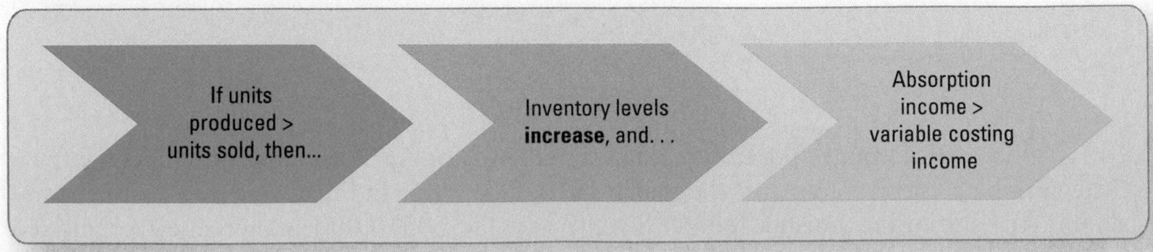

### Scenario 2: Inventory levels increase

When inventory levels increase, operating income will be greater under absorption costing than it is under variable costing. This scenario typically occurs at traditional manufacturers during times of economic growth.

In this situation, all fixed MOH incurred during the period is expensed as a period cost under variable costing. However, under absorption costing, some of the fixed MOH remains "trapped" on the balance sheet as part of the cost of inventory. This was seen in our first set of statements when 10,000 units were produced and 8,000 units were sold. As a result, *more* cost is expensed under variable costing than under absorption costing, leading to a higher operating income under absorption costing.

### Scenario 3: Inventory levels decrease

When inventory levels decrease, operating income will be greater under variable costing than it is under absorption costing. This scenario typically occurs at traditional manufacturers during times of economic recession. It also occurs when traditional manufacturers are in the process of switching to lean operations, which carry little or no inventory.

**EXHIBIT 3-25** Inventory Levels Decrease

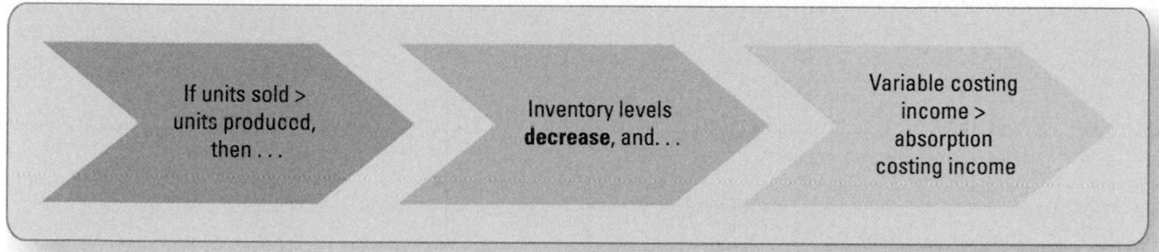


In this situation, all fixed MOH incurred during the period is expensed under variable costing. However, under absorption costing, all of the fixed MOH of the period is expensed as part of cost of goods sold *plus* some of the fixed MOH from the previous period. We saw this happen in the example where Sportade manufactured 10,000 units but sold 12,000 units. As a result, *more* cost is expensed under absorption costing than under variable costing, leading to a lower net income under absorption costing.

## Absorption Costing and Manager's Incentives

The general rule is this: When inventories increase (more units are produced than sold), absorption costing income is higher than variable costing income. When inventories decline (when fewer units are produced than sold), absorption costing income is lower than variable costing income. Suppose the Sportade manager receives a bonus based on absorption costing income. Will the manager want to increase or decrease production?

The manager knows that absorption costing assigns each case of Sportade $5 of fixed manufacturing overhead.

- For every case produced but not sold, absorption costing "hides" $5 of fixed overhead in ending inventory (an asset).
- The more cases that are added to inventory, the more fixed overhead is "hidden" in ending inventory at the end of the month.
- The more fixed overhead in ending inventory, the smaller the cost of goods sold and the higher the operating income.

To maximize the bonus under absorption costing, the manager may try to increase production to build up inventory. This incentive conflicts with the JIT philosophy, which emphasizes minimal inventory levels.

# APPENDIX 3B

## Segmented Statements

PROFESSIONAL COMPETENCY

8 Use segment reporting to utilize the contribution margin income statement format in an organization with two or more divisions. (Appendix 3B)

### Preparing Segmented Statements

Organizations need to prepare **consolidated financial statements** for external reporting purposes; however, in many instances, managers need more detailed information about an organization's operations. For example, Maplewood Equestrian Centre may produce a consolidated contribution margin statement, with all activities reported in one single column, as follows:

MAPLEWOOD EQUESTRIAN CENTRE
Income Statement (Contribution Margin Format)
for the Year Ended December 31, 2016

| | | Percentage |
|---|---|---|
| Sales | $364,000 | 100 |
| Less: Variable costs | 83,000 | 22.8 |
| Contribution margin | 281,000 | 77.2 |
| Less: Fixed costs | 239,000 | |
| operating income | $ 42,000 | |

But what if Maplewood's managers need to evaluate the different products and services that they offer? A **segmented statement** would be needed. If the statement were divided into two segments, boarding of horses and lessons, they could determine the variable and fixed costs that are attributed directly to each segment. Let's assume that the sales and costs for boarding and lessons are as follows:

| | Sales | Variable Expenses | Traceable Fixed Costs |
|---|---|---|---|
| Boarding | $115,500 | $36,000 | $27,000 |
| Lessons | $248,500 | $47,000 | $45,000 |
| Total | $364,000 | $83,000 | $72,000 |

You will note that the fixed costs in the third column have been specified as traceable fixed costs. Traceable fixed costs are costs that can be directly traced to a specific segment. In other words, if the segment disappeared, then the traceable fixed cost would disappear as well. For example, if the centre had a manager just for the Boarding Division and another manager for the Lesson Division, each manager's salary would be traceable to the segment that he or she manages. However, the salary of the administration manager, who is responsible for the accounting and administration for all of Maplewood Equestrian Centre's activities, cannot directly be traced to one or the other segment. Should one of the segments be dropped, the segment manager's position would not be needed anymore, but the administration manager's position would still be there.

Also note that the two segments' sales and variable costs total to the full amount of sales and variable costs for the farm, but the traceable fixed costs do not total to the full amount of fixed costs for Maplewood. This is due to the common fixed costs—the costs that cannot be attributed to any one segment, such as the administration manager. By incorporating the costs that can be directly traced to each segment, both variable and fixed, and the common costs that apply only to the organization as a whole, a new segmented contribution margin income statement can be created. Exhibit 3-26 demonstrates the segmented statement that is produced using the information that we have examined to this point for Maplewood.

**EXHIBIT 3-26** Maplewood Equestrian Centre Segmented Income Statement

MAPLEWOOD EQUESTRIAN CENTRE
**Segmented Income Statement**
for the Year Ended December 31, 2016

| | Boarding | Lessons | Totals |
|---|---|---|---|
| Sales | $115,500 | $248,500 | $364,000 |
| Variable costs | (36,000) | (47,000) | (83,000) |
| Contribution margin | 79,500 | 201,500 | 281,000 |
| Traceable fixed costs | (27,000) | (45,000) | (72,000) |
| Segment margin | $ 52,500 | $156,500 | 209,000 |
| Common costs | | | (167,000) |
| | | | $ 42,000 |

A new line is shown in Exhibit 3-26. The **segment margin** is the result of subtracting all of the variable costs and the traceable fixed costs for a segment. The operating income for Maplewood is found only in the Totals column since this column is the only one that incorporates all of the common costs as well as the variable and traceable fixed costs.

## Selecting Segments

There are a variety of ways to segment an organization. For example, Maplewood was segmented into Boarding and Lessons divisions as they are the major product lines for the organization. However, if the company has more than one location (a farm at the west end of Ottawa as well as the farm at the east end of Ottawa), the statement could be segmented by location. Instead of having columns for Boarding and Lessons, it would have columns for East End and West End. Depending on the needs of the owners and managers, the statements can be segmented in any way that provides better information for decision-making purposes.

## Levels of Segmentation

Along with the variety of ways to segment an organization horizontally, there are also vertical levels of segmentation. For example, the Boarding and Lessons segments can be further divided. The Boarding segment can be divided into those using indoor full-service board and those using outdoor board for horses that do not have an indoor stall. The Lessons segment can be divided into group, semiprivate, and private lessons. Each of these new segments could be further divided as well, providing as much detail as needed.

It is important to note that the determination of fixed costs as traceable or common costs depends on the level of segmentation. For example, the salary of the manager of the Boarding Division is considered a traceable fixed cost to the Boarding segment, but this same cost is a common cost of the Indoor Boarding and Outdoor Boarding segments.

# DECISION GUIDELINES

## Absorption and Variable Costing

As the CEO of Sportade, you are considering whether to use variable costing. Here are some decisions you will have to make.

| Decision | Guidelines |
|---|---|
| When should an organization use absorption costing? Variable costing? | Use absorption costing for external reporting.<br>Use variable costing only for internal reporting. |
| What is the difference between absorption and variable costing? | Fixed manufacturing costs are treated as follows:<br>■ Inventoriable product costs under absorption costing<br>■ Period costs under variable costing |
| How should an organization compute inventoriable product costs under absorption costing and variable costing? | *Absorption Costing*: Direct materials + Direct labour + Variable overhead + Fixed overhead = Product cost<br>*Variable Costing*: Direct materials + Direct labour + Variable overhead = Product cost |
| Will absorption costing income be higher than, lower than, or the same as variable costing income? | If units produced > units sold:<br>**Absorption costing income > Variable costing income**<br>If units produced < units sold:<br>**Absorption costing income < Variable costing income**<br>If units produced = units sold:<br>**Absorption costing income = Variable costing income** |
| Why should an organization use variable costing for internal reporting? | ■ Use variable costing contribution margin income statements to estimate how changes in sales or costs will affect profits.<br>■ Variable costing does not give managers incentives to build up inventory. |

# SUMMARY PROBLEM 3

Continue the Sportade illustration from Appendix 3A. In April, Sportade produces 10,000 cases of the powdered sports beverage and sells 12,000 cases (the 2,000 cases of inventory on March 31, plus the 10,000 cases produced during April). The variable costs per case and the total fixed costs are the same as in March.

### Requirements

1. Prepare an income statement for the month ended April 30, using absorption costing.
2. Prepare an income statement for the month ended April 30, using variable costing.
3. Reconcile (explain the difference between) operating income under absorption versus variable costing.

## ▪ SOLUTION

### Requirement 1

**SPORTADE**
**Income Statement (Absorption Costing)**
Month Ended April 30

| | | |
|---|---|---|
| Sales revenue (12,000 × $30) | | $360,000 |
| Deduct: Cost of goods sold: | | |
| Beginning finished goods inventory | $ 32,000* | |
| Cost of goods manufactured (10,000 × $16) | 160,000† | |
| Cost of goods available for sale | 192,000 | |
| Ending finished goods inventory | (0) | |
| Cost of goods sold | | 192,000 |
| Gross profit | | 168,000 |
| Deduct: Operating expenses [(12,000 × $2.50) + $25,000] | | (55,000) |
| Operating income | | $113,000 |

*Ending inventory from March 31 (Exhibit 3-20).
†Absorption costing cost per case = $6 + $3 + $2 + $5.

## Requirement 2

| SPORTADE<br>Contribution Margin Income Statement (Variable Costing)<br>Month Ended April 30 | | |
|---|---|---|
| Sales revenue (12,000 × $30) | | $360,000 |
| Deduct: Variable expenses: | | |
| Variable cost of goods sold: | | |
| Beginning finished goods inventory | $ 22,000* | |
| Variable cost of goods manufactured (10,000 × $11) | 110,000† | |
| Variable cost of goods available for sale | 132,000 | |
| Ending finished goods inventory | (0) | |
| Variable cost of goods sold | 132,000 | |
| Sales commission expense (12,000 × $2.50) | 30,000 | (162,000) |
| Contribution margin | | 198,000 |
| Deduct: Fixed expenses: | | |
| Fixed manufacturing overhead | 50,000 | |
| Fixed marketing and administrative expenses | 25,000 | (75,000) |
| Operating income | | $123,000 |

*Ending inventory from March 31 (Exhibit 3-21).
†Variable costing cost per case = $6 + $3 + $2.

## Requirement 3

April operating income is $10,000 higher under variable costing than under absorption costing. Why? Both methods expense all of April's $160,000 manufacturing costs ($110,000 variable + $50,000 fixed) during April. However, the two methods differ in the amount of March manufacturing cost expensed in April. Absorption costing holds $32,000 of March manufacturing costs in inventory and expenses them in April when the goods are sold. Variable costing holds only $22,000 of March manufacturing costs in inventory and expenses them in April.

Thus, absorption costing operating income is as follows:

- $10,000 higher than variable costing income in March (because absorption costing defers $10,000 more of March costs to April)
- $10,000 lower than variable costing income in April (because absorption costing expenses $10,000 more of March costs in April)

# END OF CHAPTER

## LEARNING OBJECTIVES

1. Describe key characteristics and graphs of various cost behaviours.
2. Use cost equations to express and predict costs.
3. Use account analysis and scatter plots to analyze cost behaviour.
4. Use the high-low method to analyze cost behaviour.
5. Use regression analysis to analyze cost behaviour.
6. Prepare contribution margin income statements for service firms and merchandising firms.
7. Use variable costing to prepare contribution margin income statements for manufacturers. (Appendix 3A)
8. Use segment reporting to utilize the contribution margin income statement format in an organization with two or more divisions. (Appendix 3B)



## ACCOUNTING VOCABULARY

**Absorption Costing (p. 138)** The costing method in which products "absorb" both fixed and variable manufacturing costs.

**Account Analysis (p. 125)** A method for determining cost behaviour that is based on a manager's judgment in classifying each general ledger account as a variable, fixed, or mixed cost.

**Committed Fixed Costs (p. 115)** Fixed costs that are locked in because of previous management decisions; management has little or no control over these costs in the short run.

**Consolidated Financial Statement (p. 146)** A financial statement that incorporates all of the divisions of a company in one report.

**Contribution Margin (p. 134)** Sales revenues minus variable expenses.

**Contribution Margin Income Statement (p. 133)** Income statement that organizes costs by behaviour (variable costs or fixed costs) rather than by function.

**Cost Behaviour (p. 111)** Describes how costs change as volume changes.

**Cost Equation (p. 113)** A mathematical equation for a straight line that expresses how a cost behaves.

**Curvilinear Costs (p. 121)** A cost behaviour that is not linear (not a straight line).

**Discretionary Fixed Costs (p. 115)** Fixed costs that are a result of annual management decisions; fixed costs that are controllable in the short run.

**Fixed Costs (p. 111)** Costs that do not change in total despite wide changes in volume.

**High-Low Method (p. 127)** A method for determining cost behaviour that is based on two historical data points: the highest and lowest volume of activity.

**Mixed Costs (p. 111)** Costs that change but not in direct proportion to changes in volume. Mixed costs have both variable cost and fixed cost components.

**Outliers (p. 127)** Abnormal data points; data points that do not fall in the same general pattern as the other data points.

**Regression Analysis (p. 127)** A statistical procedure for determining the line that best fits the data by using all of the historical data points, not just the high and low data points.

**Relevant Range (p. 114)** The range of operations within which the total fixed costs and the variable cost per unit remain constant.

**Segment Margin (p. 147)** The excess of sales over variable costs and traceable fixed costs for a segment of the organization.

**Segmented Statement (p. 146)** A financial statement that shows the detail of different divisions in separate columns, utilizing the contribution margin income statement format.

**Step Costs (p. 121)** A cost behaviour that is fixed over a small range of activity and then jumps to a different fixed level with moderate changes in volume.

**Variable Costs (p. 111)** Costs that change in total in direct proportion to changes in volume.

**Variable Costing (p. 138)** The costing method that assigns only variable manufacturing costs to products.

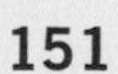

MyAccountingLab Make the grade with MyAccountingLab: Questions marked in # can be found on MyAccountingLab. You can practise them as often as you want, and most feature step-by-step guided instructions to help you find the right answer.



# QUICK CHECK

1. (Learning Objective 1) If a per-unit cost remains constant over a wide range of volume, the cost is most likely a
   a. variable cost.
   b. fixed cost.
   c. mixed cost.
   d. step cost.
2. (Learning Objective 1) The cost per unit decreases as volume increases for which of the following cost behaviours?
   a. Variable costs and fixed costs
   b. Variable costs and mixed costs
   c. Fixed costs and mixed costs
   d. Only fixed costs
3. (Learning Objective 2) In the mixed cost equation $y = vx + f$, which amount represents the total variable cost component?
   a. $y$
   b. $v$
   c. $f$
   d. $vx$
4. (Learning Objective 2) Which of the following would generally be considered a committed fixed cost for a retailing firm?
   a. Cost of a trip to Cancun given to the employee who is Employee of the Year
   b. Lease payments made on the store building
   c. Cost of sponsoring the local golf tournament for charity
   d. Cost of annual sales meeting for all employees
5. (Learning Objective 3) Which method is used to see if a relationship between the cost driver and total cost exists?
   a. Scatter plot
   b. Variance analysis
   c. Outlier
   d. Account analysis
6. (Learning Objective 4) How is the high point selected for the high-low method?
   a. The point with the highest total cost is chosen.
   b. The point with the highest volume of activity is chosen.
   c. The point that has the highest cost and highest volume of activity is always chosen.
   d. Both the high point and the low point are selected at random.
7. (Learning Objective 5) What is the advantage of using regression analysis to determine the cost equation?
   a. The method is objective.
   b. All data points are used to calculate the cost equation.
   c. It is generally more accurate than the high-low method.
   d. All of the above statements are true about regression analysis.
8. (Learning Objective 6) The contribution margin income statement
   a. provides owners with cash flow information.
   b. is required for external reporting.
   c. is useful to managers in decision making and planning.
   d. arrives at operating income by subtracting operating expenses from gross profit.
9. (Learning Objective 7) The only difference between variable costing and absorption costing lies in the treatment of
   a. fixed manufacturing overhead costs.
   b. variable manufacturing overhead costs.
   c. direct materials and direct labour costs.
   d. variable nonmanufacturing costs.
10. (Learning Objective 7) When inventories decline, operating income under variable costing is
    a. lower than operating income under absorption costing.
    b. the same as operating income under absorption costing.
    c. higher than operating income under absorption costing.
11. (Learning Objective 8) A multinational company that produces three brands of tires (in both all-season and winter varieties) and 20 different wheel designs (in both steel and alloy) in North America and Europe could segment its income statement in all of the following segments except for
    a. tires and wheels.
    b. winter tires, summer tires, steel wheels, and alloy wheels.
    c. North American region and European region.
    d. North American region and tires.

**Quick Check Answers**

1. *a* 2. *c* 3. *d* 4. *b* 5. *a* 6. *b* 7. *d* 8. *c* 9. *a* 10. *c* 11. *d*

# SHORT EXERCISES

**S3-1 Identify cost behaviour** *(Learning Objective 1)*

The following chart shows three different costs: Cost A, Cost B, and Cost C. For each cost, the chart shows the total cost and cost per unit at two different volumes within the same relevant range. Based on this information, identify each cost as fixed, variable, or mixed. Explain your answers.

| | *At 5,000 units* | | *At 6,000 units* | |
|---|---|---|---|---|
| | **Total Cost** | **Cost per Unit** | **Total Cost** | **Cost per Unit** |
| Cost A | $30,000 | $6.00 | $36,000 | $6.00 |
| Cost B | $30,000 | $6.00 | $30,000 | $5.00 |
| Cost C | $30,000 | $6.00 | $33,000 | $5.50 |

**S3-2 Sketch cost behaviour graphs** *(Learning Objective 1)*

Sketch graphs of the following cost behaviours. In each graph, the y-axis should be "total costs" and the x-axis should be "volume of activity."

a Step
b Fixed
c Curvilinear
d Mixed
e Variable

**S3-3 Compute fixed costs per unit** *(Learning Objective 2)*

Sport-Time produces high-quality basketballs. If the fixed cost per basketball is $3 when the company produces 12,000 basketballs, what is the fixed cost per basketball when it produces 15,000 basketballs? Assume that both volumes are in the same relevant range.

**S3-4 Define various cost equations** *(Learning Objective 2)*

Write the cost equation for each of the following cost behaviours. Define the variables in each equation.

a Fixed
b Mixed
c Variable

**S3-5 Predict total mixed costs** *(Learning Objective 2)*

Ritter Razors produces deluxe razors that compete with Gillette's Mach line of razors. Total manufacturing costs are $100,000 when 20,000 packages are produced. Of this amount, total variable costs are $40,000. What are the total production costs when 25,000 packages of razors are produced? Assume the same relevant range.

Check sum: Slope equals $2.00.

**S3-6 Predict and graph total mixed costs** *(Learning Objective 3)*

Suppose Telus offers an international calling plan that charges $5.00 per month plus $0.35 per minute for calls outside Canada.

1. Under this plan, what is your monthly international long-distance cost if you call Europe for
   a. 20 minutes?
   b. 40 minutes?
   c. 80 minutes?
2. Draw a graph illustrating your total cost under this plan. Label the axes and show your costs at 20, 40, and 80 minutes.

Check sum: (c) Cost for 80 minute call is $33.00.

**S3-7 Classify cost behaviour** *(Learning Objective 3)*

Ariel builds innovative loudspeakers for music and home theatre. Identify the following costs as variable or fixed:

a. Depreciation on equipment used to cut wood speaker enclosures
b. Wood for speaker enclosures
c. Patents on crossover relays (internal components)
d. Crossover relays
e. Grill cloth
f. Glue
g. Quality inspector's salary

### S3-8 Prepare and analyze a scatter plot *(Learning Objective 3)*

Lube-for-Less is a car-care centre specializing in ten-minute oil changes. Lube-for-Less has two service bays, which limits its capacity to 3,600 oil changes per month. The following information was collected over the past six months:

| Month | Number of Oil Changes | Operating Expenses |
|---|---|---|
| January | 3,400 | $36,800 |
| February | 2,700 | $32,100 |
| March | 3,000 | $33,300 |
| April | 2,900 | $32,900 |
| May | 3,500 | $37,700 |
| June | 3,100 | $34,100 |

1. Prepare a scatter plot graphing the volume of oil changes (x-axis) against the company's monthly operating expenses (y-axis). Graph by hand or use Excel.
2. How strong does the relationship appear to be between the company's operating expenses and the number of oil changes performed each month? Explain. Does there appear to be any outliers in the data? Explain.
3. Based on the graph, do the company's operating costs appear to be fixed, variable, or mixed? Explain how you can tell.

Check sum: Slope equals $7.00.

### S3-9 Use the high-low method *(Learning Objective 4)*

Refer to the Lube-for-Less data in S3-8. Use the high-low method to determine the variable and fixed cost components of Lube-for-Less's operating costs. Use this information to project the monthly operating costs for a month in which the company performs 3,600 oil changes.

Check sum: Slope equals $25.00.

### S3-10 Use the high-low method *(Learning Objective 4)*

Mason Company uses the high-low method to predict its total overhead costs. Past records show that total overhead cost was $25,000 for 800 labour hours worked and $27,500 for 900 labour hours worked. If Mason Company plans to work 825 labour hours next month, what is the expected total overhead cost?

### S3-11 Critique the high-low method *(Learning Objective 4)*

You have been assigned an intern to help you forecast your firm's costs at different volumes. He thinks he will get cost and volume data from the two most recent months, plug them in to the high-low method equations, and turn in the cost equation results to your boss before the hour is over. As his mentor, explain to him why the process is not quite as simple as he thinks. Point out some of the concerns he is overlooking, including your concerns about his choice of data and method.

### S3-12 Analyze a scatter plot *(Learning Objectives 3 & 4)*

The local Holiday Inn collected seven months of data on the number of room-nights rented per month and the monthly utilities cost. The data were graphed, resulting in the following scatter plot:

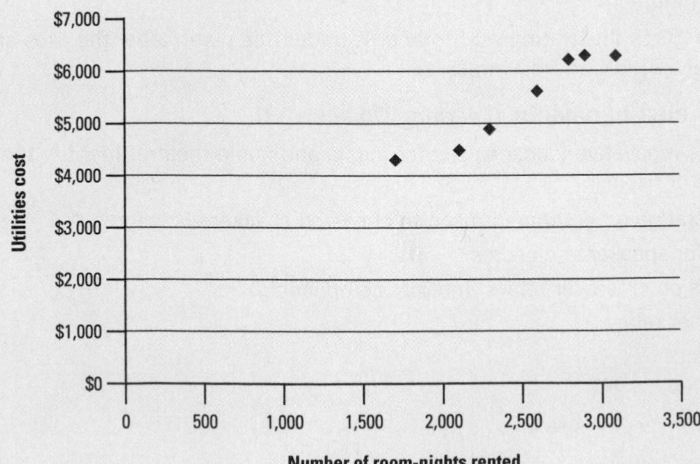

1. Based on this scatter plot, how strong does the relationship appear to be between the number of room-nights rented per month and the monthly utilities cost?
2. Do there appear to be any outliers in the data? Explain.
3. Suppose management performs the high-low method using this data. Do you think the resulting cost equation would be very accurate? Explain.

### S3-13 Make a theoretical comparison of high-low and regression analysis *(Learning Objectives 4 & 5)*

Refer to the Holiday Inn scatter plot in S3-12.

1. Would the high-low method or regression analysis result in a more accurate cost equation for the data pictured in the scatter plot? Explain.
2. A regression analysis of the data revealed an R-squared figure of 0.939. Interpret this figure in light of the lowest and highest possible R-squared values.
3. As a manager, would you be confident predicting utilities costs for other room-night volumes within the same relevant range?
4. Would you feel comfortable using this information to project operating costs for a volume of 4,000 room-nights per month? Explain.

### S3-14 Write a cost equation given regression output *(Learning Objective 5)*

Check sum: Slope is 0.92.

A firm wanted to determine the relationship between its monthly operating costs and a potential cost driver, machine hours. The output of a regression analysis performed using Microsoft Excel showed the following information:

SUMMARY OUTPUT

| *Regression Statistics* | |
|---|---|
| Multiple R | 0.87 |
| R Square | 0.86 |
| Adjusted R Square | 0.84 |
| Standard Error | 398.49 |
| Observations | 12 |

ANOVA

| | *df* | *SS* | *MS* | *F* | *Significance F* |
|---|---|---|---|---|---|
| Regression | 1 | 2365870.5 | 2365871 | 14.89886 | 0.0032 |
| Residual | 10 | 1587954.5 | 158795 | | |
| Total | 11 | 3953825 | | | |

| | *Coefficients* | *Standard Error* | *t Stat* | *P-value* | *Lower 95%* | *Upper 95%* | *Lower 95.0%* | *Upper 95.0%* |
|---|---|---|---|---|---|---|---|---|
| Intercept | 9942.83 | 406.44 | 24.46 | 2.97 | 9037.23 | 10848.43 | 9037.23 | 10848.43 |
| X Variable 1 | 0.92 | 0.23 | 3.86 | 0.00 | 0.37 | 1.40 | 0.37 | 1.40 |

1. Given this output, write the firm's monthly cost equation.
2. Should management use this equation to predict monthly operating costs? Explain your answer.

### S3-15 Prepare a contribution margin income statement *(Learning Objective 6)*

Check sum: Contribution margin is $2,600.

Pam's Quilt Shoppe sells homemade Mennonite quilts. Pam buys the quilts from local Mennonite artisans for $250 each, and her shop sells them for $300 each. Pam also pays a sales commission of 5% of sales revenue to her sales staff. Pam leases her country-style shop for $1,000 per month and pays $1,200 per month in payroll costs in addition to the sales commissions. Pam sold 80 quilts in February. Prepare Pam's traditional income statement and contribution margin income statement for the month.

Check sum: Contribution margin is $181,500.

**S3-16 Prepare an income statement using variable costing** *(Learning Objective 7)*

Consider the Sportade example in Appendix 3A. Suppose that during April, the company produces 10,000 cases of powdered drink mix and sells 11,000 cases. Sales price, variable cost per case, and total fixed expenses remain the same as in March. Prepare the April income statement using variable costing.

Check sum: Gross profit is $154,000.

**S3-17 Continuation of S3-16: absorption costing** *(Learning Objective 7)*

Refer to the Sportade example in Appendix 3A and the data and your answer to S3-16.

1. Prepare the April income statement under absorption costing.
2. Is absorption costing income higher or lower than variable costing income? Explain.
3. Reconcile the difference between the absorption costing income statement and the variable costing income statement.

Check sum: Common costs are $38,000.

**S3-18 Prepare a segmented income statement** *(Learning Objective 8)*

Use the information from the Royal Hellenic Data Set in Chapter 4, page 213. Assume that in the month of April, Northern Cruiseline sold 8,000 regular cruises and 3,500 executive cruises and that $75,000 of the fixed costs are traceable to regular cruises while $97,000 of the fixed costs are traceable to executive cruises. Prepare a segmented income statement using the contribution margin format.



# EXERCISES Group A

**E3-19A Graph specific costs** *(Learning Objective 1)*

Graph these cost behaviour patterns over a relevant range of 0–10,000 units:

a. Variable expenses of $8 per unit
b. Mixed expenses made up of fixed costs of $20,000 and variable costs of $3 per unit
c. Fixed expenses of $15,000

**E3-20A Identify cost behaviour graph** *(Learning Objective 1)*

Following are 12 cost behaviour graphs. The total cost is shown on the y-axis and the volume (activity) is shown on the x-axis.

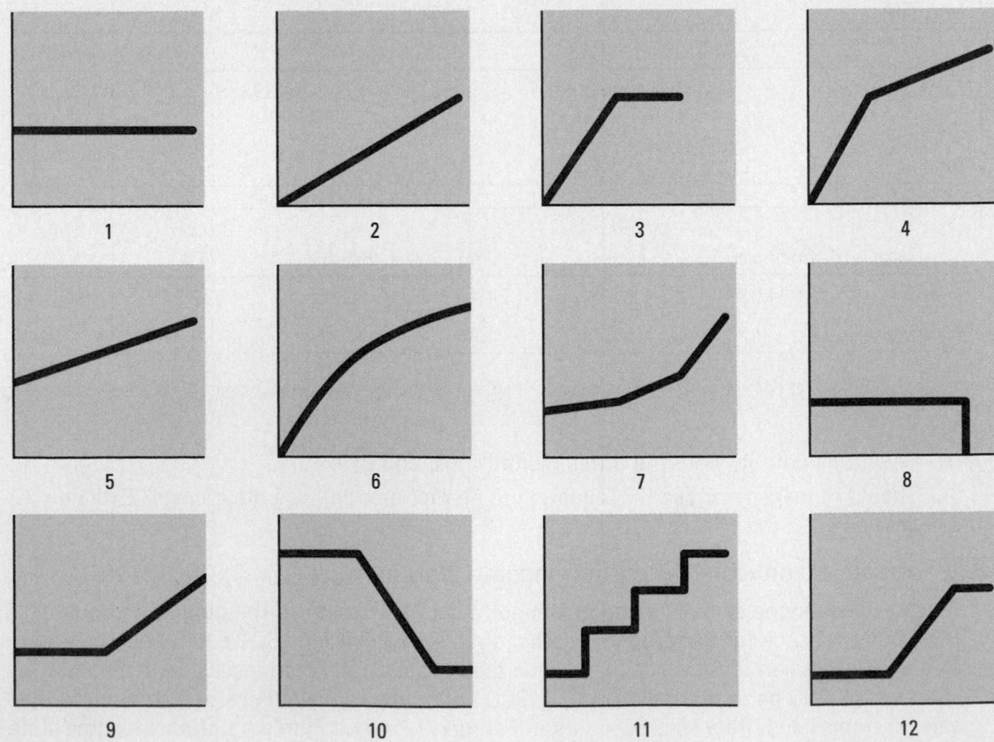

For each of the following situations, identify the graph that most closely represents the cost behaviour pattern of the cost in that situation. Some graphs may be used more than once or not at all.

a. Straight-line depreciation of equipment (based on years of life)
b. Monthly electric bill, which consists of a flat monthly service charge plus $0.002 per kilowatt hour used
c. Factory rent of $4,000 per month will be forgiven by the city (which owns the building) if the company employs twelve disadvantaged youth in the month (the activity on the x-axis is the number of disadvantaged youths employed)
d. Office rent of $1,500 per month (the activity on the x-axis is sales in units)
e. Tuition is $384 per semester credit hour up to 10 credit hours; tuition for 11 credit hours or more is a flat fee of $4,215 per semester
f. Salaries of delivery workers, where a delivery person is needed for every 200 deliveries scheduled in a given month
g. The cost of direct materials for picnic tables when the wood in each table costs $45
h. Cost of water used in plant; to encourage conservation, the water company has the following price schedule per litre of water in addition to the monthly service fee of $20:

| | |
|---|---|
| Up to 10,000 litres | $0.005 per litre |
| 10,001–20,000 litres | $0.006 per litre |
| More than 20,000 litres | $0.008 per litre |

i. Cell phone bill, which is $29.99 for 450 anytime minutes in a month plus $0.25 per minute for any minutes used above the included 450 minutes
j. Assembly-line workers are paid $15.00 per hour

### E3-21A Identify cost behaviour terms *(Learning Objectives 1, 2, 3, 4, & 5)*

Complete the following statements with one of the terms listed here. You may use a term more than once, and some terms may not be used at all.

| | | |
|---|---|---|
| Account analysis | Step cost(s) | High-low method |
| Variable cost(s) | Fixed cost(s) | Regression analysis |
| Curvilinear cost(s) | Total cost(s) | Average cost per unit |
| R-square | Mixed cost(s) | Committed fixed costs |

a. ______ remain constant in total over a wide range of volume.
b. ______ is often referred to as the goodness-of-fit statistic.
c. ______ and ______ increase in total as volume increases.
d. Graphs of ______ always begin at the origin.
e. ______ uses the manager's judgment to determine the cost behaviour of various accounts.
f. ______ remain constant in total over small ranges of activity.
g. ______ and ______ increase on a per unit basis as volume decreases.
h. ______ uses only two historical data points to determine the cost line and cost equation.
i. ______ remain constant on a per unit basis.
j. When graphing cost equations, ______ are always shown on the y-axis.
k. The ______ should not be used to predict total costs at various volumes unless it is strictly a/an ______.
l. ______ uses all historical data points provided to determine the cost equation.
m. ______ are the result of previous management decisions and are not usually controllable in the short run.

### E3-22A Forecast costs at different volumes *(Learning Objectives 1 & 2)*

Perreth Dry Cleaners has capacity to clean up to 5,000 garments per month.

**Requirements**

Check sum: Total fixed costs are $7,000.

1. Complete the following schedule for the three volumes shown.

| | 2,000 Garments | 3,500 Garments | 5,000 Garments |
|---|---|---|---|
| Total variable costs | | $2,625 | |
| Total fixed costs | ____ | ____ | ____ |
| Total operating costs | ____ | ____ | ____ |
| Variable cost per garment | | | |
| Fixed cost per garment | ____ | $ 2.00 | ____ |
| Average cost per garment | ____ | ____ | ____ |

2. Why does the average cost per garment change?
3. Suppose the owner, Dan Perreth, erroneously uses the average cost per unit *at full capacity* to predict total costs at a volume of 2,000 garments. Would he overestimate or underestimate his total costs? By how much?

Check sum: Ooperating income is $19,575.

### E3-23A Prepare an income statement in two formats *(Learning Objective 6)*

Refer to the Perreth Dry Cleaners in E3-22A. Assume that Perreth charges customers $7 per garment for dry cleaning. Prepare Perreth's *projected* income statement if 4,252 garments are cleaned in March. First, prepare the income statement using the traditional format; then, prepare Perreth's contribution margin income statement.

### E3-24A Prepare a segmented contribution margin income statement *(Learning Objective 8)*

Victor's Sporting Goods is a retailer of sporting equipment. Last year, Victor's Sporting Goods' sales revenues totalled $8,000,000. Total expenses were $2,100,000. Of this amount, approximately $1,500,000 were variable, while the remainder were fixed. Since Victor's Sporting Goods offers thousands of different products, its managers prefer to calculate the break-even point in terms of sales dollars rather than units.

Check sum: Common costs are $50,000.

Assume that Victor's Sporting Goods gathers information on the sales of its products based on two departments: Winter Sports and Summer Sports. Winter Sports revenues are $4,000,000 of the total $8,000,000 and the department has an average contribution margin of 70%, while Summer Sports brings in the remaining revenues and has a contribution margin of 85%. Of the fixed costs, $250,000 can be directly traced to Winter Sports and $300,000 can be traced to Summer Sports. Prepare a segmented contribution margin income statement for Victor's Sporting Goods.

Check sum: Slope is $2.00/MH.

### E3-25A Use the high-low method *(Learning Objective 4)*

Jackson Company, which uses the high-low method to analyze cost behaviour, has determined that machine hours best predict the company's total utilities cost. The company's cost and machine hour usage data for the first six months of the year follow.

| Month | Total Cost | Machine Hours |
|---|---|---|
| January | $3,200 | 1,000 |
| February | $3,700 | 1,150 |
| March | $3,500 | 1,075 |
| April | $3,780 | 1,200 |
| May | $4,000 | 1,350 |
| June | $4,300 | 1,400 |

**Requirements**

Using the high-low method, answer the following questions:

1. What is the variable utilities cost per machine hour?

2. What is the fixed cost of utilities each month?
3. If Jackson Company uses 1,280 machine hours in a month, what will its total costs be?

## E3-26A Use unit cost data to forecast total costs *(Learning Objective 2)*

Check sum: (b) The variable cost per unit is $6.56.

MagiPost produces decorative mailboxes. When it produces 1,000 mailboxes, the company's average cost per unit is $24.56.

a. What is the total cost of producing 1,000 mailboxes?
b. If $18,000 of the total costs are fixed, what is the variable cost of producing each mailbox?
c. Write MagiPost cost equation.
d. If the plant manager uses the average cost per unit to predict total costs, what would the forecast be for 1,200 mailboxes?
e. If the plant manager uses the cost equation to predict total costs, what would the forecast be 1,200 mailboxes?
f. What is the dollar difference between your answers to questions d and e? Which approach to forecasting costs is appropriate? Why?

## E3-27A Use account analysis to determine cost behaviour *(Learning Objective 3)*

Use your judgment (just as a manager would use his or her judgment for account analysis) to determine the cost behaviour of each of the following personal costs:

a. Apartment rental, $500 per month
b. Local phone service with unlimited local calls, $19.99 per month
c. Cell phone plan, the first 700 minutes are included for $39.99 per month and every minute thereafter costs $0.30
d. Utilities, $0.475 per kilowatt hour
e. Car payment, $350 per month
f. Car insurance, $250 per month
g. Gas, $0.98 per litre; your car averages 17 km/L
h. Cable TV, $50 per month for 120 channels plus $4.99 per pay-per-view movie
i. Commuter rail tickets, $2 per ride
j. Student activity pass, $100 plus $5 per event
k. Campus meal plan, $3 per meal



## E3-28A Sustainability and cost estimation *(Learning Objective 4)*

Check sum: Variable cost is $1.06.

Star Entertainment is a provider of cable, internet, and on-demand video services. Star currently sends monthly bills to its customers via the postal service. Because of a concern for the environment and recent increases in postal rates, Star management is considering offering an option to its customers for paperless billing. In addition to saving printing, paper, and postal costs, paperless billing will save energy and water (through reduced paper needs, reduced waste disposal, and reduced transportation needs). While Star would like to switch to 100% paperless billing, many of its customers are not comfortable with paperless billing or may not have Web access, so the paper billing option will remain, regardless of whether Star adopts a paperless billing system or not.

The cost of the paperless billing system would be $140,000 per quarter with no variable costs since the costs of the system are the salaries of the clerks and the cost of leasing the computer system. The paperless billing system being proposed would be able to handle up to 900,000 bills per quarter. (More than 900,000 bills per quarter would require a different computer system and is outside the scope of the current situation at Star.)

Star has gathered its cost data for the past year by quarter for paper, toner cartridges, printer maintenance costs, and postage costs for its billing department. The cost data is as follows:

| | Quarter 1 | Quarter 2 | Quarter 3 | Quarter 4 |
|---|---|---|---|---|
| Total paper, toner, printer maintenance, and postage costs | $627,500 | $635,000 | $770,000 | $650,000 |
| Total number of bills mailed | 575,000 | 605,000 | 725,000 | 625,000 |

### Requirements

1. Calculate the variable cost per bill mailed under the current paper-based billing system.
2. Assume that the company projects that it will have a total of 690,000 bills to mail in the upcoming quarter. If enough customers choose the paperless billing option so that 25% of the mailings can be converted to paperless, how much would the company save from the paperless billing system (be sure to consider the cost of the paperless billing system)?
3. What if only 20% of the mailings are converted to the paperless option (assume a total of 690,000 bills)? Should the company still offer the paperless billing system? Explain your rationale.

Check sum: Contribution margin is $2,600.

### E3-29A Create a scatter plot *(Learning Objective 3)*

Alice Jungemann, owner of Flower Power, operates a local chain of floral shops. Each shop has its own delivery van. Instead of charging a flat delivery fee, Jungemann wants to set the delivery fee based on the distance driven to deliver the flowers. Jungemann wants to separate the fixed and variable portions of her van operating costs so that she has a better idea how delivery distance affects these costs. She has the following data from the past seven months:

| Month | Kilometres Driven | Van Operating Costs |
|---|---|---|
| January | 15,800 | $5,460 |
| February | 17,300 | 5,680 |
| March | 14,600 | 4,940 |
| April | 16,000 | 5,310 |
| May | 17,100 | 5,830 |
| June | 15,400 | 5,420 |
| July | 14,100 | 4,880 |

February and May are always Flower Power's biggest months because of Valentine's Day and Mother's Day, respectively.

### Requirements

1. Prepare a scatter plot of Alice's volume (kilometres driven) and van operating costs.
2. Do the data appear to contain any outliers? Explain.
3. How strong is the relationship between kilometres driven and van operating costs?

Check sum: Vertical intercept is $1,355.

### E3-30A High-low method *(Learning Objective 4)*

Refer to Alice's Flower Power data in E3-29A. Use the high-low method to determine Flower Power's cost equation for van operating costs. Use your results to predict van operating costs at a volume of 15,000 kilometres.

Check sum: Slope is $0.28/km.

### E3-31A Continuation of E3-29A: Regression analysis *(Learning Objective 5)*

Refer to the Flower Power data in E3-29A. Use Microsoft Excel to do the following.

### Requirements

1. Run a regression analysis.
2. Determine the firm's cost equation (use the output from the Excel regression).
3. Determine the R-square (use the output from the Excel regression). What does Flower Power's R-square indicate?
4. Predict van operating costs at a volume of 15,000 km.

### E3-32A Perform regression analysis using Excel output *(Learning Objective 5)*

Assume that Alice's Flower Power does a regression analysis on the next year's data using Microsoft Excel. The output generated by Excel is as follows:

SUMMARY OUTPUT

| *Regression Statistics* | |
|---|---|
| Multiple R | 0.96 |
| R Square | 0.92 |
| Adjusted R Square | 0.90 |
| Standard Error | 112.91 |
| Observations | 7 |

ANOVA

| | *df* | *SS* | *MS* | *F* | *Significance F* |
|---|---|---|---|---|---|
| Regression | 1 | 689408.19 | 689408.19 | 54.08 | 0.0007 |
| Residual | 5 | 63745.52 | 12749.10 | | |
| Total | 6 | 753153.71 | | | |

| | *Coefficients* | *Standard Error* | *t Stat* | *P-value* | *Lower 95%* | *Upper 95%* | *Lower 95.0%* | *Upper 95.0%* |
|---|---|---|---|---|---|---|---|---|
| Intercept | 826.04 | 629.77 | 1.31 | 0.25 | −792.83 | 2444.91 | −792.83 | 2444.91 |
| X Variable 1 | 0.32 | 0.04 | 7.35 | 0.00 | 0.18 | 0.37 | 0.18 | 0.37 |

#### Requirements

1. Determine the firm's cost equation (use the output from the Excel regression).
2. Determine the R-square (use the output from the Excel regression). What does Flower Power's R-square indicate?
3. Predict van operating costs at a volume of 16,000 km.

### E3-33A Prepare and interpret a scatter plot *(Learning Objective 3)*

Asokan's Golden Brown Pancake Restaurant features sourdough pancakes made from a strain of sourdough dating back to the Yukon gold rush. To plan for the future, Asokan needs to figure out his cost behaviour patterns. He has the following information about his operating costs and the number of pancakes served:

| Month | Number of Pancakes | Total Operating Costs |
|---|---|---|
| July | 3,600 | $2,340 |
| August | 3,900 | $2,390 |
| September | 3,200 | $2,320 |
| October | 3,300 | $2,270 |
| November | 3,850 | $2,560 |
| December | 3,620 | $2,530 |

#### Requirements

1. Prepare a scatter plot of Asokan's pancake volume and operating costs. (*Hint:* If you use Excel, be sure to force the y-axis to zero.)
2. Do the data appear sound, or do there appear to be any outliers? Explain.
3. Based on the scatter plot, do operating costs appear to be variable, fixed, or mixed costs?
4. How strong is the relationship between pancake volume and operating costs?

Check sum: (1) Vertical intercept is $2,000.

**E3-34A High-low method** *(Learning Objective 4)*

Refer to Asokan's Golden Brown Pancake Restaurant in E3-33A.

**Requirements**

1. Use the high-low method to determine Asokan's operating cost equation.
2. Use your answer from Requirement 1 to predict total monthly operating costs if Asokan serves 4,000 pancakes in one month.
3. Can you predict total monthly operating costs if Asokan serves 10,000 pancakes a month? Explain.

**E3-35A Perform regression analysis** *(Learning Objective 5)*

Refer to Asokan's Golden Brown Pancake Restaurant in E3-33A.

**Requirements**

1. Use Microsoft Excel to perform regression analysis on Asokan's monthly data. Based on the output, write Asokan's monthly operating cost equation.
2. Based on the R-square shown on the regression output, how well does this cost equation fit the data?

**E3-36A Perform regression analysis using Excel output** *(Learning Objective 5)*

Assume that Asokan's Golden Brown Pancake Restaurant does a regression analysis on the next year's data using Excel 2007. The output generated by Excel is as follows:

SUMMARY OUTPUT

| *Regression Statistics* | |
|---|---|
| Multiple R | 0.72 |
| R Square | 0.51 |
| Adjusted R Square | 0.39 |
| Standard Error | 99.45 |
| Observations | 6 |

ANOVA

| | *df* | *SS* | *MS* | *F* | *Significance F* |
|---|---|---|---|---|---|
| Regression | 1 | 41497.60 | 41497.60 | 4.20 | 0.11 |
| Residual | 4 | 39561.23 | 9890.31 | | |
| Total | 5 | 81058.83 | | | |

| | *Coefficients* | *Standard Error* | *t Stat* | *P-value* | *Lower 95%* | *Upper 95%* | *Lower 95.0%* | *Upper 95.0%* |
|---|---|---|---|---|---|---|---|---|
| Intercept | 1,563.26 | 564.95 | 2.52 | 0.07 | −144.96 | 2992.16 | −144.96 | 2992.16 |
| X Variable 1 | 0.28 | 0.15 | 2.05 | 0.11 | −0.11 | 0.72 | −0.11 | 0.72 |

**Requirements**

1. What is the fixed cost per month?
2. What is the variable cost per pancake?
3. If Asokan's Golden Brown Pancake Restaurant serves 3,700 pancakes in a month, what would the company's total operating costs be?

**E3-37A Determine cost behaviour and predict operating costs** *(Learning Objective 4)*

Check sum: Operating costs at 60% occupancy are $191,000.

Bayview Apartments is a 500-unit apartment complex. When the apartments are 90% occupied, monthly operating costs total $200,000. When occupancy dips to 80%, monthly operating costs fall to $197,000. The owner of the apartment complex is worried because many of the apartment residents work at a nearby manufacturing plant that has just announced it will close in three months. The apartment owner fears that occupancy of her apartments will drop to 60% if residents lose their jobs and move away. Assuming the same relevant range, what can the owner expect her operating costs to be if occupancy falls to 60%?

**E3-38A Prepare a contribution margin income statement** *(Learning Objective 6)*

Check sum: Total fixed expenses are $90,900.

Precious Pets is a small e-tail business specializing in the sale of exotic pet gifts and accessories over the Web. The business is owned by a sole proprietor and operated out of her home. Results for last year are as follows:

**PRECIOUS PETS**
**Income Statement**
Year Ended December 31

| | | |
|---|---|---|
| Sales revenue | | $ 987,000 |
| Cost of goods sold | | (665,000) |
| Gross profit | | 322,000 |
| Operating expenses: | | |
| Selling and marketing expenses | $61,000 | |
| Website maintenance expenses | 56,000 | |
| Other operating expenses | 17,000 | |
| Total operating expenses | | (134,000) |
| Operating income | | $ 188,000 |

For internal planning and decision-making purposes, the owner of Precious Pets would like to translate the company's income statement into the contribution margin format. Since Precious Pets is an e-tailer, all of its cost of goods sold was variable. A large portion of the selling and marketing expenses consisted of freight-out charges ($19,000), which were also variable. Only 20% of the remaining selling and marketing expenses and 25% of the Website expenses were variable. Of the other operating expenses, 90% were fixed.

Based on this information, prepare Precious Pets' contribution margin income statement for last year.

**E3-39A Prepare a contribution margin income statement** *(Learning Objective 6)*

Check sum: Total fixed expenses are $62,500.

Quebec City Carriage Company offers guided horse-drawn carriage rides through historic Quebec City. The carriage business is highly regulated by the city. Quebec City Carriage Company has the following operating costs during April:

| | |
|---|---|
| Monthly depreciation expense on carriages and stable | $2,000 |
| Fee paid to Quebec City | 15% of ticket revenue |
| Cost of souvenir set of postcards given to each passenger | $0.50/set of postcards |
| Brokerage fee paid to independent ticket brokers (60% of tickets are issued through these brokers; 40% are sold directly by the Quebec City Carriage Company) | $1.00/ticket sold by broker |
| Monthly cost of leasing and boarding the horses | $45,000 |
| Carriage drivers (tour guides) are paid on a per-passenger basis | $3.00 per passenger |
| Monthly payroll costs of non–tour-guide employees | $7,500 |
| Marketing, Website, telephone, and other monthly fixed costs | $8,000 |

During April (a month during peak season) Quebec City Carriage Company had 12,960 passengers. Eighty-five percent of passengers were adults ($20 fare) while 15% were children ($12 fare).

### Requirements

1. Prepare the company's contribution margin income statement for the month of April. Round all figures to the nearest dollar.
2. Assume that passenger volume increases by 10% in May. Which figures on the income statement would you expect to change, and by what percentage would they change? Which figures would remain the same as in April?

Check sum: Cost of goods sold (absorption) is $4,625,000.

## E3-40A Absorption and variable costing income statements *(Learning Objective 7)*

The annual data that follow pertain to Rays, a manufacturer of swimming goggles. (Rays had no beginning inventories.)

| | |
|---|---|
| Sale price | $ 35 |
| Variable manufacturing expense per unit | 15 |
| Sales commission expense per unit | 5 |
| Fixed manufacturing overhead | 2,000,000 |
| Fixed operating expenses | 250,000 |
| Number of goggles produced | 200,000 |
| Number of goggles sold | 185,000 |

### Requirements

1. Prepare both conventional (absorption costing) and contribution margin (variable costing) income statements for Rays for the year.
2. Which statement shows the higher operating income? Why? Reconcile the difference between the two statements.
3. Rays' marketing vice president believes a new sales promotion that costs $200,000 would increase sales to 200,000 goggles. Should the company go ahead with the promotion? Give your reason.

## E3-41A Contribution format income statement *(Learning Objective 6)*

MusicTowne sells amplifiers. Information from the quarter shows income of $800,000 and cost of goods sold as $400,000. The company has $200,000 in selling expenses, which includes a 10% commission for each amplifier sold. The company also has $100,000 in administrative expenses, 80% of which are fixed. The company buys amplifiers from several suppliers with an average price of $200, and resells them with a 100% mark-up on the price.

### Requirements

1. Prepare an income statement for the quarter using the absorption costing approach.
2. Prepare an income statement for the quarter using the contribution approach.
3. How much does the sale of each amplifier contribute to covering fixed costs?
4. What is the minimum number of amplifiers MusicTowne needs to sell to break even?

## E3-42A Cost function *(Learning Objective 2)*

Wellspring produces agricultural irrigation equipment. During a year, the amount of overhead costs on a per month basis varies in relation to the machine hours used in a given year. The low for the past year was 4,500 hours, and the expense associated was $90,000. The high for the period was 6,000 hours, and the associated expense was $140,000. During the low month, the $90,000 in overhead costs consisted of indirect materials of $45,000 (a variable expense), rent of $35,000 (a fixed expense), and maintenance costs of $10,000 (a mixed expense).

### Requirements

1. Given the breakdown of expenses in the low period, what are the estimated costs for (a) indirect materials, (b) rent, and (c) maintenance during the high period?
2. What is the cost function for maintenance costs?
3. What amount of maintenance costs would expect with 8,000 machine hours of work?
4. What would be the total overhead costs at 8,000 machine hours?

# EXERCISES Group B

## E3-43B Graph specific costs *(Learning Objective 1)*

Graph these cost behaviour patterns over a relevant range of 0–10,000 units:

a. Variable expenses of $6 per unit
b. Mixed expenses made up of fixed costs of $30,000 and variable costs of $2 per unit
c. Fixed expenses of $20,000

## E3-44B Identify cost behaviour graph *(Learning Objective 1)*

Following are 12 cost behaviour graphs. The total cost is shown on the y-axis and the volume (activity) is shown on the x-axis.

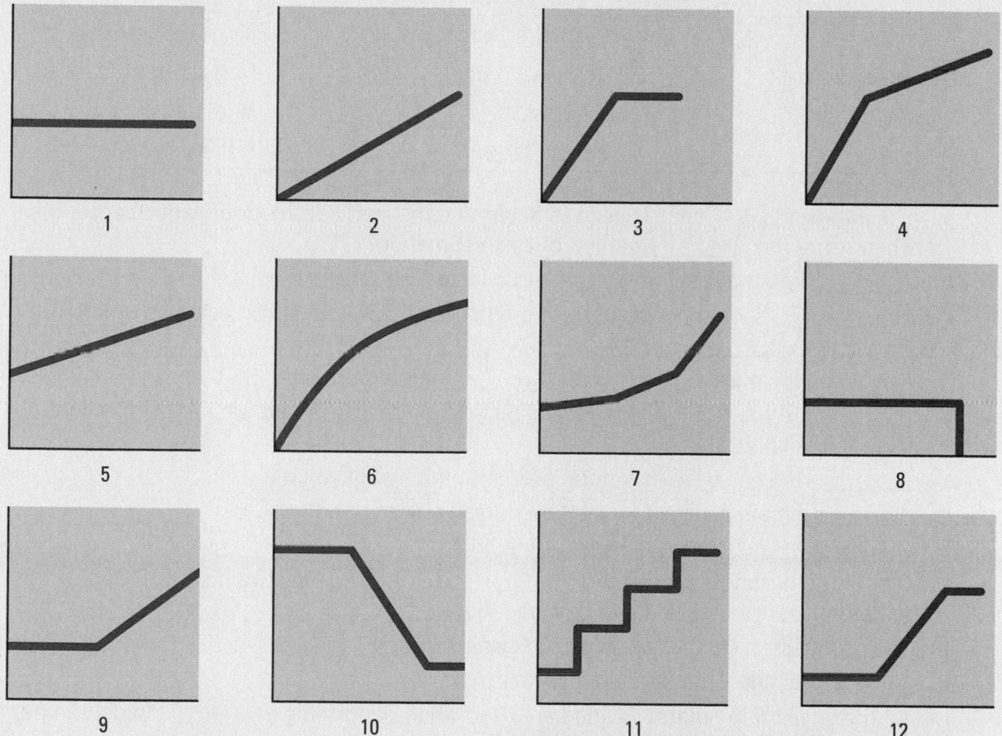


For each of the following situations, identify the graph that most closely represents the cost behaviour pattern of the cost in that situation. Some graphs may be used more than once or not at all.

a. Cell phone bill, which is $59.99 for 1,400 anytime minutes in a month plus $0.30 per minute for any minutes used above the included 1,400 minutes
b. Rent on local specialty chocolates store building of $900 per month (the activity on the x-axis is sales dollars)
c. Mortgage loan processors are paid $20.00 per hour (the activity on the x-axis is number of mortgage loans processed).
d. Tuition is $400 per semester credit hour up to 10 credit hours; tuition for 11 credit hours or more is a flat fee of $4,400 per semester.
e. Factory rent of $5,000 per month will be forgiven by the city (which owns the building) if the company employs 20 displaced workers in the month (the activity on the x-axis is the number of displaced workers employed).
f. The cost of materials for salsa chips when the ingredients in each kilogram of chips cost $0.85
g. Salaries of sales team managers, wherein a manager is needed for every 30 salespeople employed (the activity on the x-axis is the number of sales people)
h. Straight-line depreciation of computer network; depreciation is taken over a projected five-year life

i. Cost of electricity used in plant; to encourage conservation, the electric company has the following price schedule per kilowatt hour in addition to the monthly service fee of $20:

| | |
|---|---|
| Up to 1,000 kilowatt hours | $0.050 per kilowatt hour |
| 1,001–20,000 kilowatt hours | $0.055 per kilowatt hour |
| More than 20,000 kilowatt hours | $0.075 per kilowatt hour |

j. Monthly natural gas bill, which consists of a flat monthly service charge of $15.50 plus $13.01 per thousand cubic metre of natural gas used

### E3-45B Identify cost behaviour terms *(Learning Objectives 1, 2, 3, 4, & 5)*

Complete the following statements with one of the terms listed here. You may use a term more than once, and some terms may not be used at all.

| | | |
|---|---|---|
| R-square | Committed fixed costs | Regression analysis |
| Average cost per unit | Curvilinear cost(s) | Fixed cost(s) |
| Variable cost(s) | Total cost(s) | Mixed cost(s) |
| Step cost(s) | Account analysis | High-low method |



a. The manager's judgment is used to determine the cost behaviour of various accounts when using the _______ method of cost estimation.
b. _______ are always shown on the y-axis in cost equations graphs.
c. The _______ should not be used to predict total costs at various volumes unless it is strictly a/an _______.
d. As volume increases, _______ and _______ increase in total.
e. _______ are the result of previous management decisions and are not usually controllable in the short run.
f. _______ remain constant in total over a wide range of volume.
g. _______ remain constant in total over small ranges of activity.
h. Graphs of _______ always begin at the origin.
i. One of the disadvantages of the _______ is that it uses only two historical data points to determine the cost line and cost equation.
j. The goodness-of-fit statistic is also known as the _______.
k. _______ remain constant on a per unit basis.
l. All historical data points provided are used when performing a _______ to determine the cost equation.
m. As volume decreases, _______ and _______ increase on a per-unit basis.

### E3-46B Forecast costs at different volumes *(Learning Objectives 1 & 2)*

Renaud Dry Cleaners has capacity to clean up to 6,000 garments per month.

| | 3,000 Garments | 4,500 Garments | 6,000 Garments |
|---|---|---|---|
| Total variable costs | | $3,375 | |
| Total fixed costs | ____ | ____ | ____ |
| Total operating costs | ____ | ____ | ____ |
| Variable cost per garment | | | |
| Fixed cost per garment | ____ | $ 2.00 | ____ |
| Average cost per garment | ____ | ____ | ____ |

Check sum: Total fixed costs are $9,900.

#### Requirements

1. Complete the following schedule for the three volumes shown.
2. Why does the average cost per garment change?
3. The owner, Guy Renaud, uses the average cost per unit at full capacity to predict total costs at a volume of 3,000 garments. Does he overestimate or underestimate his total costs? By how much?

### E3-47B Prepare income statement in two formats *(Learning Objective 6)*

Check sum: Operating income is $29,690.

Refer to the Renaud Dry Cleaners in E3-46B. Assume that Renaud charges customers $10 per garment for dry cleaning. Prepare Renaud's projected income statement if 4,280 garments are cleaned in March. First, prepare the income statement using the traditional format; then, prepare Renaud's contribution margin income statement.

### E3-48B Segmented contribution margin income statement *(Learning Objective 8)*

Check sum: Common costs are $58,000.

Red Deer Sporting Goods is a retailer of sporting equipment. Last year, Red Deer Sporting Goods' sales revenues totalled $6,400,000. Total expenses were $2,800,000. Of this amount, approximately $1,792,000 were variable, while the remainder were fixed. Since Red Deer Sporting Goods offers thousands of different products, its managers prefer to calculate the break-even point in terms of sales dollars rather than units.

Assume that Red Deer Sporting Goods gathers information on the sales of its products based on two departments: Winter Sports and Summer Sports. Winter Sports revenues total $4,000,000 of the total $6,400,000 and the department has an average contribution margin of 75%, while Summer Sports brings in the remaining revenues and has a contribution margin of 67%. Of the fixed costs, $550,000 can be directly traced to Winter Sports and $400,000 can be traced to Summer Sports. Prepare a segmented contribution margin income statement for Red Deer Sporting Goods.

### E3-49B Use the high-low method *(Learning Objective 4)*

Check sum: (2) The vertical intercept is $2,300.

Schultz Company, which uses the high-low method to analyze cost behaviour, has determined that machine hours best predict the company's total utilities cost. The company's cost and machine hour usage data for the first six months of the year follow:

| Month | Total Cost | Machine Hours |
|---|---|---|
| January | $3,420 | 1,090 |
| February | 3,720 | 1,160 |
| March | 3,590 | 1,040 |
| April | 3,760 | 1,200 |
| May | 4,600 | 1,310 |
| June | 4,086 | 1,440 |

Using the high-low method, answer the following questions:

**Requirements**

1. What is the variable utilities cost per machine hour?
2. What is the fixed cost of utilities each month?
3. If Schultz Company uses 1,220 machine hours in a month, what will its total costs be?

### E3-50B Use unit cost data to forecast total costs *(Learning Objective 2)*

Check sum: (5) The cost of 1,700 mailboxes = $37,831.

Acme Mailboxes produces decorative mailboxes. The company's average cost per unit is $23.43 when it produces 1,500 mailboxes.

1. What is the total cost of producing 1,500 mailboxes?
2. If $15,000 of the total costs are fixed, what is the variable cost of producing each mailbox?
3. Write Acme Mailboxes' cost equation.
4. If the plant manager uses the average cost per unit to predict total costs, what would his forecast be for 1,700 mailboxes?
5. If the plant manager uses the cost equation to predict total costs, what would his forecast be for 1,700 mailboxes?
6. What is the dollar difference between your answers to Questions 4 and 5? Which approach to forecasting costs is appropriate? Why?

### E3-51B Use account analysis to determine cost behaviour *(Learning Objective 3)*

Use your judgment (just as a manager would use his or her judgment for account analysis) to determine the cost behaviour of each of the following personal costs:

a. Satellite TV, $40 per month for 150 channels plus $2.99 per pay-per-view movie
b. Bus ticket to local mall, $1 per ride
c. Condo rental, $750 per month

d. Local phone service with unlimited local calls, $19.99 per month plus $0.05 per minute for long-distance calls
e. Student activity pass, $50 plus $5 per event
f. Campus meal plan, $3 per meal
g. Pay-as-you-go cell phone plan with no monthly service fee and $0.20 per minute used
h. Utilities, $20 per month plus $0.475 per kilowatt hour
i. Car payment, $400 per month
j. Gas, $1.04 per litre and your car averages 14 km/L
k. Car insurance, $175 per month

### E3-52B Sustainability and cost estimation *(Learning Objective 4)*



Bright Entertainment is a provider of cable, internet, and on-demand video services. Bright currently sends monthly bills to its customers via the postal service. Because of a concern for the environment and recent increases in postal rates, Bright's management is considering offering an option to its customers for paperless billing. In addition to saving printing, paper, and postal costs, paperless billing will save energy and water (through reduced paper needs, reduced waste disposal, and reduced transportation needs). While Bright would like to switch to 100% paperless billing, many of its customers are not comfortable with paperless billing or may not have Web access, so the paper billing option will remain, regardless of whether Bright adopts a paperless billing system or not.

The cost of the paperless billing system would be $125,000 per quarter with no variable costs since the costs of the system are the salaries of the clerks and the cost of leasing the computer system. The paperless billing system being proposed would be able to handle up to 900,000 bills per quarter. (More than 900,000 bills per quarter would require a different computer system and is outside the scope of the current situation at Bright.)

Check sum: (3) Net savings would be $24,126.

Bright has gathered its cost data for the past year by quarter for paper, toner cartridges, printer maintenance costs, and postage costs for its billing department. The cost data is as follows:

Total paper, toner, printer maintenance, and postage costs
Total number of bills mailed

| Quarter 1 | Quarter 2 | Quarter 3 | Quarter 4 |
|---|---|---|---|
| $622,000 | $770,000 | $670,000 | $642,500 |
| 614,000 | 725,000 | 625,000 | 575,000 |

#### Requirements

1. Calculate the variable cost per bill mailed under the current paper-based billing system.
2. Assume that the company projects that it will have a total of 700,000 bills to mail in the upcoming quarter. If enough customers choose the paperless billing option so that 25% of the mailing can be converted to paperless, how much would the company save from the paperless billing system? (Be sure to consider the cost of the paperless billing system.)
3. What if only 20% of the mailings are converted to the paperless option? (Assume a total of 700,000 bills.) Should the company still offer the paperless billing system? Explain your rationale.

### E3-53B Create a scatter plot *(Learning Objective 3)*

Kent Huynh, owner of Tulip Time, operates a local chain of flower shops. Each shop has its own delivery van. Instead of charging a flat delivery fee, Kent wants to set the delivery fee based on the distance driven to deliver the flowers. Kent wants to separate the fixed and variable portions of his van operating costs so that he has a better idea how delivery distance affects these costs. He has the following data from the past seven months:

| Month | Kilometres Driven | Van Operating Costs |
|---|---|---|
| January | 15,500 | $5,400 |
| February | 17,500 | 5,350 |
| March | 14,400 | 4,980 |
| April | 16,400 | 5,280 |
| May | 16,900 | 5,580 |
| June | 15,300 | 5,010 |
| July | 13,500 | 4,590 |

February and May are always Tulip Time's biggest months because of Valentine's Day and Mother's Day, respectively.

**Requirements**

1. Prepare a scatter plot of Kent's volume (kilometres driven) and van operating costs.
2. Do the data appear to contain any outliers? Explain.
3. How strong is the relationship between kilometres driven and van operating expenses?

## E3-54B High-low method *(Learning Objective 4)*

Refer to Kent's Tulip Time data in E3-53B. Use the high-low method to determine Tulip Time's cost equation for van operating costs. Use your results to predict van operating costs at a volume of 14,500 km.

## E3-55B Continuation of E3-53B: regression analysis *(Learning Objective 5)*

Refer to the Tulip Time data in E3-53B. Use Microsoft Excel to run a regression analysis, then do the following calculations.

**Requirements**

1. Determine the firm's cost equation (use the output from the Excel regression).
2. Determine the R-square (use the output from the Excel regression). What does Tulip Time's R-square indicate?
3. Predict van operating costs at a volume of 14,500 kilometres.

## E3-56B Regression analysis using Excel output *(Learning Objective 5)*

Assume that Kent's Tulip Time does a regression analysis on the next year's data using Microsoft Excel. The output generated by Excel is as follows:

| Regression Statistics | |
|---|---|
| Multiple R | 0.85 |
| R Square | 0.72 |
| Adjusted R Square | 0.66 |
| Standard Error | 205.01 |
| Observations | 7 |

ANOVA

| | *df* | *SS* | *MS* | *F* | *Significance F* |
|---|---|---|---|---|---|
| Regression | 1 | 539222.81 | 539222.81 | 12.83 | 0.0158 |
| Residual | 5 | 210148.62 | 42029.72 | | |
| Total | 6 | 749371.43 | | | |

| | *Coefficients* | *Standard Error* | *t Stat* | *P-value* | *Lower 95%* | *Upper 95%* | *Lower 95.0%* | *Upper 95.0%* |
|---|---|---|---|---|---|---|---|---|
| Intercept | 624.10 | 1316.00 | 0.52 | 0.63 | −2704.12 | 4061.65 | −2704.12 | 4061.65 |
| X Variable 1 | 0.29 | 0.08 | 3.58 | 0.02 | 0.08 | 0.51 | 0.08 | 0.51 |

**Requirement**

1. Determine the firm's cost equation (use the output from the Excel regression).
2. Determine the R-square (use the output from the Excel regression). What does Tulip Time's R-square indicate?
3. Predict van operating costs at a volume of 15,500 kilometres.

### E3-57B Prepare and interpret a scatter plot *(Learning Objective 3)*

Cliff's Fresh Stacks Pancake Restaurant features sourdough pancakes made from a strain of sourdough dating back to Confederation. To plan for the future, Cliff needs to figure out his cost behaviour patterns. He has the following information about his operating costs and the number of pancakes served:

| Month | Number of Pancakes | Total Operating Costs |
|---|---|---|
| July | 3,900 | $2,340 |
| August | 4,200 | $2,530 |
| September | 3,600 | $2,440 |
| October | 3,700 | $2,290 |
| November | 4,000 | $2,560 |
| December | 3,850 | $2,510 |



#### Requirements

1. Prepare a scatter plot of Cliff's pancake volume and operating costs.
2. Do the data appear sound, or do there appear to be any outliers? Explain.
3. Based on the scatter plot, do operating costs appear to be variable, fixed, or mixed costs?
4. How strong is the relationship between pancake volume and operating costs?

### E3-58B Use the high-low method *(Learning Objective 4)*

Refer to Cliff's Fresh Stacks Pancake Restaurant in E3-57B.

Check sum: The slope is $0.15/ pancake.

#### Requirements

1. Use the high-low method to determine Cliff's operating cost equation.
2. Use your answer from Requirement 1 to predict total monthly operating costs if Cliff serves 4,500 pancakes a month.
3. Can you predict total monthly operating costs if Cliff serves 12,000 pancakes a month? Explain.

### E3-59B Analyze a regression analysis *(Learning Objective 5)*

Refer to Cliff's Fresh Stacks Pancake Restaurant in E3-57B. Use Microsoft Excel to run a regression analysis, then do the following calculations.

#### Requirements

1. Determine Cliff's monthly operating cost equation (use the output from the Excel regression).
2. Based on the R-square shown on the regression output, how well does this cost equation fit the data?

### E3-60B Analyze a regression analysis using Excel output *(Learning Objective 5)*

Assume that Cliff's Fresh Stack Pancake Restaurant does a regression analysis on the next year's data using Microsoft Excel. The output generated by Excel is as follows:

| Regression Statistics | |
|---|---|
| Multiple R | 0.56 |
| R Square | 0.31 |
| Adjusted R Square | 0.14 |
| Standard Error | 107.40 |
| Observations | 6 |

ANOVA

| | *df* | *SS* | *MS* | *F* | *Significance F* |
|---|---|---|---|---|---|
| Regression | 1 | 20542.55 | 20542.55 | 1.78 | 0.25 |
| Residual | 4 | 46140.78 | 11535.19 | | |
| Total | 5 | 66683.33 | | | |

| | *Coefficients* | *Standard Error* | *t Stat* | *P-value* | *Lower 95%* | *Upper 95%* | *Lower 95.0%* | *Upper 95.0%* |
|---|---|---|---|---|---|---|---|---|
| Intercept | 1626.18 | 632.59 | 2.57 | 0.06 | –130.18 | 3382.54 | –130.18 | 3382.54 |
| X Variable 1 | 0.22 | 0.16 | 1.33 | 0.25 | –0.24 | 0.67 | –0.24 | 0.67 |

**Requirements**

1. What is the fixed cost per month?
2. What is the variable cost per pancake?
3. If Cliff's Fresh Stack Pancake Restaurant serves 4,200 pancakes in a month, what would its total operating costs be?

Check sum: (2) The fixed cost per month is $1,626.18.

### E3-61B Determine cost behaviour and predict operating costs *(Learning Objective 4)*

Bayside Apartments is a 750-unit apartment complex. When the apartments are 90% occupied, monthly operating costs total $216,825. When occupancy dips to 80%, monthly operating costs fall to $212,400. The owner of the apartment complex is worried because many of the apartment residents work at a nearby manufacturing plant that has just announced it will close in three months. The apartment owner fears that occupancy of his apartments will drop to 60% if residents lose their jobs and move away. Assuming the same relevant range, what should the owner expect his operating costs to be if occupancy falls to 60%?

### E3-62B Prepare a contribution margin income statement *(Learning Objective 6)*

Pretty Pets is a small e-tail business specializing in the sale of exotic pet gifts and accessories over the Web. The business is owned by a sole proprietor and operated out of her home. Results for last year are as follows:

Check sum: The contribution margin is $144,700.

| PRETTY PETS<br>Income Statement<br>Year Ended December 31 | | |
|---|---|---|
| Sales revenue | | $861,000 |
| Cost of goods sold | | (671,000) |
| Gross profit | | 190,000 |
| Operating expenses: | | |
| Selling and marketing expenses | $61,000 | |
| Website maintenance expenses | 60,000 | |
| Other operating expenses | 17,800 | |
| Total operating expenses | | (138,800) |
| Operating income | | $ 51,200 |

For internal planning and decision-making purposes, the owner of Pretty Pets would like to translate the company's income statement into the contribution margin format. Since Pretty Pets is an e-tailer, all of its cost of goods sold were variable. A large portion of the selling and marketing expenses consisted of freight-out charges ($20,400), which were also variable. Only 20% of the remaining selling and marketing expenses and 25% of the Website expenses were variable. Of the other operating expenses, 90% were fixed. Based on this information, prepare Pretty Pets' contribution margin income statement for last year.

### E3-63B Prepare a contribution margin income statement *(Learning Objective 6)*

Chartrand Carriage Company offers guided horse-drawn carriage rides through historic old Montreal. The carriage business is highly regulated by the city. Chartrand Carriage Company has the following operating costs during April:

| | |
|---|---|
| Monthly depreciation expense on carriages and stable | $2,900 |
| Fee paid to City of Montreal | 15% of ticket revenue |
| Cost of souvenir set of postcards given to each passenger | $0.75/set of postcards |
| Brokerage fee paid to independent ticket brokers (60% of tickets are issued through these brokers; 40% are sold directly by the Chartrand Carriage Company) | $1.20/ticket sold by broker |
| Monthly cost of leasing and boarding the horses | $48,000 |
| Carriage drivers (tour guides) are paid on a per-passenger basis | $3.00 per passenger |
| Monthly payroll costs of non-tour-guide employees | $7,500 |
| Marketing, Website, telephone, and other monthly fixed costs | $7,250 |

During April (a month during peak season) Chartrand Carriage Company had 12,970 passengers. Eighty-five percent of passengers were adults ($26 fare) while 15% were children ($18 fare).

Check sum: The contribution margin is $215,432.

#### Requirements

1. Prepare the company's contribution margin income statement for the month of April. Round all figures to the nearest dollar.
2. Assume that passenger volume increases by 18% in May. Which figures on the income statement would you expect to change, and by what percentage would they change? Which figures would remain the same as in April?

**E3-64B Prepare absorption and variable costing income statements** *(Learning Objective 7)*

The annual data that follow pertain to Swim Clearly, a manufacturer of swimming goggles. (Swim Clearly has no beginning inventories.)

| | |
|---|---|
| Sale price | $ 42 |
| Variable manufacturing expense per unit | 20 |
| Sales commission expense per unit | 5 |
| Fixed manufacturing overhead | 1,935,000 |
| Fixed operating expense | 265,000 |
| Number of goggles produced | 215,000 |
| Number of goggles sold | 200,000 |

**Requirements**

1. Prepare both conventional (absorption costing) and contribution margin (variable costing) income statements for Swim Clearly for the year.
2. Which statement shows the higher operating income? Why? Reconcile the difference between the two statements.
3. Swim Clearly's marketing vice president believes a new sales promotion that costs $145,000 would increase sales to 215,000 goggles. Should the company go ahead with the promotion? Give your reason.



# PROBLEMS Group A

**P3-65A Analyze cost behaviour** *(Learning Objectives 1, 2, 3, & 4)*

Berg Industries is in the process of analyzing its manufacturing overhead costs. Berg Industries is not sure if the *number of units produced* or *number of direct labour hours* is the best cost driver to use for predicting manufacturing overhead costs. The following information is available:

| Month | Manufacturing Overhead Costs | Direct Labour Hours | Units Produced | MOH Cost per DL Hour | MOH Cost per Unit Produced |
|---|---|---|---|---|---|
| July | $460,000 | 23,000 | 3,600 | $20.00 | $127.78 |
| August | 515,000 | 26,400 | 4,320 | 19.51 | 119.21 |
| September | 425,000 | 19,000 | 4,200 | 22.37 | 101.19 |
| October | 448,000 | 21,600 | 3,400 | 20.74 | 131.76 |
| November | 527,000 | 27,000 | 5,750 | 19.52 | 91.65 |
| December | 437,000 | 19,400 | 3,250 | 22.53 | 134.46 |

**Requirements**

1. Are manufacturing overhead costs fixed, variable, or mixed? Explain.
2. Graph Berg Industries' MOH costs against DL hours. Use Excel or graph by hand.
3. Graph Berg Industries' MOH costs against units produced. Use Excel or graph by hand.
4. Do the data appear to be sound, or do you see any potential data problems? Explain.
5. Use the high-low method to determine Berg Industries' MOH cost equation using DL hours as the cost driver. Assume that management believes that all data are accurate and wants to include all of it in the analysis.
6. Estimate MOH costs if Berg Industries incurs 24,000 DL hours in January.

**P3-66A Continuation of P3-65A: regression analysis** *(Learning Objective 5)*

Refer to Berg Industries in P3-65A.

**Requirements**

1. Use Excel regression analysis to determine Berg Industries' manufacturing overhead cost equation using DL hours as the cost driver. Comment on the R-square. Estimate MOH costs if Berg Industries incurs 24,000 DL hours in January.
2. Use Excel regression analysis to determine Berg's MOH cost equation using number of units produced as the cost driver. Use all of the data provided. Project total MOH costs if Berg Industries produces 5,000 units. Which cost equation is better—this one or the one from Requirement 1? Why?
3. Use Excel regression analysis to determine Berg Industries' MOH cost equation using number of units produced as the cost driver. This time, remove any potential outliers before performing the regression. How does this affect the R-square? Project total MOH costs if 5,000 units are produced.
4. In which cost equation do you have the most confidence? Why?



**P3-67A Prepare traditional and contribution margin income statements** *(Learning Objective 6)*

Kelsey's Ice Cream Shoppe sold 9,000 servings of ice cream during June for $3 per serving. Kelsey purchases the ice cream in large tubs from the BlueBell Ice Cream Company. Each tub costs Kelsey $15 and has enough ice cream to fill 30 ice cream cones. Kelsey purchases the ice cream cones for $0.05 each from a local warehouse club. Kelsey's Shoppe is located in a local strip mall, and she pays $1,800 a month to lease the space. Kelsey expenses $250 a month for the depreciation of the shop's furniture and equipment. During June, Kelsey incurred an additional $2,500 of other operating expenses (75% of these were fixed costs).

**Requirements**

1. Prepare Kelsey's June income statement using a traditional format.
2. Prepare Kelsey's June income statement using a contribution margin format.

**P3-68A Determine financial statement components** *(Learning Objective 7)*

Violins-by-Zain produces student-grade violins for beginning violin students. The company produced 2,000 violins in its first month of operations. At month-end, 600 finished violins remained unsold. There was no inventory in work in process. Violins were sold for $112.50 each. Total costs from the month are as follows:

| | |
|---|---:|
| Direct materials used | $80,000 |
| Direct labour | 50,000 |
| Variable manufacturing overhead | 30,000 |
| Fixed manufacturing overhead | 40,000 |
| Variable selling and administrative expenses | 10,000 |
| Fixed selling and administrative expenses | 15,000 |

The company prepares traditional (absorption costing) income statements for its bankers. Zain would also like to prepare contribution margin income statements for his own management use. Compute the following amounts that would be shown on these income statements:

**Requirements**

1. Gross profit
2. Contribution margin
3. Total expenses shown below the gross profit line
4. Total expenses shown below the contribution margin line
5. Dollar value of ending inventory under absorption costing
6. Dollar value of ending inventory under variable costing

Which income statement has a higher operating income? By how much? Explain.

### P3-69A Compute absorption and variable costing income statements
*(Learning Objective 7)*

Sasha's Foods produces frozen meals, which it sells for $7 each. The company uses the FIFO inventory costing method, and it computes a new monthly fixed manufacturing overhead rate based on the actual number of meals produced that month. All costs and production levels are exactly as planned. The following data are from Sasha's first two months in business:

| | January | February |
|---|---|---|
| Sales | 1,000 meals | 1,200 meals |
| Production | 1,400 meals | 1,000 meals |
| Variable manufacturing expense per meal | $ 4 | $ 4 |
| Sales commission expense per meal | $ 1 | $ 1 |
| Total fixed manufacturing overhead | $ 700 | $ 700 |
| Total fixed marketing and administrative expenses | $ 600 | $ 600 |

#### Requirements

1. Compute the product cost per meal produced under absorption costing and under variable costing. Do this first for January and then for February.
2. Prepare separate monthly income statements for January and for February, using (a) absorption costing and (b) variable costing.
3. Is operating income higher under absorption costing or variable costing in January? In February? Explain the pattern of differences in operating income based on absorption costing versus variable costing.



## PROBLEMS Group B

### P3-70B Analyze cost behaviour *(Learning Objectives 1, 2, 3, & 4)*

Cherestal Industries is in the process of analyzing its manufacturing overhead costs. Cherestal Industries is not sure if the number of units produced or the number of direct labour hours is the best cost driver to use for predicting MOH costs. The following information is available:

| Month | Manufacturing Overhead Costs | Direct Labour Hours | Units Produced | MOH Cost per DL Hour | MOH Cost per Unit Produced |
|---|---|---|---|---|---|
| July | $463,000 | 23,100 | 3,620 | $20.04 | $127.90 |
| August | 513,000 | 26,500 | 4,300 | 19.36 | 119.30 |
| September | 435,000 | 20,000 | 4,230 | 21.75 | 102.84 |
| October | 450,000 | 21,400 | 3,380 | 21.03 | 133.14 |
| November | 562,000 | 30,000 | 5,790 | 18.73 | 97.06 |
| December | 438,000 | 20,500 | 3,300 | 21.37 | 132.73 |

#### Requirements

1. Are manufacturing overhead costs fixed, variable, or mixed? Explain.
2. Graph Cherestal Industries' MOH costs against DL hours.
3. Graph Cherestal Industries' MOH costs against units produced.
4. Do the data appear to be sound or do you see any potential data problems? Explain.
5. Use the high-low method to determine Cherestal Industries' MOH cost equation using DL hours as the cost driver. Assume that management believes that all the data are accurate and wants to include all of it in the analysis.
6. Estimate MOH costs if Cherestal Industries incurs 25,500 DL hours in January.

### P3-71B Continuation of P3-68B: regression analysis *(Learning Objective 5)*

Refer to Cherestal Industries in P3-70B.

#### Requirements

1. Use Excel regression analysis to determine Cherestal Industries' manufacturing overhead cost equation using DL hours as the cost driver. Comment on the R-square. Estimate MOH costs if Cherestal Industries incurs 25,500 DL hours in January.
2. Use Excel regression analysis to determine Cherestal's MOH cost equation using number of units produced as the cost driver. Use all of the data provided. Project total MOH costs if Cherestal Industries produces 5,200 units. Which cost equation is better—this one or the one from Question 1? Why?
3. Use Excel regression analysis to determine Cherestal Industries' MOH cost equation using number of units produced as the cost driver. This time, remove any potential outliers before performing the regression. How does this affect the R-square? Project total MOH costs if 5,200 units are produced.
4. In which cost equation do you have the most confidence? Why?

### P3-72B Prepare traditional and contribution margin income statements *(Learning Objective 6)*

Mary's Ice Cream Shoppe sold 9,100 servings of ice cream during June for $4 per serving. Mary purchases the ice cream in large tubs from the Organic Ice Cream Company. Each tub costs Mary $14 and has enough ice cream to fill 28 ice cream cones. Mary purchases the ice cream cones for $0.20 each from a local warehouse club. Mary's Shoppe is located in a local strip mall, and she pays $2,050 a month to lease the space. Mary expenses $210 a month for the depreciation of the Shoppe's furniture and equipment. During June, Mary incurred an additional $2,000 of other operating expenses (75% of these were fixed costs).

#### Requirements

1. Prepare Mary's June income statement using a traditional format.
2. Prepare Mary's June income statement using a contribution margin format.

### P3-73B Determine financial statement components *(Learning Objective 7)*

Music World produces student-grade violins for beginning violin students. The company produced 2,100 violins in its first month of operations. At month-end, 550 finished violins remained unsold. There was no inventory in work in process. Violins were sold for $122.50 each. Total costs from the month are as follows:

| | |
|---|---:|
| Direct materials used | $87,200 |
| Direct labour | 60,000 |
| Variable manufacturing overhead | 25,000 |
| Fixed manufacturing overhead | 44,100 |
| Variable selling and administrative expenses | 8,000 |
| Fixed selling and administrative expenses | 13,900 |

The company prepares traditional (absorption costing) income statements for its bankers. Hannah would also like to prepare contribution margin income statements for her own management use. Compute the following amounts that would be shown on these income statements:

#### Requirements

1. Gross profit
2. Contribution margin
3. Total expenses shown below the gross profit line
4. Total expenses shown below the contribution margin line
5. Dollar value of ending inventory under absorption costing
6. Dollar value of ending inventory under variable costing

Which income statement has a higher operating income? By how much? Explain.

### P3-75B Prepare absorption and variable costing income statements

*(Learning Objective 7)*

Marty's Entrees produces frozen meals, which it sells for $9 each. The company uses the FIFO inventory costing method, and it computes a new monthly fixed manufacturing overhead rate based on the actual number of meals produced that month. All costs and production levels are exactly as planned. The following data are from Marty's Entrees' first two months in business:

| | January | February |
|---|---|---|
| Sales | 1,400 meals | 1,800 meals |
| Production | 2,000 meals | 1,400 meals |
| Variable manufacturing expense per meal | $ 5 | $ 5 |
| Sales commission expense per meal | $ 1 | $ 1 |
| Total fixed manufacturing overhead | $ 700 | $ 700 |
| Total fixed marketing and administrative expenses | $ 500 | $ 500 |

#### Requirements

1. Compute the product cost per meal produced under absorption costing and under variable costing. Do this first for January and then for February.
2. Prepare separate monthly income statements for January and for February, using (a) absorption costing and (b) variable costing.
3. Is operating income higher under absorption costing or variable costing in January? In February? Explain the pattern of differences in operating income based on absorption costing versus variable costing.

# CAPSTONE APPLICATION PROBLEMS

## APPLICATION QUESTION

### A3-75 Appendix 3A *(Learning Objective 7)*

Suppose you serve on the board of directors of Canadian Faucet, a manufacturer of bathroom fixtures that recently adopted a lean production philosophy. Part of your responsibility is to develop a compensation contract for Toni Moen, the vice-president of manufacturing. To give her the incentive to make decisions that will increase the company's profits, the board decides to give Moen a year-end bonus if Canadian Faucet meets a target operating income.

Write a memo to Chairperson of the Board Herbert Kohler explaining whether the bonus contract should be based on absorption costing or variable costing. Use the following format:

Date: ______________________

To: ______________________

From: ______________________

Subject: ______________________

### A3-76 Analyze cost behaviour using a variety of methods *(Learning Objectives 1, 2, 3, 4, & 5)*

Braunhaus Microbrewery is in the process of analyzing its manufacturing overhead costs. Braunhaus is not sure if the number of cases produced or the number of processing hours is the best cost driver of MOH costs. The following information is available:

| Month | Manufacturing Overhead Costs | Processing Hours | Cases | MOH Cost per Processing Hour | MOH Cost per Case |
|---|---|---|---|---|---|
| January | $29,500 | 680 | 8,000 | $43.38 | $3.69 |
| February | 27,800 | 575 | 6,750 | 48.35 | 4.12 |
| March | 24,500 | 500 | 5,500 | 49.00 | 4.45 |
| April | 29,000 | 600 | 7,250 | 48.33 | 4.00 |
| May | 28,000 | 650 | 7,800 | 43.08 | 3.59 |
| June | 29,750 | 710 | 5,600 | 41.90 | 5.31 |

1. Are manufacturing overhead costs fixed, variable, or mixed? Explain.
2. Graph Braunhaus Microbrewery's MOH costs against processing hours. Use Excel or graph by hand.
3. Graph Braunhaus Microbrewery's MOH costs against cases produced. Use Excel or graph by hand.
4. Do the data appear to be sound, or do you see any potential data problems? Explain.
5. Use the high-low method to determine Braunhaus Microbrewery's MOH cost equation using processing hours as the cost driver. Assume that management believes all of the data to be accurate and wants to include all of it in the analysis.
6. Estimate MOH costs if Braunhaus Microbrewery incurs 550 processing hours in July, using the results of the high-low analysis in Question 5.
7. Use Excel regression analysis to determine Braunhaus Microbrewery's MOH cost equation using processing hours as the cost driver. Comment on the R-square. Estimate MOH costs if Braunhaus Microbrewery incurs 550 processing hours in July.
8. Use Excel regression analysis to determine Braunhaus Microbrewery's MOH cost equation using number of cases produced as the cost driver. Use all of the data provided. Project total MOH costs if Braunhaus Microbrewery produces 6,000 cases. Which cost equation is better—this one or the one from Question 7? Why?

9. Use Excel regression analysis to determine Braunhaus Microbrewery's MOH cost equation using number of cases produced as the cost driver. This time, remove any potential outliers before performing the regression. How does this affect the R-square? Project total MOH costs if Braunhaus Microbrewery produces 6,000 cases.
10. In which cost equation do you have the most confidence? Why?

# CASE ASSIGNMENT

## C3-77 WaterDogs Inc.

Nikki Castle started making lifejackets for dogs in her basement part-time 10 years ago after getting a puppy. She wanted to go canoeing but was unable to find a suitable lifejacket for her puppy, so she spent a couple of days fabricating something herself. When Nikki got to the canoe club, she was flooded with inquiries about her puppy's lifejacket and she started taking orders. Ten years later, her company now has revenues of over $5,000,000 per year, and her lifejackets are sold in 45 different countries through her online store and in specialty pet stores across North America.

Before starting her business, WaterDogs, Inc., Nikki had been working in an insurance company as a clerk. She had always made her own clothes and had taken a few fashion design courses but did not have a business background. Beginning the company was challenging, and over the first few years of getting her business going, Nikki also took a few online courses in business management and accounting. There were a couple of times that she thought that the business wasn't going to make it—especially in the beginning when she experienced a lot of growth very quickly—but after six years was confident enough with the organization to incorporate. She hires an accountant to look after the bookkeeping and goes through an audit each year, but doesn't feel as though the financial statements, and in particular the income statement, provide her with the right information for decision making.

| | 2011 | 2012 | 2013 |
|---|---|---|---|
| Revenues | 4,880,000 | 4,320,000 | 5,355,000 |
| Less cost of goods sold: | | | |
| Beginning inventory | 2,600,000 | 3,419,000 | 4,805,000 |
| Add: Cost of goods manufactured | 3,230,000 | 3,650,000 | 4,175,000 |
| Cost of goods available for sale | 5,830,000 | 7,069,000 | 8,980,000 |
| Less: Ending inventory | 3,532,000 | 5,749,500 | 7,889,600 |
| Cost of goods sold | 2,298,000 | 1,319,500 | 1,090,400 |
| Gross profit | 2,582,000 | 3,000,500 | 4,264,600 |
| Less: Operating expenses | | | |
| Selling and admin | 1,608,000 | 1,587,000 | 1,6140,00 |
| Operating income | 974,000 | 1,413,500 | 2,650,600 |

Her income statements didn't seem to fit with what she felt the company was really doing. Yes, the company was growing, but not at the rate that the profit was demonstrating, Nikki thought. In particular, Nikki felt that 2012 had been a slump year, but the income statement doesn't seem to reflect that. She dug up some additional information on the company and was looking at it when she decided she needed an advisor to help her. She didn't have enough knowledge to be able to figure out what to do.

| | 2010 | 2011 | 2012 | 2013 |
|---|---|---|---|---|
| Units beginning inventory | | 70,000 | 109,000 | 175,000 |
| Units produced | 90,000 | 100,000 | 120,000 | 145,000 |
| Units sold | | 61,000 | 54,000 | 63,000 |

Direct materials are $12 per unit, direct labour is $6 per unit, and variable manufacturing overhead is $3 per unit for each of the years. The company uses a FIFO inventory system.

# DISCUSSION & ANALYSIS

1. Briefly describe an organization with which you are familiar. Describe a situation when a manager in that organization could use cost behaviour information and how it could be used.
2. How are fixed costs similar to step fixed costs? How are fixed costs different from step fixed costs? Give an example of a step fixed cost and describe why that cost is not considered to be a fixed cost.
3. Describe a specific situation when a scatter plot could be useful to a manager.
4. What is a mixed cost? Give an example of a mixed cost. Sketch a graph of this example.
5. Compare discretionary fixed costs to committed fixed costs. Think of an organization with which you are familiar. Give two possible examples of discretionary fixed costs and two possible examples of committed fixed costs for that organization. Explain why the costs you have chosen as examples fit within the definitions of discretionary fixed costs and committed fixed costs.
6. Define the terms "independent variable" and "dependent variable" as used in regression analysis. Illustrate the concepts of independent variables and dependent variables by selecting a cost a company would want to predict and what activity it might use to predict that cost. Describe the independent variable and the dependent variable in that situation.
7. Define the term "relevant range." Why is it important to managers?
8. Describe the term "R-square." If a regression analysis for predicting manufacturing overhead using direct labour hours as the dependent variable has an R-square of 0.40, why might this be a problem? Given the low R-square value, describe the options a manager has for predicting MOH costs. Which option do you think is the best option for the manager? Defend your answer.
9. Over the past year, a company's inventory has increased significantly. For its financial statements the company uses absorption costing, but internally it uses variable costing. Which set of financial statements will show the highest operating income? What specifically causes the difference between the two sets of financial statements?
10. A company has adopted a lean production philosophy and, as a result, has cut its inventory levels significantly. Describe the impact on the company's external financial statements as a result of this inventory reduction. Also describe the impact of the inventory reduction on the company's internal financial statements, which are prepared using variable costing.

# APPLICATION & ANALYSIS

## Cost Behaviour in Real Companies

Choose a company with which you are familiar that manufactures a product or provides a service. In this activity, you will make reasonable estimates of the costs and activities associated with this company, although companies do not typically publish internal cost or process information.

## Discussion Questions

1. Describe the company you selected and the products or services it provides.
2. List 10 costs that this company would incur. Include costs from a variety of departments within the company, including human resources, sales, accounting, production (if a manufacturer), service (if a service company), and others. Make sure that you have at least one cost from each of the following categories: fixed, variable, and mixed.
3. Classify each of the costs you listed as either fixed, variable, or mixed. Justify why you classified each cost as you did.
4. Describe a potential cost driver for each of the variable and mixed costs you listed. Explain why each cost driver is appropriate for its associated cost.
5. Discuss how easy or difficult it was for you to decide whether each cost was fixed, variable, or mixed. Describe techniques a company could use to determine whether a cost is fixed, variable, or mixed.

### Classroom Applications

**Web:** Post the discussion questions on an electronic discussion board. Have small groups of students choose a company for their group.

**Classroom:** Form groups of three or four students. Your group should choose a company that manufactures a product or provides a service. After deciding upon a company, discuss each of the listed questions. Prepare a five-minute presentation about your group's company that addresses the listed questions.

**Independent:** Write a paper that addresses each of the listed questions for a company of your choice that manufacturers a product or provides a service. Turn in a two- or three-page typed paper (12-point font, double-spaced with 2.5 cm margins).

## TRY IT SOLUTIONS

**page 117:**

a. Total fixed costs do not react to wide changes in volume; therefore, total fixed costs will still be $100,000.

b. Fixed costs per unit decrease as volume increases. At the higher occupancy, the fixed cost per guest is as follows:

$$\$100{,}000 \div 16{,}000 \text{ guests} - \$6.25 \text{ per guest}$$

If only 2,000 guests stay during the month, the fixed cost per guest is much higher ($50).

**page 121:**

1. The monthly cost of belonging to the fitness club can be expressed as

$$y = \$5x + \$30$$

Where $y$ = monthly cost of belonging to the club and
$x$ = number of instructor-led exercise classes attended.

2. If you attend five classes in a month, your total cost will be $55 [= ($5 × 5 classes) + $30].
3. If you attend 10 classes in a month, your total cost will be $80 [= ($5 × 10 classes) + $30]. The cost does not double when the number of classes attended doubles. The variable portion of the bill doubles from $25 to $50, but the fixed portion of the bill ($30) stay constant.

**page 134:**

1. $32.00. Absorption costing treats all manufacturing costs as inventoriable product costs, regardless of whether they are fixed or variable.
2. $12.00 of fixed MOH will be expensed as part of cost of goods sold every time a unit is sold.
3. $20.00. Variable costing treats only variable manufacturing costs (direct materials, direct labour, and variable MOH) as inventoriable product costs. Fixed MOH is not included in the product cost.
4. $120,000 of fixed MOH will be expensed as a period cost (operating expense) of the month.

# 4 Cost-Volume-Profit Analysis

## Learning Objectives

1 Calculate the unit contribution margin and the contribution margin ratio.

2 Use CVP analysis to find break-even points and target profit volumes.

3 Perform sensitivity analysis in response to changing business conditions.

4 Find break-even and target profit volumes for multiproduct companies.

5 Determine a firm's margin of safety and operating leverage.

Chapter 4, "Cost-Volume-Profit Analysis," covers material outlined in **Section 3: Management Accounting** of the CPA Competency Map. Specifically, this chapter addresses *Section 3.3 Cost Management.* The Learning Objectives in this chapter have been aligned with the CPA Competency map to ensure the best coverage possible.

PROFESSIONAL COMPETENCY

The presence of the **coverage button** in the margin indicates focus on one or more of the specific competency areas from the competency map. The concepts in the text are building blocks to developing the competencies required in the CPA. While the chapter may address multiple areas of the competency map, the main focus will be:

Competencies:

**3.5.1** Performs sensitivity analysis*

**3.5.2** Evaluates sustainable profit maximization and capacity management performance*

© Opas Chotiphantawanon/Shutterstock

## Gallery Art Inc.

is a company based in Halifax, Nova Scotia, that provides art consultation services to companies across Canada and the world. Gallery Art's main service is to provide selection and leasing services for works of art (paintings, sculptures, etc.) that can be placed in a client's offices. Gallery Art will have a consultation with a client concerning the current décor of their offices and the theme they may want to invoke in the offices (for example, calm and relaxed or exciting and trendy) and select works of art that are consistent with this theme and general look of the office space. An added benefit is that companies do not have to pay the full price of the art, just a monthly leasing cost that is a fraction of the full cost of the artwork. Recently, Gallery Art has added a new rotation service, where clients pay a monthly flat fee and new art is automatically installed to replace art that has been in place at the office for a set period (usually six months), to keep the office looking "fresh." Gallery Art generates revenue through the lease payment (often paying between 25% and 50% of the monthly lease cost to the artist), and through the rotation service, which is a surcharge on the lease payment. (No portion of the rotation charge is shared with artist.)

Gallery Art uses cost-volume-profit (CVP) analysis to determine the number of pieces of artwork necessary at each client site to ensure that each

*Reprinted from *The Chartered Professional Accountant Competency Map - Understanding the competencies a candidate must demonstrate to become a CPA*, © 2012, with permission Chartered Professional Accountants of Canada, Toronto, Canada. Any changes to the original material are the sole responsibility of the author (and/or publisher) and have not been reviewed or endorsed by the Chartered Professional Accountants of Canada.

client reaches a target profitability/client. Gallery Art also uses CVP to establish how many clients are necessary to achieve targeted levels of overall profitability. And finally, because one of Gallery Art's missions is to provide exposure for new struggling artists, Gallery Art uses CVP to determine pricing for art that is little known (and thus, less in demand) to ensure that each client site has some new artists as well as some established artists.

In the last chapter, we discussed cost behaviour patterns and the methods managers use to determine how the company's costs behave. We showed how managers use the contribution margin income statement to separately display the firm's variable and fixed costs. In this chapter, we show how managers identify the volume of sales necessary to achieve break-even or a target profit. We also look at how changes in costs, sales price, and volume affect the firm's profit. Finally, we discuss ways to identify the firm's risk level, including ways to gauge how easily a firm's profits could turn to losses if sales volume declines.

# Cost-Volume-Profit Analysis

Cost-volume-profit analysis, or CVP, is a powerful tool that helps managers make decisions using the relationships among costs, volume, and the company's profit. Entrepreneurs and managers use CVP analysis to determine the sales volume that will be needed just to break even, or cover costs. They also use CVP to determine the sales volume that will be needed to earn a target profit, (e.g., $100,000 per month). And because business conditions are always changing, CVP can help managers prepare for and respond to economic changes, such as increases in costs from suppliers (sometimes called a sensitivity analysis).

## Data Required for Effective CVP Analysis

CVP analysis relies on the interdependency of five components, or pieces of information, as shown in Exhibit 4-1.

**EXHIBIT 4-1** Components of CVP Analysis

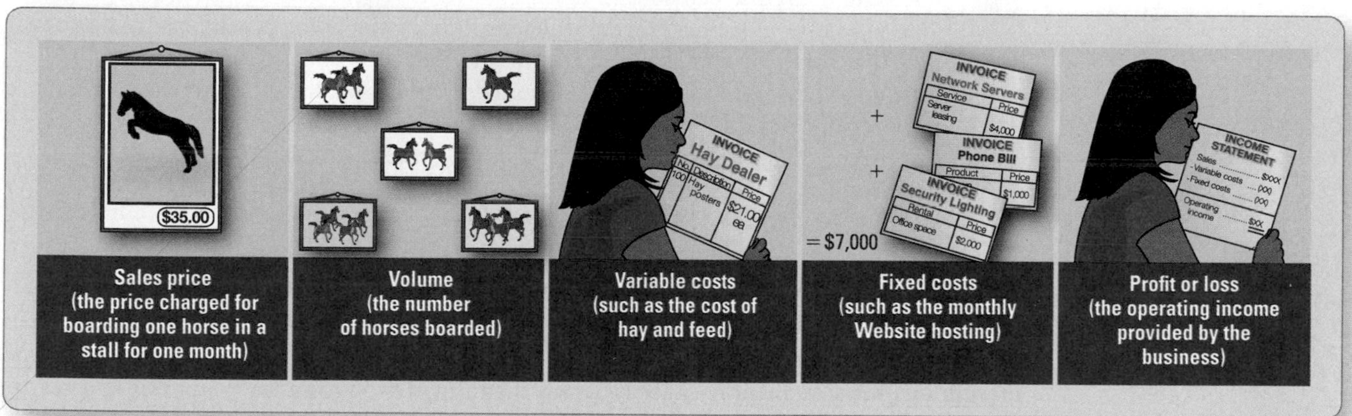


If you know or can estimate four of these five components, you can use CVP analysis to compute the remaining unknown amount. Therefore, CVP helps managers discover how changes in any of these components will affect their businesses.

## CVP Assumptions

CVP analysis assumes the following:

1. A change in volume is the only factor that affects costs.
2. Managers can classify each cost (or the components of mixed costs) as either variable or fixed. These costs are linear throughout the relevant range of volume.
3. Revenues are linear throughout the relevant range of volume.
4. Inventory levels will not change.
5. The sales mix of products will not change. Sales mix is the combination of products that make up total sales. For example, Maplewood may sell 40% boarding services, 25% summer camp lessons, and 35% riding lessons. If the contribution margin differs across products, changes in sales mix will affect CVP analysis.

## A CVP Example: Kay Martin

Kay Martin, an entrepreneur, has just started a retail business selling art posters on the internet. Kay is a "virtual retailer" and carries no inventory. Her software tabulates all customer orders each day and then automatically places the order to buy posters from a wholesaler. She buys only what she needs to fill the prior day's sales orders. The posters cost $21 each and Kay sells them for $35 each. Customers pay the shipping costs, so there are no other variable selling costs. Monthly fixed costs for server leasing and maintenance, software, and office rental total $7,000. Kay's relevant range extends from 0 to 2,000 posters a month. Beyond this volume, Kay will need to hire an employee and upgrade her Website software in order to handle the increased volume.

**Kay Martin's Business Meets the CVP Assumptions***

1. **A change in volume is the only factor that affects costs.** In Kay's business, costs are expected to increase only if volume increases. ✓
2. **Managers can classify each cost (or the components of mixed costs) as either variable or fixed. These costs are linear throughout the relevant range of volume.** In Kay's business, variable costs are $21 per poster and fixed costs are $7,000 per month. These costs are expected to remain the same unless Kay's volume exceeds 2,000 posters per month. Thus, we could draw each of these costs as a straight line on a graph. ✓
3. **Revenues are linear throughout the relevant range of volume.** In Kay's business, each poster generates $35 of sales revenue, with no volume discounts. Therefore, revenue could be graphed as a straight line beginning at the origin and sloping upward at a rate of $35 per poster sold. ✓
4. **Inventory levels will not change.** Kay keeps no inventory. If she did, CVP analysis would still work as long as Kay did not allow her inventory levels to greatly fluctuate from one period to the next. ✓
5. **The sales mix of products will not change. Sales mix is the combination of products that make up total sales. For example, Art.com may sell 15% posters, 25% unframed photographs, and 60% framed prints. If profits differ across products, changes in sales mix will affect CVP analysis.** Kay currently offers only one size of poster, so her sales mix is 100% posters. Later in this chapter we will expand her product offerings to illustrate how sales mix impacts CVP analysis. ✓

## The Unit Contribution Margin

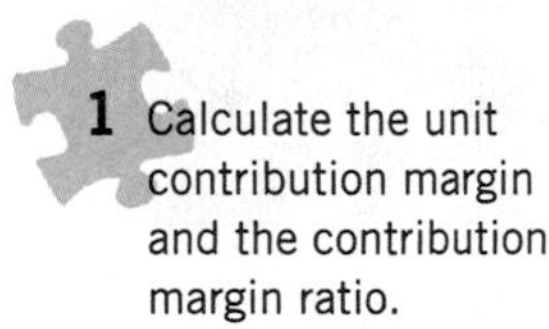

Calculate the unit contribution margin and the contribution margin ratio.

The previous chapter introduced the contribution margin income statement, which separates costs by behaviour rather than function. Many managers prefer the **contribution margin income statement** because it details the information for a CVP analysis in a ready-to-use format. On these income statements, the contribution margin is the dividing line—all variable expenses go above the line and all fixed expenses go below the line. The results of Kay's first month of operations are shown in Exhibit 4-2.

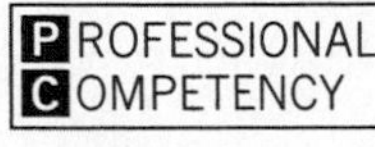


**EXHIBIT 4-2** Contribution Margin Income Statement

| KAY MARTIN POSTERS<br>**Contribution Margin Income Statement**<br>Month Ended August 31 | |
|---|---|
| Sales revenue (550 posters) | $ 19,250 |
| Less: Variable expenses | (11,550) |
| Contribution margin | 7,700 |
| Less: Fixed expenses | (7,000) |
| Operating income | $ 700 |

*From *Managerial Accounting* by Karen Wilken Braun and Wendy M. Tietz.,Published by Prentice Hall, © 2015.

Notice that the contribution margin is the excess of sales revenue over variable expenses. The contribution margin tells managers how much revenue is left—after paying variable expenses—for *contributing* toward covering fixed costs and then generating a profit, hence the name *contribution margin.*

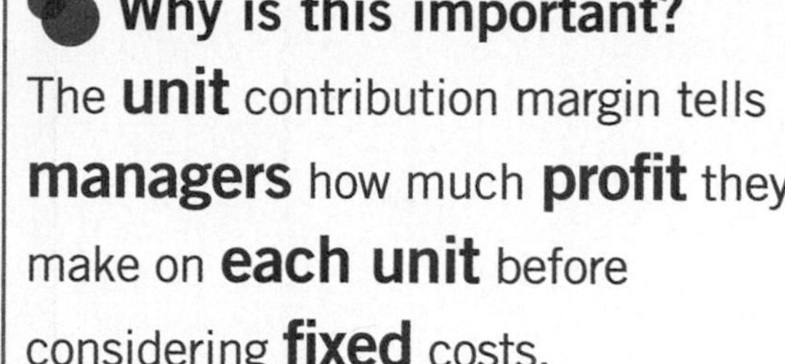


The contribution margin is stated as a total amount on the contribution margin income statement. However, managers often state the contribution margin on a per-unit basis and as a percentage or ratio. A product's **contribution margin per unit**—or **unit contribution margin**—is the excess of the selling price per unit over the variable cost of obtaining and selling each unit. Some businesses pay a sales commission on each unit or have other variable costs, such as shipping costs, for each unit sold. However, Kay's variable cost per unit is simply the price she pays for each poster. Therefore, her unit contribution margin is as follows:

| | |
|---|---|
| Sales price per poster | $ 35 |
| Less: Variable cost per poster | (21) |
| Contribution margin per poster | $ 14 |

The unit contribution margin indicates how much profit each unit provides before fixed costs are considered. Each unit first contributes this profit toward covering the firm's fixed costs. Once the company sells enough units to cover its fixed costs, the unit contribution margin contributes *directly* to profit. For example, every poster Kay sells generates $14 of contribution margin that can be used to pay for the monthly $7,000 of fixed costs. After Kay sells enough posters to cover fixed costs, each additional poster she sells will generate $14 of operating income.

Managers can use the contribution margin per unit to quickly forecast income at any volume within their relevant range. First, they project the total contribution margin by multiplying the unit contribution margin by the number of units they expect to sell. Then, they subtract fixed costs. For example, let us assume that Kay hopes to sell 650 posters next month. She can project her operating income as follows:

| | |
|---|---|
| Contribution margin (650 posters × $14 per poster) | $ 9,100 |
| Less: Fixed expenses | (7,000) |
| Operating income | $ 2,100 |

If Kay sells 650 posters next month, her operating income should be $2,100.

## The Contribution Margin Ratio

In addition to computing the unit contribution margin, managers often compute the **contribution margin ratio**, which is the ratio of contribution margin to sales revenue. Kay can compute her contribution margin ratio at the unit level as follows:

$$\text{Contribution margin ratio} = \frac{\text{Unit contribution margin}}{\text{Sales price per unit}} = \frac{\$14}{\$35} = 40\%$$

Kay could also compute the contribution margin ratio using any volume of sales. Let's use her current sales volume, shown in Exhibit 4-2:

$$\text{Contribution margin ratio} = \frac{\text{Contribution margin}}{\text{Sales revenue}} = \frac{\$7{,}700}{\$19{,}250} = 40\%$$

EXHIBIT 4-3 Breakdown of $1 of Sales Revenue

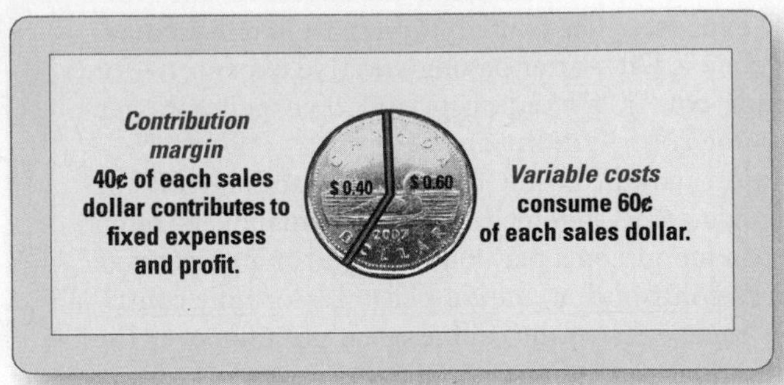


*The contribution margin ratio is the percentage of each sales dollar that is available for covering fixed expenses and generating a profit.* As shown in Exhibit 4-3, each $1.00 of sales revenue contributes $0.40 toward fixed expenses and profit, while the remaining $0.60 of each sales dollar is used to pay for variable costs.

Managers can also use the contribution margin ratio to quickly forecast operating income within the relevant range. When using the contribution margin ratio, managers project income based on sales *dollars* (revenue) rather than sales *units*. For example, if Kay generates $70,000 of sales revenue one month, she can estimate her operating income by multiplying her projected sales revenue by the contribution margin ratio to get the total contribution margin. Then she subtracts fixed expenses:

| | |
|---|---|
| Contribution margin ($70,000 sales × 40%) | $28,000 |
| Less: Fixed expenses | (7,000) |
| Operating income | $21,000 |

To verify this estimation, we can calculate Kay's contribution margin income statement. If Kay has $70,000 of sales revenue, she has sold 2,000 posters ($70,000 ÷ $35 per poster).

| | |
|---|---|
| Sales revenue (2,000 posters × $35/poster) | $ 70,000 |
| Less: Variable expenses (2,000 posters × $21/poster) | (42,000) |
| Contribution margin (2,000 posters × $14/poster) | $ 28,000 |
| Less: Fixed expenses | (7,000) |
| Operating income | $ 21,000 |

The contribution margin per unit and contribution margin ratio help managers quickly and easily project income at different sales volumes. However, when projecting profits, managers must keep in mind the relevant range. For instance, if Kay wants to project income at a volume of 5,000 posters, she should not use the existing contribution margin and fixed costs. Her current relevant range extends to only 2,000 posters per month. At a higher volume of sales, her variable cost per unit may be lower than $21 (due to volume discounts from her suppliers) and her monthly fixed costs may be higher than $7,000 (due to upgrading her system and hiring an employee to handle the extra sales volume).

Rather than using the individual unit contribution margins on each of their products, large companies that offer hundreds or thousands of products use their contribution margin *ratio* to predict profits. As long as the sales mix remains constant (a CVP assumption), the contribution margin ratio will remain constant.

We have seen how managers use the contribution margin to project income. However, managers use the contribution margin for other purposes too, such as motivating the sales force. Salespeople who know the contribution margin of each product can generate more profit by emphasizing high-margin products. This is why many companies base sales commissions on the contribution margins produced by sales rather than on sales revenue alone.

# CVP and the Break-even Point

2 Use CVP analysis to find break-even points and target profit volumes.

A company's <u>break-even point</u> is the sales level at which *operating income is zero*. Sales below the break-even point result in a loss. Sales above the break-even point provide a profit. Before Kay started her business, she wanted to figure out how many posters she would have to sell just to break even.

There are three ways to calculate the break-even point:

1. The income statement approach
2. The shortcut approach using the *unit* contribution margin
3. The shortcut approach using the contribution margin *ratio*

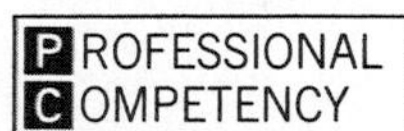


All of the approaches are based on the income statement, so they all reach the same conclusion. The first two methods find break-even in terms of sales *units*. The last approach finds break-even in terms of sales *dollars* (sales *revenue*).

Let's examine these three approaches in detail.

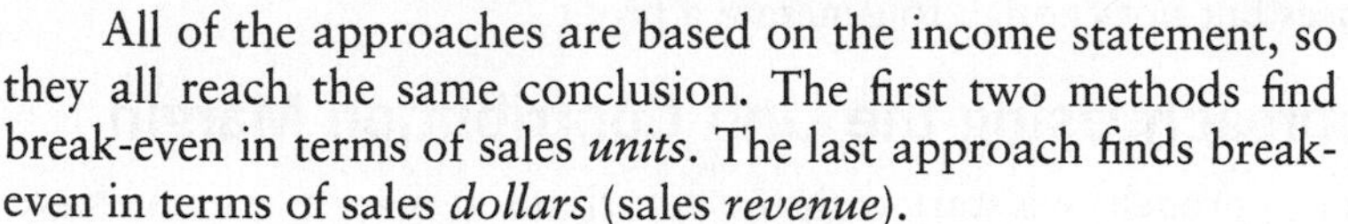

**Why is this important?**
Businesses **don't** want to operate at a **loss**. CVP analysis helps **managers** figure how many units they need to sell **just** to **break even**.

## The Income Statement Approach

The income statement approach starts with the contribution margin income statement and then breaks it down into smaller components:

| SALES REVENUE | − | VARIABLE EXPENSES | − FIXED EXPENSES | = | OPERATING INCOME |
|---|---|---|---|---|---|
| (Sales price per unit × Units sold) | − | (Variable cost per unit × Units sold) | − Fixed expenses | = | Operating income |

This approach can be used to find Kay's break-even point. Recall that Kay sells her posters for $35 each and that her variable cost is $21 per poster. Kay's fixed expenses total $7,000. At the break-even point, operating income is zero. This information can be used to solve the income statement equation for the number of posters Kay must sell to break even.

| SALES REVENUE | − | VARIABLE EXPENSES | − FIXED EXPENSES | = | OPERATING INCOME |
|---|---|---|---|---|---|
| (Sales price per unit × Units sold) | − | (Variable cost per unit × Units sold) | − Fixed expenses | = | Operating income |
| ($35 × Units sold) | − | ($21 × Units sold) − | $7,000 | = | $ 0 |
| ($35 | − | $21) × Units sold) − | $7,000 | = | $ 0 |
| | | $14 × Units sold | | = | $7,000 |
| | | Units sold | | | $7,000/$14 |
| | | Sales in units | | = | 500 Posters |

Kay must sell 500 posters to break even. Her break-even point in sales dollars is $17,500 (500 posters × $35).

Check the answer by substituting the break-even number of units into the income statement and checking that this level of sales results in zero profit:

| | |
|---|---|
| Sales revenue (500 posters × $35) | $ 17,500 |
| Less: Variable expenses (500 posters × $21) | (10,500) |
| Contribution margin | $ 7,000 |
| Less: Fixed expenses | (7,000) |
| Operating income | $ 0 |

Notice that at break-even, a firm's fixed expenses ($7,000) equal its contribution margin ($7,000). In other words, the firm has generated *just* enough contribution margin to cover its fixed expenses but *not* enough to generate a profit.

## The Shortcut Approach Using the Unit Contribution Margin

To develop the shortcut approach, we start with the contribution margin income statement and then rearrange some of its terms:

SALES REVENUE − VARIABLE EXPENSES − FIXED EXPENSES = OPERATING INCOME

| | | | |
|---|---|---|---|
| Contribution margin | − | Fixed expenses | = Operating income |
| Contribution margin | | | = Fixed expenses + Operating income |
| (Contribution margin per unit × Units sold) | | | = Fixed expenses + Operating income |

As a final step, divide both sides of the equation by the contribution margin per unit.

$$\text{Sales in units} = \frac{\text{Fixed expenses} + \text{Operating income}}{\text{Contribution margin per unit}}$$

Kay can use this approach to find her break-even point in units. Kay's fixed expenses total $7,000, and her unit contribution margin is $14. At the break-even point, operating income is zero. Thus, Kay's break-even point in units is

$$\text{Sales in units} = \frac{\$7{,}000 + \$0}{\$14}$$
$$= 500 \text{ posters}$$

Why does this approach work? Recall that each poster provides $14 of contribution margin. To break even, Kay must generate enough contribution margin to cover $7,000 of fixed expenses. At the rate of $14 per poster, Kay must sell 500 posters ($7,000 ÷ $14) to cover her $7,000 of fixed expenses. Because the shortcut formula simply rearranges the income statement equation, the break-even point is the same under both methods (500 posters).

### TRY IT!

Rachel runs her own hot dog stand on the U of A campus. The monthly cost of the cart rental and business permit is $300. Rachel spends $0.50 on each hot dog sold, including bun and condiments. She sells each hot dog for dog for $2.00.

1. What is the contribution margin per unit?
2. What is the contribution margin ratio?
3. Predict operating income for a month in which Rachel sells 1,000 hot dogs.

Please see page 243 for solutions.

## STOP & THINK

What would Kay's operating income be if she sold 501 posters? What would it be if she sold 600 posters?

**Answer:** Every poster sold provides $14 of contribution margin, which contributes first toward covering fixed costs, then to profit. Once Kay reaches her break-even point (500 posters), she has covered all fixed costs. Therefore, each additional poster sold after the break-even point contributes $14 *directly to profit.* If Kay sells 501 posters, she has sold one more poster than break-even. Her operating income is $14. If she sells 600 posters, she has sold 100 more posters than break-even. Her operating income is $1,400 ($14 per poster × 100 posters). We can verify this as follows:

| | |
|---|---|
| Contribution margin (600 posters × $14 per poster) | $ 8,400 |
| Less: Fixed expenses | (7,000) |
| Operating income | $ 1,400 |

*Once a company achieves break-even, each additional unit sold contributes its unique unit contribution margin directly to profit.*

## The Shortcut Approach Using the Contribution Margin Ratio

It is easy to compute the break-even point in *units* for a simple business like Kay's that has only one product. It is more difficult for companies that have more than one product or service such as Bombardier and Black Fly Beverage Company. Multiproduct companies usually compute break-even in terms of sales dollars (revenue).

To calculate break-even in terms of dollars, fixed expenses plus operating income are divided by the contribution margin *ratio* (not by contribution margin *per unit*) to yield sales in *dollars* (not *units*):

$$\text{Sales in dollars} = \frac{\text{Fixed expenses} + \text{Operating income}}{\text{Contribution margin ratio}}$$

Recall that Kay's contribution margin ratio is 40%. At the break-even point, operating income is $0, so Kay's break-even point in sales revenue is as follows:

$$\begin{aligned}\text{Sales in dollars} &= \frac{\$7,000 + \$0}{0.40}\\ &= \$17,500\end{aligned}$$

This is the same break-even sales revenue calculated earlier (500 posters × $35 sales price = $17,500). Each dollar of Kay's sales contributes $0.40 to fixed expenses and profit. To break even, she must generate enough contribution margin at the rate of $0.40 per sales dollar to cover the $7,000 fixed expenses ($7,000 ÷ 0.40 = $17,500).

*To recall which formula gives which result, remember this: Dividing fixed costs by the **unit** contribution margin provides break-even in sales **units**. Dividing fixed costs by the contribution margin **ratio** provides break-even in sales **dollars**.*

**TRY IT!**

Rachel runs her own hot dog stand on the U of A campus. The monthly cost of the cart rental and business permit is $300. Rachel's contribution margin per unit is $1.50 and contribution margin ratio is 75%.

1. How many hot dogs does Rachel need to sell each month to break even?
2. How much sales revenue does Rachel need to generate each month to break even?

Please see page 244 for solutions.

## Calculating the Volume Needed to Earn a Target Profit

**Why is this important?**
**Companies** want to a make profit. **CVP** analysis helps **managers** determine **how many** units they need to sell to earn a **target** amount of **profit**.

For established products and services, managers are more interested in the sales level needed to earn a target profit than in the break-even point. Managers of new business ventures are also interested in the profits they can expect to earn. For example, Kay does not want to just break even—she wants her business to be profitable. She would like the business to earn $4,900 of profit each month. How many posters must Kay sell each month to reach her target profit?

### Sales and the Target Profit

The only difference from our prior analysis is that instead of determining the sales level needed for zero profit (break-even), Kay now wants to know how many posters she must sell to earn a $4,900 profit. You will note that we substitute operating income for profit in order to eliminate the impact of taxes.[1] We can use the income statement approach or the shortcut approach to find the answer. Because Kay wants to know the number of units, we will use the shortcut formula based on the unit contribution margin. This time, instead of an operating income of zero (break-even), we will insert Kay's target operating income of $4,900:

$$\text{Sales in } \textit{units} = \frac{\text{Fixed expenses} + \text{Operating income}}{\text{Contribution margin } \textit{per unit}}$$

$$= \frac{\$7{,}000 + \$4{,}900}{\$14}$$

$$= \frac{\$11{,}900}{\$14}$$

$$= 850 \text{ posters}$$

This analysis shows that Kay must sell 850 posters each month to earn profits of $4,900 a month. Notice that this level of sales falls within Kay's current relevant range (0–2,000 posters per month), so the conclusion that she would earn $4,900 of income at this sales volume is valid. If the calculation resulted in a sales volume outside the current relevant range (greater than 2,000 units) we would need to reassess our cost assumptions.

Assume that Kay also wants to know how much sales revenue she needs in order to earn $4,900 of monthly profit. Because she already knows the number of units needed (850), she can easily translate this volume into sales revenue:

$$850 \text{ posters} \times \$35 \text{ sales price/poster} = \$29{,}750 \text{ sales revenue}$$

[1]If you are given an after-tax profit target, you need to convert that to a before-tax amount and then insert the before-tax profit amount into the formula.

If Kay only wanted to know the sales revenue needed to achieve her target profit, rather than the number of units needed, she could have found the answer directly by using the shortcut formula based on the contribution margin *ratio*:

$$\text{Sales in } \textit{dollars} = \frac{\text{Fixed expenses} + \text{Operating income}}{\text{Contribution margin } \textit{ratio}}$$

$$= \frac{\$7{,}000 + \$4{,}900}{0.40}$$

$$= \frac{\$11{,}900}{0.40}$$

$$= \$29{,}750$$

Finally, Kay could have used the income statement approach to find the same answers:

| SALES REVENUE | – | VARIABLE EXPENSES | – | FIXED EXPENSES | = | OPERATING INCOME |
|---|---|---|---|---|---|---|
| (\$35 × Units sold) | – | (\$21 × Units sold) | – | \$7,000 | = | \$ 4,900 |
| (\$35 | – | \$21) × Units sold | – | \$7,000 | = | \$ 4,900 |
| | | \$14 × Units sold | | | = | \$11,900 |
| | | | | Units sold | = | \$11,900/\$14 |
| | | | | Units sold | = | 850 posters |

We can prove that our answers (from any of the three approaches) are correct by preparing Kay's income statement for a sales volume of 850 units:

| | |
|---|---|
| Sales revenue (850 posters × \$35) | \$ 29,750 |
| Less: Variable expenses (850 posters × \$21) | (17,850) |
| Contribution margin | \$ 11,900 |
| Less: Fixed expenses | (7,000) |
| Operating income | \$ 4,900 |

## Graphing CVP Relationships

By graphing the CVP relationships for her business, Kay can see at a glance how changes in the levels of sales will affect profits. As in the previous chapter, the volume of units (posters) is placed on the x-axis, while dollars is placed on the y-axis. Then, she follows five steps to graph the CVP relations for her business, as illustrated in Exhibit 4-4.

**STEP 1: Choose a sales volume, such as 1,000 posters.**

Plot the point for total sales revenue at that volume: 1,000 posters × \$35 per poster = sales of \$35,000. Draw the *sales revenue line* from the origin (0) through the \$35,000 point. Why does the sales revenue line start at the origin? If Kay does not sell any posters, there is no sales revenue.

**STEP 2: Draw the *fixed expense line*, a horizontal line that intersects the y-axis at \$7,000.**

Recall that the fixed expense line is flat because fixed expenses are the same (\$7,000) no matter how many posters Kay sells within her relevant range (up to 2,000 posters per month).

**STEP 3: Draw the *total expense line*.**

Total expense is the sum of variable expense plus fixed expense. Thus, total expense is a mixed cost, so the total expense line follows the form of the mixed cost line. Begin by computing variable expense at the chosen sales volume: 1,000 posters × \$21 per poster = variable expense of \$21,000. Add variable expense to fixed expense: \$21,000 + \$7,000 = \$28,000. Plot the total expense point

**EXHIBIT 4-4** Cost-Volume-Profit Graph

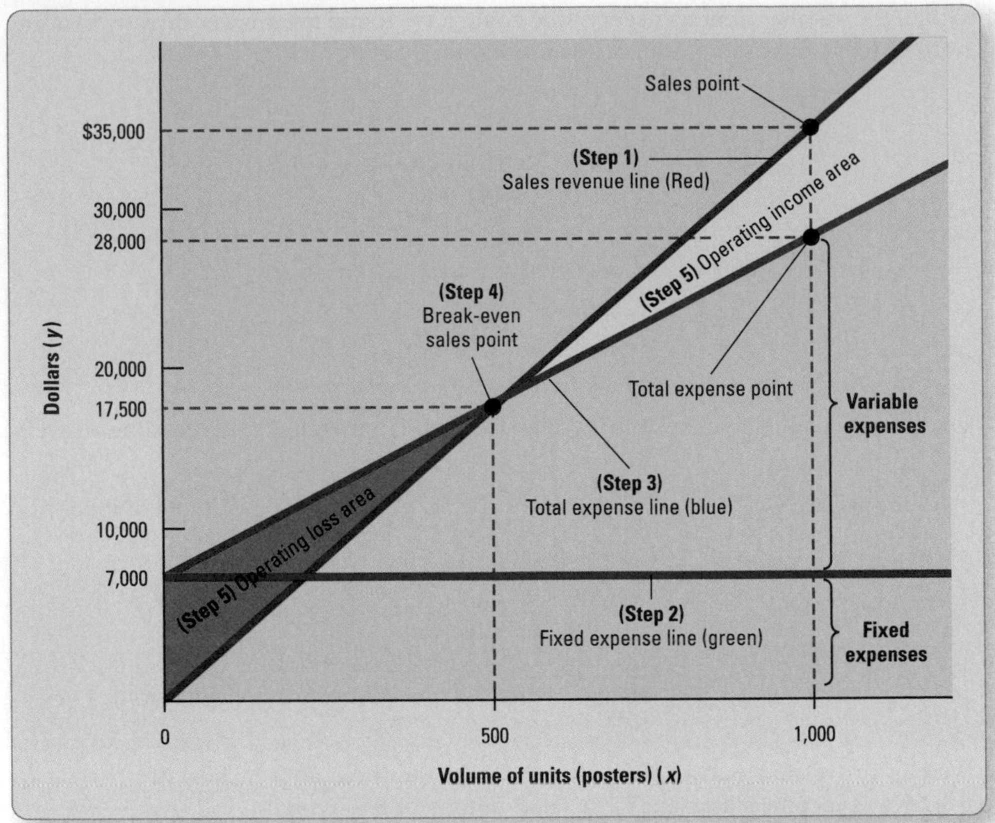


($28,000) for 1,000 units. Then, draw a line through this point from the $7,000 fixed expense intercept on the y-axis. This is the total expense line. Why does the total expense line start at the fixed expense line? If Kay sells no posters, she still incurs the $7,000 fixed cost for the server leasing, software, and office rental, but she incurs no variable costs.

**STEP 4: Identify the *break-even point.***

The break-even point is the point where the sales revenue line intersects the total expense line. This is the point where sales revenue equals total expenses. Our previous analyses told us that Kay's break-even point is 500 posters, or $17,500 in sales. The graph shows this information visually.

**STEP 5: Mark the *operating income* and the *operating loss* areas on the graph.**

To the left of the break-even point, the total expense line lies above the sales revenue line. Expenses exceed sales revenue, leading to an operating loss. If Kay sells only 300 posters, she incurs an operating loss. The amount of the loss is the vertical distance between the total expense line and the sales revenue line:

| SALES REVENUE | – | VARIABLE EXPENSES | – | FIXED EXPENSES | = | OPERATING INCOME (LOSS) |
|---|---|---|---|---|---|---|
| (300 × $35) | – | (300 × $21) | – | $7,000 | = | $(2,800) |

To the right of the break-even point, the business earns a profit. The vertical distance between the sales revenue line and the total expense line equals income. Exhibit 4-4 shows that if Kay sells 1,000 posters, she earns operating income of $7,000 ($35,000 sales revenue – $28,000 total expenses).

Why bother with a graph? Why not just use the income statement approach or the shortcut approach? Graphs like Exhibit 4-4 help managers visualize profit or loss over a range of volume. The income statement and shortcut approaches estimate income or loss for only a single sales volume.

# DECISION GUIDELINES

## CVP Analysis

Your friend wants to open her own ice cream parlour after her post-secondary education. She needs help making the following decisions.

| Decision | Guidelines |
|---|---|
| How do I determine what I will earn? | You need to determine the selling price in order to provide a specific amount of earnings on each unit. The unit contribution margin shows managers how much they earn on each unit sold after paying for variable costs *but before considering fixed expenses.* The unit contribution margin is the amount each unit earns that contributes toward covering fixed expenses and generating a profit. It is computed as follows:<br><br>Sales price per unit<br>Less: Variable cost per unit<br>Contribution margin per unit<br><br>The contribution margin ratio shows managers how much contribution margin is earned on every $1 of sales. It is computed as follows:<br><br>$\text{Contribution margin ratio} = \frac{\text{Contribution margin}}{\text{Sales revenue}}$ |
| How do I decide between using a traditional format and a contribution margin format for my income statement? | The contribution margin concept allows managers to forecast income quickly at different sales volumes. First, find the total contribution margin (by multiplying the forecasted number of units by the unit contribution margin *or* by multiplying the forecasted sales revenue by the contribution margin ratio) and then subtract all fixed expenses.<br>Using a traditional approach would require the creation of the entire financial statement. |
| I would like to at least break even or even earn a profit. How do I determine the number of ice cream cones I need to sell? | **Income Statement Approach:**<br><br>$\text{SALES REVENUE} - \text{VARIABLE EXPENSES} - \text{FIXED EXPENSES} = \text{OPERATING INCOME}$<br>$\begin{pmatrix}\text{Sale price per unit}\\ \times \text{ Units sold}\end{pmatrix} - \begin{pmatrix}\text{Variable cost per unit}\\ \times \text{ Units sold}\end{pmatrix} - \text{Fixed expenses} = \text{Operating income}$<br><br>**Shortcut Unit Contribution Margin Approach:**<br><br>$\text{Sales in } \textit{units} = \frac{\text{Fixed expenses} + \text{Operating income}}{\text{Contribution margin } \textit{per unit}}$ |
| How can I compute the dollars of sales revenue I will have to generate to break even or earn a target profit? | **Shortcut Contribution Margin Ratio Approach:**<br><br>$\text{Sales in } \textit{dollars} = \frac{\text{Fixed expenses} + \text{Operating income}}{\text{Contribution margin } \textit{ratio}}$ |
| I would like to view my profits over a range of volumes. What tool can I use to facilitate this? | CVP graphs show managers, at a glance, how different sales volumes will affect profits. |

# SUMMARY PROBLEM 1

Fleet Foot buys hiking socks for $6 a pair and sells them for $10. Management budgets monthly fixed expenses of $10,000 for sales volumes between zero and 12,000 pairs.

### Requirements

1. Use the income statement approach and the shortcut unit contribution margin approach to compute monthly break-even sales in units.
2. Use the shortcut contribution margin ratio approach to compute the break-even point in sales dollars.
3. Compute the monthly sales level (in units) required to earn a target operating income of $14,000. Use either the income statement approach or the shortcut contribution margin approach.
4. Prepare a graph of Fleet Foot's CVP relationships similar to Exhibit 4-4. Draw the sales revenue line, the fixed expense line, and the total expense line. Label the axes, the break-even point, the operating income area, and the operating loss area.

## ▪ SOLUTION

### Requirement 1

**Income Statement Approach:**

SALES REVENUE − VARIABLE EXPENSES − FIXED EXPENSES = OPERATING INCOME

$$\left(\text{Sales price per unit} \times \text{Units sold}\right) - \left(\text{Variable cost per unit} \times \text{Units sold}\right) - \text{Fixed expenses} = \text{Operating income}$$

$$(\$10 \times \text{Units sold}) - (\$6 \times \text{Units sold}) - \$10{,}000 = \$\ 0$$

$$(\$10 - \$6) \times \text{Units sold} = \$10{,}000$$

$$\$4 \times \text{Units sold} = \$10{,}000$$

$$\text{Units sold} = \$10{,}000 \div \$4$$

$$\text{Break-even sales in units} = 2{,}500 \text{ units}$$

**Shortcut Unit Contribution Margin Approach:**

$$\text{Sales in units} = \frac{\text{Fixed expenses} + \text{Operating income}}{\text{Contribution margin per unit}}$$

$$= \frac{\$10{,}000 + \$0}{(\$10 - \$6)}$$

$$= \frac{\$10{,}000}{\$4}$$

$$= 2{,}500 \text{ units}$$

### Requirement 2

$$\text{Sales in dollars} = \frac{\text{Fixed expenses} + \text{Operating income}}{\text{Contribution margin ratio}}$$

$$= \frac{\$10{,}000 + \$0}{0.40^*}$$

$$= \$25{,}000$$

$$*\text{Contribution margin ratio} = \frac{\text{Contribution margin per unit}}{\text{Sales price per unit}} = \frac{\$4}{\$10} = 0.40$$

**Requirement 3**

**Income Statement Approach:**

| SALES REVENUE | – | VARIABLE EXPENSES | – FIXED EXPENSES | = OPERATING INCOME |
|---|---|---|---|---|
| (Sales price per unit × Units sold) | – | (Variable cost per unit × Units sold) | – Fixed expenses | = Operating income |
| (\$10 × Units sold) | – | (\$6 × Units sold) | – \$10,000 | = \$14,000 |
| (\$10 | – | \$6) × Units sold | | = \$10,000 + \$14,000 |
| | | \$4 × Units sold | | = \$24,000 |
| | | Units sold | | = \$24,000 ÷ \$4 |
| | | Units sold | | = 6,000 units |

**Shortcut Unit Contribution Margin Approach:**

$$\text{Sales in units} = \frac{\text{Fixed expenses} + \text{Operating income}}{\text{Contribution margin per unit}}$$

$$= \frac{\$10,000 + \$14,000}{(\$10 - \$6)}$$

$$= \frac{\$24,000}{\$4}$$

$$= 6,000 \text{ units}$$

**Requirement 4**

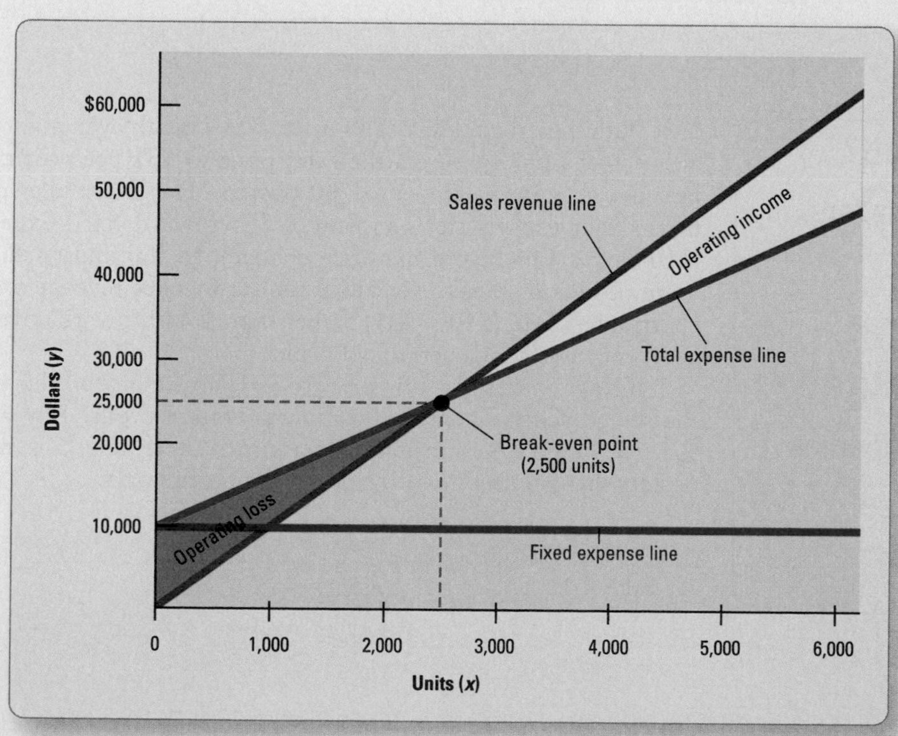

# The CVP as a Tool to Plan for Changing Business Conditions

**3** Perform sensitivity analysis in response to changing business conditions.

In today's fast-changing business world, managers need to be prepared for increasing costs, pricing pressure from competitors, and other changing business conditions.

Managers use CVP analysis to conduct **sensitivity analysis**. Sensitivity analysis is a "what-if" technique that asks what results will be if actual prices or costs change, or if an underlying assumption such as sales mix changes. For example, increased competition may force Kay to lower her sales price, while at the same time her suppliers increase poster costs. How will these changes affect Kay's break-even and target profit volumes? What will happen if Kay changes her sales mix by offering posters in two different sizes? We will tackle these issues next.

## Changing the Sales Price

Let's assume that Kay has now been in business for several months. Because of competition, Kay is considering cutting her sales price to $31 per poster. If her variable expenses remain at $21 per poster and her fixed expenses stay at $7,000, how many posters will she need to sell to break even? To answer this question, Kay calculates a new unit contribution margin using the new sales price:

| | |
|---|---|
| New sales price per poster | $ 31 |
| Less: Variable cost per poster | (21) |
| New contribution margin per poster | $ 10 |

She then uses the new unit contribution margin to compute break-even sales in units:

$$\text{Sales in units} = \frac{\text{Fixed expenses} + \text{Operating income}}{\text{Contribution margin per unit}}$$

$$= \frac{\$7{,}000 + \$0}{\$10}$$

$$= 700 \text{ posters}$$

**Why is this important?**

**CVP analysis** helps managers prepare for and respond to **economic** changes, such as increasing costs and **pressure** to drop sales prices, so companies can remain **competitive** and **profitable**.

With the original $35 sales price, Kay's break-even point was 500 posters. If Kay lowers the sales price to $31 per poster, her break-even point increases to 700 posters. The lower sales price means that each poster contributes *less* toward fixed expenses ($10 versus $14 before the price change), so Kay must sell 200 *more* posters to break even. Each dollar of sales revenue would contribute $0.32 ($10 ÷ $31) rather than $0.40 toward covering fixed expenses and generating a profit.

If Kay reduces her sales price to $31, how many posters must she sell to achieve her $4,900 monthly target profit? Kay again uses the new unit contribution margin to determine how many posters she will need to sell to reach her profit goals:

$$\text{Sales in units} = \frac{\$7{,}000 + \$4{,}900}{\$10}$$

$$= 1{,}190 \text{ posters}$$

With the original sales price, Kay needed to sell only 850 posters per month to achieve her target profit level. If Kay cuts her sales price (and, therefore, her contribution margin), she must sell more posters to achieve her financial goals. Kay could have found these same results using the income statement approach. Exhibit 4-5 shows the effect of changes in sales price on break-even and target profit volumes.

**EXHIBIT 4-5** The Effect of Changes in Sales Price on Break-even and Target Profit Volumes

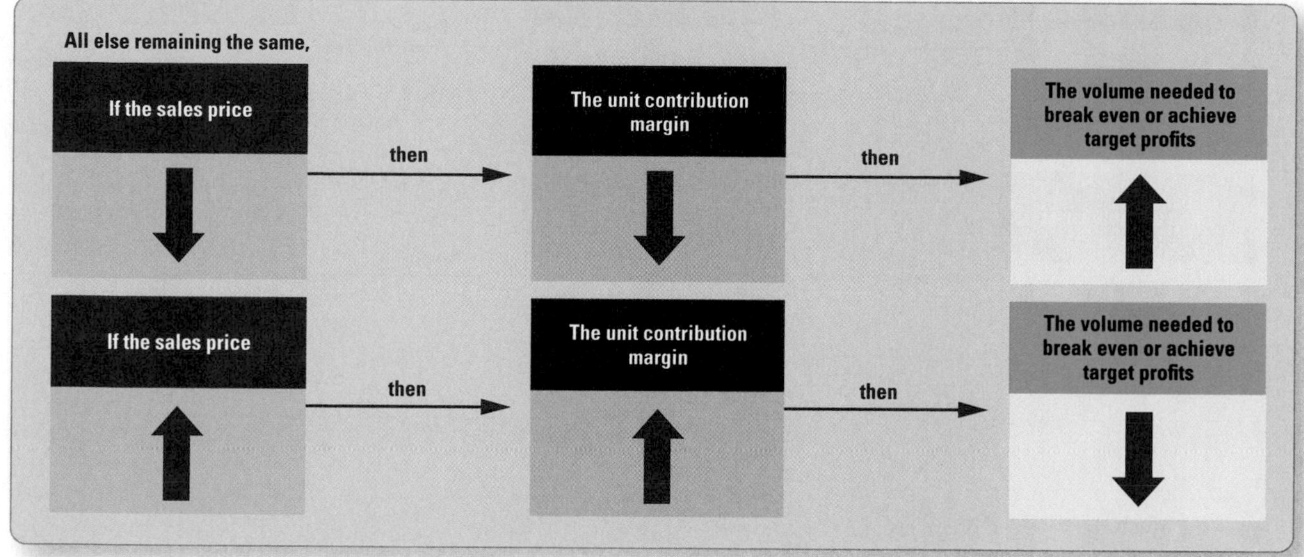


## STOP & THINK

Kay believes she could dominate the e-commerce art poster business if she cut the sales price to $20. Is this a good idea?

**Answer:** No. The variable cost per poster is $21. If Kay sells posters for $20 each, she loses $1 on each poster. Kay will incur a loss if the sales price is less than the variable cost.

## Changing Variable Costs

Let's assume that Kay does *not* lower her sales price. However, Kay's supplier raises the price for each poster to $23.80 (instead of the original $21). Kay does not want to pass this increase on to her customers, so she holds her sales price at the original $35 per poster. Her fixed costs remain $7,000. How many posters must she sell to break even after her supplier raises the prices? Kay's new contribution margin per unit drops to $11.20 ($35 sales price per poster – $23.80 variable cost per poster). So, her new break-even point is as follows:

$$\text{Sales in units} = \frac{\text{Fixed expenses} + \text{Operating income}}{\text{Contribution margin per unit}}$$

$$= \frac{\$7{,}000 + \$0}{\$11.20}$$

$$= 625 \text{ posters}$$

Higher variable costs per unit have the same effect as lower selling prices per unit—they both reduce the product's unit contribution margin. As a result, Kay has to sell *more* units to break even and achieve target profits. As shown in Exhibit 4-6, a *decrease* in variable costs has the opposite effect. Lower variable costs increase the contribution margin each poster provides and, therefore, lowers the break-even point.

**EXHIBIT 4-6** The Effect of Changes in Variable Costs on Break-even and Target Profit Volumes

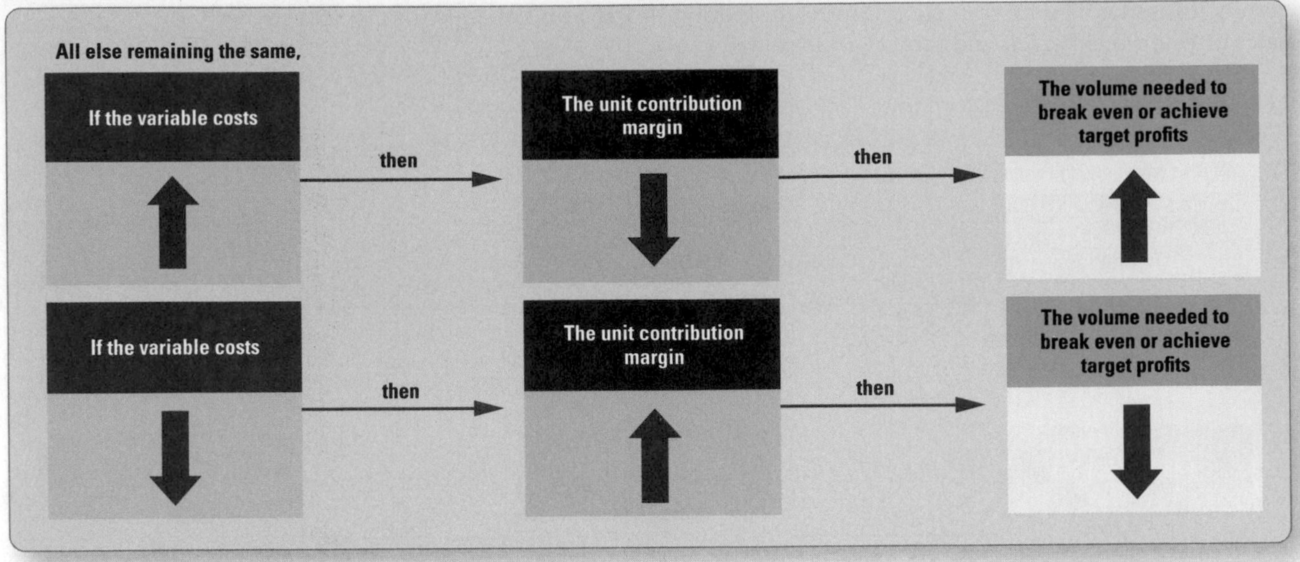


## STOP & THINK

Suppose Kay is squeezed from both sides: Her supply costs have increased to $23.80 per poster, yet she must lower her price to $31 in order to compete. Under these conditions, how many posters will Kay need to sell to achieve her monthly target profit of $4,900? If Kay does not think she can sell that many posters, how else might she attempt to achieve her profit goals?

**Answer:** Kay is now in a position faced by many companies—her unit contribution margin is squeezed by both higher supply costs and lower sales prices.

| | |
|---|---|
| New sales price per poster | $ 31.00 |
| Less: New variable cost per poster | (23.80) |
| New contribution margin per poster | $ 7.20 |

Kay's new contribution margin is about half of what it was when she started her business ($14). To achieve her target profit, her volume has to increase dramatically (yet it would still fall within her current relevant range for fixed costs—which extends to 2,000 posters per month):

$$\text{Sales in units} = \frac{\text{Fixed expenses} + \text{Operating income}}{\text{Contribution margin per unit}}$$

$$= \frac{\$7{,}000 + \$4{,}900}{\$7.20}$$

$$= 1{,}653 \text{ posters (rounded)}$$

Based on her current volume, Kay may not believe she can sell so many posters. To maintain a reasonable profit level, Kay may need to take other measures. For example, she may try to find a different supplier with lower poster costs. She may also attempt to lower her fixed costs. For example, perhaps she could negotiate a cheaper lease on her office space or move her business to a less expensive location. She could also try to increase her volume by spending more on fixed costs, such as advertising. Kay could also investigate selling other products with higher unit contribution margins, in addition to her regular-size posters. We will discuss these measures next.

## Changing Fixed Costs

Let's return to Kay's original data ($35 selling price and $21 variable cost). Kay has decided she really does not need a storefront office at the retail strip mall because she does not have many walk-in customers. She could decrease her monthly fixed costs from $7,000 to $4,200 by moving her office to an industrial park.

How will this decrease in fixed costs affect Kay's break-even point? *Changes in fixed costs do not affect the contribution margin.* Therefore, Kay's unit contribution margin is still $14 per poster. However, her break-even point changes because her fixed costs change:

$$\text{Sales in units} = \frac{\text{Fixed expenses} + \text{Operating income}}{\text{Contribution margin per unit}}$$
$$= \frac{\$4{,}200 + \$0}{\$14.00}$$
$$= 300 \text{ posters}$$

Because of the decrease in fixed costs, Kay will need to sell only 300 posters, rather than 500 posters, to break even. The volume needed to achieve her monthly $4,900 target profit will also decline. However, if Kay's fixed costs increase, she will have to sell more units to break even. Exhibit 4-7 shows the effect of changes in fixed costs on break-even and target profit volumes.

**EXHIBIT 4-7** The Effect of Changes in Fixed Costs on Break-even and Target Profit Volumes

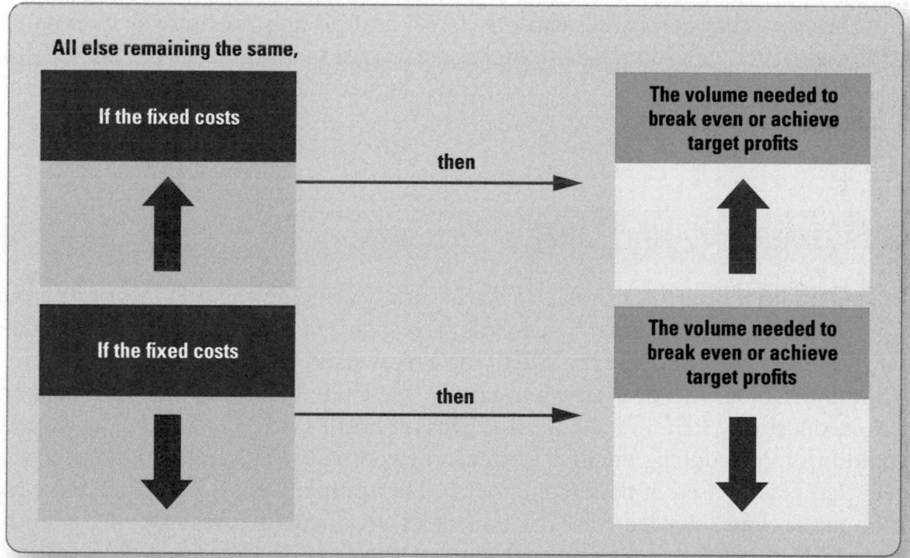


We have seen that changes in sales prices, variable costs, and fixed costs can have dramatic effects on the volume of product that companies must sell to achieve break-even and target profits. Companies often turn to automation to decrease variable costs (direct labour); but this, in turn, increases their fixed costs (equipment depreciation). Companies often move production overseas to decrease variable and fixed production costs, feeling forced to take these measures to keep their prices as low as their competitors' prices. For example, Char-Broil, the maker of gas grills, said that if it did not move production overseas, profits would decline, or worse yet, the company would go out of business.

## STOP & THINK

Kay has been considering advertising as a means to increase her sales volume. Kay could spend an extra \$3,500 per month on Website banner ads. How many *extra* posters would Kay have to sell just to pay for the advertising? (Use Kay's original data.)

**Answer:** Instead of using all of Kay's fixed costs, we can isolate just the fixed costs relating to advertising. This allows us to figure out how many extra posters Kay would have to sell each month to break even on (or pay for) the advertising cost. Advertising is a fixed cost, so Kay's contribution margin remains \$14 per unit.

$$\text{Sales in units} = \frac{\text{Fixed expenses} + \text{Operating income}}{\text{Contribution margin per unit}}$$

$$= \frac{\$3{,}500 + \$0}{\$14.00}$$

$$= 250 \text{ posters}$$

Kay must sell 250 extra posters each month just to pay for the cost of advertising. If she sells fewer than 250 extra posters, she has increased her volume but lost money on the advertising. If she sells more than 250 extra posters, her plan worked—she has increased her volume *and* her profit. Even though investing in the Website banner ads increases Kay's break-even point to 750 units (500 plus another 250 to cover the advertising costs), Kay may be willing to pay the extra \$3,500 if she expects the ads to stimulate enough extra sales to more than cover the additional advertising expense. Companies often face this issue. How many extra 12-packs of cola do you think Coca-Cola has to sell to pay for one 30-second advertisement during the Super Bowl?

Another way that companies can offset cost and pricing pressures is to expand their product lines to include products with higher contribution margins. In the next section, we will see what happens when Kay decides to sell higher-margin, large-size posters in addition to regular-size posters.

## Sustainability and CVP

Sustainability initiatives can have a significant bearing on the cost information used in CVP analysis. For example, Coca-Cola, a recognized leader in corporate sustainability, has been able to reduce the size of the cap on its PET plastic bottles by 38%, saving 18 million kilograms of plastic annually in the United States alone. The company has also reduced the PET in its Coke and Dasani bottles by 23% and 35%, respectively. In addition to reducing the PET content, the company has increased the percentage of recycled plastic used in these containers.[2] The company is also working to reduce the amount of water needed for each unit of its product. As a result of these initiatives, the variable cost of packaging each unit of product has decreased. For example, the company reports that its new ultra glass contour bottle is not only 40% stronger and 20% lighter but also 10% cheaper to produce than its traditional contour bottle.

See Exercises E4-24A and E4-48B

Coca-Cola's redesign of product packaging has had favourable environmental and financial ramifications. For example, the new ultra glass contour bottle has reduced annual $CO_2$ emissions by an amount equivalent to planting 8,000 acres of trees. From a financial standpoint, the 10% variable cost savings on the ultra glass contour design results in a 10% increase in each bottle's contribution margin. As a result, one might assume that Coca-Cola needs to sell fewer units of product to achieve its target profit. However, keep in mind that the company had to incur many

[2]The Coca-Cola Company shares its efforts at sustainability on its Website at www.coca-colacompany.com/sustainability.

fixed costs to research, develop, and design these new bottles. In addition, they probably had to invest in new production equipment to handle the new packaging design.

As the Coca-Cola example shows, sustainability initiatives often result in both cost savings *and* additional costs. These costs and cost savings may be fixed or variable in nature. Managers use CVP analysis to determine how these initiatives will impact the volume needed to achieve the company's operating income goals.

## Changing the Mix of Products Offered for Sale

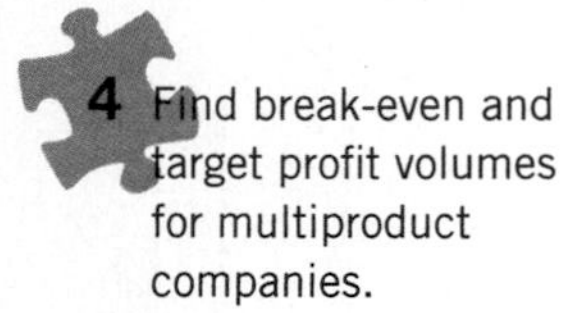

Find break-even and target profit volumes for multiproduct companies.

So far, we have assumed that Kay sold only one size of poster. What would happen if she offered different types of products? Companies that sell more than one product must consider their *sales mix* when performing CVP analysis. All else being equal, a company earns more income by selling high-contribution margin products than by selling an equal number of low-contribution margin products.

The same CVP formulas that are used to perform CVP analysis for a company with a single product can be used for any company that sells more than one product. However, the formulas use the weighted-average contribution margin of all products, rather than the contribution margin of a sole product. Each unit's contribution margin is *weighted* by the relative number of units sold. As before, the company can find the break-even or the target profit volume in terms of units or sales revenue. We will consider each in turn.

### Multiproduct Company: Finding Break-even in Terms of Sales Units

Suppose Kay plans to sell two types of posters: regular-size and large posters. Assume that none of Kay's original costs have changed. Exhibit 4-8 shows that each regular poster continues to generate \$14 of contribution margin, while each large poster generates \$30 of contribution margin. Kay is adding the large-poster line because it carries a higher unit contribution margin.

**EXHIBIT 4-8** Calculating the Weighted-average Contribution Margin per Unit

| | Regular Posters | Large Posters | Total |
|---|---|---|---|
| Sales price per unit | \$ 35 | \$ 70 | |
| Less: Variable cost per unit | (21) | (40) | |
| Contribution margin per unit | \$ 14 | \$ 30 | |
| Sales mix | × 5 | × 3 | 8 |
| Contribution margin | \$ 70 | \$ 90 | \$160 |
| Weighted-average contribution margin per unit (\$160/8) | | | \$ 20 |

For every five regular posters sold, Kay expects to sell three large posters. In other words, she expects 5/8 of the sales to be regular posters and 3/8 to be large posters. This is a 5:3 sales mix. Exhibit 4-8 shows how Kay uses this expected sales mix to find the weighted-average contribution margin per unit.

Notice that none of Kay's products actually generates \$20 of contribution margin. However, if the sales mix is 5:3, as expected, it is as if the contribution margin is \$20 per unit. Once Kay has computed the weighted-average contribution margin per unit, she uses it in the shortcut formula to determine the total number of posters that would need to be sold to break even:

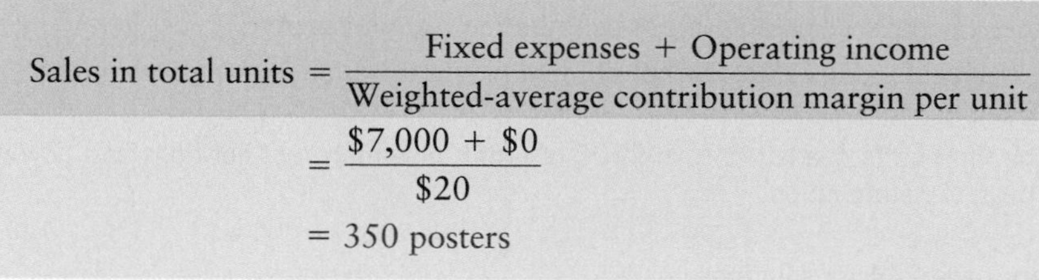

$$\text{Sales in total units} = \frac{\text{Fixed expenses} + \text{Operating income}}{\text{Weighted-average contribution margin per unit}}$$

$$= \frac{\$7{,}000 + \$0}{\$20}$$

$$= 350 \text{ posters}$$

As a final step, Kay splits the total number of posters into the regular and large sizes using the same sales-mix ratios she assumed previously:

| | |
|---|---|
| Break-even sales of regular posters (350 × 5/8) .................. | 218.75 regular posters |
| Break-even sales of large posters (350 × 3/8) ...................... | 131.25 large posters |

As is often the case in real situations, these computations do not yield round numbers. Because Kay cannot sell partial posters, she must sell 219 regular posters and 132 large posters to avoid a loss. Using these rounded numbers would lead to a small rounding error in our check figures, however, so the rest of our computations will use the exact results: 218.75 regular posters and 131.25 large posters.

If Kay wants, she can now use the number of units to find her break-even point in terms of sales revenue (amounts rounded to the nearest dollar):

| | |
|---|---|
| 218.75 regular posters at $35 each...................... | $ 7,656 |
| 131.25 large posters at $70 each........................ | 9,188 |
| Total revenues .................................................. | $16,844 |

We can prove this break-even point as follows:

| | Total |
|---|---|
| Contribution margin: | |
| Regular posters (218.75 × $14).................... | $ 3,063 |
| Large posters (131.25 × $30) ....................... | 3,937 |
| Contribution margin .......................................... | $ 7,000 |
| Less: Fixed expenses.......................................... | (7,000) |
| Operating income.............................................. | $ 0 |

We just found Kay's break-even point, but Kay can also use the same steps to calculate the number of units she must sell to achieve a target profit. The only difference, as before, is that she would use target profit, rather than zero, as the operating income in the shortcut formula.

## TRY IT!

Rachel runs her own hot dog stand on the U of A campus. The monthly cost of the cart rental and business permit is $300. Rachel's contribution margin is $1.50 per hot dog sold. She has recently added individual servings of potato chips to her product offering. Each bag of potato chips has a contribution margin of $0.75 per bag. Rachel sells 5 bags of potato chips for every 10 hot dogs.

1. What is Rachel's weighted-average contribution margin per unit?
2. How many total units must Rachel sell in a month to earn a target monthly profit of $900?
3. Of the total units needed to earn $900 of profit, how many are hot dogs and how many are bags of potato chips?

Please see page 244 for solutions.

## STOP & THINK

Suppose Kay would still like to earn a monthly profit of $4,900. Recall that she needed to sell 850 posters to achieve this profit level when she was selling only regular posters. If her sales mix is 5:3 as planned, will she need to sell *more than* or *fewer than* 850 posters to achieve her target profit? Why?

**Answer:** Kay will need to sell fewer than 850 posters because she is now selling some large posters that have a higher unit contribution margin. We can verify this as follows:

$$\text{Sales in total units} = \frac{\text{Fixed expenses} + \text{Operating income}}{\text{Weighted-average contribution margin per unit}}$$

$$= \frac{\$7,000 + \$4,900}{\$20}$$

$$= 595 \text{ posters}$$

Kay would have to sell a total of 595 posters—372 regular posters (595 × 5/8) and 223 large posters (595 × 3/8)—to achieve her target profit.

### Multiproduct Company: Finding Break-even in Terms of Sales Revenue

Companies that offer hundreds or thousands of products (such as Le Château and Lowe's) do not want to find the break-even point in terms of units. Rather, they want to know break-even (or target profit volumes) in terms of sales revenue. To find this sales volume, the company needs to know, or estimate, its weighted-average contribution margin ratio. If a company prepares contribution margin income statements, it easily calculates the contribution margin ratio by dividing the total contribution margin by total sales. The contribution margin ratio is *already* weighted by the company's *actual* sales mix! The following Stop & Think illustrates how Maplewood Equestrian Centre would use this approach to calculating break-even.

## STOP & THINK

Suppose Maplewood Equestrian Centre's total sales revenue is $450,000, its variable expenses total $315,000, and its fixed expenses total $110,000 when offering a full mix of services such as full-service indoor board for horses, outdoor board for horses, group lessons, private lessons, and day camps. What is the break-even point in sales revenue?

**Answer:** First, Maplewood computes its total contribution margin:

| | |
|---|---:|
| Sales revenue | $450, 000 |
| Less: Variable expenses | 315, 000 |
| Contribution margin | $135, 000 |

Now Maplewood is able to compute its overall contribution margin ratio, which is already weighted by the company's actual sales mix: $135,000 ÷ 450,000 = 30%.

Finally, Maplewood uses the contribution margin ratio in the shortcut formula to predict the break-even point:

$$\text{Sales in dollars} = \frac{\text{Fixed expenses} + \text{Operating income}}{\text{Contribution margin per unit}}$$

$$= \frac{\$110,000 + \$0}{0.30}$$

$$= \$366,667 \text{ (rounded)}$$

Under these circumstances, Maplewood must achieve sales revenue of $366,667 just to break even.

Unlike Maplewood, Kay's business to this point has been limited to a sole product (regular posters), which had a 40% contribution margin ratio. Once Kay starts selling large posters in addition to the regular posters, her overall weighted-average contribution margin ratio will change. Recall that Kay expects to sell five regular posters for every three large posters. Exhibit 4-9 shows how Kay weights the individual contribution margins and sales revenue, using the anticipated sales mix, to arrive at her anticipated weighted-average contribution margin ratio:

**EXHIBIT 4-9** Estimating the Weighted-average Contribution Margin Ratio

| | | |
|---|---|---|
| Expected contribution margin: | | |
| Regular posters (5 × \$14) | \$ 70 | |
| Large posters (3 × \$30) | \$ 90 | |
| Expected contribution margin | | \$160 |
| Divided by expected sales revenue: | | |
| Regular posters (5 × \$35) | \$175 | |
| Large posters (3 × \$70) | \$210 | |
| Expected sales revenue | | ÷ 385 |
| Weighted-average contribution margin ratio | | = 41.558% |

Notice how Kay's weighted-average contribution margin ratio (41.558%) is higher than it was when she sold only regular posters (40%). That is because she expects to sell some large posters that have a 42.9% contribution margin ratio (\$30/\$70) in addition to the regular-size posters. Because her sales mix is changing, she now has a different contribution margin ratio.

Once Kay knows her weighted-average contribution margin ratio, she can use the shortcut formula to estimate break-even in terms of sales revenue:

$$\text{Sales in dollars} = \frac{\text{Fixed expenses} + \text{Operating income}}{\text{Contribution margin per unit}}$$

$$= \frac{\$7{,}000 + \$0}{0.41558}$$

$$= \$16{,}844 \text{ (rounded)}$$

Notice that this is the same break-even point in sales revenue we found earlier by first finding break-even in *units*. Kay could also use the formula to find the total sales revenue she would need to meet her target monthly operating income of \$4,900.

If Kay's actual sales mix is not five regular posters to three large posters, her actual operating income will differ from the planned. The sales mix greatly influences the break-even point. When companies offer more than one product, they do not have a unique break-even point. Every sales-mix assumption leads to a different break-even point.

## STOP & THINK

Suppose Kay plans to sell 800 total posters in the 5:3 sales mix. She actually does sell 800 posters—375 regular and 425 large. The sales prices per poster, variable costs per poster, and fixed expenses are exactly as predicted. Without doing any computations, is Kay's actual operating income greater than, less than, or equal to her expected income?

**Answer:** Kay's actual sales mix did not turn out to be the 5:3 mix she expected. She actually sold *more* of the higher-margin large posters than the lower-margin regular posters. This favourable change in the sales mix causes her to earn a higher operating income than she expected.

## Common Indicators of Risk

A company's level of risk depends on many factors, including the general health of the economy and the specific industry in which the company operates. In addition, a firm's risk depends on its current volume of sales and the relative amount of fixed and variable costs that make up its total costs. Next, we discuss how a firm can gauge its level of risk, to some extent, by its **margin of safety** and its **operating leverage**.

### Margin of Safety

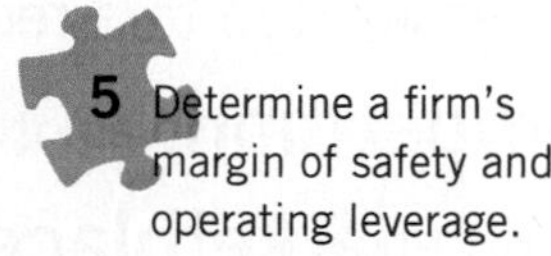

The **margin of safety** is the excess of actual or expected sales over break-even sales. This is the "cushion," or drop in sales, the company can absorb without incurring a loss. The higher the margin of safety, the greater the cushion against loss and the less risky the business plan. Managers use the margin of safety to evaluate the risk of current operations as well as the risk of new plans.

Let's continue to assume that Kay has been in business for several months and that she generally sells 950 posters a month. Kay's break-even point in our original data is 500 posters. Kay can express her margin of safety in units, as follows:

| **Margin of safety in units** | = | **Expected sales in units** | − | **Break-even sales in units** |
|---|---|---|---|---|
| | = | 950 posters | − | 500 posters |
| | = | 450 posters | | |

Kay can also express her margin of safety in sales dollars:

| **Margin of safety in dollars** | = | **Expected sales in dollars** | − | **Break-even sales in dollars** |
|---|---|---|---|---|
| | = | (950 posters × $35) | − | (500 posters × $35) |
| | = | $33,250 | − | $17,500 |
| | = | $15,750 | | |

Sales can drop by 450 posters, or $15,750 a month, before Kay incurs a loss. This is a fairly comfortable margin.

Managers can also compute the margin of safety as a percentage of sales. Simply divide the margin of safety by sales. We obtain the same percentage whether we use units or dollars.

*In units:*

$$\text{Margin of safety as a percentage} = \frac{\text{Margin of safety in units}}{\text{Expected sales in units}}$$

$$= \frac{450 \text{ posters}}{950 \text{ posters}}$$

$$= 47.4\% \text{ (rounded)}$$

*In dollars:*

$$\text{Margin of safety as a percentage} = \frac{\text{Margin of safety in units}}{\text{Expected sales in units}}$$

$$= \frac{\$15,750}{\$33,250}$$

$$= 47.4\% \text{ (rounded)}$$

**Why is this important?**

The margin of safety and **operating leverage** help managers understand their **risk** if **volume** decreases due to a recession, **competition**, or other **changes** in the **marketplace**.

The margin of safety percentage tells Kay that sales would have to drop by more than 47.4% before she would incur a loss. If sales fall by less than 47.4%, she would still earn a profit. If sales fall exactly 47.4%, she would break even. This ratio tells Kay that her business plan is not unduly risky.

## Operating Leverage

A company's operating leverage refers to the relative amount of fixed and variable costs that make up its total costs. Most companies have both fixed and variable costs. However, companies with high operating leverage have relatively more fixed costs and relatively fewer variable costs. Companies with high operating leverage include golf courses, airlines, and hotels. Because they have fewer variable costs, their contribution margin ratio is relatively high. Recall from the previous chapter that Banff Rocky Mountain Resort's variable cost of servicing each guest is low, which means that the hotel has a high contribution margin and high operating leverage.

What does high operating leverage have to do with risk? If sales volume decreases, the total contribution margin will drop significantly because each sales dollar contains a high percentage of contribution margin. Yet the high fixed costs of running the company remain. Therefore, the operating income of these companies can easily turn from profit to loss if sales volume declines. For example, airlines were financially devastated after September 11, 2001, because the number of people flying suddenly dropped, creating large reductions in contribution margin. Yet, the airlines had to continue paying their high fixed costs. High operating leverage companies are at *more* risk because their income declines drastically when sales volume declines.

What if the economy is growing and sales volume *increases*? High operating leverage companies will reap high rewards. Remember that after break-even, each unit sold contributes its unit contribution margin directly to profit. Because high operating leverage companies have high contribution margin ratios, each additional dollar of sales contributes more to the firm's operating income.

However, companies with low operating leverage have relatively *fewer* fixed costs and relatively *more* variable costs. For example, while retailers incur significant levels of fixed costs, more of every sales dollar is used to pay for the merchandise (a variable cost), so less ends up as contribution margin. If sales volume declines, these companies have relatively fewer fixed costs to cover, so they are at *less* risk of incurring a loss. If sales volume increases, their relatively small contribution margin ratios add to the bottom line, but in smaller increments. Therefore, they reap less reward than high operating leverage companies experiencing the same volume increases. *In other words, changes in sales volume at low operating leverage companies do not have as much impact on operating income as they do at high operating leverage companies.* Exhibit 4-10 summarizes the characteristics of both high operating leverage firms and low operating leverage firms.

A company's <u>**operating leverage factor**</u>[3] tells us how responsive a company's operating income is to changes in volume. The greater the operating leverage factors, the greater the impact a change in sales volume has on operating income.

The operating leverage factor, at a given level of sales, is calculated as follows:

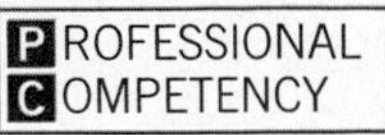

$$\text{Operating leverage factor} = \frac{\text{Contribution margin}}{\text{Operating income}}$$

Why do we say "at a given level of sales"? A company's operating leverage factor depends, to some extent, on the sales level used to calculate the contribution margin and operating income. Most companies compute the operating leverage factor at their current or expected volume of sales, which is what we will do in our examples.

[3]This is also referred to as the degree of operating leverage.

**EXHIBIT 4-10** Characteristics of High Operating Leverage Firms

| High operating leverage | Low operating leverage |
|---|---|
| ♦ High operating leverage companies have the following:<br>• *Higher* levels of fixed costs and *lower* levels of variable costs<br>• *Higher* contribution margin ratios | ♦ Low operating leverage companies have the following:<br>• *Higher* levels of variable costs and *lower* levels of fixed costs<br>• *Lower* contribution margin ratios |
| ♦ For high operating leverage companies, changes in volume significantly affect operating income, so they face the following:<br>• *Higher* risk<br>• *Higher* potential for reward | ♦ For low operating leverage companies, changes in volume do NOT have as significant an effect on operating income, so they face the following:<br>• *Lower* risk<br>• *Lower* potential for reward |
| Examples include golf courses, hotels, rental car agencies, theme parks, airlines, cruise lines, etc. | Examples include merchandising companies and fast-food restaurants. |

What does the operating leverage factor tell us?

*The operating leverage factor, at a given level of sales, indicates the percentage change in operating income that will occur from a 1% change in volume. In other words, it tells us how responsive a company's operating income is to changes in volume.*

The lowest possible value for this factor is 1, which occurs only if the company has no fixed costs (an extremely *low* operating leverage company). For a minute, let us assume that Kay has no fixed costs. Given this scenario, her unit contribution margin ($14 per poster) contributes directly to profit because she has no fixed costs to cover. In addition, she has no risk. The worst she can do is break even, and that will occur only if she does not sell any posters. Let's continue to assume that she generally sells 950 posters a month; we will calculate the operating leverage factor at this level of sales.

| | |
|---|---|
| Sales revenue (950 posters × $35/poster) | $ 33,250 |
| Less: Variable expenses (950 posters × $21/poster) | (19,950) |
| Contribution margin (950 posters × $14/poster) | $ 13,300 |
| Less: Fixed expenses | (0) |
| Operating income | $ 13,300 |

Her operating leverage factor is as follows:

$$\text{Operating leverage factor} = \frac{\$13{,}300}{\$13{,}300} = 1$$

What does this tell us? If Kay's volume changes by 1%, her operating income also changes by 1% (her operating leverage factor of 1 multiplied by a 1% change in volume). What would happen to Kay's operating income if her volume changed by 15% rather than 1%? Her operating income would then change by 15% (her operating leverage factor of 1 multiplied by a 15% change in volume).

Let's now see what happens if we assume, as usual, that Kay's fixed expenses are $7,000. We will once again calculate the operating leverage factor given Kay's current level of sales (950 posters per month):

| | |
|---|---|
| Contribution margin (950 posters × $14/poster) | $13,300 |
| Less: Fixed expenses | (7,000) |
| Operating income | $ 6,300 |

Now that we have once again assumed that Kay's fixed expenses are $7,000, her operating leverage factor is as follows:

$$\text{Operating leverage factor} = \frac{\$13,300}{\$6,300}$$
$$= 2.11 \text{ (rounded)}$$

Notice that her operating leverage factor is higher (2.11 versus 1) when she has *more* fixed costs ($7,000 versus $0). If Kay's sales volume changes by 1%, her operating income will change by 2.11% (her operating leverage factor of 2.11 multiplied by a 1% change in volume). Again, what would happen to Kay's operating income if her volume changed by 15% rather than 1%? Her operating income would then change by 31.65% (her operating leverage factor of 2.11 multiplied by a 15% change in volume).

Managers use the firm's operating leverage factor to determine how vulnerable their operating income is to changes in sales volume. The larger the operating leverage factor is, the greater the impact a change in sales volume has on operating income. This is true for both increases *and* decreases in volume. Therefore, companies with higher operating leverage factors are particularly vulnerable to changes in volume. In other words, they have both a higher risk of incurring losses if volume declines and a higher potential reward if volume increases. Hoping to capitalize on the reward side, many companies have intentionally increased their operating leverage by lowering their variable costs while at the same time increasing their fixed costs. This strategy works well during periods of economic growth but can be detrimental when sales volume slides.

## STOP & THINK

Assume Kay's original data ($14 unit contribution margin, $7,000 fixed costs, and 950 posters per month sales volume). Use Kay's operating leverage factor to determine the percentage impact of a 10% decrease in sales volume on Kay's operating income. Prove your results.

**Answer:** If sales volume decreases by 10%, Kay's operating income will decrease by 21.1% (her operating leverage factor of 2.11 multiplied by a 10% decrease in volume).

| | | |
|---|---|---|
| Proof: | Current volume of posters | 950 |
| | Less: Decrease in volume | |
| | (10% × 950) of posters | (95) |
| | New volume of posters | 855 |
| | Multiplied by: Unit contribution margin | × $ 14 |
| | New total contribution margin | $11,970 |
| | Less: Fixed expenses | (7,000) |
| | New operating income | $ 4,970 |
| | Versus operating income | |
| | before change in volume | $ 6,300* |
| | Decrease in operating income | $ (1,330) |
| | Percentage change ($1,330/$6,300) | 21.1%(rounded) |

*(950 posters × $14/unit contribution margin) − $7,000 fixed expenses

# DECISION GUIDELINES

## CVP Analysis

Your friend did decide to open an ice cream parlour. But now she is facing changing business conditions. She needs help making the following decisions.

| Decision | Guidelines |
|---|---|
| The cost of ice cream is rising, yet my competitors have lowered their prices. What will I need to do to break even or achieve my target profit? | Increases in variable costs (such as ice cream) and decreases in sales prices both decrease the unit contribution margin and contribution margin ratio. You will have to sell more units in order to achieve break-even or a target profit. You can use sensitivity analysis to better pinpoint the actual volume you will need to sell. Simply compute your new unit contribution margin and use it in the shortcut unit contribution margin formula. |
| Would it help if I could renegotiate my lease with the landlord? | Decreases in fixed costs do not affect the firm's contribution margin. However, a decrease in fixed costs means that the company has to sell fewer units to achieve break-even or a target profit. Increases in fixed costs have the opposite effect. |
| What happens to the sales volume required for a target profit if my product mix changes? | Your contribution margin ratio will change as a result of changing your sales mix. A company earns more income by selling higher-margin products than by selling an equal number of lower-margin products. If you can shift sales toward higher contribution margin products, you will have to sell fewer units to reach your target profit. |
| If the economy takes a downturn, how much risk do I face of incurring a loss? | The margin of safety indicates how far sales volume can decline before you would incur a loss: $\text{Margin of safety} = \text{Expected sales} - \text{Break-even sales}$ The operating leverage factor indicates the percentage change in operating income that will occur from a 1% change in volume. It tells you how sensitive your company's operating income is to changes in volume. At a given level of sales, the operating leverage factor is as follows: $\text{Operating leverage factor} = \frac{\text{Contribution margin}}{\text{Operating income}}$ |

# SUMMARY PROBLEM 2

Recall from Summary Problem 1 that Fleet Foot buys hiking socks for $6 a pair and sells them for $10. Monthly fixed costs are $10,000 (for sales volumes between zero and 12,000 pairs), resulting in a break-even point of 2,500 units. Assume that Fleet Foot has been selling 8,000 pairs of socks per month.

### Requirements

1. What is Fleet Foot's current margin of safety in units, in sales dollars, and as a percentage? Explain the results.
2. At this level of sales, what is Fleet Foot's operating leverage factor? If volume declines by 25% due to increasing competition, by what percentage will the company's operating income decline?

3. Competition has forced Fleet Foot to lower its sales price to $9 a pair. How will this affect Fleet Foot's break-even point?
4. To compensate for the lower sales price, Fleet Foot wants to expand its product line to include men's dress socks. Each pair will sell for $7.00 and cost $2.75 from the supplier. Fixed costs will not change. Fleet Foot expects to sell four pairs of dress socks for every one pair of hiking socks (at its new $9 sales price). What is Fleet Foot's weighted-average contribution margin per unit? Given the 4:1 sales mix, how many of each type of sock will it need to sell to break even?

## SOLUTION

### Requirement 1

| Margin of safety in units | = Expected sales in units | – Break-even sales in units |
|---|---|---|
| = | 8,000 | – 2,500 |
| = | 5,500 units | |

| Margin of safety in dollars | = Expected sales in dollars | – Break-even sales in dollars |
|---|---|---|
| = | (8,000 × $10) | – (2,500 × $10) |
| = | $55,000 | |

$$\text{Margin of safety as a percentage} = \frac{\text{Margin of safety in units}}{\text{Expected sales in units}} = \frac{5{,}500 \text{ pairs}}{8{,}000 \text{ pairs}} = 68.75\%$$

Fleet Foot's margin of safety is quite high. Sales have to fall by more than 5,500 units (or $55,000) before Fleet Foot incurs a loss. Fleet Foot will continue to earn a profit unless sales drop by more than 68.75%.

### Requirement 2

At its current level of volume, Fleet Foot's operating income is as follows:

| | |
|---|---|
| Contribution margin (8,000 pairs × $4/pair) | $ 32,000 |
| Less: Fixed expenses | (10,000) |
| Operating income | $ 22,000 |

Fleet Foot's operating leverage factor at this level of sales is computed as follows:

$$\text{Operating leverage factor} = \frac{\text{Contribution margin}}{\text{Operating income}} = \frac{\$32{,}000}{\$22{,}000} = 1.45 \text{ (rounded)}$$

If sales volume declines by 25%, operating income will decline by 36.25% (Fleet Foot's operating leverage factor of 1.45 multiplied by 25%).

**Requirement 3**

If Fleet Foot drops its sales price to \$9 per pair, its contribution margin per pair declines to \$3 (sales price of \$9 – variable cost of \$6). Each sale contributes less toward covering fixed costs. Fleet Foot's new break-even point *increases* to 3,334 pairs of socks (\$10,000 fixed costs ÷ \$3 unit contribution margin).

**Requirement 4**

| | Hiking Socks | Dress Socks | Total |
|---|---|---|---|
| Sales price per unit | \$ 9.00 | \$ 7.00 | |
| Deduct: Variable expense per unit | (6.00) | (2.75) | |
| Contribution margin per unit | \$ 3.00 | \$ 4.25 | |
| Sales mix | × 1 | × 4 | 5 |
| Contribution margin | \$ 3.00 | \$17.00 | \$20.00 |
| Weighted-average contribution margin per unit (\$20/5) | | | \$ 4.00 |

$$\text{Sales in total units} = \frac{\text{Fixed expenses} + \text{Operating income}}{\text{Weighted} - \text{average contribution margin per unit}}$$

$$= \frac{\$10{,}000 + \$0}{\$4}$$

$$= 2{,}500 \text{ pairs of socks}$$

| | |
|---|---|
| Break-even sales of dress socks (2,500 × 4/5) | 2,000 pairs dress socks |
| Break-even sales of hiking socks (2,500 × 1/5) | 500 pairs hiking socks |

By expanding its product line to include higher-margin dress socks, Fleet Foot is able to decrease its break-even point back to its original level (2,500 pairs). However, to achieve this break-even point, Fleet Foot must sell the planned ratio of four pairs of dress socks to every one pair of hiking socks.

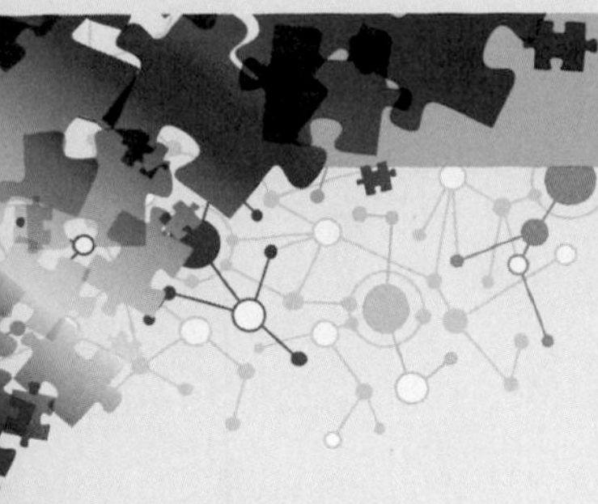

# END OF CHAPTER

## LEARNING OBJECTIVES

1 Calculate the unit contribution margin and the contribution margin ratio.

2 Use CVP analysis to find break-even points and target profit volumes.

3 Perform sensitivity analysis in response to changing business conditions.

4 Find break-even and target profit volumes for multiproduct companies.

5 Determine a firm's margin of safety and operating leverage.

## ACCOUNTING VOCABULARY

**Break-even Point (p. 187)** The sales level at which operating income is zero: Total revenues equals total expenses.

**Contribution Margin Income Statement (p. 184)** An income statement that groups costs by behaviour rather than function; it can be used only by internal management.

**Contribution Margin per Unit (p. 185)** The excess of the unit sales price over the variable cost per unit; also called unit contribution margin.

**Contribution Margin Ratio (p. 185)** Ratio of contribution margin to sales revenue.

**Cost-Volume-Profit (CVP) Analysis (p. 183)** Expresses the relationships among costs, volume, and profit or loss.

**Margin of Safety (p. 205)** Excess of actual or expected sales over break-even sales; the drop in sales a company can absorb without incurring an operating loss.

**Operating Leverage (p. 205)** The relative amount of fixed and variable costs that make up a firm's total costs.

**Operating Leverage Factor (p. 206)** At a given level of sales, the contribution margin divided by operating income; the operating leverage factor indicates the percentage change in operating income that will occur from a 1% change in sales volume. Also known as the degree of operating leverage.

**Sales Mix (p. 183)** The combination of products that make up total sales.

**Sensitivity Analysis (p. 196)** A "what-if" technique that asks what results will be if actual prices or costs change or if an underlying assumption changes.

CHAPTER 4

MyAccountingLab Make the grade with MyAccountingLab: Questions marked in # can be found on MyAccountingLab. You can practise them as often as you want, and most feature step-by-step guided instructions to help you find the right answer.

## QUICK CHECK

1. (Learning Objective 2) When a company is operating at its break-even point
   a. its selling price is equal to its variable expense per unit.
   b. its contribution margin is equal to its variable expenses.
   c. its fixed expenses are equal to its variable expenses.
   d. its total revenues are equal to its total expenses.
2. (Learning Objective 2) If a company sells one unit above its break-even sales volume, then its operating income would be equal to
   a. the unit selling price.
   b. the unit contribution margin.
   c. the fixed expenses.
   d. zero.
3. (Learning Objective 2) How do we calculate the unit sales volume necessary to reach a target profit?
   a. Target profit ÷ unit contribution margin
   b. Target profit ÷ contribution margin ratio
   c. (Fixed expenses + target profit) ÷ unit contribution margin
   d. (Fixed expenses + target profit) ÷ contribution margin ratio
4. (Learning Objective 2) The number of units to be sold to reach a certain target profit is calculated as
   a. Target profit ÷ unit contribution margin.
   b. Target profit ÷ contribution margin ratio.
   c. (Fixed expenses + target profit) ÷ unit contribution margin.
   d. (Fixed expenses + target profit) ÷ contribution margin ratio.

5. (Learning Objective 2) The break-even point on a CVP graph is
   a. the intersection of the sales revenue line and the total expense line.
   b. the intersection of the fixed expense line and the total expense line.
   c. the intersection of the fixed expense line and the sales revenue.
   d. the intersection of the sales revenue line and the y-axis.

6. (Learning Objective 3) If the sales price of a product increases while everything else remains the same, what happens to the break-even point?
   a. The break-even point increases.
   b. The break-even point decreases.
   c. The break-even point remains the same.
   d. The effect cannot be determined without further information.

7. (Learning Objective 2) Target profit analysis is used to calculate the sales volume that is needed to
   a. cover all fixed expenses.
   b. cover all expenses.
   c. avoid a loss.
   d. earn a specific amount of net operating income.

8. (Learning Objective 4) A shift in the sales mix from a product with a high contribution margin ratio toward a product with a low contribution margin ratio will cause the break-even point to
   a. increase.
   b. decrease.
   c. remain the same.
   d. increase or decrease, but the direction of change cannot be determined from the information given.

9. (Learning Objective 5) If the operating leverage factor is 3, then a 2% change in the number of units sold should result in a 6% change in
   a. sales.
   b. variable expense.
   c. unit contribution margin.
   d. operating income.

10. (Learning Objective 5) What is the margin of safety?
    a. The amount of fixed and variable costs that make up a company's total costs
    b. The difference between the sales price per unit and the variable cost per unit
    c. The excess of expected sales over break-even sales
    d. The sales level at which operating income is zero

**Quick Check Answers**

1. d 2. b 3. c 4. c 5. a 6. b 7. d 8. a 9. d 10. c



# SHORT EXERCISES

**Royal Hellenic Cruiseline Data Set used for S4-1 through S4-5 and S4-7 through S4-12.**

Royal Hellenic Cruiseline offers nightly dinner cruises off the coast of Nanaimo and Victoria. Dinner cruise tickets sell for $60 per passenger. Royal Hellenic Cruiseline's variable cost of providing the dinner is $20 per passenger, and the fixed cost of operating the vessels (depreciation, salaries, docking fees, and other expenses) is $210,000 per month. The company's relevant range extends to 15,000 monthly passengers.

### S4-1 Compute unit contribution margin and contribution margin ratio *(Learning Objective 1)*

Use the information from the Royal Hellenic Cruiseline data set to compute the following:

Check sum: (d) Operating income is $125,000.

**a.** What is the contribution margin per passenger?

**b.** What is the contribution margin ratio?

**c.** Use the unit contribution margin to project operating income if monthly sales total 10,000 passengers.

**d.** Use the contribution margin ratio to project operating income if monthly sales revenue totals $500,000.

### S4-2 Project change in income *(Learning Objective 1)*

Use the information from the Royal Hellenic Cruiseline data set. If Royal Hellenic Cruiseline sells an additional 500 tickets, by what amount will its operating income increase (or operating loss decrease)?

### S4-3 Find break-even (*Learning Objective 2*)

Check sum: (b) Fixed expenses are $215,000.

Use the information from the Royal Hellenic Cruiseline data set to compute the number of dinner cruise tickets it must sell to break even.

a. Use the income statement equation approach.
b. Using the shortcut *unit* contribution margin approach, perform a numerical proof to ensure that your answer is correct.
c. Use your answers from (a) and (b) to determine the sales revenue needed to break even.
d. Use the shortcut contribution margin *ratio* approach to verify the sales revenue needed to break even.

### S4-4 Find target profit volume (*Learning Objective 2*)

Check sum: 7,250 tickets

Use the information from the Royal Hellenic Cruiseline data set. If Royal Hellenic Cruiseline has a target operating income of $80,000 per month, how many dinner cruise tickets must the company sell?

### S4-5 Prepare a CVP graph (*Learning Objective 2*)

Use the information from the Royal Hellenic Cruiseline data set. Draw a graph of Royal Hellenic Cruiseline's CVP relationships. Include the sales revenue line, the fixed expense line, and the total expense line. Label the axes, the break-even point, the income area, and the loss area.

### S4-6 Interpret a CVP graph (*Learning Objective 2*)

Describe what each letter stands for in the CVP graph.



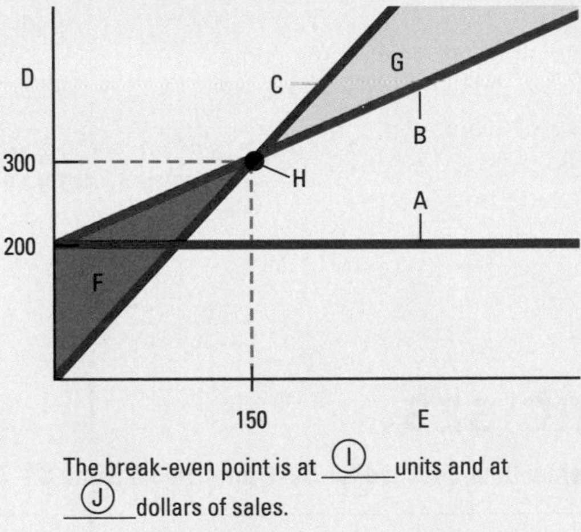


### S4-7 Changes in sales price and variable costs (*Learning Objective 3*)

Check sum: (1) 10,500 passengers

Use the information from the Royal Hellenic Cruiseline data set.

1. Suppose Royal Hellenic Cruiseline cuts its dinner cruise ticket price from $60 to $40 to increase the number of passengers. Compute the new break-even point in units and in sales dollars. Explain how changes in sales price generally affect the break-even point.
2. Assume that Royal Hellenic Cruiseline does *not* cut the price. Royal Hellenic Cruiseline could reduce its variable costs by no longer serving an appetizer before dinner. Suppose this operating change reduces the variable expense from $20 to $10 per passenger. Compute the new break-even point in units and in dollars. Explain how changes in variable costs generally affect the break-even point.

### S4-8 Compute changes in fixed costs (*Learning Objective 3*)

Check sum: (1) 4,500 passengers

Use the information from the Royal Hellenic Cruiseline data set. Suppose Royal Hellenic Cruiseline embarks on a cost-reduction drive and slashes fixed expenses from $210,000 per month to $180,000 per month.

1. Compute the new break-even point in units and in sales dollars.
2. Is the break-even point higher or lower than in S4-3? Explain how changes in fixed costs generally affect the break-even point.

**S4-9 Compute weighted-average contribution margin** *(Learning Objective 4)*

Use the information from the Royal Hellenic Cruiseline data set. Suppose Royal Hellenic Cruiseline decides to offer two types of dinner cruises: regular cruises and executive cruises. The executive cruise includes complimentary cocktails and a five-course dinner on the upper deck. Assume that fixed expenses remain at $210,000 per month and that the following ticket prices and variable expenses apply:

Check sum: Weighted-average contribution margin is $40 per passenger.

| | Regular Cruise | Executive Cruise |
|---|---|---|
| Sales price per ticket | $50 | $130 |
| Variable expense per passenger | $20 | $ 50 |

Assuming that Royal Hellenic Cruiseline expects to sell four regular cruises for every executive cruise, compute the weighted-average contribution margin per unit. Is it higher or lower than a *simple* average contribution margin? Why? Is it higher or lower than the regular cruise contribution margin calculated in S4-1? Why? Will this new sales mix cause Royal Hellenic Cruiseline's break-even point to increase or decrease from what it was when it sold only regular cruises?

**S4-10 Continuation of S4-9: break-even** *(Learning Objective 4)*

Refer to your answer to S4-9.

Check sum: (a) 5,250 passengers

a. Compute the total number of dinner cruises that Royal Hellenic Cruiseline must sell to break even.
b. Compute the number of regular cruises and executive cruises the company must sell to break even.

**S4-11 Compute margin of safety** *(Learning Objective 5)*

Use the information from the Royal Hellenic Cruiseline data set. If Royal Hellenic Cruiseline sells 10,000 dinner cruises, compute the margin of safety

Check sum: (a) 4,750 passengers

a. in units (dinner cruise tickets).
b. in sales dollars.
c. as a percentage of sales.

**S4-12 Compute and use operating leverage factor** *(Learning Objective 5)*

Use the information from the Royal Hellenic Cruiseline data set.

Check sum: (a) Operating leverage is 1.78.

a. Compute the operating leverage factor when Royal Hellenic Cruiseline sells 12,000 dinner cruises.
b. If volume increases by 10%, by what percentage will operating income increase?
c. If volume decreases by 5%, by what percentage will operating income decrease?

**S4-13 Compute margin of safety** *(Learning Objective 5)*

Kay has an e-tail poster business. Suppose Kay expects to sell 1,000 posters. Her average sales price per poster is $30 and her average cost per poster is $24. Her fixed expenses total $3,600. Compute her margin of safety

Check sum: (a) 400 posters

a. in units (posters).
b. in sales dollars.
c. as a percentage of expected sales.

**S4-14 Compute and use operating leverage factor** *(Learning Objective 5)*

Suppose Kay sells 1,000 posters. Use the data from S4-13 to compute her operating leverage factor. If sales volume increases 10%, by what percentage will her operating income change? Prove your answer.

Check sum: Operating leverage is 2.5.

# EXERCISES Group A

## E4-15A Prepare contribution margin income statements *(Learning Objectives 1 & 2)*

Check sum: (2) Break-even sales are $187,500.

First Nation Travel uses the contribution margin income statement internally. First Nation's first-quarter results follow. First Nation's relevant range is between sales of $100,000 and $700,000.

Cost-Volume-Profit Analysis

| FIRST NATION TRAVEL<br>Contribution Margin Income Statement<br>Three Months Ended March 31 | |
|---|---|
| Sales revenue | $500,000 |
| Less: Variable expenses | 100,000 |
| Contribution margin | $400,000 |
| Less: Fixed expenses | 150,000 |
| Operating income | $250,000 |

### Requirements

1. Prepare contribution margin income statements at sales levels of $150,000 and $600,000. (*Hint*: Use the contribution margin ratio.)
2. Compute break-even sales in dollars.



## E4-16A Work backward to find missing information *(Learning Objectives 1 & 2)*

Check sum: Operating income is $90,000.

Berg Dry Cleaners has determined the following about its costs: Total variable expenses are $40,000, total fixed expenses are $30,000; and the sales revenue needed to break even is $40,000. Use the contribution margin income statement and the shortcut contribution margin approaches to determine Berg Dry Cleaners' current (1) sales revenue and (2) operating income. (*Hint*: First find the contribution margin ratio, then prepare the contribution margin income statement.)

## E4-17A Find break-even and target profit volume *(Learning Objectives 1 & 2)*

Check sum: (1) Contribution margin per unit is $1.30.

Little Piggie produces sports socks. The company has fixed expenses of $75,000 and variable expenses of $1.20 per package. Each package sells for $2.50.

### Requirements

1. Compute the contribution margin per package and the contribution margin ratio.
2. Find the break-even point in units and in dollars using the contribution margin shortcut approaches.
3. Find the number of packages Little Piggie needs to sell to earn a $25,000 operating income.

## E4-18A Continuation of E4-17A: changing costs *(Learning Objective 3)*

Refer to Little Piggie in E4-17A. If Little Piggie can decrease its variable costs to $1.00 per package by increasing its fixed costs to $100,000, how many packages will it have to sell to generate $25,000 of operating income? Is this more or less than before? Why?

## E4-19A Find break-even and target profit volume *(Learning Objectives 1 & 2)*

Owner Shan Lo is considering franchising her Happy Wok restaurant concept. She believes people will pay $5 for a large bowl of noodles. Variable costs are $1.50 a bowl. Lo estimates monthly fixed costs for franchisees at $8,400.

**Requirements**

1. Use the contribution margin ratio shortcut approach to find a franchisee's break-even sales in dollars.
2. Is franchising a good idea for Lo if franchisees want a minimum monthly operating income of $8,750 and Lo believes that most locations could generate $25,000 in monthly sales?

Check sum: (1) Break-even sales in dollars is $12,000.

### E4-20A Continuation of E4-19A: changing business conditions *(Learning Objective 3)*

Refer to Happy Wok in E4-19A. Lo did franchise her restaurant concept. Because of Happy Wok's success, Noodles 'n' More has come on the scene as a competitor. To maintain its market share, Happy Wok will have to lower its sales price to $4.50 per bowl. At the same time, Happy Wok hopes to increase each restaurant's volume to 6,000 bowls per month by embarking on a marketing campaign. Each franchise will have to contribute $500 per month to cover the advertising costs. Prior to these changes, most locations were selling 5,500 bowls per month.

Check sum: (2) New operating income is $9,100.

**Requirements**

1. What was the average restaurant's operating income before these changes?
2. Assuming that the price cut and advertising campaign are successful at increasing volume to the projected level, will the franchisees still earn their target profit of $8,750 per month? Show your calculations.

### E4-21A Compute break-even and project income *(Learning Objectives 1 & 2)*

Vair's Steel Parts produces parts for the automobile industry. The company has monthly fixed expenses of $600,000 and a contribution margin of 80% of revenues.

Check sum: (1) Break-even sales in dollars is $750,000.

**Requirements**

1. Compute Vair's Steel Parts' monthly break-even sales in dollars. Use the contribution margin ratio shortcut approach.
2. Use the contribution margin ratio to project operating income (or loss) if revenues are $700,000 and if they are $1,000,000.
3. Do the results in Requirement 2 make sense given the break-even sales you computed in Requirement 1? Explain.



### E4-22A Continuation of E4-21A: changing business conditions *(Learning Objective 3)*

Refer to Vair's Steel Parts in E4-21A. Vair feels like he is in a giant squeeze play: The automotive manufacturers are demanding lower prices, and the steel producers have increased raw material costs. Vair's contribution margin has shrunk to 50% of revenues. Vair's monthly operating income, prior to these pressures, was $200,000.

Check sum: (1) Break-even in dollars is $1,600,000.

**Requirements**

1. To maintain this same level of profit, what sales volume (in sales revenue) must Vair now achieve?
2. Vair believes that his monthly sales revenue will go only as high as $1,000,000. He is thinking about moving operations overseas to cut fixed costs. If monthly sales are $1,000,000, by how much will he need to cut fixed costs to maintain his prior profit level of $200,000 per month?

### E4-23A Identify information on a CVP graph *(Learning Objective 2)*

Joseph Maksoud is considering starting a Web-based educational business, ePrep MBA. He plans to offer a short-course review of accounting for students entering MBA programs. The materials would be available on a password-protected Website, and students would complete the course through self-study. Maksoud would have to grade the course assignments, but most of the work is in developing the course materials, setting up the site, and marketing.

Unfortunately, Maksoud's hard drive crashed before he finished his financial analysis. However, he did recover the following partial CVP chart:

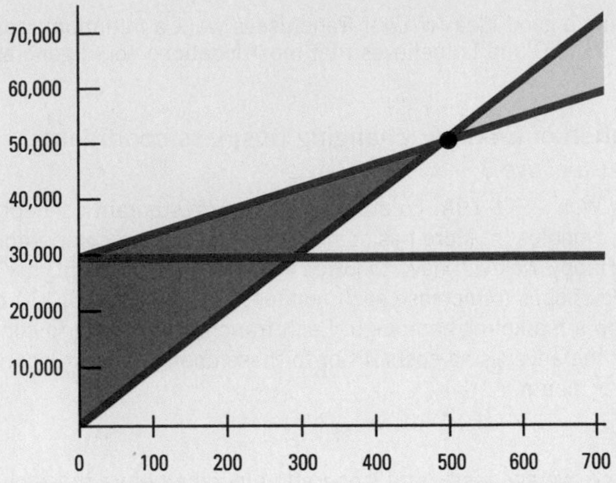


### Requirements

1. Label each axis, sales revenue line, total expense line, fixed expense line, operating income area, and operating loss area.
2. If Maksoud attracts 400 students to take the course, will the venture be profitable?
3. What are the break-even sales in students and dollars?

## E4-24A Sustainability and CVP concepts *(Learning Objective 3)*

Check sum: (1) Break-even in dollars is $480,000.

Kingston Garage Doors manufactures a premium garage door. Currently the price and cost data associated with the premium garage door are as follows:

| | |
|---|---|
| Average selling price per premium garage door | $ 1,500 |
| Average variable manufacturing cost per door | $ 600 |
| Average variable selling cost per door | $ 150 |
| Total annual fixed costs | $240,000 |

Kingston Garage Doors has undertaken several sustainability projects over the past few years. Management is currently evaluating whether to develop a comprehensive software control system for its manufacturing operations that would significantly reduce scrap and waste generated during the manufacturing process. If the company were to implement this software control system in its manufacturing operations, the use of the software control system would result in an increase of $60,000 in its annual fixed costs, while the average variable manufacturing cost per door would drop by $50.

### Requirements

1. What is the company's current break-even in units and in dollars?
2. If the company expects to sell 400 premium garage doors in the upcoming year, and it does not develop the software control system, what is its expected operating income from premium garage doors?
3. If the software control system were to be developed and implemented, what would be the company's new break-even point in units and in dollars?
4. If the company expects to sell 400 premium garage doors in the upcoming year, and it develops the software control system, what is its expected operating income from premium garage doors?
5. If the company expects to sell 400 premium garage doors in the upcoming year, do you think the company should implement the software control system? Why or why not? What factors should the company consider?

### E4-25A Prepare a CVP graph *(Learning Objective 2)*

Suppose that the Rogers Centre, home of the Toronto Blue Jays, earns total revenue that averages $24 for every ticket sold. Assume that annual fixed expenses are $24 million and that variable expenses are $4 per ticket.

Check sum: (2) Break-even in dollars is $28,800,000.

**Requirements**

1. Prepare the ballpark's CVP graph under these assumptions. Label the axes, sales revenue line, fixed expense line, total expense line, operating loss area, and operating income area on the graph.
2. Show the break-even point in dollars and in tickets.

### E4-26A Work backward to find new break-even point *(Learning Objectives 2 & 3)*

Pistone Industries is planning to purchase a new piece of equipment that will increase the quality of its production. It hopes the increased quality will generate more sales. The company's contribution margin ratio is 30%, and its current break-even point is $500,000 in sales revenue. If Pistone Industries' fixed expenses increase by $40,000 due to the equipment, what will its new break-even point be (in sales revenue)?

Check sum: Break-even in dollars is $633,333.

### E4-27A Find the consequence of rising fixed costs *(Learning Objectives 1 & 3)*

DeAnna Braun sells homemade knit scarves for $16 each at local craft shows. Her contribution margin ratio is 62.5%. Currently, the craft show entrance fees cost DeAnna $1,000 per year. The craft shows are raising their entrance fees by 15% next year. How many *extra* scarves will DeAnna have to sell next year just to pay for rising entrance fee costs?

Check sum: Break-even is 15 scarves.

### E4-28A Extension of E4-27A: multiproduct firm *(Learning Objective 4)*

Arlan Braun admired his wife's success at selling scarves at local craft shows (E4-27A), so he decided to make two types of plant stands to sell at the shows. Arlan makes twig stands from twigs he collects from a friend's farm, so his variable cost is minimal (wood screws, glue, and so forth). However, Arlan has to purchase wood to make his oak plant stands. His unit prices and costs are as follows:

Check sum: Break-even in total units is 20 units.

| | Twig Stands | Oak Stands |
|---|---|---|
| Sales price | $15.00 | $35.00 |
| Variable cost | 2.50 | 10.00 |

The twig stands are more popular, so Arlan sells four twig stands for every one oak stand. DeAnna charges her husband $300 to share her booth at the craft shows (after all, she has paid the entrance fees). How many of each plant stand does Arlan need to sell to break even? Will this affect the number of scarves DeAnna needs to sell to break even? Explain.

### E4-29A Find the break-even sales for a multiproduct firm *(Learning Objective 4)*

Racer Scooters plans to sell a motorized standard scooter for $54 and a motorized chrome scooter for $78. Racer Scooters purchases the standard scooter for $36 and the chrome scooter for $50. Racer Scooters expects to sell two chrome scooters for every three standard scooters. Racer Scooters' monthly fixed expenses are $9,680. How many of each type of scooter must Racer Scooters sell monthly to break even? To earn $6,600?

Check sum: Break-even in total units is 440 units.

### E4-30A Work backward to find missing data *(Learning Objective 4)*

Kenisha manufactures two styles of watches: the Digital and the Classic. The following data pertain to the Digital:

Check sum: Contribution margin per Classic watch is $300.

| | |
|---|---|
| Variable manufacturing cost | $120 |
| Variable operating cost | 30 |
| Sales price | 200 |

Kenisha's monthly fixed expenses total $190,000. When Digitals and Classics are sold at a ratio of 7:3, respectively, the sale of 2,000 total watches results in an operating income of $60,000. Compute the contribution margin per watch for the Classic.

### E4-31A Find the break-even point and evaluate an advertising decision at a multiproduct company *(Learning Objectives 3, 4, & 5)*

Check sum: (2) Contribution margion ratio is 70%.

Kick-A's Sporting Goods is a retailer of sporting equipment. Last year, Kick-A's sales revenues totalled $5,000,000. Total expenses were $2,100,000. Of this amount, approximately $1,500,000 were variable, while the remainder were fixed. Since Kick-A's Sporting Goods offers thousands of different products, its managers prefer to calculate the break-even point in terms of sales dollars rather than units.

**Requirements**

1. What is Kick-A's Sporting Goods' current operating income? (Prepare a contribution margin format income statement.)
2. What is Kick-A's contribution margin ratio?
3. What is Kick-A's break-even point in sales dollars? (*Hint*: The contribution margin ratio calculated in Requirement 2 is already the actual sales mix.)
4. Top management is deciding whether to embark on a $200,000 advertising campaign. The marketing firm has projected annual sales volume to increase by 15% as a result of this campaign. Assuming that the projections are correct, what effect would this advertising campaign have on Kick-A's Sporting Goods' annual operating income?

### E4-32A Compute margin of safety and operating leverage *(Learning Objective 5)*

Check sum: Operating leverage is 1.6.

Use the First Nation Travel data in E4-15A to answer the following questions:

**Requirements**

1. What is First Nation Travel's current margin of safety (in dollars)?
2. What is First Nation Travel's current operating leverage factor?
3. If sales volume increases 5% next quarter, by what percentage will First Nation Travel's operating income increase? What will the new operating income be?



### E4-33A Work backward through margin of safety *(Learning Objective 5)*

Check sum: Sales at break-even are $8,000.

Quincy's Bait Shop had budgeted bait sales for the season at $10,000, with a $2,000 margin of safety. However, due to unseasonable weather, bait sales reached only $9,200. Actual sales exceeded break-even sales by what amount?

### E4-34A Compute margin of safety and operating leverage *(Learning Objective 5)*

Check sum: (1) Margin of safety is $136,000.

Regina Repair Shop has a monthly target operating income of $32,000. Variable expenses are 75% of sales and monthly fixed expenses are $10,000.

**Requirements**

1. Compute the monthly margin of safety in dollars if the shop achieves its income goal.
2. Express Regina Repair Shop's margin of safety as a percentage of target sales.
3. What is Regina Repair Shop's operating leverage factor at the target level of operating income?
4. Assume that the repair shop reaches its target. By what percentage will Regina Repair Shop's operating income fall if sales volume declines by 10%?

### E4-35A Use operating leverage factor to find fixed costs *(Learning Objective 5)*

Check sum: Operating Income is $8,000.

Mathieu Manufacturing had a 1.25 operating leverage factor when sales were $50,000. Mathieu Manufacturing's contribution margin ratio was 20%. What were Mathieu Manufacturing's fixed expenses?

### E4-36A Make a comprehensive CVP analysis *(Learning Objectives 1, 2, 3, & 5)*

Check sum: (1) Contribution margin per unit is $50.

Dean Braknis is evaluating a business opportunity to sell grooming kits at dog shows. Dean can buy the grooming kits at a wholesale cost of $30 per set. He plans to sell the grooming kits for $80 per set. He estimates fixed costs, such as travel costs, booth rental cost, and lodging to be $900 per dog show.

**Requirements**

1. Determine the number of grooming kits Dean must sell per show to break even.
2. Assume Dean wants to earn a profit of $1,100 per show.
   a. Determine the sales volume in units necessary to earn the desired profit.
   b. Determine the sales volume in dollars necessary to earn the desired profit.
   c. Using the contribution margin format, prepare an income statement (condensed version) to confirm your answers to Requirements (a) and (b).
3. Determine the margin of safety between the sales volume at the break-even point and the sales volume required to earn the desired profit. Determine the margin of safety in sales dollars, in units, and as a percentage.

**E4-37A Make a comprehensive CVP analysis** *(Learning Objectives 1, 2, 3, & 5)*

Bowerston Company manufactures and sells a single product. The company's sales and expenses for last year follow:

| | Total | Per Unit | % |
|---|---|---|---|
| Sales | $100,000 | $20 | ? |
| Variable expenses | 60,000 | 12 | ? |
| Contribution margin | ? | ? | ? |
| Fixed expenses | 12,000 | | |
| Operating income | $28,000 | | |

**Requirements**

1. Fill in the missing numbers in the preceding table. Use the table to answer the following questions:
   a. What is the total contribution margin?
   b. What is the per-unit contribution margin?
   c. What is the operating income?
   d. How many units were sold?
2. Use the table to answer the following questions about break-even analysis:
   a. What is the annual break-even point in units?
   b. What is the annual break-even point in sales dollars?
3. Use the table to answer the following questions about target profit analysis and safety margin:
   a. How many units must the company sell in order to earn a profit of $50,000?
   b. What is the margin of safety in units?
   c. What is the margin of safety in sales dollars?
   d. What is the margin of safety as a percentage?

Check sum: (2) Break-even in units is 1,500.

CHAPTER 4

**E4-38A Make a comprehensive CVP analysis** *(Learning Objectives 1, 2, 3, 4, & 5)*

FlashCo manufactures 1GB flash drives (jump drives). Price and cost data for a relevant range extending to 200,000 units per month are as follows:

Check sum: (1) Contribution margin ratio is 25%.

| | |
|---|---|
| **Sale price per unit** | |
| (currently monthly sales volume is 120,000 units) | $ 20.00 |
| **Variable cost per unit:** | |
| Direct materials | 6,40 |
| Direct labour | 5.00 |
| Variable manufacturing overhead | 2.20 |
| Variable selling and administrative expenses | 1.40 |
| **Monthly fixed expenses:** | |
| Fixed manufacturing overhead | $191,400 |
| Fixed selling and administrative expenses | 276,600 |

**Requirements**

1. What is the company's contribution margin per unit? Contribution margin percentage? Total contribution margin?
2. What would the company's monthly operating income be if the company sold 150,000 units?
3. What would the company's monthly operating income be if the company had sales of $4,000,000?
4. What is the break-even point in units? In sales dollars?
5. How many units would the company have to sell to earn a target monthly profit of $260,000?
6. Management is currently in contract negotiations with the labour union. If the negotiations fail, direct labour costs will increase by 10% and fixed costs will increase by $22,500 per month. If these costs increase, how many units will the company have to sell each month to break even?
7. Return to the original data for this question and the remaining questions. What is the company's current operating leverage factor, rounded to two decimals?
8. If sales volume increases by 8%, by what percentage will operating income increase?
9. What is the firm's current margin of safety in sales dollars? What is its margin of safety as a percentage of sales?
10. Say FlashCo adds a second line of flash drives (2GB rather than 1GB). A 2GB flash drive will sell for $45 and have variable cost per unit of $20 per unit. The expected sales mix is three small flash drives for each large flash drive. Given this sales mix, how many of each type of flash drive will FlashCo need to sell to reach its target monthly profit of $260,000? Is this volume higher or lower than previously needed (in Requirement 5) to achieve the same target profit? Why?



# EXERCISES Group B

### E4-39B Prepare contribution margin income statements *(Learning Objectives 1 & 2)*

Check sum: (2) Contribution margin ratio is 59%.

Airborne Travel uses the contribution margin income statement internally. Airborne's first quarter results follow. Airborne's relevant range is between sales of $201,000 and $463,000.

**Airborne Travel**
**Contribution Margin Income Statement**
Three Months Ended March 31

| | |
|---|---|
| Sales revenue | $ 318,500 |
| Less: Variable expenses | (129,000) |
| Contribution margin | 189,500 |
| Less: Fixed expenses | (179,000) |
| Operating income | $ 10,500 |

**Requirements**

1. Prepare contribution margin income statements at sales levels of $251,000 and $363,000. (*Hint:* Use the contribution margin ratio.)
2. Compute break-even sales in dollars.

### E4-40B Work backward to find missing information *(Learning Objectives 1 & 2)*

Check sum: Sales are $130,000.

Arm-Bras Dry Cleaners has determined the following about its costs: Total variable expenses are $39,000; total fixed expenses are $35,000; and the sales revenue needed to break even is $50,000. Use the contribution margin income statement and the shortcut contribution margin approaches to determine Arm-Bras Dry Cleaners' current (1) sales revenue and (2) operating income. (*Hint:* First, find the contribution margin ratio, then prepare the contribution margin income statement.)

**E4-41B Find break-even and target profit volume** *(Learning Objectives 1 & 2)*

Happy Ten produces sports socks. The company has fixed expenses of $80,000 and variable expenses of $0.80 per package. Each package sells for $1.60.

Check sum: Contribution margin ratio is 50%.

**Requirements**

1. Compute the contribution margin per package and the contribution margin ratio.
2. Find the break-even point in units and in dollars, using the contribution margin shortcut approaches.
3. Find the number of packages Happy Ten needs to sell to earn a $22,000 operating income.

**E4-42B Continuation of E4-41B: changing costs** *(Learning Objective 3)*

Refer to Happy Ten in E4-41B. If Happy Ten can decrease its variable costs to $0.70 per package by increasing its fixed costs to $95,000, how many packages will it have to sell to generate $22,000 of operating income? Is this more or less than before? Why?

Check sum: Sales in units is 130,000 packages.

**E4-43B Find break-even and target profit volume** *(Learning Objectives 1 & 2)*

Owner Sunny Chadha is considering franchising her Oriental Express restaurant concept. She believes people will pay $5.50 for a large bowl of noodles. Variable costs are $2.75 a bowl. Chadha estimates monthly fixed costs for franchisees at $8,750.

Check sum: Contribution margin ratio is 50%.

**Requirements**

1. Use the contribution margin ratio shortcut approach to find a franchisee's break-even sales in dollars.
2. Is franchising a good idea for Chadha if franchisees want a minimum monthly operating income of $3,500 and Chadha believes most locations could generate $24,000 in monthly sales?

**E4-44B Continuation of E4-43B: changing business conditions** *(Learning Objective 3)*

Refer to Oriental Express in E4-43B. Since franchising, Oriental Express has not been very successful due to competition from Noodles Plus. To increase its market share, Oriental Express will have to lower its sales price to $5.00 per bowl. At the same time, Oriental Express hopes to increase each restaurant's volume to 7,000 bowls per month by embarking on a marketing campaign. Each franchise will have to contribute $500 per month to cover the advertising costs. Prior to these changes, most locations were selling 6,500 bowls per month.

Check sum: (1) Operating income was $9,125.

**Requirements**

1. What was the average restaurant's operating income before these changes?
2. Assuming the price cut and advertising campaign are successful at increasing volume to the projected level, will the franchisees earn their target profit of $3,500 per month?

**E4-45B Compute break-even and project income** *(Learning Objectives 1 & 2)*

Antigonish Steel Parts produces parts for the automobile industry. The company has monthly fixed expenses of $620,000 and a contribution margin of 75% of revenues.

Check sum: (1) Break-even sales is $826,667.

**Requirements**

1. Compute Antigonish Steel Parts' monthly break-even sales in dollars. Use the contribution margin ratio shortcut approach.
2. Use the contribution margin ratio to project operating income (or loss) if revenues are $500,000 and if they are $1,030,000.
3. Do the results in Requirement 2 make sense given the break-even sales you computed in Requirement 1? Explain.

**E4-46B Continuation of E4-45B: changing business conditions** *(Learning Objective 3)*

Refer to Antigonish Steel Parts in E4-45B. The automotive manufacturers are demanding lower prices, and the steel producers have increased raw material costs. The company's contribution margin has shrunk to 60% of revenues. Monthly operating income, prior to these pressures, was $307,000.

Check sum (1) Sales in dollars is $1,545,000.

### Requirements

1. To maintain this same level of profit, what sales volume (in sales revenue) must the company now achieve?
2. The company president believes that his monthly sales revenue will only go as high as $1,030,000. He is thinking about moving operations overseas to cut fixed costs. If monthly sales are $1,030,000, by how much will he need to cut fixed costs to maintain his prior profit level of $307,000 per month?

## E4-47B Identify information on a CVP graph *(Learning Objective 2)*

Susannah Chardon is thinking about starting an upscale gift basket service. She would create gift baskets for corporate clients and then arrange for delivery. She is trying to decide if the gift basket service would be profitable. Unfortunately, Chardon's hard drive crashed before she finished her financial analysis. However, she did recover the following partial CVP chart:

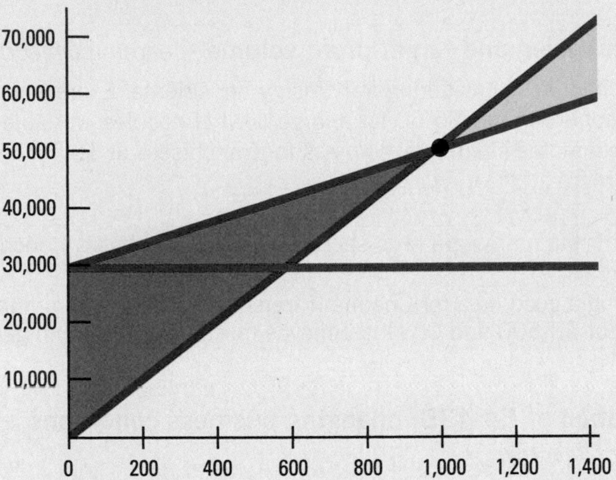


### Requirements

1. Label the axes, sales revenue line, total expense line, fixed expense line, operating income area, and operating loss area.
2. If Susannah sells 825 gift baskets in her first year, will the venture be profitable?
3. What are the break-even sales in baskets and dollars?

## E4-48B Sustainability and CVP *(Learning Objective 3)*

Lopez Garage Doors manufactures a premium garage door. Currently, the price and cost data associated with the premium garage door are as follows:

| | |
|---|---:|
| Average selling price per premium garage door | $ 1,300 |
| Average variable manufacturing cost per door | $ 550 |
| Average variable selling cost per door | $ 150 |
| Total annual fixed costs | $240,000 |

Check sum: (3) New break-even is 430.

Lopez Garage Doors has undertaken several sustainability projects over the past few years. Management is currently evaluating whether to develop a comprehensive software control system for its manufacturing operations that would significantly reduce scrap and waste generated during the manufacturing process. If the company were to implement this software control system in its manufacturing operations, the use of the software control system would result in an increase of $61,000 in its annual fixed costs while the average variable manufacturing cost per door would drop by $100.

### Requirements

1. What is the company's current break-even in units and in dollars?
2. If the company expects to sell 450 premium garage doors in the upcoming year, and it does not develop the software control system, what is its expected operating income from premium garage doors?

3. If the software control system were to be developed and implemented, what would be the company's new break-even point in units and in dollars?
4. If the company expects to sell 450 premium garage doors in the upcoming year, and it develops the software control system, what is its expected operating income from premium garage doors?
5. If the company expects to sell 450 premium garage doors in the upcoming year, do you think the company should implement the software control system? Why or why not? What factors should the company consider?

### E4-49B Prepare a CVP graph *(Learning Objective 2)*

Suppose that the Saddledome, the home of the Calgary Flames, earns total revenue that averages $28 for every ticket sold. Assume that annual fixed expenses are $22 million and that variable expenses are $6 per ticket.

**Requirements**

1. Prepare the hockey rink's CVP graph under these assumptions. Label the axes, sales revenue line, fixed expense line, total expense line, operating loss area, and operating income area on the graph.
2. Show the break-even point in dollars and in tickets.

### E4-50B Work backward to find new break-even point *(Learning Objectives 2 & 3)*

Flow Industries is planning to purchase a new piece of equipment that will increase the quality of its production. It hopes the increased quality will generate more sales. The company's contribution margin ratio is 20%, and its current break-even point is $650,000 in sales revenue. If Flow Industries' fixed expenses increase by $50,000 due to the equipment, what will its new break-even point be in sales revenue?

Check sum: Fixed expenses are $130,000.

### E4-51B Find the consequence of rising fixed costs *(Learning Objectives 1 & 3)*

Michele Quigg sells homemade knit scarves for $25 each at local craft shows. Her contribution margin ratio is 60%. Currently, the craft show entrance fees cost Michele $1,500 per year. The craft shows are raising their entrance fees by 25% next year. How many *extra* scarves will Michele have to sell next year just to pay for rising entrance fee costs?

Check sum: Break-even in units is 25 scarves.

CHAPTER 4

### E4-52B Extension of E4-51B: multiproduct firm *(Learning Objective 4)*

Sebastien Quigg admired his wife's success at selling scarves at local craft shows (E4-51B), so he decided to make two types of plant stands to sell at the shows. Sebastien makes twig stands from twigs he collects in the neighbourhood, so his variable cost is minimal (wood screws, glue, and so forth). However, Sebastien has to purchase wood to make his oak plant stands. His unit prices and costs are as follows.

Check sum: Sales are 35 units.

| | Twig Stands | Oak Stands |
|---|---|---|
| Sales price | $13.00 | $30.00 |
| Variable cost | 2.50 | 7.00 |

The twig stands are more popular, so Sebastien sells four twig stands for every one oak stand. Michele charges her husband $455 to share her booths at the craft shows (after all, she has paid the entrance fees). How many of each plant stand does Sebastien need to sell to break even? Will this affect the number of scarves Michele needs to sell to break even? Explain.

### E4-53B Find the break-even sales for a multiproduct firm *(Learning Objective 4)*

Rapid Scooters plans to sell a motorized standard scooter for $65 and a motorized chrome scooter for $75. Rapid Scooters purchases the standard scooter for $50 and the chrome scooter for $55. Rapid Scooters expects to sell two chrome scooters for every three standard scooters. Rapid Scooters' monthly fixed expenses are $15,300. How many of each type of scooter must Rapid Scooters sell monthly to break even? To earn $9,350?

Check sum: Sales in units are 900 units.

## E4-54B Work backward to find missing data *(Learning Objective 4)*

Jicky manufactures two styles of watches: the Digital and the Classic. The following data pertain to the Digital:

| | |
|---|---|
| Variable manufacturing cost | $140 |
| Variable operating cost | 20 |
| Sales price | 240 |

Jicky's monthly fixed expenses total $210,000. When Digitals and Classics are sold at a ratio of 6:4, respectively, the sale of 2,500 total watches results in an operating income of $80,000. Compute the contribution margin per watch for the Classic.

## E4-55B Find the break-even point and evaluate an advertising decision at a multiproduct company *(Learning Objectives 3, 4, & 5)*

Check sum: (2) Contribution margin ratio is 72%.

Red Deer Sporting Goods is a retailer of sporting equipment. Last year, Red Deer's sales revenues totalled $6,400,000. Total expenses were $2,800,000. Of this amount, approximately $1,792,000 were variable, while the remainder were fixed. Since Red Deer Sporting Goods offers thousands of different products, its managers prefer to calculate the break-even point in terms of sales dollars rather than units.

### Requirements

1. What is Red Deer Sporting Goods' current operating income? (Prepare a contribution margin format income statement.)
2. What is Red Deer's contribution margin ratio?
3. What is Red Deer's break-even point in sales dollars? (*Hint:* The contribution margin ratio calculated in Requirement 2 is already weighted by Red Deer Sporting Goods' actual sales mix.) What does it mean?
4. Red Deer's top management is deciding whether to embark on a $190,000 advertising campaign. The marketing firm has projected annual sales volume to increase by 20% as a result of this campaign. Assuming that the projections are correct, how would this advertising campaign affect Red Deer Sporting Goods' annual operating income?



## E4-56B Compute margin of safety and operating leverage *(Learning Objective 5)*

Check sum: (2) Operating leverage is 18.05.

Use the Airborne Travel data in E4-39B to answer the following questions.

### Requirements

1. What is Airborne Travel's current margin of safety (in dollars)?
2. What is Airborne Travel's current operating leverage factor?
3. If sales volume increases 4% next quarter, by what percent will Airborne's operating income increase? What will the new operating income be?

## E4-57B Work backward through margin of safety *(Learning Objective 5)*

Check sum: Sales at break-even are $9,000.

Tackle's Bait Shop had budgeted bait sales for the season at $15,000, with a $6,000 margin of safety. However, due to unseasonable weather, bait sales only reached $12,100. By what amount did actual sales exceed break-even sales?

## E4-58B Compute margin of safety and operating leverage *(Learning Objective 5)*

Check sum: (1) Contribution margin ratio is 20%.

Nate's Repair Shop has a monthly target operating income of $13,500. Variable expenses are 80% of sales, and monthly fixed expenses are $10,000.

### Requirements

1. Compute the monthly margin of safety in dollars if the shop achieves its income goal.
2. Express Nate's margin of safety as a percentage of target sales.
3. What is Nate's operating leverage factor at the target level of operating income?
4. Assume that Nate reaches his target. By what percentage will his operating income fall if sales volume declines by 9%?

## E4-59B Use operating leverage factor to find fixed costs *(Learning Objective 5)*

When sales were $60,000, Popley Manufacturing had a 1.40 operating leverage factor. Popley Manufacturing's contribution margin ratio was 35%. What were Popley Manufacturing's fixed expenses?

Check sum: Operating income is $15,000.

## E4-60B Make a comprehensive CVP analysis *(Learning Objectives 1, 2, 3, 4, & 5)*

Larry Stenback is evaluating a business opportunity to sell grooming kits at dog shows. Larry can buy the grooming kits at a wholesale cost of $32 per set. He plans to sell the grooming kits for $62 per set. He estimates fixed costs such as travel costs, booth rental cost, and lodging to be $600 per dog show.

Check sum: Contribution margin per is $30.

### Requirements

1. Determine the number of grooming kits Larry must sell per show to break even.
2. Assume Larry wants to earn a profit of $900 per show.
   a. Determine the sales volume in units necessary to earn the desired profit.
   b. Determine the sales volume in dollars necessary to earn the desired profit.
   c. Using the contribution margin format, prepare an income statement (condensed version) to confirm your answers to Requirements (a) and (b).
3. Determine the margin of safety between the sales volume at the break-even point and the sales volume required to earn the desired profit. Determine the margin of safety in sales dollars in units and as a percentage.

## E4-61B Make a comprehensive CVP analysis *(Learning Objectives 1, 2, 3, & 5)*

Austen Company manufactures and sells a single product. The company's sales and expenses for last year are as follows:

Check sum: (2) Break-even in units is 1,300 units.

| | Total | Per Unit | % |
|---|---|---|---|
| Sales | $81,250 | $25 | ? |
| Variable expenses | 48,750 | 15 | ? |
| Contribution margin | ? | ? | ? |
| Fixed expenses | 13,000 | | |
| Operating income | $19,500 | | |

### Requirements

1. Fill in the missing numbers in the table. Use the table to answer the following questions:
   a. What is the total contribution margin?
   b. What is the per-unit contribution margin?
   c. What is the operating income?
   d. How many units were sold?
2. Use the table to answer the following questions about break-even analysis:
   a. What is the annual break-even point in units?
   b. What is the annual break-even point in sales dollars?
3. Use the table to answer the following questions about target profit analysis and safety margin:
   a. How many units must the company sell in order to earn a profit of $53,000?
   b. What is the margin of safety in units?
   c. What is the margin of safety in sales dollars?
   d. What is the margin of safety as a percentage?

### E4-62B Comprehensive CVP analysis *(Learning Objectives 1, 2, 3, 4, & 5)*

Check sum: (1) Contribution margin ratio is 32%.

GigaCo manufactures 1GB flash drives (jump drives). Price and cost data for a relevant range extending to 200,000 units per month are as follows:

| | |
|---|---|
| **Sales price per unit** | |
| (Current monthly sales volume is 130,000 units) | $ 25.00 |
| **Variable cost per unit:** | |
| Direct materials | 6.20 |
| Direct labour | 7.00 |
| Variable manufacturing overhead | 2.00 |
| Variable selling and administrative expenses | 1.80 |
| **Monthly fixed expenses:** | |
| Fixed manufacturing overhead | $102,300 |
| Fixed selling and administrative expenses | 187,800 |

**Requirements**

1. What is the company's contribution margin per unit? Contribution margin percentage? Total contribution margin?
2. What would the company's monthly operating income be if it sold 160,000 units?
3. What would the company's monthly operating income be if it had sales of $4,000,000?
4. What is the break-even point in units? In sales dollars?
5. How many units would the company have to sell to earn a target monthly profit of $260,100?
6. Management is currently in contract negotiations with the labour union. If the negotiations fail, direct labour costs will increase by 10% and fixed costs will increase by $22,500 per month. If these costs increase, how many units will the company have to sell each month to break even?
7. Return to the original data for this question and the remaining questions. What is the company's current operating leverage factor, rounded to two decimals?
8. If sales volume increases by 7%, by what percentage will operating income increase?
9. What is the firm's current margin of safety in sales dollars? What is its margin of safety as a percentage of sales?
10. Let's say GigaCo adds a second line of flash drive (2GB as well as the 1GB drive). The 2GB flash drive will sell for $45 and has a variable cost per unit of $28. The expected sales mix is six of the smaller flash drives for every one larger flash drive. Given this sales mix, how many of each type of flash drive will GigaCo need to sell to reach its target monthly profit of $260,100? Is this volume higher or lower than previously needed (in Requirement 5) to achieve the same target profit? Why?

# PROBLEMS Group A

### P4-63A Find missing data in CVP relationships *(Learning Objectives 1 & 2)*

Check sum: Contribution margin ratio for Q is 70%.

The budgets of four companies yield the following information:

| | Company | | | |
|---|---|---|---|---|
| | **Q** | **R** | **S** | **T** |
| Target sales | $720,000 | $400,000 | $190,000 | $ ____ |
| Variable expenses | 216,000 | ____ | ____ | 270,000 |
| Fixed expenses | ____ | 156,000 | 90,000 | ____ |
| Operating income (loss) | $154,000 | $ ____ | $ ____ | 140,000 |
| Units sold | ____ | 125,000 | 12,000 | 15,750 |
| Contribution margin per unit | $ 6 | ____ | $ 9.50 | $ 40 |
| Contribution margin ratio | ____ | 0.65 | ____ | ____ |

### Requirements

1. Fill in the blanks for each company.
2. Compute break-even, in sales dollars, for each company. Which company has the lowest break-even point in sales dollars? What causes the low break-even point?

## P4-64A Find break-even and target profit and prepare income statements *(Learning Objectives 1 & 2)*

A travelling production of *The Phantom of the Opera* performs 100 shows each year. The average sales for each show are 800 tickets at $50 a ticket. The show has a cast of 40, each earning an average of $260 per show. The cast is paid only after each show. The other variable expense is program printing costs of $6 per guest. Annual fixed expenses total $942,400.

Check sum: Variable expenses for cast are $10,400.

### Requirements

1. Compute revenue and variable expenses for each show.
2. Use the income statement equation approach to compute the number of shows needed annually to break even.
3. Use the shortcut unit contribution margin approach to compute the number of shows needed annually to earn a profit of $1,438,400. Is this goal realistic? Give your reason.
4. Prepare *The Phantom of the Opera*'s contribution margin income statement for 100 shows each year. Report only two categories of expenses: variable and fixed.

## P4-65A Solve a comprehensive CVP problem *(Learning Objectives 1, 2, & 5)*

Team Spirit imprints calendars with college and university names. The company has fixed expenses of $1,035,000 each month plus variable expenses of $3.60 per carton of calendars. Of the variable expense, 70% is cost of goods sold, while the remaining 30% relates to variable operating expenses. Team Spirit sells each carton of calendars for $10.50.

Check sum: (1) Break-even in units is 150,000 cartons.

### Requirements

1. Use the income statement equation approach to compute the number of cartons of calendars that Team Spirit must sell each month to break even.
2. Use the contribution margin ratio shortcut formula to compute the dollar amount of monthly sales Team Spirit needs in order to earn $285,000 in operating income (round the contribution margin ratio to two decimal places).
3. Prepare Team Spirit's contribution margin income statement for June for sales of 450,000 cartons of calendars.
4. What is June's margin of safety (in dollars)? What is the operating leverage factor at this level of sales?
5. By what percentage will operating income change if July's sales volume is 13% higher? Prove your answer.



## P4-66A Compute break-even, prepare CVP graph, and respond to change *(Learning Objectives 1, 2, & 3)*

Personal Investors is opening an office in Whitehorse. Fixed monthly expenses are office rent ($2,500), depreciation on office furniture ($260), utilities ($280), special telephone lines ($600), a connection with an online brokerage service ($640), and the salary of a financial planner ($3,320). Variable expenses include payments to the financial planner (10% of revenue), advertising (5% of revenue), supplies and postage (2% of revenue), and usage fees for the telephone lines and computerized brokerage service (3% of revenue).

Check sum: (1) Contribution margin ratio is 80%.

### Requirements

1. Use the contribution margin ratio CVP formula to compute the investment firm's break-even revenue in dollars. If the average trade leads to $475 in revenue for Personal Investors, how many trades must it make to break even?
2. Use the income statement equation approach to compute dollar revenues needed to earn monthly operating income of $3,040.
3. Graph Personal Investors' CVP relationships. Assume that an average trade leads to $400 in revenue for Personal Investors. Show the break-even point, sales revenue line, fixed expense line, total expense line, operating loss area, operating income area, and sales in units (trades) and dollars when monthly operating income of $3,840 is earned. The graph should range from zero to 40 units (trades).
4. Assume that the average revenue that Personal Investors earns decreases to $375 per trade. How does this affect the break-even point in number of trades?

Check sum: Weighted average contribution margin/unit is $1.25.

## P4-67A Conduct a CVP analysis of a multiproduct firm *(Learning Objectives 4 & 5)*

The contribution margin income statement of Extreme Coffee for February is as follows. Extreme Coffee sells three small coffees for every large coffee. A small coffee sells for $2 with a variable expense of $1. A large coffee sells for $4 with a variable expense of $2.

**EXTREME COFFEE**
**Contribution Margin Income Statement**
**For the Month Ended February 29**

| | | |
|---|---|---|
| Sales revenue | | $90,000 |
| Variable expenses: | | |
| Cost of goods sold | $32,000 | |
| Marketing expense | 10,000 | |
| General and administrative expense | 3,000 | 45,000 |
| Contribution margin | | 45,000 |
| Fixed expenses: | | |
| Marketing expense | 16,500 | |
| General and administrative expense | 3,500 | 20,000 |
| Operating income | | $25,000 |

### Requirements

1. Determine Extreme Coffee's monthly break-even point in the numbers of small coffees and large coffees. Prove your answer by preparing a summary contribution margin income statement at the break-even level of sales. Show only two categories of expenses: variable and fixed.
2. Compute Extreme Coffee's margin of safety in dollars.
3. Use Extreme Coffee's operating leverage factor to determine its new operating income if sales volume increases 15%. Prove your results using the contribution margin income statement format. Assume that sales mix remains unchanged.

CHAPTER 4

# PROBLEMS Group B

Check sum: Contribution margin ratio for Q is 64%.

## P4-68B Find missing data in CVP relationships *(Learning Objectives 1 & 2)*

The budgets of four companies yield the following information:

| | Company | | | |
|---|---|---|---|---|
| | Q | R | S | T |
| Target sales | $828,125 | $415,625 | $181,250 | $ |
| Variable expenses | 298,125 | | | 270,000 |
| Fixed expenses | | 160,000 | 98,000 | |
| Operating income (loss) | $230,000 | $ | $ | 133,000 |
| Units sold | | 118,000 | 11,600 | 18,000 |
| Contribution margin per unit | $6.25 | | $10.00 | $ 35.00 |
| Contribution margin ratio | | 0.64 | | |

### Requirements

1. Fill in the blanks for each company.
2. Compute break-even, in sales dollars, for each company. Which company has the lowest break-even point in sales dollars? What causes the low break-even point?

### P4-69B Find break-even and target profit, and prepare income statements *(Learning Objectives 1 & 2)*

A travelling production of *Grease* performs 120 shows each year. An average of 1,000 tickets is sold for each show at $65 per ticket. The show has a cast of 45, each earning an average of $320 per show. The cast is paid only after each show. The other variable expense is program printing expenses of $6 per guest. Annual fixed expenses total $802,800.

Check sum: Total variable expenses/show are $20,400.

**Requirements**

1. Compute revenue and variable expenses for each show.
2. Use the income statement equation approach to compute the number of shows needed annually to break even.
3. Use the shortcut unit contribution margin approach to compute the number of shows needed annually to earn a profit of $5,708,800. Is this goal realistic? Give your reason.
4. Prepare *Grease*'s contribution margin income statement for 120 shows each year. Report only two categories of expenses: variable and fixed.

### P4-70B Solve a comprehensive CVP problem *(Learning Objectives 1, 2, & 5)*

Vast Spirit imprints calendars with college and university names. The company has fixed expenses of $1,045,000 each month plus variable expenses of $3.90 per carton of calendars. Of the variable expense, 66% is cost of goods sold, while the remaining 34% relates to variable operating expenses. Vast Spirit sells each carton of calendars for $11.50.

Check sum: (2) Contribution margin ratio is 66%.

**Requirements**

1. Use the income statement equation approach to compute the number of cartons of calendars that Vast Spirit must sell each month to break even.
2. Use the contribution margin ratio shortcut formula to compute the dollar amount of monthly sales Vast Spirit needs in order to earn $275,000 in operating income (round the contribution margin ratio to two decimal places).
3. Prepare Vast Spirit's contribution margin income statement for June for sales of 460,000 cartons of calendars.
4. What is June's margin of safety (in dollars)? What is the operating leverage factor at this level of sales?
5. By what percentage will operating income change if July's sales volume is 10% higher? Prove your answer.

CHAPTER 4

### P4-71B Compute break-even, prepare CVP graph, and respond to change *(Learning Objectives 1, 2, & 3)*

Personal Investors is opening an office in Ville Marie. Fixed monthly costs are office rent ($2,800), depreciation on office furniture ($310), utilities ($260), special telephone lines ($670), a connection with an online brokerage service ($700), and the salary of a financial planner ($2,760). Variable expenses include payments to the financial planner (10% of revenue), advertising (5% of revenue), supplies and postage (2% of revenue), and usage fees for the telephone lines and computerized brokerage service (23% of revenue).

Check sum: (1) Contribution margin ratio is 60%.

**Requirements**

1. Use the contribution margin ratio CVP formula to compute the investment firm's break-even revenue in dollars. If the average trade leads to $500 in revenue for Personal Investors, how many trades must be made to break even?
2. Use the income statement equation approach to compute dollar revenues needed to earn monthly operating income of $3,900.
3. Graph Personal Investors' CVP relationships. Assume that an average trade leads to $500 in revenue for Personal Investors. Show the break-even point, sales revenue line, fixed expense line, total expense line, operating loss area, operating income area, and sales in units (trades) and dollars when monthly operating income of $3,900 is earned. The graph should range from zero to 40 units (trades).
4. Assume that the average revenue Personal Investors earns decreases to $400 per trade. How does this affect the break-even point in number of trades?

### P4-72B Conduct a CVP analysis for a multiproduct firm

*(Learning Objectives 4 & 5)*

Check sum: Weighted average contribution margin/unit is $1.75.

The contribution margin income statement of Cosmic Coffee for February follows. Cosmic Coffee sells three small coffees for every large coffee. A small coffee sells for $3.00 with a variable expense of $1.50. A large coffee sells for $5.00 with a variable expense of $2.50.

| Cosmic Coffee<br>Contribution Margin Income Statement<br>For the Month Ended February 29 | | |
|---|---|---|
| Sales revenue | | $88,000 |
| Variable expenses: | | |
| Cost of goods sold | $30,000 | |
| Marketing expense | 8,000 | |
| General and administrative expense | 2,000 | 40,000 |
| Contribution margin | | 48,000 |
| Fixed expenses: | | |
| Marketing expense | 34,650 | |
| General and administrative expense | 7,350 | 42,000 |
| Operating income | | $ 6,000 |

**Requirements**

1. Determine Cosmic Coffee's monthly break-even point in numbers of small coffees and large coffees. Prove your answer by preparing a summary contribution margin income statement at the break-even level of sales. Show only two categories of expenses: variable and fixed.
2. Compute Cosmic Coffee's margin of safety in dollars.
3. Use Cosmic Coffee's operating leverage factor to determine its new operating income if sales volume increases by 15%. Prove your results using the contribution margin income statement format. Assume the sales mix remains unchanged.

# CAPSTONE APPLICATION PROBLEMS

## APPLICATION QUESTION

### A4-73 Determine the feasibility of a business plan *(Learning Objective 2)*

Brian and Nui Soon live in Sudbury. Two years ago, they visited Thailand. Nui, a professional chef, was impressed with the cooking methods and the spices used in the Thai food. Sudbury does not have a Thai restaurant, and the Soons are contemplating opening one. Nui would supervise the cooking and Brian would leave his current job to be the maître d'. The restaurant would serve dinner Tuesday through Saturday.

Brian has noticed a restaurant for lease. The restaurant has seven tables, each of which can seat four. Tables can be moved together for a large party. Nui is planning two seatings per evening, and the restaurant will be open 50 weeks per year.

The Soons have drawn up the following estimates:

| | |
|---|---|
| Average revenue, including beverages and dessert | $ 40 per meal |
| Average cost of the food | $ 12 per meal |
| Chef's and dishwasher's salaries | $50,400 per year |
| Rent (premises, equipment) | $ 4,000 per month |
| Cleaning (linen and premises) | $ 800 per month |
| Replacement of dishes, cutlery, glasses | $ 300 per month |
| Utilities, advertising, telephone | $ 1,900 per month |

**Requirement**

Compute the *annual* break-even number of meals and sales revenue for the restaurant. Also, compute the number of meals and the amount of sales revenue needed to earn operating income of $75,600 for the year. How many meals must the Soons serve each night to earn their target income of $75,600? Should the couple open the restaurant? Support your answer.

## CASE ASSIGNMENT

### C4-74 Shining Oaks Toy Company

*Source:* Laborant/Shutterstock

**CVP analysis**

Alvarez Garcia grew up always working with his father in a woodshop in their backyard. It was no surprise to the family when Alvarez decided to pursue carpentry as a career. When he was in school, he found that he much preferred the fine detail work of small objects rather than building large cabinets and furniture. Alvarez and two other students in the school began to create small wooden toys, and by selling the toys they created at fairs and local craft shows—especially just before Christmas—they were able to pay for their schooling and still put some money aside. When they graduated, only Alvarez wanted to continue. He bought out the other two students and incorporated the Shining Oaks Toy Company Inc. Alvarez made a commitment to himself to use sustainable wood sources (wood from tree farms rather than old forest logging) but still create a top-quality product. He also always wanted to remain innovative and creative. In his first year, he won the Gold Leaf Environment Award from Industry Canada and the New Toy of the Year Award from the Toy and Game Council of North America. Alvarez also got involved in local charities and was named the Business Person of the Year last year by the Chamber of Commerce for his involvement and support of charities.

After just five years, Alvarez has his toys in 350 high-end toy shops across Canada and the United States. He has a few different product lines, and they are quickly becoming highly collectible. Toy shop owners are telling him that once a customer buys a few pieces of one product line, they keep coming back to complete the set. The most popular are the sets of wooden blocks; only specific shapes are available in each set, so customers need to purchase additional sets in order to have all of the shapes and for children to be able to build larger and larger structures.

These toy-shop owners are Alvarez's best source of information for new products and demand. In order to plan for the Christmas rush, Alvarez travelled to some of the stores and sat down with the owners to get their opinions. What he discovered is as follows:

- Customers are willing to pay up to 10% more in order to have the wooden toys in higher-quality, rarer woods.
- Higher-quality packaging with a more upscale design would increase sales by about 8%.
- Increasing the regular price on the product lines by 5% will reduce the number of units sold by 5%.
- Adding a complete product line on wooden people to accompany the building sets will add 60,000 units to sales but will take away sales from each of the other lines by 14%. It is possible that the addition of the wooden people will make the lines of toys even more appealing to young girls and bring additional new sales for all of the lines, but this is still speculation.

Alvarez went back to work and dug up some additional information regarding these potential changes but didn't know how to actually turn all of this information into a decision. He looked into sourcing new, exotic woods for the toys and discovered that the cost of DM would increase by 55% in order to obtain these rarer types of wood. The packaging redesign could be done with a one-time design fee for $100,000 and an ongoing increase in shipping costs (Selling) of $0.75 per package. The new product line of wooden people would sell for $40 per set, and the costs associated with the line would be DM = $5 DL = $2 VMOH = $2. The variable selling expenses (VSell) and variable general and administrative expenses (VG&A) would remain the same per unit as for the other products. FMOH = an additional $50,000 per year, fixed selling expenses (FSelling) = an additional $25,000 per year.

The income statement for Shining Oaks Toy Company Inc. is as follows:

| | 2012 | 2013 | 2014 |
|---|---|---|---|
| Units | 350,000 | 400,000 | 500,000 |
| Sales | $14,000,000 | $16,000,000 | $20,000,000 |
| COGS | (4,150,000) | (4,700,000) | (5,800,000) |
| Gross Profit | 9,850,000 | 11,300,000 | 14,200,000 |
| | | | |
| Expenses | | | |
| Selling | 1,312,500 | 1,500,000 | 1,875,000 |
| G&A | 3,940,000 | 4,360,000 | 5,200,000 |
| Advert | 1,150,000 | 1,150,000 | 1,200,000 |
| Total Expenses | (6,402,500) | (7,010,000) | (8,275,000) |
| NOI | $ 3,447,500 | $ 4,290,000 | $ 5,925,000 |

Note: Each of these options should be examined independently with the original information. The product costs for all of the current lines are the same with the following amounts:

| | |
|---|---|
| DM | $6 |
| DL | 3 |
| VMOH | 2 |
| FMOH 0.75 | (when production is at 400,000 units) |

# ETHICAL ISSUE

## I4-75 Examine an ethical dilemma with CVP analysis error

*(Learning Objective 2)*

You have just begun your summer internship at Tmedic. The company supplies sterilized surgical instruments for physicians. To expand sales, Tmedic is considering paying a commission to its sales force. The controller, Sasha Korablina, asks you to compute (1) the new break-even sales figure and (2) the operating profit if sales increase 15% under the new sales commission plan. She thinks you can handle this task because you learned CVP analysis in your accounting class.

You spend the next day collecting information from the accounting records, performing the analysis, and writing a memo to explain the results. The company president is pleased with your memo. You report that the new sales commission plan will lead to a significant increase in operating income and only a small increase in break-even sales.

The following week, you realize that you made an error in the CVP analysis. You overlooked the sales personnel's $2,500 monthly salaries, and you did not include this fixed marketing expense in your computations. You are not sure what to do. If you tell Korablina of your mistake, she will have to tell the president. In this case, you are afraid Tmedic might not offer you permanent employment after your internship.

**Requirements**

1. How would your error affect break-even sales and operating income under the proposed sales commission plan? Could this cause the president to reject the sales commission proposal?
2. Consider your ethical responsibilities. Is there a difference between (a) initially making an error and (b) subsequently failing to inform the controller?
3. Suppose you tell Korablina of the error in your analysis. Why might the consequences not be as bad as you fear? Should Korablina take any responsibility for your error? What could Korablina have done differently?
4. After considering all of the factors, should you inform Korablina or simply keep quiet?

# TEAM PROJECT

## T4-76 Assess advertising campaign and production level decisions

*(Learning Objectives 1 & 3)*

EZPAK Manufacturing produces filament packaging tape. In 2016, EZPAK Manufacturing produced and sold 15 million rolls of tape. The company has recently expanded its capacity, so it can now produce up to 30 million rolls per year. EZPAK Manufacturing's accounting records show the following results from 2016:

| | |
|---|---|
| Sales price per roll | $ 3.00 |
| Variable manufacturing expenses per roll | 2.00 |
| Variable marketing and administrative expenses per roll | 0.50 |
| Total fixed manufacturing overhead costs | $8,400,000 |
| Total fixed marketing and administrative expenses | $ 600,000 |
| Sales | 15 million rolls |
| Production | 15 million rolls |

There were no beginning or ending inventories in 2016.

In January 2017, EZPAK Manufacturing hired a new president, Kevin McDaniel. McDaniel has a one-year contract specifying that he will be paid 10% of EZPAK Manufacturing's 2017 operating income (based on traditional absorption costing) instead of a salary. In 2017, McDaniel must make two major decisions:

1. Should EZPAK Manufacturing undertake a major advertising campaign? This campaign would raise sales to 25 million rolls. This is the maximum level of sales that EZPAK Manufacturing can expect to make in the near future. The ad campaign would add an additional $3.5 million in marketing and administrative costs. Without the campaign, sales will be 15 million rolls.
2. How many rolls of tape will EZPAK Manufacturing produce?

At the end of the year, EZPAK Manufacturing's board of directors will evaluate McDaniel's performance and decide whether to offer him a contract for the following year.

## Requirements

Within your group form two subgroups. One subgroup assumes the role of Kevin McDaniel, EZPAK Manufacturing's new president; the other subgroup assumes the role of EZPAK Manufacturing's board of directors. McDaniel will meet with the board of directors shortly after the end of 2017 to decide whether he will remain at EZPAK Manufacturing. Most of your effort should be devoted to advance preparation for this meeting. Each subgroup should meet separately to prepare for the meeting between the board and McDaniel. (*Hint:* Keep computations [other than per-unit amounts] in millions.)

*Kevin McDaniel should do the following:*

1. Compute EZPAK Manufacturing's 2016 operating income.
2. Decide whether to adopt the advertising campaign by calculating the projected increase in operating income from the advertising campaign. Do not include the salary computation in this calculation. Prepare a memo to the board of directors explaining this decision. Use the following format:

---

Date: ______________________

To: ______________________

From: ______________________

Subject: ______________________

---

Give this memo to the board of directors as soon as possible (before the joint meeting).

3. Assume that EZPAK Manufacturing adopts the advertising campaign. Decide how many rolls of tape to produce in 2017. Assume that no safety stock is considered necessary to EZPAK's business.
4. Given your response to Requirement 3, prepare an absorption costing income statement for the year ended December 31, 2017, ending with operating income before salary computation. Then, compute your salary separately. The variable cost per unit and the total fixed expenses (with the exception of the advertising campaign) remain the same as in 2016. Give this income statement and your salary computation to the board of directors as soon as possible (before your meeting with the board).
5. Decide whether you want to remain at EZPAK Manufacturing for another year. You currently have an offer from another company. The contract with the other company is identical to the one you currently have with EZPAK Manufacturing—you will be paid 10% of absorption costing operating income instead of a salary.

*The board of directors should do the following:*

1. Compute EZPAK Manufacturing's 2016 operating income.
2. Determine whether EZPAK Manufacturing should adopt the advertising campaign by calculating the projected increase in operating income from the advertising campaign. Do not include the executive salary in this calculation.
3. Determine how many rolls of tape that EZPAK Manufacturing should produce in 2017. Assume that no safety stock is considered necessary to EZPAK's business.

4. Evaluate McDaniel's performance based on his decisions and the information he provided to the board. (*Hint:* You may want to prepare a variable costing income statement.)
5. Evaluate the contract's salary provision. Are you satisfied with this provision? If so, explain why. If not, recommend how it should be changed.

After McDaniel has given the board his memo and income statement, and after the board has had a chance to evaluate McDaniel's performance, McDaniel and the board should meet. The purpose of the meeting is to decide whether it is in everyone's mutual interest for McDaniel to remain with EZPAK Manufacturing and, if so, the terms of the contract EZPAK Manufacturing will offer McDaniel.

# DISCUSSION & ANALYSIS

1. Define break-even point. Why is the break-even point important to managers?
2. Describe four different ways cost-volume-profit analysis could be useful to management.
3. The purchasing manager for Rockwell Fashion Bags has been able to purchase the material for its signature handbags for $2 less per bag. Keeping everything else the same, what effect would this reduction in material cost have on the break-even point for Rockwell Fashion Bags? Now assume that the sales manager decides to reduce the selling price of each handbag by $2. What would the net effect of both of these changes be on the break-even point in units for Rockwell Fashion Bags?
4. Describe three ways that cost-volume-profit concepts could be used by a service organization.
5. "Break-even analysis isn't very useful to a company because companies need to do more than break even to survive in the long run." Explain why you agree or disagree with this statement.
6. What conditions must be met for cost-volume-profit analysis to be accurate?
7. Why is it necessary to calculate a weighted-average contribution margin ratio for a multi-product company when calculating the break-even point for that company? Why can't all the products' contribution margin ratios just be added together and averaged?
8. Is the contribution margin ratio of a grocery store likely to be higher or lower than that of a plastics manufacturer? Explain the difference in cost structure between a grocery store and a plastics manufacturer. How does the cost structure difference affect operating risk?
9. Alston Jewellery had sales revenues last year of $2.4 million, while their break-even point (in dollars) was $2.2 million. What was Alston Jewellery's margin of safety in dollars? What does the term margin of safety mean? What can you discern about Alston Jewellery from their margin of safety?
10. Rondell Pharmacy is considering switching to the use of robots to fill prescriptions that consist of oral solids or medications in pill form. The robots will assist the human pharmacists and reduce the number of human pharmacy workers needed. This change is expected to reduce the number of prescription-filling errors, to reduce the customers' wait times, and to reduce the total overall costs. How does the use of the robots affect Rondell Pharmacy's cost structure? Explain the impact of this switch to robotics on Rondell Pharmacy's operating risk.

# APPLICATION & ANALYSIS

## 4-1 Analyze CVP for a Product

Select one product that you could make yourself. Examples could be cookies, birdhouses, jewellery, or custom T-shirts. Assume that you have decided to start a small business producing and selling this product. You will be applying the concepts of cost-volume-profit analysis to this potential venture.

## Discussion Questions

1. Describe your product. What market are you targeting this product for? What price will you sell your product for? Make projections of your sales in units over each of the upcoming five years.
2. Make a detailed list of all of the materials needed to make your product. Include quantities needed of each material. Also include the cost of the material on a per-unit basis.
3. Make a list of all of the equipment you will need to make your product. Estimate the cost of each piece of equipment that you will need.
4. Make a list of all other expenses you would incur to create your product. Examples of other expenses would be rent, utilities, and insurance. Estimate the cost of each of these expenses per year.
5. Now classify all of the expenses you have listed as being either fixed or variable. For mixed expenses, separate the expense into the fixed component and the variable component.
6. Calculate how many units of your product you will need to sell to break even in each of the five years you have projected.
7. Calculate the margin of safety in units for each of the five years in your projection.
8. Now decide how much you would like to make in before-tax operating income (target profit) in each of the upcoming five years. Calculate how many units you would need to sell in each of the upcoming years to meet these target profit levels.
9. How realistic is your potential venture? Do you think you would be able to break even in each of the projected five years? How risky is your venture (use the margin of safety to help answer this question). Do you think your target profits are achievable?

## Classroom Applications

**Web:** Post the discussion questions on an electronic discussion board. Have small groups of students choose a product for their group. Students should collaboratively answer the questions.

**Classroom:** Form groups of three or four students. Your group should choose a product. After estimating costs and making the calculations, prepare a five-minute presentation that addresses the listed questions about your group's product.

**Independent:** Research answers to each of the questions. Turn in a two- or three-page typed paper (12-point font, double-spaced with 2.5 cm margins). Include tables that include the estimated fixed costs and estimated variable costs. Also show all calculations.

# Demo Doc

Chapter 4

**MyAccountingLab** Make the grade with MyAccountingLab! Animated versions of similar Demo Docs to these can be found on MyAccountingLab.

## USING CVP FOR SENSITIVITY ANALYSIS

### Learning Objectives 1, 2, 3, & 4

Hacker Golf has developed a unique swing trainer golf club. The company currently pays a production company to produce the golf club at a cost of $32 each. Other variable costs total $6 per golf club and monthly fixed expenses are $18,000. Hacker Golf currently sells the trainer golf club for $68.

NOTE: Solve each requirement as a separate situation.

### Requirements

1. Calculate Hacker Golf's break-even point in units.
2. Hacker Golf is considering raising the club's selling price to $78. Calculate the new break-even in units.
3. Hacker Golf has found a new company to produce the golf club at a lower cost of $26. Calculate the new break-even in units.
4. Because many customers have requested a golf glove to go along with the trainer club, Hacker Golf is considering selling gloves. The company expects to sell only one glove for every four trainer clubs it sells. Hacker Golf can purchase the gloves for $4 each and sell them for $9. Total fixed costs should remain the same at $18,000 per month. Calculate the break-even point in units for trainer clubs and golf gloves.
5. Use a contribution margin income statement to prove the break-even point calculated in Requirement 4.

# Demo Doc Solution

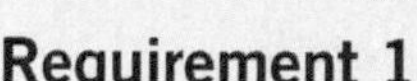

### Requirement 1

**Calculate Hacker's break-even point in units.**

To determine the break-even point, we first must calculate the contribution margin per unit. The contribution margin is calculated by subtracting variable costs from the sales revenue.

Contribution margin per unit = Sales price per unit − Variable cost per unit

Hacker Golf's variable cost per club (unit) is the price it pays for each club ($32) plus its additional variable costs per golf club ($6). Therefore, its unit contribution margin is as follows:

| | |
|---|---|
| Selling price per club | $ 68 |
| Variable cost per club ($32 + $6) | (38) |
| Contribution margin per club | $ 30 |

The contribution margin represents the amount from each unit sold that is available to cover fixed expenses. That means Hacker Golf earns $30 per club, which contributes toward fixed expenses until fixed expenses are covered. After fixed expenses are covered, each club sold contributes $30 directly to the company's operating income.

Break-even is the level of sales at which income is zero. The break-even point can be calculated as follows:

$$\text{Break-even in units} = \frac{\text{Fixed expenses} + \text{Operating income}}{\text{Contribution margin per unit}}$$

$$\text{Break-even in units} = \frac{\$18{,}000 + 0}{\$30}$$

$$= 600 \text{ trainer clubs}$$

## Requirement 2

**Hacker Golf is considering raising the club's selling price to $78. Calculate the new break-even in units.**

Even if Hacker Golf raises its sales price per club to $78, its variable costs ($38 per unit) and fixed expenses ($18,000) will stay the same. As a result of increasing the sales price, the company will now have a higher contribution margin per unit:

| | |
|---|---|
| Selling price per club | $ 78 |
| Variable cost per club ($32 + $6) | (38) |
| Contribution margin per club | $ 40 |

Once again, you can use the break-even formula to find the new break-even point:

$$\text{Break-even in units} = \frac{\text{Fixed expenses} + \text{Operating income}}{\text{Contribution margin per unit}}$$

$$\text{Break-even in units} = \frac{\$18{,}000 + 0}{\$40}$$

$$= 450 \text{ trainer clubs}$$

With the increased selling price, break-even has been reduced from 600 clubs to 450 clubs. The higher price means that each club contributes more to fixed expenses.

You can prove the answer by preparing an income statement for a sales volume of 450 units:

| | |
|---|---|
| Sales revenue (450 × $78) | $ 35,100 |
| Less: Variable expenses (450 × $38) | (17,100) |
| Total contribution margin | 18,000 |
| Less: Fixed expenses | (18,000) |
| Operating income | 0 |

If the selling price increases, the volume required to break even or achieve target profit goals decreases (provided costs do not change). Conversely, if the selling price decreases, the volume required to break even or achieve target profit goals increases.

## Requirement 3

**Hacker Golf has found a new company to produce the golf club at a lower cost of $26. Calculate the new break-even in units.**

Let's return to Hacker Golf's original sales price ($68). Assuming that Hacker Golf has found a new company to produce the golf club for $26 each, the company's variable costs per club will decrease. However, fixed expenses remain the same ($18,000). Once again,

Hacker Golf's contribution margin per unit will increase as a result of this change in business conditions:

| | |
|---|---|
| Selling price per club | $ 68 |
| Variable cost per club ($26 + $6) | (32) |
| Contribution margin per club | $ 36 |

The new break-even point is found as follows:

$$\text{Break-even in units} = \frac{\text{Fixed expenses} + \text{Operating income}}{\text{Contribution margin per unit}}$$

$$\text{Break-even in units} = \frac{\$18{,}000 + 0}{\$36}$$

$$= 500 \text{ trainer clubs}$$

With the reduced variable cost, Hacker Golf's break-even in units decreases from 600 clubs to 500 clubs. Using this information, Hacker Golf's management must decide if it is worth the risk to switch to a new producer.

You can also prove this result by preparing an income statement:

| | |
|---|---|
| Sales revenue (500 × $68) | $ 34,000 |
| Less: Variable expenses (500 × $32) | (16,000) |
| Total contribution margin | 18,000 |
| Less: Fixed expenses | (18,000) |
| Operating income | 0 |

As variable or fixed expenses increase, so does the volume needed to break even or achieve target profits. Conversely, as these expenses decrease, the volume needed to break even or achieve target profits also decreases.

## Requirement 4

**Because many customers have requested a golf glove to go along with the trainer club, Hacker Golf is considering selling gloves. The company expects to sell only one glove for every four trainer clubs it sells. Hacker Golf can purchase the gloves for $4 each and sell them for $9. Total fixed expenses should remain the same at $18,000 per month. Calculate the break-even point in units for trainer clubs and golf gloves.**

Calculating the break-even point is fairly straightforward when a company is selling only one product. But Hacker Golf is now considering selling two products. Now, break-even becomes more complicated. Different products have different effects on the contribution margins because of different costs and selling prices. So, the company needs to consider the sales mix (a combination of products that make up total sales) when determining CVP relationships.

Finding the break-even point for multiproduct firms involves a simple three-step process. The first step is to calculate a combined weighted-average contribution margin for all of the products the company sells.

**Step 1: Calculate the weighted-average contribution margin.**

Hacker Golf believes that it can sell one glove for every four clubs that it sells. This would give the company a 4:1 sales mix. So, Hacker expects that 1/5 (or 20%) of sales will be gloves and 4/5 (or 80%) of sales will be trainer clubs.

Let's return to Hacker's original selling price and variable costs for the trainer club. Recall that Hacker Golf earns a $30 contribution margin on each golf club that it sells. Hacker will also earn a $5 contribution margin on each golf glove that it sells:

| | Clubs | Gloves |
|---|---|---|
| Sales price per unit | $ 68 | $ 9 |
| Less: Variable cost per unit | (38) | (4) |
| Contribution margin per unit | $ 30 | $ 5 |

The weighted-average contribution margin is calculated by multiplying the contribution margin per unit by the sales mix expected for each product. Once we have a total contribution margin for the bundle of products ($120 + $5 = $125, in this case), we divide it by the total number of units (5) in the sales mix, as follows:

| | Clubs | Gloves | Total |
|---|---|---|---|
| Sales price per unit | $ 68 | $ 9 | |
| Less: Variable cost per unit | (38) | (4) | |
| Contribution margin per unit | $ 30 | $ 5 | |
| Sales mix in units | ×4 | ×1 | 5 |
| Contribution margin | $120 | $ 5 | $125 |
| Weighted-average contribution (margin per unit [$125 ÷ 5]) | | | $ 25 |

The $25 represents a weighted-average contribution margin for all of the products that Hacker Golf sells. The golf clubs are weighted more heavily because Hacker Golf expects to sell four times as many clubs as golf gloves.

The next step is to calculate the break-even in units for the bundle of products.

**Step 2: Calculate the break-even point in units for the total of both products combined.**

This is calculated using the break-even formula modified for the weighted-average contribution margin in the denominator:

$$\text{Sales in total units} = \frac{\text{Fixed expenses} + \text{Operating income}}{\text{Weighted-average contribution margin per unit}}$$

We know from the question that fixed expenses will not be affected, so they should remain at $18,000. The weighted-average contribution margin, as we just calculated, is $25 per unit. So, we compute total sales as follows:

$$\begin{aligned}\text{Sales in total units} &= \frac{\$18{,}000 + \$0}{\$25} \\ &= 720\end{aligned}$$

Hacker Golf must sell 720 clubs and gloves combined to break even. Management needs to know how many units of each product must be sold to break even. Therefore, the next step is to determine how many of the total sales units (720) need to be clubs and how many need to be gloves in order to break even.

**Step 3: Calculate the break-even in units for each product line.**
Because Hacker Golf believes that it will sell four trainer clubs for every one glove, the total number of units, 720, is multiplied by each product's sales mix percentage:

$$\text{Break-even sales of clubs: } [720 \times (4/5)] = 576$$
$$\text{Break-even sales of gloves: } [720 \times (1/5)] = 144$$

From this analysis, we know that Hacker Golf needs to sell 576 trainer clubs and 144 golf gloves to break even.

## Requirement 5

**Use a contribution margin income statement to prove the break-even point calculated in Requirement 4.**

To test the calculation of the break-even point, you add the revenue generated from all sales, subtract the variable costs associated with all sales, and subtract the total fixed expenses. The result should balance to zero (or close to zero in cases in which rounding occurs).

| | Clubs | Gloves | Total |
|---|---|---|---|
| Sales revenue: | | | |
| Trainer clubs (576 × $68) | $ 39,168 | | |
| Gloves (144 × $9) | | $1,296 | $ 40,464 |
| Less: Variable expenses: | | | |
| Trainer clubs (576 × $38) | (21,888) | | |
| Gloves (144 × $4) | | (576) | (22,464) |
| Contribution margin | $ 17,280 | $ 720 | $ 18,000 |
| Less: Fixed expenses | | | (18,000) |
| Operating income | | | $ 0 |

# TRY IT SOLUTIONS

**Page 188:**

1.

| | |
|---|---|
| Sales price per unit | $2.00 |
| Less: Variable cost per unit | 0.50 |
| Contribution margin per unit | $1.50 |

2.

$$\text{Contribution margin ratio} = \frac{\text{Contribution margin per unit}}{\text{Sales price per unit}} = \frac{\$1.50}{\$2.00} = 75\%$$

3.

| | |
|---|---|
| Contribution margin (1,000 hot dogs × $1.50 per hot dog) | $1,500 |
| Less: Fixed expenses | 300 |
| Operating income | $1,200 |

**Page 190:**

1.

$$\text{Sales in units to breakeven} = \frac{\text{Fixed expenses} + \text{Operating income}}{\text{Contribution margin per unit}}$$

$$= \frac{\$300 + 0}{\$1.50} = 200 \text{ hot dogs}$$

2.

$$\text{Sales in dollars to breakeven} = \frac{\text{Fixed expenses} + \text{Operating income}}{\text{Contribution margin ratio}}$$

$$= \frac{\$300 + 0}{75\%} = \$400 \text{ of sales revenue}$$

**Page 202**

1.

| | A | B | C | D |
|---|---|---|---|---|
| 1 | **Calculating Weighted-Average Contribution Margin per Unit** | **Hotdogs** | **Potato Chips** | **Total in "basket"** |
| 2 | Contribution margin per unit | $ 1.50 | $ 0.75 | |
| 3 | Multiply by: Sales mix (number of units in "basket") | 10 | 5 | 15 |
| 4 | Contribution margin | $ 15.00 | $ 3.75 | $ 18.75 |
| 5 | | | | |
| 6 | Weighted-average contribution margin per unit ($18.75/15 units) | | | $ 1.25 |
| 7 | | | | |

2.

$$\text{Sales in units} = \frac{\text{Fixed expenses} + \text{Operating income}}{\text{Contribution per unit}} = \frac{\$300 + \$900}{\$1.25} = 960 \text{ total units}$$

3.

| | |
|---|---|
| Hot dogs (960 × 10/15 sales mix) | 640 |
| Potato chips (960 × 5/15 sales mix) | 320 |
| Total units | 960 |

# Job Costing

5

## Learning Objectives

1 Distinguish between job costing and process costing.

2 Understand the flow of production and how direct materials and direct labour are traced to jobs.

3 Compute a predetermined manufacturing overhead (MOH) rate, and use it to allocate MOH to jobs.

4 Compute and dispose of overallocated or underallocated manufacturing overhead.

5 Determine the cost of a job, and use it to make business decisions.

6 Prepare journal entries for a manufacturer's job costing system.

7 Use job costing at a service firm as a basis for billing clients. (Appendix)

Chapter 5, "Job Costing," covers material outlined in **Section 3: Management Accounting** of the CPA Competency Map. Specifically, this chapter addresses *Section 3.3 Cost Management*. The Learning Objectives in this chapter have been aligned with the CPA Competency Map to ensure the best coverage possible.

PROFESSIONAL COMPETENCY

The presence of the **coverage button** in the margin indicates focus on one or more of the specific competency areas from the competency map. The concepts in the text are building blocks to developing the competencies required in the CPA. While the chapter may address multiple areas of the competency map, the main focus will be:

Competencies:

**3.3.1** Evaluates cost classifications and costing methods for management of ongoing operations*

**3.3.2** Evaluates and applies cost management techniques appropriate for specific costing decisions*

**3.4.1** Evaluates sources and drivers of revenue growth*

## It is quite likely that during your lifetime

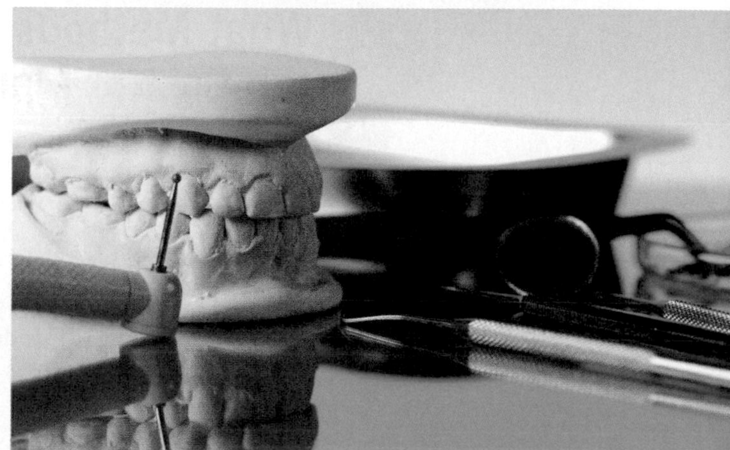

© Mariusz Szczygiel/ Shutterstock

you will use the services of a dental laboratory, but it is also likely that you won't know that you have done so. Dental laboratories manufacture a multitude of products such as retainers, dentures, mouthguards, crowns, bridges, and veneers. The laboratory receives an impression of a patient's teeth from the patient's dentist. From that impression, dental technicians create a product for the patient. Therefore, every unit made by the dental laboratory is unique. For example, the manufacture of a gold crown starts when a technician, using the impression, prepares a model of the patient's teeth using a stone product. The technician then carves a mock-up of the new tooth in wax, making sure that the wax crown fits appropriately in size and shape with the rest of the teeth on the stone model. The technician then makes a casting of the mock-up in gold. The gold crown is polished, packaged, and sent to the dentist for the patient.

The Shaw Group of Dental Laboratories[1] has been making unique dental products for 70 years and has grown to eight locations in Ontario and two in the United States. This growth would not have been possible without the ability to price its products appropriately. Not only is each product different, but each unit made (known as a "job") is unique. This makes it difficult to determine both the cost of each job and the price to charge the dentist.

The cost of each gold crown depends on the size, shape, and complexity of the job. The company's job costing system traces the direct materials (gold) and direct labour (technician's wages) required by each job. The company also allocates some manufacturing overhead (other manufacturing costs) to each job. By summing the direct materials, direct labour, and manufacturing overhead assigned to each job, the company can calculate how much it costs to make each gold crown. The company uses this cost information to make vital business decisions, such as

- Setting selling prices that will lead to profits on each product
- Identifying opportunities to cut costs
- Determining which products are most profitable and therefore deserve the most marketing emphasis

Shaw Group's managers also use cost information on each job in order to prepare the company's financial statements. From this information, they determine the following:

- The cost of goods sold for the income statement
- The cost of the inventory for the balance sheet

Whether you plan a career in marketing, engineering, production, general management, or accounting, you will need to understand how to determine the cost of your company's products or services. In the example above, we see how Shaw Group's marketing team needs to know how much it costs to produce a gold crown in order to set the selling price high enough to cover costs and provide a profit. Technicians study the materials, labour, and manufacturing overhead that go into each product to pinpoint new cost-cutting opportunities. Production managers need to know whether it is cheaper to produce each unit within the company or to *outsource* (pay another firm for) manufacturing. General managers use cost data to identify the most profitable products so they can guide marketing to boost sales of those products. The accounting department uses product costs to determine the cost of goods sold and inventory for the financial statements.

## What Methods are Used to Determine the Cost of Manufacturing a Product?

Most manufacturers use one of two product costing systems to find the cost of producing their products:

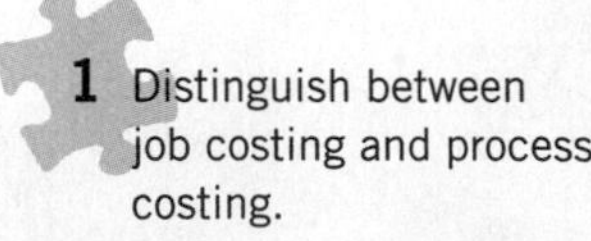

1 Distinguish between job costing and process costing.

- Process costing
- Job costing

The end goal of both product costing systems is the same: to find the cost of manufacturing one unit of product. However, the manner in which this goal is achieved differs. Management chooses the product costing system that works best for its particular environment.

### Process Costing

**Process costing** is used by manufacturing companies that produce extremely large numbers of identical units through a series of uniform production steps or processes. Because each unit is identical, in theory each unit should cost the same to make. Process costing averages manufacturing costs across all units so that each identical unit bears the same cost.

[1]All references to Shaw Group in the following hypothetical example were created by the author solely for academic purposes and are not intended, in any way, to represent the actual business practices of, or costs incurred by, Shaw Group.

For example, OMG's Candy uses two processes to make Clodhoppers: (1) preparing the chocolate, graham wafers, and other ingredients; and (2) mixing and packaging the candy. First, OMG's accumulates the costs incurred in the preparation process over a period of time. The costs incurred in this process include the cost of the ingredients as well as any chopping and processing necessary. The company averages these costs over all units passing through the process during the same period of time.

For example, let's say OMG's spends $2,000,000 on purchasing and preparing the ingredients to make one million packages of Clodhoppers during a month. The average cost per package of the preparation process, including the cost of the ingredients themselves, is as follows:

$$\text{Preparation process} = \frac{\$2,000,000}{1,000,000 \text{ packages}} = \$2.00 \text{ per package}$$

*Source:* Cindy Charles/PhotoEdit

That is the unit manufacturing cost for just the first production process. Now the prepared ingredients go through the second production process, mixing and packaging, where a similar calculation is performed to find the average cost per unit of that process. Again, this process includes any raw materials used, such as the cost of the packaging bags themselves, as well as the cost of mixing the ingredients and filling the packages with the finished candy. Let's say the average cost to mix and package each bag of Clodhoppers is $0.50.

Now OMG's can figure out the total cost to manufacture each package of Clodhoppers:

Each package of Clodhoppers is identical to every other package, so each bears the same average cost: $2.50. Once managers know the cost of manufacturing each package, they can use that information to help set sales prices and make other business decisions. To generate a profit, the sales price has to be set high enough to cover the $2.50 per package manufacturing cost, as well as the company's operating costs incurred along other areas of the value chain (marketing, distribution, and so forth) during the period.

We will delve more deeply into process costing in Chapter 6. For now, just remember that any company that mass-produces identical units of product will most likely use process costing to determine the cost of making each unit. The following industries and companies are further examples of companies that use process costing:

- Oil refining—Nanticoke Refinery (Imperial Oil), St. John Refiners (Irving Oil), BP (British Petroleum)
- Food and beverages—McCain Foods Ltd., Kellogg's, Dare Foods Ltd., General Mills, Kraft Canada Inc.
- Consumer toiletries and paper products—Cascades Tissue Group Inc., Colgate-Palmolive Canada Inc., Kruger Products Ltd. (Scotties tissues)

## Job Costing

Job costing has a different focus from process costing. It is used by companies that produce unique products or services. Job costing is best suited for custom-ordered products

**Why is this important?**

**Managers** need the most accurate **cost information** they can get in order to make good **business decisions**. They choose a costing system (usually **job costing** or **process costing**) based on which system best fits their operations.

or relatively small batches of different products, or for services provided on a contract basis, such as conducting an audit. Each unique service engagement, product, or batch of units is considered a separate "job."

Different jobs can vary considerably in their use of direct materials, direct labour, and manufacturing overhead costs, so job costing accumulates these costs separately for each individual job. For example, Edge Fitness Hydra Fit Mfg. Inc. manufactures a variety of different exercise machines. Edge Fitness has a limited number of products, but it produces them in small, separate batches for each customer. Each batch of exercise machines produced is considered a separate job. The Shaw Group of Dental Laboratories, as discussed in the opening story, custom manufactures each dental product based on the unique requirements of each patient. Since each unit is unique, Shaw Group treats each unit as an individual job. Job costing would also be used by Bombardier Inc. (airplanes), custom home builders (unique houses), high-end jewellers (unique jewellery), and any other manufacturers that build custom-ordered products.

Professional service providers such as law firms, accounting firms, consulting firms, and marketing firms use job costing to determine the cost of serving each client. People working in trades, such as mechanics, plumbers, and electricians, also use job costing to determine the cost of performing separate jobs for clients. In both cases, the job cost is used as a basis for billing the client. In the appendix to this chapter we will study a complete example of how a law firm would use job costing to bill its clients.

In summary, companies use job costing when their products or services vary in terms of materials needed, time required to complete the job, and/or the complexity of the production process. Because the jobs are so different, it would not be reasonable to assign them equal costs. Therefore, the cost of each job is compiled separately. This chapter examines how companies compile, record, and use job costs to make business decisions. Exhibit 5-1, which summarizes the key differences between job and process costing.

**EXHIBIT 5-1** Differences Between Job and Process Costing

| | Job Costing | Process Costing |
|---|---|---|
| Cost object: | Job | Process |
| Outputs: | Single units or small batches with large difference between jobs | Large quantities of identical units |
| Extent of averaging: | Less averaging—costs are averaged over the small number of units in a job (often 1 unit in a job) | More averaging—costs are averaged over the many identical units that pass through the process |

## STOP & THINK

Do all organizations use job costing or process costing systems?

**Answer:** Some manufacturers use a hybrid of these two costing systems if neither "pure" system mirrors their operational environment very well. For example, clothing manufacturers often mass produce the same product over and over (dress shirts) but use different materials in different batches (cotton fabric in one batch and silk fabric in another). Another example might be a software company that produces standard enterprise resource management software (same service), but provides unique implementation consultation services (e.g., a custom service) for each client. A hybrid costing system has some elements of a process costing system (averaging labour and manufacturing overhead costs equally across all units) and some elements of a job costing system (tracing different fabric costs to different batches).

# How Do Manufacturers Determine a Job's Cost?

2 Understand the flow of production and how direct materials and direct labour are traced to jobs.

As we have just seen, manufacturers use job costing if they produce unique products or relatively small batches of different products. Shaw Group produces each of its products individually, so each unit is a unique job. In this section, we will show you how Shaw Group determines the cost of producing Job 603, a single gold crown. Gold is used to make crowns, or "caps," to replace damaged portions of teeth because gold does not tarnish or change and wears down in a similar fashion to natural teeth.

## Overview: Flow of Inventory Through a Manufacturing System

As you learned in Chapter 2, manufacturers such as Shaw Group maintain three separate types of inventory: raw materials, work in process, and finished goods. The cost of each of these inventories is reflected on the company's balance sheet.

As shown in Exhibit 5-2, raw materials (RM) inventory is maintained in a storeroom within the manufacturing facility until the materials are needed in production. As soon as these materials are transferred to the production area, they are no longer considered raw materials because they have become part of the work in process. Work in process (WIP) inventory consists of all products that are partway through the production process. As soon as the manufacturing process is complete, the products are moved out of the manufacturing area and into a finished goods (FG) inventory storage area, where they await sale and shipment to a customer. Finally, when the products are shipped to customers, the cost of manufacturing those products becomes the cost of goods sold (CGS) shown on the company's income statement.

**EXHIBIT 5-2** Flow of Inventory Through a Manufacturing System

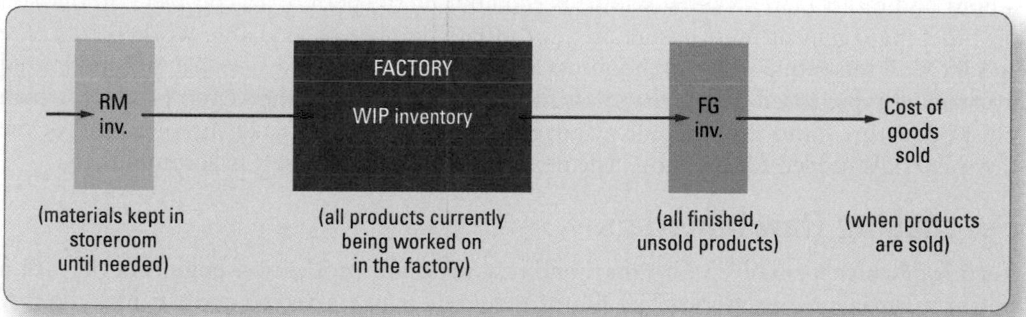


## Scheduling Production

Job costing begins with management's decision to produce a batch of units. Sometimes companies produce a batch of units just to meet a particular customer order; however, most companies also produce **stock inventory** for products they sell on a regular basis. By forecasting demand for the product, the manufacturer is able to estimate the number of units that should be produced during a given time period. For Shaw Group, forecasting is not possible as they do not know what is actually needed until the orders arrive from the dental offices. As these orders arrive, the jobs are added to the current month's **production schedule**. (Quite often, the production is done in two stages: First, the models are prepared so that the impressions of the patient's teeth do not dry out or shrink, and second, a technician creates the product when it is scheduled.) As shown in Exhibit 5-3, the production schedule indicates the number and types of inventory that are scheduled to be manufactured during the period. You should note that, for simplicity, only a portion of the scheduled jobs have been included.

Depending on the company, the types of products it offers, and the production time required, production schedules may cover periods of time as short as one day (Shaw Group, producing customized gold crowns) or as long as one year or more (Bombardier Inc., manufacturing Learjet 85 airplanes). In an environment such as a dental laboratory, scheduling the jobs can become quite complex. Since the nature of the work to be

**EXHIBIT 5-3** Monthly Production Schedule

**Production Schedule (partial)**
For the Month of December

| Job | Description | Customer # | Employee # | Scheduled Start Date | Scheduled End Date |
|---|---|---|---|---|---|
| 603 | Gold crown | 17 Dr. Waja | 3 | 12/22 | 12/23 |
| 604 | Sports mouthguard × 2 | 8 Dr. Joseph | 1 | 12/22 | 12/24 |
| 605 | Full upper denture | 34 Dr. Clissold | 5 | 12/23 | 12/24 |
| 606 | Retainer | 19 Dr. Mah | 3 | 12/23 | 12/24 |
| | FACTORY CLOSED FOR HOLIDAYS and ANNUAL MAINTENANCE | | | 12/25 | 12/31 |

completed isn't known until the job arrives from a dental office, the individual in charge of scheduling needs to continually update the production schedule with each new delivery. At the end of the month (December in Exhibit 5-3), any unfinished jobs are noted on the schedule; they will be the first entries for the next month's production schedule. New jobs in January are added to the schedule as they are received. The schedule must be updated whenever production is delayed for any reason (perhaps a technician is ill or machinery needs repairs) or when jobs are completed ahead of schedule.

The production schedule is very important in helping management determine the direct labour and direct materials that will be needed during the period. To complete production on time, management must ensure an appropriate number of available workers with the specific skill sets required for each job. At Shaw Group, technicians are usually specialized by product type, based on the materials that are used to create the dental product, which must be factored into the schedule. Management also needs to make sure it has all of the raw materials needed for each job. The next section shows how this is accomplished.

## Purchasing Raw Materials

For products that involve more than one raw material, production engineers prepare a bill of materials for each job. The bill of materials is like a recipe card: It lists the raw materials required to complete the job. At Shaw Group, the technician assigned to the job is responsible for recording the materials used in its creation. Exhibit 5-4 illustrates a bill of materials for Job 603.

**EXHIBIT 5-4** Bill of Materials (Partial Listing)

**Bill of Materials**

**Job:** 603

**Model:** Gold crown, 3-6 **Quantity:** Single

| Date Requisitioned | Item | Quantity Used |
|---|---|---|
| 12/23 | HL 5 | 2.3 g |
| | | |
| | | |
| | | |
| | | |
| | | |
| | | |

After the bill of materials has been prepared, the Purchasing Department checks the raw materials inventory to determine what raw materials are currently in stock, and what raw materials must be purchased. Each type of raw material has its own **raw materials record**. As shown in Exhibit 5-5, a raw materials record provides detailed information about each item in stock: the number of units received, the number of units used, and the balance of units currently in stock. Additionally, the raw materials record shows how much each unit costs to purchase, as well as the cost of the units used and the cost of the units still in raw materials inventory.

**EXHIBIT 5-5** Raw Materials Record

**Raw Materials Record**

**Item No.:** HL 5 **Description:** dental gold **Minimum Balance :** 25 g

| | Received | | | Used | | | | Balance | | |
|---|---|---|---|---|---|---|---|---|---|---|
| Date | g | Cost | Total | Job Number | g | Cost | Total | g | Cost | Total |
| 11-25 | 30 | $60 | $1,800 | | | | | 30 | $60 | $1,800 |
| 11-30 | | | | 580 | 1.8 | $60 | $108 | 28.2 | $60 | $1,692 |
| 12-02 | | | | 586 | 2.7 | $60 | $162 | 25.5 | $60 | $1,530 |
| 12-10 | | | | 591 | 1.9 | $60 | $114 | 23.6 | $60 | $1,416 |
| | | | | | | | | | | |

**Why is this important?**

Intentionally leaving the quantity ordered blank on the RECEIVING REPORT acts as a control to double check amounts ordered, received, and paid because it requires dock personnel to count and record the quantity of materials.

By looking at the raw materials record pictured in Exhibit 5-5, the Purchasing Department sees that only 28.2 g of HL 5 dental gold are currently in stock, and the bill of materials for Job 603 (Exhibit 5-4) shows that 2.3 g are needed for the job. There is sufficient HL 5 for the current job; however, the company requires a minimum balance of 25 g of HL 5, and the new balance is 23.6 g. Therefore, the Purchasing Department needs to buy additional HL 5. The Purchasing Department also needs to consider other jobs that will use HL 5 in the near future, as well as the time it takes to obtain the dental gold from the company's suppliers. According to the production schedule, Job 603 is scheduled to begin production on December 22; therefore, the Purchasing Department must make sure all necessary raw materials are on hand by that date.

When raw materials are needed, Shaw Group's Purchasing Department issues a **purchase order** to its suppliers. For control purposes, incoming shipments of raw materials are counted and recorded on a **receiving report**, which is typically a duplicate of the purchase order but without the quantity prelisted on the form. Shaw Group's Accounting Department will not pay the **invoice** (bill from the supplier) unless it agrees with the quantity of materials both ordered *and* received. By matching the purchase order, receiving report, and invoice, Shaw Group ensures that it pays for only those materials that were ordered and received, *and nothing more*.

In addition to tracking the current level of individual inventory items and what raw materials to buy, the raw materials records also form the basis for valuing the raw materials inventory account found on the company's balance sheet. On a given date, by adding together the balances in the individual raw materials records, the company is able to substantiate the total raw materials inventory shown on the balance sheet. For example, as shown in Exhibit 5-6, on November 30, Shaw Group had in stock $1,692 of HL 5 dental

**EXHIBIT 5-6** Individual Raw Materials Records Sum to the Raw Materials Inventory Balance

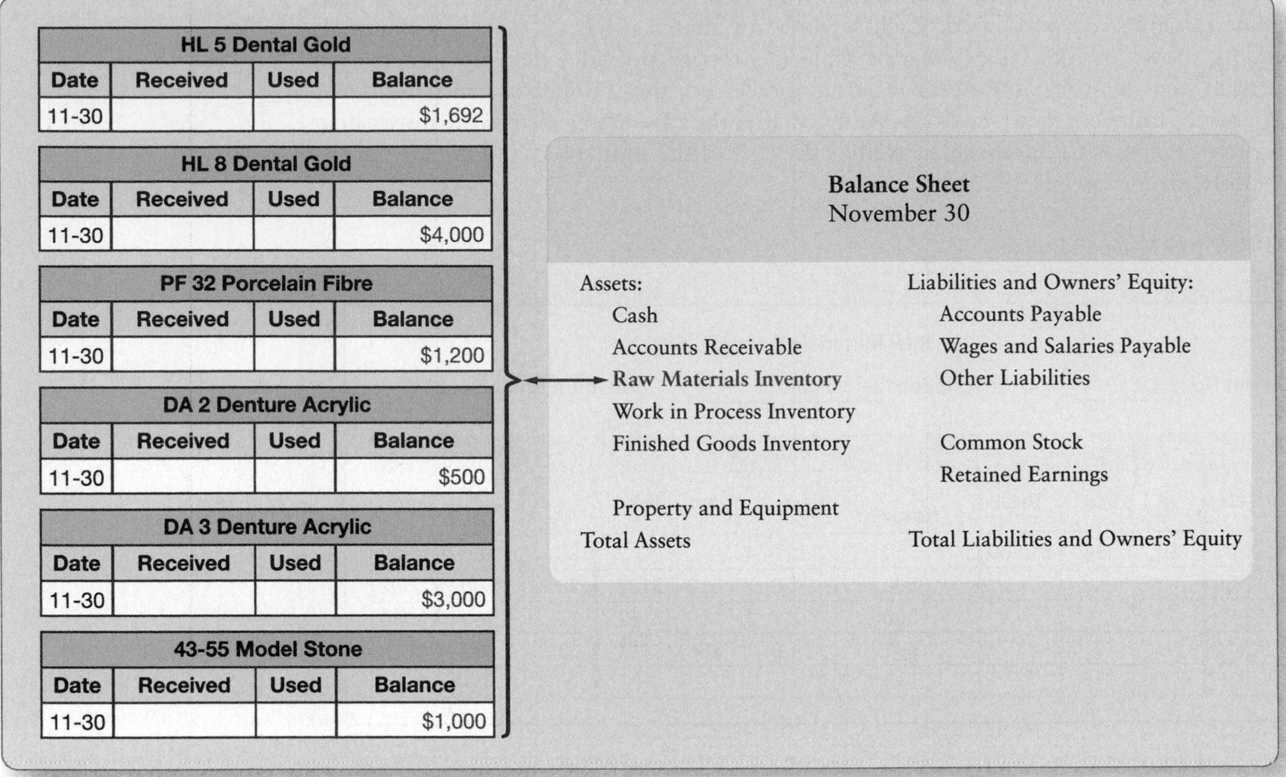


gold, $4,000 of HL 8 dental gold, $1,200 of PF 32 porcelain fibre, and so forth. When combined, these individual balances sum to the raw materials inventory balance shown on the Shaw Group's November 30 balance sheet.

## Using a Job Cost Record to Accumulate Job Costs

Once the necessary raw materials have arrived and production is ready, the technician begins Job 603. A job cost record, as pictured in Exhibit 5-7, is used to accumulate all of the direct materials and direct labour used on the job, as well as the manufacturing overhead allocated to the job.

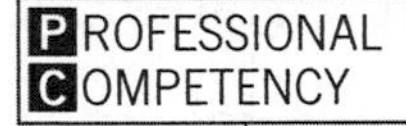


Each job has its own job cost record. Note that the job cost record is merely a form (electronic or hard copy) for tracking the costs associated with each job: direct materials, direct labour, and manufacturing overhead. As we saw in the last section, the individual raw materials records sum to the total raw materials inventory shown on the balance sheet. Similarly, as shown in Exhibit 5-8, the job cost records on all *incomplete* jobs sum to the total work in process inventory shown on the balance sheet.

**Why is this important?** **Job cost records** keep track of **all manufacturing costs** assigned to **individual jobs** so that **managers** know how much it costs to **make** each product.

As shown near the bottom of Exhibit 5-7, job cost records usually also contain details about what happens to the units in the job after it has been completed and sent to the finished goods warehouse or delivered to the customer. These details include the date and quantity of units shipped to customers, the number of units remaining in finished goods inventory, and the cost of these units. The balance of *unsold* units from *completed* job cost records sum to the total finished goods inventory on the balance sheet. For Shaw Group, the only units in finished goods inventory are those that must still be delivered, because units are not put into production unless they are ordered by the customer. That means that they do not make additional units as inventory to await sale.

**EXHIBIT 5-7** Job Cost Record

**Job Cost Record**

**Job Number:** 603

**Customer:** Dr. Waja

**Job Description:** HL 5 dental gold crown 3-6

**Date Started:** Dec. 22 **Date Completed:** ________

| Manufacturing Cost Information: | Cost Summary |
|---|---|
| Direct Materials | $ |
| Direct Labour | $ |
| Manufacturing Overhead | $ |
| Total Job Cost | $ |
| Number of Units | ÷ 1 unit |
| Cost per Unit | $ |

**Shipping Information:**

| Date | Quantity Shipped | Units Remaining | Cost Balance |
|---|---|---|---|
| | | | |
| | | | |

**EXHIBIT 5-8** Job Cost Records on *Incomplete* Jobs Sum to the WIP Inventory Balance

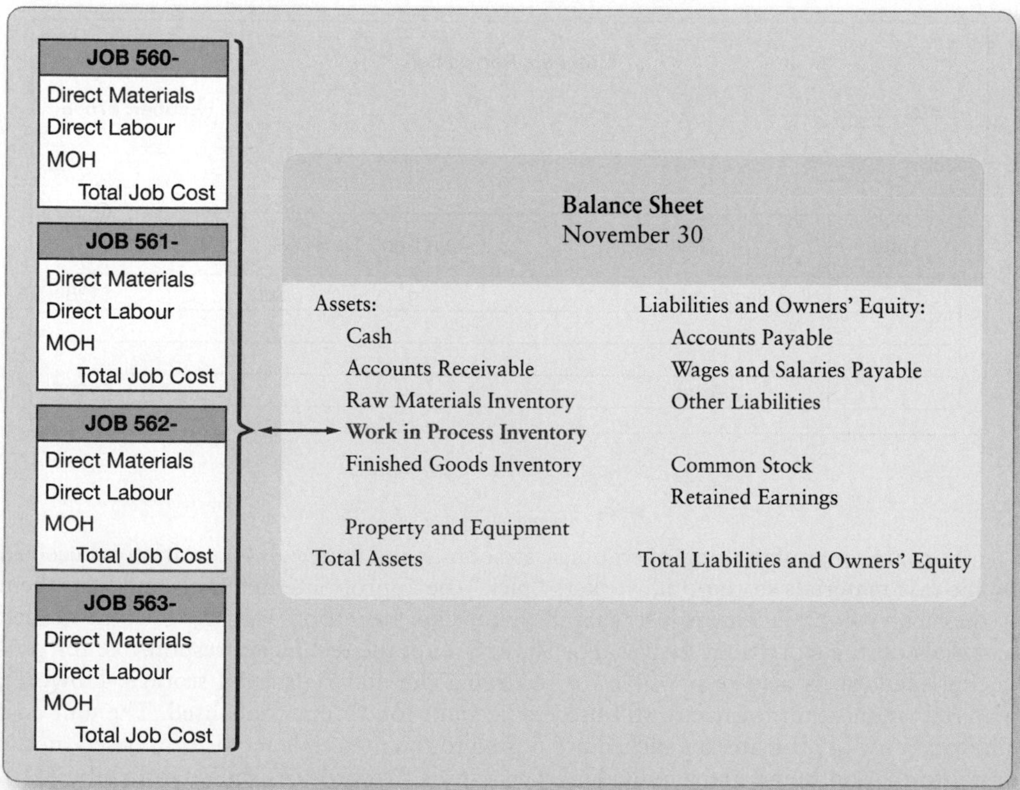

## TRY IT!

**Match the following concepts to their descriptions:**

1. Document specifying when jobs will be manufactured
2. Product costing system used by mass manufactures
3. Bill from supplier
4. Document specifying parts needed to produce a job
5. Product costing system used by manufacturers of unique products
6. Document containing the details and balance of each part in stock
7. Document for recording incoming shipments
8. Products normally kept on hand in order to fill orders quickly

a. Process costing
b. Stock inventory
c. Raw materials record
d. Production schedule
e. Receiving report
f. Invoice
g. Bill of materials
h. Job costing

Please see page 324 for solutions.

## Tracing Direct Material Costs to a Job

Once production is ready to begin Job 603, it will need the materials shown on the bill of materials (Exhibit 5-4). According to the production schedule (Exhibit 5-3), this job is scheduled to take two days to complete (the 22nd and the 23rd). The production crew will work on the preparatory steps on the 22nd, and the technician will want the requisitioned raw materials (the HL 5 gold) for the 23rd. If production can be completed in one day, the raw materials may be wanted at the beginning of the job. For longer production schedules, a **materials requisition** is filled out each time production needs some raw materials. As shown in Exhibit 5-9, the materials requisition is a form itemizing the raw materials currently needed from the storeroom.

**EXHIBIT 5-9** Materials Requisition

**Materials Requisition**

**Date:** 12/22 **Number: #7568**

**Job:** 603

| Date | Description | Quantity | Unit Cost | Amount |
|---|---|---|---|---|
| 12/22 | HL 5 dental gold | 2.3 g | $60 | $138 |
| | | | | |
| | | | | |
| | Total | | | $138 |

For large manufacturing operations, as soon as the materials requisition is received by the raw materials storeroom, workers "pick" the appropriate materials and send them to the factory floor. Picking is just what it sounds like: Storeroom workers pick the needed materials off the storeroom shelves. For Shaw Group, the technician responsible for producing each job is also responsible for retrieving the materials from storage. However, materials requisition forms are still used to account for all materials used. The unit cost and total cost of all materials picked are posted to the materials requisition based on the cost information found in the individual raw materials records. As shown in Exhibit 5-10,

**EXHIBIT 5-10** Raw Materials Record Updated for Materials Received and Used

**Raw Materials Record**

**Item No.:** HL 5 **Description:** dental gold **Minimum Balance :** 25 g

| | Received | | | Used | | | | Balance | | |
|---|---|---|---|---|---|---|---|---|---|---|
| **Date** | **g** | **Cost** | **Total** | **Job Number** | **g** | **Cost** | **Total** | **g** | **Cost** | **Total** |
| 11-25 | 30 | $60 | $1,800 | | | | | 30 | $60 | $1,800 |
| 11-30 | | | | 580 | 1.8 | $60 | $108 | 28.2 | $60 | $1,692 |
| 12-02 | | | | 586 | 2.7 | $60 | $162 | 25.5 | $60 | $1,530 |
| 12-10 | | | | 591 | 1.9 | $60 | $114 | 23.6 | $60 | $1,416 |
| 12-15 | 30 | $60 | $1,800 | | | | | 53.6 | $60 | $3,216 |
| 12-22 | | | | 603 | 2.3 | $60 | $138 | 51.3 | $60 | $3,078 |

the individual raw materials records are also updated as soon as the materials are picked. In many companies, scanning a bar code on the product can replace the manual recording.

Finally, the raw materials requisitioned for the job are posted to the job cost record as shown in Exhibit 5-11. If materials need to be requisitioned more than once for the same job number (for example, two separate teeth were being created for the same customer), the raw materials are posted to the direct materials section of the job cost record each time. They are considered direct materials as they can be traced specifically to Job 603. By using this system to trace direct materials to specific jobs, managers know the *exact* cost of direct materials incurred for each job.

**EXHIBIT 5-11** Posting Direct Materials Used to the Job Cost Record

**Job Cost Record**

**Job Number:** 603

**Customer:** 17 Dr. Waja

**Job Description:** 1 HL 5 dental gold crown

**Date Started:** Dec. 22 **Date Completed:** ________

| **Manufacturing Cost Information:** | **Cost Summary** |
|---|---|
| **Direct Materials**<br>Req. #7568: 2.3 g HL 5 $ 138 | $ 138 |
| **Direct Labour** | $ |
| **Manufacturing Overhead** | $ |
| **Total Job Cost** | $ |
| **Number of Units** | ÷ 1 unit |
| **Cost per Unit** | $ |

## Tracing Direct Labour Cost to a Job

Direct labour costs are traced to individual jobs through labour time records. As shown in Exhibit 5-12, a **labour time record** simply records the time spent by each employee on each job throughout the day. These records are usually kept electronically, rather than using old-fashioned time tickets and punch clocks. The direct labour cost to be charged to the job is calculated based on each employee's unique hourly wage rate and time spent on the job.

**EXHIBIT 5-12** Labour Time Record

**Labour Time Record**

**Employee:** Hannah Smith **Week:** 12/21 – 12/27

**Hourly Wage Rate:** $20 **Record #:** 324

| Date | Job Number | Start Time | End Time | Hours | Cost |
|---|---|---|---|---|---|
| 12/21 | 598 | 8:00 | 10:00 | 2 | $40 |
| 12/21 | 602 | 10:00 | 4:00 | 6 | $120 |
| 12/22 | 603 | 8:00 | 4:00 | 8 | $160 |
| 12/23 | 603 | 8:00 | 9:00 | 1 | $20 |
| 12/23 etc. | | | | | |

For example, in Exhibit 5-12, we see that Hannah Smith, who is paid a wage rate of $20 per hour, worked on Jobs 598, 602, and 603 during the week. Hannah spent 8 hours working on Job 603 on December 22. Therefore, $160 of direct labour cost ($20 × 1) will be charged to Job 603 for Hannah's work on that date. On December 23, Hannah's hour of work on Job 603 resulted in another $20 of direct labour being charged to the job. The cost of each direct labourer's time is computed using one employee's unique wage rate, just as is done with Hannah Smith's time.

Then, as shown in Exhibit 5-13, the information from the individual labour time records is posted to the direct labour section of the job cost record.

As you can see, by tracing direct labour cost in this fashion, jobs are charged only for the direct labour actually incurred in producing the job.

What about employee benefits, such as employee-sponsored retirement plans, health insurance, payroll taxes, and other benefits? As discussed in Chapter 2, these payroll-related benefits often add another 30% or more to the cost of gross wages and salaries. Some companies factor, or "load," these costs into the hourly wage rate charged to the jobs. For example, if a factory worker earns a wage rate of $10 per hour, the job cost records would show a loaded hourly rate of about $13 per hour, which would include all benefits associated with employing that worker. However, since coming up with an *accurate* loaded hourly rate such as this is difficult, many companies treat these extra payroll-related costs as part of manufacturing overhead, rather than loading these costs into the direct labour wage rates. We will talk about how all manufacturing overhead costs are handled in the next section.

**EXHIBIT 5-13** Posting Direct Labour Used to the Job Cost Record

**Job Cost Record**

**Job Number:** 603

**Customer:** 17 Dr. Waja

**Job Description:** 1 HL 5 dental gold crown

**Date Started:** Dec. 22 **Date Completed:** ______

| Manufacturing Cost Information: | Cost Summary |
|---|---|
| **Direct Materials**<br>Req. #7568: 2.3 g HL 5 $ 138 | $ 138 |
| **Direct Labour**<br>No. #324 (9 hours): $160, $20, etc.<br>No. #327* (1 hour): $ 15<br>No. #333* (1.5 hours): $ 30<br>Etc.<br>(a total of 11.5 direct labour hours) | $ 225 |
| **Manufacturing Overhead** | $ |
| **Total Job Cost** | $ |
| **Number of Units** | ÷ 1 unit |
| **Cost per Unit** | $ |

* The additional cost cards would be from other people who had worked on the job even though they were not on the production schedule. This would be the case if other employees had worked on doing some of the preparation work prior to the technician receiving the job or some of the finishing work after the technician had completed the job (for example, cleaning, spraying with an anti-bacterial spray, etc.). Note the hourly rate of the employees submitting job record numbers #327 and #333 was $15, and $20, respectively.

## Allocating Manufacturing Overhead to a Job

So far, we have traced the direct materials cost and direct labour cost to Job 603. Recall, however, that Shaw Group incurs many other manufacturing costs that cannot be directly traced to specific jobs. These indirect costs, otherwise known as manufacturing overhead, include depreciation on the factory plant and equipment, utilities to run the plant, property taxes and insurance on the plant, equipment maintenance, the salaries of plant janitors and supervisors, machine lubricants, and so forth. Because of the nature of these costs, we cannot tell exactly how much of these costs is attributable to producing a specific job. Therefore, we cannot trace these costs to jobs, as we did with direct materials and direct labour. Rather, we have to allocate some reasonable amount of these costs to each job. Why bother? IFRS and ASPE mandate that manufacturing overhead *must* be treated as an inventoriable product cost for financial reporting purposes. The rationale is that these costs are a *necessary* part of the production process: Jobs could not be produced without incurring these costs.

**3** Compute a predetermined manufacturing overhead (MOH) rate, and use it to allocate MOH to jobs.

**Why is this important?**

Managers use the **predetermined MOH rate** as a way to "**spread**" (allocate) **indirect** manufacturing costs, like factory utilities, **among all products** produced in the factory during the year.

### What Does Allocating Mean?

Allocating manufacturing overhead[2] to jobs simply means that we "split up" or "divide" the total manufacturing overhead costs among the jobs we produced during the year. There are many different ways to "split up" the total manufacturing overhead costs among jobs. Think about the different ways you could split up a pizza among friends. You could give equal portions to each friend, you could give larger portions to the largest friends; or you could give larger portions to the hungriest friends. All in all, you have a set amount of pizza, but you can come up with several different reasonable bases for your decisions.

Likewise, a manufacturer has a total amount of manufacturing overhead (MOH) that must be split among all of the jobs produced during the year. Since each job is unique in size and resource requirements, it would not be fair to allocate an equal amount of manufacturing overhead to each job. Rather, management needs some other reasonable basis for splitting up the total manufacturing overhead costs among jobs. In this chapter, we will discuss the most basic method of allocating MOH to jobs. This method has traditionally been used by most manufacturers.

### Steps to Allocating Manufacturing Overhead

Manufacturers follow four steps to implement this basic allocation system. The first three steps are taken ***before the year begins:***

**STEP 1: The company estimates its total manufacturing overhead costs for the coming year.**

This is the total "pie" to be allocated. For Shaw Group, let us assume management estimates total manufacturing overhead costs for the year to be $1 million.

**STEP 2: The company selects an allocation base and estimates the total amount that will be used during the year.**

This is the *basis* management has chosen for "dividing up the pie." For Shaw Group, let us assume management has selected direct labour hours as the allocation base. Furthermore, management estimates that 62,500 hours of direct labour will be used during the year.

Ideally, the allocation base should be the cost driver of the manufacturing overhead costs. As the term implies, a cost driver is the primary factor that causes a cost. For example, in many companies (like Shaw Group), manufacturing overhead costs rise and fall with the amount of work performed. Because of this, most companies in the past have used either direct labour hours or direct labour cost as their allocation base. This information was also easy to gather from the labour time records or job cost records. However, for manufacturers who have automated much of their production process, machine hours may be a more appropriate allocation base, because the amount of time spent running the machines drives the utility, maintenance, and equipment depreciation costs. As you will learn in Chapter 7, some companies even use multiple allocation bases to more accurately allocate MOH costs to individual jobs. The important point is that the allocation base selected should bear a strong relationship to the MOH costs.

**STEP 3: The company calculates its predetermined manufacturing overhead rate using the information estimated in Steps 1 and 2:**

$$\text{Predetermined MOH rate} = \frac{\text{Total estimated manufacturing overhead costs}}{\text{Total estimated amount of the allocation base}}$$

[2]The term "applying" manufacturing overhead is often used synonymously with "allocating" manufacturing overhead.

Shaw Group would calculate its predetermined manufacturing overhead rate as follows:

$$\text{Predetermined MOH rate} = \frac{\$1{,}000{,}000}{62{,}500 \text{ DL hours}} = \$16 \text{ per direct labour hour}$$

This rate will be used throughout the coming year. It is not revised unless the company finds that either the MOH costs or the total amount of the allocation base being used (direct labour hours for Shaw Group) has substantially shifted away from the estimated amounts.

Why does the company use a *predetermined* MOH rate, based on *estimated or budgeted data*, rather than an actual MOH rate based on actual data for the year? In order to get actual data, the company would have to wait until the *end of the year* to set its MOH rate. By then, the information is too late to be useful for making pricing and other decisions related to individual jobs. Managers are willing to sacrifice some accuracy in order to get timely information on how much each job costs to produce.

### Allocating Manufacturing Overhead to Individual Jobs

***During the year***, as jobs are produced, companies take the following step to calculate the amount of MOH to allocate to each job.

**STEP 4: The company allocates some manufacturing overhead to each individual job as follows:**

$$\text{MOH allocated to a job} = \text{Predetermined MOH rate} \times \text{Actual amount of allocation base used by the job}$$

Let's see how this works for Shaw Group's Job 603. Since the predetermined MOH rate is based on direct labour hours ($16 per DL hour), we will need to know how many direct labour hours were used on Job 603. From Exhibit 5-13, we see that Job 603 required a total of 11.5 DL hours. This information was collected from the individual labour time records and summarized on the job cost record. Therefore, we calculate the amount of MOH to be allocated to Job 603 as follows:

$$\begin{aligned}\text{MOH to be allocated to Job 603} &= \$16 \text{ per direct labour hour} \times 11.5 \text{ direct labour hours} \\ &= \$184\end{aligned}$$

The $184 of MOH allocated to Job 603 is now posted to the job cost record, as shown in Exhibit 5-14.

### When Is Manufacturing Overhead Allocated to Jobs?

The point in time at which manufacturing overhead is allocated to the job depends on the sophistication of the company's computer system. In most sophisticated systems, some MOH is allocated to the job each time some of the allocation base is posted to the job cost record. In less sophisticated systems, manufacturing overhead is allocated only once: as soon as the job is complete and the total amount of allocation base used by the job is known (as shown in Exhibit 5-14). However, if the balance sheet date (for example, December 31) arrives before the job is complete, Shaw Group would need to allocate some MOH to the job based on the number of direct labour hours used on the job thus far. Only by updating the job cost records will the company have the most accurate work in process inventory on its balance sheet.

**EXHIBIT 5-14** Posting Manufacturing Overhead and Completing the Job Cost Record

**Job Cost Record**

**Job Number:** 603

**Customer:** 17 Dr. Waja

**Job Description:** 1 HL 5 dental gold crown

**Date Started:** Dec. 22 **Date Completed:** Dec. 28

| **Manufacturing Cost Information:** | **Cost Summary** |
|---|---|
| **Direct Materials**<br>Req. #7568: 2.3 g HL 5 $ 138 | $ 138 |
| **Direct Labour**<br>No. #324 (9 hours): $ 160, $ 20, etc.<br>No. #327 (1 hour): $ 15<br>No. #333 (1.5 hours): $ 30<br>Etc.<br>(a total of 11.5 direct labour hours) | $ 225 |
| **Manufacturing Overhead**<br>$16/ DL hour × 11.5 DL hours = $184 | $ 184 |
| **Total Job Cost** | $ 547 |
| **Number of Units** | ÷ 1 unit |
| **Cost per Unit** | $ 547 |

# How Do Managers Deal with Underallocated or Overallocated Manufacturing Overhead?

4 Compute and dispose of overallocated or underallocated manufacturing overhead.

In job order costing, managers calculate the cost of producing a job by tracing *actual* direct materials and direct labour to each job using materials requisitions and labour time records, while manufacturing overhead is allocated to each job using a predetermined overhead rate. The *predetermined rate* is calculated using *estimates* of the company's total annual manufacturing costs and *estimates* of the total annual allocation base (such as direct labour hours). However, by the end of the period the *actual* manufacturing overhead costs incurred by the company will be known, and will no doubt differ from the total amount allocated to jobs during the period. Invariably, they will have either **underallocated manufacturing overhead** (estimated too little) or **overallocated manufacturing overhead** (estimated too much) as shown in Exhibit 5-15.

**EXHIBIT 5-15** Underallocated vs. Overallocated Manufacturing Overhead

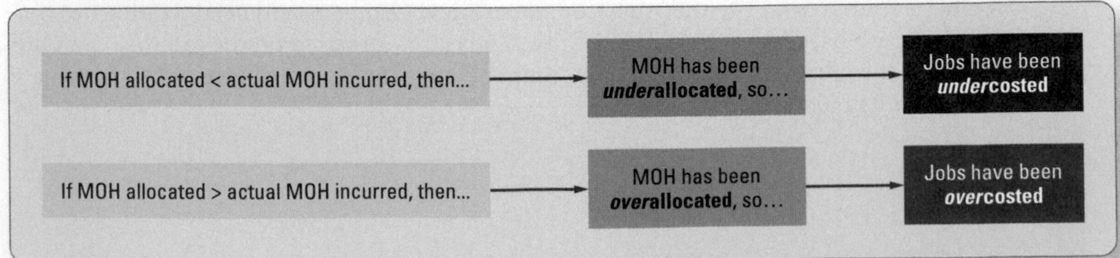

Suppose Shaw Group incurred the following *actual* manufacturing overhead costs in December:

| Manufacturing Overhead Incurred | Actual MOH Costs |
|---|---|
| Indirect materials used (janitorial supplies, machine lubricants, etc.) | $ 2,000 |
| Indirect labour (janitors' and supervisors' wages, etc.) | 13,000 |
| Other indirect manufacturing costs | |
| (Plant utilities, depreciation, property taxes, insurance, etc.) | 10,000 |
| Total actual manufacturing overhead costs incurred | $25,000 |

Now let's look at the total amount of MOH that was allocated to specific jobs during the month using the predetermined overhead rate of $16 per direct labour hour. For simplicity, we will detail Job 603 and combine all other jobs worked on in December into one total.

| Job | Amount of MOH Allocated to Job |
|---|---|
| 603 (from Exhibit 5-14) ($16 per DL hour × 11.5 DL hours) | $ 184 |
| 604 (not shown) ($16 per DL hour × 1,488.5 DL hours) | 23,816 |
| Total MOH allocated to jobs ($16 per hour × 1,500 DL hours) | $24,000 |

Notice that we do not need to have the individual job cost records available to figure out the total amount of MOH allocated to jobs during the period. Rather, we only need to do the following:

Total MOH allocated = Predetermined MOH rate × Actual *total* amount of allocation base used on all jobs
= $16 per DL hour × 1,500 direct labour hours
= $24,000 total MOH allocated to jobs during the period

The difference between the *actual MOH costs incurred* and the amount of MOH *allocated to jobs* shows that Shaw Group underallocated MOH by $1,000 during December:

| | |
|---|---|
| Actual manufacturing overhead costs **incurred** | $25,000 |
| Manufacturing overhead **allocated** to jobs | 24,000 |
| Underallocated manufacturing overhead | $ 1,000 |

By underallocating MOH, Shaw Group *did not allocate enough* MOH cost to the jobs worked on during the period. In other words, the management should have allocated, a total of $1,000 more MOH cost than the job cost records indicated to jobs worked on during the period. These jobs have been undercosted, as shown in Exhibit 5-15.

If, on the other hand, a manufacturer finds that the amount of MOH allocated to jobs is *greater* than the actual amount of MOH incurred, we would say that MOH has been overallocated, resulting in overcosting these jobs.

What do manufacturers do about this problem? Assuming that the amount of under- or overallocation is immaterial, or that most of the inventory produced during the period has been sold, manufacturers typically adjust the cost of goods sold shown on the income statement for the total amount of the under- or overallocation. Why? Because the actual cost of producing these goods differed from what was initially reported on the job cost records. Since the job cost records were used as a basis for recording cost of goods sold at the time the units were sold, the cost of goods sold will be wrong unless it is adjusted. As shown in Exhibit 5-16, by increasing cost of goods sold when MOH has been underallocated, or by decreasing cost of goods sold when MOH has been overallocated, the company actually corrects the error that exists in cost of goods sold.

**EXHIBIT 5-16** Correcting Cost of Goods Sold for Underallocated or Overallocated MOH

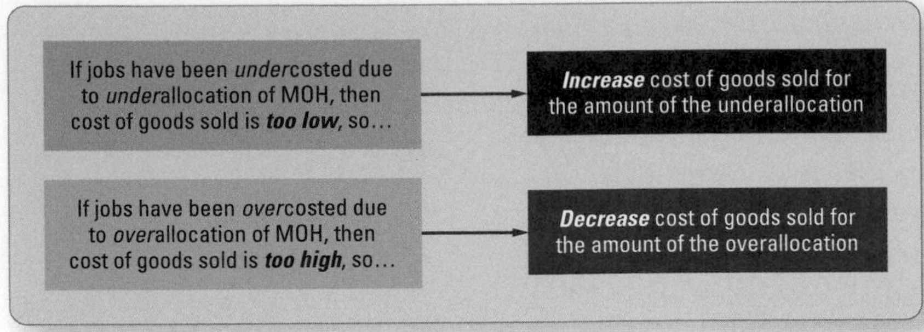


What if the amount of under- or overallocation is large, and the company has *not* sold almost all of the jobs it worked on during the period? Then the company will prorate the total amount of under- or overallocation among work in process inventory, finished goods inventory, and cost of goods sold, based on the amount of applied MOH in each of the three accounts (WIP, FG, and COGS). This can be quite complex because the amount of applied MOH becomes hidden once it moves to the FG and COGS accounts. Therefore, for simplicity, the total amount in each of the three accounts is typically used for calculating the distribution of the over- or underallocated overhead. For example, assume the three accounts had balances as follows:

| | |
|---|---|
| WIP: | $14,250 |
| FG: | $10,700 |
| COGS: | $17,300 |

In this case, the total amount of underallocation ($1,000 in the case of Shaw Group) would be roughly allocated as follows: $337 to work in process inventory (14,250/(14,250 + 10,700 + 17,300) ÷ 1,000); $253 to finished goods inventory (10,700/(14,250 + 10,700 + 17,300) ÷ 1,000); and $409 to cost of goods sold (17,300/(14,250 + 10,700 + 17,300) ÷ 1,000). You will note that rounding has meant that the total amount to be allocated equals $999 rather than the full $1,000.

## STOP & THINK

Assume Shaw Group's managers had chosen direct labour cost as its MOH allocation base, rather than direct labour *hours*. Furthermore, assume management estimated direct labour would cost $1,200,000 for the year.

1. Assuming direct labour cost as the allocation base, calculate the company's predetermined MOH rate.
2. How much MOH would have been allocated to Job 603?

**Answer:**

$$1.\ \text{Predetermined MOH rate} = \frac{\$1{,}000{,}000}{\$1{,}200{,}000 \text{ of DL cost}} = \begin{array}{c}0.8333 \textit{ or } 83.33\% \\ \text{of direct labour cost}\end{array}$$

$$2.\ \text{MOH allocated to Job 603} = 83.33\% \times \begin{array}{c}\$225 \text{ direct labour cost} \\ \text{(from Exhibit 5-14)}\end{array}$$
$$= \$187.50$$

Note that this allocation differs from that shown in Exhibit 5-14 ($184). That is because the amount of MOH allocated to an individual job depends upon the allocation base chosen by management. While there is no one "correct" allocation, the most accurate and equitable allocation occurs when the company uses the MOH cost driver as its allocation base.

## Completing the Job Cost Record and Using It to Make Business Decisions

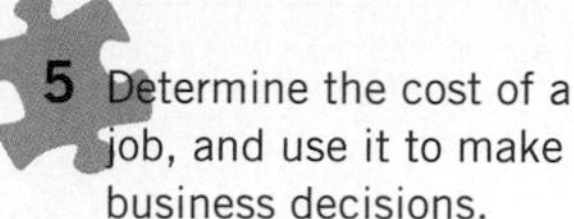

Remember, there is more than one way to determine the cost of a product, and job costing is just one of them. Some methods determine different total costs for each job, and other approaches may include more or exclude some of the costs that have been demonstrated with job costing. The method used to determine the cost will affect decision making within an organization. Other methods will be demonstrated in later chapters (ABC costing and variable costing, for example), and your first decision as a manager will be to determine which costing method is most appropriate for your own situation.

As shown in Exhibit 5-14, now that all three manufacturing costs have been posted to the job cost record, Shaw Group can determine the total cost of Job 603 ($547). If there was more than one unit in the batch, or job, Shaw Group would also calculate the cost of producing each of the identical units in the job by dividing the total cost by the number of units. For example, if a dentist orders two athletic mouthguards for the same patient, the costs of fabricating both mouthguards would be accumulated in the job cost card. Shaw Group would then take the total costs and divide by two to get an individual cost for each mouthguard.

**REDUCING FUTURE JOB COSTS** Management uses the job cost information to control costs. By examining the exact costs traced to the job, management might be able to determine ways of reducing the cost of similar jobs produced in the future. For example, is the HL 5 dental gold costing more than it did on previous jobs? Perhaps management can renegotiate its contract with its primary suppliers or identify different suppliers that are willing to sell the materials more cheaply without sacrificing quality.

What about direct labour costs? By examining the time spent by various workers on the job, management may be able to improve the efficiency of the process so that less production time is required. Management will also examine the hourly wage rates paid to the individuals who worked on the job to determine if less skilled, and therefore less costly, workers could accomplish the same production tasks, freeing up the more highly skilled employees for more challenging work.

**ASSESSING AND COMPARING THE PROFITABILITY OF EACH MODEL.** Management also uses job cost information to determine the profitability of the various models. Assume that a single gold crown (a molar, for example) is listed at a sales price of $1,000.[3] That means the company can expect the following gross profit on this job:

| | |
|---|---|
| Unit sales price | $1,000 |
| Unit cost (computed on job cost record in Exhibit 5-14) | 547 |
| Gross profit | $ 453 |

This profit analysis shows that the company generates a gross profit of $453 for this unit.[4] Keep in mind that Shaw Group incurs many operating costs, outside of its manufacturing costs, that must be covered by the gross profit earned by product sales. For example, Shaw Group needs to cover the costs of advertising, training for the technicians, and costs from the head office and training location in downtown Toronto. Managers compare the gross profit on this unit to the gross profit of other models to determine which products to emphasize selling. Management will concentrate on marketing those models that yield the higher profit margins.

**DEALING WITH PRICING PRESSURE FROM COMPETITORS** Management can also use this information to determine how it will deal with pricing pressure. If a competitor drops the

[3]Because the products made at this organization are all customized for a particular customer, it is abnormal to have one price for all versions of the same product (for example, one price for any gold crown made). We will deal with the customized situations later in the chapter; for this example, you can assume that a single selling price is used for a product.

[4]Since the cost figures used in this chapter are hypothetical, the gross profit on unit sales is also hypothetical.

price of a similar gold crown to $950, according to the profit analysis, Shaw Group could drop its sales price of a gold crown to $950 and still generate $403 of gross profit on the sale. In fact, Shaw Group could *undercut* the competitors, by charging less than $950, to generate additional sales and perhaps increase its market share.

**ALLOWING DISCOUNTS ON HIGH-VOLUME SALES** Customers often expect discounts for high-volume sales. For example, perhaps Dr. Waja has proposed that she will send all of her orders to the Shaw Group. In exchange for this exclusive arrangement, she has asked for a 25% volume discount off the regular sales price. If Shaw Group does not agree to the discount, the dentist will take her business to a competitor. Can Shaw Group agree to this discount and still earn a profit on the sale? Let us see:

| | |
|---|---|
| Discounted sales price (75% of $1,000) | $750 |
| Unit cost (computed on job cost record in Exhibit 5-14) | 547 |
| Gross profit | $203 |

These calculations show that the discounted sales price will still be profitable. We will talk more about special orders like this in Chapter 8.

**BIDDING FOR CUSTOM ORDERS** Management also uses product cost information to bid for custom orders. For Shaw Group, all orders are custom orders because each dental patient has unique needs. However, some companies have a blend of standard products and customized products. For example, kitchen cabinets can be made in standard sizes, but customers can also design their own package of kitchen cabinets. A cabinet company uses one price for each standard product; however, this is not the most effective pricing method for customized products. Let's now look at how prices are determined for Shaw Group, recognizing that each unit is a custom job.

**Why is this important?**

Once managers know how much it **costs** to make a **job**, they use that **information** to

- Find **cheaper** ways of producing similar jobs in the future
- Figure out which products are **most profitable**
- Establish prices for **custom-ordered** jobs

Management can use the job cost records from past custom jobs to determine a good estimate of how much it will cost to complete the new custom order. For example, depending on the size and shape of the tooth, each gold crown the company makes requires a different amount of gold, and complexity of the job affects the amount of labour that is required to fabricate the crown. Shaw Group factors in these additional costs to get an estimate of the total job cost before the job is produced. Shaw Group could use cost-plus pricing to determine a sales price for the custom job. When companies use cost-plus pricing, they take the cost of the job (from the estimated or actual job cost record) and add a markup to help cover operating expenses and generate a profit:

$$\text{Cost plus price} = \text{Cost} + \text{Markup on cost}$$

In many instances, the markup percentage or final bid price is agreed upon in a written contract before the company goes ahead with production. For example, a construction company may propose to build a building in a cost-plus contract at 30%. This means that the construction company will invoice the customer for the total costs, plus 30% of the total costs. In other instances, the customer is not involved in a negotiation process for the markup on the product and the company must determine a markup that will provide sufficient profit for the organization. For Shaw Group, let's assume that a markup of 50% is used. If the job cost record shows a total job cost of $547 for the crown, then the sales price is calculated as follows:

$$\begin{aligned}\text{Cost-plus price} &= \$547 + (50\% \times \$547)\\ &= \$820.50\end{aligned}$$

## Sustainability and Job Costing

Job cost records serve a vital role for manufacturers who embrace sustainability. Since job cost records contain information about the direct materials, direct labour, and manufacturing overhead assigned to each job, they capture the essential resources required to manufacture a product. The summary information on the job cost records can be enhanced to provide management with further information about how the product or production process may affect the environment, employees involved in the manufacturing process, future consumers of the product, and future disposal of the packaging materials and product itself.

For example, the direct materials section of the job cost record can be broken down into subcategories that provide management with useful environmental information. Categories might include the following:

See Exercises E5-20A and E5-40B

- Material inputs that are post-consumer-use or recycled materials
- Toxic versus non-toxic materials
- Packaging materials that can be recycled or composted versus those that will end up in a landfill
- Materials sourced from local suppliers versus those sourced from geographically distant suppliers (thereby increasing the company's carbon footprint)
- Materials that will become waste as a result of the production process
- Materials sourced from companies that embrace fair-labour practices and environmental sustainability
- Materials with heavy fossil-fuel footprints

The job cost record could also reflect the percentage of the end product that can be recycled by the consumer. Companies embracing sustainability will also need more information about the specific resources that are treated as manufacturing overhead costs, especially those that are related to energy and water consumption. To provide better information, the accounting system should contain multiple subsidiary MOH accounts based on the types of MOH incurred. For example, the company could separately track the following:

- The amount (and cost) of water used (reclaimed water versus potable water)
- Electricity generated from coal-burning power plants versus wind turbines
- The amount of fossil fuel versus biofuels used to power forklifts and equipment
- Costs related to emission control, wastewater, and garbage disposal

Even property taxes, property insurance, and employee training costs may be affected by a company's journey toward sustainability. Only by separately measuring these costs will management have the information it needs to adequately weigh the costs and benefits associated with environmental and social responsibility initiatives. To provide managers with better information with which to make decisions, job cost records could also contain a section estimating the future environmental costs associated with each job.

For example, many Canadian provinces have already put legislation in place to reduce the amount of potentially dangerous e-waste (electronic waste) in landfills by shifting the end-of-life disposal cost back to the manufacturer. The costs vary by province, so different end-of-life products will bear different costs if a manufacturer sells or ships these products to another province. By bearing the disposal cost, manufacturers should be motivated to design greener products that are repairable, are more easily recyclable, and have a longer life cycle. In response to the differing regulations in each province, an industry association, Electronic Product Stewardship Canada (EPSC), was founded and includes members such as Hewlett-Packard, Microsoft Corporation, and Apple, Inc. The goal of the association is to promote harmonization among provincial electronic waste regulatory programs and strong environmental standards for the treatment of end-of-life electronics in Canada. More information can be found on the EPSC Website: epsc.ca.

**PREPARING THE FINANCIAL STATEMENTS** Finally, the job cost information is crucial to preparing the company's financial statements. Why? Because the information is used to figure out the total cost of goods sold shown on the income statement, as well as the work in process and finished goods inventory accounts shown on the balance sheet. Once Job 603 is delivered to the dental office that ordered it, its cost ($547) becomes part of the cost of goods sold during the period. The finished goods inventory would simply be the sum of all of the job cost cards for the completed jobs. As shown earlier (Exhibit 5-8), the cost-to-date of unfinished jobs remains in the company's work in process inventory.

# DECISION GUIDELINES

## Job Costing

Shaw Group uses a job costing system that assigns manufacturing costs to each batch, or job, of dental products that it makes. These guidelines explain some of the decisions Shaw Group made in designing its costing system.

| Decision | Guidelines |
|---|---|
| Should we use job costing or process costing? | Managers use the costing system that best fits their production environment. Job costing is best suited to manufacturers that produce unique, custom-built products, such as Shaw Group, or relatively small batches of different products. Process costing is best suited to manufacturers that mass produce identical units in a series of uniform production processes. |
| How do we figure out how much each job costs to manufacture? | The exact amount of direct materials and direct labour can be traced to individual jobs using materials requisitions and labour time records. However, the exact amount of manufacturing overhead attributable to each job is unknown and therefore *cannot* be traced to individual jobs. To deal with this issue, companies *allocate* some manufacturing overhead to each job. |
| To determine the cost of each job, we need to include the costs of manufacturing overhead such as the supervisor's salary and depreciation of the equipment that is used in the fabrication of the dental products. If we don't know what they are by the time we finish a job, how can we include these costs in the total costs of a job? | While it would be more accurate to use the actual manufacturing overhead rate, companies would have to wait until the end of the year to have that information. Most companies are willing to sacrifice some accuracy for the sake of having timely information that helps them make decisions throughout the year. Therefore, most companies use a predetermined overhead rate to allocate manufacturing overhead to jobs as they are produced. |
| How do we calculate the predetermined MOH rate? | $\text{Predetermined MOH rate} = \dfrac{\text{Total estimated manufacturing overhead cost}}{\text{Total estimated amount of the allocation base}}$ |
| How do we determine the allocation base that we should use for allocating manufacturing overhead? | If possible, companies should use the cost driver of manufacturing overhead as the allocation base. The most common allocation bases are direct labour hours, direct labour cost, and machine hours. Some companies use multiple bases in order to more accurately allocate MOH. This topic will be covered in Chapter 7. |
| How should we allocate manufacturing overhead to individual jobs? | The MOH allocated to a job is calculated as follows:<br>= Predetermined MOH rate × Actual amount of allocation base used by the job |

# SUMMARY PROBLEM 1

E-Z-Boy Furniture makes sofas, love seats, and recliners. The company allocates manufacturing overhead based on direct labour hours. E-Z-Boy estimated a total of $2 million of manufacturing overhead and 40,000 direct labour hours for the year.

Job 310 consists of a batch of 10 recliners. The company's records show that the following direct materials were requisitioned for Job 310:

**Lumber:** 10 units at $30 per unit

**Padding:** 20 m at $20 per metre

**Upholstery fabric:** 60 m at $25 per metre

Labour time records show the following employees (direct labour) worked on Job 310:

**Jesse Slothower:** 10 hours at $12 per hour

**Becky Wilken:** 15 hours at $18 per hour

**Chip Lathrop:** 12 hours at $15 per hour

### Requirements

1. Compute the company's predetermined manufacturing overhead rate.
2. Compute the total amount of direct materials, direct labour, and manufacturing overhead that should be shown on Job 310's job cost record.
3. Compute the total cost of Job 310, as well as the cost of each recliner produced in Job 310.

## ■ SOLUTION

1. The predetermined MOH rate is calculated as follows:

$$\text{Predetermined MOH rate} = \frac{\text{Total estimated manufacturing overhead cost}}{\text{Total estimated amount of the allocation base}}$$

For E-Z-Boy,

$$\text{Predetermined MOH rate} = \frac{\$2{,}000{,}000}{40{,}000 \text{ direct labour hours}} = \$50 \text{ per direct labour hour}$$

2. The total amount of direct materials ($2,200) and direct labour ($570) incurred on Job 310 is determined from the materials requisitions and labour time records, as detailed next. Since the job required 37 direct labour hours, we determine the amount of manufacturing overhead to allocate to the job is as follows:

$$= \text{Predetermined MOH rate} \times \text{Actual amount of allocation base used by the job}$$
$$= \$50 \text{ per direct labour hour} \times 37 \text{ direct labour hours used on Job 310}$$
$$= \$1{,}850$$

These costs are summarized on the following job cost record:

**Job Cost Record**

**Job Number:** 310

**Job Description:** 10 recliners

| **Manufacturing Cost Information:** | | | **Cost Summary** |
|---|---|---|---|
| **Direct Materials** | | | |
| | Lumber: | 10 units × $30 = $300 | |
| | Padding: | 20 yards × $20 = $400 | |
| | Fabric: | 60 yards × $25 = $1,500 | $ 2,200 |
| **Direct Labor** | | | |
| | Slothower: | 10 hours × $12 = $120 | |
| | Wilken: | 15 hours × $18 = $270 | |
| | Lathrop: | 12 hours × $15 = $180 | |
| | Total hours: | 37 hours | $ 570 |
| **Manufacturing Overhead** | | | |
| | | 37 direct labour hours × $50 = $1,850 | $ 1,850 |
| **Total Job Cost** | | | $ 4,620 |
| **Number of Units** | | | ÷ 10 units |
| **Cost per Unit** | | | $ 462 |

3. The direct materials ($2,200), direct labour ($570), and manufacturing overhead ($1,850) sum to a total job cost of $4,620, as previously shown. When averaged over the 10 recliners in the job, the cost per recliner is $462.

## How Do Manufacturers Treat Nonmanufacturing Costs?

Job costing in manufacturing companies has *traditionally* focused on assigning only production-related costs to jobs. This is why our Shaw Group example focuses on assigning only manufacturing costs (direct materials, direct labour, and manufacturing overhead) to jobs. The focus on manufacturing costs arises because reporting standards require that the accounting records treat only inventoriable costs as assets. Costs incurred in other elements of the value chain (period costs) are not assigned to products for external financial reporting, but instead are treated as operating expenses.

However, manufacturers often want to know more than just the cost to manufacture a product; they want to know the *total* cost of researching and developing, designing, producing, marketing, distributing, and providing customer service for new or existing products. *In other words, they want to know the total cost of the product across the entire value chain.* Managers use this information to guide internal decisions, such as setting long-run average sales prices. But how do managers figure this out? The same principles of tracing direct costs and allocating indirect costs apply to all costs incurred in other elements of the value chain. Managers can add these nonmanufacturing costs to the inventoriable job costs to build *the total cost of the product across the value chain.* Keep in mind that these nonmanufacturing costs are assigned to products *only* for internal decision making, *never* for external financial reporting, because reporting standards do not allow it.

Recall that Life Fitness had estimated $1,000,000 of MOH for the year and 62,500 DL hours, resulting in a predetermined MOH rate of $16/DL hour. By the end of the year the company had actually incurred $975,000 of MOH costs and used a total of 60,000 DL hours on jobs. By how much had life Fitness overallocated or underallocated MOH for the year?

Please see page 324 for solutions.

## What Journal Entries Are Needed in a Manufacturer's Job Costing System?

6 Prepare journal entries for a manufacturer's job costing system.

Now that you know how manufacturers determine job costs and how those costs are used to make business decisions, let's look at how these costs are entered into the company's general ledger accounting system. We will consider the journal entries needed to record the flow of costs through Shaw Group's accounts during the month of December. For the sake of simplicity, we will detail only the entries required for two of the jobs and combine all other jobs:

Job 603: 1 HL 5 Dental Gold Crown

Job 604: 2 Sports Mouthguards (This is a clear plastic covering to protect the teeth during sports. We will assume the following costs associated with the job: direct materials totalling $83, direct labour of 4 hours totalling $80, and MOH totalling $64.)

All other jobs: We will assume the following information associated with the rest of the jobs worked on in December: 367 units completed using direct materials totalling $111,779, direct labour totalling $29,695, and MOH totalling $23,752.

You may wish to review the basic mechanics of journal entries, shown in Exhibit 5-17, before we begin our discussion.

**EXHIBIT 5-17** Review of Journal Entry and T-Account Mechanics

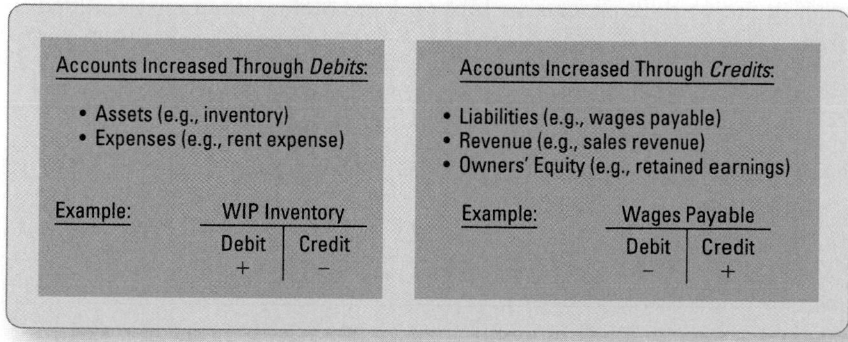


Additionally, keep in mind the flow of inventory that was first described in Exhibit 5-2. You may find this visual reminder helpful as we describe how the journal entries reflect the flow of inventory through the manufacturing system. Each arrow represents a journal entry that must be made to reflect activities that occur along the process: purchasing raw materials, using direct materials, using direct labour, recording actual MOH costs, allocating MOH to jobs, moving the jobs out of the factory after completion, and finally selling the units from a job.

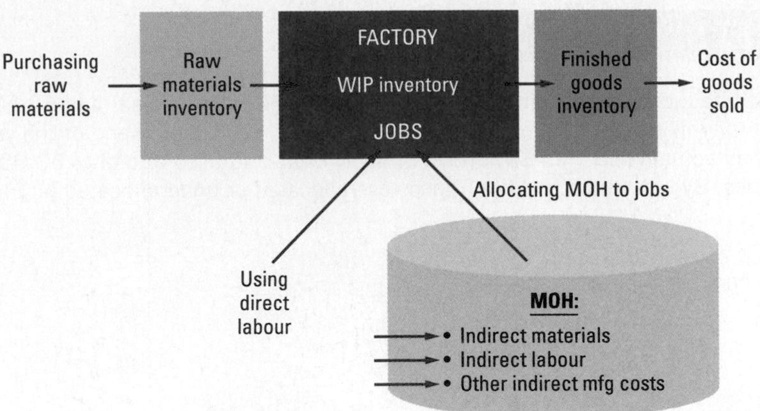


## Purchase of Raw Materials

Shaw Group's purchase manager uses the bill of materials and raw materials records to determine what raw materials to purchase. Assume that Shaw Group ordered and received $90,000 of raw materials during December. Once the materials are received and verified against the purchase order and the invoice received from the supplier, the purchase is recorded as follows:

| | | | | |
|---|---|---|---|---|
| (1) | | Raw Materials Inventory | 90,000 | |
| | | Accounts Payable | | 90,000 |
| | | *(to record purchases of raw materials)* | | |

These materials will remain in the raw materials storeroom until they are needed for production. The liability in Accounts Payable will be removed when the supplier is paid.

## Use of Direct Materials

Recall that direct materials are the primary physical components of the product. Each time production managers need particular direct materials for Jobs 603 and 604, they fill out a materials requisition informing the storeroom workers to pick the materials and send them into the manufacturing facility. Once these materials are sent into production, they become part of the work in process on Jobs 603 and 604, so their cost is added to the job cost records:

| JOB 603 HL 5 Dental Gold Crown | | JOB 604 Sport Mouthguard | | All Other Jobs | |
|---|---|---|---|---|---|
| Direct Materials................................ | $138 | Direct Materials................................ | $83 | Direct Materials................................ | $111,779 |
| Direct Labour.................................... | | Direct Labour.................................... | | Direct Labour.................................... | |
| Manufacturing Overhead.................. | | Manufacturing Overhead.................. | | Manufacturing Overhead.................. | |
| Total Job Cost............................... | | Total Job Cost............................... | | Total Job Cost............................... | |

From an accounting perspective, the cost of these materials must also be moved into the work in process inventory (through a debit) and out of raw materials inventory (through a credit). The following journal entry is made:

| | | | | |
|---|---|---|---|---|
| (2) | | Work in Process Inventory (138 + 83 + 111,779) | 112,000 | |
| | | Raw Materials Inventory | | 112,000 |
| | | *(to record the use of direct materials on jobs)* | | |

Recall from the first half of the chapter that the individual job cost records form the underlying support for the work in process inventory account shown on the Balance

Sheet.[5] Therefore, the amount posted to the general ledger account ($112,000) must be identical to the sum of the amounts posted to the individual job cost records $138 + $83 + $111,779 = $112,000.

## Use of Indirect Materials

Indirect materials are materials used in the manufacturing plant that cannot be traced to individual jobs, and therefore are not recorded on any job cost record. Examples include janitorial supplies used in the factory and machine lubricants for the factory machines. Once again, materials requisitions inform the raw materials storeroom to release these materials. However, instead of becoming part of the work in process for a particular job, the indirect materials used in the factory ($2,000) become part of the MOH account. Therefore, the MOH account is debited (to increase the account) and raw materials inventory is credited (to decrease the account) as follows:

| | | | | |
|---|---|---|---|---|
| (3) | | Manufacturing Overhead | 2,000 | |
| | | Raw Materials Inventory | | 2,000 |
| | | *(to record the use of indirect materials in the factory)* | | |

All indirect manufacturing costs, including indirect materials, indirect labour, and other indirect manufacturing costs (such as plant insurance and depreciation) are accumulated in the manufacturing overhead account. The manufacturing overhead account is a temporary account used to "store" or "pool" indirect manufacturing costs until those costs can be allocated to individual jobs.

We can summarize the flow of materials costs through the T-accounts as follows:

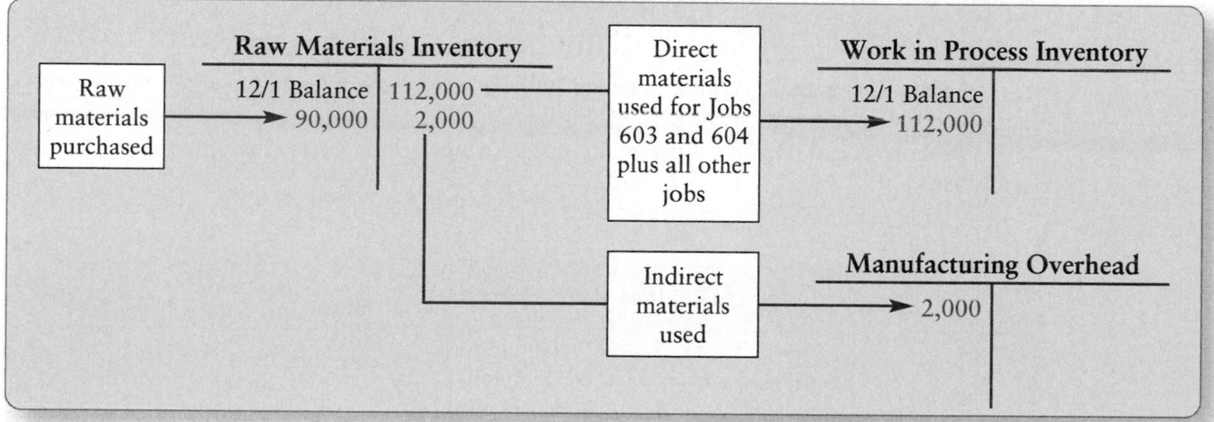


## Use of Direct Labour

The labour time records of individual factory workers are used to determine exactly how much time was spent directly working on Jobs 603 and 604. The cost of this direct labour is entered on the job cost records:

| JOB 603 HL 5 Dental Gold Crown | |
|---|---|
| Direct Materials | $138 |
| Direct Labour (11.5 DL hr) | $225 |
| Manufacturing Overhead | |
| Total Job Cost | |

| JOB 604 Sport Mouthguard | |
|---|---|
| Direct Materials | $83 |
| Direct Labour (4 DL hr) | $80 |
| Manufacturing Overhead | |
| Total Job Cost | |

| All Other Jobs | |
|---|---|
| Direct Materials | $111,779 |
| Direct Labour (1484.5 DL hr) | $ 29,695 |
| Manufacturing Overhead | |
| Total Job Cost | |

[5]The job cost records of unfinished jobs form the subsidiary ledger for the work in process inventory account. Recall that a subsidiary ledger is simply the supporting detail for a general ledger account. Many other general ledger accounts (such as Accounts Receivable, Accounts Payable, Plant & Equipment) also have subsidiary ledgers. The raw material inventory records form the subsidiary ledger for the Raw Materials Inventory account, while the job cost records on completed, unsold jobs form the subsidiary ledger for the Finished Goods Inventory account.

Again, since the job cost records form the underlying support for work in process inventory, an identical amount ($225 + $80 + $29,695 = $30,000) must be debited to the work in process inventory account. Wages Payable is credited to show that the company has a liability to pay its factory workers.

| | | | | |
|---|---|---|---|---|
| (4) | | Work in Process Inventory ($225 + $80 + $29,695 = $30,000) | 30,000 | |
| | | Wages Payable | | 30,000 |
| | | *(to record the use of direct labor on jobs)* | | |

The wages payable liability will be removed on payday, when the workers receive their paycheques.

## Use of Indirect Labour

Recall that indirect labour consists of the salary, wages, and benefits of all factory workers who are *not* directly working on individual jobs, for example, factory janitors, supervisors, and forklift operators. Since their time cannot be traced to particular jobs, the cost of employing these factory workers during the month ($13,000) cannot be posted to individual job cost records. Thus, we record the cost of indirect labour as part of MOH, *not* work in process inventory:

| | | | | |
|---|---|---|---|---|
| (5) | | Manufacturing Overhead | 13,000 | |
| | | Wages Payable | | 13,000 |
| | | *(to record the use of indirect labour in the factory)* | | |

Again, the wages payable liability will be removed on payday, when the workers receive their paycheques.

We can summarize the flow of manufacturing labour costs through the T-accounts as follows:

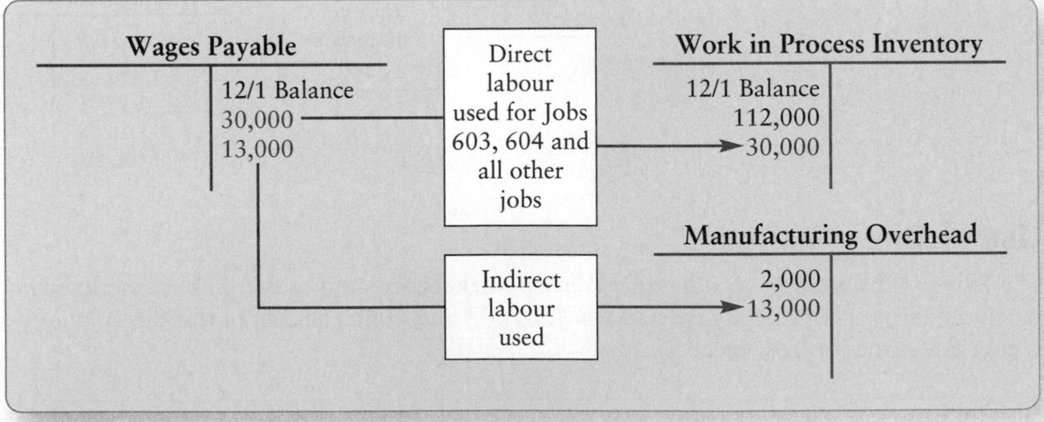


## Incurring Other Manufacturing Overhead Costs

We have already recorded the indirect materials and indirect labour used in the factory during December by debiting the MOH account. However, Shaw Group incurs other indirect manufacturing costs, such as plant utilities ($3,000), plant depreciation ($4,000), plant insurance ($1,000), and plant property taxes ($2,000) during the period. These indirect costs of operating the manufacturing plant during the month are also accumulated in the MOH account until they can be allocated to specific jobs:

| (6) | | Manufacturing Overhead | 10,000 | |
|---|---|---|---|---|
| | | Accounts Payable *(for electricity bill)* | | 3,000 |
| | | Accumulated Depreciation—Plant and Equipment | | 4,000 |
| | | Prepaid Plant Insurance *(for expiration of prepaid insurance)* | | 1,000 |
| | | Plant Property Taxes Payable *(for taxes to be paid)* | | 2,000 |
| | | *(to record other indirect manufacturing costs incurred during the month)* | | |

After recording all other indirect manufacturing costs, the manufacturing overhead account appears as follows:

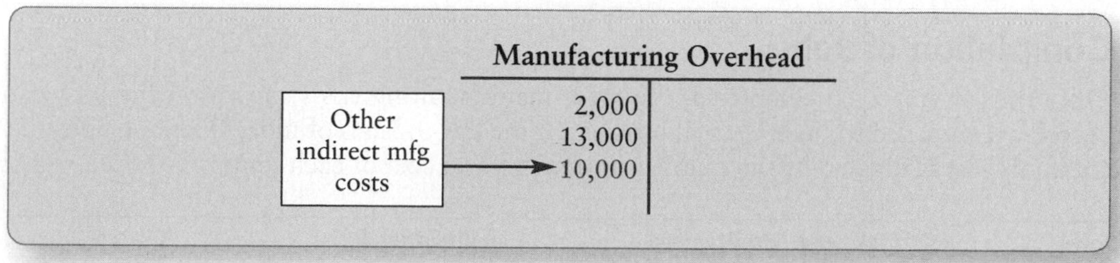


## Allocating Manufacturing Overhead to Jobs

Shaw Group allocates some MOH to each job worked on during the month using its predetermined overhead rate ($16 per direct labour hour). The total of direct labour hours used on each job is found on the labour time records and is usually summarized on the job cost records. Assume Job 603 used 11.5 DL hours and Job 604 used 4 DL hours, while all remaining jobs used 1,484.5 DL hours. Then the amount of MOH allocated to each job is determined as follows:

Job 603: $16 per DL hour × 11.5 DL hours = $184
Job 604: $16 per DL hour × 4 DL hours = $64
All other jobs: $16 per DL hour × 1,484.5 DL hours = $23,752

| JOB 603 HL 5 Dental Gold Crown | |
|---|---|
| Direct Materials............................... | $138 |
| Direct Labour (11.5 DL hr)................ | 225 |
| Manufacturing Overhead.................. | 184 |
| Total Job Cost.............................. | |

| JOB 604 Sport Mouthguard | |
|---|---|
| Direct Materials............................... | $83 |
| Direct Labour (4 DL hr)..................... | 80 |
| Manufacturing Overhead.................. | 64 |
| Total Job Cost.............................. | |

| All Other Jobs | |
|---|---|
| Direct Materials............................... | $111,779 |
| Direct Labour (1484.5 DL hr)............ | 29,695 |
| Manufacturing Overhead.................. | 23,752 |
| Total Job Cost.............................. | |

Again, since the job cost records form the underlying support for work in process inventory, an identical amount ($184 + $64 + $23,752 = $24,000) must be debited to the work in process inventory account. Since we accumulated all actual MOH costs *into* an account called MOH (through debiting the account), we now allocate MOH costs *out of* the account by crediting it.

| (7) | | Work in Process Inventory ($184 + $64 + $23,752) | 24,000 | |
|---|---|---|---|---|
| | | Manufacturing Overhead | | 24,000 |
| | | *(to allocate manufacturing overhead to specific jobs)* | | |

By looking at the MOH T-account, you can see how actual MOH costs are accumulated in the account through debits, while the amount of MOH allocated to specific jobs is credited to the account:

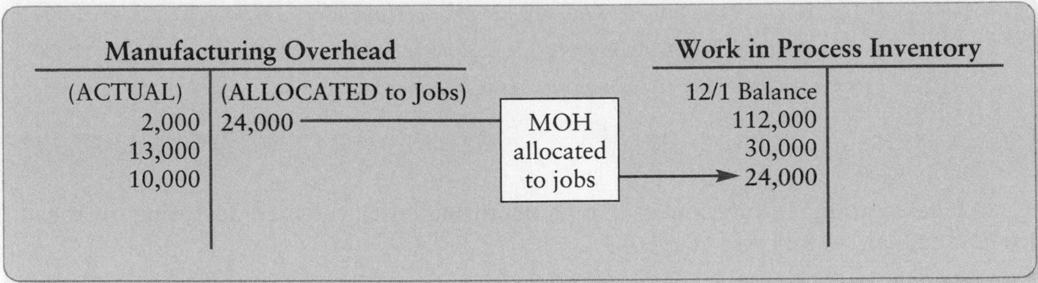


## Completion of Jobs

Once the job has been completed, the three manufacturing costs shown on the job cost record are summed to find the total job cost. If the job consists of more than one unit, the total job cost is divided by the number of units to find cost of each unit:

| JOB 603 HL 5 Dental Gold Crown | | JOB 604 Sport Mouthguard | | All Other Jobs | |
|---|---|---|---|---|---|
| Direct Materials | $138 | Direct Materials | $ 83 | Direct Materials | $111,779 |
| Direct Labour (11.5 DL hr) | 225 | Direct Labour (4 DL hr) | 80 | Direct Labour (1484.5 DL hr) | 29,695 |
| Manufacturing Overhead | 184 | Manufacturing Overhead | 64 | Manufacturing Overhead | 23,752 |
| Total Job Cost | $547 | Total Job Cost | $ 227 | Total Job Cost | 165,226 |
| Number of Units | ÷1 | Number of Units | ÷2 | Number of Units | ÷367 |
| Cost per Unit | $547 | Cost per Unit | $113.5 | Cost per Unit | 450 |

The jobs are physically moved off the plant floor and into the finished goods warehouse. (For Shaw Group, the finished goods are taken to the administration area to be recorded, boxed, and delivered.) Likewise, in the accounting records, the jobs are moved out of work in process inventory (through a credit) and into finished goods inventory (through a debit):

| | | | | |
|---|---|---|---|---|
| (8) | | Finished Goods Inventory ($547 + $227 + $165,226) | 166,000 | |
| | | Work in Process Inventory | | 166,000 |
| | | *(to move the completed jobs out of the factory and into Finished Goods)* | | |

The T-accounts show the movement of completed jobs off the factory floor:

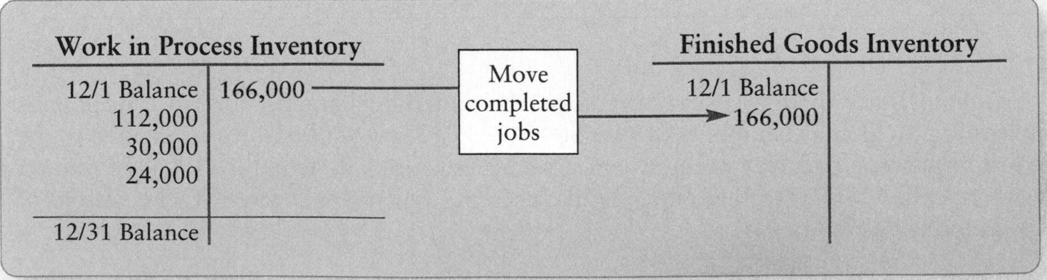


### Sale of Units

For simplicity, let us record only Job 603, understanding that we would need to make similar entries for all the units sold in December (we will assume that sales of all other jobs totalled $230,779.50). The sales price was $820.50 based on a 50% cost-plus pricing method. Two journal entries are needed. The first journal entry records the revenue generated from the sale and shows the amount due from the customer:

| | | | | |
|---|---|---|---|---|
| (9) | | Accounts Receivable ($547 × 150%) | 820.50 | |
| | | Sales Revenue | | 820.50 |
| | | *(to record the sale of HL 5 Dental Gold Crown to Dr. Waja)* | | |

The second journal entry reduces the company's finished goods inventory and records the cost of goods sold. From the job cost record, we know that Job 603 cost $547 to make. Therefore, the following entry is recorded:

| | | | | |
|---|---|---|---|---|
| (10) | | Cost of Goods Sold | 547 | |
| | | Finished Goods Inventory | | 547 |
| | | *(to reduce finished goods inventory and record cost of goods sold)* | | |

The following T-accounts show the movement of the units out of finished goods inventory and into cost of goods sold (including the additional entry for all other jobs sold in the month):

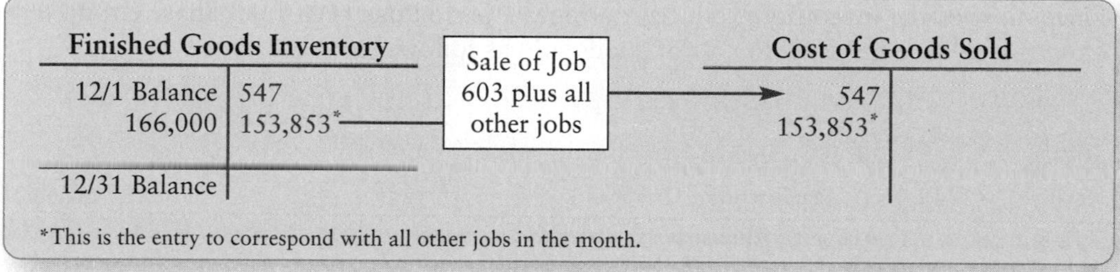


## Operating Expenses

During the month, Shaw Group also incurred $32,700 of operating expenses to run its business. For example, Shaw Group incurred salaries and commissions ($20,000) for its sales people, office administrators, research and design staff, and customer service representatives. It paid rent ($3,300) for its office headquarters. The company also received a bill from its advertising agency for marketing expenses incurred during the month ($9,400). *All costs incurred outside of the manufacturing function of the value chain* are expensed in the current month and shown as "operating expenses" on the company's income statement:

| | | | | |
|---|---|---|---|---|
| (11) | | Salaries and Commission Expense | 20,000 | |
| | | Rent Expense | 3,300 | |
| | | Marketing Expenses | 9,400 | |
| | | Salaries and Commissions Payable | | 20,000 |
| | | Cash | | 3,300 |
| | | Accounts Payable | | 9,400 |
| | | *(to record all nonmanufacturing costs incurred during the month)* | | |

## Closing Manufacturing Overhead

As a final step, Shaw Group must deal with the balance in the manufacturing overhead account. Since the company uses a *predetermined* overhead rate to allocate MOH to individual jobs, the total amount allocated to jobs will most likely differ from the amount of MOH incurred.

Let us see how this plays out in the manufacturing overhead T-account:

1. All MOH costs *incurred* by Shaw Group were recorded as *debits* to the MOH account. These debits total $25,000 of actual MOH incurred.
2. On the other hand, all MOH *allocated* to specific jobs ($248 + $23,752) were recorded as *credits* to the MOH account.

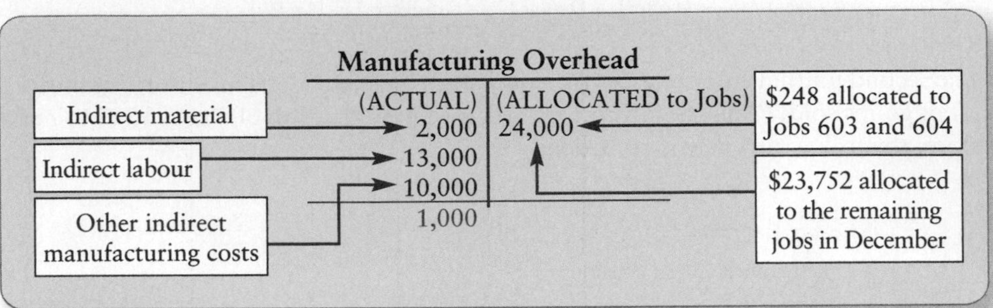


This leaves a debit balance of $1,000 in the MOH account, which means that MOH has been *underallocated* during the month. Since MOH is a temporary account, not shown on any of the company's financial statements, it must be closed out (zeroed out). Since most of the inventory produced during the period has been sold, Shaw Group will close the balance in MOH to cost of goods sold as follows:

| | | | | |
|---|---|---|---|---|
| (12) | | Cost of Goods Sold | 1,000 | |
| | | Manufacturing Overhead | | 1,000 |
| | | *(to close the manufacturing overhead account)* | | |

As a result of this entry, (1) the MOH account now has a zero balance and (2) the balance in cost of goods sold has increased, to correct for the fact that the jobs had been undercosted during the month (noting that the cost of goods sold amount in the T-account includes the cost of all jobs sold in December).

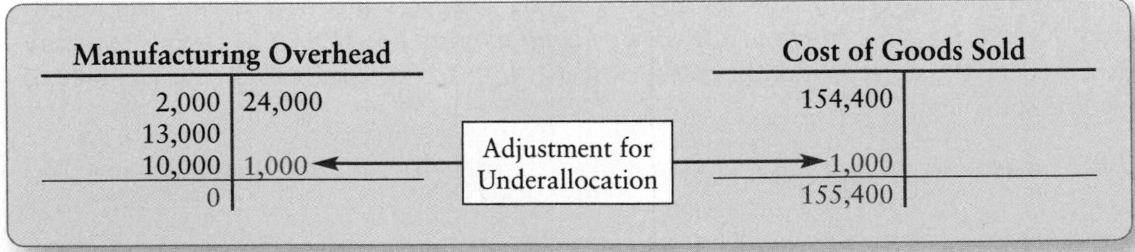


If, in some period, Shaw Group overallocates its overhead, the journal entry to close manufacturing overhead would be the opposite of that shown: You would debit manufacturing overhead to zero it out and credit cost of goods sold to reduce it as a result of having overcosted jobs during the period.

Now you have seen how all of the costs flowed through Shaw Group's accounts during December. Exhibit 5-18 shows the company's income statement that results from these journal entries, and the journal entries from the units produced and sold that we have not included in the examples:

**EXHIBIT 5-18** Income Statement after Adjusting for Underallocated Manufacturing Overhead

| Shaw Group<br>Income Statement<br>December 31 | |
|---|---|
| Sales Revenue | $231,600 |
| Less: Cost of Goods Sold | 155,400 |
| Gross Profit | 76,200 |
| Less: Operating Expenses | 32,700 |
| Operating Income | $ 43,500 |

# DECISION GUIDELINES

## Job Costing

As a result of using a predetermined manufacturing overhead rate to allocate manufacturing overhead to jobs, manufacturers will invariably either underallocate or overallocate manufacturing overhead. The following decision guidelines describe the implications as well as other decisions that need to be made in a job costing environment.

| Decision | Guidelines |
|---|---|
| If we have underallocated (or overallocated) manufacturing overhead, what does it mean about the cost of the jobs produced during the period? | If manufacturing overhead has been *underallocated*, it means that the jobs have been *undercosted*. In other words, not enough manufacturing overhead cost was posted on the job cost records.<br>On the other hand, if manufacturing overhead has been *overallocated*, it means that the jobs have been *overcosted*. Too much manufacturing overhead cost was posted on the job cost records.<br>Since the costs that are allocated to each job may impact the selling price (particularly with cost-plus pricing), overallocated and underallocated manufacturing overhead can have an impact on product sales in the long term. |
| What do we do about overallocated or underallocated manufacturing overhead? | Assuming most of the inventory produced during the period has been sold, manufacturers generally adjust the cost of goods sold for the total amount of the under- or overallocation. If a significant portion of the inventory is still on hand, then the adjustment will be prorated between WIP, finished goods, and cost of goods sold. |
| How do we know whether to increase or decrease cost of goods sold? | If manufacturing overhead has been overallocated, then cost of goods sold is too high and must be decreased.<br>If manufacturing overhead has been underallocated, then cost of goods sold is too low and must be increased. |
| How does job costing work at a service firm? | Job costing at a service firm is very similar to job costing at a manufacturer. The main difference is that the company is allocating operating expenses, rather than manufacturing costs, to each client job. In addition, since there are no inventory or cost of goods sold accounts, no journal entries are needed to move costs through the system. |
| Can manufacturers also allocate operating expenses to jobs? | For *internal decision making only*, operating expenses can also be assigned to jobs. However, operating expenses are *never* assigned to jobs for external financial reporting purposes. Direct operating costs are traced to jobs (such as the sales commission on a particular job or the design costs related to a particular job), while indirect operating costs (such as the lease of the corporate headquarters) are allocated to jobs. |

# SUMMARY PROBLEM 2

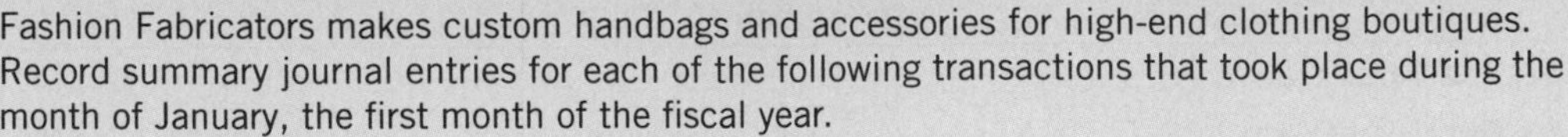

Fashion Fabricators makes custom handbags and accessories for high-end clothing boutiques. Record summary journal entries for each of the following transactions that took place during the month of January, the first month of the fiscal year.

**Requirements**

1. $150,000 of raw materials were purchased on account.
2. During the month, $140,000 of raw materials were requisitioned. Of this amount, $135,000 was traced to specific jobs, while the remaining materials were for general factory use.
3. Manufacturing labour (both direct and indirect) for the month totalled $80,000. It has not yet been paid. Of this amount, $60,000 was traced to specific jobs.
4. The company recorded $9,000 of depreciation on the plant building and machinery. In addition, $3,000 of prepaid property tax expired during the month. The company also received the plant utility bill for $6,000.
5. Manufacturing overhead was allocated to jobs using a predetermined manufacturing overhead rate of 75% of direct labour *cost*. (*Hint:* Total direct labour cost is found in Requirement 3.)
6. Several jobs were completed during the month. According to the job cost records these jobs cost $255,000 to manufacture.
7. Sales (all on credit) for the month totalled $340,000. According to the job cost records, the units sold cost $250,000 to manufacture. Assume the company uses a perpetual inventory system.
8. The company incurred operating expenses of $60,000 during the month. Assume that 80% of these were for marketing and administrative salaries and the other 20% were lease and utility bills related to the corporate headquarters.
9. In order to prepare its January financial statements, the company had to close its manufacturing overhead account.
10. Based on the transactions previously incurred, prepare the January income statement for Fashion Fabrics.

## ■ SOLUTION

1. Raw materials worth $150,000 were purchased on account.

| | | | |
|---|---|---|---|
| | Raw Materials Inventory | 150,000 | |
| | Accounts Payable | | 150,000 |
| | *(to record purchases of raw materials)* | | |

2. During the month $140,000 of raw materials were requisitioned. Of this amount, $135,000 was traced to specific jobs, while the remaining materials were for general factory use.

| | | | |
|---|---|---|---|
| | Work in Process Inventory | 135,000 | |
| | Manufacturing Overhead | 5,000 | |
| | Raw Materials Inventory | | 140,000 |
| | *(to record the use of direct materials and indirect materials)* | | |

3. Manufacturing labour (both direct and indirect) for the month totalled $80,000. It has not yet been paid. Of this amount, $60,000 was traced to specific jobs.

| | | | |
|---|---|---|---|
| | Work in Process Inventory *(for direct labour)* | 60,000 | |
| | Manufacturing Overhead *(for indirect labour)* | 20,000 | |
| | Wages Payable | | 80,000 |
| | *(to record the use of direct labour and indirect labour)* | | |

4. The company recorded $9,000 of depreciation on the plant building and machinery. In addition, $3,000 of prepaid property tax expired during the month. The company also received the plant utility bill for $6,000.

| | | | |
|---|---|---|---|
| | Manufacturing Overhead | 18,000 | |
| | Accumulated Depreciation—Plant and Equipment | | 9,000 |
| | Prepaid Plant Property Tax *(for expiration of property tax)* | | 3,000 |
| | Accounts Payable *(for electricity bill)* | | 6,000 |
| | *(to record other indirect manufacturing costs incurred during the month)* | | |

5. Manufacturing overhead was allocated to jobs using a predetermined manufacturing overhead rate of 75% of direct labour cost. (*Hint:* Total direct labour cost is found in Requirement 3.)

| | | | |
|---|---|---|---|
| | Work in Process Inventory (75% × $60,000 of direct labour) | 45,000 | |
| | Manufacturing Overhead | | 45,000 |
| | *(to allocate manufacturing overhead to jobs)* | | |

6. Several jobs were completed during the month. According to the job cost records these jobs cost $255,000 to manufacture.

| | | | |
|---|---|---|---|
| | Finished Goods Inventory | 255,000 | |
| | Work in Process Inventory | | 255,000 |
| | *(to move the completed jobs out of the factory and into Finished Goods)* | | |

7. Sales (all on credit) for the month totalled $340,000. According to the job cost records, the units sold cost $250,000 to manufacture. Assume the company uses a perpetual inventory system.

| | | | |
|---|---|---|---|
| | Accounts Receivable | 340,000 | |
| | Sales Revenue | | 340,000 |
| | *(to record the sales and receivables)* | | |

| | | | |
|---|---|---|---|
| | Cost of Goods Sold | 250,000 | |
| | Finished Goods Inventory | | 250,000 |
| | *(to reduce finished goods inventory and record cost of goods sold)* | | |

8. The company incurred operating expenses of $60,000 during the month. Assume that 80% of these were for marketing and administrative salaries and the other 20% were lease and utility bills related to the corporate headquarters.

| | | | |
|---|---|---|---|
| | Salaries Expense | 48,000 | |
| | Lease and Utilities Expense | 12,000 | |
| | Salaries and Wages Payable | | 48,000 |
| | Accounts Payable | | 12,000 |
| | *(to record all nonmanufacturing costs incurred during the month)* | | |

9. In order to prepare its January financial statements, the company had to close its manufacturing overhead account. An analysis of the manufacturing overhead account *prior to closing* shows the following:

| Manufacturing Overhead | |
|---|---|
| (ACTUAL) | (ALLOCATED) |
| 5,000 | 45,000 |
| 20,000 | |
| 18,000 | |
| | 2,000 |

| | | | |
|---|---|---|---|
| | Manufacturing Overhead | 2,000 | |
| | Cost of Goods Sold | | 2,000 |
| | *(to close the manufacturing overhead account to CGS)* | | |

10. Based on the transactions previously incurred, prepare the January income statement for Fashion Fabrics.

| Fashion Fabrics Income Statement | |
|---|---|
| Sales Revenue | $340,000 |
| Less: Cost of Goods Sold* | 248,000 |
| Gross Profit | 92,000 |
| Less: Operating Expenses | 60,000 |
| Operating Income | $ 32,000 |

*$250,000 – 2,000 closing adjustment

# APPENDIX 5A

## How Do Service Firms Use Job Costing to Determine the Amount to Bill Clients?

7 Use job costing at a service firm as a basis for billing clients.

So far in this chapter we have illustrated job costing in a manufacturing environment. However, job costing is also commonly used by service firms (such as law firms, accounting firms, marketing firms, and consulting firms) and by tradespeople (such as plumbers, electricians, and auto mechanics). At these firms, the work performed for each individual client is considered a separate job. Service firms need to keep track of job costs so that they have a basis for billing their clients. As shown in Exhibit 5-19, the direct costs of serving the client are traced to the job, whereas the indirect costs of serving the client are allocated to the job.

**EXHIBIT 5-19** Assigning Cost to Client Jobs

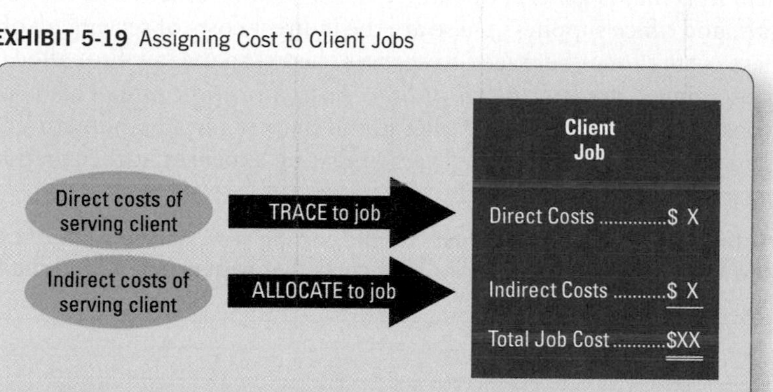


The amount billed to the client is determined by adding a profit markup to the total job cost. The main difference between job costing at a manufacturer and job costing at a service firm is that for the service firm the indirect costs of serving the client are all *operating expenses* rather than inventoriable product costs. In the next section, we will illustrate how job costing is used at Barnett & Associates law firm to determine how much to bill Client 367.

## What Costs Are Considered Direct Costs of Serving the Client?

The most significant direct cost at service firms is direct professional labour. In our example, direct professional labour is the lawyer's time spent on clients' cases. Lawyers use labour time records to keep track of the amount of time they spend working on each client. Firms estimate the hourly cost of employing their professionals based on the number of hours the professionals are expected to work on client jobs during the year. For example, say lawyer Sophia Mirza is paid a salary of $100,000 per year. The law firm expects her to spend 2,000 hours a year performing legal work for clients (50 weeks × 40 hours per week). Therefore, for job costing purposes, the law firm converts her annual salary to an hourly cost rate as follows:

$$\frac{\$100{,}000 \text{ annual salary}}{2{,}000 \text{ hours per year}} = \$50 \text{ per hour}$$

If the labour time record indicates that Mirza has spent 14 hours on Client 367, then the direct professional labour cost traced to the client is calculated as follows:

14 hours × $50 per hour = $700 of direct professional labour

At a law firm, very few other costs will be directly traceable to the client. Examples of other traceable costs might include travel and entertainment costs, long-distance phone charges, postage and courier fees, or court filing fees related directly to specific clients. When tradespeople such as auto mechanics or plumbers use job costing, they trace their time to specific client jobs, just like lawyers do. They also trace the direct materials costs (such as the cost of new tires, an exhaust pipe, or garbage disposal) to the jobs on which those materials were used.

## What Costs Are Considered Indirect Costs of Serving the Client?

The law firm also incurs general operating costs, such as office rent, the salaries of office support staff, and office supplies. These are the indirect costs of serving *all* of the law firm's clients. These costs cannot be traced to specific clients, so the law firm allocates these costs to client jobs using a *predetermined indirect cost allocation rate*. This is done using the same four basic steps that we used earlier in the chapter for a manufacturer. The only real difference is that we are allocating indirect operating expenses, rather than indirect manufacturing costs (manufacturing overhead).

**Step 1: Estimate the total indirect costs for the coming year. Before the fiscal year begins, the law firm estimates the total indirect costs that will be incurred in the coming year:**

| | |
|---|---|
| Office rent | $190,000 |
| Office supplies, telephone, internet access, and copier lease | 10,000 |
| Office support staff | 70,000 |
| Maintaining and updating law library for case research | 25,000 |
| Advertising | 3,000 |
| Sponsorship of the symphony | 2,000 |
| Total indirect costs | $300,000 |

**Step 2: Choose an allocation base and estimate the total amount that will be used during the year.**

Next, the law firm chooses a cost allocation base. Service firms typically use professional labour hours as the cost allocation base because the time spent on client jobs is probably the main driver of indirect costs. For example, Barnett & Associates estimates that its lawyers will spend a total of 10,000 professional labour hours working on client jobs throughout the coming year.

**Step 3: Compute the predetermined indirect cost allocation rate. The predetermined indirect cost allocation rate is found as follows:**

$$\text{Predetermined indirect cost allocation rate} = \frac{\text{Total estimated indirect costs}}{\text{Total estimated amount of the allocation base}}$$

$$= \frac{\$300{,}000 \text{ total indirect costs}}{10{,}000 \text{ professional labour hours}}$$

$$= \$30 \text{ per professional labour hour}$$

**Step 4:** **Allocate indirect costs to client jobs using the predetermined rate.**

Throughout the year, indirect costs are allocated to individual client jobs using the predetermined indirect cost allocation rate. For example, assume Sophia Mirza was the only lawyer who worked on Client 367. Since Mirza spent 14 hours working on Client 367, the amount of indirect cost allocated to the job is computed as follows:

= Predetermined indirect cost allocation rate × Actual amount of allocation base used by the job
= $30 per professional labour hour × 14 professional labour hours
= $420

## Finding the Total Cost of the Job and Adding a Profit Markup

Barnett & Associates can now determine the total cost of serving Client 367:

| | |
|---|---|
| Direct costs traced to Client 367 ($50 per hour × 14 hours) | $ 700 |
| Indirect costs allocated to Client 367 ($30 per hour × 14 hours) | 420 |
| Total cost of serving Client 367 | $1,120 |

Once the total job cost is known, Barnett & Associates can determine the amount to bill the client. Let us assume that Barnett & Associates wants to achieve a 25% profit over its costs. To achieve this profit, Barnett would bill Client 367 as follows:

Job cost + Markup for Profit = Amount to bill the client
$1,120 + (25% × $1,120) = $1,400

## Invoicing the Client Using a Professional Billing Rate

When service firms and tradespeople bill their clients, they rarely show the actual direct costs of providing the service, the allocation of indirect costs, or the profit they earned on the job. Rather, these figures are "hidden" from the client's view. How is this done? By incorporating these costs and profit components in the labour rate, often known as the billing rate, charged to the customer. Consider the last time you had your vehicle repaired. A typical mechanic billing rate exceeds $48 per hour, yet the mechanic employed by the auto repair shop does not actually earn a $48 per hour wage rate.

**Why is this important?**
**Service** companies and trades (such as **law firms**, auto repair shops, and plumbers) use **job costing** to determine how much to **bill** their clients.

Let us look at the calculations a service firm performs "behind the scenes" to determine its hourly billing rates. Barnett & Associates determines Sophia Mirza's billing rate as follows:

| | |
|---|---|
| Professional labour cost per hour | $ 50 |
| Plus: Indirect cost allocation rate per hour | 30 |
| Total hourly cost | $ 80 |
| Multiplied by the 25% profit markup | × 1.25 |
| Hourly billing rate for Sophia Mirza | $ 100 |

Whenever Sophia Mirza performs legal work for a client, her time will be billed at $100 per hour. Remember, this is the *price* Barnett & Associates charges its clients for any work performed by Sophia Mirza. The actual invoice to Client 367 would be similar to Exhibit 5-20.

**EXHIBIT 5-20** Invoice to Client

**Barnett & Associates Law Firm**

**Invoice:** Client 367

Work performed the week of July 23: Researching and filing patent application

| | |
|---|---|
| Lawyer Sophia Mirza: 14 hours × $100 hourly billing rate | $1,400 |

## What Journal Entries Are Needed in a Service Firm's Job Costing System?

The journal entries required for job costing at a service firm are much simpler than those used at a manufacturing company. Service firms typically have no inventory, so there is no need to record the movement of inventory through the system. Rather, all costs at a service company are treated as period costs, meaning they are immediately recorded as operating expenses when they are incurred (for example, salaries expense, rent expense, supplies expense, etc.). The tracing of direct costs and allocation of indirect costs is performed *only* on the client's job cost record, *not* through journal entries to the company's general ledger.

### TRY IT!

Sarah Haymeyer, CPA, pays her new staff accountant, Hannah, a salary equivalent to $25 per hour while Sarah receives a salary equivalent to $40 per hour. The firm's predetermined indirect cost allocation rate for the year is $12 per hour. Haymeyer bills for the firm's services at 30% over cost. Assume Sarah works 5 hours and Hannah works 10 hours preparing a tax return for Michele Meckfessel.

1. What is the total cost of preparing Meckfessel's tax return?
2. How much will Sarah bill Meckfessel for the tax work?

Please see page 324 for solutions.

# END OF CHAPTER

## LEARNING OBJECTIVES

1 Distinguish between job costing and process costing.

2 Understand the flow of production and how direct materials and direct labour are traced to jobs.

3 Compute a predetermined manufacturing overhead (MOH) rate, and use it to allocate MOH to jobs.

4 Compute and dispose of overallocated or underallocated manufacturing overhead.

5 Determine the cost of a job, and use it to make business decisions.

6 Prepare journal entries for a manufacturer's job costing system.

7 Use job costing at a service firm as a basis for billing clients.

## ACCOUNTING VOCABULARY

**Bill of Materials (p. 250)** A list of all of the raw materials needed to manufacture a job.

**Billing Rate (p. 283)** A cost, usually presented on an hourly basis, that reflects the labour rate (cost); costs associated with overhead and profit.

**Cost Driver (p. 258)** The primary factor that causes a cost.

**Invoice (p. 251)** A bill from a supplier for purchases. An invoice is also used to bill a customer for goods or services sold.

**Job Cost Record (p. 252)** A written or electronic document that lists the direct materials, direct labour, and manufacturing overhead costs assigned to each individual job.

**Job Costing (p. 247)** A system for assigning costs to products or services that differ in the amount of materials, labour, and overhead required. Typically used by manufacturers that produce unique or custom-ordered products in small batches; also used by professional service firms.

**Labour Time Record (p. 256)** A written or electronic document that identifies the employee, the amount of time spent on a particular job, and the labour cost charged to a job.

**Materials Requisition (p. 254)** A written or electronic document requesting that specific materials be transferred from the raw materials inventory storeroom to the production floor.

**Overallocated Manufacturing Overhead (p. 260)** The amount of manufacturing overhead allocated to jobs is more than the amount of manufacturing overhead costs actually incurred; this results in jobs being overcosted.

**Predetermined Manufacturing Overhead Rate (p. 259)** The rate used to allocate manufacturing overhead to individual jobs, calculated before the year begins as follows: total estimated manufacturing overhead costs divided by total estimated amount of allocation base.

**Process Costing (p. 246)** A system for assigning costs to large numbers of identical units that typically pass through a series of uniform production steps. Costs are averaged over the units produced such that each unit bears the same unit cost.

**Production Schedule (p. 249)** A written or electronic document indicating the quantity and types of inventory that will be manufactured during a specified time frame.

**Purchase Order (p. 251)** A written or electronic document authorizing the purchase of specific raw materials from a specific supplier. A purchase order can also be used by a customer when purchasing goods and services.

**Raw Materials Record (p. 251)** A written or electronic document listing the number and cost of all units of raw materials received and used, and the balance currently in stock; a separate record is maintained for each type of raw material kept in stock.

**Receiving Report (p. 251)** A written or electronic document listing the quantity and type of raw materials received in an incoming shipment; the report is typically a duplicate of the purchase order without the quantity prelisted on the form.

**Stock Inventory (p. 249)** Products in finished goods inventory that are normally kept on hand in order to quickly fill customer orders instead of being made for a specific customer order.

**Underallocated Manufacturing Overhead (p. 260)** The amount of manufacturing overhead allocated to jobs is less than the amount of manufacturing overhead costs actually incurred; this results in jobs being undercosted.

# QUICK CHECK

1. (Learning Objective 1) Which of the following companies would be most likely to use a job costing system rather than a process costing system?
   a. Steel manufacturer
   b. Legal firm
   c. Beverage bottler
   d. Paint manufacturer
2. (Learning Objective 1) Would the advertising agency Saatchi & Saatchi use job or process costing? What about a Tembec paper mill?
   a. Saatchi & Saatchi—job costing
      Tembec—job costing
   b. Saatchi & Saatchi—process costing
      Tembec—process costing
   c. Saatchi & Saatchi—process costing
      Tembec—job costing
   d. Saatchi & Saatchi—job costing
      Tembec—process costing
3. (Learning Objective 2) In a job costing system, all of the following statements about materials are correct except for one. Which of the following is incorrect?
   a. A materials requisition is used to request materials needed from the storeroom.
   b. The job cost record for a job contains all direct material used for that particular job.
   c. Materials that cannot be traced to a particular job are treated as manufacturing overhead.
   d. All materials are always classified as direct materials.
4. (Learning Objective 3) How does Dell's management use product cost information?
   a. To set the prices of its products
   b. To decide which products to emphasize
   c. To identify ways to cut production costs
   d. All of the above
5. (Learning Objective 3) The formula to calculate the amount of manufacturing overhead to allocate to jobs is
   a. predetermined overhead rate times the actual amount of the allocation base used by the specific job.
   b. predetermined overhead rate divided by the actual allocation base used by the specific job.
   c. predetermined overhead rate times the actual manufacturing overhead used on the specific job.
   d. predetermined overhead rate times the estimated amount of the allocation base used by the specific job.
6. (Learning Objective 3) Averaging is involved in computing unit product costs when
   a. using process costing but not when using job order costing.
   b. using job order costing but not when using process costing.
   c. using both job order costing and process costing.
   d. averaging is not involved when using either job costing or process costing.
7. (Learning Objective 5) For which of the following reasons would John Barnett, owner of the Barnett & Associates law firm, want to know the total costs of a job (serving a particular client)?
   a. To determine the fees charged to the client
   b. For inventory valuation
   c. For external reporting
   d. All of the above
8. (Learning Objective 4) If the company underestimates the amount of allocation base when calculating its predetermined manufacturing overhead rate but estimates the amount of manufacturing overhead costs correctly, the amount of manufacturing overhead allocated for the year will be
   a. underallocated.
   b. overallocated.
   c. exactly equal to the actual manufacturing overhead for the year.
   d. cannot be determined from the information given
9. (Learning Objective 4) If manufacturing overhead is overallocated for the period at $200, then
   a. the $200 should be prorated between work in process inventory, finished goods inventory, and cost of goods sold.
   b. actual manufacturing overhead is greater than allocated manufacturing overhead.
   c. jobs have been overcosted during the period.
   d. cost of goods sold should be adjusted with an increase of $200.
10. (Learning Objective 6) When Dell uses direct labour, it traces the cost to the job by debiting
    a. direct labour.
    b. wages payable.
    c. manufacturing overhead.
    d. work in process inventory.

**Quick Check Answers**

1. *b* 2. *d* 3. *d* 4. *d* 5. *a* 6. *c* 7. *a* 8. *b* 9. *c* 10. *d*

# SHORT EXERCISES

**S5-1 Decide on a product costing system** *(Learning Objective 1)*

Would the following companies use job costing or process costing?

a. A manufacturer of cellulose (recycled paper) insulation
b. A residential plumbing contractor
c. A manufacturer of fibre-optic cabling
d. A custom home builder
e. A hospital

**S5-2 Determine the flow of costs between inventory accounts** *(Learning Objective 2)*

Parker's Wood Amenities is a manufacturing plant that makes picnic tables, benches, and other outdoor furniture. Indicate which inventory account(s) would be affected by the following actions, which occur at Parker's in the process of manufacturing its standard picnic tables. Also indicate whether the inventory account would increase or decrease as a result of the action.

| Action | Raw Materials Inventory | Work in Process Inventory | Finished Goods Inventory |
|---|---|---|---|
| a. Lumber is delivered by the supplier to the plant, where it is stored in a materials storeroom until needed. | | | |
| b. Lumber is requisitioned from the storeroom to be used for tops and seats for the tables. | | | |
| c. Factory workers cut the lumber for the tables. | | | |
| d. Ten tables are completed and moved to the inventory storage area to await sale. | | | |
| e. A customer purchases a table and takes it home. | | | |

**S5-3 Compute various manufacturing overhead rates** *(Learning Objective 3)*

Dodds Aquatics manufactures swimming pool equipment. The company estimates total manufacturing costs next year to be $2,400,000. Dodds also estimates it will use 50,000 direct labour hours and incur $1,000,000 of direct labour cost next year. In addition, the machines are expected to be run for 40,000 hours. Compute the predetermined manufacturing overhead rate for next year under the following independent situations:

1. Assume that Dodds uses direct labour hours as its manufacturing overhead allocation base.
2. Assume that Dodds uses direct labour cost as its manufacturing overhead allocation base.
3. Assume that Dodds uses machine hours as its manufacturing allocation base.

**S5-4 Continuation of S5-3: compute total allocated overhead** *(Learning Objective 3)*

Use your answers from S5-3 to determine the total manufacturing overhead allocated to Dodds's manufacturing jobs in the following independent situations:

1. Assume that Dodds actually used 52,000 direct labour hours.
2. Assume that Dodds actually incurred $1,030,000 of direct labour cost.
3. Assume that Dodds actually ran the machines 46,500 hours.
4. Briefly explain what you have learned about the total manufacturing overhead allocated to production.

**S5-5** **Continuation of S5-4: determine over- or underallocation** *(Learning Objectives 3 & 4)*

Use your answers from S5-4 to determine the total overallocation or underallocation of manufacturing overhead during the year. Actual manufacturing costs for the year totalled $2,600,000.

1. Assume that Dodds used direct labour hours as the allocation base.
2. Assume that Dodds used the direct labour cost as the allocation base.
3. Assume that Dodds used machine hours as the allocation base.
4. Were there any situations in which jobs were costed correctly? If not, when were they overcosted? When were they undercosted?

**S5-6** **Calculate rate and analyze year-end results** *(Learning Objectives 3 & 4)*

Rainbow manufactures wooden backyard playground equipment. Rainbow estimated $1,785,000 of manufacturing overhead and $2,100,000 of direct labour cost for the year. After the year was over, the accounting records indicated that the company had actually incurred $1,700,000 of manufacturing overhead and $2,200,000 of direct labour cost.

1. Calculate Rainbow's predetermined manufacturing overhead rate assuming that the company uses direct labour cost as an allocation base.
2. How much manufacturing overhead would have been allocated to manufacturing jobs during the year?
3. At year-end, was manufacturing overhead overallocated or underallocated? By how much? (*Hint:* Use a T-account to aid in your analysis.)

**S5-7** **Calculate job cost and billing** *(Learning Objectives 2 & 5)*

Troy James is the owner of a business that sells and installs home theatre systems. He just completed a job for a builder consisting of the installation of 12 home theatre systems in a new condominium complex. The installations required materials totalling $17,400 and 72 hours of direct labour hours at a wage rate of $20 per hour. Overhead is allocated to jobs using a predetermined overhead rate of $5 per direct labour hour.

1. What is the total cost of the job?
2. What is the average unit cost (per theatre system installed)?
3. If Troy charges a price to the builder that is 150% of the total job cost, what price will he charge for the job?

**S5-8** **Calculate job cost and billing for A-1 Appliance's repair service** *(Learning Objectives 2 & 5)*

A-1 Appliance provides repair services for all makes and models of home appliances. A-1 Appliance charges customers for labour on each job at a rate of $50 per hour. The labour rate is high enough to cover actual technician wages of $20 per hour and shop overhead (allocated at a cost of $12 per hour), and to provide a profit. A-1 Appliance charges the customer "at cost" for parts and materials. A recent customer job consisted of $37 in parts and materials and two hours of technician time.

1. What was A-1 Appliance's cost for this job? Include shop overhead in the cost calculation.
2. How much was charged to the customer for this repair job?

**S5-9** **Ramifications of overallocating and underallocating jobs** *(Learning Objectives 2 & 4)*

Answer the following questions:

1. Why do managers use a *predetermined* manufacturing overhead allocation rate rather than the *actual* rate to cost jobs?
2. Jobs will typically be overcosted or undercosted. Is one worse than the other? Explain your thoughts.

**S5-10** **Record the purchase and use of materials** *(Learning Objective 6)*

Trekker manufactures backpacks. Its plant records include the following materials-related transactions:

| | |
|---|---|
| Purchases of canvas (on account) | $70,000 |
| Purchases of thread (on account) | 1,100 |
| Material requisition: | |
| Canvas | 63,000 |
| Thread | 280 |

Make the journal entries to record these transactions. Post these transactions to the raw materials inventory account. If the company had $35,680 of raw materials inventory at the beginning of the period, what is the ending balance of raw materials inventory?

**S5-11** **Record manufacturing labour costs** *(Learning Objective 6)*

Art Glass reports the following labour-related transactions at its plant in St. Andrew's, New Brunswick.

| | |
|---|---|
| Plant janitor's wages | 600 |
| Plant supervisor's wages | 900 |
| Glassblowers' wages | 76,000 |

Record the journal entries for the incurrence of these wages.

**S5-12** **Recompute job cost at a legal firm** *(Learning Objectives 3, 5, & 7)*

In the Barnett & Associates example on page 281–284, suppose Mirza's annual salary is $110,000 rather than $100,000. Also suppose the Barnett's lawyers are expected to work a total of 12,000 direct labour hours rather than 10,000 direct labour hours.

1. What would be the hourly (cost) rate to Barnett & Associates of employing Mirza?
2. What direct labour cost would be traced to Client 367?
3. What is the indirect cost allocation rate?
4. What indirect costs will be allocated to Client 367?
5. What is the total job cost for client 367?

# EXERCISES Group A

**E5-13A** **Identify the type of costing system** *(Learning Objective 1)*

Specify whether each of the following companies would be more likely to use job costing or process costing.

a. Jumbo airline manufacturer
b. Oil refinery
c. Custom cabinet manufacturer
d. Cereal manufacturer
e. Dental office
f. Auto-body repair shop
g. Mainframe computer manufacturer
h. CA firm
i. Print shop
j. Paper manufacturer
k. Movie production company
l. Hospital
m. Prescription eyewear retailer with on-site lab
n. Brewery

**E5-14A** **Describe the flow of costs in a job cost shop** *(Learning Objective 2)*

Hender Doors is a manufacturer of exterior doors made from recycled plastic lumber (HDPE). The following table contains events that occur in the manufacture and sale of the company's products. Put the events in the order in which they would occur by designating the step number in the Order column. Also, indicate with a "+" or a "–" whether that account would increase or decrease as a result of the event.

| Event | Order | Raw Materials Inventory | WIP Inventory | FG Inventory | Cost of Goods Sold | No Effect on Inventory or COGS |
|---|---|---|---|---|---|---|
| a. Eight basic "Entrance" doors are completed and are stored in the finished goods warehouse. | | | | | | |
| b. Six HDPE sheets are taken from the stockroom to be cut down into 12 half sheets, which is a common dimension for doors. | | | | | | |
| c. The customer is billed for five basic "Entrance" doors. | | | | | | |
| d. Pamela Kajjouni, an employee of Hender Doors, sets up the machining process to manufacture the doors. | | | | | | |
| e. An order of recycled plastic lumber (HDPE) sheets, the primary component in making the interior doors, is received. The HDPE sheets are stored in the stockroom until needed in production. | | | | | | |
| f. An order is received for five basic "Entrance" doors, and the doors are shipped to the customer. | | | | | | |

## E5-15A Understand key document terms in a job cost shop

*(Learning Objective 2)*

Fill in the blanks in the following sentences using the correct document term.

1. Incoming shipments of raw materials are counted and recorded on this document, a(n) __________, which does not include preprinted quantities or prices.
2. The time spent by each employee on each job he or she worked on throughout the day is detailed on a(n) __________.
3. A supplier would issue a(n) __________ to bill the customer for product the customer ordered and received.
4. Information about each item in stock, including number of units received and the balance of units currently in stock, would be found on a(n) __________.
5. A listing of all of the raw materials needed to manufacture a job would be found in a(n) __________.
6. A(n) __________ itemizes the raw materials currently needed from the storeroom and provides documentation of authorization for the request.
7. The __________ indicates the quantity and types of inventory that are planned to be manufactured during the given time period.
8. A(n) __________ is used to accumulate all of the direct materials and direct labour used on a job, as well as the manufacturing overhead allocated to the job.
9. A(n) __________ is authorization for a supplier to ship products at a given price.

a. Bill of materials
b. Job cost record
c. Production schedule
d. Purchase order
e. Raw materials record
f. Labour time record
g. Receiving report
h. Materials requisition
i. Invoice



## E5-16A Understand the flow of costs in a job cost shop *(Learning Objective 2)*

Smythe Feeders manufactures bird feeders for wild bird specialty stores. In September, Smythe Feeders received an order from Wild Birds, Inc. for 20 platform bird feeders. The order from Wild Birds, Inc. became Job Number 1102 at Smythe Feeders.

The following charts show a materials requisition for Job 1102, along with the materials requisition and the labour time records (partial) for the week that these feeders were made. Other products were also being produced during that week, so not all of the labour belongs to Job 1102.

**Materials Requisition**
**Number: #1250**

**Date:** 9/14

**Job:** 1102

| Part Number | Description | Quantity | Unit Cost | Amount |
|---|---|---|---|---|
| WOCD06 | Rough-hewn cedar planks | 40 | $2.50 | |
| SSF0304 | Stainless steel fasteners | 80 | $0.50 | |
| AS222 | Reinforced aluminum screens | 20 | $1.50 | |
| | **Total** | | | |

**Labour Time Record**

**Employee:** Greg Henderson **Week:** 9/14 – 9/20

**Hourly Wage Rate:** $12 **Record #:** 912

| Date | Job Number | Start Time | End Time | Hours | Cost |
|---|---|---|---|---|---|
| 9/14 | 1102 | 9:00 | 2:00 | | |
| 9/14 | 1103 | 2:00 | 5:00 | | |
| 9/15 etc. | | | | | |

**Labour Time Record**

**Employee:** Andrew Peck **Week:** 9/14 – 9/20

**Hourly Wage Rate:** $8 **Record #:** 913

| Date | Job Number | Start Time | End Time | Hours | Cost |
|---|---|---|---|---|---|
| 9/14 | 1101 | 8:00 | 12:00 | | |
| 9/14 | 1102 | 12:00 | 4:00 | | |
| 9/15 | 1103 | 8:00 | 10:00 | | |
| 9/15 etc. | | | | | |

**Job Cost Record**

**Job Number:** 1102

**Customer:** Wild Birds, Inc.

**Job Description:** 20 Model 3F (platform bird feeders)

**Date Started:** Sep. 14 **Date Completed:** ______

| Manufacturing Cost Information: | Cost Summary |
|---|---|
| **Direct Materials**<br>Req. # : | |
| **Direct Labour**<br>No. #<br>No. # | |
| **Manufacturing Overhead**<br>9 hours × $2 per direct labour hour | $ 18 |
| **Total Job Cost** | |
| **Number of Units** | ÷ |
| **Cost per Unit** | |

### Requirements

Check sum: Cost per unit is $14.

1. Calculate the total for the Materials Requisition form. Post the information (cost and requisition number) from the Materials Requisition form to the Job Cost Record in the appropriate boxes.
2. Complete the labour time records for each of the employees. Once the labour time record is completed, post the information relevant to Job #1102 to the Job Cost Record for Job #1102.
3. Manufacturing overhead has already been added to the Job Cost Record. Complete the Job Cost Record by calculating the total job cost and the cost per unit. Remember that this job consisted of 20 feeders (units).



## E5-17A Compute a predetermined overhead rate and calculate cost of jobs

*(Learning Objectives 3 & 5)*

Lakeland Heating & Cooling installs and services commercial heating and cooling systems. Lakeland uses job costing to calculate the cost of its jobs. Overhead is allocated to each job based on the number of direct labour hours spent on that job. At the beginning of the current year, Lakeland estimated that its overhead for the coming year would be $60,000. It also anticipated using 5,000 direct labour hours for the year. In November, Lakeland started and completed the following two jobs:

| | Job 101 | Job 102 |
|---|---|---|
| Direct materials used | $18,000 | $12,000 |
| Direct labour hours used | 120 | 80 |

Lakeland paid a $22-per-hour wage rate to the employees who worked on these two jobs.

### Requirements

Check sum: Direct Labour costs for Job #101 are $2,640.

1. What is Lakeland's predetermined overhead rate based on direct labour hours?
2. Calculate the overhead to be allocated based on direct labour hours to each of the two jobs.
3. What is the total cost of Job 101? What is the total cost of Job 102?

## E5-18A Compute a predetermined manufacturing overhead rate and calculate the cost of a job *(Learning Objectives 3 & 5)*

Dellroy Restaurant Supply manufactures commercial stoves and ovens for restaurants and bakeries. Dellroy uses job costing to calculate the costs of its jobs with direct labour cost as its manufacturing overhead allocation base. At the beginning of the current year, Dellroy estimated that its overhead for the coming year would be $300,000. It also anticipated using 25,000 direct labour hours for the year. Dellroy pays its employees an average of $20 per direct labour hour. Dellroy just finished Job 371, which consisted of two large ovens for a regional bakery. The costs for Job 371 were as follows:

| | Job 371 |
|---|---|
| Direct materials used | $13,000 |
| Direct labour hours used | 110 |

### Requirements

1. What is Dellroy's predetermined manufacturing overhead rate based on direct labour cost?
2. Calculate the manufacturing overhead to be allocated based on direct labour cost to Job 371.
3. What is the total cost of Job 371?

Check sum: Total cost for Job 371 is $16,520.

## E5-19A Determine the cost of a job and use it for pricing *(Learning Objectives 2 & 5)*

Saturn Park manufactures custom-designed playground equipment for schools and city parks. Saturn Park expected to incur $664,000 of manufacturing overhead cost, 41,500 of direct labour hours, and $830,000 of direct labour cost during the year (the cost of direct labour is $20 per hour). The company allocates manufacturing overhead on the basis of direct labour hours. During May, Saturn Park completed Job 301. The job used 155 direct labour hours and required $12,700 of direct materials. The City of Dartifax has contracted to purchase the playground equipment at a price of 30% over manufacturing cost.

1. Calculate the manufacturing cost of Job 301.
2. How much will the City of Dartifax pay for this playground equipment?

Check sum: Predetermined overhead rate is $16 per direct labour hour.

## E5-20A Sustainability and job costing *(Learning Objectives 2 & 5)*

Lincoln Plastics manufactures custom park furniture and signage from recycled plastics (primarily shredded plastic containers). Many of the company's customers are municipalities that are required by law to purchase goods that meet certain recycled-content guidelines. (Recycled content can include post-consumer waste materials, pre-consumer waste materials, and recovered materials.) As a result, Lincoln includes two types of direct material charges in its job cost for each job: (1) virgin materials (nonrecycled); and (2) recycled-content materials. Lincoln also keeps track of the weight of each type of direct material so that the final recycled-content percentage for the job can be reported to the customer. In its internal report system, Lincoln also reports on the percentage of recycled content as a total of plastic used each month to help to encourage managers to use recycled content whenever possible.

Lincoln Plastics uses a predetermined manufacturing overhead rate of $10 per direct labour hour. Here is a summary of the materials and labour used on a recent job for Dartmouth:

| **Description** | | |
|---|---|---|
| Virgin materials | Recycled-content materials | Direct labour |
| **Quantity** | | |
| 50 kg | 75 kg | 12 hours |
| **Cost** | | |
| $7.00 per kg | $ 6.00 per kg | $15.00 per hour |

Check sum: Total job cost is $1,100.

### Requirements

1. Calculate the total cost of the Dartmouth job.
2. Calculate the percentage of recycled content used in the Dartmouth job (in kg). If items purchased by Dartmouth are required by bylaws to contain at least 50% recycled content, does this job meet that requirement?

## E5-21A Calculate job cost, billing, and profit at a car care centre *(Learning Objectives 2, 5, & 7)*

Check sum: Labour for Cory's job is $105.00.

Conrad's Car Care Centre specializes in providing car tune-ups, brake jobs, and tire replacements for most vehicle makes and models. Conrad's charges customers for materials "at cost" but charges labour at a rate of $84 per hour. The labour rate is high enough to cover actual mechanic wages ($24 per hour) and shop overhead (allocated at a cost of $16 per hour), and to provide a profit. Cory recently had a 100,000 km service performed on his Honda Pilot. Materials used on the job included $9.95 for oil and filter, $60.45 for transmission fluid exchange, $20.86 for the air filter, and $33.02 for the cabin filter. The mechanic spent 1.25 hours on the job.

### Requirements

1. How much was charged to the customer for this work?
2. What was Conrad's cost for this job?
3. How much profit did Conrad's earn on this job?

## E5-22A Understand key terms *(Learning Objectives 1, 2, 3, & 5)*

Complete the following statements with one of the key terms. You may use a term more than once, and some terms may not be used at all.

| Cost allocation | Cost driver | Job costing | Process costing |
|---|---|---|---|
| Cost tracing | Job cost record | Materials requisition | |

a. A _____shows the accumulation of costs of an individual job.
b. _____is used by companies that produce small quantities of many different products.
c. A _____is the primary factor that causes costs.
d. Resolute Forest Products Inc. pulverizes wood into pulp to manufacture cardboard. This company would use a _____system.
e. To record costs of maintaining thousands of identical mortgage files, financial institutions such as Mortgage Alliance Company of Canada would use a _____system.
f. _____is assigning direct costs to cost objects.
g. Companies that produce large numbers of identical products use _____systems for product costing.
h. The computer repair service that visits your home and repairs your computer would use a _____system.
i. A _____is manufacturing personnel's request that materials be moved to the production floor.
j. _____is assigning indirect costs to cost objects.



## E5-23A Determine the cost of a job *(Learning Objectives 2, 3, & 5)*

E-Z-Boy started and finished Job 310 during April. The company's records show that the following direct materials were requisitioned for Job 310:

Lumber: 50 units at $9 per unit
Padding: 15 m at $20 per metre
Upholstery fabric: 30 m at $25 per metre

Labour time records show the following employees (direct labour) worked on Job 310:

Vince Owens: 10 hours at $10 per hour
Patrick Erin: 15 hours at $15 per hour

E-Z-Boy allocates manufacturing overhead at a rate of $9 per direct labour hour.

**Requirements**

1. Compute the total amount of direct materials, direct labour, and manufacturing overhead that should be shown on Job 310's job cost record.
2. Job 310 consists of five recliners. If each recliner sells for $600, what is the gross profit per recliner?

Check sum: Total job cost is $2,050.

### E5-24A Compare bid prices under two different allocation bases
*(Learning Objectives 3 & 5)*

Hillsboro Recycling recycles newsprint, cardboard, etc., into recycled packaging materials. For the coming year, Hillsboro Recycling estimates total manufacturing overhead to be $360,000. The company's managers are not sure if direct labour hours (estimated to be 10,000) or machine hours (estimated to be 15,000 hours) is the best allocation base to use for allocating manufacturing overhead. Hillsboro Recycling bids for jobs using a 30% markup over total manufacturing cost.

After the new fiscal year began, B.C. Paper Supply asked Hillsboro Recycling to bid for a job that would take 3,000 machine hours and 1,600 direct labour hours to produce. The direct labour cost for this job would be $12 per hour, and the direct materials would total $25,000.

**Requirements**

1. Compute the total job cost and bid price if Hillsboro Recycling decides to use direct labour hours as the manufacturing overhead allocation base for the year.
2. Compute the total job cost and bid price if Hillsboro Recycling decides to use machine hours as the manufacturing overhead allocation base for the year.
3. In addition to the bid from Hillsboro Recycling, B.C. Paper Supply received a bid of $125,000 for this job from Sun Prairie Recycling. What are the ramifications for Hillsboro Recycling?

Check sum: Direct labour costs are $19,200.

### E5-25A Compute job cost and bid price at a consulting firm
*(Learning Objectives 3, 5, & 7)*

Black Consulting, a real estate consulting firm, specializes in advising companies on potential new plant sites. Black Consulting uses a job cost system with a predetermined indirect cost allocation rate computed as a percentage of expected direct labour costs.

At the beginning of the year, managing partner Jada Black prepared the following plan, or budget, for the year:

| | |
|---|---|
| Direct labour hours (professionals) | 17,000 hours |
| Direct labour costs (professionals) | $2,669,000 |
| Office rent | 350,000 |
| Support staff salaries | 1,194,300 |
| Utilities | 324,000 |

Land Resources is inviting several consulting firms to bid for work. Black estimates that this job will require about 220 direct labour hours.

**Requirements**

1. Compute Black Consulting's (a) hourly direct labour cost rate and (b) indirect cost allocation rate.
2. Compute the predicted cost of the Land Resources job.
3. If Black wants to earn a profit that equals 50% of the job's cost, how much should she bid for the Land Resources job?

Check sum: Total indirect costs are $1,868,300.

### E5-26A Analyze manufacturing overhead *(Learning Objectives 3 & 4)*

Freeman Foundry uses a predetermined manufacturing overhead rate to allocate overhead to individual jobs based on the machine hours required. At the beginning of the year, the company expected to incur the following:

| | |
|---|---|
| Manufacturing overhead cost | $ 600,000 |
| Direct labour cost | 1,500,000 |
| Machine hours | 75,000 hours |

At the end of the year, the company had actually incurred the following:

| | |
|---|---|
| Direct labour cost | $1,210,000 |
| Depreciation on manufacturing plant and equipment | 480,000 |
| Property taxes on plant | 20,000 |
| Sales salaries | 25,000 |
| Delivery drivers' wages | 15,000 |
| Plant janitors' wages | 10,000 |
| Machine hours | 55,000 hours |

Check sum: Predetermined manufacturing overhead rate is $8/machine hour.

### Requirements

1. Compute Freeman's predetermined manufacturing overhead rate.
2. How much manufacturing overhead was allocated to jobs during the year?
3. How much manufacturing overhead was incurred during the year? Is manufacturing overhead underallocated or overallocated at the end of the year? By how much?
4. Were the jobs overcosted or undercosted? By how much?

## E5-27A Record manufacturing overhead *(Learning Objectives 4 & 6)*

Refer to the data in Exercise 5-26A. Freeman's accountant found an error in the expense records from the year reported. Depreciation on manufacturing plant and equipment was actually $400,000, not the $480,000 originally reported. The unadjusted cost of goods sold balance at year end was $600,000.

### Requirements

1. Prepare the journal entry(s) to record manufacturing overhead costs incurred.
2. Prepare the journal entry to record the manufacturing overhead allocated to jobs in production.
3. Use a T-account to determine whether manufacturing overhead is underallocated or overallocated, and by how much.
4. Record the entry to close out the underallocated or overallocated manufacturing overhead.
5. What is the adjusted ending balance of cost of goods sold?

## E5-28A Determine transactions from T-accounts *(Learning Objectives 2 & 6)*

Use the following T-accounts to determine the cost of direct materials used and indirect materials used.

**Raw Materials Inventory**

| | | | |
|---|---|---|---|
| Balance | 16 | | |
| Purchases | 230 | X | |
| Balance | 24 | | |

**Work in Process Inventory**

| | | | |
|---|---|---|---|
| Balance | 32 | | |
| Direct materials | Y | Cost of goods manufactured | 744 |
| Direct labour | 320 | | |
| Manufacturing overhead | 200 | | |
| Balance | 8 | | |

**E5-29A** **Record journal entries** *(Learning Objectives 2, 3, 4, & 6)*

The following transactions were incurred by French Fabricators during January, the first month of its fiscal year.

### Requirements

1. Record the proper journal entry for each transaction.
   a. $190,000 of materials were purchased on account.
   b. $174,000 of materials were used in production; of this amount, $152,000 were used on specific jobs.
   c. Manufacturing labour and salaries for the month totalled $225,000. A total of $190,000 of manufacturing labour and salaries was traced to specific jobs, while the remainder was indirect labour used in the factory.
   d. The company recorded $20,000 of depreciation on the plant and plant equipment. The company also received a plant utility bill for $10,000.
   e. $81,000 of manufacturing overhead was allocated to specific jobs.
2. By the end of January, was manufacturing overhead overallocated or underallocated? By how much?

**E5-30A** **Analyze T-accounts** *(Learning Objectives 2, 3, 4, & 6)*

Touch Enterprises produces LCD touch-screen products. The company reports the following information at December 31. Touch Enterprises began operations 11 months before, on January 31.

| Work in Process Inventory | | Wages Payable | | Manufacturing Overhead | | Finished Goods Inventory | | Raw Materials Inventory | |
|---|---|---|---|---|---|---|---|---|---|
| 30,000 | 123,000 | 70,000 | 70,000 | 2,000 | 48,000 | 123,000 | 111,000 | 52,000 | 32,000 |
| 80,000 | | | | 10,000 | | | | | |
| 48,000 | | Balance 0 | | 37,000 | | | | | |

### Requirements

1. What is the cost of direct materials used?
2. What is the cost of indirect materials used?
3. What is the cost of direct labour?
4. What is the cost of indirect labour?
5. What is the cost of goods manufactured?
6. What is the cost of goods sold (before adjusting for any under- or overallocated manufacturing overhead)?
7. What is the actual manufacturing overhead?
8. How much manufacturing overhead was allocated to jobs?
9. What is the predetermined manufacturing overhead rate as a percentage of direct labour cost?
10. Is manufacturing overhead underallocated or overallocated? By how much?

Check sum: Manufacturing overhead is underallocated.



**E5-31A** **Prepare journal entries** *(Learning Objectives 2, 3, & 6)*

Record the following transactions in Micro Speakers' general journal.

a. Received bill for Website expenses, $3,400.
b. Incurred manufacturing wages, $15,000, 70% of which was direct labour and 30% of which was indirect labour.
c. Purchased materials on account, $14,750.
d. Used in production: direct materials, $7,000; indirect materials, $3,000.

e. Recorded manufacturing overhead: depreciation on plant, $13,000; prepaid plant insurance expired, $1,700; plant property tax, $4,200 (credit Property Tax Payable).
f. Allocated manufacturing overhead to jobs: 200% of direct labour costs.
g. Cost of jobs completed during the month: $33,000.
h. Sold all jobs (on account) completed during the month for $52,000. Assume a perpetual inventory system.

**E5-32A Record completion and sale of jobs** *(Learning Objectives 2 & 6)*

September production generated the following activity in TechStore's work in process inventory:

| Work in Process Inventory | | |
|---|---|---|
| Sep 1 Bal | 20,000 | |
| Direct materials used | 29,000 | |
| Direct labour assigned to jobs | 32,000 | |
| Manufacturing overhead allocated to jobs | 12,000 | |

Production was completed in September, but is not recorded yet; it consists of Jobs B-78 and G-65, with total costs of $41,000 and $37,000, respectively.

**Requirements**

1. Compute the balance of work in process inventory at September 30.
2. Prepare the journal entry for the production completed in September.
3. Prepare the journal entry to record the sale (on credit) of Job G-65 for $40,000. Assume a perpetual inventory system.
4. What is the gross profit of Job G-65? What other costs must this gross profit cover?

# EXERCISES Group B

**E5-33B Identify type of costing system** *(Learning Objective 1)*

Specify whether each of the following companies would be more likely to use job costing or process costing.

a. Optometrist's office
b. Hospital
c. Oil refinery
d. Textile (fabric) manufacturer
e. Corporate caterer
f. Ice cream manufacturer
g. Advertising agency
h. Computer chip manufacturer
i. Small engine repair shop
j. Soft drink bottler
k. Photography studio
l. Satellite manufacturer
m. Sugar manufacturer
n. Menswear custom tailor

**E5-34B Describe the flow of costs in a job cost shop** *(Learning Objective 2)*

Outdoor Furniture Company manufactures outdoor furniture from recycled plastic lumber (HDPE). The following table contains events that occur in the manufacture and sale of tables by Outdoor Furniture Company. Put the events in the order in which they would occur by designating the step number in the Order column. Also indicate with a "+" or a "–" whether that account would increase or decrease as a result of the event.

| Event | Order | Raw Materials Inventory | WIP Inventory | FG Inventory | Cost of Goods Sold | No Effect on Inventory or COGS |
|---|---|---|---|---|---|---|
| a. John Hosbach, an employee of Outdoor Furniture Company, drills holes into the cut lumber so that these pieces can be used in building the basic model of an outdoor table. | | | | | | |
| b. An order of recycled plastic lumber, the primary component in making the outdoor tables, is received by Outdoor Furniture Company. The plastic lumber is stored in the stockroom until needed in production. | | | | | | |
| c. An order is received for five of the basic model outdoor tables and the tables are shipped to the customer. | | | | | | |
| d. Several of the plastic lumber boards are taken from the stockroom to be cut down into the lengths used in the basic model of the outdoor table. | | | | | | |
| e. The customer is billed for the five basic model outdoor tables. | | | | | | |
| f. Twelve of the basic model outdoor tables are completed and are stored in the finished goods warehouse. | | | | | | |

## E5-35B Understanding key document terms in a job cost shop *(Learning Objective 2)*

Use the list of terms to fill in the blanks of each of the following statements.

1. A supplier would issue a(n) __________ to bill the customer for products the customer ordered and received.
2. The quantity and types of inventory that are planned to be manufactured during the given time period are indicated on the __________.
3. On a(n) __________ would be a listing of all the raw materials needed to manufacture the job.
4. A(n) __________ itemizes the raw materials currently needed from the storeroom and provides documentation of authorization for the request.
5. A(n) __________ details the time spent by each employee on the job he or she worked on throughout the day.
6. Information about each item in stock, including number of units received and the balance of units currently in stock, would be found on a(n) __________.
7. A(n) __________ is used to accumulate all of the direct materials and direct labour used on a job, as well as the manufacturing overhead allocated to the job.
8. Authorization for a supplier to ship products at a given price is a(n) __________.
9. A(n) __________ is where incoming shipments of raw materials are counted and recorded, but it does not include pre-printed quantities or prices.

a. Invoice
b. Receiving report
c. Labour time record
d. Purchase order
e. Production schedule
f. Bill of materials
g. Raw materials record
h. Materials requisition
i. Job cost record



## E5-36B Understand the flow of costs in a job cost shop *(Learning Objective 2)*

Alberta River manufactures feeders for dairy farms. In September, Alberta River received an order from Wild Steer Farms for 24 platform feeders. The order from Wild Steer Farms, became Job 1102.

The following charts show a materials requisition for Job 1102 along with the labour time records (partial) for the week that these feeders were made and a job cost record. Other products were also produced during that week, so not all of the labour belongs to Job 1102.

**Materials Requisition**
**Number: #1250**

**Date:** 9/14

**Job:** 1102

| Part Number | Description | Quantity | Unit Cost | Amount |
|---|---|---|---|---|
| WOCD06 | Rough-hewn cedar planks | 50 | $2.00 | |
| SSF0304 | Stainless steel fasteners | 84 | $1.00 | |
| AS222 | Reinforced aluminum screens | 28 | $1.50 | |
| | **Total** | | | |

**Labour Time Record**

**Employee:** Greg Henderson **Week:** 9/14 – 9/20

**Hourly Wage Rate:** $14 **Record #:** 912

| Date | Job Number | Start Time | End Time | Hours | Cost |
|---|---|---|---|---|---|
| 9/14 | 1102 | 8:00 | 12:00 | | |
| 9/14 | 1103 | 12:00 | 4:00 | | |
| 9/15 etc. | | | | | |

**Labour Time Record**

**Employee:** Andrew Peck **Week:** 9/14 – 9/20

**Hourly Wage Rate:** $6 **Record #:** 913

| Date | Job Number | Start Time | End Time | Hours | Cost |
|---|---|---|---|---|---|
| 9/14 | 1101 | 9:00 | 12:00 | | |
| 9/14 | 1102 | 12:00 | 5:00 | | |
| 9/15 | 1103 | 9:00 | 11:00 | | |
| 9/15 etc. | | | | | |

**Job Cost Record**

**Job Number:** 1102

**Customer:** Wild Steer Farms.

**Job Description:** 20 Model 3F (platform feeders)

**Date Started:** Sep. 14 **Date Completed:** ________

| Manufacturing Cost Information: | Cost Summary |
|---|---|
| **Direct Materials** | |
| Req. #: | |
| **Direct Labour** | |
| No. # | |
| No. # | |
| **Manufacturing Overhead** | |
| 9 hours × $2 per direct labour hour | $ 18 |
| **Total Job Cost** | |
| **Number of Units** | |
| **Cost per Unit** | |

### Requirements

1. Calculate the total for the Materials Requisition form. Post the information (cost and requisition number) from the Materials Requisition form to the Job Cost Record in the appropriate boxes.
2. Complete the labour time records for each of the employees. Once the labour time record is completed, post the relevant information to the Job Cost Record for Job 1102.
3. Manufacturing overhead has already been added to the Job Cost Record. Complete the Job Cost Record by calculating the total job cost and the cost per unit. Remember that this job consisted of 24 feeders (units).

Check sum: Total direct labour costs are $86.

## E5-37B Compute a predetermined overhead rate and calculate cost of jobs

*(Learning Objectives 3 & 5)*

Dansville Heating & Cooling installs and services commercial heating and cooling systems. Dansville uses job costing to calculate the cost of its jobs. Overhead is allocated to each job based on the number of direct labour hours spent on that job. At the beginning of the current year, Dansville estimated that its overhead for the coming year would be $64,800. It also anticipated using 4,050 direct labour hours for the year. In May, Dansville started and completed the following two jobs:

| | Job 101 | Job 102 |
|---|---|---|
| Direct materials used | $16,000 | $13,500 |
| Direct labour hours used | 175 hours | 82 hours |

Dansville paid a $20 per hour wage rate to the employees who worked on these two jobs.

### Requirements

1. What is Dansville's predetermined overhead rate based on direct labour hours?
2. Calculate the overhead to be allocated based on direct labour hours to each of the two jobs.
3. What is the total cost of Job 101? What is the total cost of Job 102?

Check sum: Direct labour hours for job #102 are $1,312.

### E5-38B Compute a predetermined overhead rate and calculate the cost of a job *(Learning Objectives 3 & 5)*

Aeki Restaurant Supply manufactures commercial stoves and ovens for restaurants and bakeries. Aeki uses job costing to calculate the costs of its jobs with direct labour cost as its manufacturing overhead allocation base. At the beginning of the current year, Aeki estimated that its overhead for the coming year would be $292,600. It also anticipated using 27,500 direct labour hours for the year. Aeki pays its employees an average of $19 per direct labour hour. Aeki just finished Job 371, which consisted of two large ovens for a regional bakery. The costs for Job 371 were as follows:

| | Job 371 |
|---|---|
| Direct materials used | $17,500 |
| Direct labour hours used | 200 hours |

**Requirements**

Check sum: Direct labour costs are $3,800.

1. What is Aeki's predetermined manufacturing overhead rate based on direct labour cost?
2. Calculate the manufacturing overhead to be allocated based on direct labour hours to Job 371.
3. What is the total cost of Job 371?

### E5-39B Determine the cost of a job and use it for pricing *(Learning Objectives 2 & 4)*

Check sum: Contracted billing price is $27,724.

All Wood Industries manufactures custom-designed playground equipment for schools and city parks. All Wood expected to incur $637,500 of manufacturing overhead cost, 42,500 of direct labour hours, and $860,000 of direct labour cost during the year (the cost of direct labour is $38 per hour). The company allocates manufacturing overhead on the basis of direct labour hours. During May, All Wood completed Job 305. The job used 180 direct labour hours and required $13,000 of direct materials. The City of Ogdenville has contracted to purchase the playground equipment at a price of 23% over manufacturing cost.

**Requirements**

1. Calculate the manufacturing cost of Job 305.
2. How much will the City of Ogdenville pay for this playground equipment?



### E5-40B Sustainability and job costing *(Learning Objectives 2 & 5)*

Woodfree Plastics manufactures custom park furniture and signage from recycled plastics (primarily shredded plastic containers). Many of the company's customers are municipalities that are required by law to purchase goods that meet certain recycled-content guidelines. (Recycled content can include post-consumer waste materials, pre-consumer waste materials, and recovered materials.) As a result, Woodfree Plastics includes two types of direct material charges in their job cost for each job: (1) virgin materials (non-recycled); and (2) recycled-content materials. Woodfree Plastics also keeps track of the weight of each type of direct material so that the final recycled-content percentage for the job can be reported to the customer. The company also reports on the percentage of recycled content as a total of plastics used each month on its own internal reporting system to help encourage managers to use recycled content whenever possible.

Woodfree Plastics uses a predetermined manufacturing overhead rate of $15 per direct labour hour. Here is a summary of the materials and labour used on a recent job for Regina:

Check sum: Total quantity equals 275 kg.

| **Description** | | |
|---|---|---|
| Virgin materials | Recycled-content materials | Direct labour |
| **Quantity** | | |
| 125 kg | 150 kg | 12 hours |
| **Cost** | | |
| $7.00 per kg | $ 6.00 per kg | $18.00 per hour |

**Requirements**

1. Calculate the total cost of the Regina job.
2. Calculate the percentage of recycled content used in the Regina job (in kg) If items purchased by Regina are required by bylaws to contain at least 50% recycled content, does the job meet that requirement?

## E5-41B Calculate job cost, billing, and profit at Alan's Car Care Centre

*(Learning Objectives 2, 5, & 7)*

Alan's Car Care Centre specializes in providing car tune-ups, brake jobs, and tire replacements for most vehicle makes and models. Alan's charges customers for materials "at cost" but charges labour at a rate of $87 per hour. The labour rate is high enough to cover actual mechanic wages ($29 per hour) and shop overhead (allocated at a cost of $18 per hour), and to provide a profit. Giles recently had a 72,000 km service performed on his car. Materials used on the job included $15.50 for oil and filter, $65.45 for transmission fluid exchange, $21.35 for the air filter, and $32.78 for the cabin filter. The mechanic spent 1.75 hours on the job.

**Requirements**

1. How much was charged to the customer for this work?
2. What was Alan's cost for this job?
3. How much profit did Alan's earn on this job?

(Round all your answers to two decimal places.)

Check sum: Labour for Giles' job is $152.25.

## E5-42B Understand key terms *(Learning Objectives 1, 2, 3, & 5)*

Complete the following statements with one of the key terms. You may use a term more than once, and some terms may not be used at all.

| | | | |
|---|---|---|---|
| Materials requisition | Cost allocation | Job cost record | Job costing |
| Process costing | Job cost record | Cost driver | Cost tracing |

a. The process of assigning direct costs to cost objects is called ________.
b. The local hospital would use a ________system.
c. A paint manufacturer would use a ________system.
d. A ________is manufacturing personnel's request that materials be moved to the production floor.
e. Companies that produce small qualities of many different products would use ________.
f. The process of assigning indirect costs to cost objects is called ________.
g. A ________is the primary factor that causes costs.
h. To record costs of maintaining thousands of identical mortgage files, lending companies would use a ________system.
i. Companies that produce large numbers of identical products use ________systems for product costing.
j. The direct materials, direct labour, and manufacturing overhead associated with an individual job are accumulated on a ________.

## E5-43B Determine the cost of a job *(Learning Objectives 2, 3, & 5)*

Labico Furniture started and finished Job 310 during March. The company's records show that the following direct materials were requisitioned for Job 310:

Lumber: 47 units at $10 per unit
Padding: 17 m at $18 per metre
Upholstery fabric: 32 m at $23 per metre

Labour time records show the following employees (direct labour) worked on Job 310:

Billal Ghadie: 8 hours at $12 per hour
Angel Beath: 12 hours at $14 per hour.

Labico Furniture allocates manufacturing overhead at a rate of $8 per direct labour hour.

Check sum: Total direct labour is $264.

**Requirements**

1. Compute the total amount of direct materials, direct labour, and manufacturing overhead that should be shown on 310's job cost record.
2. Job 310 consists of seven recliners. If each recliner sells for $700, what is the gross profit per recliner?

### E5-44B Compare bid prices under two different allocation bases *(Learning Objectives 3 & 5)*

Wellington Recycling recycles newsprint, cardboard, etc., into packaging materials. For the coming year, Wellington Recycling estimates total manufacturing overhead to be $360,360. The company's managers are not sure if direct labour hours (estimated to be 10,010) or machine hours (estimated to be 18,018 hours) is the best allocation base to use for allocating manufacturing overhead. Wellington Recycling bids for jobs using a 29% markup over total manufacturing cost.

After the new fiscal year began, Lundy Paper Supply asked Wellington Recycling to bid for a job that would take 1,995 machine hours and 1,750 direct labour hours to produce. The direct labour cost for this job would be $12 per hour, and the direct materials would total $25,400.

Check sum: Predetermined overhead rate is $36 per direct labour hour.

1. Compute the total job cost and bid price if Wellington Recycling decides to use direct labour hours as the manufacturing overhead allocation base for the year.
2. Compute the total job cost and bid price if Wellington Recycling decides to use machine hours as the manufacturing overhead allocation base for the year.
3. In addition to the bid from Wellington Recycling, Lundy Paper Supply received a bid of $124,500 for this job from Kearns Recycling. What are the ramifications for Wellington Recycling?

### E5-45B Compute job cost and bid price at a consulting firm *(Learning Objectives 3, 5, & 7)*

Quah Consulting, a real estate consulting firm, specializes in advising companies on potential new plant sites. Quah Consulting uses a job costing system with a predetermined indirect cost allocation rate computed as a percentage of direct labour costs. At the beginning of the year, managing partner Adora Quah prepared the following plan, or budget, for the year:

| | |
|---|---|
| Direct labour hours (professionals) | 14,000 hours |
| Direct labour costs (professionals) | $2,150,000 |
| Office rent | 250,000 |
| Support staff salaries | 870,000 |
| Utilities | 350,000 |

Chance Resources is inviting several consultants to bid for work. Quah estimates that this job will require about 200 direct labour hours.

Check sum: Direct labour cost rate is $154/hour.

**Requirements**

1. Compute Quah Consulting's (1) hourly direct labour cost rate and (2) indirect cost allocation rate.
2. Compute the predicted cost of the Chance Resources job.
3. If Quah wants to earn a profit that equals 35% of the job's cost, how much should she bid for the Chance Resources job?

### E5-46B Analyze manufacturing overhead *(Learning Objectives 3 & 5)*

Smith Foundry in Sarnia, Ontario, uses a predetermined manufacturing overhead rate to allocate overhead to individual jobs based on the machine hours required. At the beginning of the year, the company expected to incur the following:

| | |
|---|---|
| Manufacturing overhead costs | $ 560,000 |
| Direct labour costs | 1,700,000 |
| Machine hours | 80,000 hours |

At the end of the year, the company had actually incurred the following:

| | |
|---|---|
| Direct labour cost | $1,230,000 |
| Depreciation on manufacturing plant and equipment | 490,000 |
| Property taxes on plant | 18,500 |
| Sales salaries | 24,000 |
| Delivery drivers' wages | 16,000 |
| Plant janitors' wages | 11,000 |
| Machine hours | 57,000 hours |

### Requirements

1. Compute Smith's predetermined manufacturing overhead rate.
2. How much manufacturing overhead was allocated to jobs during the year?
3. How much manufacturing overhead was incurred during the year? Is manufacturing overhead underallocated or overallocated at the end of the year? By how much?
4. Were the jobs overcosted or undercosted? By how much?

Check sum: Predetermined overhead rate is $7 per machine hour.

## E5-47B Record manufacturing overhead *(Learning Objectives 4 & 6)*

Refer to the data in Exercise E5-46B. Smith's accountant found an error in the expense records from the year reported. Depreciation on manufacturing plant and equipment was actually $305,000, not the $490,000 it originally reported. The unadjusted cost of goods sold balance at year end was $630,000.

### Requirements

1. Prepare the journal entry(s) to record manufacturing overhead costs incurred.
2. Prepare the journal entry to record the manufacturing overhead allocated to jobs in production.
3. Use a T-account to determine whether manufacturing overhead is underallocated or overallocated, and by how much.
4. Record the entry to close out the underallocated or overallocated manufacturing overhead.
5. What is the adjusted ending balance of cost of goods sold?

## E5-48B Determine transactions from T-accounts *(Learning Objectives 2 & 6)*

Use the following T-accounts to determine the cost of direct materials used and indirect materials used.

**Raw Materials Inventory**

| | | |
|---|---|---|
| Balance | 30 | |
| Purchases | 235 | X |
| Balance | 65 | |

**Work in Process Inventory**

| | | | |
|---|---|---|---|
| Balance | 20 | | |
| Direct materials | Y | Cost of goods manufactured | 550 |
| Direct labour | 305 | | |
| Manufacturing overhead | 130 | | |
| Balance | 20 | | |

### E5-49B Record journal entries *(Learning Objectives 2, 3, 4, & 6)*

The following transactions were incurred by Whooley Fabricators during January, the first month of its fiscal year.

a. $205,000 of materials were purchased on account.
b. $174,000 of materials were used in production; of this amount, $146,000 was used on specific jobs.
c. Manufacturing labour and salaries for the month totalled $210,000, and $200,000 of the total manufacturing labour and salaries was traced to specific jobs. The remainder was indirect labour used in the factory.
d. The company recorded $16,000 of depreciation on the plant and plant equipment. The company also received a plant utility bill for $14,000.
e. $56,000 of manufacturing overhead was allocated to specific jobs.

**Requirements**

1. Record the proper journal entry for each transaction.
2. By the end of January, was manufacturing overhead overallocated or underallocated? By how much?

### E5-50B Analyze T-accounts *(Learning Objectives 2, 3, 4, & 6)*

LCDs For You produces LCD touch screen products. The company reports the following information at December 31. LCDs For You began operations on January 31 earlier that same year.

| Work in Process Inventory | | Wages Payable | | Manufacturing Overhead | | Finished Goods Inventory | | Raw Materials Inventory | |
|---|---|---|---|---|---|---|---|---|---|
| 28,000 | 125,500 | 73,000 | 73,000 | 7,500 | 42,000 | 125,500 | 111,500 | 57,500 | 35,500 |
| 60,000 | | | | 13,000 | | | | | |
| 42,000 | | Balance 0 | | 41,500 | | | | | |

1. What is the cost of direct materials used?
2. What is the cost of indirect materials used?
3. What is the cost of direct labour?
4. What is the cost of indirect labour?
5. What is the cost of goods manufactured?
6. What is the cost of goods sold (before adjusting for any under- or overallocated manufacturing overhead)?
7. What is the actual manufacturing overhead?
8. How much manufacturing overhead was allocated to jobs?
9. What is the predetermined manufacturing overhead rate as a percentage of direct labour cost?
10. Is manufacturing overhead underallocated or overallocated? By how much?

### E5-51B Prepare journal entries *(Learning Objectives 2, 3, & 6)*

Record the following transactions in general journal.

a. Received bill for Website expenses, $2,200.
b. Incurred manufacturing wages, $19,000, 55% of which was direct labour and 45% of which was indirect labour.
c. Purchased materials on account, $18,000.
d. Used in production: direct materials, $9,500; indirect materials, $4,000.

e. Recorded manufacturing overhead: depreciation on plant, $14,000; prepaid plant insurance expired, $1,700; plant property tax, $3,500 (credit Property Tax Payable).
f. Allocated manufacturing overhead to jobs, 190% of direct labour costs.
g. Cost of jobs completed during the month, $38,000.
h. Sold all jobs (on account) completed during the month for $62,000. Assume a perpetual inventory system.

## E5-52B Record completion and sale of jobs *(Learning Objectives 2 & 6)*

July production generated the following activity in Blegro Piano's work in process inventory. Production was completed in July, but is not recorded yet; it consists of Jobs C-55 and G-72, with total costs of $42,600 and $36,900, respectively.

| Work in Process Inventory | | |
|---|---|---|
| Jul 1 Bal | 15,750 | |
| Direct materials used | 28,600 | |
| Direct labour assigned to jobs | 32,150 | |
| Manufacturing overhead allocated to jobs | 12,250 | |

**Requirements**

1. Compute the balance of work in process inventory at July 31.
2. Prepare the journal entry for the production completed in July.
3. Prepare the journal entry to record the sale (on credit) of Job G-72 for $43,900. Assume a perpetual inventory system.
4. What is the gross profit of Job G-72? What other costs must this gross profit cover?

# PROBLEMS Group A

## P5-53A Analyze Manufacturing Overhead *(Learning Objectives 3 & 4)*

HawkEye produces uniforms. The company allocates manufacturing overhead based on the machine hours each job uses. HawkEye reports the following cost data for the past year:

| | Budget | Actual |
|---|---|---|
| Direct labour hours | 7,000 hours | 6,200 hours |
| Machine hours | 6,920 hours | 6,400 hours |
| Depreciation on salespeople's autos | $22,000 | $22,000 |
| Indirect materials | 50,000 | 52,000 |
| Depreciation on trucks used to deliver uniforms to customers | 14,000 | 12,000 |
| Depreciation on plant and equipment | 65,000 | 67,000 |
| Indirect manufacturing labour | 40,000 | 43,000 |
| Customer service hotline | 19,000 | 21,000 |
| Plant utilities | 18,000 | 20,000 |
| Direct labour cost | 70,000 | 85,000 |

**Requirements**

1. Compute the predetermined manufacturing overhead rate.
2. Calculate the allocated manufacturing overhead for the past year.
3. Compute the underallocated or overallocated manufacturing overhead. How will this underallocated or overallocated manufacturing overhead be disposed of?
4. How can managers use accounting information to help control manufacturing overhead costs?

**P5-54A Use job costing at an advertising agency** *(Learning Objectives 3, 5, & 7)*

Adnet.com is an internet advertising agency. The firm uses a job cost system in which each client is a different "job." Adnet.com traces direct labour, software licensing costs, and travel costs directly to each job. The company allocates indirect costs to jobs based on a predetermined indirect cost allocation rate based on direct labour hours.

At the beginning of the current year, managing partner Ricky Buena prepared a budget:

| | |
|---|---|
| Direct labour hours (professional) | 17,500 hours |
| Direct labour costs (professional) | $1,750,000 |
| Support staff salaries | 305,000 |
| Rent and utilities | 95,000 |
| Supplies | 15,000 |
| Lease payments on computer hardware | 285,000 |

During January of the current year, Adnet.com served several clients. Records for two clients appear here:

| | GoVacation .com | Port Armour Golf Resort |
|---|---|---|
| Direct labour hours | 460 hours | 40 hours |
| Software licensing costs | $1,490 | $280 |
| Travel costs | $9,000 | $ 0 |

**Requirements**

1. Compute Adnet.com's predetermined indirect cost allocation rate for the current year based on direct labour hours.
2. Compute the total cost of each job.
3. If Adnet.com wants to earn profits equal to 20% of sales revenue, how much (what total fee) should it charge each of these two clients?
4. Why does Adnet.com assign costs to jobs?

**P5-55A Use job costing at a consulting firm** *(Learning Objectives 3, 5, & 7)*

WB Design is a Website design and consulting firm. The firm uses a job cost system in which each client is a different "job." WB Design traces direct labour, licensing, and travel costs directly to each job. It allocates indirect costs to jobs based on a predetermined indirect cost allocation rate computed as a percentage of direct labour costs.

At the beginning of the current year, managing partner Mary Milici prepared the following budget:

| | |
|---|---|
| Direct labour hours (professional) | 8,000 hours |
| Direct labour costs (professional) | $1,000,000 |
| Support staff salaries | 80,000 |
| Computer lease payments | 46,000 |
| Office supplies | 25,000 |
| Office rent | 49,000 |

Later that same year, in November, WB Design served several clients. Records for two clients appear here:

| | Organic Foods | SunNow.com |
|---|---|---|
| Direct labour hours | 750 hours | 50 hours |
| Licensing costs | $ 1,850 | $160 |
| Travel costs | $14,150 | $ 0 |

### Requirements

1. Compute WB Design's predetermined indirect cost allocation rate for the current year.
2. Compute the total cost of each of the two jobs listed.
3. If Milici wants to earn profits equal to 20% of sales revenue, how much (what total fee) should she charge each of these two clients?
4. Why does WB Design assign costs to jobs?

## P5-56A Prepare a job cost record *(Learning Objectives 2, 3, & 5)*

Geolander manufactures tires for all-terrain vehicles. Geolander uses job costing and has a perpetual inventory system.

On September 22, Geolander received an order for 100 TX tires from ATV Corporation at a price of $55 each. The job, assigned number 298, was promised for October 10. After purchasing the materials, Geolander began production on September 30 and incurred the following direct labour and direct materials costs in completing the order:

| Date | Labour Time Record # | Description | Amount |
|---|---|---|---|
| 9/30 | 1896 | 12 hr @ $20 per hour | $240 |
| 10/3 | 1904 | 30 hr @ $19 per hour | 570 |

| Date | Materials Requisition # | Description | Amount |
|---|---|---|---|
| 9/30 | 437 | 60 kg rubber @ $18 per kg | $1,080 |
| 10/2 | 439 | 40 m polyester fabric @ $12 per metre | 480 |
| 10/3 | 501 | 100 m steel cord @ $10 per metre | 1,000 |

Geolander allocates manufacturing overhead to jobs on the basis of the relation between expected overhead costs ($540,000) and expected direct labour hours (20,000). Job 298 was completed on October 3 and shipped to ATV on October 5.

### Requirements

1. Prepare a job cost record for Job 298 similar to Exhibit 5-7.
2. Calculate the total profit and the per-unit profit for Job 298.

## P5-57A Determine and record job costs *(Learning Objectives 2, 3, 5, & 6)*

Getaway Homes manufactures prefabricated chalets in Alberta. The company uses a perpetual inventory system and a job cost system in which each chalet is a job. The following events occurred during May:

a. Purchased materials on account, $405,000.
b. Incurred total manufacturing wages of $111,600, which included both direct labour and indirect labour. Used direct labour in manufacturing as follows:

| | |
|---|---|
| Chalet 13 | $14,800 |
| Chalet 14 | 28,500 |
| Chalet 15 | 19,200 |
| Chalet 16 | 21,000 |

c. Requisitioned direct materials in manufacturing as follows:

| | |
|---|---|
| Chalet 13 | $41,100 |
| Chalet 14 | 56,800 |
| Chalet 15 | 62,100 |
| Chalet 16 | 66,000 |

d. Depreciation of manufacturing equipment used on different chalets, $20,000.

e. Other overhead costs incurred on Chalets 13–16:

| | |
|---|---|
| Equipment rentals paid in cash | $10,400 |
| Prepaid plant insurance expired | 6,000 |

f. Allocated overhead to jobs at the predetermined rate of 60% of direct labour cost.

g. Chalets completed: 13, 15, and 16.

h. Chalets sold on account: #13 for $99,000 and #16 for $141,900.

### Requirements

1. Record the preceding events in the general journal.
2. Open T-accounts for work in process inventory and finished goods inventory. Post the appropriate entries to these accounts, identifying each entry by letter. Determine the ending account balances assuming that the beginning balances were zero.
3. Summarize the job costs of the unfinished chalet and show that this equals the ending balance in work in process inventory.
4. Summarize the job cost of the completed chalet that has not yet been sold and show that this equals the ending balance in finished goods inventory.
5. Compute the gross profit on each chalet that was sold. What costs must the gross profit cover for Getaway Homes?

## P5-58A Determine flow of costs through accounts *(Learning Objectives 2 & 6)*

CarNut reconditions engines. Its job cost records yield the following information. CarNut uses a perpetual inventory system.

| | Date | | | | |
|---|---|---|---|---|---|
| **Job #** | **Started** | **Finished** | **Sold** | **Total Cost of Job at March 31** | **Total Manufacturing Cost Added in April** |
| 1. | 2/26 | 3/7 | 3/9 | $1,400 | |
| 2. | 2/3 | 3/12 | 3/13 | 1,600 | |
| 3. | 3/29 | 3/31 | 4/3 | 1,300 | |
| 4. | 3/31 | 4/1 | 4/1 | 500 | $ 400 |
| 5. | 4/8 | 4/12 | 4/14 | | 700 |
| 6. | 4/23 | 5/6 | 5/9 | | 1,200 |

### Requirements

1. Compute CarNut's cost of (1) work in process inventory at March 31 and April 30, (2) finished goods inventory at March 31 and April 30, and (3) cost of goods sold for March and April.
2. Make summary journal entries to record the transfer of completed jobs from work in process inventory to finished goods inventory for March and April.
3. Record the sale of Job 5 on account for $1,600.
4. Compute the gross profit for Job 5. What costs must the gross profit cover?

## P5-59A Determine Job Costs and Analyze Manufacturing Overhead

*(Learning Objectives 3 & 4)*

Hi-Tek is a small software firm that builds and installs custom business applications for clients and uses a job-order costing system. The costs for each client are organized into two departments: Development and Implementation. The firm uses pre-determined overhead rates to charge clients. At the beginning of the year, the following estimates were made:

| | Development | Implementation |
|---|---|---|
| Programming hours | 10,000 | |
| Consultant hours | 5,000 | 15,000 |
| Materials/supplies | $10,000 | $4,000 |
| Consultant cost | $100,000 | $400,000 |
| Overhead costs | $400,000 | $150,000 |

The predetermined overhead rate in the Development department is based on programming hours, in the Implementation department it is based on consultant hours (but only those in the Implementation department). The cost for any particular job is based on direct consultant costs, materials and supplies, and an applied overhead cost.

A job for client 1812 was completed with the following costs:

| | Development | Implementation |
|---|---|---|
| Programming hours | 80 | |
| Consultant hours | 50 | 200 |
| Materials/supplies | $1000 | $500 |
| Consultant cost | $18,000 | $90,000 |

At the end of the year, the following were the actual hours expended and costs incurred for Hi-Tek

| | Development | Implementation |
|---|---|---|
| Programming hours | 9,000 | |
| Consultant hours | 6,000 | 16,000 |
| Materials/supplies | $11,000 | $6,000 |
| Consultant cost | $110,000 | $450,000 |
| Overhead Costs | $450,000 | $200,000 |

**Required:**

1. Calculate the predetermined overhead rates for the Development and Implementation departments.
2. Calculate the total cost of the job for client 1812.
3. Calculate whether the overhead for both departments was overapplied or underapplied.

# PROBLEMS Group B

## P5-60B Analyze Manufacturing Overhead *(Learning Objectives 3 & 4)*

Root Company produces uniforms. The company allocates manufacturing overhead based on the machine hours each job uses. Root Company reports the following cost data for the past year:

| | Budget | Actual |
|---|---|---|
| Direct labour hours | 7,400 hours | 6,600 hours |
| Machine hours | 7,125 hours | 6,800 hours |
| Depreciation on salespeople's autos | $21,500 | $21,500 |
| Indirect materials | 48,500 | 54,500 |
| Depreciation on trucks used to deliver uniforms to customers | 13,500 | 11,000 |
| Depreciation on plant and equipment | 63,500 | 65,000 |
| Indirect manufacturing labour | 40,500 | 42,500 |
| Customer service hotline | 18,000 | 20,500 |
| Plant utilities | 18,500 | 19,500 |
| Direct labour cost | 72,500 | 84,000 |

### Requirements

1. Compute the predetermined manufacturing overhead rate.
2. Calculate the allocated manufacturing overhead for the past year.
3. Compute the underallocated or overallocated manufacturing overhead. How will this underallocated or overallocated manufacturing overhead be disposed of?
4. How can managers use accounting information to help control manufacturing overhead costs?

## P5-61B Use job costing at an advertising agency *(Learning Objectives 3, 4, & 7)*

Gettem and Init, PLC is an advertising agency. The firm uses a job cost system in which each client is a different "job." The company traces direct labour, software licensing costs, and travel costs directly to each job (client). The company allocates indirect costs to jobs based on a predetermined indirect cost allocation rate computed as a percentage of direct labour costs.

At the beginning of the current year, managing partner Isolda Carr prepared a budget:

| | |
|---|---|
| Direct labour hours (professional) | 8,000 hours |
| Direct labour costs (professional) | $1,600,000 |
| Support staff salaries | 190,000 |
| Rent and utilities | 41,000 |
| Supplies | 23,000 |
| Less payment on computer hardware | 66,000 |

During January of the current year, Gettem and Init, PLC served several clients. Records for two clients appear here:

| | AllVacation.com | Port Adak Golf Resort |
|---|---|---|
| Direct labour hours | 760 hours | 60 hours |
| Software licensing costs | $2,000 | $150 |
| Travel costs | $9,000 | $ 0 |

**Requirements**

1. Compute the company's predetermined indirect cost allocation rate for the current year based on direct labour hours.
2. Compute the total cost of each job.
3. If the company wants to earn profits equal to 20% of sales revenue, how much (what total fee) should it charge each of these two clients?
4. Why does the company assign costs to jobs?

## P5-62B Use job costing at a consulting firm *(Learning Objectives 3, 5, & 7)*

Cardinal Design is a Website design and consulting firm. The firm uses a job cost system in which each client is a different job. Cardinal Design traces direct labour, licensing costs, and travel costs directly to each job. It allocates indirect costs to jobs based on a predetermined indirect cost allocation rate computed as a percentage of direct labour costs.

At the beginning of the current year, managing partner Jane Snow prepared the following budget:

| | |
|---|---|
| Direct labour hours (professional) | 6,250 hours |
| Direct labour costs (professional) | $1,000,000 |
| Support staff salaries | 120,000 |
| Computer leases | 45,000 |
| Office supplies | 25,000 |
| Office rent | 50,000 |

Later that same year in November, Cardinal Design served several clients. Records for two clients appear here:

| | Delicious Treats | GoGreen.com |
|---|---|---|
| Direct labour hours | 770 hours | 55 hours |
| Software licensing costs | $ 2,500 | $500 |
| Travel costs | 10,000 | $ 0 |

**Requirements**

1. Compute Cardinal Design's predetermined indirect cost allocation rate for the current year.
2. Compute the total cost of each of the two jobs listed.
3. If Snow wants to earn profits equal to 20% of sales revenue, how much (what total fee) should she charge each of these two clients?
4. Why does Cardinal Design assign costs to jobs?

## P5-63B Prepare job cost record *(Learning Objectives 2, 3, & 5)*

Great Quality manufactures tires for all-terrain vehicles. Great Quality uses job costing and has a perpetual inventory system. On November 22, Great Quality received an order for 170 TX tires from ATV Corporation at a price of $60 each. The job, assigned number 298, was promised for December 10. After purchasing the materials, Great Quality began production on November 30 and incurred the following direct labour and direct materials costs in completing the order:

| Date | Labour Time Record # | Description | Amount |
|---|---|---|---|
| 11/30 | 1896 | 12 hr @ $20 per hour | $240 |
| 12/3 | 1904 | 30 hr @ $14 per hour | 420 |

| Date | Materials Requisition No. | Description | Amount |
|---|---|---|---|
| 11/30 | 437 | 60 kg rubber @ $12 per kg | $720 |
| 12/2 | 439 | 40 m polyester fabric @ $16 per metre | 640 |
| 12/3 | 501 | 100 m steel cord @ $10 per metre | 1,000 |

Great Quality allocates manufacturing overhead to jobs on the basis of the relation between expected overhead costs ($529,000) and expected direct labour hours (23,000). Job 298 was completed on December 3 and shipped to ATV on December 5.

### Requirements

1. Prepare a job cost record for Job 298 similar to Exhibit 5-7.
2. Calculate the total profit and the per-unit profit for Job 298.

## P5-64B Determine and record job costs *(Learning Objectives 2, 3, 5, & 6)*

Divine Homes manufactures prefabricated chalets in Colorado. The company uses a perpetual inventory system and a job cost system in which each chalet is a job. The following events occurred during May:

a. Purchased materials on account, $480,000.

b. Incurred total manufacturing wages of $116,000, which included both direct labour and indirect labour. Used direct labour in manufacturing as follows:

| | Direct Labour |
|---|---|
| Chalet 13 | $14,300 |
| Chalet 14 | 28,700 |
| Chalet 15 | 19,100 |
| Chalet 16 | 21,500 |

c. Requisitioned direct materials in manufacturing as follows:

| | Direct Materials |
|---|---|
| Chalet 13 | $41,900 |
| Chalet 14 | 56,900 |
| Chalet 15 | 62,400 |
| Chalet 16 | 66,800 |

d. Depreciation of manufacturing equipment used on different chalets, $6,700.

e. Other overhead costs incurred on Chalets 13–16:

| | |
|---|---|
| Equipment rentals paid in cash | $10,800 |
| Prepaid plant insurance expired | 3,000 |

f. Allocated overhead to jobs at the predetermined rate of 60% of direct labour cost.

g. Chalets completed: 13, 15, and 16.

h. Chalets sold on account: #13 for $97,000; #16 for $149,000.

### Requirements

1. Record the events in the general journal.
2. Post the appropriate entries to the T-accounts, identifying each entry by letter. Determine the ending account balances, assuming that the beginning balances were zero.
3. Add the costs of the unfinished chalet, and show that this total amount equals the ending balance in the work in process inventory account.
4. Summarize the job cost of the completed chalet that has not yet been sold and show that this equals the ending balance in finished goods inventory.
5. Compute gross profit on each chalet that was sold. What costs must gross profit cover for Divine Homes?

## P5-65B Determine flow of costs through accounts *(Learning Objectives 2 & 6)*

EnginePro reconditions engines. Its job costing records yield the following information. EnginePro uses a perpetual inventory system.

| Job # | Date | | | Total Cost of Job at April 30 | Total Manufacturing Cost Added in May |
|---|---|---|---|---|---|
| | Started | Finished | Sold | | |
| 1. | 3/26 | 4/7 | 4/9 | $1,400 | |
| 2. | 3/3 | 4/12 | 4/13 | 1,200 | |
| 3. | 4/29 | 4/30 | 5/3 | 1,600 | |
| 4. | 4/30 | 5/1 | 5/1 | 700 | $ 700 |
| 5. | 5/8 | 5/12 | 5/14 | | 900 |
| 6. | 5/23 | 6/6 | 6/9 | | 1,700 |

### Requirements

1. Compute EnginePro's cost of (1) work in process inventory at April 30 and May 31, (2) finished goods inventory at April 30 and May 31, and (3) cost of goods sold for April and May.
2. Make summary journal entries to record the transfer of completed jobs from work in process to finished goods for April and May.
3. Record the sale of Job 5 for $2,100.
4. Compute the gross profit for Job 5. What costs must the gross profit cover?

# CAPSTONE APPLICATION PROBLEMS

## APPLICATION QUESTION

### A5-66 Analyze issues with cost of job *(Learning Objectives 2, 3, & 5)*

Hegy Chocolate is located in Montreal. The company prepares gift boxes of chocolates for private parties and corporate promotions. Each order contains a selection of chocolates determined by the customer, and the box is designed to the customer's specifications. Accordingly, Hegy Chocolate uses a job cost system and allocates manufacturing overhead based on direct labour cost.

One of Hegy Chocolate's largest customers is the Bailey and Choi law firm. This organization sends chocolates to its clients each Christmas and also provides them to employees at the firm's gatherings. The law firm's managing partner, Genevieve Bailey, placed the client gift order in September for 500 boxes of cream-filled dark chocolates. But Bailey and Choi did not place its December staff party order until the last week of November. This order was for an additional 100 boxes of chocolates identical to the ones to be distributed to clients.

Hegy Chocolate budgeted the cost per box for the original 500-box order as follows:

| | |
|---|---:|
| Chocolate, filling, wrappers, box | $14.00 |
| Employee time to fill and wrap the box (10 min.) | 2.00 |
| Manufacturing overhead | 1.00 |
| Total manufacturing cost | $17.00 |

Estephan Hegy, president of Hegy Chocolate, priced the order at $20 per box.

In the past few months, Hegy Chocolate has experienced price increases for both dark chocolate and direct labour. *All other costs have remained the same.* Hegy budgeted the cost per box for the second order as follows:

| | |
|---|---:|
| Chocolate, filling, wrappers, box | $15.00 |
| Employee time to fill and wrap the box (10 min.) | 2.20 |
| Manufacturing overhead | 1.10 |
| Total manufacturing cost | $18.30 |

#### Requirements

1. Do you agree with the cost analysis for the second order? Explain your answer.
2. Should the two orders be accounted for as one or two jobs in Hegy Chocolate's system?
3. What sales price per box should Hegy set for the second order? What are the advantages and disadvantages of this price?

### A5-67 Analyze issues with the manufacturing overhead rate *(Learning Objectives 2, 3, & 5)*

All Natural manufactures organic fruit preserves sold primarily through health food stores and on the Web. The company closes for two weeks each December to allow employees to spend time with their families over the holiday season. All Natural's manufacturing overhead is mostly straight-line depreciation on its plant and air-conditioning costs for keeping the berries cool during the summer months. The company uses direct labour hours as the allocation base. President Kara Wise has just approved new accounting software and is telling Controller Melissa Kokelj about her decision.

"I think this new software will be great," Wise says. "It will save you time in preparing all of those reports."

"Yes, and having so much more information just a click away will help us make better decisions and help control costs," replies Kokelj. "We need to consider how we can use the new system to improve our business practices."

"And I know just where to start," says Wise. "You complain each year about having to predict the weather months in advance for estimating air-conditioning costs and direct labour hours for the denominator of the predetermined manufacturing overhead rate. I think we should calculate the predetermined overhead rate on a monthly basis."

Controller Kokelj is not so sure this is a good idea.

**Requirements**

1. What are the advantages and disadvantages of Wise's proposal?
2. Should All Natural compute its predetermined manufacturing overhead rate on an annual basis or a monthly basis? Explain.

# CASE ASSIGNMENT

*Source:* Dmitry Vereshchagin/Fotolia

## C5-68 Draper Automotive

Draper Automotive started business in April 2011. Since opening a couple of years ago, it has been able to serve some people more than once as they come back for repeat service and additional work. Dawn Draper is in charge of all the scheduling of jobs, billing, and customer relations. In the last six months, Dawn has received a number of complaints from customers about the billing. Strangely, however, she would receive a flurry of complaints in one month, then cards and thank-you notes the next month. She does the billing the same way every month, so she can't understand the fluctuations in satisfaction levels.

The process for the billing is to start with the cost of the automotive parts used in the repair or upgrade. These costs are taken from the purchase order price lists from the suppliers. To the amount for the parts is added a labour amount. The labour amount is calculated so that it includes the cost of the mechanics' labour ($25) plus an amount for overhead. The amount for overhead is the previous month's actual overhead amount divided by the estimated number of jobs for the upcoming month. Dawn's estimations for the number of upcoming jobs is usually pretty good.

Peggy Olsen came to see Dawn today to complain about the billing. She brought in two invoices, one from five months ago and one from a week ago. Both were for oil and filter changes. The invoices are below:

Draper Automotive
1209 Mobile Lane
Cumberland, ON
(613) 555-1234

**PAID**

INVOICE

February 10, 2013

| | |
|---|---|
| Parts | $24 |
| Labour 2 @ $56 | $112 |
| Total | $136 |

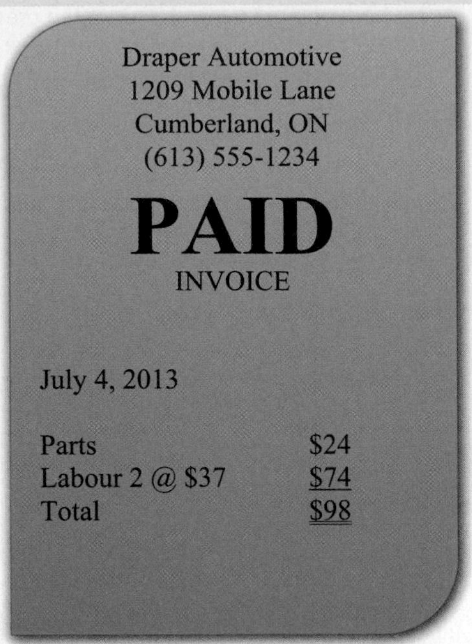

Draper Automotive
1209 Mobile Lane
Cumberland, ON
(613) 555-1234

**PAID**

INVOICE

July 4, 2013

| | |
|---|---|
| Parts | $24 |
| Labour 2 @ $37 | $74 |
| Total | $98 |

Once Dawn saw them side by side, she knew there was a problem, but since she was working from actual numbers for the overhead, she wasn't sure what could be done. She knew that if something didn't change they would begin to lose customers, so she went through her records to see if she could see where any mistakes were made. Dawn summarized the last six months' overhead calculations as follows:

| | Jan | Feb | Mar | Apr | May | June | July |
|---|---|---|---|---|---|---|---|
| Actual overhead costs | $4309 | $5735 | $4725 | $3842 | $3731 | $3576 | $3690 |
| Estimated # labour hours for current month | | 139 | 155 | 189 | 226 | 287 | 298 |
| OH rate for current month | | 4309/139 = $31 / hour | 5735/155 = $37 / hour | 4725/189 = $25 / hour | 3842/226 = $17 / hour | 3731/287 = $13 / hour | 3576/298 = $12 / hour |

Dawn didn't find any errors in the calculations, so she was at a loss to explain what to do next.

# TEAM PROJECT

## T5-69 Find the cost of flight routes *(Learning Objectives 2, 3, & 5)*

Major airlines such as Air Canada, Delta, and Lufthansa are struggling to meet the challenges of budget carriers such as Southwest and WestJet. Suppose Air Canada's CFO Michael Rousseau has just returned from a meeting on strategies for responding to competition from budget carriers. The vice president of operations suggests doing nothing: "We just need to wait until these new airlines run out of money. They cannot be making money with their low fares." In contrast, the vice president of marketing, not wanting to lose market share, suggests cutting Air Canada's fares to match the competition. "If WestJet charges only $75 for that flight from Toronto, so must we!" Others, including Rousseau, emphasize the potential for cutting costs. Another possibility is starting a new budget airline within Air Canada. Imagine that CEO Calin Rovinescu cuts the meeting short and directs Rousseau to "get some hard data."

As a start, Rousseau decides to collect cost and revenue data for a typical Air Canada flight and then compare it to the data for a competitor. He prepares the following schedule:

| | Air Canada | WestJet |
|---|---|---|
| Route: Toronto to Fredericton | Flight 1247 | Flight 53 |
| Distance | 1,011 kilometres | 1,011 kilometres |
| Seats per plane | 142 | 162 |
| One-way ticket price | $80–$621* | 75 |
| Food and beverage | Meal | Meal |

*The highest price is first-class airfare.

Excluding food and beverage, Rousseau estimates that the cost per available seat kilometre is $0.084 for Air Canada, compared to $0.053 for WestJet. ("Cost per available seat kilometre" is the cost of flying a seat for one kilometre—whether or not the seat is occupied.) Assume that the average cost of food and beverage is $5 per passenger for snacks and $10 for a meal.

Split your team into two groups. Group 1 should prepare its response to Requirement 1, and Group 2 should prepare its response to Requirement 2 before the entire team meets to consider Requirements 3–6.

### Requirements

1. Group 1 uses the data to determine the following for Air Canada:
   a. The total cost of Flight 1247 assuming a full plane (100% load factor)
   b. The revenue generated by Flight 1247 assuming a 100% load factor and average revenue per one-way ticket of $102
   c. The profit per Flight 1247 given the responses to (a) and (b)
2. Group 2 uses the data to determine for WestJet:
   a. The total cost of Flight 53 assuming a full plane (100% load factor)
   b. The revenue generated by Flight 53 assuming a 100% load factor
   c. The profit per Flight 53 given the responses to (a) and (b)
3. When the entire team meets, combine your analyses. Based on the responses to Requirements 1 and 2, carefully evaluate each of the four alternative strategies discussed in Air Canada's executive meeting.
4. The analysis in this project is based on several simplifying assumptions. As a team, brainstorm factors that your quantitative evaluation does not include but that may affect a comparison of Air Canada's operations with those of budget carriers.
5. Prepare a memo from CFO Rousseau addressed to Air Canada CEO Rovinescu summarizing the results of your analyses. Be sure to include the limitations of your analyses identified in Requirement 5. Use the following format for your memo:

**Date:** ____________________

**To:** CEO Calin Rovinescu

**From:** CFO Michael Rousseau

**Subject:** Air Canada's Response to Competition from WestJet Airlines

## DISCUSSION & ANALYSIS

1. Why would it be inappropriate for a custom home builder to use process costing?
2. What types of products is job costing appropriate for? Why? For what types of products is process costing appropriate? Why?
3. What product costs must be allocated to jobs? Why must these costs be allocated rather than assigned?
4. When the predetermined manufacturing overhead rate is calculated, why are estimated costs and cost driver levels used instead of actual dollars and amounts?
5. Why should manufacturing overhead be allocated to a job even though the costs cannot be directly traced to a job? Give at least two reasons.
6. Why does management need to know the cost of a job? Discuss at least five reasons.

7. Why is it acceptable to close overallocated or underallocated manufacturing overhead to cost of goods sold rather than allocating it proportionately to work in process inventory, finished goods inventory, and cost of goods sold? Under what circumstances would it be advisable to allocate the overallocated or underallocated manufacturing overhead to work in process inventory, finished goods inventory, and cost of goods sold?
8. Describe a situation that may cause manufacturing overhead to be overallocated in a given year. Also describe a situation that may cause manufacturing overhead to be underallocated in a given year.
9. Explain why cost of goods sold should be lower if manufacturing overhead is overallocated. Should operating income be higher or lower if manufacturing overhead is overallocated? Why?
10. What account is credited when manufacturing overhead is allocated to jobs during the period? What account is debited when manufacturing overhead costs are incurred during the period? Would you expect these two amounts (allocated and incurred manufacturing overhead) to be the same amount? Why or why not?

# APPLICATION & ANALYSIS

## 5-1 *Unwrapped* or *How It's Made*

### Product Costs and Job Costing Versus Process Costing

Go to YouTube.com and search for clips from the show *Unwrapped* on the Food Network or *How It's Made* on the Discovery Channel. Watch a clip for a product you find interesting.

### Discussion Questions

1. Describe the product being produced (and the company that makes it).
2. Summarize the production process used in making this product.
3. What raw materials are used to make this product?
4. What indirect materials are used to make this product?
5. Describe the jobs of the workers who would be considered "direct labour" in making this product.
6. Describe the jobs of the workers who would be considered "indirect labour" in making this product.
7. Define manufacturing overhead. In addition to the indirect materials and indirect labour previously described, what other manufacturing overhead costs would be incurred in this production process? Be specific and thorough. Make reasonable "guesses" if you do not know for sure.
8. Would a job order costing system or a process costing system be used for this production process? Give specific reasons for your choice of which costing system would be most appropriate for this manufacturer.

### Classroom Applications

**Web:** Post the discussion questions on an electronic discussion board. Have small groups of students choose a product for their group. Each student should watch the clip for the product for their group.

**Classroom**: Form groups of three or four students. Each group should choose a product and its clip to view. After viewing the clip, prepare a five-minute presentation about your group's product, addressing the listed questions.

**Independent**: Research answers to each of the questions. Turn in a two- to three-page typed paper (12-point font, double spaced with 2.5 cm margins). Include references, including the URL for the clip that you viewed.

# Demo Doc

Chapter 5

**MyAccountingLab** Make the grade with MyAccountingLab! Animated versions of similar Demo Docs to these can be found on MyAccountingLab.

## JOB COSTING FOR MANUFACTURERS

### Learning Objectives 1, 2, & 6

Douglas Art manufactures specialized art for customers. Suppose Douglas has the following transactions during the month:

a. Raw materials were purchased on account for $67,000.

b. Materials costing $45,000 were requisitioned for production. Of this total, $40,000 was traced to individual jobs, while $5,000 was requisitioned for general factory use.

c. $32,000 of labour was incurred in the factory. Of the total labour costs, $30,000 was traced to specific jobs worked on during the month. The remainder of the factory labour cost related to indirect labour.

d. Manufacturing overhead is allocated to production using the predetermined overhead rate of 75% of direct labour cost.

e. Jobs costing $67,000 were completed during the month.

f. Douglas sold several jobs during the month for a total price of $106,000. These jobs cost $65,000 to produce. Assume all sales are made on account. Also assume that Douglas uses a perpetual inventory system.

### Requirements

1. What type of product costing system would Douglas use? Justify your answer.
2. What document would Douglas use to show the direct materials, direct labour, and manufacturing overhead costs assigned to each individual job?
3. Prepare journal entries for each transaction.

# Demo Doc Solutions

### Requirement 1

**What type of product costing system would Douglas use?**

Job costing system—companies that manufacture batches of unique or specialized products would use a job costing system to accumulate costs for each job or batch.

### Requirement 2

**What document would Douglas use to show the direct materials, direct labour, and manufacturing overhead costs assigned to each individual job?**

Douglas would use a job cost record to show the direct materials, direct labour, and manufacturing overhead costs assigned to each individual job. Managers use the job cost record to see how they can use materials and labour more efficiently. For example, if a job's costs exceed its budget, managers must either do a better job of controlling costs on future jobs or raise the sales price on similar jobs to be sure that the company remains profitable.

### Requirement 3

**Prepare journal entries for each transaction.**

**a. Raw materials were purchased on account for $67,000.**

When materials are purchased you need to record an increase in raw materials inventory, so you would debit raw materials inventory (an asset) for the cost of the materials, $67,000.

Since the materials were purchased on account, you also need to record a liability to your suppliers, so you would credit Accounts Payable (a liability) for $67,000.

| | | | |
|---|---|---|---|
| | Raw Materials Inventory | 67,000 | |
| | Accounts Payable | | 67,000 |

**b. Materials costing $45,000 were requisitioned for production. Of this total, $40,000 was traced to individual jobs, while $5,000 was requisitioned for general factory use.**

When materials are requisitioned, it means that they are moved from raw materials inventory into production.

The direct materials traced to specific jobs are posted to individual job cost records. Since the job cost records form the supporting detail for the work in process inventory account, the cost of these direct materials is debited directly to work in process inventory, increasing the asset by $40,000.

The materials that cannot be traced to a specific job (indirect materials) would be debited to manufacturing overhead (an increase of $5,000).

Because we are taking the materials out of the raw materials inventory, we reduce this asset with a credit for the total amount of the materials requisitioned ($45,000).

| | | | |
|---|---|---|---|
| | Work in Process Inventory | 40,000 | |
| | Manufacturing Overhead | 5,000 | |
| | Raw Materials Inventory | | 45,000 |

**c. $32,000 of labour was incurred in the factory. Of the total labour costs, $30,000 was traced to specific jobs worked on during the month. The remainder of the factory labour cost related to indirect labour.**

The amount of direct labour traced to individual jobs is posted to individual job cost records. Once again, since the job cost records form the supporting detail for the work in process inventory account; the cost of direct labour is debited to work in process inventory. The rest of the labour, $2,000, is for indirect labour, such as factory supervisors, forklift operators, and janitors. Indirect labour cannot be traced to specific jobs; therefore, it is debited to manufacturing overhead.

We credit wages payable to show a liability to our factory employees until they are paid on the company's payday.

| | | | |
|---|---|---|---|
| | Work in Process Inventory | 30,000 | |
| | Manufacturing Overhead | 2,000 | |
| | Wages Payable | | 32,000 |

**d. Manufacturing overhead is allocated to production using the predetermined overhead rate of 75% of direct labour cost.**

Manufacturing overhead consists of all of the indirect costs of running the manufacturing plant, such as depreciation on the plant and equipment, salaries of the janitors, utilities, and property taxes and insurance on the plant. It is impossible to trace these costs to each job; therefore, manufacturers allocate some of these costs to each job using a predetermined overhead rate. Since Douglas Art's predetermined manufacturing overhead rate is 75% of direct labour cost, the total amount of manufacturing overhead allocated to production for the month is as follows:

$$75\% \times \$30{,}000 \text{ of direct labour (from part c)} = \$22{,}500$$

Keep in mind that each individual job cost record would show the amount of manufacturing overhead allocated to that particular job (75% of the direct labour cost traced to the job). Here, we just computed the *total* amount of manufacturing overhead allocated to *all jobs* worked on during the month.

All actual manufacturing overhead costs are recorded as debits to the manufacturing overhead account. To take cost *out* of the account and assign it to specific jobs in production, we credit the manufacturing overhead account:

| Manufacturing Overhead | |
|---|---|
| (Actual Costs) | (Allocated to Jobs) |

To record the amount of manufacturing overhead allocated to jobs, we debit the work in process inventory. We then take this cost out of the manufacturing overhead account through a credit, as shown in the previous T-account.

| | | | |
|---|---|---|---|
| | Work in Process Inventory | 22,500 | |
| | Manufacturing Overhead | | 22,500 |

**e. Jobs costing $67,000 were completed during the month.**

When jobs are completed, the direct materials, direct labour, and manufacturing overhead costs shown on the job cost records are added together to determine the total cost of the jobs. Then the jobs are moved off the plant floor and into the finished goods storage area until they are shipped to customers. In the accounting records, we also show the movement of these completed jobs by transferring the cost of the jobs from one inventory account to the next. Since all inventory accounts are assets, we debit the accounts to increase them and credit the accounts to decrease them. Thus, the following entry shows an increase in the finished goods inventory and a decrease in the work in process inventory:

| | | | |
|---|---|---|---|
| | Finished Goods Inventory | 67,000 | |
| | Work in Process Inventory | | 67,000 |

**f. Douglas sold several jobs during the month for a total price of $106,000. These jobs cost $65,000 to produce. Assume all sales are made on account. Also assume that Douglas uses a perpetual inventory system.**

We need to make two journal entries here. The first journal entry records the sale of the art to customers at a sales price of $106,000. Therefore, the following entry records an increase in the accounts receivable and an increase in sales revenue for the year:

| | | | |
|---|---|---|---|
| | Accounts Receivable | 106,000 | |
| | Sales Revenue | | 106,000 |

The second entry is made assuming that Douglas has a perpetual inventory system. In a perpetual inventory system, companies show the costs of goods sold at the time they make a sale. They also show that the inventory sold is no longer theirs—it has been sold to the customer. So they make the following journal entry to increase the cost of goods sold (through a debit) and decrease the amount of inventory they have on hand (through a credit):

| | | | |
|---|---|---|---|
| | Cost of Goods Sold | 65,000 | |
| | Finished Goods Inventory | | 65,000 |

# TRY IT SOLUTIONS

**page** 254: 1. d 2. a 3. f 4. g 5. h 6. c 7. e 8. b

**page** 269:

| | |
|---|---|
| Actual MOH incurred during the year | $975,000 |
| MOH allocated to jobs during the year ($16/DL hour × 60,000 DL hours) | 960,000 |
| Difference: Underallocated MOH | $ 15,000 |

Since the company allocated less MOH to jobs than was actually incurred during the year, it has underallocated MOH. Notice that the $1 million of estimated MOH at the beginning of the year is only used to calculate the predermined MOH rate.

**page** 284:

**1.**

| | |
|---|---|
| Direct cost: Sarah's time (5 hrs × $40/hr) + Hannah's time (10 hrs × $25/hr) | $450 |
| Indirect cost: (15 hrs × $12/hr) | 180 |
| Total cost of preparing tax return | $630 |

**2.**

| | |
|---|---|
| Total cost of preparing tax return | $630 |
| Plus profit markup ($630 × 30%) | 189 |
| Amount to bill Meckfessel | $819 |

# Process Costing

## Learning Objectives

1. Distinguish between the flow of costs in process costing and job costing.
2. Compute equivalent units.
3. Use process costing in the first production department.
4. Prepare journal entries for a process costing system.
5. Use process costing in a second or later production department.

Chapter 6, "Process Costing," covers material outlined in **Section 3: Management Accounting** of the CPA Competency Map. Specifically, this chapter addresses *Section 3.1 Cost Management*, component *e – Process Costing*. The Learning Objectives in this chapter have been aligned with the CPA Competency Map to ensure the best coverage possible.

PROFESSIONAL COMPETENCY — The presence of the **coverage button** in the margin indicates focus on one or more of the specific competency areas from the competency map. The concepts in the text are building blocks to developing the competencies required in the CPA. While the chapter may address multiple areas of the competency map, the main focus will be:

Competencies:

**3.3.1** Evaluates cost classifications and costing methods for management of ongoing operations*

**3.3.2** Evaluates and applies cost management techniques appropriate for specific costing decisions*

**3.4.1** Evaluates sources and drivers of revenue growth*

## Black Fly Beverage Company, Ontario's

first microdistillery, was founded by husband and wife Rob Kelly and Cathy Siskind-Kelly.[†] Having spent the summers of his youth in Muskoka, Rob drew the name Black Fly from the reputation of the small but determined Canadian insect that, like this micro-business, might be small but delivers a mighty bite. The pure wild blueberry juice used in two of the vodka cooler flavours—Cranberry/Wild Blueberry and Black Currant/Wild Blueberry—also links with the Black Fly name, as the black fly pollinates wild blueberries.

Each bottle of Black Fly cooler spends many days going through seven different processes:

© Black Fly Beverage Company

1. Hot mix: Mixing many of the ingredients in a hot process in order to dissolve the sugars
2. Cold mix: Mixing the remaining ingredients in a cold process
3. Blending: Incorporating the hot and the cold mixes together
4. Carbonation: Adding just the right amount of bubbles
5. Chilling: Getting the beverage to the right temperature

*Reprinted from *The Chartered Professional Accountant Competency Map - Understanding the competencies a candidate must demonstrate to become a CPA*, © 2012, with permission Chartered Professional Accountants of Canada, Toronto, Canada. Any changes to the original material are the sole responsibility of the author (and/or publisher) and have not been reviewed or endorsed by the Chartered Professional Accountants of Canada.

†Black Fly Beverage Company Inc, © 2015. Used with permission.

6. Bottling: Putting the beverage in individual bottles
7. Packaging: Inserting four bottles into an environmentally friendly cardboard package and then into shipping cases, which are palletized and shrinkwrapped for loading onto a truck

The company needs to know how much it costs to make each batch, which helps them set selling prices and measure profits. They also want to know how efficiently each process is operating, which helps them control costs. Black Fly uses accounting information to answer these questions.

Black Fly produces its coolers in a sequence of processes and accumulates the costs for each process. Then the company spreads these costs over the number of bottles of coolers passing through each process. Black Fly uses a process costing approach well suited to its operations, producing a large quantity of similar products. This is in contrast to operations that are based on unique, individual, or custom-ordered products or services, such as the business of Shaw Group, discussed in Chapter 5.

## Process Costing: An Overview

1 Distinguish between the flow of costs in process costing and job costing.

Chapter 5 discusses job costing, the technique companies such as Shaw Group and Bombardier use to determine the cost of producing unique goods in relatively small batches. Service companies, such as law firms and hospitals, also use job costing to determine the cost of serving individual clients. In contrast, companies such as Black Fly Beverage Company and Saint John Refinery (Irving Oil) use a series of steps (called processes) to make large quantities of identical units. These companies typically use *process costing* systems.

To simplify our discussion, we will consolidate Black Fly's seven separate processes into three processes. We will combine the hot mix, cold mix, and blending into a single process called Blending. We will also combine the carbonation and chilling steps into a second process called Carbonation. The third and final process is Packaging, which will incorporate both the bottling and packaging into four-packs.[1] Black Fly produces a variety of beverages, but we will focus our analysis on the production of bottles of Strawberry/Rhubarb beverage.

Black Fly accumulates the costs of each process and then assigns these costs to the units (each bottle of Strawberry/Rhubarb) passing through that process.

Suppose the Blending process incurs $1,350,000 of costs to produce enough liquid for 1,000,000 bottles of Strawberry/Rhubarb, the Carbonation process incurs $800,000, and Packaging incurs $700,000. The total cost to produce each bottle of Strawberry/Rhubarb is the sum of the cost per bottle for each of the three processes.

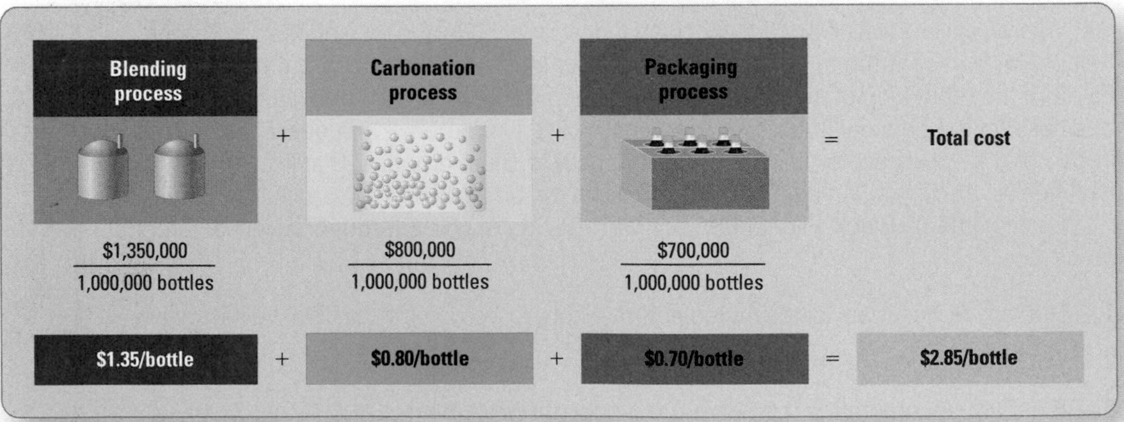


Black Fly's managers use the cost per bottle of each process to help control costs. For example, they can compare the actual cost of producing the blended Strawberry/Rhubarb liquid for a bottle (assumed to be $1.35 in our example) to the budget or plan. If the actual cost of the Blending process exceeds the budget, they can look for ways to cut costs in that process. Black Fly's managers also consider the total cost of making a

[1]The example we use is created from fictional data.

bottle of Strawberry/Rhubarb (assumed to be $2.85 in our example) when setting selling prices. The price should be high enough to cover costs and to return a profit. Black Fly also uses the total cost of making a bottle of Strawberry/Rhubarb for financial reporting:

- To value the ending inventory of Strawberry/Rhubarb for the balance sheet ($2.85 per bottle still in ending inventory)
- To value cost of goods sold for the income statement ($2.85 per bottle sold)

The simple computation of the cost to make a bottle of Strawberry/Rhubarb is correct only if there are no work in process inventories, but it takes 7 to 10 days to complete all of the processes. So, Black Fly *does* have inventories of partially complete Strawberry/Rhubarb. These inventories make the costing more complicated. In the rest of this chapter, you will learn how to do process costing when there are work in process inventories.

## How Does the Flow of Costs Differ Between Job and Process Costing?

Exhibit 6-1 compares the flow of costs in

- A job costing system for Shaw Group Inc. (Panel A)
- A process costing system for Black Fly Beverage Company (Panel B)

Panel A shows that Shaw Group's job costing system has a single work in process inventory control account supported by individual job cost records for each job that is being worked on. Shaw Group assigns direct materials, direct labour, and manufacturing overhead to individual jobs, as explained in Chapter 5. When a job is finished, its costs flow directly into finished goods inventory. When the job is sold, the cost flows out of finished goods inventory and into cost of goods sold.

In contrast to Shaw Group's individual jobs, Black Fly uses a series of three manufacturing processes to produce Strawberry/Rhubarb beverages. The movement of Strawberry/Rhubarb through these three processes is shown in Exhibit 6-2.

Take a moment to follow along as we describe Exhibit 6-2. In the first process (Blending) Black Fly converts raw cane sugar, fruit, and other ingredients (the direct materials) into the beverage liquid, using both a hot mix (dissolving the sugar) and a cold mix. This process uses direct labour and manufacturing overhead, such as depreciation on the mixing vats. Once the beverage liquid is made, it is transferred to the Carbonation process. In the Carbonation process, Black Fly uses different labour and equipment to incorporate the carbonation (the direct materials), adding a champagne-like bubble to the beverage. Once that process is complete, the finished Strawberry/Rhubarb liquid is transferred to the Packaging process. In the Packaging process, Black Fly bottles the beverage and then puts the finished bottles by hand into environmentally friendly, glueless cardboard packaging, using other labour and equipment. The bottled and boxed Strawberry/Rhubarb beverages are then transferred to finished goods inventory until they are sold.

Now, let's see how Panel B of Exhibit 6-1 summarizes the flow of costs through this process costing system. Study the exhibit carefully, paying particular attention to the following key points:

1. Each process (Blending, Carbonation, and Packaging) has its own separate work in process inventory account.
2. Direct materials, direct labour, and manufacturing overhead are assigned to each processing department's work in process inventory account based on the manufacturing costs incurred by that process. Exhibit 6-2 shows that each of Black Fly's processes uses different direct materials, direct labour, and manufacturing overhead costs.
3. Recall from Exhibit 6-2 that when the Blending process is complete, the Strawberry/Rhubarb liquid is physically transferred out of the Blending process and transferred into the Carbonation process. Likewise, the cost of the liquid is also transferred out of work in process inventory—blending and transferred into Work in Process Inventory—Carbonation. The transfer of costs between accounts is pictured in

Panel B of Exhibit 6-1 as a series of green X's. Consider the next passage as a rule of thumb:

PROFESSIONAL COMPETENCY

> In process costing, the manufacturing costs assigned to the product must always follow the physical movement of the product. Therefore, when units are physically transferred out of one process and into the next, the *costs* assigned to those units must *also* be transferred out of the appropriate Work in Process Inventory account and into the next.

**EXHIBIT 6-1** Flow of Costs in Job Costing

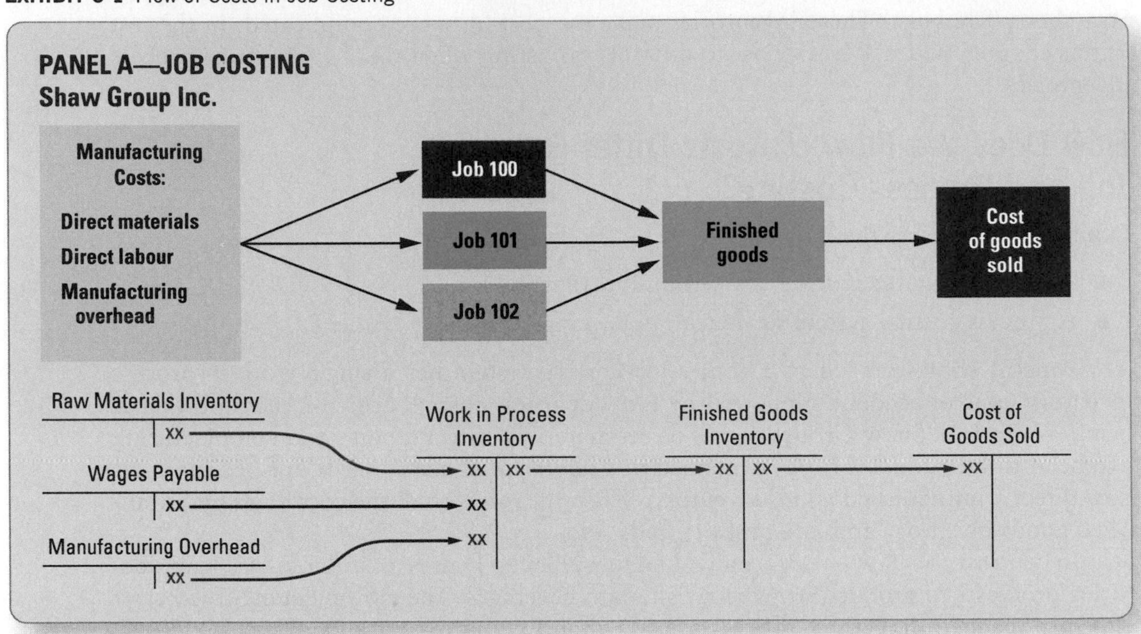


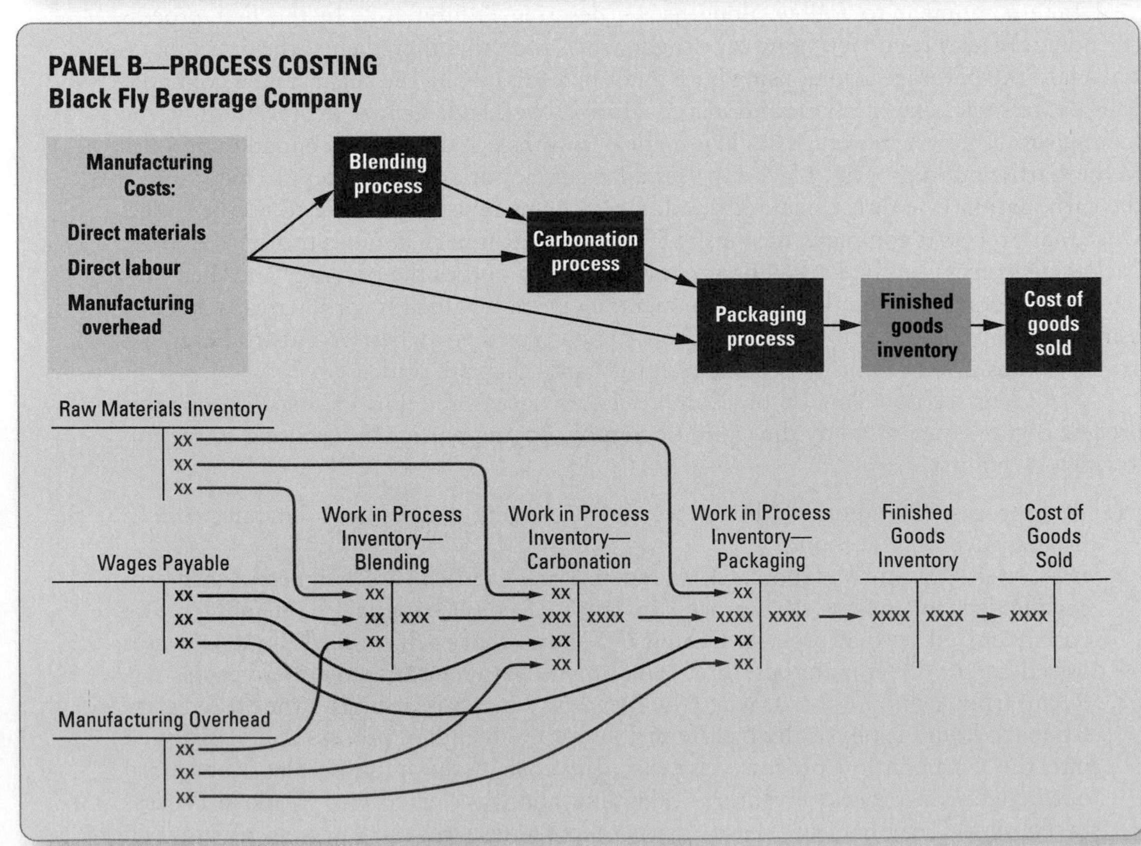

EXHIBIT 6-2 Flow of Costs in Production of Beverages

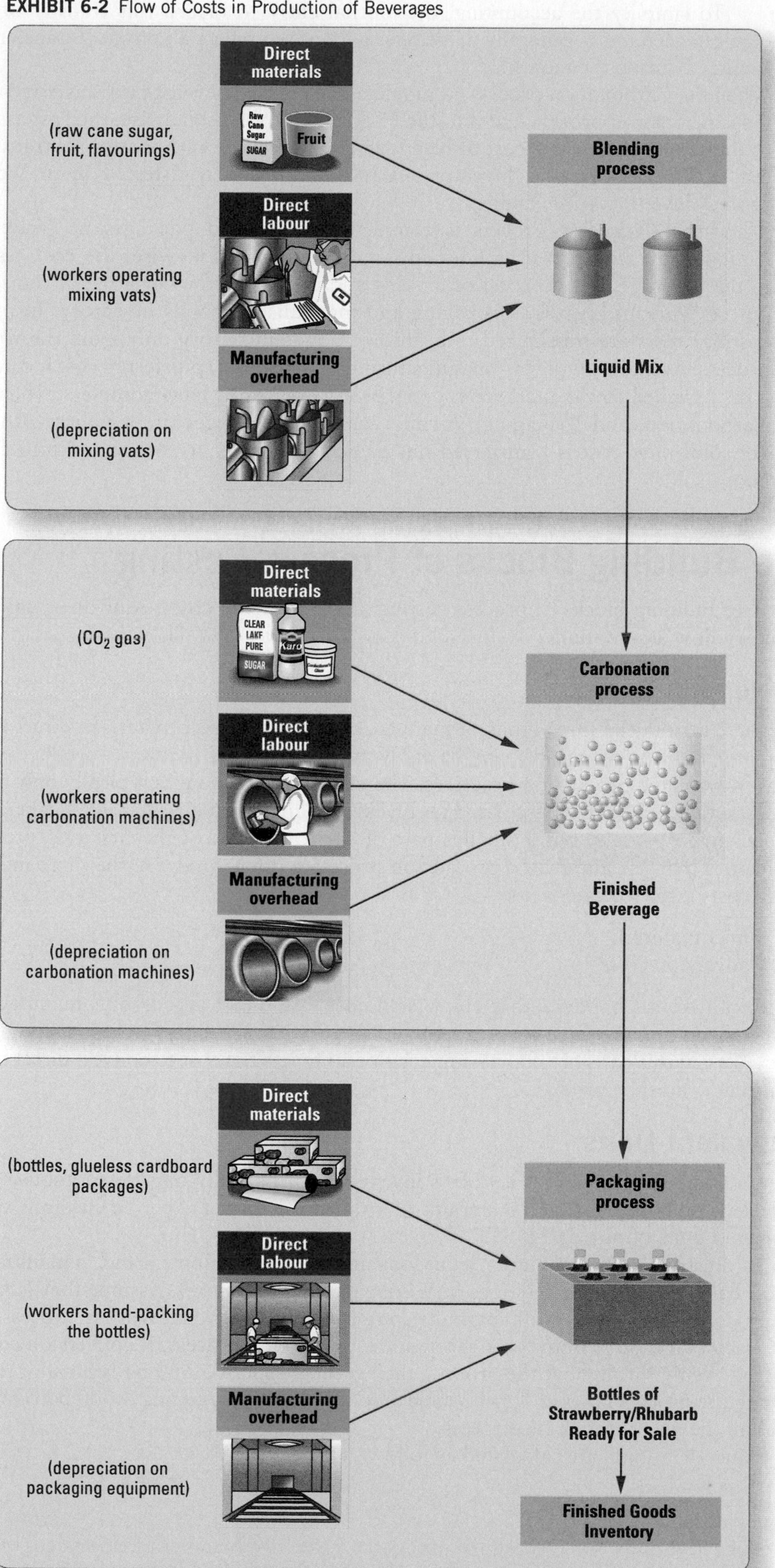

To simplify the accounting, the journal entry to record this transfer of costs between accounts is generally made once a month to reflect all physical transfers that occurred during the month.

4. When the Carbonation process is complete, the finished beverage is transferred out of the Carbonation process and into the Packaging process. Likewise, the cost assigned to the beverage thus far (cost of blending and adding the carbonation) is transferred out of Work in Process Inventory—Carbonation and **transferred in** to Work in Process Inventory—Packaging.
5. When the Packaging process is complete, the finished packages of Strawberry/Rhubarb are transferred to finished goods inventory. Likewise, the cost assigned to the beverage thus far (cost of making and packaging the beverage) is transferred out of Work in Process—Packaging and into finished goods inventory. In process costing, costs are transferred into finished goods inventory only from the work in process inventory of the last manufacturing process. The transferred cost includes all costs assigned to the units from every process the units have completed (Blending, Carbonation, and Packaging). Finally, when the packages of Strawberry/Rhubarb are sold, their cost is transferred out of finished goods inventory and into cost of goods sold.

# The Building Blocks of Process Costing

The three building blocks of process costing are: conversion costs, **equivalent units**, and inventory flow assumptions.

## Conversion Costs

Chapter 2 introduced three kinds of manufacturing costs: direct materials, direct labour, and manufacturing overhead. Like Black Fly, most companies that mass-produce a product use automated production processes. Therefore, direct labour is typically only a small part of total manufacturing costs. For Black Fly, direct labour is a significant cost in the packaging process, but a smaller part of the total costs of the first two processes. Companies that use automated production processes often condense the three manufacturing costs into two categories:

1. Direct materials
2. Conversion costs

Recall from Chapter 2 that conversion costs are direct labour plus manufacturing overhead. Combining these costs in a single category simplifies the process costing procedures. We call this category conversion costs because it is the cost to convert direct materials into new finished products.

## Equivalent Units

2 Compute equivalent units.

When a company has work in process inventories of partially completed goods, we use equivalent units to express the amount of work done during a period in terms of fully completed units of output.

To illustrate equivalent units, let us look at Jazz Golf Equipment Inc., a manufacturer of golf balls, clubs, and accessories in Winnipeg. See Exhibit 6-3. Assume that Jazz's golf ball production plant has 5,000 partially completed balls in ending work in process inventory. Each ball is 80% of the way through the production process. If conversion costs are incurred evenly throughout the process, then getting each of 5,000 balls 80% of the way through the process takes about the same amount of work as getting 4,000 balls (5,000 × 80%) all the way through the process.

Equivalent units are calculated as follows:

Number of partially complete physical units × Percentage of process completed = Number of equivalent units

**EXHIBIT 6-3** Jazz Production Plant Time Line

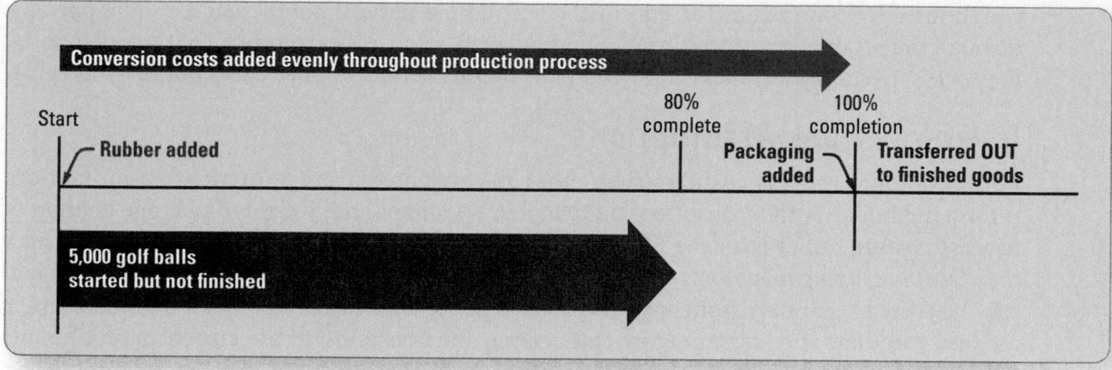


So, the number of equivalent units of conversion costs in Jazz's ending work in process inventory is calculated as follows:

$$5{,}000 \times 80\% = 4{,}000$$

Conversion costs are usually incurred evenly throughout production. However, direct materials are often added at a particular point in the process. For example, Jazz adds rubber at the beginning of the production process but does not add packaging materials until the end. How many equivalent units of rubber and packaging materials are in the ending inventory of 5,000 balls?

All 5,000 balls are 80% complete, so they all have passed the point at which rubber is added. Each ball has its full share of rubber (100%), so the balls have 5,000 equivalent units of rubber. In contrast, the time line in Exhibit 6-3 shows that none of the 5,000 balls has made it to the end of the process, where the packaging materials are added. The ending inventory, therefore, has zero equivalent units of packaging materials.

To summarize, the 5,000 balls in ending work in process inventory have the following:

- 5,000 equivalent units of rubber (5,000 units 100% of rubber)
- Zero equivalent units of packaging materials (5,000 units × 0% of packaging materials)
- 4,000 equivalent units of conversion costs (5,000 units × 80% converted)

Be careful to distinguish the *end of the production process* from the *end of the accounting period*. Goods at the end of the production process are transferred to the next process

## STOP & THINK

Colleges and universities use the equivalent-unit concept to describe the number of faculty as well as the number of students. Assume that the University of Alberta has about 2,000 full-time faculty and 400 part-time faculty. Assume the following:

1. A full-time faculty member teaches six courses per year.
2. 100 part-time faculty teach three courses per year.
3. 300 part-time faculty teach two courses per year.

What is the "full-time equivalent" faculty—the number of equivalent units of faculty?

**Answer:** Compute the full-time equivalent faculty as follows:

| | |
|---|---|
| Full-time faculty | 2,000 × 6/6 = 2,000 |
| Half-time faculty | 100 × 3/6 = 50 |
| One-third-time faculty | 300 × 2/6 = 100 |
| Full-time equivalent faculty | 2,150 |

or to finished goods. For example, Jazz's completed golf balls proceed to the finished goods warehouse. By contrast, at the end of the accounting period, goods that are only partway through the production process are the ending work in process inventory. Jazz's ending work in process inventory includes 5,000 golf balls that have their rubber cores but no packaging.

## Inventory Flow Assumptions

Firms compute process costing using either the weighted-average or the first-in, first-out (FIFO) method. For the majority of this chapter, we will use the **weighted-average method of process costing** rather than the FIFO method. *The two costing methods differ only in how they treat beginning inventory.* The FIFO method requires that any units in beginning inventory be costed separately from any units started in the current period. The weighted-average method combines any beginning inventory units (and costs) with the current period's units (and costs) to get a weighted-average cost. From a cost–benefit standpoint, many firms prefer to use the weighted-average method because the extra cost of calculating the FIFO method does not justify the additional benefits they gain from using FIFO information. The FIFO method of calculating equivalent units will be demonstrated in the appendix to this chapter.

### TRY IT!

Dairymaid makes organic yogourt. The only ingredients, milk and bacteria cultures, are added at the very beginning of the fermentation process. At month end, Dairymaid has 100,000 cups of yogourt that are only 25% of the way through the fermentation process. Use the equivalent unit formula to answer the following:

1. How many equivalent units of direct materials are in ending work in process?
2. How many equivalent units of conversion costs are in ending work in process?

Please see page 392 for solutions.

# Process Costing in the First Processing Department

3 Use process costing in the first production department.

To illustrate process costing, we will follow GogglesPlus, a manufacturer that mass produces swim masks. We will see how GogglesPlus could use the weighted-average method of process costing to measure (1) the average cost of producing each swim mask and (2) the costs of the two major processes it uses to make the masks (shaping and insertion).

Exhibit 6-4 illustrates GogglesPlus' production process. The Shaping Department begins with plastic and metal fasteners (direct materials) and uses labour and equipment (conversion costs) to transform the materials into shaped masks. The direct materials are added at the beginning of the process, but conversion costs are incurred evenly throughout the process. After shaping, the masks move to the Insertion Department, where the shaped masks are polished and the clear faceplates are inserted.

Let's assume that the Shaping Department begins October with no work in progress inventory. During October, the Shaping Department incurs the following costs while working on 50,000 masks:

| | | |
|---|---|---|
| Beginning work in process inventory | | $ 0 |
| Direct materials | | 140,000 |
| Conversion costs: | | |
| Direct labour | $21,250 | |
| Manufacturing overhead | 46,750 | |
| Total conversion costs | | 68,000 |
| Total costs to account for | | $208,000 |

**EXHIBIT 6-4** GogglesPlus' Production Process

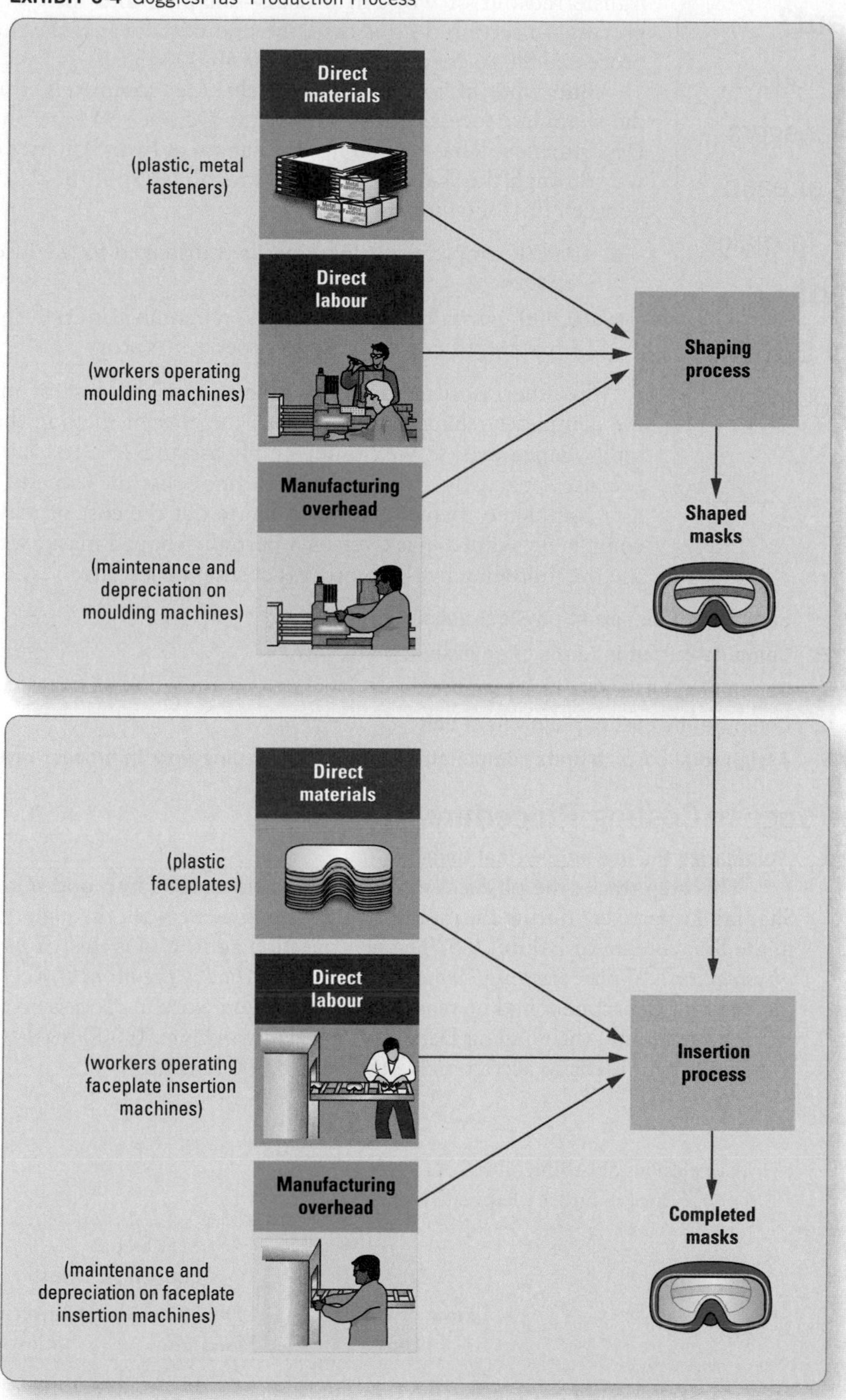


How did GogglesPlus arrive at these costs? GogglesPlus traces direct materials and direct labour to each processing department using materials requisitions and labour time records (just as we used these documents to trace direct materials and direct labour to individual jobs in Chapter 5). GogglesPlus allocates manufacturing overhead to each processing department.

If, at the end of October, all 50,000 masks have been completely shaped and transferred out of the Shaping Department and into the Insertion Department, the entire $208,000 of manufacturing cost associated with these masks should likewise be

**Why is this important?**

Most food and consumer products are **mass produced**. Managers need to know (1) the **cost** of each **manufacturing** process to make each one as **cost-efficient** as possible and (2) the cost of **each unit** to aid in **pricing** and other business decisions.

transferred out of work in process—shaping and into work in process—insertion. In this case, the unit cost for *just* the shaping process is $4.16 per mask ($208,000/50,000 masks).

But what if only 40,000 masks are completely through the shaping process? Let's say that at October 31, the Shaping Department still has 10,000 masks that are only one-quarter of the way through the shaping process. How do we split the $208,000 between the following?

- 40,000 completely shaped masks transferred to the Insertion Department
- 10,000 partially shaped masks remaining in the Shaping Department's ending work in process inventory

In other words, how do we determine the cost of making the completely shaped masks versus the cost of making the partially shaped masks? We cannot simply assign $4.16 to each mask because a partially shaped mask does not cost the same to make as a completely shaped mask. To figure out the cost of making a completely shaped mask versus a partially shaped mask, we must use the following five-step process costing procedure:

**STEP 1: Summarize the flow of physical units.**
**STEP 2: Compute output in terms of equivalent units.**
**STEP 3: Summarize total costs to account for.**
**STEP 4: Compute the cost per equivalent unit.**
**STEP 5: Assign total costs to units completed and to units in ending work in process inventory.**

## The Process Costing Procedure

**STEP 1: Summarize the flow of physical units.**

This step tracks the physical movement of swim masks into and out of the Shaping Department during the month. Follow along as we walk through this step in the first column of Exhibit 6-5. The first question addressed is this: *How many physical units did the Shaping Department work on during the month?* Recall that the Shaping Department had no masks in the beginning work in process inventory. During the month, the Shaping Department began work on 50,000 masks. Thus, the department needs to account for a total of 50,000 masks.

**EXHIBIT 6-5** Step 1: Summarize the Flow of Physical Units

GogglesPlus SHAPING DEPARTMENT
Month Ended October 31

| | Step 1 | Step 2 Equivalent Units | |
|---|---|---|---|
| Flow of Production | Flow of Physical Units | Direct Materials | Conversion Costs |
| Units to account for: | | | |
| Beginning work in process, October 1 | 0 | | |
| Started in production during October | 50,000 | | |
| Total physical units to account for | 50,000 | | |
| Units accounted for: | | | |
| Completed and transferred out during October | 40,000 | 40,000 | 40,000 |
| Ending work in process, October 31 | 10,000 | 10,000 | 2,500* |
| Total physical units | 50,000 | | |
| Total equivalent units | | 50,000 | 42,500 |

*10,000 units each 25% complete = 2,500 equivalent units

**STEP 2: Compute output in terms of equivalent units.**

The second question addressed is, *What happened to those masks?* The Shaping Department reports that it completed and transferred out 40,000 masks to the Insertion Department during October. The remaining 10,000 partially shaped masks are still in the Shaping Department's ending work in process inventory on October 31. Notice that the *Total physical units to account for* (50,000) must equal the *Total physical units accounted for* (50,000). In other words, the Shaping Department must account for the whereabouts of every mask it worked on during the month.

Step 2 computes all of the Shaping Department's output for the month in terms of equivalent units. Step 2 is shown in the last two columns of Exhibit 6-5. First, let us consider the 40,000 masks that were completed and transferred out to the Insertion Department during October. These units have been fully completed in the Shaping Department; therefore, these 40,000 completed masks have incurred 40,000 equivalent units of direct materials (40,000 masks × 100% of direct materials) and 40,000 equivalent units of conversion costs (40,000 masks × 100% of conversion costs).

Consider the 10,000 masks still in ending work in process, which are only 25% of the way through the shaping process on October 31. The timeline in Exhibit 6-6 reminds us that all direct materials are added at the *beginning* of the shaping process. Therefore, the partially shaped masks have made it past the point where direct materials are added. As a result, these masks have incurred 10,000 equivalent units of direct materials (10,000 masks × 100% of direct materials).

**EXHIBIT 6-6** GogglesPlus' Shaping Department Timeline

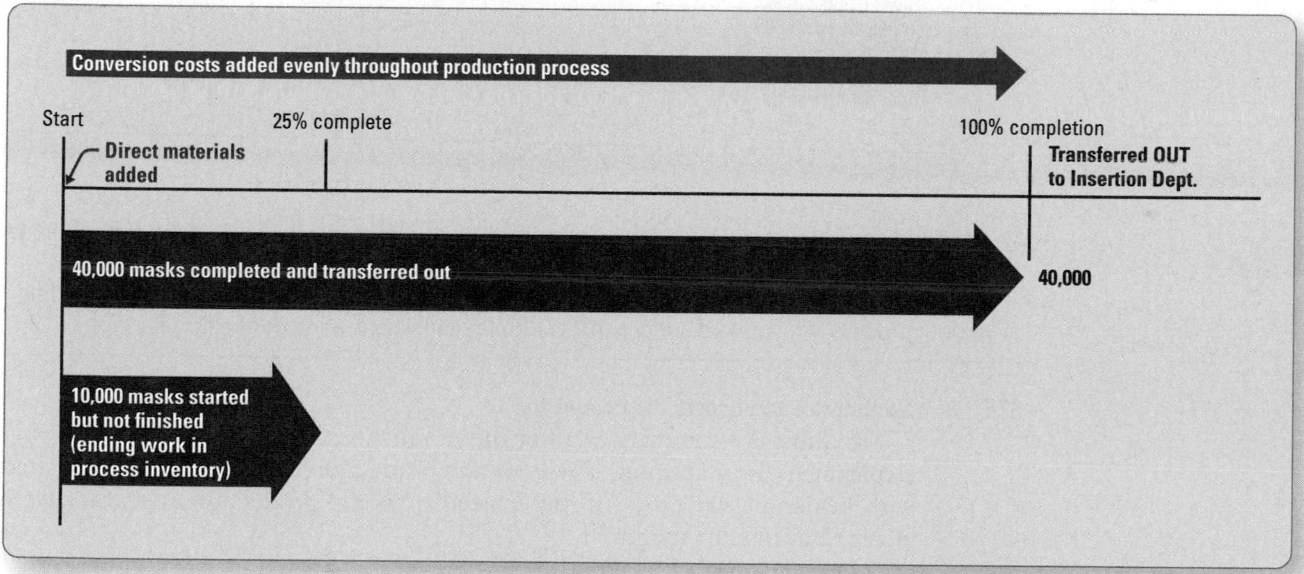


Unlike direct materials, the conversion costs are added *evenly* throughout the shaping process. For these partially shaped masks, the equivalent units of conversion costs are as follows:

10,000 × 25% = 2,500 equivalent units of conversion costs

The final part of Step 2 is to calculate the Shaping Department's output in terms of *total equivalent units* for the month. We must calculate totals separately for direct materials and conversion costs because they will differ in most circumstances. To find the totals, we simply add the equivalent units of all masks worked on during the month. For example, the total equivalent units of direct materials (50,000 as shown in Exhibit 6-5) is simply the sum of the 40,000 equivalent units completed and transferred out *plus* the 10,000 equivalent units still in ending work in process. Likewise, the total equivalent units of conversion costs (42,500 as shown in Exhibit 6-5) is the sum of the 40,000 equivalent units completed and transferred out plus the 2,500 equivalent units still in ending work in process.

## STOP & THINK

Suppose the Shaping Department adds direct materials at the end of the shaping process rather than at the beginning.

1. Draw a new timeline similar to the one in Exhibit 6-6.
2. Use the timeline to determine the number of equivalent units of direct materials.

**Answer:**

1.

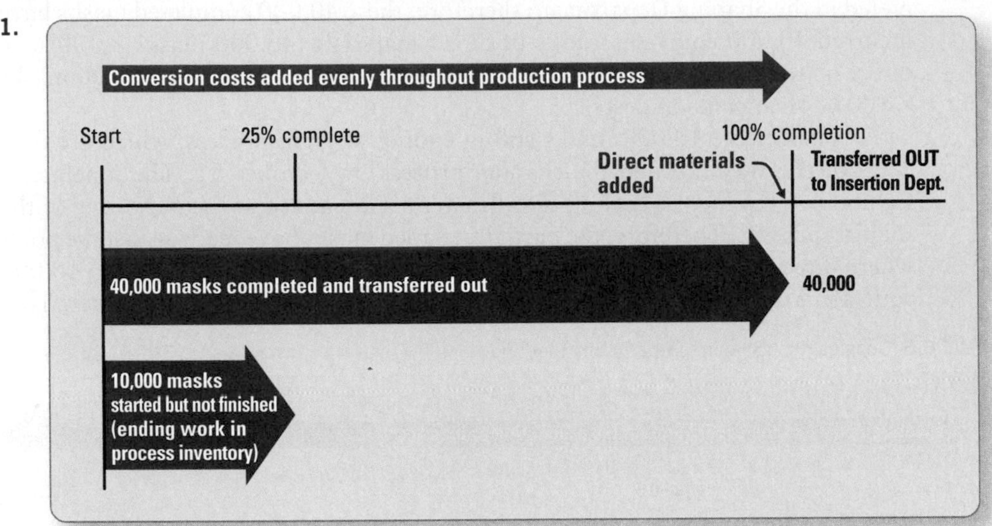


2. The timeline shows that the 10,000 masks in ending work in process inventory have not made it to the end of the shaping process where materials are added. Materials have been added only to the 40,000 masks completed and transferred out, not to the 10,000 masks in ending work in process. Thus, there are only 40,000 total equivalent units of direct materials.

---

**STEP 3: Summarize total costs to account for.**

Exhibit 6-7 summarizes all of the production costs for which the Shaping Department must account. These are the production costs that were associated with beginning inventory (if any existed) plus the production costs that were incurred during the month.[2]

**EXHIBIT 6-7** Step 3: Summarize Total Costs to Account For

GogglesPlus SHAPING DEPARTMENT
Month Ended October 31

| | Direct Materials | Conversion Costs | Total |
|---|---|---|---|
| Beginning work in process, October 1 | $ 0 | $ 0 | $ 0 |
| Costs added during October: | 140,000 | 68,000* | 208,000 |
| **Total costs to account for** | $140,000 | $68,000 | $208,000 |

*21,250 of direct labour plus $46,750 of manufacturing overhead = $68,000 of conversion costs

[2] The Shaping Department did not have a beginning inventory. Summary Problem 1 illustrates a department that does have a beginning inventory. As long as we assume the weighted-average method of process costing, we include the beginning balance to arrive at total costs to account for, as shown in Exhibit 6-7.

Once again, we must show separate totals for each of the two cost categories: direct materials and conversion costs. Because the Shaping Department did not have any beginning inventory of partially shaped masks, the beginning balance in the Work in Process Inventory—Shaping account is zero. During the month, the Shaping Department used $140,000 of direct material and $68,000 of conversion costs ($21,250 of direct labour plus $46,750 of manufacturing overhead).

We have calculated the Shaping Department's total equivalent units (Step 2) and summarized its total costs to account for (Step 3). Our next step is to calculate the cost per equivalent unit.

**STEP 4: Compute the cost per equivalent unit.**

The *cost per equivalent unit* is the *total costs* (from Step 3) divided by the *total equivalent units* (from Step 2). Because the total equivalent units for direct materials (50,000) and conversion costs (42,500) differ, we must compute a separate cost per equivalent unit for each cost category: direct materials and conversion costs. Exhibit 6-8 shows the computations:

**EXHIBIT 6-8** Step 4: Compute the Cost per Equivalent Unit

GogglesPlus SHAPING DEPARTMENT
Month Ended October 31

| | Direct Materials | Conversion Costs |
|---|---|---|
| Total costs to account for (from Exhibit 6-7) | $140,000 | $68,000 |
| Divided by total equivalent units (from Exhibit 6-5) | ÷50,000 | ÷42,500 |
| **Cost per equivalent unit** | $ 2.80 | $ 1.60 |

The calculations indicate that during October, GogglesPlus' Shaping Department incurred an average of $2.80 of direct materials cost and $1.60 of conversion costs to completely shape the equivalent of one mask. In addition to using the cost per equivalent unit in the five-step process costing procedure, managers also use this information to determine how well they have controlled costs. Managers compare the actual cost per equivalent unit to the budgeted cost per equivalent unit for both direct materials and conversion costs. If the cost per equivalent unit is the same as or lower than budgeted, the manager has successfully controlled costs.

**STEP 5: Assign total costs to units completed and to units in ending work in process inventory.**

The goal of Step 5 (Exhibit 6-9) is to determine how much of the Shaping Department's $208,000 total costs should be assigned to (1) the 40,000 completely shaped masks transferred out to the Insertion Department and (2) the 10,000 partially shaped masks remaining in the Shaping Department's ending

**EXHIBIT 6-9** Step 5: Assign Total Costs to Units Completed and to Units in Ending Work in Process Inventory

GogglesPlus SHAPING DEPARTMENT
Month Ended October 31

| | Direct Materials | Conversion Costs | Total |
|---|---|---|---|
| Completed and transferred out (40,000) | [40,000 × ($2.80 + $1.60)] | | = $176,000 |
| Ending work in process inventory (10,000): | | | |
| Direct materials | [10,000 × $2.80] | | = $ 28,000 |
| Conversion costs | | [2,500 × $1.60] | = 4,000 |
| Total cost of ending work in process inventory | | | $ 32,000 |
| Total costs accounted for | | | $208,000 |

Note: Equivalent units are from Exhibit 6-5; Costs per equivalent are from Exhibit 6-8.

work in process inventory. Exhibit 6-9 shows how the equivalent units computed in Step 2 (Exhibit 6-5) are costed at the cost per equivalent unit computed in Step 4 (Exhibit 6-8).

First, consider the 40,000 masks completed and transferred out. Exhibit 6-5 shows 40,000 equivalent units for both direct materials and conversion costs. In Exhibit 6-8 we learned that the company spent $2.80 on direct materials for each equivalent unit and $1.60 on conversion costs for each equivalent unit. Thus, the total cost of these completed masks is 40,000 × ($2.80 + $1.60) = $176,000, as shown in Exhibit 6-9. We have accomplished our first goal—now we know how much cost ($176,000) should be assigned to the completely shaped masks transferred to the Insertion Department.

Next, consider the 10,000 masks still in ending work in process. These masks have 10,000 equivalent units of direct materials (which cost $2.80 per equivalent unit), so the direct material cost is $28,000 (= 10,000 × $2.80). These masks also have 2,500 equivalent units of conversion costs (which cost $1.60 per equivalent unit), so the conversion cost is $4,000 (= 2,500 × $1.60). Therefore, the total cost of the 10,000 partially completed masks in the Shaping Department's ending work in process inventory is the sum of these direct material and conversion costs: $28,000 + $4,000 = $32,000. Now, we have accomplished our second goal—we know how much cost ($32,000) should be assigned to the partially shaped masks still in ending work in process inventory.

In summary, Exhibit 6-9 represents the division of the total costs of $208,000 between the 40,000 masks completed and transferred out to the Insertion Department and the 10,000 partially shaped masks remaining in work in process inventory.

## Average Unit Costs

The average cost of making one completely shaped unit is $4.40 ($176,000 transferred to insertion ÷ 40,000 completely shaped masks transferred to insertion). This average unit cost ($4.40) is the sum of the direct material cost per equivalent unit ($2.80) and the conversion cost per equivalent unit ($1.60). The average cost of one partially shaped unit that is 25% of the way through the production process is $3.20 ($32,000 in ending inventory of shaping ÷ 10,000 partially shaped masks).

The five-step process costing procedure is necessary to calculate these average costs per unit. If the Shaping Department manager ignored the five-step process and simply spread the entire production cost over all units worked on during the period, each unit would be assigned a cost of $4.16 ($208,000 ÷ 50,000 masks)—whether completely shaped or not. That would be wrong. The average cost per unit should be (and is) higher for completely shaped units transferred to the Insertion Department than it is for partially shaped units remaining in the Shaping Department's ending work in process inventory.

Recall that once the masks are shaped, they still need to have the faceplates inserted. Later in this chapter, we will discuss how the second process—insertion—uses the same five-step procedure to find the *total* unit cost of making a completed mask, from start to finish.

### STOP & THINK

Assume that the Shaping Department manager incorrectly assigned all of October's production costs ($208,000) to the completely shaped masks rather than using the five-step process to divide the costs between the completely shaped and partially shaped masks. What would be the results of this error?

**Answer:** If the manager incorrectly assigned all production costs to the completely shaped masks, the unit cost of completely shaped masks would be too high ($208,000 ÷ 40,000 = $5.20). In addition, the unit cost of the partially shaped masks would be too low ($0.00). In essence, the manager would be saying that the partially shaped units were "free" to make because he or she assigned all of the production costs to the completely shaped units. To assign production costs properly, managers must use the five-step process.

# Journal Entries in a Process Costing System

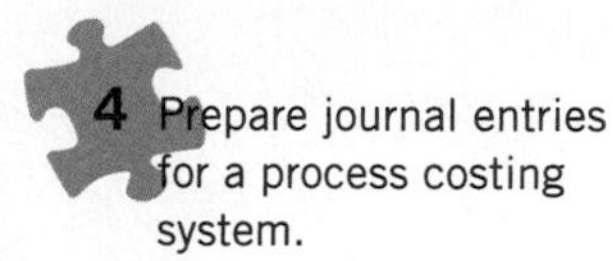


The journal entries used in a process costing system are very similar to those in a job costing system. The basic difference is that the manufacturing costs (direct materials, direct labour, and manufacturing overhead) are assigned to processing departments, rather than jobs. In addition, at the end of the month a journal entry must be made to transfer costs to the next processing department. Let us now look at the journal entries that would have been made in October for the Shaping Department.

During October, $140,000 of direct materials were requisitioned for use by the Shaping Department. In the following journal entry, notice how these costs are recorded specifically to the Shaping Department's work in process inventory account. In process costing, each processing department maintains a separate work in process inventory account.

| | Account | Debit | Credit |
|---|---|---|---|
| | Work in Process Inventory—Shaping | 140,000 | |
| | Raw Materials Inventory | | 140,000 |
| | *(To record direct materials used by the Shaping Department in October)* | | |

Labour time records show that $21,250 of direct labour was used in the Shaping Department during October, resulting in the following journal entry:

| | Account | Debit | Credit |
|---|---|---|---|
| | Work in Process Inventory—Shaping | 21,250 | |
| | Wages Payable | | 21,250 |
| | *(To record direct labour used in the Shaping Department in October)* | | |

Manufacturing overhead is allocated to the Shaping Department using the company's predetermined overhead rate(s). Just as in a job costing environment, the company may use a single plantwide rate, departmental overhead rates, or activity-based costing (discussed in Chapter 7 to allocate its manufacturing overhead costs. For example, let us say that the Shaping Department's overhead rate is $50 per machine hour and the department used 935 machine hours during the month. That means $46,750 ($50 × 935) of MOH should be allocated to the Shaping Department during October:

| | Account | Debit | Credit |
|---|---|---|---|
| | Work in Process Inventory—Shaping | 46,750 | |
| | Manufacturing Overhead | | 46,750 |
| | *(To record manufacturing overhead allocated to the Shaping Department in October.)* | | |

After making these journal entries during the month, the Work in Process Inventory—Shaping T-account appears as follows:

| Work in Process Inventory—Shaping | |
|---|---|
| Balance, October 1 | $ 0 |
| Direct materials | 140,000 |
| Direct labour | 21,250 |
| Manufacturing overhead | 46,750 |
| Total value | $208,000 |

Notice how the sum of the costs currently in the T-account is $208,000. This is the same total costs to account for summarized in Exhibit 6-7. By performing the five-step process at the end of the month, GogglesPlus was able to determine how much of the $208,000 should be assigned to units still being completed ($32,000) and how much should be assigned to the units completed and transferred out to the Insertion Department ($176,000). The company uses this information (pictured in Exhibit 6-9) to make the following journal entry:

| | Account | Debit | Credit |
|---|---|---|---|
| | Work in Process Inventory—Insertion | 176,000 | |
| | Work in Process Inventory—Shaping | | 176,000 |
| | *(To record the transfer of cost out of the Shaping Department and into the Insertion Department)* | | |

After this journal entry is posted, the Work in Process Inventory—Shaping account appears as follows:

**Work in Process Inventory—Shaping**

| | | | |
|---|---|---|---|
| Balance, October 1 | 0 | Transferred to Insertion | 176,000 |
| Direct materials | 140,000 | | |
| Direct labour | 21,250 | | |
| Manufacturing overhead | 46,750 | | |
| Balance, October 31 | 32,000 | | |

Notice that the new ending balance in the account—$32,000—agrees with the amount assigned to the partially shaped masks in Exhibit 6-9.

In the next half of the chapter, we will look at the journal entries made by the Insertion Department to record the completion and sale of the swim masks.

## Sustainability and Process Costing

As we have seen, process costing is suitable for manufacturers that produce large volumes of product using a set of standardized production processes. These manufacturing environments are conducive to employing lean practices, which eliminate economic waste from the manufacturing process, and green practices, which minimize or eliminate harmful environmental consequences.

For example, GogglesPlus employs two standardized production processes: Shaping and Insertion. Management should be continually asking, "Is each of these production processes as efficient and environmentally friendly as it can be?" If not, then changes are warranted.

See Exercises E6-34A and E6-45B

Management should study each of the production processes to discover the quantities and types of solid waste, airborne emissions, and waste water that are generated, as well as the types and quantities of energy used. Solid waste and scrap can be identified simply by studying the contents of the company's trash. These studies are known as trash audits, waste audits, or waste sorts. After conducting trash audits, many companies have discovered they can reclaim and repurpose the scraps into new products, or sell them to a third-party recycler. For example, Parma Plastics recovers unwanted vinyl scraps from manufacturers across North America and recycles the scraps into re-compounded vinyl.[3]

[3] www.iisd.org/business/viewcasestudy.aspx?id=84

Many parties benefit:

- Manufacturers reduce their waste disposal costs and generate new revenue from selling their vinyl scraps.
- Manufacturers reduce their raw material costs by buying recompounded vinyl rather than virgin vinyl.
- Parma Plastics creates jobs and profit by manufacturing and selling the recompounded vinyl.
- Landfills are spared from receiving vinyl scraps.

Air and water discharges should also be examined to determine if any environmentally damaging substances are released into the environment.

While switching to environmentally friendly production equipment, energy sources, and production processes may be costly in the short run, companies may recognize long-term economic benefits as a result. For example, as carbon-trading schemes (otherwise known as "cap and trade") become more prevalent across the globe, those companies that manage to reduce their carbon emissions may be able to profit from selling their carbon credits. In searching for greener ways to manufacture and recycle their products, some companies may eventually profit from developing, patenting, and selling their own environmentally neutral production systems and technologies.

# DECISION GUIDELINES

## Process Costing—First Processing Department

Here are some of the key decisions GogglesPlus made in setting up its costing system.

| Decision | Guidelines |
|---|---|
| Should GogglesPlus use job or process costing? | GogglesPlus mass-produces identical swim masks using two production processes: shaping and insertion. It uses process costing to do the following:<br>1. *Accumulate* the cost of each process<br>2. *Assign* these costs to the masks passing through that process |
| What types of accounts will GogglesPlus need to incorporate into its costing system for the swim masks? | In GogglesPlus' process costing system, costs flow from the following:<br>Work in Process Inventory—Shaping<br>↓<br>Work in Process Inventory—Insertion<br>↓<br>Finished Goods Inventory<br>More generally, costs flow from one work in process inventory account to the next until the last process, after which they flow into finished goods inventory. Therefore, GogglesPlus will need to set up work in process accounts for each processing department in addition to raw materials inventory and finished goods inventory. |
| In order to set up a costing system, the managerial accountant needs to decide on the number of work in process inventory accounts that GogglesPlus should have. How is this determined? | GogglesPlus uses a separate work in process inventory account for each of its two major processes: shaping and insertion. |

| Decision | Guidelines |
|---|---|
| GogglesPlus doesn't fully complete each unit in production. How does GogglesPlus account for partially completed products? | GogglesPlus uses equivalent units. |
| Which costs require separate equivalent-unit computations? | Compute equivalent units separately for each input added at a different point in the production process. GogglesPlus computes equivalent units separately for direct materials and conversion costs because it adds direct materials at a particular point in the production process but incurs conversion costs evenly throughout the process. |
| How does GogglesPlus compute equivalent units of conversion costs? | GogglesPlus' conversion costs are incurred evenly throughout the production process, so the equivalent units are computed as follows: $$\text{Equivalent units} = \text{Number of partially complete units} \times \text{Percentage of process completed}$$ |
| How does GogglesPlus compute equivalent units of direct materials? | GogglesPlus' materials are added at specific points in the production process, so the equivalent units are computed using the following percentages:<br>■ If physical units have passed the point at which materials are added, then the units are 100% complete with respect to materials.<br>■ If physical units have *not* passed the point at which materials are added, then the units are 0% complete with respect to materials. |
| How do you compute the cost per equivalent unit? | For each category (direct materials and conversion), divide the total cost to account for by the total equivalent units. |
| How do you split the costs of the shaping process between the following?<br>• Swim masks completed and transferred out<br>• Partially completed swim masks in ending work in process inventory | Multiply the cost per equivalent unit by the following:<br>• Number of equivalent units completed and transferred out<br>• Number of equivalent units in the ending work in process inventory |
| The owner of GogglesPlus evaluates each department's manager in part by how well the manager controls costs. How well did the manager of the Shaping Department control the department's costs? | If direct material and conversion cost per equivalent unit is the same or lower than the target unit cost per equivalent unit, the manager has done a good job controlling costs. |

# SUMMARY PROBLEM 1

Drimo Tile in New Westminster, B.C., produces ceramic tiles using two sequential production departments: Tile-Forming and Tile-Finishing. The following information was created for Drimo Tile's first production process, the Tile-Forming Department.

DRIMO TILE
TILE-FORMING DEPARTMENT
Month Ended May 31

| | |
|---|---|
| **Information about units:** | |
| Beginning work in process, May 1 | 2,000 units |
| Started in production during May | 18,000 units |
| Completed and transferred to Finishing Department during May | 16,000 units |
| Ending work in process, May 31 (25% complete as to direct materials, 55% complete as to conversion cost) | 4,000 units |
| **Information about costs:** | |
| Beginning work in process, May 1 (consists of $800 of direct materials cost and $4,000 of conversion costs) | $ 4,800 |
| Direct materials used in May | $ 6,000 |
| Conversion costs incurred in May | $32,400 |

## Requirement

Use the five steps of process costing to calculate the cost that should be assigned to (1) units completed and transferred out and (2) units still in ending work in process inventory. Then prepare the journal entry needed at month-end to transfer the costs associated with the formed tiles to the next department, Tile Finishing.

## SOLUTION

**Step 1:** Summarize the flow of physical units.

**Step 2:** Compute output in terms of equivalent units using the weighted average method.

DRIMO TILE
TILE-FORMING DEPARTMENT
Month Ended May 31

| | Step 1 | Step 2: Equivalent Units | |
|---|---|---|---|
| **Flow of Production** | **Flow of Physical Units** | **Direct Materials** | **Conversion Costs** |
| Units to account for: | | | |
| Beginning work in process, May 1 | 2,000 | | |
| Started in production during May | 18,000 | | |
| Total physical units to account for | 20,000 | | |
| Units accounted for: | | | |
| Completed and transferred out in May | 16,000 | 16,000 | 16,000 |
| Ending work in process, May 31 | 4,000 | 1,000* | 2,200** |
| Total physical units accounted for | 20,000 | | |
| **Total equivalent units** | | 17,000 | 18,200 |

*Direct materials: 4,000 units each 25% complete = 1,000 equivalent units.
**Conversion costs: 4,000 units each 55% complete = 2,200 equivalent units.

**Step 3:** Summarize total costs to account for.

DRIMO TILE
TILE-FORMING DEPARTMENT
Month Ended May 31

| | Direct Materials | Conversion Costs | Total |
|---|---|---|---|
| Beginning work in process, May 1 | $ 800 | $ 4,000 | $ 4,800 |
| Costs added during May | 6,000 | 32,400 | 38,400 |
| Total costs to account for | $6,800 | $36,400 | $43,200 |

Note: All cost information is from the summary problem data set.

**Step 4:** Compute the cost per equivalent unit.

DRIMO TILE
TILE-FORMING DEPARTMENT
Month Ended May 31

| | Direct Materials | Conversion Costs |
|---|---|---|
| Total costs to account for (from Step 3) | $ 6,800 | $ 36,400 |
| Divided by total equivalent units (from Step 2) | ÷ 17,000 | ÷ 18,200 |
| Cost per equivalent unit | $ 0.40 | $ 2.00 |

**Step 5:** Assign total costs to units completed and to units in ending work in process inventory.

DRIMO TILE
TILE-FORMING DEPARTMENT
Month Ended May 31

| | Direct Materials | Conversion Costs | Total |
|---|---|---|---|
| Units completed and transferred out (16,000) | [16,000 × ($0.40 + $2.00)] | | = $38,400 |
| Units in ending work in process inventory (4,000): | | | |
| Direct materials | [1,000 × $0.40] | | = $ 400 |
| Conversion costs | | [2,200 × $2.00] | = 4,400 |
| Total cost of ending work in process inventory | | | $ 4,800 |
| Total costs accounted for | | | $43,200 |

The journal entry needed to transfer costs is as follows:

| | | |
|---|---|---|
| Work in Process Inventory—Finishing | 38,400 | |
| Work in Process Inventory—Tile Forming | | 38,400 |

The cost of making one completely formed tile in the Forming Department is $2.40. This is the sum of the direct materials cost per equivalent unit ($0.40) and the conversion cost per equivalent unit ($2.00). The completely formed tiles must still be finished in the Finishing Department before we will know the final cost of making one tile from start to finish.

# Process Costing in a Second or Later Processing Department

5 Use process costing in a second or later production department.

PROFESSIONAL COMPETENCY

Most products require a series of processing steps. Recall that Black Fly uses seven processing steps to make its Strawberry/Rhubarb beverage. In the last section, we saw how much it costs GogglesPlus to shape one mask. In this section, we consider a second department, GogglesPlus' Insertion Department. After units pass through the final department (Insertion, in GogglesPlus' case), managers can determine the entire cost of making one unit—from start to finish. In the second or later department, we use the same five-step process costing procedure used for the Shaping Department, with one major difference: We separately consider the costs transferred in to the Insertion Department from the Shaping Department when calculating equivalent units and the cost per equivalent unit. Transferred-in costs are incurred in a previous process (the Shaping Department, in the GogglesPlus example) and are carried forward as part of the product's cost when it moves to the next process.

**Why is this important?**
Most products are **manufactured** through a **series** of production processes. To find the **total cost** of making one unit—from **start to finish**—managers must perform the five-step process costing procedure in **each** production department.

The concept of transferred-in costs is particularly important when service companies adopt process costing. For example, the dental office of Matheson and Podge provides dental cleaning and dental X-rays as part of a regular hygiene appointment. While each patient may have individual health characteristics, the practices of dental cleaning and X-rays in a regular appointment is somewhat standardized. After the patient passes through the first "department" of dental cleaning, they proceed to the next phase, the X-ray "department." Thus, the dental office can account for the costs that occur in these two distinct phases of a regular hygiene appointment. The costs of the first phase (cleaning) are carried forward and included with the separate cost of X-rays to constitute the total cost of the service.

To account for transferred-in costs, we will add one more column to our calculations in Steps 2–5. Let us walk through the Insertion Department's process costing to see how this is done.

## Process Costing in GogglesPlus' Insertion Department

The Insertion Department receives the shaped masks and polishes them before inserting the faceplates at the end of the process. Exhibit 6-10 shows the following:

- Shaped masks are transferred in from the Shaping Department at the beginning of the Insertion Department's process.
- The Insertion Department's conversion costs are added evenly throughout the process.
- The Insertion Department's direct materials (faceplates) are not added until the end of the process.

Keep in mind that *direct materials* in the Insertion Department refer *only* to the faceplates and not to the materials (the plastic and metal fasteners) added in the Shaping Department. Likewise, *conversion costs* in the Insertion Department refer to the direct labour and manufacturing overhead costs incurred *only* in the Insertion Department.

Exhibit 6-11 lists GogglesPlus' Insertion Department data for October. The top portion of the exhibit lists the unit information, while the lower portion lists the costs. Let us walk through this information together.

Exhibit 6-11 shows that GogglesPlus' Insertion Department started the October period with 5,000 masks that had made it partway through the insertion process in September. During October, the Insertion Department started work on the 40,000 masks received from the Shaping Department. By the end of the month, the Insertion Department had completed 38,000 masks, while 7,000 remained partially complete.

Exhibit 6-11 also shows that the Insertion Department started October with a beginning balance of $23,100 in its work in process inventory account, which is associated

**EXHIBIT 6-10** GogglesPlus' Insertion Department Timeline

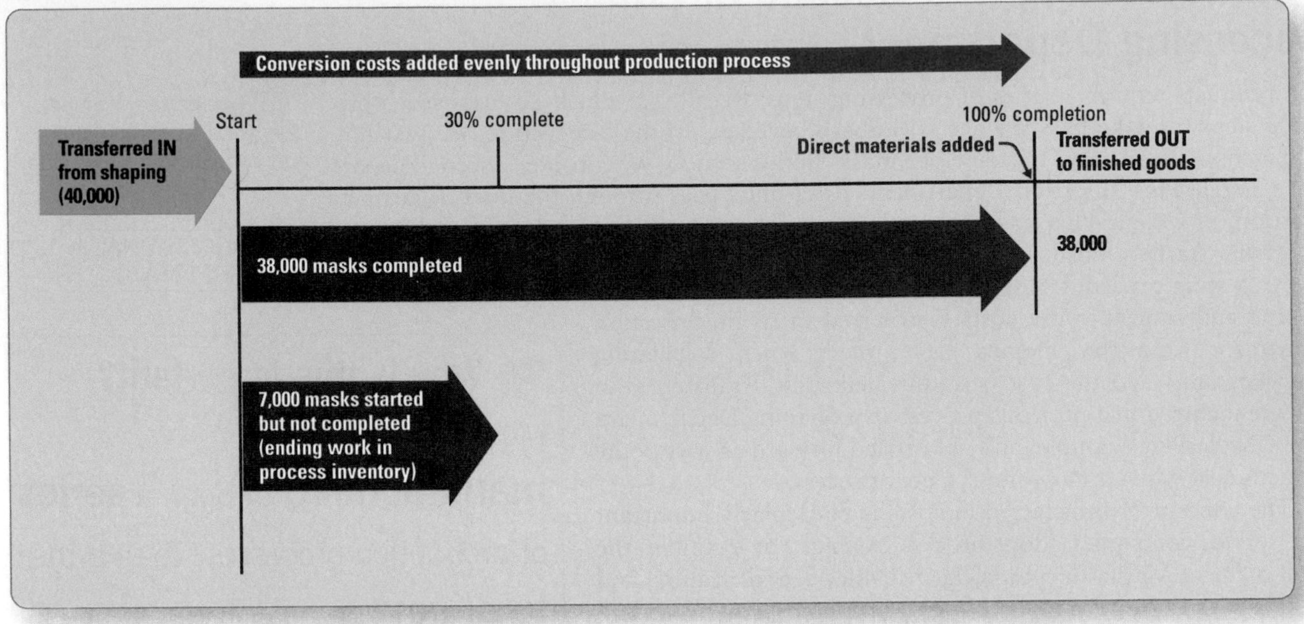


**EXHIBIT 6-11** GogglesPlus' Insertion Department Data for October

| | | |
|---|---|---|
| **Information about units:** | | |
| Beginning work in process, October 1 (0% complete as to direct materials, 60% complete as to conversion work) | | 5,000 masks* |
| Transferred in from Shaping Department during October (from Exhibit 6-6) | | 40,000 masks |
| Completed and transferred out to Finished Goods Inventory during October | | 38,000 masks |
| Ending work in process, October 31 (0% complete as to direct materials, 30% complete as to conversion work) | | 7,000 masks |
| **Information about costs:** | | |
| Beginning work in process, October 1 | | |
| Transferred-in costs | $ 22,000 | |
| Conversion costs | 1,100* | |
| Beginning balance | | $ 23,100 |
| Transferred in from Shaping Department during October | | $176,000 |
| Direct materials added during October in Insertion Department | | $ 19,000 |
| Conversion costs added during October in Insertion Department: | | |
| Direct labour | $ 3,710 | |
| Manufacturing overhead | 9,225 | |
| Conversion costs | | $ 12,935 |
| Total costs to account for | | $231,035 |

*This information would have been obtained from Step 5 of the process costing procedure from September. The September 30 balance in work in process becomes the October 1 balance.

with the 5,000 partially completed masks in its beginning inventory. During the month, $176,000 was transferred in from the Shaping Department for the 40,000 masks transferred into the department from shaping. Additionally, the Insertion Department incurred $19,000 in direct material costs (faceplates) and $12,935 in conversion costs during the month.

Just as in the Shaping Department, our goal is to split the total cost in the Insertion Department ($231,035) between the following:

- The 38,000 masks that the Insertion Department completed and transferred out (this time, to finished goods inventory)
- The 7,000 partially complete masks remaining in the Insertion Department's ending work in process inventory at the end of October

After splitting the total cost, we will be able to determine the cost of making one complete mask—from start to finish. We use the same five-step process costing procedure that we used for the Shaping Department.

## Steps 1 and 2: Summarize the Flow of Physical Units and Compute Output in Terms of Equivalent Units

**STEP 1: Summarize the flow of physical units.**

This step is the same as in the Shaping Department—we must track the movement of swim masks into and out of the Insertion Department. Exhibit 6-12 shows that the Insertion Department had a beginning work in process inventory of 5,000 masks that were partway through the insertion process at the start of the period. Recall that during October, the Shaping Department finished 40,000 masks and transferred them into the Insertion Department. Thus, Exhibit 6-12 shows that the Insertion Department has 45,000 masks to account for (5,000 + 40,000).

Where did these 45,000 masks go? Exhibits 6-10 and 6-11 show that the Insertion Department completed and transferred 38,000 masks to finished goods inventory while the remaining 7,000 masks were only partway through the insertion process on October 31. Thus, Exhibit 6-12 shows that the department has

**EXHIBIT 6-12** Step 1: Summarize the Flow in Physical Units and Step 2: Compute Output in Terms of Equivalent Units

GogglesPlus' INSERTION DEPARTMENT
Month Ended October 31

| | Step 1 | Step 2: Equivalent Units | | |
|---|---|---|---|---|
| Flow of Production | Flow of Physical Units | Transferred-in | Direct Materials | Conversion Costs |
| Units to account for: | | | | |
| Beginning work in process, October 1 | 5,000 | | | |
| Transferred in during October | 40,000 | | | |
| Total physical units to account for | 45,000 | | | |
| Units accounted for: | | | | |
| Completed and transferred out during October | 38,000 | 38,000 | 38,000* | 38,000* |
| Ending work in process, October 31 | 7,000 | 7,000 | 0† | 2,100† |
| Total physical units accounted for | 45,000 | | | |
| Total equivalent units | | 45,000 | 38,000 | 40,100 |

In the Insertion Department:
*Units completed and transferred out
Direct materials: 38,000 units each 100% completed = 38,000 equivalent units
Conversion costs: 38,000 units each 100% completed = 38,000 equivalent units
†Ending inventory
Direct materials: 7,000 units each 0% completed = 0 equivalent units
Conversion costs: 7,000 units each 30% completed = 2,100 equivalent units

accounted for all 45,000 masks (38,000 completed and transferred out + 7,000 in ending work in process inventory).

**STEP 2: Compute Output in Terms of Equivalent Units**

As mentioned earlier, process costing in a second or later department must separately calculate equivalent units for transferred-in costs, much like they separately calculate equivalent units for direct materials and conversion costs. Therefore, Step 2 in Exhibit 6-12 shows three columns for the Insertion Department's three categories of equivalent units: transferred in, direct materials, and conversion costs. Let us consider each in turn.

Exhibit 6-10 shows that transferred-in masks are added at the very beginning of the insertion process. You might think of the shaped masks transferred in as raw materials added at the very beginning of the insertion process. All masks worked on in the Insertion Department—whether completed or not by the end of the month—started in the department as a shaped mask. Therefore, they are all 100% complete with respect to transferred-in work and costs. So, the Transferred In column of Exhibit 6-12 shows 38,000 equivalent units completed and transferred out (38,000 physical units × 100%) and 7,000 equivalent units still in ending inventory (7,000 physical units × 100%).

The following rule holds: *All physical units, whether completed and transferred out or still in ending work in process, are considered 100% complete with respect to transferred-in work and costs.*

The Insertion Department calculates equivalent units of direct material the same way as the Shaping Department. However, in the Insertion Department, the direct materials (faceplates) are added at the *end* of the process rather than at the beginning of the process. The 38,000 masks completed and transferred out contain faceplates (have 100% of the Insertion Department's direct materials). On the other hand, the 7,000 masks in the ending work in process inventory have *not* made it to the end of the process, so they *do not* contain faceplates. As we see in Exhibit 6-12, these unfinished masks have zero equivalent units of the Insertion Department's direct materials (7,000 physical units × 0%).

Now, consider the conversion costs. The 38,000 finished masks are 100% complete with respect to the Insertion Department's conversion costs. However, the 7,000 unfinished masks are only 30% converted (see Exhibits 6-10 and 6-11), so the equivalent units of conversion costs equal 2,100 (7,000 × 30%).

Now, the equivalent units in each column are summed to find the *total* equivalent units for each of the three categories: transferred in (45,000), direct materials (38,000), and conversion costs (40,100). We will use these equivalent units in Step 4.

## Steps 3 and 4: Summarize Total Costs to Account For and Compute the Cost per Equivalent Unit

Exhibit 6-13 accumulates the Insertion Department's total costs to account for based on the data in Exhibit 6-11.

In addition to direct material and conversion costs, the Insertion Department must account for transferred-in costs. Recall that transferred-in costs are incurred in a previous process (the Shaping Department, in the GogglesPlus example) and are carried forward as part of the product's cost when the physical product is transferred to the next process.

If the Insertion Department had bought these shaped masks from an outside supplier, it would have to account for the costs of purchasing the masks. However, the Insertion Department receives the masks from an internal supplier—the Shaping Department. Thus, the Insertion Department must account for the costs the Shaping Department incurred to

**EXHIBIT 6-13** Step 3: Summarize Total Costs to Account For and Step 4: Compute the Cost per Equivalent Unit

**GogglesPlus' INSERTION DEPARTMENT**
Month Ended October 31

| | Transferred-in | Direct Materials | Conversion Costs | Total |
|---|---|---|---|---|
| Beginning work in process, October 1 (from Exhibit 6-11) | $ 22,000 | $ 0 | $ 1,100 | $ 23,100 |
| Costs added during October (from Exhibit 6-11) | 176,000 | 19,000 | 12,935 | 207,935 |
| Total costs to account for | $198,000 | $19,000 | $14,035 | $231,035 |
| Divide by total equivalent units (from Exhibit 6-12) | ÷ 45,000 | ÷ 38,000 | ÷ 40,100 | |
| Cost per equivalent unit | $ 4.40 | $ 0.50 | $ 0.35 | |

provide the shaped masks (the Insertion Department's transferred-in costs) as well as the Insertion Department's own direct materials (faceplates) and conversion costs (labour and overhead to insert the faceplates).

Exhibit 6-13 shows that in Step 3, the Insertion Department's total costs to account for ($231,035) is the sum of the following:

- The cost incurred in September to start the insertion process on the 5,000 masks in the Insertion Department's beginning work in process inventory ($23,100)
- The costs added to Work in Process Inventory—Insertion during October ($207,935 = $176,000 transferred in from the Shaping Department + $19,000 direct materials incurred in the Insertion Department + $12,935 conversion costs incurred in the Insertion Department)

Exhibit 6-13 also shows the results of Step 4—the cost per equivalent unit. For each of the three cost categories, GogglesPlus divides the total cost of that category by the total number of equivalent units in that category.

## Step 5: Assign Total Costs to Units Completed and to Units in Ending Work in Process Inventory

Exhibit 6-14 shows how GogglesPlus assigns the Insertion Department's total costs to account for ($231,035, from Exhibit 6-13) to (1) units completed and transferred out to finished goods inventory and (2) units remaining in the Insertion Department's ending work in process inventory. GogglesPlus uses the same approach as it used for the Shaping Department in Exhibit 6-9. GogglesPlus multiplies the number of equivalent units from Step 2 (Exhibit 6-12) by the cost per equivalent unit from Step 4 (Exhibit 6-13).

**EXHIBIT 6-14** Step 5: Assign Total Costs to Units Completed and to Units in Ending Work in Process Inventory

**GogglesPlus' INSERTION DEPARTMENT**
Month Ended October 31

| | Transferred-in | Direct Materials | Conversion Costs | Total |
|---|---|---|---|---|
| Units completed and transferred out to Finished Goods Inventory (38,000) | [38,000 × ($4.40 + $0.50 + $0.35)] | | | $199,500 |
| Ending work in process, October 31 (7,000): | | | | |
| Transferred-in costs | [7,000 × $4.40] | | | $ 30,800 |
| Direct materials | | [0 × $0.50] | | 0 |
| Conversion costs | | | [2,100 × $0.35] | 735 |
| Total ending work in process, October 31 | | | | 31,535 |
| Total costs accounted for | | | | $231,035 |

Exhibit 6-15 illustrates how the costs were assigned in Step 5.

**EXHIBIT 6-15** Assign Insertion Department's Costs to Units Completed and Transferred Out and to Ending Work in Process Inventory

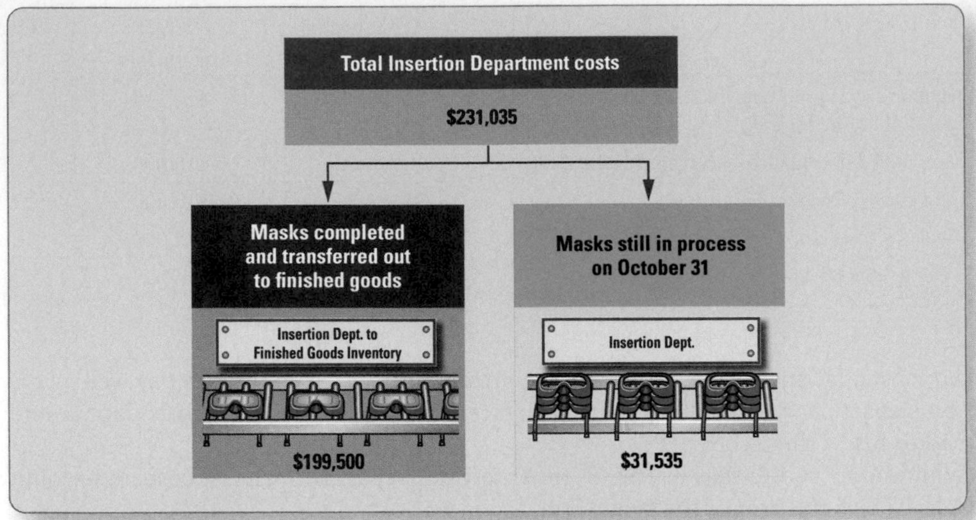


## Unit Costs and Gross Profit

GogglesPlus' managers can now compute the cost of manufacturing one swim mask, from start to finish. Step 5 shows that $199,500 should be transferred to the finished goods inventory account for the 38,000 masks completed during the month. Therefore, GogglesPlus's cost of making one completed mask is $5.25 ($199,500 ÷ 38,000 finished masks). Exhibit 6-14 shows that this cost includes the costs from both processing departments:

- $4.40 from the Shaping Department[4]
- $0.85 from the Insertion Department ($0.50 for direct materials and $0.35 for conversion costs)

GogglesPlus' managers use this information to help control costs, set prices, and assess the profitability of the swim masks. Let us assume GogglesPlus is able to charge customers $10 for each mask. If so, the gross profit on the sale of each of these masks will be as follows:

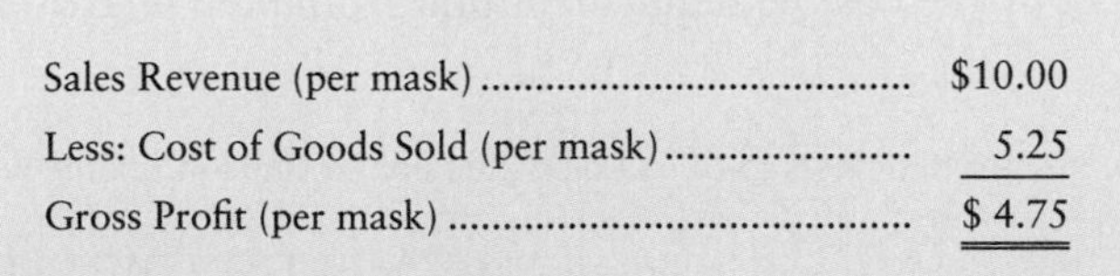

| | |
|---|---|
| Sales Revenue (per mask) | $10.00 |
| Less: Cost of Goods Sold (per mask) | 5.25 |
| Gross Profit (per mask) | $ 4.75 |

For GogglesPlus to be profitable, the total gross profit (gross profit per mask × number of masks sold) will need to exceed all of GogglesPlus' operating expenses, such as marketing and distribution expenses, incurred in nonmanufacturing elements of the value chain. In addition to using the unit cost for valuing cost of goods sold (on the income statement), the unit cost will also be used to value ending finished goods inventory ($5.25 for each mask still in finished goods inventory at the end of October).

[4]This is the same $4.40 per unit we saw the Shaping Department transfer out to the Insertion Department in the first half of the chapter. Notice how the transferred-in cost carries through from one department to the next. The weighted average method of process costing *combines* the current period's costs ($176,000) with any costs in beginning inventory ($23,100) to yield a weighted average cost per unit ($4.40). Therefore, the weighted average cost could be different than $4.40 if the beginning inventory had cost more or less than $4.40 per unit to make in September.

Dairymaid's yogourt goes through two sequential processes in two departments: Fermenting and Packaging. Assume that in the Packaging Department, Step 4 of the process costing procedure indicated the following costs per equivalent unit (cases of yogourt):

| | Transferred-in | Direct Materials | Conversion Costs |
|---|---|---|---|
| Cost per equivalent unit | $6.50 | $1.15 | $1.25 |

a. How much did each case of yogourt cost to make, from start to finish?

b. If each case sells for $20, what is the gross profit per case?

Please see page 392 for solutions.

## Production Cost Reports

Most companies prepare a **production cost report**, which summarizes the entire five-step process on one schedule. Notice how the production cost report for the Insertion Department shown in Exhibit 6-16 simply brings together all of the steps that we showed separately in Exhibits 6-12, 6-13, and 6-14. The top half of the schedule focuses on units (Steps 1 and 2), while the bottom half of the schedule focuses on costs (Steps 3, 4, and 5). Each processing department prepares its own production cost report each month. The transferred-in costs, direct materials cost, and conversion costs assigned to the units in ending work in process inventory become the beginning work in process inventory balances on the next month's cost report.

GogglesPlus' managers monitor production costs by comparing the actual direct materials and conversion costs—particularly the equivalent-unit costs—with expected amounts. If actual costs are higher than expected, managers will try to uncover the reason for the increase and look for ways to cut costs in the future without sacrificing quality.

## Journal Entries in a Second Processing Department

The Insertion Department's journal entries are similar to those of the Shaping Department.

The following summary entry records the manufacturing costs incurred in the Insertion Department during the month of October (data from Exhibit 6-11):

| | | | | |
|---|---|---|---|---|
| | | Work in Process Inventory—Insertion | 31,935 | |
| | | Raw Materials Inventory | | 19,000 |
| | | Wages Payable | | 3,710 |
| | | Manufacturing Overhead | | 9,225 |
| | | *(To record manufacturing costs incurred in the Insertion Department during October)* | | |

Next, recall the journal entry made to transfer the cost of shaped masks out of the Shaping Department and into the Insertion Department at the end of October. This journal entry would be made only once, but it is repeated here simply as a reminder:

| | | | | |
|---|---|---|---|---|
| | | Work in Process Inventory—Insertion | 176,000 | |
| | | Work in Process Inventory—Shaping | | 176,000 |
| | | *(To record the transfer cost out of the Shaping Department and into the Insertion Department)* | | |

**EXHIBIT 6-16** Production Cost Report

**GogglesPlus' INSERTION DEPARTMENT**
**Production Cost Report**
Month Ended October 31

| Flow of Production | Step 1 Flow of Physical Units | Step 2: Equivalent Units Transferred-in | Direct Materials | Conversion Costs | |
|---|---|---|---|---|---|
| Units to account for: | | | | | |
| Beginning work in process, Oct. 1 | 5,000 | | | | |
| Transferred in during October | 40,000 | | | | |
| Total physical units to account for | 45,000 | | | | |
| Units accounted for: | | | | | |
| Completed and transferred out during October | 38,000 | 38,000 | 38,000 | 38,000 | |
| Ending work in process, Oct. 31 | 7,000 | 7,000 | 0 | 2,100 | |
| Total physical units accounted for | 45,000 | | | | |
| Total equivalent units | | 45,000 | 38,000 | 40,100 | |
| **Flow of Costs** | | **Step 3, 4, and 5 Transferred-in** | **Direct Materials** | **Conversion Costs** | **Total** |
| Beginning work in process, October 1 | | $ 22,000 | $ 0 | $ 1,100 | $ 23,100 |
| Costs added during October | | 176,000 | 19,000 | 12,935 | 207,935 |
| Total costs to account for | | $198,000 | $19,000 | $14,035 | $231,035 |
| ÷ Total equivalent units | | ÷ 45,000 | ÷38,000 | ÷40,100 | |
| Cost per equivalent unit | | $ 4.40 | $ 0.50 | $ 0.35 | |
| *Assignment of total costs:* | | | | | |
| Units completed during October | | [38,000 × ($4.40 + $0.50 + $0.35)] | | | $199,500 |
| Ending work in process, October 31: | | | | | |
| Transferred-in costs | | [7,000 × $4.40] | | | $ 30,800 |
| Direct materials | | | [0 × $0.50] | | 0 |
| Conversion costs | | | | [2,100 × $0.35] | 735 |
| Total ending work in process, October 31 | | | | | 31,535 |
| Total costs accounted for | | | | | $231,035 |

After completing the fifth step of the process costing procedure (shown in Exhibit 6-14), the Insertion Department knows that $199,500 should be assigned to the completed masks, while $31,535 should be assigned to the units still being worked on in the Insertion Department. Therefore, the following journal entry is made to transfer cost out of the Insertion Department and into finished goods inventory:

| | | | |
|---|---|---|---|
| | Finished Goods Inventory | 199,500 | |
| | Work in Process Inventory—Insertion | | 199,500 |
| | *(To record transfer of cost out of the Insertion Department and into Finished Goods Inventory)* | | |

After posting, the key accounts appear as follows:

| Work in Process Inventory—Shaping | | | |
|---|---|---|---|
| Balance, September 30 | 0 | Transferred to Insertion | 176,000 |
| Direct materials | 140,000 | | |
| Direct labour | 21,250 | | |
| Manufacturing overhead | 46,750 | | |
| Balance, October 31 | 32,000 | | |

| Work in Process Inventory—Insertion | | | |
|---|---|---|---|
| Balance, September 30 | 23,100 | Transferred to Finished Goods Inventory | 199,500 |
| Transferred in from Shaping | 176,000 | | |
| Direct materials | 19,000 | | |
| Direct labour | 3,710 | | |
| Manufacturing overhead | 9,225 | | |
| Balance, October 31 | 31,535 | | |

| Finished Goods Inventory | | | |
|---|---|---|---|
| Balance, September 30 | 0 | | |
| Transferred in from Shaping | 199,500 | | |

## STOP & THINK

Assume that GogglesPlus sells 36,000 of the masks for $10 each. Assuming that GogglesPlus uses a perpetual inventory system, what journal entries would GogglesPlus make to record the sales transaction?

**Answer:** The unit cost of making one mask from start to finish is $5.25 ($199,500 transferred to Finished Goods ÷ 38,000 finished masks). GogglesPlus will make one journal entry to record the sales revenue and a second journal entry to record the cost of goods sold:

| | | | |
|---|---|---|---|
| | Accounts Receivable (36,000 × $10.00) | 360,000 | |
| | Sales Revenue | | 360,000 |

| | | | |
|---|---|---|---|
| | Cost of Goods Sold (36,000 × 5.25) | 189,000 | |
| | Finished Goods Inventory | | 189,000 |

# DECISION GUIDELINES

## Process Costing—Second Process

Let us use GogglesPlus' Insertion Department to review some of the key process costing decisions that arise in a second (or later) process.

| Decision | Guidelines |
|---|---|
| At what point in the insertion process are transferred-in costs (from the shaping process) incurred? | Transferred-in costs are incurred at the *beginning* of the insertion process. The masks must be completely shaped before the insertion process begins. |
| What percentage of completion is used to calculate equivalent units in the Transferred-In column? | All units, whether completed and transferred out or still in ending work in process, are considered 100% complete with respect to transferred-in work and costs. |
| What checks and balances does the five-step process costing procedure provide? | The five-step procedure provides two important checks:<br>**1.** The total units to account for (beginning inventory + units started or transferred in) *must equal* the total units accounted for (units completed and transferred out + units in ending inventory).<br>**2.** The total costs to account for (cost of beginning inventory + costs incurred in the current period) must equal the total costs accounted for (cost of units completed and transferred out + cost of ending inventory). |
| What are the two main goals of the Insertion Department's process costing? | The first goal is to split total costs between swim masks completed and transferred out to finished goods inventory and the masks that remain in the Insertion Department's ending work in process inventory.<br>The second goal is to determine the cost of making each swim mask—from start to finish. |
| What is a production cost report, and how do managers use the information found on it? | A production cost report simply summarizes all five steps on one schedule. GogglesPlus managers use the cost per equivalent unit to determine the cost of producing a swim mask. These costs provide a basis for setting selling prices, performing profitability analysis to decide which products to emphasize, and so forth. These costs are also the basis for valuing inventory on the balance sheet and cost of goods sold on the income statement.<br>Managers also use the cost per equivalent unit to control material and conversion costs and to evaluate the performance of production department managers. |

## SUMMARY PROBLEM 2

This problem extends the Summary Problem 1 to a second department. During May, Drimo Tile reports the following in its Finishing Department:

| Drimo Tile: Finishing Department Data for May | |
|---|---|
| **Information about units:** | |
| Beginning work in process, May 1 (20% complete as to direct materials, 70% complete as to conversion work) | 4,000 units |
| Transferred in from Tile-Forming Department during May | 16,000 units |
| Completed and transferred out to Finished Goods Inventory during May | 15,000 units |
| Ending work in process, May 31 (36% complete as to direct materials, 80% complete as to conversion work) | 5,000 units |
| **Information about costs:** | |
| Work in process, May 1 (transferred-in costs, $10,000; direct materials costs, $488; conversion costs, $5,530) | $16,018 |
| Transferred in from Tile-Forming Department during May (page 344) | 38,400 |
| Finishing Department direct materials added during May | 6,400 |
| Finishing Department conversion costs added during May | 24,300 |

### Requirements

Using the weighted average method:

1. Assign the Finishing Department's Total Costs to Account For to units completed and to units in ending work in process inventory.

   (*Hint:* Do not confuse the Finishing Department with finished goods inventory. The Finishing Department is Drimo Tile's second process. The tiles do not become part of finished goods inventory until they have completed the second process, which happens to be called the Finishing Department.)
2. Make the journal entry to transfer the appropriate amount of cost to finished goods inventory.
3. What is the cost of making one unit of product from start to finish?

## ▪ SOLUTION

**Steps 1 and 2:** Summarize the flow of physical units; compute output in terms of equivalent units.

DRIMO TILE
FINISHING DEPARTMENT
Month Ended May 31

| | Step 1 | Step 2: Equivalent Units | | |
|---|---|---|---|---|
| Flow of Production | Flow of Physical Units | Transferred-in | Direct Materials | Conversion Costs |
| Units to account for: | | | | |
| Beginning work in process, May 1 | 4,000 | | | |
| Transferred in from Tile-Forming Department during May | 16,000 | | | |
| Total physical units to account for | 20,000 | | | |
| Units accounted for: | | | | |
| Completed and transferred out during May | 15,000 | 15,000 | 15,000 | 15,000 |
| Ending work in process, May 31 | 5,000 | 5,000 | 1,800* | 4,000* |
| Total physical units accounted for | 20,000 | | | |
| Total equivalent units | | 20,000 | 16,800 | 19,000 |

*Ending inventory:
Direct materials: 5,000 units each 36% completed = 1,800 equivalent units
Converted costs: 5,000 units each 80% completed = 4,000 equivalent units

**Steps 3 and 4:** Summarize total costs to account for; compute the cost per equivalent unit.

DRIMO TILE
FINISHING DEPARTMENT
Month Ended May 31

| | Step 1 | Step 2: Equivalent Units | | |
|---|---|---|---|---|
| | Transferred-in | Direct Materials | Conversion Costs | Total |
| Beginning work in process, May 1 | $10,000 | $ 488 | $ 5,530 | $16,018 |
| Costs added during May | 38,400 | 6,400 | 24,300 | 69,100 |
| Total costs to account for | $48,400 | $6,888 | $29,830 | $85,118 |
| Divide by total equivalent units | ÷ 20,000 | ÷ 16,800 | ÷ 19,000 | |
| Cost per equivalent unit | $ 2.42 | $ 0.41 | $ 1.57 | |

**Step 5:** Assign total costs to units completed and to units in ending work in process inventory.

DRIMO TILE
FINISHING DEPARTMENT
Month Ended May 31

| Flow of Production | Transferred-in | Direct Materials | Conversion Costs | Total |
|---|---|---|---|---|
| Units completed and transferred out to | | | | |
| Finished Goods Inventory | [15,000 × ($2.42 + $0.41 + $1.57)] | | | $66,000 |
| Ending work in process, May 31: | | | | |
| Transferred-in costs | [5,000 × $2.42] | | | 12,100 |
| Direct materials | | [1,800 × $0.41] | | 738 |
| Conversion costs | | | [4,000 × $1.57] | 6,280 |
| Total ending work in process, May 31 | | | | 19,118 |
| Total costs accounted for | | | | $85,118 |

### Requirement 2

Journal entry:

| | | | |
|---|---|---|---|
| | Finished Goods Inventory | 66,000 | |
| | Work in Process Inventory—Finishing Department | | 66,000 |
| | *(To record the transfer of cost out of the Finishing* | | |
| | *Department and into Finished Goods Inventory.)* | | |

### Requirement 3

The cost of making one unit from start to finish is $4.40 ($66,000 transferred to finished goods inventory divided by the 15,000 completed tiles). This consists of $2.42[5] of cost incurred in the Tile-Forming Department and transferred in and $1.98 of cost incurred in the Finishing Department ($0.41 of direct materials and $1.57 of conversion costs).

[5] In Summary Problem 1, we saw that the average cost per unit in May was $2.40. The weighted-average method combines the current period's costs (May's costs) with any costs in beginning inventory to yield a weighted-average cost of $2.42 per unit.

APPENDIX 6A

# Process Costing Using the First-In, First-Out Method

The weighted average method for calculating equivalent units assumes a blending of the units so that the work is distributed over all units. In contrast, the FIFO method assumes that the *first units in* (the ones that are in the beginning inventory) are completed before work is done on the next units. The *physical* flow of units is not affected by the choice in costing method.

The following section will demonstrate how to determine the equivalent units using either the weighted average method or the FIFO method so that you can compare the results.

At Best Toys, the Shaping Department had the following data from November 2015:

| | | % Complete | |
|---|---|---|---|
| | Units | Materials | Conversion |
| WIP, November 1 | 3,000 | 75% | 40% |
| Units started in production in November | 26,000 | | |
| Units completed and transferred to the next department | 25,000 | 100% | 100% |
| WIP, November 30 | 4,000 | 30% | 15% |

The way to read these data is to see that the WIP that was worked on in October, but not finished, is the WIP on November 1. There are 3,000 units, and they are 75% complete with respect to materials and 40% complete with respect to conversion. That means that 75% of the direct materials have already been added and 40% of the direct labour and MOH have been completed for these units before the beginning of November. In other words, to complete these 3,000 units, Best Toys will need to add the remaining 25% of the direct materials and complete the remaining 60% of direct labour and MOH during November.

In November, 26,000 units were started into production, so these are not the same units from the November 1 WIP. That means that a total of 29,000 units (3,000 WIP + 26,000 started) were worked on in November. From the third row in the chart above, we can see that 25,000 of these units were transferred to the next department. It is somewhat redundant that they are shown to be 100% complete for materials and conversion costs because they would not be transferred to the next department if the work on them were not complete for this department.

This leaves 4,000 units (29,000 total – 25,000 transferred) that must still be in the Shaping Department at the end of November, which we can see in the last row of the data. These 4,000 units had some work done on them, but not enough for them to be completed. They have had 30% of the direct materials added and 15% of the conversion costs added.

Now that we understand the data that we are going to be working with, we can move on to calculating the equivalent units.

**Weighted Average**

| | | Materials | Conversion |
|---|---|---|---|
| Units transferred to the next department | | 25,000 | 25,000 |
| WIP, November 30 | 4,000 × 30% | 1,200 | |
| | 4,000 × 15% | | 600 |
| Total equivalent units | | 26,200 | 25,600 |

For the weighted average calculation, we took the 29,000 units that were worked on in November and divided them into units transferred out of the department and those that were still remaining in the ending inventory at the end of November.

**FIFO**

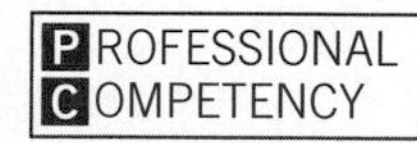


| | | Materials | Conversion |
|---|---|---|---|
| WIP, November 1 | 3,000 × 25% | 750 | |
| | 3,000 × 60% | | 1,800 |
| Units started and completed (25,000 − 3,000) | | 22,000 | 22,000 |
| WIP, November 30 | 4,000 × 30% | 1,200 | |
| | 4,000 × 15% | | 600 |
| Total equivalent units | | 23,950 | 24,400 |

In the FIFO calculation, the difference is in the treatment of the 25,000 units that had been transferred to the next department. When using weighted average, we simply included 100% of the units. However, with FIFO, we calculated how much of the 3,000 beginning inventory needed to be completed first and then included all of the 22,000 units that had been started *and* completed in November. This is different from the number of units that were started in November from the original data, because these needed not only to have been started in November, but also to be fully complete. The treatment of the WIP ending balance is the same in either method.

## Comparing Weighted Average and FIFO costing

The FIFO approach assumes that all the units from a previous period in *beginning work in process* are the first to be completed and transferred out of the process. It is only following this that costs from *current* work in process is included. Thus, the total cost will reflect cost differences between work from a previous period and current work in process. By contrast, the weighted-average method "smooths out" cost per equivalent unit by assuming there is no chronological order to the transfer of work in process to ending inventory.

As a result, the cost of completed units can differ between the weighted-average and FIFO methods when costs for materials and conversion per equivalent unit vary from period to period; or, if inventory levels of work in process are large relative to the total number of units transferred out. This can have an impact on the operating impact for a period: If, over time, costs are *falling*, the FIFO method will result in a *higher* cost per equivalent unit than the weighted average method, causing a *lower* operating income to be reported. Conversely, if, over time, costs are *increasing*, the FIFO method will result in a *lower* cost per equivalent unit than the weighted average method, causing a *higher* operating income to be reported.

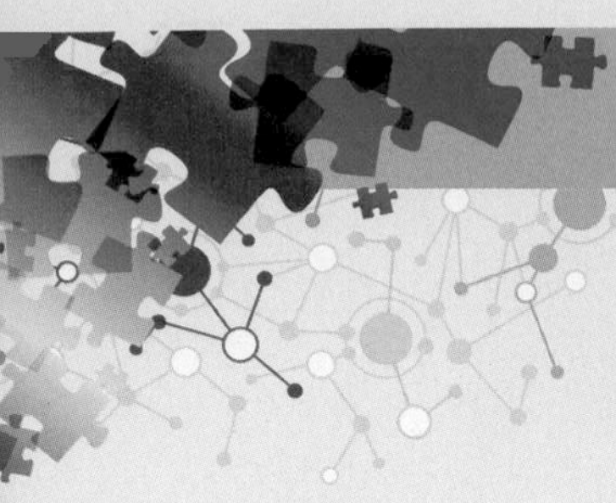

# END OF CHAPTER

## LEARNING OBJECTIVES

1. Distinguish between the flow of costs in process costing and job costing.
2. Compute equivalent units.
3. Use process costing in the first production department.
4. Prepare journal entries for a process costing system.
5. Use process costing in a second or later production department.

## ACCOUNTING VOCABULARY

**Equivalent Units (p. 330)** An expression of the amount of work done during a period in terms of fully completed units of output.

**Production Cost Report (p. 351)** Summary of a processing department's operations for a period.

**Transferred-in Costs (p. 330)** Costs incurred in a previous process that are carried forward as part of the product's cost when it moves to the next process.

**Weighted-average Method of Process Costing (p. 332)** A process costing method that combines any beginning inventory units (and costs) with the current period's units (and costs) to get a weighted-average cost.

MyAccountingLab Make the grade with MyAccountingLab: Questions marked in # can be found on MyAccountingLab. You can practise them as often as you want, and most feature step-by-step guided instructions to help you find the right answer.

## QUICK CHECK

1. (Learning Objective 1) Which of these companies would use process costing?
   a. Cartier Communication Marketing, advertising firm in Quebec
   b. McCain Foods, producer of sweet potato fries
   c. Auld & Company Management Consultants, headquarters in Calgary
   d. Amazon.com
2. (Learning Objective 1) Which of these companies would use job costing?
   a. An oil refinery
   b. A dairy farm
   c. A paint manufacturer
   d. A hospital
3. (Learning Objective 1) All of the following statements are correct except one. Which one is incorrect?
   a. Costs are accumulated by department when using process costing.
   b. Units produced are indistinguishable from each other in a process costing system.
   c. Process costing has the same basic purposes as job costing.
   d. Process costing would be appropriate for a custom cabinetmaker.
4. (Learning Objective 2) Tucker Manufacturing uses weighted-average process costing. All materials at Tucker are added at the beginning of the production process. The equivalent units for materials at Tucker would be
   a. the units started plus the units in beginning work in process.
   b. the units completed and transferred out plus the units in beginning work in process.
   c. the units started plus the units in ending work in process.
   d. the units started and completed plus the units in ending work in process.
5. (Learning Objective 2) An equivalent unit of conversion costs is equal to
   a. an equivalent unit of material costs.
   b. the amount of conversion costs needed to produce one unit.
   c. the amount of conversion costs necessary to start a unit into work in process.
   d. half of the conversion costs necessary to produce one unit.
6. (Learning Objective 2) When using the weighted-average method of process costing, the computation of the cost per equivalent unit includes
   a. costs incurred during the current period only.

b. costs incurred during the current period plus the cost of the beginning work in process inventory.

c. costs incurred during the current period plus the cost of the ending work in process inventory.

d. costs incurred during the current period plus all of the costs incurred in the prior period.

**7.** (Learning Objective 3) All of the following statements about process costing are true except for one. Which one is untrue?

a. Process costing is appropriate for those production processes where similar units are produced in a continuous flow.

b. Equivalent units for materials and equivalent units for conversion costs are the same.

c. Units in beginning work in process plus the units started into production should equal units in ending work in process plus units completed.

d. Each process will have its own separate work in process inventory account.

**8.** (Learning Objective 3) Which of the following statements describes Black Fly's process costing system?

a. Direct materials and direct labour are traced to each specific order.

b. Costs flow directly from a single work in process inventory account to finished goods inventory.

c. Costs flow through a sequence of work in process inventory accounts and then into finished goods inventory from the final work in process inventory account.

d. The subsidiary work in process inventory accounts consist of separate records for each individual order, detailing the materials, labour, and overhead assigned to that order.

**9.** (Learning Objective 4) The journal entry to record the transfer of units from Department A to the next processing department, Department B, includes a debit to

a. Work in Process Inventory for Dept. B and a credit to Raw Materials Inventory.

b. Work in Process Inventory for Dept. A and a credit to Work in Process Inventory for Dept. B.

c. Work in Process Inventory for Dept. B and a credit to Work in Process Inventory for Dept. A.

d. Finished Goods Inventory and a credit to work in process for Dept. A.

**10.** (Learning Objective 5) In general, transferred-in costs include

a. costs incurred in the previous period.

b. costs incurred in all prior periods.

c. costs incurred in only the previous process.

d. costs incurred in all prior processes.

**Quick Check Answers**

1. *b* 2. *d* 3. *d* 4. *a* 5. *b* 6. *b* 7. *b* 8. *c* 9. *c* 10. *d*

## SHORT EXERCISES

### S6-1 Compare flow of costs *(Learning Objective 1)*

Use Exhibit 6-1 to help you describe in your own words the major difference in the flow of costs between a job costing system and a process costing system.

### S6-2 Prepare flow of costs through work in process inventory *(Learning Objective 1)*

As shown in Exhibits 6-1 and 6-2, Black Fly produces bottles of Strawberry/Rhubarb in three sequential processing departments: Blending, Carbonation, and Packaging. Assume that the Carbonation Department began September with $18,340 of unfinished liquid. During September, the carbonation process used $42,600 of direct materials and $12,130 of direct labour, and was allocated $17,260 of manufacturing overhead. In addition, during September, $126,400 was transferred out of the Blending Department and $196,420 was transferred out of the Carbonation Department. These transfers represent the cost of the Strawberry/Rhubarb liquid transferred from one process to another.

1. Prepare a T-account for the Work in Process Inventory—Carbonation showing all activity that took place in the account during September.
2. What is the ending balance in the Work in Process Inventory—Carbonation on September 30? What does this figure represent?

### S6-3 Recompute GogglesPlus' equivalent units *(Learning Objective 2)*

Look at GogglesPlus' Shaping Department's equivalent-unit computation in Exhibit 6-5. Suppose the ending work in process inventory is 30% of the way through the shaping process rather than 25% of the way through. Compute the total equivalent units of direct materials and conversion costs.

**S6-4 Determine the physical flow of units (process costing Step 1)** *(Learning Objective 1)*

Summerhill Estate Winery's Bottling Department had 30,000 units in the beginning inventory of work in process on June 1. During June, 110,000 units were started into production. On June 30, 30,000 units were left in ending work in process inventory. Summarize the physical flow of units in a schedule similar to Exhibit 6-5 (Step 1 column).

**S6-5 Compute equivalent units using the weighted average method (process costing Step 2)** *(Learning Objective 2)*

Blumhoff's Packaging Department had the following information at March 31. All direct materials are added at the *end* of the conversion process. The units in ending work in process inventory were only 30% of the way through the conversion process.

| | | Equivalent Units | |
|---|---|---|---|
| | Physical Units | Direct Materials | Conversion Costs |
| Units accounted for: | | | |
| Completed and transferred out | 115,000 | | |
| Ending work in process, March 31 | 15,000 | | |
| Total physical units accounted for: | 130,000 | | |
| Total equivalent units | | | |

**Requirement**

Complete the schedule by computing the total equivalent units (weighted average method) of direct materials and conversion costs for the month.

**S6-6 Compute equivalent units using the weighted average method (process costing Step 2)** *(Learning Objective 2)*

The Frying Department of Lay's Potato Chips had 100,000 partially completed units in work in process at the end of August. All of the direct materials had been added to these units, but the units were only 50% of the way through the conversion process. In addition, 1,200,000 units had been completed and transferred out of the Frying Department to the Packaging Department during the month.

1. How many equivalent units of direct materials and equivalent units of conversion costs are associated with the 1,200,000 units completed and transferred out?
2. Compute the equivalent units of direct materials and the equivalent units of conversion costs associated with the 100,000 partially completed units still in ending work in process.
3. What are the total equivalent units of direct materials and the total equivalent units of conversion costs for the month?

**S6-7 Summarize total costs to account for (process costing Step 3)** *(Learning Objective 3)*

McIntyre Industries' work in process inventory account had a $68,000 beginning balance on May 1. ($40,000 of this related to direct materials used during April, while $28,000 related to conversion costs incurred during April.) During May, the following costs were incurred in the department:

| | |
|---|---|
| Direct materials used | $106,000 |
| Direct labour | 18,000 |
| Manufacturing overhead allocated to the department | 154,000 |

Summarize the department's Total Costs to Account For. Prepare a schedule (similar to Exhibit 6-7) that summarizes the department's total costs to account for by direct materials and conversion costs.

**S6-8** **Compute the cost per equivalent unit (process costing Step 4)** *(Learning Objective 3)*

At the end of July, Jolly Doughnuts' Mixing Department had total costs to account for of $752,420. Of this amount, $287,045 related to direct materials costs, while the remainder related to conversion costs. The department had 62,340 total equivalent units of direct materials and 45,625 total equivalent units of conversion costs for the month. Compute the cost per equivalent unit for direct materials and the cost per equivalent unit for conversion costs.

**S6-9** **Recompute GogglesPlus' cost per equivalent unit** *(Learning Objective 3)*

Return to the original GogglesPlus example in Exhibits 6-5 and 6-7. Suppose direct labour is $34,000 rather than $21,250. Now what is the conversion cost per equivalent unit? (Use Exhibit 6-8 to format your answer.)

**S6-10** **Assign costs (process costing Step 5)** *(Learning Objective 3)*

Tabor Industries produces its product using a single production process. For the month of December, Tabor Industries determined its cost per equivalent unit to be as follows:

| | Direct Materials | Conversion Costs |
|---|---|---|
| Cost per equivalent unit: | $4.10 | $3.25 |

During the month, Tabor completed and transferred out 410,000 units to finished goods inventory. At month-end, 80,000 partially complete units remained in ending work in process inventory. These partially completed units were equal to 70,000 equivalent units of direct materials and 50,000 equivalent units of conversion costs.

**Requirements**

1. Determine the total cost that should be assigned to the following:
   a. Units completed and transferred out
   b. Units in ending work in process inventory
   (*Hint:* Use Exhibit 6-9 as a guide.)
2. What was the total cost accounted for?
3. What was Tabor's average cost of making one unit of its product?

**S6-11** **Flow of costs through Work in Process Inventory** *(Learning Objective 4)*

Manitoba Tile produces its product in two processing departments: Forming and Finishing. The following T-account shows the Forming Department's work in process inventory at August 31 prior to completing the five-step process costing procedure:

| Work in Process Inventory—Forming Department | | |
|---|---|---|
| Beginning balance | $ 53,250 | |
| Direct materials used | 78,360 | |
| Direct labour | 14,920 | |
| Manufacturing overhead allocated | 126,250 | |

**Requirements**

1. What is the Forming Department's Total Costs to Account For for the month of August?
2. Assume that after using the five-step process costing procedure, the company determines that the cost to be assigned to units completed and transferred out is $243,800. What journal entry is needed to record the transfer of costs to the Finishing Department?
3. After the journal entry is made, what will be the new ending balance in the Forming Department's work in process inventory account?

**S6-12** **Assign total costs in a second processing department** *(Learning Objective 5)*

After completing Steps 1–4 of the process costing procedure, Chip Corp. arrived at the following equivalent units and costs per equivalent unit for its final production department for the month of February:

| | Equivalent Units | | |
|---|---|---|---|
| | **Transferred-in** | **Direct Materials** | **Conversion Costs** |
| Units completed and transferred out.... | 70,000 | 70,000 | 70,000 |
| Units in ending work in process, | | | |
| February 28............................. | 10,000 | 6,000 | 4,000 |
| Total equivalent units............ | 80,000 | 76,000 | 74,000 |
| Cost per equivalent unit................ | $2.64 | $0.20 | $1.26 |

**Requirements**

1. How much cost should be assigned to the
   a. Units completed and transferred out to finished goods inventory during February?
   b. Partially complete units still in ending work in process inventory at the end of February?
3. What was the Total Cost Accounted For during February? What other important figure must this match? What does this figure tell you?
4. What is the average cost of making *each unit* of its product from the first production department all the way through the final production department?

**S6-13** **Find unit cost and gross profit on a final product** *(Learning Objective 5)*

Ockham Kitchens produces granite countertops in two sequential production departments: Forming and Polishing. The Polishing Department calculated the following costs per equivalent unit (square metres) on its April production cost report:

| | Transferred-in | Direct Materials | Conversion Costs |
|---|---|---|---|
| Cost per equivalent unit: | $2.64 | $0.10 | $1.26 |

During April, 250,000 square metres were completed and transferred out of the Polishing Department to finished goods inventory. The countertops were subsequently sold for $12 per square metre.

**Requirements**

1. What was the cost per square metre of the finished product?
2. Did most of the production cost occur in the Forming Department or in the Polishing Department? Explain how you can tell.
3. What was the gross profit per square metre?
4. What was the total gross profit on the countertops produced in April?

**The following data set is used for S6-14 through S6-18.**

**Canadian Springs Data Set: Filtration Department**
Canadian Springs produces premium bottled water. Canadian Springs purchases artesian water, stores the water in large tanks, and then runs the water through two processes:

- Filtration, where workers microfilter and ozonate the water
- Bottling, where workers bottle and package the filtered water

During February, the filtration process incurs the following costs in processing 200,000 litres:

| | |
|---|---|
| Wages of workers operating the filtration equipment | $ 11,100 |
| Wages of workers operating ozonation equipment | 12,850 |
| Manufacturing overhead allocated to filtration | 24,050 |
| Water | 120,000 |

Canadian Springs has no beginning inventory in the Filtration Department.

### S6-14 Compute cost per litre *(Learning Objective 1)*

Refer to the Canadian Springs Filtration Department data set.

**Requirements**

1. Compute the February conversion costs in the Filtration Department.
2. If the Filtration Department completely processed 200,000 litres, what would be the average filtration cost per litre?
3. Now, assume that the total costs of the filtration process listed in the previous chart yield 160,000 litres that are completely filtered and ozonated, while the remaining 40,000 litres are only partway through the process at the end of February. Is the cost per completely filtered and ozonated litre higher, lower, or the same as in Requirement 2? Why?

### S6-15 Summarize physical flow and compute equivalent units using the weighted average method *(Learning Objective 2)*

Refer to the Canadian Springs Filtration Department data set. At Canadian Springs, water is added at the beginning of the filtration process. Conversion costs are added evenly throughout the process, and in February, 160,000 litres have been completed and transferred out of the Filtration Department to the Bottling Department. The 40,000 litres remaining in the Filtration Department's ending work in process inventory are 80% of the way through the filtration process. Recall that Canadian Springs has no beginning inventories.

**Requirements**

1. Draw a timeline for the filtration process similar to the one in Exhibit 6-6.
2. Complete the first two steps of the process costing procedure for the Filtration Department: Summarize the physical flows of units and then compute the equivalent units (weighted average method) of direct materials and conversion costs. Your answer should look similar to Exhibit 6-5.

### S6-16 Continuation of S6-15: Summarize total costs to account for and compute cost per equivalent unit *(Learning Objective 3)*

Refer to the Canadian Springs Filtration Department data set and your answer to S6-15. Complete Steps 3 and 4 of the process costing procedure: Summarize total costs to account for and then compute the cost per equivalent unit for both direct materials and conversion costs.

### S6-17 Continuation of S6-15 and S6-16: assign costs *(Learning Objective 3)*

Refer to the Canadian Springs Filtration Department data set and your answer to S6-15 and S6-16. Complete Step 5 of the process costing procedure: Assign costs to units completed and to units in ending inventory. Prepare a schedule similar to Exhibit 6-9 that answers the following questions.

### Requirements

1. What is the cost of the 160,000 litres completed and transferred out of the Filtration Department?
2. What is the cost of 40,000 litres remaining in the Filtration Department's ending work in process inventory?

### S6-18 Continuation of S6-17: Record journal entry and post to T-account

*(Learning Objective 4)*

Refer to the Canadian Springs Filtration Department data set and your answer to S6-17.

### Requirements

1. Record the journal entry to transfer the cost of the 160,000 litres completed and transferred out of the Filtration Department and into the Bottling Department.
2. Record all of the transactions in the "Work in Process Inventory—Filtration" T-account.

## The following data set is used for S6-19 through S6-22.

**Canadian Springs Data Set: Bottling Department**

Canadian Springs produces premium bottled water. The preceding short exercises considered Canadian Springs' first process—filtration. We now consider Canadian Springs' second process—bottling. In the Bottling Department, workers bottle the filtered water and pack the bottles into boxes. Conversion costs are incurred evenly throughout the bottling process, but packaging materials are not added until the end of the process.

| February data from the Bottling Department follow: | |
|---|---|
| Beginning work in process inventory | |
| (40% of the way through the process) | 8,000 litres |
| Transferred in from Filtration* | 160,000 litres |
| Completed and transferred out to Finished Goods | |
| Inventory in February | 154,000 litres |
| Ending work in process inventory | |
| (70% of the way through the bottling process) | 14,000 litres |

| **Costs in beginning work in process inventory** | | **Costs added during February** | |
|---|---|---|---|
| Transferred in | $1,760 | Transferred in* | $136,000 |
| Direct materials | 0 | Direct materials | 30,800 |
| Direct labour | 600 | Direct labour | 33,726 |
| Manufacturing overhead | 520 | Manufacturing overhead | 22,484 |
| Total beginning work in process inventory as of February 1 | $ 2,880 | Total costs added during February | $223,010 |

*S6-17 showed that Canadian Springs Filtration Department completed and transferred out 160,000 litres at a total cost of $136,000.

### S6-19 Compute equivalent units in second department

*(Learning Objectives 2 & 5)*

Refer to the Canadian Springs Bottling Department data set.

### Requirements

1. Draw a timeline similar to the one in Exhibit 6-10.
2. Complete the first two steps of the process costing procedure for the Bottling Department: Summarize the physical flow of units and then compute the equivalent units using the weighted average method of direct materials and conversion costs. Your answer should look similar to Exhibit 6-12.

**S6-20** **Continuation of S6-19: Compute cost per equivalent unit in second department** *(Learning Objective 5)*

Refer to the Canadian Springs Bottling Department data set and your answer to S6-19. Complete Steps 3 and 4 of the process costing procedure: Summarize total costs to account for and then compute the cost per equivalent unit for both direct materials and conversion costs. Your answer should look similar to Exhibit 6-13.

**S6-21** **Continuation of S6-19 and S6-20: Assign costs in second department** *(Learning Objective 5)*

Refer to the Canadian Springs Bottling Department data set and your answers to S6-19 and 6-20. Complete Step 5 of the process costing procedure: Assign costs to units completed and to units in ending inventory. Your answer should look similar to Exhibit 6-14.

**S6-22** **Continuation of S6-21: Record journal entry and post to T-account** *(Learning Objective 4)*

Refer to the Canadian Springs Bottling Department data set and your answer to S6-21.

**Requirements**

1. Prepare the journal entry to record the cost of units completed and transferred to finished goods.
2. Post all transactions to the "Work in Process Inventory—Bottling" T-account. What is the ending balance?

# EXERCISES Group A

**E6-23A** **Diagram flow of costs** *(Learning Objective 1)*

Sael Inc. produces kitchen cabinets in a three-stage process that includes milling, assembling, and finishing, in that order. Direct materials are added in the Milling and Finishing Departments. Direct labour and overhead are incurred in all three departments. The company's general ledger includes the following accounts:

| | |
|---|---|
| Cost of Goods Sold | Materials Inventory |
| Manufacturing Wages | Finished Goods Inventory |
| Work in Process Inventory—Milling | Manufacturing Overhead |
| Work in Process Inventory—Assembling | |
| Work in Process Inventory—Finishing | |

Outline the flow of costs through the company's accounts, including a brief description of each flow. Include a T-account for each account title given.

**E6-24A** **Analyze flow of costs through inventory T-accounts** *(Learning Objective 1)*

Warm Hearth Bakery mass-produces bread using three sequential processing departments: Mixing, Baking, and Packaging. The following transactions occurred during January:

| | |
|---|---:|
| 1. Direct materials used in the Packaging Department | $ 40,000 |
| 2. Costs assigned to units completed and transferred out of Mixing | 225,000 |
| 3. Direct labour incurred in the Mixing Department | 11,000 |
| 4. Beginning balance: Work in Process Inventory—Baking | 15,000 |
| 5. Manufacturing overhead allocated to the Baking Department | 75,000 |
| 6. Beginning balance: Finished Goods Inventory | 4,000 |
| 7. Costs assigned to units completed and transferred out of Baking | 301,000 |
| 8. Beginning balance: Work in Process Inventory—Mixing | 12,000 |
| 9. Direct labour incurred in the Packaging Department | 8,000 |
| 10. Manufacturing overhead allocated to the Mixing Department | 60,000 |
| 11. Direct materials used in the Mixing Department | 152,000 |

| | |
|---|---|
| 12. Beginning balance: Raw Materials Inventory | 23,000 |
| 13. Costs assigned to units completed and transferred out of Packaging | 381,000 |
| 14. Beginning balance: Work in Process Inventory—Packaging | 8,000 |
| 15. Purchases of Raw Materials | 170,000 |
| 16. Direct labour incurred in the Baking Department | 4,000 |
| 17. Manufacturing overhead allocated to the Packaging Department | 40,000 |
| 18. Cost of goods sold | 382,000 |

Note: No direct materials were used by the Baking Department.

**Requirements**

1. Post each of these transactions to the company's inventory T-accounts. You should set up separate T-accounts for the following:
   - Raw Materials Inventory
   - Work in Process Inventory—Mixing Department
   - Work in Process Inventory—Baking Department
   - Work in Process Inventory—Packaging Department
   - Finished Goods Inventory
2. Determine the balance at month-end in each of the inventory accounts.
3. Assume that 3,175,000 loaves of bread were completed and transferred out of the Packaging Department during the month. What was the cost per unit of making each loaf of bread (from start to finish)?

Check sum: Ending Work in Process Inventory—Mixing Department) is $10,000.

### E6-25A Summarize physical units and compute equivalent units (process costing Steps 1 and 2) *(Learning Objective 2)*

Alice's Apple Pies collected the following production information relating to June's baking operations:

| | Physical Units | Direct Materials (% complete) | Conversion Costs (% complete) |
|---|---|---|---|
| Beginning work in process | 200,000 | — | — |
| Ending work in process | 150,000 | 75% | 80% |
| Units started during the month | 1,000,000 | | |

**Requirements**

Complete the first two steps in the process costing procedure:

1. Summarize the flow of physical units.
2. Compute output in terms of equivalent units using the weighted average method (*Hint:* Your answer should look similar to Exhibit 6-5.)

Check sum: Finished goods inventory ending balance is $3,000.

### E6-26A Compute equivalent units *(Learning Objective 2)*

Lili Lime manufactures yoga mats. The Pressing Department had the following data from the end of the most recent period.

| | | % Complete | |
|---|---|---|---|
| | **Units** | **Materials** | **Conversion** |
| WIP, July 1 | 500 | 90% | 30% |
| Units started in production in July | 9,800 | | |
| Units completed and transferred to the next department | 10,000 | 100% | 100% |
| WIP, July 31 | 400 | 60% | 40% |

Calculate the equivalent units using both the weighted average and FIFO methods.

| Weighted Average | Materials | Conversion |
|---|---|---|
| Units transferred to the next department | | |
| WIP, July 31 | | |
| Total equivalent units | | |

| FIFO | Materials | Conversion |
|---|---|---|
| WIP, July 1 | | |
| Units started and completed | | |
| WIP, July 31 | | |
| Total equivalent units | | |

Check sum: Weighted average equivalent units (materials) is $10,240.

### E6-27A Compute equivalent units in a second processing department

*(Learning Objectives 2 & 5)*

Mogyardy's Mayonnaise uses a process costing system to determine its product's cost. The last of the three processes is packaging. The Packaging Department reported the following information for the month of May:

The units in ending work in process inventory were 90% complete with respect to direct materials but only 60% complete with respect to conversion.

| | | Equivalent Units | | |
|---|---|---|---|---|
| | Physical Units | Transferred-in | Direct Materials | Conversion Costs |
| Units to account for: | | | | |
| Beginning work in process .......... | 25,000 | | | |
| Transferred in during May .......... | 225,000 | | | |
| Total units to account for ............ | (a) | | | |
| Units accounted for: | | | | |
| Completed and transferred out | (b) | (d) | (g) | (j) |
| Ending work in process ............... | 30,000 | (e) | (h) | (k) |
| Total units accounted for: | (c) | | | |
| Total equivalent units ................. | | (f) | (i) | (l) |

Check sum: Total units to account for is $250,000.

**Requirement**

Summarize the flow of physical units and compute output in terms of equivalent units using the weighted average method in order to arrive at the missing figures (a) through (l).

### E6-28A Complete five-step procedure in first department *(Learning Objective 3)*

Rainbow Vision prepares and packages paint products. Rainbow Vision has two departments: Blending and Packaging. Direct materials are added at the beginning of the blending process (dyes) and at the end of the packaging process (cans). Conversion costs are added evenly throughout each process. Data from the month of May for the Blending Department are as follows:

| Litres: | |
|---|---|
| Beginning work in process inventory ............................................... | 0 |
| Started production ........................................................................ | 8,000 litres |
| Completed and transferred out to Packaging in May ............................ | 6,000 litres |
| Ending work in process inventory (30% of the way through the blending process) ................................................................ | 2,000 litres |

CHAPTER 6

| Costs: | |
|---|---|
| Beginning work in process inventory | $ 0 |
| Costs added during May: | |
| Direct materials (dyes) | 4,800 |
| Direct labour | 1,000 |
| Manufacturing overhead | 1,840 |
| Total costs added during May | $7,440 |

### Requirements

Check sum: Total equivalent units for conversion costs is $6,600.

1. Draw a timeline for the Blending Department similar to Exhibit 6-6.
2. Summarize the physical flow of units and compute total equivalent units using the weighted average method for direct materials and for conversion costs.
3. Summarize total costs to account for and find the cost per equivalent unit for direct materials and conversion costs.
4. Assign total costs to units (litres):
   a. Completed and transferred out to the Packaging Department
   b. In the Blending Department ending work in process inventory
5. What is the average cost per litre transferred out of the Blending Department to the Packaging Department? Why would Rainbow Vision's managers want to know this cost?

## E6-29A Continuation of E6-28A: journal entries *(Learning Objective 4)*

Return to the Blending Department data for Rainbow Vision in E6-28A.

### Requirements

Check sum: Raw materials is a credit in the amount of $4,800.

1. Present the journal entry to record the use of direct materials and direct labour and the allocation of manufacturing overhead to the Blending Department. Also, give the journal entry to record the costs of the litres completed and transferred out to the Packaging Department.
2. Post the journal entries to the Work in Process Inventory—Blending T-account. What is the ending balance?

## E6-30A Record journal entries *(Learning Objective 4)*

Record the following process costing transactions in the general journal:

a. Purchase of raw materials on account, $9,000
b. Requisition of direct materials to
   Assembly Department, $4,000
   Finishing Department, $2,000
c. Incurrence and payment of manufacturing labour, $10,800
d. Incurrence of manufacturing overhead costs:
   Property taxes—plant, $1,900
   Utilities—plant, $4,500
   Insurance—plant, $1,100
   Depreciation—plant, $3,400
e. Assignment of conversion costs to the Assembly Department:
   Direct labour, $4,700
   Manufacturing overhead, $2,900
f. Assignment of conversion costs to the Finishing Department:
   Direct labour, $4,400
   Manufacturing overhead, $6,200
g. Cost of goods completed and transferred out of the Assembly Department to the Finishing Department, $10,250
h. Cost of goods completed and transferred out of the Finishing Department into Finished Goods Inventory, $15,600

**E6-31A Compute equivalent units using the weighted average method and assign costs** *(Learning Objectives 2, 3, & 4)*

The Assembly Department of ZAP Surge Protectors began September with no work in process inventory. During the month, production that cost $39,860 (direct materials, $9,900, and conversion costs, $29,960) was started on 23,000 units. ZAP completed and transferred to the Testing Department a total of 15,000 units. The ending work in process inventory was 37.5% complete as to direct materials and 80% complete as to conversion work.

### Requirements

1. Compute the equivalent units for direct materials and conversion costs.
2. Compute the cost per equivalent unit.
3. Assign the costs to units completed and transferred out and ending work in process inventory.
4. Record the journal entry for the costs transferred out of the Assembly Department to the Testing Department.
5. Post all of the transactions in the Work in Process Inventory—Assembly T-account. What is the ending balance?

Check sum: Cost per equivalent unit for direct materials is $.55.

**E6-32A Complete five-step procedure in first department** *(Learning Objective 3)*

Gaspereau Vineyards in Nova Scotia has two departments: Fermenting and Packaging. Direct materials are added at the beginning of the fermenting process (grapes) and at the end of the packaging process (bottles). Conversion costs are added evenly throughout each process. Data from the month of March for the Fermenting Department are as follows:

| | |
|---|---|
| Litres: | |
| Beginning work in process inventory | 2,000 litres |
| Started production | 6,000 litres |
| Completed and transferred out to Packaging in March | 6,550 litres |
| Ending work in process inventory (80% of the way through the fermenting process) | 1,450 litres |
| Costs: | |
| Beginning work in process inventory ($2,800 of direct materials and $2,855 of conversion cost) | $ 5,655 |
| Costs added during March: | |
| Direct materials | 8,800 |
| Direct labour | 1,600 |
| Manufacturing overhead | 2,484 |
| Total costs added during March | $12,884 |

### Requirements

1. Draw a timeline for the Fermenting Department similar to Exhibit 6-6.
2. Summarize the flow of physical units and compute the total equivalent units using the weighted average method.
3. Summarize total costs to account for and compute the cost per equivalent unit for direct materials and conversion costs.
4. Assign total costs to units (litres):
   a. Completed and transferred out to the Packaging Department
   b. In the Fermenting Department ending work in process inventory
5. What is the average cost per litre transferred out of Fermenting into Packaging? Why would Gaspereau Vineyard's managers want to know this cost?

Check sum: Average cost per litre is $2.35.

### E6-33A Continuation of E6-32A: journal entries *(Learning Objective 4)*

Return to the Fermenting Department data for Gaspereau Vineyard in E6-32A.

#### Requirements

1. Present the journal entries to record the use of direct materials and direct labour and the allocation of manufacturing overhead to the Fermenting Department. Also, give the journal entry to record the cost of the litres completed and transferred out to the Packaging Department.
2. Post the journal entries to the Work in Process Inventory—Fermenting T-account. What is the ending balance?

### E6-34A Sustainability and process costing *(Learning Objective 3)*

Woodlan Industries manufactures plastic bottles for the food industry. On average, Sylvan pays $75 per tonne for its plastics. Sylvan's waste disposal company has increased its waste disposal charge to $55 per tonne for solid and inert waste. Sylvan generates a total of 500 tonnes of waste per month.

Woodlan managers have been evaluating the production processes for areas to cut waste. In the process of making plastic bottles, a certain amount of machine "drool" occurs. Machine drool is the excess plastic that drips off the machine between moulds. In the past, Woodlan has discarded the machine drool. In an average month, 150 tonnes of machine drool is generated. Management has arrived at three possible courses of action for the machine drool issue:

1. Do nothing and pay the increased waste disposal charge.
2. Sell the machine drool waste to a local recycler for $12 per tonne.
3. Re-engineer the production process at an annual cost of $50,000. This change in the production process would reduce the amount of machine drool by 50% each month. The remaining machine drool would then be sold to a local recycler for $12 per tonne.

#### Requirements

Check sum: Total annual costs for Option #1 are $234,000.

1. What is the annual cost of the machine drool currently? Include both the original plastic cost and the waste disposal cost.
2. How much would the company save per year (net) if the machine drool were to be sold to the local recycler?
3. How much would the company save per year (net) if the production process were to be re-engineered?
4. What do you think the company should do? Explain your rationale.

### E6-35A Complete five-step procedure and journalize result *(Learning Objectives 3 & 4)*

The following information was taken from the ledger of Wawa Roping:

| Work in Process—Forming | | | |
|---|---|---|---|
| Beginning inventory, October 1 | $ 47,820 | Transferred to Finishing | $? |
| Direct materials | 193,620 | | |
| Conversion costs | 168,640 | | |
| Ending inventory | ? | | |



The Forming Department had 10,000 partially complete units in beginning work in process inventory. The department started work on 70,000 units during the month and ended the month with 8,000 units still in work in process. These unfinished units were 60% complete as to direct materials but 20% complete as to conversion work. The beginning balance of $47,820 consisted of $21,420 of direct materials and $26,400 of conversion costs.

Check sum: Total units to account for in the Mixing Department are 90,000.

#### Requirements

Journalize the transfer of costs to the Finishing Department. (*Hint:* Complete the five-step process costing procedure to determine how much cost to transfer.)

**E6-36A Compute equivalent units in two later departments**
*(Learning Objectives 2 & 5)*

Selected production and cost data of Martha's Fudge follow for May:

| | Flow of Physical Units | |
|---|---|---|
| **Flow of Production** | **Mixing Department** | **Heating Department** |
| Units to account for: | | |
| Beginning work in process, May 1 | 20,000 | 6,000 |
| Transferred in during May | 70,000 | 80,000 |
| Total physical units to account for | 90,000 | 86,000 |
| Units accounted for: | | |
| Completed and transferred out during May | 80,000 | 76,000 |
| Ending work in process, May 31 | 10,000 | 10,000 |
| Total physical units accounted for | 90,000 | 86,000 |

On May 31, the Mixing Department's ending work in process inventory was 70% complete as to materials and 20% complete as to conversion costs.

On May 31, the Heating Department's ending work in process inventory was 65% complete as to materials and 55% complete as to conversion costs.

**Requirement**

Compute the equivalent units using the weighted average method for transferred-in costs, direct materials, and conversion costs for both the Mixing and the Heating Departments.

**E6-37A Complete five-step procedure in second department**
*(Learning Objective 5)*

Alpha Semiconductors experienced the following activity in its Photolithography Department during December. Materials are added at the beginning of the photolithography process.

| | |
|---|---|
| Units: | |
| Work in process, December 1 (80% of the way through the process | 8,000 units |
| Transferred in from the Polishing and Cutting Department during December | 27,000 units |
| Completed during December | ? units |
| Work in process, December 31 (70% of the way through the process) | 9,000 units |
| Costs: | |
| Work in process, December 1 (transferred-in costs, $20,050; direct materials costs, $20,250; and conversion costs, $19,816) | $60,116 |
| Transferred in from the Polishing and Cutting Department during December | 97,200 |
| Direct materials added during December | 74,250 |
| Conversion costs added during December | 90,650 |

**Requirements**

(*Hint:* Use Exhibits 6-12, 6-13, and 6-14 as guides if needed.)

1. Summarize flow of physical units and compute total equivalent units using the weighted average method for three cost categories: transferred-in, direct materials, and conversion costs.
2. Summarize total costs to account for and compute the cost per equivalent unit for each cost category.
3. Assign total costs to (a) units completed and transferred to Finished Goods Inventory and (b) units in December 31 Work in Process Inventory.

Check sum: Total costs accounted for is $322,216.

# EXERCISES Group B

## E6-38B Diagram flow of costs *(Learning Objective 1)*

Wood Again Inc. produces tables from recycled wood in a three-stage process that includes cutting, assembling, and finishing, in that order. Direct materials are added in the Cutting and Finishing Departments. Direct labour and overhead are incurred in all three departments. The company's general ledger includes the following accounts:

| | |
|---|---|
| Cost of Goods Sold | Materials Inventory |
| Manufacturing Wages | Finished Goods Inventory |
| Work in Process Inventory—Cutting | Manufacturing Overhead |
| Work in Process Inventory—Assembling | |
| Work in Process Inventory—Finishing | |

Outline the flow of costs through the company's accounts, including a brief description of each flow. Include a T-account for each account title given.

## E6-39B Analyze flow of costs through inventory T-accounts *(Learning Objective 1)*

Best Friends Bakery mass-produces bread using three sequential processing departments: Mixing, Baking, and Packaging. The following transactions occurred during May:

| | |
|---|---|
| 1. Direct materials used in the Packaging Department | $ 35,000 |
| 2. Costs assigned to units completed and transferred out of Mixing | 228,000 |
| 3. Direct labour incurred in the Mixing Department | 11,600 |
| 4. Beginning balance: Work in Process Inventory—Baking | 15,600 |
| 5. Manufacturing overhead allocated to the Baking Department | 70,000 |
| 6. Beginning balance: Finished Goods Inventory | 4,700 |
| 7. Costs assigned to units completed and transferred out of Baking | 302,000 |
| 8. Beginning balance: Work in Process Inventory—Mixing | 12,700 |
| 9. Direct labour incurred in the Packaging Department | 8,400 |
| 10. Manufacturing overhead allocated to the Mixing Department | 62,000 |
| 11. Direct materials used in the Mixing Department | 153,000 |
| 12. Beginning balance: Raw Materials Inventory | 23,500 |
| 13. Costs assigned to units completed and transferred out of Packaging | 382,000 |
| 14. Beginning balance: Work in Process Inventory—Packaging | 8,000 |
| 15. Purchases of Raw Materials | 178,000 |
| 16. Direct labour incurred in the Baking Department | 4,000 |
| 17. Manufacturing overhead allocated to the Packaging Department | 43,000 |
| 18. Cost of goods sold | 383,000 |

### Requirements

1. Post each of these transactions to the company's inventory T-accounts. You should set up separate T-accounts for the following:
   - Raw Materials Inventory
   - Work in Process Inventory—Mixing Department
   - Work in Process Inventory—Baking Department
   - Work in Process Inventory—Packaging Department
   - Finished Goods Inventory
2. Determine the balance at month-end in each of the inventory accounts.

3. Assume 3,375,000 loaves of bread were completed and transferred out of the Packaging Department during the month. What was the cost per unit of making each loaf of bread (from start to finish)?

### E6-40B Summarize physical units and compute equivalent units (process costing Steps 1 and 2) *(Learning Objective 2)*

Nigel's Pecan Pies collected the following production information relating to September's baking operations:

| | Physical Units | Direct Materials (% complete) | Conversion Costs (% complete) |
|---|---|---|---|
| Beginning work in process ................ | 206,000 | — | — |
| Ending work in process .................... | 156,000 | 65% | 80% |
| Units started during the month .......... | 1,015,000 | | |

**Requirements**

Complete the first two steps in the process costing procedure:

1. Summarize the flow of physical units.
2. Compute output in terms of equivalent units using the weighted average method. (*Hint:* Your answer should look similar to Exhibit 6-5).

### E6-41B Compute equivalent units *(Learning Objective 2)*

Vroom Inc. makes miniature toy cars. The Plastic Moulding Department had the following data from the most recent period end.

| | | % Complete | |
|---|---|---|---|
| | **Units** | **Materials** | **Conversion** |
| WIP, February 1 | 8,000 | 20% | 10% |
| Units started in production in Feb. | 124,000 | | |
| Units completed and transferred to the next department | 125,000 | 100% | 100% |
| WIP, February 28 | 7,000 | 50% | 20% |

Calculate the equivalent units using both the weighted average and FIFO methods.

| **Weighted Average** | **Materials** | **Conversion** |
|---|---|---|
| Units transferred to the next department | | |
| WIP, February 28 | | |
| Total equivalent units | | |

| **FIFO** | **Materials** | **Conversion** |
|---|---|---|
| WIP, February 1 | | |
| Units started and completed | | |
| WIP, February 28 | | |
| Total equivalent units | | |

Check sum: Total equivalent units of materials under FIFO is 122,100.

CHAPTER 6

### E6-42B Compute equivalent units in a second processing department *(Learning Objectives 2 & 5)*

Maxwell's Mayonnaise uses a process costing system to determine its product's cost. The last of the three processes is packaging. The Packaging Department reported the following information for the month of July:

| | | Equivalent Units | | |
|---|---|---|---|---|
| | Physical Units | Transferred-in | Direct Materials | Conversion Costs |
| Units to account for: | | | | |
| Beginning work in process ........... | 23,000 | | | |
| Transferred in during July ............ | 229,000 | | | |
| Total units to account for ............. | (a) | | | |
| Units accounted for: | | | | |
| Completed and transferred out | (b) | (d) | (g) | (j) |
| Ending work in process................ | 28,000 | (e) | (h) | (k) |
| Total units accounted for: | (c) | | | |
| Total Equivalent Units.................... | | (f) | (i) | (l) |

The units in ending work in process inventory were 90% complete with respect to direct materials, but only 60% complete with respect to conversion.

**Requirement**

Summarize the flow of physical units and compute output in terms of equivalent units in order to arrive at the missing figures (a) through (l).

### E6-43B Complete five-step procedure in first department *(Learning Objective 3)*

You Can Paint Too prepares and packages paint products. You Can Paint Too has two departments: Blending and Packaging. Direct materials are added at the beginning of the blending process (dyes) and at the end of the packaging process (cans). Conversion costs are added evenly throughout each process. Data from the month of May for the Blending Department are as follows:

| | |
|---|---|
| Litres: | |
| Beginning work in process inventory.................................................. | 0 |
| Started production ........................................................................ | 8,500 litres |
| Completed and transferred out to Packaging in May............................ | 6,400 litres |
| Ending work in process inventory (30% of the way through the blending process)...................................................... | 2,100 litres |
| Costs: | |
| Beginning work in process inventory.................................................. | $ 0 |
| Costs added during May: | |
| Direct materials (dyes)..................................................................... | 4,200 |
| Direct labour.................................................................................... | 750 |
| Manufacturing overhead.................................................................. | 2,500 |
| Total costs added during May............................................................ | $7,450 |

**Requirements**

1. Fill in the time line for the Blending Department similar to Exhibit 6-6.
2. Summarize the physical flow of units and compute total equivalent units using the weighted average method for direct materials and for conversion costs.
3. Summarize total costs to account for and find the cost per equivalent unit for direct materials and for conversion costs.
4. Assign total costs to units (litres):
   a. Completed and transferred out to the Packaging Department
   b. In the Blending Department ending work in process inventory
5. What is the average cost per litre transferred out of the Blending Department to the Packaging Department? Why would You Can Paint Too's managers want to know this cost?

Check sum: The average cost per litre is $.95 litre.

**E6-44B Continuation of E6-43B: journal entries** *(Learning Objective 4)*

Return to the Blending Department data for You Can Paint Too in E6-43B.

YOU CAN PAINT TOO
BLENDING DEPARTMENT
Assignment of Costs

| Assign Costs | Direct Materials | Conversion Costs | | Total |
|---|---|---|---|---|
| Completed and transferred out | [6,400 × ($0.49 + $0.46)] | | = | $6,080 |
| Ending work in process inventory: | | | | |
| Direct materials | [2,100 × $0.49] | | = | 1,029 |
| Conversion costs | | [630 × $0.46] | = | 290 |
| Total ending work in process inventory, May 31 | | | | 1,319 |
| Total cost accounted for | | | | $7,399 |

**Requirements**

1. Present the journal entry to record the use of direct materials and direct labour and the allocation of manufacturing overhead to the Blending Department. Also, give the journal entry to record the costs of the litres completed and transferred out to the Packaging Department.
2. Post the journal entries to the Work in Process Inventory—Blending T-account. What is the ending balance?

**E6-45B Sustainability and process costing** *(Learning Objective 3)*

Redstar Plastics manufactures plastic bottles for the food industry. On average, Redstar Plastics pays $95 per tonne for its plastics. Redstar's waste disposal company has increased its waste disposal charge to $65 per tonne for solid and inert waste. Redstar generates a total of 1,000 tonnes of waste per month.

Redstar's managers have been evaluating the production processes for areas to cut waste. In the process of making plastic bottles, a certain amount of machine "drool" occurs. Machine drool is the excess plastic that drips off the machine between moulds. In the past, Redstar Plastics has discarded the machine drool. In an average month, 300 tonnes of machine drool are generated.

Management has arrived at three possible courses of action for the machine drool issue:

1. Do nothing and pay the increase waste disposal charge.
2. Sell the machine drool waste to a local recycler for $25 per tonne.
3. Re-engineer the production process at an annual cost of $120,000. This change in the production process would cause the amount of machine drool generated to be reduced by 50% each month. The remaining machine drool would then be sold to a local recycler for $25 per tonne.

**Requirements**

1. What is the annual cost of the machine drool currently? Include both the original plastics cost and the waste disposal cost.
2. How much would the company save per year (net) if the machine drool were to be sold to the local recycler?
3. How much would the company save per year (net) if the production process were to be re-engineered?
4. What do you think the company should do? Explain your rationale.

Check sum: The annual total cost for Option 3 is $321,000.



**E6-46B Record journal entries** *(Learning Objective 4)*

Record the following process costing transactions in the general journal:

a. Purchase of raw materials on account, $9,900
b. Requisition of direct materials to:
   Assembly Department, $4,500
   Finishing Department, $2,900

c. Incurrence and payment of manufacturing labour, $10,100

d. Incurrence of manufacturing overhead costs:
Property taxes—plant, $1,600
Utilities—plant, $4,600
Insurance—plant, $1,400
Depreciation—plant, $3,700

e. Assignment of conversion costs to the Assembly Department:
Direct labour, $5,000
Manufacturing overhead, $2,100

f. Assignment of conversion costs to the Finishing Department:
Direct labour, $4,200
Manufacturing overhead, $6,200

g. Cost of goods completed and transferred out of the Assembly Department to the Finishing Department, $10,500

h. Cost of goods completed and transferred out of the Finishing Department into Finished Goods Inventory, $15,500

### E6-47B Compute equivalent units using the weighted average method and assign costs *(Learning Objectives 2, 3, & 4)*

The Assembly Department of Best Surge Protectors began September with no work in process inventory. During the month, production that cost $41,400 (direct materials, $9,000, and conversion costs, $32,400) was started on 22,000 units. Best completed and transferred to the Testing Department a total of 17,000 units. The ending work in process inventory was 37.5% complete as to direct materials and 80% complete as to conversion work.

**Requirements**

Check sum: The cost per equivalent unit of direct materials is $.477.

1. Compute the equivalent units for direct materials and conversion costs.
2. Compute the cost per equivalent unit.
3. Assign the costs to units completed and transferred out and ending work in process inventory.
4. Record the journal entry for the costs transferred out of the Assembly Department to the Testing Department.
5. Post all of the transactions in the Work in Process Inventory—Assembly T-account. What is the ending balance?

### E6-48B Complete five-step procedure in first department *(Learning Objective 3)*

Petite Rivière Vineyard in Nova Scotia has two departments: Fermenting and Packaging. Direct materials are added at the beginning of the fermenting process (grapes) and at the end of the packaging process (bottles). Conversion costs are added evenly throughout each process. Data from the month of March for the Fermenting Department are as follows:

| | |
|---|---|
| Litres: | |
| Beginning work in process inventory | 2,000 litres |
| Started production | 6,000 litres |
| Completed and transferred out to Packaging in March | 6,500 litres |
| Ending work in process inventory (80% of the way through the fermenting process) | 1,500 litres |
| Costs: | |
| Beginning work in process inventory ($2,900 of direct materials and $3,000 of conversion cost) | $ 5,900 |
| Costs added during March: | |
| Direct materials | 10,300 |
| Direct labour | 2,000 |
| Manufacturing overhead | 4,100 |
| Total costs added during March | $16,400 |

**Requirements**

1. Draw a timeline for the Fermenting Department similar to Exhibit 6-6.
2. Summarize the flow of physical units and compute the total equivalent units using the weighted average method.
3. Summarize total costs to account for and compute the cost per equivalent unit for direct materials and conversion costs.
4. Assign total costs to units (litres):
   a. Completed and transferred out to the Packaging Department
   b. In the Fermenting Department ending work in process inventory
5. What is the average cost per litre transferred out of fermenting into packaging? Why would Petite Rivière's managers want to know this cost?

## E6-49B Continuation of E6-48B: journal entries *(Learning Objective 4)*

Return to the Fermenting Department data for Petite Rivière Vineyard in E6-48B, assuming the following information.

Check sum: The average cost per litre is $2.83 litre.

PETITE RIVIÈRE VINEYARD
FERMENTING DEPARTMENT
Assignment of Costs

| Assign Costs: | Direct Materials | Conversion Costs | | Total |
|---|---|---|---|---|
| Completed and transferred out | [6,500 × ($1.65 + $1.18)] | | = | $18,395 |
| Ending work in process inventory: | | | | |
| Direct materials | [1,500 × $1.65] | | = | 2,475 |
| Conversion costs | | [1.200 × $1.18] | = | 1,416 |
| Total ending work in process inventory, May 31 | | | | 3,891 |
| Total cost accounted for | | | | $22,286 |

**Requirements**

1. Present the journal entries to record the use of direct materials and direct labour and the allocation of manufacturing overhead to the Fermenting Department. Also, give the journal entry to record the cost of the litres completed and transferred out to the Packaging Department.
2. Post the journal entries to the Work in Process Inventory—Fermenting T-account. What is the ending balance?

## E6-50B Complete five-step procedure and journalize result *(Learning Objectives 3 & 4)*

The following information was taken from the ledger of Evans Roping:

| Work in Process—Forming | | | |
|---|---|---|---|
| Beginning inventory, October 1 | 47,200 | Transferred to Finishing | ? |
| Direct materials | 193,700 | | |
| Conversion costs | 168,500 | | |
| Ending inventory | ? | | |

The Forming Department had 8,000 partially complete units in beginning work in process inventory. The department started work on 69,000 units during the month and ended the month with 7,000 units still in work in process. These unfinished units were 60% complete as to direct materials but 20% complete as to conversion work. The beginning balance of $47,200 consisted of $21,000 of direct materials and $26,200 of conversion costs.

**Requirement**

Journalize the transfer of costs to the Finishing Department. (*Hint*: Complete the five-step process costing procedure to determine how much cost to transfer.)

### E6-51B Compute equivalent units in two later departments

*(Learning Objectives 2 & 5)*

Selected production and cost data of Abdi's Fudge follow for May:

| | Flow of Physical Units | |
|---|---|---|
| **Flow of Production** | **Mixing Department** | **Heating Department** |
| Units to account for: | | |
| Beginning work in process, May 1 | 24,000 | 6,000 |
| Transferred in during May | 79,000 | 84,000 |
| Total physical units to account for | 103,000 | 90,000 |
| Units accounted for: | | |
| Completed and transferred out during May | 89,000 | 78,000 |
| Ending work in process, May 31 | 14,000 | 12,000 |
| Total physical units accounted for | 103,000 | 90,000 |

On May 31, the Mixing Department's ending work in process inventory was 70% complete as to materials and 20% complete as to conversion costs. On May 31, the Heating Department's ending work in process inventory was 75% complete as to materials and 65% complete as to conversion costs.

Check sum: The total equivalent units for transferred in costs is 103,000 units.

**Requirement**

Compute the equivalent units for transferred-in costs, direct materials, and conversion costs for both the Mixing and the Heating Departments.

### E6-52B Complete five-step procedure in second department

*(Learning Objective 5)*

Brookstein Semiconductors experienced the following activity in its Photolithography Department during December. Materials are added at the beginning of the photolithography process.

| | |
|---|---|
| Units: | |
| Work in process, December 1 (80% of the way through the process | 5,500 units |
| Transferred in from the Polishing and Cutting Department during December | 30,000 units |
| Completed during December | ? units |
| Work in process, December 31 (70% of the way through the process) | 9,000 units |
| Costs: | |
| Work in process, December 1 (transferred-in costs, $20,200; direct materials costs, $20,400; and conversion costs, $19,100) | $59,700 |
| Transferred in from the Polishing and Cutting Department during December | 97,200 |
| Direct materials added during December | 73,360 |
| Conversion costs added during December | 90,500 |

**Requirements**

(*Hint*: Use Exhibits 6-12, 6-13, and 6-14 as guides if needed.)

1. Summarize flow of physical units and compute total equivalent units using the weighted average method for three cost categories: transferred in, direct materials, and conversion costs.

2. Summarize total costs to account for and compute the cost per equivalent unit for each cost category.
3. Assign total costs to (a) units completed and transferred to finished goods inventory and (b) units in December 31 work in process inventory.

Check sum: The total costs accounted for are $320,760.

# PROBLEMS Group A

## P6-53A Process costing in a single processing department

*(Learning Objectives 1, 2, & 3)*

Winter Lips produces a lip balm used for cold-weather sports. The balm is manufactured in a single processing department. No lip balm was in process on May 31, and Winter Lips started production on 20,400 lip balm tubes during June. Direct materials are added at the beginning of the process, but conversion costs are incurred evenly throughout the process. Completed production for June totalled 15,200 units. The June 30 work in process was 40% of the way through the production process. Direct materials costing $4,080 were placed in production during June, and direct labour of $3,315 and manufacturing overhead of $1,005 were assigned to the process.

### Requirements

1. Draw a timeline for Winter Lips that is similar to Exhibit 6-6.
2. Use the timeline to help you compute the total equivalent units using the weighted average method and the cost per equivalent unit for June.
3. Assign total costs to (a) units completed and transferred to Finished Goods and (b) units still in process at June 30.
4. Prepare a T-account for work in process inventory to show activity during June, including the June 30 balance.

## P6-54A Process costing in a first department *(Learning Objectives 1, 3, & 4)*

The Newfoundland Furniture Company produces dining tables in a three-stage process: sawing, assembly, and staining. Costs incurred in the Sawing Department during September are summarized as follows:

| Work in Process Inventory—Sawing | | |
|---|---|---|
| September 1 balance | 0 | |
| Direct materials | 1,860,000 | |
| Direct labour | 139,100 | |
| Manufacturing overhead | 153,400 | |

Direct materials (lumber) are added at the beginning of the sawing process, while conversion costs are incurred evenly throughout the process. September activity in the Sawing Department included sawing of 11,000 metres of lumber, which were transferred to the Assembly Department. Also, work began on 1,000 metres of lumber, which on September 30 were 70% of the way through the sawing process.

### Requirements

1. Draw a timeline for the Sawing Department similar to Exhibit 6-6.
2. Use the timeline to help you compute the number of equivalent units and the cost per equivalent unit in the Sawing Department for September.
3. Show that the sum of (a) cost of goods transferred out of the Sawing Department and (b) ending Work in Process Inventory—Sawing equals the total cost accumulated in the department during September.
4. Journalize all transactions affecting the company's sawing process during September, including those already posted.

**P6-55A Five-step process: materials added at different points**
*(Learning Objectives 1, 2, & 3)*

Kun Pow produces canned chicken à la king. The chicken à la king passes through three departments: Mixing, Retort (sterilization), and Packing. In the Mixing Department, chicken and cream are added at the beginning of the process, the mixture is partly cooked, and chopped green peppers and mushrooms are added at the end of the process. Conversion costs are added evenly throughout the mixing process. November data from the Mixing Department are as follows:

| Litres | | Costs | |
|---|---|---|---|
| Beginning work in process inventory | 0 litres | Beginning work in process inventory | $ 0 |
| Started production | 15,000 litres | Costs added during November: | |
| Completed and transferred out to Retort in November | 12,900 litres | Chicken | 12,500 |
| | | Cream | 4,000 |
| Ending work in process inventory (60% of the way through the mixing process) | 2,100 litres | Green peppers and mushrooms | 11,610 |
| | | Direct labour | 11,108 |
| | | Manufacturing overhead | 3,052 |
| | | Total costs | $42,270 |

**Requirements**

1. Draw a timeline for the Mixing Department similar to Exhibit 6-6.
2. Use the timeline to help you summarize the flow of physical units and compute the equivalent units. (*Hint:* Each direct material added at a different point in the production process requires its own equivalent-unit computation.)
3. Compute the cost per equivalent units using the weighted average method for each cost category.
4. Compute the total costs of the units (litres):
   a. Completed and transferred out to the Retort Department
   b. In the Mixing Department's ending work in process inventory

**P6-56A Prepare a production cost report and journal entries**
*(Learning Objectives 4 & 5)*

Off Road manufactures auto roof racks in a two-stage process that includes shaping and plating. Steel alloy is the basic raw material of the shaping process. The steel is moulded according to the design specifications of automobile manufacturers (Ford and General Motors). The Plating Department then adds an anodized finish.

At March 31, before recording the transfer of cost from the Plating Department to Finished Goods Inventory, the Off Road general ledger included the following account:

| Work in Process Inventory—Plating | | |
|---|---|---|
| March 1 balance | 30,480 | |
| Transferred in from Shaping | 36,000 | |
| Direct materials | 24,200 | |
| Direct labour | 21,732 | |
| Manufacturing overhead | 35,388 | |

The direct materials (rubber pads) are added at the end of the plating process. Conversion costs are incurred evenly throughout the process. Work in process of the Plating Department on March 1 consisted of 1,200 racks. The $30,480 beginning balance of Work in Process—Plating includes $18,000 of transferred-in cost and $12,480 of conversion cost. During March, 2,400 racks were transferred in from the Shaping Department. The Plating Department transferred 2,200 racks to finished goods inventory in March and 1,400 were still in process on March 31. This ending inventory was 50% of the way through the plating process.

### Requirements

1. Draw a timeline for the Plating Department, similar to Exhibit 6-10.
2. Prepare the March production cost report for the Plating Department.
3. Journalize all transactions affecting the Plating Department during March, including the entries that have already been posted.

### P6-57A Complete five-step process in a later department (equivalent units using the weighted average method) *(Learning Objective 5)*

Sidcrome uses three departments to produce plastic handles for screwdrivers: Mixing, Moulding, and Drying. The Assembly Department attaches the screwdriver shanks to the handles.

Sidcrome's Drying Department requires no direct materials. Conversion costs are incurred evenly throughout the drying process. Other process costing information follows:

| | |
|---|---|
| Units: | |
| Beginning work in process | 7,000 units |
| Transferred in from the Moulding Department during the period | 28,000 units |
| Completed during the period | 16,000 units |
| Ending work in process (20% complete as to conversion work) | 19,000 units |
| Costs: | |
| Beginning work in process (transferred in costs, \$140; conversion cost, \$231) | \$371 |
| Transferred in from the Moulding Department during the period | 4,760 |
| Conversion costs added during the period | 1,947 |

After the drying process, the screwdrivers are completed by assembling the handles and shanks and packaging for shipment to retail outlets.

### Requirements

1. Draw a timeline of the Drying Department's process, similar to the one in Exhibit 6-10.
2. Use the timeline to compute the number of equivalent units of work performed by the Drying Department during the period, the cost per equivalent unit, and the total costs to account for.
3. Assign total costs to (a) units completed and transferred to the assembly operation and (b) units in the Drying Department's ending work in process inventory.

## PROBLEMS Group B

### P6-58B Process costing in a single processing department *(Learning Objectives 1, 2, & 3)*

Beautiful Lips produces a lip balm to prevent chapped lips. The balm is manufactured in a single processing department. No lip balm was in process on May 31, and Beautiful Lips started production on 20,100 lip balm tubes during June. Direct materials are added at the beginning of the process, but conversion costs are incurred evenly throughout the process. Completed production for June totalled 15,500 units. The June 30 work in process was 45% of the way through the production process. Direct materials costing \$4,060 were placed in production during June, and direct labour of \$3,375 and manufacturing overhead of \$2,425 were assigned to the process.

### Requirements

1. Draw the timeline for Beautiful Lips.
2. Use the timeline to help you compute the total equivalent units and the cost per equivalent unit for June.

3. Assign total costs to (a) units completed and transferred to Finished Goods and (b) units still in process at June 30.
4. Prepare a T-account for work in process inventory to show activity during June, including the June 30 balance.

## P6-59B Process costing in a first department

*(Learning Objectives 1, 3, & 4)*

The Yukon Table Company produces dining tables in a three-stage process: sawing, assembly, and staining. Costs incurred in the Sawing Department during September are summarized as follows:

| Work in Process Inventory—Sawing | | |
|---|---|---|
| September 1 balance | 0 | |
| Direct materials | 1,863,000 | |
| Direct labour | 137,100 | |
| Manufacturing overhead | 157,400 | |

Direct materials (lumber) are added at the beginning of the sawing process, while conversion costs are incurred evenly throughout the process. September activity in the Sawing Department included sawing of 10,000 metres of lumber, which were transferred to the Assembly Department. Also, work began on 3,500 metres of lumber, which on September 30 were 80% of the way through the sawing process.

### Requirements

1. Draw a timeline for the Sawing Department similar to Exhibit 6-6.
2. Use the timeline to help you compute the number of equivalent units using the weighted average method and the cost per equivalent unit in the Sawing Department for September.
3. Show that the sum of (a) cost of goods transferred out of the Sawing Department and (b) ending "Work in Process Inventory—Sawing" equals the total cost accumulated in the department during September.
4. Journalize all transactions affecting the company's sawing process during September, including those already posted.

## P6-60B Five-step process: materials added at different points

*(Learning Objectives 1, 2, & 3)*

Happy Giant produces canned chicken à la king. The chicken à la king passes through three departments: Mixing, Retort (sterilization), and Packing. In the Mixing Department, chicken and cream are added at the beginning of the process, the mixture is partly cooked, and chopped green peppers and mushrooms are added at the end of the process. Conversion costs are added evenly throughout the mixing process. November data from the Mixing Department are as follows:

| Litres | | Costs | |
|---|---|---|---|
| Beginning work in process inventory | 0 litres | Beginning work in process inventory | $ 0 |
| Started production | 14,800 litres | Costs added during November: | |
| Completed and transferred out to Retort in November | 13,200 litres | Chicken | 12,500 |
| | | Cream | 4,200 |
| Ending work in process inventory (60% of the way through the mixing process) | 1,600 litres | Green peppers and mushrooms | 11,110 |
| | | Direct labour | 11,808 |
| | | Manufacturing overhead | 3,112 |
| | | Total costs | $42,730 |

**Requirements**

1. Draw a timeline for the Mixing Department similar to Exhibit 6-6.
2. Use the timeline to help you summarize the flow of physical units and compute the equivalent units. (*Hint:* Each direct material added at a different point in the production process requires its own equivalent-unit computation.)
3. Compute the cost per equivalent units using the weighted average method for each cost category.
4. Compute the total costs of the units (litres):
   a. Completed and transferred out to the Retort Department
   b. In the Mixing Department's ending work in process inventory

## P6-61B Prepare a production cost report and journal entries

*(Learning Objectives 4 & 5)*

Classic Accessories manufactures auto roof racks in a two-stage process that includes shaping and plating. Steel alloy is the basic raw material of the shaping process. The steel is moulded according to the design specifications of automobile manufacturers (Ford and General Motors). The Plating Department then adds an anodized finish.

At March 31, before recording the transfer of cost from the Plating Department to Finished Goods Inventory, the Classic Accessories general ledger included the following account:

| Work in Process Inventory—Plating | | |
|---|---|---|
| March 1 balance | 26,370 | |
| Transferred in from Shaping | 28,800 | |
| Direct materials | 28,600 | |
| Direct labour | 20,867 | |
| Manufacturing overhead | 36,763 | |

The direct materials (rubber pads) are added at the end of the plating process. Conversion costs are incurred evenly throughout the process. Work in process of the Plating Department on March 1 consisted of 600 racks. The $26,370 beginning balance of Work in Process—Plating includes $14,400 of transferred-in cost and $11,970 of conversion cost. During March, 3,000 racks were transferred in from the Shaping Department. The Plating Department transferred 2,200 racks to Finished Goods Inventory in March and 1,400 were still in process on March 31. This ending inventory was 50% of the way through the plating process.

**Requirements**

1. Draw a timeline for the Plating Department, similar to Exhibit 6-10.
2. Prepare the March production cost report for the Plating Department.
3. Journalize all transactions affecting the Plating Department during March, including the entries that have already been posted.

## P6-62B Complete five-step process in a later department

*(Learning Objective 5)*

Brookman uses three departments to produce plastic handles for screwdrivers: Mixing, Moulding, and Drying. The Assembly Department attaches the screwdriver shanks to the handles.

Brookman's Drying Department requires no direct materials. Conversion costs are incurred evenly throughout the drying process. Other process costing information follows:

| | |
|---|---|
| Units: | |
| Beginning work in process | 8,000 units |
| Transferred in from the Moulding Department during the period | 29,000 units |
| Completed during the period | 17,000 units |
| Ending work in process (20% complete as to conversion work) | 20,000 units |
| Costs: | |
| Beginning work in process (transferred-in costs, $120; conversion cost, $240) | $ 360 |
| Transferred in from the Moulding Department during the period | 5,800 |
| Conversion costs added during the period | 2,700 |

After the drying process, the screwdrivers are completed by assembling the handles and shanks and packaging them for shipment to retail outlets.

## Requirements

1. Draw a timeline of the Drying Department's process, similar to the one in Exhibit 6-10.
2. Use the timeline to compute the number of equivalent units of work performed by the Drying Department during the period, the cost per equivalent unit, and the total costs to account for.
3. Assign total costs to (a) units completed and transferred to the assembly operation and (b) units in the Drying Department's ending work in process inventory.

# CAPSTONE APPLICATION PROBLEMS

## APPLICATION QUESTION

### A6-63 Cost per unit and gross profit *(Learning Objective 5)*

Yaovi Akpawu operates Yaovi's Cricket Farm in Thunder Bay, Ontario. Yaovi's raises about 18 million crickets a month. Most are sold to pet stores at $12.60 for a box of 1,000 crickets. Pet stores sell the crickets for $0.05 to $0.10 each as live feed for reptiles.

Raising crickets requires a two-step process: incubation and brooding. In the first process, employees place cricket eggs on mounds of peat moss to hatch. In the second process, employees move the newly hatched crickets into large boxes filled with cardboard dividers. Depending on the desired size, the crickets spend approximately 2 weeks in brooding before being shipped to pet stores. In the brooding process, Yaovi's crickets consume about 16 tonnes of food and produce 12 tonnes of manure.

Akpawu has invested $400,000 in the cricket farm, and he had hoped to earn a 24% annual rate of return, which works out to a 2% monthly return on his investment. After looking at the farm's bank balance, Akpawu fears he is not achieving this return. To get more accurate information on the farm's performance, Akpawu bought new accounting software that provides weighted-average process cost information. After Akpawu input the data, the software provided the following reports. However, Akpawu needs help interpreting these reports.

Akpawu does know that a unit of production is a box of 1,000 crickets. For example, in June's report, the 7,000 physical units of beginning work in process inventory are 7,000 boxes (each one of the 7,000 boxes contains 1,000 immature crickets). The finished goods inventory is zero because the crickets ship out as soon as they reach the required size. Monthly operating expenses total $2,000 (in addition to the costs that follow).

**YAOVI'S CRICKET FARM**
**Brooding Department**
**Production Cost Report (part 1 of 2)**
Month Ended June 30

| | | Equivalent Units | | |
|---|---|---|---|---|
| **Flow of Production** | **Flow of Physical Units** | **Transferred-in** | **Direct Materials** | **Conversion Costs** |
| Units to account for: | | | | |
| Beginning work in process inventory, June 1 | | | | |
| Transferred in during June | 7,000 | | | |
| Total units to account for | 21,000 | | | |
| Units accounted for: | 28,000 | | | |
| Completed and shipped out during June | | | | |
| Ending work in process, June 30 | 19,000 | 19,000 | 19,000 | 19,000 |
| Total physical units accounted for | 9,000 | 9,000 | 7,200 | 3,600 |
| Total equivalent units | 28,000 | | | |
| | | 28,000 | 26,200 | 22,600 |

**YAOVI'S CRICKET FARM**
**Brooding Department**
**Production Cost Report (part 2 of 2)**
Month Ended June 30

| | Transferred-in | Direct Materials | Conversion Costs | Total |
|---|---|---|---|---|
| Unit costs: | | | | |
| Beginning work in process, June 1 | $21,000 | $ 39,940 | $ 5,020 | $ 65,960 |
| Costs added during June | 46,200 | 156,560 | 51,480 | 254,240 |
| Total costs to account for | $67,200 | $196,500 | $56,500 | $320,200 |
| Divide by total equivalent units | ÷ 28,000 | ÷ 26,200 | ÷ 22,600 | |
| Cost per equivalent unit | $ 2.40 | $ 7.50 | $ 2.50 | |
| Assignment of total cost: | | | | |
| Units completed and shipped out during June | [19,000 × ($2.40 + $7.50 + $2.50)] | | | $235,600 |
| Ending work in process, June 30: | | | | |
| Transferred-in costs | [9,000 × $2.40] | | | 21,600 |
| Direct materials | | [7,200 × $7.50] | | 54,000 |
| Conversion costs | | | [3,600 × $2.50] | 9,000 |
| Total ending work in process, June 30 | | | | 84,600 |
| Total cost accounted for | | | | $320,200 |

### Requirements

Yaovi Akpawu has the following questions about the farm's performance during June:

1. What is the cost per box of crickets sold? (*Hint:* This is the cost of the boxes completed and shipped out of brooding.)
2. What is the gross profit per box?
3. How much operating income did Yaovi's Cricket Farm make in June?
4. What is the return on Akpawu's investment of $400,000 for the month of June? (Compute this as June's operating income divided by Akpawu's $400,000 investment, expressed as a percentage.)
5. What monthly operating income would provide a 2% monthly rate of return? What price per box would Yaovi's Cricket Farm have had to charge in June to achieve a 2% monthly rate of return?

# CASE ASSIGNMENT

*Source:* paulos1/Fotolia

## C6-64 Boggs and Button Custom Guitars

Walter Boggs and Sydney Button have been friends their whole lives. They started playing guitar as young boys and performed together for 30 years all over the world as a singer/

songwriter duo. They never struck it rich, but they had a wonderful career and were able to put away enough money to retire comfortably. They retired and bought homes beside each other on the same block of the neighbourhood they grew up in. Their retirement lasted for two years before they started feeling restless. They didn't want to go on the road to perform anymore, but over the years they had started to make their own guitars. They had sold a few to other musicians and the idea started to form that they should make guitars. Word spread quickly, and six months before they started they already had more orders than they could fill.

Their only problem was making sure that the cost of the guitars was calculated correctly in order to satisfy income tax purposes. They'd had a bit of a problem with income taxes during their performing career, and they didn't want to get into trouble with their new business. So they sent some of their information to a friend to look at:

Finishing Department for the month of June:

Cost per unit = $1,605.86 (total cost in the Finishing Department of $93,140, divided by the total number of units that were moved into Finished Goods and able to be sent to customers)

At the beginning of June, 30 units were already started and they had a total of $22,270 in costs associated with them ($12,000 transferred in and $1,350 in DM). Sixty-five guitars were transferred into the Finishing Department from the Fabrications Department in June.

The Finishing Department added $3,880 in direct materials and $19,600 in conversion costs during June. $47,390 was transferred in from the Fabrications Department.

Once Walter and Sydney's friend had looked at the information, he sent a message requesting more detail on the percentage of work already done on the guitars that had been started at the beginning of June and on the ones that were still being worked on at the end of June. Walter and Sydney hadn't kept track of that, but they said they could reasonably estimate that the ones at the beginning of the month already had 70% of the DM added and 50% of the rest of the costs, while the guitars that they were still working on at the end of June had about 80% of the DM added and about 60% of the rest of the costs. Their friend thanked them and said that they would hear from him shortly with some recommendations.

# ETHICAL ISSUE

## 16-65 Evaluate an ethical dilemma regarding percentage of completion

*(Learning Objectives 2 & 5)*

Danielle Bazinet and Annadine Lue are the plant managers for Pacific Lumber's particle board division. Pacific Lumber has adopted a JIT management philosophy. Each plant combines wood chips with chemical adhesives to produce particle board to order, and all production is sold as soon as it is completed. Din Nguyen is Pacific Lumber's regional controller. All of Pacific Lumber's plants and divisions send Nguyen their production and cost information. While reviewing the numbers of the two particle board plants, he is surprised that both plants estimate their ending work in process inventories at 80% complete, which is higher than usual. Nguyen calls Lue, whom he has known for some time. She admits that to ensure that their division met its profit goal and that both she and Bazinet would make their bonus (which is based on division profit), she and Bazinet agreed to inflate the percentage completion. Lue explains, "Determining the percentage completion always requires judgment. Whatever the percentage completion, we will finish the work in process inventory first thing next year."

### Requirements

1. How would inflating the percentage completion of ending work in process inventory help Bazinet and Lue get their bonus?
2. The particle board division is the largest of Pacific Lumber's divisions. If Nguyen does not correct the percentage completion of this year's ending work in process inventory, how will the misstatement affect Pacific Lumber's financial statements?
3. Evaluate Lue's justification, including the effect, if any, on next year's financial statements.
4. In considering what Nguyen should do, answer the following questions:
   a. What is the ethical question?
   b. What are the options?
   c. What are the possible consequences?
   d. What should Nguyen do?

# TEAM PROJECT

## T6-66 Calculate costs for a customer order *(Learning Objective 5)*

Hamilton Food Processors in Hamilton, Ontario, processes potatoes into french fries. Production requires two processes: cutting and cooking. The cutting process begins as scalding steam explodes the potatoes' brown skins. Workers using paring knives gouge out black spots before high-pressure water blasts potatoes through a pipe and into blades arranged in a half-centimetre grid. In the cooking process, the raw shoestring fries are cooked in a blancher, dried, partially fried at 193°C, and immediately flash-frozen at minus 24°C before being dropped into 5 kg bags. Direct materials are added at the beginning of the cutting process (potatoes) and at the end of the cooking process (bags). Conversion costs are incurred evenly throughout each process.

Assume that McDonald's offers Hamilton $0.40 per kilogram to supply restaurants in the Far East. If Hamilton accepts McDonald's offer, the cost (per equivalent unit) that Hamilton will incur to fill the McDonald's order equals the April cost per equivalent unit.

Sue Davis, COO, must prepare a report explaining whether Hamilton should accept the offer. She speaks to J. R. Simlott, manager of the cooking process, and Lola Mendez, who manages the cutting process to get their input on the decision.

Simlott gathers the following information for April's cooking operations:

**HAMILTON FOOD PROCESSORS**
**Cooking Department**
April Activity and Costs

| | |
|---|---|
| Beginning work in process inventory, April 1 | 21,000 kg |
| Potatoes started during April | 121,000 kg |
| Cut fries completed and transferred out | 129,000 kg |
| Ending work in process inventory (60% complete), April 30 | 13,000 kg |
| Costs related to the beginning WIP inventory: | |
| Direct materials | $ 1,260 |
| Conversion costs | $ 840 |
| Costs added during April: | |
| Direct materials | $ 8,680 |
| Conversion costs | $12,840 |

Split your team into two groups. Each group should meet separately before a meeting of the entire team.

### Requirements

1. The first group takes the role of Simlott, manager of the cooking production process. Before meeting with the entire team, determine the maximum transferred-in cost per kilogram of raw shoestring fries the Cooking Department can incur from the Cutting Department if Hamilton is to make a profit on the McDonald's order. (*Hint:* You may find it helpful to prepare a timeline and to use Exhibits 6-10 to 6-13 as a guide for your analysis.)
2. The second group takes the role of Mendez, manager of the cutting process. Before meeting with the entire team, determine the April cost per kilogram of raw shoestring fries in the cutting process. (Hint: You may find it helpful to prepare a timeline and to use Exhibits 6-10 to 6-14 as a guide for your analysis.)
3. After each group meets, the entire team should meet and take the role of Sue Davis, COO, to decide whether Hamilton should accept or reject the McDonald's offer.

# DISCUSSION & ANALYSIS

1. What characteristics of the product or manufacturing process would lead a company to use a process costing system? Give two examples of companies that are likely to use process costing. What characteristics of the product or manufacturing process would lead a company to use a job costing system? Give two examples of companies that are likely to use job costing.
2. How are process costing and job costing similar? How are they different?
3. What are conversion costs? In a job costing system, at least some conversion costs are assigned directly to products. Why do all conversion costs need to be assigned to processing departments in a process costing system?
4. Why not assign all costs of production during a period to only the completed units? What happens if a company does this? Why are the costs of production in any period allocated between completed units and units in work in process? Is there any situation in which a company can assign all costs of production during a period to the completed units? If so, when?
5. What information generated by a process costing system can be used by management? How can management use this process costing information?
6. Why are the equivalent units for direct materials often different from the equivalent units for conversion costs in the same period?
7. Describe the flow of costs in a process costing system. List each type of journal entry that would be made, and describe the purpose of that journal entry.
8. If a company has very little or no inventory, what effect does that lack of inventory have on its process costing system? What other benefits result from having very little or no inventory?
9. How does process costing differ between a first processing department and a second or later processing department?
10. "Process costing is easier to use than job costing." Do you agree or disagree with this statement? Explain your reasoning.

# APPLICATION & ANALYSIS

## Process Costing in Real Companies

Go to YouTube.com and search for clips from the show *Unwrapped* on the Food Network or *How It's Made* on the Discovery Channel. Watch a clip for a product that would use process costing. For some of the questions, you may need to make assumptions about the production process (i.e., companies may not publicize their entire production process). If you make any assumptions, be sure to disclose both the assumption and your rationale for that assumption.

## Discussion Questions

1. Describe the product selected.
2. Summarize the production process.
3. Justify why you think this production process would dictate the use of a process costing system.
4. List at least two separate processes that are performed in creating this product. What departments would house these processes?
5. Describe at least one department that would have ending work in process. What do the units look like as they are "in process"?

## Classroom Applications

**Web:** Post the discussion questions on an electronic discussion board. Have small groups of students choose a product for their group. Each student should watch the clip for the product for their group.

**Classroom:** Form groups of three or four students. Your group should choose a product and its clip to view. After viewing the clip, prepare a 5-minute presentation about your group's product and production process that addresses the listed questions.

Independent: Research answers to each of the questions. Turn in a two- or three-page typed paper (12-point font, double-spaced with 2.5 cm margins). Include references, including the URL of the clip viewed.

# TRY IT SOLUTIONS

Page 332:

1. 100,000 units × 100% of direct materials = 100,000 equivalent units of direct materials.
2. 100,000 units × 25% of the way through fermentation process = 25,000 equivalent units of conversion costs.

Page 351:

a. The total cost of making each unit can be found by looking at Step 4 of the process costing procedure in the final production department. The total cost is the sum of the cost per equivalent unit transferred in from earlier departments and the costs per equivalent unit incurred in the final department. In this example, those figures add up to $8.90 per case ($6.50 + $1.15 + $1.25).

b. The gross profit per case is $11.10, which is the sales price per case ($20.00) minus the cost to manufacture each case ($8.90).

# Demo Doc
Chapter 6

MyAccountingLab Make the grade with MyAccountingLab! Animated versions of similar Demo Docs to these can be found on MyAccountingLab.

## ILLUSTRATING PROCESS COSTING

### Learning Objectives 2 & 3

Clear Bottled Water produces bottled water. Clear Bottled Water has two production departments: Blending and Packaging. In the Blending Department, materials are added at the beginning of the process. Conversion costs are added evenly throughout the process for blending. Data for the month of April for the Blending Department are as follows:

| | |
|---|---|
| Units: | |
| Beginning work in process | 0 |
| Started in production during April | 116,000 units |
| Completed and transferred out to Packaging in April | 98,000 units |
| Ending work in process inventory (70% completed) | 18,000 units |
| Costs: | |
| Beginning work in process | 0 |
| Costs added during April: | |
| Direct materials | $54,520 |
| Conversion costs | 32,074 |
| Total costs added during April | $86,594 |

### Requirement

Use the five-step process to calculate (1) the cost of the units completed and transferred out to the Packaging Department and (2) the total cost of the units in the Blending Department's ending work in process inventory.

# Demo Doc Solutions

### Requirement

Use the five-step process costing procedure to calculate (1) the cost of the units completed and transferred out to the Packaging Department and (2) the total cost of the units in the Blending Department's ending work in process inventory.

#### Step 1: Summarize the flow of physical units.

The first step tracks the physical movement of units into and out of the Blending Department during the month. We first ask ourselves, "How many physical units did the Blending Department work on during the month?" That is the total number of units the Blending Department must account for. Total units to account for (116,000) is the sum of the units in beginning work in process (zero) plus the units started in production during the month (116,000).

Next we ask ourselves, "What happened to those units?" The Blending Department accounts for the whereabouts of every unit it worked on during the month by showing that the total units accounted for equals the total units to account for. Total units accounted for (116,000) is the sum of units completed and transferred out of the Blending Department in April (98,000) plus the units in ending work in process at April 30 (18,000).

| Flow of Production | Step 1<br>Flow of Physical Units |
|---|---|
| Units to account for: | |
| Beginning work in process, April 1 | 0 |
| Started in production during April | 116,000 |
| Total physical units to account for | 116,000 |
| Units accounted for: | |
| Completed and transferred out during April | 98,000 |
| Ending work in process, April 30 | 18,000 |
| Total physical units accounted for | 116,000 |
| Total equivalent units | |

### Step 2: Compute output in terms of equivalent units.

Now that we have analyzed the flow of physical units, we compute the output in terms of equivalent units. First, the units completed and transferred out during April have 100% of their direct material and conversion costs. Therefore, the equivalent units for direct materials and conversion are the same as their physical units (98,000).

Next, consider the physical units (18,000) still in ending work in process. Materials are added at the beginning of the blending process, so 100% of the direct materials have been added. Therefore, the direct materials equivalent units are also 18,000 (18,000 physical units × 100%).

Conversion costs include both direct labour and manufacturing overhead. Conversion costs are added evenly throughout the blending process, so the conversion equivalent units for the ending work in process are the physical units in ending work in process (18,000) × the percentage complete (70%), which equals 12,600.

| Flow of Production | Step 1 | Step 2 Equivalent Units | |
|---|---|---|---|
| | Flow of Physical Units | Direct Materials | Conversion Costs |
| Units to account for: | | | |
| Beginning work in process, April 1 | 0 | | |
| Started in production during April | 116,000 | | |
| Total physical units to account for | 116,000 | | |
| Units accounted for: | | | |
| Completed and transferred out during April | 98,000 | 98,000 | 98,000 |
| Ending work in process, April 30 | 18,000 | 18,000 | 12,600 |
| Total physical units accounted for | 116,000 | | |
| Total equivalent units | | 116,000 | 110,600 |

The total equivalent units for direct materials is 116,000 (98,000 completed units + 18,000 in work in process). The total equivalent units for conversion costs is 110,600 (98,000 completed units + 12,600 in work in process).

### Steps 3 and 4: Summarize total costs to account for and compute the cost per equivalent unit.

The next step is to summarize the total costs to account for, which consists of the costs in beginning work in process inventory plus the manufacturing costs incurred during April. The beginning inventory was zero. Direct materials of $54,520 and conversion costs of $32,074 were added during April. The total costs to account for is $86,594:

| | Direct Materials | Conversion Costs | Total |
|---|---|---|---|
| Beginning work in process, April 1 | $ 0 | $ 0 | $ 0 |
| Costs added during April | 54,520 | 32,074 | 86,594 |
| Total costs to account for | $54,520 | $32,074 | $86,594 |
| Divide by total equivalent units | ÷ 116,000 | ÷ 110,600 | |
| Cost per equivalent unit | $ 0.47 | $ 0.29 | |

The cost per equivalent unit is computed by dividing the total costs to account for by the total equivalent units for each of the cost categories.

To calculate the cost per equivalent unit for direct materials, we divide the total direct materials costs of $54,520 by the equivalent units of direct materials, determined in Step 2 as 116,000 units. The result is $0.47 per equivalent unit for direct materials.

To calculate the cost per equivalent unit for conversion costs, we divide the total conversion cost of $32,074 by the number of equivalent units for conversion (which was determined in Step 2 to be 110,600). Dividing $32,074 by 110,600 gives us $0.29 per equivalent unit for conversion costs.

The cost of completing one unit in the Blending Department is $0.76 ($0.47 for direct materials plus $0.29 for conversion costs).

### Step 5: Assign costs to units completed and to units in ending work in process inventory.

Because the units completed and transferred out were finished in the month of April, each unit is assigned the full unit cost of $0.76. Thus, the total cost to be assigned to the units completed and transferred out is $74,480 (98,000 units × $0.76). Shown another way, the total cost to be assigned to the units completed and transferred out is computed by multiplying the number of equivalent units (found in Step 2) by the cost per equivalent unit (found in Step 4):

98,000 × $0.47 = $46,060 (direct materials)
98,000 × $0.29 = $28,420 (conversion costs)
$74,480

The total cost to be assigned to the units still in work in process inventory is computed in a similar manner. The number of equivalent units still in ending work in process (from Step 2) is multiplied by the cost per equivalent unit (found in Step 4):

18,000 × $0.47 = $ 8,460 (direct materials)
12,600 × $0.29 = $ 3,654 (conversion costs)
$12,114

The total costs to account for ($86,594) is now properly divided between the units completed and transferred out to the Packaging Department ($74,480) and the units still in the Blending Department ending work in process inventory ($12,114).

| | Direct Materials | Conversion Costs | | Total |
|---|---|---|---|---|
| Completed and transferred out (98,000) | 98,000 × ($0.47 + $0.29) | | = | $74,480 |
| Ending work in process inventory: | | | | |
| Direct materials | 18,000 × $0.47 | | = | $ 8,460 |
| Conversion costs | | 12,600 × $0.29 | = | 3,654 |
| Total cost of ending work in process inventory | | | | $12,114 |
| Total costs accounted for | | | | $86,594 |

7

# Activity Based Costing

7

## Learning Objectives

1 Develop and use departmental overhead rates to allocate indirect costs.

2 Develop and use activity based costing (ABC) to allocate indirect costs.

3 Understand the benefits and limitations of activity based costing and activity based management systems.

Chapter 7, "Activity Based Costing," covers material outlined in **Section 3: Management Accounting** of the CPA Competency Map. Specifically, this chapter addresses *Section 3.3 Cost Management*. The Learning Objectives in this chapter have been aligned with the CPA Competency Map to ensure the best coverage possible.

PROFESSIONAL COMPETENCY

The presence of the **coverage button** in the margin indicates focus on one or more of the specific competency areas from the competency map. The concepts in the text are building blocks to developing the competencies required in the CPA. While the chapter may address multiple areas of the competency map, the main focus will be:

Competencies:

**3.3.1** Evaluates cost classifications and costing methods for management of ongoing operations*

**3.3.2** Evaluates and applies cost management techniques appropriate for specific costing decisions*

**3.4.1** Evaluates sources and drivers of revenue growth*

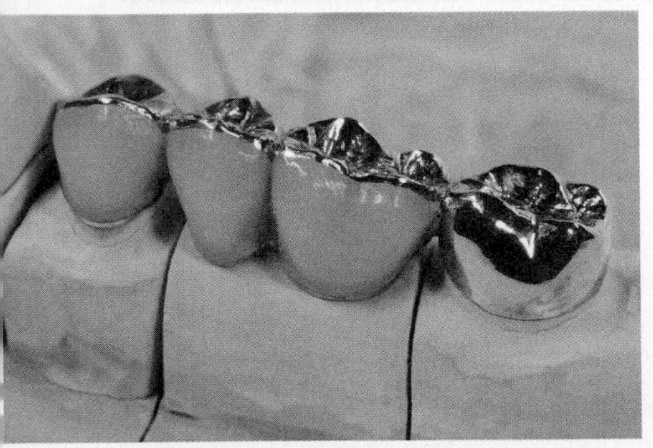

© PHOTO FUN/Shutterstock

## Early attempts at making replacements

for missing teeth used natural materials such as bone, animal teeth, and metal.[1] With the advancement of synthetic materials and new technologies, dentists can now offer a wide variety of products that are almost impossible to distinguish from your natural teeth. Dental laboratories, such as the Shaw Group of Dental Laboratories introduced in Chapter 5, provide a service to dentists by specializing in the manufacture of these products.

Let's suppose that, as a result of the increase in competition and product diversity, managers of dental labs found that they needed better, more accurate product cost information to help guide their business decisions and to remain competitive.[2] A traditional job costing system ensures that the direct material and direct labour costs traced to each product are correct. However, the traditional method of allocating manufacturing overhead

*Reprinted from *The Chartered Professional Accountant Competency Map - Understanding the competencies a candidate must demonstrate to become a CPA*, © 2012, with permission Chartered Professional Accountants of Canada, Toronto, Canada. Any changes to the original material are the sole responsibility of the author (and/or publisher) and have not been reviewed or endorsed by the Chartered Professional Accountants of Canada.

[1] National Board for Certification in Dental Laboratory Technology at www.nbccert.org/dent_tech_history.cfm

[2] All references to Shaw Group in the following hypothetical example were created by the author solely for academic purposes and are not intended, in any way, to represent the actual business practices of, or costs incurred by, Shaw Group.

costs may not do a sufficiently good job of matching overhead costs to each product that used those overhead resources.

Shaw Group's managers may need a more refined cost allocation system: one that isn't based on a single, predetermined manufacturing overhead rate. By using either departmental overhead rates or activity based costing (ABC) to allocate manufacturing overhead, the company could determine the cost of individual jobs or products more accurately. ABC could also help managers cut costs by highlighting the cost of each activity performed during production. It could also help them identify the costs associated with providing high-quality products to their customers. With more accurate cost information in hand, managers could ensure Shaw Group's continuing focus on providing a quality product at the right price.

To thrive in a globally competitive market, Shaw Group must provide value to the customer by delivering a high-quality product at an attractive price, while managing costs so the company still earns a profit. This chapter will introduce refined costing systems, such as departmental overhead rates and activity based costing (ABC) that today's managers use to make their companies competitive.

## Simple Cost Systems and the Potential for Distortion

Simple cost allocation systems do not always do a good job of matching the cost of overhead resources with the products that consume those resources. An example can be seen in something as simple as sharing the utilities and rent of a shared apartment:

David, Abdi, and Marc are three college friends who share an apartment. They agree to split the following monthly costs equally, with each roommate's share being $300 ($900 ÷ 3):

| | |
|---|---|
| Rent and utilities | $570 |
| Cable TV | 50 |
| High-speed internet access | 40 |
| Groceries | 240 |
| Total monthly costs | $900 |

Things go smoothly for the first few months. But then David calls a meeting: "Since I started having dinner at Amy's each night, I shouldn't have to chip in for the groceries." Abdi then pipes up: "I'm so busy studying and using the internet that I never have time to watch TV. I don't want to pay for the cable TV anymore. And Marc, since your friend Jennifer eats here most evenings, you should pay a double share of the grocery bill." Marc replies, "If that's the way you feel, Abdi, then you should pay for the internet access, since you're the only one around here who uses it!"

What happened? The friends originally agreed to share the costs equally. But they are not participating equally in watching cable TV, using the internet, and eating the groceries. Splitting these costs equally is not equitable.

The roommates could use a cost allocation approach that better matches costs with the people who participate in the activities that cause those costs. This means splitting the cable TV costs between David and Marc, assigning the internet access cost to Abdi, and allocating the grocery bill one-third to Abdi and two-thirds to Marc. Exhibit 7-1 compares the results of this refined cost allocation system with the original cost allocation system.

No wonder David called a meeting! The original cost allocation system charged him $300 a month, but the refined system shows that a more equitable share would be only $215. The new system allocates Marc $375 a month instead of $300. David was paying for resources he did not use (internet and groceries), while Marc was not paying for all of the resources (groceries) he and his guest consumed. The simple system ended up distorting the cost that should be charged to each roommate: David was overcharged by $85, while Abdi and Marc were undercharged by an equal but offsetting amount ($10 + $75 = $85).

**EXHIBIT 7-1** More-Refined versus Less-Refined Cost Allocation System

| | David | Abdi | Marc | Total |
|---|---|---|---|---|
| **More-refined cost allocation system:** | | | | |
| Rent and utilities | $190 | $190 | $190 | $570 |
| Cable TV | 25 | 0 | 25 | 50 |
| High-speed internet access | 0 | 40 | 0 | 40 |
| Groceries | 0 | 80 | 160 | 240 |
| Total costs allocated | $215 | $310 | $375 | $900 |
| **Less-refined original cost allocation system** | $300 | $300 | $300 | $900 |
| Difference | $ (85) | $ 10 | $ 75 | $ 0 |

**Why is this important?**

With better **cost information**, managers are able to make more **profitable** decisions. One company reported triple sales and a **five-fold increase** in profits after it implemented a **refined costing system**. By using better cost information for quoting jobs, **management** was able to generate a more **profitable mix** of job contracts.[3]

[3]Douglas Hicks, "Yes, ABC Is for Small Business, Too," *Journal of Accountancy*, Aug. 1999, p. 41.

Notice the total "pool" of monthly costs ($900) is the same under both allocation systems. The only difference is *how* the pool of costs is allocated among the three roommates.

Just as the simple allocation system had resulted in overcharging David and undercharging Abdi and Marc, many companies find that the simple overhead cost allocation system described in Chapter 5 results in overcosting some of their jobs or products while undercosting others. This is called **cost distortion**. As we will see in the following sections, companies often refine their cost allocation systems to minimize the amount of cost distortion caused by simpler cost allocation systems. By refining their costing systems, companies can more equitably assign indirect costs (such as manufacturing overhead) to individual jobs, products, or services. When less cost distortion occurs, managers have more accurate information for making vital business decisions. For example, each of the roommates now has better information about his actual living costs. This information will be useful if they ever consider moving out on their own.

In the following section, we will describe how cost allocation systems can be refined to better allocate manufacturing overhead (indirect manufacturing costs) to specific products to reduce cost distortion. However, keep in mind that the same principles apply to allocating *any* indirect costs to *any* cost objects. Thus, even merchandising and service companies, as well as governmental agencies, can use these refined cost allocation systems to provide their managers with better cost information.

## Review: Using a Plantwide Overhead Rate to Allocate Indirect Costs

In the Chapter 5, we assumed that Shaw Group allocated its manufacturing overhead costs using one predetermined MOH rate ($16 per DL hour). This rate was based on management's estimate of the total MOH costs for the year ($1 million) and estimate of the total amount of the allocation base (62,500 DL hours) for the year. The rate was calculated as follows:

$$\text{Predetermined MOH rate} = \frac{\$1{,}000{,}000}{62{,}500 \text{ DL hours}} = \$16 \text{ per direct labour hour}$$

This rate is also known as a **plantwide overhead rate**, because any job produced in the plant, whether it be gold crowns, mouthguards, or dentures, is allocated MOH using this single rate. It does not matter whether the job is worked on in one department or many departments during the production process: The same rate is used throughout the plant.

Let's see how this works for Shaw Group. In Chapter 5, we followed a job in which a gold crown required about 11.5 direct labour hours to make.[4] We will continue to assume that each gold crown made by the company requires 11.5 direct labour hours to make. Let's also assume that each mouthguard requires 2 direct labour hours to make.[5] Exhibit 7-2 shows how MOH is allocated to a job in which one gold crown was made and another job in which one mouthguard was made, using the plantwide overhead rate.

**EXHIBIT 7-2** Allocating Manufacturing Overhead Using a Plantwide Overhead Rate

| | Plantwide Overhead Rate | | Actual Use of Allocation Base | | MOH Allocated to One Unit |
|---|---|---|---|---|---|
| Gold Crown | $16 per DL hour | × | 11.5 DL hours | = | $184 |
| Mouthguard | $16 per DL hour | × | 2 DL hours | = | $ 32 |

The plantwide allocation system is illustrated in Exhibit 7-3.

**EXHIBIT 7-3** Plantwide Allocation System

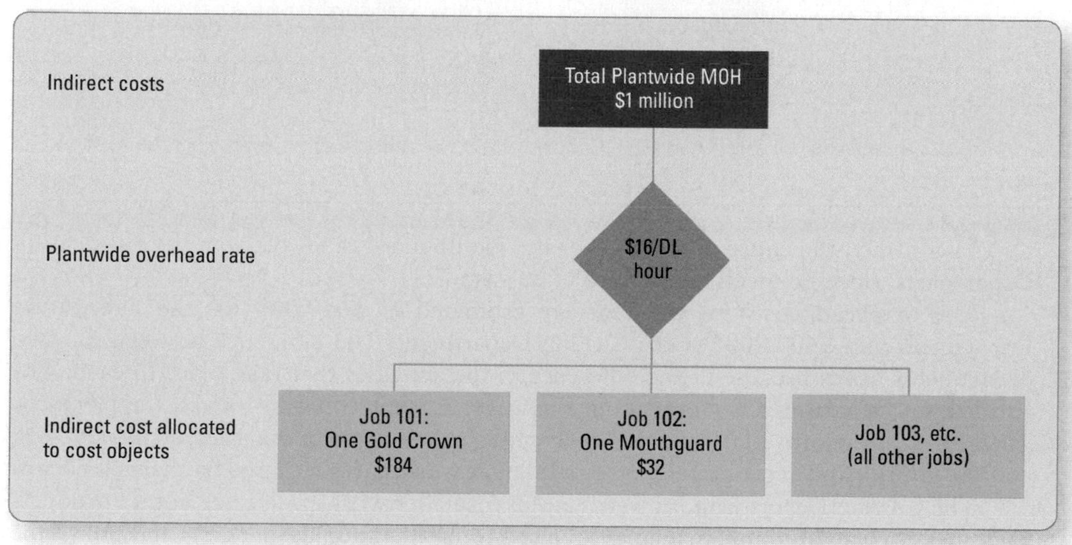


## Using Departmental Overhead Rates to Allocate Indirect Costs

1 Develop and use departmental overhead rates to allocate indirect costs.

The plantwide allocation system described above works well for some companies. However, it may end up distorting costs if the following conditions exist:

1. Different departments incur different amounts and types of manufacturing overhead.
2. Different jobs or products use the departments to a different extent.

If these circumstances exist, the company should strongly consider refining its cost allocation system. Let's see if these conditions exist at Shaw Group.

[4] Job 603, a job with one HL 5 dental gold crown, required 11.5 DL hours to complete.

[5] Job 604, a job with two sports mouthguards, required 4 DL hours to complete. Therefore, it takes on average 2 DL hours to make one mouthguard.

**CONDITION 1: DO DIFFERENT DEPARTMENTS HAVE DIFFERENT AMOUNTS AND TYPES OF MOH COSTS?** As shown in Exhibit 7-4, let's assume Shaw Group has two primary production departments: Fabrication and Casting. The Fabrication Department takes care of the customized designing and forming of the gold crown through a process of carving the crown in wax. The crown then moves to the Casting Department, where it is encased in stone, fired to remove the wax, and then cast in gold.

**EXHIBIT 7-4** Machining and Casting Departments' Manufacturing Overhead

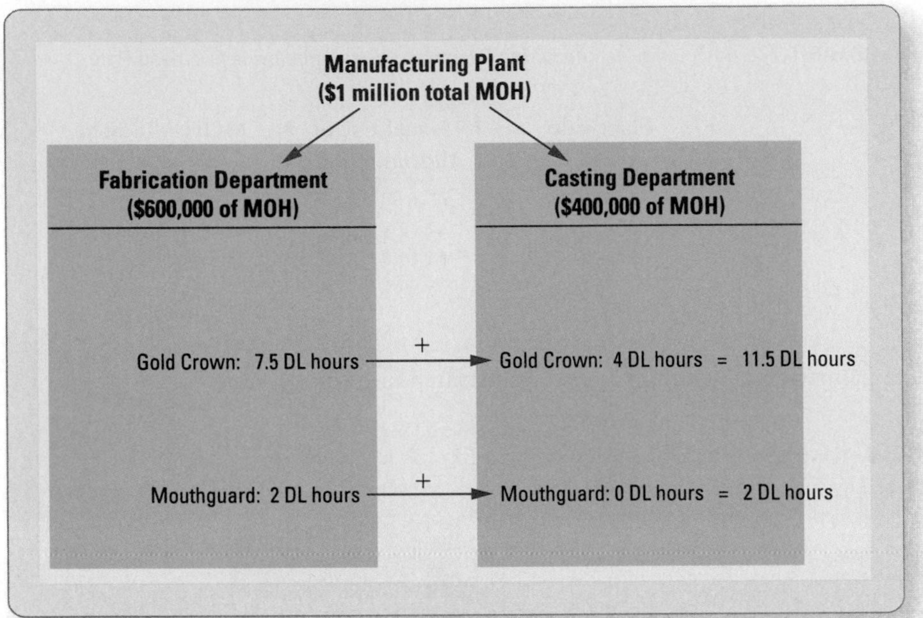

In contrast, the entire production of the mouthguard takes place in the Fabrication Department, since no metal pieces need to be cast.

The overhead costs for the year are estimated at $600,000 for the Fabrication Department and $400,000 for the Casting Department. The difference between the two departments arises because of the difference in the activities that take place in each. The Fabrication Department is more labour intensive, as the technicians design the products. Therefore, the majority of its overhead costs come from supervisory salaries, quality control, and the utilities and expenses relating to the larger workspaces required by the technicians.

The Casting Department, however, needs a smaller workspace since not all products need metal work, but more machines are used to fire the moulds and cool and polish the final product. The Casting Department's overhead costs consist of the depreciation and maintenance of the machines and the expenses relating to the smaller workspace allocated.

Exhibit 7-4 shows that the first condition is present: Each department incurs different types and amounts of MOH. Shaw Group expects to incur a total of $1 million of manufacturing overhead: $600,000 relating to the Fabrication Department and $400,000 relating to the Casting Department.

**CONDITION 2: DO DIFFERENT PRODUCTS USE THE DEPARTMENTS TO DIFFERENT EXTENTS?** Exhibit 7-4 also shows that gold crowns and mouthguards spend different amounts of time in each production department. Each gold crown requires 7.5 DL hours in the Fabrication Department and 4 DL hours in the Casting Department. Contrast that with a mouthguard, which spends its entire production time (2 DL hours) in the Fabrication Department. As a result of these differences, the second condition is also present. The company's cost allocation system would be much more accurate if it took these differences into account when determining how much manufacturing overhead to allocate to each product.

Since both Conditions 1 and 2 are present, the company should consider fine-tuning its cost allocation systems by establishing separate MOH rates, known as **departmental overhead rates**, for each department. This means that Shaw Group will establish one

MOH rate for the Fabrication Department and another overhead rate for the Casting Department. These rates are then used to allocate MOH to jobs or products based on the extent to which each product uses the different manufacturing departments.

Exhibit 7-5 shows the circumstances under which departmental overhead rates do better than a plantwide rate when allocating MOH costs.

**EXHIBIT 7-5** Circumstances Favouring Departmental Overhead Rates

**Departmental overhead rates increase the accuracy of job costs when....**

- Each department incurs different types and amounts of manufacturing overhead
- Each product, or job, uses the departments to a different extent

## Four Basic Steps to Compute and Use Departmental Overhead Rates

In Chapter 5, we used four steps in allocating manufacturing overhead. These steps are summarized in Exhibit 7-6.

**EXHIBIT 7-6** Four Basic Steps to Allocate Manufacturing Overhead

1. Estimate the total manufacturing overhead (MOH) costs for the coming year.
2. Select an allocation base and estimate the total amount that will be used during the year.
3. Calculate the predetermined overhead rate by dividing the total estimated MOH costs by the total estimated amount of the allocation base.
4. Allocate some MOH cost to each job worked on during the year by multiplying the predetermined MOH rate by the actual amount of the allocation base used by the job.

The same four basic steps are used to allocate MOH using departmental overhead rates. The only real difference is that we will be calculating separate rates for each department. Let us now take a look at how the four basic steps outlined in Exhibit 7-6 are modified slightly to implement a refined costing system.

**STEP 1: The company estimates the total manufacturing overhead costs that will be incurred in each department in the coming year. These estimates are known as departmental overhead cost pools.**

Some of these costs are easy to identify or trace to different departments. For example, management can trace the cost of lease payments and repairs to the machines used in the Casting Department. Management can also trace the cost of employing supervisors and quality control inspectors to the Fabrication Department.

However, other overhead costs are more difficult to identify with specific departments. For example, the depreciation, property taxes, and insurance on the entire plant would have to be split, or allocated, between the individual departments, most likely based on the square metres occupied by each department in the plant.

As shown in Exhibit 7-4, Shaw Group has determined that $400,000 of its total estimated MOH relates to its Casting Department, while the remaining $600,000 relates to its Fabrication Department.

| Department | Total Departmental Overhead Cost Pool |
|---|---|
| Casting | $ 400,000 |
| Fabrication | $ 600,000 |
| TOTAL MOH | $1,000,000 |

**STEP 2: The company selects an allocation base for each department and estimates the total amount that will be used during the year.**

The allocation base selected for each department should be the cost driver of the costs in the departmental overhead pool. Often, manufacturers use different allocation bases for different departments. For example, machine hours might be the best allocation base for a very automated Machining Department that uses machine robotics extensively. However, direct labour hours might be the best allocation base for an Assembly Department.

Assume that Shaw Group's Fabrication Department uses a lot of human-operated tools and machinery. This would mean the number of direct labour hours used in the department is the best indicator of how costs accumulate in the department. The Casting Department incorporates more machinery. However, the machines are run by technicians, which means that machine hours and labour hours are the same for the Casting Department. As a result, management has selected direct labour hours as the allocation base for both departments. Recall that Shaw Group estimates using a total of 62,500 direct labour hours during the year. Of this amount, management expects to use 50,000 in the Fabrication Department and 12,500 in the Casting Department.

| Department | Total Amount of Departmental Allocation Base |
|---|---|
| Casting | 12,500 DL hours |
| Fabrication | 50,000 DL hours |

**STEP 3: The company calculates its departmental overhead rates using the information estimated in Steps 1 and 2:**

$$\text{Departmental overhead rate} = \frac{\text{Total estimated departmental overhead cost pool}}{\text{Total estimated amount of the departmental allocation base}}$$

PROFESSIONAL COMPETENCY

Therefore, Shaw Group calculates its departmental overhead rates as follows:

$$\text{Casting Department overhead rate} = \frac{\$400{,}000}{12{,}500\text{ DL hours}} = \$32\text{ per DL hour}$$

$$\text{Fabrication Department overhead rate} = \frac{\$600{,}000}{50{,}000\text{ DL hours}} = \$12\text{ per DL hour}$$

These first three steps are performed before the year begins, using estimated data for the year. Thus, departmental overhead rates are also predetermined, just like the plantwide predetermined MOH rate discussed in Chapter 5. The first three steps are summarized in Exhibit 7-7.

**EXHIBIT 7-7** Steps to Calculating Departmental Overhead Rates

| Department | Step 1: Total Departmental Overhead Cost Pool | | Step 2: Total Amount of Departmental Allocation Base | | Step 3: Departmental Overhead Rate |
|---|---|---|---|---|---|
| Casting | $400,000 | ÷ | 12,500 DL hours | = | $32 per DL hour |
| Fabrication | $600,000 | ÷ | 50,000 DL hours | = | $12 per DL hour |

Once these rates have been established, the company uses them throughout the year to allocate MOH to each job as it is produced, as shown in Step 4.

**STEP 4: The company allocates some manufacturing overhead from *each department* to the individual jobs that use those departments. The amount of MOH allocated from each department is calculated as follows:**

MOH allocated to job = Departmental overhead rate × Actual amount of departmental allocation base used by job

Exhibit 7-8 shows how these departmental overhead rates are used to allocate manufacturing to a job in which one gold crown is produced.

**EXHIBIT 7-8** Allocating MOH to One Gold Crown Using Departmental Overhead Rates

| Department | Departmental Overhead Rate (from Exhibit 7-7) | | Actual Use of Departmental Allocation Base (from Exhibit 7-4) | | MOH Allocated to One Gold Crown |
|---|---|---|---|---|---|
| Fabrication | $12 per DL hour | × | 7.5 DL hours | = | $ 90 |
| Casting | $32 per DL hour | × | 4 DL hours | = | 128 |
| Total | | | | | $218 |

Exhibit 7-9 shows how the same rates are used to allocate MOH to another job in which one mouthguard is produced. Notice, because it is not required for the mouthguard to go through the casting process, no hours are allocated to this activity (and the cost equals zero).

**EXHIBIT 7-9** Allocating MOH to One Mouthguard Using Departmental Overhead Rates

| Department | Departmental Overhead Rate (from Exhibit 7-7) | | Actual Use of Departmental Allocation Base (from Exhibit 7-4) | | MOH Allocated to One Mouthguard |
|---|---|---|---|---|---|
| Fabrication | $12 per DL hour | × | 2 DL hours | = | $24 |
| Casting | $32 per DL hour | × | 0 DL hours | = | 0 |
| Total | | | | | $24 |

## Did the Plantwide Overhead Rate Distort Product Costs?

We have just seen that Shaw Group's refined cost allocation system allocates $218 of MOH to each gold crown and $24 of MOH to each mouthguard (Exhibit 7-10). This differs from the amount that would have been allocated to each unit using Shaw Group's original plantwide rate. Recall from Exhibit 7-2 that if Shaw Group used a plantwide overhead rate, $184 of MOH would be allocated to the gold crown and $32 to the mouthguard, demonstrating that the refined system allocates the MOH differently from the plantwide overhead rate.

The plantwide allocation system does not pick up on the nuances of the number of direct labour hours used by the products in *each* department. Therefore, it could not do a very good job of matching MOH costs to the products that use those costs. As a result,

**EXHIBIT 7-10** Departmental Cost Allocation System

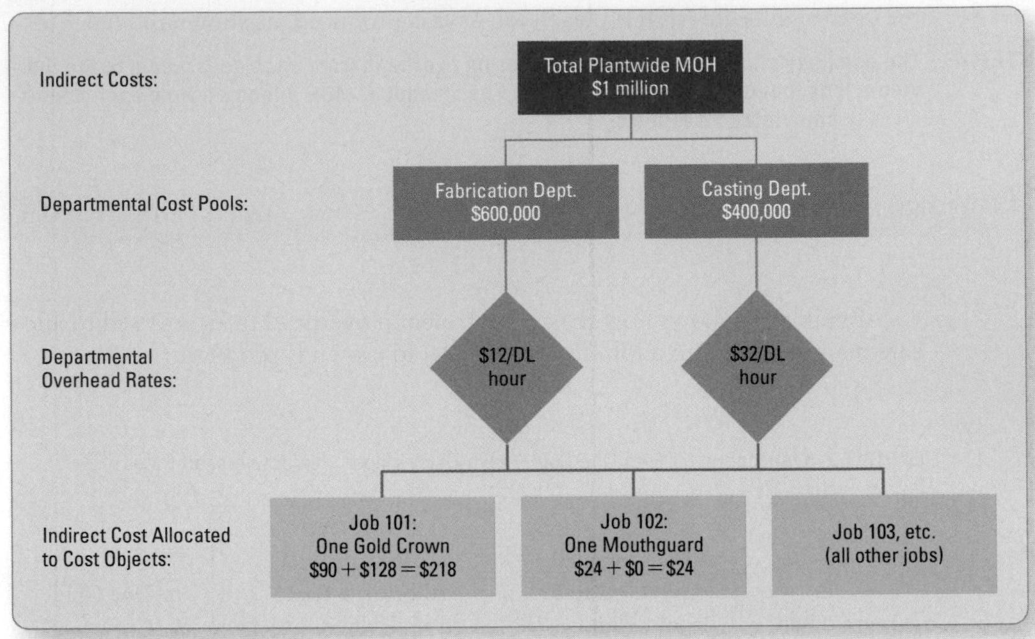


the plantwide rate would have undercosted each gold crown and overcosted each mouthguard, as shown in Exhibit 7-11.

**EXHIBIT 7-11** Cost Distortion Caused by Plantwide Overhead Rate

| | Plantwide Overhead Rate MOH Allocation (from Exhibit 7-2) | Departmental Overhead Rates MOH Allocation (from Exhibit 7-10) | Amount of Cost Distortion |
|---|---|---|---|
| Gold Crown........................ | $184 | $218 | $34 *undercosted* |
| Mouthguard........................ | $ 32 | $ 24 | $ 8 *overcosted* |

On the other hand, the refined cost allocation system recognizes the cost differences between departments and the usage difference between jobs. Therefore, the refined costing system does a better job of matching each department's overhead costs to the products that use the department's resources. This is the same thing we saw with the three roommates: The refined costing system did a better job of matching the cost of resources (cable, internet, groceries) to the roommates who used those resources. Because of this better matching, we can believe that the departmental overhead rates more accurately allocate MOH costs.

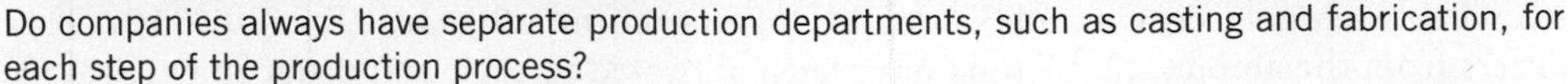

## STOP & THINK

Do companies always have separate production departments, such as casting and fabrication, for each step of the production process?

**Answer:** No. Rather than basing production departments on separate processing steps, some companies have separate production departments for each of their products. For example, Shaw Group could have one department for producing gold crowns, another department for producing mouthguards, and yet another department for producing dentures. Each department would have all of the equipment necessary for producing its unique product. The porcelain fibre crowns and bridges require a dust-free environment; therefore, production for these specialized products is usually separated from the rest of production. Departmental overhead rates would be formulated by using the same four basic steps discussed above to determine a unique departmental overhead rate for each department. The only difference is that each product (for example, a gold crown) would travel through only one department (the Gold Crown Department) rather than travelling through separate production departments (Fabrication and Casting). Always keep in mind that the accounting system should reflect the actual production environment.

---

## Using Activity Based Costing to Allocate Indirect Costs

**2** Develop and use activity based costing (ABC) to allocate indirect costs.

Activity based costing (ABC) focuses on activities, rather than departments, as the fundamental cost objects. ABC recognizes that activities are costly to perform, and each product manufactured may require different types and amounts of activities. Thus, activities become the building blocks for compiling the indirect costs of products, services, and customers. Companies such as Coca-Cola and Scotiabank use ABC to more accurately estimate the cost of resources required to produce different products, to render different services, and to serve different customers.

The most equitable and accurate cost allocation system for the roommates in the example discussed at the beginning of the chapter is one in which the roommates are charged only for the activities in which they participate and for the extent to which they participate in those activities. Likewise, activity-based costing generally causes the least amount of cost distortion among products because indirect costs are allocated to the products based on (1) the types of activities used by the product and (2) the extent to which the activities are used.

### Four Basic Steps to Computing and Using Activity Cost Allocation Rates

ABC requires the same four basic steps listed in Exhibit 7-6. The main difference between an ABC system and a plantwide or departmental cost allocation system is that ABC systems have separate cost allocation rates for each activity identified by the company.

**STEP 1: The company first identifies its primary activities and then estimates the total manufacturing overhead costs associated with each activity. These are known as the activity cost pools.**

Let's assume that Shaw Group has determined that the following activities occur in its plant. First the purchase orders and patient tooth impressions are received from the dental office. The impressions are cleaned and scheduled into production. If the order was delivered with completed models (stone replicas of the patient's teeth and gums) that are ready for production, then the models wait for their allocated time in production. If the order was delivered with only impressions (moulds of the patient's teeth and gums), then the moulds are prepared and stone models are cast.

The models then move to the appropriate production area, depending on the type of product. Different products require different amounts of fabrication time with the technicians. Models for any gold or metal work then go to the casting area, where they are cast into the appropriate metal. All products then go through a finishing phase where quality is double-checked and the product is polished. The final phase incorporates cleaning and packaging the product for delivery to the appropriate dental office.

As part of this step, management must determine how much of the total estimated $1 million of MOH relates to each activity. Exhibit 7-12 shows some of the specific MOH costs that management has identified with each activity, along with the total estimated amount of each activity cost pool. Keep in mind that all of the costs in the activity costs pools are MOH costs. The activity cost pool totals are determined through a process of reviewing financial statements and operations of an organization to determine how much of general overhead costs can be attributed to each of the activities that make up the various cost pools.

**EXHIBIT 7-12** Activity Cost Pools

| Activity | MOH Costs Related to the Activity | Total Activity Cost Pool |
|---|---|---|
| Receiving | Depreciation of scheduling equipment, cleaning chemicals, indirect labour for set-up of production equipment | $ 80,000 |
| Preparation | Indirect materials (stone powders), equipment depreciation, utilities, cutting and grinding machines for shaping the stone models | 200,000 |
| Fabrication | Indirect materials (blue wax for carving, lubricants), machinery and equipment depreciation, supervisory labour, utilities | 300,000 |
| Casting | Materials for casting, casting equipment, utilities | 150,000 |
| Finishing | Sandblasting equipment, polishing equipment, inspection labour | 170,000 |
| Packaging | Cleaning equipment and chemicals, packaging equipment | 100,000 |
| | TOTAL MOH | $1,000,000 |

Direct labour costs and direct materials costs are not included because they are directly traced to specific jobs and therefore do not need to be allocated. That is why we include only supervisory labour in the overhead cost pool for the casting activity. The machine operators and casting workers are considered direct labour, so their cost is traced to individual jobs, not allocated as part of MOH.

**STEP 2: The company selects an allocation base for each activity and estimates the total amount that will be used during the year.**

When selecting an allocation base for each activity, the company should keep the following in mind:

- The allocation base selected for each activity should be the cost driver of the costs in that particular activity cost pool.
- The company must keep track of how much of the allocation base each job or product uses. Therefore, the company must have the means to collect usage information about each allocation base. Thankfully, bar coding and other technological advances have helped make data collection easier and less costly in recent years.

Let's assume that Shaw Group has identified a cost driver for each activity and has plans for how it will collect usage data. Exhibit 7-13 shows the selected allocation bases, along with the total estimated amounts for the year.

**EXHIBIT 7-13** Activity Allocation Bases and Total Estimated Amount of Each

| Activity | Activity Allocation Base | Total Estimated Amount of Allocation Base |
|---|---|---|
| Receiving | Number of jobs | 8,000 jobs |
| Preparation | Number of moulds | 16,000 moulds |
| Fabrication | Direct labour hours | 50,000 DL hours |
| Casting | Direct labour hours | 12,500 DL hours |
| Finishing | Number of units | 34,000 units |
| Packaging | Number of jobs | 8,000 jobs |

**STEP 3: The company calculates its activity cost allocation rates using the information estimated in Steps 1 and 2.**

The formula for calculating the activity cost allocation rates is as follows:

$$\text{Activity cost allocation rate} = \frac{\text{Total estimated activity cost pool}}{\text{Total estimated activity allocation base}}$$

Exhibit 7-14 shows how this formula is used to compute a unique cost allocation rate for each of the company's production activities.

**EXHIBIT 7-14** Computing Activity Cost Allocation Rates

| Activity | Step 1: Total Activity Cost Pool (from Exhibit 7-12) | | Step 2: Total Amount of Activity Allocation Base (from Exhibit 7-13) | | Step 3: Activity Cost Allocation Rate |
|---|---|---|---|---|---|
| Receiving | $ 80,000 | ÷ | 8,000 jobs | = | $ 10 per job |
| Preparation | 200,000 | ÷ | 16,000 moulds | = | $ 12.50 per mould |
| Fabrication | 300,000 | ÷ | 50,000 DL hours | = | $ 6 per DL hour |
| Casting | 150,000 | ÷ | 12,500 DL hours | = | $ 12 per DL hour |
| Finishing | 170,000 | ÷ | 34,000 units | = | $ 5 per unit |
| Packaging | 100,000 | ÷ | 8,000 jobs | = | $ 12.50 per job |

Once again, these rates are calculated based on estimated, or budgeted, costs for the year. Hence, they are also "predetermined" before the year begins. Then, during the year, the company uses them to allocate MOH to specific jobs, as shown in Step 4.

**STEP 4: The company allocates some manufacturing overhead from each activity to the individual jobs that use the activities.**

The formula is as follows:

$$\text{MOH allocated to job} = \text{Activity cost allocation rate} \times \text{Actual amount of activity allocation base used by job}$$

Exhibit 7-15 shows how these activity cost allocation rates are used to allocate MOH to a job in which one gold crown was produced, needing two moulds prepared, 7.5 DL hours of fabrication, 4 DL hours of casting, and one unit of finishing. Since only one gold crown is needed, the number of units is the same as the number of jobs.

**EXHIBIT 7-15** Allocating MOH to One Gold Crown Using ABC

| Activity | Activity Cost Allocation Rate (from Exhibit 7-14) | | Actual Use of Activity Allocation Base (information collected on job) | | MOH Allocated to One Gold Crown |
|---|---|---|---|---|---|
| Receiving | $ 10 per job | × | 1 job | = | $ 10.00 |
| Preparation | $ 12.50 per mould | × | 2 moulds | = | 25.00 |
| Fabrication | $ 6 per DL hour | × | 7.5 DL hours | = | 45.00 |
| Casting | $ 12 per DL hour | × | 4 DL hours | = | 48.00 |
| Finishing | $ 5 per unit | × | 1 unit | = | 5.00 |
| Packaging | $ 12.50 per job | × | 1 job | = | 12.50 |
| Total | | | | | $145.50 |

Exhibit 7-16 shows how the same activity cost allocation rates are used to allocate MOH to a job in which one mouthguard was produced. It required no moulds, 2 hours of DL for fabrication, no casting, and one unit of finishing.

**EXHIBIT 7-16** Allocating MOH to One Mouthguard Using ABC

| Activity | Activity Cost Allocation Rate (from Exhibit 7-14) | | Actual Use of Departmental Allocation Base (information collected on job) | | MOH Allocated to One Mouthguard |
|---|---|---|---|---|---|
| Receiving | $ 10 per job | × | 1 job | = | $ 10.00 |
| Preparation | $ 12.50 per mould | × | 0 moulds | = | 0 |
| Fabrication | $ 6 per DL hour | × | 2 DL hours | = | 12.00 |
| Casting | $ 12 per DL hour | × | 0 DL hours | = | 0 |
| Finishing | $ 5 per unit | × | 1 unit | = | 5.00 |
| Packaging | $ 12.50 per job | × | 1 job | = | 12.50 |
| Total | | | | | $ 39.50 |

Exhibit 7-17 illustrates the company's ABC system, showing the allocation of indirect costs to different jobs, based on the activities in which the company engages.

**EXHIBIT 7-17** Illustration of the Company's ABC System

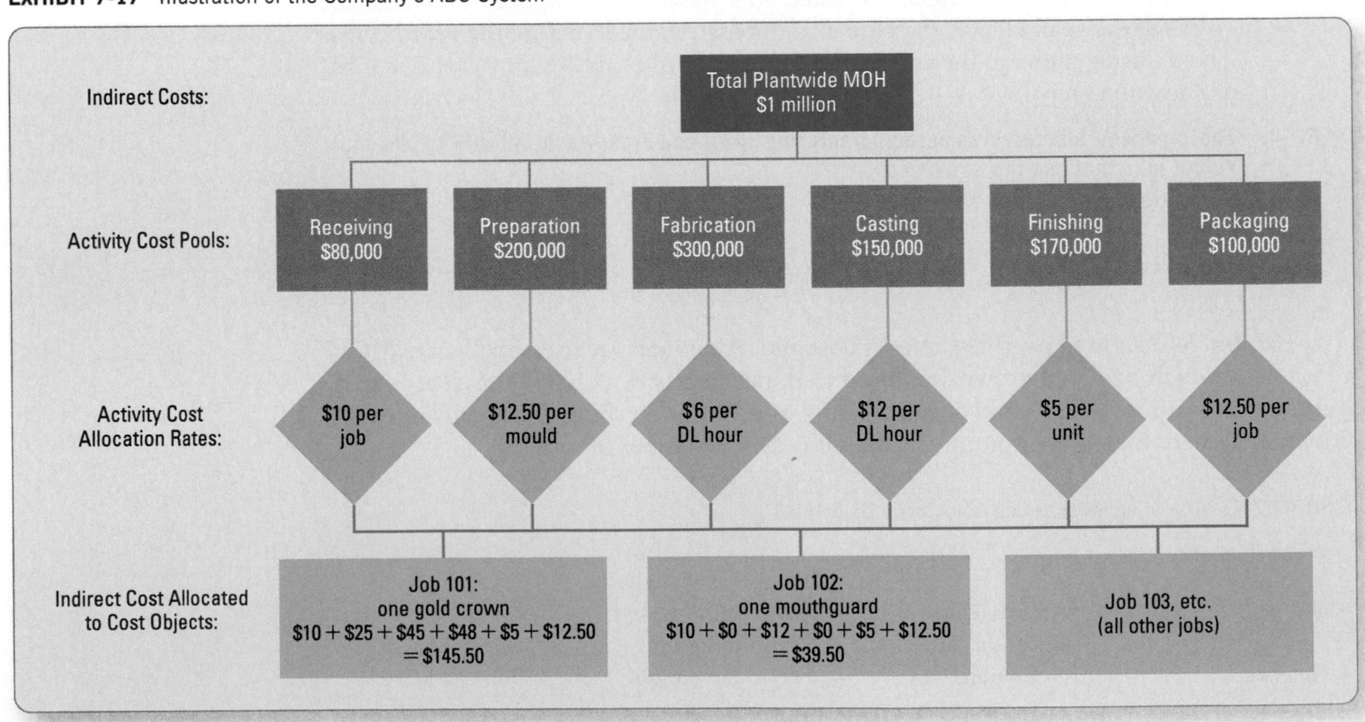


## One Last Look at Cost Distortion: Comparing the Three Allocation Systems

Exhibit 7-18 compares the amount of MOH that would have been allocated to each gold crown and each mouthguard, using the three cost allocation systems that we have discussed: (1) a single plantwide overhead rate, (2) departmental overhead rates, and (3) ABC.

**EXHIBIT 7-18** Comparing the Three Cost Allocation Processes

| | Plantwide Overhead Rate MOH Allocation (from Exhibit 7-2) | Departmental Overhead Rates MOH Allocation (from Exhibit 7-10) | Activity Based Costing (from Exhibit 7-18) |
|---|---|---|---|
| Gold Crown.............................. | $184 | $218 | $145.50 |
| Mouthguard.............................. | $ 32 | $ 24 | $ 39.50 |

This example of three distinct cost allocation systems discusses the production and resulting MOH costs allocation of two units, and results in *three different allocations*. The same would be true if we considered all of the products the company produces during the year. However, the total amount by which some products have been overcosted will always equal the total amount by which other products have been undercosted. This is because cost systems do not change the total amount of overhead spending; they merely change how those expenditures are allocated. In this example, the three different methods of costing are allocating the $1 million in three different ways. In Exhibit 7-18 the gold crown has been overcosted by $38.50 ($184.00 – $145.50) when the plantwide overhead rate is applied. Similarly, the mouthguard is undercosted by $7.50 ($32.00 – $39.50) when using the plantwide rate.

ABC costs are generally thought to be the most accurate because ABC takes into account (1) the specific resources each product uses (for example, casting resources) and (2) the extent to which they use these resources (for example, 4 DL hours of casting for the gold crown, but no DL hours of casting for the mouthguard).

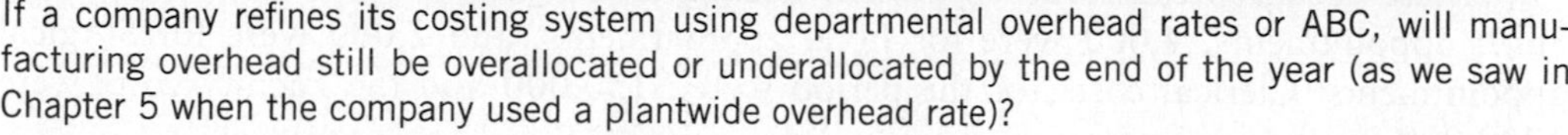


If a company refines its costing system using departmental overhead rates or ABC, will manufacturing overhead still be overallocated or underallocated by the end of the year (as we saw in Chapter 5 when the company used a plantwide overhead rate)?

**Answer:** Yes. The use of *any predetermined* allocation rate will result in the over- or underallocation of MOH. That is because predetermined rates are developed using budgeted data, before the actual MOH costs and actual cost driver activity for the year are known. Refined costing systems decrease cost distortion between products, but do not eliminate the issue of over- or underallocation.[6] As described in Chapter 5, cost of goods sold will need to be adjusted at year-end for the total amount of over- or underallocation.

## ABC in the Service Industry: Dan's Dentist Service

Through the majority of the chapter, ABC has been discussed in the context of manufacturing. An ABC system is also well suited to the service industry, as illustrated here by the example of Dan's Dentist Service (DDS). Dan is a dentist and owns a large practice, employing many dentists, hygienists, and dental technicians. DDS offers a variety of services that fall into three categories: Simple (a short appointment, such as dental cleaning); Long (a more complicated procedure such as filling a cavity); and Surgical (which includes dental surgeries and some orthodontic work).

[6] In some cases, ABC may reduce the total amount of over- or underallocation. How? Some activity cost pools may be overallocated, while others are underallocated, resulting in an offsetting total effect.

At DDS every patient is seen by a dentist. Patients in for Short appointments see a hygienist; and patients at DDS for Long appointments are seen by a Dental Technician (Tech). In addition, all patients go through an intake and discharge process with clerical staff. As a result of reviewing the operations, DDS has established the following activities and cost drivers:

| Activity | Cost Driver |
|---|---|
| Dentist Time | Time with patient (minutes) |
| Hygienist Time | Time with patient (minutes) |
| Tech Time | Time with patient (minutes) |
| Clerical Time | Number of appointments |
| Facility Maintenance | Number of appointments |

During the previous year, the total costs for dentists, hygienists, and techs and the amount of time (minutes) spent in each of Short, Long, and Surgical is outlined in the following table.

| | Time (minutes) Spent with Patient in each Service | | | Total Cost |
|---|---|---|---|---|
| | *Short* | *Long* | *Surgical* | |
| **Dentist** | 60,000 | 80,000 | 60,000 | $1,000,000 |
| **Hygienist** | 50,000 | 20,000 | | $ 210,000 |
| **Tech** | | 30,000 | 50,000 | $ 320,000 |

These costs represent 12,000 patient visits over the year, of which 6,000 were for Short appointments, 4,000 were for Long appointments, and 2,000 were for Surgical appointments. Clerical costs for the period were $150,000 and the Facility costs were $200,000.

In order to understand the cost of each kind of appointment (Short, Long, or Surgical), we first have to determine the activity pool rate for each activity. To do that, it is necessary to divide the total costs of an activity by the total amount of the cost driver of the activity.

| A | B | C | D | E |
|---|---|---|---|---|
| Activity | Activity Cost | Cost Driver | Activity Cost | Activity Rate |
| | | | | B/D |
| Dentist Time | $1,000,000 | Time with patient (minutes) | 200,000 | $ 5.00 |
| Hygienist Time | $ 210,000 | Time with patient (minutes) | 70,000 | $ 3.00 |
| Tech Time | $ 320,000 | Time with patient (minutes) | 80,000 | $ 4.00 |
| Clerical Time | $ 150,000 | Number of appointments | 12,000 | $12.50 |
| Facility | $ 240,000 | Number of appointments | 12,000 | $20.00 |

Once the activity pool rates are determined, the costs for each patient service can be established. First, the costs for each activity in a service are calculated (Column D, below). Then these costs are totalled to determine the total cost of each service.

For Short appointments, the calculation would be

| A | B | C | D |
|---|---|---|---|
| Activity | Activity Rate | Amount of Activity | Activity Cost |
| | | | B × C |
| Dentist Time | $ 5.00 | 60,000 | $300,000 |
| Hygienist Time | $ 3.00 | 50,000 | $150,000 |
| Tech Time | $ 4.00 | 0 | $ 0 |
| Clerical Time | $12.50 | 6,000 | $ 75,000 |
| Facility | $20.00 | 6,000 | $120,000 |
| Total Cost | $61.50 | | $645,000 |
| | | | *total cost of service* |

For Long appointments, the calculation would be

| A | B | C | D |
|---|---|---|---|
| Activity | Activity Rate | Amount of Activity | Activity Cost |
| | | | B × C |
| Dentist Time | $ 5.00 | 80,000 | $400,000 |
| Hygienist Time | $ 3.00 | 20,000 | $ 60,000 |
| Tech Time | $ 4.00 | 30,000 | $120,000 |
| Clerical Time | $12.50 | 4,000 | $ 50,000 |
| Facility | $20.00 | 4,000 | $ 80,000 |
| Total Cost | | | $710,000 |
| | | | *total cost of service* |

For Surgical Appointments, the calculation would be

| A | B | C | D |
|---|---|---|---|
| Activity | Activity Rate | Amount of Activity | Activity Cost |
| | | | B × C |
| Dentist Time | $ 5.00 | 60,000 | $300,000 |
| Hygienist Time | $ 3.00 | 0 | $ 0 |
| Tech Time | $ 4.00 | 50,000 | $200,000 |
| Clerical Time | $12.50 | 2,000 | $ 25,000 |
| Facility | $20.00 | 2,000 | $ 40,000 |
| Total Cost | | | $565,000 |
| | | | *total cost of service* |

To examine the cost for each appointment, it is necessary to divide the activity cost for each appointment type by the number of appointments (clerical time and facility maintenance are already on a per appointment basis).

*Cost of a Short Appointment*

| A | B | C | D |
|---|---|---|---|
| | | *Short Appointments* | |
| Activity | Activity Cost | # appointments | Cost / Appointment |
| | | | B / C |
| Dentist Time | $300,000 | 6,000 | $ 50.00 |
| Hygienist Time | $150,000 | 6,000 | $ 25.00 |
| Tech Time | $ 0 | 6,000 | $ 0.00 |
| Clerical Time | $75,000 | 6,000 | $ 12.50 |
| Facility | $120,000 | 6,000 | $ 20.00 |
| Total Cost | | | $107.50 |

*Cost of a Long Appointment*

| A | B | C | D |
|---|---|---|---|
| | | *Long Appointments* | |
| Activity | Activity Cost | # appointments | Cost / Appointment |
| | | | B / C |
| Dentist Time | $400,000 | 4,000 | $100.00 |
| Hygienist Time | $ 60,000 | 4,000 | $ 15.00 |
| Tech Time | $120,000 | 4,000 | $ 30.00 |
| Clerical Time | $ 50,000 | 4,000 | $ 12.50 |
| Facility | $ 80,000 | 4,000 | $ 20.00 |
| Total Cost | | | $177.50 |

*Cost of a Surgical Appointment*

| A | B | C | D |
|---|---|---|---|
| | | *Surgical Appointments* | |
| Activity | Activity Cost | # appointments | Cost / Appointment |
| | | | B / C |
| Dentist Time | $300,000 | 2,000 | $150.00 |
| Hygienist Time | $ 0 | 2,000 | $ 0.00 |
| Tech Time | $200,000 | 2,000 | $100.00 |
| Clerical Time | $ 25,000 | 2,000 | $ 12.50 |
| Facility | $ 40,000 | 2,000 | $ 20.00 |
| Total Cost | | | $282.50 |

It is interesting to note the most expensive service, when taken as a whole, is Long appointments, costing $710,000. However, Surgical appointments have the highest cost of $282.50 (and the lowest overall cost when the cost of the service is considered as a whole). This information can be used alongside pricing information to determine which parts of the operations of DDS are most profitable.

## The Cost Hierarchy: A Useful Guide for Setting Up Activity Cost Pools

Some companies use a classification system, called the cost hierarchy, to establish activity cost pools. Companies often have hundreds of different activities. To keep the ABC system manageable, companies need to keep the system as simple as possible, yet refined enough to accurately determine product costs.[7] The cost hierarchy, pictured in Exhibit 7-19, helps managers understand the nature of each activity cost pool and what drives it.

**EXHIBIT 7-19** The Cost Hierarchy

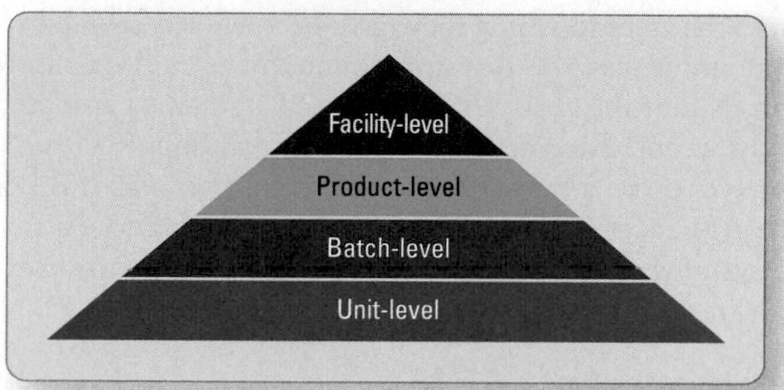


There are four categories of activity costs in this hierarchy, each determined by the underlying factor that drives its costs:

1. Unit-level activities—activities and costs incurred for every unit. Examples include inspecting and packaging each unit the company produces.
2. Batch-level activities—activities and costs incurred for every batch, regardless of the number of units in the batch. One example is machine set-up. Once the machines are set up for the specifications of the production run, the company could produce a batch of 1, 10, or 100 units, yet the company incurs the machine set-up cost only once for the entire batch.
3. Product-level activities—activities and costs incurred for a particular product, regardless of the number of units or batches of the product produced. Examples include the cost to research, develop, design, and market new models.
4. Facility-level activities—activities and costs incurred no matter how many units, batches, or products are produced in the plant. An example is facility upkeep: the cost of depreciation, insurance, property tax, and maintenance on the entire production plant.

By considering how the costs of different activities are consumed (at the unit, batch, product, or facility level), managers are often able to maintain a relatively simple, yet accurate, ABC system. After initially identifying perhaps 100 different activities, managers may be able to settle on 5 to 15 cost pools by combining activities that behave the same way (for example, batch-level activities) into the same cost pools.

### STOP & THINK

Do the journal entries used to record job costing differ if a manufacturer uses a refined cost allocation system rather than a single, plantwide overhead rate?

**Answer:** The journal entries used for a refined costing system are essentially the same as those described in Chapter 5 for a traditional job costing system. The only difference is that the company may decide to use several MOH accounts (one for each department or activity cost pool) rather than one MOH account. By using several MOH accounts, the manufacturer obtains more detailed information on each cost pool. This information may help managers make better estimates when calculating allocation rates the next year.

[7] When ABC system implementations fail, it is often due to managers' development of an overly complex system with too many cost pools and too many different cost drivers. After several redesigns of their ABC systems, Coca-Cola and Allied Signal both found that the simpler designs resulted in just as much accuracy. G. Cokins, "Learning to Love ABC," *Journal of Accountancy*, August 1999, pp. 37–39.

### Limitations and Impediments to Adopting ABC Systems

The development of ABC systems in organizations is a substantial project that requires a great deal of investment in terms of time and money. Further, ABC systems are more expensive to operate than traditional costing system due to the volume of data that must be tracked and measured. The advantage of better cost accuracy may not justify this expense and effort. In addition to the obvious elements of cost and benefit, ABC also raises concerns with respect to organizational buy-in. Managers who are familiar with traditional costing systems in the operations of their unit, or more importantly in the calculation of their bonuses, may resist a new system that changes the rules to which they have become accustomed.

Another factor that influences the decisions of many organizations regarding the adoption of ABC systems is that the cost calculations ABC systems generate are not compliant with most generally accepted accounting principles including IFRS and ASPE. Thus, an organization would have to run a parallel costing system that was IFRS or ASPE compliant in addition to the ABC approach. As the power of information systems increases, the cost of running two systems will continue to decline, but an organization is still forced to pay for the operations of two costing systems rather than one.

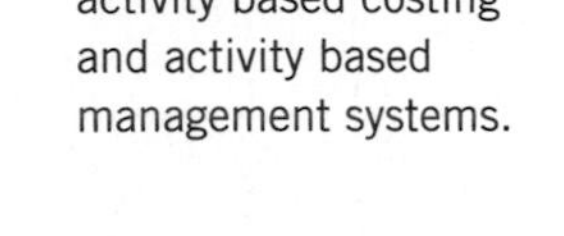
3 Understand the benefits and limitations of activity based costing and activity based management systems.

## Activity Based Management (ABM)

Activity based management (ABM) is an approach to managing organizational activities with a focus on eliminating waste, delays, defects, and any identifiable non-value added activities to make decisions that increase profits while satisfying customers' needs. Shaw Group can use ABC information for pricing and product mix decisions, for helping to identify ways of cutting costs, and for routine planning and control decisions as part of its ABM strategy.

### Pricing and Product Mix Decisions

The information provided by ABC showed Shaw Group's managers that gold crowns cost less to make and mouthguards cost more to make than indicated by the original plantwide cost allocation system. As a result, managers may decide to change pricing on these products. For example, the company may be able to reduce its price on gold crowns to become more price competitive. Or the company may decide to leave the price where it is, yet try to increase demand for this product since it is more profitable than originally assumed. Of course, managers will want to reevaluate the price charged for mouthguards. The price must be high enough to cover the cost of producing and selling the mouthguards and earn Shaw Group a reasonable profit but low enough to compete with other companies.

After implementing ABC, companies often realize they were overcosting their high-volume products and undercosting their low-volume products. Plantwide overhead rates based on volume-sensitive allocation bases (such as direct labour hours) end up allocating more cost to high-volume products and less cost to low-volume products. However, ABC recognizes that not all indirect costs are driven by the number of units produced. That is to say, not all costs are unit-level costs. Rather, many costs are incurred at the batch-level or product-level, where they can be spread over the number of units in the batch or in the product line. As shown in Exhibit 7-20, ABC tends

**EXHIBIT 7-20** Typical Result of ABC Costing

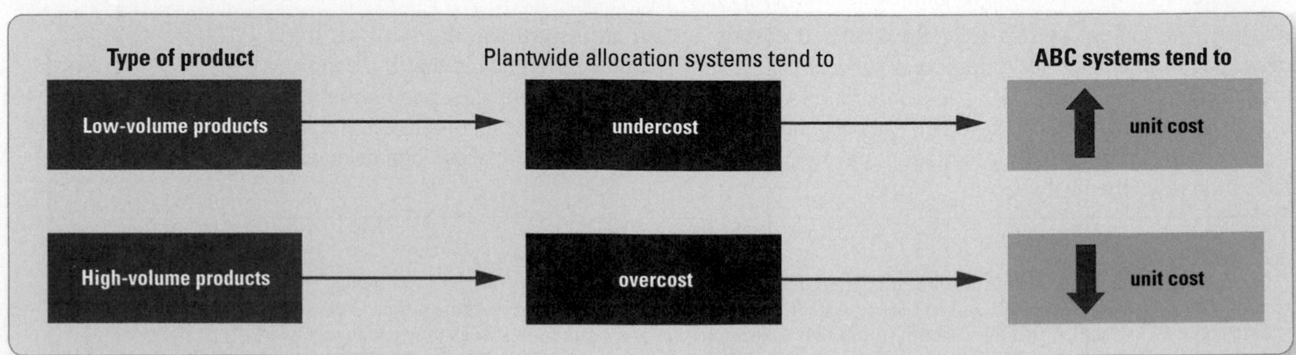

to increase the unit cost of low-volume products (that have fewer units over which to spread batch-level and product-level costs) and decrease the unit cost of high-volume products.

As a result of using ABC, many companies have found that they were actually losing money on some of their products, while earning much more profit than they had realized on other products! By shifting the mix of products offered away from the less profitable and toward the more profitable, companies are able to generate a higher operating income.

## Cutting Costs

Most companies adopt ABC to get more accurate product costs for pricing and product mix decisions, but they often reap even greater benefits by using ABM to pinpoint opportunities to cut costs. For example, using ABC allowed Shaw Group to better understand what drives its manufacturing overhead costs. The plantwide allocation system failed to pinpoint this, so managers could not effectively determine which costs could be minimized. Once the company switched to ABC, managers realized that it costs $12.50 each time a mould needs to be prepared, $5 for finishing each unit, and so forth. Now, production managers have a "starting place" for cutting costs.

Once managers identify the company's activities and their related costs, they can analyze whether all of the activities are really necessary. As the term suggests, **value-added activities** are activities that enhance the value of the product or service such that the customer is willing to pay for this benefit. Value-added services can include tangible activities such as processing raw bitumen into fuel. Activities can also be less tangible, such as the addition of a company's branding to an already manufactured product. In other words, these activities help satisfy the customer's expectations of the product or service. For example, fabricating units and finishing the units are value-added activities because they are necessary for changing raw materials into high-quality gold crowns and mouthguards.

On the other hand, **non-value-added activities** (also referred to as waste activities), are activities that neither enhance the customer's image of the product or service nor provide a competitive advantage. These types of activities, such as storage of inventory and wait time for production to begin, could be reduced or removed from the process with no ill effect on the end product or service. The goal of **value engineering**, as described in Exhibit 7-21, is to eliminate all waste in the system by making the company's processes as effective and efficient as possible. That means eliminating, reducing, or simplifying all non-value-added activities and examining whether value-added activities could be improved.

**EXHIBIT 7-21** The Goal of Value Engineering

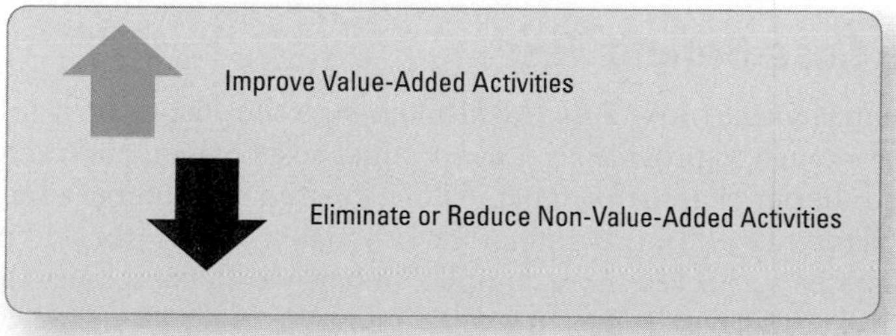


One way of determining whether an activity adds value is to ask if it could be eliminated or reduced by improving another part of the process. For example, could the movement of parts be eliminated or reduced by changing the factory layout? Could inventory storage be eliminated if the company purchased only the raw materials that were needed for each day's production run? Could inspection be reduced if more emphasis were placed on improving the production process, training employees, or using better-quality inputs? We will now discuss tools that many companies have adopted to identify and eliminate these costly non-value-added activities. Keep in mind the discussion on lean manufacturing and the costs of quality from Chapter 1 as you proceed.

### Routine Planning and Control Decisions

In addition to pricing, product mix, and cost-cutting decisions, Shaw Group can use ABC in routine planning and control. Activity based budgeting uses the costs of activities to create budgets. Managers can compare actual activity costs to budgeted activity costs to determine how well they are achieving their goals.

### Using ABC Outside of Manufacturing

We have discussed how ABC can be used in multiple settings—both manufacturing and service-based organizations—to more accurately allocate MOH. For example, The Bay may use ABC to allocate the cost of store operating activities such as ordering, stocking, and customer service among its housewares, clothing, and electronics departments. An accounting firm may use ABC to allocate secretarial support, software costs, and travel costs between its tax, audit, and consulting clients. Even manufacturers may use ABC to allocate operating activities, such as research and development, marketing, and distribution costs, to different product lines. ABC has been used to determine customer profitability, not just product or service profitability. Firms use the same four basic steps discussed above but apply them to indirect *operating* costs rather than indirect *manufacturing* costs (MOH). Once again, managers can use the data generated by ABC to determine which products or services to emphasize, to set prices, to cut costs, and to make other routine planning and control decisions.

**STOP & THINK**

Can governmental agencies use ABC/ABM to run their operations more efficiently?

**Answer:** ABC/ABM is not just for private-sector companies. A governmental agency, such as Canada Post or the City of Regina, could successfully use ABC/ABM to run its operations more cost effectively. For example, in the past Canada Post accepted customer payments only in the form of cash or cheques. An ABC analysis may have been used to study the cost of its revenue collection procedures (activities). This could have revealed that it was cheaper to accept debit and credit card sales. Enabling debit and credit card sales may also produce higher customer satisfaction, allowing Canada Post to better compete with private mail and package carriers.

The City of Regina could use ABC to study the cost of providing city services (activities) to local citizens. Once the city determines the cost of its activities, it could obtain competitive bids for those same services from private businesses. As a result, the city could outsource many activities to private-sector firms for a lower cost and save taxpayers millions of dollars.

## Passing the Cost–Benefit Test

Like all other management tools, ABC/ABM must pass the cost–benefit test. The system should be refined enough to provide accurate product costs but simple enough for managers to understand. In our chapter example, ABC increased the number of allocation rates from the single plantwide allocation rate in the original system to six activity cost allocation rates. ABC systems are even more complex in real-world companies that have many more activities and cost drivers.

## Sustainability and Refined Costing Systems

See Exercises E7-19A and E7-30B

Refined costing systems are almost always a necessity for companies that wish to move toward environmental sustainability. Why? Because jobs and product lines do not drive environmental overhead costs equally. Even a smaller manufacturing company with two to three product lines will often find that environmental costs, such as solid waste disposal, water and energy consumption, hazardous material training, and so forth, are not driven equally between each product line. If a

*continued*

company uses a plantwide overhead rate, environmental and nonenvironmental overhead costs will be combined within one cost pool, where they will be allocated to each of the company's product lines using the same rate. However, refined costing systems allow companies to identify and separately pool overhead costs affecting the environment and properly allocate each of those cost pools to the activities and products that drive those costs. The use of refined costing systems creates better transparency, thus giving management a clear plan for reducing the company's environmental impact.

## Circumstances Favouring ABC/ABM Systems

ABC and ABM pass the cost–benefit test when the benefits of adopting ABC/ABM exceed the costs.

***The benefits of adopting ABC/ABM are higher for companies in competitive markets because***

- Accurate product cost information is essential for setting competitive sales prices that still allow the company to earn a profit.
- ABM can pinpoint opportunities for cost savings, which increase the company's profit or are passed on to customers through lower prices.

***The benefits of adopting ABC/ABM are higher when the risk of cost distortion is high, for example, when***

- The company produces many different products that use different types and amounts of resources. (If all products use similar types and amounts of resources, a simple plantwide allocation system works fine.)
- The company has high indirect costs. (If the company has relatively low indirect costs, it matters less how they are allocated.)
- The company produces high volumes of some products and low volumes of other products. (Plantwide allocation systems based on a volume-related driver, such as direct labour hours, tend to overcost high-volume products and undercost low-volume products.)

We have seen that ABC offers many benefits. However, the cost and time required to implement and maintain an ABC system are often quite high. Some companies report spending up to four years to design and implement their ABC systems. The larger the company, the longer it usually takes. Top management support is crucial for the success of such an expensive and time-consuming initiative. Without such support, ABC implementations might easily be abandoned for an "easier" allocation system. Since we know ABC systems are costly to implement, how can a company judge the costs involved with setting one up?

***The costs of adopting ABC are generally lower when the company has***

- Accounting and information system expertise to develop the system. However, even "canned" accounting packages offer ABC modules. Small companies often find that Excel spreadsheets can be used to implement ABC, rather than integrating ABC into their general ledger software.
- Information technology such as bar coding, optical scanning, web-based data collection, or data warehouse systems to record and compile cost driver data.

***Are real-world companies glad they adopted ABC?***

Usually, but not always. A survey shows that 89% of the companies using ABC data say that it was worth the cost.[8] Adoption is on the rise among financial companies,

[8]K. Krumwiede, "ABC: Why It's Tried and How It Succeeds," *Management Accounting*, April 1998, pp. 32–38.

utilities, and nonprofits, but ABC is not a cure-all. As the controller for one manufacturer said, "ABC will not reduce cost; it will only help you understand costs better to know what to correct."

### Signs that the Old System May Be Distorting Costs

Broken cars or computers simply stop running. But unlike cars and computers, even broken or outdated costing systems continue to report "product costs." How can you tell whether a cost system is broken and needs repair? In other words, how can you tell whether an existing cost system is distorting costs and needs to be refined by way of departmental rates or ABC?

A company's product cost system may need repair in the following situations.

***Managers don't understand costs and profits.***

- In bidding for jobs, managers lose bids they expected to win and win bids they expected to lose.
- Competitors with similar high-volume products price their products below the company's costs but still earn good profits.
- Employees do not believe the cost numbers reported by the accounting system.

***The cost system is outdated.***

- The company has diversified its product offerings since the allocation system was first developed.
- The company has reengineered its production process but has not changed its accounting system to reflect the new production environment.

## Sustainability and Lean Thinking

Sustainability and lean thinking have many similarities: Both practices seek to reduce waste. However, lean operations focus on eliminating waste and empowering employees in an effort to increase economic profits. "Lean and green" operations focus on eliminating waste and empowering employees not only to increase economic profits but also to preserve the planet and improve the lives of *all* people touched by the company. While lean practices tend to centre on *internal* operational waste, green practices also consider the *external* waste that may occur as a result of the product. To become greener, a lean company should be particularly cognizant of all waste that could harm the planet: packaging waste, water waste, energy waste, and emissions waste that occur both from manufacturing the product *and* from consumers using and eventually disposing of the product.

See Exercises E7-19A and E7-30B

## TRY IT!

Which of the following would you expect to see at a company that espouses lean thinking?

1. Larger inventories
2. Smaller batch sizes
3. More organized workstations
4. Longer setup times
5. Lower-level small-team problem solving
6. Centralized storage cribs
7. Pull system

Please see page 451 for solutions

# DECISION GUIDELINES

## Refined Costing Systems

The new managers of Maplewood Equestrian Centre just outside Ottawa, Ontario, are looking at how to determine the cost of the products and services that the centre offers, such as the production of hay, boarding of horses, and lessons for students. They need to decide what costing system to use. These are some of the questions that they considered in their decision making.

| Decision | Guidelines |
|---|---|
| How do we develop an ABC system? | 1. Identify the activities and estimate the total MOH associated with each activity. These are known as the activity cost pools.<br>2. Select a cost allocation base for each activity, and estimate the total amount that will be used during the year.<br>3. Calculate an activity cost allocation rate for each activity.<br>4. Allocate some MOH from each activity to the individual jobs that use the activities. |
| How do we compute an activity cost allocation rate? | $\frac{\text{Total estimated activity cost pool}}{\text{Total estimated activity allocation base}}$ |
| How do we allocate an activity's cost to a job? | $\text{Activity cost allocation rate} \times \text{Actual amount of activity allocation base used by job}$ |
| What types of decisions would benefit from the use of ABC? | Managers use ABC data in ABM to make decisions on the following:<br>• Pricing and product mix<br>• Cost cutting<br>• Routine planning and control |
| What are the main benefits of ABC? | • More accurate product cost information<br>• More detailed information on costs of activities and associated cost drivers to help managers control costs |
| When is ABC most likely to pass the cost–benefit test? | • The company is in a competitive environment and needs accurate product costs.<br>• The company makes different products that use different amounts of resources.<br>• The company has high indirect costs.<br>• The company produces high volumes of some products and lower volumes of other products.<br>• The company has accounting and information technology expertise to implement the system.<br>• The old cost system appears to be "broken." |
| How do we tell when a cost system needs to be refined? | • Managers lose bids they expected to win and win bids they expected to lose.<br>• Competitors earn profits despite pricing high-volume products below the company's costs.<br>• Employees do not believe cost numbers.<br>• The company uses a single allocation base system, developed long ago.<br>• The company has reengineered the production process but not the accounting system. |

# SUMMARY PROBLEM 1

Edmonton Auto Parts (EAP) has a Seat Manufacturing Department that uses ABC. EAP's activity cost allocation rates include the following:

| Activity | Allocation Base | Activity Cost Allocation Rate |
|---|---|---|
| Machining | Number of machine hours | $30.00 per machine hour |
| Assembling | Number of parts | 0.50 per part |
| Packaging | Number of finished seats | 0.90 per finished seat |

Suppose Ford Canada has asked for a bid on 50,000 built-in baby seats that would be installed as an option on some Ford SUVs. Each seat has 20 parts, and the direct materials cost per seat is $11. The job would require 10,000 direct labour hours at a labour wage rate of $25 per hour. In addition, EAP will use a total of 400 machine hours to fabricate some of the parts required for the seats.

### Requirements

1. Compute the total cost of producing and packaging 50,000 baby seats. Also compute the average cost per seat.
2. For bidding, EAP adds a 30% markup to total cost. What price will the company bid for the Ford order?
3. Suppose that instead of an ABC system, EAP has a traditional product costing system that allocates manufacturing overhead at a plantwide overhead rate of $65 per direct labour hour. The baby-seat order will require 10,000 direct labour hours. Compute the total cost of producing the baby seats and the average cost per seat. What price will EAP bid using this system's total cost?
4. Use your answers to Requirements 2 and 3 to explain how ABC can help EAP make a better decision about the bid price it will offer Ford.

## ▪ SOLUTION

### Requirement 1

Total Cost of Order and Average Cost per Seat

| | |
|---|---|
| Direct materials: 50,000 seats × $11.00 per seat | $ 550,000 |
| Direct labour: 10,000 DL hours × $25.00 per DL hour | 250,000 |
| Manufacturing overhead: | |
| Machining, 400 machine hours × $30 per machine hour | 12,000 |
| Assembling, (50,000 × 20 parts) × $0.50 per part | 500,000 |
| Packaging, 50,000 seats × $0.90 per seat | 45,000 |
| Total cost of order | $1,357,000 |
| Divide by number of seats | ÷ 50,000 |
| Average cost per seat | $ 27.14 |

### Requirement 2

Bid Price (ABC System)

Bid price ($1,357,000 × 130%) = $1,764,100

**Requirement 3**

Bid Price (Traditional System)

| | |
|---|---|
| Direct materials: 50,000 seats × $11.00 | $ 550,000 |
| Direct labour: 10,000 DL hours × $25.00 per DL hour | 250,000 |
| Manufacturing overhead: 10,000 DL hours × $65 per DL hour | 650,000 |
| Total cost of order | $1,450,000 |
| Divide by number of seats | ÷ 50,000 |
| Average cost per seat | $ 29.00 |
| Bid price ($1,450,000 × 130%) | $1,885,000 |

**Requirement 4**

EAP's bid would be $120,900 higher using the plantwide overhead rate than using ABC ($1,885,000 versus $1,764,100). Assuming that the ABC system more accurately captures the costs caused by the order, the traditional plantwide overhead system overcosts the order. This leads to a higher bid price that reduces EAP's chance of winning the bid. The ABC system shows that EAP can increase its chance of winning the bid by bidding a lower price and still make a profit.

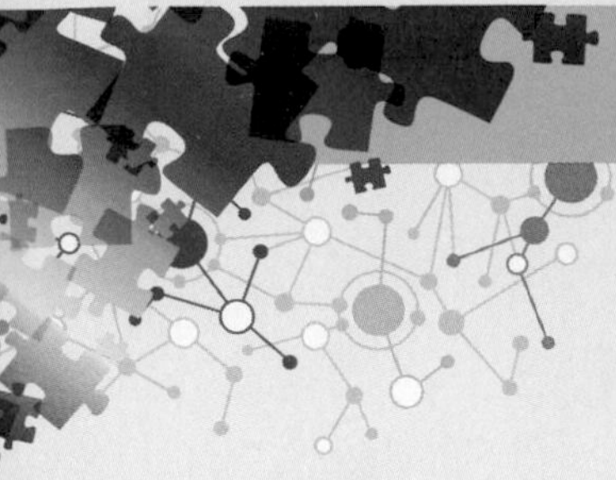

# END OF CHAPTER

## LEARNING OBJECTIVES

1 Develop and use departmental overhead rates to allocate indirect costs.

2 Develop and use activity based costing (ABC) to allocate indirect costs.

3 Understand the benefits and limitations of activity based costing and activity based management systems.

## ACCOUNTING VOCABULARY

**Activity Based Costing (ABC) (p. 405)** Focuses on *activities* as the fundamental cost objects. The costs of those activities become building blocks for compiling the indirect costs of products, services, and customers.

**Activity Based Management (ABM) (p. 414)** Using activity based cost information to make decisions that increase profits while satisfying customers' needs.

**Batch-level Activities (p. 413)** Activities and costs incurred for every batch, regardless of the number of units in the batch.

**Cost Distortion (p. 398)** Overcosting some products while undercosting other products.

**Departmental Overhead Rates (p. 400)** Separate manufacturing overhead rates established for each department.

**Facility-level Activities (p. 413)** Activities and costs incurred no matter how many units, batches, or products are produced in the plant.

**Non-value-added Activities (p. 415)** Activities that neither enhance the customer's image of the product or service nor provide a competitive advantage; also known as waste activities.

**Plantwide Overhead Rate (p. 398)** The single rate used to allocate all overhead incurred in the entire plant among the jobs and products produced.

**Product-level Activities (p. 413)** Activities and costs incurred for a particular product, regardless of the number of units or batches of the product produced.

**Unit-level Activities (p. 413)** Activities and costs incurred for every unit produced.

**Value Engineering (p. 415)** Eliminating waste in the system by making the company's processes as effective and efficient as possible.

**Value-added Activities (p. 415)** Activities that enhance the value of the product or service such that the customer is willing to pay for this benefit.



## QUICK CHECK

1. (Learning Objective 1) Which of the following reasons would indicate that a company should consider using departmental overhead rates rather than using a single plantwide overhead rate?
   a. Each product is in each department for a different length of time.
   b. Each department spends different amounts on manufacturing overhead.
   c. Each department incurs different types of manufacturing overhead.
   d. All of the above statements are correct.

2. (Learning Objective 2) Which of the following statements regarding steps in computing ABC cost allocation rates is correct?
   a. Costs from each activity are allocated to individual jobs that use those activities.
   b. Manufacturing overhead costs associated with each primary production activity are estimated.
   c. The amounts of the allocation base to be used for each primary production activity are estimated.
   d. All of the above statements are correct regarding steps in calculating ABC cost allocation rates.

3. (Learning Objective 3) Manufacturing overhead is allocated to jobs in an ABC system by using which following formula?
   a. Activity cost allocation rate × Estimated amount of activity allocation base used by the job
   b. Activity cost allocation rate ÷ Estimated amount of activity allocation base used by the job
   c. Activity cost allocation rate = Actual amount of activity allocation base used by the job
   d. Activity cost allocation rate ÷ Actual amount of activity allocation base used by the job
4. (Learning Objective 2) The legal costs associated with filing a patent for a new model of oven at an appliance manufacturer is an example of which type of activity?
   a. Unit-level
   b. Batch-level
   c. Product-level
   d. Facility-level
5. (Learning Objective 3) Which of the following is *false*?
   a. ABC focuses on allocating indirect costs.
   b. Advances in information technology have made it feasible for more companies to adopt ABC.
   c. ABC is only for manufacturing firms.
   d. A system that uses ABC is more refined than one that uses departmental overhead rates.
6. (Learning Objective 3) Companies can use ABC information for what decisions?
   a. Pricing
   b. Cost cutting
   c. Evaluating managers' performance
   d. All of the above
7. (Learning Objective 3) Which of the following is *not* a good reason for a computer company to use ABC?
   a. The computer industry is highly competitive.
   b. The computer company produces many more desktops than servers, and servers are more difficult to assemble.
   c. Most costs are direct; indirect costs are a small proportion of total costs.
   d. The computer company has advanced information technology, including bar-coded materials and labour.

**Quick Check Answers**

1. *d* 2. *d* 3. *c* 4. *c* 5. *c* 6. *d* 7. *c* 8. *d* 9. *a* 10. *c*

# SHORT EXERCISES

## S7-1 Understand key terms *(Learning Objectives 1, 2, & 3)*

Listed below are several terms. Complete the following statements with one of these terms. You may use a term more than once, and some terms may not be used at all.

| | | | |
|---|---|---|---|
| Plantwide overhead rate | Unit-level costs | Overcosted | Batch-level costs |
| Non-value-added activities | Cost distortion | Value-added activities | Facility-level costs |
| Undercosted | Product-level costs | Activity based costing | |

a. The more detailed information provided by ______________ helps managers control costs.

b. ______________ are incurred for every individual unit.

c. ______________ are activities for which the customer is willing to pay.

d. The cost to design a new product is an example of ______________.

e. ______________ include storage, moving, and inspecting activities.

f. ______________ are incurred for each batch of products.

g. Total manufacturing overhead is divided by one cost allocation base to calculate a ______________.

h. It is likely that ______________ will result if a single plantwide overhead rate is used when products vary widely in their usage of various MOH activities.

i. ______________ are incurred to support the entire organization and cannot be traced to any particular product or batch.

**S7-2 Use departmental overhead rates to allocate manufacturing overhead** *(Learning Objective 1)*

Offbraugh Furniture uses departmental overhead rates (rather than a plantwide overhead rate) to allocate its manufacturing overhead to jobs. The company's two production departments have the following departmental overhead rates:

| | |
|---|---|
| Cutting Department: | $12 per machine hour |
| Finishing Department: | $17 per direct labour hour |

Job 392 used the following direct labour hours and machine hours in the two manufacturing departments:

| Job 392 | Cutting Department | Finishing Department |
|---|---|---|
| Direct labour hours | 2 | 6 |
| Machine hours | 8 | 1 |

1. How much MOH should be allocated to Job 392?
2. Assume that direct labour is paid at a rate of $25 per hour and Job 392 used $2,500 of direct materials. What was the total manufacturing cost of Job 392?

**S7-3 Compute departmental overhead rates** *(Learning Objective 1)*

Pack's Snacks makes potato chips, corn chips, and cheese puffs using three different production lines within the same manufacturing plant. Currently, Pack's uses a single plantwide overhead rate to allocate its $3,500,000 of annual manufacturing overhead. Of this amount, $1,800,000 is associated with the potato chip line, $1,000,000 with the corn chip line, and $700,000 with the cheese puff line. Pack's plant is currently running a total of 17,500 machine hours: 11,250 in the potato chip line, 3,450 in the corn chip line, and 2,800 in the cheese puff line. Pack's considers machine hours to be the cost driver of MOH costs.

1. What is Pack's plantwide overhead rate?
2. Calculate the departmental overhead rates for Pack's three production lines. Round all answers to the nearest cent.
3. Which products are overcosted by the plantwide rate? Which products are undercosted by the plantwide rate?

**S7-4 Compute activity cost allocation rates** *(Learning Objective 2)*

Stufft produces different styles of potato chips (ruffled, flat, thick-cut, gourmet) for different corporate customers. Each style of potato chip requires different preparation times, different cooking and draining times (depending on desired fat content), and different packaging (single serving versus bulk). Therefore, Stufft has decided to try ABC costing to better capture the manufacturing overhead costs incurred by each style of chip. Stufft has identified the following activities related to yearly MOH costs and cost drivers associated with producing potato chips:

| Activity | Machine Overhead | Cost Driver |
|---|---|---|
| Preparation | $600,000 | Preparation time |
| Cooking and draining | $900,000 | Cooking and draining time |
| Packaging | $300,000 | Units packaged |

Compute the activity cost allocation rates for each activity assuming the following total estimated activity for the year: 15,000 preparation hours, 30,000 cooking and draining hours, and 6 million packages.

**S7-5** **Continuation of S7-4: Use ABC to allocate overhead** *(Learning Objective 2)*

Stufft just received an order to produce 12,000 single-serving bags of gourmet, fancy-cut, low-fat potato chips. The order will require 16 preparation hours and 32 cooking and draining hours. Use the activity rates you calculated in S7-4 to compute the following:

1. What is the total amount of MOH that should be allocated to this order?
2. How much MOH should be assigned to each bag?
3. What other costs will Stufft need to consider to determine the total manufacturing costs of this order?

**S7-6** **Calculate a job cost using ABC** *(Learning Objective 2)*

Berg Industries, a family-run small manufacturer, has adopted an ABC costing system. The following manufacturing activities, indirect manufacturing costs, and usage of cost drivers have been estimated for the year:

| Activity | Estimated Total Manufacturing Overhead Costs | Estimated Total Usage of Cost Driver |
|---|---|---|
| Machine set-up | $ 150,000 | 3,000 set-ups |
| Machining | $1,000,000 | 5,000 machine hours |
| Quality control | $ 337,500 | 4,500 tests run |

During May, Evan and Sajiah Berg machined and assembled Job 624. Evan worked a total of 10 hours on the job, while Sajiah worked 5 hours on the job. Evan is paid a $25 per hour wage rate, while Sajiah is paid $30 per hour because of her additional experience level. Direct materials requisitioned for Job 624 totalled $1,050. The following additional information was collected on Job 624: The job required 1 machine set-up, 5 machine hours, and 2 quality control tests.

1. Compute the activity cost allocation rates for the year.
2. Complete the following job cost record for Job 624:

| Job Cost Record JOB 624 | Manufacturing Costs |
|---|---|
| Direct materials | ? |
| Direct labour | ? |
| Manufacturing overhead | ? |
| Total job cost | $ ? |

**S7-7** **Apply activity cost allocation rates** *(Learning Objective 2)*

Narnia Technology uses ABC to allocate all of its manufacturing overhead. Narnia's Cell Phone Department, which assembles and tests digital processors, reports the following data regarding processor G27:

| | |
|---|---|
| Direct materials cost | $14.00 |
| Direct labour cost | $42.00 |
| Manufacturing overhead allocated | ? |
| Manufacturing product cost | $ ? |

The activities required to build the processors are as follows:

| Activity | Allocation Base | Cost Allocated to Each Unit |
|---|---|---|
| Start station | Number of processor boards | 1 × \$ 0.90 = \$ 0.90 |
| Dip insertion | Number of dip insertions | 40 × \$ 0.25 = ? |
| Manual insertion | Number of manual insertions | 5 × \$ ? = 2.00 |
| Wave solder | Number of processor boards soldered | 1 × \$ 4.50 = 4.50 |
| Backload | Number of backload insertions | ? × \$ 0.70 = 2.80 |
| Test | Standard time each processor board is in test activity (hours) | 0.15 × \$90.00 = ? |
| Defect analysis | Standard time for defect analysis and repair (hours) | 0.16 × \$ ? = 8.00 |
| Total | | \$ ? |

1. Fill in the blanks in both the opening schedule and the list of activities.
2. Why might managers favour this ABC system instead of the older system that allocated all MOH costs on the basis of direct labour?

**S7-8 Classifying costs within the cost hierarchy** *(Learning Objective 2)*

Classify each of the following costs as unit-level, batch-level, product-level, or facility-level.

a. Product line manager salary
b. CEO salary
c. Machine set-up costs that are incurred whenever a new production order is started
d. Direct materials
e. Order processing
f. Factory utilities
g. Patent for new product
h. Direct labour
i. Cost to inspect each product as it is finished
j. Depreciation on factory
k. Engineering costs for new product
l. Shipment of an order to a customer

**S7-9 Classifying costs within the cost hierarchy** *(Learning Objective 2)*

Halliwell Manufacturing produces a variety of plastic containers using an extrusion blow-moulding process. The following activities are part of Halliwell Manufacturing's operating process. Classify each activity as unit-level, batch-level, product-level, or facility-level.

1. Each container is cut from the mould once the plastic has cooled and hardened.
2. Patents are obtained for each new type of container mould.
3. Plastic resins are used as the main direct material for the containers.
4. A plant manager oversees the entire manufacturing operation.
5. The sales force incurs travel expenses to attend various trade shows throughout the country to market the containers.
6. Each container product line has a product line manager.
7. The extrusion machine is calibrated for each batch of containers made.
8. Each type of container has its own unique moulds.
9. Routine maintenance is performed on the extrusion machines.
10. Rent is paid for the building that houses the manufacturing processes.

**S7-10 Determine the usefulness of refined costing systems in various situations** *(Learning Objective 3)*

In each of the following situations, determine whether the company would be (1) more likely or (2) less likely to benefit from refining its costing system.

1. The company has reengineered its production process but has not changed its accounting system.

2. The company produces few products, and each product consumes resources in a similar manner.
3. The company operates in a very competitive industry.
4. The company has very few indirect costs.
5. The company produces high volumes of some of its products and low volumes of other products.
6. In bidding for jobs, managers lost bids they expected to win and won bids they expected to lose.

**Mission Inc. Data Set for S7-11 through S7-14:**

Mission Inc. is a technology consulting firm focused on website development and integration of internet business applications. President Susan Nelson's ear is ringing after an unpleasant call from client Jerry Webb. Webb was irate after opening his bill for Mission's redesign of his company's website. Webb said that Mission's major competitor, Delta Applications, charged much lower fees to another company for which Webb serves on the board of directors.

Nelson is puzzled for two reasons. First, she is confident that her firm knows website design and support as well as any of Mission's competitors. Nelson cannot understand how Delta Applications can undercut Mission's rates and still make a profit. But Delta Applications is reputed to be very profitable. Second, just yesterday Nelson received a call from client Keith Greg. Greg was happy with the excellent service and reasonable fees Nelson charged him for adding a database-driven job-posting feature to his company's website. Nelson was surprised by Greg's compliments because this was an unusual job for Mission that required development of complex database management and control applications, and she had felt a little uneasy accepting it.

Like most consulting firms, Mission traces direct labour to individual engagements (jobs). Mission allocates indirect costs to engagements using a budgeted rate based on direct labour hours. Nelson is happy with this system, which she has used since she established Mission in 1995.

Nelson expects to incur $706,000 of indirect costs this year, and she expects her firm to work 5,000 direct labour hours. Nelson and the other systems consultants earn $350 per hour. Clients are billed at 150% of direct labour cost. Last month, Mission's consultants spent 100 hours on Webb's engagement. They also spent 100 hours on Greg's engagement.

**S7-11 Compute and use traditional allocation rate** *(Learning Objective 1)*

Refer to the Mission data set.

1. Compute Mission's indirect cost allocation rate.
2. Compute the total costs assigned to the Webb and Greg engagements.
3. Compute the operating income from the Webb and Greg engagements.

**S7-12 Identify clues that the old system is broken** *(Learning Objective 3)*

Refer to the Mission data set. List all of the signals or clues indicating that Mission's cost system may be "broken."

**S7-13 Compute activity cost allocation rates** *(Learning Objective 2)*

Refer to the Mission data set. Nelson suspects that her allocation of indirect costs could be giving misleading results, so she decides to develop an ABC system. She identifies three activities: documentation preparation, information technology support, and training. Nelson figures that documentation costs are driven by the number of pages, information technology support costs are driven by the number of software applications used, and training costs are most closely associated with the number of direct labour hours worked. Estimates of the costs and quantities of the allocation bases follow:

| Activity | Estimated Cost | Allocation Base | Estimated Quantity of Cost Driver |
|---|---|---|---|
| Documentation preparation | $100,000 | Pages | 3,125 pages |
| Information technology support | 156,000 | Applications used | 780 applications |
| Training | 450,000 | Direct labour hours | 5,000 hours |
| Total indirect costs | $706,000 | | |

Compute the cost allocation rate for each activity.

**S7-14** **Continuation of S7-13: compute job costs using ABC** *(Learning Objective 2)*

Refer to the Mission data set and the activity cost allocation rates you computed in S7-13. The Webb and Greg engagements used the following resources last month:

| Cost Driver | Webb | Greg |
|---|---|---|
| Direct labour hours | 100 | 100 |
| Pages | 50 | 300 |
| Application used | 1 | 78 |

1. Compute the cost assigned to the Webb engagement and to the Greg engagement using the ABC system.
2. Compute the operating income from the Webb engagement and from the Greg engagement using the ABC system.

**S7-15** **Identifying costs as value-added or non-valued-added** *(Learning Objective 3)*

Identify which of the following manufacturing overhead costs are value-added and which are non-value-added:

a. Cost of moving raw materials into production
b. Product inspection
c. Engineering design costs for a new product
d. Costs arising from backlog in production
e. Costs of warehousing raw materials
f. Wages of the workers assembling products
g. Salary for supervisor on the factory floor
h. Costs of reworking of defective units

**S7-16** **Identifying activities as value-added or non-valued-added** *(Learning Objective 3)*

Identify which of the following manufacturing overhead costs are value-added and which are non-value-added.

1. Moving raw materials from the receiving area to the storage area
2. Storing raw materials until needed in production
3. Inspecting raw materials when they arrive to make sure that they meet specifications
4. Assembling parts into a completed product
5. Stacking partially completed units while awaiting the next production step
6. Breaking some of the raw materials while in storage
7. Performing product warranty work on units that malfunctioned for customers
8. Delivering the product to the customer

# EXERCISES Group A

Check sum: Plantwide allocation is $44 per direct labour hour.

**E7-17A** **Compare traditional and departmental cost allocations** *(Learning Objective 1)*

Heisenburg Furnishings manufactures upscale custom furniture. Heisenburg Furnishings currently uses a plantwide overhead rate based on direct labour hours to allocate its $1,100,000 of manufacturing overhead to individual jobs. However, Werner Heisenburg, owner and CEO, is considering refining the company's costing system by using departmental overhead rates. Currently, the Machining Department incurs $900,000 of MOH while the Finishing Department incurs $350,000 of MOH. Ernie has identified machine hours (MH) as the primary MOH cost driver in the Machining Department and direct labour (DL) hours as the primary cost driver in the Finishing Department.

The Heisenburg Furnishings plant completed Jobs 450 and 455 on May 15. Both jobs incurred a total of 6 DL hours throughout the entire production process. Job 450 incurred 2 MH in the Machining Department and 5 DL hours in the Finishing Department. (The other DL hour occurred in the Machining Department.) Job 455 incurred 6 MH in the Machining

Department and 4 DL hours in the Finishing Department. (The other 2 DL hours occurred in the Machining Department.)

**Requirements**

1. Compute the plantwide overhead rate assuming that the company expects to incur 25,000 total DL hours during the year.
2. Compute departmental overhead rates assuming that the company expects to incur 15,000 MH in the Machining Department and 17,500 DL hours in the Finishing Department during the year.
3. If the company continues to use the plantwide overhead rate, how much manufacturing overhead would be allocated to Job 450 and Job 455?
4. If the company uses departmental overhead rates, how much MOH would be allocated to Job 450 and Job 455?
5. Based on your answers to Requirements 3 and 4, does the plantwide overhead rate overcost or undercost either job? Explain. If the company sells its furniture at 125% of cost, will his choice of allocation systems affect product pricing? Explain.

### E7-18A Compute activity rates and apply to jobs *(Learning Objective 2)*

Betelgeuse Inc. uses ABC to account for its chrome wheel manufacturing process. Company managers have identified four manufacturing activities that incur manufacturing overhead costs: materials handling, machine set-up, insertion of parts, and finishing. The budgeted activity costs for the upcoming year and their allocation bases are as follows:

| Activity | Total Budgeted Manufacturing Overhead Cost | Allocation Base |
|---|---|---|
| Materials handling | $ 12,000 | Number of parts |
| Machine set-up | 3,400 | Number of set-ups |
| Insertion of parts | 48,000 | Number of parts |
| Finishing | 80,000 | Finishing direct labour hours |
| Total | $143,400 | |

Check sum: Total manufacturing overhead assigned to job 420 is $81,40.

Betelgeuse Inc. expects to produce 1,000 chrome wheels during the year. The wheels are expected to use 3,000 parts, require 10 set-ups, and consume 2,000 hours of finishing time.

Job 420 used 150 parts, required 1 set-up, and consumed 120 finishing hours.
Job 510 used 400 parts, required 2 set-ups, and consumed 320 finishing hours.

**Requirements**

1. Compute the cost allocation rate for each activity.
2. Compute the MOH cost that should be assigned to Job 420.
3. Compute the MOH cost that should be assigned to Job 510.

### E7-19A Apply activity cost allocation rates *(Learning Objective 2)*

Scofield Industries manufactures a variety of custom products. The company has traditionally used a plantwide manufacturing overhead rate based on machine hours to allocate manufacturing overhead to its products. The company estimates that it will incur $790,000 in total manufacturing overhead costs in the upcoming year and will use 10,000 machine hours.

Up to this point, hazardous waste disposal fees have been absorbed into the plantwide manufacturing overhead rate and allocated to all products as part of the manufacturing overhead process. Recently, the company has been experiencing significantly increased waste disposal fees for hazardous waste generated by certain products, and as a result, profit margins on all products have been negatively impacted. Company management wants to implement an activity based costing system so that managers know the cost of each product, including its hazardous waste disposal costs.

Expected usage and costs for manufacturing overhead activities for the upcoming year are as follows:

Check sum: Req. 1 Total cost of job is $24,000.

| Description of Cost Pool | Estimated Cost | Cost Driver | Estimated Activity for this Year |
|---|---|---|---|
| Machine maintenance costs | $250,000 | Number of machine hours | 10,000 |
| Engineering change orders | $240,000 | Number of change orders | 4,000 |
| Hazardous waste disposal | $300,000 | Kg of hazardous materials generated | 1,000 |
| Total overhead cost | $790,000 | | |

During the year, Job 356 is started and completed. Usage for this job is as follows:

300 kg of direct materials at $50 per kg
55 direct labour hours used at $20 per labour hour
100 machine hours used
6 change orders
50 kg of hazardous waste generated

**Requirements**

1. Calculate the cost of Job 356 using the traditional plantwide manufacturing overhead rate based on machine hours.
2. Calculate the cost of Job 356 using activity based costing.
3. If you were a manager, which cost estimate would provide you more useful information? How might you use this information?

### E7-20A Apply activity cost allocation rates *(Learning Objective 2)*

The Electronics Manufacturing Department of Envision uses ABC to allocate all of its manufacturing overhead. The company assembles and tests electronic components used in handheld video phones. Consider the following data regarding component T24:

Check sum: Total activity costs allocated are $66.80.

| | |
|---|---|
| Direct materials cost | $60.00 |
| Direct labour cost | $30.00 |
| Manufacturing overhead allocated | ? |
| Manufacturing product cost | $ ? |

The activities required to build the component follow:

| Activity | Allocation Base | | | Cost Allocated to Each Unit |
|---|---|---|---|---|
| Start station | Number of raw component chassis | 2 | × $ 1.30 = | $ 2.60 |
| Dip insertion | Number of dip insertions | ? | × $ 0.40 = | 12.00 |
| Manual insertion | Number of manual insertions | 12 | × $ 0.80 = | ? |
| Wave solder | Number of components soldered | 1 | × $ 1.40 = | 1.40 |
| Backload | Number of backload insertions | 7 | × $ ? = | 4.20 |
| Test | Standard time each component is in test activity | 0.40 | × $80.00 = | ? |
| Defect analysis | Standard time for defect analysis and repair | 0.10 | × $ ? = | 5.00 |
| Total | | | | $ ? |

**Requirements**

1. Fill in the blanks in both the opening schedule and the list of activities.
2. Why might managers favour this ABC system instead of the older system, which allocated all MOH costs on the basis of direct labour?

## E7-21A Using ABC to bill clients at a service firm *(Learning Objective 2)*

Curtis & Company is an architectural firm specializing in home remodelling for private clients and new office buildings for corporate clients.

Curtis & Company charges customers at a billing rate equal to 135% of the client's total job cost. A client's total job cost is a combination of (1) professional time spent on the client ($65 per hour cost of employing each professional) and (2) operating overhead allocated to the client's job. Curtis allocates operating overhead to jobs based on professional hours spent on the job. Curtis estimates its five professionals will incur a total of 10,000 professional hours working on client jobs during the year.

All operating costs other than professional salaries (travel reimbursements, copy costs, secretarial salaries, office lease, and so forth) can be assigned to the three activities. Total activity costs, cost drivers, and total usage of those cost drivers are estimated as follows:

| Activity | Total Activity Cost | Cost Driver | Total Usage by Corporate Clients | Total Usage by Private Clients |
|---|---|---|---|---|
| Transportation to clients | $ 9,000 | Round-trip mileage to clients | 3,000 kilometres | 12,000 km |
| Blueprint copying | 35,000 | Number of copies | 300 copies | 700 copies |
| Office support | 190,000 | Secretarial time | 2,200 secretarial hours | 2,800 secretarial hours |
| **Total operating overhead** | $234,000 | | | |

Amy Lee hired Curtis & Company to remodel her kitchen. A total of 24 professional hours were incurred on this job. In addition, Amy's remodelling job required one of the professionals to travel back and forth to her house for a total of 125 km. The blueprints had to be copied four times because Amy changed the plans several times. In addition, 18 hours of secretarial time were used lining up the subcontractors for the job.

Check sum: Activity allocation rate for transportation to clients is $.60/km.

### Requirements

1. Calculate the current indirect cost allocation rate per professional hour.
2. Calculate the amount that would be billed to Amy Lee given the current costing structure.
3. Calculate the activity cost allocation rates that could be used to allocate operating overhead costs to client jobs.
4. Calculate the amount that would be billed to Amy Lee using ABC costing.
5. Which type of billing system is fairer to clients? Explain.

## E7-22A Reassess product costs using ABC *(Learning Objective 2)*

Evans Inc. manufactures only two products, Medium (42-inch) and Large (63-inch) plasma screen TVs. To generate adequate profit and cover its expenses throughout the value chain, Evans prices its TVs at 300% of manufacturing cost. The company is concerned because the Large model is facing severe pricing competition, whereas the Medium model is the low-price leader in the market. The CEO questions whether the cost numbers generated by the accounting system are correct. He has just learned about ABC and wants to reanalyze this past year's product costs using an ABC system.

Information about the company's products this past year are as follows:

Medium (42-inch) Plasma TVs

Total direct material cost: $660,000
Total direct labour cost: $216,000
Production volume: 3,000 units

Large (63-inch) Plasma TVs

Total direct material cost: $1,240,000
Total direct labour cost: $384,000
Production volume: 4,000 units

Currently, the company applies manufacturing overhead on the basis of direct labour hours. The company incurred $800,000 of MOH this year and 25,000 direct labour hours (9,000 direct labour hours making Medium TVs and 16,000 making Large TVs). The ABC team identified three primary production activities that generate MOH costs:

| |
|---|
| Material Handling ($150,000); driven by number of material orders handled |
| Machine Processing ($560,000); driven by machine hours |
| Packaging ($90,000); driven by packaging hours |

The company's only two products required the following activity levels during the year:

Check sum: Req. 1 Plantwide overhead rate is $32 per direct labour hour.

| | Machine Orders Handled | Machine Hours | Packaging Hours |
|---|---|---|---|
| Medium | 400 | 20,000 | 4,000 |
| Large | 200 | 20,000 | 6,000 |

### Requirements

1. Use the company's current costing system to find the total cost of producing all Medium TVs and the total cost of producing all Large TVs. What was the average cost of making each unit of each model? Round your answers to the nearest cent.
2. Use ABC to find the total cost of producing all Medium TVs and the total cost of producing all Large TVs. What was the average cost of making each unit of each model? Round your answers to the nearest cent.
3. How much cost distortion was occurring between Evans' two products? Calculate the cost distortion in total and on a per unit basis. Could the cost distortion explain the CEO's confusion about pricing competition? Explain.

### E7-23A Use ABC to allocate manufacturing overhead *(Learning Objective 2)*

Several years after reengineering its production process, Enke Corp. hired a new controller, Natalie Babin. She developed an ABC system very similar to the one used by Enke's chief rival, Northstar. Part of the reason Babin developed the ABC system was that Enke's profits had been declining even though the company had shifted its product mix toward the product that had appeared most profitable under the old system. Before adopting the new ABC system, Enke had used a plantwide overhead rate based on direct labour hours that was developed years ago.

For the upcoming year, Enke's budgeted ABC manufacturing overhead allocation rates are as follows:

| Activity | Allocation Base | Activity Cost Allocation Rate |
|---|---|---|
| Materials handling | Number of parts | $3.75 per unit |
| Machine set-up | Number of set-ups | 400 per set-up |
| Insertion of parts | Number of parts | 24.00 per part |
| Finishing | Finishing direct labour hours | 50.00 per hour |

The number of parts is now a feasible allocation base because Enke recently purchased bar-coding technology. Enke produces two wheel models: Standard and Deluxe. Budgeted data for the upcoming year are as follows:

| | Standard | Deluxe |
|---|---|---|
| Parts per wheel | 4.0 | 6.0 |
| Set-ups per 1,000 wheels | 15.0 | 15.0 |
| Finishing direct labour hours per wheel | 1.0 | 2.5 |
| Total direct labour hours per wheel | 2.0 | 3.0 |

The company's managers expect to produce 1,000 units of each model during the year.

Check sum: Total budgeted indirect cost are $464,500.

**Requirements**

1. Compute the total budgeted MOH cost for the upcoming year.
2. Compute the MOH cost per wheel of each model using ABC.
3. Compute Enke's traditional plantwide overhead rate. Use this rate to determine the MOH cost per wheel under the traditional system.

### E7-24A Continuation of E7-23A: determine product profitability

*(Learning Objectives 2 & 3)*

Refer to your answers in E7-23A. In addition to the manufacturing overhead costs, the following data are budgeted for the company's Standard and Deluxe models for next year:

| | Standard | Deluxe |
|---|---|---|
| Sales price per wheel | $300.00 | $440.00 |
| Direct materials per wheel | 30.00 | 46.00 |
| Direct labour per wheel | 45.00 | 50.00 |

**Requirements**

Check sum: Gross profit for the Standard is $59.50.

1. Compute the gross profit per wheel if managers rely on the ABC unit cost data computed in E7-23A.
2. Compute the gross profit per wheel if the managers rely on the plantwide allocation cost data.
3. Which product line is more profitable for Enke?
4. Why might controller Natalie Babin have expected ABC to pass the cost–benefit test? Were there any warning signs that Enke's old direct-labour-based allocation system was broken?

### E7-25A Work backward to determine ABC rates *(Learning Objective 2)*

Channell Fabricators completed two jobs in June. Channell Fabricators recorded the following costs assigned to the jobs by the company's activity based costing system:

| | | Allocated Cost | |
|---|---|---|---|
| **Activity** | **Allocation Base** | **Job 409** | **Job 622** |
| Materials handling | Number of parts | $ 500 | $1,500 |
| Lathe work | Number of lathe turns | 5,000 | 15,000 |
| Milling | Number of machine hours | 4,000 | 28,000 |
| Grinding | Number of parts | 300 | 1,500 |
| Testing | Number of output units | 126 | 2,700 |

Job 622 required 3,000 parts, 60,000 lathe turns, and 1,400 machine hours. All 300 of the job's output units were tested. All units of Job 409 were tested.

Check sum: Activity cost allocation rate is $9 for testing.

**Requirements**

1. How do you know that at least one of the costs recorded for the two jobs is inaccurate?
2. Disregard materials handling costs. How many parts were used for Job 409? How many lathe turns did Job 409 require? How many machine hours? How many units were produced in Job 409?
3. A nearby company has offered to test all product units for $13 each. On the basis of ABC data, should Channell Fabricators accept or reject the offer? Give your reason.

### E7-26A ABC in a service organization *(Learning Objective 2)*

Check sum: Actviity rate for the property manager is $12.50.

Haddleburg Property Management (HPM) offers a variety of services to homeowners. The services include: *Outside Care,* which includes grass-cutting, snow shovelling, tending of gardens, and so forth; and *Inside Care,* which includes house cleaning services. These services are ongoing and are based on yearly contracts. In addition, HPM offers short-term services for people who are travelling or will otherwise be away from their homes. This service, *Absent Care,* includes maintaining a property inside and outside while a client is away to ensure the house is kept in good order and appears "lived in."

At HPM every contract has a *property manager.* In terms of completing the work, Outside Care appointments have a *grounds keeper* and Inside Care appointments have a *major domo. Absent Care* appointments have both a *grounds keeper* and a *major domo.* In addition, the office staff maintains all records and completes billing activity. Another important activity that HPM must perform is general equipment maintenance. As a result of reviewing the operations, HPM has established the following cost drivers for these activities:

| Activity | Cost Driver |
|---|---|
| Property Manager | Time (minutes) |
| Grounds Keeper | Time (minutes) |
| Major Domo | Time (minutes) |
| Clerical Time | Number of visits |
| Equipment Maintenance | Number of visits |

For the previous year, the total costs for property managers, grounds keepers, and major domos and the amount of time (minutes) spent on each of Outside Care, Inside Care, and Absent Care are outlined in the following table.

| | Time (minutes) Spent on Each Service | | | Total Cost |
|---|---|---|---|---|
| | Outside Care | Inside Care | Absent Care | |
| Property Manager | 2500 | 2500 | 1000 | 75000 |
| Grounds Keeper | 4000 | 0 | 500 | 35000 |
| Major Domo | | 5000 | 1000 | 50000 |

These costs represent 8,000 appointments over the year, of which 3,000 were for Outside Care, 2,000 were for Inside Care, and 3,000 were for Absent Care. Clerical costs for the period were $75,000 and the Equipment Maintenance costs were $50,000.

**Requirements:**

1. Calculate the activity rate for all identified activities of the organization
2. Calculate the total cost of providing each service.
3. Calculate the cost of each client visit for each type of service.

### E7-27A ABC in a service organization *(Learning Objective 2)*

Blackfish and Corr (B&C) is a small accounting firm that offers services to businesses in the area. The services include *Assurance Services,* which include reviews of controls to help companies establish a good internal control environment; *Valuation Services,* which involve the valuation of an entire business or a segment of a business; and finally, *Tax Strategy Services,* which involve tax consultancy and preparation services.

At B&C every engagement involves a Partner overseeing the completion of the contract, client contact, and the provision of expertise. All engagements also involve the work of both Junior and Senior Associates, but not at the same level of involvement. B&C also has identified *support staff* and *office operations* as two important activities in completing an engagement. *Support Staff* work consists of secretarial work that is directly involved in client contact, such as issuing invoices. *Office Operations* are other essential tasks that keep the company's operations running smoothly, for example, maintaining subscriptions to tax law update services. As a result of reviewing the operations, B&C has established the following cost drivers for these activities:

Check sum: Activity cost for partners is $3200.

| Activity | Cost Driver |
|---|---|
| Partner | Time (minutes) |
| Senior Associate | Time (minutes) |
| Junior Associate | Time (minutes) |
| Support Staff | Number of visits to engagements |
| Office Operations | Number of visits to engagements |

For the previous year, the total costs for Partners, Senior Associates, and Junior Associates and the amount of time (minutes) spent on Assurance Services, Valuation Services, and Tax Strategy Services are outlined in the following table.

| | Time (minutes) Spent on Each Service | | | Total Cost |
|---|---|---|---|---|
| | Assurance Services | Valuation Services | Tax Strategy Services | |
| Partner | 400 | 1800 | 1000 | $250000 |
| Senior Associate | 1100 | 1200 | 2500 | $280000 |
| Junior Associate | 4600 | 500 | 500 | $270000 |

These costs represent 400 engagements over the year, of which 160 were for Assurance Services, 140 were for Valuation Services, and 100 were for Strategy Services. Support Staff costs for the period were $125,000 and the Office Operations costs were $75,000.

### Requirements

1. Calculate the activity rate for all identified activities of the organization.
2. Calculate the total cost of providing each service.
3. Calculate the cost of each client visit for each type of service.

# EXERCISES Group B

## E7-28B Compare traditional and departmental cost allocations

*(Learning Objective 1)*

Garvey's Fine Furnishings manufactures upscale custom furniture. Garvey's Fine Furnishings currently uses a plantwide overhead rate, based on direct labour hours, to allocate its $1,200,000 of manufacturing overhead to individual jobs. However, Ernie Garvey, owner and CEO, is considering refining the company's costing system by using departmental overhead rates. Currently, the Machining Department incurs $800,000 of MOH while the Finishing Department incurs $400,000 of MOH. Ernie has identified machine hours (MH) as the primary MOH cost driver in the Machining Department and direct labour (DL) hours as the primary cost driver in the Finishing Department.

Garvey's plant completed Jobs 450 and 455 on May 15. Both jobs incurred a total of 7 DL hours throughout the entire production process. Job 450 incurred 3 MH in the Machining Department and 6 DL hours in the Finishing Department. (The other DL hour occurred in the Machining Department.) Job 455 incurred 4 MH in the Machining Department and 5 DL hours in the Finishing Department. (The other 2 DL hours occurred in the Machining Department.)

### Requirements

1. Compute the plantwide overhead rate, assuming Garvey's expects to incur 25,000 total DL hours during the year.
2. Compute departmental overhead rates, assuming Garvey's expects to incur 15,400 MH in the Machining Department and 17,800 DL hours in the Finishing Department during the year.

Check sum: Plantwide allocation rate is $48 per hour.

3. If Garvey continues to use the plantwide overhead rate, how much MOH would be allocated to Job 450 and Job 455?
4. If Garvey uses departmental overhead rates, how much MOH would be allocated to Job 450 and Job 455?
5. Based on your answers to Requirements 3 and 4, does the plantwide overhead rate overcost or undercost either of the jobs? Explain. If Garvey sells his furniture at 125% of cost, will his choice of allocation systems affect product pricing?

### E7-29B Compute activity rates and apply to jobs *(Learning Objective 2)*

Central Plain uses ABC to account for its chrome wheel manufacturing process. Company managers have identified four manufacturing activities that incur manufacturing overhead costs: materials handling, machine set-up, insertion of parts, and finishing. The budgeted activity costs for the upcoming year and their allocation bases are as follows:

| Activity | Total Budgeted Manufacturing Overhead Cost | Allocation Base |
|---|---|---|
| Materials handling | $ 5,600 | Number of parts |
| Machine set-up | 6,400 | Number of set-ups |
| Insertion of parts | 39,200 | Number of parts |
| Finishing | 96,800 | Finishing direct labour hours |
| Total | $148,000 | |

Check sum: Finishing costs activity rate is $44.00 per hour.

Central Plain expects to produce 1,000 chrome wheels during the year. The wheels are expected to use 2,800 parts, require 20 set-ups, and consume 2,200 hours of finishing time.

Job 420 used 250 parts, required 3 set-ups, and consumed 130 finishing hours.

Job 510 used 475 parts, required 6 set-ups, and consumed 300 finishing hours.

#### Requirements

1. Compute the cost allocation rate for each activity.
2. Compute the MOH cost that should be assigned to Job 420.
3. Compute the MOH cost that should be assigned to Job 510.

### E7-30B Apply activity cost allocation rates *(Learning Objective 2)*

Castle Industries manufactures a variety of custom products. The company has traditionally used a plantwide manufacturing overhead rate based on machine hours to allocate manufacturing overhead to its products. The company estimates that it will incur $1,310,000 in total manufacturing overhead costs in the upcoming year and will use 10,000 machine hours.

Up to this point, hazardous waste disposal fees have been absorbed into the plantwide manufacturing overhead rate and allocated to all products as part of the manufacturing overhead process. Recently the company has been experiencing significantly increased waste disposal fees for hazardous waste generated by certain products and, as a result, profit margins on all products have been negatively impacted. Company management wants to implement an activity based costing system so that managers know the cost of each product, including its hazardous waste disposal costs.

Expected usage and costs for manufacturing overhead activities for the upcoming year are as follows:

| Description of Cost Pool | Estimated Cost | Cost Driver | Estimated Activity for this Year |
|---|---|---|---|
| Machine maintenance costs | $ 350,000 | Number of machine hours | 10,000 |
| Engineering change orders | 360,000 | Number of change orders | 3,000 |
| Hazardous waste disposal | 600,000 | Kg of hazardous materials generated | 1,000 |
| Total overhead cost | $1,310,000 | | |

During the year, Job 356 is started and completed. Usage data for this job are as follows:

| |
|---|
| 400 kg of direct materials at $40 per kg |
| 75 direct labour hours used at $20 per labour hour |
| 100 machine hours used |
| 8 change orders |
| 60 kg of hazardous waste generated |

### Requirements

Check sum: Hazardous waste handling allocation rate $600.

1. Calculate the cost of Job 356 using the traditional plantwide manufacturing overhead rate based on machine hours.
2. Calculate the cost of Job 356 using activity-based costing.
3. If you were a manager, which cost estimate would provide you more useful information? How might you use this information?

## E7-31B Apply activity cost allocation rates *(Learning Objective 2)*

The Electronics Manufacturing Department of Best Gadgets uses ABC to allocate all of its conversion costs (direct labour and manufacturing overhead). The company assembles and tests electronic components used in handheld video phones. Consider the following data regarding component T24:

| | |
|---|---|
| Direct materials cost | $44.00 |
| Direct labour cost | 32.00 |
| Manufacturing overhead allocated | ? |
| Manufacturing product cost | $ ? |

The activities required to build the component follow:

| Activity | Allocation Base | Cost Allocated to Each Unit |
|---|---|---|
| Start station | Number of raw component chassis | 8 × $ 1.80 = $14.40 |
| Dip insertion | Number of dip insertions | ? × $ 0.40 = 16.00 |
| Manual insertion | Number of manual insertions | 18 × $ 1.60 = ? |
| Wave solder | Number of components soldered | 7 × $ 2.20 = 15.40 |
| Backload | Number of backload insertions | 15 × $ ? = 5.10 |
| Test | Standard time each component is in test activity | 0.70 × $110.00 = ? |
| Defect analysis | Standard time for defect analysis and repair | 0.50 × $ ? = 11.00 |
| Total | | $ ? |

### Requirements

Check sum: Manufacturing product cost is $243.70.

1. Fill in the blanks in both the opening schedule and the list of activities.
2. Why might managers favour this ABC system over the older system, which allocated all conversion costs on the basis of direct labour?

## E7-32B Using ABC to bill clients at a service firm *(Learning Objective 2)*

Grenier & Company is an architectural firm specializing in home remodelling for private clients and new office buildings for corporate clients.

Grenier & Company charges customers at a billing rate equal to 131% of the client's total job cost. A client's total job cost is a combination of (1) professional time spent on the client ($63 per hour cost of employing each professional) and (2) operating overhead allocated to the client's job. Grenier allocates operating overhead to jobs based on professional hours spent on the job. Grenier estimates its five professionals will incur a total of 10,000 professional hours working on client jobs during the year.

All operating costs other than professional salaries (travel reimbursements, copy costs, secretarial salaries, office lease, and so forth) can be assigned to the three activities. Total activity costs, cost drivers, and total usage of those cost drivers are estimated as follows:

| Activity | Total Activity Cost | Cost Driver | Total Usage by Corporate Clients | Total Usage by Private Clients |
|---|---|---|---|---|
| Transportation to clients | $ 11,000 | Round-trip mileage to clients | 4,000 kilometres | 11,000 km |
| Blueprint copying | 31,000 | Number of copies | 500 copies | 500 copies |
| Office support | 194,000 | Secretarial time | 2,200 secretarial hours | 2,800 secretarial hours |
| Total operating overhead | $236,000 | | | |

Amy Lee hired Grenier & Company to remodel her kitchen. A total of 21 professional hours were incurred on this job. In addition, Amy's remodelling job required one of the professionals to travel back and forth to her house for a total of 123 km. The blueprints had to be copied four times because Amy changed the plans several times. In addition, 13 hours of secretarial time were used lining up the subcontractors for the job.

Check sum: Req. 1 Plantwide allocation rate is $31.25 per direct labour hour.

### Requirements

1. Calculate the current operating overhead allocation rate per professional hour.
2. Calculate the amount that would be billed to Amy Lee given the current costing structure.
3. Calculate the activity cost allocation rates that could be used to allocate operating overhead costs to client jobs.
4. Calculate the amount that would be billed to Amy Lee using ABC costing.
5. Which type of billing system is fairer to clients? Explain.

## E7-33B Reassess product costs using ABC *(Learning Objective 2)*

Jefferis Inc. manufactures only two products, Medium (42-inch) and Large (63-inch) plasma screen TVs. To generate adequate profit and cover its expenses throughout the value chain, Jefferis prices its TVs at 300% of manufacturing cost. The company is concerned because the Large model is facing severe pricing competition, whereas the Medium model is the low-price leader in the market. The CEO questions whether the cost numbers generated by the accounting system are correct. He has just learned about ABC and wants to reanalyze this past year's product costs using an ABC system. Information about the company's products this past year is as follows:

Medium (42-inch) Plasma TVs

Total direct material cost: $661,000
Total direct labour cost: $223,000
Production volume: 3,180 units

Large (63-inch) Plasma TVs

Total direct material cost: $1,240,000
Total direct labour cost: $386,000
Production volume: 4,120 units

Currently, the company applies manufacturing overhead on the basis of direct labour hours. This year, the company incurred $828,000 of MOH and 26,500 direct labour hours (9,600 direct labour hours making Medium TVs and 16,900 making Large TVs). The ABC team identified three primary production activities that generate MOH costs:

Materials Handling ($156,000); driven by number of material orders handled
Machine Processing ($570,00); driven by machine hours
Packaging ($112,000); driven by packaging hours

The company's only two products required the following activity levels during the year:

| | Material Orders Handled | Machine Hours | Packaging Hours |
|---|---|---|---|
| Medium | 340 | 20,000 | 4,040 |
| Large | 240 | 23,400 | 6,040 |

**Requirements**

Check sum: Total activity allocation base for packaging is 10,080 hours.

1. Use the company's current costing system to find the total cost of producing all Medium TVs and the total cost of producing all Large TVs. What was the average cost of making each unit of each model? Round your answers to the nearest cent.
2. Use ABC to find the total cost of producing all Medium TVs and the total cost of producing all Large TVs. What was the average cost of making each unit of each model? Round your answers to the nearest cent.
3. How much cost distortion was occurring between Jefferis' two products? Calculate the cost distortion in total and on a per unit basis. Could the cost distortion explain the CEO's confusion about pricing competition? Explain.

### E7-34B Use ABC to allocate manufacturing overhead *(Learning Objective 2)*

Several years after reengineering its production process, Zeke Corp. hired a new controller, Jen Nguyen. She developed an ABC system very similar to the one used by Zeke's chief rival, Hotbeach. Part of the reason Nguyen developed the ABC system was that Zeke's profits had been declining even though the company had shifted its product mix toward the product that had appeared most profitable under the old system. Before adopting the new ABC system, Zeke had used a plantwide overhead rate that was developed years ago, based on direct labour hours.

For the upcoming year, Zeke's budgeted ABC manufacturing overhead allocation rates are as follows:

| Activity | Allocation Base | Activity Base Allocation Rate |
|---|---|---|
| Materials handling | Number of parts | $ 3.85 per part |
| Machine set-up | Number of set-ups | 345.00 per set-up |
| Insertion of parts | Number of parts | 27.00 per part |
| Finishing | Finishing direct labour hours | 55.00 per hour |

The number of parts is now a feasible allocation base because Zeke recently purchased bar-coding technology. Zeke produces two wheel models: Standard and Deluxe. Budgeted data for the upcoming year are as follows:

| | Standard | Deluxe |
|---|---|---|
| Parts per wheel | 4.0 | 6.0 |
| Set-ups per 1,000 wheels | 10.0 | 10.0 |
| Finishing direct labour hours per wheel | 1.1 | 3.5 |
| Total direct labour hours per wheel | 2.7 | 3.8 |

The company's managers expect to produce 1,000 units of each model during the year.

**Requirements**

Check sum: Budgeted total manufacturing overhead cost is $568,400.

1. Compute the total budgeted MOH cost for the upcoming year.
2. Compute the MOH cost per wheel of each model using ABC.
3. Compute Zeke's traditional plantwide overhead rate. Use this rate to determine the MOH cost per wheel under the traditional system.

### E7-35B Continuation of E7-34B: determine product profitability
*(Learning Objectives 2 & 3)*

Refer to your answers in E7-34B. In addition to the manufacturing overhead costs, the following data are budgeted for the company's Standard and Deluxe models for next year:

| | Standard | Deluxe |
|---|---|---|
| Sales price per wheel | $470.00 | $640.00 |
| Direct materials per wheel | 31.00 | 47.00 |
| Direct labour per wheel | 45.50 | 51.50 |

Check sum: Gross profit for deluxe is $160.45.

**Requirements**

1. Compute the gross profit per wheel if managers rely on the ABC unit cost data.
2. Compute the gross profit per unit if the managers rely on the plantwide allocation cost data.
3. Which product line is more profitable for Zeke?
4. Why might controller Jen Nguyen have expected ABC to pass the cost–benefit test? Were there any warning signs that Zeke's old direct-labour-based allocation system was broken?

### E7-36B Work backward to determine ABC rates *(Learning Objective 2)*

Burke Fabricators completed two jobs in June. Burke Fabricators recorded the following costs assigned to the jobs by the company's activity based costing system:

| | | Allocated Cost | |
|---|---|---|---|
| **Activity** | **Allocation Base** | **Job 409** | **Job 622** |
| Materials handling | Number of parts | $ 400 | $ 1,200 |
| Lathe work | Number of lathe turns | 4,700 | 15,500 |
| Milling | Number of machine hours | 3,600 | 26,000 |
| Grinding | Number of parts | 336 | 1,680 |
| Testing | Number of output units | 125 | 2,500 |

Check sum: Burke's cost of performing this activity is only $6.25 per unit.

Job 622 required 2,400 parts, 77,500 lathe turns, and 1,625 machine hours. All 400 of the job's output units were tested. All units of Job 409 were tested.

**Requirements**

1. How do you know that at least one of the costs recorded for the two jobs is inaccurate?
2. Disregard materials handling costs. How many parts were used for Job 409? How many lathe turns did Job 409 require? How many machine hours did Job 409 require? How many units were produced in Job 409?
3. A nearby company has offered to test all product units for $10 each. On the basis of ABC data, should Burke Fabricators accept or reject the offer? Give your reason.

## PROBLEMS Group A

### P7-37A Implementation and analysis of departmental rates *(Learning Objective 1)*

Perreth Products manufactures its products in two separate departments: machining and assembly. Total manufacturing overhead costs for the year are budgeted at $1 million. Of this amount, the Machining Department incurs $600,000 (primarily for machine operation and depreciation) while the Assembly Department incurs $400,000. Perreth Products estimates that it will incur 4,000 machine hours (all in the Machining Department) and 12,500 direct labour hours (2,500 in the Machining Department and 10,000 in the Assembly Department) during the year.

Perreth Products currently uses a plantwide overhead rate based on direct labour hours to allocate overhead. However, the company is considering refining its overhead allocation system by using departmental overhead rates. The Machining Department would allocate its overhead using machine hours (MH), but the Assembly Department would allocate its overhead using direct labour (DL) hours.

The following chart shows the machine hours (MH) and direct labour (DL) hours incurred by Jobs 500 and 501 in each production department:

| | Machine Department | Assembly Department |
|---|---|---|
| Job 500 | 3 MH | 12 DL hours |
| | 2 DL hours | |
| Job 501 | 6 MH | 12 DL hours |
| | 2 DL hours | |

Both Jobs 500 and 501 used $1,000 of direct materials. Wages and benefits total $25 per direct labour hour. Perreth Products prices its products at 110% of total manufacturing costs.

### Requirements

1. Compute Perreth Products' current plantwide overhead rate.
2. Compute refined departmental overhead rates.
3. Which job (Job 500 or Job 501) uses more of the company's resources? Explain.
4. Compute the total amount of overhead allocated to each job if Perreth Products uses its current plantwide overhead rate.
5. Compute the total amount of overhead allocated to each job if Perreth Products uses departmental overhead rates.
6. Do both allocation systems accurately reflect the resources that each job used? Explain.
7. Compute the total manufacturing cost and sales price of each job using Perreth Products' current plantwide overhead rate.
8. Based on the current (plantwide) allocation system, how much profit did Perreth Products *think* it earned on each job? Based on the departmental overhead rates and the sales price determined in Requirement 7, how much profit did it *really* earn on each job?
9. Compare and comment on the results you obtained in Requirements 7 and 8.

### P7-38A Use ABC to compute full product costs *(Learning Objective 2)*

Hone's Office Department manufactures computer desks in its Moosejaw, Saskatchewan, plant. The company uses activity based costing to allocate all manufacturing conversion costs (direct labour and manufacturing overhead). Its activities and related data follow:

| Activity | Budgeted Cost of Activity | Allocation Base | Cost Allocation Rate |
|---|---|---|---|
| Materials handling | $ 300,000 | Number of parts | $ 0.60 |
| Assembling | 2,500,000 | Direct labour hours | 15.00 |
| Painting | 170,000 | Number of painted desks | 5.00 |

Hone produced two styles of desks in March: the Standard desk and the Unpainted desk. Data for each follow:

| Product | Total Units Produced | Total Direct Materials Costs | Total Number of Parts | Total Assembling Direct Labour Hours |
|---|---|---|---|---|
| Standard desk | 6,000 | $96,000 | 120,000 | 6,000 |
| Unpainted desk | 1,500 | 21,000 | 30,000 | 900 |

### Requirements

1. Compute the per-unit manufacturing product costs of Standard desks and Unpainted desks.
2. Premanufacturing activities, such as product design, were assigned to the Standard desks at $5 each and to the Unpainted desks at $3 each. Similar analyses were conducted of postmanufacturing activities, such as distribution, marketing, and customer service. The postmanufacturing costs were $25 per Standard and $22 per Unpainted desk. Compute the full product costs per desk.
3. Which product costs are reported in the external financial statements? Which costs are used for management decision making? Explain the difference.
4. What price should Hone's managers set for Standard desks to earn a $42 profit per desk?

## P7-39A Comprehensive ABC implementation *(Learning Objectives 2 & 3)*

ACom develops software for internet applications. The market is very competitive, and ACom's competitors continue to introduce new products at low prices. The company offers a wide variety of software—from simple programs that enable new users to create personal webpages to complex commercial search engines. Like most software companies, ACom's raw material costs are insignificant.

ACom has just hired Nicole Merrell, a recent university graduate in accounting. Merrell asks Software Department Manager Jeff Gire to join her in a pilot activity based costing study. Merrell and Gire identify the following activities, related costs, and cost allocation bases:

| Activity | Estimated Indirect Activity Costs | Allocated Base | Estimated Quantity of Allocation Base |
|---|---|---|---|
| Applications development | $1,600,000 | New applications | 4 new applications |
| Content production | 2,400,000 | Lines of code | 18 million lines |
| Testing | 288,000 | Testing hours | 1,800 testing hours |
| Total indirect costs | $4,288,000 | | |

ACom is planning to develop the following new applications:

- X-Page—software for developing personal webpages
- X-Secure—commercial security and firewall software

X-Page requires 500,000 lines of code and 100 hours of testing, while X-Secure requires 7.5 million lines of code and 600 hours of testing. ACom expects to produce and sell 30,000 units of X-Page and 10 units of X-Secure.

### Requirements

1. Compute the cost allocation rate for each activity.
2. Use the activity based cost allocation rates to compute the indirect cost of each new application, X-Page and X-Secure. (*Hint:* Compute the total activity costs allocated to each product line and then compute the cost per unit.)
3. ACom's original single-allocation-based cost system allocated indirect costs to products at $100 per programmer hour. X-Page requires 10,000 programmer hours, while X-Secure requires 15,000 programmer hours. Compute the total indirect costs allocated to X-Page and X-Secure under the original system. Then, compute the indirect cost per unit for each product.
4. Compare the activity-based costs per unit to the costs from the simpler original system. How have the unit costs changed? Explain why the costs changed as they did.
5. What are the clues that ACom's ABC system is likely to pass the cost–benefit test?

## P7-40A Comprehensive ABC implementation *(Learning Objectives 2 & 3)*

HCI Pharmaceuticals manufactures an over-the-counter allergy medication called Breathe and is trying to win market share from Sudafed and Claritin. HCI Pharmaceuticals has developed several different Breathe products tailored to specific markets. For example, the company sells large commercial containers of 1,000 capsules to health-care facilities and travel packs of 20 capsules to shops in airports, train stations, and hotels.

HCI Pharmaceuticals' controller, Sandra Dean, has just returned from a conference on ABC. She asks Keith Yeung, supervisor of the Breathe product line, to help her develop an ABC system. Dean and Yeung identify the following activities, related costs, and cost allocation bases:

| Activity | Estimated Indirect Activity Costs | Allocation Base | Estimated Quantity of Allocation Base |
|---|---|---|---|
| Materials handling | $190,000 | Kilograms | 19,000 kg |
| Packaging | 400,000 | Machine hours | 2,000 hours |
| Quality assurance | 112,500 | Samples | 1,875 samples |
| Total indirect costs | $702,500 | | |

The commercial-container Breathe product line had a total weight of 8,000 kilograms, used 1,200 machine hours, and required 200 samples. The travel-pack line had a total weight of 6,000 kilograms, used 400 machine hours, and required 300 samples. HCI produced 2,500 commercial containers of Breathe and 50,000 travel packs.

### Requirements

1. Compute the cost allocation rate for each activity.
2. Use the activity based cost allocation rates to compute the indirect cost of each unit of the commercial containers and the travel packs. (*Hint:* Compute the total activity costs allocated to each product line and then compute the cost per unit.)
3. HCI Pharmaceuticals' original single-allocation-based cost system allocated indirect costs to products at $300 per machine hour. Compute the total indirect costs allocated to the commercial containers and to the travel packs under the original system. Then, compute the indirect cost per unit for each product.
4. Compare the activity based costs per unit to the costs from the original system. How have the unit costs changed? Explain why the costs changed as they did.

## P7-41A Using ABC in conjunction with quality decisions *(Learning Objective 2)*

Real Toys is using a costs of quality approach to evaluate design engineering efforts for a new toy robot. The company's senior managers expect the engineering work to reduce appraisal, internal failure, and external failure activities. The predicted reductions in activities over the two-year life of the toy robot follow. Also shown is the cost allocation rate for each activity.

| Activity | Predicted Reduction in Activity Units | Activity Cost Allocations Rate per Unit |
|---|---|---|
| Inspection of incoming materials | 300 | $20 |
| Inspection of finished goods | 300 | 30 |
| Number of defective units discovered in-house | 3,200 | 15 |
| Number of defective units discovered by customers | 900 | 35 |
| Lost sales to dissatisfied customers | 300 | 55 |

### Requirements

1. Calculate the predicted quality cost savings from the design engineering work.
2. Real Toys spent $60,000 on design engineering for the new toy robot. What is the net benefit of this "preventive" quality activity?
3. What major difficulty would Real Toys' managers have had in implementing this costs of quality approach? What alternative approach could they use to measure quality improvement?

# PROBLEMS Group B

## P7-42B Implementation and analysis of departmental rates *(Learning Objective 1)*

Cortana Products manufactures its products in two separate departments: Machining and Assembly. Total manufacturing overhead costs for the year are budgeted at $1.09 million. Of this amount, the Machining Department incurs $670,000 (primarily for machine operation and depreciation), while the Assembly Department incurs $420,000. Cortana Products estimates it will incur 4,000 machine hours (all in the Machining Department) and 14,000 direct labour hours (2,000 in the Machining Department and 12,000 in the Assembly Department) during the year.

Cortana Products currently uses a plantwide overhead rate based on direct labour hours to allocate overhead. However, the company is considering refining its overhead allocation system by using departmental overhead rates. The Machining Department would allocate its overhead using machine hours (MH), but the Assembly Department would allocate its overhead using direct labour (DL) hours.

The following chart shows the machine hours (MH) and direct labour (DL) hours incurred by Jobs 500 and 501 in each production department.

| | Machine Department | Assembly Department |
|---|---|---|
| Job 500 | 8 MH | 15 DL hours |
| | 5 DL hours | |
| Job 501 | 16 MH | 20 DL hours |
| | 5 DL hours | |

Both Jobs 500 and 501 used $1,200 of direct materials. Wages and benefits total $30 per direct labour hour. Cortana Products prices its products at 130% of total manufacturing costs.

### Requirements

1. Compute Cortana Products' current plantwide overhead rate.
2. Compute refined departmental overhead rates.
3. Which job (Job 500 or Job 501) uses more of the company's resources? Explain.
4. Compute the total amount of overhead allocated to each job based on the current plantwide overhead rate.
5. Compute the total amount of overhead allocated to each job based on the departmental overhead rates.
6. Do both allocation systems accurately reflect the resources that each job used? Explain.
7. Compute the total manufacturing cost and sales price of each job based on the current plantwide overhead rate.
8. Based on the current (plantwide) allocation system, how much profit did Cortana Products *think* it earned on each job? Based on the departmental overhead rates and the sales price determined in Requirement 7, how much profit did it *really* earn on each job?
9. Compare and comment on the results you obtained in Requirements 7 and 8.

## P7-43B Use ABC to compute full product costs *(Learning Objective 2)*

Johnston's Office Department manufactures computer desks in its Brandon, Manitoba, plant. The company uses activity-based costing to allocate all manufacturing conversion costs (direct labour and manufacturing overhead). Its activities and related data follow:

| Activity | Budgeted Cost of Activity | Allocation Base | Cost Allocation Rate |
|---|---|---|---|
| Materials handling | $ 300,000 | Number of parts | $ 0.60 |
| Assembling | 2,500,000 | Direct labour hours | 13.00 |
| Painting | 170,000 | Number of painted desks | 5.30 |

Johnston's produced two styles of desks in March: the Standard desk and Unpainted desk. Data for each follow:

| Product | Total Units Produced | Total Direct Materials Costs | Total Number of Parts | Total Assembling Direct Labour Hours |
|---|---|---|---|---|
| Standard desk | 6,500 | $98,000 | 120,500 | 6,300 |
| Unpainted desk | 2,000 | 18,000 | 30,500 | 1,000 |

### Requirements

1. Compute the per-unit manufacturing product cost of Standard desks and Unpainted desks.
2. Premanufacturing activities, such as product design, were assigned to the Standard desks at $4 each and to the Unpainted desks at $3 each. Similar analyses were conducted of postmanufacturing activities such as distribution, marketing, and customer service. The postmanufacturing costs were $22 per Standard and $19 per Unpainted desk. Compute the full product costs per desk.
3. Which product costs are reported in the external financial statements? Which costs are used for management decision making? Explain the difference.
4. What price should Johnston's managers set for Standard desks to earn a $39 profit per desk?

## P7-44B Comprehensive ABC implementation *(Learning Objectives 2 & 3)*

Gibson Networking develops software for internet applications. The market is very competitive, and Gibson Networking's competitors continue to introduce new products at low prices. Gibson Networking offers a wide variety of software, from simple programs that enable new users to create personal webpages to complex commercial search engines. Like most software companies, Gibson Networking's raw material costs are insignificant.

Gibson Networking has just hired Nicole Merrell, a recent accounting graduate. Merrell asks Software Department Manager Jeff Gire to join her in a pilot activity-based costing study. Merrell and Gire identify the following activities, related costs, and cost allocation bases:

| Activity | Estimated Indirect Activity Costs | Allocated Base | Estimated Quantity of Allocation Base |
|---|---|---|---|
| Applications development | $1,500,000 | New applications | 3 new applications |
| Content production | 2,700,000 | Lines of code | 9 million lines |
| Testing | 270,000 | Testing hours | 1,500 testing hours |
| Total indirect costs | $4,470,000 | | |

Gibson Networking is planning to develop the following new applications:

- X-Page software for developing personal webpages
- X-Secure commercial security and firewall software

X-Page requires 480,000 lines of code and 70 hours of testing, while X-Secure requires 7.2 million lines of code and 420 hours of testing. Gibson Networking expects to produce and sell 25,000 units of X-Page and 9 units of X-Secure.

### Requirements

1. Compute the cost allocation rate for each activity.
2. Use the activity based cost allocation rates to compute the indirect cost of each unit of X-Page and X-Secure. (*Hint:* Compute the total activity costs allocated to each product line and then compute the cost per unit.)

3. Gibson Networking's original single-allocation-base costing system allocated indirect costs to products at $104 per programmer hour. X-Page requires 14,000 programmer hours, while X-Secure requires 21,000 programmer hours. Compute the total indirect costs allocated to X-Page and X-Secure under the original system. Then, compute the indirect cost per unit for each product.
4. Compare the activity based costs per unit to the costs from the simpler original system. How have the unit costs changed? Explain why the costs changed as they did.
5. What are the clues that Gibson Networking's ABC system is likely to pass the cost-benefit test?

## P7-45B Comprehensive ABC implementation *(Learning Objectives 2 & 3)*

Maloney Pharmaceuticals manufactures an over-the-counter allergy medication called Breathe and is trying to win market share from Sudafed and Claritin. Maloney Pharmaceuticals has developed several different Breathe products tailored to specific markets. For example, the company sells large commercial containers of 1,000 capsules to health-care facilities and travel packs of 20 capsules to shops in airports, train stations, and hotels.

Maloney Pharmaceuticals' controller, Sandra Dean, has just returned from a conference on ABC. She asks Keith Yeung, supervisor of the Breathe product line, to help her develop an ABC system. Dean and Yeung identify the following activities, related costs, and cost allocation bases:

| Activity | Estimated Indirect Activity Costs | Allocated Base | Estimated Quantity of Allocation Base |
|---|---|---|---|
| Materials handling | $160,000 | Kilograms | 20,000 kg |
| Packaging | 390,000 | Machine hours | 2,000 hours |
| Quality assurance | 110,000 | Samples | 2,200 samples |
| Total indirect costs | $660,000 | | |

The commercial-container Breathe product line had a total weight of 8,200 kilograms, used 1,200 machine hours, and required 270 samples. The travel-pack line had a total weight of 6,500 kg, used 400 machine hours, and required 370 samples. Maloney produced 2,700 commercial containers of Breathe and 40,000 travel packs.

### Requirements

1. Compute the cost allocation rate for each activity.
2. Use the activity based cost allocation rates to compute the indirect cost of each unit of the commercial containers and the travel packs. (*Hint:* Compute the total activity costs allocated to each product line and then compute the cost per unit.)
3. Maloney Pharmaceuticals' original single-allocation-based cost system allocated indirect costs to products at $350 per machine hour. Compute the total indirect costs allocated to the commercial containers and to the travel packs under the original system. Then, compute the indirect cost per unit for each product.
4. Compare the activity based costs per unit to the costs from the simpler original system. How have the unit costs changed? Explain why the costs changed as they did.

## P7-46B Using ABC in conjunction with quality decisions *(Learning Objective 2)*

Teensy Toys is using a costs of quality approach to evaluate design engineering efforts for a new toy robot. The company's senior managers expect the engineering work to reduce appraisal, internal failure, and external failure activities. The predicted reductions in activities over the two-year life of the toy robot follow. Also shown are the cost allocation rates for each activity.

| Activity | Predicted Reduction in Activity Units | Activity Cost Allocations Rate per Unit |
|---|---|---|
| Inspection of incoming materials | 310 | $16 |
| Inspection of finished goods | 310 | 26 |
| Number of defective units discovered in-house | 3,200 | 15 |
| Number of defective units discovered by customers | 850 | 42 |
| Lost sales to dissatisfied customers | 330 | 61 |

## Requirements

1. Calculate the predicted quality cost savings from the design engineering work.
2. Teensy Toys spent $75,000 on design engineering for the new toy robot. What is the net benefit of this "preventive" quality activity?
3. What major difficulty would Teensy Toys' managers have had in implementing this costs of quality approach? What alternative approach could they use to measure quality improvement?

# CAPSTONE APPLICATION PROBLEMS

## APPLICATION QUESTION

### A7-47 Comprehensive ABC *(Learning Objectives 2 & 3)*

Axis Systems specializes in servers for work-group, e-commerce, and ERP applications. The company's original job cost system has two direct cost categories: direct materials and direct labour. Overhead is allocated to jobs at the single rate of $22 per direct labour hour.

A task force headed by Axis's CFO recently designed an ABC system with four activities. The ABC system retains the current system's two direct cost categories. Thus, it budgets only overhead costs for each activity. Pertinent data are as follows:

| Activity | Allocation Base | Cost Allocation Rate |
|---|---|---|
| Materials handling | Number of parts | $ 0.85 |
| Machine set-up | Number of set-ups | 500.00 |
| Assembling | Assembly hours | 80.00 |
| Shipping | Number of shipments | 1,500.00 |

Axis Systems has been awarded two new contracts that will be produced as Job A and Job B. Budget data relating to the contracts are as follows:

| | Job A | Job B |
|---|---|---|
| Number of parts | 15,000 | 2,000 |
| Number of set-ups | 6 | 4 |
| Number of assembly hours | 1,500 | 200 |
| Number of shipments | 1 | 1 |
| Total direct labour hours | 8,000 | 600 |
| Number of output units | 100 | 10 |
| Direct materials cost | $210,000 | $30,000 |
| Direct labour cost | $160,000 | $12,000 |

#### Requirements

1. Compute the product cost per unit for each job using the original costing system (with two direct cost categories and a single overhead allocation rate).
2. Suppose Axis Systems adopts the ABC system. Compute the product cost per unit for each job using ABC.
3. Which costing system more accurately assigns to jobs the costs of the resources consumed to produce them? Explain.
4. A dependable company has offered to produce both jobs for Axis for $5,400 per output unit. Axis may outsource (buy from the outside company) Job A only, Job B only, or both jobs. Which course of action will Axis's managers take if they base their decision on (1) the original system or (2) ABC system costs? Which course of action will yield more income? Explain.

### A7-48 Continues A7-47: meeting target costs

To remain competitive, Axis Systems' management believes the company must produce Job B-type servers (from A7-47) at a target cost of $5,400. Axis Systems has just joined a business-to-business (B2B) e-marketing site that management believes will enable the firm to cut direct material costs by 10%. Axis's management also believes that a value-engineering team can reduce assembly time.

**Requirements**

Compute the assembly cost savings per Job B-type server required to meet the $5,400 target cost. (*Hint:* Begin by calculating the direct material, direct labour, and allocated activity costs per server.)

# ETHICAL ISSUE

### 17-49 ABC and ethical dilemma *(Learning Objectives 2 & 3)*

Cynthia Tse is assistant controller at Stone Packaging, a manufacturer of cardboard boxes and other packaging materials. Tse has just returned from a packaging industry conference on ABC. She realizes that ABC may help Stone meet its goal of reducing costs by 5% over each of the next three years.

Stone Packaging's Order Department is a likely candidate for ABC. While orders are entered into a computer that updates the accounting records, clerks manually check customers' credit history and hand-deliver orders to shipping. This process occurs whether the sales order is for a dozen specialty boxes worth a total of $80 or 10,000 basic boxes worth a total of $8,000.

Tse believes that identifying the cost of processing a sales order would justify (1) further computerizing the order process and (2) changing the way the company processes small orders. However, the significant cost savings would arise from elimination of two positions in the Order Department. The company's sales order clerks have been with the company many years. Tse is uncomfortable with the prospect of proposing a change that will likely result in terminating these employees.

**Requirements**

Refer to the CPA Canada Principles of Ethical Conduct discussed in Chapter 1 to consider Tse's responsibility when cost comes at the expense of employees' jobs.

# CASE ASSIGNMENT

### C7-50 Oak Leaf Embroidery

Dale Gauthier and Randy "Chip" Charters were sitting at lunch at the beginning of April looking at the financial statements for January, February, and March and wondering why their profit was decreasing even though their sales were increasing. Their costs had remained stable, so an increase in costs was eliminated as a cause. The only difference that they noticed was that customers seemed to be redesigning what they wanted embroidered to encompass more colours, and most of the increase in revenues came from new customers.

For quoting orders, Dale and Chip have determined their costs for embroidering a logo on a T-shirt as follows:

| | |
|---|---:|
| Direct Materials | $4.00 |
| Direct labour | 2.00 |
| MOH | 3.50 |
| Total | 9.50 |

The manufacturing overhead was estimated using last year's financial statements. The selling price was then determined by taking the total cost and adding a 30% markup.

Dale and Chip are the owners and the only employees of the company. They pay themselves $20 per hour. They each share in the administrative work and the embroidery work for the production of the finished product. They can embroider 10 shirts per hour, but this is complicated when there are additional colours. Each job needs 6 minutes of set-up time and each colour change requires 12 minutes of labour to reconfigure the embroidery machine. The largest amount of time is taken up by the design work, though. Each new design or redesign of a logo requires 4 hours of Chip or Dale's day in order to produce the electronic code required for the embroidery machine. Dale and Chip incur administrative costs of $0.70 per order, as well.

While at the sales counter this morning, Dale spoke with four customers, and he needs to produce a quote for each of them. Two of the jobs are for repeat customers who do not need any design work, and of the other two, one is for a repeat customer who wants to redesign the logo and the other is for a brand-new customer who will need the logo designed before any work can be done. The jobs also have different colour requirements and volumes as follows:

Job 1: repeat customer (2 colours, 25 shirts)

Job 2: repeat customer (5 colours, 200 shirts)

Job 3: repeat customer with a redesign (2 colours, 200 shirts)

Job 4: new customer (5 colours, 25 shirts)

Before lunch, Dale would simply have quoted $9.50 per shirt, but now she is second-guessing the amount, based on the trends of decreasing profits. She and Chip head back to work without a clear idea of how to write up the new quotes.

# DISCUSSION & ANALYSIS

## Discussion Questions

1. Explain why departmental overhead rates might be used instead of a single plantwide overhead rate.
2. Using activity based costing, why are indirect costs allocated while direct costs are not allocated?
3. Compare and contrast activity based costing (ABC) and activity based management (ABM).
4. How can using a single predetermined manufacturing overhead rate based on a unit-level cost driver cause a high-volume product to be overcosted?
5. Assume a company uses a plantwide predetermined manufacturing overhead rate, which is calculated using direct labour hours as the cost driver. The use of this plantwide predetermined MOH rate has resulted in cost distortion. The company's high-volume products are overcosted and its low-volume products are undercosted. What effects of this cost distortion will the company most likely be experiencing? Why might the cost distortion be harmful to the company's competitive position in the market?
6. A hospital can use activity based costing (ABC) for costing its services. In a hospital, what activities might be considered to be value-added activities? What activities at that hospital might be considered to be non-value-added?
7. A company makes shatterproof, waterproof cases for iPhones. It makes only one model and has been very successful in marketing its case; no other company in the market has a similar product. The only customization available to the customer is the colour of the case. There is no manufacturing cost difference between different case colours. Since this company has a high-volume product, its controller thinks that the company should adopt activity based costing. Why might activity based costing not be as beneficial for this company as for other companies?

# APPLICATION & ANALYSIS

## 7-1 ABC in Real Companies

Choose a company in any of the following categories: airline, florist, bookstore, bank, grocery store, restaurant, college or university, retail clothing shop, movie theatre, or lawn service. In this activity, you will have to make reasonable estimates of the types of costs and activities associated with this company; companies do not typically publish internal cost or process information. Be reasonable in your cost estimates and include the assumptions you used in selecting costs.

## Discussion Questions

1. Describe the company selected, including its products or services.
2. List eight key activities performed at this company. Choose at least one activity in the areas of production, sales, human resources, and accounting.
3. For each of the key activities, list a potential cost driver for that activity, and describe why this cost driver would be appropriate for the associated activity.

## Classroom Applications

**Web:** Post the discussion questions on an electronic discussion board. Have small groups of students choose a product for their group. Each student should watch the clip for the product for their group.

**Classroom:** Form groups of three to four students. Each group should choose a company from one of the listed categories. After deciding upon a company, groups discuss each of the listed questions and then prepare a 5-minute presentation about the group's company that addresses the listed questions.

**Independent:** Students write a paper that addresses each of the listed questions for the company of their choice from one of the given categories and then turn in a two- or three-page typed paper (12-point font, double-spaced, with 2.5 cm margins).

# TRY IT SOLUTIONS

**page 418:**

2, 3, 5, 7.

# 8 Short-Term Business Decisions

## Learning Objectives

1. Describe and identify information relevant to short-term business decisions.
2. Make pricing decisions.
3. Make target costing decisions.
4. Make special-order decisions.
5. Make decisions about dropping a product or segment.
6. Make product mix decisions.
7. Make outsourcing (make-or-buy) decisions.
8. Make sell as is or process-further decisions.
9. Make transfer-pricing decisions.

Chapter 8 "Short-Term Business Decisions" covers material outlined in **Section 3: Management Accounting** of the CPA Competency Map. Specifically, this chapter addresses competencies from a number of sections, including *Section 3.4 Revenue Management, Section 3.5 Profitability Management,* and *Section 3.6 Organizational Performance Measurement*. The Learning Objectives in this chapter have been aligned with the CPA Competency Map to ensure the best coverage possible.

PROFESSIONAL COMPETENCY

The presence of the **coverage button** in the margin indicates focus on one or more of the specific competency areas from the competency map. The concepts in the text are building blocks to developing the competencies required in the CPA. While the chapter may address multiple areas of the competency map, the main focus will be:

**Competencies:**

**3.4 Revenue Management***

**3.4.1** Evaluates sources and drivers of revenue growth*

**3.5 Profitability Management***

**3.5.1** Performs sensitivity analysis*

**3.5.2** Evaluates sustainable profit maximization and capacity management performance*

**3.6 Organizational Performance Measurement***

**3.6.1** Evaluates performance using accepted frameworks*

**3.6.2** Evaluates performance of responsibility centres*

**3.6.3** Evaluates root causes of performance issues*

*Source:* Charles Polidano/Touch The Skies/Alamy

## Major airlines, such as Air Canada,

outsource a portion of their aircraft maintenance, repair, and overhaul (MRO). Many costs in the airline industry are rising (e.g., the costs of qualified pilots and mechanics), and other costs have a high degree of unpredictability (e.g., fuel). In an effort to manage costs and maintain some level of predictability for planning and control purposes, many airlines outsource multiple functions in addition to MRO, such as finance, accounting, and customer service. Through outsourcing, Air Canada is able to reduce annual labour costs; avoid costly investments in facilities, equipment, and parts inventories; and better manage cost forecasts. However, costs are not everything. Some companies that have chosen to outsource their customer service to third-party providers have experienced dramatic increases in customer dissatisfaction, prompting companies to "re-insource." Outsourcing enables companies to concentrate on their core competencies—the operating activities at which they excel—while at the same time make use of the expertise and best-practices of firms that excel at other areas of operations. For companies like Air Canada, it is important to understand which core functions should remain within the company, and which are best performed through partners.

*Reprinted from *The Chartered Professional Accountant Competency Map - Understanding the competencies a candidate must demonstrate to become a CPA*, © 2012, with permission Chartered Professional Accountants of Canada, Toronto, Canada. Any changes to the original material are the sole responsibility of the author (and/or publisher) and have not been reviewed or endorsed by the Chartered Professional Accountants of Canada.

In the previous chapter, we saw how managers use cost behaviour to determine the company's break-even point and to estimate the sales volume needed to achieve target profits. In this chapter, we'll see how managers use their knowledge of cost behaviour to make special business decisions, such as whether to outsource operating activities. The decisions in this chapter usually pertain to short periods of time, so managers do not need to worry about the time value of money. In other words, they do not need to compute the present value of the revenues and expenses relating to the decision. In Chapter 12, we will discuss longer-term decisions (such as buying equipment and undertaking plant expansions) in which the time value of money becomes important. Before we look at these seven business decisions in detail, let's consider a manager's decision-making process and the information managers need to evaluate their options.

## How Do Managers Make Decisions?

Exhibit 8-1 illustrates how managers decide among alternative courses of action. Management accountants gather and analyze relevant information to compare alternatives and help with comparing the actual results of a decision to those originally anticipated. This feedback informs management as it faces similar types of decisions in the future. It also helps management adjust current operations if the actual results of its decisions are markedly different from those anticipated.

**EXHIBIT 8-1** How Managers Make Decisions

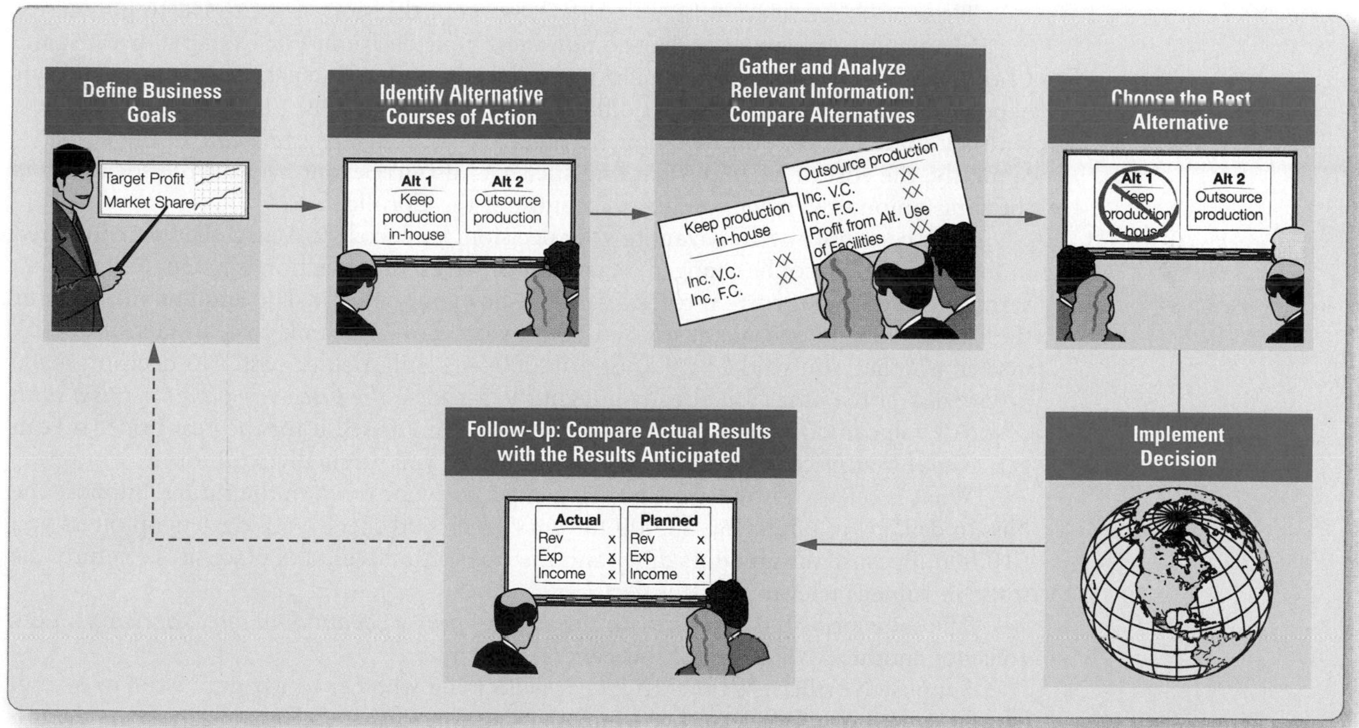


## Relevant Information

When managers make decisions, they focus on costs and revenues that are relevant to the decisions. Exhibit 8-2 shows that the <u>**relevant information**</u>

**1** Describe and identify information relevant to short-term business decisions.

1. Is expected *future* data
2. Differs among alternatives

**EXHIBIT 8-2** Relevant Information

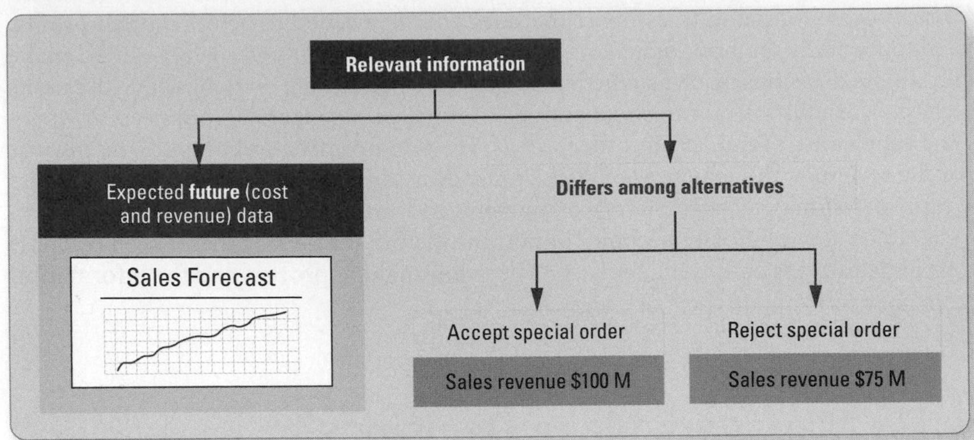


PROFESSIONAL COMPETENCY

Recall our discussion of relevant costs in Chapter 2. In deciding whether to purchase a Toyota Corolla or Nissan Sentra, the cost of the car, the sales tax, and the insurance premium are relevant because these costs

- Are incurred in the future (after you decide to buy the car)
- Differ between alternatives (each car has a different invoice price, sales tax, and insurance premium)

These costs are relevant because they affect your decision of which car to purchase.

Irrelevant costs are costs that do not affect your decision. For example, because the Corolla and Sentra both have similar fuel efficiency and maintenance ratings, we do not expect the car operating costs to differ between them. Because these costs do not differ, they do not affect your decision. In other words, they are *irrelevant* to the decision. Similarly, the cost of a campus parking sticker is also irrelevant because the sticker costs the same amount whether you buy the Sentra or the Corolla.

**Sunk costs** are also irrelevant to your decision. Sunk costs are costs that were incurred in the past and cannot be changed, regardless of which future action is taken. Perhaps you want to trade in your current truck when you buy your new car. The amount you paid for the truck—which you bought for $15,000 a year ago—is a sunk cost. In fact, it doesn't matter whether you paid $15,000 or $50,000—it's still a sunk cost. No decision made *now* can alter the past. You already bought the truck, so *the price you paid for it is a sunk cost.* All you can do *now* is keep the truck, trade it in, or sell it for the best price you can get, even if that price is substantially less than what you originally paid for it.

What *is* relevant is the amount you can get for your truck in the future. Suppose the Nissan dealership offers you $8,000 for your truck and the Toyota dealership offers you $10,000. Because the amounts differ and the transaction will take place in the future, the trade-in value is relevant to your decision.

The same principle applies to all situations—*only relevant data affect decisions.* Let's consider another application of this general principle.

Suppose Northern Watters Knitwear is deciding whether to use pure wool or a wool blend in a new line of sweaters. Assume that Northern Watters Knitwear predicts the following costs under the two alternatives:

| | *Expected Materials and Labour Cost per Sweater* | | |
|---|---|---|---|
| | Wool | Wool Blend | Cost Difference |
| Direct materials | $10 | $6 | $4 |
| Direct labour | 2 | 2 | 0 |
| Total cost of direct materials and direct labour | $12 | $8 | $4 |

The cost of direct materials is relevant because this cost differs between alternatives (the wool costs $4 more than the wool blend). The labour cost is irrelevant because that cost is the same for both kinds of wool.

 **Why is this important?**

The accounting information used to make **business decisions** in this chapter considers only one factor: **profitability**. However, in real life, managers should consider **many** more **factors**, including the effect of the decision on **employees**, the local **community**, and the **environment**.

## Relevant Nonfinancial Information

Nonfinancial, or qualitative, factors also play a role in managers' decisions. For example, closing manufacturing plants or laying off employees can seriously hurt the local community and employee morale. **Outsourcing** can reduce control over delivery time and product quality. Offering discounted prices to select customers can upset regular customers and tempt them to take their business elsewhere. Managers must think through the likely quantitative *and* qualitative effects of their decisions.

Managers who ignore qualitative factors can make serious mistakes. For example, the City of Nottingham, England, spent $1.6 million on 215 solar-powered parking meters after seeing how well the parking meters worked in countries along the Mediterranean Sea. However, the city did not adequately consider that British skies are typically overcast. The result? Because of the lack of sunlight, the meters didn't always work. The city lost money because people ended up parking for free!

Relevant qualitative information has the same characteristics as relevant financial information: The qualitative factor occurs in the *future*, and it *differs* between alternatives. The amount of future sunshine required differed between alternatives: The mechanical meters didn't require any sunshine, but the solar-powered meters needed a great deal.

Likewise, in deciding between the Corolla and Sentra, you will likely consider qualitative factors that differ between the cars (legroom, trunk capacity, dashboard design, and so forth) before making your final decision. Since you must live with these factors in the future, they become relevant to your decision.

# Regular-Pricing Decisions

**2** Make pricing decisions.

Managers typically start with three basic questions when setting regular prices for their products or services (see Exhibit 8-3).

PROFESSIONAL COMPETENCY

**EXHIBIT 8-3** Regular-Pricing Considerations

- What is our target profit?
- How much will customers pay?
- Are we a price-taker or a price-setter for this product?

The answers to these questions are often complex and ever-changing. Economic conditions, historical company earnings, industry risk, competition, and new business developments all affect the level of profit that shareholders expect. Shareholders usually tie their profit expectations to the amount of assets invested in the company. For example, shareholders may expect a 10% annual return on their investment. A company's share price tends to decline if the company does not meet target profits, so managers must keep costs low while generating enough revenue to meet target profits.

This leads to the second question: How much will customers pay? Managers cannot set prices above what customers are willing to pay, or sales will decline. The amount customers will pay depends on the competition, the product's uniqueness, the effectiveness of marketing campaigns, general economic conditions, and so forth.

**EXHIBIT 8-4** Price-Takers versus Price-Setters

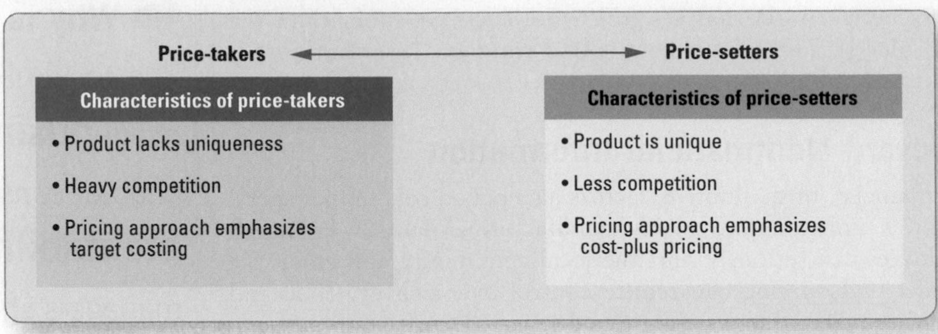


**Why is this important?**

Both **branding** and product **differentiation** give managers more control over pricing. Without such features, a **company** must often settle for selling its **product** at the same price as its competitors.

To address the third pricing question, imagine a continuum with price-takers at one end and price-setters at the other end. A company's products and services fall somewhere along this continuum, shown in Exhibit 8-4. Companies are price-takers when they have little or no control over the prices of their products or services. This occurs when their products and services are *not* unique or when competition is heavy. Examples include food commodities (milk and corn), natural resources (oil and lumber), and generic consumer products and services (paper towels, dry cleaning, and banking).

Companies are price-setters when they have more control over pricing—in other words, they can "set" prices to some extent. Companies are price-setters when their products are unique, which results in less competition. Unique products such as original art and jewellery, specially manufactured machinery, patented perfume scents, and custom-made furniture can command higher prices.

To gain more control over pricing, companies try to differentiate their products in terms of features, service, or quality.

Firms must also consider their capability to provide a service or product when considering pricing decisions. This capability is often discussed in terms of *throughput.* Throughput is the rate at which something can be processed. This could refer to the amount of product an organization can manufacture based on accessibility or conversion time of raw materials. An example in terms of service organizations might be the amount of person-hours that a software company can dedicate to the development of software. An organization's ability to produce or provide a service is governed by throughput, and analyzing operations from this perspective can help to identify what is commonly called a *bottleneck*.

The *theory of constraints* focuses on throughput analysis and conceives of a bottleneck as a constrained resource, which is the component of the service or production process that dictates the performance or capacity of the entire system. For example, Carol is a senior partner in an audit firm, and must review all final reports before they are released to the client. Carol has 10 audit managers submitting reports for review, resulting in a bottleneck. The constrained resource for the audit firm will be the time it takes for Carol, the senior partner, to review all 10 completed audit reports before they are released, regardless of how quickly the audit managers are able to complete and submit the report to her.

A company's approach to pricing depends on whether its product or service is on the price-taking or price-setting end of the spectrum. Price-takers emphasize a target-costing approach; price-setters emphasize a **cost-plus pricing** approach. Keep in mind that many products fall somewhere along the continuum. Therefore, managers tend to use both approaches to some extent. We'll now discuss each approach in turn.

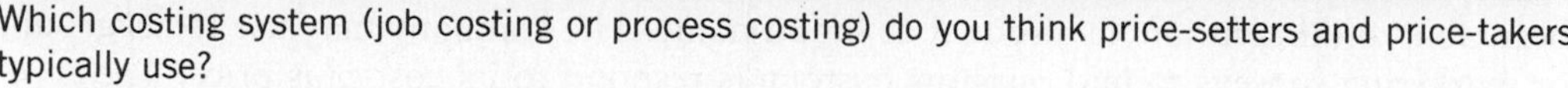

Which costing system (job costing or process costing) do you think price-setters and price-takers typically use?

**Answer:** Companies tend to be price-setters when their products are unique. Unique products are produced as single items or in small batches. Therefore, these companies use job costing to determine the product's cost. However, companies are price-takers when their products are high-volume commodities. Process costing better suits this type of product.

## Cost-Plus Pricing

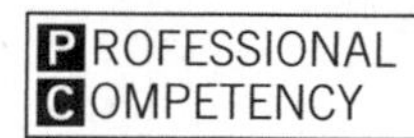

When a company is a price-setter, it emphasizes a cost-plus approach to pricing. This pricing approach is essentially the *opposite* of the target-pricing approach. Cost-plus pricing starts with the product's total costs (as a given) and *adds* its desired profit to determine a cost-plus price.

Total cost
Plus: Desired profit
Cost-plus price

When the product is unique, the company has more control over pricing. However, the company still needs to make sure that the cost-plus price is not higher than customers are willing to pay. Exhibit 8-5 provides data for an air filter company named Electro Breeze. Let's assume that the air filters benefit from brand recognition, so the company has some control over the price it charges for its filters. Exhibit 8-6 takes a cost-plus pricing approach assuming the current level of sales.

**EXHIBIT 8-5** Traditional (Absorption Costing) Format and Contribution Margin Format Income Statements

INCOME STATEMENT
(at a production and sales level of 250,000 units)
Year Ended December 31

| Traditional (Absorption Costing) Format | | Contribution Margin Format | | |
|---|---|---|---|---|
| Sales revenue | $800,000 | Sales revenue | | $800,000 |
| Less cost of goods sold | (500,000) | Less variable expenses: | | |
| Gross profit | 300,000 | Manufacturing | $(300,000) | |
| Less marketing and administrative expenses | (200,000) | Marketing and administrative | (75,000) | (375,000) |
| | | Contribution margin | | 425,000 |
| | | Less fixed expenses: | | |
| | | Manufacturing | $(200,000) | |
| | | Marketing and administrative | (125,000) | (325,000) |
| Operating income | $100,000 | Operating income | | $100,000 |

**EXHIBIT 8-6** Calculating Cost-Plus Price

| | Calculations | Total |
|---|---|---|
| Current variable costs | 250,000 units × $1.50 per unit = | $375,000 |
| Plus: Current fixed costs | | +325,000 |
| Current total costs | | $700,000 |
| Plus: Desired revenue | 10% × $1,000,000 of assets | +100,000 |
| Target revenue | | $800,000 |
| Divided by number of units | | ÷250,000 |
| Cost-plus price per unit | | $ 3.20 |

If the current market price for generic air filters is $3.00, can Electro Breeze sell its brand-name filters for $3.20 apiece? The answer depends on how well the company has been able to differentiate its product or brand name. The company may use focus groups or marketing surveys to find out how customers respond to its cost-plus price. The company may find out that its cost-plus price is too high, or it may find that it could set the price even higher without jeopardizing sales.

## Target Costing

3 Make target costing decisions.

When a company is a price-taker, it emphasizes a **target costing** approach to pricing. Target costing starts with the market price of the product (the price customers are willing to pay) and subtracts the company's desired profit to determine the product's target total cost—the *total* cost to develop, design, produce, market, deliver, and service the product (Exhibit 8-7). In other words, the total cost includes every cost incurred throughout the value chain relating to the product.

| |
|---|
| Revenue at market price |
| Less: Desired profit |
| Target total cost |

**EXHIBIT 8-7**

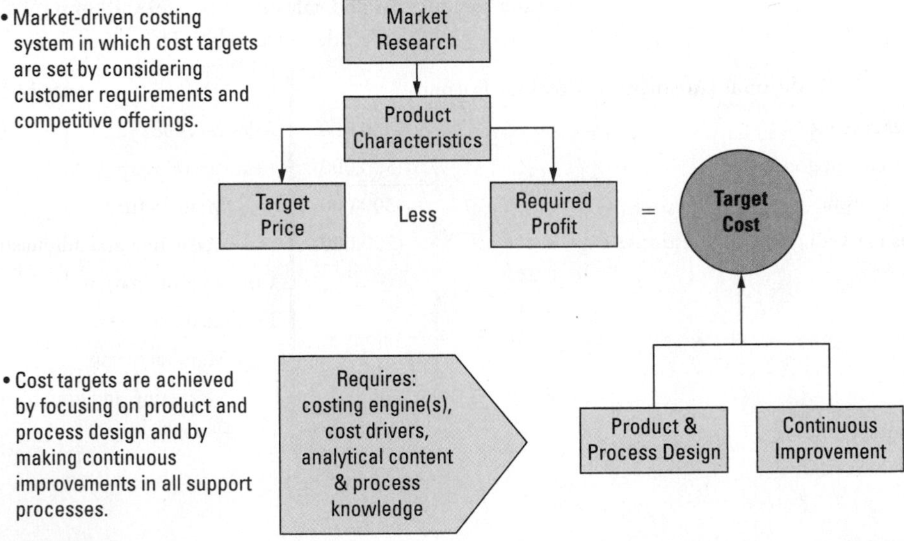


In this relationship, the market price is "taken." If the product's current cost is higher than the target cost, the company must find ways to reduce costs; otherwise it will not meet its profit goals. Managers often use ABC along with value engineering (discussed in Chapter 7) to find ways to cut costs.

Let's look at an example of target costing. Let's assume that air filters are a commodity and that the current market price is $3.00 per filter (not the $3.20 sales price assumed in the earlier Electro Breeze example). Because the air filters are a commodity, Electro Breeze will emphasize a target-costing approach. Let's assume that Electro Breeze's shareholders expect a 10% annual return on the company's assets. If the company has $1,000,000 in assets, the desired profit is $100,000 ($1,000,000 × 10%).

Exhibit 8-8 calculates the target total cost at the current sales volume (250,000 units). Once we know the target total cost, we can analyze the fixed and variable cost components separately.

**EXHIBIT 8-8** Calculating Target Full Cost

| | Calculations | Total |
|---|---|---|
| Revenue at market price | 250,000 units × $3.00 price = | $ 750,000 |
| Less: Desired profit | 10% × $1,000,000 of assets | (100,000) |
| Target total cost | | $ 650,000 |

Can Electro Breeze make and sell 250,000 air filters at a target total cost of $650,000 or less? We know from Electro Breeze's contribution margin income statement (Exhibit 8-5) that the company's variable costs are $1.50 per unit ($375,000 ÷ 250,000 units). This variable cost per unit includes both manufacturing costs ($1.20 per unit) and marketing and administrative costs ($0.30 per unit). We also know that the company incurs $325,000 in fixed costs in its current relevant range. Again, some fixed cost stems from manufacturing and some from marketing and administrative activities. *In setting regular sales prices, companies must cover all of their costs—it doesn't matter if these costs are inventoriable product costs or period costs, or whether they are fixed or variable.*

Making and selling 250,000 filters currently costs the company $700,000 [(250,000 units × $1.50 variable cost per unit) + $325,000 of fixed costs], which is more than the target total cost of $650,000 (shown in Exhibit 8-8). So, what are Electro Breeze's options?

1. Accept a lower profit
2. Cut fixed costs
3. Cut variable costs
4. Use other strategies

For example, as an alternate strategy, Electro Breeze could attempt to increase sales volume. Recall that the company has excess capacity, so making and selling more units would affect only variable costs. The company could also consider changing or adding to its product mix. Finally, it could attempt to differentiate its air filters (or strengthen its name brand) to gain more control over sales prices.

Let's look at some of these options. Electro Breeze may first try to cut fixed costs. As shown in Exhibit 8-9, the company has to reduce fixed costs to $275,000 to meet its target profit. Since current fixed costs are $325,000 (Exhibit 8-5), that means the company has to cut fixed costs by $50,000.

**EXHIBIT 8-9** Calculating Target Fixed Cost

| | Calculations | Total |
|---|---|---|
| Target total cost | | $ 650,000 |
| Less: Current variable costs | 250,000 units × $1.50 | (375,000) |
| Target fixed cost | | $ 275,000 |

The company starts by considering whether any discretionary fixed costs could be eliminated without harming the company. Since committed fixed costs are nearly impossible to change in the short run, Electro Breeze probably cannot reduce this type of fixed cost.

## STOP & THINK

Suppose Electro Breeze can reduce its current fixed costs, but only by $25,000. If it wants to meet its target profit, by how much will it have to reduce the variable cost of each unit? Assume that sales volume remains at 250,000 units.

**Answer:** Companies typically try to cut both fixed and variable costs. Because Electro Breeze can cut its fixed costs only by $25,000, it also has to cut its variable costs to meet its target profit:

| | |
|---|---|
| Target total cost | $ 650,000 |
| Less: Reduced fixed costs ($325,000 – $25,000) | (300,000) |
| Target total variable costs | $ 350,000 |
| Divided by number of units | ÷ 250,000 |
| Target variable cost per unit | $ 1.40 |

In addition to cutting its fixed costs by $25,000, the company must reduce its variable costs by $0.10 per unit ($1.50 – $1.40) to meet its target profit at the existing volume of sales.

If the company cannot reduce its fixed costs by $50,000, it has to lower its variable cost to $1.30 per unit, as shown in Exhibit 8-10.

**EXHIBIT 8-10** Calculating Target Unit Variable Cost

| | Total |
|---|---|
| Target total cost | $ 650,000 |
| Less: Current fixed costs | (325,000) |
| Target total variable costs | $ 325,000 |
| Divided by number of units | ÷ 250,000 |
| Target variable cost per unit | $ 1.30 |

Perhaps the company could renegotiate raw materials costs with its suppliers, or find a less costly way of packaging or shipping the air filters.

However, if Electro Breeze can't reduce variable costs to $1.30 per unit, could it meet its target profit through a combination of lowering both fixed costs and variable costs?

Another strategy is to increase sales. Electro Breeze's managers can use CVP analysis, as you learned in Chapter 4, to figure out how many air filters the company has to sell to achieve its target profit. How could the company increase demand for the air filters? Perhaps it could reach new markets or advertise. How much does the advertising cost—and how many extra air filters would the company have to sell to cover that cost? These are only some of the questions managers must ask. As you can see, managers do not have an easy task when the current total cost exceeds the target total cost. Sometimes, companies just cannot compete given the current market price. If that is the case, they may have no other choice than to exit the market for that product.

Notice how pricing decisions used our two keys to decision making: (1) Focus on relevant information, and (2) use a contribution margin approach that separates variable costs from fixed costs. In pricing decisions all cost information is relevant because the company must cover *all* costs along the value chain before it can generate a profit. However, we still needed to consider variable costs and fixed costs separately because they behave differently at different volumes.

Our pricing decision rule is as follows:

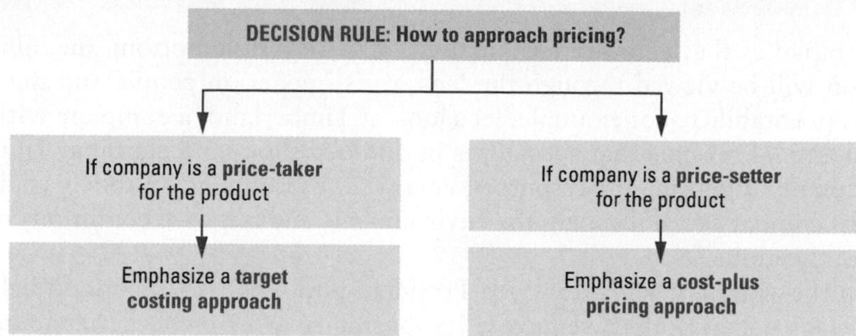


## Keys to Making Short-term Special Decisions

Our approach to making short-term special decisions is called the *relevant information approach* or the *incremental analysis approach*. Instead of looking at the company's entire income statement under each decision alternative, we'll just look at how operating income would change or differ under each alternative. Using this approach, we'll leave out irrelevant information—the costs and revenues that won't differ between alternatives.

We'll consider six kinds of decisions in this chapter:

1. Special sales orders
2. Dropping products, departments, and territories
3. Product mix
4. Outsourcing (make or buy)
5. Selling as-is or processing further
6. Transfer-pricing decisions

As you study these decisions, keep in mind the two keys in analyzing short-term special business decisions shown in Exhibit 8-11:

1. **Focus on relevant revenues, costs, and profits.** Irrelevant information only clouds the picture and creates information overload. That's why we'll use the incremental analysis approach.
2. **Use a contribution margin approach that separates variable costs from fixed costs.** Because fixed costs and variable costs behave differently, they must be analyzed separately. Traditional (absorption costing) income statements, which blend fixed and variable costs, can mislead managers. Contribution margin (CM) income statements, which isolate costs by behaviour (variable or fixed), help managers gather the cost-behaviour information they need. Keep in mind that unit manufacturing costs are mixed costs, too, so they can also mislead managers. If you use unit manufacturing costs in your analysis, make sure you separate the costs' fixed and variable components first.

We'll use these two keys in each decision.

**EXHIBIT 8-11** Two Keys to Making Short-term Special Decisions

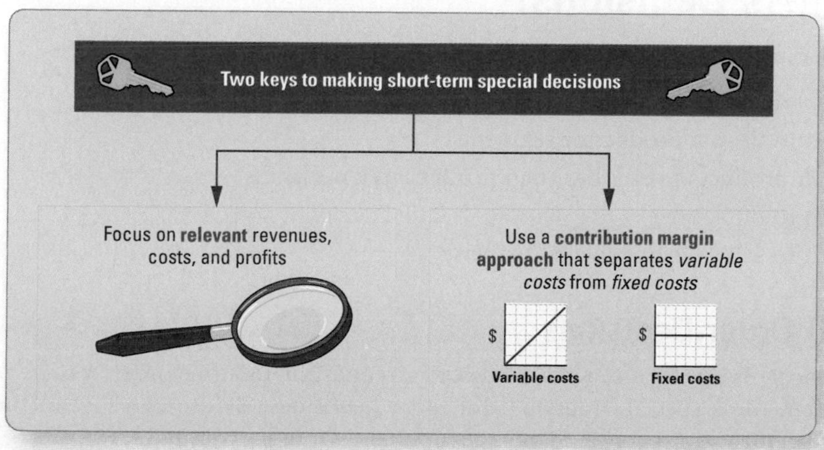

## Sustainability and Short-Term Business Decisions

See Exercises E8-18A and E8-33B

For companies that embrace sustainability and the triple bottom line, almost every decision will be viewed through the lens of its impact on people and the planet, as well as profitability. For example, let's look at Timberland, a company with $1.4 billion in annual revenue that specializes in outdoor shoes and clothing. Timberland is intentionally "focusing the resources, energy, and profits of a publicly traded...company to combat social ills, help the environment, and improve conditions of laborers around the globe."

In the words of Jeffrey Swartz, President and CEO, "Timberland believes, and has always believed, that we have a responsibility to help effect change in the communities where we work and live." The company is committed to "doing well and doing good." But how does the company work toward such lofty goals? Here are a few examples of the company's many initiatives:

- Employees are given up to 40 hours of paid leave each year to perform community service work.
- The company's strict Code of Conduct ensures that domestic and overseas workers are employed at fair wage rates, work reasonable shifts, and work in safe factories.
- The company is committed to being environmentally conscious in the production of its products. The company labels its footwear with a Green Index rating system. The index educates consumers about the product's climate impact, chemicals used, and materials (percentage of organic, recycled, or renewable materials) used.
- The company uses solar panels on its California distribution centre to provide 60% of its energy. This $3.5 million investment was made, even though cost models showed it might take 20 years for the investment to earn a return.
- By the end of 2013, Timberland met its 2015 goal to reduce GHG emissions by 50% by 2015, based on 2006 baseline.

In 2013 alone, the brand reported a 22% reduction in GHG emissions as compared to 2012. A second goal related to climate change, to source 30% of energy from clean, renewable sources by 2015, based on 2006 baseline, is also on track. By the end of 2013, Timberland derived 26% of its energy from renewable sources, exceeding its 2013 target of 23%, and just 1% shy of its 27% goal for 2014. In 2013 alone, the brand increased its use of renewable energy by 28% versus 2012.

# How Do Managers Make Special Business Decisions?

A *segment* is an independent or semi-independent unit within an organization. A segment could be a department, a division, or a geographical territory

In this part of the chapter we'll consider five more special business decisions:

- Accept a special order
- When to drop a product or segments
- Which products to emphasize in product mix decisions
- When to outsource
- When to sell as-is or process further

## Special Order Decisions

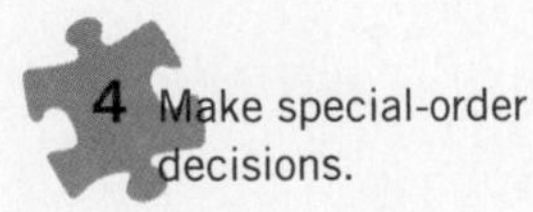


4 Make special-order decisions.

A special order is an instance when a customer requests a one-time order at a *reduced* sales price. Often, these special orders are for large quantities. Before agreeing to the special deal, management must consider the questions shown in Exhibit 8-12.

**EXHIBIT 8-12** Special-Order Considerations

- Do we have excess capacity available to fill this order?
- Will the reduced sales price be high enough to cover the *incremental* costs of filling the order (the variable costs and any additional fixed costs)?
- Will the special order affect regular sales in the long run?

First, managers must consider available capacity. If the company is already making as many units as possible and selling them all at its regular sales price, it wouldn't make sense to fill a special order at a *reduced* sales price. Therefore, available excess capacity is a necessity for accepting a special order. This is true for service firms (law firms, caterers, and so forth) as well as manufacturers.

Second, managers need to consider whether the special reduced sales price is high enough to cover the incremental costs of filling the order. The special price must exceed the variable costs of filling the order or the company will lose money on the deal. In other words, the special order must provide a positive contribution margin.

Next, the company must consider fixed costs. If the company has excess capacity, fixed costs probably won't be affected by producing more units (or delivering more service). However, in some cases, management may need to hire a consultant or incur some other fixed cost to fill the special order. If so, management will need to consider whether the special sales price is high enough to generate a positive contribution margin *and* cover the additional fixed costs.

Finally, managers need to consider whether the special order will affect regular sales in the long run. Will regular customers find out about the special order and demand a lower price or take their business elsewhere? Will the special-order customer come back again and again, asking for the same reduced price? Will the special-order price start a price war with competitors? Any decision on accepting a *special order* must consider if the benefit of accepting the order is worth these risks.

Let's consider a special sales order example. Suppose Electro Breeze sells air filters for \$3.20 each. Assume that a mail-order company has offered Electro Breeze \$35,000 for 20,000 air filters, or \$1.75 per filter (\$35,000 ÷ 20,000 = \$1.75). This sale will

- Use manufacturing capacity that would otherwise be idle
- Not change fixed costs
- Not require any variable *nonmanufacturing* expenses (because no extra marketing costs are incurred with this special order)
- Not affect regular sales

We have addressed every consideration except one: Is the special sales price high enough to cover the variable *manufacturing* costs associated with the order? Let's take a look at the *wrong* way and then the *right* way to figure out the answer to that question.

Recall Electro Breeze made and sold 250,000 air filters before considering the special order. Using the traditional (absorption costing) income statement on the left side of Exhibit 8-5, the manufacturing cost per unit is \$2.00 (\$500,000 ÷ 250,000). A manager who does not examine these numbers carefully may believe that Electro Breeze should *not* accept the special order at a sale price of \$1.75 because each air filter costs \$2.00 to manufacture. However, this would be an error, and a bad decision. Remember that the unit manufacturing cost of a product (\$2.00) is a *mixed* cost containing both fixed and variable cost components. To correctly answer the question, we should adopt an incremental analysis to valuate the variable portion of the manufacturing unit cost.

The right-hand side of Exhibit 8-5 shows the contribution margin income statement that separates variable expenses from fixed expenses. The contribution margin income statement shows that the *variable* manufacturing cost per unit is only $1.20 ($300,000 ÷ 250,000). The special sales price of $1.75 is higher than the variable manufacturing cost of $1.20. Therefore, the special order will provide a positive contribution margin of $0.55 per unit ($1.75 − $1.20). Since the special order is for 20,000 units, Electro Breeze's total contribution margin should increase by $11,000 (20,000 units × $0.55 per unit) if it accepts this order. Remember that in this example, Electro Breeze's variable marketing expenses are irrelevant because the company will not incur the usual variable marketing expenses on this special order. However, this won't always be the case. Often, companies incur variable operating expenses (such as freight-out or sales commissions) on special orders.

Using an incremental analysis approach, Electro Breeze compares the additional revenues from the special order with the incremental expenses to see if the special order will contribute to profits. Exhibit 8-13 shows that the special sales order will increase revenue by $35,000 (20,000 × $1.75), but it will also increase variable manufacturing costs by $24,000 (20,000 × $1.20). As a result, Electro Breeze's contribution margin will increase by $11,000, as previously anticipated.

**EXHIBIT 8-13** Incremental Analysis of Special Sales Order

| | |
|---|---|
| Expected increase in revenues—sale of 20,000 oil filters × $1.75 each | $ 35,000 |
| Expected increase in expenses—variable manufacturing costs: | |
| 20,000 oil filters × $1.20 each | (24,000) |
| Expected increase in operating income | $ 11,000 |

The other costs shown in Exhibit 8-5 are irrelevant. Variable marketing and administrative expenses will be the same whether or not Electro Breeze accepts the special order because Electro Breeze made no marketing efforts to get this sale. Fixed manufacturing expenses won't change because Electro Breeze has enough idle capacity to produce 20,000 extra air filters without requiring additional facilities. Fixed marketing and administrative expenses won't be affected by this special order, either. Because there are no additional fixed costs, the total increase in contribution margin flows directly to operating income. As a result, the special sales order will increase operating income by $11,000.

Notice that the analysis follows the two keys to making short-term special business decisions discussed earlier: (1) Focus on relevant data (revenues and costs that *will change* if Electro Breeze accepts the special order), and (2) use a contribution margin approach that separates variable costs from fixed costs.

To summarize, for special sales orders, the decision rule is as follows:

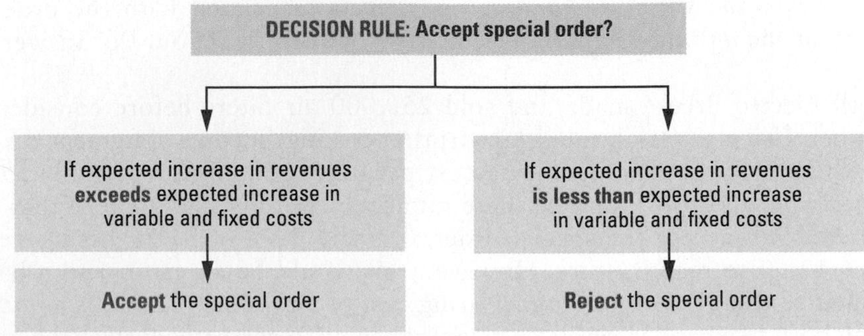

Now let's change the situation by assuming that full capacity for Electro Breeze is 250,000 units. Since Electro Breeze is already selling 250,000 units, this means that for each unit it sells as a special order, the company must give up one unit of regular sales. Therefore, an opportunity cost becomes a part of the equation. If Electro Breeze is operating at full capacity, the minimum selling price for the special order would be

$$\text{Minimum selling price} = \text{variable costs (of the special order)} + \text{opportunity cost of lost sales}$$

The **opportunity cost** is the contribution margin that is lost for each regular sale that cannot be fulfilled. Therefore, the total contribution margin lost is equal to

$$\text{Contribution margin lost} = \frac{\text{CM}}{\text{Unit}}\text{(for regular sales)} \times \text{\# regular sales lost}$$

At full capacity, the number of regular sales lost due to the special order is 20,000. The contribution margin per unit of regular sales is \$1.70 (\$3.20 – ((300,000 + 75,000) ÷ 250,000)). That means that the total contribution margin lost is \$34,000 (\$1.70 × 20,000 units).

There is one more consideration to factor into this equation. The total contribution margin lost due to lost regular sales needs to be distributed among the number of units of the special order because each unit of the special order shares in the opportunity cost. We can now complete the formula to show the minimum selling price for a special order as

$$\text{Minimum selling price} = \text{variable costs (of the special order)} + \frac{\left[\frac{\text{CM}}{\text{Unit}}\text{(regular sales)} \times \text{\#regular sales lost}\right]}{\text{\# units of special order}}$$

When Electro Breeze is operating at full capacity, the number of regular sales lost is the same as the number of special-order units. In this instance, the regular sales lost and the units of special order cancel each other out, and the formula is simply variable cost + lost CM/unit. For this example, the minimum selling price for the special order would be \$2.90 per unit (\$1.20 + \$1.70). Since the minimum selling price is greater than the special-order offer, it would not be in Electro Breeze's best interest, numerically speaking, to accept the special order.

The two extremes we have seen so far are when there is plenty of capacity to fulfill the special order and when there is no leftover capacity so that all of the units of the special order would have to replace units of regular sales. However, this formula also works in a situation between these two extremes. Let's see how that works.

Let's assume that capacity for Electro Breeze is 250,000 units and it is operating at 235,000 units. Therefore, there are 15,000 units of leftover capacity available. This means that only 5,000 units of regular sales would be lost (20,000 – 5,000). With this information, we can complete the equation.

$$\begin{aligned}\text{Minimum selling price} &= \frac{\$1.20 + \$1.70(5{,}000)}{20{,}000} \\ &= \$1.20 + \$0.425 \\ &= \$1.63\end{aligned}$$

You will note that the contribution margin for the 5,000 units of lost regular sales is spread out over all of the 20,000 units for the special order, thereby lowering the impact on the minimum selling price. With only 5,000 lost regular sales, the minimum selling price becomes $1.63. Since the minimum selling price is less than the special-order price, it would be in Electro Breeze's best interest, numerically speaking, to accept the special order.

Management should also consider qualitative elements. For example, would the details of the special order remain confidential, or could they potentially affect regular sales? There could be many reasons why Electro Breeze would not want to take on the special order even if the calculations show that it should be accepted. The numerical calculations are only the first step to the decision-making processes that managers will undertake.

## TRY IT!

Assume that a Campbell's soup plant is running at 90% of its monthly capacity. Campbell's has just received a special order to produce 40,000 cases of chicken noodle soup for a national supermarket. The supermarket will sell the soup under its own private brand label. The soup will be the same in all respect, except for the label, which will cost Campbell's an extra $5,000 in total to design. The supermarket has offered to pay only $19.00 per case, which is well under Campbell's normal sales price.

Costs at the current production level (450,000 cases) are as follows:

| | Total Cost | Cost per Case (450,000 cases) |
|---|---|---|
| Direct Materials | $4,500,000 | $10.00 |
| Direct Labour | 1,350,000 | 3.00 |
| Variable MOH | 900,000 | 2.00 |
| Fixed MOH | 2,700,000 | 6.00 |
| Total | $9,450,000 | $21.00 |

1. Is there enough excess capacity to fill this order?
2. Will Campbell's operating income increase or decrease if it accepts this special order? By how much?

Please see page 513 for solution.

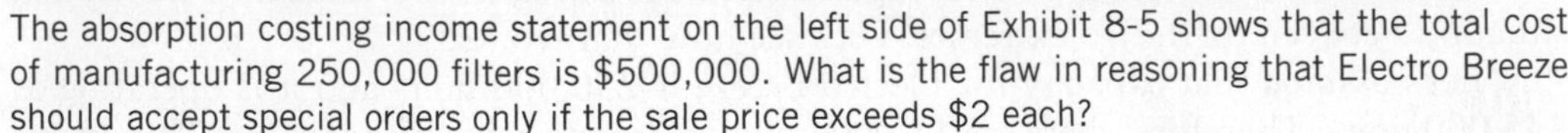


The absorption costing income statement on the left side of Exhibit 8-5 shows that the total cost of manufacturing 250,000 filters is $500,000. What is the flaw in reasoning that Electro Breeze should accept special orders only if the sale price exceeds $2 each?

**Answer:** The flaw in this analysis arises from treating a mixed cost as though it were variable. Manufacturing one extra air filter will cost only $1.20—the variable manufacturing cost. Fixed expenses are irrelevant because Electro Breeze will incur $200,000 of fixed manufacturing overhead expenses whether or not the company accepts the special order. Producing 20,000 more air filters will not increase *total* fixed expenses, so manufacturing costs increase at the rate of $1.20 per unit, not $2.00 per unit.

# DECISION GUIDELINES

## Relevant Information for Business Decisions

Nike makes special-order and regular-pricing decisions. Even though it sells mass-produced shoes and sports clothing, Nike has differentiated its products with advertising. Nike's managers consider both quantitative and qualitative factors as they make pricing decisions. Here are key guidelines that Nike's managers follow in making their decisions.

| Decision | Guidelines |
|---|---|
| What information is relevant for my short-term special business decisions? | Relevant information is as follows:<br>1. Pertains to the *future*<br>2. *Differs* between alternatives |
| What are two key guidelines that I should keep in mind while making short-term special business decisions? | 1. Focus on relevant data.<br>2. Use a contribution margin approach that separates variable costs from fixed costs. |
| Should I accept a lower sales price than the regular price for a large order from a customer in São Paulo, Brazil? | If the revenue from the order exceeds the extra variable and fixed costs incurred to fill the order, then accepting the order will increase operating income. |
| What should I consider when setting regular product prices? | You should consider the following:<br>1. What profit shareholders expect<br>2. What price customers will pay<br>3. Whether you are a price-setter or a price-taker |
| What approach should I take to pricing? | If you have differentiated your products through advertising, you tend to be a price-setter. Your managers can emphasize a cost-plus approach to pricing. |
| What approach to pricing should I take if I do not have a highly branded product? | As a price-taker, your managers should use a target-costing approach to pricing. |

# SUMMARY PROBLEM 1

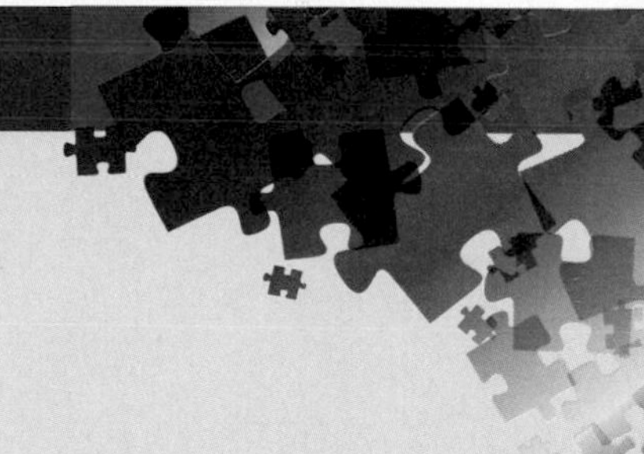

Linger Industries makes tennis balls. Linger's only plant can produce up to 2.5 million cans of balls per year. Current production is 2 million cans. Annual manufacturing, selling, and administrative fixed costs total $700,000. The variable cost of making and selling each can of balls is $1. Stockholders expect a 12% annual return on the company's $3 million of assets.

### Requirements

1. What is Linger Industries' current total cost of making and selling 2 million cans of tennis balls? What is the current cost per unit of each can of tennis balls?
2. Assume that Linger Industries is a price-taker and the current market price is $1.45 per can of balls. (This is the price at which manufacturers sell to retailers.) What is the *target* total cost of producing and selling two million cans of balls? Given Linger Industries' current total costs, will the company reach shareholders' profit goals?
3. If Linger Industries cannot reduce its fixed costs, what is the target variable cost per can of balls?
4. Suppose Linger Industries could spend an extra $100,000 on advertising to differentiate its product so that it could be more of a price-setter. Assuming the original volume and costs plus the $100,000 of new advertising costs, what cost-plus price will Linger Industries want to charge for a can of balls?

5. Nike has just asked Linger Industries to supply 400,000 cans of balls at a special-order price of $1.20 per can. Nike wants Linger Industries to package the balls under the Nike label. (Linger will imprint the Nike logo on each ball and can.) As a result, Linger Industries will have to spend $10,000 to change the packaging machinery. Assuming the original volume and costs, should Linger Industries accept this special order? (Unlike the chapter problem, assume that Linger will incur variable selling costs as well as variable manufacturing costs related to this order.)

## ▪ SOLUTION

### Requirement 1

The current total cost, and cost per unit are calculated as follows:

| | |
|---|---|
| Fixed costs | $ 700,000 |
| Plus: Total variable costs (2 million cans × $1 per unit) | + 2,000,000 |
| Current total costs | $2,700,000 |
| Divided by number of units | ÷ 2,000,000 |
| Current cost per can | $ 1.35 |

### Requirement 2

The target total cost is as follows:

| | |
|---|---|
| Revenue at market price (2,000,000 cans × $1.45 price) | $2,900,000 |
| Less: Desired profit (12% × $3,000,000 of assets) | (360,000) |
| Target total cost | $2,540,000 |

Linger Industries' *current* total costs ($2,700,000 from Requirement 1) are $160,000 higher than the *target* total costs ($2,540,000). If Linger Industries can't cut costs, it won't be able to meet shareholders' profit expectations.

### Requirement 3

Assuming that Linger Industries cannot reduce its fixed costs, the target variable cost per can is as follows:

| | |
|---|---|
| Target total cost (from Requirement 2) | $ 2,540,000 |
| Less: Fixed costs | (700,000) |
| Target total variable costs | $ 1,840,000 |
| Divided by number of units | ÷ 2,000,000 |
| Target variable cost per unit | $ 0.92 |

Since Linger Industries cannot reduce its fixed costs, it needs to reduce variable costs by $0.08 per can ($1.00 – $0.92) to meet its profit goals. This would require an 8% cost reduction in variable costs, which may not be possible.

**Requirement 4**

If Linger Industries can differentiate its tennis balls, it will gain more control over pricing. The company's new cost-plus price would be as follows:

| | |
|---|---|
| Current total costs (from Requirement 1) | $ 2,700,000 |
| Plus: Additional cost of advertising | + 100,000 |
| Plus: Desired profit (from Requirement 2) | + 360,000 |
| Target revenue | $ 3,160,000 |
| Divided by number of units | ÷2,000,000 |
| Cost-plus price per unit | $ 1.58 |

Linger Industries must study the market to determine whether retailers would pay $1.58 per can of balls.

**Requirement 5**

First, Linger determines that it has enough extra capacity (500,000 cans) to fill this special order (400,000). Next, Linger compares the revenue from the special order with the extra costs that will be incurred to fill the order. Notice that Linger shouldn't compare the special-order price ($1.20) with the current unit cost of each can ($1.35) because the unit cost contains both a fixed and variable component. Since the company has excess capacity, the existing fixed costs won't be affected by the order. The correct analysis is as follows:

| | |
|---|---|
| Revenue from special order (400,000 × $1.20 per unit) | $ 480,000 |
| Less: Variable cost of special order (400,000 × $1.00) | (400,000) |
| Contribution margin from special order | $ 80,000 |
| Less: Additional fixed costs of special order | (10,000) |
| Operating income provided by special order | $ 70,000 |

Linger Industries should accept the special order because it will increase operating income by $70,000. However, Linger Industries also needs to consider whether its regular customers will find out about the special price and demand lower prices, too. If Linger had simply compared the special-order price of $1.20 to the current unit cost of each can ($1.35), it would have rejected the special order and missed out on the opportunity to make an additional $70,000 of profit.

## Decisions to Drop Products or Segments

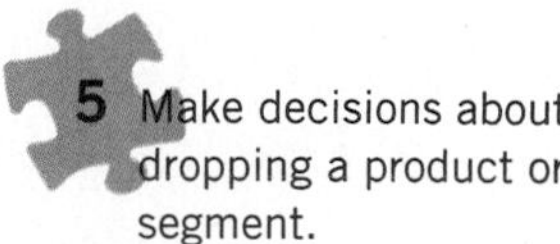

Make decisions about dropping a product or segment.

Managers often must decide whether to drop products, departments, stores, or territories that are not as profitable as desired. In recent years many companies have had to make difficult decisions about adding or dropping operating segments. Canadian Tire decided to eliminate its credit card division in 2009; RBC decided to eliminate is US consumer banking division in 2011, and to re-start the segment in 2015 with the purchase of City National, a California bank.[1] In some cases, companies have divested segments that were formerly core business operations; EMI sold Abbey Road recording studios—the

[1] http://www.thestar.com/business/2015/01/22/rbc-buys-us-bank-for-54-billion-us.html

legendary U.K. recording studio for the Beatles,[2] and Air Canada sold Aeroplan, its successful customer loyalty division.[3] How do managers make these decisions? Exhibit 8-14 shows some questions managers must consider when deciding whether to drop a product line, department, retail store location, or territory.

**EXHIBIT 8-14** Considerations for Dropping Products, Departments, or Territories

- Does the product provide a positive contribution margin?
- Will fixed costs continue to exist even if we drop the product?
- Are there any direct fixed costs that can be avoided if we drop the product?
- Will dropping the product affect sales of the company's other products?
- What could we do with the freed capacity?

In the first half of the chapter we assumed that Electro Breeze offered only one product—air filters. Now, let's assume that it also makes and sells UV air cleaners. Exhibit 8-15 shows the company's contribution margin income statement by product line. Because the UV air cleaner product line has an operating loss of $19,074, management is considering discontinuing it.

**EXHIBIT 8-15** Contribution Margin Income Statements by Product Line

| | | Product Line | |
|---|---|---|---|
| | Total (270,000 units) | Air Filters (250,000 units) | UV Air Cleaners (20,000 units) |
| Sales revenue | $ 835,000 | $ 800,000 | $ 35,000 |
| Less: Variable expenses | (405,000) | (375,000) | (30,000) |
| Contribution margin | 430,000 | 425,000 | 5,000 |
| Less: Fixed expenses: | | | |
| Manufacturing | (200,000) | (185,185)* | (14,815)* |
| Marketing and administrative | (125,000) | (115,741)† | (9,259)† |
| Total fixed expenses | (325,000) | (300,926) | (24,074) |
| Operating income (loss) | $ 105,000 | $ 124,074 | $(19,074) |

*$200,000 ÷ 270,000 units = $0.74074 per unit; 250,000 units × $0.74074 = $185,185; 20,000 units × $0.74074 = $14,815
†$125,000 ÷ 270,000 units = $0.462963 per unit; 250,000 units × $0.462963 = $115,741; 20,000 units × $0.462963 = $9,259

The first question management should ask is, Does the product provide a positive contribution margin? If the product line has a negative contribution margin, the product is not even covering its variable costs. Therefore, the company should drop the product line. However, if the product line has a positive contribution margin, it is *helping* to cover at least some of the company's fixed costs. In Electro Breeze's case, the UV air cleaners provide a $5,000 positive contribution margin. Electro Breeze's managers now need to consider fixed costs.

Suppose Electro Breeze allocates fixed expenses between product lines in proportion to the number of units sold. Dividing the fixed manufacturing expense of $200,000 by 270,000 total units (air filters, 250,000; UV air cleaners, 20,000) yields a fixed manufacturing cost of $0.74074 per unit. Allocating this unit cost to the 250,000 air filters assigns

[2] Reuters, "Debt-Laden EMI Seeks Buyers for Abbey Road Studios in U.K.," *National Post*, February 17, 2010, www.nationalpost.com/story.html?id=2573716
[3] Bova, F. (2005) "The spin-offs that followed Air Canada's bankruptcy" *Financial Times*, July 2014, www.ft.com/cms/s/0/7f494142-dc60-11e3-9016-00144feabdc0.html

a fixed manufacturing cost of $185,185 to this product, as shown in Exhibit 8-15. The same procedure allocates $14,815 to the 20,000 UV air cleaners. Fixed marketing and administrative expenses are allocated in the same manner.

It is important to note that this allocation method is arbitrary. Electro Breeze could allocate fixed costs in many different ways and in each way allocate a different amount of fixed costs to each product line. Since the amount of fixed costs allocated to each product line differs depending on the allocation method used, we need to look at fixed costs in a different light. What matters is this:

1. Will the total fixed costs continue to exist even if the product line is dropped?
2. Can any direct fixed costs of the air cleaners be avoided if the product line is dropped?

### Fixed Costs Continue to Exist (Unavoidable Fixed Costs)

As seen in Appendix 3B, fixed costs that continue to exist even after a product is dropped are often called common or unavoidable fixed costs. Unavoidable fixed costs are irrelevant to the decision because they *will not* differ between alternatives—they are incurred regardless of whether the product line is dropped. Let's assume that all of Electro Breeze's fixed costs ($325,000) will continue to exist even if the company drops the UV air cleaners. Perhaps Electro Breeze makes the UV air cleaners in the same manufacturing facilities as the air filters and uses the same administrative overhead. If that is the case, only the contribution margin the UV air cleaners provide is relevant. If Electro Breeze drops the UV air cleaners, it will lose the $5,000 contribution margin that they provide.

The incremental analysis shown in Exhibit 8-16 verifies the loss. If Electro Breeze drops the UV air cleaners, revenue will decrease by $35,000; but variable expenses will decrease by only $30,000, resulting in a net $5,000 decrease in operating income. Because the company's total fixed costs are unaffected, they aren't included in the analysis. This analysis suggests that management should *not* drop the air cleaners.

**EXHIBIT 8-16** Incremental Analysis for Dropping a Product When Fixed Costs Continue to Exist

| | | |
|---|---|---|
| | Expected decrease in revenues: | |
| | Sale of UV air cleaners (20,000 × $1.75) | $35,000 |
| | Expected decrease in expenses: | |
| | Variable manufacturing expenses (20,000 × $1.50) | 30,000 |
| | Expected *decrease* in operating income | $ (5,000) |

We could also verify that our analysis is correct by looking at what would remain if the UV air cleaners were dropped:

| | |
|---|---|
| Contribution margin from air filters | $ 425,000 |
| Less: Company's fixed expenses (all unavoidable) | (325,000) |
| Remaining operating income | $ 100,000 |

The company's operating income after dropping the UV air cleaners ($100,000) is $5,000 less than before ($105,000). This verifies our earlier conclusion: Electro Breeze's income decreases by $5,000 if it drops the UV air cleaners. Keep in mind that most companies have many product lines. Therefore, analyzing the decision to drop a particular product line is accomplished more easily by performing an incremental analysis (as we did in Exhibit 8-16) rather than adding up all of the revenues and expenses that would remain after dropping one product line. We simply show this second analysis as a means of proving our original result.

### Direct Fixed Costs that Can Be Avoided

Even though Electro Breeze allocates its fixed costs between product lines, some of the fixed costs might belong strictly to the UV air cleaner product line. As seen in Appendix 3B, these are traceable or direct fixed costs of the UV air cleaners.[4] For example, suppose Electro Breeze employs a part-time supervisor to oversee *just* the UV air cleaner product line. The supervisor's $13,000 salary is a direct fixed cost that Electro Breeze can avoid if it stops producing UV air cleaners. Avoidable fixed costs, such as the supervisor's salary, are relevant to the decision because they differ between alternatives. (They will be incurred if the company keeps the product line; they will *not* be incurred if the company drops the product line.)

Exhibit 8-17 shows that in this situation, operating income *will* increase by $8,000 if Electro Breeze drops UV air cleaners. Why? Because revenues will decline by $35,000 but expenses will decline even more—by $43,000. The result is a net increase to operating income of $8,000. This analysis suggests that management should drop the air cleaners.

**EXHIBIT 8-17** Incremental Analysis for Dropping a Product When Direct Fixed Costs Can Be Avoided

| | | |
|---|---|---|
| Expected decrease in revenues: | | |
| Sale of UV air cleaners (20,000 × $1.75) | | $35,000 |
| Expected decrease in expenses: | | |
| Variable manufacturing expenses (20,000 × $1.50) | $30,000 | |
| Direct fixed expenses—supervisor's salary | 13,000 | |
| Expected decrease in total expenses | | 43,000 |
| Expected *increase* in operating income | | $ 8,000 |

## TRY IT!

Assume Sobey's grocery store is deciding whether to eliminate the salad bar section of its stores. The product line income statement shows the following quarterly data for the salad bar operations:

Sales revenue = $750,000
Fixed costs = $100,000
Variable costs = $600,000

1. Only $20,000 of fixed costs can be eliminated if the salad bar is eliminated. The remaining $80,000 of fixed costs are unavoidable. What will happen to Sobey's operating income if it discontinues the salad bars and does nothing with the freed capacity?
2. Management is thinking about replacing the salad bar section of the stores with a specialty olive bar, which is projected to bring in $200,000 of contribution margin each quarter while incurring no additional fixed costs. What will happen to Sobey's operating income if it replaces the salad bars with olive bars?

Please see page 513 for solutions.

### Other Considerations

Management must also consider whether dropping the product line, department, or territory will hurt other sales. In the examples given so far, we assumed that discontinuing the UV air cleaners would not affect air filter sales. However, think about a grocery store. If the Produce Department is not profitable, would managers still drop it? Probably not,

[4] To aid in decision making, companies should separate direct fixed costs from indirect fixed costs on their contribution margin income statements. Companies should trace direct fixed costs to the appropriate product line and allocate only indirect fixed costs among product lines. As in the Electro Breeze example, companies do not always make this distinction on the income statement.

because if they did, they would lose customers who want one-stop shopping. In such situations, managers must also include the loss of contribution margin from *other* departments affected by the change when performing the financial analysis shown previously.

Management should also consider what it could do with freed capacity. In the Electro Breeze example, we assumed that the company produces air filters and UV air cleaners using the same manufacturing facilities. If Electro Breeze drops the UV air cleaners, could it make and sell another product using the freed capacity? Managers should consider whether using the facilities to produce a different product would be more profitable than using the facilities to produce UV air cleaners.

## STOP & THINK

Assume that all of Electro Breeze's fixed costs are unavoidable. If the company drops UV air cleaners, they could make water filters with the freed capacity. The company expects water filters would provide $50,000 of sales, incur $30,000 of variable costs, and incur $10,000 of new direct fixed costs. Should Electro Breeze drop the UV air cleaners and use the freed capacity to make water filters?

**Answer:** If all fixed costs are unavoidable, Electro Breeze would lose $5,000 of contribution margin if it dropped UV air cleaners. Electro Breeze should compare this loss with the expected gain from producing and selling water filters with the freed capacity:

| | |
|---|---|
| Sales of water filters | $ 50,000 |
| Less: Variable cost of water filters | (30,000) |
| Less: Direct fixed costs of water filters | (10,000) |
| Operating income gained from water filters | $ 10,000 |

The gain from producing water filters ($10,000) outweighs the loss from dropping UV air cleaners ($5,000). This suggests that management should replace UV air cleaner production with water filter production.

Business decisions should take into account all costs affected by the choice of action. Managers must ask what total costs—variable and fixed—will change. As Exhibits 8-16 and 8-17 show, the key to deciding whether to drop products, departments, or territories is to compare the lost revenue against the costs that can be saved and to consider what would be done with the freed capacity. The decision rule is as follows:

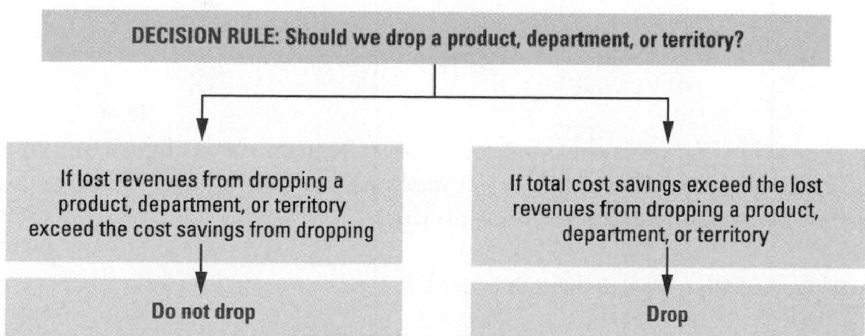


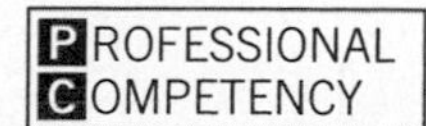


## Product Mix Decisions

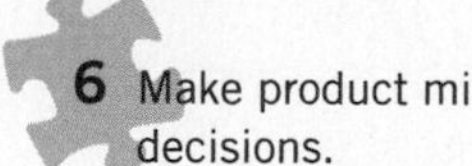


Companies do not have unlimited resources. <u>Constraints</u>, which restrict production or sale of a product, vary from company to company. For a manufacturer, the production constraint is often the number of available machine hours. For a merchandiser such as

The Bay, the primary constraint is volume of display space. In order to determine which products to emphasize producing or displaying, companies facing constraints consider the questions shown in Exhibit 8-18.

**EXHIBIT 8-18** Product Mix Considerations

- What constraint(s) stops us from making (or displaying) all of the units we can sell?
- Which products offer the highest contribution margin per unit of the constraint?
- Would emphasizing one product over another affect fixed costs?

Consider Silver Jeans, a manufacturer of shirts and jeans. Let's say the company can sell all of the shirts and jeans it produces, but it has only 2,000 machine hours of capacity. The company uses the same machines to produce both jeans and shirts. In this case, machine hours is the constraint. Note that this is a short-term decision, because in the long run, Silver Jeans could expand its production facilities to meet sales demand if it made financial sense to do so. The following data suggest that shirts are more profitable than jeans:

| | *Per Unit* | |
|---|---|---|
| | **Shirts** | **Jeans** |
| Sales price | \$ 30 | \$ 60 |
| Less: Variable expenses | (12) | (48) |
| Contribution margin | \$ 18 | \$ 12 |
| Contribution margin ratio: | | |
| Shirts—\$18 ÷ \$30 | 60% | |
| Jeans—\$12 ÷ \$60 | | 20% |

However, an important piece of information is missing—the time it takes to make each product. Let's assume that Silver Jeans can produce either 20 pairs of jeans *or* 10 shirts per machine hour. *The company will incur the same fixed costs either way, so fixed costs are irrelevant.* Which product should it emphasize?

To maximize profits when fixed costs are irrelevant, follow this decision rule:

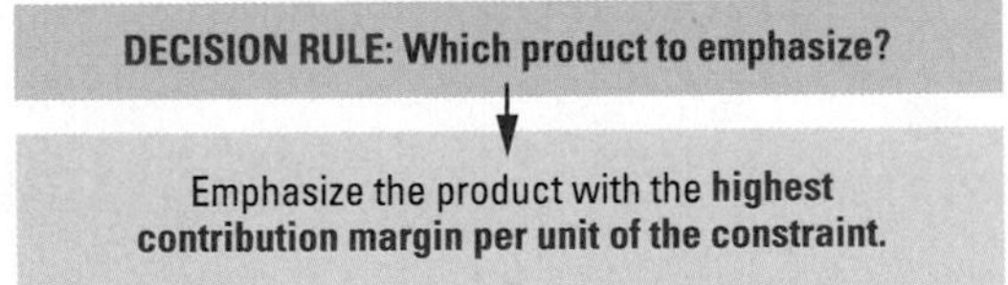


Because *machine hours* is the constraint, Silver Jeans needs to figure out which product has the *highest contribution margin per machine hour.* Exhibit 8-19 shows the contribution margin per machine hour for each product.

**EXHIBIT 8-19** Product Mix—Which Product to Emphasize

| | Shirts | Jeans |
|---|---|---|
| (1) Units that can be produced each machine hour | 10 | 20 |
| (2) Contribution margin per unit | × \$ 18 | × \$ 12 |
| Contribution margin per machine hour (1) × (2) | \$180 | \$240 |
| Available capacity—number of machine hours | × 2,000 | × 2,000 |
| Total contribution margin at full capacity | \$ 360,000 | \$ 480,000 |

Jeans have a higher contribution margin per machine hour ($240) than shirts ($180). Therefore, Silver Jeans will earn more profit by producing jeans. Why? Because even though jeans have a lower contribution margin *per unit*, Silver Jeans can make twice as many jeans as shirts in the available machine hours. Exhibit 8-19 also proves that Silver Jeans earns more total profit by making jeans. Multiplying the contribution margin per machine hour by the available number of machine hours shows that Silver Jeans can earn $480,000 of contribution margin by producing jeans but only $360,000 by producing shirts.

To maximize profit, Silver Jeans should make 40,000 jeans (2,000 machine hours × 20 jeans per hour) and zero shirts. Why zero shirts? Because for every machine hour spent making shirts, Silver Jeans *gives up* $60 of contribution margin ($240 per hour for jeans versus $180 per hour for shirts).

### Changing Assumptions: Product Mix When Demand Is Limited

We made two assumptions about Silver Jeans: (1) Silver Jeans' sales of other products, if any, won't be hurt by this decision, and (2) Silver Jeans can sell as many jeans and shirts as it can produce. Let's challenge these assumptions. First, how could making only jeans (and not shirts) hurt sales of the company's other products? Using other production equipment, Silver Jeans also makes ties and jackets that coordinate with their shirts. Tie and jacket sales might fall if Silver Jeans no longer offers coordinating shirts.

Let's challenge our second assumption. A new competitor has decreased the demand for Silver Jeans' jeans. Now, the company can sell only 30,000 pairs of jeans. Silver Jeans should make only as many jeans as it can sell and use the remaining machine hours to produce shirts. Let's see how this constraint in sales demand changes profitability.

Recall from Exhibit 8-19 that Silver Jeans earns $480,000 of contribution margin from using all 2,000 machine hours to produce jeans. However, if Silver Jeans makes only 30,000 jeans, it uses only 1,500 machine hours (30,000 jeans ÷ 20 jeans per machine hour). That leaves 500 machine hours available for making shirts. Silver Jeans' new contribution margin is as follows:

| | Shirts | Jeans | Total |
|---|---|---|---|
| Contribution margin per machine hour (from Exhibit 8-19) | $ 180 | $ 240 | |
| Machine hours devoted to product | × 500 | × 1,500 | 2,000 |
| Total contribution margin at full capacity | $90,000 | $360,000 | $450,000 |

Because of the change in product mix, Silver Jeans' total contribution margin falls from $480,000 to $450,000, a $30,000 decline. Silver Jeans has to give up $60 of contribution margin per machine hour ($240 − $180) on the 500 hours it spends producing shirts rather than jeans. However, Silver Jeans has no choice—the company would incur an *actual loss* from producing jeans that it could not sell. If Silver Jeans had produced 40,000 jeans but sold only 30,000, the company would have spent $480,000 to make the unsold jeans (10,000 jeans × $48 variable cost per pair of jeans) yet received no sales revenue from them.

What about fixed costs? In most cases, changing the product mix emphasis in the short run will not affect fixed costs, so fixed costs are irrelevant. However, fixed costs could differ when a different product mix is emphasized. What if Silver Jeans had a month-to-month lease on a zipper machine used only for making jeans? If Silver Jeans made only shirts, it could *avoid* the lease cost. However, if Silver Jeans makes any jeans, it needs the machine. In this case, the fixed costs become relevant because they differ between alternative product mixes (shirts only *versus* jeans only or jeans and shirts).

Notice that the analysis again follows the two guidelines for special business decisions: (1) Focus on relevant data (only those revenues and costs that differ), and (2) use a contribution margin approach, which separates variable from fixed costs.

## STOP & THINK

Would Silver Jeans' product mix decision change if it had a $20,000 cancellable lease on a zipper machine needed only for jean production? Assume that the company can sell as many units as it makes.

**Answer:** Compare the profitability as follows:

| | Shirts | Jeans |
|---|---|---|
| Total contribution margin at full capacity (from Exhibit 8-18) | $360,000 | $480,000 |
| Less: Avoidable fixed costs | -0- | (20,000) |
| Net benefit | $360,000 | $460,000 |

Even considering the zipper machine lease, producing jeans is more profitable than producing shirts. Silver Jeans would prefer to produce jeans over shirts unless demand for jeans drops so low that the net benefit from jeans is less than $360,000 (the benefit gained from producing solely shirts).

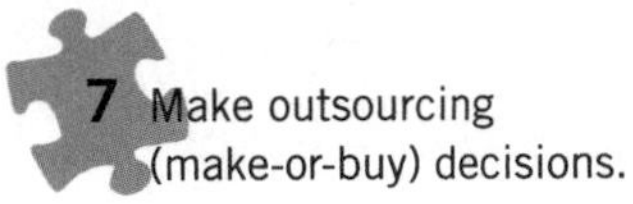


7 Make outsourcing (make-or-buy) decisions.

PROFESSIONAL COMPETENCY

## Outsourcing Decisions (Make-or-Buy)

Recall from the chapter's opening vignette that the Bank of Canada outsources much of its information technology work for retail products such as Canada Savings Bonds. *Outsourcing* decisions are sometimes called make-or-buy decisions because managers must decide whether to buy a product or service or produce it in-house. The heart of these decisions is *how best to use available resources.*

Let's see how managers make outsourcing decisions. ExoMedia Inc., a manufacturer of music CDs, is deciding whether to make paper liners for CD jewel boxes (the plastic cases in which CDs are sold) in-house or whether to outsource them to Mūz-Art, a company that specializes in producing paper liners. ExoMedia's cost to produce 250,000 liners is as follows:

| | Total Cost (250,000 liners) |
|---|---|
| Direct materials | $ 40,000 |
| Direct labour | 20,000 |
| Variable manufacturing overhead | 15,000 |
| Fixed manufacturing overhead | 50,000 |
| Total manufacturing cost | $ 125,000 |
| Number of liners | ÷ 250,000 |
| Cost per liner | $ 0.50 |

Mūz-Art offers to sell ExoMedia the liners for $0.37 each. Should ExoMedia make the liners or buy them from Mūz-Art? ExoMedia's $0.50 cost per unit to make the liner is $0.13 higher than the cost of buying it from Mūz-Art. It first appears that ExoMedia should outsource the liners. But the correct answer is not so simple. Why? Because manufacturing unit costs contain both fixed and variable components. In deciding whether to outsource, managers must consider fixed and variable costs separately. Exhibit 8-20 shows some of the questions management must consider when deciding whether to outsource.

**EXHIBIT 8-20** Outsourcing Considerations

- How do our variable costs compare to the outsourcing cost?
- Are any fixed costs avoidable if we outsource?
- What could we do with the freed capacity?

Let's see how these considerations apply to ExoMedia. By purchasing the liners, ExoMedia can avoid all variable manufacturing costs—$40,000 of direct materials, $20,000 of direct labour, and $15,000 of variable manufacturing overhead. In total, the company will save $75,000 in variable manufacturing costs, or $0.30 per liner ($75,000 ÷ 250,000 liners). However, ExoMedia will have to pay the variable outsourcing cost of $0.37 per unit, or $92,500 for the 250,000 liners. Based only on variable costs, the lower cost alternative is to manufacture the liners in-house. However, managers must still consider fixed costs.

Assume that ExoMedia cannot avoid any of the fixed costs by outsourcing. In this case, the company's fixed costs are irrelevant to the decision because ExoMedia would continue to incur $50,000 of fixed costs regardless of whether the company outsources the liners. The fixed costs are irrelevant because they do not differ between alternatives. ExoMedia should continue to make its own liners because the variable cost of outsourcing the liners ($92,500) exceeds the variable cost of making the liners ($75,000).

**Why is this important?**
Almost any **business activity** can be **outsourced** (for example, manufacturing, marketing, payroll). **Companies** often choose to retain only their **core competencies**—things they are really good at doing—and **outsource** just about everything else to companies that can do it better for them.

However, what if ExoMedia can avoid some fixed costs by outsourcing the liners? Let's assume that management can reduce fixed overhead cost by $10,000 by outsourcing the liners. ExoMedia will still incur $40,000 of fixed overhead ($50,000 – $10,000) even if they outsource the liners. In this case, fixed costs become relevant to the decision because they differ between alternatives. Exhibit 8-21 shows the differences in costs between the make and buy alternatives under this scenario.

**EXHIBIT 8-21** Incremental Analysis for Outsourcing Decision

| Liner Costs | Make Liners | Buy Liners | Difference |
|---|---|---|---|
| Variable costs: | | | |
| Direct materials | $ 40,000 | — | $40,000 |
| Direct labour | 20,000 | — | 20,000 |
| Variable overhead | 15,000 | — | 15,000 |
| Purchase cost from Mūz-Art | | | |
| (250,000 × $0.37) | — | $ 92,500 | (92,500) |
| Fixed overhead | 50,000 | 40,000 | 10,000 |
| Total cost of liners | $125,000 | $132,500 | $ (7,500) |

Exhibit 8-21 shows that it would still cost ExoMedia less to make the liners than to buy them from Mūz-Art, even with the $10,000 reduction in fixed costs. The net savings from making 250,000 liners is $7,500. Exhibit 8-21 also shows that outsourcing decisions follow our two key guidelines for special business decisions: (1) Focus on relevant data (differences in costs in this case), and (2) use a contribution margin approach that separates variable costs from fixed costs.

Note how the unit cost—which does not separate costs according to behaviour—can be deceiving. If ExoMedia's managers made their decision by comparing the total manufacturing cost per liner ($0.50) to the outsourcing unit cost per liner ($0.37), they would have incorrectly decided to outsource. Recall that the manufacturing unit cost ($0.50) contains both fixed and variable components whereas the outsourcing cost ($0.37) is strictly variable. To make the correct decision, ExoMedia has to separate the two cost components and analyze them separately.

Our decision rule for outsourcing is as follows:

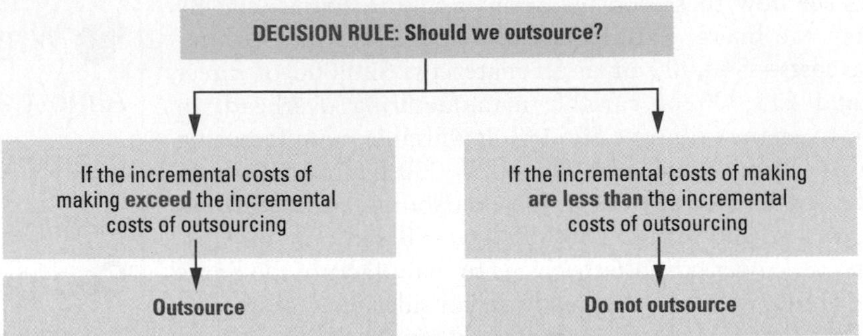


## STOP & THINK

Assuming that ExoMedia could save $10,000 in fixed costs by outsourcing, what is the most the company would be willing to pay per liner to outsource production of 250,000 liners?

**Answer:** To answer that question, we must find the outsourcing price at which ExoMedia would be *indifferent* making the liners or outsourcing the liners. ExoMedia would be indifferent if the total costs were the same either way:

$$\text{Costs if making liners} = \text{Costs if outsourcing liners}$$
$$\text{Variable manufacturing costs} + \text{Fixed costs} = \text{Variable outsourcing costs} + \text{Fixed costs}$$
$$(250{,}000 \text{ units} \times \$0.30 \text{ per unit}) + \$50{,}000 = (250{,}000 \times \text{outsourcing cost per unit}) + \$40{,}000$$
$$\$75{,}000 + \$50{,}000 - \$40{,}000 = (250{,}000 \times \text{outsourcing cost per unit})$$
$$\$85{,}000 = (250{,}000 \times \text{outsourcing cost per unit})$$
$$\$85{,}000 \div 250{,}000 = \text{outsourcing cost per unit}$$
$$\$0.34 = \text{outsourcing cost per unit}$$

ExoMedia would be indifferent about making or outsourcing the liners if the outsourcing cost price is $0.34 per unit. At that price, ExoMedia incurs the same cost to manufacture or outsource the liners. ExoMedia saves money only if the outsourcing price is less than $0.34 per unit. Therefore, the most ExoMedia would pay to outsource is $0.33 per liner.

---

We haven't considered what ExoMedia could do with the freed capacity it would have if it decided to outsource the liners. The analysis in Exhibit 8-21 assumes no other use for the production facilities if ExoMedia buys the liners from Mūz-Art. But suppose ExoMedia has an opportunity to use its freed capacity to make more CDs for an additional profit of $18,000. Now, ExoMedia must consider its opportunity cost—the benefit forgone by not choosing an alternative course of action. In this case, ExoMedia's opportunity cost of making the liners is the $18,000 profit it forgoes if it does not free its production facilities to make the additional CDs.

Let's see how ExoMedia's managers decide among three alternatives:

1. Use the facilities to make the liners.
2. Buy the liners and leave facilities idle (continue to assume $10,000 of avoidable fixed costs from outsourcing liners).
3. Buy the liners and use facilities to make more CDs (continue to assume $10,000 of avoidable fixed costs from outsourcing liners).

The alternative with the lowest *net* cost is the best use of ExoMedia's facilities. Exhibit 8-22 compares the three alternatives.

**EXHIBIT 8-22** Best Use of Facilities Given Opportunity Costs

| | | Buy Liners | |
|---|---|---|---|
| | Make Liners | Facilities Idle | Make Additional CDs |
| Expected cost of 250,000 liners (from Exhibit 8-20) | $125,000 | $132,500 | $132,500 |
| Expected *profit* from additional CDs | — | — | (18,000) |
| Expected net cost of obtaining 250,000 liners | $125,000 | $132,500 | $114,500 |

ExoMedia should buy the liners from Mūz-Art and use the vacated facilities to make more CDs. If ExoMedia makes the liners or buys the liners from Mūz-Art but leaves its production facilities idle, it forgoes the opportunity to earn $18,000.

## STOP & THINK

How does the $18,000 opportunity cost change the *maximum* amount ExoMedia is willing to pay to outsource each liner?

**Answer:** ExoMedia is now willing to pay *more* to outsource its liners. In essence, the company is willing to pay for the opportunity to make more CDs.

ExoMedia's managers should consider qualitative factors as well as revenue and cost differences in making their final decision. For example, ExoMedia managers may believe they can better control quality or delivery schedules by making the liners themselves. This argues for making the liners, even if the cost is slightly higher.

## TRY IT!

Rossignol makes downhill ski equipment. Assume that Atomic has offered to produce ski poles for Rossignol for $18 per pair. Rossignol needs 100,000 pairs of poles per period. Rossignol can avoid only $125,000 of fixed costs if it outsources; the remaining fixed costs are unavoidable. Rossignol currently has the following costs at a production level of 100,000 pairs of poles:

| Manufacturing Costs | Total Cost | Cost per pair(100,000 pairs) |
|---|---|---|
| Direct Materials | $ 750,000 | $ 7.50 |
| Direct Labour | 80,000 | 0.80 |
| Variable MOH | 520,000 | 5.20 |
| Fixed MOH | 650,000 | 6.50 |
| Total | $2,000,000 | $20.00 |

1. Should Rossignol outsource ski pole production if the next best use of the freed capacity is to leave it idle? What affect will outsourcing have on Rossignol operating income?
2. If the freed capacity could be used to produce ski boots that would provide $500,000 of operating income, should Rossignol outsource ski pole production?

Please see page 513 for solutions.

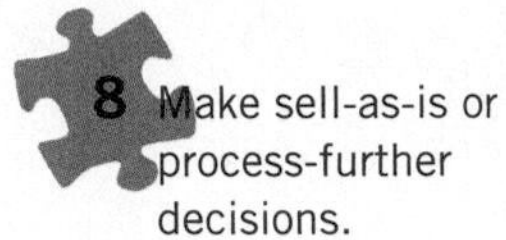
8 Make sell-as-is or process-further decisions.

PROFESSIONAL COMPETENCY

## Sell-As-Is or Process-Further Decisions

At what point in processing should a company sell its product? Many companies, especially in the food processing and natural resource industries, face this business decision. Companies in these industries process a raw material (milk, corn, livestock, crude oil, lumber, and so forth) to a point before it is saleable. For example, Maple Leaf Foods processes raw meat products before they are saleable. Maple Leaf Foods must then decide whether it should sell the raw meat as-is or process it further into other products (lunch meats, ready-to-serve-meals, and so forth). Managers consider the questions shown in Exhibit 8-23 when deciding whether to sell as-is or process further.

**EXHIBIT 8-23** Sell-As-Is or Process-Further Considerations

- How much revenue will we receive if we sell the product as-is?
- How much revenue will we receive if we sell the product *after* processing it further?
- How much will it cost to process the product further?

**Why is this important?**

Some companies are able to sell their products at **different points** of completion. For example, some furniture **manufacturers** sell flat-packed bookshelves, TV stands, and home office furniture that the consumer must assemble. A **cost-benefit analysis** helps managers choose the most **profitable point** at which to sell the company's products.

Let's consider Bertolli, a manufacturer of Italian food products. Suppose Bertolli spends $100,000 to process raw olives into 50,000 litres of plain virgin olive oil. Should Bertolli sell the olive oil as-is or should it spend more to process the olive oil into gourmet dipping oils, such as a basil and garlic infused dipping oil? In making the decision, Bertolli's managers consider the following relevant information:[5]

- Bertolli could sell the plain olive oil for $5 per litre, for a total of $250,000 (50,000 × $5).
- Bertolli could sell the gourmet dipping oil for $7 per litre, for a total of $350,000 (50,000 × $7).
- Bertolli would have to spend $0.75 per litre, or $37,500 (50,000 litres × $0.75), to further process the plain olive oil into the gourmet dipping oil. This cost would include the extra direct materials required (such as basil, garlic, and the incremental cost of premium glass containers) as well as the extra conversion costs incurred (the cost of any *additional* machinery and labour that the company would need to purchase in order to complete the extra processing).

By examining the incremental analysis shown in Exhibit 8-24, Bertolli's managers can see that they can increase operating income by $62,500 by further processing the plain olive oil into the gourmet dipping oil. The extra $100,000 of revenue greatly exceeds the incremental $37,500 of cost incurred to further process the olive oil.

**EXHIBIT 8-24** Incremental Analysis for Sell-As-Is or Process-Further Decision

| | Sell As-Is | Process Further | Difference |
|---|---|---|---|
| Expected revenue from selling 50,000 L of plain olive oil at $5.00/L | $250,000 | | |
| Expected revenue from selling 50,000 L of gourmet dipping oil at $7.00/L | | $350,000 | $100,000 |
| Additional costs of $0.75/L to convert 50,000 L of plain olive oil into gourmet dipping oil | | (37,500) | (37,500) |
| Total net benefit | $250,000 | $312,500 | $ 62,500 |

[5]All references to Bertolli in this hypothetical example were created by the author solely for academic purposes and are not intended, in any way, to represent the actual business practices of or costs incurred by Bertolli.

Notice that Bertolli's managers do *not* consider the $100,000 originally spent on processing the olives into olive oil. Why? It is a sunk cost. Recall from our previous discussion that a sunk cost is a past cost that cannot be changed regardless of which future action the company takes. Bertolli has incurred $100,000 regardless of whether it sells the olive oil as-is or processes it further into gourmet dipping oils. Therefore, the cost is *not* relevant to the decision.

Thus, the decision rule is as follows:

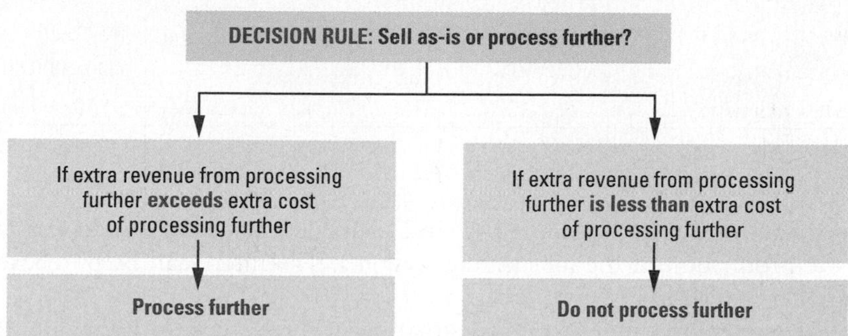


## Transfer-Pricing Decisions

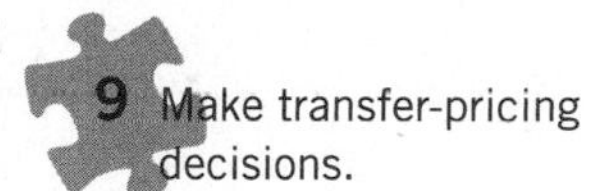

An extension of the make-or-buy decision is the decision on transfer pricing. A **transfer price** refers to the selling price of a product or service from one division of an organization to another division of the same organization. For example, Maple Leaf Foods processes raw chicken breasts for sale to grocery stores, but the division of Maple Leaf Foods that produces ready to eat meals also needs raw chicken breasts. At what price should these raw chicken breasts be transferred from the Raw Meat Processing Department to the Meal Production Department? Should they be transferred at cost? Should the Raw Meat Processing Department make a profit on the transfer? If so, how much profit?

Let's assume that Electro Breeze's air filter is sold to hardware stores and also used in the manufacture of an air cleaning system that is manufactured in the Air Cleaner System Department.

Selling Division's Perspective: The manager of the Air Filter Department would want to maximize the selling price of the air filters, even those transferred to the Air Cleaning System Department. This manager will be evaluated on a number of measures, including department profit. This motivates the manager of the Air Filter Department to request a transfer price equal to the selling price on the retail market.

Purchasing Division's Perspective: The manager of the Air Cleaner System Department wants to purchase the air filters for the system's manufacture at as low a price as possible. A low price means that the department will be able to maximize its profit for the sale of the air cleaning systems on the market.

You will note that these perspectives are contrary to each other. It is not possible for both managers to achieve their optimal goal at the same time. In order to determine the actual transfer price, the two managers will need to consider the points identified in Exhibit 8-25.

**EXHIBIT 8-25** Transfer-Pricing Considerations

- Does the selling department have excess capacity to supply what is needed by the purchasing department?
- Will the transfer price be high enough to cover the incremental costs of the transfer order?
- Will the transfer price be low enough for the purchasing department to reach target profit goals?

Now let's work through an example. We'll refer to the original information regarding Electro Breeze's air filters:

| | |
|---|---|
| Market selling price of air filters | $ 3.20 |
| Variable manufacturing costs per air filter | $ 1.20 |
| Variable marketing and administrative costs per air filter | $ 0.30 |
| Fixed manufacturing costs | $200,000 |
| Fixed marketing and administrative costs | $125,000 |
| Capacity | 300,000 air filters |
| Current sales volume | 250,000 units |

The manager of the Air Cleaning System Department needs to purchase 50,000 air filters for the production of the air cleaning systems. The filters can be purchased from another supplier for $1.40 per unit.

We will complete the analysis of this situation in three steps: 1) Calculate the minimum selling price for the selling division; 2) calculate the maximum purchasing price for the purchasing division; 3) determine the range of possible transfer prices in which a transfer could take place.

**STEP 1: Minimum selling price**

In order for a transfer to take place, the selling division must be able to cover its costs. If the selling division has sufficient capacity to do the order without interfering with the other orders, the transfer price would simply need to cover the variable manufacturing costs (assuming that no variable selling and administrative expenses are incurred).

Minimum transfer price = variable manufacturing costs

Therefore, in this situation, the minimum transfer price would be $1.20.

**STEP 2: Maximum purchasing price**

The purchasing division would not make a transfer deal at a price greater than what they could purchase elsewhere. If there is no other supplier, then the market price becomes the maximum price, but if the purchasing division can purchase the product elsewhere, this outside price becomes the maximum price.

Maximum transfer price = market price or external purchase price

Therefore, in this situation, the maximum transfer price is $1.40, the amount they would pay to the other supplier.

**STEP 3: Determine the range of possible transfer prices**

Since the minimum transfer price is $1.20 and the maximum transfer price is $1.40, the ranges of the two divisions overlap. This can be expressed as

$$\$1.20 \leqq \text{transfer price} \leqq 1.40$$

A transfer should take place for the 50,000 units. At what price, exactly? This would need to be negotiated by the two division managers, but it should be between $1.20 and $1.40 per unit.

## Insufficient Capacity

If the selling division does not have sufficient capacity to prepare the order, then an opportunity cost comes into play. For each unit that the selling division manufactures for the purchasing department, the selling division foregoes the selling price on the market.

In the example for Electro Breeze, the minimum transfer price becomes $3.20, the market price of the filters. No overlap occurs since the minimum selling price is greater than the maximum purchase price of $1.40. No transfer would take place.

Thus, the decision rule is as follows:

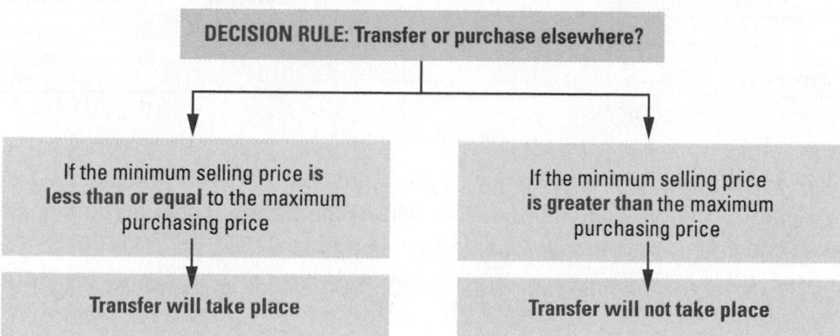


# DECISION GUIDELINES

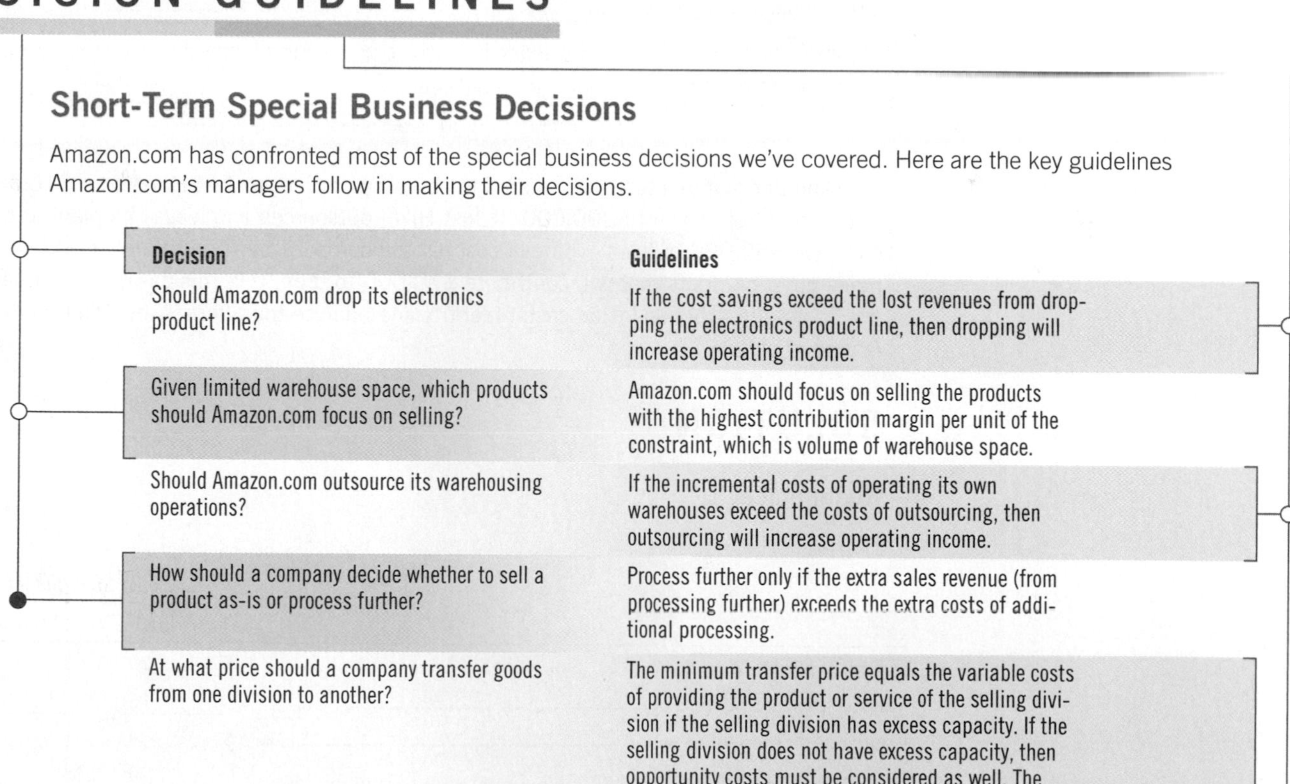

## Short-Term Special Business Decisions

Amazon.com has confronted most of the special business decisions we've covered. Here are the key guidelines Amazon.com's managers follow in making their decisions.

| Decision | Guidelines |
|---|---|
| Should Amazon.com drop its electronics product line? | If the cost savings exceed the lost revenues from dropping the electronics product line, then dropping will increase operating income. |
| Given limited warehouse space, which products should Amazon.com focus on selling? | Amazon.com should focus on selling the products with the highest contribution margin per unit of the constraint, which is volume of warehouse space. |
| Should Amazon.com outsource its warehousing operations? | If the incremental costs of operating its own warehouses exceed the costs of outsourcing, then outsourcing will increase operating income. |
| How should a company decide whether to sell a product as-is or process further? | Process further only if the extra sales revenue (from processing further) exceeds the extra costs of additional processing. |
| At what price should a company transfer goods from one division to another? | The minimum transfer price equals the variable costs of providing the product or service of the selling division if the selling division has excess capacity. If the selling division does not have excess capacity, then opportunity costs must be considered as well. The maximum transfer price equals the market price of the product or the external price of the product or service should the purchasing division purchase the product or service elsewhere. If the minimum price for the selling division is less than the maximum price that the purchasing division will pay, a transfer should take place at a negotiated price between the two limits. |

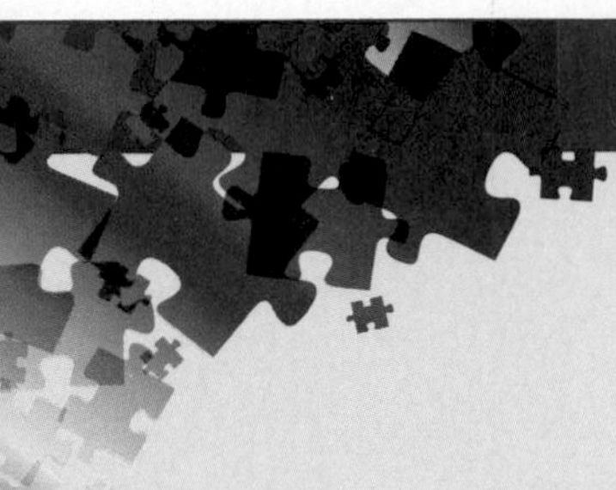

# SUMMARY PROBLEM 2

## Requirements

1. Aziz produces Standard and Deluxe sunglasses:

| | Per Pair | |
|---|---|---|
| | Standard | Deluxe |
| Sales price | $20 | $30 |
| Variable expenses | 16 | 21 |

The company has 15,000 machine hours available. In one machine hour, Aziz can produce 70 pairs of the Standard model or 30 pairs of the Deluxe model. Assuming machine hours is a constraint, which model should Aziz emphasize?

2. Just Hike! incurs the following costs for 20,000 pairs of its high-tech hiking socks:

| | |
|---|---|
| Direct materials | $ 20,000 |
| Direct labour | 80,000 |
| Variable manufacturing overhead | 40,000 |
| Fixed manufacturing overhead | 80,000 |
| Total manufacturing cost | $220,000 |
| Cost per pair ($220,000 ÷ 20,000) | $ 11 |

Another manufacturer has offered to sell socks similar to Just Hike!'s for $10 a pair, a total purchase cost of $200,000. If Just Hike! outsources *and* leaves its plant idle, it can save $50,000 of fixed overhead cost. Or the company can use the released facilities to make other products that will contribute $70,000 to profits. In this case, the company will not be able to avoid any fixed costs. Identify and analyze the alternatives. What is the best course of action?

## ■ SOLUTION

### Requirement 1

| | Style of Sunglasses | |
|---|---|---|
| | Standard | Deluxe |
| Sale price per pair | $ 20 | $ 30 |
| Variable expense per pair | (16) | (21) |
| Contribution margin per pair | $ 4 | $ 9 |
| Units produced each machine hour | × 70 | × 30 |
| Contribution margin per machine hour | $ 280 | $ 270 |
| Capacity—number of machine hours | × 15,000 | × 15,000 |
| Total contribution margin at full capacity | $4,200,000 | $4,050,000 |

*Decision:* Emphasize the Standard model because it has the higher contribution margin per unit of the constraint—machine hours—resulting in a higher contribution margin for the company.

**Requirement 2**

| | Make Socks | *Buy Socks* | |
|---|---|---|---|
| | | Facilities Idle | Make Other Products |
| Relevant costs: | | | |
| Direct materials | $ 20,000 | — | — |
| Direct labour | 80,000 | — | — |
| Variable overhead | 40,000 | — | — |
| Fixed overhead | 80,000 | $ 30,000 | $ 80,000 |
| Purchase cost from outsider (20,000 × $10) | — | 200,000 | 200,000 |
| Total cost of obtaining socks | 220,000 | 230,000 | 280,000 |
| Profit from other products | — | — | (70,000) |
| Net cost of obtaining 20,000 pairs of socks | $220,000 | $230,000 | $210,000 |

*Decision:* Just Hike! should buy the socks from the outside supplier and use the released facilities to make other products.

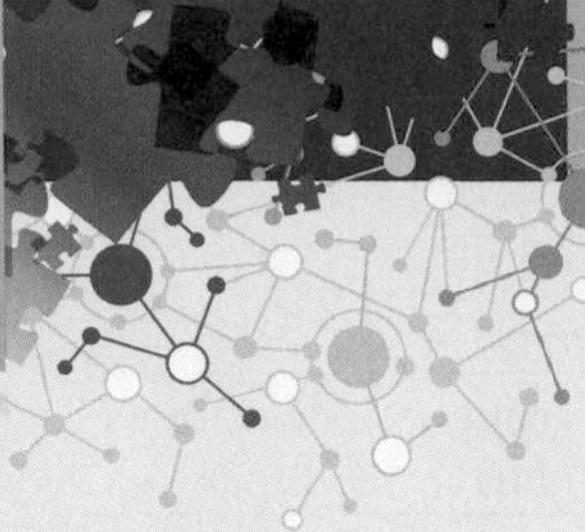

# END OF CHAPTER

## LEARNING OBJECTIVES

1 Describe and identify information relevant to short-term business decisions.

2 Make pricing decisions.

3 Make target costing decisions.

4 Make special-order decisions.

5 Make decisions about dropping a product or segment.

6 Make product mix decisions.

7 Make outsourcing (make-or-buy) decisions.

8 Make sell-as-is or process-further decisions.

9 Make transfer-pricing decisions.

## ACCOUNTING VOCABULARY

**Constraint (p. 473)** A factor that restricts production or sale of a product.

**Cost-Plus Pricing (p. 456)** An approach to pricing used by price-setters. Cost-plus pricing begins with the product's total costs and adds the company's desired profit to determine a cost-plus price.

**Opportunity Cost (p. 465)** The benefit forgone by not choosing an alternative course of action.

**Outsourcing (p. 455)** A make-or-buy decision; managers decide whether to buy a product or service or produce it in-house.

**Relevant Information (p. 453)** Expected *future* data that *differ* among alternatives.

**Sunk Cost (p. 454)** A past cost that cannot be changed regardless of which future action is taken.

**Target Costing (p. 458)** An approach to pricing used by price-takers. Target costing begins with the revenue at market price and subtracts the company's desired profit to arrive at the target total cost.

**Transfer Price (p. 481)** The price at which one division sells a product or service to another division of the same company.



## QUICK CHECK

1. (Learning Objective 1) When making short-term special decisions, you should
   a. focus on total costs.
   b. separate variable from fixed costs.
   c. use a traditional absorption costing approach.
   d. focus only on quantitative factors.
2. (Learning Objective 1) When making decisions, managers should
   a. consider sunk costs.
   b. consider costs that do not differ between alternatives.
   c. consider only variable costs.
   d. consider revenues that differ between alternatives.
3. (Learning Objective 1) Which of the following costs are irrelevant to business decisions?
   a. Sunk costs
   b. Costs that differ between alternatives
   c. Variable costs
   d. Avoidable costs
4. (Learning Objective 4) Which of the following is relevant to Amazon.com's decision to accept a special order at a lower sale price from a large customer in China?
   a. The cost of Amazon.com's warehouses in the United States
   b. Amazon.com's investment in its website
   c. The cost of shipping the order to the customer
   d. Founder Jeff Bezos's salary
5. (Learning Objective 2) When companies are price-setters, their products and services
   a. are priced by managers using a target-pricing emphasis.
   b. tend to be unique.
   c. tend to have a great many competitors.
   d. tend to be commodities.

6. (Learning Objective 2) When pricing a product or service, managers must consider which of the following?
   a. Only variable costs
   b. Only period costs
   c. Only manufacturing costs
   d. All costs
7. (Learning Objective 5) In deciding whether to drop its electronics product line, Amazon.com would consider
   a. the costs it could save by dropping the product line.
   b. the revenues it would lose from dropping the product line.
   c. how dropping the electronics product line would affect sales of its other products, such as CDs.
   d. all of the above.
8. (Learning Objective 6) In deciding which product lines to emphasize, Amazon.com should focus on the product line that has the highest
   a. contribution margin per unit of the constraining factor.
   b. contribution margin per unit of product.
   c. contribution margin ratio.
   d. profit per unit of product.
9. (Learning Objective 7) When making outsourcing decisions
   a. the manufacturing full unit cost of making the product in-house is relevant.
   b. the variable cost of producing the product in-house is relevant.
   c. avoidable fixed costs are irrelevant.
   d. expected use of the freed capacity is irrelevant.
10. (Learning Objective 8) When deciding whether to sell as-is or process a product further, managers should ignore which of the following?
    a. The revenue if the product is processed further
    b. The cost of processing further
    c. The costs of processing the product thus far
    d. The revenue if the product is sold as-is
11. (Learning Objective 9) A transfer should take place between two divisions of the same company when
    a. transfer price ≥ selling price ≥ purchasing price.
    b. selling price ≤ transfer price ≤ purchasing price.
    c. purchasing price ≤ transfer price ≤ selling price.
    d. purchasing price ≥ selling price ≥ transfer price.

**Quick Check Answers**

*1. b 2. d 3. a 4. c 5. b 6. d 7. d 8. a 9. b 10. c 11. b*

# SHORT EXERCISES

### S8-1 Determine relevance of information *(Learning Objective 1)*

You are trying to decide whether to trade in your ink-jet printer for a more recent model. Your usage pattern will remain unchanged, but the old and new printers use different ink cartridges. Are the following items relevant or irrelevant to your decision?

**a.** The price of the new printer
**b.** The price you paid for the old printer
**c.** The trade-in value of the old printer
**d.** Paper costs
**e.** The difference between the cost of ink cartridges

### S8-2 Make special-order decision given revised data *(Learning Objective 4)*

Consider the Electro Breeze special sales order example on pages 463–464. Suppose Electro Breeze's variable manufacturing cost is $1.35 per air filter (instead of $1.20). In addition, Electro Breeze would have to buy a special stamping machine that costs $7,000 to mark the customer's logo on the special-order air filters. The machine would be scrapped when the special order is complete.

Would you recommend that Electro Breeze accept the special order under these conditions? Show your analysis.

### S8-3 Determine pricing approach and target price *(Learning Objectives 2 & 3)*

SnowDreams operates a Rocky Mountain ski resort. The company is planning its lift-ticket pricing for the coming ski season. Investors would like to earn a 15% return on the company's $100 million of assets. The company incurs primarily fixed costs to groom the runs and operate the lifts. SnowDreams projects fixed costs to be $33,750,000 for the ski season. The resort serves about 750,000 skiers and snowboarders each season. Variable costs are about $10 per guest. Currently, the resort has such a favourable reputation among skiers and snowboarders that it has some control over the lift-ticket prices.

**1.** Would SnowDreams emphasize target costing or cost-plus pricing? Why?
**2.** If other resorts in the area charge $70 per day, what price should SnowDreams charge?

**S8-4 Use target costing to analyze data** *(Learning Objectives 2 & 3)*

Consider SnowDreams from S8-3. Assume that SnowDreams' reputation has diminished and other resorts in the vicinity are charging only $65 per lift ticket. SnowDreams has become a price-taker and won't be able to charge more than its competitors. At the market price, SnowDreams managers believe they will still serve 750,000 skiers and snowboarders each season.

1. If SnowDreams can't reduce its costs, what profit will it earn? State your answer in dollars and as a percent of assets. Will investors be happy with the profit level? Show your analysis.
2. Assume that SnowDreams has found ways to cut its fixed costs to $30 million. What is its new target variable cost per skier/snowboarder? Compare this to the current variable cost per skier/snowboarder. Comment on your results.

**S8-5 Decide whether to drop a department** *(Learning Objective 5)*

Knight Fashion store operates three departments: Men's, Women's, and Accessories. Knight Fashion allocates all fixed expenses (unavoidable building depreciation and utilities) based on each department's floor space. Departmental operating income data for the third quarter of the current year are as follows:

| | Department | | | |
|---|---|---|---|---|
| | **Men's** | **Women's** | **Accessories** | **Total** |
| Sales revenue | $105,000 | $54,000 | $100,000 | $259,000 |
| Variable expenses | 60,000 | 30,000 | 80,000 | 170,000 |
| Fixed expenses | 25,000 | $30,000 | 25,000 | 70,000 |
| Total expenses | 85,000 | 50,000 | 105,000 | 240,000 |
| Operating income (loss) | $ 20,000 | ($6,000) | $ (5,000) | $ 19,000 |

The store will remain in the same building regardless of whether any of the departments are dropped. Should Knight Fashion drop any of the departments? Give your reason.

**S8-6 Drop a department: revised information** *(Learning Objective 5)*

Consider Knight Fashion from S8-5. Assume that the fixed expenses assigned to each department include only direct fixed costs of the department (rather than unavoidable fixed costs as given in S8-5):

- Salary of the department's manager
- Cost of advertising directly related to that department

If Knight Fashion drops a department, it will not incur these fixed expenses. Under these circumstances, should Knight Fashion drop any of the departments? Give your reason.

**S8-7 Replace a department** *(Learning Objective 5)*

Consider Knight Fashion from S8-5. Assume once again that all fixed costs are unavoidable. If Knight Fashion drops one of the current departments, it plans to replace the dropped department with a Shoe Department. The company expects the Shoe Department to produce $80,000 in sales and have $50,000 of variable costs. Because the shoe business would be new to Knight Fashion, the company would have to incur an additional $7,000 of fixed costs (advertising, new shoe display racks, and so forth) per quarter related to the department. What should Knight Fashion do now?

**S8-8 Making a product mix decision: unlimited demand** *(Learning Objective 6)*

StoreAll produces plastic storage bins for household storage needs. The company makes two sizes of bins: Large (200 L) and Regular (140 L). Demand for the product is so high that StoreAll can sell as many of each size as it can produce. The company uses the same machinery to produce both sizes. The machinery can be run for only 3,000 hours per period. StoreAll can produce 10 Large bins or 15 Regular bins every hour.

Fixed expenses amount to $100,000 per period. Sales prices and variable costs are as follows:

| | **Regular** | **Large** |
|---|---|---|
| Sales price per unit | $8.00 | $10.00 |
| Variable cost per unit | $3.00 | $ 4.00 |

1. Which product should StoreAll emphasize? Why?
2. To maximize profits, how many of each size bin should StoreAll produce?
3. Given this product mix, what will the company's operating income be?

**S8-9 Making a product mix decision: limited demand** *(Learning Objective 6)*

Consider StoreAll in S8-8. Assume that demand for Regular bins is limited to 30,000 units and demand for Large bins is limited to 25,000 units.

1. How many of each size bin should StoreAll make now?
2. Given this product mix, what will be the company's operating income?
3. Explain why the operating income is less than it was when StoreAll was producing its optimal product mix.

**S8-10 Making an outsourcing production decision** *(Learning Objectives 1 & 7)*

Suppose Sally's Restaurant is considering whether to bake bread for its restaurant in-house or buy the bread from a local bakery. The chef estimates that variable costs of making each loaf include $0.50 of ingredients, $0.45 of variable overhead (electricity to run the oven), and $0.75 of direct labour for kneading and forming the loaves. Allocating fixed overhead (depreciation on the kitchen equipment and building) based on direct labour assigns $1.00 of fixed overhead per loaf. None of the fixed costs are avoidable. The local bakery would charge Sally's $1.75 per loaf.

1. What is the unit cost of making the bread in-house (use absorption costing)?
2. Should Sally's bake the bread in-house or buy from the local bakery? Why?
3. In addition to the financial analysis, what else should Sally's consider when making this decision?

**S8-11 Relevant information for outsourcing delivery function** *(Learning Objectives 1 & 7)*

Frito-Lay manufactures and markets snack foods. Betsy Gonzalez manages the company's fleet of 200 delivery trucks. Gonzalez has been charged with "reengineering" the fleet-management function. She has an important decision to make.

- Should she continue to manage the fleet in-house with the five employees reporting to her? To do so, she will have to acquire new fleet-management software to streamline Frito-Lay's fleet-management process.
- Should she outsource the fleet-management function to Fleet Management Services, a company that specializes in managing fleets of trucks for other companies? Fleet Management Services would take over the maintenance, repair, and scheduling of Frito-Lay's fleet (but Frito-Lay would retain ownership). This alternative would require Gonzalez to lay off her five employees. However, her own job would be secure, as she would be Frito-Lay's liaison with Fleet Management Services.

Assume that Gonzalez's records show the following data concerning Frito-Lay's fleet:

| | |
|---|---|
| Book value of Frito-Lay's trucks, with an estimated five-year life | $3,500,000 |
| Annual leasing fee for new fleet-management software | 8,000 |
| Annual maintenance of trucks | 145,500 |
| Fleet Supervisor Gonzalez's annual salary | 60,000 |
| Total annual salaries of Frito-Lay's five other fleet-management employees | 150,000 |

Suppose that Fleet Management Services offers to manage Frito-Lay's fleet for an annual fee of $290,000.

Which alternative will maximize Frito-Lay's short-term operating income?

**S8-12 Assess outsourcing qualitative considerations** *(Learning Objectives 1 & 7)*

Refer to Frito-Lay in S8-11. What qualitative factors should Gonzalez consider before making a final decision?

**S8-13 Make a scrap or process-further decision** *(Learning Objective 8)*

Auto Components has an inventory of 500 obsolete remote-entry keys that are carried in inventory at a manufacturing cost of $100,000. Production Supervisor Natasha Buss must decide to do one of the following:

- Process the inventory further at a cost of $20,000, with the expectation of selling it for $28,000
- Scrap the inventory for a sale price of $6,000

What should Buss do? Present figures to support your decision.

**S8-14 Determine the most profitable final product** *(Learning Objective 8)*

Chocolite processes cocoa beans into cocoa powder at a processing cost of $10,000 per batch. Chocolite can sell the cocoa powder as-is, or it can process the cocoa powder further into chocolate syrup or boxed assorted chocolates. Once processed, each batch of cocoa beans would result in the following sales revenue:

| | |
|---|---|
| Cocoa powder | $ 15,000 |
| Chocolate syrup | $100,000 |
| Boxed assorted chocolates | $200,000 |

The cost of transforming the cocoa powder into chocolate syrup is $70,000. Likewise, the company would incur $180,000 to transform the cocoa powder into boxed chocolates. The company president has decided to make boxed chocolates owing to its high sales value and to the fact that the $10,000 cost of processing cocoa beans "eats up" most of the cocoa powder profits. Has the president made the right or wrong decision? Explain your answer. Be sure to include the correct financial analysis in your response.

**S8-15 Determine transfer prices** *(Learning Objective 9)*

TK Electronics is a manufacturer with two departments: computer chips and cell phones. The computer chip that is produced in the Chips Department can be sold to customers at $5.00 per chip. The costs associated with the computer chips are as follows:

| | |
|---|---|
| Variable manufacturing costs | $ 2.40 |
| Variable selling and administrative costs | $ 0.80 |
| Capacity | 500,000 units |
| Current production | 500,000 units |

The Cell Phone Department has been purchasing the chips that it needs for $2.75 per chip from Chips R Us, but the manager was thinking that if the Chips Department could supply the chips for less than what Chips R Us is asking, then it would arrange a transfer between departments instead of giving the business to an external company.

**Requirements**

1. Should the Chips Department supply the chips to the Cell Phone Department under these circumstances?
2. If the Chips Department had sufficient capacity, would this make a difference?

# EXERCISES Group A

**E8-16A Determine relevant and irrelevant information** *(Learning Objective 1)*

The Plastic Lumber Company is considering whether it should replace an extrusion machine. The new machine will produce 40% more finished lumber than the old machine. The increase in production will cause fixed selling costs to increase, but variable selling costs will not increase. The new machine will require installation by an engineering firm; the old machine had required a similar installation. If the new machine is purchased, the old machine can be sold as scrap. The old machine requires frequent repairs and maintenance to keep it running, while the new machine will require maintenance once a year. The new machine will be paid for by signing a notes payable with the bank that will cover the cost of the new machine. The

Plastic Lumber Company will pay interest on the notes payable. The notes payable that was used to pay for the old machine was fully paid off last year.

In the following chart, indicate whether each of the costs described would be relevant or not to Plastic Lumber Company's decision about whether to purchase the new extrusion machine or to keep using the old extrusion machine.

| Item | Relevant | Not Relevant |
|---|---|---|
| a. Cost of new machine | | |
| b. Cost of old machine | | |
| c. Added profits from increase in production from new machine | | |
| d. Fixed selling costs | | |
| e. Variable selling costs | | |
| f. Scrap value of old machine | | |
| g. Interest expense on new machine | | |
| h. Interest expense on old machine | | |
| i. Book value of old machine | | |
| j. Maintenance cost of new machine | | |
| k. Repairs and maintenance costs of old machine | | |
| l. Installation cost of new machine | | |
| m. Installation costs of old machine | | |
| n. Salary of company's CEO | | |
| o. Accumulated depreciation of old machine | | |

**E8-17A Analyze special-order decisions given two scenarios** *(Learning Objective 4)*

Suppose the Hockey Hall of Fame in Toronto has approached Sports-Cardz with a special order. The Hall of Fame wants to purchase 60,000 hockey card packs for a special promotional campaign and offers $0.40 per pack, a total of $20,000. Sports-Cardz's total production cost is $0.60 per pack, as follows:

| | |
|---|---|
| Variable costs: | |
| Direct materials | $0.14 |
| Direct labour | 0.08 |
| Variable overhead | 0.13 |
| Fixed overhead | 0.25 |
| Total cost | $0.60 |

Sports-Cardz has enough excess capacity to handle the special order.

**Requirements**

1. Prepare an incremental analysis to determine whether Sports-Cardz should accept the special sales order assuming fixed costs would not be affected by the special order.
2. Now assume that the Hall of Fame wants special hologram hockey cards. Sports-Cardz must spend $2,000 to develop this hologram, which will be useless after the special order is completed. Should Sports-Cardz accept the special order under these circumstances? Show your analysis.

Check sum: Req. 1 expected increase in operating income $3,000.

**E8-18A Sustainability and short-term decision making** *(Learning Objective 8)*

Over the past several years, decommissioned U.S. warships have been turned into artificial reefs in the ocean by towing them out to sea and sinking them. The thinking was that sinking the ship would conveniently dispose of it while providing an artificial reef environment for aquatic life. In reality, some of the sunken ships have released toxins into the ocean and have been costly to decontaminate. Now the U.S. government is taking bids to dismantle and recycle ships that have recently been decommissioned (but have not been sunk yet).

Assume that a recently decommissioned aircraft carrier, the USS *Forrestal*, is estimated to contain approximately 40 tonnes of recyclable materials able to be sold for approximately $32.3 million. The low bid for dismantling and transporting the ship materials to appropriate facilities is $33.7 million. Recycling and dismantling the ship would create about 500 jobs for about a year in the Rust Belt. This geographic area has been experiencing record-high unemployment rates in recent years.

Check sum: Cost to sink ship is $200,000 more favourable.

- Is it more financially advantageous to sink the ship (assuming that it costs approximately $1.2 million to tow a ship out to sea and sink it) or to dismantle and recycle it? Show your calculations.
- From a sustainability standpoint, what should be done with the decommissioned aircraft carrier? List some of the qualitative factors that should enter into this analysis.
- As a taxpayer, which action would you prefer (sink or recycle)? Defend your answer.

### E8-19A Assess special-order decision and considerations *(Learning Objective 4)*

Maui Jane Sunglasses sell for about $150 per pair. Suppose the company incurs the following average costs per pair:

| | |
|---|---|
| Direct materials | $40 |
| Direct labour | 12 |
| Variable manufacturing overhead | 8 |
| Variable marketing expenses | 4 |
| Fixed manufacturing overhead | 20* |
| Total costs | $84 |

$$^*\frac{\$2{,}000{,}000 \text{ total fixed manufacturing overhead}}{100{,}000 \text{ pairs of sunglasses}}$$

Check sum: Req. 2 Total additional costs are $60.

Maui Jane has enough idle capacity to accept a one-time-only special order from Vision Lenses for 20,000 pairs of sunglasses at $76 per pair. Maui Jane will not incur any variable marketing expenses for the order.

#### Requirements

1. How would accepting the order affect Maui Jane's operating income? In addition to the special order's effect on profits, what other (longer-term qualitative) factors should Maui Jane's managers consider in deciding whether to accept the order?
2. Maui Jane's marketing manager, Jim Revo, argues against accepting the special order because the offer price of $76 is less than Maui Jane's $84 cost to make the sunglasses. Revo asks you, as one of Maui Jane's staff accountants, to write a memo explaining whether his analysis is correct.

### E8-20A Analyze pricing decisions given two scenarios *(Learning Objectives 2 & 3)*

Bennett Builders builds townhomes in a new subdivision just outside of Calgary. Land and labour are cheap, and competition among developers is fierce. The homes in the subdivision are identical to one another, but buyers can upgrade features by paying the difference. Bennett Builders' costs per developed sublot are as follows:

Check sum: Cost-plus price is $232,200.

| | |
|---|---|
| Land | $ 50,000 |
| Construction | $125,000 |
| Landscaping | $ 5,000 |
| Variable marketing costs | $ 2,000 |

Bennett Builders would like to earn a profit of 15% of the variable cost of each home sale. Similar homes offered by competing builders sell for $200,000 each.

#### Requirements

1. Which approach to pricing should Bennett Builders emphasize? Why?
2. Will Bennett Builders be able to achieve its target profit levels? Show your computations.

3. Bathrooms and kitchens are typically the most important selling features of a home. Bennett Builders could differentiate the homes by upgrading bathrooms and kitchens. The upgrades would cost $20,000 per home but would enable Bennett Builders to increase the selling prices by $35,000 per home. (In general, kitchen and bathroom upgrades typically add at least 150% of their cost to the value of any home.) If Bennett Builders upgrades, what will the new cost-plus price per home be? Should the company differentiate its product in this manner? Show your analysis.

**E8-21A Decide whether to drop a product line** *(Learning Objective 5)*

Top managers of Video Avenue are alarmed by their operating losses. They are considering dropping the DVD product line. Company accountants have prepared the following analysis to help make this decision. Total fixed costs will not change if the company stops selling DVDs.

| | Total | Blu-ray Discs | DVDs |
|---|---|---|---|
| Sales revenue | $420,000 | $300,000 | $120,000 |
| Variable expenses | 230,000 | 150,000 | 80,000 |
| Contribution margin | 190,000 | 150,000 | 40,000 |
| Fixed expenses: | | | |
| Manufacturing | 125,000 | 70,000 | 55,000 |
| Marketing and administrative | 85,000 | 55,000 | 30,000 |
| Total fixed expenses | 205,000 | 125,000 | 85,000 |
| Operating income (loss) | $(20,000) | $ 25,000 | $(45,000) |

### Requirements

Check sum: Req. 1 Expected decrease in operating income is $40,000.

1. Prepare an incremental analysis to show whether Video Avenue should drop the DVD product line. Will dropping DVDs add to operating income? Explain.
2. Assume that Video Avenue can avoid $30,000 of fixed expenses by dropping the DVD product line. (These costs are direct fixed costs of the DVD product line.) Prepare an incremental analysis to show whether Video Avenue should stop selling DVDs.
3. Now, assume that all $70,000 of fixed costs assigned to DVDs are direct fixed costs and can be avoided if the company stops selling DVDs. However, marketing has concluded that Blu-ray disc sales would be adversely affected by discontinuing the DVD line. (Retailers want to buy both from the same supplier.) Blu-ray disc production and sales would decline 10%. What should the company do?

**E8-22A Dropping a product line** *(Learning Objective 5)*

Suppose McCain is considering dropping its sweet potato fries product line. Assume that during the past year, the sweet potato fries product line income statement showed the following:

| | |
|---|---|
| Sales | $7,600,000 |
| Cost of goods sold | 6,400,000 |
| Gross profit | 1,200,000 |
| Operating expenses | 1,400,000 |
| Operating loss | $ (200,000) |

Fixed manufacturing overhead costs account for 40% of the cost of goods, while only 30% of the operating expenses are fixed. Since the sweet potato fries line is only one of McCain's french fries, only $750,000 of direct fixed costs (the majority of which is advertising) will be eliminated if the product line is discontinued. The remainder of the fixed costs will still be incurred by McCain. If the company decides to drop the product line, what will happen to the company's operating income? Should McCain drop the product line?

Check sum: Contribution margin is $2.78 million.

**E8-23A Identify constraint, then determine product mix** *(Learning Objective 6)*

Lifemaster produces two types of exercise treadmills: Regular and Deluxe. The exercise craze is such that Lifemaster could use all of its available machine hours producing either model. The two models are processed through the same Production Department.

Check sum: Contribution margin of Deluxe is $275 per unit.

| | Per Units | |
|---|---|---|
| | Deluxe | Regular |
| Sales price | $1,000 | $ 550 |
| Costs: | | |
| Direct materials | $ 290 | $ 100 |
| Direct labour | 80 | 180 |
| Variable manufacturing overhead | 240 | 80 |
| Fixed manufacturing overhead* | 120 | 40 |
| Variable operating expenses | 115 | 65 |
| Total cost | 845 | 465 |
| Operating income | $ 155 | $ 85 |

**Allocated on the basis of machine hours.*

What product mix will maximize operating income? (*Hint:* Use the allocation of fixed manufacturing overhead to determine the proportion of machine hours used by each product.)

### E8-24A Determine product mix for retailer *(Learning Objective 6)*

Vivace sells both designer and moderately priced fashion accessories. Top management is deciding which product line to emphasize. Accountants have provided the following data:

Check sum: Designer model total contribution margin at capacity is $34,500.

| | Per Item | |
|---|---|---|
| | Designer | Moderately Priced |
| Average sales price | $200 | $84 |
| Average variable expenses | 85 | 24 |
| Average fixed expenses (allocated) | 20 | 10 |
| Average operating income | $ 95 | $50 |

The Vivace store in Ottawa has 950 m² of floor space. If Vivace emphasizes moderately priced goods, it can display 650 items in the store. If Vivace emphasizes designer wear, it can display only 300 designer items to create more of a boutique-like atmosphere. These numbers are also the average monthly sales in units.

Prepare an analysis to show which product to emphasize.

### E8-25A Determine product mix for retailer—two stocking scenarios *(Learning Objective 6)*

Each morning, Max Imery stocks the drink case at Max's Beach Hut in the Muskokas. Max's Beach Hut has 33 linear metres of refrigerated display space for cold drinks. Each linear metre can hold either 18 341-mL cans or 12 551-mL plastic or glass bottles. Max's Beach Hut sells three types of cold drinks:

1. Coca-Cola in 341-mL cans for $1.50 per can
2. A&W Root Beer in 551-mL plastic bottles for $1.75 per bottle
3. Mountain Dew in 551-mL glass bottles for $2.20 per bottle

Max's Beach Hut pays its suppliers the following:

1. $0.25 per 341-mL can of Coca-Cola
2. $0.40 per 551-mL bottle of A&W Root Beer
3. $0.75 per 551-mL bottle of Mountain Dew

Max's Beach Hut's monthly fixed expenses include the following:

| | |
|---|---|
| Hut rental | $ 375 |
| Refrigerator rental | 75 |
| Max's salary | 1,550 |
| Total fixed expenses | $2,000 |

Each day, Max's Beach Hut can sell all the drinks in the display case.

**Requirements**

1. What is Max's Beach Hut's constraining factor? What should Max stock to maximize profits? What is the maximum contribution margin he could generate from refrigerated drinks each day?
2. To provide variety to customers, suppose Max refuses to devote more than 20 linear metres and no fewer than 3 linear metres to any individual product. Under this condition, how many linear metres of each drink should Max stock? How many units of each product will be available for sale each day?
3. Assuming the product mix calculated in Requirement 2, what contribution margin will Max generate each day?

Check sum: Contribution margin is $742.50.

### E8-26A Make-or-buy product component *(Learning Objective 7)*

Fibre Systems manufactures an optical switch that it uses in its final product. Fibre Systems incurred the following manufacturing costs when it produced 70,000 units last year:

| | |
|---|---|
| Direct materials | $ 630,000 |
| Direct labour | 105,000 |
| Variable overhead | 140,000 |
| Fixed overhead | 455,000 |
| Total manufacturing cost for 70,000 units | $1,330,000 |

Fibre Systems does not yet know how many switches it will need this year; however, another company has offered to sell Fibre Systems the switch for $14 per unit. If Fibre Systems buys the switch from the outside supplier, the manufacturing facilities that become idle cannot be used for any other purpose, yet none of the fixed costs are avoidable.

**Requirements**

1. Given the same cost structure, should Fibre Systems make or buy the switch? Show your analysis.
2. Now, assume that Fibre Systems can avoid $80,000 of fixed costs a year by outsourcing production. In addition, because sales are increasing, Fibre Systems needs 75,000 switches a year rather than 70,000. What should Fibre Systems do now?
3. Given the last scenario, what is the most Fibre Systems would be willing to pay to outsource the switches?

Check sum: Net cost to make is $1.50 per unit less advantageous.

### E8-27A Assess make-or-buy with alternative use of facilities *(Learning Objective 7)*

Check sum: The more cost effective decision is to outsource.

Refer to E8-26A. Fibre Systems needs 80,000 optical switches next year (assume same relevant range). By outsourcing them, Fibre Systems can use its idle facilities to manufacture another product that will contribute $220,000 to operating income, but none of the fixed costs will be avoidable. Should Fibre Systems make or buy the switches? Show your analysis.

### E8-28A Determine maximum outsourcing price *(Learning Objective 7)*

Check sum: Cost of making unit is $.305/unit.

As a result of increased sales, ExoMedia needs 400,000 jewel-case liners rather than 250,000. ExoMedia has enough existing capacity to make all of the liners it needs. In addition, due to volume discounts, its variable costs of making each liner will decline to $0.28 per liner. Assume that by outsourcing, ExoMedia can reduce its current fixed costs ($50,000) by $10,000. There is no alternative use for the factory space freed through outsourcing, so it will just remain idle. What is the maximum ExoMedia will pay to outsource production of its CD liners?

### E8-29A Decide to sell as-is or process further *(Learning Objective 8)*

Check sum: Sell as 4-L containers results in $2,950.

HappyCow processes organic milk into plain yogourt. HappyCow sells plain yogourt to hospitals, nursing homes, and restaurants in bulk, 4-L containers. Each batch, processed at a cost of $800, yields 2,000 (500 4-L) containers of plain yogourt, which are sold for $6.00 each and spends $0.10 for each plastic tub.

HappyCow has recently begun to reconsider its strategy to sell individual-sized portions of fruited organic yogourt at local food stores. HappyCow could further process each batch of plain yogourt into 10,526 individual portions (190 mL each) of fruited yogourt. A recent market analysis indicates that demand for the product exists. Each individual portion would sell for $0.50. Packaging would cost $0.08 per portion, and fruit would cost $0.10 per portion. Fixed costs would not change. Should HappyCow continue to sell only the 4-L tubs of plain yogourt (sell as-is) or convert the plain yogourt into individual-sized portions of fruited yogourt (process further)? Why?

Check sum: Minimum transfer price is $2.75.

### E8-30A Compute transfer prices *(Learning Objective 9)*

Refer to the TK Electronics information in S8-15. If the Cell Phone Department needs 150,000 computer chips and current production in the Chips Department is 300,000 chips, should a transfer take place? If so, at what price? (*Note*: For internal transfers, the selling and administrative costs are reduced to $0.25 per unit.)

What other qualitative factors might need to be considered?

# EXERCISES Group B

### E8-31B Determine relevant and irrelevant information *(Learning Objective 1)*

Emerson Trotman, production manager for Fabricut, invested in computer-controlled production machinery last year. He purchased the machinery from Advanced Design at a cost of $2 million. A representative from Advanced Design recently contacted Emerson because the company has designed an even more efficient piece of machinery. The new design would double the production output of the year-old machinery but would cost Fabricut another $3 million. The old machinery was installed by an engineering firm; the same firm will be required to install the new machinery. Fixed selling costs would not increase if Fabricut purchased the new machinery, but variable selling costs would increase.

Fabricut paid off the notes payable it used to pay for the machinery last year. If Fabricut purchases the new machinery, it will sign a new notes payable. Maintenance costs for the new machinery would be the same as for the current machinery. If Fabricut purchases the new machinery, it can trade in the old machinery; Advanced Design will credit Fabricut's account for the trade-in value.

In the following chart, indicate whether each of the costs described would be relevant or not to Fabricut's decision about whether to purchase the new machinery or to keep using the older machinery.

| Item | Relevant | Not Relevant |
|---|---|---|
| a. Cost of new machinery | | |
| b. Cost of old machinery | | |
| c. Book value of old machinery | | |
| d. Maintenance cost of new machinery | | |
| e. Maintenance cost of old machinery | | |
| f. Trade-in value of old machinery | | |
| g. Interest expense on new machinery | | |
| h. Interest expense on old machinery | | |
| i. Added profits from increase in production from new machinery | | |
| j. Fixed selling costs | | |
| k. Variable selling costs | | |
| l. Accumulated depreciation on old machinery | | |
| m. Installation costs of new machinery | | |
| n. Installation costs of old machinery | | |
| o. Salary of company's CEO | | |

**E8-32B Analyze special-order decisions given two scenarios** *(Learning Objective 4)*

Suppose the Hockey Hall of Fame in Toronto has approached Star-Cardz with a special order. The Hall of Fame wishes to purchase 54,000 hockey card packs for a special promotional campaign and offers $0.38 per pack, a total of $20,520. Star-Cardz's total production cost is $0.68 per pack, as follows:

| | |
|---|---|
| Variable costs: | |
| Direct materials | $0.11 |
| Direct labour | 0.07 |
| Variable overhead | 0.10 |
| Fixed overhead | 0.40 |
| Total cost | $0.68 |

Star-Cardz has enough excess capacity to handle the special order.

**Requirements**

1. Prepare an incremental analysis to determine whether Star-Cardz should accept the special sales order. Assume that fixed costs would not be affected by the special order.
2. Now assume that the Hall of Fame wants special hologram hockey cards. Star-Cardz would spend $5,300 to develop this hologram, which will be useless after the special order is completed. Should Star-Cardz accept the special order under these circumstances? Show your analysis.

**E8-33B Sustainability and short-term decision making** *(Learning Objective 8)*

Over the past several years, decommissioned U.S. warships have been turned into artificial reefs in the ocean by towing them out to sea and sinking them. The thinking was that sinking the ship would conveniently dispose of it while providing an artificial reef environment for aquatic life. In reality, some of the sunken ships have released toxins into the ocean and have been costly to decontaminate. Now the U.S. government is taking bids to dismantle and recycle ships that have recently been decommissioned (but have not been sunk yet).

Assume that a recently decommissioned aircraft carrier, the USS *Independence,* is estimated to contain approximately 40 tonnes of recyclable materials able to be sold for approximately $30.8 million. The low bid for dismantling and transporting the ship materials to appropriate facilities is $32.3 million. Recycling and dismantling the ship would create about 500 jobs for about a year in the Rust Belt. This geographic area has been experiencing record-high unemployment rates in recent years.

**Requirements**

1. Is it more financially advantageous to sink the ship (assume that it costs approximately $1.2 million to tow a ship out to sea and sink it) or to dismantle and recycle it? Show your calculations.
2. From a sustainability standpoint, what should be done with the decommissioned aircraft carrier? List some of the qualitative factors that should enter into this analysis.
3. As a taxpayer, which action would you prefer (sink or recycle)? Defend your answer.

**E8-34B Analyze a special-order decision and considerations** *(Learning Objective 4)*

Maui Juda Sunglasses sell for about $154 per pair. Suppose the company incurs the following average costs per pair:

| | |
|---|---|
| Direct materials | $38 |
| Direct labour | 10 |
| Variable manufacturing overhead | 8 |
| Variable marketing expenses | 2 |
| Fixed manufacturing overhead | 16* |
| Total cost | $74 |

**$2,200,000 total fixed manufacturing overhead ÷ 137,500 pairs of sunglasses*

Maui Juda has enough idle capacity to accept a one-time-only special order from East Coast Glasses for 19,000 pairs of sunglasses at $49 per pair. Maui Juda will not incur any variable marketing expenses for the order.

### Requirements

1. How would accepting the order affect Maui Juda's operating income? In addition to the special order's effect on profits, what other (longer-term, qualitative) factors should Maui Juda's managers consider in deciding whether to accept the order?
2. Maui Juda's marketing manager, Jim Revo, argues against accepting the special order because the offer price of $49 is less than Maui Juda's $74 cost to make the sunglasses. Revo asks you, as one of Maui Juda's staff accountants, to explain whether his analysis is correct.

## E8-35B Make pricing decisions given two scenarios *(Learning Objectives 2 & 3)*

Rouse Builders builds starter homes in the fast-growing suburbs of Saint John, New Brunswick. Land and labour are cheap, and competition among developers is fierce. The homes are "cookie-cutter," with any upgrades added by the buyer after the sale. Rouse Builders' costs per developed sublot are as follows:

| | |
|---|---|
| Land | $ 51,000 |
| Construction | $123,000 |
| Landscaping | $ 6,000 |
| Variable marketing costs | $ 1,000 |

Rouse Builders would like to earn a profit of 16% of the variable cost of each home sale. Similar homes offered by competing builders sell for $201,000 each.

### Requirements

1. Which approach to pricing should Rouse Builders emphasize? Why?
2. Will Rouse Builders be able to achieve its target profit levels? Show your computations.
3. Bathrooms and kitchens are typically the most important selling features of a home. Rouse Builders could differentiate the homes by upgrading bathrooms and kitchens. The upgrades would cost $16,000 per home but would enable Rouse Builders to increase the selling prices by $28,000 per home. (In general, kitchen and bathroom upgrades typically add at least 150% of their cost to the value of any home.) If Rouse Builders upgrades, what will the new cost-plus price per home be? Should the company differentiate its product in this manner? Show your analysis.

## E8-36B Decide whether to drop a product line *(Learning Objective 5)*

Top managers of City Video are alarmed by their operating losses. They are considering dropping the DVD product line. Company accountants have prepared the following analysis to help make this decision. Total fixed costs will not change if the company stops selling DVDs.

| | Total | Blu-ray Discs | DVDs |
|---|---|---|---|
| Sales revenue | $428,000 | $308,000 | $120,000 |
| Variable expenses | 238,000 | 150,000 | 88,000 |
| Contribution margin | 190,000 | 158,000 | 32,000 |
| Fixed expenses: | | | |
| Manufacturing | 133,000 | 76,000 | 57,000 |
| Marketing and administrative | 65,000 | 54,000 | 11,000 |
| Total fixed expenses | 198,000 | 130,000 | 68,000 |
| Operating income (loss) | $ (8,000) | $ 28,000 | $ (36,000) |

**Requirements**

1. Prepare an incremental analysis to show whether City Video should drop the DVD product line. Will dropping the DVDs add $36,000 to operating income? Explain.
2. Assume that City Video can avoid $36,000 of fixed expenses by dropping the DVD product line. (These costs are direct fixed costs of the DVD product line). Prepare an incremental analysis to show whether City Video should stop selling DVDs.
3. Now, assume that all $68,000 of fixed costs assigned to DVDs are direct fixed costs and can be avoided if the company stops selling DVDs. However, marketing has concluded that Blu-ray disc sales would be adversely affected by discontinuing the DVD line. (Retailers want to buy both from the same supplier.) Blu-ray disc production and sales would decline 10%. What should the company do?

## E8-37B Consider dropping a product line *(Learning Objective 5)*

Suppose Crispy Pops is considering dropping its Special Oats product line. Assume that during the past year, Special Oats' product line income statement showed the following:

| | |
|---|---|
| Sales | $ 7,400,000 |
| Cost of goods sold | 6,150,000 |
| Gross profit | 1,250,000 |
| Operating expenses | 1,350,000 |
| Operating loss | $ (100,000) |

Fixed manufacturing overhead costs account for 40% of the cost of goods, while only 30% of the operating expenses are fixed. Since the Special Oats line is only one of Crispy Pops' breakfast cereals, only $730,000 of direct fixed costs (the majority of which is advertising) will be eliminated if the product line is discontinued. The remainder of the fixed costs will still be incurred by Crispy Pops. If the company decides to drop the product line, what will happen to the company's operating income? Should Crispy Pops drop the product line?

## E8-38B Identify constraint, then determine product mix *(Learning Objective 6)*

BiGGym produces two types of exercise treadmills: Regular and Deluxe. The exercise craze is such that BiGGym could use all of its available machine hours producing either model. The two models are processed through the same Production Department.

| | Per Unit | |
|---|---|---|
| | **Deluxe** | **Regular** |
| Sales price | $990 | $560 |
| Costs: | | |
| Direct materials | $290 | $100 |
| Direct labour | 86 | 188 |
| Variable manufacturing overhead | 172 | 86 |
| Fixed manufacturing overhead* | 80 | 40 |
| Variable operating expenses | 115 | 61 |
| Total cost | 743 | 475 |
| Operating income | $247 | $ 85 |

**Allocated on the basis of machine hours.*

What product mix will maximize operating income? (*Hint:* Use the allocation of fixed manufacturing overhead to determine the proportion of machine hours used by each product.)

### E8-39B Determine product mix for retailer *(Learning Objective 5)*

Bellicose sells both designer and moderately priced fashion accessories. Top management is deciding which product line to emphasize. Accountants have provided the following data:

| | Per Item | |
|---|---|---|
| | Designer | Moderately Priced |
| Average sales price | $205 | $78 |
| Average variable expenses | 80 | 27 |
| Average fixed expenses (allocated) | 15 | 5 |
| Average operating income | $110 | $46 |

The Bellicose store in Montreal has 1,556 $m^2$ of floor space. If Bellicose emphasizes moderately priced goods, it can display 840 items in the store. If Bellicose emphasizes designer wear, it can display only 560 designer items to create more of a boutique-like atmosphere. These numbers also are the average monthly sales in units. Prepare an analysis to show which product to emphasize.

### E8-40B Determine product mix for retailer—two stocking scenarios *(Learning Objective 6)*

Each morning, Iriza Sandoval stocks the drink case at Iriza's Beach Hut on Vancouver Island. Iriza's Beach Hut has 35 linear metres of refrigerated display space for cold drinks. Each linear metre can hold either 15 341-mL cans or 12 551-mL plastic or glass bottles.

Iriza's Beach Hut sells three types of cold drinks:

1. Grand-Cola in 341-mL cans for $1.50 per can
2. Fizzle Pop in 551-mL plastic bottles for $1.75 per bottle
3. Value-Soda in 551-mL glass bottles for $2.30 per bottle

Iriza's Beach Hut pays its suppliers the following:

1. $0.25 per 341-mL can of Grand-Cola
2. $0.40 per 551-mL bottle of Fizzle Pop
3. $0.80 per 551-mL bottle of Value-Soda

Iriza's Beach Hut's monthly fixed expenses include the following:

| | |
|---|---|
| Hut rental | $ 365 |
| Refrigerator rental | 65 |
| Iriza's salary | 1,750 |
| Total fixed expenses | $2,180 |

Each day, Iriza's Beach Hut can sell all the drinks in the display case.

#### Requirements

1. What is Iriza's Beach Hut's constraining factor? What should Iriza stock to maximize profits? What is the maximum contribution margin she could generate from refrigerated drinks each day?
2. To provide variety to customers, suppose Iriza refuses to devote more than 20 linear metres and no fewer than 2 linear metres to any individual product. Under this condition, how many linear metres of each drink should Iriza stock? How many units of each product will be available for sale each day?
3. Assuming the product mix calculated in Requirement 2, what contribution margin will Iriza generate each day?

## E8-41B Decide to make or buy product component *(Learning Objective 7)*

Tech Systems manufactures an optical switch that it uses in its final product. Tech Systems incurred the following manufacturing costs when it produced 68,000 units last year:

| | |
|---|---|
| Direct materials | $ 680,000 |
| Direct labour | 136,000 |
| Variable overhead | 68,000 |
| Fixed overhead | 386,000 |
| Manufacturing cost for 68,000 units | $1,270,000 |

Tech Systems does not yet know how many switches it will need this year; however, another company has offered to sell Tech Systems the switch for $11.00 per unit. If Tech Systems buys the switch from the outside supplier, the manufacturing facilities that will be idle cannot be used for any other purpose, yet none of the fixed costs are avoidable.

### Requirements

1. Given the same cost structure, should Tech Systems make or buy the switch? Show your analysis.
2. Now, assume that Tech Systems can avoid $120,000 of fixed costs a year by outsourcing production. In addition, because sales are increasing, Tech Systems needs 73,000 switches a year rather than 68,000. What should Tech Systems do now?
3. Given the last scenario, what is the most Tech Systems would be willing to pay to outsource the switches?

## E8-42B Analyze make-or-buy decision with alternative use of facilities *(Learning Objective 7)*

Refer to E8-41B. Tech Systems needs 80,000 optical switches next year (assume same relevant range). By outsourcing them, Tech Systems can use its idle facilities to manufacture another product that will contribute $130,000 to operating income, but none of the fixed costs will be avoidable. Should Tech Systems make or buy the switches? Show your analysis.

**Tech Systems**
**Incremental Analysis for Outsourcing Decision**

| | Make Unit | Buy Unit | Cost to Make Minus Cost to Buy |
|---|---|---|---|
| Variable cost per unit: | | | |
| Direct materials | $10.00 | $ — | $ 10.00 |
| Direct labour | 2.00 | — | 2.00 |
| Variable overhead | 1.00 | — | 1.00 |
| Purchase price from outsider | — | 11.00 | (11.00) |
| Variable cost per unit | $13.00 | $11.00 | $ 2.00 |

## E8-43B Determine maximum outsourcing price *(Learning Objective 7)*

CoolMedia's sales have increased; as a result, the company needs 430,000 jewel-case liners rather than 280,000. CoolMedia has enough existing capacity to make all of the liners it needs. In addition, due to volume discounts, its variable costs of making each liner will decline to $0.26 per liner. Assume that by outsourcing, CoolMedia can reduce its current fixed costs ($58,800) by $8,600. There is no alternative use for the factory space freed through outsourcing, so it will just remain idle. What is the maximum CoolMedia will pay to outsource production of its CD liners?

### E8-44B Decide to sell as-is or process further *(Learning Objective 8)*

Organicplus processes organic milk into plain yogourt. Organicplus sells plain yogourt to hospitals, nursing homes, and restaurants in bulk, 4-L containers. Each batch, processed at a cost of $810, yields 550 4-L tubs of plain yogourt. Organicplus sells the 4-L tubs for $8.00 each, and spends $0.12 for each plastic tub.

Organicplus has recently begun to reconsider its strategy. The manager wonders if it would be more profitable to sell individual-sized portions of fruited organic yogourt at local food stores. Organicplus could further process each batch of plain yogourt into 11,579 individual portions (190 mL each) of fruited yogourt. A recent market analysis indicates that demand for the product exists. Organicplus would sell each individual portion for $0.50. Packaging would cost $0.05 per portion, and fruit would cost $0.10 per portion. Fixed costs would not change. Should Organicplus continue to sell only the 4-L tubs of plain yogourt (sell as-is) or convert the plain yogourt into individual-sized portions of fruited yogourt (process further)? Why?

### E8-45B Compute transfer pricing *(Learning Objective 9)*

Refer to the TK Electronics information in S8-15. The Cell Phone Department needs 90,000 computer chips but half of the Chips Department's variable selling and administrative costs would still be incurred. Current production in the Chips Department is 400,000 chips. Should a transfer take place? If so, at what price?

What other qualitative factors might need to be considered?

## PROBLEMS Group A

### P8-46A Analyze special-order decision and considerations *(Learning Objective 4)*

Float-All manufactures flotation vests in Guelph. Float-All's contribution margin income statement for the most recent month contains the following data:

| | |
|---|---|
| Sales in units | 31,000 |
| Sales revenue | $434,000 |
| Variable expenses: | |
| Manufacturing | $ 93,000 |
| Marketing and administrative | 107,000 |
| Total variable expenses | 200,000 |
| Contribution margin | 234,000 |
| Fixed expenses: | |
| Manufacturing | 126,000 |
| Marketing and administrative | 90,000 |
| Total fixed expenses | 216,000 |
| Operating income | $ 18,000 |

Suppose Overton's wants to buy 5,000 vests from Float-All. Acceptance of the order will not increase Float-All's variable marketing and administrative expenses or any of its fixed expenses. The Float-All plant has enough unused capacity to manufacture the additional vests. Overton's has offered $12 per vest, which is below the normal sale price of $14.

#### Requirements

1. Prepare an incremental analysis to determine whether Float-All should accept this special sales order.
2. Identify long-term factors Float-All should consider in deciding whether to accept the special sales order.

**P8-47A** **Analyze pricing of nursery plants** *(Learning Objectives 2 & 3)*

GreenThumb operates a commercial plant nursery where it propagates plants for garden centres throughout the region. GreenThumb has $5 million in assets. Its yearly fixed costs are $600,000, and the variable costs for the potting soil, container, label, seedling, and labour for each plant total $1.25. GreenThumb's volume is currently 500,000 units. Competitors offer the same quality plants to garden centres for $3.50 each. Garden centres then mark them up to sell to the public for $8 to $10, depending on the type of plant.

### Requirements

1. GreenThumb's owners want to earn a 12% return on the company's assets. What is GreenThumb's target full cost?
2. Given GreenThumb's current costs, will its owners be able to achieve their target profit? Show your analysis.
3. Assume that GreenThumb has identified ways to cut its variable costs to $1.10 per unit. What is its new target fixed cost? Will this decrease in variable costs allow the company to achieve its target profit? Show your analysis.
4. GreenThumb started an aggressive advertising campaign strategy to differentiate its plants from those grown by other nurseries. Plant City made this strategy work, so GreenThumb has decided to try it too. GreenThumb doesn't expect volume to be affected, but it hopes to gain more control over pricing. If GreenThumb has to spend $100,000 this year to advertise and its variable costs continue to be $1.10 per unit, what will its cost-plus price be? Do you think GreenThumb will be able to sell its plants to garden centres at the cost-plus price? Why or why not?

**P8-48A** **Prepare and use contribution margin statements to decide whether to drop a line** *(Learning Objective 5)*

Members of the board of directors of Security Systems have received the following operating income data for the year just ended:

| | *Product Line* | | |
|---|---|---|---|
| | **Industrial Systems** | **Household Systems** | **Total** |
| Sales revenue | $300,000 | $310,000 | $610,000 |
| Cost of goods sold: | | | |
| Variable | $ 38,000 | $ 42,000 | $ 80,000 |
| Fixed | 210,000 | 69,000 | 279,000 |
| Total cost of goods sold | 248,000 | 111,000 | 359,000 |
| Gross profit | 52,000 | 199,000 | 251,000 |
| Marketing and administrative expenses: | | | |
| Variable | 66,000 | 71,000 | 137,000 |
| Fixed | 40,000 | 22,000 | 62,000 |
| Total marketing and administrative expenses | 106,000 | 93,00 | 199,000 |
| Operating income (loss) | $ (54,000) | $106,000 | $ 52,000 |

Members of the board are surprised that the industrial systems product line is losing money. They commission a study to determine whether the company should drop the line. Company accountants estimate that dropping industrial systems will decrease fixed cost of goods sold by $80,000 and decrease fixed marketing and administrative expenses by $12,000.

### Requirements

1. Prepare an incremental analysis to show whether Security Systems should drop the industrial systems product line.
2. Prepare contribution margin income statements to show Security Systems' total operating income under the two alternatives: (a) with the industrial systems line and (b) without the line. Compare the difference between the two alternatives' income numbers to your answer to Requirement 1. What have you learned from this comparison?

**P8-49A Product mix decision under constraint** *(Learning Objective 6)*

Bolton Dental Manufacturer, located in Cambridge, produces two lines of electric toothbrushes: Deluxe and Standard. Because Bolton can sell all of the toothbrushes it produces, the owners are expanding the plant. They are deciding which product line to emphasize. To make this decision, they assemble the following data:

| | Per Unit | |
|---|---|---|
| | Deluxe Toothbrush | Standard Toothbrush |
| Sales price | $ 80 | $48 |
| Variable expenses | 20 | 18 |
| Contribution margin | $ 60 | $30 |
| Contribution margin ratio | 75% | 62.5% |

After expansion, the factory will have a production capacity of 4,500 machine hours per month. The plant can manufacture either 60 Standard electric toothbrushes or 24 Deluxe electric toothbrushes per machine hour.

**Requirements**

1. Identify the constraining factor for Bolton.
2. Prepare an analysis to show which product line to emphasize.

**P8-50A Outsourcing decision given alternative use of capacity** *(Learning Objective 7)*

Krass Snowboard Mfg. Inc. manufactures snowboards. Its cost of making 1,800 bindings is as follows:

| | |
|---|---|
| Direct materials | $17,520 |
| Direct labour | 3,100 |
| Variable manufacturing overhead | 2,080 |
| Fixed manufacturing overhead | 6,800 |
| Total manufacturing costs | $29,500 |
| Cost per binding ($29,500 ÷ 1,800) | $ 16.39 (rounded) |

Suppose O'Brien will sell bindings to Krass for $14 each. Krass will pay $1.00 per unit to transport the bindings to its manufacturing plant, where it will add its own logo at a cost of $0.20 per binding.

**Requirements**

1. Krass's accountants predict that purchasing the bindings from O'Brien will enable the company to avoid $3,200 of fixed overhead. Prepare an analysis to show whether Krass should make or buy the bindings.
2. The facilities freed by purchasing bindings from O'Brien can be used to manufacture another product that will contribute $3,100 to profit. Total fixed costs will be the same as if Krass had produced the bindings. Show which alternative makes the best use of Krass' facilities: (a) make bindings, (b) buy bindings and leave facilities idle, or (c) buy bindings and make another product.

**P8-51A Analyze sell-as-is or process-further decisions** *(Learning Objective 8)*

Vision Chemical has spent $240,000 to refine 72,000 L of acetone, which can be sold for $2.16/L. Alternatively, Vision Chemical can process the acetone further to yield a total of 60,000 L of lacquer thinner that can be sold for $3.20/L. The additional processing will cost $0.62/L of lacquer thinner. To sell the lacquer thinner, Vision Chemical must pay shipping of $0.22/L and administrative expenses of $0.10/L on the thinner.

**Requirements**

1. Diagram Vision's decision, using Exhibit 8-24 as a guide.
2. Identify the sunk cost. Is the sunk cost relevant to Vision's decision? Why or why not?
3. Should Vision sell the acetone or process it into lacquer thinner? Show the expected net revenue difference between the two alternatives.

# PROBLEMS Group B

## P8-52B Special-order decision and considerations *(Learning Objective 4)*

Deep Blue manufactures flotation vests in New Brunswick. Deep Blue's contribution margin income statement for the most recent month contains the following data:

| | |
|---|---|
| Sales in units | 31,000 |
| Sales revenue | $434,000 |
| Variable expenses: | |
| Manufacturing | $186,000 |
| Marketing and administrative | 110,000 |
| Total variable expenses | 296,000 |
| Contribution margin | 138,000 |
| Fixed expenses: | |
| Manufacturing | 130,000 |
| Marketing and administrative | 92,000 |
| Total fixed expenses | 222,000 |
| Operating income | $ (84,000) |

Suppose Boats-n-More wishes to buy 4,600 vests from Deep Blue. Acceptance of the order will not increase Deep Blue's variable marketing and administrative expenses. The Deep Blue plant has enough unused capacity to manufacture the additional vests. Boats-n-More has offered $5 per vest, which is below the normal sale price of $14.

**Requirements**

1. Prepare an incremental analysis to determine whether Deep Blue should accept this special sales order.
2. Identify long-term factors Deep Blue should consider in deciding whether to accept the special sales order.

## P8-53B Analyze pricing of nursery plants *(Learning Objectives 2 & 3)*

Plant City operates a commercial plant nursery where it propagates plants for garden centres throughout the region. Plant City has $5.25 million in assets. Its yearly fixed costs are $668,500, and the variable costs for the potting soil, container, label, seedling, and labour for each plant total $1.20. Plant City's volume is currently 490,000 units. Competitors offer the same quality plants to garden centres for $3.70 each. Garden centres then mark them up to sell to the public for $8 to $9, depending on the type of plant.

**Requirements**

1. Plant City's owners want to earn a 12% return on the company's assets. What is Plant City's target full cost?
2. Given Plant City's current costs, will its owners be able to achieve their target profit? Show your analysis.
3. Assume that Plant City has identified ways to cut its variable costs to $1.05 per unit. What is its new target fixed cost? Will this decrease in variable costs allow the company to achieve its target profit? Show your analysis.

4. Plant City started an aggressive advertising campaign strategy to differentiate its plants from those grown by other nurseries. GreenThumb made this strategy work, so Plant City has decided to try it too. Plant City doesn't expect volume to be affected, but it hopes to gain more control over pricing. If Plant City has to spend $53,900 this year to advertise and its variable costs continue to be $1.05 per unit, what will its cost-plus price be? Do you think Plant City will be able to sell its plants to garden centres at the cost-plus price? Why or why not?

## P8-54B Prepare and use contribution margin statements to decide whether to drop a line *(Learning Objective 5)*

Members of the board of directors of Security Force have received the following operating income data for the year just ended:

| | *Product Line* | | |
|---|---|---|---|
| | **Industrial Systems** | **Household Systems** | **Total** |
| Sales revenue | $360,000 | $370,000 | $730,000 |
| Cost of goods sold: | | | |
| Variable | $ 35,000 | $ 42,000 | $ 77,000 |
| Fixed | 260,000 | 66,000 | 326,000 |
| Total cost of goods sold | 295,000 | 108,000 | 403,000 |
| Gross profit | 65,000 | 262,000 | 327,000 |
| Marketing and administrative expenses: | | | |
| Variable | 66,000 | 71,000 | 137,000 |
| Fixed | 42,000 | 22,000 | 64,000 |
| Total marketing and administrative expenses | 108,000 | 93,000 | 201,000 |
| Operating income (loss) | $(43,000) | $169,000 | $126,000 |

Members of the board are surprised that the industrial systems product line is losing money. They commission a study to determine whether the company should drop the line. Company accountants estimate that dropping industrial systems will decrease fixed cost of goods sold by $82,000 and decrease fixed marketing and administrative expenses by $15,000.

### Requirements

1. Prepare an incremental analysis to show whether Security Force should drop the industrial systems product line.
2. Prepare contribution margin income statements to show Security Force's total operating income under the two alternatives: (a) with the industrial systems line and (b) without the line. Compare the difference between the two alternatives' income numbers to your answer to Requirement 1. What have you learned from this comparison?

## P8-55B Make a product mix decision under constraint *(Learning Objective 6)*

Bandin Dental Products, located in Moosonee, produces two lines of electric toothbrushes: Deluxe and Standard. Because Bandin can sell all the toothbrushes it can produce, the owners are expanding the plant. They are deciding which product line to emphasize. To make this decision, they assemble the following data:

| | *Per Unit* | |
|---|---|---|
| | **Deluxe Toothbrush** | **Standard Toothbrush** |
| Sales price | $98 | $50 |
| Variable expenses | 19 | 16 |
| Contribution margin | 79 | 34 |
| Contribution margin ratio | 80.6% | 68% |

After expansion, the factory will have a production capacity of 4,000 machine hours per month. The plant can manufacture either 55 Standard electric toothbrushes or 25 Deluxe electric toothbrushes per machine hour.

### Requirements

1. Identify the constraining factor for Bandin.
2. Prepare an analysis to show which product line to emphasize.

## P8-56B Outsourcing decision given alternative use of capacity *(Learning Objective 7)*

Winter Sports manufactures snowboards. Its cost of making 23,600 bindings is as follows:

| | |
|---|---|
| Direct materials | $ 24,000 |
| Direct labour | 82,000 |
| Variable manufacturing overhead | 48,000 |
| Fixed manufacturing overhead | 82,000 |
| Total manufacturing cost | $236,000 |
| Cost per binding ($236,000 / 23,600) | $ 10.00 |

Suppose Monroe will sell bindings to Winter Sports for $11 each. Winter Sports would pay $2.00 per unit to transport the bindings to its manufacturing plant, where it would add its own logo at a cost $0.50 of per binding.

### Requirements

1. Winter Sports' accountants predict that purchasing the bindings from Monroe will enable the company to avoid $10,000 of fixed overhead. Prepare an analysis to show whether Winter Sports should make or buy the bindings.
2. The facilities freed by purchasing bindings from Monroe can be used to manufacture another product that will contribute $25,000 to profit. Total fixed costs will be the same as if Winter Sports had produced the bindings. Show which alternative makes the best use of Winter Sports' facilities: (a) make bindings, (b) buy bindings and leave facilities idle, or (c) buy bindings and make another product.

## P8-57B Analyze sell-as-is or process-further decisions *(Learning Objective 8)*

Preston Chemical has spent $243,000 to refine 73,000 L of acetone, which can be sold for $2.00/L. Alternatively, Preston Chemical can process the acetone further to yield a total of 58,000 L of lacquer thinner that can be sold for $3.30/L. The additional processing will cost $0.40/L of lacquer thinner. To sell the lacquer thinner, Preston Chemical must pay shipping of $0.24/L and administrative expenses of $0.14/L on the thinner.

### Requirements

1. Diagram Preston's decision, using Exhibit 8-24 as a guide.
2. Identify the sunk cost. Is the sunk cost relevant to Preston's decision? Why or why not?
3. Should Preston sell the acetone or process it into lacquer thinner? Show the expected net revenue difference between the two alternatives.

# CAPSTONE APPLICATION PROBLEMS

## APPLICATION QUESTIONS

### A8-58 Assess opportunity for outsourcing e-mail *(Learning Objective 7)*

BKFin.com provides banks access to sophisticated financial information and analysis systems via the Web. The company combines these tools with benchmarking data access, including e-mail and wireless communications, so that banks can instantly evaluate individual loan applications and entire loan portfolios.

BKFin.com's CEO, Eugene Mikoula, is happy with the company's growth. To better focus on client service, Mikoula is considering outsourcing some functions. CFO Jenny Lee suggests that the company's e-mail may be the place to start. She recently attended a conference and learned that companies such as Air Canada, Nipissing University, GTE, and NBC were outsourcing their e-mail function. Mikoula asks Lee to identify costs related to BKFin.com's in-house Microsoft Exchange e-mail application, which has 2,300 mailboxes. This information follows:

| | |
|---|---|
| Variable costs: | |
| E-mail licence | $7 per mailbox per month |
| Virus protection licence | $1 per mailbox per month |
| Other variable costs | $8 per mailbox per month |
| Fixed costs: | |
| Computer hardware costs | $94,300 per month |
| $8,050 monthly salary for two information technology staff members who work only on e-mail | $16,100 per month |

### Requirements

1. Compute the total cost per mailbox per month of BKFin.com's current e-mail function.
2. Suppose Mail.com, a leading provider of internet messaging outsourcing services, offers to host BKFin.com's email function for $9 per mailbox per month. If BKFin.com outsources its e-mail to Mail.com, BKFin.com will still need the virus protection software, its computer hardware, and one information technology staff member who would be responsible for maintaining virus protection, quarantining suspicious e-mails, and managing content (e.g., screening e-mails for objectionable content). Should CEO Mikoula accept Mail.com's offer? Why or why not?
3. Suppose for an additional $5 per mailbox per month, Mail.com will also provide virus protection, quarantine, and content-management services. Outsourcing these additional functions would mean that BKFin.com would not need an e-mail information technology staff member or the separate virus protection license. Should CEO Mikoula outsource these extra services to Mail.com? Why or why not?

# CASE ASSIGNMENT

## C8-59 Downtown Architecture and Design

*Source:* Igorsky/Shutterstock

Tony Li just heard that the Interior Design Department of Downtown Architecture is being considered for closure. Tony has been with Downtown for eight years and has managed the department well. He has increased revenues steadily over the years, has raised the quality of design being done by recruiting and retaining some of the most qualified and sought-after interior designers, and has even had several of its designs in the past two years featured in national style and interior design magazines.

He knows that every quarter the owners inform him that the Interior Design Department isn't covering its costs, but that doesn't make sense to him. He has streamlined operations by cutting out any wasted efforts and resources and, through conversations with managers at other firms, believes that he has one of the most efficient teams going. He was also told by a few customers that the only reason that they had Downtown Architecture design their building was so that they would have the Downtown Design Department on their project as well.

So Tony decided to be proactive and asked to see the financial statements. He wanted to look them over and see how the numbers were adding up. And he was shocked. It was true. The Design Department had net losses each quarter so far this year. Now Tony doesn't know what to do. He doesn't want to go to the manager of the Architecture Department because he and Lucinda have had a rivalry ever since he started at Downtown. Tony has always suspected that Lucinda was sabotaging his efforts and trying to get him fired, but he never had any concrete proof.

Lucinda, as the manager for the Architecture Department, which is the owner's pride and joy, is responsible for financial decisions for the firm such as the allocations of the costs that are shared between the two divisions (the leased equipment, utilities, insurance, rent, and other general expenses). But those are split 50/50 between the departments, so there can't be anything wrong with that. Now it looks as though he may lose not only his job, but the entire department. Tony asks the controller for a set of financial statements for the entire firm and goes home to look them over. Frustrated, he puts them away and starts looking at job postings.

| | Quarter 1 | | | Quarter 2 | | | Quarter 3 | | |
|---|---|---|---|---|---|---|---|---|---|
| | Total | Architecture | Interior Design | Total | Architecture | Interior Design | Total | Architecture | Interior Design |
| **Sales** | $200,000 | $150,000 | $50,000 | $210,000 | $156,000 | $54,000 | $500,000 | $410,000 | $ 90,000 |
| Direct Cost of Sales | $ 1,251 | $ 938 | $ 313 | $ 1,313 | $ 975 | $ 338 | $ 3,126 | $ 2,563 | $ 563 |
| **Gross Margin Expenses** | $198,749 | $149,062 | $49,687 | $208,687 | $155,025 | $53,662 | $496,874 | $407,437 | $ 89,437 |
| Payroll | $120,200 | $ 90,000 | $30,200 | $120,200 | $ 90,000 | $30,200 | $286,000 | $231,000 | $ 55,000 |
| Sales and Marketing and Other Expenses | $ 10,000 | $ 7,000 | $ 3,000 | $ 10,800 | $ 7,800 | $ 3,000 | $ 34,500 | $ 30,500 | $ 4,000 |
| Leased Equipment | $ 1,440 | $ 720 | $ 720 | $ 1,680 | $ 840 | $ 840 | $ 1,920 | $ 960 | $ 960 |
| Utilities | $ 600 | $ 300 | $ 300 | $ 620 | $ 310 | $ 310 | $ 650 | $ 325 | $ 325 |
| Insurance | $ 2,500 | $ 1,250 | $ 1,250 | $ 2,800 | $ 1,400 | $ 1,400 | $ 3,500 | $ 1,750 | $ 1,750 |
| Rent | $ 17,030 | $ 8,515 | $ 8,515 | $ 23,400 | $ 11,700 | $11,700 | $ 23,400 | $ 11,700 | $ 11,700 |
| Other General and Administrative | $ 25,000 | $ 12,500 | $12,500 | $ 26,750 | $ 13,375 | $13,375 | $ 58,600 | $ 29,300 | $ 29,300 |
| **Total Operating Expenses** | $176,770 | $120,285 | $56,485 | $186,250 | $125,425 | $60,825 | $408,570 | $305,535 | $103,035 |
| Profit Before Interest and Taxes | $ 21,979 | $ 28,777 | ($ 6,798) | $ 22,437 | $ 29,600 | ($ 7,163) | $ 88,304 | $101,902 | ($ 13,598) |
| Interest Expense | $ 1,518 | $ 759 | $ 759 | $ 1,098 | $ 549 | $ 549 | $ 660 | $ 330 | $ 330 |
| Taxes Incurred | $ 11,746 | $ 5,873 | $ 5,873 | $ 11,538 | $ 5,769 | $ 5,769 | $ 37,330 | $ 18,665 | $ 18,665 |
| **Net Profit** | $ 8,715 | $ 22,145 | ($13,430) | $ 9,801 | $ 23,282 | ($13,481) | $ 50,314 | $ 82,907 | ($ 32,593) |

# ETHICAL ISSUE

## 18-60 Analyze outsourcing and ethics *(Learning Objective 7)*

Mary Tan is the controller for Duck Associates, a property management company in Saskatoon. Each year, Tan and payroll clerk Toby Stock meet with the external auditors about payroll accounting. This year, the auditors suggest that Tan consider outsourcing Duck Associates' payroll accounting to a company specializing in payroll processing services. This would allow Tan and her staff to focus on their primary responsibility: accounting for the properties under management. At present, payroll requires 1.5 employee positions—payroll clerk Toby Stock and a bookkeeper who spends half her time entering payroll data in the system.

As Tan considers this suggestion, she lists the following items relating to outsourcing payroll accounting:

a. The current payroll software that was purchased for $4,000 three years ago would not be needed if payroll processing were outsourced.

b. Duck Associates' bookkeeper would spend half her time preparing the weekly payroll input form that is given to the payroll processing service. She is paid $450 a week.

c. Duck Associates would no longer need payroll clerk Toby Stock, whose annual salary is $42,000.

d. The payroll processing service would charge $2,000 a month.

### Requirements

1. Would outsourcing the payroll function increase or decrease Duck Associates' operating income?
2. Tan believes that outsourcing payroll would simplify her job, but she does not like the prospect of having to lay off Stock, who has become a close personal friend. She does not believe there is another position available for Stock at his current salary. Can you think of other factors that might support keeping Stock rather than outsourcing payroll processing? How should each of the factors affect Tan's decision if she wants to do what is best for Duck Associates and act ethically?

# TEAM PROJECT

## T8-61 Assess information relevant to outsourcing decision *(Learning Objective 7)*

Shyhrete Berisha is the founder and sole owner of Berisha. Analysts have estimated that his chain of home improvement stores scattered throughout the provinces and territories generate about $3 billion in annual sales. But how can Berisha compete with giant Home Depot?

Suppose Berisha is trying to decide whether to invest $45 million in a state-of-the-art manufacturing plant in the Okanagan. Berisha expects the plant would operate for 15 years, after which it would have no residual value. The plant would produce Berisha's own line of formica countertops, cabinets, and picnic tables.

Suppose Berisha incurred the following unit costs in producing its own product lines:

| | *Per Unit* | | |
|---|---|---|---|
| | **Countertops** | **Cabinets** | **Picnic Tables** |
| Direct materials | $15 | $10 | $25 |
| Direct labour | 10 | 5 | 15 |
| Variable manufacturing overhead | 5 | 2 | 6 |

Rather than Berisha making these products, assume that he can buy them from outside suppliers. Suppliers would charge Berisha $40 per countertop, $25 per cabinet, and $65 per picnic table.

Whether Berisha makes or buys these products, assume that he expects the following annual sales:

- Countertops—487,200 at $130 each
- Picnic tables—100,000 at $225 each
- Cabinets—150,000 at $75 each

If making the products is sufficiently more profitable than outsourcing, Berisha will build the new plant. Shyhrete Berisha has asked your consulting group for a recommendation. Berisha uses the straight-line depreciation method.

### Requirements

1. Are the following items relevant or irrelevant in Berisha's decision to build a new plant that will manufacture his own products?
   a. The unit sale prices of the countertops, cabinets, and picnic tables (the sale prices that Berisha charges its customers)
   b. The prices that outside suppliers would charge Berisha for the three products if Berisha decides to outsource the products rather than make them
   c. The $45 million to build the new plant
   d. The direct materials, direct labour, and variable overhead that Berisha would incur to manufacture the three product lines
   e. Berisha's salary

6. Determine whether Berisha should make or outsource the countertops, cabinets, and picnic tables *assuming that the company has already built the plant and, therefore, has the manufacturing capacity to produce these products.* In other words, what is the annual difference in cash flows if Berisha decides to make rather than outsource each of these three products?

7. Write a memo giving your recommendation to Berisha. The memo should clearly state your recommendation and briefly summarize the reasons for your recommendation.

# DISCUSSION & ANALYSIS

1. A beverage company is considering whether to drop its line of grape soda. What factors will affect the company's decision? What is a qualitative factor? Which of the factors you listed are qualitative?
2. What factors would be relevant to a restaurant that is considering whether to make its own dinner rolls or to purchase dinner rolls from a local bakery?
3. How would outsourcing change a company's cost structure? How might this change in cost structure help or harm a company's competitive position?
4. What is an opportunity cost? List possible opportunity costs associated with a make-or-buy decision.
5. What undesirable result can arise from allocating common fixed costs to product lines?
6. Why could a manager be justified in ignoring fixed costs when making a decision about a special order? When would fixed costs be relevant when making a decision about a special order?
7. What is the difference between segment margin and contribution margin? When would each be used?
8. Do sunk costs affect a sell or process-further decision? Why or why not?
9. How can make-or-buy concepts be applied to decisions at a service organization? What types of make-or-buy decisions might a service organization face?
10. Oscar Company builds outdoor furniture using a variety of woods and plastics. What is a constraint? List at least four possible constraints at Oscar Company.

# APPLICATION & ANALYSIS

## 8-1 Making an outsourcing decision at a real company

Go to the *Financial Post* website (www.financialpost.com) or to CTV News (www.ctv.ca/news) and search for the term "outsource." Find an article about a company making a decision to outsource a part of its business operations.

### Discussion Questions

1. Describe the company that is making the decision to outsource. What area of the business is the company either looking to outsource or did it already outsource?
2. Why did the company decide to outsource (or is considering outsourcing)?
3. List the revenues and costs that might be affected by this outsourcing decision. The article will not list many, if any, of these revenues and costs; you should make reasonable guesses about what revenues and/or costs would be associated with the business operation being outsourced.
4. List the qualitative factors that could influence the company's decision whether to outsource this business operation or not. Again, you need to make reasonable guesses about the qualitative factors that might influence the company's decision to outsource or not.

### Classroom Applications

**Web:** Post the discussion questions on an electronic discussion board. Have small groups of students choose a news article for their groups. Each student should read the article for the product for his or her group.

**Classroom:** Form groups of three or four students. Your group should choose a news article as described. After reading the article, prepare a five-minute presentation about your group's company and its outsourcing decision, which addresses the listed questions.

**Independent:** Research answers to each of the questions. Turn in a two- or three-page typed paper (12-point font, double-spaced with 2.5 cm margins). Include references, including the URL for the article that you referenced.

# TRY IT SOLUTIONS

**page 466:**

1. Yes, there is enough capacity to fill this special order. If the plant is producing 450,000 cases a month, yet only operating at 90% of capacity, it must have a capacity level of 500,000 cases per month (= 450,000 ÷ 90%). This means the plant has excess capacity of 50,000 cases per month, which is enough to fill the special order of 40,000 cases without increasing the current level of fixed costs ($2,700,000). Thus, the current level of fixed costs is irrelevant to the decision. Campbell's will *not* incur an additional $6.00 of fixed MOH for every case produced in this order.
2. Take a contribution margin approach to determining whether the special order is profitable:

| | A | B | C |
|---|---|---|---|
| 1 | **Incremental Analysis for Special Order Decision** | **Per Unit** | **Total Order (40,000 units)** |
| 2 | Revenue from special order | $ 19.00 | $ 760,000 |
| 3 | Less: Variable expenses associated with the order (DM, DL, Variable MOH) | 15.00 | 600,000 |
| 4 | Contribution margin | $ 4.00 | $ 160,000 |
| 5 | Less: Additional fixed expenses associated with the order | | 5,000 |
| 6 | Increase in operating income from the special order | | $ 155,000 |
| 7 | | | |

**page 472:**

1. Analyze the revenues and costs that would be lost if the salad bar operation is discontinued:

| | A | B | C |
|---|---|---|---|
| 1 | **Incremental Analysis for Discontinuation Decision** | **Total** | |
| 2 | Sales revenue from salad bars | $ 750,000 | |
| 3 | Less: Variable expenses related to salad bars | 600,000 | |
| 4 | Contribution margin lost if salad bars are discontinued | $ 150,000 | |
| 5 | Less: Fixed cost savings if salad bars are discontinued | 20,000 | |
| 6 | Operating income lost if salad bars are discontinued | $ 130,000 | |
| 7 | | | |
| 8 | | | |
| 9 | **If Salad Bars Are Replaced with Olive Bars** | **Total** | |
| 10 | Contribution margin provided by olive bar | $ 200,000 | |
| 11 | Less: Operating income lost if salad bars are discontinued | 130,000 | ← |
| 12 | Increase in operating income from replacing salad bars with olive bars | $ 70,000 | |
| 13 | | | |

**page 479:**

1. As shown below, the total cost of outsourcing the ski poles and leaving the freed capacity idle is $325,000 greater than the cost to produce the poles in-house. Rossignol should not outsource production because its operating income would decline by $325,000.
2. However, Rossignol's income would increase by $175,000 if it outsources production and uses the freed capacity to make ski boots.

| | A | B | C | D |
|---|---|---|---|---|
| 1 | **Incremental Analysis Outsourcing Decision** | **Make Ski Poles** | **Outsource Ski Poles** | **Difference** |
| 2 | Variable Costs: | | | |
| 3 | If make: $13.50 × 100,000 units<br>If outsource: $18.00 × 100,000 units | $ 1,350,000 | $ 1,800,000 | $ 450,000 |
| 4 | Plus: Fixed costs | 650,000 | 525,000 | (125,000) |
| 5 | Total cost of producing 100,000 units | $ 2,000,000 | $ 2,325,000 | $ 325,000 |
| 6 | Less: Income from ski boots if outsource | 0 | 500,000 | 500,000 |
| 7 | Net cost | $ 2,000,000 | $ 1,825,000 | $ (175,000) |
| 8 | | | | |

# The Master Budget and Responsibility Accounting

Chapter 9, "The Master Budget and Responsibility Accounting," covers material outlined in **Section 3: Management Accounting** of the CPA Competency Map. Specifically, this chapter addresses *Section 3.2 Planning, Budgeting, and Forecasting* and *Section 3.6 Organizational Performance Measurement*. The Learning Objectives in this chapter have been aligned with the CPA Competency Map to ensure the best coverage possible.

PROFESSIONAL COMPETENCY — The presence of the **coverage button** in the margin indicates focus on one or more of the specific competency areas from the competency map. The concepts in the text are building blocks to developing the competencies required in the CPA. While the chapter may address multiple areas of the competency map, the main focus will be:

Competencies:

**3.2.1** Develops or evaluates information inputs for operational plans, budgets, and forecasts*

**3.2.2** Prepares, analyzes, or evaluates operational plans, budgets, and forecasts*

**3.2.3** Computes, analyzes, or assesses implications of variances*

**3.4.1** Evaluates sources and drivers of revenue growth*

**3.6.2** Evaluates performance of responsibility centres*

© ssuaphotos/Shutterstock
*Source:* www.solgate.ca

## Learning Objectives

1. Describe how and why managers use budgets.
2. Prepare the operating budgets.
3. Prepare the financial budgets.
4. Describe the four types of responsibility centres, and prepare performance reports.
5. Prepare a merchandiser's cost of goods sold, inventory, and purchases budget. (Appendix 9A)

## SolGate Inc. is the first large-scale photo-

voltaic panel manufacturer in Canada. According to the company's website (solgate.ca/about), it is "strongly committed to continually produce the highest quality solar panels in the world." How will the company attain this goal? First, it identifies key strategies. SolGate has created a strategic alliance with a silicon cell producer that assists the company in reaching its objectives. Other key strategies could include increasing margins through improving productivity and advancing its commitment to organizational excellence and social responsibility.

These strategies require that detailed plans be put into place. The company's managers express these plans, in financial terms, through budgets. The company's budgets reflect and support each of these key strategies. For example, management has budgeted for extensive quality control measures to ensure that the solar panels adhere to the quality standards of the company and are able to fit with any mounting system. Management may also budget millions of dollars for new, more productive manufacturing equipment and an enterprise resource planning (ERP) information system that could improve profit margins and increase organizational excellence. The company's budget is a vital tool in making it all happen.

*Reprinted from *The Chartered Professional Accountant Competency Map - Understanding the competencies a candidate must demonstrate to become a CPA*, © 2012, with permission Chartered Professional Accountants of Canada, Toronto, Canada. Any changes to the original material are the sole responsibility of the author (and/or publisher) and have not been reviewed or endorsed by the Chartered Professional Accountants of Canada.

# How and Why Do Managers Use Budgets?

1 Describe how and why managers use budgets.

Budgeting is perhaps the most widely used management accounting tool employed by companies, organizations, and governments. Budgets show how resources are intended to be used, and how they are *actually* used, making them powerful techniques for planning and control as well as performance measurement. In this chapter, we'll take a closer look at how budgets are used and developed, the benefits of budgeting, and the particular budgets that are prepared as part of the company's master budget.

Exhibit 9-1 shows how managers use budgets in fulfilling their major responsibilities of planning, directing, and controlling operations. Budgeting is an ongoing cycle: Company strategies lead to detailed plans, which in turn lead to actions. Results are then compared to the budget to provide feedback. This feedback allows managers to take corrective actions and, if necessary, revise strategies, which starts the cycle over.

**EXHIBIT 9-1** Managers Use Budgets to Plan and Control Business Activities

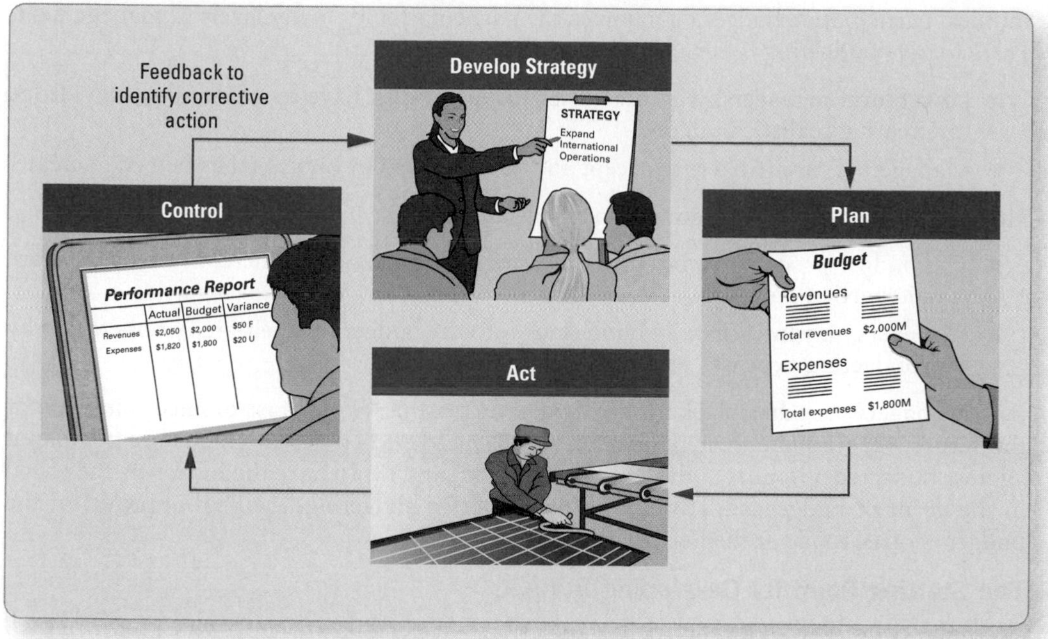


## Developing Budgets

Let's assume that a few years ago SolGate was not performing up to expectations. The first step toward getting the company back on track would have been management's decision to create long-term strategic goals. **Strategic planning** involves setting long-term goals that may extend 5 to 10 years into the future. Long-term, loosely detailed budgets are often created to reflect expectations for these long-term goals.

Once the goals are set, management designs key strategies for attaining the goals. These strategies, such as SolGate's alliance with a European company that produces silicone cells, are then put into place through the use of shorter-term budgets for an entire fiscal year. However, even a yearly budget is not detailed enough to guide many management decisions. For example, Solgate's solar panel production managers must know what month of the year they will receive and start using new production machinery. They must also decide how much of each raw material (low-iron glass, aluminum, and so forth) to purchase each month to meet production requirements for both existing and new products. In turn, this will affect monthly cash needs. Therefore, companies usually prepare a budget for every month of the fiscal year.

Many companies set aside time during the last two quarters of the fiscal year to create their budget for the upcoming fiscal year. Other companies prepare rolling, or continuous, budgets. A **rolling budget** is a budget that is continuously updated so that the next 12 months of operations are always budgeted. For example, as soon as January is over, the next January is added to the budget. The benefit of a rolling budget is that managers always have a budget for the next 12 months.

## Participants in the Budget Process

In most organizations, the **budget committee** is at the centre of the formal process that reviews budgets, suggests revisions, and approves the final budget (sometimes after several cycles of revision). The budget committee often includes upper management, such as the CEO and CFO, as well as managers from every area of the value chain (such as Research and Development, Marketing, Distribution, and so forth). Overseen by a cross-functional budget committee, the final budget is more likely to reflect a comprehensive view of the organization and be accepted by managers than if the budget were prepared by one person or department for the entire organization.

Instead of using a top-down approach, in which top management determines the budget, some organizations use some degree of **participative budgeting**. As the term implies, participative budgeting involves the participation of many levels of management. Participative budgeting is beneficial because

- Lower-level managers, who are closer to operations, have more detailed knowledge for creating realistic budgets.
- Managers are more likely to accept and be motivated by budgets they helped to create.

However, participative budgeting also has disadvantages:

- The budget process can become much more complex and time consuming as more people participate.
- Managers may intentionally build **slack** into the budget for their area of operation by overbudgeting expenses or underbudgeting revenue.

Managers introduce slack for three possible reasons: (1) because of uncertainty about the future, (2) to make their performance look better when actual results are compared against budgeted amounts at the end of the period, and (3) to have the resources they need in the event of budget cuts. Even with participative budgeting, the final approval of the budget is often made at the budget committee.

## The Starting Point for Developing Budgets

After the overall strategy for the organization is determined (which will then drive all decision-making for the budgets), the next step is to determine what approach will be used to guide the creation of specific elements of the budgets. Many companies use the prior year's budgeted figures, or actual results, as the starting point for creating the budget for the coming year. Information needs to be gathered from past income statements and balance sheets. Of course, those figures will then be modified to reflect the following:

- New products, customers, or geographical areas
- Changes in the marketplace caused by competitors
- Changes in labour contracts, raw material, and fuel costs
- Inflation and general economic conditions
- Any new strategies

For example, SolGate Inc. may have a strategy to focus on monocrystalline solar panels. Because of this strategy, it estimates that it should be able to increase its sales of monocrystalline panels by 10%. Managers can then take the previous year's sales figures in units and increase this by 10%. However, this approach to budgeting may cause year-after-year increases that, after time, grow out of control. To prevent perpetual increases in budgeted expenses, many companies intermittently use **zero-based budgeting**. When a company implements zero-based budgeting, all managers begin with a budget of zero and must justify every dollar they put in the budget. For example, SolGate Inc., instead of assuming a 10% increase in sales, could take its current customer list and estimate how many units will be sold to each customer (perhaps based on discussions with the sales team, which would have a good sense of what each customer will likely need in the upcoming year) and add to this any new customers that it feels it will attract based on its strategy and marketing plan. It would then total all of the unit sales from new sales to current and new customers. This budgeting approach is very time consuming and labour intensive. Therefore, companies use it only from time to time in order to keep their numbers in check.

## What Are the Benefits of Budgeting?

Exhibit 9-2 summarizes three key benefits of budgeting. Budgeting forces managers to plan, promotes coordination and communication, and provides a benchmark for motivating employees and evaluating actual performance.

**EXHIBIT 9-2** Benefits of Budgeting

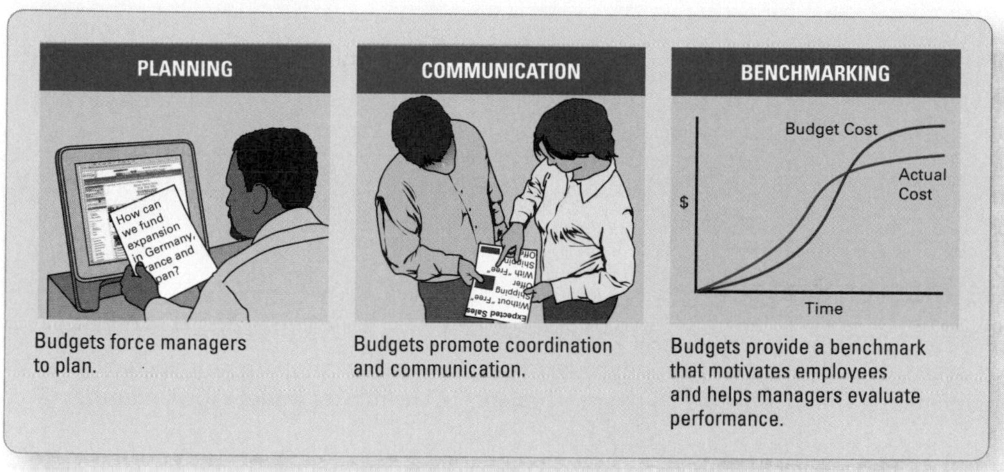


### Planning

Business managers are extremely busy directing the day-to-day operations of the company. The budgeting process forces managers to spend time planning for the future, rather than concerning themselves only with daily operations. The sooner companies develop a plan and have time to act on the plan, the more likely they will achieve their goals.

### Coordination and Communication

The budget coordinates a company's activities. It forces managers to consider relations among operations across the entire value chain. For example, SolGate's decision to expand its product line will first affect the research and development function. However, once new products are developed, the design and production teams will need to focus on how and where the products will be mass produced. The marketing team will need to develop attractive labelling and create a successful advertising campaign. The distribution team may need to alter its current distribution system to accommodate the new products. And customer service will need to be ready to handle any complaints or warranty issues. All areas of the value chain are ultimately affected by management's plans. The budget process helps to communicate the plan and coordinate its effects.

### Benchmarking

Budgets provide a benchmark that motivates employees and helps managers evaluate performance. The budget provides a target that most managers will try to achieve, especially if they participated in the budgeting process and the budget has been set at a realistic level. Budgets should be achievable with effort. Budgets that are too tight (too hard to achieve) or too loose (too easy to achieve) do not provide managers with much motivation.

Think about exams for a moment. Some professors have a reputation for giving "impossible" exams, while others may be known for giving "easy" exams. In either of these cases, students are rarely motivated to put much effort into learning the material because they feel they won't be rewarded for their additional efforts. However, if students feel that a professor's exam can be achieved with effort, they will be more likely to devote themselves to learning the material. In other words, the perceived fairness of the exam affects how well the exam motivates students to study. Likewise, if a budget is perceived to be fair, employees are likely to be motivated by it.

Budgets also provide a benchmark for evaluating performance. At the end of the period, companies use performance reports, such as the one pictured in Exhibit 9-3, to compare actual revenues and expenses against budgeted revenues and expenses. The **variance**, or difference between actual and budgeted figures, is used to evaluate how well the manager controlled operations and to determine whether the plan needs to be revised. The second half of this chapter delves more deeply into this aspect of budgeting.

**EXHIBIT 9-3** Summary Performance Report

| | Actual | Budget | Variance (Actual – Budget) |
|---|---|---|---|
| Sales revenue | $550 | $600 | $(50) |
| Less: Total expenses | 90 | 68 | (22) |
| Net income | $460 | $532 | $(72) |

## The Master Budget

The **master budget** is the comprehensive planning document for the entire organization. It consists of all of the supporting budgets needed to create the company's budgeted financial statements. Exhibit 9-4 shows all the components of the master budget for a manufacturer

**EXHIBIT 9-4** Master Budget for a Manufacturing Company

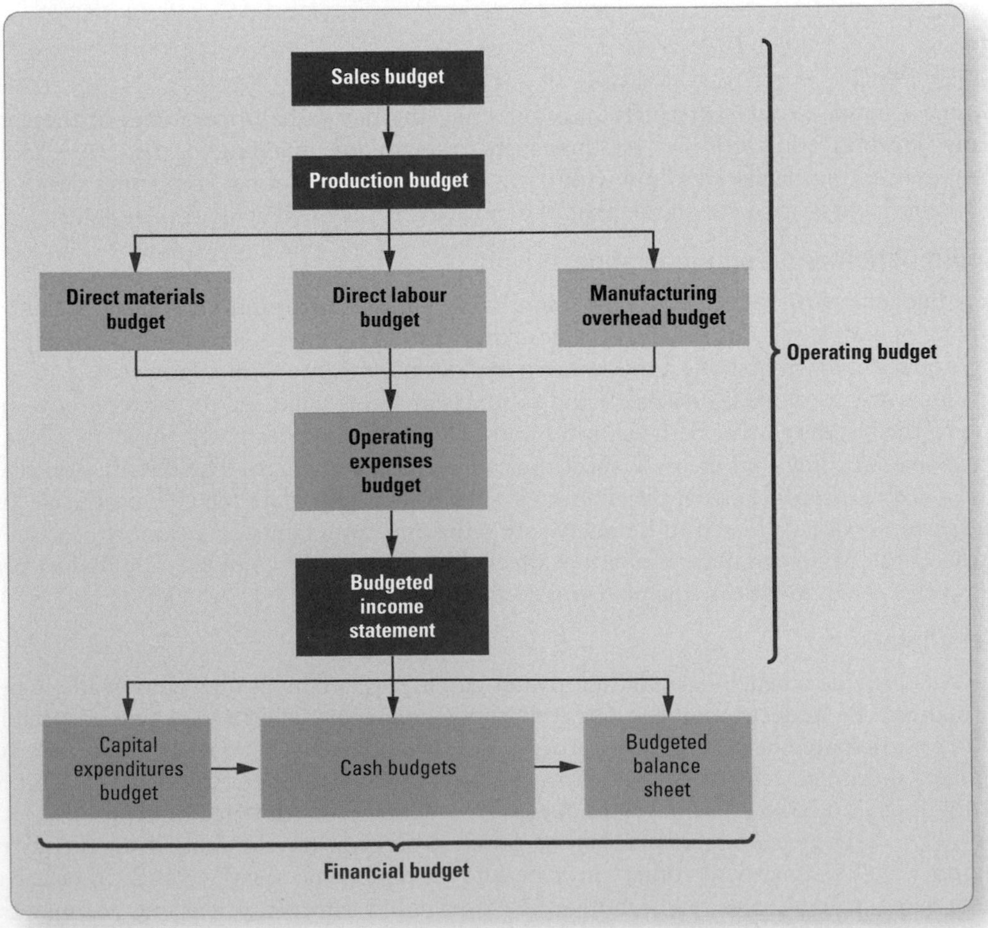

and the order in which they are usually prepared. The master budgets of service and merchandising firms are less complex, and are described in Appendix 9A.

The **operating budgets** are the budgets needed to run the daily operations of the company. The operating budgets culminate in a budgeted income statement. As Exhibit 9-4 shows, the starting point of the operating budgets is the sales budget, because it affects most other components of the master budget. After estimating sales, manufacturers prepare the production budget, which determines how many units need to be produced. Once production volume is established, managers prepare the budgets that determine the amounts of direct materials, direct labour, and manufacturing overhead that will be needed to meet production. Next, managers prepare the operating expenses budget. After all of these budgets are prepared, management will be able to prepare the budgeted income statement.

As you'll see throughout the chapter, cost behaviour is important in forming most of the operating budgets. Total fixed costs do not change as volume changes within the relevant range. However, total variable costs change in direct proportion to changes in volume.

The **financial budgets** project the collection and payment of cash, as well as forecast the company's budgeted balance sheet. The capital expenditure budget shows the company's plan for purchasing property, plant, and equipment. The cash budget projects the cash that will be available to run the company's operations and determines whether the company will have extra funds to invest or will need to borrow cash. Finally, the budgeted balance sheet forecasts the company's position at the end of the budget period.

# How Are the Operating Budgets Prepared?

2 Prepare the operating budgets.

We will follow the budget process for Tasty Tortilla, a fairly small, independently owned manufacturer of tortilla chips just outside Cornwall, Ontario. The company sells its product, by the case, to restaurants, grocery stores, and convenience stores. To keep our example simple, we will show just the budgets for the first 3 months of the fiscal year, rather than all 12 months. Since many companies prepare quarterly budgets (budgets that cover a three-month period), we'll also show the quarterly figures on each budget. For every budget, we'll walk through the calculations for the month of January. Then we'll show how the same pattern is used to create budgets for the months of February and March.

## Sales Budget

The sales budget is the starting place for budgeting. Managers multiply the expected number of unit sales by the expected sales price per unit to arrive at the expected total sales revenue.

For example, Tasty Tortilla expects to sell 30,000 cases of tortilla chips in January, at a sales price of $20 per case, so the estimated sales revenue for January is as follows:

30,000 cases × $20 per case = $600,000

The sales budget for the first three months of the year is shown in Exhibit 9-5. As you can see, the monthly sales volume is expected to fluctuate. January sales are expected to be higher than February sales due to the extraordinary number of chips purchased for Super Bowl parties. Also, since more tortilla chips are sold when the weather warms up, the company expects sales to begin their seasonal upward climb beginning in March.

As shown in the lower portion of Exhibit 9-5, managers may also indicate the type of sale they can expect. Tasty Tortilla expects 20% of its sales to be cash (COD) sales.

**EXHIBIT 9-5** Sales Budget

| Tasty Tortilla<br>Sales Budget<br>For the Quarter Ended March 31 | | | | |
|---|---|---|---|---|
| | Month | | | |
| | January | February | March | 1st Quarter |
| Unit sales (cases) | 30,000 | 20,000 | 25,000 | 75,000 |
| Unit selling price | × $ 20 | × $ 20 | × $ 20 | × $ 20 |
| Total sales revenue | $600,000 | $400,000 | $500,000 | $1,500,000 |
| | | | | |
| Type of Sale: | | | | |
| Cash sales (20%) | $120,000 | $ 80,000 | $100,000 | $ 300,000 |
| Credit sales (80%) | 480,000 | 320,000 | 400,000 | 1,200,000 |
| Total sales revenue | $600,000 | $400,000 | $500,000 | $1,500,000 |

**Why is this important?**

The **sales budget** is the **basis** for every other budget. If sales are not projected as **accurately** as possible, all other budgets will be **off target**.

Companies often use COD ("collect on delivery"[1]) collection terms if the customer is new, has a poor credit rating, or has not paid on time in the past. Tasty Tortilla will still sell to these customers, but will demand payment immediately when the inventory is delivered.

The managers expect the remaining 80% of sales will be made on credit. Tasty Tortilla's credit terms are "net 30," meaning the customer has up to 30 days to pay for its purchases. Having this information available on the sales budget will help managers prepare the cash collections budget later.

## Production Budget

Once managers have estimated how many units they expect to sell, they can figure out how many units they need to produce. Most manufacturers maintain some ending finished goods inventory, or <u>safety stock</u>, which is inventory kept on hand in case demand is higher than predicted or problems in the factory slow production (such as machine breakdown, employees off sick, and so forth). As a result, managers need to factor in the desired level of ending inventory when deciding how much inventory to produce. They do so as follows:

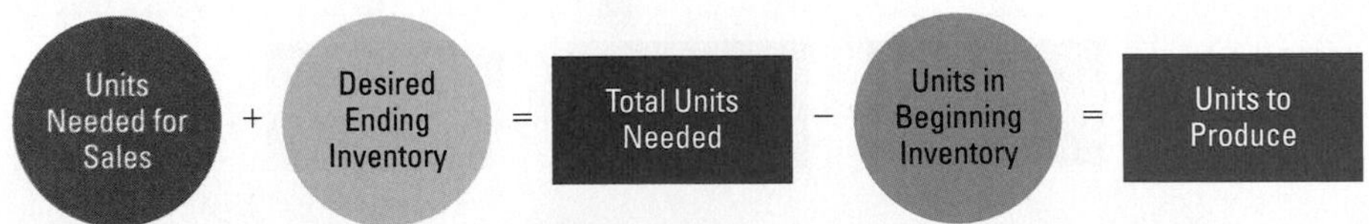


Let's walk through this calculation step by step.

**STEP 1. Managers figure out how many total units they need.**

To do this, they add the number of units they plan to sell to the number of units they want on hand at the end of the month. Let's assume Tasty Tortilla wants to maintain an ending inventory equal to 10% of the next month's expected sales (20,000 cases in February). Thus, the total number of cases needed in January is as follows:

30,000 cases for January sales + (10% × 20,000) = 32,000 total cases needed

[1]In the past, COD meant "cash on delivery." However, as other forms of payment (such as cheques, credit cards, and debit cards) have become more common, the word "cash" has been replaced with the word "collect" to incorporate these additional types of payments.

**STEP 2. Managers calculate the amount of inventory they expect to have on hand at the beginning of the month.**

Since Tasty Tortilla desires ending inventory to be 10% of the next month's sales, managers expect to have 10% of January's sales on hand on December 31, which becomes the beginning balance on January 1:

10% × 30,000 cases = 3,000 cases in beginning inventory on January 1

**STEP 3. Managers calculate how many units to produce.**

By subtracting what the company already has in stock at the beginning of the month from the total units needed, the company is able to calculate how many units to produce:

32,000 cases needed − 3,000 cases in beginning inventory = 29,000 cases to produce

Exhibit 9-6 shows Tasty Tortilla's production budget for the first three months of the year. As the red arrows show, the ending inventory from one month (January 31) always becomes the beginning inventory for the next month (February 1).

**EXHIBIT 9-6** Production Budget

Tasty Tortilla
Production Budget
For the Quarter Ended March 31

| | Month | | | |
|---|---|---|---|---|
| | January | February | March | 1st Quarter |
| Unit sales (from Sales Budget) | 30,000 | 20,000 | 25,000 | 75,000 |
| Plus: Desired end inventory | 2,000 | 2,500 | 3,200* | 3,200** |
| Total needed | 32,000 | 22,500 | 28,200 | 78,200 |
| Less: Beginning inventory | (3,000) | (2,000) | (2,500) | (3,000)** |
| Units to produce | 29,000 | 20,500 | 25,700 | 75,200 |

*April sales are projected to be 32,000 units.

**Since the quarter begins January 1 and ends March 31, the beginning inventory for the quarter is the balance on January 1 and the ending inventory for the quarter is the balance on March 31.

Now that the company knows how many units it plans to produce every month, it can figure out the amount of direct materials, direct labour, and manufacturing overhead that will be needed. As shown in the following sections, the company will create separate budgets for each of these three manufacturing costs. Each budget will be driven by the number of units to be produced each month.

## TRY IT!

Assume Tucson Tortilla's sales budget shows projected sales of 32,000 cases in April and 40,000 cases in May. The company's manager would like to maintain ending safety stock equal to 10% of the next month's projected sales. How many units should be produced in April?

Please see page 591 for solutions.

## Direct Materials Budget

The format of the direct materials budget (DM) is quite similar to the production budget:

Let's walk through the process using January as an example.

**STEP 1. Management figures out the quantity of direct materials needed for production.**

Let's assume Tasty Tortilla's only direct material is masa harina, the special corn flour used to make tortilla chips. Each case of tortilla chips requires 5 kg of this corn flour. Therefore, the quantity of direct materials needed for January production is as follows:

$$29{,}000 \text{ cases to be produced} \times 5 \text{ kg per case} = 145{,}000 \text{ kg}$$

**STEP 2. The managers add in the desired ending inventory of direct materials.**

Some amount of direct materials safety stock is usually needed in case suppliers do not deliver all of the direct materials needed on time. Let's assume that Tasty Tortilla wants to maintain an ending inventory of direct materials equal to 10% of the materials needed for next month's production (102,500 required in February, as shown in Exhibit 9-7):

$$145{,}000 \text{ kg} + (10\% \times 102{,}500) = 155{,}250 \text{ total kg needed}$$

**STEP 3. Managers determine the direct material inventory they expect to have on hand at the beginning of the month.**

Tasty Tortilla expects to have 10% of the materials needed for January's production in stock on December 31, which becomes the opening balance on January 1:

$$10\% \times 145{,}000 \text{ kg} = 14{,}500 \text{ kg in beginning inventory}$$

**STEP 4. Subtract what the company already has in stock at the beginning of the month from the total quantity needed.**

This way, the managers calculate the quantity of direct materials they need to purchase:

$$155{,}250 \text{ kg needed} - 14{,}500 \text{ kg in beginning inventory} = 140{,}750 \text{ kg to buy}$$

**STEP 5. Finally, management calculates the expected cost of purchasing those direct materials.**

Let's say Tasty Tortilla can buy the masa harina corn flour in bulk for $1.50 per kilogram:

$$140{,}750 \text{ kg} \times \$1.50 = \$211{,}125$$

Exhibit 9-7 shows Tasty Tortilla's direct materials budget for the first three months of the year.

**EXHIBIT 9-7** Direct Materials Budget

Tasty Tortilla
Direct Materials Budget for Masa Harina Corn Flour
For the Quarter Ended March 31

| | Month | | | |
|---|---|---|---|---|
| | January | February | March | 1st Quarter |
| Unit to be produced (from Production Budget) | 29,000 | 20,500 | 25,700 | 75,200 |
| × Quantity (kg) of DM needed per unit | × 5 kg | × 5 kg | × 5 kg | × 5 kg |
| Quantity (kg) needed for production | 145,000 | 102,500 | 128,500 | 376,000 |
| Plus: Desired end inventory of DM | 10,250 | 12,850 | 16,150* | 16,150** |
| Total quantity (kg) needed | 155,250 | 115,350 | 144,650 | 392,150 |
| Less: Beginning inventory of DM | (14,500) | (10,250) | (12,850) | (14,500)** |
| Quantity (kg) to purchase | 140,750 | 105,100 | 131,800 | 377,650 |
| × Cost per kg | × $1.50 | × $1.50 | × $1.50 | × $1.50 |
| Total cost of DM purchases | $211,125 | $157,650 | $197,700 | $566,475 |

(Arrows: ×10% of next month's quantity needed for production → desired end inventory; end inventory → next month's beginning inventory.)

*161,500 kg are needed for production in April.
**Since the quarter begins January 1 and ends March 31, the beginning inventory for the quarter is the balance on January 1 and the ending inventory for the quarter is the balance on March 31.

## Direct Labour Budget

The direct labour (DL) budget is determined as follows:

Tasty Tortilla's factory is fairly automated, so very little direct labour is required. Let's assume that each case requires only 0.05 of an hour. Direct labourers are paid $22 per hour. Thus, the direct labour cost for January is projected to be as follows:

29,000 cases × 0.05 hours per case = 1,450 hours required × $22 per hour = $31,900

The direct labour budget for the first three months of the year is shown in Exhibit 9-8:

**EXHIBIT 9-8** Direct Labour Budget

Tasty Tortilla
Direct Labour Budget
For the Quarter Ended March 31

| | Month | | | |
|---|---|---|---|---|
| | January | February | March | 1st Quarter |
| Units to be produced (from Production Budget) | 29,000 | 20,500 | 25,700 | 75,200 |
| × Direct labour hours per unit | × 0.05 | × 0.05 | × 0.05 | × 0.05 |
| Total hours required | 1,450 | 1,025 | 1,285 | 3,760 |
| × Direct labour cost per hour | × $ 22 | × $ 22 | × $ 22 | × $ 22 |
| Total Direct labour cost | $31,900 | $22,550 | $28,270 | $82,720 |

## Manufacturing Overhead Budget

The manufacturing overhead (MOH) budget is highly dependent on cost behaviour. Some overhead costs, such as indirect materials, are variable. For example, Tasty Tortilla considers the oil used for frying the tortilla chips to be an indirect material. Since a portion of the oil is absorbed into the chips, the amount of oil required increases as production volume increases. Thus, the cost is variable. The company also considers salt and cellophane packaging to be variable indirect materials. Tasty Tortilla expects to spend $1.25 on indirect materials for each case of tortilla chips produced, so January's budget for indirect materials is as follows:

29,000 cases × $1.25 = $36,250 of indirect materials

Costs such as utilities and indirect labour are mixed costs. Mixed costs are usually separated into their variable and fixed components using one of the cost behaviour estimation methods discussed in Chapter 3. Based on engineering and cost studies, Tasty Tortilla has determined that each case of chips requires $0.75 of variable indirect labour and $0.50 of variable utility costs as a result of running the production machinery. These variable costs are budgeted as follows for January:

29,000 cases × $0.75 = $21,750 of variable indirect labour
29,000 cases × $0.50 = $14,500 of variable factory utilities

Finally, many manufacturing overhead costs are fixed. Tasty Tortilla's fixed costs include depreciation, insurance, and property taxes on the factory. The company also incurs some fixed indirect labour (salaried production engineers who oversee the daily manufacturing operation) and a fixed amount of utilities just to keep the lights, heat, or air conditioning on in the plant regardless of the production volume.

Exhibit 9-9 shows that the manufacturing overhead budget usually has separate sections for variable and fixed overhead costs so that managers can easily see which costs will change as production volume changes.

**EXHIBIT 9-9** Manufacturing Overhead Budget

Tasty Tortilla
Manufacturing Overhead Budget
For the Quarter Ended March 31

| | Month | | | |
|---|---|---|---|---|
| | January | February | March | 1st Quarter |
| Units to be Produced (from Production Budget) | 29,000 | 20,500 | 25,700 | 75,200 |
| Variable Costs: | | | | |
| Indirect materials ($1.25 per case) | $ 36,250 | $25,625 | $32,125 | $ 94,000 |
| Indirect labour—variable portion ($0.75 per case) | 21,750 | 15,375 | 19,275 | 56,400 |
| Utilities—variable portion ($0.50 per case) | 14,500 | 10,250 | 12,850 | 37,600 |
| Total variable MOH | $ 72,500 | $51,250 | $64,250 | $188,000 |
| Fixed MOH Costs: | | | | |
| Depreciation on factory and production equipment | $ 10,000 | $10,000 | $10,000 | $ 30,000 |
| Insurance and property taxes on the factory | 3,000 | 3,000 | 3,000 | 9,000 |
| Indirect labour—fixed portion | 15,000 | 15,000 | 15,000 | 45,000 |
| Utilities—fixed portion | 2,000 | 2,000 | 2,000 | 6,000 |
| Total fixed MOH | $ 30,000 | $30,000 | $30,000 | $ 90,000 |
| Total manufacturing overhead | $102,500 | $81,250 | $94,250 | $278,000 |

Now that we have completed budgets for each of the three manufacturing costs (direct materials, direct labour, and manufacturing overhead), we turn our attention to operating expenses.

## Operating Expenses Budget

Recall that all costs incurred in every area of the value chain, except production, must be expensed as operating expenses in the period incurred. Thus all research and development, design, marketing, distribution, and customer service costs will be shown on the operating expenses budget.

Some operating expenses are variable, based on how many units are sold (not produced). For example, to motivate its sales force to generate sales, Tasty Tortilla pays its sales representatives a \$1.50 sales commission for every case they sell.

30,000 sales units × \$1.50 = \$45,000 sales commission expense in January

The company also incurs \$2.00 of shipping costs on every case sold.

30,000 sales units × \$2.00 = \$60,000 shipping expense in January

Finally, the company knows that not all of the sales made on credit will eventually be collected. Based on experience, Tasty Tortilla expects monthly bad debt expense to be 1% of its credit sales. Since January credit sales are expected to be \$480,000 (from Sales Budget, Exhibit 9-5), the company's bad debt expense for January is as follows:

\$480,000 of credit sales in January × 1% = \$4,800 bad debt expense for January

Other operating expenses are fixed: They will stay the same each month even though sales volume fluctuates. For example, Tasty Tortilla's fixed expenses include salaries, office rent, depreciation on office equipment and the company's vehicles, advertising, telephone, and internet service.

As shown in Exhibit 9-10, operating expenses are usually shown according to their cost behaviour.

**EXHIBIT 9-10** Operating Expenses Budget

Tasty Tortilla
Operating Expenses Budget
For the Quarter Ended March 31

| | Month | | | |
|---|---|---|---|---|
| | January | February | March | 1st Quarter |
| Sales units (from Sales Budget) | 30,000 | 20,000 | 25,000 | 75,000 |
| Variable Operating Expenses: | | | | |
| Sales commissions expense (\$1.50 per case sold) | \$ 45,000 | \$ 30,000 | \$ 37,500 | \$112,500 |
| Shipping expense (\$2.00 per case sold) | 60,000 | 40,000 | 50,000 | 150,000 |
| Bad debt expense (1% of credit sales) | 4,800 | 3,200 | 4,000 | 12,000 |
| Variable operating expenses | \$109,800 | \$ 73,200 | \$ 91,500 | \$274,500 |
| Fixed Operating Expenses: | | | | |
| Salaries | \$ 20,000 | \$ 20,000 | \$ 20,000 | \$ 60,000 |
| Office rent | 4,000 | 4,000 | 4,000 | 12,000 |
| Depreciation | 6,000 | 6,000 | 6,000 | 18,000 |
| Advertising | 2,000 | 2,000 | 2,000 | 6,000 |
| Telephone and internet | 1,000 | 1,000 | 1,000 | 3,000 |
| Fixed operating expenses | \$ 33,000 | \$ 33,000 | \$ 33,000 | \$ 99,000 |
| Total operating expenses | \$142,800 | \$106,200 | \$124,500 | \$373,500 |

## Budgeted Income Statement

A budgeted income statement looks just like a regular income statement, except for the fact that it uses budgeted data. Recall the general format for an income statement:

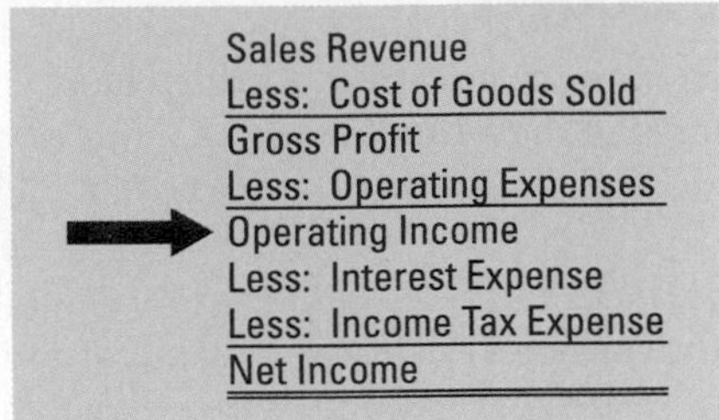


**Why is this important?**
The **budgeted income statement** helps managers know in advance whether their plans will result in an **acceptable** level of **income**. If not, **management** will need to consider how it can cut expenses or increase **sales revenues**.

This textbook has focused on a company's operating income, rather than net income. However, a complete income statement would include any interest expense (and/or interest income) as well as a provision for income taxes. These additional costs are subtracted from operating income to arrive at net income.

We have already computed the budgeted sales revenue and operating expenses on separate budgets. But we still need to calculate the cost of goods sold before we can prepare the income statement.

Tasty Tortilla computes its cost of goods sold as follows:

This will be relatively simple for Tasty Tortilla since the company produces only one product.

The cost of manufacturing each case of tortilla chips is shown in Exhibit 9-11. Almost all of the information presented has already been used to prepare the budgets for direct materials, direct labour, and manufacturing overhead. The only new piece of information is the total production volume for the year, budgeted to be 400,000 cases.

**EXHIBIT 9-11** Budgeted Manufacturing Cost per Unit

| Tasty Tortilla<br>Budgeted Manufacturing Cost per Unit | |
|---|---|
| Direct materials (5 kilograms of corn flour per case × \$1.50 per kilogram) | \$ 7.50 |
| Direct labour (0.05 hours per case × \$22 per hour) | 1.10 |
| Manufacturing overhead: | |
| Variable—indirect materials (\$1.25 per case), variable indirect labour | |
| (\$0.75 per case), and variable utilities (\$0.50 per case) | 2.50 |
| Fixed—\$30,000 per month × 12 months = \$360,000 for the year | |
| So, the fixed cost per unit is \$360,000 ÷ 400,000* cases | .90 |
| Cost of manufacturing each case | \$12.00 |

*Recall that companies base their predetermined MOH rate on the total estimated cost and volume for the *entire year*, rather than on monthly costs and volumes that will fluctuate.

Exhibit 9-12 shows the company's budgeted income statement for January. Interest expense is budgeted to be zero since the company has no outstanding debt. The income tax expense is budgeted to be 35% of income before taxes. The company will prepare budgeted income statements for each month and quarter, as well as for the entire year.

**EXHIBIT 9-12** Budgeted Income Statement

| Tasty Tortilla<br>Budgeted Income Statement<br>For the month ended January 31 | |
|---|---|
| Sales (30,000 cases × $20 per case, from Exhibit 9-5) | $ 600,000 |
| Less: Cost of goods sold (30,000 cases × $12.00 per case, from Exhibit 9-11) | (360,000) |
| Gross profit | 240,000 |
| Less: Operating expenses (from Exhibit 9-10) | (142,800) |
| Operating income | $ 97,200 |
| Less: Interest expense (or add interest income) | 0 |
| Less: Income tax expense* | (34,020) |
| Net income | $ 63,180 |

*The corporate income tax rate for most companies is currently 35% of income before tax ($97,200 × 35% = $34,020).

We have now completed the operating budgets for Tasty Tortilla. In the second half of the chapter we'll prepare Tasty Tortilla's financial budgets.

# DECISION GUIDELINES

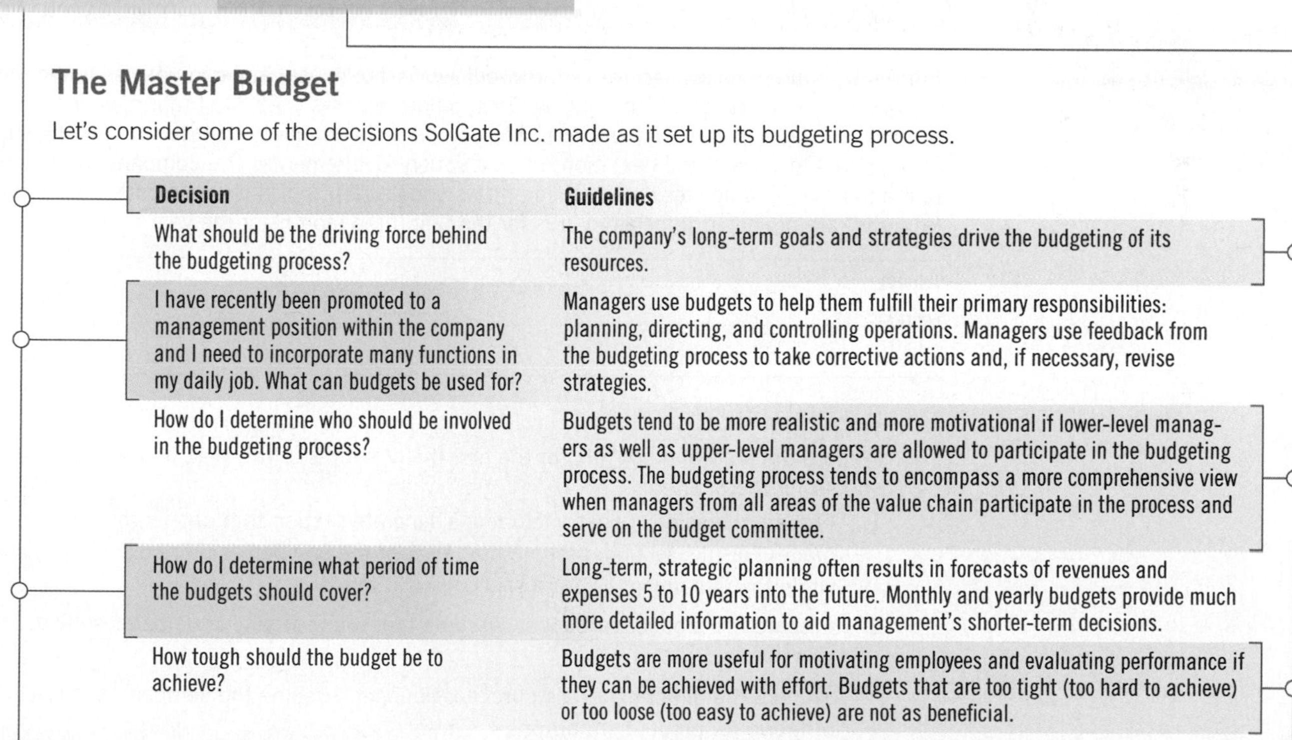

## The Master Budget

Let's consider some of the decisions SolGate Inc. made as it set up its budgeting process.

| Decision | Guidelines |
|---|---|
| What should be the driving force behind the budgeting process? | The company's long-term goals and strategies drive the budgeting of its resources. |
| I have recently been promoted to a management position within the company and I need to incorporate many functions in my daily job. What can budgets be used for? | Managers use budgets to help them fulfill their primary responsibilities: planning, directing, and controlling operations. Managers use feedback from the budgeting process to take corrective actions and, if necessary, revise strategies. |
| How do I determine who should be involved in the budgeting process? | Budgets tend to be more realistic and more motivational if lower-level managers as well as upper-level managers are allowed to participate in the budgeting process. The budgeting process tends to encompass a more comprehensive view when managers from all areas of the value chain participate in the process and serve on the budget committee. |
| How do I determine what period of time the budgets should cover? | Long-term, strategic planning often results in forecasts of revenues and expenses 5 to 10 years into the future. Monthly and yearly budgets provide much more detailed information to aid management's shorter-term decisions. |
| How tough should the budget be to achieve? | Budgets are more useful for motivating employees and evaluating performance if they can be achieved with effort. Budgets that are too tight (too hard to achieve) or too loose (too easy to achieve) are not as beneficial. |

| Decision | Guidelines |
|---|---|
| There is resistance to the budgeting process from some of the managers because of the time involved in preparing all of the budgets. What benefits can I highlight to describe what a company should expect to obtain from developing a budget? | Benefits of budgeting include the following:<br>• Planning<br>• Coordination and communication<br>• Benchmarking (used for both motivation and performance evaluation) |
| What budgets should be included in the master budget? | The *operating budgets* include all budgets necessary to create a budgeted income statement. For a manufacturer, this includes the following:<br>• Sales budget<br>• Production budget<br>• Direct materials budget<br>• Direct labour budget<br>• Manufacturing overhead budget<br>• Operating expenses budget<br>• Budgeted income statement<br>The operating budgets for merchandising and service companies are less complex (see Appendix 9A).<br>The *financial budgets* include the capital expenditures budget, the cash budgets, and the budgeted balance sheet. |

## SUMMARY PROBLEM 1

Pillows Unlimited makes decorative throw pillows for home use. The company sells the pillows to home décor retailers for $14 per pillow. Each pillow requires 1.25 m of fabric, which the company obtains at a cost of $6 per metre. The company would like to maintain an ending stock of fabric equal to 10% of the next month's production requirements. The company would also like to maintain an ending stock of finished pillows equal to 20% of the next month's sales. Sales (in units) are projected to be as follows for the first three months of the year:

| | |
|---|---|
| January | 100,000 |
| February | 110,000 |
| March | 115,000 |

### Requirements

Prepare the following budgets for the first three months of the year, as well as a summary budget for the quarter:

1. Prepare the sales budget, including a separate section that details the types of sales made. For this section, assume that 10% of the company's pillows are cash sales, while the remaining 90% are sold on credit terms.
2. Prepare the production budget. Assume that the company anticipates selling 120,000 units in April.
3. Prepare the direct materials purchases budget. Assume the company needs 150,000 m of fabric for production in April.

# ▪ SOLUTIONS

## Requirement 1

Pillows Unlimited
Sales Budget
For the Quarter ended March 31

| | Month | | | |
|---|---|---|---|---|
| | January | February | March | 1st Quarter |
| Unit sales | 100,000 | 110,000 | 115,000 | 325,000 |
| Unit selling price | × $ 14 | × $ 14 | × $ 14 | × $ 14 |
| Total sales revenue | $1,400,000 | $1,540,000 | $1,610,000 | $4,550,000 |
| | | | | |
| Type of Sale: | | | | |
| Cash sales (10%) | $ 140,000 | $ 154,000 | $ 161,000 | $ 455,000 |
| Credit sales (90%) | 1,260,000 | 1,386,000 | 1,449,000 | 4,095,000 |
| Total sales revenue | $1,400,000 | $1,540,000 | $1,610,000 | $4,550,000 |

## Requirement 2

Pillows Unlimited
Production Budget
For the Quarter ended March 31

| | Month | | | |
|---|---|---|---|---|
| | January | February | March | 1st Quarter |
| Unit sales | 100,000 | 110,000 | 115,000 | 325,000 |
| Plus: Desired end inventory (20% of next month's unit sales) | 22,000 | 23,000 | 24,000 | 24,000 |
| Total needed | 122,000 | 133,000 | 139,000 | 349,000 |
| Less: Beginning inventory | (20,000)* | (22,000) | (23,000) | (20,000) |
| Units to produce | 102,000 | 111,000 | 116,000 | 329,000 |

*January 1 balance (equal to December 31 balance) is 20% of the projected unit sales in January (100,000).

**Requirement 3**

Pillows Unlimited
Direct Materials Budget
For the Quarter ended March 31

| | Month | | | |
|---|---|---|---|---|
| | January | February | March | 1st Quarter |
| Units to be produced (from Production Budget) | 102,000 | 111,000 | 116,000 | 329,000 |
| × Quantity (metres) of DM needed per unit | × 1.25 | × 1.25 | × 1.25 | × 1.25 |
| Quantity (metres) needed for production | 127,500 | 138,750 | 145,000 | 411,250 |
| Plus: Desired end inventory of DM (10% of the amount needed for next month's production) | 13,875 | 14,500 | 15,000 | 15,000 |
| Total quantity (metres) needed | 141,375 | 153,250 | 160,000 | 426,250 |
| Less: Beginning inventory of DM | (12,750)* | (13,875) | (14,500) | (12,750) |
| Quantity (metres) to purchase | 128,625 | 139,375 | 145,500 | 413,500 |
| × Cost per metre | × $ 6.00 | × $ 6.00 | × $ 6.00 | × $ 6.00 |
| Total cost of DM purchases | $771,750 | $836,250 | $873,000 | $2,481,000 |

*January 1 balance (equal to December 31 balance) is 10% of the quantity needed for January's production (127,500).

# How Are Financial Budgets Prepared?

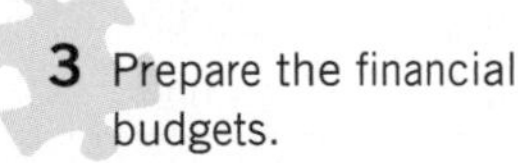
3 Prepare the financial budgets.

In the first half of the chapter, we prepared Tasty Tortilla's operating budgets, culminating with the company's budgeted income statement. In this part of the chapter we turn our attention to Tasty Tortilla's financial budgets. Managers typically prepare a capital expenditures budget as well as three separate cash budgets:

1. Cash collections (or receipts) budget
2. Cash payments (or disbursements) budget
3. Combined cash budget, complete with financing arrangements

Finally, managers prepare the budgeted balance sheet. Each of these budgets is illustrated next.

## Capital Expenditure Budget

The capital expenditure budget shows the company's intentions to invest in new property, plant, or equipment (capital investments). When planned capital investments are significant, this budget must be developed early in the process because the additional investments may affect depreciation expense, interest expense (if funds are borrowed to pay for the investments), or dividend payments (if stock is issued to pay for the investments). Chapter 12 contains a detailed discussion of the capital budgeting process, including the techniques managers use in deciding whether to make additional investments.

Exhibit 9-13 shows Tasty Tortilla's capital expenditure budget for the first three months of the year. *Tasty Tortilla expects to purchase a new piece of production equipment in January. The equipment will cost $125,000. No other capital investments are planned in the first quarter of the year.*

**EXHIBIT 9-13** Capital Expenditure Budget

| Tasty Tortilla<br>Capital Expenditure Budget<br>For the Quarter Ended March 31 | | | | |
|---|---|---|---|---|
| | Month | | | |
| | January | February | March | 1st Quarter |
| New investments in property, plant, and equipment | $125,000 | 0 | 0 | $125,000 |

## Cash Collections Budget

The cash collections budget is all about timing: *When* does Tasty Tortilla expect to receive cash from its sales? Of course, Tasty Tortilla will receive cash immediately on its COD sales. From the sales budget (Exhibit 9-5), we see that the company expects the following cash sales in January:

Cash (COD) sales = $120,000

However, most of the company's sales are made on credit. Recall that Tasty Tortilla's credit terms are net 30 days, meaning customers have 30 days to pay. Therefore, most customers will wait nearly 30 days (a full month) before paying. However, some companies may be experiencing cash flow difficulties and may not be able to pay Tasty Tortilla on time. Because of this, Tasty Tortilla doesn't expect to receive payment on all of its credit sales the month after the sale.

Based on collection history, Tasty Tortilla expects 85% of its credit sales to be collected in the month after the sale, and 14% to be collected two months after the sale. Tasty Tortilla expects that 1% of credit sales will never be collected, and therefore has recognized a 1% bad debt expense in its operating expenses budget. Furthermore, assume that December credit sales were $500,000 and November credit sales were $480,000.

Anticipated January Collections of Credit Sales:

85% × $500,000 (December credit sales) = $425,000

14% × $480,000 (November credit sales) = $ 67,200

Exhibit 9-14 shows Tasty Tortilla's expected cash collections for the first three months of the year:

**EXHIBIT 9-14** Cash Collection Budget

| Tasty Tortilla<br>Cash Collections Budget<br>For the Quarter Ended March 31 | | | | |
|---|---|---|---|---|
| | Month | | | |
| | January | February | March | 1st Quarter |
| Cash sales (from Sales Budget) | $120,000 | $ 80,000 | $100,000 | $ 300,000 |
| Collections on Credit Sales: | | | | |
| 85% of credit sales made last month | 425,000 | 408,000[A] | 272,000[C] | 1,105,000 |
| 14% of credit sales made two months ago | 67,200 | 70,000[B] | 67,200[D] | 204,400 |
| Total cash collections | $612,200 | $558,000 | $439,200 | $1,609,400 |

[A]85% × $480,000 (January credit sales, Exhibit 9-5) = $408,000
[B]14% × $500,000 (December credit sales) = $70,000
[C]85% × $320,000 (February credit sales, Exhibit 9-5) = $272,000
[D]14% × $480,000 (January credit sales, Exhibit 9-5) = $67,200

## TRY IT!

Assume Georgio's has the following budgeted sales for the quarter:

| | January | February | March |
|---|---|---|---|
| COD sales | $ 10,000 | $ 20,000 | $ 15,000 |
| Credit sales | 100,000 | 110,000 | 120,000 |
| Total Sales | $110,000 | $130,000 | $135,000 |

Determine Georgio's budget for March cash collections assuming credit sales are collected as follows: 90% is collected the month after sale, 8% is collected two months after the month of sale, and 2% is never collected.

Please see page 591 for solutions.

## Cash Payments Budget

The cash payments budget is also about timing: *When* will Tasty Tortilla pay for its direct materials purchases, direct labour costs, manufacturing overhead costs, operating expenses, capital expenditures, and income taxes? Let's tackle each cost, one at a time.

**DIRECT MATERIALS PURCHASES** Tasty Tortilla has been given "net 30 days" payment terms from its suppliers of the corn flour used to make the tortilla chips. Therefore, Tasty Tortilla waits a month before it pays for the direct material purchases shown in the direct materials budget (Exhibit 9-7). So the company will pay for its December purchases (projected to be $231,845) in January, its January purchases of $211,125 (Exhibit 9-7) in February, its February purchases of $157,650 (Exhibit 9-7) in March, and so forth:

| | January | February | March | 1st Quarter |
|---|---|---|---|---|
| Cash payments for DM purchases | $231,845 | $211,125 | $157,650 | $600,620 |

**DIRECT LABOUR** Tasty Tortilla's factory employees are paid twice a month for the work they perform during the month. Therefore, January's direct labour cost of $31,900 (Exhibit 9-8) will be paid in January, and likewise for each month.

| | January | February | March | 1st Quarter |
|---|---|---|---|---|
| Cash payments for direct labour | $31,900 | $22,550 | $28,270 | $82,720 |

**MANUFACTURING OVERHEAD** Tasty Tortilla must consider when it pays for its manufacturing overhead costs. Let's assume that the company pays for all manufacturing overhead costs (other than depreciation), insurance, and property taxes in the month in which they are incurred. Depreciation is a noncash expense, so it never appears on the cash disbursements budget. Insurance and property taxes are typically prepaid on a semiannual basis. While Tasty Tortilla budgets a cost of $3,000 per month for factory insurance and property tax, it doesn't actually pay these costs on a monthly basis. Rather, Tasty Tortilla prepays its insurance and property tax twice a year, in January and July. The amount of these semiannual payments is calculated as shown:

$3,000 monthly cost × 12 months = $36,000 ÷ 2 = $18,000 payments in January and July

So, the cash payments for manufacturing overhead costs are expected to be as follows:

| | January | February | March | 1st Quarter |
|---|---|---|---|---|
| Total manufacturing overhead (from Exhibit 9-9) | $102,500 | $ 81,250 | $ 94,250 | $278,000 |
| Less: Depreciation (not a cash expense) | (10,000) | (10,000) | (10,000) | (30,000) |
| Less: Property tax and insurance (paid twice a year, not monthly) | (3,000) | (3,000) | (3,000) | (9,000) |
| Plus: Semiannual payments for property taxes and insurance | 18,000 | 0 | 0 | 18,000 |
| Cash payments for MOH costs | $107,500 | $ 68,250 | $ 81,250 | $257,000 |

**OPERATING EXPENSES** Let's assume that the company pays for all operating expenses, except depreciation and bad debt expense, in the month in which they are incurred. Both depreciation and bad debt expense are noncash expenses, so they never appear on the cash payments budget. Bad debt expense simply recognizes the sales revenue that will never be collected. Therefore, these noncash expenses need to be deducted from the total operating expenses to arrive at cash payments for operating expenses:

| | January | February | March | 1st Quarter |
|---|---|---|---|---|
| Total operating expenses (from Exhibit 9-10) | $142,800 | $106,200 | $124,500 | $373,500 |
| Less: Depreciation expense | (6,000) | (6,000) | (6,000) | (18,000) |
| Less: Bad debt expense | (4,800) | (3,200) | (4,000) | (12,000) |
| Cash payments for operating expenses | $132,000 | $ 97,000 | $114,500 | $343,500 |

**CAPITAL EXPENDITURES** The timing of these cash payments has already been scheduled on the capital expenditures budget in Exhibit 9-13.

**INCOME TAXES** Corporations must file their income tax returns within six months of their fiscal year end. Payments for their estimated income tax liability are typically due quarterly, or monthly if they do not qualify for quarterly payments. For corporations like Tasty Tortilla that have a December 31 fiscal year end and meet the criteria for quarterly payments, the income tax return is not due until June 30; however, the first payment is due by April 15. *As a result, Tasty Tortilla will not show any income tax payments in the first quarter of the year.* It is important to note that other organization structures are subject to different income tax rules. For example, sole proprietorships must file their return prior to June 15 with payment due before April 30, while partnerships are required to file and pay income taxes before March 31.

**DIVIDENDS** Like many corporations, Tasty Tortilla pays dividends to its shareholders on a quarterly basis. Tasty Tortilla plans to pay $25,000 in cash dividends in January for the company's earnings in the fourth quarter of the previous year.

Finally, we pull all of these cash payments together onto a single budget, as shown in Exhibit 9-15.

**EXHIBIT 9-15** Cash Payment Budget

Tasty Tortilla
Cash Payments Budget
For the Quarter Ended March 31

| | Month | | | |
|---|---|---|---|---|
| | January | February | March | 1st Quarter |
| Cash payments for direct materials purchases | $231,845 | $211,125 | $157,650 | $ 600,620 |
| Cash payments for direct labour | 31,900 | 22,550 | 28,270 | 82,720 |
| Cash payments for manufacturing overhead | 107,500 | 68,250 | 81,250 | 257,000 |
| Cash payments for operating expenses | 132,000 | 97,000 | 114,500 | 343,500 |
| Cash payments for capital investments | 125,000 | 0 | 0 | 125,000 |
| Cash payments for income taxes | 0 | 0 | 0 | 0 |
| Cash dividends | 25,000 | 0 | 0 | 25,000 |
| Total cash payments | $653,245 | $398,925 | $381,670 | $1,433,840 |

## Combined Cash Budget

The combined cash budget simply merges the budgeted cash collections and cash payments to project the company's ending cash position. Exhibit 9-16 shows the following:

- Budgeted cash collections for the month are added to the beginning cash balance to determine the total cash available.
- Budgeted cash payments are then subtracted to determine the ending cash balance before financing.
- Based on the ending cash balance before financing, the company knows whether it needs to borrow money or whether it has excess funds with which to repay debt or invest.

By looking at Exhibit 9-16, we see that Tasty Tortilla expects to begin the month with \$36,100 of cash. However, by the end of the month, it will be short of cash. Therefore, the company's managers must plan for how they will handle this shortage. One strategy would be to delay the purchase of equipment planned for January. Another strategy would be to borrow money. Let's say Tasty Tortilla has prearranged a **line of credit** that carries an interest rate of prime plus 1%. A line of credit is a lending arrangement from a bank in which a company is allowed to borrow money as needed, up to a specified maximum amount, yet pay interest on only the portion that is actually borrowed until it is repaid.

**EXHIBIT 9-16** Combined Cash Budget

Tasty Tortilla
Combined Cash Budget
For the Quarter Ended March 31

| | Month | | | |
|---|---|---|---|---|
| | January | February | March | 1st Quarter |
| Beginning balance of cash | \$ 36,100 | \$ 15,055 | \$ 153,980 | \$ 36,100 |
| Cash collections (Exhibit 9-14) | 612,200 | 558,000 | 439,200 | 1,609,400 |
| Total cash available | 648,300 | 573,055 | 593,180 | 1,645,500 |
| Less: Cash payments (Exhibit 9-15) | (653,245) | (398,925) | (381,670) | (1,433,840) |
| Ending cash balance before financing | (4,945) | 174,130 | 211,510 | 211,660 |
| Financing: | | | | |
| Borrowings | 20,000 | 0 | 0 | 20,000 |
| Repayments | 0 | (20,000) | 0 | (20,000) |
| Interest payments | 0 | (150) | 0 | (150) |
| End cash balance | \$ 15,055 | \$ 153,980 | \$ 211,510 | \$ 211,510 |

The line of credit will enable Tasty Tortilla to borrow funds to meet its short-term cash deficiencies. Let's say that Tasty Tortilla wants to maintain an ending cash balance of at least \$15,000. By borrowing \$20,000 on its line of credit at the end of January, the company will have slightly more (\$15,055) than its minimum desired balance.

The cash budget also shows that Tasty Tortilla will be able to repay this borrowing, along with the accrued interest, in February. Assuming Tasty Tortilla borrows the \$20,000 for a full month at an interest rate of 9%, February's interest payment would be calculated as follows:

$$\$20,000 \text{ loan} \times 1/12 \text{ of the year} \times 9\% \text{ interest rate} = \$150$$

Exhibit 9-16 also shows that Tasty Tortilla expects to have a fairly substantial cash balance at the end of both February and March. The company's managers use the cash budgets to determine when this cash will be needed and to decide how to invest it accordingly. Since the first quarterly income tax payment is due April 15, management will want to invest most of this excess cash in a safe, short-term investment, such as a money-market fund or short-term certificate of deposit. The company will also need cash in April to pay shareholders a quarterly dividend. Any cash not needed in the short run can be invested in longer-term investments. Managers exercising good cash management should have a plan in place for both cash deficiencies and cash excesses.

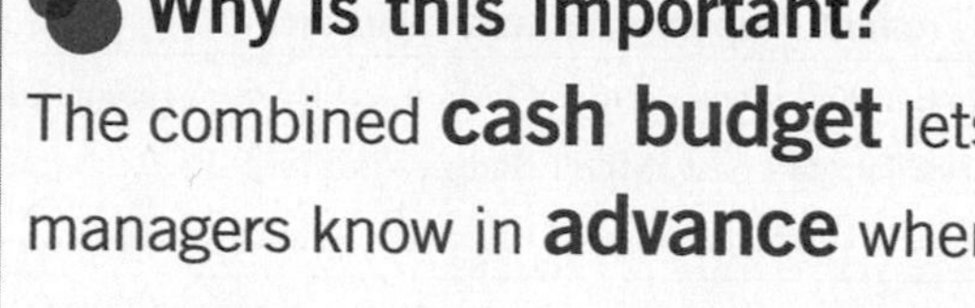


The combined **cash budget** lets managers know in **advance** when they will be short on cash and need to **borrow** money, or when they may have **extra funds** to invest.

## Budgeted Balance Sheet

Exhibit 9-17 shows Tasty Tortilla's budgeted balance sheet as of January 31. The company will prepare a budgeted balance sheet for each month of the year.

**EXHIBIT 9-17** Budgeted Balance Sheet

| Tasty Tortilla<br>Budgeted Balance Sheet<br>January 31 | | |
|---|---|---|
| **Assets** | | |
| Cash (from Cash Budget, Exhibit 9-16) | $ 15,055 | |
| Accounts receivable, net of allowance[A] | 549,450 | |
| Raw materials inventory (from Direct Materials Budget: 10,250 kg end inventory × $1.50) | 15,375 | |
| Finished goods inventory (from Production Budget: 2,000 cases × $12.00 unit cost) | 24,000 | |
| Prepaid property taxes and insurance[B] | 15,000 | |
| Total current assets | | $ 618,880 |
| Property, plant, and equipment[C] | 6,350,000 | |
| Less: Accumulated depreciation[D] | (1,920,000) | |
| Property, plant, and equipment, net | | 4,430,000 |
| Total assets | | $5,048,880 |
| **Liabilities and Stockholders' Equity** | | |
| Accounts payable[E] | $ 211,125 | |
| Income tax liability (from income statement, Exhibit 9-12) | 34,020 | |
| Other current liabilities (line of credit) (from Cash Budget, Exhibit 9-16) | 20,000 | |
| Total liabilities | | $ 265,145 |
| Stockholders' equity[F] | | 4,783,735 |
| Total liabilities and owner's equity | | $5,048,880 |

| [A] Accounts Receivable, Net of Allowance | |
|---|---|
| January credit sales (from Sales Budget, Exhibit 9-5) | $480,000 |
| 15% of December's credit sales ($500,000) yet to be collected | 75,000 |
| Accounts receivable, January 31 | $555,000 |
| Less: Allowance for uncollectible accounts (Assume $750 balance prior to additional $4,800 bad debt expense, Exhibit 9-10) | (5,550) |
| Accounts receivable, net of allowance for uncollectible accounts | $549,450 |

| [B] **Prepaid Property Tax and Insurance** | |
|---|---|
| Semiannual payment made in January (cash payments for MOH, p. 533) | $18,000 |
| Less: January cost (MOH Budget, Exhibit 9-9) | 3,000 |
| Prepaid property tax and insurance, January 31 | $15,000 |

| [C] **Property, Plant, and Equipment** | |
|---|---|
| December 31 balance (assumed) | $6,225,000 |
| Plus: January's investment in new equipment (Capital Expenditure Budget, Exhibit 9-13) | 125,000 |
| Property, plant, and equipment, January 31 | $6,350,000 |

| [D] **Accumulated Depreciation** | |
|---|---|
| December 31 balance (assumed) | $1,904,000 |
| Plus: January's depreciation from Manufacturing Overhead Budget, Exhibit 9-9 | 10,000 |
| Plus: January's depreciation from Operating Expenses Budget, Exhibit 9-10 | 6,000 |
| Accumulated depreciation, January 31 | $1,920,000 |

| [E] **Accounts Payable** | |
|---|---|
| January's DM purchases to be paid in February (p. 523 and Exhibit 9-15) | 211,125 |
| Accounts payable, January 31 | $211,125 |

| [F] **Stockholders' Equity** | |
|---|---|
| December 31 balance of common stock and retained earnings (assumed) | $4,720,555 |
| Plus: January's net income (Budgeted Income Statement, Exhibit 9-12) | 63,180 |
| Stockholders' equity, January 31 | $4,783,735 |

## Sensitivity Analysis

The master budget models the company's *planned* activities. Managers try to use the best estimates possible when creating budgets. However, some of the key assumptions (such as sales volume) used to create the budgets may turn out to be different than originally predicted. Managers prepare themselves for potentially different scenarios using **sensitivity analysis**.

As shown in Exhibit 9-18, sensitivity analysis is a *what if* technique that asks *what* a result will be *if* a predicted amount is not achieved or *if* an underlying assumption changes. *What if* demand for tortilla chips is less than expected? *What if* shipping costs increase due to increases in gasoline prices? *What if* the cost of the corn flour increases or union workers negotiate a wage increase? *What if* sales are 15% cash and 85% credit, rather than 20% cash and 80% credit? How will any or all of these changes in key assumptions affect Tasty Tortilla's budgeted income and budgeted cash position? Will Tasty Tortilla have to borrow more cash? On the other hand, *what if* sales are greater than expected? Management must be prepared to meet the additional demand for its product, or its customers may turn to competing suppliers.

**EXHIBIT 9-18** Sensitivity Analysis

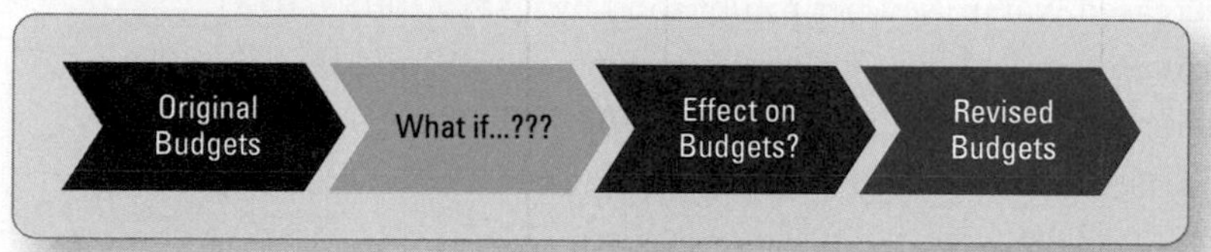


Technology makes it cost effective to perform comprehensive sensitivity analyses. Most companies use computer spreadsheet programs or special budget software to prepare the master budget and all of its components. Managers perform sensitivity analyses by simply changing one or several of the underlying assumptions in the budgets, such as sales quantity, direct material cost, and collection terms. The budget software automatically computes a complete set of revised budgets based on the changes.

Armed with a better understanding of how changes in key assumptions will affect the company's bottom line and cash position, today's managers can be prepared to lead the company when business conditions change.

## Sustainability and Budgeting

Budgets reflect and communicate management's goals and objectives. Managers leading their companies toward more sustainable practices will want to reflect those goals in the company's budgets. For example, the Campbell Soup Company,[2] which has been on the Dow Jones Sustainability Index for the last three years, has set long-term environmental goals for 2020 that include

- Cutting water use and greenhouse gas emissions per ton of food produced
- Recycling 95% of waste generated
- Reducing packaging material and delivering 100% of packaging from sustainable materials
- Sourcing 40% of energy used from renewable or alternative energy sources

See Exercises E9-18A and E9-40B

The adoption of these long-term goals will affect most, if not all, of the company's short-term budgets. For example, the operating expenses budget should reflect additional resources devoted to researching and developing more sustainable packaging materials. Once developed, the new packaging will impact the direct materials budget. The operating expenses budget should also include additional resources for marketing the sustainably packaged products, which should in turn create additional sales to be included in the sales budget. The capital expenditures budget will reflect plans to purchase new energy saving production equipment. The company's MOH budget will in turn be affected by depreciation of the new equipment, as well as the reduction of water cost, the recycling of waste, and the use of alternative forms of energy. All of these measures will impact the cash budget, as well as the company's projected income statement and balance sheet.

In addition to environmental goals, the company also has social impact goals, that will be reflected in the company's budgets. These goals include

- Increasing the nutritional value of its products
- Reducing childhood obesity and hunger
- Promoting volunteerism

[2] *Campbell Soup Company 2012 Corporate Social Responsibility Report*

*continued*

Recall that budgets also serve as benchmarks for judging performance. By developing strategic environmental and social goals that span several years, and then tracking yearly performance, Campbell can see how well it is working toward achieving those longer-term goals. For example, from an environmental perspective Campbell has

- Decreased water used per ton of food by 15% (2008–2011)
- Decreased greenhouse gas emissions per ton of food by 6% (2008–2011)
- Decreased packaging materials used by 73% (2009–2011)
- Increased its recycling rate to 80% of waste (2011)

From a social impact perspective Campbell has

- Increased the number of products defined as "healthy"
- Increased the percentage of products sold with reduced amounts of negative nutrients, such as reduced levels of sugars and saturated fats
- Donated over $50 million in food and cash to charitable causes
- Encouraged employee volunteerism through its "Make a Difference" week

## What Is Responsibility Accounting?

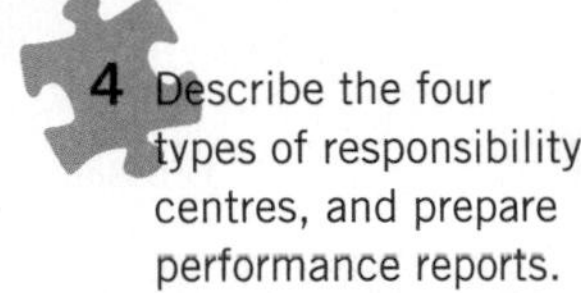
4 Describe the four types of responsibility centres, and prepare performance reports.

You've seen how managers set strategic goals and develop plans and budgets that help reach those goals. Let's return to SolGate Inc. and look more closely at how managers use budgets to control operations.

**Why is this important?** **Responsibility accounting** allows upper management to "divide and conquer." The company's operations are divided into various **responsibility centres**, and a manager is held responsible for making sure the centre is run as effectively and efficiently as possible.

Each manager is responsible for planning and controlling some part of the firm's activities. A <u>responsibility centre</u> is a part or subunit of an organization whose manager is accountable for specific activities. Lower-level managers are often responsible for budgeting and controlling costs of a single value chain function. For example, one manager is responsible for planning and controlling the *production* of SolGate's solar panels at the plant, while another is responsible for planning and controlling the *distribution* of the product to customers. Lower-level managers report to higher-level managers, who have broader responsibilities. Managers in charge of production and distribution report to senior managers responsible for profits earned by an entire product line.

### Four Types of Responsibility Centres

<u>Responsibility accounting</u> is a system for evaluating the performance of each responsibility centre and its manager. Responsibility accounting performance reports compare plans (budgets) with actions (actual results) for each centre. Superiors then evaluate how well each manager controlled the operations for which he or she was responsible.

Exhibit 9-19 illustrates four types of responsibility centres. We'll briefly describe each type.

#### Cost Centre

In a <u>cost centre</u>, managers are accountable for costs only. Manufacturing operations, such as the SolGate photovoltaic cell manufacturing plant, are cost centres. The plant manager controls costs by ensuring that the entire production process runs efficiently. The plant manager is *not* responsible for generating revenues because he or she is not involved in selling the product. The plant manager is evaluated on his or her ability to control *costs* by comparing actual costs to budgeted costs. If quality and volume remain constant, the plant manager is likely to receive a more favourable evaluation when actual costs are less than budgeted costs.

**EXHIBIT 9-19** Four Types of Responsibility Centres

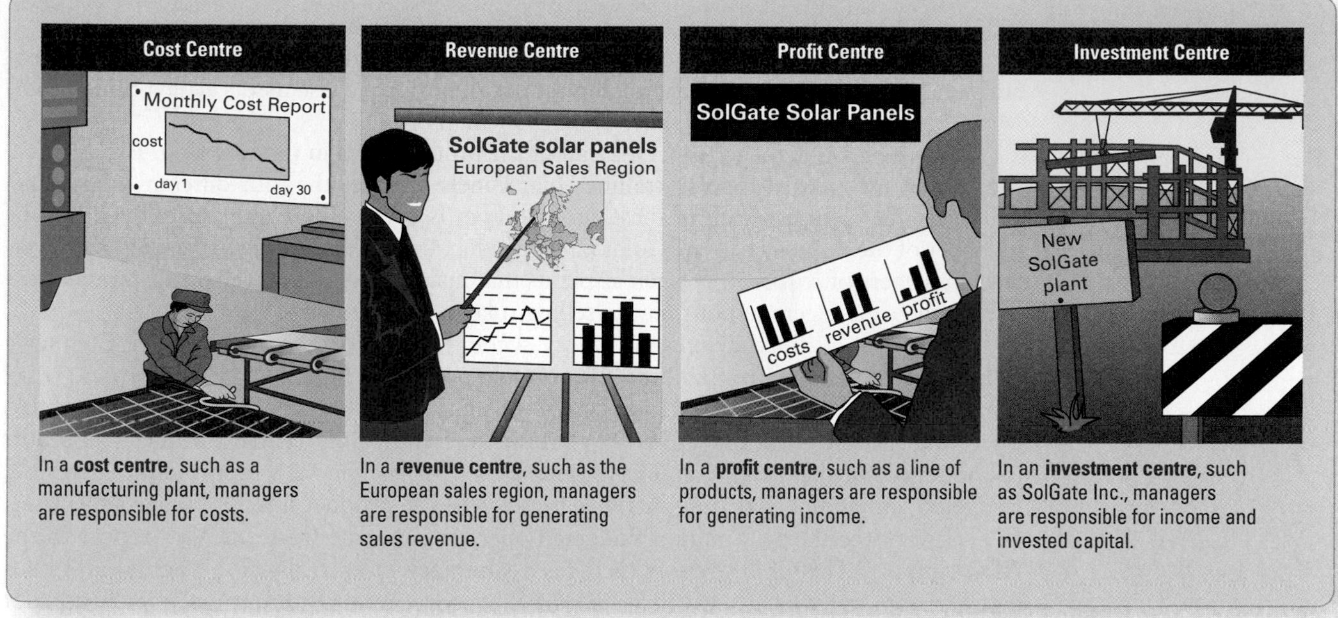


In a **cost centre**, such as a manufacturing plant, managers are responsible for costs.

In a **revenue centre**, such as the European sales region, managers are responsible for generating sales revenue.

In a **profit centre**, such as a line of products, managers are responsible for generating income.

In an **investment centre**, such as SolGate Inc., managers are responsible for income and invested capital.

## Revenue Centre

In a revenue centre, managers are accountable primarily for revenues. Revenue centres are often sales territories, such as SolGate's European and North American sales regions. Managers of revenue centres may also be responsible for the costs of their own sales operations. Revenue centre performance reports compare actual with budgeted revenues. All else being equal, the manager is likely to receive a more favourable evaluation when actual revenues exceed the budget.

## Profit Centre

In a profit centre, managers are accountable for both revenues and costs and, therefore, profits. For example, in the SolGate MonoCrystalline Solar Panel division, a (higher-level) manager is responsible for increasing sales revenue and controlling costs to achieve the profit goals for the entire line of MonoCrystalline solar panels. Profit centre reports include both revenues *and* expenses to show the profit centre's income. Superiors evaluate the manager's performance by comparing actual revenues, expenses, and profits to the budget. All else being equal, the manager is likely to receive a more favourable evaluation when actual profits exceed the budget.

## Investment Centre

In an **investment centre**, managers are accountable for investments, revenues, and costs. Investment centres are generally large divisions of a corporation. For example, SolGate Inc. has four different divisions based on the type of solar panel and the geographic regions. Managers of investment centres are responsible for (1) generating sales, (2) controlling costs, and (3) efficiently managing the division's assets (the company's investment in the division). Investment centres are treated almost as if they were stand-alone companies. Managers have decision-making authority over how the division's assets are used. As a result, managers are held responsible for generating as much income as they can with those assets.

In addition to using performance reports, top management often evaluates investment centre managers based on performance measures such as return on investment (ROI), residual income, and economic value added (EVA). Chapter 11 explains how these measures are calculated and used. All else being equal, the manager will receive a more favourable evaluation if the division's actual ROI, residual income, or EVA exceeds the amount budgeted.

## Responsibility Accounting Performance Reports

Exhibit 9-20 shows how an organization such as SolGate Inc. assigns responsibility.

At the top level, the CEO oversees each of the four divisions. Division managers generally have broad responsibility, including deciding how to use assets to maximize ROI. Most companies consider divisions as *investment centres*.

Each division manager supervises all of the product lines in that division. Exhibit 9-20 shows that the VP of MonoCrystalline Solar Panels oversees the four different solar panel wattages and voltages. Each of these product lines is considered to be a profit centre. The manager of the 180-watt 24-volt solar panel product line is responsible for evaluating lower-level managers of *cost centres* (such as plants that make photovoltaic cells) and *revenue centres* (such as managers responsible for selling solar panel products).

Exhibit 9-21 illustrates responsibility accounting performance reports for each level of management shown in Exhibit 9-20, using hypothetical figures.

Start with the lowest level and move to the top. Follow the $25 million budgeted operating income from the 175W 24V MonoCrystalline Solar Panel product line report to the report of the VP—MonoCrystalline Solar Panels. The VP's report summarizes the budgeted and actual operating incomes for each of the product lines he or she supervises.

Now, trace the $70 million budgeted operating income from the VP's report to the CEO's report. The CEO's report includes a summary of each division's actual and budgeted profits, as well as the costs incurred by corporate headquarters, which are not assigned to any of the divisions.

**EXHIBIT 9-20** Partial Organization Chart

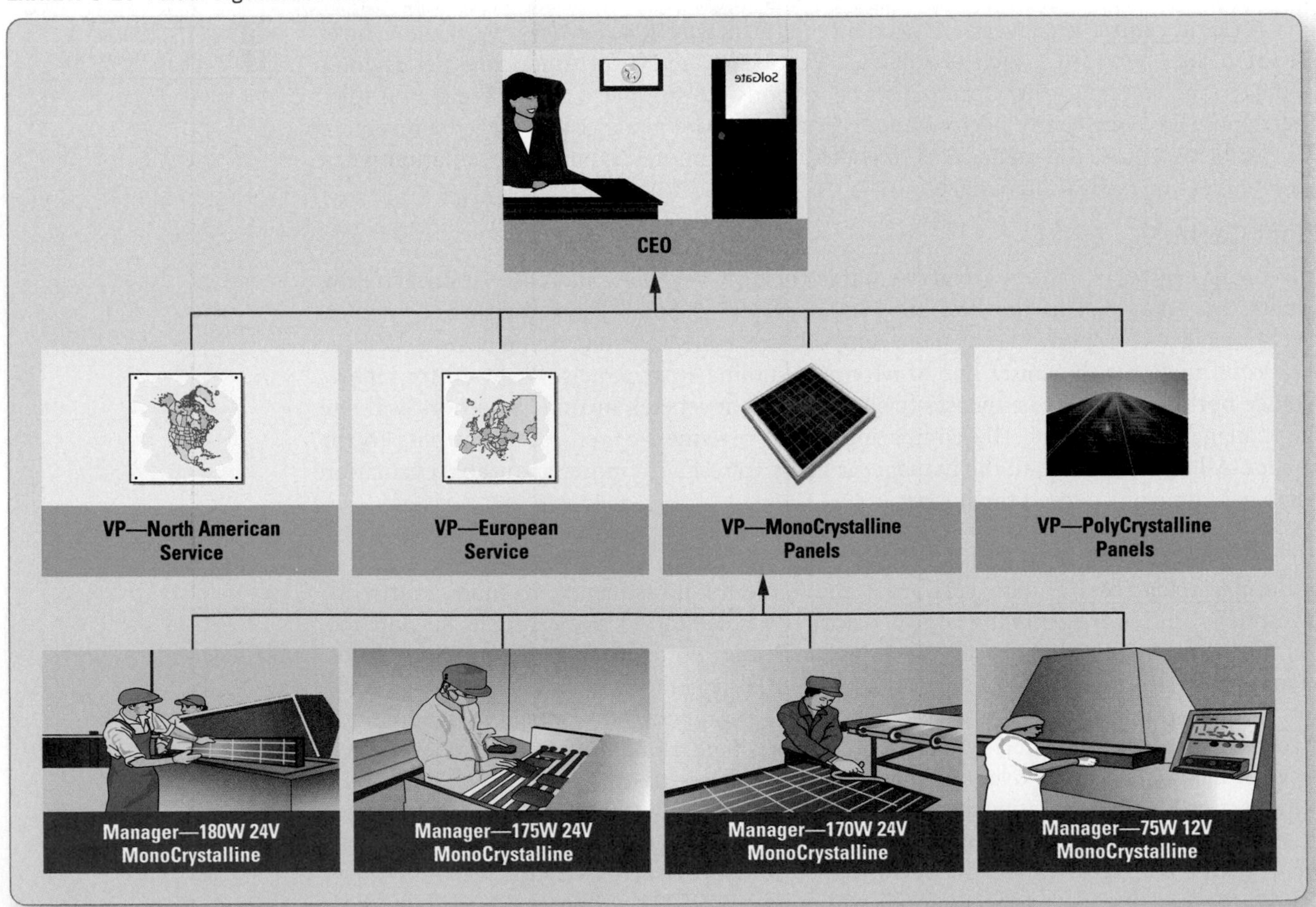


*Source:* ssuaphotos/Shutterstock

**EXHIBIT 9-21** Responsibility Accounting Performance Reports at Various Levels

**CEO'S QUARTERLY RESPONSIBILITY REPORT**
**(in millions of dollars*)**

| Operating Income of Divisions and Corporate Headquarters Expense | Actual | Budget | Variance Favourable/ (Unfavourable) |
|---|---|---|---|
| North American Service | $209 | $218 | $ (9) |
| European Service | 87 | 79 | 8 |
| MonoCrystalline Panels | 84 | 70 | 14 |
| PolyCrystalline Panels | 34 | 35 | (1) |
| Corporate Headquarters Expense | (29) | (33) | 4 |
| Operating Income | $385 | $369 | $16 |

**VP—MonoCrystalline Panels**
**QUARTERLY RESPONSIBILITY REPORT**
**(in millions of dollars)**

| Operating Income of Product Lines | Actual | Budget | Variance Favourable/ (Unfavourable) |
|---|---|---|---|
| 180W 24V MonoCrystalline Panels | $18 | $20 | $ (2) |
| 175W 24V MonoCrystalline Panels | 38 | 25 | 13 |
| 170W 24V MonoCrystalline Panels | 15 | 10 | 5 |
| 75W 12V MonoCrystalline Panels | 13 | 15 | (2) |
| Operating Income | $84 | $70 | $14 |

**MANAGER—175W 24V MonoCrystalline Panels**
**QUARTERLY RESPONSIBILITY REPORT**
**(in millions of dollars)**

| Revenue and Expenses | Actual | Budget | Variance Favourable/ (Unfavourable) |
|---|---|---|---|
| Sales revenue | $84 | $80 | $ 4 |
| Cost of goods sold | (30) | (36) | 6 |
| Gross profit | 54 | 44 | 10 |
| Marketing expenses | (9) | (12) | 3 |
| Research and development expenses | (3) | (2) | (1) |
| Other expenses | (4) | (5) | 1 |
| Operating income | $38 | $25 | $13 |

*All figures are hypothetical.

## Management by Exception

Managers use a technique called **management by exception** when they analyze performance reports. Management by exception means that managers will investigate only budget variances that are material in amount, meaning they are a relatively large deviation from what was expected (in terms of a percentage or dollar amount). Look at the CEO's report. The PolyCrystalline Division's actual operating income of $34 million is very close to the budgeted $35 million. Unless there are other signs of trouble, the CEO will not waste time investigating such a relatively small variance.

In contrast, the MonoCrystalline Solar Panel Division earned a great deal more profit than budgeted. The CEO will want to know why. Suppose the VP of the division believes that a national sales promotion was especially effective. That promotion may be repeated or adapted by other divisions. One reason managers investigate large, favourable variances (not just large, unfavourable ones) is to identify the reason for exceptional results so that other parts of the organization may benefit. Another is to ensure that employees are not skimping on materials, marketing, or R&D, which could hurt the company's long-term success. Also, it's possible that large variances are the result of unrealistic budgets.

The CEO would likely focus on improving the North American Service Division because its actual income fell $9 million below budget. The CEO would want to see which services caused the shortfall so that he or she and the VP of the division can work together to correct any problems.

Exhibit 9-21 also shows how summarized data can hide problems. Although as a whole, the MonoCrystalline Solar Panel Division performed well, the 180W 24V and 75W 12V lines did not. If the CEO received only the condensed report at the top of the exhibit, he or she would rely on division managers to spot and correct problems in individual product lines.

### Not a Question of Blame

Responsibility accounting assigns managers responsibility for their unit's actions and provides a way to evaluate both the managers and their unit's performance. But superiors should not misuse responsibility accounting to find fault or place blame. The question is not who is to blame for an unfavourable variance; instead, it is who can best explain why a specific variance occurred. Consider the North American Service Division in Exhibit 9-21. Suppose a tornado devastated a distribution facility. The remaining facilities may have operated very efficiently and this efficiency kept the income variance down to $9 million. If so, the North American Service Division and its VP actually did a good job.

### Flexible Budgets

The performance report pictured in Exhibit 9-21 compares actual costs to the amounts that were originally budgeted. One potential problem with this type of performance report is that the actual volume may differ from that which was originally budgeted. For example, say the budgeted cost was for 100 million units, yet 120 million units were actually produced. Is it "fair" to compare the actual cost (which is probably higher) to the budgeted cost in such a situation? In the next chapter, we discuss a different type of performance report that adjusts the budgeted amounts to reflect the actual volume produced and sold (these are called flexible budgets). Some companies prefer these types of performance reports since they provide more of an "apples to apples" comparison.

### Other Performance Measures

Top management uses responsibility accounting performance reports to assess each responsibility centre's *financial* performance. Top management also often assesses each responsibility centre's nonfinancial *operating* performance. Typical nonfinancial performance measures include customer satisfaction ratings, delivery time, product quality, and employee expertise. Chapter 11 discusses the broader view of performance evaluation, known as the "balanced scorecard." In that chapter, we will look at how managers use both financial and nonfinancial performance measures to form a "balanced view" of each responsibility centre's performance.

# DECISION GUIDELINES

## The Master Budget and Responsibility Accounting

Let's consider some additional decisions with respect to budgeting.

| Decision | Guidelines |
|---|---|
| What is the key to preparing the cash collections and cash payments budgets? | The key to preparing the cash budgets is timing. *When* will cash be received, and *when* will cash be paid? The timing of cash collections and cash payments often differs from the period in which the related revenues and expenses are recognized on the income statement. |
| What can be done to prepare for possible changes in key underlying budget assumptions? | Management uses sensitivity analysis to understand how changes in key underlying assumptions might affect the company's financial results. This awareness helps managers cope with changing business conditions when they occur. |
| As a new manager, what should I expect to be held responsible for? | **Cost centre:** Manager is responsible for costs.<br>**Revenue centre:** Manager is responsible for revenues.<br>**Profit centre:** Manager is responsible for both revenues and costs and, therefore, profits.<br>**Investment centre:** Manager is responsible for revenues, costs, and the efficient use of the assets invested in the division. |
| How should upper management evaluate the performance of the responsibility centres and their managers? | Actual performance should be compared with the budget. Using management by exception, any large variances should be investigated, with an emphasis on uncovering information, rather than placing blame. |

# SUMMARY PROBLEM 2

The following information was taken from Pillows Unlimited sales budget, found in Summary Problem 1 on pages 528–530:

Pillows Unlimited
Sales Budget—Type of Sale
For the Quarter Ended March 31

| | Month | | | |
|---|---|---|---|---|
| Type of Sale: | January | February | March | 1st Quarter |
| Cash sales (10%) | $ 140,000 | $ 154,000 | $ 161,000 | $ 455,000 |
| Credit sales (90%) | 1,260,000 | 1,386,000 | 1,449,000 | 4,095,000 |
| Total sales revenue | $1,400,000 | $1,540,000 | $1,610,000 | $4,550,000 |

The company's collection history indicates that 75% of credit sales are collected in the month after the sale, 15% are collected two months after the sale, 8% are collected three months after the sale, and the remaining 2% are never collected.

Assume the following additional information was gathered about the types of sales made in the fourth quarter (October through December) of the previous year:

Pillows Unlimited
Sales Budget—Type of Sale
For the Quarter Ended December 31

| | Month | | | |
|---|---|---|---|---|
| Type of Sale: | October | November | December | 4th Quarter |
| Cash sales (10%) | $ 142,800 | $ 151,200 | $ 137,200 | $ 431,200 |
| Credit sales (90%) | 1,285,200 | 1,360,800 | 1,234,800 | 3,880,800 |
| Total sales revenue | $1,428,000 | $1,512,000 | $1,372,000 | $4,312,000 |

The following information was taken from Pillows Unlimited direct materials budget, found in Summary Problem 1 on pages 528–530:

| | January | February | March | 1st Quarter |
|---|---|---|---|---|
| Total cost of DM purchases | $771,750 | $836,250 | $873,000 | $2,481,000 |

Assume that the total cost of direct materials purchases in December was $725,000. The company pays 40% of its direct materials purchases in the month of purchase and pays the remaining 60% in the month after purchase.

### Requirements

1. Prepare the cash collections budget for January, February, and March, as well as a summary for the first quarter.
2. Prepare the cash disbursements budget for direct materials purchases for the months of January, February, and March, as well as a summary for the quarter.

## SOLUTIONS

### Requirement 1

**Pillows Unlimited**
**Cash Collections Budget**
For the Quarter Ended March 31

| | Month | | | |
|---|---|---|---|---|
| | January | February | March | 1st Quarter |
| Cash sales | $ 140,000 | $ 154,000 | $ 161,000 | $ 455,000 |
| Collections on credit sales: | | | | |
| 75% of credit sales made last month | 926,100[A] | 945,000[D] | 1,039,500[G] | 2,910,600 |
| 15% of credit sales made two months ago | 204,120[B] | 185,220[E] | 189,000[H] | 578,340 |
| 8% of credit sales made two months ago | 102,816[C] | 108,864[F] | 98,784[I] | 310,464 |
| Total cash collections | $1,373,036 | $1,393,084 | $1,488,284 | $4,254,404 |

[A]December credit sales ($1,234,800) × 75% = $ 926,100
[B]November credit sales ($1,360,800) × 15% = $ 204,120
[C]October credit sales ($1,285,200) × 8% = $ 102,816

[D]January credit sales ($1,260,000) × 75% = $ 945,000
[E]December credit sales ($1,234,800) × 15% = $ 185,220
[F]November credit sales ($1,360,800) × 8% = $ 108,864

[G]February credit sales ($1,386,000) × 75% = $1,039,500
[H]January credit sales ($1,260,000) × 15% = $ 189,000
[I]December credit sales ($1,234,800) × 8% = $ 98,784

### Requirement 2

**Pillows Unlimited**
**Cash Payment Budget—Direct Materials**
For the Quarter Ended March 31

| | Month | | | |
|---|---|---|---|---|
| | January | February | March | 1st Quarter |
| 40% of current month DM purchases | $308,700[A] | $334,500[C] | $349,200[E] | $ 992,400 |
| 60% of last month's DM purchases | 435,000[B] | 463,050[D] | 501,750[F] | 1,399,800 |
| Total cash payments for DM | $743,700 | $797,550 | $850,950 | $2,392,200 |

[A]January DM purchases ($771,750) × 40% = $308,700
[B]December DM purchases ($725,000) × 60% = $435,000

[C]February DM purchases ($836,250) × 40% = $334,500
[D]January DM purchases ($771,750) × 60% = $463,050

[E] March DM purchases ($873,000) × 40% = $349,200
[F] February DM purchases ($836,250) × 60% = $501,750

# APPENDIX 9A

## The Master Budget for Service and Merchandising Companies

5 Prepare a merchandiser's cost of goods sold, inventory, and purchases budget.

In this chapter, we presented the master budget for a manufacturing company. The components of the master budget were summarized in Exhibit 9-4. The master budgets for service companies and merchandising companies are somewhat less complex.

- *Service companies*: Since service companies have no merchandise inventory,[3] their operating budgets only include the sales budget, the operating expenses budget, and the budgeted income statement. The financial budgets are the same as those shown in Exhibit 9-4: the capital expenditures budget, cash budgets, and budgeted balance sheet.
- *Merchandising companies:* Since merchandising companies purchase ready-made products, they do not need to prepare the production, direct materials, direct labour, or manufacturing overhead budgets. Replacing these budgets is a combined **cost of goods sold, inventory, and purchases budget**. This budget follows the same general format as the manufacturer's production budget except that it is calculated at cost (in dollars) rather than in units:[4]

| | |
|---|---|
| Cost of Goods Sold | (the inventory we plan to sell during the month, at cost) |
| Plus: Desired Ending Inventory | (the amount of inventory we want on hand at month's end) |
| = Total Inventory Needed | (the total amount of inventory needed) |
| Less: Beginning Inventory | (the amount of inventory we have on hand) |
| Purchases of Inventory | the amount of inventory we need to purchase) |

Let's try an example:

Let's say one Mac's Convenience Store expects sales of $500,000 in January, $520,000 in February, $530,000 in March, and $550,000 in April. Let's also assume that management sets its prices to achieve a 40% gross profit. As a result, cost of goods sold is 60% of the sales revenue (100% – 40%). Finally, management wishes to have ending inventory equal to 10% of the next month's cost of goods sold. Exhibit 9-22 shows the cost of goods sold, inventory, and purchases budget for the months of January through March. Keep in mind that all figures (other than sales revenue) are shown at cost.

Figures from this budget are then used as follows:

- *Cost of goods sold* is used in preparing the budgeted income statement.
- *Ending inventory* is used in preparing the budgeted balance sheet.
- *Purchases of inventory* is used in preparing the cash payments budget.

[3]Refer to the discussion in Chapter 2 regarding service organizations and inventory. Services do not require inventory; however, many service organizations combine both the sale of services and the sale of products. For example, a lawn care company sells lawn maintenance services, and possibly products such as grass seed, sod, and lawn edging materials. In this situation, the service organization has an inventory, but not for the services.

[4]A merchandiser could first prepare this budget in units and then convert it to dollars. However, merchandisers usually have hundreds or thousands of products for sale, so it is often simpler to directly state it in dollars.

In summary, a merchandising company's *operating* budgets include the following:

- Sales budget
- Cost of goods sold, inventory, and purchases budget
- Operating expenses budget
- Budgeted income statement

The *financial* budgets are the same as those shown in Exhibit 9-4: the capital expenditures budget, cash budgets, and budgeted balance sheet.

**EXHIBIT 9-22** Merchandiser's Cost of Goods Sold, Inventory, and Purchases Budget

**Mac's Convenience Store**
**Cost of Goods Sold, Inventory, and Purchases Budget**
For the months of January, February, and March

| | Month | | |
|---|---|---|---|
| | **January** | **February** | **March** |
| Sales revenue (from Sales Budget) | $500,000 | $520,000 | $530,000 |
| Cost of goods sold (60% of sales revenue) | $300,000 | $312,000 | $318,000 |
| Plus: Desired ending inventory 10% of next month's cost of goods sold) | 31,200 | 31,800 | 33,000[B] |
| Total inventory required | 331,200 | 343,800 | 351,000 |
| Less: Beginning inventory | (30,000)[A] | (31,200) | (31,800) |
| Purchases of inventory | $301,200 | $312,600 | $319,200 |

[A]December 31 balance (equal to January 1 balance) is 10% of January's Cost of Goods Sold.
[B]April sales of $550,000 × 60% = $330,000; April Cost of Goods Sold × 10% = $33,000.

# END OF CHAPTER

CHAPTER 9

## LEARNING OBJECTIVES

1 Describe how and why managers use budgets.

2 Prepare the operating budgets.

3 Prepare the financial budgets.

4 Describe the four types of responsibility centres, and prepare performance reports.

5 Prepare a merchandiser's cost of goods sold, inventory, and purchases budget. (Appendix 9A)

## ACCOUNTING VOCABULARY

**Budget Committee (p. 516)** A committee comprising upper management, as well as cross-functional managers, who review, revise, and approve the final budget.

**COD (p. 519)** Collect on Delivery or Cash on Delivery. A sales term indicating that the inventory must be paid for at the time of delivery.

**Cost Centre (p. 538)** A responsibility centre for which the manager is responsible for costs only.

**Cost of Goods Sold, Inventory, and Purchases Budget (p. 545)** A merchandiser's budget that computes the cost of goods sold, the amount of desired ending inventory, and amount of merchandise to be purchased.

**Financial Budgets (p. 519)** The budgets that project the collection and payment of cash, as well as forecast the company's budgeted balance sheet.

**Investment Centre (p. 539)** A responsibility centre for which the manager is accountable for revenues, costs, and the efficient use of the assets.

**Line of Credit (p. 534)** A lending arrangement from a bank in which a company is allowed to borrow money as needed, up to a specified maximum amount, yet pay interest on only the portion that is actually borrowed until it is repaid.

**Management by Exception (p. 541)** Directs management's attention to important differences between actual and budgeted amounts.

**Master Budget (p. 518)** The comprehensive planning document for the entire organization. The master budget includes the operating budgets and the financial budgets.

**Operating Budgets (p. 519)** The budgets needed to run the daily operations of the company. The operating budgets culminate in a budgeted income statement.

**Participative Budgeting (p. 516)** Budgeting that involves the participation of many levels of management.

**Profit Centre (p. 539)** A responsibility centre for which the manager is responsible for both costs and revenues, and therefore, profit.

**Responsibility Accounting (p. 538)** A system for evaluating the performance of each responsibility centre and its manager.

**Responsibility Centre (p. 538)** A part or subunit of an organization whose manager is accountable for specific activities.

**Revenue Centre (p. 539)** A responsibility centre for which the manager is accountable for revenues only.

**Rolling Budget (p. 516)** A budget that is continuously updated so that the next 12 months of operations are always budgeted; also known as a continuous budget.

**Safety Stock (p. 520)** Extra inventory kept on hand in case demand is higher than expected or problems in the factory slow production.

**Sensitivity Analysis (p. 536)** A "what if" technique that asks what a result will be if a predicted amount is not achieved or if an underlying assumption changes.

**Slack (p. 516)** Intentionally overstating budgeted expenses or understating budgeted revenues in order to cope with uncertainty, make performance appear better, or make room for potential budget cuts.

**Strategic Planning (p. 515)** Setting long-term goals that may extend 5 to 10 years into the future.

**Variance (p. 518)** The difference between actual and budgeted figures (revenues and expenses).

**Zero-Based Budgeting (p. 516)** A budgeting approach in which managers begin with a budget of zero and must justify every dollar put into the budget.

MyAccountingLab Make the grade with MyAccountingLab: Questions marked in # can be found on MyAccountingLab. You can practise them as often as you want, and most feature step-by-step guided instructions to help you find the right answer.

# QUICK CHECK

1. (Learning Objective 1) Mac's Convenience expects to receive which of the following benefits when it uses its budgeting process?
   a. The planning required to develop the budget helps managers foresee and avoid potential problems before they occur.
   b. The budget helps motivate employees to achieve Mac's sales growth and cost reduction goals.
   c. The budget provides Mac's managers with a benchmark against which to compare actual results for performance evaluation.
   d. All of the above.

2. (Learning Objective 1) Budgets are
   a. required by International Financial Reporting Standards (IFRS) or Accounting Standards for Private Enterprises (ASPE).
   b. future oriented.
   c. only used by large corporations.
   d. prepared by the controller for the entire company.

3. (Learning Objective 1) Technology has made it easier for managers to perform all of the following tasks except
   a. sensitivity analyses.
   b. combining individual units' budgets to create the company-wide budget.
   c. removing slack from the budget.
   d. preparing responsibility centre performance reports that identify variances between actual and budgeted revenues and costs.

4. (Learning Objective 2) Which of the following is the starting point for the master budget?
   a. The sales budget
   b. The direct materials budget
   c. The production budget
   d. The operating expenses budget

5. (Learning Objective 2) The income statement is part of which element of a company's master budget?
   a. The operating budgets
   b. The capital expenditures budget
   c. The financial budgets
   d. The cash budgets

6. (Learning Objective 2) The usual starting point for a direct labour budget for a manufacturer is the
   a. direct materials budget.
   b. sales budget.
   c. cash budget.
   d. production budget.

7. (Learning Objective 3) The following budgets are all financial budgets except for the
   a. combined cash budget.
   b. budgeted balance sheet.
   c. budgeted income statement.
   d. capital expenditures budget.

8. (Learning Objective 3) Which of the following expenses would never appear in a cash budget?
   a. Depreciation expense
   b. Wages expense
   c. Interest expense
   d. Marketing expense

9. (Learning Objective 4) Which of the following responsibility centres is a profit centre?
   a. The Accounting Department for a local bank
   b. The sales office of a charter airline service
   c. The headquarters of an international tire manufacturer
   d. The local branch office for a national bank

10. (Learning Objective 4) Which of the following managers is at the highest level of the organization?
    a. Cost centre manager
    b. Revenue centre manager
    c. Profit centre manager
    d. Investment centre manager

**Quick Check Answers**

*1. d 2. b 3. c 4. a 5. a 6. d 7. c 8. a 9. d 10. d*

# SHORT EXERCISES

**S9-1 Identify the order of preparation and components of master budget**
*(Learning Objective 1)*

Identify the order in which a manufacturer would prepare the following budgets. Also note whether each budget is an operating budget or a financial budget.

**a.** Budgeted income statement
**b.** Combined cash budget
**c.** Sales budget
**d.** Budgeted balance sheet

e. Cash payments budget
f. Direct materials budget
g. Production budget

**S9-2 Understand key terms and definitions** *(Learning Objectives 1 & 2)*

Complete the following statements with one of these terms. You may use a term more than once, and some terms may not be used at all.

| | | | |
|---|---|---|---|
| Operating budgets | Production budget | Master budget | Participative budgeting |
| Financial budgets | Slack | Zero-based | Strategic planning |
| Safety stock | Variance | Budget committee | Rolling budget |

a. ______ is a budget that is continuously updated by adding months to the end of the budgeting period.
b. ______ is the comprehensive planning document for the entire organization.
c. These budgets, ______, project both the collection and payment of cash and forecast the company's budgeted balance sheet.
d. The ______ is used to forecast how many units should be made to meet the sales projections.
e. When an organization builds its budgets from the ground up, it is using ______ budgeting.
f. ______ is the process of setting long-term goals that may extend several years into the future.
g. Managers will sometimes build ______ into their budgets to protect themselves against unanticipated expenses or lower revenues.
h. The ______ is the difference between actual and budgeted figures and is used to evaluate how well the manager controlled operations during the period.
i. ______ are often used by companies to review submitted budgets, make revisions as needed, and approve the final budgets.
j. ______ is extra inventory of finished goods that is kept on hand in case demand is higher than predicted or problems in the factory slow production.
k. The sales budget and production budget are examples of ______.
l. ______ is a budgeting process that begins with departmental managers and flows up through middle management to top management.

**S9-3 Prepare a sales budget** *(Learning Objective 2)*

Gibbs Company manufactures two sizes of cargo containers. The small model sells for $100, while the large containers sell for $700. In the second quarter of the upcoming year, Gibbs Company expects to sell 1,000 small containers and 450 large containers in April, 1,300 small and 500 large containers in May, and 1,500 small and 670 large containers in June. Prepare the sales budget for the second quarter, with a column for each month and for the quarter in total.

**S9-4 Prepare a production budget** *(Learning Objective 2)*

Thomas Cycles manufactures chainless bicycles. On March 31, Thomas Cycles had 200 bikes in inventory. The company's policy is that the ending inventory in any month must be 20% of the following month's expected sales. Thomas Cycles expects to sell the following number of bikes in each of next four months:

| | |
|---|---|
| April | 1,000 bikes |
| May | 1,100 bikes |
| June | 1,300 bikes |
| July | 1,300 bikes |

Prepare a production budget for the second quarter, with a column for each month and for the quarter.

**S9-5 Direct materials budget** *(Learning Objective 2)*

Mountain Breads produces organic bread that is sold by the loaf. Each loaf requires 0.5 kg of flour. The company pays $3.00 per kilogram of the organic flour used in its loaves. Mountain Breads expects to produce the following number of loaves in each of the upcoming four months:

| | |
|---|---|
| July | 1,500 loaves |
| August | 1,800 loaves |
| September | 1,600 loaves |
| October | 1,500 loaves |

The company's policy is to have 10% of the following month's flour needs on hand at the end of each month. At the end of June, there were 75 kg of flour on hand. Prepare the direct materials budget for the third quarter, with a column for each month and for the quarter.

**S9-6 Calculate a direct labour budget** *(Learning Objective 2)*

The Production Department of Lauren Manufacturing has prepared the following schedule of units to be produced over the first quarter of the upcoming year:

| | January | February | March |
|---|---|---|---|
| Units to be produced | 500 | 600 | 800 |

Each unit requires 2.0 hours of direct labour. Direct labour workers are paid an average of $15 per hour. How many hours will be required in January? In February? In March?

**S9-7 Prepare a manufacturing overhead budget** *(Learning Objective 2)*

Probe Corporation is preparing its manufacturing overhead budget. The direct labour budget for the upcoming quarter is as follows:

| | April | May | June |
|---|---|---|---|
| Budgeted direct labour hours | 400 | 700 | 600 |

The company's variable manufacturing overhead rate is $1.50 per direct labour hour and the company's fixed manufacturing overhead is $3,500 per month. How much manufacturing overhead will be budgeted for April? For May? For June?

**S9-8 Prepare an operating expenses budget** *(Learning Objective 2)*

Davenport Corporation is preparing its operating expenses budget. The budgeted unit sales for the upcoming quarter are as follows:

| | July | August | September |
|---|---|---|---|
| Budgeted unit sales | 1,200 | 1,400 | 1,700 |

The company's variable operating expenses are $4.00 per unit. Fixed monthly operating expenses include $5,000 for salaries, $5,000 for office rent, and depreciation of $2,500. How much operating expenses will be budgeted for July? For August? For September?

**S9-9 Prepare a budgeted income statement** *(Learning Objective 2)*

Sound Beginnings manufactures hearing aid devices. For January, Sound Beginnings expects to sell 600 hearing aid devices at an average price of $2,300 per unit. Sound Beginnings' average manufacturing cost of each unit sold is $1,400. Variable operating expenses for Sound Beginnings will be $1.50 per unit sold, and fixed operating expenses are expected to be $7,500 for the month. Monthly interest expense is $3,700. Sound Beginnings has a tax rate of 30% of income before taxes. Prepare Sound Beginnings' budgeted income statement for January.

### S9-10 Cash collections budget *(Learning Objective 3)*

Diamond Service anticipates the following sales revenue over a five-month period:

| | November | December | January | February | March |
|---|---|---|---|---|---|
| Sales revenue | $16,000 | $10,000 | $15,000 | $12,000 | $14,000 |

Diamond Service's sales are 25% cash and 75% credit. Its collection history indicates that credit sales are collected as follows:

| |
|---|
| 30% in the month of the sale |
| 60% in the month after the sale |
| 6% two months after the sale |
| 4% are never collected |

How much cash will be collected in January? In February? In March?

### S9-11 Prepare a cash payments budget *(Learning Objective 3)*

Sentinel Corporation is preparing its cash payments budget for next month. The following information pertains to the cash payments:

a. Sentinel Corporation pays for 50% of its direct materials purchases in the month of purchase and the remainder the following month. The current month's direct material purchases were $70,000, while Sentinel Corporation anticipates $80,000 of direct material purchases next month.

b. Direct labour for the upcoming month is budgeted to be $32,000 and will be paid at the end of the upcoming month.

c. Manufacturing overhead is estimated to be 150% of direct labour cost each month and is paid in the month in which it is incurred. This monthly estimate includes $11,000 of depreciation on the plant and equipment.

d. Monthly operating expenses for next month are expected to be $43,000, which includes $2,000 of depreciation on office equipment and $1,000 of bad debt expense. These monthly operating expenses are paid during the month in which they are incurred.

e. Sentinel Corporation will make an estimated tax payment of $7,000 next month.

How much cash will be paid out next month?

### S9-12 Prepare a cash budget *(Learning Objective 3)*

Grippers Manufacturing has $10,300 cash on hand on January 1. The company requires a minimum cash balance of $7,500. January cash collections are $548,330. Total cash payments for January are $583,200. Prepare a cash budget for January. How much cash, if any, will Grippers need to borrow by the end of January?

### S9-13 Prepare a budgeted balance sheet *(Learning Objective 3)*

Ireland Company's budgeted data for the upcoming year showed total projected assets of $1,275,500 and total projected liabilities of $812,000. The balance of common shares for the year is projected to remain stable at $250,000. The shareholders' equity section of the balance sheet is made up of common shares and retained earnings. No cash dividends will be paid during the year. Ireland Company is budgeting net income for the year of $158,500. Prepare a budgeted balance sheet for end of the year. What was the balance of retained earnings at the beginning of the year?

### S9-14 Identify responsibility centres *(Learning Objective 4)*

Fill in the blanks with the word or phrase that best completes the sentence.

| | | |
|---|---|---|
| A cost centre | A responsibility centre | Lower |
| An investment centre | A revenue centre | Higher |
| A profit centre | | |

CHAPTER 9

a. The Maintenance Department at the Calgary Zoo is _____.
b. The concession stand at the Calgary Zoo is _____.
c. The Menswear Department at The Bay, which is responsible for buying and selling merchandise, is _____.
d. A production line at a BlackBerry plant is _____.
e. _____ is any segment of the business whose manager is accountable for specific activities.
f. Quaker, a division of PepsiCo, is _____.
g. The sales manager in charge of Nike's Northwest sales territory oversees _____.
h. Managers of cost and revenue centres are at _____ levels of the organization than are managers of profit and investment centres.



**S9-15 Identify types of responsibility centres** *(Learning Objective 4)*

Identify each responsibility centre below as a cost centre, a revenue centre, a profit centre, or an investment centre.

a. The Bakery Department of a Sobey's supermarket reports income for the current year.
b. Pace Foods is a subsidiary of Campbell Soup Company.
c. The Personnel Department of RBC Insurance prepares its budget and subsequent performance report on the basis of its expected expenses for the year.
d. The Shopping Section of Burpee.com reports both revenues and expenses.
e. Burpee.com's investor relations Website provides operating and financial information to investors and other interested parties.
f. The manager of an Irving Oil service station is evaluated based on the station's revenues and expenses.
g. A charter airline records revenues and expenses for each airplane each month. Each airplane's performance report shows its ratio of operating income to average book value.
h. The manager of the Maritimes sales territory is evaluated based on a comparison of current period sales against budgeted sales.

**S9-16 Analyze inventory, purchases, and cost of goods sold** *(Learning Objective 5)*

Grippers sells its rock-climbing shoes worldwide. Grippers expects to sell 5,000 pairs of shoes for $185 each in January and 3,500 pairs of shoes for $220 each in February. All sales are cash only. Grippers expects cost of goods sold to average 65% of sales revenue, and the company expects to sell 4,300 pairs of shoes in March for $240 each. Grippers' target ending inventory is $10,000 plus 50% of the next month's cost of goods sold.

**Requirements**

1. Prepare the sales budget for January and February.
2. Prepare Grippers' inventory, purchases, and cost of goods sold budget for January and February.

# EXERCISES Group A

**E9-17A Prepare summary performance report** *(Learning Objective 1)*

Check sum: $20,000 net income

Priya Bali owns a chain of travel goods stores. Management anticipated selling 10,000 suitcases at an average sales price of $150. Variable expenses were budgeted to be 80% of sales revenue, and the total fixed expense was budgeted to be $100,000. The actual results for the year showed that 8,000 suitcases were sold at an average price of $200. The actual variable expense percentage was 80% of sales revenue and the total fixed expenses were as budgeted.

**Requirement**

1. Prepare a performance report for this year, similar to Exhibit 9-3. How would you improve Bali's performance evaluation system to better analyze this year's results?

**E9-18A Budgeting and sustainability** *(Learning Objective 2)*

Dudley Beverages manufactures its own soda pop bottles. The bottles are made from polyethylene terephthalate (PET), a lightweight yet strong plastic. Dudley uses as much PET recycled resin pellets in its bottles as it can, both because using recycled PET helps Dudley to meet its sustainability goals and because recycled PET is less expensive than virgin PET.

Dudley is continuing to search for ways to reduce its costs and its impact on the environment. PET plastic is melted and blown over soda bottle molds to produce the bottles. One idea Dudley's engineers have suggested is to retrofit the soda bottle moulds and change the plastic formulation slightly so that 20% less PET plastic is used for each bottle. The average kilograms of PET per soda bottle before any redesign is 0.005 kg. The cost of retrofitting the soda bottle moulds will result in a one-time charge of $18,000, while the plastic reformulation will cause the average cost per kilogram of PET plastic to change from $2.00 to $2.20.

Check sum: $13730 annual savings from redesign

Dudley's management is analyzing whether the change to the bottle moulds to reduce PET plastic usage should be made. Management expects the following number of soda bottles to be used in the upcoming year:

| | Quarter 1 | Quarter 2 | Quarter 3 | Quarter 4 |
|---|---|---|---|---|
| Number of soda pop bottles to be produced | 2,500,000 | 2,900,000 | 3,200,000 | 2,300,000 |

For the upcoming year, management expects the beginning inventory of PET to be 1,250 kilograms, while ending inventory (before any redesign) is expected to be 1,700 kilograms. During the first three quarters of the year, management wants to keep the ending inventory of PET at the end of each quarter equal to 10% of the following quarter's PET needs.

**Requirements**

1. Using the original data (before any redesign of soda bottles), prepare a direct materials budget to calculate the cost of PET purchases in each quarter for the upcoming year and for the year in total.
2. Assume that the company retrofits the soda bottle moulds and changes the plastic formulation slightly so that less PET plastic is used in each bottle. Now prepare a direct materials budget to calculate the cost of PET purchases in each quarter for the upcoming year and for the year in total for this possible scenario.
3. Compare the cost of PET plastic for Requirement 1 (original data) and for Requirement 2 (making the change to using less PET). What is the direct material cost savings from making the change to using less PET? Compare the total of those savings to the cost of retrofitting the soda bottle moulds. Should the company make the change? Explain your rationale.



**E9-19A Prepare a sales budget for a retail organization** *(Learning Objective 2)*

Harding College Bookstore, a campus bookstore, shows the following sales projections in units by quarter for the upcoming year:

Check sum: Book revenue for the year is $368,000.

| Quarter | Books | School Supplies | Apparel | Miscellaneous |
|---|---|---|---|---|
| 1st | 1,500 | 200 | 500 | 660 |
| 2nd | 800 | 150 | 350 | 520 |
| 3rd | 1,700 | 240 | 800 | 840 |
| 4th | 600 | 140 | 550 | 490 |

The average price of an item in each of the departments is as follows:

| | Average sales per unit |
|---|---|
| Books | $80 |
| School supplies | $10 |
| Apparel | $25 |
| Miscellaneous | $ 5 |

**Requirement**

1. Prepare a sales budget for the upcoming year by quarter for the Harding College Bookstore, with sales categorized by the four product groupings (books, school supplies, apparel, and miscellaneous).

### E9-20A Prepare a sales budget for a not-for-profit organization *(Learning Objective 2)*

Bright Star Preschool operates a not-for-profit morning preschool. Each family pays a nonrefundable registration fee of $120 per child per school year. Monthly tuition for the nine-month school year varies depending on the number of days per week that the child attends preschool. The monthly tuition is $115 for the two-day program, $130 for the three-day program, $145 for the four-day program, and $160 for the five-day program. The following enrolment has been projected for the coming year:

Check sum: Total revenue $233,520

| | |
|---|---|
| Two-day program | 56 children |
| Three-day program | 32 children |
| Four-day program | 48 children |
| Five-day program | 16 children |

In addition to the morning preschool, Bright Star Preschool offers a Lunch Bunch program where kids have the option of staying an extra hour for lunch and playtime. Bright Star Preschool charges an additional $5 per child for every Lunch Bunch attended. Historically, half the children stay for Lunch Bunch an average of 10 times a month.

**Requirement**

1. Calculate Bright Star Preschool's budgeted revenue for the school year.

### E9-21A Prepare a production budget *(Learning Objective 2)*

Ringer Foods produces specialty soup sold in jars. The projected sales in dollars and jars for each quarter of the upcoming year are as follows:

Check sum: Yearly units to produce is 717,500.

| | Total sales revenue | Number of jars sold |
|---|---|---|
| 1st quarter | $180,000 | 150,000 |
| 2nd quarter | $216,000 | 180,000 |
| 3rd quarter | $252,000 | 210,000 |
| 4th quarter | $192,000 | 160,000 |

Ringer anticipates selling 220,000 jars, with total sales revenue of $264,000, in the first quarter of the year following the year given in the preceding table. Ringer has a policy that the ending inventory of jars must be 25% of the following quarter's sales. Prepare a production budget for the year that shows the number of jars to be produced each quarter and for the year in total.

### E9-22A Prepare a direct materials budget *(Learning Objective 2)*

Beckett Industries manufactures a popular interactive stuffed animal for children that requires three computer chips inside each toy. Beckett Industries pays $2 for each computer chip. To help guard against stockouts of the computer chip, Beckett Industries has a policy that states that the ending inventory of computer chips should be at least 20% of the following month's production needs. The production schedule for the first four months of the year is as follows:

Check sum: Units to be produced for the quarter is 14,200.

| | Number of toys to be purchased |
|---|---|
| January | 5,000 |
| February | 4,400 |
| March | 4,800 |
| April | 4,200 |

**Requirement**

1. Prepare a direct materials budget for the first quarter that shows both the number of computer chips needed and the dollar amount of the purchases in the budget.

### E9-23A Prepare production and direct materials budgets *(Learning Objective 2)*

Mason Manufacturing produces self-watering planters for use in upscale retail establishments. Sales projections for the first five months of the upcoming year show the estimated unit sales of the planters each month to be as follows:

| | Number of planters to be sold |
|---|---|
| January | 3,500 |
| February | 3,400 |
| March | 3,600 |
| April | 4,000 |
| May | 4,200 |

Inventory at the start of the year was 350 planters and 1,396 kg of polypropylene (a type of plastic). The desired inventory of planters at the end of each month should be equal to 10% of the following month's budgeted sales. Each planter requires 2 kg of polypropylene. The company wants to have 20% of the polypropylene required for next month's production on hand at the end of each month. The polypropylene costs $0.25 per kilogram.

Check sum: Units needed in January is 3,840.

**Requirements**

1. Prepare a production budget for each month in the first quarter of the year, including production in units for each month and for the quarter.
2. Prepare a direct materials budget for the polypropylene for each month in the first quarter of the year, including the kilograms of polypropylene required and the total cost of the polypropylene to be purchased.

Check sum: Quantity needed for the quarter is 21,100 kg.

### E9-24A Prepare a direct labour budget *(Learning Objective 2)*

Madden Industries manufactures three models of a product in a single plant with two departments: Cutting and Assembly. The company has estimated costs for each of the three product models: the Zip, the Flash, and the Royal. The company is currently analyzing direct labour hour requirements for the upcoming year.

| | Cutting | Assembly |
|---|---|---|
| Estimated hours per unit: | | |
| Zips | 1.0 | 2.0 |
| Flashes | 1.5 | 2.4 |
| Royals | 1.2 | 2.3 |
| Direct labour hour rate | $10 | $12 |

Budgeted unit production for each of the products is as follows:

| | Number of units to be produced |
|---|---|
| Product model: | |
| Zips | 500 |
| Flashes | 700 |
| Royals | 800 |

**Requirement**

1. Prepare a direct labour budget for the upcoming year that shows the budgeted direct labour costs for each department and for the company as a whole.

## E9-25A Preparing a manufacturing overhead budget *(Learning Objective 2)*

The Harris Company is in the process of preparing its manufacturing overhead budget for the upcoming year. Sales are projected to be 40,000 units. Information about the various manufacturing overhead costs follows:

Check sum: Budgeted DL cost for ZIPS is $5,000.

| | Variable rate per unit | Total fixed costs |
|---|---|---|
| Indirect materials | $1.00 | |
| Supplies | $0.80 | |
| Indirect labour | $0.50 | $60,000 |
| Plant utilities | $0.10 | $30,000 |
| Repair and maintenance | $0.40 | $12,000 |
| Depreciation on plant and equipment | | $48,000 |
| Insurance on plant and equipment | | $20,000 |
| Plant supervision | | $65,000 |



### Requirement

1. Prepare the manufacturing overhead budget for the Harris Company for the upcoming year.

## E9-26A Prepare an operating expenses budget and an income statement *(Learning Objective 2)*

Great Start Preschool operates a not-for-profit morning preschool that operates nine months of the year. Great Start has 152 kids enrolled in its various programs. Great Start's primary expense is payroll. Teachers are hired so that there are no more than eight kids per teacher. Teachers are paid a flat salary each of the nine months as follows:

Check sum: Total monthly operating expenses are $22,252.

| | |
|---|---|
| Teachers of two-day program: | $ 432 per month |
| Teachers of three-day program: | $ 648 per month |
| Teachers of four-day program: | $ 864 per month |
| Teachers of five-day program: | $1,080 per month |
| Preschool director's salary: | $1,500 per month |

Great Start has seven two-day program teachers, four three-day program teachers, six four-day program teachers, and two five-day program teachers. Great Start also has one director.

In addition to the salary expense, Great Start must pay payroll taxes in the amount of 7.65% of salary expense. Great Start leases its facilities from a local church, paying $4,012 every month it operates. Fixed operating expenses (telephone, internet access, bookkeeping services, and so forth) amount to $850 per month over the nine-month school year. Variable monthly expenses (over the nine-month school year) for art supplies and other miscellaneous supplies are $12 per child. Revenue for the entire nine-month school year from tuition and registration fees is projected to be $219,840.

### Requirements

1. Prepare Great Start Preschool's monthly operating budget. Round all amounts to the nearest dollar.
2. Using your answer from Requirement 1, create Great Start Preschool's budgeted income statement for the entire nine-month school year. Assume that the operating revenue is $219,840. You may group all operating expenses together.
3. Great Start is a not-for-profit preschool. What might Great Start do with its projected income for the year?

**E9-27A Prepare a budgeted income statement** *(Learning Objective 2)*

Grandma's Touch Specialty Foods produces a specialty chocolate chip cookie that is sold to hotel chains by the case for $50 per case. For the upcoming quarter, Grandma's Touch is projecting the following sales:

| | January | February | March |
|---|---|---|---|
| Cases of cookies | 5,000 | 4,500 | 5,700 |

Check sum: Net income for the quarter is $166,880.

The budgeted cost of manufacturing each case is $23. Operating expenses are projected to be $58,000 in January, $53,000 in February, and $61,000 in March. Grandma's Touch is subject to a corporate tax rate of 30%.

**Requirement**

1. Prepare a budgeted income statement for the first quarter, with a column for each month and for the quarter.



**E9-28A Prepare a budgeted income statement** *(Learning Objective 2)*

Wheels is an exotic car dealership. Sales in the fourth quarter of last year were $4,000,000. Suppose its Sherbrooke office projects that its current year's quarterly sales will increase by 3% in quarter 1, by another 4% in quarter 2, by another 6% in quarter 3, and by another 5% in quarter 4. Management expects cost of goods sold to be 50% of revenues every quarter, while operating expenses should be 30% of revenues during each of the first two quarters, 25% of revenues during the third quarter, and 35% during the fourth quarter.

Check sum: Sales for the first quarter are $4,120,000.

**Requirement**

1. Prepare a budgeted income statement for each of the four quarters and for the entire year.

**E9-29A Prepare a cash collections budget** *(Learning Objective 3)*

Brandon Wholesalers has found that 80% of its sales in any given month are credit sales, while the remainder are cash sales. Of the credit sales, Brandon Wholesalers has experienced the following collection pattern:

| |
|---|
| 25% paid in the month of the sale |
| 50% paid in the month after the sale |
| 20% paid two months after the sale |
| 5% of the sales are never collected |

November sales for last year were $80,000, while December sales were $120,000. Projected sales for the next three months are as follows:

Check sum: Total cash collections in January are $92,800.

| | |
|---|---|
| January | $160,000 |
| February | $125,000 |
| March | $180,000 |

**Requirement**

1. Prepare a cash collections budget for the first quarter, with a column for each month and for the quarter.

**E9-30A Prepare a cash payments budget** *(Learning Objective 3)*

DB Corporation is preparing its cash payments budget. The following items relate to cash payments that DB Corporation anticipates making during the second quarter of the upcoming year.

a. DB Corporation pays for 50% of its direct materials purchases in the month of purchase and the remainder the following month. DB Corporation's direct material purchases for March through June are anticipated to be as follows:

Check sum: Total cash payments in January are $270,550.

| March | April | May | June |
|---|---|---|---|
| $112,000 | $135,000 | $128,000 | $145,000 |



b. Direct labour is paid in the month in which it is incurred. Direct labour for each month of the second quarter is budgeted as follows:

| April | May | June |
|---|---|---|
| $50,000 | $60,000 | $75,000 |

c. Manufacturing overhead is estimated to be 150% of direct labour cost each month. This monthly estimate includes $35,000 of depreciation on the plant and equipment. All manufacturing overhead (excluding depreciation) is paid in the month in which it is incurred.

d. Monthly operating expenses for March through June are projected to be as follows:

| March | April | May | June |
|---|---|---|---|
| $72,000 | $87,000 | $84,000 | $93,000 |

Monthly operating expenses are paid in the month after they are incurred. Monthly operating expenses include $12,000 for monthly depreciation on administrative offices and equipment, and $3,000 for bad debt expense.

e. DB Corporation plans to pay $5,000 (cash) for a new server in May.

f. DB Corporation must make an estimated tax payment of $12,500 on June 15.

**Requirement**

1. Prepare a cash payments budget for April, May, and June, and for the quarter.

**E9-31A Prepare a combined cash budget** *(Learning Objective 3)*

Woodlawn Manufacturing produces a variety of industrial valves. The company is preparing its cash budget for the upcoming third quarter. The following transactions are expected to occur:

a. Cash collections from sales in July, August, and September are projected to be $90,000, $152,000, and $121,000, respectively.

b. Cash payments for the upcoming third quarter are projected to be $140,000 in July, $100,000 in August, and $135,000 in September.

Check sum: Borrowings in July are $45,000.

c. The cash balance as of the first day of the third quarter is projected to be $30,000.

d. Woodlawn Manufacturing has a policy that it must maintain a minimum cash balance of $25,000.

The company has a line of credit with the local bank that allows it to borrow funds in months where it would not otherwise have a minimum balance of $25,000. If the company has more than $25,000 at the end of any given month, it uses the excess funds to pay off any outstanding line of credit balance. Each month, Woodlawn Manufacturing pays interest on the prior month's line of credit ending balance. The actual interest rate that Woodlawn Manufacturing will pay floats since it is tied to the prime rate. However, the interest rate paid during the budget period is expected to be 1% of the prior month's line of credit ending balance. (If the company did not have an outstanding balance at the end of the prior month, then Woodlawn Manufacturing does not have to pay any interest.) All line of credit borrowings are taken or paid off on the first day of the month. As of the first day of the third quarter, Woodlawn Manufacturing did not have a balance on its line of credit.

**Requirement**

1. Prepare a combined cash budget for Woodlawn Manufacturing for the third quarter, with a column for each month and for the quarter total.

**E9-32A Compute cash receipts and payments** *(Learning Objective 3)*

Aqua Pure is a distributor of bottled water. For each item below, compute the amount of cash receipts or payments Aqua Pure will budget for September. The solution to one item may depend on the answer to an earlier item.

a. The company expenses $5,000 per month for insurance on its fleet of delivery vehicles. The insurance premium is paid semiannually in September and March.
b. Management expects to sell 7,500 cases of water in August and 9,200 in September. Each case sells for $12. Cash sales average 30% of total sales, and credit sales make up the rest. On average, three-fourths of credit sales are collected in the month of sale, with the balance collected the following month.
c. The company pays commissions and other expenses of $4,200 per month.
d. A depreciation expense of $4,500 is recognized each month.
e. Aqua Pure declares $100,000 in dividends to shareholders of record as of September 14.
f. The payment date for the dividends declared in part e is September 30.

Check sum: Cash payment for insurance in September is $30,000.



**E9-33A Prepare sales and cash collections budgets** *(Learning Objectives 2 & 3)*

Horns and More, Ltd., a manufacturer of saxophone, oboe, and clarinet reeds, has projected sales to be $890,000 in October, $950,000 in November, $1,025,000 in December, and $920,000 in January. The company's sales are 25% cash and 75% credit, and collection history indicates that credit sales are collected as follows:

| |
|---|
| 25% in the month of the sale |
| 65% in the month after the sale |
| 8% two months after the sale |
| 2% are never collected |

Check sum: Total sales in January are $920,000.

**Requirements**

1. Prepare a sales budget for all four months, showing the breakdown between cash and credit sales.
2. Prepare a cash collections budget for December and January. Round all answers up to the nearest dollar.

**E9-34A Prepare a budgeted balance sheet** *(Learning Objective 3)*

Use the following information to prepare a budgeted balance sheet for Marine.com at March 31. Show computations for the cash and owners' equity amounts.

a. March 31 inventory balance, $15,000
b. March payments for inventory, $4,600
c. March payments of accounts payable and accrued liabilities, $8,200
d. March 31 accounts payable balance, $4,300
e. February 28 furniture and fixtures balance, $34,800; accumulated depreciation balance, $29,870
f. February 28 owners' equity, $26,700
g. March depreciation expense, $600
h. Cost of goods sold, 60% of sales
i. Other March expenses, including income tax, total $5,000; paid in cash
j. February 28 cash balance, $11,400
k. March budgeted sales, $12,200
l. March 31 accounts receivable balance, one-fourth of March sales
m. March cash receipts, $14,300

Check sum: Owners' equity is $25,980.

### E9-35A Prepare a cash budget *(Learning Objective 3)*

Check sum: November ending cash balance is $9,600.

Battery Power, a family-owned battery store, began October with $10,500 cash. Management forecasts that collections from credit customers will be $11,000 in October and $15,000 in November. The store is scheduled to receive $6,000 cash on a business note receivable in October. Projected cash payments include inventory purchases ($13,000 in October and $13,900 in November) and operating expenses ($3,000 each month).

Battery Power's bank requires a $8,000 minimum balance in the store's chequing account. At the end of any month when the account balance dips below $8,000, the bank automatically extends credit to the store in multiples of $1,000. Battery Power borrows as little as possible and pays back loans in quarterly instalments of $2,000 plus 4% interest on the entire unpaid principal. The first payment occurs three months after the loan.

**Requirement**

1. Prepare Battery Power's cash budget for October and November.

### E9-36A Finish an incomplete cash budget *(Learning Objective 3)*

Check sum: Borrowing at end of month in March is $0.

You recently began a job as an accounting intern at Outdoor Adventures. Your first task was to help prepare the cash budget for February and March. Unfortunately, the computer with the budget file crashed, and you did not have a backup or even a hard copy. You ran a program to salvage bits of data from the budget file. After entering the following data in the budget, you may have just enough information to reconstruct the budget.

Outdoor Adventures eliminates any cash deficiency by borrowing the exact amount needed from Caisse Populaire, where the current interest rate is 8%. Outdoor Adventures pays interest on its outstanding debt at the end of each month. The company also repays all borrowed amounts at the end of the month as cash becomes available.

**Requirement**

1. Complete the following cash budget:

**OUTDOOR ADVENTURES LTD.**
**Cash Budget**
**February and March**

| | February | March |
|---|---|---|
| Beginning cash balance | $ 16,900 | $ ? |
| Cash collections | ? | 79,600 |
| Cash from sale of plant assets | 0 | 1,800 |
| Cash available | 106,900 | ? |
| Cash payments: | | |
| Purchase of inventory | $ ? | $41,000 |
| Operating expenses | 47,200 | ? |
| Total payments | 98,000 | ? |
| (1) Ending cash balance before financing | ? | 25,100 |
| Minimum cash balance desired | 20,000 | 20,000 |
| Cash excess (deficiency) | $ ? | $ ? |
| Financing of cash deficiency: | | |
| Borrowing (at end of month) | $ ? | $ ? |
| Principal repayments (at end of month) | ? | ? |
| Interest expense | ? | ? |
| (2) Total effects of financing | ? | ? |
| Ending cash balance (1) + (2) | $ ? | $ ? |

### E9-37A Prepare performance reports at different organizational levels
*(Learning Objective 4)*

InTouch is a Lethbridge company that sells cell phones and tablets on the Web. InTouch has assistant managers for its digital and video cell phone operations. These assistant managers report to the manager of the total cell phone product line, who, with the manager of tablets, reports to the manager for all sales of handheld devices, Rima Bouagada. Bouagada received the following data for November operations:

| | *Cell Phones* | | |
|---|---|---|---|
| | **Digital** | **Video** | **Tablets** |
| Revenues, budget | $204,000 | $800,000 | $300,000 |
| Expenses, budget | 140,000 | 390,000 | 225,000 |
| Revenues, actual | 214,000 | 840,000 | 290,000 |
| Expenses, actual | 135,000 | 400,000 | 230,000 |

Check sum: Actual operating income from PDAs is $60.



**Requirement**

1. Arrange the data in a performance report similar to Exhibit 9-21. Show November results, in thousands of dollars, for digital cell phones, for the total cell phone product line, and for all devices. Should Bouagada investigate the performance of digital cell phone operations? Why or why not?

### E9-38A Prepare an inventory, purchases, and cost of goods sold budget
*(Learning Objective 5)*

Leno sells tire rims. Its sales budget for the nine months ended September 30 follows:

| | *Quarter Ended* | | | Nine-Month |
|---|---|---|---|---|
| | **Mar 31** | **Jun 30** | **Sep 30** | **Total** |
| Cash sales, 30% | $ 30,000 | $ 45,000 | $ 37,500 | $112,500 |
| Credit sales, 70% | 70,000 | 105,000 | 87,500 | 262,500 |
| Total sales, 100% | $100,000 | $150,000 | $125,000 | $375,000 |

In the past, cost of goods sold has been 60% of total sales. The director of marketing and the financial vice president agree that each quarter's ending inventory should not be below $20,000 plus 10% of cost of goods sold for the following quarter. The marketing director expects sales of $220,000 during the fourth quarter. The January 1 inventory was $19,000.

**Requirement**

1. Prepare an inventory, purchases, and cost of goods sold budget for each of the first three quarters of the year. Compute cost of goods sold for the entire nine-month period (use Exhibit 9-22 as a model).

# EXERCISES Group B

### E9-39B Prepare a summary performance report *(Learning Objective 1)*

Daniel Kyler owns a chain of travel goods stores. Management anticipated selling 10,500 suitcases at an average sale price of $180. Variable expenses were budgeted to be 65% of sales revenue, and the total fixed expenses were budgeted to be $115,000. The actual results for the year showed that 9,000 suitcases were sold at an average price of $280. The actual variable expense percentage was 65% of sales revenue and the total fixed expenses were as budgeted. Prepare a performance report for this year. How would you improve Kyler's performance evaluation system to better analyze this year's results?

### E9-40B Budgeting and Sustainability *(Learning Objective 2)*

Crawford Beverages manufactures its own soda pop bottles. The bottles are made from polyethylene terephthalate (PET), a lightweight yet strong plastic. Crawford uses as much PET recycled resin pellets in its bottles as it can, both because using recycled PET helps Crawford to meet its sustainability goals and because recycled PET is less expensive than virgin PET. Crawford is continuing to search for ways to reduce its costs and its impact on the environment.

PET plastic is melted and blown over soda bottle moulds to produce the bottles. One idea Crawford's engineers have suggested is to retrofit the soda bottle moulds and change the plastic formulation slightly so that 20% less PET plastic is used for each bottle. The average kilograms of PET per soda bottle before any redesign is 0.005 kg. The cost of retrofitting the soda bottle moulds will result in a one-time charge of $24,000, while the plastic reformulation will cause the average cost per kilogram of PET plastic to change from $2.50 to $2.60.

Crawford's management is analyzing whether the change to the bottle moulds to reduce PET plastic usage should be made. Management expects the following number of soda bottles to be used in the upcoming year:

| | Quarter 1 | Quarter 2 | Quarter 3 | Quarter 4 |
|---|---|---|---|---|
| Number of soda pop bottles to be produced.......................... | 2,000,000 | 3,000,000 | 2,700,000 | 2,500,000 |

For the upcoming year, management expects the beginning inventory of PET to be 1,000 kilograms, while ending inventory (before any redesign) is expected to be 1,700 kilograms. During the first three quarters of the year, management wants to keep the ending inventory of PET at 10% of the following quarter's PET needs.

#### Requirements

1. Using the original data (before any redesign of soda bottles), prepare a direct materials budget to calculate the cost of PET purchases in each quarter for the upcoming year and for the year in total.
2. Assume that the company retrofits the soda bottle moulds and changes the plastic formulation slightly so that less PET plastic is used in each bottle. Now prepare a direct materials budget to calculate the cost of PET purchases in each quarter for the upcoming year and for the year in total for this possible scenario.
3. Compare the cost of PET plastic for Requirement 1 (original data) and for Requirement 2 (making the change to using less PET). What is the direct material cost saving from making the change to using less PET? Compare the total of those savings to the cost of retrofitting the soda bottle moulds. Should the company make the change? Explain your rationale.

### E9-41B Prepare a sales budget for a retail organization *(Learning Objective 2)*

The Scholar CoOp Bookstore, a campus bookstore, shows the following sales projections in units by quarter for the upcoming year:

| Quarter | Books | School Supplies | Apparel | Miscellaneous |
|---|---|---|---|---|
| 1st.................................. | 1,580 | 260 | 520 | 620 |
| 2nd.................................. | 890 | 110 | 380 | 510 |
| 3rd.................................. | 1,790 | 280 | 870 | 800 |
| 4th.................................. | 610 | 160 | 560 | 450 |

The average price of an item in each of the departments is as follows:

| | Average sales per unit |
|---|---|
| Books | $84 |
| School supplies | $19 |
| Apparel | $23 |
| Miscellaneous | $ 8 |



**Requirement**

1. Prepare a sales budget for the upcoming year by quarter, with sales categorized by the four product groupings (books, school supplies, apparel, and miscellaneous).

## E9-42B Prepare a sales budget for a not-for-profit organization *(Learning Objective 2)*

Wonderland Preschool operates a not-for-profit morning preschool. Each family pays a nonrefundable registration fee of $100 per child per school year. Monthly tuition for the eight-month school year varies depending on the number of days per week that the child attends preschool. The monthly tuition is $130 for the two-day program, $150 for the three-day program, $175 for the four-day program, and $190 for the five-day program. The following enrolment has been projected for the coming year:

| | |
|---|---|
| Two-day program: 80 children | Four-day program: 54 children |
| Three-day program: 42 children | Five-day program: 12 children |

In addition to the morning preschool, Wonderland Preschool offers a Lunch Bunch program where kids have the option of staying an extra hour for lunch and playtime. Wonderland Preschool charges an additional $3 per child for every Lunch Bunch attended. Historically, half the children stay for Lunch Bunch an average of 15 times a month.

**Requirement**

1. Calculate Wonderland Preschool's budgeted revenue for the school year.

## E9-43B Prepare a production budget *(Learning Objective 2)*

Epicuria Foods produces specialty soup sold in jars. The projected sales in dollars and jars for each quarter of the upcoming year are as follows:

| | Total sales revenue | Number of jars sold |
|---|---|---|
| 1st quarter | $182,000 | 150,000 |
| 2nd quarter | $210,000 | 180,500 |
| 3rd quarter | $251,000 | 213,500 |
| 4th quarter | $195,000 | 164,500 |

Epicuria anticipates selling 223,000 jars with total sales revenue of $265,000, in the first quarter of the year following the year given in the preceding table. Epicuria has a policy that the ending inventory of jars must be 30% of the following quarter's sales. Prepare a production budget for the year that shows the number of jars to be produced each quarter and for the year in total.

## E9-44B Prepare a direct materials budget *(Learning Objective 2)*

Gable Industries manufactures a popular interactive stuffed animal for children that requires two computer chips inside each toy. Gable Industries pays $3 for each computer chip. To help guard against stockouts of the computer chip, Gable Industries has a policy that states that the ending inventory of computer chips should be at least 30% of the following month's production needs. The production schedule for the first four months of the year is as follows:

| | Stuffed animals to be produced |
|---|---|
| January | 5,700 |
| February | 4,600 |
| March | 4,300 |
| April | 4,900 |



**Requirement**

1. Prepare a direct materials budget for the first quarter that shows both the number of computer chips needed and the dollar amount of the purchases in the budget.

## E9-45B Prepare production and direct materials budgets *(Learning Objective 2)*

Green Thumb Manufacturing produces self-watering planters for use in upscale retail establishments. Sales projections for the first five months of the upcoming year show the estimated unit sales of the planters each month to be as follows:

| | Number of planters to be sold |
|---|---|
| January | 3,300 |
| February | 3,100 |
| March | 3,500 |
| April | 4,800 |
| May | 4,600 |

Inventory at the start of the year was 330 planters and 3,936 kg of polypropylene (a type of plastic). The desired inventory of planters at the end of each month should be equal to 10% of the following month's budgeted sales. Each planter requires 4 kg of polypropylene. The company wants to have 30% of the polypropylene required for next month's production on hand at the end of each month. The polypropylene costs $0.30 per kilogram.

**Requirements**

1. Prepare a production budget for each month in the first quarter of the year, including production in units for each month and for the quarter.
2. Prepare a direct materials budget for the polypropylene for each month in the first quarter of the year, including the kilograms of polypropylene required, and the total cost of the polypropylene to be purchased.

## E9-46B Prepare direct labour budget *(Learning Objective 2)*

AZ Industries manufactures three models of a product in a single plant with two departments: Cutting and Assembly. The company has estimated costs for each of the three product models, which are the Imperial, the Zip, and the Zoom models.

The company is currently analyzing direct labour hour requirements for the upcoming year.

| | Cutting | Assembly |
|---|---|---|
| Estimated hours per unit: | | |
| Imperials | 1.6 | 2.1 |
| Zips | 1.1 | 2.4 |
| Zooms | 1.7 | 2.9 |
| Direct labour hour rate | $10 | $11 |

Budgeted unit production for each of the products is as follows:

| | Number of units to be produced |
|---|---|
| Imperials | 540 |
| Zips | 770 |
| Zooms | 830 |



### Requirement

1. Prepare a direct labour budget for the upcoming year that shows the budgeted direct labour costs for each department and for the company as a whole.

## E9-47B Prepare manufacturing overhead budget *(Learning Objective 2)*

The Schulman Company is in the process of preparing its manufacturing overhead budget for the upcoming year. Sales are projected to be 44,000 units. Information about the various manufacturing overhead costs follows:

| | Variable rate per unit | Total fixed costs |
|---|---|---|
| Indirect materials | $0.80 | |
| Supplies | $0.90 | |
| Indirect labour | $0.60 | $68,000 |
| Plant utilities | $0.20 | $30,000 |
| Repairs and maintenance | $0.30 | $14,000 |
| Depreciation on plant and equipment | | $45,000 |
| Insurance on plant and equipment | | $20,000 |
| Plant supervision | | $66,000 |

### Requirement

1. Prepare the manufacturing overhead budget for the Schulman Company for the upcoming year.

## E9-48B Prepare an operating expenses budget and an income statement *(Learning Objective 2)*

Nice Place Preschool operates a not-for-profit morning preschool that operates nine months of the year. Nice Place has 161 kids enrolled in its various programs. Nice Place's primary expense is payroll. Teachers are paid a flat salary each of the nine months as follows:

| Salary data | |
|---|---|
| Teachers of two-day program: | $ 438 per month |
| Teachers of three-day program: | $ 651 per month |
| Teachers of four-day program: | $ 872 per month |
| Teacher of five-day program: | $1,040 per month |
| Preschool director's salary | $1,250 per month |

Nice Place has eight two-day program teachers, five three-day program teachers, seven four-day program teachers, and three five-day program teachers. Nice Place also has one director.

In addition to the salary expense, Nice Place must pay payroll taxes in the amount of 7.65% of salary expense. Nice Place leases its facilities from a local church, paying $2,200 per month plus 10.75% of monthly tuition revenue. Fixed operating expenses (telephone, internet access, bookkeeping services, and so forth) amount to $890 per month over the nine-month school year. Variable monthly expenses (over the nine-month school year) for art supplies and other miscellaneous supplies are $10 per child.

Revenue for the entire nine-month school year from tuition and registration fees is projected to be $291,865. The monthly tuition revenue is $26,710.

### Requirements

1. Prepare Nice Place Preschool's monthly operating budget. Round all amounts to the nearest dollar.
2. Using your answer from Requirement 1, create Nice Place Preschool's budgeted income statement for the entire nine-month school year. Assume that the operating revenue is $291,865. You may group all operating expenses together.
3. Nice Place is a not-for-profit preschool. What might Nice Place do with its projected income for the year?



## E9-49B Prepare a budgeted income statement *(Learning Objective 2)*

Cloutier Foods produces a specialty brownie that is sold to hotel chains by the case for $55 per case. For the upcoming quarter, Cloutier Foods is projecting the following sales:

| | January | February | March |
|---|---|---|---|
| Cases of brownies | 5,700 | 4,900 | 5,500 |

The budgeted cost of manufacturing each case is $27. Operating expenses are projected to be $61,000 in January, $57,000 in February, and $64,000 in March. Cloutier Foods is subject to a corporate tax rate of 30%.

### Requirement

1. Prepare a budgeted income statement for the first quarter, with a column for each month and for the quarter in total.

## E9-50B Prepare a budgeted income statement *(Learning Objective 2)*

Warm Wheels is an exotic car dealership. Sales in the fourth quarter of last year were $4,400,000. Suppose its Vancouver office projects that its current year's quarterly sales will increase by 2% in quarter 1, by another 6% in quarter 2, by another 4% in quarter 3, and by another 3% in quarter 4. Management expects cost of goods sold to be 45% of revenues every quarter, while operating expenses should be 35% of revenues during each of the first two quarters, 20% of revenues during the third quarter, and 25% during the fourth quarter.

### Requirement

1. Prepare a budgeted income statement for each of the four quarters and for the entire year.

## E9-51B Prepare a cash collections budget *(Learning Objective 3)*

Won Wholesalers has found that 60% of its sales in any given month are credit sales, while the remainder are cash sales. Of the credit sales, Won Wholesalers has experienced the following collection pattern:

| |
|---|
| 25% paid in the month of the sale |
| 50% paid in the month after the sale |
| 15% paid two months after the sale |
| 10% of the sales are never collected |

November sales for last year were $90,000, while December sales were $125,000. Projected sales for the next 3 months are as follows:

| | |
|---|---|
| January sales | $180,000 |
| February sales | $135,000 |
| March sales | $190,000 |

### Requirement

1. Prepare a cash collections budget for the first quarter, with a column for each month and for the quarter.

## E9-52B Prepare a cash payments budget *(Learning Objective 3)*

Monachino Corporation is preparing its cash payments budget. The following items relate to cash payments Monachino Corporation anticipates making during the second quarter of the upcoming year.

a. Monachino Corporation pays for 55% of its direct materials purchases in the month of purchase and the remainder the following month. Monachino Corporation's direct material purchases for March through June are anticipated to be as follows:

| March | April | May | June |
|---|---|---|---|
| $117,000 | $134,000 | $129,000 | $148,000 |

b. Direct labour is paid in the month in which it is incurred. Direct labour for each month of the second quarter is budgeted as follows:

| April | May | June |
|---|---|---|
| $54,000 | $64,000 | $79,000 |

c. Manufacturing overhead is estimated to be 130% of direct labour cost each month. This monthly estimate includes $34,000 of depreciation on the plant and equipment. All manufacturing overhead (excluding depreciation) is paid in the month in which it is incurred.

d. Monthly operating expenses for March through June are projected to be as follows:

| March | April | May | June |
|---|---|---|---|
| $77,000 | $84,000 | $86,000 | $97,000 |

Monthly operating expenses are paid in the month after they are incurred. Monthly operating expenses include $13,000 for monthly depreciation on administrative offices and equipment and $3,500 for bad debt expense.

e. Monachino Corporation plans to pay $10,000 (cash) for a new server in May.

f. Monachino Corporation must make an estimated tax payment of $12,500 on June 15.

### Requirement

1. Prepare a cash payments budget for April, May, and June, and for the quarter.

## E9-53B Prepare a combined cash budget *(Learning Objective 3)*

Zhang Manufacturing produces a variety of industrial valves. The company is preparing its cash budget for the upcoming third quarter. The following transactions are expected to occur:

a. Cash collections from sales in July, August, and September are projected to be $93,000, $158,000, and $120,000, respectively.

b. Cash payments for the upcoming third quarter are projected to be $143,000 in July, $108,000 in August, and $132,000 in September.

c. The cash balance as of the first day of the third quarter is projected to be $34,000.

Zhang Manufacturing has a policy that it must maintain a minimum cash balance of $27,000. The company has a line of credit with the local bank that allows it to borrow funds in months that it would not otherwise have a minimum balance of $27,000. If the company has more than $27,000 at the end of any given month, it uses the excess funds to pay off any outstanding line of credit balance.

Each month, Zhang Manufacturing pays interest on the prior month's line of credit ending balance. The actual interest rate floats since it is tied to the prime rate. However, the interest rate paid during the budget period is expected to be 1% of the prior month's line of credit ending balance. (If it did not have an outstanding balance at the end of the prior month, then Zhang Manufacturing does not have to pay any interest.) All line of credit borrowings are taken or paid off on the first day of the month. As of the first day of the third quarter, Zhang Manufacturing did not have a balance on its line of credit.

**Requirement**

1. Prepare a combined cash budget for Zhang Manufacturing for the third quarter, with a column for each month and for the quarter total.

### E9-54B Compute cash receipts and payments *(Learning Objective 3)*

Aqua Cool is a distributor of bottled water. For each item below, compute the amount of cash receipts or payments Aqua Cool will budget for September. The solution to one item may depend on the answer to an earlier item.

a. The company expenses $5,200 per month for insurance on its fleet of delivery vehicles. The insurance premium is paid semiannually, in September and March.
b. Management expects to sell 7,900 cases of water in August and 9,600 in September. Each case sells for $13. Cash sales average 30% of total sales, and credit sales make up the rest. Three-fourths of credit sales are collected in the month of sale, with the balance collected the following month.
c. The company pays commissions and other expenses of $4,100 per month.
d. Depreciation expense of $3,500 is recognized each month.
e. Aqua Cool declares $106,000 in dividends to shareholders of record as of September 14.
f. The payment date for the dividends declared in part (e) is September 30.

### E9-55B Prepare sales and cash collections budgets *(Learning Objectives 2 & 3)*

Yung Reeds, a manufacturer of saxophone, oboe, and clarinet reeds, has projected sales to be $900,000 in October, $954,000 in November, $1,040,000 in December, and $924,000 in January. Yung's sales are 20% cash and 80% credit. Yung's collection history indicates that credit sales are collected as follows:

| |
|---|
| 25% paid in the month of the sale |
| 60% paid in the month after the sale |
| 14% paid two months after the sale |
| 1% of the sales are never collected |

**Requirements**

1. Prepare a sales budget for all four months, showing the breakdown between cash and credit sales.
2. Prepare a cash collection budget for December and January. Round all answers up to the nearest dollar.

### E9-56B Prepare a budgeted balance sheet *(Learning Objective 3)*

Use the following information to prepare a budgeted balance sheet for Rescue.com at March 31. Show computations for the cash and owners' equity amounts.

a. March 31 inventory balance, $17,535
b. March payments for inventory, $4,400
c. March payments of accounts payable and accrued liabilities, $8,300
d. March 31 accounts payable balance, $2,200
e. February 28 furniture and fixtures balance, $34,600; accumulated depreciation balance, $29,880
f. February 28 owners' equity, $28,510
g. March depreciation expense, $800
h. Cost of goods sold, 40% of sales
i. Other March expenses, including income tax, total $6,000; paid in cash

j. February 28 cash balance, $11,400
k. March budgeted sales, $12,700
l. March 31 accounts receivable balance, one-fourth of March sales
m. March cash receipts, $14,200

### E9-57B Prepare a cash budget *(Learning Objective 3)*

Energy Power, a family-owned battery store, began October with $10,000 cash. Management forecasts that collections from credit customers will be $11,400 in October and $14,800 in November. The store is scheduled to receive $4,500 cash on a business note receivable in October. Projected cash payments include inventory purchases ($9,700 in October and $13,200 in November) and operating expenses ($4,200 each month).

Energy Power's bank requires a $11,000 minimum balance in the store's chequing account. At the end of any month when the account balance dips below $11,000, the bank automatically extends credit to the store in multiples of $2,000. Energy Power borrows as little as possible and pays back loans in quarterly instalments of $4,000, plus 6% interest on the entire unpaid principal. The first payment occurs three months after the loan.

**Requirement**

1. Prepare Energy Power's cash budget for October and November.

### E9-58B Finish an incomplete cash budget *(Learning Objective 3)*

You recently began a job as an accounting intern at Backyard Adventures. Your first task was to help prepare the cash budget for February and March. Unfortunately, the computer with the budget file crashed, and you did not have a backup or even a hard copy. You ran a program to salvage bits of data from the budget file. After entering the following data in the budget, you may have just enough information to reconstruct the budget.

Backyard Adventures eliminates any cash deficiency by borrowing the exact amount needed from a local bank, where the current interest rate is 6%. Backyard Adventures pays interest on its outstanding debt at the end of each month. The company also repays all borrowed amounts at the end of the month, as cash becomes available.

**Requirement**

1. Complete the following cash budget:

**Backyard Adventures, LTD.**
**Cash Budget**
February and March

| | February | March |
|---|---|---|
| Beginning cash balance | $ 16,500 | $ ? |
| Cash collections | ? | 80,000 |
| Cash from sale of plant assets | 0 | 1,900 |
| Cash available | 106,500 | ? |
| Cash payments: | | |
| Purchase of inventory | $ ? | $41,100 |
| Operating expenses | 47,400 | ? |
| Total payments | 98,300 | ? |
| (1) Ending cash balance before financing | ? | 23,700 |
| Minimum cash balance desired | 21,000 | 21,000 |
| Cash excess (deficiency) | $ ? | $ ? |
| Financing of cash deficiency: | | |
| Borrowing (at end of month) | $ ? | $ ? |
| Principal repayments (at end of month) | ? | ? |
| Interest expense | ? | ? |
| (2) Total effects of financing | ? | ? |
| Ending cash balance (1) + (2) | $ ? | $ ? |

CHAPTER 9

### E9-59B Prepare performance reports at different organizational levels

*(Learning Objective 4)*

iHere-U is a Halifax company that sells cell phones and tablets on the Web. iHere-U has assistant managers for its digital and video cell phone operations. These assistant managers report to the manager of the total cell phone product line, who, with the manager of tablets reports to the manager for sales of all handheld devices, Mary Burton. Burton received the following data for November operations:

| | *Cell Phones* | | |
|---|---|---|---|
| | **Digital** | **Video** | **Tablets** |
| Revenues, budget | $205,000 | $805,000 | $300,000 |
| Expenses, budget | 144,000 | 430,000 | 228,000 |
| Revenues, actual | 217,000 | 865,000 | 280,000 |
| Expenses, actual | 134,000 | 400,000 | 240,000 |

**Requirement**

1. Arrange the data in the performance reports. Show November results, in thousands of dollars, for digital cell phones, for the total cell phone product line, and for all handheld devices. Should management investigate the performance of digital cell phone operations? Why or why not?

### E9-60B Prepare an inventory, purchases, and cost of goods sold budget

*(Learning Objective 5)*

Sullivan sells tire rims. Its sales budget for the nine months ended September 30 follows:

| | *Quarter Ended* | | | |
|---|---|---|---|---|
| | **Mar 31** | **Jun 30** | **Sep 30** | **Nine-Month Total** |
| Cash sales, 40% | $ 40,000 | $ 60,000 | $ 50,000 | $150,000 |
| Credit sales, 60% | 60,000 | 90,000 | 75,000 | 225,000 |
| Total sales, 100% | $100,000 | $150,000 | $125,000 | $375,000 |

In the past, cost of goods sold has been 65% of total sales. The director of marketing and the financial vice president agree that each quarter's ending inventory should not be below $10,000 plus 15% of cost of goods sold for the following quarter. The marketing director expects sales of $200,000 during the fourth quarter. The January 1 inventory was $17,000.

**Requirement**

1. Prepare an inventory, purchases, and cost of goods sold budget for each of the first three quarters of the year. Compute cost of goods sold for the entire nine-month period (use Exhibit 9-22 as a model).

# PROBLEMS Group A

**P9-61A Solve a comprehensive budgeting problem** *(Learning Objectives 2 & 3)*

Cicek Manufacturing is preparing its master budget for the first quarter of the upcoming year. The following data pertain to Cicek Manufacturing's operations:

| Current Assets as of December 31 (prior year): | |
|---|---|
| Cash | $ 4,500 |
| Accounts receivable, net | $ 49,000 |
| Inventory | $ 15,320 |
| Property, plant, and equipment, net | $121,500 |
| Accounts payable | $ 42,400 |
| Capital stock | $125,000 |
| Retained earnings | $ 22,920 |

a. Actual sales in December were $70,000. Selling price per unit is projected to remain stable at $10 per unit throughout the budget period. Sales for the first five months of the upcoming year are budgeted to be as follows:

| | |
|---|---|
| January | $80,000 |
| February | $92,000 |
| March | $99,000 |
| April | $97,000 |
| May | $85,000 |

b. Sales are 30% cash and 70% credit. All credit sales are collected in the month following the sale.

c. Cicek Manufacturing has a policy that states that each month's ending inventory of finished goods should be 25% of the following month's sales (in units).

d. Of each month's direct material purchases, 20% are paid for in the month of purchase, while the remainder is paid for in the month following purchase. Two kilograms of direct material is needed per unit at $2/kg. Ending inventory of direct materials should be 10% of next month's production needs.

e. Monthly manufacturing conversion costs are $5,000 for factory rent, $3,000 for other fixed manufacturing expenses, and $1.20 per unit for variable manufacturing overhead. No depreciation is included in these figures. All expenses are paid in the month in which they are incurred.

f. Computer equipment for the administrative offices will be purchased in the upcoming quarter. In January, Cicek Manufacturing will purchase equipment for $5,000 (cash), while February's cash expenditure will be $12,000 and March's cash expenditure will be $16,000.

g. Operating expenses are budgeted to be $1 per unit sold plus fixed operating expenses of $1,000 per month. All operating expenses are paid in the month in which they are incurred.

h. Depreciation on the building and equipment for the general and administrative offices is budgeted to be $6,000 for the entire quarter, which includes depreciation on new acquisitions.

i. Cicek Manufacturing has a policy that the ending cash balance in each month must be at least $4,000. It has a line of credit with a local bank. The company can borrow in increments of $1,000 at the beginning of each month, up to a total outstanding loan balance of $100,000. The interest rate on these loans is 1% per month simple interest (not compounded). Cicek Manufacturing pays down on the line of credit balance if it has excess funds at the end of the quarter. The company also pays the accumulated interest at the end of the quarter on the funds borrowed during the quarter.

CHAPTER 9

j. The company's income tax rate is projected to be 30% of operating income less interest expense. The company pays $10,000 cash at the end of February in estimated taxes.

## Requirements

1. Prepare a schedule of cash collections for January, February, and March, and for the quarter in total. Use the following format:

**Cash Collections Budget**

| | January | February | March | Quarter |
|---|---|---|---|---|
| Cash sales | | | | |
| Credit sales | | | | |
| Total cash collections | | | | |

2. Prepare a production budget, using the following format:

**Production Budget**

| | January | February | March | Quarter |
|---|---|---|---|---|
| Unit sales* | | | | |
| Plus: Desired ending inventory | | | | |
| Total needed | | | | |
| Less: Beginning inventory | | | | |
| Units to produce | | | | |

**Hint:* Unit sales = Sales in dollars ÷ Selling price per unit

3. Prepare a direct materials budget, using the following format:

**Direct Materials Budget**

| | January | February | March | Quarter |
|---|---|---|---|---|
| Units to be produced | | | | |
| × kg of DM needed per unit | | | | |
| Quantity (kg) needed for production | | | | |
| Plus: Desired ending inventory of DM | | | | |
| Total quantity (kg) needed | | | | |
| Less: Beginning inventory of DM | | | | |
| Quantity (kg) to purchase | | | | |
| × Cost per kg | | | | |
| Total cost of DM purchases | | | | |

4. Prepare a cash payments budget for the direct material purchases from Requirement 3, using the following format:

| Cash Payments for Direct Material Purchases Budget | | | | |
|---|---|---|---|---|
| | January | February | March | Quarter |
| December purchases (from Accounts Payable) | | | | |
| January purchases | | | | |
| February purchases | | | | |
| March purchases | | | | |
| Total cash payments for direct material purchases | | | | |

5. Prepare a cash payments budget for conversion costs, using the following format:

| Cash Payments for Conversion Costs Budget | | | | |
|---|---|---|---|---|
| | January | February | March | Quarter |
| Variable conversion costs | | | | |
| Rent (fixed) | | | | |
| Other fixed MOH | | | | |
| Total payments for conversion costs | | | | |

6. Prepare a cash payments budget for operating expenses, using the following format:

| Cash Payments for Operating Expenses Budget | | | | |
|---|---|---|---|---|
| | January | February | March | Quarter |
| Variable operating expenses | | | | |
| Fixed operating expenses | | | | |
| Total payments for operating expenses | | | | |

7. Prepare a combined cash budget, using the following format:

| Combined Cash Budget | | | | |
|---|---|---|---|---|
| | January | February | March | Quarter |
| Cash balance, beginning | | | | |
| Add cash collections | | | | |
| Total cash available | | | | |
| Less cash payments: | | | | |
| Direct material purchases | | | | |
| Conversion costs | | | | |
| Operating expenses | | | | |
| Equipment purchases | | | | |
| Tax payment | | | | |
| Total cash payments | | | | |
| Ending cash balance before financing | | | | |
| Financing: | | | | |
| Borrowings | | | | |
| Repayments | | | | |
| Interest payments | | | | |
| Ending cash balance | | | | |

8. Calculate the budgeted manufacturing cost per unit, using the following format (assume that fixed manufacturing overhead is budgeted to be $0.80 per unit for the year):

| Budgeted Manufacturing Cost per Unit | |
|---|---|
| Direct materials cost per unit | |
| Conversion costs per unit | |
| Fixed manufacturing overhead per unit | |
| Budgeted cost of manufacturing each unit | |

9. Prepare a budgeted income statement for the quarter ending March 31, using the following format:

| Budgeted Income Statement<br>For the Quarter Ending March 31 |  |
|---|---|
| Sales | ........ |
| Cost of goods sold* | ........ |
| Gross profit | ........ |
| Operating expenses | ........ |
| Depreciation | ........ |
| Operating income | ........ |
| Less interest expense | ........ |
| Less provision for income taxes | ........ |
| Net income | ........ |

*Cost of goods sold = Budgeted cost of manufacturing each unit × Number of units sold

10. Prepare a partial budgeted balance sheet for March 31. Follow the same format as the original balance sheet provided for December 31, adding Loans Payable and Income Tax Payable.

CHAPTER 9

### P9-62A Prepare budgeted income statement *(Learning Objective 2)*

The budget committee of Vinning Office Supply has assembled the following data. As the business manager, you must prepare the budgeted income statements for May and June.

a. Sales in April were $50,000. You forecast that monthly sales will increase 10% in May and 3% in June.

b. Vinning Office Supply maintains inventory of $9,000 plus 30% of sales revenues budgeted for the following month. Monthly purchases average 50% of sales revenues in that same month. Actual inventory on April 30 is $14,000. Sales budgeted for July are $55,000.

c. Monthly salaries amount to $4,000. Sales commissions equal 10% of sales for that month. Combine salaries and commissions into a single figure.

d. Other monthly expenses are as follows:

| | |
|---|---|
| Rent expense | $3,000, paid as incurred |
| Depreciation expense | $ 600 |
| Insurance expense | $ 200, expiration of prepaid amount |
| Income tax | 20% of operating income |

### P9-63A Prepare cash budgets *(Learning Objective 3)*

Veeran's Manufacturing is preparing its cash budgets for the first two months of the upcoming year. The following information concerns the company's upcoming cash receipts and cash disbursements.

a. Sales are 70% cash and 30% credit. Credit sales are collected 20% in the month of sale and the remainder in the month after sale. Actual sales in December were $55,000. Schedules of budgeted sales for the two months of the upcoming year are as follows:

| | Budgeted Sales Revenue |
|---|---|
| January | $60,000 |
| February | $68,000 |

b. Actual purchases of direct materials in December were $24,000. Veeran's purchases of direct materials in January are budgeted to be $22,000 and $26,000 in February. All purchases are paid 50% in the month of purchase and 50% the following month.

c. Salaries and sales commissions are also paid half in the month earned and half the next month. Actual salaries were $8,000 in December. Budgeted salaries in January are $9,000, and February budgeted salaries are $10,500. Sales commissions each month are 10% of that month's sales.

d. Rent expense is $3,000 per month.

e. Depreciation is $2,500 per month.

f. Estimated income tax payments are made at the end of January. The estimated tax payment is projected to be $12,500.

g. The cash balance at the end of the prior year was $21,000.

### Requirements

1. Prepare schedules of (a) budgeted cash collections, (b) budgeted cash payments for purchases, and (c) budgeted cash payments for operating expenses. Show amounts for each month and totals for January and February.
2. Prepare a combined cash budget similar to Exhibit 9-16. If no financing activity took place, what is the budgeted cash balance on February 28?

### P9-64A Prepare a combined cash budget and a budgeted balance sheet

*(Learning Objective 3)*

Alliance Printing of Fredericton has applied for a loan. Scotiabank has requested a budgeted balance sheet as of April 30 and a combined cash budget for April. As Alliance Printing's controller, you have assembled the following information:

a. March 31 equipment balance, $52,400; accumulated depreciation, $41,300

b. April capital expenditures of $42,800 budgeted for cash purchase of equipment

c. April depreciation expense, $900

d. Cost of goods sold, 60% of sales

e. Other April operating expenses, including income tax, total $13,200, 25% of which will be paid in cash and the remainder accrued at April 30

f. March 31 owners' equity, $93,700

g. March 31 cash balance, $40,600

h. April budgeted sales, $90,000, 70% of which is for cash; of the remaining 30%, half will be collected in April and half in May

i. April cash collections on March sales, $29,700

j. April cash payments of March 31 liabilities incurred for March purchases of inventory, $17,300

k. March 31 inventory balance, $29,600

l. April purchases of inventory, $10,000 for cash and $36,800 on credit; half of the credit purchases will be paid in April and half in May

### Requirements

1. Prepare the budgeted balance sheet for Alliance Printing at April 30. Show separate computations for cash, inventory, and owners' equity balances.
2. Prepare the combined cash budget for April.
3. Suppose Alliance Printing has become aware of more efficient (and more expensive) equipment than it budgeted for purchase in April. What is the total amount of cash available for equipment purchases in April, before financing, if the minimum desired ending cash balance is $21,000? (For this requirement, disregard the $42,800 initially budgeted for equipment purchases.)
4. Before granting a loan to Alliance Printing, Scotiabank asks for a sensitivity analysis assuming that April sales are only $60,000 rather than the $90,000 originally budgeted. (While the cost of goods sold will change, assume that purchases, depreciation, and the other operating expenses will remain the same as in the earlier requirements.)

   a. Prepare a revised budgeted balance sheet for Alliance Printing, showing separate computations for cash, inventory, and owners' equity balances.

   b. Suppose Alliance Printing has a minimum desired cash balance of $23,000. Will the company need to borrow cash in April?

   c. In this sensitivity analysis, sales declined by 33 1/3% ($30,000 ÷ $90,000). Is the decline in expenses and income more or less than 33 1/3%? Explain.



## P9-65A Prepare performance reports for various organizational levels

*(Learning Objective 4)*

Winnie's World operates a chain of pet stores in the Prairies. The manager of each store reports to the regional manager, who, in turn, reports to the headquarters in Regina. The *actual* income statements for the Winnipeg store, the Manitoba region (including the Winnipeg store), and the company as a whole (including the Manitoba region) for July are as follows:

| | Winnipeg | Manitoba | Companywide |
|---|---|---|---|
| Revenue | $148,900 | $1,647,000 | $4,200,000 |
| Expenses: | | | |
| Regional manager/headquarters office | $ — | $ 60,000 | $ 116,000 |
| Cost of materials | 81,100 | 871,900 | 1,807,000 |
| Salary expense | 38,300 | 415,100 | 1,119,000 |
| Depreciation expense | 7,200 | 91,000 | 435,000 |
| Utilities expense | 4,000 | 46,200 | 260,000 |
| Rent expense | 2,400 | 34,700 | 178,000 |
| Total expenses | $133,000 | $1,518,900 | $3,915,000 |

*Budgeted* amounts for July were as follows:

| | Winnipeg | Manitoba | Companywide |
|---|---|---|---|
| Revenue | $162,400 | $1,769,700 | $4,450,000 |
| Expenses: | | | |
| Regional manager/headquarters office | $ — | $ 65,600 | $ 118,000 |
| Cost of materials | 86,400 | 963,400 | 1,972,000 |
| Salary expense | 38,800 | 442,000 | 1,095,000 |
| Depreciation expense | 7,200 | 87,800 | 449,000 |
| Utilities expense | 4,400 | 54,400 | 271,000 |
| Rent expense | 3,600 | 32,300 | 174,000 |
| Total expenses | $140,400 | $1,645,500 | $4,079,000 |

**Requirements**

1. Prepare a report for July that shows the performance of the Winnipeg store, the Manitoba region, and the company as a whole. Follow the format of Exhibit 9-21.
2. As the Manitoba region manager, would you investigate the Winnipeg store on the basis of this report? Why or why not?
3. Briefly discuss the benefits of budgeting. Base your discussion on Winnie's World's performance report.

**P9-66A Prepare an inventory, purchases, and cost of goods sold budget** *(Learning Objective 5)*

University Logos buys logo-imprinted merchandise and then sells it to university bookstores. Sales are expected to be $2,000,000 in September, $2,160,000 in October, $2,376,000 in November, and $2,400,000 in December. University Logos sets its prices to earn an average 30% gross profit on sales revenue. The company does not want inventory to fall below $400,000 plus 15% of the next month's cost of goods sold.

**Requirement**

1. Prepare an inventory, purchases, and cost of goods sold budget for the months of October and November.

# PROBLEMS Group B

## P9-67B Comprehensive budgeting problem *(Learning Objectives 2 & 3)*

Osborne Manufacturing is preparing its master budget for the first quarter of the upcoming year. The following data pertain to Osborne Manufacturing's operations:

| Current Assets as of December 31 (prior year): | |
|---|---|
| Cash | $ 4,640 |
| Accounts receivable, net | $ 57,600 |
| Inventory | $ 15,600 |
| Property, plant, and equipment, net | $121,500 |
| Accounts payable | $ 42,800 |
| Capital stock | $124,500 |
| Retained earnings | $ 22,800 |

a. Actual sales in December were $72,000. Selling price per unit is projected to remain stable at $12 per unit throughout the budget period. Sales for the first five months of the upcoming year are budgeted to be as follows:

| | |
|---|---|
| January | $104,400 |
| February | $108,000 |
| March | $112,800 |
| April | $109,200 |
| May | $105,600 |

b. Sales are 20% cash and 80% credit. All credit sales are collected in the month following the sale.

c. Osborne Manufacturing has a policy that states that each month's ending inventory of finished goods should be 10% of the following month's sales (in units).

d. Of each month's direct material purchases, 20% are paid for in the month of purchase, while the remainder is paid for in the month following purchase. Three kilograms of direct material is needed per unit at $2.00 per kilogram. Ending inventory of direct materials should be 30% of next month's production needs.

e. Monthly manufacturing conversion costs are $4,500 for factory rent, $2,800 for other fixed manufacturing expenses, and $1.10 per unit for variable manufacturing overhead. No depreciation is included in these figures. All expenses are paid in the month in which they are incurred.

f. Computer equipment for the administrative offices will be purchased in the upcoming quarter. In January, Osborne Manufacturing will purchase equipment for $6,000 (cash), while February's cash expenditure will be $12,800, and March's cash expenditure will be $15,600.

g. Operating expenses are budgeted to be $1.30 per unit sold plus fixed operating expenses of $1,800 per month. All operating expenses are paid in the month in which they are incurred.

h. Depreciation on the building and equipment for the general and administrative offices is budgeted to be $4,600 for the entire quarter, which includes depreciation on new acquisitions.

i. Osborne Manufacturing has a policy that the ending cash balance in each month must be at least $4,200. The company has a line of credit with a local bank. It can borrow in increments of $1,000 at the beginning of each month, up to a total outstanding loan balance of $130,000. The interest rate on these loans is 2% per month simple interest (not compounded). Osborne Manufacturing pays down on the line of credit balance if it has excess funds at the end of the quarter. The company also pays the accumulated interest at the end of the quarter on the funds borrowed during the quarter.

j. The company's income tax rate is projected to be 30% of operating income less interest expense. The company pays $10,800 cash at the end of February in estimated taxes.



## Requirements

1. Prepare a schedule of cash collections for January, February, and March, and for the quarter in total.

**Cash Collections Budget**

| | January | February | March | Quarter |
|---|---|---|---|---|
| Cash sales | | | | |
| Credit sales | | | | |
| Total cash collections | | | | |

2. Prepare a production budget. (*Hint:* Unit sales = Sales in dollars/Selling price per unit.)

**Production Budget**

| | January | February | March | Quarter |
|---|---|---|---|---|
| Unit sales | | | | |
| Plus: Desired ending inventory | | | | |
| Total needed | | | | |
| Less: Beginning inventory | | | | |
| Units to produce | | | | |

3. Prepare a direct materials budget.

| Direct Materials Budget | January | February | March | Quarter |
|---|---|---|---|---|
| Units to be produced | | | | |
| × kg of DM needed per unit | | | | |
| Quantity (kg) needed for production | | | | |
| Plus: Desired ending inventory of DM | | | | |
| Total quantity (kg) needed | | | | |
| Less: Beginning inventory of DM | | | | |
| Quantity (kg) to purchase | | | | |
| × Cost per kg | | | | |
| Total cost of DM purchases | | | | |

4. Prepare a cash payments budget for the direct material purchases from Requirement 3.

| Cash Payments for Direct Material Purchases Budget | January | February | March | Quarter |
|---|---|---|---|---|
| December purchases (from Accounts Payable) | | | | |
| January purchases | | | | |
| February purchases | | | | |
| March purchases | | | | |
| Total cash payments for DM purchases | | | | |

5. Prepare a cash payments budget for conversion costs.

| Cash Payments for Conversion Costs Budget | January | February | March | Quarter |
|---|---|---|---|---|
| Variable conversion costs | | | | |
| Rent (fixed) | | | | |
| Other fixed MOH | | | | |
| Total payments for conversion costs | | | | |

6. Prepare a cash payments budget for operating expenses.

| Cash Payments for Operating Expenses Budget | January | February | March | Quarter |
|---|---|---|---|---|
| Variable operating expenses | | | | |
| Fixed operating expenses | | | | |
| Total payments for operating expenses | | | | |

7. Prepare a combined cash budget.

**Combined Cash Budget**

| | January | February | March | Quarter |
|---|---|---|---|---|
| Cash balance, beginning | | | | |
| Add cash collections | | | | |
| Total cash available | | | | |
| Less cash payments: | | | | |
| Direct material purchases | | | | |
| Conversion costs | | | | |
| Operating expenses | | | | |
| Equipment purchases | | | | |
| Tax payment | | | | |
| Total disbursements | | | | |
| Ending cash balance before financing | | | | |
| Financing: | | | | |
| Borrowings | | | | |
| Repayments | | | | |
| Interest payments | | | | |
| Total financing | | | | |
| Cash balance, ending | | | | |

8. Calculate the budgeted manufacturing cost per unit (assume that fixed manufacturing overhead is budgeted to be $0.80 per unit for the year).

**Budgeted Manufacturing Cost per Unit**

| | |
|---|---|
| Direct materials cost per unit | |
| Conversion costs per unit | |
| Fixed manufacturing overhead per unit | |
| Budgeted cost of manufacturing each unit | |

9. Prepare a budgeted income statement for the quarter ending March 31. (*Hint:* Cost of goods sold = Budgeted cost of manufacturing each unit × Number of units sold)

**Budgeted Income Statement**
**For the Quarter Ended March 31**

| | |
|---|---|
| Sales | |
| Cost of goods sold | |
| Gross profit | |
| Operating expenses | |
| Depreciation expense | |
| Operating income | |
| Less interest expense | |
| Less provision for income taxes | |
| Net income | |

10. Prepare a partial budgeted balance sheet for March 31. Follow the same format as the original balance sheet provided for December 31, adding Loans Payable and Income Tax Payable.



### P9-68B Prepare budgeted income statement *(Learning Objective 2)*

The budget committee of Binders Office Supply has assembled the following data. As the business manager, you must prepare the budgeted income statements for May and June.

a. Sales in April were $42,000. You forecast that monthly sales will increase 12% in May and 3% in June.
b. Binders Office Supply maintains inventory of $8,000 plus 30% of the sales revenue budgeted for the following month. Monthly purchases average 50% of sales revenue in that same month. Actual inventory on April 30 is $15,000. Sales budgeted for July are $45,000.
c. Monthly salaries amount to $6,000. Sales commissions equal 12% of sales for that month. Combine salaries and commissions into a single figure.
d. Other monthly expenses are as follows:

| | |
|---|---|
| Rent expense | $2,200, paid as incurred |
| Depreciation expense | $ 300 |
| Insurance expense | $ 100, expiration of prepaid amount |
| Income tax | 20% of operating income |

**Requirement**

1. Prepare Binder's budgeted income statements for May and June. Show cost of goods sold computations.

### P9-69B Prepare cash budgets *(Learning Objective 3)*

Amelia Manufacturing is preparing its cash budgets for the first two months of the upcoming year. The following information concerns the company's upcoming cash receipts and cash disbursements.

a. Sales are 65% cash and 35% credit. Credit sales are collected 30% in the month of sale and the remainder in the month after sale. Actual sales in December were $51,000. Schedules of budgeted sales for the two months of the upcoming year are as follows:

| | Budgeted sales revenue |
|---|---|
| January | $60,000 |
| February | $69,000 |

b. Actual purchases of direct materials in December were $25,500. Purchases of direct materials in January are budgeted to be $23,500 and $28,000 in February. All purchases are paid 30% in the month of purchase and 70% the following month.
c. Salaries and sales commissions are also paid half in the month earned and half the next month. Actual salaries were $8,000 in December. Budgeted salaries in January are $9,000, and February budgeted salaries are $10,500. Sales commissions each month are 8% of that month's sales.
d. Rent expense is $3,300 per month.
e. Depreciation is $2,800 per month.
f. Estimated income tax payments are made at the end of January. The estimated tax payment is projected to be $12,000.
g. The cash balance at the end of the prior year was $18,000.

**Requirements**

1. Prepare schedules of (a) budgeted cash collections, (b) budgeted cash payments for purchases, and (c) budgeted cash payments for operating expenses. Show amounts for each month and totals for January and February.
2. Prepare a combined cash budget. If no financing activity took place, what is the budgeted cash balance on February 28?



## P9-70B Prepare a combined cash budget and a budgeted balance sheet

*(Learning Objective 3)*

Sheet Printing of Whitehorse has applied for a loan. The Royal Bank of Canada has requested a budgeted balance sheet at April 30 and a combined cash budget for April. As Sheet Printing's controller, you have assembled the following information:

a. March 31 equipment balance, $52,600; accumulated depreciation, $41,700
b. April capital expenditures of $42,000 budgeted for cash purchase of equipment
c. April depreciation expense, $900
d. Cost of goods sold, 65% of sales
e. Other April operating expenses, including income tax, total $14,000, 20% of which will be paid in cash and the remainder accrued at April 30
f. March 31 owners' equity, $91,700
g. March 31 cash balance, $40,100
h. April budgeted sales, $84,000, 60% of which is for cash; of the remaining 40%, half will be collected in April and half in May
i. April cash collections on March sales, $29,200
j. April cash payments of March 31 liabilities incurred for March purchases of inventory, $17,600
k. March 31 inventory balance, $29,100
l. April purchases of inventory, $10,300 for cash and $36,300 on credit; half of the credit purchases will be paid in April and half in May

**Requirements**

1. Prepare the budgeted balance sheet for Sheet Printing at April 30. Show separate computations for cash, inventory, and owners' equity balances.
2. Prepare the combined cash budget for April.
3. Suppose Sheet Printing has become aware of more efficient (and more expensive) equipment than it budgeted for purchase in April. What is the total amount of cash available for equipment purchases in April, before financing, if the minimum desired ending cash balance is $14,000? (For this requirement, disregard the $42,000 initially budgeted for equipment purchases.)
4. Before granting a loan to Sheet Printing, the Royal Bank of Canada asks for a sensitivity analysis assuming that April sales are only $56,000 rather than the $84,000 originally budgeted. (While the cost of goods sold will change, assume that purchases, depreciation, and the other operating expenses will remain the same as in the earlier requirements.)

   a. Prepare a revised budgeted balance sheet for Sheet Printing, showing separate computations for cash, inventory, and owners' equity balances.
   b. Suppose Sheet Printing has a minimum desired cash balance of $16,000. Will the company need to borrow cash in April?
   c. In this sensitivity analysis, sales declined by 33 1/3% ($28,000 ÷ $84,000). Is the decline in expenses and income more or less than 33 1/3%? Explain.

## P9-71B Prepare performance reports for various organizational levels

*(Learning Objective 4)*

HappyPet operates a chain of pet stores in the Prairies. The manager of each store reports to the regional manager, who, in turn, reports to headquarters in Red Deer, Alberta. The actual and budgeted income statements for the Saskatoon store, the Saskatchewan region (including the Saskatoon store), and the company as a whole (including the Saskatchewan region) for July are as follows:

| | Saskatoon | Saskatchewan | Companywide |
|---|---|---|---|
| Revenue | $148,400 | $1,645,000 | $4,300,000 |
| Expenses: | | | |
| Regional manager/ headquarters office | $ — | $ 55,000 | $ 118,000 |
| Cost of materials | 81,800 | 871,800 | 1,808,000 |
| Salary expense | 38,800 | 415,700 | 1,121,000 |
| Depreciation expense | 7,700 | 93,000 | 439,000 |
| Utilities expense | 4,600 | 46,500 | 265,000 |
| Rent expense | 2,500 | 34,400 | 178,000 |
| Total expenses | 135,400 | 1,516,400 | 3,929,000 |
| Operating income | $ 13,000 | $ 128,600 | $ 371,000 |

*Budgeted* amounts for July were as follows:

| | Saskatoon | Saskatchewan | Companywide |
|---|---|---|---|
| Revenue | $162,400 | $1,768,000 | $4,550,000 |
| Expenses: | | | |
| Regional manager/ headquarters office | $ — | $ 60,600 | $ 120,000 |
| Cost of materials | 86,700 | 963,600 | 1,974,000 |
| Salary expense | 38,900 | 440,000 | 1,092,000 |
| Depreciation expense | 7,700 | 87,400 | 447,000 |
| Utilities expense | 4,700 | 54,400 | 274,000 |
| Rent expense | 4,000 | 32,700 | 172,000 |
| Total expenses | 142,000 | 1,638,700 | 4,079,000 |
| Operating income | $ 20,400 | $ 129,300 | $ 471,000 |

**Requirements**

1. Prepare a report for July that shows the performance of the Saskatoon store, the Saskatchewan region, and the company as a whole.
2. As the Saskatchewan regional manager, would you investigate the Saskatoon store on the basis of this report? Why or why not?
3. Briefly discuss the benefits of budgeting. Base your discussion on HappyPet's performance report.

## P9-72B Prepare an inventory, purchases, and cost of goods sold budget *(Learning Objective 5)*

Cool Logos buys logo-imprinted merchandise and then sells it to university bookstores. Sales are expected to be $2,006,000 in September, $2,240,000 in October, $2,381,000 in November, and $2,570,000 in December. Cool Logos sets its prices to earn an average 40% gross profit on sales revenue. The company does not want inventory to fall below $420,000 plus 15% of the next month's cost of goods sold.

**Requirement**

1. Prepare an inventory, purchases, and cost of goods sold budget for the months of October and November.

# CAPSTONE APPLICATION PROBLEMS

## APPLICATION QUESTION

### A9-73 Suggest performance improvements *(Learning Objective 1)*

Donna Tse recently joined Cycle World, a bicycle store in Dartmouth, as an assistant manager. She recently finished her accounting courses. Cycle World's manager and owner, Jeff Towry, asks Tse to prepare a budgeted income statement for the upcoming year based on the information he has collected. Tse's budget follows:

| CYCLE WORLD<br>**Budgeted Income Statement**<br>For the Year Ending July 31 | | |
|---|---|---|
| Sales revenue | | $244,000 |
| Cost of goods sold | | 177,000 |
| Gross profit | | 67,000 |
| Operating expenses: | | |
| Salary and commission expense | $46,000 | |
| Rent expense | 8,000 | |
| Depreciation expense | 2,000 | |
| Insurance expense | 800 | |
| Miscellaneous expenses | 12,000 | (68,800) |
| Operating loss | | (1,800) |
| Interest expense | | (225) |
| Net loss | | $ (2,025) |

**Requirement**

1. Tse does not want to give Towry this budget without making constructive suggestions for steps Towry could take to improve expected performance. Write a memo to Towry outlining your suggestions. Your memo should take the following form:

**Date:** ____________________

**To:** Mr. Jeff Towry, Manager
Cycle World

**From:** Donna Tse

**Subject:** Cycle World's budgeted income statement

### A9-74 Prepare cash budgets under two alternatives *(Learning Objectives 2 & 3)*

Each autumn, as a hobby, Suzanne De Angelo weaves cotton placemats to sell at a local crafts shop. The mats sell for $20 per set of four. The shop charges a 10% commission and remits the net proceeds to De Angelo at the end of December. De Angelo has woven and sold 25 sets each of the last two years. She has enough cotton in inventory to make another 25 sets. She paid $7 per set for the cotton. De Angelo uses a four-harness loom that she purchased for cash exactly two years ago. It is depreciated at the rate of $10 per month. The accounts payable relate to the cotton inventory and are payable by September 30.

De Angelo is considering buying an eight-harness loom so that she can weave more intricate patterns in linen. The new loom costs $1,000; it would be depreciated at $20 per month. Her bank has agreed to lend her $1,000 at 18% interest, with $200 principal plus accrued interest payable each December 31. De Angelo believes she can weave 15 linen placemat sets in time for the Christmas rush if she does not weave any cotton mats. She predicts that each linen set will sell for $50. Linen costs $18 per set. De Angelo's supplier will sell her linen on credit, payable December 31.

De Angelo plans to keep her old loom whether or not she buys the new loom. The balance sheet for her weaving business at August 31 is as follows:

**SUZANNE DE ANGELO, WEAVER**
**Balance Sheet**
**August 31**

| | | | |
|---|---|---|---|
| Current assets: | | Current liabilities: | |
| Cash | $ 25 | Accounts payable | $ 74 |
| Inventory of cotton | 175 | | |
| | 200 | | |
| Fixed assets: | | | |
| Loom | 500 | Owner's equity | 386 |
| Accumulated depreciation | (240) | | |
| | 260 | | |
| Total assets | $ 460 | Total liabilities and owner's equity | $460 |

### Requirements

1. Prepare a combined cash budget for the four months ending December 31 for two alternatives: weaving the placemats in cotton using the existing loom and weaving the placemats in linen using the new loom. For each alternative, prepare a budgeted income statement for the four months ending December 31 and a budgeted balance sheet at December 31.
2. On the basis of financial considerations only, what should De Angelo do? Give your reason.
3. What nonfinancial factors might De Angelo consider in her decision?

# CASE ASSIGNMENT

## C9-75 SecurForce Inc.

*Source:* Federico Rostagno/Shutterstock

SecurForce specializes in residential security alarm system installations and monitoring. It has been in business for just over 25 years, and for the most part things have been good. It has experienced steady growth over the years and now provides monitoring services for

500,000 homes across Canada. Its target is to install new systems in 30,000 homes in the upcoming year. It has had a few growing pains, though, especially when it seems to be difficult to hold on to management-level employees.

The other concern for the CEO has been the cash flow. In the past, the CEO and CFO have simply taken the previous year's budget and adjusted for inflation and an estimated percentage increase in sales. This has, unfortunately, led to some cash flow problems, and a couple of times in the previous year the company came close to not being able to cover the costs of payroll and had to scurry to the bank to arrange for emergency financing. They know that they will not be able to continue to access funds at the last minute but are unsure how to anticipate their cash shortfalls over the year. They are looking at making some large purchases in the first quarter of 2017 of $3,500,000, but they're not sure if they will need to borrow that much. They anticipate having $820,000 at the end of 2016, so are assuming that they will need to borrow at least $2,680,000.

Both the CEO and CFO were part of the founding team for the company. Chanelle, the CEO, and Frederik, the CFO, along with a couple of friends, were able to put some money together to buy a small security system 25 years ago when they had graduated from high school, and they have slowly been building the company to a national corporation. They had both been working for the security company over the summers and part-time throughout the year as installers before buying the company when the owner told them he was going to retire. So they have learned pretty well everything they needed to know about running the company through experience, trial and error, and a lot of guidance from friends and family.

Last week, they were describing their cash flow problem to Di, a CPA friend of theirs, and she said that she would help them out with forecasting their cash needs and gave them a list of information that she would need. They gathered everything together and sent it to Di. They are hoping that this year they will be able to improve the strained relationship that they have with their bank.

| **Sales:** | |
|---|---|
| New installations | $400 |
| Monitoring package | $30 per month |
| Repairs | $100 on average |

Cash is received for revenues, with 60% received in the quarter in which the work was done, 2% never collected, and the remainder received in the quarter after the revenues are recorded.

**They anticipate the following workload:**

| | Q4 (2016) | Q1 (2017) | Q2 | Q3 | Q4 | Total | Q1 2018 |
|---|---|---|---|---|---|---|---|
| Monitoring | 495,000 | 500,000 | 506,000 | 513,500 | 521,000 | | 530,000 |
| New installs | 5,000 | 6,000 | 7,500 | 7,500 | 9,000 | 30,000 | 8,000 |
| Repairs (1%) | 4,990 | 5,000 | 5,060 | 5,135 | 5,210 | 20,405 | 5,300 |

**Labour:**

Installations are done in teams of two technicians who work full-time. Each team has one senior installer and one junior installer. The senior installer earns $35 per hour, and the junior installer earns $25 per hour (on an assumption of 160 hours per month). They need a technician team for every 300 installations or repair jobs that need to be done. They do the hiring at the beginning of the quarter in which they are needed.

The monitoring centre is housed in one location and serves all customers across Canada. They hire one full-time employee for every 5,000 customers. Monitoring-centre staff earn $15 per hour.

One manager and 0.5 of an administrative person are needed for each region. There are 20 regions across Canada. Managers earn $45,000 per year, and administrative staff earn a total of $22,500 for their part-time work.

All employees are part of a benefits plan that costs SecurForce an additional 30% (including the costs of provincial and federal mandatory payroll benefits such as CPP, EI, health insurance, etc.).

Cash is paid to employees, with 87.5% of payroll paid in the quarter in which the employee worked and 12.5% in the following quarter. Benefits are paid 100% in the quarter after the employee worked.

**Expenses:**
SecurForce purchases one complete system of hardware at $150 each for each new system to be installed, and they order one complete system for every five repairs that need to be done. They have found it cheaper to purchase the system that will then typically provide enough hardware to do five repairs than to purchase individual parts for repairs. They order enough to have a buffer of 5% of the next quarter's new installations and 20% of the next quarter's repairs. A/P for the systems is $625,000 at the end of 2016, and they pay 40% of the purchases in the quarter of purchase and 60% in the following quarter.

Other expenses, including depreciation, selling costs, and all administrative and general costs, are expected to be as follows:

Q4 (2016) = $11,870,000
Q1 (2017) = $12,025,000
Q2 (2017) = $12,673,000
Q3 (2017) = $13,224,000
Q4 (2017) = $13,576,000

90% of the other expenses are paid in the quarter in which they are incurred, with the remaining 10% being paid in the following quarter.

# ETHICAL ISSUE

## I9-76 Assess ethical considerations for padded budgets

*(Learning Objectives 1 & 5)*

Residence Suites operates a regional hotel chain. Each hotel is operated by a manager and an assistant manager/controller. Many of the staff who run the front desk, clean the rooms, and prepare the breakfast buffet work part-time or have a second job, so turnover is high.

Assistant Manager/Controller Jalaluddin Romi asked the new bookkeeper to help prepare the hotel's master budget. The master budget is prepared once a year and submitted to company headquarters for approval. Once approved, the master budget is used to evaluate the hotel's performance. These performance evaluations affect hotel managers' bonuses; they also affect company decisions about which hotels deserve extra funds for capital improvements.

When the budget was almost complete, Romi asked the bookkeeper to increase amounts budgeted for labour and supplies by 15%. When asked why, Romi responded that hotel manager Leanna Quach told him to do this when he began working at the hotel. Quach explained that this budgetary cushion gave him flexibility in running the hotel. For example, because company headquarters tightly controls capital improvement funds, Quach can use the extra money budgeted for labour and supplies to replace broken televisions or to pay "bonuses" to keep valued employees. Romi initially accepted this explanation because he had observed similar behaviour at her previous place of employment.

Put yourself in Romi's position. In deciding how to deal with the situation, answer the following questions:

1. What is the ethical issue?
2. What are my options?
3. What are the possible consequences?
4. What should I do?

# TEAM PROJECT

## T9-77 Analyze and discuss budget concerns *(Learning Objectives 1, 2, & 3)*

Xellnet provides e-commerce software for the pharmaceuticals industry. Xellnet is organized into several divisions. A companywide planning committee sets general strategy and goals for the company and its divisions, but each division develops its own budget.

Rick Watson is the new division manager of wireless communications software. His division has two departments: Development and Sales. Carrie Pronai manages the 20 or so programmers and systems specialists typically employed in the Development Department to create and update the division's software applications. Fernande Girarde manages the Sales Department.

Xellnet considers the divisions to be investment centres. To earn his bonus next year, Watson must achieve a 30% return on the $3 million invested in his division. This amounts to $900,000 of income (30% × $3 million). Within the wireless division, development is a cost centre, while sales is a revenue centre.

Budgeting is in progress. Pronai met with her staff and is now struggling with two sets of numbers. Alternative A is her best estimate of next year's costs. However, unexpected problems can arise in the writing of software, and finding competent programmers is an ongoing challenge. She knows that Watson was a programmer before he earned an MBA, so he should be sensitive to this uncertainty. Consequently, she is thinking of increasing her budgeted costs (Alternative B). Her department's bonuses largely depend on whether the department meets its budgeted costs.

**XELLNET**
**Wireless Division**
Development Budget

| | Alternative A | Alternative B |
|---|---|---|
| Salaries expense (including overtime and part-time) | $2,400,000 | $2,640,000 |
| Software expense | 120,000 | 132,000 |
| Travel expense | 65,000 | 71,500 |
| Depreciation expense | 255,000 | 255,000 |
| Miscellaneous expense | 100,000 | 110,000 |
| Total expense | $2,940,000 | $3,208,500 |

Fernande Girarde is also struggling with her sales budget. Companies have made their initial investments in communications software, so it is harder to win new customers. If things go well, she believes her sales team can maintain the level of growth achieved over the past few years. This is Alternative A in the sales budget. However, if Girarde is too optimistic, sales may fall short of the budget. If this happens, her team will not receive bonuses. Therefore, Girarde is considering reducing the sales numbers and submitting Alternative B.

**XELLNET**
**Wireless Division**
Sales Budget

| | Alternative A | Alternative B |
|---|---|---|
| Sales revenue | $5,000,000 | $4,500,000 |
| Salaries expense | 360,000 | 360,000 |
| Travel expense | 240,000 | 210,500 |

Split your team into three groups. Each group should meet separately before the entire team meets.

**Requirements**

1. Group 1 plays the role of Development Manager Carrie Pronai. Before meeting with the entire team, determine which set of budget numbers to present to Rick Watson. Write a memo supporting the decision. Give this memo to Group 3 before the team meeting.
2. Group 2 plays the role of Sales Manager Fernande Girarde. Before meeting with the entire team, determine which set of budget numbers to present to Rick Watson. Write a memo supporting the decision. Give this memo to Group 3 before the team meeting.
3. Group 3 plays the role of Division Manager Rick Watson. Before meeting with the entire team, use the memos that Pronai and Girarde provided to prepare a division budget based on the sales and development budgets. Divisional overhead costs (additional costs beyond those incurred by the Development and Sales Departments) are approximately $390,000. Determine whether the wireless division can meet its targeted 30% return on assets given the budgeted alternatives submitted by the department managers.

During the meeting of the entire team, Group 3 presents the division budget and considers its implications. Each group should take turns discussing its concerns with the proposed budget. The team as a whole should consider whether the division budget must be revised. The team should prepare a report that includes the division budget and a summary of the issues covered in the team meeting.

# DISCUSSION & ANALYSIS

1. "The sales budget is the most important budget." Do you agree or disagree? Explain your answer.
2. List at least four reasons why a company would use budgeting.
3. Describe the difference between an operating budget and a capital budget.
4. Describe the process for developing a budget.
5. Compare and contrast "participative budgeting" with "top-down" budgeting.
6. What is a budget committee? What is the budget committee's role in the budgeting process?
7. What are operating budgets? List at least four operating budgets.
8. What are financial budgets? List at least three financial budgets.
9. What is a responsibility centre? List the four types of responsibility centres. Describe an example of each of the four types of responsibility centres.
10. How does the master budget for a service company differ from a master budget for a manufacturing company? Which (if any) operating budgets differ, and how specifically do they differ? Which (if any) financial budgets differ, and how specifically do they differ?

# APPLICATION & ANALYSIS

## 9-1 Budgeting for a Single Product

In this activity, you will create budgets for a single product for each of the months in an upcoming quarter. Select a product that you could purchase in large quantities (e.g., at a warehouse retail chain) and repackage into smaller quantities to offer for sale at a sidewalk café, sporting event, flea market, or other similar venue. Investigate the price and quantity at which this product is available at the warehouse. Choose a selling price for the smaller (repackaged) package. Make reasonable assumptions about how many of the smaller units you can sell in each of the next four months. (You will need the fourth month's sales in units for the operating budgets).

## Discussion Questions

1. Describe your product. What is your cost of this product? What size (quantity) will you purchase? At what price will you sell your repackaged product? Make projections of your sales in units in each of the upcoming four months.
2. Estimate how many hours you will spend in each of the upcoming three months doing the purchasing, repackaging, and selling. Select a reasonable wage rate for yourself. What will your total labour costs be in each of the upcoming three months?
3. Prepare a sales budget for each of the upcoming three months.
4. Prepare the direct material budgets for the upcoming three months, assuming that you need to keep 10% of the direct materials needed for next month's sales on hand at the end of each month. (This requirement is why you needed to estimate unit sales for four months.)
5. Prepare a direct labour budget (for your labour) for each of the upcoming three months.
6. Think about any other expenses you are likely to have (i.e., booth rental at a flea market or a vendor licence). Prepare the operating expenses budget for each of the upcoming three months.
7. Prepare a budgeted income statement that reflects the budgets you prepared, including the sales budget, direct materials budget, direct labour budget, and the operating expenses budget. This budgeted income statement should include one column for each of the three months in the quarter and it should also include a total column that represents the totals of the three months. What is your projected profit by month and for the quarter?

## Classroom Applications

**Web:** Post the activity description and discussion questions on an electronic discussion board. Have small groups of students choose a product for their groups. The group should collaborate on estimating selling price, sales volume, and costs and on preparing the budgets. The group should discuss the results of the budget and the budgeting process.

**Classroom:** Form groups of three or four students. Your group should choose a product. Your group should collaborate on estimating selling price, sales volume, and costs and on preparing the budgets. Discuss the results of the budget and the budgeting process itself. Prepare a five-minute presentation about your group's product and its budgets.

**Independent:** Select a product as described in the introduction for this activity. Prepare the budgets as listed. Be sure to include your assumptions about estimated selling price, estimated sales volume, and your estimates of all of your costs. Turn in a three- to four-page paper (12-point font, double-spaced with 2.5 cm margins). The paper should include your budgets for each of the three months and for the quarter in total. These budgets can be tables within your Word document.

# TRY IT SOLUTIONS

**Page 521:**

The company should produce 32,800 cases, calculated as follows:

| | |
|---|---|
| Unit sales for April | 32,000 |
| Plus: Desired ending inventory (10% of May sales of 40,000) | 4,000 |
| Total units needed | 36,000 |
| Less: Beginning inventory (March ending inventory = 10% of April sales of 32,000) | 3,200 |
| Units to produce | 32,800 |

**Page 532:**

$122,000, calculated as follows:

| | March Budgeted Collections |
|---|---|
| COD sales in March | $ 15,000 |
| Credit sales from February ($110,000 × 90%) | 99,000 |
| Credit sales from January ($100,000 × 8%) | 8,000 |
| Total cash collections | $122,000 |

# PRODUCTION AND DIRECT MATERIALS BUDGETS

## Learning Objective 2

Collegiate Basket Company makes high-quality picnic baskets that it markets to the enthusiastic tailgater. The baskets are hand-painted in school colours with the college or university mascot on the top. The company's sales budget for the third quarter of the fiscal year is as follows:

**Collegiate Basket Company**
Sales Budget
For the Quarter ended September 30

| | Month | | | |
|---|---|---|---|---|
| | July | August | September | 3rd Quarter |
| Unit Sales (baskets) | 1,225 | 1,300 | 1,350 | 3,875 |
| Unit Selling Price | × $70 | × $70 | × $70 | × $70 |
| Total Sales Revenue | $85,750 | $91,000 | $94,500 | $271,250 |

Additionally, the company has estimated October sales to be 1,400 units.

Collegiate doesn't want its inventory to fall below 10% of the next month's unit sales, but it started July with only 100 completed baskets in stock.

Collegiate buys the wood it uses to make the baskets from a local lumber company at a price of $3 per metre. Each basket requires 4 m of wood strips. Collegiate wants to maintain an ending inventory of direct materials equal to 20% of the materials needed for next month's production. On July 1, the company had 1,000 m of wood strips on hand.

## Requirement

1. Prepare the following budgets for July, August, and September, as well as a budget for the third quarter:

   a. Production budget

   b. Direct material budget

# Demo Doc Solutions

## Requirement 1

a. **Production budget**

To prepare the production budget, we start with the unit sales (baskets) from the sales budget and add the amount of inventory that Collegiate wants to have on hand at the end of the month. We know that Collegiate doesn't want its inventory to fall below 10% of the next month's unit sales. Consequently, we can calculate the company's desired ending inventory each month as follows:

| | | |
|---|---|---|
| July: 1,300 | (August unit sales) × 10% | = 130 units |
| August: 1,350 | (September unit sales) × 10% | = 135 units |
| September: 1,400 | (October unit sales) × 10% | = 140 units |

We begin to build our production budget with these data:

**Collegiate Basket Company**
Production Budget
For the Quarter ended September 30

| | Month | | | |
|---|---|---|---|---|
| | **July** | **August** | **September** | **3rd Quarter** |
| Unit Sales (baskets) | 1,225 | 1,300 | 1,350 | 3,875 |
| Plus: Desired Ending Inventory | 130 | 135 | 140 → | 140 |
| Total Needed | 1,355 | 1,435 | 1,490 | 4,015 |

Notice that we do not add up the desired ending inventory for each month and put that amount in the quarter column. The third quarter begins on July 1 and ends on September 30, so the ending inventory for the quarter is the balance at September 30, as shown by the blue arrow in the budget.

Now we know the total number of units needed each month. To complete the production budget, we need to subtract what the company already has in stock at the beginning of the month. After doing so, we'll know how many units the company will need to produce each month.

We were told that the company had 100 completed baskets on July 1. To determine the beginning inventory for August and September, we simply take the ending inventory from the previous month. (The ending inventory one month becomes the beginning inventory the next month.) This is shown by the red arrows in the budget below.

**Collegiate Basket Company**
Production Budget
For the Quarter ended September 30

| | Month | | | |
|---|---|---|---|---|
| | **July** | **August** | **September** | **3rd Quarter** |
| Unit Sales (baskets) | 1,225 | 1,300 | 1,350 | 3,875 |
| Plus: Desired Ending Inventory | 130 | 135 | 140 → | 140 |
| Total Needed | 1,355 | 1,435 | 1,490 | 4,015 |
| Less: Beginning Inventory | (100) | (130) | (135) | (100) |
| Units to produce | 1,255 | 1,305 | 1,355 | 3,915 |

Finally, we subtract the beginning inventory from the total units needed to determine the number of units to produce each month.

Notice from the orange arrow that the beginning inventory for the third quarter is the July 1 balance of 100 units. This is because the third quarter of the fiscal year begins on July 1. Avoid the mistake of adding up all of the beginning inventory units and placing that in the third quarter column.

b. **Direct materials budget**

Now that we know how many baskets Collegiate needs to produce, we are ready to prepare the direct materials budget. Each basket requires 4 m of wood strips, so we figure out the quantity of direct materials (DM) needed for production each month as follows:

**Collegiate Basket Company**
Direct Materials Budget
For the Quarter ended September 30

| | Month | | | |
|---|---|---|---|---|
| | July | August | September | 3rd Quarter |
| Units to be produced (from Production Budget) | 1,255 | 1,305 | 1,355 | 3,915 |
| × Quantity (metres) of DM needed per unit | × 4 | × 4 | × 4 | × 4 |
| Quantity (metres) needed for production | 5,020 | 5,220 | 5,420 | 15,660 |

Let's also assume that the fourth quarter production budget indicates that 1,408 units will be produced in October, resulting in 5,632 m of wood strips needed for production in October (1,408 × 4 m = 5,632 m).

Next, we need to calculate the amount of wood strips that Collegiate wants to have on hand at the end of each month. We know that Collegiate wants to maintain an ending stock of wood strips equal to 20% of the materials needed for next month's production. So the desired ending inventory of wood strips for each month can be calculated as follows:

July: 5,220 metres (August quantity needed) × 20% = 1,044 metres
August: 5,420 metres (September quantity needed) × 20% = 1,084 metres
September: 5,632 metres (October quantity needed) × 20% = 1,126 metres

By adding the desired ending inventory to the amount of wood strips needed for production, we are able to figure out the total amount of wood strips needed each month:

**Collegiate Basket Company**
Direct Materials Budget
For the Quarter ended September 30

| | Month | | | |
|---|---|---|---|---|
| | July | August | September | 3rd Quarter |
| Units to be produced (from Production Budget) | 1,255 | 1,305 | 1,355 | 3,915 |
| × Quantity (metres) of DM needed per unit | × 4 | × 4 | × 4 | × 4 |
| Quantity (metres) needed for production | 5,020 | 5,220 | 5,420 | 15,660 |
| Plus: Desired End Inventory of DM | 1,044 | 1,084 | 1,126 → | 1,126 |
| Total Quantity (metres) Needed | 6,064 | 6,304 | 6,546 | 16,786 |

Notice again from the blue arrow that the ending inventory for the quarter is the ending inventory on September 30.

Will Collegiate need to buy all of this inventory? No, because it begins each month with some wood strips on hand. So the next step is to subtract the beginning inventory of wood strips from the total needed in order to arrive at the amount of wood strips to purchase.

We were told that the company had 1,000 m of wood strips in stock on July 1. To determine the beginning inventory for August and September, we just take the ending inventory from the previous month. This is shown by the red arrows in the budget below.

**Collegiate Basket Company**
Direct Materials Budget
For the Quarter ended September 30

| | Month | | | |
|---|---|---|---|---|
| | July | August | September | 3rd Quarter |
| Units to be produced (from Production Budget) | 1,255 | 1,305 | 1,355 | 3,915 |
| × Quantity (metres) of DM needed per unit | × 4 | × 4 | × 4 | × 4 |
| Quantity (metres) needed for production | 5,020 | 5,220 | 5,420 | 15,660 |
| Plus: Desired End Inventory of DM | 1,044 | 1,084 | 1,126 → | 1,126 |
| Total Quantity (metres) Needed | 6,064 | 6,304 | 6,546 | 16,786 |
| Less: Beginning Inventory of DM | (1,000) | (1,044) | (1,084) | (1,000) |
| Quantity (metres) to purchase | 5,064 | 5,260 | 5,462 | 15,786 |

Notice again from the orange arrow that the beginning inventory for the quarter is the July 1 inventory balance.

Now we know the total amount of wood strips that Collegiate needs to purchase each month. The final step is to figure out how much these purchases will cost. To do so, we simply multiply the total metres of wood strips to purchase by the $3 cost per metre:

**Collegiate Basket Company**
Direct Materials Budget
For the Quarter ended September 30

| | Month | | | |
|---|---|---|---|---|
| | July | August | September | 3rd Quarter |
| Units to be produced (from Production Budget) | 1,255 | 1,305 | 1,355 | 3,915 |
| × Quantity (metres) of DM needed per unit | × 4 | × 4 | × 4 | × 4 |
| Quantity (metres) needed for production | 5,020 | 5,220 | 5,420 | 15,660 |
| Plus: Desired End Inventory of DM | 1,044 | 1,084 | 1,126 → | 1,126 |
| Total Quantity (metres) Needed | 6,064 | 6,304 | 6,546 | 16,786 |
| Less: Beginning Inventory of DM | (1,000) | (1,044) | (1,084) | (1,000) |
| Quantity (metres) to purchase | 5,064 | 5,260 | 5,462 | 15,786 |
| × Cost per metre | × $ 3 | × $ 3 | × $ 3 | × $ 3 |
| Total Cost of DM purchases | $15,192 | $15,780 | $16,386 | $47,358 |

# 10 Flexible Budgets and Standard Costs

Chapter 10, "Flexible Budgets and Standard Costs," covers material outlined in **Section 3: Management Accounting** of the CPA Competency Map. Specifically, this chapter addresses *Section 3.2 Planning, Budgeting, and Forecasting* and *Section 3.6 Organizational Performance Measurement.* The Learning Objectives in this chapter have been aligned with the CPA Competency Map to ensure the best coverage possible.

PROFESSIONAL COMPETENCY The presence of the **coverage button** in the margin indicates focus on one or more of the specific competency areas from the competency map. The concepts in the text are building blocks to developing the competencies required in the CPA. While the chapter may address multiple areas of the competency map, the main focus will be:

**Competencies:**

**3.2.1** Develops or evaluates information inputs for operational plans, budgets, and forecasts*

**3.2.2** Prepares, analyzes, or evaluates operational plans, budgets, and forecasts*

**3.2.3** Computes, analyzes, or assesses implications of variances*

**3.4.1** Evaluates sources and drivers of revenue growth*

## Learning Objectives

1. Prepare a flexible budget for planning purposes.
2. Use the sales volume variance and flexible budget variance to explain why actual results differ from the master budget.
3. Identify the benefits of standard costs, and learn how to set standards.
4. Compute standard cost variances for direct materials and direct labour.
5. Compute manufacturing overhead variances.
6. Record transactions at standard cost, and prepare a standard cost income statement. (Appendix 10A)

© Kevin Wheal/Alamy
*Source:* www.mccain.ca.

## From coast to coast in Canada, McCain is

one of the most popular and trusted consumer brands. The company offers a wide range of potato products, beverages, juices, pizzas, and desserts. So how does McCain make sure that its 55 plants spread across six continents deliver the same levels of quality, service, and value to its customers worldwide at all times? One of the ways it does so is by using budgets, standards, and variances. Managers budget sales, schedule just enough workers, and purchase or grow the right amount of direct materials (ingredients) and other resources to handle the budgeted level of sales. As they calculate the actual results, managers can then compute variances (the difference between actual results and budgeted figures). These variances provide the feedback that managers need in order to control costs and determine any adjustments or improvements to the processes.

*Reprinted from *The Chartered Professional Accountant Competency Map - Understanding the competencies a candidate must demonstrate to become a CPA*, © 2012, with permission Chartered Professional Accountants of Canada, Toronto, Canada. Any changes to the original material are the sole responsibility of the author (and/or publisher) and have not been reviewed or endorsed by the Chartered Professional Accountants of Canada.

The feedback that allows McCain to control costs also gives it the opportunity to live up to its vision, "It's all good," by focusing on incorporating healthy ingredients that are found in your own kitchen at a price that offers good value to the customer. All this leads to McCain's goal of producing not only new and innovative products but also putting smiles on the faces of its customers and consumers every day.

In the previous chapter, we saw how managers use budgets for planning and performance evaluation. We saw that managers compare actual results to budgeted figures and investigate any variances they deem to be significant. This chapter builds on your knowledge of budgeting to show how managers can use more in-depth variance analysis techniques to learn *why* actual results differ from budgets. Why is this important? Because you must know *why* actual costs differ from the budget in order to identify problems and to decide what, if any, action to take.

In this chapter, you'll learn how managers of companies can use flexible budgets, standard costs, and variance analysis to better pinpoint *why* actual results differ from the budget. This is the first step in determining how to correct problems.

# How Do Managers Use Flexible Budgets?

In this chapter we'll see how Kool-Time Pools, an installer of in-ground swimming pools, uses flexible budgets and standard costs to help control its operations. Kool-Time uses direct materials, direct labour, and manufacturing overhead (such as the monthly lease on the earth-moving equipment) to manufacture swimming pools directly on the customer's site. In addition to manufacturing costs, the company incurs selling and administrative expenses in conjunction with its marketing and sales efforts. As with most companies, some of these costs are variable, while others are fixed.

## The Static Budget

At the beginning of the year, Kool-Time's managers prepared a master budget like the one in Chapter 9. The master budget is a **static budget**, which means that it is prepared for *one* level of sales volume. Once the master budget is developed, it does not change.

Exhibit 10-1 compares June's actual results with the static (master) budget for June. The difference between actual results and the budget is called a **variance**. In this case, because we are comparing actual results against the static budget, this particular variance is called the **static budget variance**. Variances are considered favourable (F) when a higher actual amount increases operating income and unfavourable (U) when a higher actual amount decreases operating income. Favourable variances should not necessarily be interpreted as "good." Likewise, unfavourable variances should not be interpreted as "bad." Rather, they simply indicate the variance's effect on operating income. Exhibit 10-1 shows that Kool-Time's revenues were $25,000 higher than expected and its expenses were $21,000 higher than expected. Together, these variances resulted in a $4,000 favourable static budget variance for operating income.

**EXHIBIT 10-1** Actual Results versus Static Budget

KOOL-TIME POOLS
**Comparison of Actual Results with Static Budget**
Month Ended June 30

| | Actual Results | Static (Master) Budget | Static Budget Variance |
|---|---|---|---|
| Output units (pools installed) | 10 | 8 | 2 F |
| Sales revenue | $ 121,000 | $ 96,000 | $ 25,000 F |
| Expenses | (105,000) | (84,000) | (21,000) U |
| Operating income | $ 16,000 | $ 12,000 | $ 4,000 F |

1 Prepare a flexible budget for planning purposes.

## The Flexible Budget

The static budget variance in Exhibit 10-1 is hard to analyze because the static budget is based on eight pools, but actual results are for 10 pools. Trying to compare actual results against a budget prepared for a different volume is like comparing apples to oranges. The comparison presented in Exhibit 10-1 does not give managers enough information to answer important questions, such as, Why did the $21,000 unfavourable expense variance occur? Were materials wasted? Did the cost of materials suddenly increase? How much of the additional expense and revenues arose because Kool-Time installed 10 pools rather than eight?

However, flexible budgets can help managers answer such questions. Exhibit 10-2 shows that in contrast to the static budget developed for a single level of sales volume, **flexible budgets** are summarized budgets prepared for different levels of volume. Flexible budgets can be used to help managers plan for future periods *and* to evaluate performance after the period has ended. We'll consider both uses and then get back to the question of why the $21,000 unfavourable expense variance occurred.

**EXHIBIT 10-2** Static versus Flexible Budgets

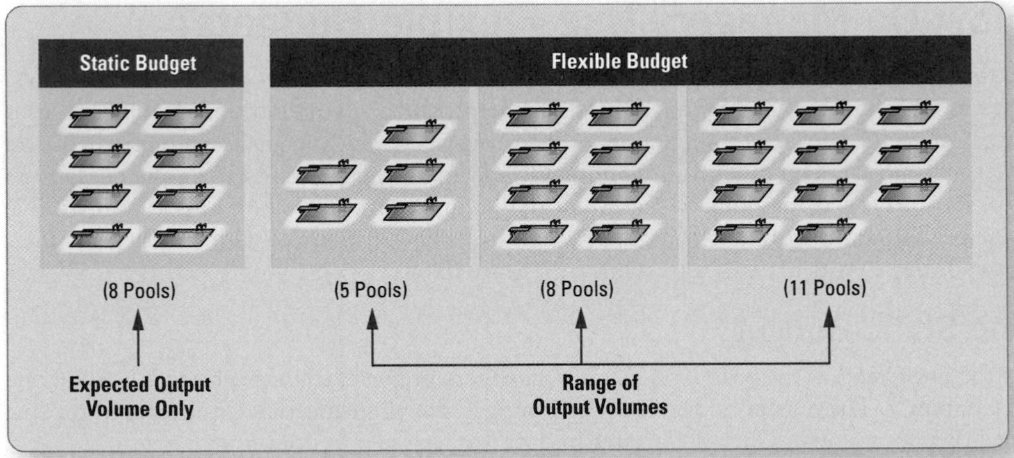


## Using Flexible Budgets for Planning

Managers can use flexible budgets for planning revenues and expenses at different sales volumes. Even though Kool-Time's managers believe the company will install eight pools in June, they also know that they might not be correct about this estimate. Pool sales could be higher or lower during the month, and managers need to be prepared for both possibilities. Flexible budgets show how Kool-Time's revenues and expenses *should* vary as the number of pools installed varies.

Let's prepare flexible budgets for Kool-Time, assuming pool sales for the month could be as low as 5 or as high as 11. We'll start with revenues: The budgeted sales price per pool is $12,000, so each additional pool sale should yield another $12,000 of revenue. Exhibit 10-3 shows projected revenues at three possible volumes: 5 pools, 8 pools, and 11 pools.

To project expenses at different volumes, managers must know how the company's costs behave. Total fixed costs will be the same regardless of volume as long as the volume is within the same relevant range. However, total variable costs will change as volume changes. Managers use a mixed cost equation, such as the one we discussed in Chapter 3, to budget expenses at different volumes. This is sometimes referred to as a flexible budget formula:

Flexible budget total cost = (Number of output units × Variable cost per output unit) + Total fixed cost

**EXHIBIT 10-3** Flexible Budgets

| KOOL-TIME POOLS<br>Flexible Budget<br>Month Ended June 30 | | | | |
|---|---|---|---|---|
| | | Output Units (Pools Installed) | | |
| | Flexible Budget per Output Unit | 5 | 8 | 11 |
| Sales revenue | $ 12,000 | $ 60,000 | $ 96,000 | $ 132,000 |
| Variable expenses | 8,000 | (40,000) | (64,000) | (88,000) |
| Fixed expenses | | (20,000) | (20,000) | (20,000) |
| Total expenses | | (60,000) | (84,000) | (108,000) |
| Operating income | | $ 0 | $ 12,000 | $ 24,000 |

Kool-Time's variable costs are $8,000 per pool. Of this amount, $7,000 is for variable manufacturing costs (direct materials, direct labour, and variable manufacturing overhead such as gasoline to operate the earth-moving equipment), while $1,000 is for variable selling and administrative expenses (such as the commission paid to sales staff on every pool sold). It is these variable expenses that put the "flex" in the flexible budget because budgeted total monthly fixed costs remain constant. Kool-Time's monthly fixed costs are $20,000. This includes $12,000 of fixed monthly manufacturing overhead (such as the monthly lease of earth-moving equipment), while $8,000 relates to fixed selling and administrative expenses (sales and administrative salaries, lease of sales office, telephone and internet service, and so forth).

Using this information on cost behaviour, managers can predict costs at different volumes, just as we did in Chapter 3. For example, the total budgeted cost for five pools is as follows:

$60,000 = (5 pools × $8,000 variable cost per pool) + $20,000 fixed cost

Likewise, the total budgeted cost for 11 pools is as follows:

$108,000 = (11 pools × $8,000 variable cost per pool) + $20,000 fixed cost

Exhibit 10-3 shows the revenues and expenses anticipated if Kool-Time sells 5, 8, or 11 pools during the month. Kool-Time's best estimate is 8 pools, but by acknowledging that sales could be as low as 5 or as high as 11, Kool-Time's managers will be better prepared for any differences in volume that may arise.

Managers develop flexible budgets like Exhibit 10-3 for any number of volumes using a simple Excel spreadsheet or more sophisticated Web-based budget management software. However, managers must be careful: *They must consider the company's relevant range* because total monthly fixed costs and the variable cost per pool change outside this range. Kool-Time's relevant range is 0 to 11 pools. If the company installs 12 pools, it will have to lease additional equipment, so fixed monthly costs will exceed $20,000. Kool-Time also will have to pay workers an overtime premium, so the variable cost per pool will be more than $8,000.

## Graphing Flexible Budget Costs

Sometimes it's helpful for managers to see a graph of the flexible budget costs. Exhibit 10-4 shows budgeted total costs for the entire relevant range of 0 to 11 pools. Because Kool-Time has both fixed and variable costs, its total costs are mixed. Kool-Time's flexible

**EXHIBIT 10-4** Kool-Time Pools' Monthly Flexible Budget Graph

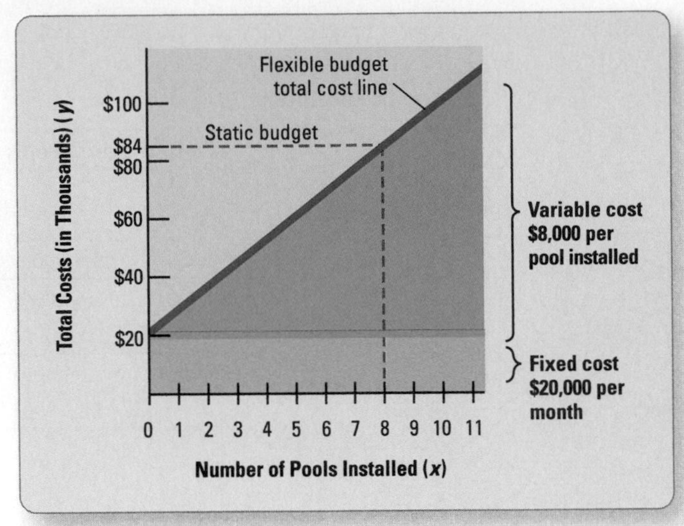


budget graph has the same characteristics as the mixed cost graphs we discussed in Chapter 3. The total cost line intersects the vertical axis at the level of total fixed cost ($20,000) that Kool-Time will incur whether it installs 0 pools or 11 pools. The total cost line also slopes upward at the rate of $8,000 per pool, which is Kool-Time's variable cost per pool. Each additional pool, up to 11 pools, should cost Kool-Time an extra $8,000.

As shown by the dotted line in Exhibit 10-4, Kool-Time expects to install eight pools in June (at a total cost of $84,000). But managers also can use this graph to *plan* costs for anywhere from 0 to 11 pools.

## Using Flexible Budgets to Evaluate Performance

We just saw how managers can use flexible budgets for planning purposes. But managers can also use flexible budgets at the end of the period to evaluate the company's financial performance and help control costs. Rather than comparing actual revenues and expenses against the static budget (as shown in Exhibit 10-1), managers can compare the actual results against the flexible budget *for the actual volume of output* that occurred during the period.

Consider June, when Kool-Time actually installed 10 pools. The flexible budget graph in Exhibit 10-5 shows that flexible budgeted total costs for 10 pools are as follows:

| | |
|---|---|
| Variable costs (10 × $8,000) | $ 80,000 |
| Fixed costs | 20,000 |
| Total costs | $100,000 |

June's actual costs were $105,000 (Exhibit 10-1). Consequently, June's actual costs for 10 pools ($105,000) slightly exceed the budget for 10 pools ($100,000). Managers can use graphs such as Exhibit 10-5 to see at a glance whether actual costs are either of the following:

- Higher than budgeted for the actual volume of output (as in April, June, and August)
- Lower than budgeted for the actual volume of output (as in May and July)

**EXHIBIT 10-5** Kool-Time Pools' Graph of Actual and Budgeted Monthly Costs

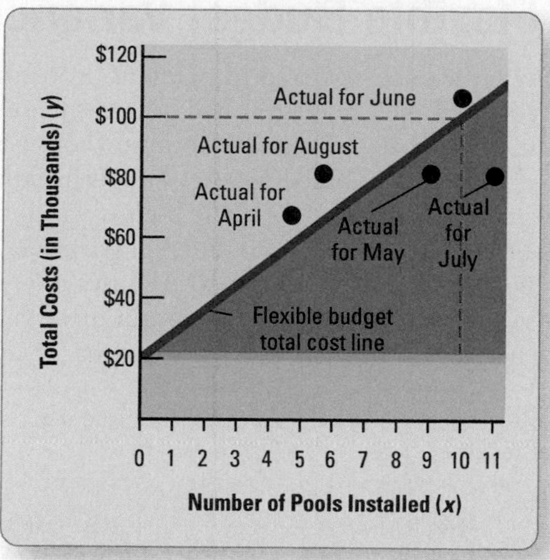


The above graph illustrates how Kool-Time's managers can compare actual costs against flexible budgeted costs. Comparing actual costs against flexible budgeted costs allows managers to make a comparison based on the *same actual volume of activity* (10 pools). By comparing the actual costs with the flexible budgeted costs for 10 pools, Kool-Time's managers see that their expenses were only $5,000 higher than anticipated for this volume. This explains a portion of the $21,000 unfavourable expense variance shown in Exhibit 10-1. In the next section, we'll see how managers can perform a more in-depth analysis to find out more about why that $21,000 unfavourable expense variance occurred.

**Why is this important?**

Flexible budgets allow managers to compare **actual results** with the results they would have expected for the particular volume achieved.

## STOP & THINK

Use the graph in Exhibit 10-5 and Kool-Time's flexible budget mixed cost equation to answer the following questions:

1. How many pools did Kool-Time install in July?
2. What were Kool-Time's actual costs in July?
3. Using Kool-Time's flexible budget mixed cost equation, what is the flexible budget total cost for the month of July?
4. Is Kool-Time's variance for total costs favourable or unfavourable in July?

**Answer:**

1. Exhibit 10-5 shows that Kool-Time installed 11 pools in July.
2. Exhibit 10-5 shows that Kool-Time's actual costs in July were about $80,000.
3. Using Kool-Time's flexible budget mixed cost equation, the flexible budget total cost for the month of July is as follows:

| | |
|---|---|
| Variable costs (11 × $8,000) | $ 88,000 |
| Fixed costs | 20,000 |
| Total costs | $108,000 |

4. Kool-Time's July variance for total costs is $28,000 ($108,000 – $80,000) favourable because actual costs are less than the budget.

# How Do Managers Compute the Sales Volume Variance and Flexible Budget Variance?

2 Use the sales volume variance and flexible budget variance to explain why actual results differ from the master budget.

Managers must know *why* a variance occurred to pinpoint problems and to identify corrective action. Recall that Kool-Time's managers had a hard time understanding why the static budget variances in Exhibit 10-1 occurred because they were based on different operating levels: The actual results were based on the 10 pools installed, yet the budget was for 8 pools. To get more answers as to why the static budget variance occurred, managers often separate the static budget variance into two different parts: (1) the **sales volume variance** and (2) the **flexible budget variance**. Exhibit 10-6 shows how the static budget variance can be separated into these two variances. To obtain these variances managers first need to prepare a flexible budget for the actual level of output for the period (10 pools).

**EXHIBIT 10-6** The Static Budget Variance, the Sales Volume Variance, and the Flexible Budget Variance

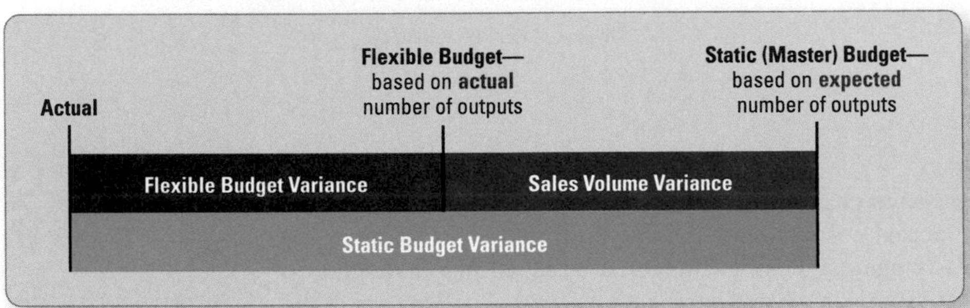


Exhibit 10-6 shows the following:

- The sales volume variance is the difference between the *static* (master) budget and the *flexible* budget (for the actual number of outputs). As the name suggests, this variance arises only because the number of units actually sold differs from the volume originally planned for in the static master budget.
- The flexible budget variance is the difference between the flexible budget and the actual results. This variance arises because the company actually earned more or less revenue or incurred more or less expense than expected for the actual level of output (10 pools). In other words, this variance is due to factors *other* than volume.

Let's see how Kool-Time's managers calculate and interpret these two different variances. Exhibit 10-7 shows Kool-Time's performance report for June. Column 1 shows Kool-Time's actual results for the period. This information is gathered from the general ledger. Now, consider the static master budget amounts presented in Column 5. Recall that at the beginning of the period, Kool-Time expected to sell eight pools. For these eight pools, Kool-Time's

- Budgeted sales revenue is \$96,000 (8 × \$12,000)
- Budgeted variable expenses are \$64,000 (8 × \$8,000)
- Budgeted fixed expenses are \$20,000

Notice that the amounts shown in Columns 1 and 5 are the same as those shown in Exhibit 10-1. The only difference is that here we show a little more detail: Variable and fixed costs are shown separately; they are not lumped together.

Finally, consider Column 3. In contrast to the static budget, which is developed *before* the period, the flexible budget used in the performance report is not developed until the *end* of the period, because it is based on the actual number of outputs, which is not known until the end of the period. For Kool-Time, this flexible budget is based on the 10 pools actually installed:

- Budgeted sales revenue is \$120,000 (10 × \$12,000)
- Budgeted variable expenses are \$80,000 (10 × \$8,000)
- Budgeted fixed expenses are \$20,000

**EXHIBIT 10-7** Income Statement Performance Report

| KOOL-TIME POOLS<br>Income Statement Performance Report<br>Month Ended June 30 | | | | | |
|---|---|---|---|---|---|
| | (1)<br>Actual Results at Actual Prices | (2)<br>(1)–(3)<br>Flexible Budget Variance | (3)<br>Flexible Budget for Actual Number of Output Units* | (4)<br>(3)–(5)<br>Sales Volume Variance | (5)<br>Static (Master) Budget* |
| Output units (pools installed) | 10 | –0– | 10 | 2 F | 8 |
| Sales revenue | $121,000 | $ 1,000 F | $120,000 | $24,000 F | $96,000 |
| Variable expenses | 83,000 | 3,000 U | 80,000 | 16,000 U | 64,000 |
| Fixed expenses | 22,000 | 2,000 U | 20,000 | –0– | 20,000 |
| Total expenses | 105,000 | 5,000 U | 100,000 | 16,000 U | 84,000 |
| Operating income | $ 16,000 | $ 4,000 U | $ 20,000 | $ 8,000 F | $12,000 |

*Flexible budget variance, $4,000 U* — *Sales volume variance, $8,000 F*

*Static budget variance, $4,000 F*

*Budgeted sales price is $12,000 per pool; budgeted variable expense is $8,000 per pool; and budgeted total monthly fixed expenses are $20,000.

Now that you know how this performance report was developed, let's take a look at the variances in more detail.

**Why is this important?**

This type of performance report allows managers to see, at a glance, how much of the overall variance is due to a difference in sales volume and how much is due to other factors, such as unexpected increases in the cost of materials or labour.

## Sales Volume Variance

The sales volume variance (shown in Column 4 of Exhibit 10-7) is the difference between the static master budget (Column 5) and the flexible budget (Column 3). The only difference between the static and flexible budgets in the performance report is the *number of outputs on which the budget is based* (8 pools versus 10 pools). Both budgets use the same

- Budgeted sales price per unit ($12,000 per pool)
- Budgeted variable cost per unit ($8,000 per pool)
- Budgeted total fixed costs ($20,000 per month)

Holding selling price per unit, variable cost per unit, and total fixed costs constant highlight the effects of differences in sales volume—the variance shown in Column 4. Exhibit 10-7 shows that by installing two more pools than initially expected, Kool-Time's

- Sales revenue *should* increase from $96,000 (8 × $12,000) to $120,000 (10 × $12,000)—a $24,000 favourable sales volume variance
- Variable costs *should* increase from $64,000 (8 × $8,000) to $80,000 (10 × $8,000)—a $16,000 unfavourable sales volume variance

Budgeted total fixed expenses are unaffected because 8 pools and 10 pools are within the relevant range where fixed expenses total $20,000. Consequently, installing two more pools should increase operating income by $8,000 ($24,000 F − $16,000 U). So, Kool-Time's June sales volume variance is $8,000 F.

**STOP & THINK**

When is there a sales volume variance for fixed expenses?

**Answer:** The only time managers would see a sales volume variance for fixed expenses is when the number of units actually sold falls within a different relevant range than the static budget sales volume. When actual and expected number of units sold fall in the same relevant range, there is no sales volume variance for fixed expenses.

## Flexible Budget Variance

As the name suggests, the flexible budget variance (shown in Column 2 of Exhibit 10-7) is the difference between the *flexible* budget (Column 3) and the *actual* results (Column 1). Recall that the flexible budget is based on the actual level of output (10 pools), so it shows the revenues and expenses that Kool-Time's managers expect for a volume of 10 pools. Therefore, the flexible budget variance highlights unexpected revenues and expenses.

Exhibit 10-7 shows a $1,000 favourable flexible budget variance for sales revenue. Kool-Time actually received $121,000 for installing 10 pools rather than the $120,000 expected for 10 pools (10 pools × $12,000). This variance means that the average sales price was $12,100 per pool ($121,000 ÷ 10 pools), which is $100 higher than the budgeted sales price of $12,000 per pool.

Exhibit 10-7 also shows a $3,000 unfavourable flexible budget variance for variable expenses. Kool-Time actually incurred $83,000 of variable expenses rather than the $80,000 expected for 10 pools (10 pools × $8,000 per pool). The company also spent $2,000 more on fixed expenses than was budgeted ($22,000 − $20,000). Consequently, the flexible budget variance for total expenses is $5,000 unfavourable ($3,000 U + $2,000 U). In other words, Kool-Time spent $5,000 more than it would expect to spend to install 10 pools. This is the same $5,000 flexible budget expense variance we saw graphed in Exhibit 10-5.

## Interpreting the Variances

The favourable sales volume variance reveals that strong sales should have increased Kool-Time's income by $8,000. In addition, the sales staff increased sales without discounting prices: The favourable $1,000 flexible budget variance for sales revenue shows that the sales price was, on average, higher than budgeted. These favourable variances, due to the quantity of pools sold (the $8,000 favourable sales volume variance) and the sales price per pool (the $1,000 favourable sales revenue **price variance**), suggest that Kool-Time's marketing staff did a better-than-expected job in selling pools and maintaining sales prices. Perhaps the high sales commission paid on each pool sale is doing a good job of motivating the sales staff.

However, higher-than-expected expenses offset much of the favourable sales volume variance. Exhibit 10-7 shows a $5,000 unfavourable flexible budget variance for expenses. The reason might be an uncontrollable increase in the cost of materials. Or higher costs might have resulted from more-controllable factors, such as employees wasting materials or working inefficiently. If so, managers can take action to reduce waste or inefficiency. Although Kool-Time does not have any favourable expense variances, in general, managers can benefit from examining favourable as well as unfavourable expense variances. Favourable variances may be the result of some type of efficiency that could also be used in other areas of the company.

Let's get back to Kool-Time's original question from Exhibit 10-1: Why did the company have an unfavourable static budget variance of $21,000 for expenses? The *sales volume variance* shows that $16,000 of this amount is due to the fact that Kool-Time installed two more pools than it originally planned to install. The *flexible budget variance* shows that the remaining $5,000 (of the $21,000 variance) is due to cost overruns caused by other factors. In the second part of this chapter, we will see how managers drill down deeper to find the root cause(s) of this $5,000 flexible budget expense variance. Once managers identify the reason for the cost overruns, they can decide what action to take to avoid similar overruns in the future.

# DECISION GUIDELINES

## Flexible Budgets

You and your roommate have started a business printing T-shirts for special customer requests (for example, with school or student organization logos). How can you use flexible budgets to plan and control your costs?

| Decision | Guidelines |
|---|---|
| How should we estimate sales revenues, costs, and profits over the range of likely sales (output) levels? | Prepare a set of flexible budgets for different sales levels. The set of budgets can include a realistic projection, a worst-case scenario, and a best-case scenario, for example. |
| How should we prepare a flexible budget for total costs? | Use a mixed cost equation to predict costs at different volumes within the relevant range: $\text{Flexible budget total cost} = \left(\text{Number of T-shirts} \times \text{Variable cost per T-shirt}\right) + \text{Fixed cost}$ |
| How should we use budgets to help evaluate performance? | • Graph actual costs versus flexible budget costs, as in Exhibit 10-5.<br>• Prepare an income statement performance report, as in Exhibit 10-7. |
| On which output level is the budget based? | Static (master) budget—*expected* number of T-shirts, estimated before the period.<br>Flexible budget—*actual* number of T-shirts, not known until the end of the period. |
| How can we better understand why actual results differed from the master budget? | Prepare an income statement performance report comparing actual results, the flexible budget for actual number of T-shirts sold, and the static (master) budget, as in Exhibit 10-7. |
| How do we interpret favourable and unfavourable variances? | • Favourable variances increase operating income.<br>• Unfavourable variances decrease operating income. |
| How much of the static budget variance is due to the fact that the actual number of T-shirts sold does not equal budgeted sales? | Compute the sales volume variance (SVV) by comparing the flexible budget with the static budget.<br>• Favourable SVV—Actual number of T-shirts sold > Expected<br>• Unfavourable SVV—Actual number of T-shirts sold < Expected |
| How much of the static budget variance occurs because actual revenues and costs are not what they should have been for the actual number of T-shirts sold? | Compute the flexible budget variance (FBV) by comparing actual results with the flexible budget.<br>• Favourable FBV—Actual sales revenue > Flexible budget sales revenue<br>OR<br>Actual expenses < Flexible budget expenses<br>• Unfavourable FBV—Actual sales revenue < Flexible budget sales revenue<br>OR<br>Actual expenses > Flexible budget expenses |
| What actions can we take to avoid an unfavourable sales volume variance? | • Design more-attractive T-shirts to increase demand.<br>• Provide marketing incentives to increase the number of T-shirts sold. |

# SUMMARY PROBLEM 1

Exhibit 10-7 indicates that Kool-Time installed 10 swimming pools during June. Now assume that Kool-Time installed 7 pools (instead of 10) and that the actual sales price averaged $12,500 per pool. Actual variable expenses were $57,400 and actual fixed expenses were $19,000.

### Requirements

1. Prepare a revised income statement performance report using Exhibit 10-7 as a guide.
2. Show that the sum of the flexible budget variance and the sales volume variance for operating income equals the static budget variance for operating income.
3. What should be done with the information provided by the performance report?

## ▪ SOLUTION

### Requirements 1 and 2

KOOL-TIME POOLS
**Income Statement Performance Report—Revised**
Month Ended June 30

| | (1)<br>Actual Results at Actual Prices | (2)<br>(1)–(3)<br>Flexible Budget Variance | (3)<br>Flexible Budget for Actual Number of Output Units | (4)<br>(3)–(5)<br>Sales Volume Variance | (5)<br>Static (Master) Budget |
|---|---|---|---|---|---|
| Output units | 7 | -0- | 7 | 1 U | 8 |
| Sales revenue | $ 87,500 | $ 3,500 F | $ 84,000 | $12,000 U | $ 96,000 |
| Variable expenses | 57,400 | 1,400 U | 56,000 | 8,000 F | 64,000 |
| Fixed expenses | 19,000 | 1,000 F | 20,000 | — | 20,000 |
| Total expenses | 76,400 | 400 U | 76,000 | 8,000 F | 84,000 |
| Operating income | $ 11,100 | $ 3,100 F | $ 8,000 | $ 4,000 U | $ 12,000 |

*Flexible budget variance,*
*$3,100 F*

*Sales volume variance,*
*$4,000 U*

*Static budget variance,*
*$900 U*

### Requirement 3

The performance report helps managers determine the amount of the static budget variance that is due to sales volume and the amount of the variance that is due to other factors (the flexible budget variance). The manager will want to investigate the cause of any significant variances and determine whether they were due to controllable factors. For example, the largest variance was the unfavourable sales volume variance. This variance could be due to insufficient advertising (a controllable factor) or a general recession in the economy (an uncontrollable factor). The manager uses this feedback to adjust operations as necessary.

## Standard Costs

3 Identify the benefits of standard costs, and learn how to set standards.

**Standard costs** are budgeted amounts for a single unit of a product or service. They are often used as benchmarks in control system and as the bases for flexible budgets. Recall that Kool-Time developed its flexible budget using a standard variable cost per pool of $8,000 (see Exhibit 10-3). Of the total standard variable cost per pool, $7,000 relates to the cost of variable manufacturing inputs: the direct materials, direct labour, and variable manufacturing overhead costs necessary to install one pool. The other $1,000 relates to selling and administrative costs associated with *selling* each pool (sales commission, for example). For the rest of this chapter, we are going to concentrate on *standard manufacturing costs*, although the same concepts apply to selling, general, and administrative costs.

In a standard cost system, each manufacturing input (such as direct materials) has a quantity standard and a price standard. For example, McCain has a standard for the amount of pepperoni used per pizza and a standard for the price paid per kilogram of pepperoni. Likewise, Kool-Time has a standard for the amount of gunite (a concrete-like material) used per pool and a standard for the price it pays per cubic metre of gunite. Let's see how managers set these quantity and price standards.

**Why is this important?**

Standard costs give managers a benchmark, or goal, for how much each unit should cost.

### Quantity Standards

Engineers and production managers set direct material and direct labour quantity standards, usually allowing for unavoidable waste and spoilage. For example, each pool that Kool-Time installs requires 24 m³ of gunite. As part of the normal installation process, an additional cubic metre of gunite is typically wasted due to unavoidable spoilage (hardened, unusable gunite). Kool-Time calculates the standard quantity of gunite per pool as follows:

| | |
|---|---|
| Gunite required | 24 m³ per pool |
| Unavoidable waste and spoilage | 1 m³ per pool |
| Standard quantity of gunite | 25 m³ per pool |

Kool-Time also develops quantity standards for direct labour based on time records from past pool installations and current installation requirements. In setting labour standards, managers usually allow for unavoidable work interruptions and normal downtime for which the employee is still paid. Considering these factors, Kool-Time has set its direct labour quantity standard at 400 direct labour hours per pool.

### Price Standards

Now, let's turn our attention to price standards. Accountants help managers set direct material price standards after considering the base purchase price of materials, early payment discounts, receiving costs, and freight-in. For example, the manager in charge of purchasing gunite for Kool-Time indicates that the purchase price, net of discounts, is $76.00 per cubic metre and that freight-in costs $4.00 per cubic metre. Kool-Time calculates its price standard for gunite as follows:

| | |
|---|---|
| Purchase price, net of discounts | $76.00 /m³ |
| Freight-in | $ 4.00 /m³ |
| Standard cost of gunite | $80.00 /m³ |

For direct labour, accountants work with personnel or human resources managers to determine standard labour rates, taking into account payroll taxes and fringe benefits as well as the hourly wage rate. Kool-Time's Human Resources Department indicates that the hourly wage rate for production workers is $8.00 and that payroll taxes and fringe benefits total $2.50 per direct labour hour. Kool-Time's direct labour price (or rate) standard is as follows:

| | |
|---|---|
| Hourly wage rate | $ 8.00 per direct labour hour |
| Payroll taxes and fringe benefits | 2.50 per direct labour hour |
| Standard direct labour rate | $10.50 per direct labour hour |

## Standard Manufacturing Overhead Rates

In addition to direct materials and direct labour price and quantity standards, companies also set standard manufacturing overhead rates. The standard predetermined manufacturing overhead rates are calculated as you learned in Chapter 5 except that two rates are calculated: one for fixed overhead and one for variable overhead. Isolating the variable overhead component helps managers create flexible budgets for different volumes. For setting standard overhead rates, accountants work with production managers to estimate variable and fixed manufacturing overhead expenses. Managers then identify an appropriate allocation base for computing the standard manufacturing overhead rates.

For example, recall that Kool-Time's fixed manufacturing overhead costs are expected to be $12,000 per month (the other $8,000 of fixed costs are related to selling and administrative expenses). Production managers also estimate variable manufacturing overhead costs to be $800 per pool, or a total of $6,400 for the eight pools they plan to produce during the month ($800 × 8 = $6,400). Kool-Time has decided to use direct labour hours as its overhead allocation base, so managers estimate the total number of direct labour hours they expect to incur during the month:

8 pools × 400 standard direct labour hours per pool = 3,200 direct labour hours

Kool-Time computes the standard variable overhead rate as follows:

$$\text{Standard } \textit{variable} \text{ overhead rate} = \frac{\text{Estimated total } \textit{variable} \text{ overhead cost}}{\text{Estimated total quality of allocation base}}$$

$$= \frac{\$6{,}400}{3{,}200 \text{ direct labour hours}}$$

$$= \underline{\underline{\$2.00}} \text{ per direct labour hour}$$

Kool-Time computes the standard fixed overhead rate in a similar way:

$$\text{Standard } \textit{fixed} \text{ overhead rate} = \frac{\text{Estimated total } \textit{fixed} \text{ overhead cost}}{\text{Estimated total quality of allocation base}}$$

$$= \frac{\$12{,}000}{3{,}200 \text{ direct labour hours}}$$

$$= \underline{\underline{\$3.75}} \text{ per direct labour hour}$$

The standard total overhead rate is the sum of the standard variable overhead and the standard fixed overhead rates:

| Variable overhead rate | + | Fixed overhead rate | = | Standard overhead rate |
|---|---|---|---|---|
| $2.00 per direct labour hour | + | $3.75 per direct labour hour | = | $5.75 per direct labour hour |

Notice that the standard manufacturing overhead rate ($5.75 per direct labour hour) is the rate we would have computed in Chapter 5 based on all anticipated manufacturing overhead costs, regardless of cost behaviour ($5.75 = $18,400 total estimated manufacturing overhead costs ÷ 3,200 total estimated direct labour hours).

## Standard Cost of Inputs

Once managers have developed quantity and price standards, they calculate the standard cost of *each input* (such as direct materials, direct labour, and manufacturing overhead) by multiplying the quantity standard by the price standard:

Quantity standard × Price standard = Standard cost of input

For example, Kool-Time's standard direct materials cost per pool is as follows:

25 $m^3$ of gunite × \$80.00 / $m^3$ = \$2,000 of direct materials per pool

Likewise, Kool-Time's standard direct labour cost per pool is as follows:

400 direct labour hours × \$10.50 per direct labour hour = \$4,200 of direct labour per pool

Exhibit 10-8 shows Kool-Time's standard costs for variable and fixed overhead. The exhibit also shows that by adding the standard cost of all of the inputs, Kool-Time can find the standard cost of manufacturing one pool (\$8,500). However, this cost can be misleading to managers because it contains a fixed overhead component. It is valid only when Kool-Time installs exactly eight pools in a month.

**EXHIBIT 10-8** Kool-Time's Standard Manufacturing Cost per Pool

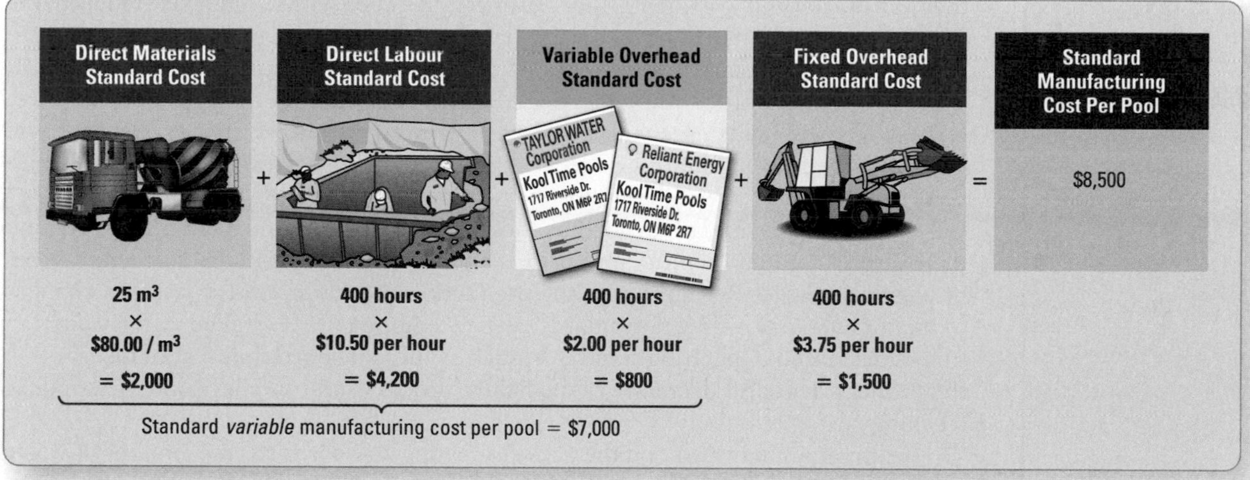


Rather than run the risk of misleading managers, it is often more helpful to highlight just the standard *variable* manufacturing cost per pool. Exhibit 10-8 shows that Kool-Time's standard costs for direct materials (\$2,000), direct labour (\$4,200), and variable overhead (\$800) amount to \$7,000 variable manufacturing cost per pool. In addition to variable *manufacturing* costs, recall that Kool-Time expects to incur \$1,000 of variable *selling and administrative* expenses per pool (for sales commissions, for example). Added together, these two costs total the \$8,000 variable cost per pool that Kool-Time used for flexible budgeting in Exhibit 10-3.

Kool-Time is not alone in its use of standards. International surveys show that over half of responding companies in the United Kingdom, Ireland, Sweden, and Japan use standard costs, while over 80% of responding U.S. companies use standard costs. Why? Companies believe that the benefits from using standard costs outweigh the costs of developing the standards and periodically revising them as business conditions change.

Companies should reassess their price standards when input prices such as the price of raw materials or labour rates change due to nontemporary market conditions. They should also reassess quantity standards when the product or production process is modified and, as a result, different quantities of materials or labour are required. Exhibit 10-9 shows five benefits that companies, such as McCain, obtain from using standard costs.

**EXHIBIT 10-9** The Benefits of Standard Costs

## Sustainability and Standard Costs

See Exercises E10-35A and E10-58B

In order to advance environmental sustainability, many companies are reengineering their products and packaging. For example, in 2009, J.M. Smucker reduced the amount of resin in its JIF peanut butter jars by 2.2 million pounds—enough resin to produce 34 million jars! Likewise, Kraft reduced the amount of plastic in the lids of its salad dressing bottles and Coca-Cola reduced the amount of plastic in its beverage bottles. These packaging changes not only reduced the amount of plastic that will eventually end up in landfills or recycling plants but also saved the companies millions of dollars.

Sustainability initiatives such as these will also require management to rethink their direct material quantity and price standards, as less plastic and different types of plastic are used. Reengineering the production process may also result in changes to manufacturing overhead standards, as new equipment is installed and production time is decreased. Operating standards, such as the transportation cost of distributing the product, will also decrease, as the lighter products and smaller containers reduce trucking costs.

Companies may also find themselves creating standards for the amount of waste that leaves the production process in the form of air pollution, scrap, or wastewater. Government regulations are forcing companies to cap, or limit, the amount of $CO_2$ and other pollutants that result from the production process. Therefore, companies will have standards for the maximum pollutants allowed to leave their plants.

## TRY IT!

Hannah owns a fruit smoothie shop at the local mall. Each smoothie requires ¼ pound of mixed berries, which are expected to cost $4 per pound during the summer months. Shop employees are paid $10 per hour. Variable overhead consists of utilities and supplies. The variable overhead rate is $0.05 per minute of DL time. Each smoothie should require 3 minutes of DL time.

1. What is the standard cost of direct materials for each smoothie?
2. What is the standard cost of direct labour for each smoothie?
3. What is the standard cost of variable overhead for each smoothie?

Please see page 666 for solutions.

# How Do Managers Use Standard Costs to Analyze Direct Material and Direct Labour Variances?

Exhibit 10-7 showed that the main cause for concern at Kool-Time is the $5,000 unfavourable flexible budget variance for expenses. The first step in identifying the causes of this variance is to take a more detailed look at what is included in the *expenses*.

Panel A of Exhibit 10-10 does just this. Note that Panel A of Exhibit 10-10 is different from Exhibit 10-7 in three ways: (1) It shows only expenses (it leaves out all

**EXHIBIT 10-10** Data for Standard Costing Example

KOOL-TIME POOLS
Data for Standard Costing Example
Month Ended June 30

**PANEL A—Comparison of Actual Results with Flexible Budget for 10 Swimming Pools**

| | (1) Actual Results at Actual Prices | (2) Flexible Budget for 10 Pools | (1) – (2) Flexible Budget Variance |
|---|---|---|---|
| Variable expenses: | | | |
| Direct materials | $ 23,100* | $ 20,000† | $3,100 U |
| Direct labour | 41,800* | 42,000† | 200 F |
| Variable overhead | 9,000 | 8,000† | 1,000 U |
| Marketing and administrative expenses | 9,100 | 10,000 | 900 F |
| Total variable expenses | 83,000 | 80,000 | 3,000 U |
| Fixed expenses: | | | |
| Fixed overhead | 12,300 | 12,000‡ | 300 U |
| Marketing and administrative expenses | 9,700 | 8,000 | 1,700 U |
| Total fixed expenses | 22,000 | 20,000 | 2,000 U |
| Total expenses | $105,000 | $100,000 | $5,000 U |

**PANEL B—Computation of Flexible Budget for Direct Materials, Direct Labour, and Variable Overhead for 10 Swimming Pools**

| | (1) Standard Quantity of Inputs Allowed for 10 Pools | (2) Standard Price per Unit of Input | (1) × (2) Flexible Budget for 10 Pools |
|---|---|---|---|
| Direct materials | 25 $m^3$ per pool × 10 pools = 250 $m^3$ | × $ 80.00 | = $ 20,000 |
| Direct labour | 400 hours per pool × 10 pools = 4,000 hours | × 10.50 | = 42,000 |
| Variable overhead | 400 hours per pool × 10 pools = 4,000 hours | × 2.00 | = 8,000 |

**PANEL C—Computation of Actual Costs for Direct Materials and Direct Labour for 10 Swimming Pools**

| | (1) Actual Quantity of Inputs Used for 10 Pools | | (2) Actual Price per Unit of Input | (1) × (2) Actual Cost for 10 Pools |
|---|---|---|---|---|
| Direct materials | 300 $m^3$ actually used | × | $77 actual cost/$m^3$ | = $ 23,100 |
| Direct labour | 3,800 hours actually used | × | $11.00 actual cost/hour | = 41,800 |

*See Panel C.
†See Panel B.
‡Fixed overhead was budgeted at $12,000 per month.

revenue data), (2) it contains only actual and flexible budget data (it leaves out the static master budget and sales volume variance), and (3) it shows the components of Kool-Time's variable and fixed expenses (detailed production costs are shown separately from marketing and administrative expenses). Take a moment to see that the total variable expenses ($83,000 actual versus $80,000 budgeted), total fixed expenses ($22,000 actual versus $20,000 budgeted), and total expenses ($105,000 actual versus $100,000 budgeted) agree with Exhibit 10-7. The total $5,000 unfavourable flexible budget variance for expenses also agrees with Exhibit 10-7.

Study Exhibit 10-10 carefully because we will continue to refer to it throughout the rest of the chapter. Panel B shows how we used Kool-Time's price and quantity standards to compute the flexible budget amounts shown in Panel A. Panel C shows how we computed the actual direct materials and direct labour costs shown in Panel A.

## Direct Material Variances

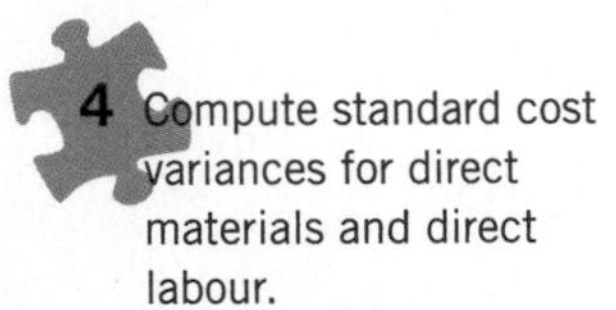

Compute standard cost variances for direct materials and direct labour.

The largest single component of the flexible budget variance in Panel A of Exhibit 10-10 is the $3,100 unfavourable variance in direct materials. Recall that the flexible budget variance is the difference between the actual cost incurred and the flexible budget (as shown in Exhibits 10-6 and 10-7). Exhibit 10-11 shows that Kool-Time computes the direct materials flexible budget variance as the difference between (1) the actual amount paid for gunite and (2) the flexible budget amount (not the static budget amount) that Kool-Time should have spent on gunite for the 10 pools that it actually installed.

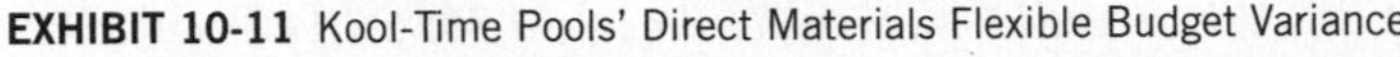
**EXHIBIT 10-11** Kool-Time Pools' Direct Materials Flexible Budget Variance

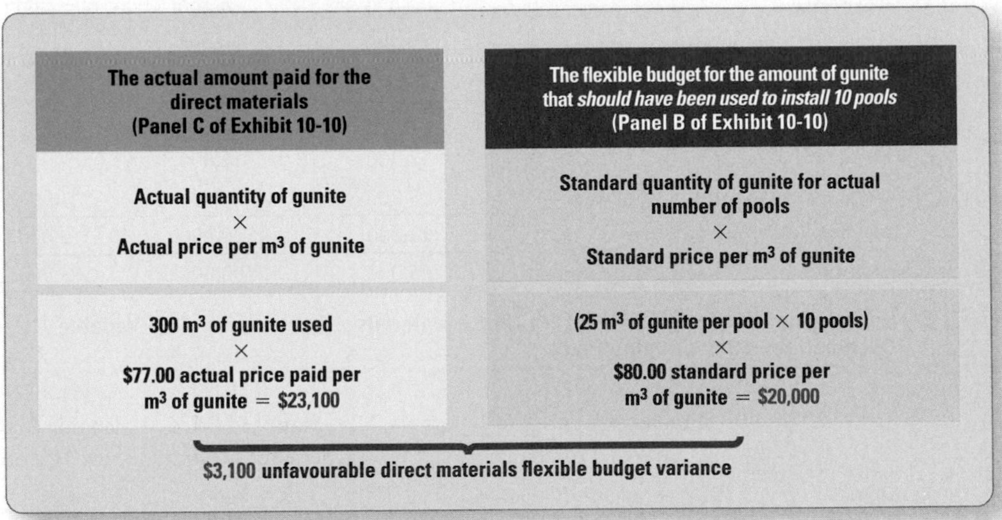


Now that Kool-Time knows that it spent $3,100 more than it should have on gunite, the next question is why. Did the $3,100 unfavourable variance arise because

- Kool-Time did not meet the price standard because it paid too much for each cubic metre of gunite?
- Kool-Time did not meet the quantity standard because workers used more gunite than they should have used to install 10 pools?

To answer those questions, Kool-Time's managers separate the flexible budget variance for direct materials into price and efficiency components, as shown in Exhibit 10-12.

Exhibit 10-12 emphasizes two points. First, added together, the price and efficiency variances equal the flexible budget variance. Second, static budgets (such as Column 5 of Exhibit 10-7) play no role in computing the flexible budget variance or in determining how it is split into price and efficiency variances. The static budget is used *only* in computing the sales volume variance—never in computing the flexible budget variance or its component price and efficiency variances.

**EXHIBIT 10-12** The Relations among Price, Efficiency, Flexible Budget, Sales Volume, and Static Budget Variances

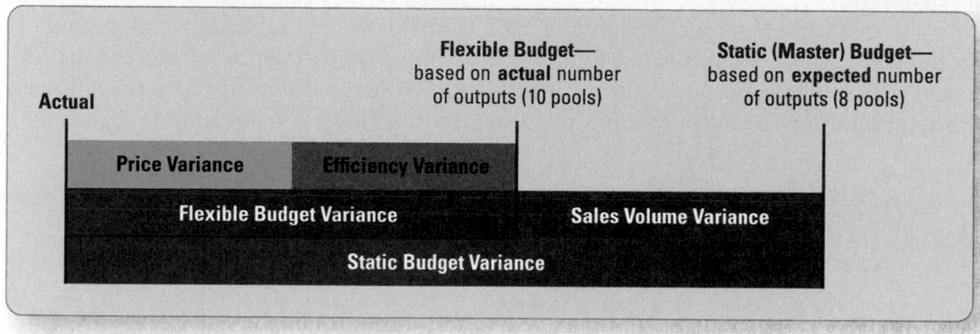


## Direct Materials Price Variance

A price variance measures how well the business keeps unit prices of material and labour inputs within standards. As the name suggests, the price variance is the *difference in price* (actual price per unit – standard price per unit) of an input, multiplied by the *actual quantity* of the input:

Price variance = (Actual price per input unit − Standard price per input unit) × (Actual quantity of input)

For Kool-Time, the direct materials price variance for gunite is

$$\begin{aligned}\text{Direct materials price variance} &= (\$77.00/\text{m}^3 - \$80.00/\text{m}^3) \times 300\ \text{m}^3 \\ &= (\$3.00/\text{m}^3) \times 300\ \text{m}^3 \\ &= \$900\ \text{F}\end{aligned}$$

The $900 direct materials price variance is *favourable* because the purchasing manager spent $3.00 less per cubic metre of gunite than budgeted ($77.00 actual price – $80.00 standard price).

The purchasing manager is responsible for the price variance on the *actual quantity* of materials he or she buys, so we multiply the $3.00 favourable price variance per cubic metre by the 300 m$^3$ of gunite he or she *actually purchased.* Thus, Kool-Time's June operating income is $900 higher [($77.00 – $80.00) × 300] than the flexible budget because the purchasing manager paid less than the standard price for gunite. (If the purchasing manager had paid *more* than the $80.00 per cubic metre standard price, the direct materials price variance would have been *unfavourable.*)

*Answer:* Purchasing

### Direct Materials Efficiency Variance

An efficiency variance measures whether the firm meets its quantity standards. It measures whether the quantity of materials actually used to make the actual number of outputs is within the standard allowed for that number of outputs. The efficiency variance is the *difference in quantities* (actual quantity of input used – standard quantity of input allowed for the actual number of outputs) multiplied by the *standard price per unit* of the input.

$$\text{Efficiency variance} = \left(\text{Actual quantity of input} - \text{Standard quantity of input allowed for the actual number of outputs}\right) \times \text{Standard price per input unit}$$

The standard quantity of inputs is the quantity that should have been used, or the standard quantity of inputs *allowed*, for the actual output. For Kool-Time, the standard quantity of inputs (gunite) that workers should have used for the actual number of outputs (10 pools) is as follows:

$$25\ m^3 \text{ of gunite per pool} \times 10 \text{ pools installed} = 250\ m^3 \text{ of gunite}$$

Thus, the direct materials efficiency variance is as follows:

$$\begin{aligned}\text{Direct materials efficiency variance} &= (300\ m^3 - 250\ m^3) \times \$80.00/m^3 \\ &= (50\ m^3) \times \$80.00/m^3 \\ &= \$4{,}000\ U\end{aligned}$$

The $4,000 direct materials efficiency variance is *unfavourable* because workers actually used 50 *more* cubic metres of gunite than they should have used to install 10 pools (300 actual cubic metres – 250 standard cubic metres).

The manager in charge of installing the pools is responsible for the variance in the quantity of the materials (gunite) used—in this case, the extra 50 m³ of gunite. However, this manager generally is not the person who purchases the gunite. The manager who installs the pools often has no control over the actual price paid for the gunite. Thus, we multiply the extra 50 m³ of gunite his or her workers used by the *standard price* of $80 per cubic metre to obtain the direct materials efficiency variance. Kool-Time's operating income is $4,000 lower [(300 – 250) × $80] than the flexible budget because workers used more gunite than they should have to install the 10 pools in June. (If workers had used *less* than the standard 250 m³ to install the 10 pools, the direct materials efficiency variance would have been *favourable*.)

**Why is this important?**

By separating the flexible budget variance into its price and efficiency components, managers can better pinpoint why the variance occurred. This information helps managers to better control costs in the future.

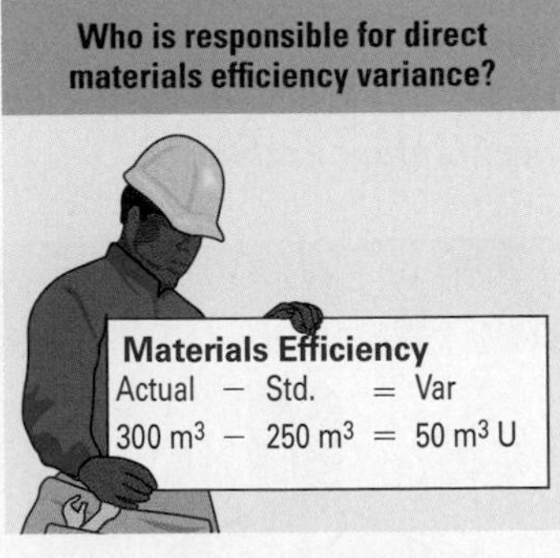


*Answer:* Pool Installation Manager

### Summary of Direct Material Variances

Exhibit 10-13 summarizes how Kool-Time splits the $3,100 unfavourable direct materials flexible budget variance, first identified in Panel A of Exhibit 10-10, into price and efficiency variances.

**EXHIBIT 10-13** Kool-Time Pools' Direct Materials Variances

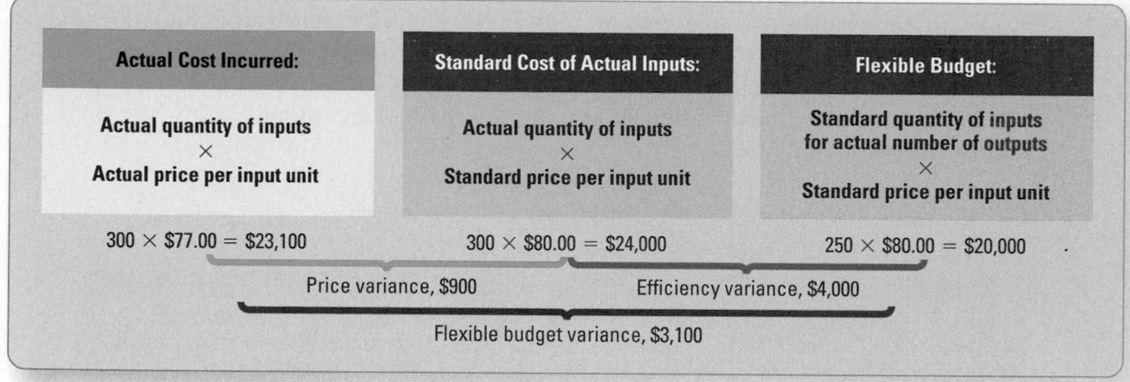


Kool-Time actually spent $3,100 more than it should have for gunite because a good price for the gunite increased profits by $900, but inefficient use of the gunite reduced profits by $4,000.

Let's review who is responsible for each of these variances and consider why each variance may have occurred.

1. *Purchasing managers typically are responsible for direct materials price variances* because they should know why the actual price differs from the standard price. Kool-Time's purchasing manager may have negotiated a good price for gunite, or perhaps the supplier did not increase the price of gunite as much as expected when Kool-Time developed its standard cost. In either case, the purchasing manager is in the best position to explain the favourable price variance.
2. *Production managers typically are responsible for direct materials efficiency variances* because they are responsible for ensuring that workers use materials efficiently and effectively. The manager in charge of installing pools should be able to explain why workers used more gunite than they should have to install the 10 pools. Was the gunite of lower quality? Did workers waste materials? Did their equipment malfunction? Kool-Time's top management needs answers to those questions in order to decide what corrective action to take. Should management require the purchase of higher-quality gunite, that workers be trained and supervised more closely to reduce waste, or that equipment maintenance be improved?

Smart managers know that these variances raise questions that can help pinpoint problems. However, a favourable variance does not necessarily mean that a manager did a good job; nor does an unfavourable variance mean that a manager did a poor job. Perhaps Kool-Time's purchasing manager obtained a lower price by purchasing inferior-quality gunite, which, in turn, led to waste and spoilage. If so, the purchasing manager's decision hurt the company, because the $900 favourable price variance is more than offset by the $4,000 unfavourable efficiency variance. This illustrates why good managers (1) use variances as a guide for investigation rather than as a simple tool to assign blame and (2) investigate favourable as well as unfavourable variances.

## TRY IT!

Hannah owns a fruit smoothie shop at the local mall. Each smoothie requires ¼ pound of mixed berries, which are expected to cost $4 per pound during the summer months. During the month of June, Hannah purchased and used 1,300 pounds of mixed berries at a cost of $3.75 per pound. Hannah's shop sold 5,000 smoothies during the month.

1. Calculate the DM price variance. Is the variance favourable or unfavourable?
2. Calculate the DM efficiency variance. Is the variance favourable or unfavourable?
3. Calculate the total DM variance. Is the variance favourable or unfavourable?

Please see page 666 for solutions.

## Direct Labour Variances

Kool-Time uses a similar approach to analyze the direct labour flexible budget variance. Using the information from Panels B and C of Exhibit 10-10, Exhibit 10-14 shows how Kool-Time computes this variance as the difference between the actual amount paid for direct labour and the flexible budget amount that Kool-Time should have spent on direct labour for 10 pools.

**EXHIBIT 10-14** Kool-Time Pools' Direct Labour Flexible Budget Variance

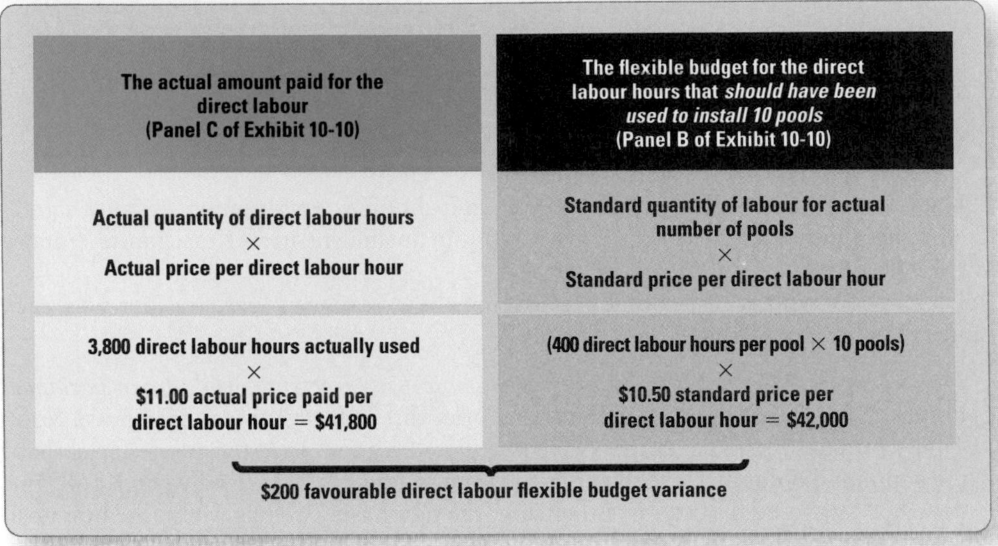


Why did Kool-Time spend $200 less on labour than it should have to install 10 pools? To answer that question, Kool-Time splits the direct labour flexible budget variance into price and efficiency variances the same way it did for direct materials.

### Direct Labour Price Variance

The direct labour price variance is computed the same way as the direct materials price variance, so we use the same formula for price variance shown earlier:

$$\text{Price variance} = (\text{Actual price per input unit} - \text{Standard price per input unit}) \times (\text{Actual quantity of input})$$

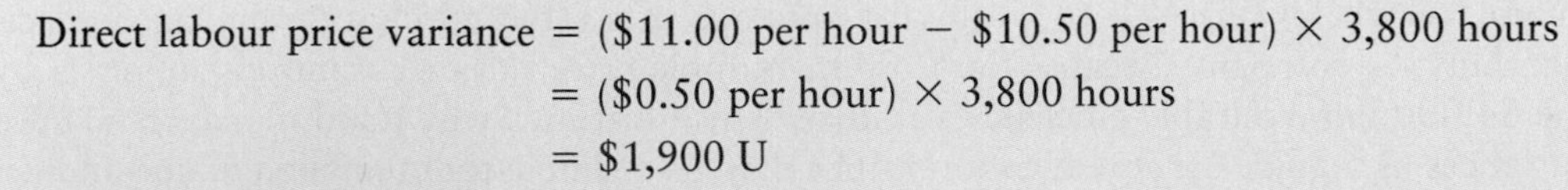

$$\begin{aligned}\text{Direct labour price variance} &= (\$11.00 \text{ per hour} - \$10.50 \text{ per hour}) \times 3{,}800 \text{ hours}\\ &= (\$0.50 \text{ per hour}) \times 3{,}800 \text{ hours}\\ &= \$1{,}900 \text{ U}\end{aligned}$$

*Answer:* HR Department

The $1,900 direct labour price variance is *unfavourable* because the Human Resources (or Personnel) Department hired workers at $0.50 *more* per direct labour hour than budgeted ($11.00 actual price – $10.50 standard price).

The human resources manager is responsible for the price variance on the actual *quantity* of labour he or she hires, so we multiply the $0.50 unfavourable price variance per direct labour hour by the 3,800 hours of labour he or she actually *purchased*.

### Direct Labour Efficiency Variance

The direct labour efficiency variance is computed the same way as the direct materials efficiency variance, so once again, we use the same formula for efficiency variance shown earlier:

$$\text{Efficiency variance} = \left(\text{Actual quantity of input} - \text{Standard quantity of input allowed for the actual number of outputs}\right) \times \text{Standard price per input unit}$$

For Kool-Time, the standard quantity of direct labour hours that workers should have used for the actual number of outputs (10 pools) is as follows:

400 direct labour hours per pool × 10 pools installed = 4,000 direct labour hours

Thus, the direct labour efficiency variance is as follows:

$$\begin{aligned}\text{Direct labour efficiency variance} &= (3{,}800 \text{ hours} - 4{,}000 \text{ hours}) \times \$10.50 \text{ per hour}\\ &= (200 \text{ hours}) \times \$10.50 \text{ per hour}\\ &= \$2{,}100 \text{ F}\end{aligned}$$

The $2,100 direct labour efficiency variance is *favourable* because installers actually worked 200 *fewer* hours than they should have to install 10 pools (3,800 actual hours – 4,000 standard hours).

### Summary of Direct Labour Variances

Exhibit 10-15 summarizes how Kool-Time splits the $200 favourable direct labour flexible budget variance into price and efficiency variances. Had they looked only at the $200 favourable direct labour flexible budget variance, Kool-Time's managers might have thought direct labour costs were close to expectations. But this illustrates the danger in ending the analysis after computing only the flexible budget variance. "Peeling the onion" to examine the price and efficiency variances yields more insight:

- The unfavourable direct labour price variance means that Kool-Time's operating income is $1,900 lower than expected because the company paid its employees an average of $11.00 per hour in June instead of the standard rate of $10.50. But this unfavourable variance was more than offset by the favourable direct labour efficiency variance.
- The favourable direct labour efficiency variance means that Kool-Time's operating income is $2,100 higher than expected because workers installed 10 pools in 3,800 hours instead of the budgeted 4,000 hours.

**EXHIBIT 10-15** Kool-Time Pools' Direct Labour Variances

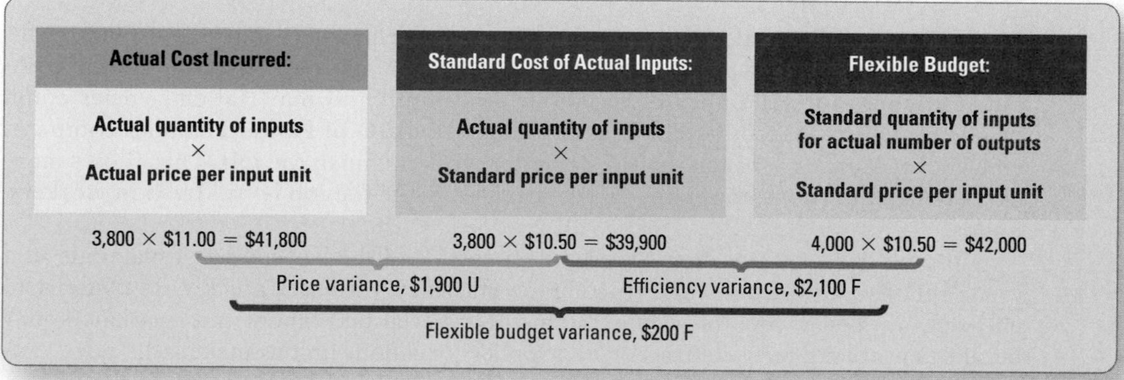

Kool-Time's top management will ask the Human Resources Department to explain the unfavourable labour price variance, and will ask the manager in charge of installing the pools to explain the favourable labour efficiency variance. Once again, there might have been a trade-off. Kool-Time might have hired more-experienced (and thus more highly paid) workers and traded off an unfavourable price variance for a favourable efficiency variance. If so, the strategy was successful—the overall effect on profits was favourable. This possibility reminds us that managers should be careful when using variances to evaluate performance.

You have now seen how Kool-Time analyzes flexible budget variances for direct materials and direct labour. Variances for variable marketing and administrative expenses could be calculated the same way, but for simplicity, we limit our detailed analysis to the variances in the production element of the value chain.

## Price and Efficiency Variances: Three Common Pitfalls

Here are three common pitfalls to avoid when computing price and efficiency variances for direct materials and direct labour.

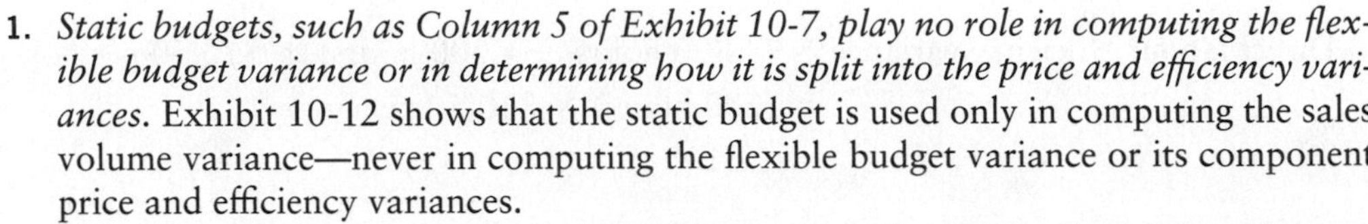

1. *Static budgets, such as Column 5 of Exhibit 10-7, play no role in computing the flexible budget variance or in determining how it is split into the price and efficiency variances.* Exhibit 10-12 shows that the static budget is used only in computing the sales volume variance—never in computing the flexible budget variance or its component price and efficiency variances.
2. In the efficiency variance, the standard quantity is the *standard quantity of inputs allowed for the actual number of outputs*—the basis for the flexible budget. To compute the standard quantity of inputs allowed, determine the actual number of outputs. For Kool-Time, the actual number of outputs is 10 pools. Next, compute how many inputs should have been used to produce the actual number of outputs (10 pools). For example, each pool should use 400 direct labour hours, so the standard quantity of direct labour hours allowed for 10 pools is $10 \times 400$ hours = 4,000 hours.
3. In the direct materials price variance, the difference in prices is multiplied by the *actual quantity* of materials. In the direct materials efficiency variance, the difference in quantities is multiplied by the *standard price* of the materials. The following explanation can help you remember this difference:
   - The materials price variance is usually the responsibility of purchasing personnel; they purchase the actual quantity used, not just the amount of materials that should have been used (the standard quantity). So, the price variance is the difference in prices multiplied by the *actual quantity* of materials purchased.
   - The materials efficiency variance is usually the responsibility of production personnel; they have no influence over the actual price paid. So, the efficiency variance is computed as the difference in quantities multiplied by the *standard* price (the price that should have been paid).

## Using Variances

Many firms monitor sales volume, direct materials efficiency, and direct labour efficiency variances day to day, or even hour to hour. A fast-food restaurant could compute variances for sales and direct labour each hour, and material efficiencies could be computed for each shift. The Brass Products Division of Parker Hannifin computes efficiency variances for each job the day after workers finish the job. This allows managers to ask questions about any large variances while the job is still fresh in workers' minds.

Technology—such as computerized data entry and the bar coding of materials, and even labour—allows companies to compute efficiency variances quickly. In contrast to efficiency variances, monthly computations of material and labour price variances may be sufficient if long-term contracts with suppliers or labour unions make large price variances unlikely.

### Using Variances to Evaluate Employees' Performance

Good managers use variances as a way to raise questions for further investigation, not as simple indicators of performance. Why should you take care in using variances to evaluate performance?

- Some variances are caused by factors that managers cannot control. For example, perhaps Kool-Time used more gunite than budgeted because workers had to repair cracked foundations resulting from an earthquake.
- Sometimes, variances are the result of inaccurate or outdated standards. Management must take care to review and update standards on a regular basis. If the production process changes or if supply prices change, the standards will need to be updated to reflect current operating conditions.
- Managers often make trade-offs among variances. Chrysler intentionally accepted a large order for customized Dodge vans because it expected that the favourable sales volume variance would more than offset the unfavourable direct labour price variance from the overtime premium and the unfavourable sales revenue price variance from extra rebates offered to the customer. Similarly, managers often trade off price variances against efficiency variances. Purchasing personnel may decide to buy higher-quality (but more expensive) direct materials to reduce waste and spoilage. The unfavourable price variance may be more than offset by a favourable efficiency variance.
- Evaluations based primarily on one variance can encourage managers to take actions that make the variance look good but hurt the company in the long run. For example, Kool-Time's managers could do the following:
  - Purchase low-quality gunite or hire less-experienced labour to get favourable price variances.
  - Use less gunite or less labour (resulting in lower-quality installed pools) to get favourable efficiency variances.

One approach to expand performance analysis beyond variance calculations is to include *nonfinancial* measures, such as quality indicators (for example, variances in the grade of gunite or labour used) or customer satisfaction measures. For instance, McCain is committed to continuous improvement in quality, which may come at the expense of efficiency variances. An unfavourable labour efficiency variance could be caused if McCain workers spent a little extra time to ensure the quality of a batch of pizzas by reworking some of the pizzas, but the high standard set by McCain would be maintained. In Chapter 11, we'll discuss nonfinancial performance evaluation in more detail.

## STOP & THINK

Why might an auto assembly plant experience a favourable direct labour efficiency variance? Should managers investigate favourable as well as unfavourable efficiency variances? Why or why not?

**Answer:**

1. The plant may have redesigned the manufacturing process to avoid wasted motion. For example, a Dodge van plant in Canada specifically reduced direct labour by reorganizing production so employees reach for raw materials as needed rather than carry armloads of materials across the plant floor.
2. Employees may have worked harder or more intensely than budgeted.
3. Employees may have rushed through the work and skimped on quality.

There are two reasons managers should investigate favourable efficiency variables. First, managers want to maximize improvements that increase profits. For example, can they capitalize on the first two answers above to further improve labour efficiency at this and/or other plants? Second, managers want to prevent employees from achieving favourable variances at the expense of long-run profits through strategies like the third one above.

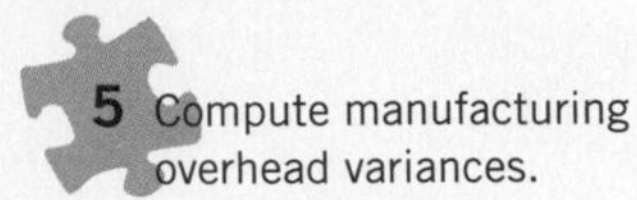


# How Do Managers Use Standard Costs to Analyze Manufacturing Overhead Variances?

In the previous section, we looked at how managers analyze direct materials and direct labour variances. In this section, we look at manufacturing overhead variances. A company's total manufacturing overhead variance *is the difference between the actual overhead incurred and the standard overhead allocated to production.* In other words, this is the amount by which manufacturing overhead has been overallocated or underallocated to production. The total manufacturing overhead variance can be broken into variable and fixed overhead variances, and each of these can be separated into two components.

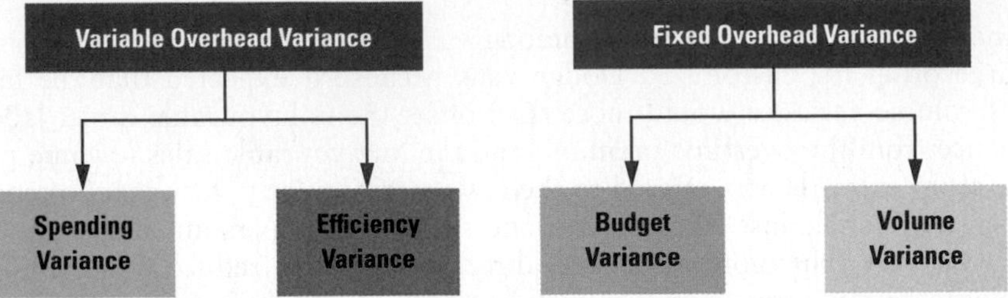


## Overhead Flexible Budget Variance

The overhead flexible budget variance shows how well management has controlled overhead costs. Therefore, this variance is often referred to as the overhead controllable variance. It is computed the same way as the flexible budget variances for direct materials and direct labour. It is the *difference between actual overhead costs and the flexible budget overhead for the actual number of outputs* (10 pools).

The following information about Kool-Time's overhead is taken directly from Exhibit 10-10.

| | (1)<br>Actual Results | (2)<br>Flexible Budget for 10 Pools | (1) − (2)<br>Flexible Budget Variance |
|---|---|---|---|
| Variable overhead ($800 per pool) | $ 9,000 | $ 8,000 | $1,000 U |
| Fixed overhead | 12,300 | 12,000 | 300 U |
| Total overhead | $21,300 | $20,000 | $1,300 U |

Before continuing, let's quickly review how we arrived at the flexible budget numbers shown previously. The amount of *variable* overhead budgeted for the actual output is calculated as follows:

(400 direct labour hours allowed per pool × $2.00 per direct labour hour variable overhead rate) × 10 pools = $8,000

Since 10 pools falls within the relevant range of 0 to 11, *fixed* production overhead for the month is budgeted at $12,000. Therefore, the total flexible budget for overhead is $20,000. Actual overhead for the month is $21,300. Therefore, Kool-Time calculates the overhead flexible budget variance as follows:

Overhead flexible budget variance = Actual overhead − Flexible budget overhead for actual output
= $21,300 − $20,000
= $1,300 U

Why did Kool-Time spend $1,300 more on overhead items than it should have to install the 10 pools in June? You can see that $1,000 ($9,000 – $8,000) of the variance is due to higher-than-expected spending on variable overhead items and that the remaining $300 ($12,300 – $12,000) is due to higher spending on fixed overhead items. Kool-Time will investigate the reason for each of these variances.

### Variable Overhead Spending Variance

The variable overhead spending variance is calculated in the same manner that the direct material and direct labour price variances are calculated, so we will again use the same formula:

$$\text{Price variance} = (\text{Actual price per input unit} - \text{Standard price per input unit}) \times (\text{Actual quantity of input})$$

$$\begin{aligned}\text{VOH spending variance} &= ((9{,}000/3{,}800) - 2) \times (3{,}800)\\ &= 0.36842 \times 3{,}800\\ &= \$1{,}400\ \text{U}\end{aligned}$$

You need to remember that the actual quantity that is referred to in this formula relates to the actual quantity of the cost driver for variable overhead, which in this scenario is direct labour hours. The standard price refers to the predetermined overhead rate that was calculated earlier in the chapter ($2.00 per direct labour hour). The $1,400 unfavourable variance can be explained by either the increases in the price of certain variable overhead elements or in the usage of the variable overhead elements. Either of those changes could result in the total variable overhead costs increasing to $9,000.

### Variable Overhead Efficiency Variance

The variable overhead efficiency variance is computed the same way as the direct material and direct labour efficiency variances:

$$\text{Efficiency variance} = (\text{Actual quantity of input} - \text{Standard quantity of input allowed for the actual number of outputs}) \times \text{Standard price per input unit}$$

$$\begin{aligned}\text{VOH efficiency variance} &= (3{,}800 - (400 \times 10)) \times 2\\ &= 200 \times 2\\ &= 400\ \text{F}\end{aligned}$$

The variance is favourable because the company used less of the cost driver than it should have in order to produce the amount of output that was made. This means that the company was efficient in the use of the cost driver. It is interesting that this variance relates more to the usage of the cost driver than it does to the elements of the variable overhead. In fact, when the cost driver is direct labour hours, the direction of the variable overhead efficiency variance is the same as the direction of the direct labour efficiency variance. In this example, the direct labour efficiency variance was favourable, therefore, it is expected that the variable overhead efficiency variance would also be favourable.

### Summary of Variable Overhead Variances

Exhibit 10-16 summarizes how Kool-Time's variable overhead variances are determined. The unfavourable spending variance shows that variable overhead costs were higher through either higher unit costs for the elements or higher usage of the elements, because the total variable overhead expenses were $9,000 when the anticipated cost was only $8,000.

**EXHIBIT 10-16** Kool-Time Pools' Variable Overhead Variances

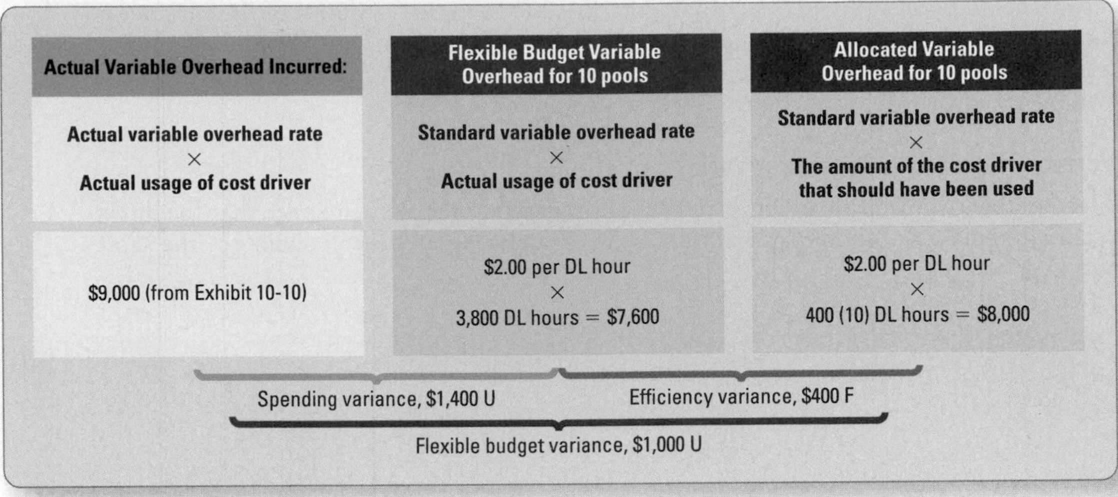


The favourable efficiency variance demonstrates that the cost driver (direct labour hours) was used efficiently because 10 pools were installed using only 3,800 direct labour hours when the anticipated direct labour was 4,000 hours.

## Fixed Overhead Budget Variance

The calculation for this variance is a little bit different from that of the price variances discussed earlier, simply because of the nature of fixed costs. The flexible budget amount for fixed overhead is not dependent on the level of production, which is different from the flexible budget amounts for direct materials, direct labour, and variable overhead. Therefore the formula for the fixed overhead budget variance is

Fixed overhead budget variance = Actual fixed overhead incurred − Budgeted fixed overhead
= (The amount actually spent on fixed overhead) − (Estimated cost driver × fixed portion of the predetermined overhead rate)
= $12,300 − $12,000
= $300 U

The most difficult part of the calculations in Exhibit 10-17 is to remember that you want the budgeted fixed overhead amount, and the amount of budgeted fixed overhead does not change with a change in production. For example, Fixed overhead for Kool-Time was budgeted to be $12,000 for eight pools, and is still budgeted at $12,000 even if 10 pools are built. The total amount of fixed overhead does not change with an increase or decrease in the number of pools built. Therefore, the calculation for the flexible budget fixed overhead amount is the estimated amount of direct labour hours (the cost driver) times the estimated rate for fixed overhead (or the fixed portion of the predetermined overhead rate). The meaning of this variance is simply that the company has spent more ($300) than what it had budgeted to spend on fixed overhead.

The total of the two variable overhead variances and the fixed overhead budget variance is equal to the total flexible budget variance. Most companies compile actual and budget cost information for the individual component items that make up overhead, such as indirect materials, indirect labour, utilities, and depreciation on plant and equipment. Managers "drill down" by comparing actual costs to budgeted costs for each of these items. For example, Kool-Time's drill-down analysis might reveal that variable overhead costs were higher than expected because the price of gasoline for the earth-moving equipment increased. Perhaps spending on fixed overhead increased because Kool-Time's monthly lease on its earth-moving equipment expired and it had to negotiate a new lease. Advanced books on cost accounting explain this drill-down variance analysis in more detail.

## Production Volume Variance

The second component of the total manufacturing overhead variance is the **production volume variance**. *The production volume variance is the difference between the flexible budget overhead and the standard overhead allocated to production.* As the name suggests, this variance arises when actual production volume differs from expected production volume. The production volume variance arises because companies treat fixed overhead as if it were variable in order to allocate it.

Recall from our discussion on standard costs that Kool-Time allocates overhead at a rate of $5.75 per direct labour hour. The total standard overhead rate consists of $2.00 per direct labour hour for variable overhead and $3.75 per direct labour hour for fixed overhead. Kool-Time computed these standard overhead rates based on the assumption that it would sell eight pools. Because Kool-Time actually installed 10 pools, the amount of standard overhead allocated to production was as follows:

| | |
|---|---|
| Standard overhead rate per direct labour hour | $ 5.75 |
| Standard direct labour hours (400 DL hours per pool × 10 pools) | × 4,000 |
| Standard overhead allocated to production | $23,000 |

Notice that when companies use standard costing, they allocate manufacturing overhead to the units produced using the standard overhead rate multiplied by the standard quantity of the allocation base allowed (400 DL hours per pool 10 pools), *not* by the actual quantity of the allocation base used (3,800 hours for the 10 pools), as you did in Chapter 5.

The production volume variance is calculated as follows:

Production volume variance = Flexible budget overhead for actual output − Standard overhead allocated to production
= $20,000 − $23,000
= $3,000 F

The production volume variance is favourable whenever actual output (10 pools for Kool-Time) exceeds expected output (8 pools). By installing 10 pools instead of 8, Kool-Time used its production capacity more fully than originally planned. In other words, it used its capacity more efficiently, resulting in a favourable variance. If Kool-Time had installed seven or fewer pools, the production volume variance would have been unfavourable because the company would have used less production capacity than expected.

The production volume variance is due only to *fixed* overhead. Why? Because the amount of *variable* overhead in the flexible budget ($8,000) is the same as the variable overhead allocated to production ($8,000 = 10 pools × 400 DL hours/pool × $2/DL hour). In essence, the production volume variance arises because companies treat fixed overhead ($12,000) as if it were variable ($3.75 per DL hour) to allocate it. The $3,000 favourable production volume variance arises because Kool-Time budgeted fixed overhead of $12,000 (Exhibit 10-10) but allocated $15,000 of fixed overhead to the 10 pools it installed (10 pools × 400 DL hours/pool × $3.75 *fixed* overhead per DL hour).

Fixed overhead volume variance = budgeted fixed overhead − applied fixed overhead
= (estimated cost driver × fixed portion of the predetermined overhead rate) − (the amount of the cost driver that should have been used for 10 pools × fixed portion of the predetermined overhead rate)
= $12,000 − ((400 × 10) × 3.75)
= $12,000 − $15,000
= $3,000 F

**EXHIBIT 10-17** Kool-Time's Fixed Overhead Variances

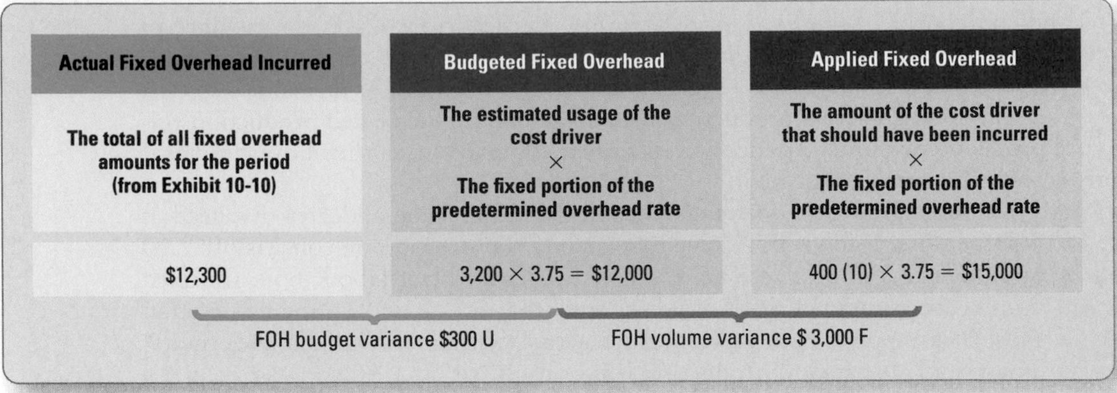


Another way to see this is by examining the hours used to determine the overhead allocation rate versus the hours used to actually allocate overhead. Since the variance is due strictly to the fixed overhead, we multiply the difference in hours by the fixed overhead rate:

| | |
|---|---|
| Total hours used to determine allocation rate (*8 pools* × 400 direct labour hours) | = 3,200 |
| Total hours used to allocate overhead (*10 pools* × 400 direct labour hours) | = 4,000 |
| Difference in hours (additional hours of overhead allocated) | 800 |
| Fixed overhead rate per hour | × $ 3.75 |
| Production volume variance | $3,000 |

As you can see, the production volume variance is due to the fact that Kool-Time allocated more fixed overhead than it had budgeted.

Now that we have seen both of the fixed overhead variance calculations, we can summarize them as shown in Exhibit 10-17.

## Overview of Kool-Time's Manufacturing Overhead Variances

Kool-Time's overhead variances are summarized as follows:

| | |
|---|---|
| **Total overhead variance:** | |
| Actual overhead cost | |
| ($9,000 variable + $12,300 fixed) | $21,300 |
| Standard overhead allocated to production | |
| (10 pools × 400 standard direct labour hours per pool × $5.75) | 23,000 |
| Total overhead variance | $ 1,700 F |
| **Overhead flexible budget variance:** | |
| Actual overhead cost (from above) | $21,300 |
| Flexible budget overhead for actual outputs | |
| ($8,000 variable + $12,000 fixed) | 20,000 |
| Overhead flexible budget variance | $ 1,300 U |
| **Production volume variance:** | |
| Flexible budget overhead for actual outputs (from above) | $20,000 |
| Standard overhead allocated to production (from above) | 23,000 |
| Production volume variance | $ 3,000 F |

This can also be done by totalling the separate variable and fixed overhead variances as follows:

| | |
|---|---|
| Variable overhead spending variance | $1,400 U |
| Variable overhead efficiency variance | $ 400 F |
| Fixed overhead budget variance | $ 300 U |
| Fixed overhead volume variance | $3,000 F |
| Total overhead variances | $1,700 F |

It is interesting to note that the total of the four overhead variances also equals the balance in the manufacturing overhead account. For example, with Kool-Time Pools' overhead variances totalling $1,700 F, there is a $1,700 balance in the manufacturing overhead account and that it was over-applied (a credit balance). If there had been an unfavourable total, overhead would have been under-applied (a debit balance).

As we have just seen, many companies use standard costs independent of the general ledger accounting system to develop flexible budgets and evaluate performance through variance analysis. Once managers know the causes of the variances, they can use that information to improve operations.

Other companies integrate standards directly into their general ledger accounting. This method of accounting, called standard costing, is discussed in Appendix 10A.

## TRY IT!

Hannah owns a fruit smoothie shop at the local mall. The budgeted monthly fixed overhead costs consist of the store lease payment ($1,000), advertising ($250), equipment depreciation ($125), and store Wi-Fi ($80). Actual fixed overhead expenses for June were $1,600. When calculating the fixed overhead rate, Hannah anticipated selling 4,800 smoothies during each summer month. She actually sold 5,000 in June.

1. What is the fixed overhead budget variance for the month of June? Is the variance favourable or unfavourable?
2. Will Hannah's fixed overhead volume variance for the month of June be favourable or unfavourable? Explain.

Please see page 666 for solutions.

# DECISION GUIDELINES

## Standard Costs and Variance Analysis

You've seen how managers use standard costs and variances in actual and budgeted costs to identify potential problems. Variances help managers see *why* actual costs differ from the budget. This is the first step in determining how to correct problems.

Let's review how Kool-Time made some of the key decisions in setting up and using its standard cost system.

| Decision | Guidelines |
|---|---|
| I would like to initiate a standard costing system in Kool-Time. How do I go about setting standards? | Historical performance data<br>Engineering analysis/time-and-motion studies |

*continued*

| Decision | Guidelines |
|---|---|
| I would like to evaluate how effectively materials were purchased and the mix of labourers was managed. How does Kool-Time compute a price variance for materials or labour? | $\text{Price variance} = \left(\text{Actual price per input unit} - \text{Standard price per input unit}\right) \times \text{Actual quantity of input}$ |
| I would like to evaluate how effectively materials and human resources were used or allocated. How does Kool-Time compute an efficiency variance for materials or labour? | $\text{Efficiency variance} = \left(\text{Actual quantity of input} - \text{Standard quantity of input allowed for the actual number of outputs}\right) \times \text{Standard price per input unit}$ |
| I need to be able to evaluate the various managers at Kool-Time. Who is most likely responsible for the: | |
| Sales volume variance? | Marketing Department |
| Sales revenue flexible budget variance? | Marketing Department |
| Direct materials price variance? | Purchasing Department |
| Direct materials efficiency variance? | Production Department |
| Direct labour price variance? | Human Resources or Personnel Department |
| Direct labour efficiency variance? | Production Department |
| How does Kool-Time allocate manufacturing overhead in a standard costing system? | $\text{Manufacturing overhead allocated} = \left(\text{Standard predetermined manufacturing overhead rate}\right) \times \left(\text{Standard quantity of allocation base allowed for actual outputs}\right)$ |
| How does Kool-Time analyze overallocated or underallocated manufacturing overhead? | Split overallocated or underallocated overhead as follows:<br>$\text{Flexible budget variance} = \text{Actual overhead} - \text{Flexible budget overhead for actual outputs}$<br>$\text{Production volume variance} = \text{Flexible budget overhead for actual outputs} - \text{Standard overhead allocated to actual outputs}$ |

## SUMMARY PROBLEM 2

Suppose Kool-Time had installed seven pools in June and that actual expenses were as follows:

| | |
|---|---|
| Direct materials (gunite) | 185 m$^3$ at \$80.00 / m$^3$ |
| Direct labour | 2,740 hours at \$10 per hour |
| Variable overhead | \$ 5,400 |
| Fixed overhead | \$11,900 |

Recall from Exhibit 10-8 that Kool-Time has the following quantity and price standards:

| | | |
|---|---|---|
| Direct materials (gunite) | 25 $m^3$ per pool, \$80.00 / $m^3$ | |
| Direct labour | 400 hours per pool at \$10.50 per hour | |
| Variable overhead rate | \$2.00 per hour | \$5.75 per hour overhead rate |
| Fixed overhead rate | \$3.75 per hour | |

### Requirements

1. Compute price variances for direct materials and direct labour.
2. Compute efficiency variances for direct materials and direct labour.
3. Compute the total overhead variance, the overhead flexible budget variance, and the production volume variance. Prepare a summary similar to the one on page 624.

## SOLUTION

### Requirement 1

$$\text{Price variance} = (\text{Actual price per input unit} - \text{Standard price per input unit}) \times \text{Actual quantity of input}$$

Direct materials:

$$\text{Price variance} = (80.00 - \$80.00) \times 185\ \text{m}^3 = 0$$

Direct labour:

$$\text{Price variance} = (\$10.00 - \$10.50) \times 2{,}740\ \text{hours} = \$1{,}370\ \text{F}$$

### Requirement 2

$$\begin{array}{c}\text{Efficiency}\\ \text{variance}\end{array} = \left(\text{Actual quantity of input} - \begin{array}{c}\text{Standard quantity of input allowed}\\ \text{for the actual number of outputs}\end{array}\right) \times \left(\begin{array}{c}\text{Standard price}\\ \text{per input unit}\end{array}\right)$$

Direct materials:
Since seven pools were installed, the standard quantity of material allowed for the actual output is 175 $m^3$ (25 $m^3$ per pool × 7 pools). Thus, the efficiency variance is as follows:

$$\text{Efficiency variance} = (185\ \text{m}^3 - 175\ \text{m}^3) \times \$80.00/\text{m}^3 = \$800\ \text{U}$$

Direct labour:
Since seven pools were installed, the standard quantity of labour allowed for the actual output is 2,800 hours (400 direct labour hours per pool × 7 pools). Thus, the efficiency variance is as follows:

$$\text{Efficiency variance} = (2{,}740\ \text{hours} - 2{,}800\ \text{hours}) \times \$10.50\ \text{per hour} = \$630\ \text{F}$$

## Requirement 3

| | |
|---|---|
| **Total overhead variance:** | |
| Actual overhead cost ($5,400 variable + $11,900 fixed) | $17,300 |
| Standard overhead allocated to production (2,800 standard direct labour hours × $5.75) | 16,100 |
| Total overhead variance | $ 1,200 U |
| **Overhead flexible budget variance:** | |
| Actual overhead cost ($5,400 + $11,900) | $17,300 |
| Flexible budget overhead for actual outputs ($5,600* + $12,000) | 17,600 |
| Overhead flexible budget variance | $ 300 F |
| **Production volume variance:** | |
| Flexible budget overhead for actual outputs ($5,600* variable + $12,000 fixed) | $17,600 |
| Standard overhead allocated to (actual) production (2,800 standard direct labour hours × $5.75) | 16,100 |
| Production volume variance | $ 1,500 U |

*2,800 standard DL hours × $2.00 variable overhead rate = $5,600

# APPENDIX 10A

## Standard Cost Accounting Systems

6 Record transactions at standard cost, and prepare a standard cost income statement.

Many companies integrate standards directly into their general ledger accounting by recording inventory-related costs at standard cost rather than actual cost. This method of accounting is called standard costing or standard cost accounting. Standard costing not only saves on bookkeeping costs but also isolates price and efficiency variances as soon as they occur. Before we go through the journal entries, keep the following key points in mind:

1. Each type of variance discussed has its own general ledger account. A debit balance means that the variance is unfavourable since it decreases income (just like an expense). A credit balance means that the variance is favourable since it increases income (just like a revenue).
2. Just as in job costing, the manufacturing costs flow through the inventory accounts in the following order: raw materials ≥ work in process ≥ finished goods ≥ cost of goods sold. The difference is that *standard* costs, rather than actual costs, are used to record the manufacturing costs put into the inventory accounts.
3. At the end of the period, the variance accounts are closed to cost of goods sold to "correct" for the fact that the standard costs recorded in the accounts were different from actual costs. Assuming that most inventory worked on during the period has been sold, any "error" from using standard costs rather than actual costs is contained in cost of goods sold. Closing the variances to cost of goods sold corrects the account balance.

**Why is this important?**

By incorporating standard costing into the company's general ledger, managers have immediate information about the **variances** as they are occurring.

### Journal Entries

We use Kool-Time's June transactions to demonstrate standard costing in a job-costing context.

1. **Recording Raw Materials Purchases**—Kool-Time debits raw materials inventory for the *actual quantity* purchased (300 m$^3$) costed at the *standard price* ($80 per cubic metre). It credits accounts payable for the *actual quantity* of gunite purchased (300 m$^3$) costed at the *actual price* ($77.00 per cubic metre) because this is the amount owed to Kool-Time's suppliers. The difference is the direct materials price variance. When Kool-Time purchases raw materials, it is immediately able to tell whether it paid more or less than the standard price for the materials; therefore, the direct materials price variance "pops out" when the purchase is recorded:

| | | | | |
|---|---|---|---|---|
| (1) | | Raw materials inventory (300 × $80.00) | 24,000 | |
| | | Direct materials price variance | | $900 |
| | | Accounts payable (300 × $77.00) | | 23,100 |
| | | *(to record purchases of direct materials)* | | |

Recall that Kool-Time's direct materials price variance was $900 favourable (page 615). So, the variance has a credit balance and increases Kool-Time's June profits.

2. **Recording Use of Direct Materials**—When Kool-Time uses direct materials, it debits its work in process inventory for the *standard price* × *standard quantity* of direct materials that should have been used for the actual output of 10 pools. This maintains work in process inventory at a purely standard cost. Raw materials inventory is credited for the *actual quantity* of materials put into production (300 $m^3$) costed at the *standard price* at which journal entry 1 entered them into the raw materials inventory account ($80). The difference is the direct materials *efficiency* variance. The direct materials efficiency variance "pops out" when Kool-Time records the *use* of direct materials:

| | | | | |
|---|---|---|---|---|
| (2) | | Work in process inventory (250 × $80.00) | 20,000 | |
| | | Direct materials efficiency variance | 4,000 | |
| | | Raw materials inventory (300 × $80.00) | | 24,000 |
| | | *(to record use of direct materials)* | | |

Kool-Time's direct materials efficiency variance was $4,000 unfavourable (page 615), which decreases June profits. See how a debit to the variance account corresponds with an unfavourable variance.

3. **Recording Direct Labour Costs**—Since work in process inventory is maintained at standard cost, Kool-Time debits work in process inventory for the *standard price* of direct labour × *standard quantity* of direct labour that should have been used for the actual output of 10 pools (just like it did for direct materials in journal entry 2). Kool-Time credits wages payable for the actual hours worked at the actual wage rate since this is the amount owed to employees. At the same time, Kool-Time records the direct labour price and efficiency variances (calculated on pages 616 and 617). The *unfavourable* price variance is recorded as a *debit*, while the *favourable* efficiency variance is recorded as a *credit*.

| | | | | |
|---|---|---|---|---|
| (3) | | Work in process inventory (4,000 × $10.50) | 42,000 | |
| | | Direct labour price variance | 1,900 | |
| | | Direct labour efficiency variance | | 2,100 |
| | | Wages payable (3,800 × $11.00) | | 41,800 |
| | | *(to record direct labour costs incurred)* | | |

4. **Recording Manufacturing Overhead Costs Incurred**—Kool-Time Pools records manufacturing overhead costs as usual, debiting the manufacturing overhead account and crediting various accounts:

| | | | | |
|---|---|---|---|---|
| (4) | | Manufacturing overhead | 21,300 | |
| | | Accounts payable, accumulated depreciation, and so forth | | 21,300 |
| | | *[to record actual overhead costs incurred (from Exhibit 10-10)]* | | |

5. **Allocating Overhead**—In standard costing, the overhead allocated to work in process inventory is computed as the standard overhead rate ($5.75 per DL hour) × standard quantity of the allocation base allowed for the actual output (10 pools × 400 DL hours per pool). As usual, the manufacturing overhead account is credited when assigning overhead:

| | | | | |
|---|---|---|---|---|
| (5) | | Work in process inventory (4,000 × $5.75) | 23,000 | |
| | | Manufacturing overhead | | 23,000 |
| | | *(to allocate overhead)* | | |

This journal entry corresponds with our calculation, on page 623, of the standard overhead allocated to production.

6. **Recording the Completion of Pools**—So far, work in process has been debited with $85,000 of manufacturing cost ($20,000 of direct materials + $42,000 of direct labour + $23,000 of manufacturing overhead). Does this make sense? According to Exhibit 10-8, the standard manufacturing cost of one pool is $8,500 ($2,000 direct material + $4,200 direct labour + $2,300 overhead). The sum of 10 pools, costed at *standard* rather than actual cost, is $85,000. As the pools are completed, the standard cost of each is transferred out of work in process and into finished goods:

| | | | | |
|---|---|---|---|---|
| (6) | | Finished goods inventory | 85,000 | |
| | | Work in process inventory | | 85,000 |
| | | *(to record completion of 10 pools)* | | |

7. **Recording the Sale and Release of Inventory**—When the pools are sold, sales revenue is recorded at the standard sales price, but accounts receivable is recorded at the actual sales price. The difference between the standard sales price and actual sales price received is the flexible budget sales revenue variance shown in Exhibit 10-7. It is favourable (a credit) because the company sold the pools for a higher price than it anticipated.

| | | | | |
|---|---|---|---|---|
| (7a) | | Cash or accounts receivable (at actual price) | 121,000 | |
| | | Flexible budget sales revenue variance | | 1,000 |
| | | Sales revenue (at standard) | | 120,000 |
| | | *(to record the sale of 10 pools)* | | |

Kool-Time must also release inventory for the pools it has sold. Since these pools were recorded at standard cost ($8,500 each), they must be removed from finished goods inventory and go into cost of goods sold at the same (standard) cost:

| | | | | |
|---|---|---|---|---|
| (7b) | | Cost of goods sold | 85,000 | |
| | | Finished goods inventory | | 85,000 |
| | | *(to record the cost of sales of 10 pools)* | | |

8. **Closing Manufacturing Overhead**—Kool-Time Pools closes manufacturing overhead to the two overhead variance accounts using the calculations performed on pages 630 and 623 ($1,300 unfavourable overhead flexible budget variance and $3,000 favourable production volume variance).

| | | | | |
|---|---|---|---|---|
| (8) | | Manufacturing overhead | 1,700 | |
| | | Overhead flexible budget variance | 1,300 | |
| | | Production volume variance | | 3,000 |
| | | *(to record overhead variances and close the Manufacturing Overhead account)* | | |

Exhibit 10-18 shows selected Kool-Time accounts after posting these entries.

**EXHIBIT 10-18** Kool-Time Pools' Flow of Costs in Standard Costing System

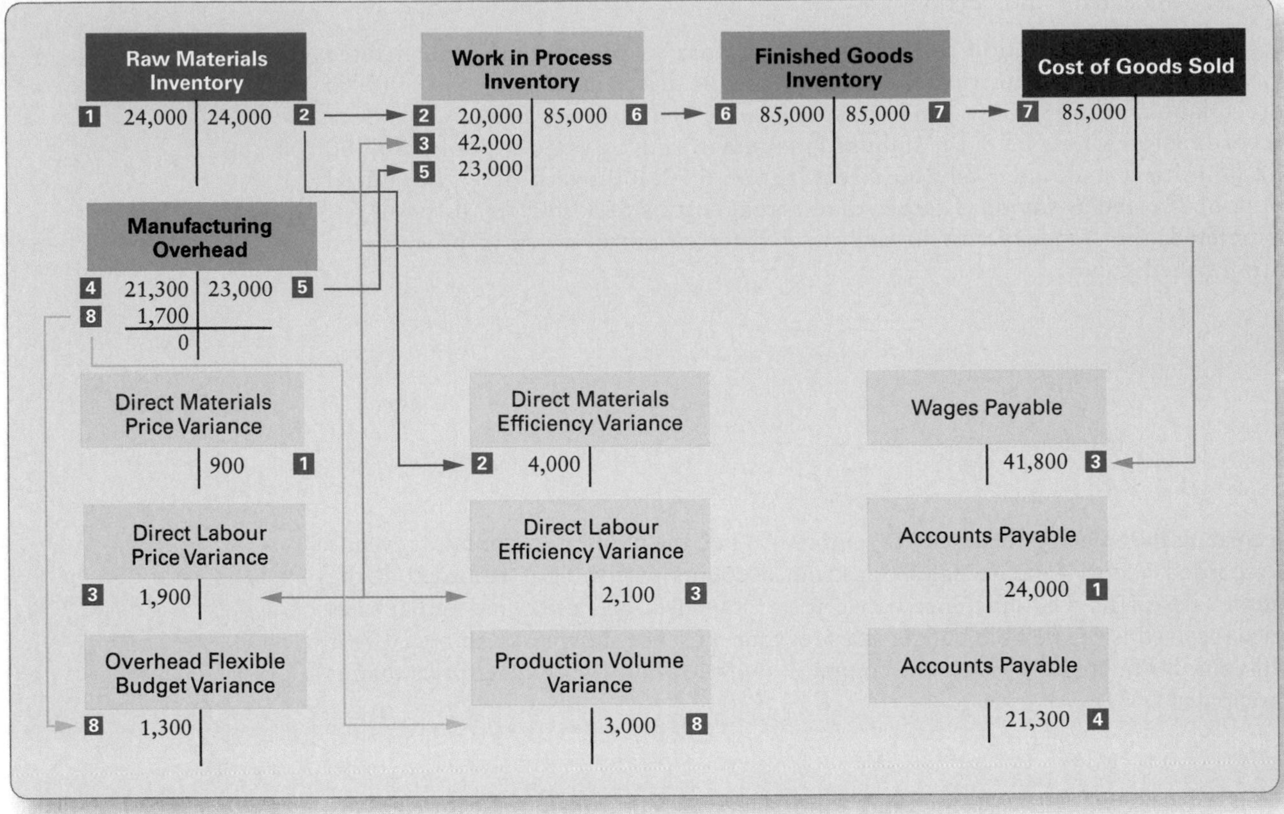


## Standard Cost Income Statement for Management

Exhibit 10-19 shows a standard cost income statement that highlights the variances for Kool-Time's management. The statement shows sales revenue at standard and then adds the favourable flexible budget sales revenue variance to yield actual sales revenue. Next,

**EXHIBIT 10-19** Standard Cost Income Statement

**KOOL-TIME POOLS**
**Standard Cost Income Statement**
**Month Ended June 30**

| | | |
|---|---|---|
| Sales revenue at standard (10 × $12,000) | | $120,000 |
| Flexible budget sales revenue variance | | 1,000 |
| Sales revenue at actual | | 121,000 |
| Cost of goods sold at standard cost | | 85,000 |
| Manufacturing cost variances: | | |
| Direct materials price variance | $ (900) | |
| Direct materials efficiency variance | 4,000 | |
| Direct labour price variance | 1,900 | |
| Direct labour efficiency variance | (2,100) | |
| Manufacturing overhead flexible budget variance | 1,300 | |
| Production volume variance | (3,000) | |
| Total manufacturing variances | | 1,200 |
| Cost of goods sold at actual cost | | 86,200 |
| Gross profit | | 34,800 |
| Marketing and administrative expenses* | | (18,800) |
| Operating income | | $ 16,000 |

*$9,100 + $9,700 from Exhibit 10-10.

the statement shows the cost of goods sold at standard cost. Then, the statement separately lists each manufacturing cost variance, followed by the cost of goods sold at actual cost. (Recall that since Kool-Time had no raw materials, work in process, or finished goods inventories, all of the variances relate to June's sales.)

The income statement shows that the net effect of all of the manufacturing cost variances is $1,200 unfavourable. Thus, June's operating income is $1,200 lower than it would have been if all actual costs had been equal to standard amounts.

At the end of the period, all of the cost variance accounts are closed to zero-out their balances. Why? For two reasons: (1) The financial statements prepared for *external* users never show variances (variances are only for internal management's use), and (2) the general ledger must be "corrected" for the fact that standard rather than actual costs were used to record manufacturing costs. Since all the pools were sold, the "error" in costing currently exists in the cost of goods sold account. Therefore, the cost variance accounts are closed to cost of goods sold.

9. **Closing the Cost Variance Accounts to Cost of Goods Sold**—To close, or zero-out, the variance accounts, all unfavourable variances (debit balances) must be credited, while all favourable variances (credit balances) must be debited:

| | | | | |
|---|---|---|---|---|
| (9a) | | Cost of goods sold | 1,200 | |
| | | Direct materials price variance | 900 | |
| | | Direct labour efficiency variance | 2,100 | |
| | | Production volume variance | 3,000 | |
| | | Direct labour price variance | | 1,900 |
| | | Direct materials efficiency variance | | 4,000 |
| | | Overhead flexible budget variance | | 1,300 |
| | | *(to close cost variance accounts to cost of goods sold)* | | |

Similar to the discussion in Chapter 5 regarding the closing of under- or overallocated manufacturing overhead at the end of a period, if the amount is significant and not all of the product has been sold, the balance in the account, or the variance, should be closed out to the work in process inventory, finished goods inventory, and cost of goods sold accounts on a prorated basis.

Likewise, the favourable flexible budget sales revenue variance ($1,000) is closed to sales revenue (to zero-out the variance account and correct the revenue account).

| | | | | |
|---|---|---|---|---|
| (9b) | | Flexible budget sales revenue variance | 1,000 | |
| | | Sales revenue | | 1,000 |
| | | *(to close the revenue variance account)* | | |

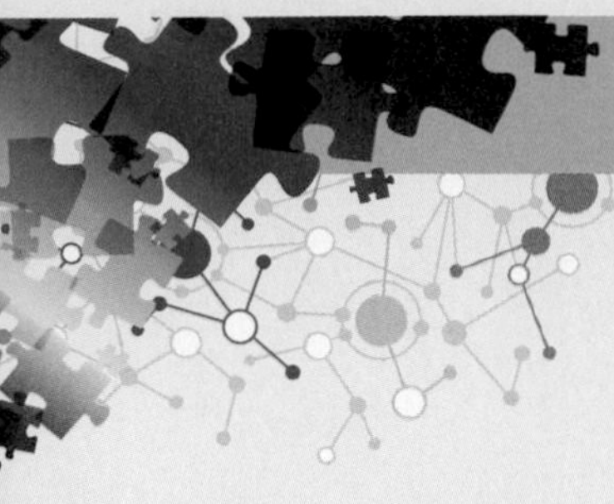

# END OF CHAPTER

## LEARNING OBJECTIVES

1 Prepare a flexible budget for planning purposes.

2 Use the sales volume variance and flexible budget variance to explain why actual results differ from the master budget.

3 Identify the benefits of standard costs, and learn how to set standards.

4 Compute standard cost variances for direct materials and direct labour.

5 Compute manufacturing overhead variances.

6 Record transactions at standard cost, and prepare a standard cost income statement. (Appendix 10A)



## ACCOUNTING VOCABULARY

**Efficiency Variance (p. 614)** Measures whether the quantity of materials or labour used to make the actual number of outputs is within the standard allowed for that number of outputs.

**Flexible Budget (p. 598)** A summarized budget prepared for different levels of volume.

**Flexible Budget Variance (p. 602)** The difference arising because the company actually earned more or less revenue, or incurred more or less cost, than expected for the actual level of output.

**Overhead Flexible Budget Variance (p. 620)** The difference between the actual overhead cost and the flexible budget overhead for the actual number of outputs.

**Price Variance (p. 604)** The difference in prices (actual price per unit minus standard price per unit) of an input multiplied by the actual quantity of the input.

**Production Volume Variance (p. 623)** The difference between the manufacturing overhead cost in the flexible budget for actual outputs and the standard overhead allocated to production.

**Sales Volume Variance (p. 602)** The difference between a static budget amount and a flexible budget amount arising only because the number of units actually sold differs from the static budget units.

**Standard Cost (p. 607)** A budget for a single unit.

**Static Budget (p. 597)** The budget prepared for only one level of sales volume; also called the master budget.

**Static Budget Variance (p. 597)** The difference between actual results and the static budget.

**Variance (p. 597)** The difference between an actual amount and a budgeted amount.



## QUICK CHECK

1. (Learning Objective 1) A budget that is based on the actual activity level of a period is a
   a. static budget.
   b. rolling budget.
   c. master budget.
   d. flexible budget.
2. (Learning Objective 1) A flexible budget
   a. contains a plan for a range of activity levels so that the plan can be adjusted to reflect changes in activity levels.
   b. is the plan for one level of activity and cannot be adjusted for changes in the level of activity.
   c. can be used to evaluate performance after the period has ended but is not used for planning.
   d. contains only variable costs but does not include fixed costs since fixed costs do not change.
3. (Learning Objective 2) Assuming that all activity is within the relevant range, an increase in the activity level in a flexible budget will
   a. increase total fixed costs.
   b. increase the variable cost per unit.
   c. increase total costs.
   d. decrease the variable cost per unit.

4. (Learning Objective 3) Advantages of using standard costs include all of the following except that
   a. standard costing allows companies to create flexible budgets.
   b. managers can evaluate the efficiency of production workers.
   c. differences between the static budget and the flexible budget can be broken down into price and quantity components.
   d. the price sensitivity of consumers can be analyzed.
5. (Learning Objective 2) A sales volume variance occurs when
   a. the actual selling price of a unit is lower than the selling price originally planned for in the master budget.
   b. the number of units actually sold differs from the volume originally planned for in the master budget.
   c. the actual cost of the inputs differ from the costs originally planned for in the master budget.
   d. the actual selling price of a unit is higher than the selling price originally planned for in the master budget.
6. (Learning Objective 4) A favourable material efficiency variance indicates that
   a. the standard material price is less than the actual material price.
   b. the actual material price is less than the standard material price.
   c. the actual quantity of material used is less than the standard material allowed for the actual quantity of output.
   d. the standard material allowed for the actual quantity of output is less than the actual quantity of material used.
7. (Learning Objective 4) The formula for calculating a direct materials efficiency variance is
   a. (actual price per input unit – standard price per input unit) × actual quantity of input.
   b. (actual quantity of input – standard quantity of input allowed for the actual number of outputs) × standard price per input unit.
   c. (actual price per input unit – actual quantity of input) × standard price per input unit.
   d. (actual quantity of input – standard price per input unit) × standard quantity of input allowed for the actual number of outputs.
8. (Learning Objective 5) The production volume variance is favourable whenever
   a. actual output exceeds expected output.
   b. expected output exceeds actual output.
   c. the actual variable overhead rate exceeds the standard variable overhead rate.
   d. the standard variable overhead rate exceeds the actual variable overhead rate.
9. (Learning Objective 5) The total manufacturing overhead variance is composed of
   a. price variance and efficiency variance.
   b. price variance and production volume variance.
   c. efficiency variance and production volume variance.
   d. flexible budget variance and production volume variance.
10. (Learning Objective 6: Appendix 10A) When a company uses direct materials, the amount of the debit to work in process inventory is based on the
   a. actual quantity of the materials used × actual price per unit of the materials.
   b. standard quantity of the materials allowed for the actual production × actual price per unit of the materials.
   c. standard quantity of the materials allowed for the actual production × standard price per unit of the materials.
   d. actual quantity of the materials used × standard price per unit of the materials.

CHAPTER 10

**Quick Check Answers**

1. d 2. a 3. c 4. d 5. b 6. c 7. b 8. a 9. d 10. c

# SHORT EXERCISES

**S10-1 Prepare a flexible budget** *(Learning Objective 1)*

Turn to Kool-Time's flexible budget in Exhibit 10-3.

1. Using the data from Exhibit 10-3, develop flexible budgets for four- and nine-pool levels of output.
2. Would Kool-Time's managers use the flexible budgets you developed in Requirement 1 for planning or for controlling? What specific insights can Kool-Time's managers gain from the flexible budgets you prepared in Requirement 1?

**S10-2 Interpret a flexible budget graph** *(Learning Objective 1)*

Look at Kool-Time's graph of actual and budgeted monthly costs in Exhibit 10-5.

1. How many pools did Kool-Time install in May?
2. How much were Kool-Time's actual expenses in May?

3. Using Kool-Time's flexible budget formula, what is the flexible budget total cost for May?
4. What is Kool-Time's flexible budget variance for total costs? Is the variance favourable or unfavourable in May?

**S10-3 Interpret a performance report** *(Learning Objective 2)*

The following is a partially completed performance report for Surf-Side Pools, one of Kool-Time's competitors:

SURF-SIDE POOLS
Income Statement Performance Report
Year Ended April 30

| | Actual Results at Actual Prices | Flexible Budget Variance | Flexible Budget for Actual Number of Output Units | Sales Volume Variance | Static (Master) Budget |
|---|---|---|---|---|---|
| Output units (pools installed) | 6 | ? | ? | ? | 5 |
| Sales revenue | $102,000 | ? | $108,000 | ? | $90,000 |
| Variable expenses | 57,000 | ? | 60,000 | ? | 50,000 |
| Fixed expenses | 21,000 | ? | 25,000 | ? | 25,000 |
| Total expenses | 78,000 | ? | 85,000 | ? | 75,000 |
| Operating income | $ 24,000 | ? | $ 23,000 | ? | $15,000 |

1. How many pools did Surf-Side originally think it would install in April?
2. How many pools did Surf-Side actually install in April?
3. How many pools is the flexible budget based on? Why?
4. What was the budgeted sales price per pool?
5. What was the budgeted variable cost per pool?
6. Define the sales volume variance. What causes it?
7. Define the flexible budget variance. What causes it?

**S10-4 Complete a performance report** *(Learning Objective 2)*

Complete the performance report shown in S10-3 by filling in all missing values. Be sure to label each variance as favourable (F) or unfavourable (U). Then, answer the following questions:

1. What was the *total* static budget variance?
2. What was the *total* sales volume variance?
3. What was the *total* flexible budget variance?
4. Show that the total sales volume variance and total flexible budget variance sum to the total static budget variance.
5. Interpret the variances and then give one plausible explanation for the variances shown in this performance report.

**S10-5 Interpret the sales volume variance** *(Learning Objective 2)*

Recall that Kool-Time's relevant range is 0 to 11 pools per month. Explain whether Kool-Time would have a sales volume variance for fixed expenses in Exhibit 10-7 if

a. Kool-Time installs 14 pools per month.
b. Kool-Time installs seven pools per month.

**S10-6 Understand key terms** *(Learning Objectives 1 & 2)*

Fill in the blank with the phrase that best completes the sentence.

| | | |
|---|---|---|
| Actual number of outputs | Beginning of the period | Static budget variance |
| Expected number of outputs | End of the period | |
| Sales volume variance | Flexible budget variance | |

a. The static budget is developed at the ______.
b. The flexible budget used in an income statement performance report is based on the ______.
c. The master budget is based on the ______.
d. The flexible budget used in an income statement performance report is developed at the ______.
e. The difference between actual costs and the costs that should have been incurred for the actual number of outputs is the ______.

**S10-7 Calculate a standard price** *(Learning Objective 3)*

The Bolognese Corporation is in the process of setting price standards for its direct materials. Polymer clay is used in one product. The polymer clay is purchased for $15 per kilogram. The Bolognese Corporation always pays its suppliers within 10 days, so it is able to take advantage of a 5% early payment discount offered by the vendor. Freight-in for the clay is $0.25 per kilogram, while receiving costs are $0.05 per kilogram. What is the standard price per kilogram of polymer clay?

**Weber's Data Set used for S10-8 through S10-12:**

The standard direct materials for a regular Weber's hamburger are as follows:

| | | |
|---|---|---|
| 1 bun | 1 pickle slice | 1/4 teaspoon of mustard |
| 1 hamburger patty | 1/8 teaspoon of onion | 25 g of ketchup |

Assume that the company has set the following standard materials prices:

| | | | |
|---|---|---|---|
| Buns | $0.10 each | Onion | $0.08 per teaspoon |
| Hamburger patties | $0.20 each | Mustard | $0.04 per teaspoon |
| Pickle slices | $0.03 per slice | Ketchup | $0.20 per 100 g |

In addition to the direct materials standards, the company sets standards for direct labour. The standard labour wage rate is $12 per hour. Since the griddles are so large, the restaurants cooks the hamburgers in batches of 20. The standard time allotted to cook, apply condiments, and wrap each batch of 20 hamburgers is four minutes.

Assume that a Halifax, N.S., Weber's sold 5,000 hamburgers yesterday and actually used the following materials:

| | | |
|---|---|---|
| 5,150 buns | 4,800 pickles slices | 1,400 teaspoons of mustard |
| 5,100 hamburger patties | 800 teaspoons of onion | 137.5 kg of ketchup |

**S10-8 Compute standard cost of direct materials** *(Learning Objective 3)*

Refer to the Weber's data set above. Compute the standard direct materials cost per hamburger.

**S10-9 Compute standard cost of direct labour** *(Learning Objective 3)*

Refer to the Weber's data set above. Compute the standard direct labour cost per hamburger. (*Hint:* Find the quantity and price standards in minutes.)

**S10-10 Compute direct materials efficiency variances** *(Learning Objective 4)*

Refer to the Weber's data set above.

1. Compute the direct materials efficiency variance for buns, hamburger patties, and pickle slices.
2. As a manager, what would you learn from the variances and supporting data?

**S10-11 Compute more direct materials efficiency variances** *(Learning Objective 4)*

Refer to the Weber's data set above.

1. Compute the direct materials efficiency variance for onion, mustard, and ketchup.
2. As a manager, what would you learn from the variances and supporting data?

**S10-12 Compute direct materials price variances** *(Learning Objective 4)*

Refer to the Weber's data set above.

Actual prices paid for ingredients purchased during the week were as follows:

| | | | |
|---|---|---|---|
| Buns | $0.12 each | Onion | $0.07 per teaspoon |
| Hamburger patties | $0.25 each | Mustard | $0.01 per teaspoon |
| Pickle slices | $0.02 per slice | Ketchup | $0.24 per 100 g |

1. Compute the direct materials price variance for each ingredient.
2. As a manager, what would you learn from the variances and supporting data?

**S10-13 Compute standard overhead allocation rates** *(Learning Objective 3)*

Homewood Farms supplies restaurants with many premanufactured ingredients (such as bags of frozen french fries). Assume that the manufacturing plant processing the fries anticipated incurring a total of $3,080,000 of manufacturing overhead during the year. Of this amount, $1,320,000 is fixed. Manufacturing overhead is allocated based on machine hours. The plant anticipates running the machines 220,000 hours next year.

1. Compute the standard *variable* overhead rate.
2. Compute the *fixed* overhead rate.
3. Compute the standard *total* overhead rate.

**S10-14 Compute manufacturing overhead variances** *(Learning Objective 5)*

Assume that the Homewood Farms french fry manufacturing facility actually incurred $2,800,000 of manufacturing overhead for the year ($1,700,000 variable overhead and $1,200,000 fixed overhead). Based on the actual output of french fries, the flexible budget indicated that total manufacturing overhead should have been $2,982,500. Using a standard costing system, the company allocated $3,045,000 of manufacturing overhead to production. ($1,890,000 variable overhead and $1,155,000 fixed overhead). The actual machine hours during the year were 200,000, which was 10,000 hours less than the standard. Homewood Farms' managers had estimated 215,000 hours when it created the budget.

1. Calculate the total manufacturing overhead variance. What does this tell managers?
2. Determine the overhead flexible budget variance. Determine the three separate variances that are involved in the flexible budget variance (the variable overhead spending and efficiency variances plus the fixed overhead budget variance). What does this tell managers?
3. Determine the production volume variance. What does this tell managers?
4. Double-check: Do the two variances (computed in Requirements 2 and 3) sum to the total overhead variance computed in Requirement 1?

**S10-15 Compute manufacturing overhead variances** *(Learning Objective 5)*

Rovnovsky Industries produces high-end flutes for professional musicians across the globe. Actual manufacturing overhead for the year was $1,240,000. The flexible budget indicated that fixed overhead should have been $800,000 and variable overhead should have been $400,000 for the number of flutes actually produced. Using a standard costing system, the company allocated $1,300,000 of overhead to production.

1. Calculate the total overhead variance. What does this tell managers?
2. Determine the overhead flexible budget variance. What does this tell managers?
3. Determine the production volume variance. What does this tell managers?

**S10-16 Record direct materials purchase and use** *(Learning Objective 6)*

During the week, Homewood Farms' french fry manufacturing facility purchased 10,000 kilograms of potatoes (transferred from its potato farming operations) at a price of $1.10 per kilogram. The standard price per kilogram is $1.05. During the week, 9,760 kg of potatoes were used. The standard quantity of potatoes that should have been used for the actual volume of output was 9,700 kg. Record the following transactions using a standard cost accounting system:

1. The purchase of potatoes
2. The use of potatoes

Are the variances favourable or unfavourable? Explain.

**S10-17 Record direct labour purchase and use** *(Learning Objective 6)*

During the week, Homewood Farms' french fry manufacturing facility incurred 2,000 hours of direct labour. Direct labourers were paid $12.50 per hour. The standard hourly labour rate is $12. Standards indicate that for the volume of output actually achieved, the factory should have used 2,100 hours. Record the following transactions using a standard cost accounting system:

1. The accumulation of labour costs
2. The assignment of direct labour to production

Are the variances favourable or unfavourable? Explain.

# EXERCISES Group A

**E10-18A Prepare flexible budgets for planning** *(Learning Objective 1)*

Logiclik sells its main product, ergonomic mouse pads, for $11 each. Its variable cost is $5 per pad. Fixed expenses are $200,000 per month for volumes up to 60,000 pads. Above 60,000 pads, monthly fixed expenses are $250,000.

Check sum: Operating income for 70,000 units is $170,000.

**Requirement**

1. Prepare a monthly flexible budget for the product, showing sales, variable expenses, fixed expenses, and operating income or loss for volume levels of 40,000, 50,000, and 70,000 pads.



**E10-19A Graph flexible budget costs** *(Learning Objective 1)*

Graph the flexible budget total cost line for Logiclik in Exercise 10-18A. Show total costs for volume levels of 40,000, 50,000, and 70,000 pads.

**E10-20A Complete and interpret a performance report** *(Learning Objective 2)*

Joe Boxer Company's managers received the following incomplete performance report:

Check sum: Flexible budget variance for operating income is $9,000 U.

JOE BOXER COMPANY
Income Statement Performance Report
Year Ended July 31

| | Actual Results at Actual Prices | Flexible Budget Variance | Flexible Budget for Actual Number of Output Units | Sales Volume Variance | Static (Master) Budget |
|---|---|---|---|---|---|
| Output units | 36,000 | ? | 36,000 | 4,000 F | ? |
| Sales revenue | $216,000 | ? | $216,000 | $24,000 F | ? |
| Variable expenses | 84,000 | ? | 81,000 | 9,000 U | ? |
| Fixed expenses | 106,000 | ? | 100,000 | –0– | ? |
| Total expenses | 190,000 | ? | 181,000 | 9,000 U | ? |
| Operating income | $ 26,000 | ? | $ 35,000 | $15,000 F | ? |

Complete the performance report. Identify the employee group that may deserve praise and the group that may be subject to criticism. Give your reasons.

**E10-21A Prepare an income statement performance report** *(Learning Objective 2)*

Check sum: Sales volume variance on revenue is $12,000 F.

Kool-Time installed nine pools during May. Prepare an income statement performance report for Kool-Time for May, using Exhibit 10-7 as a guide. Assume that the actual sales price per pool is $12,000, actual variable expenses total $61,000, and actual fixed expenses are $19,000 in May. The master budget was prepared with the following assumptions: variable cost of $8,000 per pool, fixed expenses of $20,000 per month, and anticipated sales volume of eight pools at $12,000 per pool.

**Requirement**

1. Compute the sales volume variance and flexible budget variance. Use these variances to explain to Kool-Time's management why May's operating income differs from the operating income shown in the static budget.

## E10-22A Compute sales volume and flexible budget variances *(Learning Objective 2)*

Check sum: Flexible budget variance in operating income is $176,000.

Top managers of Foodiun Ltd. predicted the following year's sales of 145,000 units of its product at a unit price of $8. Actual sales for the year were 140,000 units at $9.50 each. Variable expenses were budgeted at $2.20 per unit, and actual variable expenses were $2.30 per unit. Actual fixed expenses of $420,000 exceeded budgeted fixed expenses by $20,000. Prepare Foodiun Ltd.'s income statement performance report in a format similar to E10-20. What variance contributed most to the year's favourable results? What caused this variance?

## E10-23A Work backward to find missing values *(Learning Objective 2)*



Hanco has a relevant range extending to 30,000 units each month. The following performance report provides information about Hanco's budget and actual performance for April.

Check sum: Operating income is $74,500.

HANCO
Income Statement Performance Report
Month Ended April 30

| | Actual Results at Actual Prices | (A) | Flexible Budget for Actual Number of Output Units | (B) | Static (Master) Budget |
|---|---|---|---|---|---|
| Output units | 25,000 | | (C) | | 30,000 |
| Sales revenue | $240,000 | $ 5,000 (F) | (D) | | |
| Variable cost | | | (E) | | $187,500 |
| Fixed cost | $ 15,000 | (F) | | | $ 20,000 |
| Operating income | | | | | (G) |

**Requirement**

1. Find the missing data for letters A–G. Be sure to label any variances as favourable or unfavourable. (*Hint:* A and B are titles.)

## E10-24A Calculate standard costs *(Learning Objective 3)*

Check sum: Gross profit is $3.61.

Rachel's Bakery makes desserts for local restaurants. Each pan of gourmet brownies requires 500 g flour, 125 mL chopped pecans, 60 mL cocoa, 250 g sugar, 125 mL chocolate chips, 2 eggs, and 90 mL oil. Each pan requires 10 minutes of direct labour for mixing, cutting, and packaging. Each pan must bake for 30 minutes. Restaurants purchase the gourmet brownies by the pan, not by the individual serving. Each pan is currently sold for $12. Standard costs are $1.92 per bag of flour (4 kg in a bag), $6.00 per bag of pecans (750 mL per bag), $2.50 per tin of cocoa (500 mL per tin), $2.40 per bag of sugar (4 kg in a bag), $1.80 per bag of chocolate chips (500 mL per bag), $1.08 per dozen eggs, $1.17 per bottle of oil (1.5 L per bottle), and $0.50 for packaging materials. The standard wage rate is $12 per hour. Rachel allocates bakery overhead at $7.00 per oven hour.

**Requirements**

1. What is the standard cost per pan of gourmet brownies?
2. What is the standard gross profit per pan of gourmet brownies?
3. How often should Rachel reassess her standard quantities and standard prices for inputs?

### E10-25A Calculate materials and labour variances *(Learning Objective 4)*

Homewood Farms manufactures the bags of frozen french fries used at many restaurants. Last week, Homewood Farms purchased (transferred in from its potato farms) and used 100,000 kg of potatoes at a price of $0.75 per kilogram. During the week, 2,200 direct labour hours were incurred in the plant at a rate of $12.25 per hour. The standard price per kilogram of potatoes is $0.85, and the standard direct labour rate is $12.00 per hour. Standards indicate that for the number of bags of frozen fries produced, the factory should have used 97,000 kg of potatoes and 1,900 hours of direct labour.

Check sum: Direct materials efficiency variance is $2,550.

**Requirements**

1. Determine the direct materials price and efficiency variances. Be sure to label each variance as favourable or unfavourable.
2. Think of a plausible explanation for the variances found in Requirement 1.
3. Determine the direct labour price and efficiency variances. Be sure to label each variance as favourable or unfavourable.
4. Could the explanation for the labour variances be tied to the material variances? Explain.



### E10-26A Compute direct materials variance *(Learning Objective 4)*

The following direct materials variance computations are incomplete:

Check sum: Actual price is $10.50.

$$\text{Price variance} = (\$? - \$10) \times 9{,}600 \text{ kg} = \$4{,}800 \text{ U}$$

$$\text{Efficiency variance} = (? - 10{,}400 \text{ kg}) \times \$10 = ?\ \text{F}$$

$$\text{Flexible budget variance} = \$\ ?$$

**Requirement**

1. Fill in the missing values, and identify the flexible budget variance as favourable or unfavourable.

### E10-27A Calculate materials and labour variances *(Learning Objective 4)*

Dock Guard, which uses a standard cost accounting system, manufactured 200,000 boat fenders during the year, using 1,450,000 m of extruded vinyl purchased at $1.05 per metre. Production required 4,500 direct labour hours that cost $14 per hour. The materials standard was 7 m of vinyl per fender at a standard cost of $1.10 per metre. The labour standard was 0.025 direct labour hour per fender at a standard cost of $13 per hour. Compute the price and efficiency variances for direct materials and direct labour. Does the pattern of variances suggest that Dock Guard's managers have been making trade-offs? Explain.

Check sum: Standard quantity of material allowed is 1,400,000 metres.

### E10-28A Compute standard manufacturing overhead rates *(Learning Objective 3)*

Fresh-Cut processes bags of frozen organic vegetables sold at specialty grocery stores. It allocates manufacturing overhead based on direct labour hours. Fresh-Cut has projected total overhead for the year to be $800,000. Of this amount, $600,000 relates to fixed overhead expenses. Fresh-Cut expects to process 160,000 cases of frozen organic vegetables this year. The direct labour standard for each case is 15 minutes.

Check sum: Total standard predetermined overhead rate is $20/hr.

**Requirements**

1. Compute the standard *variable* overhead rate.
2. Compute the *fixed* overhead rate.
3. Compute the standard *total* overhead rate.

### E10-29A Continuation of E10-28A: Compute overhead variances *(Learning Objective 5)*

Fresh-Cut actually processed 180,000 cases of frozen organic vegetables during the year and incurred $840,000 of manufacturing overhead. Of this amount, $610,000 was fixed.

Check sum: Total manufacturing overhead is $825,000.

**Requirements**

1. What is the flexible budget (for the actual output) for variable overhead? For fixed overhead? For total overhead?
2. How much overhead would have been allocated to production?
3. Use your answer from Requirement 1 to determine the overhead flexible budget variance. What does this tell managers?
4. Use your answer from Requirements 1 and 2 to determine the production volume variance. What does this tell managers?
5. What is the total overhead variance?

### E10-30A Compute manufacturing overhead variances *(Learning Objective 5)*

Check sum: Production volume variance $3,000 F.

Bar-Gun manufactures paint. The company charges the following standard unit costs to production on the basis of static budget volume of 30,000 cans of paint per month:

| | |
|---|---|
| Direct materials | $2.50 |
| Direct labour | 2.00 |
| Manufacturing overhead | 1.50 |
| Standard unit cost | $6.00 |

Bar-Gun allocates overhead based on standard machine hours and uses the following monthly flexible budget for overhead:

| | *Number of Outputs (cans)* | | |
|---|---|---|---|
| | 27,000 | 30,000 | 33,000 |
| Standard machine hours | 2,700 | 3,000 | 3,300 |
| Budgeted manufacturing overhead cost: | | | |
| Variable | $13,500 | $15,000 | $16,500 |
| Fixed | 30,000 | 30,000 | 30,000 |

Bar-Gun actually produced 33,000 cans of paint using 3,100 machine hours. Actual variable overhead was $16,200, and fixed overhead was $32,500. Compute the total overhead variance, the overhead flexible budget variance, and the production volume variance.

**Watermate Data Set used for E10-31A through E10-37A (excluding 10-35A):**

Watermate is a manufacturer of ceramic bottles. The company has these standards:

| | |
|---|---|
| Direct materials (clay) | 1 kg per bottle, at a cost of $0.40 per kg |
| Direct labour | 1/5 hour per bottle, at a cost of $14 per hour |
| Static budget variable overhead | $70,000 |
| Static budget fixed overhead | $30,000 |
| Static budget direct labour hours | 10,000 hours |
| Static budget number of bottles | 50,000 |

Watermate allocated manufacturing overhead to production based on standard direct labour hours. Last month, Watermate reported the following actual results for the production of 70,000 bottles.

| | |
|---|---|
| Direct materials | 1.1 kg per bottle, at a cost of $0.50 per kg |
| Direct labour | 1/4 hour per bottle, at a cost of $13 per hour |
| Actual variable overhead | $104,000 |
| Actual fixed overhead | $ 28,000 |

**E10-31A Compute the standard cost of one unit** *(Learning Objective 3)*

Refer to the Watermate data set above.

Check sum: Standard cost of one bottle is $5.25.

**Requirements**

1. Compute the standard predetermined variable manufacturing overhead rate, the standard predetermined fixed manufacturing overhead rate, and the total standard predetermined overhead rate.
2. Compute the standard cost of each of the following inputs: direct materials, direct labour, variable manufacturing overhead, and fixed manufacturing overhead.
3. Determine the standard cost of one ceramic bottle.

**E10-32A Compute and interpret direct materials variances** *(Learning Objective 4)*

Refer to the Watermate data set above.

Check sum: Direct materials variance is $7,700 U.

**Requirements**

1. Compute the direct materials price variance and the direct materials efficiency variance.
2. What is the total flexible budget variance for direct materials?
3. Who is generally responsible for each variance?
4. Interpret the variances.



**E10-33A Compute and interpret direct labour variances** *(Learning Objective 4)*

Refer to the Watermate data set above.

Check sum: Direct labour price variance is $17,500 F.

**Requirements**

1. Compute the direct labour price variance and the direct labour efficiency variance.
2. What is the total flexible budget variance for direct labour?
3. Who is generally responsible for each variance?
4. Interpret the variances.

**E10-34A Compute and interpret manufacturing overhead variances** *(Learning Objective 5)*

Refer to the Watermate data set above.

Check sum: Total overhead variance is $8,000 F.

**Requirements**

1. Compute the total manufacturing overhead variance. What does this tell management?
2. Compute the overhead flexible budget variance. What does this tell management?
3. Compute the production volume variance. What does this tell management?

**E10-35A Calculate the standard cost of a product before and after proposed sustainability effort changes** *(Learning Objective 1 & 4)*

Wolanin Containers currently uses a recycled plastic to make bottles for the food industry.

**Current bottle production information**

The cost and time standards per batch of 10,000 bottles are as follows:

Plastic 300 kilograms at $5.00 per kg
Direct labour 2.0 hours at $20.00 per hour

The variable manufacturing overhead rate is based on total estimated variable manufacturing overhead of $500,000 and estimated total DLH of 10,000. Wolanin allocates its variable manufacturing overhead based on direct labour hours (DLH).

Check sum: Req. 1 standard cost is $1,640.

**Proposed changes to bottle design and production process**

The container division manager is considering having both the bottle redesigned and the bottle production process reengineered so that the plastic usage would drop by 20% overall due both to generating less scrap in the manufacturing process and using less plastic in each bottle. In addition to decreasing the amount of plastic used in producing the bottles, the additional following benefits would be realized:

a. Direct labour hours would be reduced by 10% because less scrap would be handled in the production process.
b. Total estimated variable manufacturing overhead would be reduced by 5% because less scrap would need to be hauled away, less electricity would be used in the production process, and less inventory would need to be stocked.

### E10-36A Record journal entries in a standard costing system *(Learning Objective 6)*

Check sum: Actual quantity of direct materials is 77,000 kg.

Refer to the Watermate data set above. Use a standard cost accounting system to do the following:

**Requirements**

1. Record Watermate's direct materials and direct labour journal entries.
2. Record Watermate's journal entries for manufacturing overhead, including the entry that records the overhead variances and closes the manufacturing overhead account.
3. Record the journal entries for the completion and sale of the 70,000 bottles, assuming Watermate sold (on account) all of the 70,000 bottles at a sales price of $8 each (there were no beginning or ending inventories).



### E10-37A Prepare a standard cost income statement *(Learning Objective 6)*

Check sum: Operating income is $85,500.

Refer to the Watermate data set above. Prepare a standard cost income statement for Watermate's management, using Exhibit 10-19 as a guide. Assume that sales were $560,000 and actual marketing and administrative expenses were $76,500.

### E10-38A Record materials and labour transactions *(Learning Objective 6)*

Check sum: Direct labour price variance is $4,500.

Make the journal entries to record the purchase and use of direct materials and direct labour made by Dock Guard in E10-27A.

### E10-39A Interpret a standard cost income statement *(Learning Objective 6)*

The managers of SeeScan, a contract manufacturer of DVD drives, are seeking explanations for the variances in the following report. Explain the meaning of each of SeeScan's materials, labour, and overhead variances.

Check sum: The favourable price variance occurred because SeeScan paid less than the standard price for raw materials.

**SEESCAN CO.**
**Standard Cost Income Statement**
Year Ended December 31

| | | |
|---|---|---|
| Sales revenue | | $1,200,000 |
| Cost of goods sold at standard cost | | 700,000 |
| Manufacturing cost variances: | | |
| Direct materials price variance | $ 8,000 F | |
| Direct materials efficiency variance | 32,000 U | |
| Direct labour price variance | 24,000 F | |
| Direct labour efficiency variance | 10,000 U | |
| Manufacturing overhead flexible budget variance | 28,000 U | |
| Production volume variance | 8,000 F | |
| Total manufacturing variances | | 30,000 |
| Cost of goods sold at actual cost | | 730,000 |
| Gross profit | | 470,000 |
| Marketing and administrative expenses | | 418,000 |
| Operating income | | $ 52,000 |

**E10-40A Prepare a standard cost income statement** *(Learning Objective 6)*

Western Outfitters' revenue and expense information for April follows:

| | |
|---|---|
| Sales revenue | $ 560,000 |
| Cost of goods sold (standard) | 442,000 |
| Direct materials price variance | 2,000 F |
| Direct materials efficiency variance | 6,000 F |
| Direct labour price variance | 4,000 U |
| Direct labour efficiency variance | 2,000 F |
| Overhead flexible budget variance | 3,500 U |
| Production volume variance | 8,000 F |

Check sum: Gross profit is $128,500.

**Requirement**

1. Prepare a standard cost income statement for management through gross profit. Report all standard cost variances for management's use. Has management done a good or poor job of controlling costs? Explain.



# EXERCISES Group B

**E10-41B Prepare flexible budgets for planning** *(Learning Objective 1)*

SmartWorx sells its main product, ergonomic mouse pads, for $8 each. Its variable cost is $2 per pad. Fixed costs are $200,000 per month for volumes up to 80,000 pads. Above 80,000 pads, monthly fixed costs are $265,000.

**Requirement**

1. Prepare a monthly flexible budget for the product, showing sales revenue, variable costs, fixed costs, and operating income for volume levels of 60,000, 70,000, and 90,000 pads.

Check sum: Operating income of 90,000 units is $275,000.

**E10-42B Graph flexible budget costs** *(Learning Objective 1)*

Graph the flexible budget total cost line for SmartWorx in Exercise 10-41B. Show total cost for volume levels of 60,000, 70,000, and 90,000 pads.

**E10-43B Complete and interpret a performance report** *(Learning Objective 2)*

McKnight Company's managers received the following incomplete performance report:

Check sum: Static budget operating income is $25,000.

McKnight Company
Income Statement Performance Report
Year Ended July 31

| | Actual Results at Actual Prices | Flexible Budget Variance | Flexible Budget for Actual Number of Output Units | Sales Volume Variance | Static (Master) Budget |
|---|---|---|---|---|---|
| Output units | 38,000 | — | 38,000 | 2,000 F | — |
| Sales revenue | $219,000 | — | $219,000 | $24,000 F | — |
| Variable cost | 81,000 | — | 80,000 | 10,000 U | — |
| Fixed cost | 107,000 | — | 100,000 | 0 | — |
| Total cost | 188,000 | — | 180,000 | 10,000 U | — |
| Operating income | $ 31,000 | — | $ 39,000 | $14,000 F | — |

**Requirement**

1. Complete the performance report. Identify the employee group that may deserve praise and the group that may be subject to criticism. Give your reasons.

## E10-44B Prepare an income statement performance report

*(Learning Objective 2)*

Time 2 Kool installed 10 pools during June. Prepare an income statement performance report for Time 2 Kool for June, using the following table as a guide.

Check sum: Operating income for static master budget is $10,800

Time 2 Kool Pools
Income Statement Performance Report
Month Ended June 30

| | (1) Actual Results at Actual Prices | (2) = [(1)–(3)] Flexible Budget Variance | (3) Flexible Budget for Actual Number of Output Units* | (4) = [(3)–(5)] Sales Volume Variance | (5) Static (Master) Budget |
|---|---|---|---|---|---|
| Output units (pools installed) | 10 | –0– | 10 | 2 F | 8 |
| Sales revenue | $121,000 | $1,000 F | $120,000 | $24,000 F | $96,000 |
| Variable expenses | 83,000 | 3,000 U | 80,000 | 16,000 F | 64,000 |
| Fixed expenses | 22,000 | 2,000 U | 20,000 | –0– | 20,000 |
| Total expenses | 105,000 | 5,000 U | 100,000 | 16,000 U | 84,000 |
| Operating income | $ 16,000 | $4,000 U | $ 20,000 | $ 8,000 F | $12,000 |

*Flexible budget variance, $4,000 U* — *Sales volume variance, $8,000 F*

*Static budget variance, $4,000 F*

*Budgeted sales price is $12,000 per pool, budgeted variable expense is $8,000 per pool, and budgeted total monthly fixed expenses are $20,000.

Assume that the actual sale price per pool is $13,000, actual variable expenses total $65,500, and actual fixed expenses are $19,100 in June. The master budget was prepared with the following assumptions: variable cost of $8,900 per pool, fixed expenses of $20,700 per month, and anticipated sales volume of nine pools at $12,400 per pool.

**Requirement**

1. Compute the sales volume variance and flexible budget variances. Use these variances to explain to Time 2 Kool's management why June's operating income differs from the operating income shown in the static budget.

## E10-45B Compute sales volume and flexible budget variances

*(Learning Objective 2)*

Check sum: Flexible budget variance for sales revenue is $345,600 F.

Top managers of Lortan Industries predicted the following year's sales of 147,000 units of its product at a unit price of $9.20. Actual sales for the year were 144,000 units at $11.60 each. Variable expenses were budgeted at $2.35 per unit, and actual variable expenses were $2.80 per unit. Actual fixed expenses of $430,000 exceeded budgeted fixed expenses by $27,500. Prepare Lortan Industries' income statement performance report. What variance contributed most to the year's favourable results? What caused this variance?

## E10-46B Work backward to find missing values *(Learning Objective 2)*

Manco has a relevant range extending to 31,000 units each month. The following performance report provides information about Manco's budget and actual performance for November.

Check sum: Static budget operating income is $79,300.

Manco
Income Statement Performance Report
Month Ended November 30

| | Actual Results at Actual Prices | (A) | Flexible Budget for Actual Number of Output Units | (B) | Static (Master) Budget |
|---|---|---|---|---|---|
| Output units | 26,000 | | (C) | | 31,000 |
| Sales revenue | $251,000 | $5,300 (F) | (D) | | |
| Variable expenses | | | (E) | | $190,650 |
| Fixed expenses | $ 15,000 | (F) | | | $ 23,000 |
| Operating income | | | | | (G) |

**Requirement**

1. Find the missing data for letters A–G. Be sure to label any variances as favourable or unfavourable. (*Hint*: A and B are titles.)

## E10-47B Calculate standard costs *(Learning Objective 3)*

Check sum: Gross profit in Req. 2 is $3.07.

Barrie's Bakery makes desserts for local restaurants. Each pan of gourmet bars requires 750 g of flour, 125 mL chopped pecans, 60 mL cocoa, 250 g sugar, 125 mL chocolate chips, 3 eggs, and 85 mL oil. Each pan requires 15 minutes of direct labour for mixing, cutting, and packaging. Each pan must bake for 30 minutes. Restaurants purchase the gourmet bars by the pan, not by the individual serving. Each pan is currently sold for $12. Standard costs are as follows: $1.60 per bag of flour (4 kg in a bag), $3.00 per bag of pecans (750 mL per bag), $4.38 per tin of cocoa (750 mL per tin), $3.00 per bag of sugar (3.75 kg in a bag), $1.80 per bag of chocolate chips (500 mL per bag), $0.84 per dozen eggs, $1.65 per bottle of oil (2 L per bottle), and $0.60 for packaging materials. The standard wage rate is $15 per hour. Barrie's Bakery allocates bakery overhead at $5.00 per oven hour.

**Requirements**

1. What is the standard cost per pan of gourmet bars?
2. What is the standard gross profit per pan of gourmet bars?
3. How often should Barrie's Bakery reassess the standard quantities and standard prices for inputs?

## E10-48B Calculate materials and labour variances *(Learning Objective 4)*

Curly's manufactures the bags of frozen french fries used at its franchised restaurants. Last week, Curly's purchased and used 99,000 kg of potatoes at a price of $0.70 per kilogram. During the week, 2,300 direct labour hours were incurred in the plant at a rate of $12.30 per hour. The standard price per kilogram of potatoes is $0.90, and the standard direct labour rate is $12.05 per hour. Standards indicate that for the number of bags of frozen fries produced, the factory should have used 97,000 kg of potatoes and 2,200 hours of direct labour.

**Requirements**

1. Determine the direct materials price and efficiency variances. Be sure to label each variance as favourable or unfavourable.

Check sum: Direct materials efficiency variance is $1,800 U.

2. Think of a plausible explanation for the variances found in Requirement 1.
3. Determine the direct labour price and efficiency variances. Be sure to label each variance as favourable or unfavourable.
4. Could the explanation for the labour variances be tied to the material variances? Explain.

### E10-49B Compute direct materials variance *(Learning Objective 4)*

The following direct materials variance computations are incomplete:

Check sum: Actual price variance is $7.50.

$$\text{Price variance} = (\$? - \$7) \times 10{,}800 \text{ kg} = \$5{,}400 \text{ U}$$
$$\text{Efficiency variance} = (? - 10{,}400 \text{ kg}) \times \$7 = ? \text{ U}$$
$$\text{Flexible budget variance} = \$?$$

**Requirement**

1. Fill in the missing values, and identify the flexible budget variance as favourable or unfavourable.

### E10-50B Calculate materials and labour variances *(Learning Objective 4)*

Check sum: Standard quantity allowed is 4,830.

Great Guard, which uses a standard cost accounting system, manufactured 210,000 boat fenders during the year, using 1,730,000 m of extruded vinyl purchased at $1.45 per metre. Production required 4,500 direct labour hours that cost $15.00 per hour. The materials standard was 8 m of vinyl per fender at a standard cost of $1.60 per metre. The labour standard was 0.023 direct labour hour per fender at a standard cost of $13.00 per hour. Compute the price and efficiency variances for direct materials and direct labour. Does the pattern of variances suggest that Great Guard's managers have been making trade-offs? Explain.



### E10-51B Compute standard manufacturing overhead rates *(Learning Objective 3)*

Check sum: Total standard predetermined overhead rate is $18.00/hr.

Great-Cut processes bags of frozen organic vegetables sold at specialty grocery stores. Great-Cut allocates manufacturing overhead based on direct labour hours. Great-Cut has projected total overhead for the year to be $765,000. Of this amount, $595,000 relates to fixed overhead expenses. Great-Cut expects to process 170,000 cases of frozen organic vegetables this year. The direct labour standard for each case is 1/4 hour.

**Requirements**

1. Compute the standard *variable* overhead rate.
2. Compute the *fixed* overhead rate.
3. Compute the standard *total* overhead rate.

### E10-52B Continuation of E10-51B: Compute overhead variances *(Learning Objective 5)*

Check sum: Total manufacturing overhead is $790,000.

Great-Cut actually processed 195,000 cases of frozen organic vegetables during the year and incurred $795,000 of manufacturing overhead. Of this amount, $605,000 was fixed.

**Requirements**

1. What is the flexible budget (for the actual output) for variable overhead? For fixed overhead? For total overhead?
2. How much overhead would have been allocated to production?
3. Use your answer from Requirement 1 to determine the overhead flexible budget variance. What does this tell managers?
4. Use your answer from Requirements 1 and 2 to determine the production volume variance. What does this tell managers?
5. What is the total overhead variance?

### E10-53B Compute manufacturing overhead variances *(Learning Objective 5)*

Canvas Company manufactures paint. The company charges the following standard unit costs to production on the basis of static budget volume of 35,000 cans of paint per month:

| | |
|---|---|
| Direct materials | $2.60 |
| Direct labour | 2.30 |
| Manufacturing overhead | 1.60 |
| Standard unit cost | $6.50 |

Canvas allocates overhead based on standard machine hours and uses the following monthly flexible budget for overhead:

| | Number of Outputs (cans) | | |
|---|---|---|---|
| | 32,000 | 35,000 | 40,000 |
| Standard machine hours | 3,200 | 3,500 | 4,000 |
| Budgeted manufacturing overhead cost: | | | |
| Variable | $22,400 | $24,500 | $28,000 |
| Fixed | 35,000 | 35,000 | 35,000 |

Check sum: Production volume variance is $1,000 F.

Canvas actually produced 40,000 cans of paint, using 3,180 machine hours. Actual variable overhead was $16,400, and fixed overhead was $33,000. Compute the total overhead variance, the overhead flexible budget variance, and the production volume variance.

### E10-54B Compute the standard cost of one unit *(Learning Objective 3)*

HippieJug is a manufacturer of ceramic bottles. The company has the following standards:

| | |
|---|---|
| Direct materials (clay) | 1.3 kg per bottle, at a cost of $0.40 per kg |
| Direct labour | 1/5 hour per bottle, at a cost of $14.80 per hour |
| Static budget variable overhead | $70,500 |
| Static budget fixed overhead | $30,500 |
| Static budget direct labour hours | 10,000 hours |
| Static budget number of bottles | 52,000 |

HippieJug allocates manufacturing overhead to production based on standard direct labour hours. Last month the company reported the following actual results for the production of 69,000 bottles:

| | |
|---|---|
| Direct materials | 1.5 kg per bottle, at a cost of $0.70 per kg |
| Direct labour | 1/4 hour per bottle, at a cost of $12.90 per hour |
| Actual variable overhead | $104,600 |
| Actual fixed overhead | $ 28,700 |

Check sum: Standard cost of one bottle is $5.50.

#### Requirements

1. Compute the standard predetermined variable manufacturing overhead rate, the standard predetermined fixed manufacturing overhead rate, and the total standard predetermined overhead rate.
2. Compute the standard cost of each of the following inputs: direct materials, direct labour, variable manufacturing overhead, and fixed manufacturing overhead.
3. Determine the standard cost of one ceramic bottle.

### E10-55B Compute and interpret direct materials variances *(Learning Objective 4)*

Refer to the HippieJug data set in E10-54B.

Check sum: Direct materials price variance is $31,050 U.

#### Requirements

1. Compute the direct materials price variance and the direct materials efficiency variance.
2. What is the total flexible budget variance for direct materials?
3. Who is generally responsible for each variance?
4. Interpret the variances.

### E10-56B Compute and interpret direct labour variances *(Learning Objective 4)*

Refer to the HippieJug data set in E10-54B.

Check sum: Direct labour price variance is $32,775 F.

**Requirements**

1. Compute the direct labour price variance and the direct labour efficiency variance.
2. What is the total flexible budget variance for direct labour?
3. Who is generally responsible for each variance?
4. Interpret the variances.

### E10-57B Compute and interpret manufacturing overhead variances *(Learning Objective 5)*

Check sum: Total overhead variance is $6,080 F.

Refer to the HippieJug data set in E10-54B.

**Requirements**

1. Compute the total manufacturing overhead variance. What does this tell management?
2. Compute the overhead flexible budget variance. What does this tell management?
3. Compute the production volume variance. What does this tell management?

### E10-58B Calculate the standard cost of a product before and after proposed sustainability effort changes *(Learning Objective 1 & 4)*

Gerbig Containers currently uses a recycled plastic to make bottles for the food industry.

**Current bottle production information**

The cost and time standards per batch of 10,000 bottles are as follows:

Plastic 300 kilograms at $5.00 per kg
Direct labour 2.0 hours at $20.00 per hour

The variable manufacturing overhead rate is based on total estimated variable manufacturing overhead of $400,000 and estimated total DLH of 40,000. Gerbig allocates its variable manufacturing overhead based on direct labour hours (DLH).

**Proposed changes to bottle design and production process**

The container division manager is considering having both the bottle redesigned and the bottle production process reengineered so that the plastic usage would drop by 30% overall due both to generating less scrap in the manufacturing process and using less plastic in each bottle. In addition to decreasing the amount of plastic used in producing the bottles, the additional following benefits would be realized:

Check sum: Req. 3 cost savings is $458.

a. Direct labour hours would be reduced by 10% because less scrap would be handled in the production process.
b. Total estimated variable manufacturing overhead would be reduced by 20% because less scrap would need to be hauled away, less electricity would be used in the production process, and less inventory would need to be stocked.

**Requirements**

1. Calculate the standard cost per batch of 10,000 bottles using the current data (before the company makes any changes). Include direct materials, direct labour, and variable manufacturing overhead in the standard cost per unit.
2. Calculate the standard cost per batch of 10,000 bottles if the company makes the changes to the bottle design and production process so that less plastic is used. Include direct materials, direct labour, and variable manufacturing overhead in the standard cost per unit.
3. Calculate the cost savings per batch by comparing the standard cost per batch under each scenario (current versus proposed change). Assume that the total cost to implement the changes would be $141,980. How many batches of bottles would need to be produced after the change to have the cost savings total equal the cost to make the changes?
4. What other benefits might arise from making this change to using less plastic in the manufacture of the bottles? Are there any risks? What would you recommend the company do?

### E10-59B Record journal entries in a standard costing system
*(Learning Objective 6)*

Refer to the HippieJug data set in E10-54B. The standard predetermined variable manufacturing overhead rate is $7.05, and the standard predetermined fixed manufacturing overhead rate is $3.05. Use a standard cost accounting system to do the following:

Check sum: Wages payable is $222,525.

**Requirements**

1. Record HippieJug's direct materials and direct labour journal entries.
2. Record HippieJug's journal entries for manufacturing overhead, including the entry that records the overhead variances and closes the manufacturing overhead account.
3. Record the journal entries for the completion and sale of the 69,000 bottles, assuming that HippieJug sold (on account) all of the 69,000 bottles at a sale price of $8.70 each (there were no beginning or ending inventories).

### E10-60B Prepare a standard cost income statement *(Learning Objective 6)*

Refer to the HippieJug data set in E10-54B. The cost of goods sold at standard cost totalled $379,500. Prepare a standard cost income statement for HippieJug's management, using Exhibit 10-19 as a guide. Assume that sales were $600,300 and actual marketing and administrative expenses were $80,500.

Check sum: Operating income is $91,525.



### E10-61B Record materials and labour transactions *(Learning Objective 6)*

Make the journal entries to record the purchase and use of direct materials and direct labour made by Great Guard in E10-50B.

Check sum: Manufacturing wages is $58,500.

### E10-62B Interpret a standard cost income statement *(Learning Objective 6)*

The managers of Monachino, a contract manufacturer of DVD drives, are seeking explanations for the variances in the following report. Explain the meaning of each of Monachino's materials, labour, and overhead variances.

| Monachino Company<br>Standard Cost Income Statement<br>Year Ended December 31 | | |
|---|---|---|
| Sales revenue | | $1,180,000 |
| Cost of goods sold at standard cost | | 700,000 |
| Manufacturing cost variances: | | |
| Direct materials price variance | $32,000 U | |
| Direct materials efficiency variance | 8,000 F | |
| Direct labour price variance | 10,000 U | |
| Direct labour efficiency variance | 24,000 F | |
| Manufacturing overhead flexible budget variance | 9,000 F | |
| Production volume variance | 30,000 U | |
| Total manufacturing variances | | 31,000 |
| Cost of goods sold at actual cost | | 731,000 |
| Gross profit | | 449,000 |
| Marketing and administrative expenses | | 426,000 |
| Operating income | | $ 23,000 |

### E10-63B Prepare a standard cost income statement *(Learning Objective 6)*

Special Outfitters' revenue and expense information for April follows:

Check sum: Operating income is $129,050.

| | |
|---|---|
| Sales revenue | $561,000 |
| Cost of goods sold (standard) | 444,000 |
| Direct materials price variance | 2,950 F |
| Direct materials efficiency variance | 6,400 F |
| Direct labour price variance | 4,300 U |
| Direct labour efficiency variance | 2,200 F |
| Overhead flexible budget variance | 3,650 U |
| Production volume variance | 8,450 F |

**Requirement**

1. Prepare a standard cost income statement for management through gross profit. Report all standard cost variances for management's use. Has management done a good or poor job of controlling costs? Explain.



## PROBLEMS Group A

### P10-64A Prepare a flexible budget for planning *(Learning Objective 1)*

Lasting Bubbles, Inc., produces multicoloured bubble solution used for weddings and other events. The company's static budget income statement for August is as follows. It is based on expected sales volume of 55,000 bubble kits.

| LASTING BUBBLES, INC.<br>Static Budget Income Statement<br>Month Ended August 31 | |
|---|---|
| Sales revenue | $165,000 |
| Variable expenses: | |
| Cost of goods sold | 63,250 |
| Sales commissions | 13,750 |
| Utilities expense | 11,000 |
| Fixed expenses: | |
| Salary expense | 32,000 |
| Depreciation expense | 20,000 |
| Rent expense | 11,000 |
| Utilities expense | 5,000 |
| Total expenses | 156,000 |
| Operating income | $ 9,000 |

Lasting Bubbles' plant capacity is 62,500 kits. If actual volume exceeds 62,500 kits, the company must expand the plant. In that case, salaries will increase by 10%, depreciation by 15%, and rent by $5,800. Fixed utilities will be unchanged by any volume increase.

**Requirements**

1. Prepare flexible budget income statements for the company, showing output levels of 55,000, 60,000, and 65,000 kits.
2. Graph the behaviour of the company's total costs.
3. Why might Lasting Bubbles' managers want to see the graph you prepared in Requirement 2 as well as the columnar format analysis in Requirement 1? What is the disadvantage of the graphic approach?

**P10-65A Prepare and interpret a performance report** *(Learning Objective 2)*

Refer to the Lasting Bubbles data in P10-64A. The company sold 60,000 bubble kits during August, and its actual operating income was as follows:

| LASTING BUBBLES, INC.<br>Income Statement<br>Month Ended August 31 | |
|---|---|
| Sales revenue | $185,000 |
| Variable expenses: | |
| Cost of goods sold | $ 69,500 |
| Sales commissions | 18,000 |
| Utilities expense | 12,000 |
| Fixed expenses: | |
| Salary expense | 34,000 |
| Depreciation expense | 20,000 |
| Rent expense | 10,000 |
| Utilities expense | 5,000 |
| Total expenses | 168,500 |
| Operating income | $ 16,500 |



### Requirements

1. Prepare an income statement performance report for August in a format similar to Exhibit 10-7.
2. What accounts for most of the difference between actual operating income and static budget operating income?
3. What is Lasting Bubbles' static budget variance? Explain why the income statement performance report provides Lasting Bubbles' managers with more useful information than the simple static budget variance. What insights can Lasting Bubbles' managers draw from this performance report?

**P10-66A Solve a comprehensive flexible budget, standards, and variances problem** *(Learning Objectives 2, 3, 4, & 5)*

One System assembles PCs and uses flexible budgeting and a standard cost system. One System allocates overhead based on the number of direct materials parts. The company's performance report includes the following selected data:

| | Static Budget (20,000 PCs) | Actual Results (22,000 PCs) |
|---|---|---|
| Sales (20,000 PCs × $400) | $8,000,000 | |
| (22,000 PCs × $420) | | $9,240,000 |
| Variable manufacturing expenses: | | |
| Direct materials (200,000 parts × $10.00) | 2,000,000 | |
| (214,200 parts × $9.80) | | 2,099,160 |
| Direct labour (40,000 hr × $14.00) | 560,000 | |
| (42,500 hr × $14.60) | | 620,500 |
| Variable overhead (200,000 parts × $4.00) | 800,000 | |
| (214,200 parts × $4.10) | | 878,220 |
| Fixed manufacturing expenses: | | |
| Fixed overhead | 900,000 | 930,000 |
| Total cost of goods sold | 4,260,000 | 4,527,880 |
| Gross profit | $3,740,000 | $4,712,120 |

### Requirements

1. Determine the company's standard cost for one unit.
2. Prepare a flexible budget based on the actual number of PCs sold.
3. Compute the price variance for direct materials and for direct labour.
4. Compute the efficiency variances for direct materials and direct labour.
5. For manufacturing overhead, compute the total variance, the flexible budget variance, and the production volume variance.
6. What is the total flexible budget variance for One System's manufacturing costs? Show how the total flexible budget variance is divided into materials, labour, and overhead variances.
7. Have One System's managers done a good job or a poor job controlling material and labour costs? Why?
8. Describe how One System's managers can benefit from the standard costing system.



## P10-67A Work backward through labour variances *(Learning Objective 4)*

Northern Music, a harmonica manufacturer, uses standard costs to judge performance. Recently, a clerk mistakenly threw away some of the records, and the manager has only partial data for October. She knows that the direct labour flexible budget variance for the month was $330 F and that the standard labour price was $10 per hour. A recent pay cut caused a favourable labour price variance of $0.50 per hour. The standard direct labour hours for actual October output were 5,600.

### Requirements

1. Find the actual number of direct labour hours worked during October. First, find the actual direct labour price per hour. Then, determine the actual number of direct labour hours worked by setting up the computation of the direct labour flexible budget variance of $330 F.
2. Compute the direct labour price and efficiency variances. Do these variances suggest that the manager may have made trade-offs? Explain.

## P10-68A Determine all variances *(Learning Objectives 4 & 5)*

Avanti manufactures embroidered jackets. The company prepares flexible budgets and uses a standard cost system to control manufacturing costs. The following standard unit cost of a jacket is based on the static budget volume of 14,000 jackets per month:

| | | |
|---|---|---|
| Direct materials (3.0 m² × $4.00 per m²) | | $12.00 |
| Direct labour (2 hours × $9.40 per hour) | | 18.80 |
| Manufacturing overhead: | | |
| Variable (2 hours × $0.65 per hour) | $1.30 | |
| Fixed (2 hours × $2.20 per hour) | 4.40 | 5.70 |
| Total cost per jacket | | $36.50 |

Data for November of the current year include the following:

a. Actual production was 13,600 jackets.
b. Actual direct materials usage was 2.70 m² per jacket at an actual cost of $4.15 per m².
c. Actual direct labour usage of 24,480 hours cost $235,008.
d. Total actual overhead cost was $79,000.

### Requirements

1. Compute the price and efficiency variances for direct materials and direct labour.
2. For manufacturing overhead, compute the total variance, the flexible budget variance, and the production volume variance.
3. Avanti's management intentionally purchased superior materials for November production. How did this decision affect the other cost variances? Overall, was the decision wise? Explain.

### P10-69A Journalize standard cost transactions *(Learning Objective 6)*

Refer to the data in P10-68A. Journalize the usage of direct materials and the assignment of direct labour, including the related variances.

### P10-70A Compute variances and prepare standard cost income statement *(Learning Objectives 4, 5, & 6)*

Happ Garden Supplies makes ground covers to prevent weed growth. During May, the company produced and sold 44,000 rolls and recorded the following cost data:

| | | Standard Unit Cost | Actual Total Cost |
|---|---|---|---|
| Direct materials: | | | |
| Standard (3 kg × $1.10 per kg) | | $3.30 | |
| Actual (136,600 kg × $1.05 per kg) | | | $143,430 |
| Direct labour: | | | |
| Standard (0.1 hr × $9.00 per hr) | | 0.90 | |
| Actual (4,600 hrs × $8.80 per hr) | | | 40,480 |
| Manufacturing overhead: | | | |
| Standard: | | | |
| Variable (0.2 machine hr × $9.00 per hr) | $1.80 | | |
| Fixed ($96,000 for static budget volume of 40,000 units and 8,000 machine hours) | 2.40 | | |
| Actual | | 4.20 | 168,800 |
| Total manufacturing costs | | $8.40 | $352,710 |

#### Requirements

1. Compute the price and efficiency variances for direct materials and direct labour.
2. For manufacturing overhead, compute the total variance, the flexible budget variance, and the production volume variance.
3. Prepare a standard cost income statement through gross profit to report all variances to management. Sales price was $10.60 per roll.
4. Happ Garden Supplies intentionally purchased cheaper materials during May. Was the decision wise? Discuss the trade-off between the two materials variances.

## PROBLEMS Group B

### P10-71B Prepare a flexible budget for planning *(Learning Objective 1)*

Creative Bubbles produces multicoloured bubble solution used for weddings and other events.

Creative Bubbles' plant capacity is 72,500 kits. If actual volume exceeds 72,500 kits, the company must expand the plant. In that case, salaries will increase by 10%, depreciation by 15%, and rent by $6,000. Fixed utilities will be unchanged by any volume increase.

The company's static budget income statement for December follows. It is based on expected sales volume of 65,000 bubble kits.

| Creative Bubbles, Inc.<br>Static Budget Income Statement<br>Month Ended December 31 | |
|---|---|
| Sales revenue | $201,500 |
| Variable expenses: | |
| Cost of goods sold | 81,250 |
| Sales commissions | 13,000 |
| Utilities expense | 9,750 |
| Fixed expenses: | |
| Salary expense | 33,000 |
| Depreciation expense | 18,000 |
| Rent expense | 9,000 |
| Utilities expense | 3,000 |
| Total expenses | 167,000 |
| Operating income | $ 34,500 |

**Requirements**

1. Prepare flexible budget income statements for the company, showing output levels of 65,000, 70,000, and 75,000 kits.
2. Graph the behaviour of the company's total costs.
3. Why might Creative Bubbles' managers want to see the graph you prepared in Requirement 2 as well as the columnar format analysis in Requirement 1? What is the disadvantage of the graphic approach?

**P10-72B Prepare and interpret a performance report** *(Learning Objective 2)*

Refer to the Creative Bubbles data in P10-71B. The company sold 70,000 bubble kits during December, and its actual operating income was as follows:

| Creative Bubbles, Inc.<br>Income Statement<br>Month Ended December 31 | |
|---|---|
| Sales revenue | $226,000 |
| Variable expenses: | |
| Cost of goods sold | $ 87,800 |
| Sales commissions | 16,500 |
| Utilities expense | 10,500 |
| Fixed costs: | |
| Salary expense | 35,100 |
| Depreciation expense | 18,000 |
| Rent expense | 8,250 |
| Utilities expense | 3,000 |
| Total expenses | 179,150 |
| Operating income | $ 46,850 |

**Requirements**

1. Prepare an income statement performance report for December.
2. What accounts for most of the difference between actual operating income and static budget operating income?

3. What is Creative Bubbles' static budget variance? Explain why the income statement performance report provides Creative Bubbles' managers with more useful information than the simple static budget variance. What insights can Creative Bubbles' managers draw from this performance report?

### P10-73B Analyze a comprehensive flexible budget, standards, and variances problem *(Learning Objectives 2, 3, 4, & 5)*

Gray System assembles PCs and uses flexible budgeting and a standard cost system. Gray System allocates overhead based on the number of direct materials parts. The company's performance report includes the following selected data:

| | Static Budget (20,500 PCs) | Actual Results (22,500 PCs) |
|---|---|---|
| Sales (20,500 PCs × $415) | $8,507,500 | |
| (22,500 PCs × $435) | | $9,787,500 |
| Variable manufacturing expenses: | | |
| Direct materials (205,000 parts × $9.50) | 1,947,500 | |
| (218,500 parts × $9.30) | | 2,032,050 |
| Direct labour (41,000 hr × $14.00) | 574,000 | |
| (43,500 hr × $14.60) | | 635,100 |
| Variable overhead (205,000 parts × $3.90) | 799,500 | |
| (218,500 parts × $4.00) | | 874,000 |
| Fixed manufacturing expenses: | | |
| Fixed overhead | 902,000 | 932,000 |
| Total cost of goods sold | 4,223,000 | 4,473,150 |
| Gross profit | $4,284,500 | $5,314,350 |

#### Requirements

1. Determine the company's standard cost for one unit.
2. Prepare a flexible budget based on the actual number of PCs sold.
3. Compute the price variance for direct materials and for direct labour.
4. Compute the efficiency variances for direct materials and direct labour.
5. For manufacturing overhead, compute the total variance, the flexible budget variance, and the production volume variance.
6. What is the total flexible budget variance for Gray System's manufacturing costs? Show how the total flexible variance is divided into materials, labour, and overhead variances.
7. Have Gray System's managers done a good job or a poor job controlling material and labour costs? Why?
8. Describe how Gray System's managers can benefit from the standard costing system.

### P10-74B Work backward through labour variances *(Learning Objective 4)*

Lorng's Music, a harmonica manufacturer, uses standard costs to judge performance. Recently, a clerk mistakenly threw away some of the records, and Lorng has only partial data for May. She knows that the direct labour flexible budget variance for the month was $360 F and that the standard labour price was $9 per hour. A recent pay cut caused a favourable labour price variance of $0.70 per hour. The standard direct labour hours for actual May output were 5,850.

#### Requirements

1. Find the actual number of direct labour hours worked during May. First, find the actual direct labour price per hour. Then, determine the actual number of direct labour hours worked by setting up the computation of the direct labour flexible budget variance of $360 F.
2. Compute the direct labour price and efficiency variances. Do these variances suggest that the manager may have made trade-offs? Explain.

CHAPTER 10

### P10-75B Determine all variances *(Learning Objectives 4 & 5)*

Preston manufactures embroidered jackets. The company prepares flexible budgets and uses a standard cost system to control manufacturing costs. The following standard unit cost of a jacket is based on the static budget volume of 13,800 jackets per month:

| | | |
|---|---|---|
| Direct materials (3.0 m² × $3.90 per m²) | | $11.70 |
| Direct labour (2 hours × $9.00 per hour) | | 18.00 |
| Manufacturing overhead: | | |
| Variable (2 hours × $0.67 per hour) | $1.34 | |
| Fixed (2 hours × $2.40 per hour) | 4.80 | 6.14 |
| Total cost per jacket | | $35.84 |

Data for November of the current year include the following:

a. Actual production was 13,400 jackets.
b. Actual direct materials usage was 2.80 m² per jacket at an actual price of $4.00 per m².
c. Actual direct labour usage of 24,600 hours cost $223,860.
d. Total actual overhead cost was $83,000.

#### Requirements

1. Compute the price and efficiency variances for direct materials and direct labour.
2. For manufacturing overhead, compute the total variance, the flexible budget variance, and the production volume variance.
3. Preston's management intentionally purchased superior materials for November production. How did this decision affect the other cost variances? Overall, was the decision wise?

### P10-76B Journalize standard cost transactions *(Learning Objective 6)*

Refer to the data in P10-75B. Journalize the usage of direct materials and the assignment of direct labour, including the related variances.

### P10-77B Compute variances and prepare standard cost income statement *(Learning Objectives 4, 5, & 6)*

Green Garden Supplies makes ground covers to prevent weed growth. During May, the company sold 44,300 rolls and recorded the following cost data:

| | | Standard Unit Cost | Actual Total Cost |
|---|---|---|---|
| Direct materials: | | | |
| Standard (3 kg × $1.25 per kg) | | $3.75 | |
| Actual (136,800 kg × $1.20 per kg) | | | $164,160 |
| Direct labour: | | | |
| Standard (0.1 hr × $7.00 per hr) | | 0.70 | |
| Actual (4,630 hrs × $6.80 per hr) | | | 31,484 |
| Manufacturing overhead: | | | |
| Standard: | | | |
| Variable (0.2 machine hr × $8.00 per hr) | $1.60 | | |
| Fixed ($99,000 for static budget volume of 39,600 units and 8,060 machine hours) | 2.50 | | |
| Actual | | 4.10 | 168,400 |
| Total manufacturing costs | | $8.55 | $364,044 |

## Requirements

1. Compute the price and efficiency variances for direct materials and direct labour.
2. For manufacturing overhead, compute the total variance, the flexible budget variance, and the production volume variance.
3. Prepare a standard cost income statement through gross profit to report all variances to management. Sales price was $10.60 per roll.
4. Green Garden Supplies intentionally purchased cheaper materials during May. Was the decision wise? Discuss the trade-off between the two materials variances.

## P10-78B Comprehensive variance review *(Learning Objectives 3, 4, & 5)*

Charlie Beagle noted a small variance on the income statement of Daribund Inc. The company manufactured 17,000 units last year using a total of 75,000 kilograms of material purchased at a cost of $4.25 per kg. The material was used in full for the manufacturing process for the 17,000 units, and there were no beginning or ending inventories for the year. Manufacturing required 33,000 direct labour-hours (against a budget of 34,000 DLH) during the year at a cost of $12.00 per hour. Overhead cost is applied to products on the basis of standard direct labour hours.

### Cost Data

| Standard Cost Card–Per Unit | | | | | |
|---|---|---|---|---|---|
| | | kilograms | | | |
| Direct materials, | 3 | at | $4.00 | Per kg | $ 12 |
| Direct labour, | 2 | DLH at | $ 11 | Per direct labour hour | $ 22 |
| Variable overhead, | 2 | DLH at | $ 3 | Per direct labour hour | $ 6 |
| Fixed overhead | 2 | DLH at | $ 5 | Per direct labour hour | $ 10 |
| **Standard cost per unit** | | | | | $ 50 |
| | | | | | |
| Fixed OH DLH expected. | | | | | 28,000 |
| Budgeted fixed overhead costs | | | | | $175,000 |
| Actual fixed overhead costs | | | | | $152,000 |
| Actual variable overhead costs | | | | | $ 79,200 |

## Requirements

1. Compute the direct materials price and quantity variances for the year.
2. Compute the direct labour rate and efficiency variances for the year.
3. For manufacturing overhead, compute the following:
   a. The variable overhead spending and efficiency variances for the year
   b. The fixed overhead budget and volume variances for the year
3. Compute the aggregate variance
4. Based on the variance analysis, what comments can you make on the stability of operations and the effectiveness of budgeting and operations?

CHAPTER 10

# CAPSTONE APPLICATION PROBLEMS

## APPLICATION QUESTIONS

### A10-79 Compute flexible budget and sales volume variances *(Learning Objective 2)*

ReelTime distributes DVDs to movie retailers, including dot-coms. ReelTime's top management meets monthly to evaluate the company's performance. Controller Jairo Munoz prepared the following performance report for the meeting.

**REELTIME, INC.**
**Income Statement Performance Report**
Month Ended July 31

| | Actual Results | Static Budget | Variance |
|---|---|---|---|
| Sales revenue | $1,640,000 | $1,960,000 | $320,000 U |
| Variable expenses: | | | |
| Cost of goods sold | 773,750 | 980,000 | 206,250 F |
| Sales commissions | 77,375 | 107,800 | 30,425 F |
| Shipping expense | 42,850 | 53,900 | 11,050 F |
| Fixed expenses: | | | |
| Salary expense | 311,450 | 300,500 | 10,950 U |
| Depreciation expense | 208,750 | 214,000 | 5,250 F |
| Rent expense | 128,250 | 108,250 | 20,000 U |
| Advertising expense | 81,100 | 68,500 | 12,600 U |
| Total expenses | 1,623,525 | 1,832,950 | 209,425 F |
| Operating income | $ 16,475 | $ 127,050 | $110,575 U |

Munoz also revealed that the actual sales price of $20 per movie was equal to the budgeted sales price and that there were no changes in inventories for the month.

Management is disappointed by the operating income results. CEO Philippe Gollin exclaims, "How can actual operating income be roughly 13% of the static budget amount when there are so many favourable variances?"

#### Requirements

1. Prepare a more informative performance report. Be sure to include a flexible budget for the actual number of DVDs bought and sold.
2. As a member of ReelTime's management team, which variances would you want investigated? Why?
3. Gollin believes that many consumers are postponing purchases of new movies until after the introduction of a new format for recordable DVD players. In light of this information, how would you rate the company's performance?

### A10-80 Calculate efficiency variances *(Learning Objective 4)*

Assume that you manage your local Marble Slab Creamery ice cream parlour. In addition to selling ice cream cones, you make large batches of a few flavours of milk shakes to sell throughout the day. Your parlour is chosen to test the company's "Made-for-You" system. The system allows patrons to customize their milk shakes by choosing different flavours.

Customers like the new system and your staff appears to be adapting, but you wonder whether this new made-to-order system is as efficient as the old system where you made just a few large batches. Efficiency is a special concern because your performance is evaluated in part on the restaurant's efficient use of materials and labour. Assume that your superiors consider that efficiency variances greater than 5% are unacceptable.

You decide to look at your sales for a typical day. You find that the parlour used 390 kilograms of ice cream and 72 hours of direct labour to produce and sell 2,000 shakes. Assume that the standard quantity allowed for a shake is 0.2 kg of ice cream and 0.03 hours (1.8 minutes) of direct labour. Further, assume that standard costs are $1.50 per kilogram for ice cream and $8.00 an hour for labour.

### Requirements

1. Compute the efficiency variances for direct labour and direct materials.
2. Provide likely explanations for the variances. Do you have reason to be concerned about your performance evaluation? Explain.
3. Write a memo to Marble Slab Creamery's national office explaining your concern and suggesting a remedy. Use the following format for your memo:

**Date:**____________________

**To:** Marble Slab Creamery's National Office

**From:** ____________________

**Subject:** "Made-for-You" System

## CASE ASSIGNMENT

### C10-81 Grantham Roses

*Source:* Lsantilli / Fotolia

Grantham Roses has been in the business of growing rosebush starter plants for 50 years. Its rosebushes are started in greenhouses in British Columbia and shipped across North America every spring in time for the new planting season each year. It specializes in Hybrid Tea rosebushes, which are the most common and come in a variety of colours and have a single rose on each stem, and the Floribunda rosebush, which has roses in clusters of three or four per stem. Grantham Roses ships its rosebush starter plants to specialty gardening centres all across North America.

Growing of the starter bushes is timed so that the majority of the bushes are ready for the spring planting season but also so that there is a supply of fresh starter bushes throughout the summer and into the fall. Ten percent of the plants that are started do not meet quality control, and so they are turned into mulch and composted. It is a great source of pride that a Grantham rosebush has never been returned from a customer for being of poor quality.

Both rosebush varieties are grown in a special pot that can be planted with the rosebush by the final customer, but because of some differences between the two types of rosebushes, there are slight differences in the resources that are needed for their growth. The Floribunda, for example, requires a support structure (a green post) to be included with the starter plant to provide support for the stems that have multiple blooms.

| | Hybrid Tea | Floribunda |
|---|---|---|
| Recycled paper pot | 1 | 1 |
| Soil | 0.1 $m^3$ | 0.15 $m^3$ |
| Fertilizer | 45 g | 80 g |
| Support structure | | 1 |
| DL | 0.5 h | 0.6 h |

Each new rosebush also requires a cutting from an existing bush in order to start the plant. It takes nine months for the cut stem to germinate and develop into a new plant, so the gardeners are constantly monitoring the young plants to ensure that they develop properly. Grantham Roses has a garden of approximately 100 acres of mature rosebushes that are maintained to provide the millions of cuttings needed for the germination of the new plants. The company is famous for its summer garden, and tourists travel from around the world to walk the gardens for free and enjoy the acres of blooms.

The only concern of management is that the purchasing department has had a considerable amount of turnover in the past year. One of its employees, Arla, who had been with them the longest (over 30 years), retired from the purchasing manager's position. Her husband was also a member of the purchasing team and left at the same time as she did, since they decided to move to Arizona for their retirement.

They promoted one of the remaining two people in the purchasing department to manager and hired two new employees. One of these new employees only stayed for a couple of months and the other person quit after six months to go back to school at the local university. Two more people were hired, and they have now been with Grantham Roses for four and five months, respectively. But with all this turnover, it is hard to keep consistency with the purchasing of important resources. The company is thankful that it does not need to source the cuttings—the most important element of its product—but it isn't sure that the other elements are being purchased appropriately. Before Arla retired, she prepared a report to show what she typically purchased as follows:

| | $ | Unit |
|---|---|---|
| Recycled paper pot | 0.1 | each |
| Soil | 3 | per $m^3$ |
| Fertilizer | 35 | per kg |
| Support structure | 0.23 | each |
| Labour | 18 | per hour |

Planned production of the rosebushes is 5,000,000 units of the Hybrid Tea and 3,000,000 units of the Floribunda variety. Everything that was purchased was used, and it turned out that they were able to produce 5,150,000 Hybrid Tea plants and 3,200,000 Floribunda plants, and the purchases for the year are as follows:

| | $ | Unit | Total Purchases |
|---|---|---|---|
| Recycled paper pot | 0.12 | each | $ 1,102,200 |
| Soil | 3.1 | per cubic m | $ 2,825,650 |
| Fertilizer | 32 | per kg | $16,552,000 |
| Support structure | 0.23 | each | $ 736,000 |
| Labour | 19.5 | per hour | $71,370,000 |

The operations manager stated that it turned out that the direct labour needed was 0.4 hours for each Hybrid Tea and 0.5 hours for the Floribunda. They needed to use 47 g of fertilizer for the Hybrid Tea and 86 g for the Floribunda. And they were able to reduce the amount of soil needed for each bush by 0.01 cubic metres.

# ETHICAL ISSUE

## I10-82 Analyze ethical dilemmas relating to standards *(Learning Objective 3)*

Austin Landers is the accountant for Sun Coast, a manufacturer of outdoor furniture that is sold through specialty stores and internet companies. Annually, Landers is responsible for reviewing the standard costs for the following year. While reviewing the standard costs for the coming year, two ethical issues arise. Use the CPA Guidelines for Ethical Behaviour to identify the ethical dilemma in each situation. Identify the relevant factors in each situation, and suggest what Landers should recommend to the controller.

**Issue 1:** Landers has been approached by Minji Chung, a former colleague who worked with Landers when they were both employed by a public accounting firm. Chung recently started her own firm, Chung Benchmarking Associates, which collects and sells data on industry benchmarks. She offers to provide Landers with benchmarks for the outdoor furniture industry free of charge if he will provide her with the last three years of Sun Coast's standard and actual costs. Chung explains that this is how she obtains most of her firm's benchmarking data. Landers always has a difficult time with the standard-setting process and believes that the benchmark data would be very useful.

**Issue 2:** Sun Coast's management is starting a continuous improvement policy that requires a 10% reduction in standard costs each year for the next three years. Adil Hassan, manufacturing supervisor of the Teak furniture line, asks Landers to set loose standard costs this year before the continuous improvement policy is implemented. Hassan argues that there is no other way to meet the tightening standards while maintaining the high quality of the Teak line.

# TEAM PROJECT

## T10-83 Evaluate approaches to setting standards *(Learning Objective 3)*

EnerGuard Windows and Doors is a window and door manufacturer in Saskatchewan. Since the company began in 2006, EnerGuard has introduced many product lines. Suppose EnerGuard has been using a standard cost system that bases price and quantity standards on EnerGuard's historical long-run average performance. Assume EnerGuard's controller has engaged your team of management consultants to recommend whether EnerGuard should use some basis other than historical performance for setting standards.

### Requirements

1. List the types of variances you recommend that EnerGuard compute (for example, direct materials price variance for glass). For each variance, what specific standards would EnerGuard need to develop? In addition to cost standards, do you recommend that EnerGuard develop any nonfinancial standards? Explain.

2. There are many approaches to setting standards other than simply using long-run average historical prices and quantities.
   a. List three alternative approaches that EnerGuard could use to set standards, and explain how EnerGuard could implement each alternative.
   b. Evaluate each alternative method of setting standards, including the pros and cons of each method.
   c. Write a memo to EnerGuard's controller detailing your recommendations. First, should EnerGuard retain its historical data-based standard cost approach? If not, which alternative approach should it adopt? Use the following format for your memo:

**Date:**____________________

**To:** Controller, EnerGuard

**From:** ____________________, Management Consultants

**Subject:** Standard Costs

# DISCUSSION & ANALYSIS

1. Compare and contrast a static budget and a flexible budget.
2. Describe two ways managers can use flexible budgets.
3. How is the sales volume variance calculated? What does it measure? Who within the organization is typically held responsible for the sales volume variance?
4. How is the flexible budget variance calculated? What does it measure? Who within the organization is typically held responsible for the flexible budget variance?
5. What does the direct materials price variance measure? Who is generally responsible for the direct materials price variance? Describe two situations that could result in a favourable materials price variance. Describe two situations that could result in an unfavourable materials price variance.
6. What does the direct materials efficiency variance measure? Who is generally responsible for the direct materials efficiency variance? Describe two situations that could result in a favourable direct materials efficiency variance and two situations that could result in an unfavourable direct materials efficiency variance.
7. What does the direct labour price variance measure? Who is generally responsible for the direct labour price variance? Describe two situations that could result in a favourable direct labour price variance and two situations that could result in an unfavourable direct labour price variance.
8. What does the direct labour efficiency variance measure? Who is generally responsible for the direct labour efficiency variance? Describe two situations that could result in a favourable labour efficiency variance and two situations that could result in an unfavourable labour efficiency variance.
9. Describe at least four ways a company could use standard costing and variance analysis.
10. What are the two manufacturing overhead variances? What does each measure? Who within the organization would be responsible for each of these variances?

# APPLICATION & ANALYSIS

## 10-1 Analyzing Variances and Potential Causes

Go to YouTube.com and search for clips from the show *Unwrapped* on the Food Network or *How It's Made* on the Discovery Channel. Watch a clip for a product you find interesting. Companies are not likely to disclose everything about their production process and other trade secrets. When you answer the following questions, you may have to make reasonable assumptions or guesses about the manufacturing process, materials, and labour.

## Discussion Questions

1. Describe the product and briefly outline the production process.
2. What direct materials are used to make this product? In general, what has happened to the cost of these materials over the past year? To find information about the price of materials, you might try one or more of these sources:
   a. Go to the *Edmonton Sun* website (www.edmontonsun.com) or to Canada AM (canadaam.ctvnews.ca) and search for each of the materials.
   b. Find the company's annual report on its Website, and read its discussion about its costs of production.
3. Given what you have discovered about the cost of materials for this product, were the price variances for each material likely to be favourable or unfavourable? Answer separately for each individual material.
4. In general, what has probably occurred to the cost of direct labour for this company? Again, to find clues about its labour costs, you might try one of the options listed in Question 2. If you cannot find anything specific about this company, then discuss what has happened to the cost of labour in general over the past year.
5. Given what you have discovered about the cost of labour, was the labour price variance likely to be favourable or unfavourable?
6. It is unlikely that the company has released information about its efficiency variances. In general, though, what could cause this company's material efficiency variances to be favourable? What could cause these material efficiency variances to be unfavourable?
7. In general, what could cause this company's labour efficiency variances to be favourable? What could cause these labour efficiency variances to be unfavourable?

## Classroom Applications

**Web:** Post the discussion questions on an electronic discussion board. Have small groups of students choose a product for their groups. Each student should watch the clip for the product for his or her group. The students should then collaborate to form answers for all of the discussion questions for their product/company.

**Classroom:** Form groups of three or four students. Your group should choose a product. After viewing its clip, prepare a five-minute presentation about your group's product that addresses the questions above.

**Independent:** Research answers to each of the questions. Turn in a two- to three-page typed paper (12-point font, double-spaced with 2.5 cm margins). Include references, including the URL for the clip that you viewed.

# TRY IT SOLUTIONS

**page 610:**

1. Standard cost of direct materials = Standard quantity of DM × Standard price of DM
   = 0.25 lbs × $4.00/lb
   = $1.00
2. Standard cost of direct labour = Standard quantity of DL × Standard price of DL
   = 3 minutes × ($10 per hour ÷ 60 minutes per hour)
   = $0.50
3. Standard cost of variable overhead = Standard quantity of time × Variable overhead rate
   = 3 minutes × $0.05 per minute
   = $0.15

**page 615:**

1. DM price variance = Actual Quantity Purchased × (Actual Price − Standard Price)
   = AQP × (AP − SP)
   = 1,300 lbs × ($3.75/lb − $4.00/lb)
   = $325 F

The price variance is favourable since the berries cost less per pound than anticipated.

2. DM quantity variance = Standard Price
   × (Actual Quantity Used − Standard Quantity Allowed)
   = SP × (AQU − SQA)
   = $4.00/lb × [1,300 lbs − (5,000 smoothies × 0.25 lbs/smoothie)]
   = $4.00/lb × (1,300 lbs − 1,250 lbs)
   = $200 U

The efficiency variance is unfavourable since the business used more berries than anticipated.

3. The total DM variance is $125 F. The total DM variance is the difference between the actual DM cost of $4,875 (= 1,300 lbs × $3.75/lb) and the flexible budget for DM of $5,000 [5,000 smoothies × standard DM cost per smoothie of $1.00 (= 0.25 lbs × $4.00 per pound)]. If the company both purchased and used the same quantity of DM, it is also the combination of the DM price variance ($325 F) and the DM efficiency variance ($200 U). The lower-than-expected price of berries more than offset the additional quantity the shop used, thus resulting in an overall favourable variance.

**page 625:**

1. The fixed overhead budget variance is $145 U. It is the difference between what was budgeted for fixed overhead ($1,455) and what was actually incurred ($1,600). The variance is unfavourable since actual fixed overhead was higher than budgeted.
2. Since Hannah's actual store volume was higher than anticipated, the fixed overhead volume variance will be favourable. By producing at a higher volume, Hannah was able to use the store's fixed overhead costs more efficiently.

# Performance Evaluation and the Balanced Scorecard

## Learning Objectives

1 Explain why and how companies decentralize.

2 Explain why companies use performance evaluation systems.

3 Describe the balanced scorecard, and identify key performance indicators for each perspective.

4 Use performance reports to evaluate cost, revenue, and profit centres.

5 Use return on investment (ROI), residual income (RI), and economic value added (EVA) to evaluate investment centres.

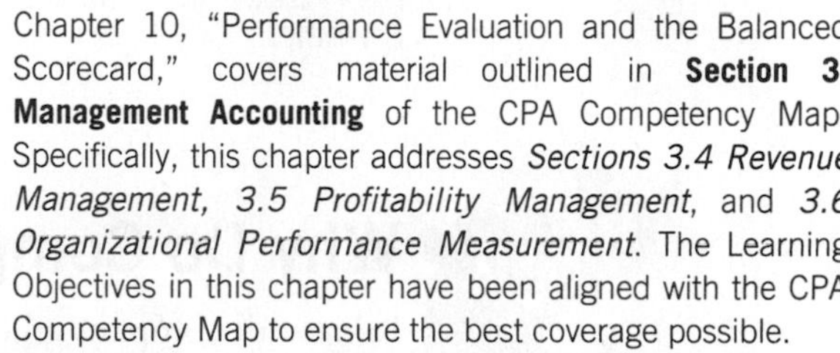

Chapter 10, "Performance Evaluation and the Balanced Scorecard," covers material outlined in **Section 3: Management Accounting** of the CPA Competency Map. Specifically, this chapter addresses *Sections 3.4 Revenue Management, 3.5 Profitability Management*, and *3.6 Organizational Performance Measurement*. The Learning Objectives in this chapter have been aligned with the CPA Competency Map to ensure the best coverage possible.

**P**ROFESSIONAL **C**OMPETENCY The presence of the **coverage button** in the margin indicates focus on one or more of the specific competency areas from the competency map. The concepts in the text are building blocks to developing the competencies required in the CPA. While the chapter may address multiple areas of the competency map, the main focus will be:

Competencies:

**3.4.1** Evaluates sources and drivers of revenue growth*

**3.5.1** Performs sensitivity analysis*

**3.5.2** Evaluates sustainable profit maximization and capacity management performance*

**3.6.1** Evaluates performance using accepted frameworks*

**3.6.2** Evaluates performance of responsibility centres*

**3.6.3** Evaluates root causes of performance issues*

## The Ministry of Health and Long-Term

Care of Ontario is responsible for five distinct areas of care: acute, emergency, rehabilitation, complex continuing care, and mental health and addictions. As the ministry with the largest anticipated expenses, the Ministry of Health and Long-Term Care has a budget of approximately $45 billion per year. This constitutes 40% of the programming budget for the Province of Ontario. Two hundred and ten hospital sites in Ontario are grouped into four categories: Public Hospitals, Private Hospitals, Federal Hospitals, and Cancer Care Ontario Hospitals. With almost 100,000 employees at only 100 of those hospitals, it is evident that a great many people are needed to effectively provide health services in Ontario.

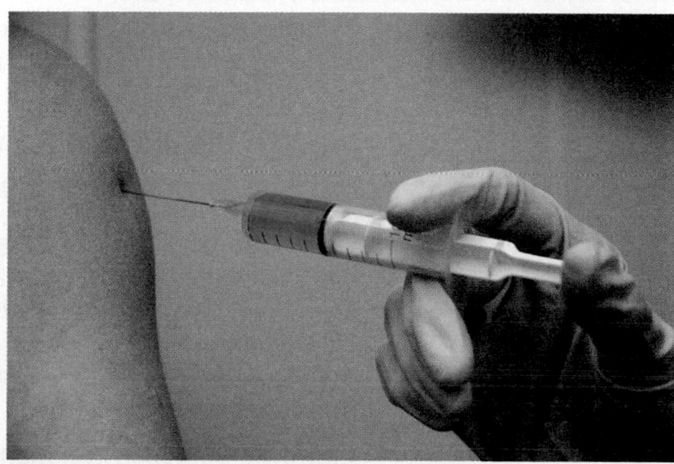

© David Cole/Alamy

*Reprinted from *The Chartered Professional Accountant Competency Map - Understanding the competencies a candidate must demonstrate to become a CPA*, © 2012, with permission Chartered Professional Accountants of Canada, Toronto, Canada. Any changes to the original material are the sole responsibility of the author (and/or publisher) and have not been reviewed or endorsed by the Chartered Professional Accountants of Canada.

Keeping all of these people organized and focused on the same goals can be a daunting task. The Ministry of Health and Long-Term Care has to put the overall strategy of the entire organization into understandable, achievable milestones for any individual. It needs an approach that helps monitor the quality of inpatient care in the five service areas. A balanced scorecard is the tool that enables the ministry to achieve these goals.

Many organizations such as the Ministry of Health and Long-Term Care decentralize their operations into subunits. Decentralization provides large companies with many advantages. But once a company decentralizes its operations, top management is no longer directly involved in running the day-to-day operations of each subunit. Therefore, upper management needs a system—such as the **balanced scorecard**—for communicating the company's strategy to subunit managers and for measuring how well the subunits are achieving their goals.

As you'll see in this chapter, the balanced scorecard helps management view the performance of company subunits from several different perspectives. Each perspective gives management unique insight into the factors that will drive the success of the company as a whole.

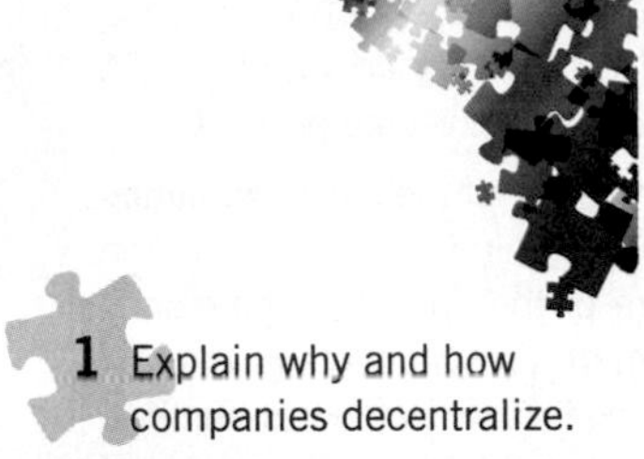

1 Explain why and how companies decentralize.

PROFESSIONAL COMPETENCY

# Why Do Companies Decentralize Operations?

In a small company, the owner or top manager often makes all the planning and operating decisions. Small companies can use centralized decision making because of the smaller scope of their operations. However, when a company grows, it becomes impossible for a single person to manage the entire organization's daily operations. Therefore, most companies decentralize as they grow.

Companies that decentralize split their operations into different divisions or operating units and delegate decision-making responsibility to the unit managers. Top management determines the type of decentralization that best suits the company's strategy. For example, decentralization may be based on geographic area, product line, customer base, business function, or some other business characteristic. McCain segments its operations by position on the value chain (food service, retail, transportation, produce production, and fertilizers). Shaw Group segments by geographic area (location of the laboratory). Bombardier segments by type of product (aerospace or rail). And the Ministry of Health and Long-Term Care segments both by service area (emergency care, for example) and hospital type (cancer care, for example).

## Advantages of Decentralization

### Frees Top Management's Time

By delegating responsibility for daily operations to unit managers, top management can concentrate on long-term strategic planning and higher-level decisions that affect the entire company.

### Supports Use of Expert Knowledge

Decentralization allows top management to hire the expertise each business unit needs to excel in its specific operations. For example, decentralizing by customer type (boarders and students) allows Maplewood Equestrian Centre to hire managers with specialized knowledge and skills for the needs of each group (such as equine health and care practices for the Boarding Division, and dressage, hunter, and jumper training knowledge for the Students Division). Such specialized knowledge can help unit managers make better decisions than the company's top managers could make about product and business improvements within the business unit.

### Improves Customer Relations

Unit managers focus on just one segment of the company; therefore, they can maintain close contact with important customers. Thus, decentralization often leads to improved customer relations and quicker customer response time.

### Provides Training

Decentralization also provides unit managers with the training and experience necessary to become effective top managers. Companies often choose CEOs based on their past performance as division managers.

### Improves Motivation and Retention

Empowering unit managers to make decisions increases managers' motivation and retention, and improves job performance and satisfaction.

## Disadvantages of Decentralization

### Duplication of Costs

Decentralization may cause the company to duplicate certain costs or assets. For example, each business unit may hire its own Payroll Department and purchase its own payroll software. Companies can often avoid such duplications by providing centralized services. For example, Shaw Group segments its business by location of the laboratory, yet each location shares one centralized Human Resources Department and one centralized Website.

### Problems Achieving Goal Congruence

**Goal congruence** occurs when unit managers' goals align with top management's goals. **Decentralized** companies often struggle to achieve goal congruence. Unit managers may not fully understand the company's big picture. They may make decisions that are good for their division but may harm another division or the rest of the company. For example, the Purchasing Department may buy cheaper components to decrease product cost. However, cheaper components may hurt the product line's quality, and the company's brand, *as a whole*, may suffer. Later in this chapter, we'll see how management accountants can design performance evaluation systems that foster goal congruence.

## Responsibility Centres

Decentralized companies delegate responsibility for specific decisions to each subunit, creating responsibility centres. Recall from Chapter 9 that a *responsibility centre* is a part or subunit of an organization whose manager is accountable for specific activities. Exhibit 11-1 reviews the four most common types of responsibility centres.

**EXHIBIT 11-1** The Four Most Common Types of Responsibility Centres

| Responsibility Centre | Manager is responsible for... | Examples |
|---|---|---|
| Cost centre | Controlling costs | Human Resources Department at Shaw Group; Accounting Department at Maplewood Equestrian Centre |
| Revenue centre | Generating sales revenue | North American Sales Division at Bombardier; European Sales Division at McCain |
| Profit centre | Producing profit through generating sales and controlling costs | Product line at Bombardier; individual corporate Prime restaurants |
| Investment centre | Producing profit and managing the division's invested capital | Company Divisions at McCain such as Production, Transportation, and Commercial Sales |

# Performance Evaluation Systems

2 Explain why companies use performance evaluation systems.

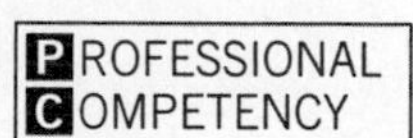


Once a company decentralizes operations, top management is no longer involved in running the subunits' day-to-day operations. Performance evaluation systems provide top management with a framework for maintaining control over the entire organization.

## Goals of Performance Evaluation Systems

When companies decentralize, top management needs a system to communicate its goals to subunit managers. In addition, top management needs to determine whether the decisions being made at the subunit level are effectively meeting company goals.

### Promoting Goal Congruence and Coordination

As previously mentioned, decentralization increases the difficulty of achieving goal congruence. Unit managers may not always make decisions consistent with the overall goals of the organization. A company will be able to achieve its goals only if each unit moves in a synchronized fashion toward the overall company goals. Like a flock of birds or a school of fish, each individual subunit must move in harmony with the other subunits. The performance measurement system should provide incentives for coordinating the subunits' activities and direct them toward achieving the overall company goals.

### Communicating Expectations

To make decisions that are consistent with the company's goals, unit managers must know the goals and the specific part that their units play in attaining those goals. The performance measurement system should spell out the unit's most critical objectives. Without a clear picture of what management expects, unit managers have little to guide their daily operating decisions.

### Motivating Unit Managers

Unit managers are usually motivated to make decisions that will help to achieve top management's expectations. For additional motivation, upper management may offer bonuses to unit managers who meet or exceed performance targets. Top management must exercise extreme care in setting performance targets. For example, a manager measured solely by his or her ability to control costs may take whatever actions are necessary to achieve that goal, including sacrificing quality or customer service. But such actions would *not* be in the best interests of the company as a whole. Therefore, upper management must consider the ramifications of the performance targets it sets for unit managers.

### Providing Feedback

In decentralized companies, top management is no longer involved in the day-to-day operations of each subunit. Performance evaluation systems provide upper management with the feedback it needs to maintain control over the entire organization, even though it has delegated responsibility and decision-making authority to unit managers. If targets are not met at the unit level, upper management will take corrective actions, ranging from modifying unit goals (if the targets are unrealistic) to replacing the unit manager (if the targets are achievable but the manager fails to reach them).

> **Why is this important?**
>
> Performance evaluation systems help managers identify operations that fall short of **company goals**, focusing their attention on what needs to be improved.

### Benchmarking

Performance evaluation results are often used for **benchmarking**, which is the practice of comparing the unit's achievements with other company subunits, other companies in the same industry, the best practices in the industry, or the subunit's past performance. By comparing current results with past performance, managers can assess whether their decisions are improving, having no effect, or adversely affecting subunit performance. However, comparing current results against industry benchmarks is often more revealing than comparing results against budgets or past performance. To survive, a company must keep up with its competitors.

## Limitations of Financial Performance Measurement

In the past, performance evaluation systems revolved almost entirely around *financial* performance. For example, before 1996, most of the performance measures of Nova Scotia Power were financial. On the one hand, this focus makes sense because the ultimate goal of a company is to generate profit. On the other hand, *current* financial performance tends to reveal the results of *past* actions rather than indicate *future* performance. For this reason, financial measures tend to be **lagging indicators** rather than **leading indicators**. Lagging measures reveal the results of past actions, while leading measures project future performance. Management needs to know the results of past decisions, as well as how current decisions may affect the future. To adequately assess the performance of subunits, managers need leading indicators in addition to lagging indicators.

Another limitation of financial performance measures is that they tend to focus on the company's short-term achievements rather than on long-term performance. Why is this the case? Because financial statements are prepared on a monthly, quarterly, or annual basis. To remain competitive, top management needs clear signals that assess and predict the company's performance over longer periods of time.

## The Balanced Scorecard

3 Describe the balanced scorecard, and identify key performance indicators for each perspective.

In the early 1990s, Robert Kaplan and David Norton introduced the balanced scorecard.[1] The balanced scorecard recognizes that management must consider *both* financial performance measures (which tend to measure the results of actions already taken) and operational performance measures (which tend to drive future performance) when judging the performance of a company and its subunits. These measures should be linked with the company's goals and its strategy for achieving those goals.

The balanced scorecard represents a major shift in corporate performance measurement: Financial indicators are no longer the sole measure of performance; they are now only one measure among a broader set of performance measures. For example, Nova Scotia Power adopted the balanced scorecard in 1996. Keeping score of operating measures *and* traditional financial measures gives management a balanced, comprehensive view of the organization.

Kaplan and Norton use the analogy of an airplane pilot to illustrate the necessity for a balanced scorecard approach to performance evaluation. Pilots cannot rely on only one factor, such as wind speed, to fly a plane. Rather, they must consider other critical factors, such as altitude, direction, and fuel level. Likewise, management cannot rely on only financial measures to guide the company. Management needs to consider other critical factors, such as customer satisfaction, operational efficiency, and employee excellence. Similar to the way pilots use cockpit instruments to measure critical factors, management uses **key performance indicators (KPIs)**—such as customer satisfaction ratings and market share—to measure critical factors that affect the success of the company. As shown in Exhibit 11-2, key performance indicators are summary performance measures that help managers assess whether the company is achieving its goals.

**EXHIBIT 11-2** Linking Company Goals to Key Performance Indicators

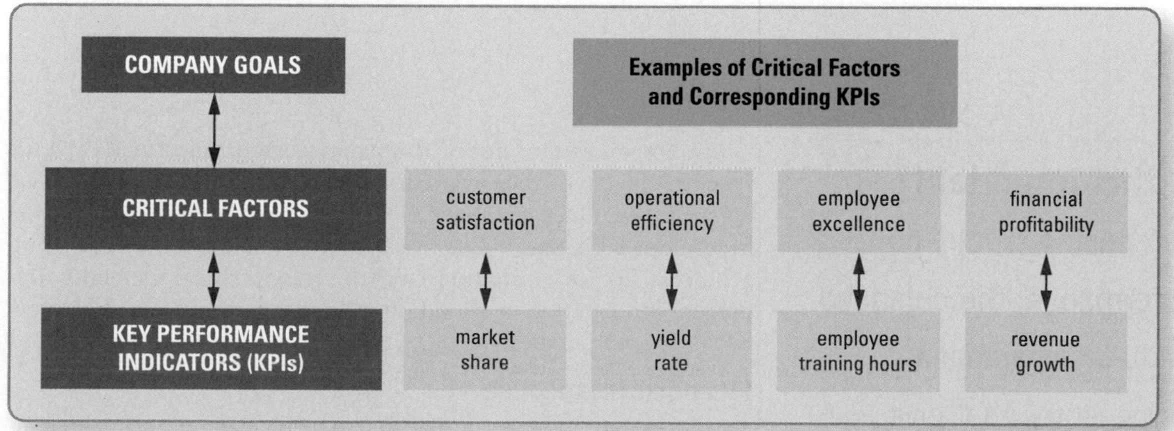


[1]Kaplan, R.S. and D.P. Norton (1992) The Balanced Scorecard: Measures that Drive Performance, *Harvard Business Review*, (January-February): 71–79; Robert Kaplan and David Norton, *Translating Strategy into Action: The Balanced Scorecard* (Boston: Harvard Business School Press, 1996).

## The Four Perspectives of the Balanced Scorecard

The balanced scorecard views the company from four different perspectives, each of which evaluates a specific aspect of organizational performance:

1. Financial perspective
2. Customer perspective
3. Internal business perspective
4. Learning and growth perspective

Exhibit 11-3 illustrates how the company's strategy affects, and in turn is affected by, all four perspectives. In addition, it shows the cause-and-effect relationship linking the four perspectives.

**EXHIBIT 11-3** The Four Perspectives of the Balanced Scorecard

Financial Perspective

Income Statement
Revenue
− Expenses
= Operating income

How do we look to shareholders?

Customer Perspective

How do customers see us?

Company Strategy

Learning and Growth

Employee Training

Can we continue to improve and create value?

Internal Business

At what business processes must we excel?

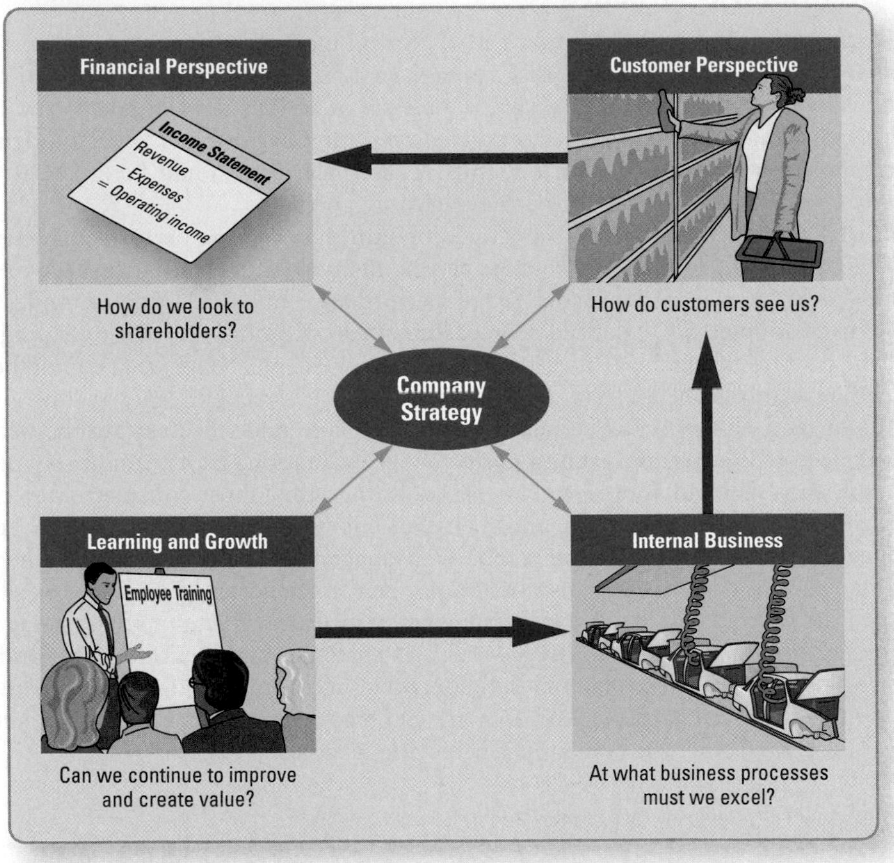

### Why is this important?

Rather than focusing strictly on financial performance, the balanced scorecard includes **operational performance** measures that give managers a holistic view of the company's performance.

Companies that adopt the balanced scorecard usually have specific objectives they want to achieve within each of the four perspectives. Once management clearly identifies the objectives, it develops KPIs that will assess how well the objectives are being achieved. To focus attention on the most critical elements and prevent information overload, management should use only a few KPIs for each perspective.

### Financial Perspective

The financial perspective helps managers answer this question: How do we look to shareholders? The ultimate goal of a for-profit company is to generate income for its owners. Therefore, company strategy revolves around increasing the company's profits through increasing revenue, controlling costs, and increasing productivity.

Companies grow revenue through introducing new products, gaining new customers, and increasing sales to existing customers. At the same time, companies must carefully monitor their costs. Companies increase productivity by using the company's assets more efficiently. For example, CVS, a U.S. drugstore chain, simply changed the direction of its store aisles and lowered its shelves to create a more user-friendly store layout. As a result, profits increased. Managers may implement seemingly sensible strategies and initiatives, but the test of their judgment is whether these decisions increase company profits.

**Financial Perspective**

Financial result and growth

Key financial parameters and performance (ROE, ROCE)

Higher profit margin

Improved cash flow

Lower bad loans and lower debt

Net interest margin

Reduced overhead expenses

Proper revenue mix

The financial perspective focuses management's attention on KPIs that assess financial objectives such as revenue growth and cost cutting. Some commonly used KPIs include sales revenue growth, gross margin growth, and return on investment. Later in the chapter, the most commonly used financial perspective KPIs will be discussed in detail.

### Customer Perspective

The customer perspective helps managers evaluate this question: How do customers see us? Customer satisfaction is a top priority for long-term company success. If customers aren't happy, they won't come back. Therefore, customer satisfaction is critical for the company to achieve its financial goals. Notice in Exhibit 11-3 how the customer perspective influences the financial perspective.

Customers are typically concerned with four specific product or service attributes: (1) the product's price, (2) the product's quality, (3) the sales service quality, and (4) the product's delivery time (the shorter the better). Since each of these attributes is crucial to making the customer happy, most companies have specific targets for each of them.

**Customer Perspective**

Increase customer satisfaction

Increase customer loyalty

Retention of key customers

Sales revenue per customer

Competitive pricing and product offering

High-quality service

Customer preference compared to competitors

Businesses commonly use customer satisfaction ratings to assess how they are performing on these attributes. No doubt you have filled out a customer satisfaction survey. Because customer satisfaction is crucial, customer satisfaction ratings are used often to determine the extent to which bonuses are granted. For example, Toyota service centres frequently conduct surveys with its service customers. The results of these surveys will affect the overall evaluation of the service department for that location. In addition to customer satisfaction ratings, the customer perspective is often measured using KPIs such as percentage of market share, increase in the number of customers, number of repeat customers, and rate of on-time deliveries.

### Internal Business Perspective

The internal business perspective helps managers address this question: At what business processes must we excel to satisfy customer and financial objectives? The answer to that question incorporates three factors: (1) innovation, (2) operations, and (3) post-sales service. All three factors substantially affect customer satisfaction, which will affect the company's financial success, as shown in Exhibit 11-3.

**Internal Business Perspective**

Cross-sell products

Improve operational efficiency and minimize problems

Proper customer relationship management

Higher success rate in converting business opportunities

Fast business decisions and approvals

Proper work culture and higher employee confidence

Satisfying customers once does not guarantee future success, which is why the first important factor of the internal business perspective is innovation. Customers' needs and wants change as the world around them changes. Not all that long ago, digital cameras, flat-panel computer monitors, plasma screen televisions, and digital video recorders (DVRs) did not exist. Companies must continually improve existing products (such as adding cameras to cell phones) and develop new products (such as the iPhone and the Xbox) to succeed in the future. Companies commonly assess innovation using KPIs such as the number of new products developed or new-product development time.

The second important factor of the internal business perspective is operations. Efficient and effective internal operations allow the company to meet customers' needs and expectations. For example, the time it takes to manufacture a product (manufacturing cycle time) affects the company's ability to deliver quickly to meet a customer's demand. Production efficiency (number of units produced per hour) and product quality (defect rate) also affect the price charged to the customer. To remain competitive, companies must be as good as the industry leader at those internal operations that are essential to their businesses.

The third factor of the internal business perspective is post-sales service. Claims of excellent post-sales service help to generate more sales. Management assesses post-sales service through the following typical KPIs: number of warranty claims received, average repair time, and average wait time on the phone for a customer service representative.

### Learning and Growth Perspective

The learning and growth perspective helps managers assess this question: Can we continue to improve and create value? The learning and growth perspective focuses on three factors: (1) employee capabilities, (2) information system capabilities, and (3) the company's "climate for action." As shown in Exhibit 11-3, the learning and growth perspective lays the foundation needed to improve internal business operations, sustain customer satisfaction, and generate financial success. Without skilled employees, updated technology, and a positive corporate culture, the company will not be able to meet the objectives of the other perspectives.

**Learning and Growth Perspective**

Develop critical skills and knowledge
Proper knowledge management
Provide strategic information to all
Align personal goals with company goals
Employee growth and turnover
Employee satisfaction and retention

Because most routine work is automated, employees are free to be critical and creative thinkers who help achieve the company's goals. The learning and growth perspective measures employees' skills, knowledge, motivation, and empowerment. KPIs typically include hours of employee training, employee satisfaction, employee turnover, and number of employee suggestions implemented.

Additionally, employees need timely and accurate information on customers, internal processes, and finances; therefore, other KPIs measure the maintenance and improvement of the company's information system. For example, KPIs might include the percentage of employees having online access to information about customers and the percentage of processes with real-time feedback on quality, cycle time, and cost.

Finally, management must create a corporate culture that supports communication, change, and growth. For example, the Ministry of Health and Long-Term Care uses the balanced scorecard to communicate strategy to all employees and to show them how their daily work contributes to overall success.

In summary, the balanced scorecard focuses performance measurement on progress toward the company's goals in each of the four perspectives. In designing the scorecard, managers start with the company's goals and its strategy for achieving those goals and then identify the most important measures of performance that will predict long-term success. Some of these measures are operational leading indicators, while others are financial lagging indicators. Managers must consider the linkages between strategy and operations and the way those operations will affect finances now and in the future.

So far, we have looked at why companies decentralize, why they need to measure subunit performance, and how the balanced scorecard can help. The second half of the chapter focuses on how companies measure the financial perspective of the balanced scorecard.

# DECISION GUIDELINES

## Performance Evaluation and the Balanced Scorecard

The Ministry of Health and Long-Term Care had to make the following types of decisions when it decentralized and developed its balanced scorecard for performance evaluation.

| Decision | Guidelines |
|---|---|
| How should we decentralize? | The manner of decentralization should fit the organization's strategy. Many companies decentralize based on geographic region, product line, business function, or customer type. |
| What negative factors need to be considered when implementing a decentralization structure? | Decentralization usually provides many benefits; however, decentralization also has potential drawbacks:<br>• Subunits may duplicate costs or assets.<br>• Subunit managers may not make decisions that are favourable to the entire company or consistent with top managers' goals. |
| How can responsibility accounting be incorporated at decentralized companies? | Subunit managers are given responsibility for specific activities and are held accountable only for the results of those activities. Subunits generally fall into one of the following four categories according to their responsibilities:<br>1. **Cost centres**—responsible for controlling costs<br>2. **Revenue centres**—responsible for generating revenue<br>3. **Profit centres**—responsible for controlling costs and generating revenue<br>4. **Investment centres**—responsible for controlling costs, generating revenue, and efficiently managing the division's invested capital (assets) |
| I need to evaluate the activities and behaviours of my managers. How should I do this? | While it is not mandatory, most companies reap many benefits from implementing a well-designed performance evaluation system. Such systems promote goal congruence, communicate expectations, motivate managers, provide feedback, and enable benchmarking. |
| Financial accounting systems typically report on the past. How do I ensure that I have forward-looking evaluation techniques? | Better performance evaluation systems include *both* lagging and leading measures. Lagging measures reveal the results of past actions, while leading measures project future performance. |
| I am preparing to implement a balanced scorecard approach. How do I ensure that I have all essential perspectives covered? | The balanced scorecard should incorporate four perspectives:<br>1. Financial perspective<br>2. Customer perspective<br>3. Internal business perspective<br>4. Learning and growth perspective. |
| I know of another company that has implemented a balanced scorecard. Can this balanced scorecard simply be used for my organization? If not, what is the first step? | Every company's balanced scorecard is unique to its business and strategy; therefore, it is unlikely that one company would be able to use the balanced scorecard from another company. To start the process, managers need to remember that the four perspectives are causally linked; they need to develop performance measures for each of the four perspectives. Quite often this is done through extensive data gathering and surveys, which is the process that the Ministry of Health and Long-Term Care completed. |

# SUMMARY PROBLEM 1

**Requirements**

1. Each of the following describes a key performance indicator. Determine which of the balanced scorecard perspectives is being addressed (financial, customer, internal business, or learning and growth).
   a. Employee turnover
   b. Earnings per share
   c. Percentage of on-time deliveries
   d. Revenue growth rate
   e. Percentage of defects discovered during manufacturing
   f. Number of warranties claimed
   g. New product development time
   h. Number of repeat customers
   i. Number of employee suggestions implemented
2. Read the following company initiatives, and determine which of the balanced scorecard perspectives is being addressed (financial, customer, internal business, or learning and growth).
   a. Purchasing efficient production equipment
   b. Providing employee training
   c. Updating retail store lighting
   d. Paying quarterly dividends
   e. Updating the company's information system

## SOLUTION

**Requirement 1**

a. Learning and growth
b. Financial
c. Customer
d. Financial
e. Internal business
f. Internal business
g. Internal business
h. Customer
i. Learning and growth

**Requirement 2**

a. Internal business
b. Learning and growth
c. Customer
d. Financial
e. Learning and growth

## Sustainability and Performance Evaluation

Companies that embrace sustainability and social responsibility incorporate relevant KPIs in their performance evaluation systems. Some companies will integrate sustainability-related KPIs into the four traditional balanced scorecard perspectives. For example, KPIs for each perspective might include the following:[2]

See Exercises E11-20A and E11-33B

- Financial: *water cost, recycling revenues, waste disposal costs*
- Customer: *number of green products, percentage of products reclaimed after use*
- Internal Business: *energy consumption, water consumption, greenhouse gas emissions*
- Learning and Growth: *number of functions with environmental responsibilities, management attention to environmental issues*

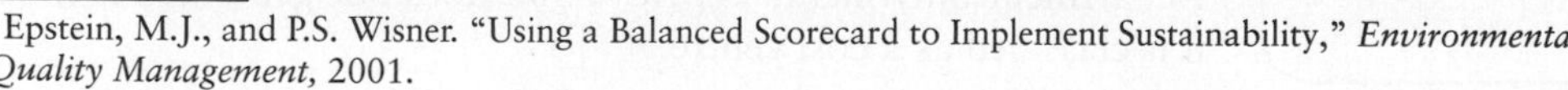

[2] Epstein, M.J., and P.S. Wisner. "Using a Balanced Scorecard to Implement Sustainability," *Environmental Quality Management*, 2001.

Other companies add a fifth perspective, sustainability, or even add a sixth perspective, community, to reflect triple bottom line goals. The sustainability perspective could include any of the examples given in the blue box on the previous page, while the community perspective might include the following:

- Community: *percentage of profit donated to local schools and organizations, percentage of materials sourced locally, product safety ratings, number of hours devoted to local volunteering*

KPIs relating to sustainability and social responsibility should be objective and measurable, with both short-term and long-term targets specified. A long-term outlook is especially important regarding sustainability, since most operational changes related to sustainability require substantial investment in the short run that should result in cost savings in the long run (for example, investing in a fleet of delivery trucks that run on alternative fuels). Baseline measurements should also be taken at the time the targets are adopted, so that managers can determine whether improvements are being made.

The environmental performance metrics also serve as a way for corporations to report their journey toward sustainability to stakeholders. For example, many companies, including Bombardier, Inc., which is recognized for its sustainability commitment by the Dow Jones Sustainability Index, now publish an annual Activity Report in addition to their annual financial report. This report includes financial data for Bombardier Inc. and its subsidiaries as well as updates on societal, environmental, governance, and economic issues that are important to the company. Bombardier, Inc., includes all of this information on its Sustainability Website at www.bombardier.com/en/sustainability.html

## Evaluating the Financial Performance of Cost, Revenue, and Profit Centres

4 Use performance reports to evaluate cost, revenue, and profit centres.

PROFESSIONAL COMPETENCY

Each type of responsibility centre is unique and requires specific and targeted performance measures. Responsibility accounting performance reports capture the financial performance of cost, revenue, and *profit centres*. Recall from Chapter 9 that responsibility accounting performance reports compare *actual* results with *budgeted* amounts and display a variance, or difference, between the two amounts. Because *cost centres* are responsible only for controlling costs, the only information their performance reports include is the actual versus budgeted costs. Likewise, performance reports for *revenue centres* contain only the actual versus budgeted revenue. However, profit centres are responsible for controlling costs and generating revenue. Therefore, performance reports contain actual and budgeted information on both revenues and costs. In addition to the performance report, a cost centre may be evaluated on KPIs such as cost per unit of output.

**Why is this important?**

Performance reports should hold managers responsible only for the **operations** that are directly under their control.

### Cost Centre Performance Reports

Cost centre performance reports typically focus on the *flexible budget variance*—the difference between actual results and the flexible budget (as described in Chapter 10). Exhibit 11-4 shows an example of a cost centre performance report for a regional Payroll Processing Department of House and Garden Depot, a home improvement warehouse chain. Because the Payroll Processing Department only incurs expenses and does not generate revenue, it is classified as a cost centre.

**EXHIBIT 11-4** Examples of Cost Centre Performance Report

HOUSE AND GARDEN DEPOT—QUEBEC REGION
Payroll Processing Department Performance Report
July 2014

| | Actual | Flexible Budget | Flexible Budget Variance (U or F) | % Variance* (U or F) |
|---|---|---|---|---|
| Salary and wages | $ 18,500 | $ 18,000 | $ 500 U | 2.8% U |
| Payroll benefits | 6,100 | 5,000 | 1,100 U | 22.0% U |
| Equipment depreciation | 3,000 | 3,000 | 0 | 0% |
| Supplies | 1,850 | 2,000 | 150 F | 7.5% F |
| Other | 1,900 | 2,000 | 100 F | 5.0% F |
| Total Expenses | $ 31,350 | $ 30,000 | $1,350 U | 4.5% U |

*Flexible budget variance ÷ flexible budget.

Managers use *management by exception* to determine which variances in the performance report are worth investigating. For example, management may investigate only those variances that exceed a certain dollar amount (say, over $1,000) or a certain percentage of the budgeted figure (say, over 10%). Smaller variances signal that operations are close to target and do not require management's immediate attention. For example, in the cost centre performance report illustrated in Exhibit 11-4, management might investigate "payroll benefits" because the variance exceeds $1,000 and 10%. As discussed in Chapter 10, management should investigate favourable as well as unfavourable variances that meet its investigation criteria. Companies that use standard costs can compute price and efficiency variances, as described in Chapter 10, to better understand why significant flexible budget variances occurred.

## Revenue Centre Performance Reports

Revenue centre performance reports often highlight both the flexible budget variance and the sales volume variance. The revenue centre performance report for the Paint Department at House and Garden Depot's Sherbrooke store might look similar to Exhibit 11-5, with detailed sales volume and revenue shown for each brand and type of

**EXHIBIT 11-5** Example of Revenue Centre Performance Report

HOUSE AND GARDEN DEPOT—Sherbrooke Store
Paint Department Performance Report
July 2014

| Sales Revenue | Actual Sales | Flexible Budget Variance | Flexible Budget | Sales Volume Variance | Static (Master) Budget |
|---|---|---|---|---|---|
| Benjamin Moore—Flat: | | | | | |
| Volume (3.6 L cans) | 2,480 | –0– | 2,480 | 155 F | 2,325 |
| Revenue | $40,920 | $3,720 U | $44,640 | $2,790 F | $41,850 |
| Benjamin Moore—Semigloss: | | | | | |
| Volume (3.6 L cans) | | | | | |
| Revenue | | | | | |
| Benjamin Moore—Glossy: | | | | | |
| Volume (3.6 L cans) | | | | | |
| Revenue | | | | | |

paint sold (for simplicity, the exhibit shows volume and revenue for only one item). The cash register bar-coding system provides management with the sales volume and sales revenue generated by individual products.

Recall from Chapter 10 that the sales volume variance is due strictly to volume differences—selling more or fewer units (3.6 L cans of paint) than originally planned. The flexible budget variance, however, is due strictly to differences in the sales price—selling units for a higher or lower price than originally planned. Both the sales volume variance and the flexible budget variance help revenue centre managers understand why they have exceeded or fallen short of budgeted revenue. In addition to the performance report, revenue centres may be evaluated on KPIs such as revenue growth percentage for different product lines.

## Profit Centre Performance Reports

Managers of profit centres are responsible for generating revenue and controlling costs, so their performance reports include both revenues and expenses. Exhibit 11-6 shows an example of a profit centre performance report for the Sherbrooke House and Garden Depot store.

**EXHIBIT 11-6** Example of Profit Centre Performance Report

HOUSE AND GARDEN DEPOT
Sherbrooke Store—Performance Report
July 2014

| | Actual | Flexible Budget | Flexible Budget Variance | % Variance |
|---|---|---|---|---|
| Sales revenue | $ 5,243,600 | $ 5,000,000 | $ 243,600 F | 4.9% F |
| Operating expenses | 4,183,500 | 4,000,000 | 183,500 U | 4.6% U |
| Income from operations before service department charges | 1,060,100 | 1,000,000 | 60,100 F | 6.0% F |
| Service department charges (allocated) | 84,300 | 75,000 | 9,300 U | 12.4% U |
| Income from operations | $ 975,800 | $ 925,000 | $ 50,800 F | 5.5% F |

Notice how this profit centre performance report contains the line "Service department charges." Recall that one drawback of decentralization is that subunits may duplicate costs or assets. Many companies avoid this problem by providing centralized service departments for which several subunits, such as profit centres, share assets or costs.

For example, the payroll processing cost centre shown in Exhibit 11-4 serves all of the House and Garden Depot stores in the Quebec region. In addition to centralized payroll departments, companies often provide centralized human resource departments, legal departments, and information systems.

When subunits share centralized services, should those services be "free" to the subunits? If they are free, the subunits' performance reports will not include any charge for using those services. However, if they are not free, the performance reports will show a charge, as you see in Exhibit 11-6. Most companies charge subunits for their use of centralized services because the subunit would otherwise have to buy those services on its own. For example, if House and Garden Depot didn't operate a Centralized Payroll Department, the Sherbrooke store would have to hire its own payroll department personnel and purchase any computers, payroll software, and supplies necessary to process the store's payroll.

As an alternative, it could outsource payroll to a company such as Payworks or ADP Canada. In either event, the store would incur a cost for processing payroll. It only seems fair that the store is charged for using the Centralized Payroll Processing Department. In addition, subunits tend to use centralized services more judiciously when they are charged for using the services. Appendix 11A describes how companies allocate service department costs between subunits. Because the charges are the result of allocation rather than a direct cost of the profit centre, they are usually shown on a separate line rather than "buried" in the subunit's other operating expenses.

Exhibit 11-7 shows the basic decisions management must make regarding centralized service departments.

**EXHIBIT 11-7** Centralized Services Decision Tree

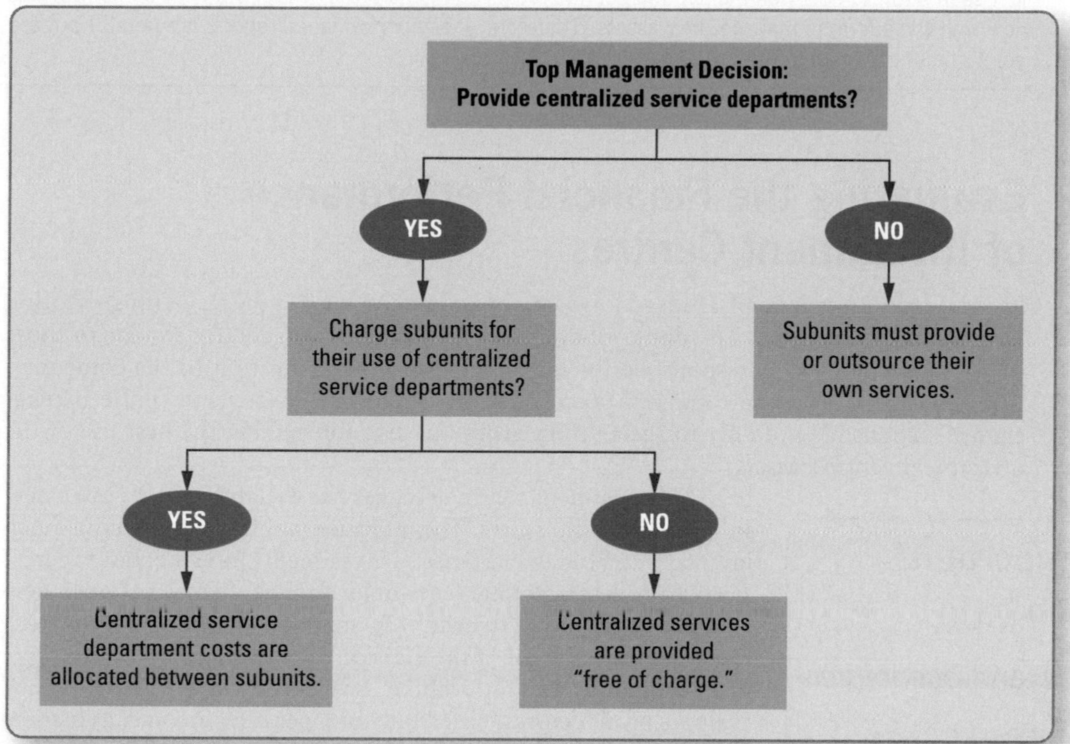


Regardless of the type of responsibility centre, performance reports should focus on information, not blame. Analyzing budget variances helps managers understand the underlying reasons for the unit's performance. Once management understands these reasons, it may be able to take corrective actions. But some variances are uncontrollable. For example, the 1998 ice storm in Quebec and Eastern Ontario increased the price of building materials (as people repaired homes damaged from fallen trees) and the price of utilities. For the maple syrup industry, the significant damage to maple trees resulted in increased syrup prices for many years following the storm. These price increases resulted in unfavourable cost variances for many companies. Managers should not be responsible for conditions they cannot control. Responsibility accounting can help management identify the causes of variances, thus allowing it to determine what was controllable and what was not.

We have just looked at the *detailed* financial information presented in responsibility accounting performance reports. In addition to these detailed reports, upper management often uses *summary* measures—financial KPIs—to assess the financial performance and address the financial perspective of the balanced scorecard of cost, revenue, and profit centres. Examples of these KPIs include the cost per unit of output (for cost centres), revenue growth (for revenue centres), and gross margin growth (for profit centres). In the next section, we'll look at the most commonly used KPIs for *investment centres*.

## STOP & THINK

We have just seen that companies like House and Garden Depot use responsibility accounting performance reports to evaluate the financial performance of cost, revenue, and profit centres. Are these types of performance reports sufficient for evaluating the financial performance of investment centres? Why or why not?

**Answer:** Investment centres are responsible not only for generating revenue and controlling costs but also for efficiently managing the subunit's invested capital. The performance reports we have just seen address how well the subunits control costs and generate revenue, but they do not address how well the subunits manage their assets. Therefore, these performance reports are helpful but are not sufficient for evaluating investment centre performance.

PROFESSIONAL COMPETENCY

# Evaluating the Financial Performance of Investment Centres

5 Use return on investment (ROI), residual income (RI), and economic value added (EVA) to evaluate investment centres.

Investment centres are typically large divisions of a company, such as the Rail Transportation Division of Bombardier. The duties of an investment centre manager are similar to those of a CEO. The CEO is responsible for maximizing income in relation to the company's invested capital by using company assets efficiently. Likewise, investment centre managers are responsible not only for generating profit but also for making the best use of the investment centre's assets.

**Why is this important?**

*Return on investment (ROI), residual income (RI),* and *economic value added (EVA)* measure how well large **company divisions** are using their assets to generate profit.

An investment centre manager has the authority to open new stores or close old stores. The manager may also decide how much inventory to hold, what types of investments to make, how aggressively to collect accounts receivable, and whether to invest in new equipment. In other words, the manager has decision-making responsibility over all of the division's assets.

Companies cannot evaluate investment centres the way they evaluate profit centres, based only on operating income, as income does not indicate how *efficiently* the division is using its assets. The financial evaluation of investment centres must measure two factors: (1) how much income the division is generating and (2) how efficiently the division is using its assets.

Consider House and Garden Depot. In addition to its home improvement warehouse stores, House and Garden Depot operates a Landscaping Division and a Design Division. Operating income, total assets, and sales for the two divisions follow (in thousands of dollars):

| House and Garden Depot | Landscaping Division | Design Division |
|---|---|---|
| Operating income | $ 450,000 | $ 600,000 |
| Total assets | 2,500,000 | 4,000,000 |
| Sales | 7,500,000 | 10,000,000 |

Based on operating income alone, the Design Division (with operating income of $600,000) appears to be more profitable than the Landscaping Division (with operating income of $450,000). However, this comparison is misleading because it does not consider the assets invested in each division. The Design Division has more assets to use for generating income than does the Landscaping Division.

To adequately evaluate an investment centre's financial performance, companies need summary performance measures—or KPIs—that include *both* the division's operating income *and* its assets. In the next sections, we discuss three commonly used performance measures: return on investment (ROI), residual income (RI), and economic value added (EVA). As shown in Exhibit 11-8, all three measures incorporate both the division's assets and its operating income. For simplicity, we will leave the word *divisional* out of the equations. However, keep in mind that all of the equations use divisional data when evaluating a division's performance.

**EXHIBIT 11-8** Summary Performance Measures (KPIs) for Investment Centres

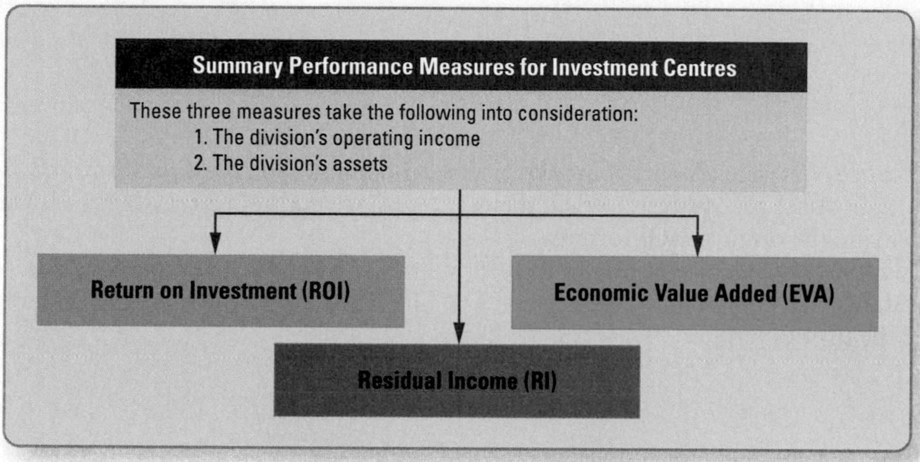


## Return on Investment (ROI)

Return on investment (ROI) is one of the most commonly used KPIs for evaluating an investment centre's financial performance. Companies typically define ROI as follows:

$$\text{ROI} = \frac{\text{Operating income}}{\text{Total assets}}$$

ROI measures the amount of income an investment centre earns relative to the size of its assets. Let's calculate each division's ROI:

$$\text{Landscaping Division ROI} = \left(\frac{\$450{,}000}{\$2{,}500{,}000}\right) = 18\%$$

$$\text{Design Division ROI} = \left(\frac{\$600{,}000}{\$4{,}000{,}000}\right) = 15\%$$

Although the Design Division has a higher operating income than the Landscaping Division, the Design Division is actually *less* profitable than the Landscaping Division when we consider that the Design Division has more assets from which to generate its profit.

The Design Division earns a profit of \$0.15 on every \$1.00 of assets, but the Landscaping Division earns \$0.18 on every \$1.00 of assets. When top management decides how to invest excess funds, it often considers each division's ROI. A division with a higher ROI is more likely to receive extra funds because it has a track record of providing a higher return.

In addition to comparing ROI across divisions, management compares a division's ROI across time to determine whether the division is becoming more or less profitable in relation to its assets. In addition, management often benchmarks divisional ROI with other companies in the same industry to determine how each division is performing compared with its competitors.

To determine what is driving a division's ROI, management often restates the ROI equation in its expanded form:

$$\text{ROI} = \frac{\text{Operating income}}{\text{Sales}} \times \frac{\text{Sales}}{\text{Total assets}} = \frac{\text{Operating income}}{\text{Total assets}}$$

Notice that sales is incorporated in the denominator of the first term and in the numerator of the second term. When the two terms are multiplied together, sales cancels out, leaving the original ROI formula.

Why do managers rewrite the ROI formula this way? Because it helps them better understand how they can improve their ROI. The first term in the expanded equation is called the **profit margin**:

$$\text{Profit margin} = \frac{\text{Operating income}}{\text{Sales}}$$

The profit margin shows how much operating income the division earns on every \$1 of sales, so this term focuses on profitability.

$$\text{Landscaping Division's profit margin} = \left(\frac{\$450{,}000}{\$7{,}500{,}000}\right) = 6\%$$

$$\text{Design Division's profit margin} = \left(\frac{\$600{,}000}{\$10{,}000{,}000}\right) = 6\%$$

Both the Landscaping Division and the Design Division have a profit margin of 6%, meaning that both divisions earn a profit of \$0.06 on every \$1.00 of sales.

If both divisions have identical profit margins, why do their ROIs differ (18% for Landscaping versus 15% for Design)? The answer is found in the second term of the expanded ROI equation, **asset turnover**:

$$\text{Asset turnover} = \frac{\text{Sales}}{\text{Total assets}}$$

Asset turnover shows how efficiently a division uses its assets to generate sales. Rather than focusing on profitability, asset turnover focuses on efficiency.

$$\text{Landscaping Division's asset turnover} = \left(\frac{\$7{,}500{,}000}{\$2{,}500{,}000}\right) = 3$$

$$\text{Design Division's asset turnover} = \left(\frac{\$10{,}000{,}000}{\$4{,}000{,}000}\right) = 2.5$$

The Landscaping Division has an asset turnover of 3. This means that the Landscaping Division generates $3 of sales with every $1 of assets. The Design Division's asset turnover is only 2.5. The Design Division generates only $2.50 of sales with every $1.00 of assets. The Landscaping Division uses its assets more efficiently in generating sales than does the Design Division.

The two terms can be combined in the expanded ROI equation:

| | Profit margin | × | Asset turnover | = | ROI |
|---|---|---|---|---|---|
| Landscaping Division: | 6% | × | 3 | = | 18% |
| Design Division: | 6% | × | 2.5 | = | 15% |

As you can see, the expanded ROI equation gives management more insight into the division's ROI. Management can now see that both divisions are equally profitable on their sales (6%), but the Landscaping Division is doing a better job of generating sales with its assets than is the Design Division. Consequently, the Landscaping Division has a higher ROI.

If a manager is not satisfied with the division's asset turnover rate, how can the manager improve it? He or she might try to eliminate nonproductive assets—for example, by being more aggressive in collecting accounts receivable or decreasing inventory levels. The manager might decide to change the layout of retail stores to generate sales. Recall that CVS successfully increased sales just by lowering shelves and changing the direction of the aisles.

What if management is not satisfied with the current profit margin? To increase the profit margin, management must increase the operating income earned on every dollar of sales. Management may cut product costs or selling and administrative costs, but it needs to be careful when trimming costs. Cutting costs in the short term can hurt long-term ROI. For example, sacrificing quality or cutting back on research and development could decrease costs in the short run but may hurt long-term sales. The balanced scorecard helps management carefully consider the consequences of cost-cutting measures before acting on them.

ROI has one major drawback. Evaluating division managers based solely on ROI gives them an incentive to adopt *only* projects that maintain or increase their current ROI. Assume that top management of House and Garden Depot has set a company-wide target ROI of 16%. Both divisions are considering investing in in-store video display equipment that shows customers how to use featured products. This equipment will increase sales because customers are more likely to buy the products after they see these infomercials. The equipment would cost each division $100,000 and is expected to provide each division with $17,000 of annual income. The *equipment's* ROI is as follows:

$$\text{Equipment ROI} = \frac{\$17{,}000}{\$100{,}000} = 17\%$$

Upper management wants the divisions to invest in this equipment since the equipment will provide a 17% ROI, which is higher than the 16% target rate. But what will the managers of the divisions do? Because the Design Division currently has an ROI of 15%, the new equipment (with its 17% ROI) will *increase* the division's *overall* ROI. Therefore, the Design Division manager will buy the equipment. However, the Landscaping Division currently has an ROI of 18%. If the Landscaping Division invests in the equipment, its *overall* ROI will *decrease*. Therefore, the manager of the Landscaping Division will probably turn down the investment. In this case, goal congruence is *not* achieved—only one division invests in equipment. Yet, top management wants both divisions to invest in the equipment because the equipment return exceeds the 16% target ROI.

## Residual Income (RI)

**Residual income (RI)** is another commonly used KPI for evaluating an investment centre's financial performance. Essentially, RI looks at whether the division has created any excess (or residual) income above and beyond management's expectations. Similar to ROI, RI incorporates the division's operating income and its total assets, thereby measuring the division's profitability and the efficiency with which it uses its assets. RI also incorporates another piece of information: top management's target rate of return (such as the 16% target return in the previous example). The target rate of return is the minimum acceptable rate of return that top management expects a division to earn with its assets. Management's target rate of return is based on many factors—for example, the risk level of the division's business, interest rates, investor's expectations, return being earned by other divisions, and general economic conditions. Since these factors change over time, management's target rate of return may also change over time.

RI compares the division's operating income with the minimum operating income that top management expects *given the size of the division's assets.* A positive RI means that the division's operating income exceeds top management's target rate of return. A negative RI means the division is not meeting the target rate of return. Let's look at the RI equation and calculate the RI for both divisions of House and Garden Depot using the 16% target rate of return from the previous example.

RI = Operating income − Minimum acceptable income

In this equation, the minimum acceptable income is defined as top management's target rate of return multiplied by the division's total assets. Thus,

RI = Operating income − (Target rate of return × Total assets)

The residual income for the Landscaping Division is

Landscaping Division RI = \$450,000 − (16% × \$2,500,000)
= \$450,000 − \$400,000
= \$50,000

The positive RI indicates that the Landscaping Division exceeded top management's 16% target return expectations. The RI calculation also confirms what we learned about the Landscaping Division's ROI: It is 18%, which is higher than the targeted 16%.

The RI for the Design Division is

Design Division RI = \$600,000 − (16% × \$4,000,000)
= \$600,000 − \$640,000
= (\$40,000)

The Design Division's RI is negative. This means that the Design Division did not use its assets as effectively as top management expected. Recall that the Design Division's ROI of 15% fell short of the target rate of 16%.

Why would a company prefer to use RI over ROI for performance evaluation? The answer is that RI is more likely to lead to goal congruence than is ROI. Let's once again consider the video display equipment that both divisions could buy. In both divisions, the equipment is expected to generate a 17% return. If the divisions are evaluated based on ROI, the Design Division will buy the equipment because doing so will increase the division's ROI. The Landscaping Division will probably not buy the equipment because doing so will lower the division's ROI.

However, if management evaluates divisions based on RI rather than ROI, what will the divisions do? The answer depends on whether the project yields a positive or negative RI. Recall that the equipment would cost each division $100,000 but would provide $17,000 of operating income each year. The RI provided by *just* the equipment would be as follows:

$$\begin{aligned}\text{Equipment RI} &= \$17{,}000 - (\$100{,}000 \times 16\%)\\ &= \$17{,}000 - \$16{,}000\\ &= \$1{,}000\end{aligned}$$

If purchased, this equipment will *improve* each division's current RI by $1,000. As a result, both divisions will be motivated to invest in the equipment. Goal congruence is achieved because both divisions take the action that top management desires. That is, both divisions invest in the equipment.

Another benefit of RI is that management may set different target returns for different divisions. For example, management might require a higher target rate of return from a division operating in a riskier business environment. If the design industry were riskier than the landscape industry, top management might decide to set a higher target return—perhaps 17%—for the Design Division.

**TRY IT!**

Quaker Foods North America is one of PepsiCo's divisions. For the most recent fiscal year-end, the division had assets of $966 million, operating income of $695 million, and sales revenue of $2,636 million.

1. Computer Quaker's ROI, sales margin, and capital turnover.
2. Computer Quaker's residual income, assuming the minimum acceptable rate of return is 25%.

Please see page 718 for solution.

## Economic Value Added (EVA)

**Economic value added (EVA)** is a special type of RI calculation. Unlike the RI calculation we've just discussed, EVA looks at a division's RI through the eyes of the company's primary stakeholders: its investors and long-term creditors (such as bondholders). Since these stakeholders provide the company's capital, management often wants to evaluate how efficiently a division is using its assets from these two stakeholders' viewpoints. EVA calculates RI for these stakeholders by specifically considering the following:

1. The income available to these stakeholders
2. The assets used to generate income for these stakeholders
3. The minimum rate of return required by these stakeholders, referred to as the **weighted average cost of capital (WACC)**

Let's compare the EVA equation with the RI equation and then look at the differences in more detail:

$$\text{RI} = \text{Operating income} - (\text{Total assets} \times \text{Target rate of return})$$

$$\text{EVA} = \text{After-tax operating income} - [(\text{Total assets} - \text{Current liabilities}) \times \text{WACC\%}]$$

Both equations calculate whether the division created any income above and beyond expectations. They do this by comparing actual income with the minimum acceptable income. But note the differences in the EVA calculation:

1. The EVA calculation uses after-tax operating income, which is the income left over after income taxes are subtracted. Why? Because the portion of income paid to the government is not available to investors and long-term creditors.
2. Total assets are reduced by current liabilities. Why? Because funds owed to short-term creditors, such as suppliers (accounts payable) and employees (wages payable), will be paid in the immediate future and will not be available for generating income in the long run. The division is not expected to earn a return for investors and long-term creditors on funds that will soon be paid out to short-term creditors.
3. The WACC replaces management's target rate of return. Since EVA focuses on investors and creditors, it's *their* expected rate of return that should be used, not management's expected rate of return. The WACC, which represents the minimum rate of return that investors and long-term creditors expect, is based on the company's cost of raising capital from both groups of stakeholders. The riskier the business, the higher the expected return. Detailed WACC computations are discussed in advanced accounting and finance courses.

In summary, EVA incorporates elements of RI from the perspective of investors and long-term creditors. To calculate EVA for the Landscape and Design Divisions, the following additional information is needed:

| | |
|---|---|
| Effective income tax rate | 30% |
| WACC | 13% |
| Landscaping Division's current liabilities | $150,000 |
| Design Division's current liabilities | $250,000 |

A 30% effective income tax rate means that the government takes 30% of the company's income, leaving only 70% to the company's stakeholders. Therefore, we calculate after-tax operating income by multiplying the division's operating income by 70%, or (100% - effective tax rate of 30%).

EVA = After-tax operating income − [(Total assets − Current liabilities) × WACC%]

Landscaping Division EVA = ($450,000 × 70%) − [($2,500,000 − $150,000) × 13%]
= $315,000 − ($2,350,000) × 13%)
= $315,000 − $305,500
= $9,500

Design Division EVA = ($600,000 × 70%) − [($4,000,000 − $250,000) × 13%]
= $420,000 − ($3,750,000) × 13%)
= $420,000 − $487,500
= ($67,500)

These EVA calculations show that the Landscaping Division has generated income in excess of expectations for its investors and long-term debtholders, whereas the Design Division has not.

Many firms, such as Coca-Cola, measure the financial performance of their investment centres using EVA. EVA promotes goal congruence, just as RI does. In addition, EVA looks at the income generated by the division in excess of expectations solely from the perspective of investors and long-term creditors. Therefore, EVA specifically addresses the financial perspective of the balanced scorecard that asks the question: How do we look to shareholders?

Exhibit 11-9 summarizes the three performance measures and some of their advantages.

**EXHIBIT 11-9** Three Investment Centre Performance Measures: A Summary

**ROI:**

| | |
|---|---|
| Equation | $\text{ROI} = \frac{\text{Operating income}}{\text{Sales}} \times \frac{\text{Sales}}{\text{Total assets}} = \frac{\text{Operating income}}{\text{Total assets}}$ |
| Advantages | • The expanded equation provides management with additional information on profitability and efficiency<br>• Management can compare ROI across divisions and with other companies<br>• ROI is useful for resource allocation |

**RI:**

| | |
|---|---|
| Equation | RI = Operating income − (Total assets × Target rate of return) |
| Advantages | • Promotes goal congruence better than ROI<br>• Incorporates management's minimum required rate of return<br>• Management can use different target rates of return for divisions with different levels of risk |

**EVA:**

| | |
|---|---|
| Equation | EVA = (After-tax operating income) − [(Total assets − Current liabilities) × WACC%] |
| Advantages | • Considers income generated for investors and long-term creditors in excess of their expectations<br>• Promotes goal congruence |

## Limitations of Financial Performance Measures

We have just finished looking at three KPIs (ROI, RI, and EVA) commonly used to evaluate the financial performance of investment centres. The ROI, RI, and EVA calculations appear to be very straightforward; however, management must make some decisions before these calculations can be made. For example, all three equations use the term *total assets*. Recall that total assets is a balance sheet figure, which means that it is a snapshot at any given point in time. Because the total assets figure will be different at the beginning of the period than at the end of the period, many companies choose to use a simple average of the two figures in their ROI, RI, and EVA calculations.

Management must also decide if it really wants to include *all* assets in the total assets figure. Many firms frequently buy land on which to build future retail outlets. Until those stores are built and opened, the land (including any construction in progress) is a nonproductive asset, one that does not add to the company's operating income. Including nonproductive assets in the total asset figure drives down the ROI, RI, and EVA figures. Therefore, some firms do not include nonproductive assets in these calculations.

### Basis of Valuation

Another asset measurement issue is whether to use the gross book value of assets (the historical cost of the assets) or the net book value of assets (historical cost less accumulated depreciation). Many firms use the net book value of assets because the figure is consistent with and easily pulled from the balance sheet. Because depreciation expense factors into the firm's operating income, the net book value concept is consistent with the measurement of operating income. However, using the net book value of assets has a definite drawback. Over time, the net book value of assets decreases because accumulated depreciation continues to grow until the assets are fully depreciated. Therefore, ROI, RI, and EVA increase over time simply because of depreciation rather than from actual improvements in operations. In addition, the rate of this depreciation effect depends on the depreciation method used.

In general, calculating ROI based on the net book value of assets gives managers incentive to continue using old, outdated equipment because its low net book value results in a higher ROI. However, top management may want the division to invest in new technology to create operational efficiency (internal business perspective of the balanced scorecard) or to enhance its information systems (learning and growth perspective). The long-term effects of using outdated equipment may be devastating as competitors begin to use new technology to produce cheaper products and sell at lower prices. Thus, to create goal congruence, some firms prefer calculating ROI based on the gross book value of assets or even based on their current replacement cost. The same general rule holds true for RI and EVA calculations: All else being equal, using the net book value will increase RI and EVA over time.

### Short-Term Focus

One serious drawback of financial performance measures is their short-term focus. Companies usually prepare performance reports and calculate ROI, RI, and EVA figures using a time frame of one year or less. If upper management uses a short time frame, division managers have an incentive to take actions that will lead to an immediate increase in these measures, even if such actions may not be in the company's long-term interest (such as cutting back on R&D or advertising). On the other hand, it may take longer than one year for some potentially positive actions to generate income at the targeted level. Many **product life cycles** start slowly, even incurring losses in the early stages before generating profit. If managers are measured on short-term financial performance only, they may not introduce new products because they are not willing to wait several years for the positive effect to show up in their financial performance measures.

As a potential remedy, management can measure financial performance using a longer time horizon, such as three to five years. Extending the time frame gives subunit managers the incentive to think long term rather than short term and make decisions that will positively affect the company over the next several years.

The limitations of financial performance measures confirm the importance of the balanced scorecard. The deficiencies of financial measures can be overcome by taking a broader view of performance—including KPIs from all four balanced scorecard perspectives, both quantitative and qualitative measures—rather than concentrating only on the financial measures.

# DECISION GUIDELINES

## Performance Evaluation and the Balanced Scorecard

The focus for the Ministry of Health and Long-Term Care's balanced scorecard is on nonfinancial indicators for priorities such as the quality of patient care. However, because it is the ministry with the largest expense budget in Ontario, accountability is essential for the continuing effectiveness of the organization. Therefore, the financial perspective of the balanced scorecard is used and applicable for this organization, especially for the Private Hospitals (even though they receive public funding as well). When the Ontario hospitals developed the financial perspective of their balanced scorecard, they would have had to make decisions such as these.

| Decision | Guidelines |
|---|---|
| I need to evaluate the financial performance of the division for which I am responsible. How do I decide which evaluation tools will be most effective? | Responsibility accounting performance reports measure the financial performance of cost, revenue, and profit centres. These reports typically highlight the variances between budgeted and actual performance. Investment centres require measures that take into account the division's operating income and the division's assets. Typical measures include the following:<br>• Return on investment (ROI)<br>• Residual income (RI)<br>• Economic value added (EVA) |
| Should I incorporate ROI in my evaluation? | ROI is calculated as follows:<br>ROI = Operating income ÷ Total assets<br>By including ROI in the evaluation, you receive a measure of the amount of income earned by a division relative to the size of its assets—the higher, the better. |
| Should I use the regular ROI formula or the ROI formula in its expanded form? | In its expanded form, ROI is written as follows:<br>ROI = Profit margin × Asset turnover<br>where<br>Profit margin = Operating income ÷ Sales<br>Asset turnover = Sales ÷ Total assets<br>Profit margin focuses on profitability (the amount of income earned on every dollar of sales), while asset turnover focuses on efficiency (the amount of sales generated with every dollar of assets). Therefore, by using the expanded formula, you are able to discover specific elements that are doing well or need improvement. |
| Should I incorporate the RI calculation in my evaluation? | RI is calculated by the following formula:<br>RI = Operating income − (Target rate of return × Total assets)<br>By including RI, you can discover if the division is earning income at a rate that exceeds management's minimum expectations (i.e., if the result is positive). This can help eliminate the instances of having a division manager foregoing an investment that would benefit the organization as a whole while not increasing the division's ROI. |
| Should I include EVA in my evaluation? | The calculation for EVA is as follows:<br>EVA = After-tax operating income − [(Total assets − Current liabilities) × WACC%]<br>EVA is a special type of RI calculation that focuses on the income (in excess of expectations) the division created for two specific stakeholders: investors and long-term creditors. Therefore, EVA enables an organization to look at itself from the perspective of outside stakeholders. |
| When calculating ROI, RI, or EVA, what, if any, measurement issues are of concern? | **1.** What date should be used to measure the assets? Many firms use the average balance of total assets rather than the beginning or ending balance of assets.<br>**2.** Should the net book value or gross book value of the assets be used? If the net book value of assets is used to measure total assets, ROI, RI, and EVA will "artificially" rise over time due to the depreciation of the assets. Using gross book value to measure total assets eliminates this measurement issue. |

# SUMMARY PROBLEM 2

Assume that House and Garden Depot expects each division to earn a 16% target rate of return. House and Garden Depot's weighted average cost of capital (WACC) is 13%, and its effective tax rate is 30%. Assume that the company's original Retail Division had the following results last year (in millions of dollars):

| | |
|---|---|
| Operating income | $ 1,450 |
| Total assets | 16,100 |
| Current liabilities | 3,600 |
| Sales | 26,500 |

### Requirements

1. Compute the Retail Division's profit margin, asset turnover, and ROI. Round your results to three decimal places. Interpret the results in relation to the Landscaping and Design Divisions discussed in the chapter.
2. Compute and interpret the Retail Division's RI.
3. Compute the Retail Division's EVA. What does this tell you?
4. What can you conclude based on all three financial performance KPIs?

## ▪ SOLUTION

### Requirement 1

| ROI = | Profit margin | × | Asset turnover |
|---|---|---|---|
| | = (Operating income ÷ Sales) | × | (Sales ÷ Total assets) |
| | = ($1,450 ÷ $26,500) | × | ($26,500 ÷ $16,100) |
| | = 0.091 | × | 1.646 |

The original Retail Division is far from meeting top management's expectations. Its ROI is only 9.1%. The profit margin (5.5%) is slightly lower than those of the Landscaping and Design Divisions (6% each), but the asset turnover (1.646) is much lower than those of the other divisions (3.0 and 2.5). This means that the original Retail Division is not generating sales from its assets as efficiently as the Landscaping and Design Divisions. Division management needs to consider ways to increase the efficiency of its use of divisional assets.

### Requirement 2

| RI = | Operating income | − | (Target rate of return × Total assets) |
|---|---|---|---|
| | = $1,450 | − | (16% × $16,100) |
| | = $1,450 | − | $2,576 |
| | = ($1,126) | | |

The negative RI confirms the ROI results: The division is not meeting management's target rate of return.

**Requirement 3**

$$
\begin{aligned}
\text{EVA} &= \text{After-tax operating income} &&- [(\text{Total assets} - \text{Current liabilities}) \times \text{WACC\%}] \\
&= (\$1{,}450 \times 70\%) &&- [(\$16{,}100 - \$3{,}600) \times 13\%] \\
&= \$1{,}015 &&- \$1{,}625 \\
&= (\$610)
\end{aligned}
$$

The negative EVA means that the division is not generating income for investors and long-term creditors at the rate that these stakeholders desire.

**Requirement 4**

All three investment centre performance measures (ROI, RI, and EVA) point to the same conclusion: The original Retail Division is not meeting financial expectations. Either top management and stakeholders' expectations are unrealistic or the division is not *currently* performing up to par. Recall, however, that financial performance measures tend to be lagging indicators—measuring the results of decisions made in the past. The division's managers may currently be implementing new initiatives to improve the division's future profitability. Leading indicators should be used to project whether such initiatives are pointing the company in the right direction.

# APPENDIX 11A

## Allocating Service Department Costs

How do companies charge subunits for their use of service departments? For example, suppose House and Garden Depot incurs $30,000 per month to operate the Quebec Region's centralized Payroll Department. To simplify the illustration, let's assume that the region has only three stores: Sherbrooke, Montreal, and Quebec City. How should the company split, or allocate, the $30,000 cost among the three stores? Splitting the cost equally—charging each store $10,000—may not be fair, especially if the three units don't use the services equally.

Ideally, the company should allocate the $30,000 based on each subunit's use of centralized payroll services. The company should use the primary activity that drives the cost of central payroll services as the allocation base. As you may recall from Chapter 7, companies identify cost drivers when they implement activity based costing (ABC). Thus, a company that has already implemented ABC should know what cost drivers would be suitable for allocating service department charges. For example, payroll processing cost may be driven by the number of employee payroll cheques or direct deposits processed. The cost driver chosen for allocating the $30,000 might be the number of employees at each store, as shown in the following table.

| Subunits Sharing Central Payroll Services | Number of Employees (allocation base) | Percentage of Total Employees | Service Department Charge ($30,000 × %) |
|---|---|---|---|
| Sherbrooke | 100 | 25% | $ 7,500 |
| Montreal | 140 | 35% | 10,500 |
| Quebec City | 160 | 40% | 12,000 |
| Total | 400 | 100% | $30,000 |

Most companies use some type of usage-related cost driver to allocate service department costs. The following table lists additional centralized services and common allocation bases.

| Centralized Service Departments | Typical Allocation Base |
|---|---|
| Human resources | Number of employees |
| Legal | Number of hours spent on legal matters |
| Travel | Number of business trips booked |

However, when usage data are not available or are too costly to collect, companies resort to allocating service department costs based on each subunit's ability to bear the cost. In such cases, companies allocate the service department cost based on the relative amount of revenue or operating income each subunit generates. This type of allocation is like a tax: The higher the subunit's income, the higher the charge. The following table illustrates this type of allocation.

| Subunits Sharing Central Payroll Services | Unit Operating Income Before Service Department Charges | Percentage of Total Operating Income | Service Department Charge ($30,000 × %) |
|---|---|---|---|
| Sherbrooke | $ 320,000 | 20% | $ 6,000 |
| Montreal | 480,000 | 30% | 9,000 |
| Quebec City | 800,000 | 50% | 15,000 |
| Total | $1,600,000 | 100% | $30,000 |

Even usage-related allocation systems have limitations. What if the cost of running the service department is fixed rather than variable? In that case, much of the cost cannot be attributed to a specific cost driver. In our payroll example, suppose $20,000 of the total $30,000 is straight-line depreciation on the equipment and software. Should the company still use the number of employees to allocate the entire $30,000 of cost? As another example, suppose the Sherbrooke store downsizes and its relative percentage of employees drops from 25% to 10% while the number of employees in each of the other two stores stays constant. If that happens, the Montreal and Quebec City stores will be charged higher costs even though they did nothing to cause an increase. These are just two examples of how the best allocation systems are still subject to inherent flaws. The process of producing segmented statements was covered in Chapter 3 (Appendix 3B) and discussed an alternative to allocating all of the common costs of the service department(s).

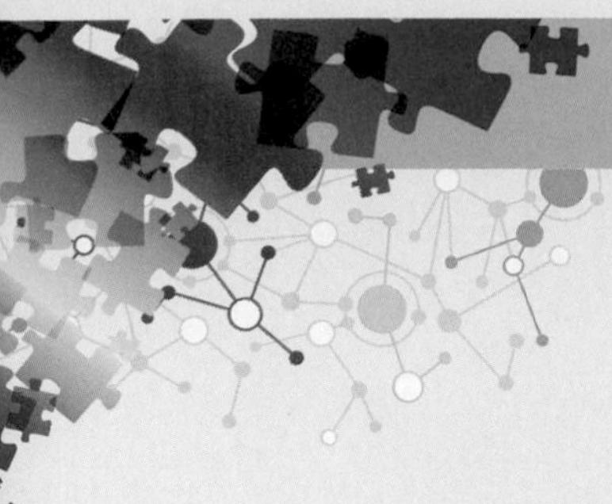

# END OF CHAPTER

## LEARNING OBJECTIVES

1 Explain why and how companies decentralize.

2 Explain why companies use performance evaluation systems.

3 Describe the balanced scorecard, and identify key performance indicators for each perspective.

4 Use performance reports to evaluate cost, revenue, and profit centres.

5 Use return on investment (ROI), residual income (RI), and economic value added (EVA) to evaluate investment centres.

## ACCOUNTING VOCABULARY

**Asset Turnover (p. 684)** The amount of sales revenue generated for every dollar of invested assets; a component of the ROI calculation computed as sales divided by total assets.

**Balanced Scorecard (p. 668)** Measures that recognize that management must consider financial performance measures and operational performance measures when judging the performance of a company and its subunits.

**Benchmarking (p. 670)** Comparing actual performance to similar companies in the same industry, to other divisions, or to world-class standards.

**Centralized (p. 668)** Refers to companies in which all major planning and operating decisions are made by top management.

**Decentralized (p. 669)** Refers to companies that are segmented into smaller operating units; unit managers make planning and operating decisions for their units.

**Economic Value Added (EVA) (p. 687)** A residual income measure calculating the amount of income generated by the company or its divisions in excess of shareholders' and long-term creditors' expectations.

**Goal Congruence (p. 669)** Aligning the goals of subunit managers with the goals of top management.

**Key Performance Indicators (KPIs) (p. 671)** Summary performance measures that help managers assess whether the company is achieving its long-term and short-term goals.

**Lagging Indicators (p. 671)** Performance measures that indicate past performance.

**Leading Indicators (p. 671)** Performance measures that forecast future performance.

**Product Life Cycle (p. 690)** The length of time between a product's initial development and its discontinuance in the market.

**Profit Margin (p. 684)** The amount of income earned on every dollar of sales; a component of the ROI calculation computed as operating income divided by sales.

**Residual Income (RI) (p. 686)** A measure of profitability and efficiency computed as the excess of actual income over a specified minimum acceptable income.

**Return on Investment (ROI) (p. 683)** A measure of profitability and efficiency computed as operating income divided by total assets.

**Weighted Average Cost of Capital (WACC) (p. 687)** The company's cost of capital; the target rate of return used in EVA calculations to represent the return that investors and long-term creditors expect.

# QUICK CHECK

1. (Learning Objective 1) Which is *not* one of the potential advantages of decentralization?
   a. Improves customer relations
   b. Increases goal congruence
   c. Improves motivation and retention
   d. Supports use of expert knowledge
2. (Learning Objective 1) The Day & Ross Transportation Division of McCain is most likely treated as a(n)
   a. cost centre.
   b. revenue centre.
   c. profit centre.
   d. investment centre.
3. (Learning Objective 1) Decentralization is often based on all of the following *except*
   a. geographic region.
   b. product line.
   c. revenue size.
   d. business function.
4. (Learning Objective 2) Which of the following is *not* a reason for a company to use a performance evaluation system?
   a. Controlling assets
   b. Communicating expectations
   c. Motivating managers
   d. Providing feedback
5. (Learning Objective 3) Manufacturing yield rate (number of units produced per unit of time) would be a typical measure for which of the following balanced scorecard perspectives?
   a. Financial
   b. Customer
   c. Internal business
   d. Learning and growth
6. (Learning Objective 3) Which of the following balanced scorecard perspectives essentially asks the question, "Can we continue to improve and create value?"
   a. Financial
   b. Customer
   c. Internal business
   d. Learning and growth
7. (Learning Objective 4) The performance evaluation of a cost centre is typically based on its
   a. sales volume variance.
   b. ROI.
   c. flexible budget variance.
   d. static budget variance.
8. (Learning Objective 5) Which of the following is a disadvantage of financial performance measures such as return on investment (ROI), residual income (RI), and economic value added (EVA)?
   a. Not readily understood by managers
   b. Focus on short-term performance
   c. Cannot be used in a balanced scorecard
   d. Cannot be used to evaluate division performance
9. (Learning Objective 5) Which performance measurement tool is most likely to cause goal incongruence between division managers and the corporate headquarters?
   a. Return on investment (ROI)
   b. Residual income
   c. Economic value added (EVA)
   d. Balanced scorecard
10. (Learning Objective 5) For which type of responsibility centre would it be appropriate to measure performance using return on investment (ROI)?
    a. Cost centre
    b. Revenue centre
    c. Profit centre
    d. Investment centre



**Quick Check Answers**

1. *b* 2. *d* 3. *c* 4. *a* 5. *c* 6. *d* 7. *c* 8. *b* 9. *a* 10. *d*

# SHORT EXERCISES

**S11-1 Explain how and why companies decentralize** *(Learning Objective 1)*

Explain why companies decentralize. Describe some typical methods of decentralization.

**S11-2 Give advice about decentralization** *(Learning Objective 1)*

Grandma Jones's Cookie Company sells homemade cookies made with organic ingredients. Her sales are strictly Web-based. The business is exceeding Grandma Jones's expectations, with orders coming in from consumers and corporate event planners across the country. Even by employing a full-time baker and a Web designer, Grandma Jones can no longer handle the business on her own. She wants your advice on whether she should decentralize and, if so, how she should do it. Explain some of the advantages and disadvantages of decentralization, and offer her three ways she might decentralize her company.

**S11-3 Describe each type of responsibility centre** *(Learning Objective 1)*

Most decentralized subunits can be described as one of four types of responsibility centres. List the four most common types of responsibility centres, and describe their responsibilities.

**S11-4 Classify types of subunits** *(Learning Objective 1)*

Each of the following managers has been given certain decision-making authority. Classify each manager according to the type of responsibility centre he or she manages.

1. Manager of Holiday Inn's central reservation office
2. Managers of various corporate-owned Holiday Inn locations
3. Manager of the Holiday Inn Corporate Division
4. Manager of the Housekeeping Department at a Holiday Inn
5. Manager of the Holiday Inn Express Corporate Division
6. Manager of the complimentary breakfast buffet at a Holiday Inn Express

**S11-5 Goals of performance evaluation systems** *(Learning Objective 2)*

Well-designed performance evaluation systems accomplish many goals. State which goal is being achieved by the following actions:

a. Comparing targets to actual results
b. Providing subunit managers with performance targets
c. Comparing actual results with industry standards
d. Providing bonuses to subunit managers who achieve performance targets
e. Aligning subunit performance targets with company strategy
f. Comparing actual results to the results of competitors
g. Using the adage "you get what you measure" when designing the performance evaluation system

**S11-6 Classify KPIs by balanced scorecard perspective** *(Learning Objective 3)*

Classify each of the following key performance indicators according to the balanced scorecard perspective it addresses. Choose from financial perspective, customer perspective, internal business perspective, or learning and growth perspective.

a. Number of employee suggestions implemented
b. Revenue growth
c. Number of on-time deliveries
d. Percentage of sales force with access to real-time inventory levels
e. Customer satisfaction ratings
f. Number of defects found during manufacturing
g. Number of warranty claims
h. ROI

**S11-7 Classify KPIs by balanced scorecard perspective** *(Learning Objective 3)*

Classify each of the following key performance indicators according to the balanced scorecard perspective it addresses. Choose from financial perspective, customer perspective, internal business perspective, or learning and growth perspective.

a. Variable cost per unit
b. Percentage of market share
c. Number of hours of employee training
d. Number of new products developed
e. Yield rate (number of units produced per hour)
f. Average repair time
g. Employee satisfaction
h. Number of repeat customers

**S11-8 Describe management by exception** *(Learning Objective 4)*

Describe management by exception and how it is used in the evaluation of cost, revenue, and profit centres.

**S11-9 Assess profitability** *(Learning Objective 5)*

Which of the following corporate divisions is more profitable? Explain.

| | Domestic | International |
|---|---|---|
| Operating income | $ 8 million | $10 million |
| Total assets | $24 million | $35 million |

**BlueHill Data Set used for S11-10 through S11-14:**

BlueHill Company makes snowboards, downhill skis, cross-country skis, skateboards, surfboards, and in-line skates. The company has found it beneficial to split operations into two divisions based on the climate required for the sport: Snow Sports and Non-Snow Sports. The following divisional information is available for the past year:

| | Sales | Operating Income | Total Assets | Current Liabilities |
|---|---|---|---|---|
| Snow Sports | $5,000,000 | $800,000 | $4,000,000 | $350,000 |
| Non-Snow Sports | 9,000,000 | 1,440,000 | 6,000,000 | 600,000 |

BlueHill management has specified a target 15% rate of return. The company's weighted average cost of capital (WACC) is 12%, and its effective tax rate is 35%.

**S11-10 Calculate ROI** *(Learning Objective 5)*

Refer to the BlueHill data set.

1. Calculate each division's ROI.
2. Top management has extra funds to invest. Which division will most likely receive those funds? Why?
3. Can you explain why one division's ROI is higher? How could management gain more insight?

**S11-11 Compute profit margin** *(Learning Objective 5)*

Refer to the BlueHill data set. Compute each division's profit margin. Interpret your results.

**S11-12 Continuation of S11-10 and S11-11: asset turnover** *(Learning Objective 5)*

Refer to the BlueHill data set.

1. Compute each division's asset turnover (round to two decimal places). Interpret your results.
2. Use your answers to Question 1 along with your answers to S11-11 to recalculate ROI using the expanded formula. Do your answers agree with your ROI calculations in S11-10?

**S11-13 Compute RI** *(Learning Objective 5)*

Refer to the BlueHill data set. Compute each division's RI. Interpret your results. Are your results consistent with each division's ROI?

**S11-14 Compute EVA** *(Learning Objective 5)*

Refer to the BlueHill data set. Compute each division's EVA. Interpret your results.

# EXERCISES Group A

**E11-15A Identify centralized and decentralized organizations** *(Learning Objective 1)*

Following is a series of descriptions of organizations. Indicate whether each scenario is more typical of a decentralized organization or a centralized organization.

a. Lawrence Company has a policy of promoting from within the company whenever possible. It has formal training programs for lower-level managers.
b. Balayet Corporation is divided into several operating units.

c. Two Turtles is a small independent store in Lethbridge, Alberta. The owner is also the manager of the store.

d. The managers at Veeson Company have been given the authority to make decisions about product offerings and pricing because Veeson Company wants its managers to be able to respond quickly to changes in local market demand.

e. Bobbins Crafts, Inc., empowers its managers to make decisions so that the managers' motivation is increased and retention of managers increases.

f. Duplication of services caused the Baroud Company to "flatten" its organization structure. The Baroud Company now has a single Payroll Department, a single Human Resources Department, and a single administrative headquarters.

g. The Plastic Lumber Company, Inc., is managed by its owner, who oversees production, sales, engineering, and the other administrative functions.

### E11-16A Identify the type of responsibility centre *(Learning Objective 1)*

Each of the following situations describes an organizational unit. Identify the type of responsibility centre of the italicized part in each item (cost, revenue, profit, or investment centre).

a. *Benjamin Moore Store #1933* is located in Grand Forks, B.C. The store sells paints, wallpapers, and supplies to do-it-yourself customers and to professional wall covering installers.

b. The *Accounting Research and Compliance Department* at FirstEnergy is responsible for researching how new accounting pronouncements and rules will affect FirstEnergy's financial statements.

c. The *North American Sales Region* of McCain Foods is responsible for selling the various product lines of McCain.

d. The *Taxation Department* at Bell Canada is responsible for preparing the federal, provincial, and local income and franchise tax returns for the corporation.

e. The *Roseville Chipotle Restaurant* in Toronto is owned by its parent Chipotle Mexican Grill, Inc. The Roseville Chipotle, like other Chipotle restaurants, serves burritos, fajitas, and tacos and competes in the "fast-casual" dining category.

f. *Trek Bicycle Corporation* manufactures and distributes bicycles and cycling products under the Trek, Gary Fisher, Bontrager, and Klein brand names.

g. *Rogers' Chocolates* is one of the oldest chocolate companies in Canada. Its product lines include chocolate and caramel sauces, chocolate gift baskets, and High Tea chocolate bars.

h. The *Human Resources Department* is responsible for recruiting and training for The Bay.

i. The *reservations office* for Air Canada is responsible for both Web sales and counter sales.

j. The *Disney Store* at the West Edmonton Mall is owned by The Walt Disney Company.

k. H & R Block Tax Services, H & R Block Bank, and RSM McGladrey are all divisions of their parent corporation, *H & R Block*.

### E11-17A Differentiate between lagging and leading indicators *(Learning Objective 2)*

Explain the difference between lagging and leading indicators. Are financial performance measures typically referred to as lagging or leading indicators? Explain, using Le Château as an example. Are operational measures (such as customer satisfaction ratings, defect rate, and number of on-time deliveries) typically referred to as lagging or leading indicators? Explain using Le Château as an example.

### E11-18A Construct a balanced scorecard *(Learning Objective 3)*

Sarvan Corporation is preparing its balanced scorecard for the past quarter. The balanced scorecard contains four perspectives: financial, customer, internal business process, and learning and growth. Through its strategic management planning process, Sarvan Corporation has selected two specific objectives for each of the four perspectives. These are listed in the following table.

| Specific Objective |
| --- |
| Improve post-sales service |
| Increase market share |
| Increase profitability of core product line |
| Improve employee job satisfaction |
| Increase sales of core product line |
| Develop new core products |
| Improve employee product knowledge |
| Increase customer satisfaction |

Sarvan Corporation has collected key performance indicators (KPIs) to measure progress toward achieving its specific objectives. The following table contains the KPIs and corresponding data that Sarvan Corporation has collected for the past quarter.

| KPI | Goal | Actual |
| --- | --- | --- |
| Core product line profit as a percentage of core product line sales | 15 % | 13 % |
| Market share percentage | 17 % | 18 % |
| Number of new core products | 15 | 21 |
| Customer satisfaction rating (1–5, with 1 being most satisfied) | 1.3 | 1.2 |
| Hours of employee training provided | 2,200 | 2,350 |
| Average repair time (number of days) | 1.0 | 1.4 |
| Sales revenue growth—Core product line | $ 2,000,000 | $ 2,200,000 |
| Employee turnover rate (number of employees leaving company/number of total employees) | 5 % | 7 % |

**Requirement**

1. Prepare a balanced scorecard report for Sarvan Corporation, using the following format.

**Sarvan Corporation**
**Balance Scoreboard Report**
**For Quarter Ended December 31**

| Perspective | Objective | KPI | Goal | Actual | Goal Achieved? (√ if met) |
| --- | --- | --- | --- | --- | --- |
| Financial | | | | | |
| Customer | | | | | |
| Internal Business Process | | | | | |
| Learning and Growth | | | | | |

Place each of the specific objectives listed under the appropriate perspective heading in the report. Select a KPI from the list of KPIs that would be appropriate to measure progress toward each objective. (There are two specific objectives for each perspective and one KPI for each of the specific objectives.) In the last column in the balanced scorecard report, place a checkmark if the associated KPI goal has been achieved.

CHAPTER 11

**E11-19A Classify KPIs by balanced scorecard perspective** *(Learning Objective 3)*

Classify each of the following key performance indicators according to the balanced scorecard perspective it addresses. Choose from financial perspective, customer perspective, internal business perspective, or learning and growth perspective.

a. Number of customer complaints
b. Number of information system upgrades completed
c. Economic value added (EVA)
d. New product development time
e. Employee turnover rate
f. Percentage of products with online help manuals
g. Customer retention
h. Percentage of compensation based on performance
i. Percentage of orders filled each week
j. Gross margin growth
k. Number of new patents
l. Employee satisfaction ratings

**E11-20A Sustainability and the balanced scorecard** *(Learning Objective 3)*

Classify each of the following sustainability key performance indicators (KPIs) according to the balanced scorecard perspective it addresses. Choose from the following five perspectives:

- Financial perspective
- Customer perspective
- Internal business perspective
- Learning and growth perspective
- Community perspective

**KPI**

a. Revenue from recycling packaging materials
b. Total litres of water used
c. Number of sustainability training hours
d. Number of employee hours devoted to local volunteering
e. Charitable contributions as a percent of income
f. Customer survey rating company's green reputation
g. Number of employees on sustainability teams
h. Cubic metres of natural gas used for heating facilities
i. Total megawatt hours of electricity purchased
j. Percentage of bottles and cans sold recovered through company-supported recovery programs
k. Cost of water used
l. Indirect greenhouse gas emissions from electricity purchased and consumed
m. Number of functions with environmental responsibilities
n. Number of green products
o. Percentage of profit donated to local schools
p. Volume of Global Greenhouse Gas (GHG) emissions
q. Waste disposal costs
r. Percentage of products reclaimed after customer use

## E11-21A Complete and analyze a performance report *(Learning Objective 4)*

One subunit of BlueHill Company had the following financial results last month:

Check sum: Flexible budget variance of materials is $1,500 U.

| BlueHill—Subunit X | Actual | Flexible Budget | Flexible Budget Variance (U or F) | % Variance* (U or F) |
|---|---|---|---|---|
| Direct materials | $ 21,500 | $ 20,000 | | |
| Direct labour | 14,250 | 15,000 | | |
| Indirect labour | 29,250 | 25,000 | | |
| Utilities | 10,950 | 10,000 | | |
| Depreciation | 25,000 | 25,000 | | |
| Repairs and maintenance | 4,200 | 5,000 | | |
| Total | $105,150 | $100,000 | | |

**Flexible budget variance ÷ Flexible budget*

### Requirements

1. Complete the performance evaluation report for this subunit (round to four decimals).
2. Based on the data presented, what type of responsibility centre is this subunit?
3. Which items should be investigated if part of management's decision criteria is to investigate all variances exceeding $3,000 or 10%?
4. Should only unfavourable variances be investigated? Explain.

## E11-22A Complete and analyze a performance report *(Learning Objective 4)*

The accountant for a subunit of BlueHill Company went on vacation before completing the subunit's monthly performance report. This is as far as she got:

| BlueHill—Subunit X Revenue by Product | Actual | Flexible Budget Variance | Flexible Budget | Sales Volume Variance | Static (Master) Budget |
|---|---|---|---|---|---|
| Downhill | | | | | |
| Model RI | $ 326,000 | | | $20,000 (F) | $ 300,000 |
| Model RII | 155,000 | | $165,000 | | 150,000 |
| Cross-Country | | | | | |
| Model EXI | 283,000 | $2,000 (U) | 285,000 | | 300,000 |
| Model EXII | 252,000 | | 245,000 | 17,500 (U) | 262,500 |
| Snowboard | | | | | |
| Model LXI | 425,000 | 5,000 (F) | | | 400,000 |
| Total | $1,441,000 | | | | $1,412,500 |

### Requirements

Check sum: Sales volume variance for Downhill model RI is $20,000 F.

1. Complete the performance evaluation report for this subunit.
2. Based on the data presented, what type of responsibility centre is this subunit?
3. Which items should be investigated if part of management's decision criteria is to investigate all variances exceeding $15,000? Interpret your results. (What could cause these variances? What impact might these variances have on company inventory levels and operations?)

## E11-23A Compute and interpret the expanded ROI equation *(Learning Objective 5)*

Benchmark, Home Hardware's manufacturing division of lawn-mowing and snowblowing equipment, segments its business according to customer type: Professional and Residential. The following divisional information was available for the past year:

Check sum: ROI for professional is 44%.

| | Sales | Operating Income | Total Assets | Current Liabilities |
|---|---|---|---|---|
| Residential | $ 635,500 | $ 63,500 | $205,000 | $ 70,000 |
| Professional | $1,031,250 | $165,000 | $375,000 | $150,000 |

Assume that management has a 25% target rate of return for each division. Also, assume that Benchmark's weighted average cost of capital is 15% and its effective tax rate is 30%.

### Requirements

Round all of your answers to four decimal places.

1. Calculate each division's ROI.
2. Calculate each division's profit margin. Interpret your results.
3. Calculate each division's asset turnover. Interpret your results.
4. Use the expanded ROI formula to confirm your results from Requirement 1. What can you conclude?

## E11-24A Compute RI and EVA *(Learning Objective 5)*

Check sum: Professional RI is $71,250.

Refer to the data about Benchmark in E11-23A.

### Requirements

1. Calculate each division's RI. Interpret your results.
2. Calculate each division's EVA. Interpret your results.
3. Describe the conceptual and computational similarities and differences between RI and EVA.



## E11-25A Find the relationship between ROI and RI *(Learning Objective 5)*

Data on three unrelated companies are given in the following table.

Check sum: Asset turn-over for Alston company is 1.5.

| | Alston Company | Baxter Industries | Calloway Inc. |
|---|---|---|---|
| Sales | $120,000 | ? | $500,000 |
| Operating income | $ 40,000 | $120,000 | ? |
| Total assets | $ 80,000 | ? | ? |
| Profit margin | ? | 15 % | 10% |
| Asset turnover | ? | 5.00 | ? |
| Return on investment (ROI) | ? | ? | 25% |
| Target rate of return | 10% | 20 % | ? |
| Residual income | ? | ? | $ 12,000 |

### Requirement

1. Fill in the missing information in the preceding table.

## E11-26A Compute ROI, RI, and EVA *(Learning Objective 5)*

Results from First Corporation's most recent year of operations are presented in the following table.

| | |
|---|---|
| Operating income | $ 9,000 |
| Total assets | $15,000 |
| Current liabilities | $ 4,000 |
| Sales | $36,000 |
| Target rate of return | 15% |
| Weighted average cost of capital | 12% |
| Tax rate | 30% |

Check sum: Req. 1 ROI is 60%.

### Requirements

1. Calculate the profit margin, asset turnover, and return on investment (ROI).
2. Calculate the residual income.
3. Calculate the economic value added (EVA).

## E11-27A Comparison of ROI and RI *(Learning Objective 5)*

Hawkins Ceramics, a division of Piper Corporation, has an operating income of $64,000 and total assets of $400,000. The required rate of return for the company is 12%. The company is evaluating whether it should use ROI or RI as a measurement of performance for its division managers.

The manager of Hawkins Ceramics has the opportunity to undertake a new project that will require an investment of $100,000. This investment would earn $14,000 for Hawkins Ceramics.

Check sum: Req. 1 ROI is 16%.

### Requirements

1. What is the original ROI for Hawkins Ceramics (before making any additional investment)?
2. What would the ROI be for Hawkins Ceramics if this investment opportunity were undertaken? Would the manager of the Hawkins Ceramics division want to make this investment if she were evaluated based on ROI? Why or why not?
3. What is the ROI of the investment opportunity? Would the investment be desirable from the standpoint of Piper Corporation? Why or why not?
4. What would the RI be for Hawkins Ceramics if this investment opportunity were undertaken? Would the manager of the Hawkins Ceramics division want to make this investment if she were evaluated based on RI? Why or why not?
5. What is the RI of the investment opportunity? Would the investment be desirable from the standpoint of Piper Corporation? Why or why not?
6. Which performance measurement method, ROI or RI, promotes goal congruence? Why?



# EXERCISES Group B

## E11-28B Identify centralized and decentralized organizations *(Learning Objective 1)*

Following is a series of descriptions of organizations. Indicate whether each scenario is more typical of a decentralized organization or a centralized organization.

a. Fulton Holdings wants its managers to be able to respond quickly to changes in local market demand, so the managers have been given the authority to make decisions about product offerings and pricing.

b. Craft Supplies & More is a small independent craft shop and is managed by its owner.

c. Didic Corporation now has a single Payroll Department, a single Human Resources Department, and a single administrative headquarters since Didic Corporation "flattened" its organizational structure.

d. Khan Resorts and Hotels, Inc., empowers its managers to make decisions so that the managers' motivation is increased and retention of managers increases.

e. Tse Corporation has formal training programs for lower-level managers and has a policy of promoting from within the company whenever possible.
f. The Plastic Lumber Company, Inc., is managed by its owner, who oversees production, sales, engineering, and the other administrative functions.
g. Daniels Furniture, Inc., is divided into several operating units.

### E11-29B Identify the type of responsibility centre *(Learning Objective 1)*

Each of the following situations describes an organizational unit. Identify the type of responsibility centre of each item in italics (cost, revenue, profit, or investment centre).

a. *The Goodyear Tire & Rubber Company* is one of the oldest tire companies in the world. Its geographic regions include North America, Europe, Africa, South America, Asia, and Australia.
b. The *Pasta Group Account Team* of Maple Leaf Foods is responsible for sales and servicing for the Sobey's, No Frills, and Costco accounts.
c. The Fairmont Banff Springs, The Fairmont Royal York in Toronto, and The Fairmont Le Château Frontenac are all hotels owned by their parent corporation, *Fairmont Hotels & Resorts*.
d. *Cow's Prince Edward Island* is located in Charlottetown. The store sells a variety of company products, while the café offers its ice cream and dairy bar products.
e. The *3M Company* manufactures and distributes products under the Post-it, Scotch, Nexcare, and Thinsulate brands.
f. The *Chapters* bookstore in Kelowna, B.C., is owned by its parent, Indigo Books and Music, Inc. The Kelowna bookstore, like other Chapters bookstores, sells books, magazines, music CDs, coffee, and a variety of other items.
g. The *Human Resources Department* at Hallmark Canada is responsible for hiring and training new associates.
h. *The Bay* store in the Place d'Orleans Shopping Centre in Ottawa is owned by the Hudson Bay Company.
i. The *Information Systems Department* is responsible for designing, installing, and servicing the information systems throughout Kohl's Corporation.
j. The *reservation office* for WestJet is responsible for both Web sales and counter sales.
k. In addition to other accounting duties, the *Financial Reporting and Control & Analysis Department* at RBC Insurance is responsible for performing a monthly analysis of general ledger accounts and fluctuations as a control mechanism.



### E11-30B Differentiate between lagging and leading indicators *(Learning Objective 2)*

Explain the difference between lagging and leading indicators. Are financial performance measures typically referred to as lagging or leading indicators? Explain, using BlackBerry (a manufacturer of mobile communication devices such as BlackBerry smartphones) as an example. Are operational measures (such as customer satisfaction ratings, defect rate, and number of on-time deliveries) typically referred to as lagging or leading indicators? Explain, again using BlackBerry as an example.

### E11-31B Construct a balanced scorecard *(Learning Objective 3)*

Byrne Corporation is preparing its balanced scorecard for the past quarter. The balanced scorecard contains four perspectives: financial, customer, internal business process, and learning and growth. Through its strategic management planning process, Byrne Corporation has selected two specific objectives for each of the four perspectives. These are listed in the following table.

| Specific Objectives |
|---|
| 1. Improve post-sales service |
| 2. Increase number of customers |
| 3. Increase gross margin |
| 4. Improve employee morale |
| 5. Increase profitability of core product line |
| 6. Increase plant safety |
| 7. Improve employee job satisfaction |
| 8. Increase customer retention |

Byrne Corporation has collected key performance indicators (KPIs) to measure progress toward achieving its specific objectives. The following table contains the KPIs and corresponding data that Byrne Corporation has collected for the past quarter.

| KPI | Goal | Actual |
|---|---|---|
| Gross margin growth percentage | 24 % | 23 % |
| Number of customers | 130,000 | 135,000 |
| Number of plant accidents | 1 | 3 |
| Number of repeat customers | 105,000 | 98,000 |
| Employee turnover rate (number of employees leaving/number of total employees) | 6 % | 9 % |
| Average repair time (number of days) | 1.2 | 1.1 |
| Core product line profit as a percentage of core product line sales | 18 % | 12 % |
| Employee satisfaction survey (1–5, with 1 as most satisfied) | 1.7 | 1.9 |

**Requirement**

1. Prepare a balanced scorecard report for Byrne Corporation, using the following format:

**Performance Evaluation and the Balanced Scorecard**

**Byrne Corporation**
**Balanced Scorecard Report**
**For Quarter Ended December 31**

| Perspective | Objective | KPI | Goal | Actual | Goal Achieved? (√ if met) |
|---|---|---|---|---|---|
| Financial | | | | | |
| Customer | | | | | |
| Internal Business Process | | | | | |
| Learning and Growth | | | | | |

Place each of the specific objectives listed under the appropriate perspective heading in the report. Select a KPI from the list of KPIs that would be appropriate to measure progress toward each objective. (There are two specific objectives for each perspective and one KPI for each of the specific objectives.) In the last column in the balanced scorecard report, place a checkmark if the associated KPI goal has been achieved.

### E11-32B Classify KPIs by balanced scorecard perspective *(Learning Objective 3)*

Classify each of the following key performance indicators according to the balanced scorecard perspective it addresses. Choose from financial perspective, customer perspective, internal business perspective, or learning and growth perspective.

a. Manufacturing cycle time (average length of production process)
b. Earnings growth
c. Average machine setup time
d. Number of new customers
e. Employee promotion rate
f. Cash flow from operations
g. Customer satisfaction ratings
h. Machine downtime
i. Finished products per day per employee
j. Percentage of employees with access to upgraded system
k. Wait time per order prior to start of production
l. Asset turnover

### E11-33B Sustainability and the balanced scorecard *(Learning Objective 3)*

Classify each of the following sustainability key performance indicators (KPIs) according to the balanced scorecard perspective it addresses. Choose from the following five perspectives:

- Financial perspective
- Customer perspective
- Internal business perspective
- Learning and growth perspective
- Community perspective

a. KPI
b. Product safety ratings
c. Total mega joules of energy used
d. Number of functions with environmental responsibilities
e. Percentage of recycled content in products
f. Revenue from recycling packaging materials
g. Cost of water used
h. Direct greenhouse gas emissions
i. Waste disposal costs
j. Number of employee hours devoted to volunteering at Habitat for Humanity
k. Percent of bottles and cans sold recovered through company-supported recovery programs
l. Percentage of products sourced locally
m. Percent of plants in compliance with internal wastewater treatment standards
n. Number of sustainability training hours
o. Number of employees on sustainability teams
p. Percentage of products reclaimed after customer use
q. Number of green products
r. Packaging use ratio defined as grams of materials used per litre of product produced
s. Customer survey rating company's green reputation

### E11-34B Complete and analyze a performance report *(Learning Objective 4)*

One subunit of Speed Sports Company had the following financial results last month:

Check sum: Total flexible budget variance is $5,235 U.

| Speed—Subunit X | Actual | Flexible Budget | Flexible Budget Variance (U or F) | % Variance (U or F) |
|---|---|---|---|---|
| Direct materials | $ 12,930 | $12,000 | | |
| Direct labour | 13,265 | 14,000 | | |
| Indirect labour | 23,380 | 20,000 | | |
| Utilities | 16,455 | 15,000 | | |
| Depreciation | 30,250 | 30,250 | | |
| Repairs and maintenance | 4,205 | 6,000 | | |
| Total | $100,485 | $97,250 | | |

**Requirements**

1. Complete the performance evaluation report for this subunit (round to four decimals).
2. Based on the data presented, what type of responsibility centre is this subunit?
3. Which items should be investigated if part of management's decision criteria is to investigate all variances exceeding $2,900 or 11%?
4. Should only unfavourable variances be investigated? Explain.

### E11-35B Complete and analyze a performance report *(Learning Objective 4)*

The accountant for a subunit of Speed Sports Company went on vacation before completing the subunit's monthly performance report. This is as far as she got:

| Speed—Subunit X Revenue by Product | Actual | Flexible Budget Variance | Flexible Budget | Sales Volume Variance | Static (Master) Budget |
|---|---|---|---|---|---|
| Downhill | | | | | |
| Model RI | $ 324,000 | | | $ 19,000 (F) | $ 301,000 |
| Model RII | 152,000 | | $162,000 | | 145,000 |
| Cross-Country | | | | | |
| Model EXI | 289,000 | $3,000 (U) | 292,000 | | 308,000 |
| Model EXII | 255,000 | | 248,000 | 20,500 (U) | 268,500 |
| Snowboard | | | | | |
| Model LXI | 423,000 | 4,000 (F) | | | 401,000 |
| Total | $1,443,000 | | | | $1,423,500 |

**Requirements**

Check sum: Downhill model RI sales volume variance is $19,000 F.

1. Complete the performance evaluation report for this subunit.
2. Based on the data presented, what type of responsibility centre is this subunit?
3. Which items should be investigated if part of management's decision criteria is to investigate all variances exceeding $16,000? Interpret your results. (What could cause these variances? What impact might these variances have on company inventory levels and operations?)

### E11-36B Compute and interpret the expanded ROI equation *(Learning Objective 5)*

Zuds, a national manufacturer of lawn-mowing and snowblowing equipment, segments its business according to customer type: Professional and Residential. The following divisional information was available for the past year (in thousands of dollars):

| | Sales | Operating Income | Total Assets | Current Liabilities |
|---|---|---|---|---|
| Residential | $ 925,000 | $ 64,750 | $185,000 | $ 76,000 |
| Professional | $1,794,000 | $179,400 | $390,000 | $165,000 |

Management has a 26% target rate of return for each division. Zuds' weighted average cost of capital is 17%, and its effective tax rate is 32%.

Check sum: Req. 1 Professional ROI is 46%.

**Requirements**

1. Calculate each division's ROI. Round all of your answers to four decimal places.
2. Calculate each division's profit margin. Interpret your results.
3. Calculate each division's asset turnover. Interpret your results.
4. Use the expanded ROI formula to confirm your results from Requirement 1. What can you conclude?

### E11-37B Compute RI and EVA *(Learning Objective 5)*

Refer to the data about Zuds in E11-36B.

**Requirements**

Check sum: Req. 1 Residential RI is $16,650.

1. Calculate each division's RI. Interpret your results.
2. Calculate each division's EVA. Interpret your results.
3. Describe the conceptual and computational similarities and differences between RI and EVA.

### E11-38B Relationship between ROI and RI *(Learning Objective 5)*

Data on three unrelated companies are given in the following table.

Check sum: Asset turnover for Sesnie is 2.9.

| | Juda Company | Gammaro Industries | Sesnie Inc. |
|---|---|---|---|
| Sales | $108,000 | ? | $522,000 |
| Operating income | $ 43,200 | $117,900 | ? |
| Total assets | $ 72,000 | ? | ? |
| Profit margin | ? | 15 % | 10% |
| Asset turnover | ? | 4.80 | ? |
| Return on investment (ROI) | ? | ? | 29% |
| Target rate of return | 9% | 20 % | ? |
| Residual income | ? | ? | $ 21,600 |

**Requirement**

1. Fill in the missing information.

### E11-39B Compute ROI, RI, and EVA *(Learning Objective 5)*

Results from Extreme Corporation's most recent year of operations are presented in the following table:

Check sum: Req. 1 Asset turnover is 2.5.

| | |
|---|---|
| Operating income | $ 9,100 |
| Total assets | $14,000 |
| Current liabilities | $ 4,600 |
| Sales | $35,000 |
| Target rate of returns | 14% |
| Weighted average cost of capital | 12% |
| Tax rate | 30% |

**Requirements**

1. Calculate the profit margin, asset turnover, and ROI.
2. Calculate the residual income.
3. Calculate the EVA.

### E11-40B Comparison of ROI and RI *(Learning Objective 5)*

Lin Ceramics, a division of Sesnie Corporation, has an operating income of $63,000 and total assets of $360,000. The required rate of return for the company is 13%. The company is evaluating whether it should use ROI or RI as a measurement of performance for its division managers.

The manager of Lin Ceramics has the opportunity to undertake a new project that will require an investment of $90,000. This investment would earn $9,000 for Lin Ceramics.

**Requirements**

1. What is the original ROI for Lin Ceramics (before making any additional investment)?
2. What would the ROI be for Lin Ceramics if this investment opportunity were undertaken? Would the manager of the Lin Ceramics division want to make this investment if she were evaluated based on ROI? Why or why not?
3. What is the ROI of the investment opportunity? Would the investment be desirable from the standpoint of Sesnie Corporation? Why or why not?
4. What would the RI be for Lin Ceramics if this investment opportunity were undertaken? Would the manager of the Lin Ceramics division want to make this investment if she were evaluated based on RI? Why or why not?
5. What is the RI of the investment opportunity? Would the investment be desirable from the standpoint of Sesnie Corporation? Why or why not?
6. Which performance measurement method, ROI or RI, promotes goal congruence? Why?

## PROBLEMS Group A

### P11-41A Evaluate subunit performance *(Learning Objectives 3 & 4)*

One subunit of BlueHill Company had the following financial results last month:

| BlueHill—Subunit X | Actual | Flexible Budget | Flexible Budget Variance (U or F) | % Variance* (U or F) |
|---|---|---|---|---|
| Sales | $486,000 | $450,000 | | |
| Cost of goods sold | 260,000 | 250,000 | | |
| Gross margin | $226,000 | $200,000 | | |
| Operating expenses | 52,000 | 50,000 | | |
| Operating income before service department charges | $174,000 | $150,000 | | |
| Service department charges (allocated) | 35,000 | 35,000 | | |
| Operating income | $139,000 | $125,000 | | |

**Flexible budget variance ÷ Flexible budget*

**Requirements**

1. Complete the performance evaluation report for this subunit (round to three decimal places).
2. Based on the data presented, what type of responsibility centre is this subunit?
3. Which items should be investigated if part of management's decision criteria is to investigate all variances equal to or exceeding $10,000 and exceeding 10% (both criteria must be met)?
4. Should only unfavourable variances be investigated? Explain.
5. Is it possible that the variances are due to a higher-than-expected sales volume? Explain.
6. Do you think management will place equal weight on each of the $10,000 variances? Explain.
7. Which balanced scorecard perspective is being addressed through this performance report? In your opinion, is this performance report a leading or lagging indicator? Explain.
8. Give one key performance indicator for the other three balanced scorecard perspectives. Indicate which perspective is being addressed by the indicators you list. Are they leading or lagging indicators? Explain.

### P11-42A Evaluate divisional performance *(Learning Objective 5)*

Benjamin Moore is a national paint manufacturer and retailer. The company is segmented into five divisions: Paint Stores (branded retail locations), Consumer (paint sold through stores such as Canadian Tire, Home Hardware, and Lowe's), Automotive (sales to auto manufacturers), International, and Administration. The following is selected divisional information for the company's two largest divisions: Paint Stores and Consumer (in thousands of dollars).

| | Sales | Operating Income | Total Assets | Current Liabilities |
|---|---|---|---|---|
| Paint stores | $3,920,000 | $490,000 | $1,400,000 | $350,000 |
| Consumer | $1,200,000 | $180,000 | $1,600,000 | $600,000 |

Assume that management has specified a 20% target rate of return. Further assume that the company's weighted average cost of capital is 15% and its effective tax rate is 32%.

**Requirements**

Round all calculations to two decimal places.

1. Calculate each division's ROI.
2. Calculate each division's profit margin. Interpret your results.
3. Calculate each division's asset turnover. Interpret your results.
4. Use the expanded ROI formula to confirm your results from Requirement 1. Interpret your results.
5. Calculate each division's RI. Interpret your results and offer recommendations for any division with negative RI.
6. Calculate each division's EVA. Interpret your results.
7. Describe the conceptual and computational similarities and differences between RI and EVA.
8. Total asset data were provided in this problem. If you were to gather this information from an annual report, how would you measure total assets? Describe your measurement choices and some of the pros and cons of those choices.
9. Describe some of the factors that management considers when setting its minimum target rate of return.
10. Explain why some firms prefer to use RI rather than ROI for performance measurement.
11. Explain why budget versus actual performance reports are insufficient for evaluating the performance of investment centres.

### P11-43A Collect and analyze division data from an annual report

*(Learning Objective 5)*

HardyCo segments its company into four distinct divisions. The net revenues, operating profit, and total assets for these divisions are disclosed in the footnotes to HardyCo's consolidated financial statements, which are presented here.



**Notes to Consolidated Financial Statements**

**Note 1—Basis of Presentation and Our Divisions:**

We manufacture, market, and sell a variety of products through our divisions, including furniture and fixtures for the home, office, and health-care facilities. The accounting policies are the same for each division. There is, however, one exception. HardyCo centrally manages commodity derivatives and does not allocate any gains and losses incurred by these contracts to individual divisions. These derivatives are used to hedge the underlying price risk to the commodities used in production. The resulting gains and losses from these contracts are recorded under corporate expenses rather than allocated to specific divisions.

| | Net Revenue | | | Operating Profit | | |
|---|---|---|---|---|---|---|
| | 2018 | 2017 | 2016 | 2018 | 2017 | 2016 |
| Home furnishings | $10,500 | $ 9,400 | $ 9,000 | $2,625 | $2,350 | $1,800 |
| Office furniture | 9,000 | 8,100 | 7,800 | 1,800 | 1,620 | 1,560 |
| Store displays | 12,200 | 11,000 | 10,500 | 1,464 | 1,320 | 1,260 |
| Health-care furnishings | 1,750 | 1,600 | 1,500 | 525 | 500 | 480 |
| Total division | 33,450 | 30,100 | 28,800 | 6,414 | 5,790 | 5,100 |
| Corporate | — | — | — | (300) | (260) | (215) |
| Total | $33,450 | $30,100 | $28,800 | $6,114 | $5,530 | $4,885 |

| | Total Assets | | | Capital Spending | | |
|---|---|---|---|---|---|---|
| | 2018 | 2017 | 2016 | 2018 | 2017 | 2016 |
| Home furnishings | $ 6,250 | $ 5,000 | $ 4,500 | $ 500 | $ 510 | $ 470 |
| Office furniture | 6,000 | 5,400 | 5,200 | 490 | 320 | 265 |
| Store displays | 10,000 | 8,800 | 8,400 | 835 | 665 | 530 |
| Health-care furnishings | 1,000 | 800 | 750 | 30 | 30 | 35 |
| Total division | 23,250 | 20,000 | 18,850 | 1,855 | 1,525 | 1,300 |
| Corporate | 1,740 | 5,300 | 3,500 | 200 | 205 | 90 |
| Total | $24,990 | $25,300 | $22,350 | $2,055 | $1,730 | $1,390 |

Corporate assets consist of cash, short-term investments, and property, plant, and equipment. The corporate property, plant, and equipment include the headquarters building, equipment within, and the surrounding property.

### Requirements

1. What are HardyCo's four business divisions? Make a table listing each division, its net revenues, operating profit, and total assets.
2. Use the data you collected in Requirement 1 to calculate each division's profit margin. Interpret your results.
3. Use the data you collected in Requirement 1 to calculate each division's asset turnover. Interpret your results.
4. Use the data you collected in Requirement 1 to calculate each division's ROI. Interpret your results.
5. Can you calculate RI and/or EVA using the data presented? Why or why not?

## PROBLEMS Group B

### P11-44B Evaluate subunit performance *(Learning Objectives 3 & 4)*

One subunit of Speed Sports Company had the following financial results last month:

| Speed Sports—Subunit X | Actual | Flexible Budget | Flexible Budget Variance (U or F) | Percentage Variance* (U or F) |
|---|---|---|---|---|
| Sales | $486,000 | $450,000 | | |
| Cost of goods sold | 259,500 | 250,000 | | |
| Gross margin | $227,400 | $200,000 | | |
| Operating expenses | 51,750 | 50,000 | | |
| Operating income before service department charges | $175,650 | $150,000 | | |
| Service department charges (allocated) | 40,750 | 31,250 | | |
| Operating income | $134,900 | $118,750 | | |

**Flexible budget variance ÷ Flexible budget*

### Requirements

1. Complete the performance evaluation report for the subunit (round to three decimal places).
2. Based on the data presented, what type of responsibility centre is this subunit?
3. Which items should be investigated if part of management's decision criteria is to investigate all variances equal to or exceeding $9,500 *and* exceeding 16% (both criteria must be met)?

4. Should only unfavourable variances be investigated? Explain.
5. Is it possible that the variances are due to a higher-than-expected sales volume? Explain.
6. Do you think management will place equal weight on each of the $9,500 variances? Explain.
7. Which balanced scorecard perspective is being addressed through this performance report? In your opinion, is this performance report a leading or lagging indicator? Explain.
8. List one key performance indicator for the other three balanced scorecard perspectives. Indicate which perspective is being addressed by the indicators you list. Are they leading or lagging indicators? Explain.

### P11-45B Evaluate divisional performance *(Learning Objective 5)*

Aurora Borealis Paints is a national paint manufacturer and retailer. The company is segmented into five divisions: Paint Stores (branded retail locations), Consumer (paint sold through stores like Canadian Tire, Home Hardware, and Lowe's), Automotive (sales to auto manufacturers), International, and Administration. The following is selected divisional information for its two largest divisions: Paint Stores and Consumer (in thousands of dollars).

| | Sales | Operating Income | Total Assets | Current Liabilities |
|---|---|---|---|---|
| Paint stores......................... | $3,950,000 | $553,000 | $1,975,000 | $350,000 |
| Consumer ........................... | $1,300,000 | $221,000 | $2,600,000 | $590,000 |

Assume that management has specified a 23% target rate of return. Further assume that the company's weighted average cost of capital is 14% and its effective tax rate is 32%.

**Requirements**

Round all calculations to four decimal places.

1. Calculate each division's ROI.
2. Calculate each division's profit margin. Interpret your results.
3. Calculate each division's asset turnover. Interpret your results.
4. Use the expanded ROI formula to confirm your results from Requirement 1. Interpret your results.
5. Calculate each division's RI. Interpret your results and offer recommendations for any division with negative RI.
6. Calculate each division's EVA. Interpret your results.
7. Describe the conceptual and computational similarities and differences between RI and EVA.
8. Total asset data were provided in this problem. If you were to gather this information from an annual report, how would you measure total assets? Describe your measurement choices and some of the pros and cons of those choices.
9. Describe some of the factors that management considers when setting its minimum target rate of return.
10. Explain why some firms prefer to use RI rather than ROI for performance measurement.
11. Explain why budget versus actual performance reports are insufficient for evaluating the performance of investment centres.

### P11-46B Collect and analyze division data from an annual report *(Learning Objective 5)*

GlennCo segments its company into four distinct divisions. The net revenues, operating profit, and total assets for these divisions are disclosed in the footnotes to GlennCo's consolidated financial statements, which are presented here.

**Notes to Consolidated Financial Statements**

**Note 1—Basis of Presentation and Our Divisions:**

We manufacture, market, and sell a variety of products through our divisions, including furniture and fixtures for the home, office, stores, and health-care facilities. The accounting policies are the same for each division. There is, however, one exception. GlennCo centrally manages commodity derivatives and does not allocate any gains and losses incurred by these contracts to individual divisions. These derivatives are used to hedge the underlying price risk to the commodities used in production. The resulting gains and losses from these contracts are recorded under corporate expenses rather than allocated to specific divisions. Corporate includes the cost of our corporation headquarters, centrally managed initiatives, and certain gains and losses that cannot be accurately allocated to specific divisions, such as derivative gains and losses. Corporate Assets consist of cash, short-term investments, and property, plant, and equipment. The corporate property, plant, and equipment includes the headquarters, building, equipment within, and the surrounding property.

**Net Revenue Operating Profit**

| | Net Revenue | | | Operating Profit | | |
|---|---|---|---|---|---|---|
| | **2018** | **2017** | **2016** | **2018** | **2017** | **2016** |
| Home furnishings | $11,250 | $10,150 | $ 9,750 | $3,150 | $2,875 | $2,325 |
| Office furniture | 9,500 | 8,600 | 8,300 | 1,995 | 1,815 | 1,755 |
| Store displays | 12,750 | 11,550 | 11,050 | 1,785 | 1,645 | 1,585 |
| Health-care furnishings | 1,500 | 1,350 | 1,250 | 480 | 455 | 435 |
| Total division | 35,000 | 31,650 | 30,350 | 7,410 | 6,790 | 6,100 |
| Corporate | - | - | - | (330) | (290) | (245) |
| Total | $35,000 | $31,650 | $30,350 | $7,080 | $6,500 | $5,855 |

| | Amortization of Intangible Assets | | | Depreciation & Other Amortization | | |
|---|---|---|---|---|---|---|
| | **2018** | **2017** | **2016** | **2018** | **2017** | **2016** |
| Home furnishings | $ 10 | $ 11 | $ 11 | $ 425 | $ 415 | $ 420 |
| Office furniture | 82 | 77 | 77 | 280 | 260 | 255 |
| Store displays | 72 | 67 | 65 | 465 | 410 | 370 |
| Health-care furnishings | - | - | 5 | 45 | 50 | 47 |
| Total division | 170 | 155 | 158 | 1,215 | 1,135 | 1,092 |
| Corporate | - | - | - | 15 | 20 | 19 |
| Total | $170 | $155 | $158 | $1,230 | $1,155 | $1,111 |

| | Total Assets | | | Capital Spending | | |
|---|---|---|---|---|---|---|
| | **2018** | **2017** | **2016** | **2018** | **2017** | **2016** |
| Home furnishings | $ 7,500 | $ 6,250 | $ 5,750 | $ 495 | $ 505 | $ 465 |
| Office furniture | 7,600 | 7,000 | 6,800 | 500 | 330 | 275 |
| Store displays | 10,625 | 9,425 | 9,025 | 865 | 695 | 560 |
| Health-care furnishings | 750 | 550 | 500 | 20 | 20 | 25 |
| Total division | 26,475 | 23,225 | 22,075 | 1,880 | 1,550 | 1,325 |
| Corporate | 1,710 | 5,270 | 3,470 | 210 | 215 | 100 |
| Total | $28,185 | $28,495 | $22,545 | $2,090 | $1,7365 | $1,425 |



## Requirements

1. What are GlennCo's four business divisions? Make a table listing each division, its net revenues, operating profit, and total assets.
2. Use the data you collected in Requirement 1 to calculate each division's profit margin. Interpret your results.
3. Use the data you collected in Requirement 1 to calculate each division's asset turnover. Interpret your results.
4. Use the data you collected in Requirement 1 to calculate each division's ROI. Interpret your results.
5. Can you calculate RI and/or EVA using the data presented? Why or why not?

# CAPSTONE APPLICATION PROBLEMS

## APPLICATION QUESTION

### A11-47 Collect and analyze division data *(Learning Objective 5)*

Colgate-Palmolive operates two product segments. Using the company's Website, locate segment information in the company's most recent annual report. (*Hint:* Look under investor relations.) Then, look in the financial statement footnotes.

**Requirements**

1. What are the two segments (ignore geographical subsets of the one product segment)? Gather data about each segment's net sales, operating income, and identifiable assets.
2. Calculate ROI for each segment.
3. Which segment has the highest ROI? Explain why.
4. If you were on the top management team and could allocate extra funds to only one division, which division would you choose? Why?

## CASE ASSIGNMENT

### C11-48 Ethics and performance evaluation *(Learning Objectives 2 & 4)*

Grommet Company has several divisions. The controller, Kayla Collins, prepares monthly segment reports for each division. Each division manager is evaluated annually, based largely on the segment margin for the manager's division. The segment margin for the division determines whether the manager receives a bonus, the amount of any bonus, and whether the division will even continue to be operated. Since operating losses reflect common fixed costs being allocated to a division, company management allows a division to show an operating loss in one or more years. However, the division is likely to be closed if its segment margin is negative for three consecutive years, since management feels that the division is then a drain on the overall company's profits.

The past few years have been tough years for the Small Engines division. The economy has caused sales to shrink. In addition, the production manager, Craig Tatter, has had some personal problems and has not been focused on work. Tatter thinks his personal issues are behind him now, and he is looking forward to better results in future years—as long as his division is not discontinued due to its poor operating results in the past few years. Here is an excerpt from the segment report for the Small Engines division for the past three years:

**Grommet Company—Small Engines Division**
**Segment Margin Performance Report for the Fiscal Years**
**Ending December 31, 2013, 2012, and 2011**
**(all figures in thousands of dollars)**

| Product | 2013 | 2012 | 2011 |
|---|---|---|---|
| Sales revenue | $6,098 | $6,501 | $6,652 |
| Less: Variable expenses | | | |
| Variable cost of goods sold | 4,728 | 5,319 | 5,412 |
| Variable operating expenses | 693 | 517 | 564 |
| Contribution margin | $ 677 | $ 665 | $ 676 |
| Less: Direct fixed expenses | | | |
| Fixed manufacturing overhead | 652 | 621 | 639 |
| Fixed operating expenses | 79 | 57 | 54 |
| Segment margin | $ (54) | $ (13) | $ (17) |
| Less: Common fixed expenses | 30 | 72 | 41 |
| Operating income (loss) | $ (84) | $ (85) | $ (58) |

Collins, the controller, is in a relationship with Tatter, the division manager of Small Engines. She wants to do whatever she can to help him with his work situation; she knows he is a good person and works hard. Once she sees the segment margin report for the Small Engines division, she realizes that there is a strong possibility that the Small Engines division will be closed due to segment margin losses over the past three years. She analyzes the preliminary segment margin performance report and realizes that there is an easy way that she could help. She could move some of the direct fixed expenses listed on the Small Engine segment report into the common fixed expenses allocated to the Small Engine division. She reasons that the overall operating income for the Small Engine division will remain the same, and it really isn't hurting anyone to do this. In fact, she actually feels that she is helping the company and its employees. By the simple act of shifting some of the direct fixed costs to the common fixed expenses, she will be saving people's jobs by preventing the division from being closed.

There is very little chance of this shift between fixed expense categories being caught because the segment reports are hard to understand. No one in the company outside of the Accounting Department understands what is included in "Segment fixed expenses" versus "Common fixed costs." Collins has used a convoluted allocation system for years, and company management has given up on understanding it and just accepts the monthly reports. Company management figures that overall the company does well, so the hard-to-understand accounting reports are just a necessary evil.

### Requirements

1. Do you agree with Collins' reasoning that no one would get hurt by her actions? Why or why not?
2. Do you agree with Collins' assessment that she is actually helping the company, and that this justifies her actions?

# DISCUSSION & ANALYSIS

1. Describe at least four advantages and at least two disadvantages of decentralization.
2. Describe at least four reasons a company would use a performance evaluation system.
3. Explain why using financial statements as the sole performance evaluation tool for a company is probably not a good idea. What issues can arise from using only financial measures for performance evaluation?
4. Define key performance indicator (KPI). What is the relationship between KPIs and a company's objectives? Select a company of any size with which you are familiar. List at least four examples of specific objectives that company might have and one potential KPI for each of those specific objectives.
5. List and describe the four perspectives found on a balanced scorecard. For each perspective, list at least two examples of KPIs that might be used to measure performance on that perspective.
6. Compare and contrast a cost centre, a revenue centre, a profit centre, and an investment centre. List a specific example of each type of responsibility centre. How is the performance of managers evaluated in each type of responsibility centre?
7. Contrast lagging indicators with leading indicators. Provide an example of each type of indicator.
8. Explain the potential problem that could arise from using ROI as the incentive measure for managers. What are some specific actions a company might take to resolve this potential problem?
9. Describe at least two specific actions that a company could take to improve its ROI.
10. Define residual income. How is it calculated? Describe the major weakness of residual income.

# APPLICATION & ANALYSIS

## 11-1 Segmented Financial Information

Select a company you are interested in and obtain its annual reports by going to the company's Website. Download the annual report for the most recent year. (On many company Websites, you will need to visit the Investor Relations section to obtain the company's financial statements.) You may also collect the information from the company's public security filings, which can be found at www.sedar.com for companies listed on Canadian stock markets. For companies listed on the United States stock markets, visit www.sec.gov/edgar/searchedgar/webusers.htm

## Discussion Questions

1. Locate the company's annual report as outlined previously. Find the company's segment information; it should be in the "Notes to Consolidated Financial Statements" or other similarly named section. Look for the word *segment* in a heading—that is usually the section you need.
2. List the segments as reported in the annual report. Make a table listing each operating segment, its revenues, income, and assets.
3. Use the data you collected in Requirement 2 to calculate each segment's profit margin. Interpret your results.
4. Use the data you collected in Requirement 2 to calculate each segment's asset turnover. Interpret your results.
5. Use the data you collected in Requirement 2 to calculate each segment's ROI. Interpret your results.
6. Can you calculate RI and/or EVA using the data presented? Why or why not?
7. The rules for how segments should be presented in the annual report are governed by external financial accounting rules. The information you gathered for the previous requirements would be used by investors and other external stakeholders in their analysis of the company and its stock. Internally, the company most likely has many segments. Based on what you know about the company and its products or services, list at least five potential segments that the company might use for internal reporting. Explain why this way of segmenting the company for internal reporting could be useful to managers.

## Classroom Applications

**Web:** Post the discussion questions on an electronic discussion board. Have small groups of students choose a company for their groups. The students should answer the listed questions in their discussion.

**Classroom:** Form groups of three or four students. Your group should choose a company. Prepare a five-minute presentation about your group's company that addresses the listed questions.

**Independent:** Research answers to each of the questions. Turn in a two- or three-page typed paper (12-point font, double-spaced with 2.5 cm margins). Include references, including the URL for the annual report you used for this activity.

# TRY IT SOLUTIONS

**page 696:**

1. ROI = Operating income/Total assets = \$695/966 = \$71.9%
   Sales margin = Operating income/Sales revenue = \$695/2,636 = \$26.4%
   Capital turnover = Sales revenue/Total assets = \$2,636/966 = \$2.73
2. Residual income = Operating income − (Target rate of return × Total assets)
   = \$695 million − (25% × \$966 million) = \$453.5 million

# Capital Investment Decisions and the Time Value of Money

## Learning Objectives

1. Describe the importance of capital investments and the capital budgeting process.
2. Use the payback and accounting rate of return methods to make capital investment decisions.
3. Use the time value of money to compute the present and future values of single lump sums and annuities.
4. Use discounted cash flow models to make capital investment decisions.
5. Compare and contrast the four capital budgeting methods.

Chapter 12 "Capital Investment Decisions and the Time Value of Money" covers material outlined in **Section 3: Management Accounting** of the CPA Competency Map. Specifically, this chapter addresses concepts from *Sections 5.3 Capital Budgeting; 5.2 Treasury Management; 3.2 Planning, Budgeting, and Forecasting;* and *3.6 Organizational Performance Measurement.* The Learning Objectives in this chapter have been aligned with the CPA Competency Map to ensure the best coverage possible.

PROFESSIONAL COMPETENCY The presence of the **coverage button** in the margin indicates focus on one or more of the specific competency areas from the competency map. The concepts in the text are building blocks to developing the competencies required in the CPA. While the chapter may address multiple areas of the competency map, the main focus will be:

Competencies:

**5.3.1** Develops or evaluates capital budgeting processes and decisions*

**5.2.4** Evaluates decisions affecting capital structure*

**5.2.3** Evaluates sources of financing*

**3.2.1** Develops or evaluates information inputs for operational plans, budgets, and forecasts*

**3.6.1** Evaluates performance using accepted frameworks*

## Arctic char, a member of the salmon family,

has been acclaimed as a world-class food product not only for its taste but also for its colour (pink-red flesh with luminescent blue-and-green skin and violet spots along its sides) and texture. Fishing quotas for Arctic char are determined only after the subsistence needs of the Nunavut communities are met. Therefore, production of Arctic char in Nunavut is typically limited to just over 100,000 kilograms per year.

The sign on the front of the store for Iqaluit Enterprises has both the English name of the company and the Inuktitut name—the bold black syllabics that translate into "the place to buy fish"—prominently

© Lehtikuva/CP Images

*Reprinted from *The Chartered Professional Accountant Competency Map - Understanding the competencies a candidate must demonstrate to become a CPA*, © 2012, with permission Chartered Professional Accountants of Canada, Toronto, Canada. Any changes to the original material are the sole responsibility of the author (and/or publisher) and have not been reviewed or endorsed by the Chartered Professional Accountants of Canada.

featured on the sign. Iqaluit Enterprises specializes in smoked Arctic char, with approximately eight employees and sales under $1 million per year.[1]

If Jim Currie, the owner of Iqaluit Enterprises, wants to take advantage of the global appeal of Arctic char and reach a larger customer base, he will have to make some investments in capital assets, such as an online store. But before he does this, he should evaluate the potential returns. Any additional medium for reaching customers is great as long as it is able to generate sufficient returns in years to come.

Companies must continually evaluate whether they need to invest in new property, buildings, equipment, or projects in order to remain competitive or increase their revenue stream. Many companies also initiate capital improvements in order to save on existing costs, such as the cost of manual labour. Management must carefully consider whether the additional revenues or cost savings will be worth the high price of these new capital investments. In this chapter, we'll see how companies such as Iqaluit Enterprises use net present value, payback period, and other capital investment analysis techniques to decide which long-term capital investments to make.

## What Is Capital Budgeting?

The process of making capital investment decisions is often referred to as <u>capital budgeting</u>. Companies make capital investments when they acquire capital assets—assets used for a long period of time. Capital investments include buying new equipment, building new plants, automating production, and developing major commercial Websites. In addition to affecting operations for many years, capital investments usually require large sums of money. A decision to develop an online store for Iqaluit Enterprises could tie up resources for years to come. This was the case when, on the advice of the North American Industry Classification System, Canadian companies in the Management of Companies and Enterprises sector (NAICS 55) invested $142 million in new machinery and equipment in 2008 and $215.7 million in 2011.[2]

> **Why is this important?**
>
> The **four methods** of analyzing capital investments outlined below help managers **decide** whether it would be wise to **invest** large sums of money in **new projects**, buildings, or equipment.

Capital investment decisions affect all types of businesses as they try to become more efficient by automating production and implementing new technologies. Grocers and retailers such as Home Outfitters have invested in expensive self-scan checkout machines, while airlines such as Air Canada and WestJet have invested in self-check-in kiosks. These new technologies cost money. How do managers decide whether these expansions in plant and equipment will be good investments? They use capital budgeting analysis. Some companies employ staff dedicated solely to capital budgeting analysis. They spend thousands of hours a year determining which capital investments to pursue.

### Four Popular Methods of Capital Budgeting Analysis

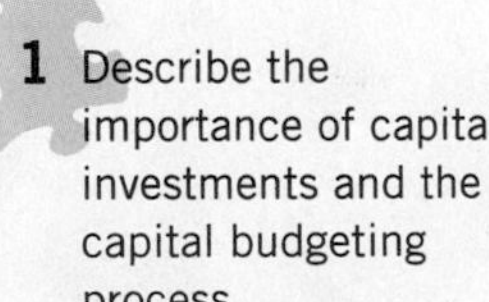

1 Describe the importance of capital investments and the capital budgeting process.

PROFESSIONAL COMPETENCY

In this chapter, we discuss four popular methods of analyzing potential capital investments:

1. Payback period
2. Accounting rate of return (ARR)
3. Net present value (NPV)
4. Internal rate of return (IRR)

The first two methods, <u>payback</u> period and <u>accounting rate of return</u>, are fairly quick and easy to calculate and work well for capital investments that have a relatively short

[1]www.profilecanada.com/companydetail.cfm?company=2340074_Iqaluit_Enterprises_Iqaluit_NT

[2]Innovation, Science and Economic Development Canada, www.ic.gc.ca

life span, such as computer equipment and software that may have a useful life of only two to three years. Management often uses the payback period and accounting rate of return to screen investments and highlight those that are less desirable. The payback period provides management with valuable information on how fast the cash invested will be recouped. The accounting rate of return shows the effect of the investment on the company's accrual-based income.

However, these two methods are inadequate if the capital investments have a longer life span. Why? Because these methods do not consider the **time value of money**,[3] which means that they are nondiscounted methods. The last two methods (discounted methods), **net present value (NPV)** and **internal rate of return (IRR)**, factor in the time value of money. Consequently, they are more appropriate for longer-term capital investments such as Iqaluit Enterprises' online store.

Management often uses a combination of methods to make final capital investment decisions. To provide an idea of the usage of each of the methods, a survey of universities in the United Kingdom found that 29% of the universities use the payback method, 11% use ARR, 41% use NPV, and 23% use IRR.[4]

Capital budgeting is not an exact science. Although the calculations these methods require may appear precise, remember that they are based on predictions about an uncertain future. These predictions must consider many unknown factors, such as changing consumer preferences, competition, and government regulations. The farther into the future the decision extends, the more likely actual results will differ from predictions. Long-term decisions are riskier than short-term decisions.

## Focus on Cash Flows

International Financial Reporting Standards (IFRS) and Accounting Standards for Private Enterprises (ASPE) are based on accrual accounting, but capital budgeting focuses on cash flows. The desirability of a capital asset depends on its ability to generate net cash inflows—that is, inflows in excess of outflows—over the asset's useful life. Recall that operating income based on accrual accounting contains noncash expenses such as depreciation expense and bad debt expense. The capital investment's net cash inflows, therefore, differ from its operating income. Of the four capital budgeting methods covered in this chapter, only the accounting rate of return method uses accrual-based accounting income. The other three methods use the investment's projected *net cash inflows*. It should also be mentioned that, for simplicity, income taxes have been ignored throughout this chapter. Cash flows are affected by income taxes, whether they be tax inflows or outflows, and noncash elements such as depreciation also affect cash flows through the impact on income taxes. The complications to capital budgeting calculations that arise from income taxes are more appropriate for more advanced managerial accounting courses.

What do the projected net cash inflows include? Cash *inflows* include future cash revenue generated from the investment, any future savings in ongoing cash operating costs resulting from the investment, and any future residual value of the asset. To determine the investment's net cash inflows, the inflows are netted against the investment's future cash outflows, such as the investment's ongoing cash operating costs and refurbishment, repairs, and maintenance costs. The initial investment itself is also a significant cash outflow. However, in our calculations, we refer to the amount of the investment separately from all other cash flows related to the investment. The projected net cash inflows are "given" in our examples and in the assignment material. In reality, much of capital investment analysis revolves around projecting these figures as accurately as possible using input from employees throughout the organization (production, marketing, and so forth, depending on the type of capital investment).

---

[3]The payback period can be expanded to incorporate the time value of money, which is known as the discounted payback period. The simplicity of the payback period calculation is traded for a little more accuracy.

[4]Cooper, P., "Management Accounting Practices in Universities," *Management Accounting (U.K.)*, February 1996, pp. 28–30.

## Capital Budgeting Process

As shown in Exhibit 12-1, the first step in the capital budgeting process is to identify potential investments—for example, new technology and equipment that may make the company more efficient, competitive, and profitable. Employees, consultants, and outside sales vendors often offer capital investment proposals to management. After identifying potential capital investments, the second step for managers is to project the investments' net cash inflows. As discussed previously, this step can be very time consuming and difficult. However, managers make the best projections possible given the information they have.

**EXHIBIT 12-1** Capital Budgeting Process

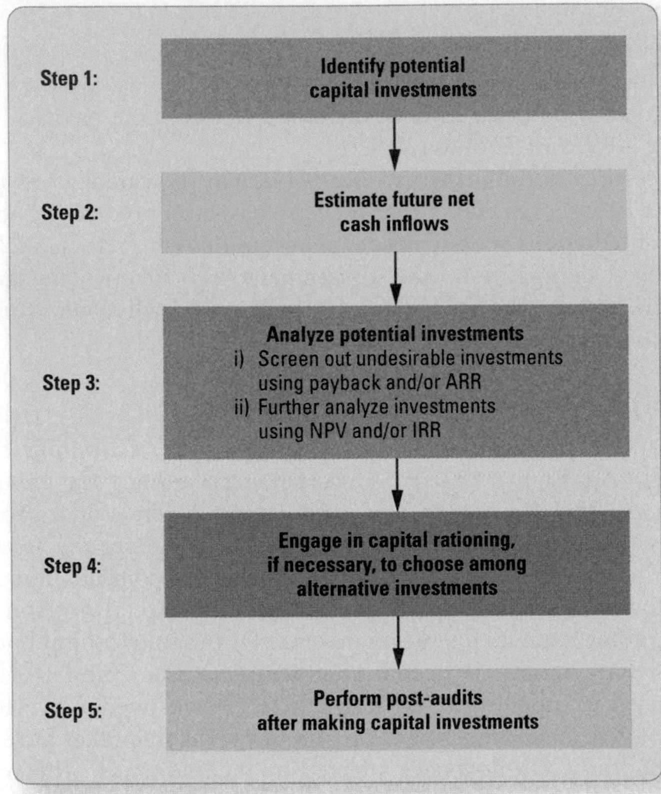


The third step is to analyze the investments using one or more of the four methods listed previously. Sometimes the analysis involves a two-stage process. In the first stage, managers screen the investments using one or both of the methods that do *not* incorporate the time value of money: payback period or accounting rate of return. These simple methods quickly weed out undesirable investments. Potential investments that pass the initial test go on to a second stage of analysis, in which managers further analyze the potential investments using either the net present value or internal rate of return method. Because these methods consider the time value of money, they provide more accurate information about the potential investment's profitability. Since each method evaluates the potential investment from a different angle, some companies use all four methods to get the most complete picture they can about the investment.

Some companies can pursue all of the potential investments that meet or exceed their decision criteria. However, because of limited resources, other companies must engage in a fourth step, **capital rationing**, choosing among alternative capital investments. Based on the availability of funds, managers determine if and when to make specific capital investments. For example, management may decide to wait three years to buy a certain piece of equipment because it considers other investments to be more important. In the intervening three years, the company will reassess whether it should still invest in the equipment. Perhaps technology has changed and even better equipment is available. Perhaps consumer tastes have changed, so the company no longer needs the equipment. Because of changing factors, long-term capital budgets are rarely set in stone.

As a final step, most companies perform **post-audits** of their capital investments. After investing in the assets, they compare the actual net cash inflows generated by the investment to the projected net cash inflows. Post-audits help companies determine whether the investments are going as planned and deserve continued support or whether they should abandon the project and sell the assets (if possible). Managers also use feedback from post-audits to better estimate net cash inflow projections for future projects. If managers expect routine post-audits, they will more likely submit realistic net cash inflow estimates with their capital investment proposals.

## Sustainability and Capital Investments

Investments in "green" technologies often require large capital outlays that are subject to capital investment analysis. Investments in clean energy have risen dramatically in recent years, especially with respect to wind and solar power projects. In 2015 alone, $329 billion was invested globally in clean energy.[5] Companies deciding whether to invest in solar paneling on retail outlets (Target)[6], a fleet of electric vehicles (Continental Airlines)[7], or LEED certified buildings (Best Buy)[8] will want to assess how quickly payback will occur and how prudent the investment will be. Their analysis should consider all of the future revenues and cost savings that may occur as a result of using greener technology.

See Exercises E12-23A and E12-44B

For example, companies need to be aware of grants and tax breaks offered by government agencies for investing in green technology. These government-sponsored incentives should be treated as reductions in the initial cost of the investment or as periodic cost savings, depending on how the incentive is structured and when it is received. Companies should also factor in future cost savings from having fewer lawsuits, regulatory fines, and clean-up costs as a result of investing in green technology. Furthermore, as the supply of fossil fuels decreases and the cost rises, greener technology may also result in lower annual operating costs.

[5]Clean energy defies fossil fuel price crash to attract record $329bn global investment in 2015, Bloomberg New Energy Finance, press release, January 14, 2016, www.bloomberg.com/company/clean-energy-investment/#form

[6]www.environmentalleader.com/2007/04/30/target-begins-solar-power-rollout

[7]www.continental.com/web/en-US/content/company/globalcitizenship/environment.aspx

[8]www.jetsongreen.com/2007/08/best-buy-to-bui.html

# Calculating the Payback Period and Accounting Rate of Return

## Payback Period

2 Use the payback and accounting rate of return methods to make capital investment decisions.

Payback period is the length of time it takes to recover, in net cash inflows, the cost of the capital outlay. The payback model measures how quickly managers expect to recover their investment dollars. The quicker an investment pays itself back, the less inherent risk that the investment will become unprofitable. Therefore, the shorter the payback period, the more attractive the asset, *all else being equal*. Computing the payback period depends on whether net cash inflows are equal each year or whether they differ over time.

### Payback with Equal Annual Net Cash Inflows

Parlee Manufacturing, in Milton, Nova Scotia, makes outdoor gear. Let's assume that the company is considering investing $240,000 in hardware and software to develop a

> **Why is this important?**
> Companies want to **recover their cash** as quickly as possible. The **payback period** tells managers **how long** it will take before the investment is **recouped**.

business-to-business (B2B) portal. Employees throughout the company will use the B2B portal to access company-approved suppliers. Parlee Manufacturing expects the portal to save $60,000 each year for the six years of its useful life. The savings will arise from a reduction in the number of purchasing personnel the company employs and from lower prices on the goods and services purchased. Net cash inflows arise from an increase in revenues, a decrease in expenses, or both. In Parlee Manufacturing's case, the net cash inflows result from lower expenses.

When net cash inflows are equal each year, managers compute the payback period as follows:

$$\text{Payback period} = \frac{\text{Amount invested}}{\text{Expected annual net cash inflow}}$$

Parlee Manufacturing computes the investment's payback as follows:

$$\text{Payback period for B2B portal} = \frac{\$240{,}000}{\$60{,}000} = 4\text{ years}$$

Exhibit 12-2 verifies that Parlee Manufacturing expects to recoup the $240,000 investment in the B2B portal by the end of Year 4, when the accumulated net cash inflows total $240,000.

**EXHIBIT 12-2** Payback—Equal Annual Net Cash Inflows

| | | Net Cash Inflows | | | |
|---|---|---|---|---|---|
| | | B2B Portal | | Website Development | |
| Year | Amount Invested | Annual | Accumulated | Annual | Accumulated |
| 0 | $240,000 | — | — | — | — |
| 1 | — | $60,000 | $ 60,000 | $80,000 | $ 80,000 |
| 2 | — | 60,000 | 120,000 | 80,000 | 160,000 |
| 3 | — | 60,000 | 180,000 | 80,000 | 240,000 |
| 4 | — | 60,000 | 240,000 | | |
| 5 | — | 60,000 | 300,000 | | |
| 6 | — | 60,000 | 360,000 | | |

(Useful Life arrows: B2B Portal Years 1–6; Website Development Years 1–3)

Parlee Manufacturing is also considering investing $240,000 to develop a Website. The company expects the Website to generate $80,000 in net cash inflows each year of its three-year life. The payback period is computed as follows:

$$\text{Payback period for Website development} = \frac{\$240{,}000}{\$80{,}000} = 3\text{ years}$$

Exhibit 12-2 verifies that Parlee Manufacturing will recoup the $240,000 investment for Website development by the end of Year 3, when the accumulated net cash inflows total $240,000.

## Payback with Unequal Net Cash Inflows

The payback equation works only when net cash inflows are the same each period. When periodic cash flows are unequal, a company must accumulate net cash inflows until the amount invested is recovered. Assume that Parlee Manufacturing is considering an alternate investment, the Z80 portal. The Z80 portal differs from the B2B portal and Website in two respects: (1) It has *unequal* net cash inflows during its life, and (2) it has a $30,000 residual value at the end of its life. The Z80 portal will generate net cash inflows of $100,000 in Year 1, $80,000 in Year 2, $50,000 each year in Years 3–5, $30,000 in Year 6, and $30,000 when it is sold at the end of its life. Exhibit 12-3 shows the payback schedule for these unequal annual net cash inflows.

**EXHIBIT 12-3** Payback—Unequal Annual Net Cash Inflows

| | | Net Cash Inflows Z80 Portal | |
|---|---|---|---|
| Year | Amount Invested | Annual | Accumulated |
| 0 | $240,000 | — | — |
| 1 | — | 100,000 | $100,000 |
| 2 | — | 80,000 | 180,000 |
| 3 | — | 50,000 | 230,000 |
| 4 | — | 50,000 | 280,000 |
| 5 | — | 50,000 | 330,000 |
| 6 | — | 30,000 | 360,000 |
| Residual Value | | 30,000 | 390,000 |

*Useful Life* (Years 1–6)

By the end of Year 3, the company has recovered $230,000 of the $240,000 initially invested and is only $10,000 short of payback. Because the expected net cash inflow in Year 4 is $50,000, by the end of Year 4, the company will have recovered *more* than the initial investment. Therefore, the payback period is somewhere between three and four years. Assuming that the cash flow occurs evenly throughout the fourth year, the payback period is calculated as follows:

$$\text{Payback} = 3 \text{ years} + \frac{\$10{,}000 \text{ (amount needed to complete recovery in Year 4)}}{\$50{,}000 \text{ (projected net cash inflow in Year 4)}}$$

$$= 3.2 \text{ years}$$

## Criticism of the Payback Period Method

A major criticism of the payback method is that it focuses only on time, not on profitability. The payback period method considers only those cash flows that occur *during* the payback period. This method ignores any cash flows that occur *after* that period, including any residual value. For example, Exhibit 12-2 shows that the B2B portal will continue to generate net cash inflows for two years after its payback period. These additional net cash inflows amount to $120,000 ($60,000 × 2 years), yet the payback method ignores this extra cash. A similar situation occurs with the Z80 portal. As shown in Exhibit 12-3, the Z80 portal will provide an additional $150,000 of net cash inflows, including residual value, after its payback period of 3.2 years. In contrast, the Website's useful life, as shown in Exhibit 12-2, is the *same* as its payback period (three years). Since no additional cash flows occur after the payback period, the Website will merely cover its cost and provide no profit. Because this is the case, the company has little or no reason to invest in the Website even though its payback period is the shortest of all three investments.

**EXHIBIT 12-4** Comparing Payback Periods Between Investments

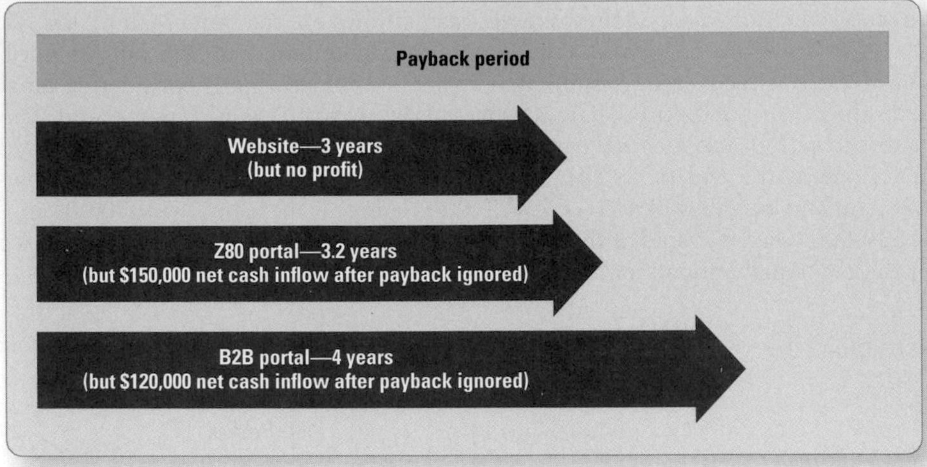


Exhibit 12-4 compares the payback period of the three investments. As the exhibit illustrates, the payback method does not consider the asset's profitability. *The method only tells management how quickly it will recover its cash.* Even though the Website has the shortest payback period, both the B2B portal and the Z80 portal are better investments because they provide profit. The key point is that the investment with the shortest payback period is best only when all other factors are the same. Therefore, managers usually use the payback method as a screening device to "weed out" investments that will take too long to recoup. They rarely use payback period as the sole method for deciding whether to invest in the asset.

When using the payback period method, managers are guided by the following decision rule:

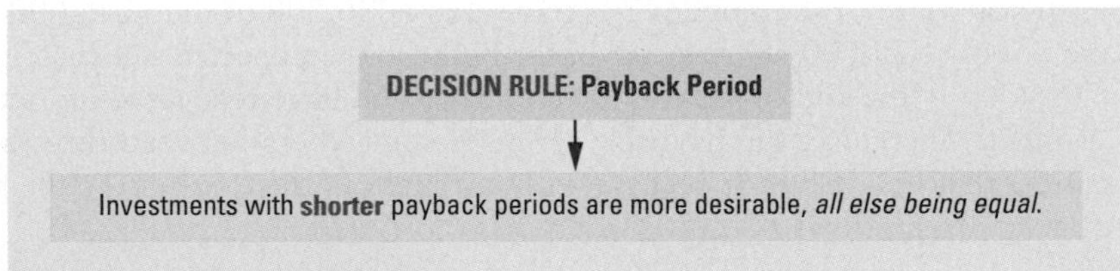


## TRY IT!

The Bruce Company is considering investing in a wind turbine to generate its own power. Any unused power will be sold back to the local utility company. Between cost savings and new revenues, the company expects to generate $750,000 per year in net cash inflows from the turbine. The turbine would cost $4 million and is expected to have a 20-year useful life with no residual value. Calculate the payback period.

Please see page 772 for solution.

## Accounting Rate of Return (ARR)

Companies are in business to earn profits. One measure of profitability is the accounting rate of return (ARR) on an asset:

$$\text{Accounting rate of return} = \frac{\text{Average annual operating income from asset}}{\text{Initial investment}^{9}}$$

[9]Some managers prefer to use the average investment, rather than the initial investment, as the denominator. For simplicity, we will use the initial investment.

The ARR focuses on the operating income that an asset generates. The ARR measures the average annual rate of return over the asset's life. Recall that operating income is based on accrual accounting. Therefore, any noncash expenses, such as depreciation expense, must be subtracted from the asset's net cash inflows to arrive at its operating income. Assuming that depreciation expense is the only noncash expense relating to the investment, we can rewrite the ARR formula as follows:

$$\text{ARR} = \frac{\text{Average annual net cash flow} - \text{Annual depreciation expense}}{\text{Initial investment}}$$

Exhibit 12-5 reviews how to calculate annual depreciation expense using the straight-line method.

**EXHIBIT 12-5** Review of Straight-Line Depreciation Expense Calculation

$$\text{Annual depreciation expense} = \frac{\text{Initial cost of asset} - \text{Residual value}}{\text{Useful life of asset (in years)}}$$

## Investments with Equal Annual Net Cash Inflows

Recall that the B2B portal, which costs \$240,000, has equal annual net cash inflows of \$60,000, a six-year useful life, and no residual value.

First, we must find the B2B portal's annual depreciation expense:

$$\text{Annual depreciation expense} = \frac{\$240{,}000 - 0}{6 \text{ years}} = \$40{,}000$$

Now, we can complete the ARR formula:

$$\text{ARR} = \frac{\$60{,}000 - \$40{,}000}{\$240{,}000} = \frac{\$20{,}000}{\$240{,}000} = 8.33\% \text{ (rounded)}$$

The B2B portal will provide an average annual accounting rate of return of 8.33%.

## Investments with Unequal Net Cash Inflows

Now, consider the Z80 portal. Recall that the Z80 portal would also cost \$240,000, but it had unequal net cash inflows during its life (as pictured in Exhibit 12-3) and a \$30,000 residual value at the end of its life. Since the yearly cash inflows vary in size, we need to first calculate the Z80's *average* annual net cash inflows:

| | |
|---|---|
| Total net cash inflows *during* operating life of asset (does not include the residual value at the end of life)[10] (Year 1 + Year 2, and so forth) from Exhibit 12-3 | \$360,000 |
| Divide by: Asset's operating life (in years) | ÷ 6 years |
| Average annual net cash inflow from asset | \$ 60,000 |

[10] The residual value is not included in the net cash inflows during the asset's operating life because we are trying to find the asset's average annual operating income. We assume that the asset will be sold for its expected residual value (\$30,000) at the end of its life, resulting in no additional accounting gain or loss.

Now, let's calculate the asset's annual depreciation expense:

$$\text{Annual depreciation expense} = \frac{\$240{,}000 - \$30{,}000}{6 \text{ years}} = \$35{,}000$$

Finally, we can complete the ARR calculation:

$$\text{ARR} = \frac{\$60{,}000 - \$35{,}000}{\$240{,}000} = \frac{\$25{,}000}{\$240{,}000} = 10.42\% \text{ (rounded)}$$

Notice that the Z80 portal's average annual operating income ($25,000) is higher than the B2B portal's average operating income ($20,000). Since the Z80 asset has a residual value at the end of its life, less depreciation is expensed each year, leading to a higher average annual operating income and a higher ARR.

Companies that use the ARR model set a minimum required accounting rate of return. If Parlee Manufacturing required an ARR of at least 10%, its managers would not approve an investment in the B2B portal but would approve an investment in the Z80 portal.

The decision rule is as follows:

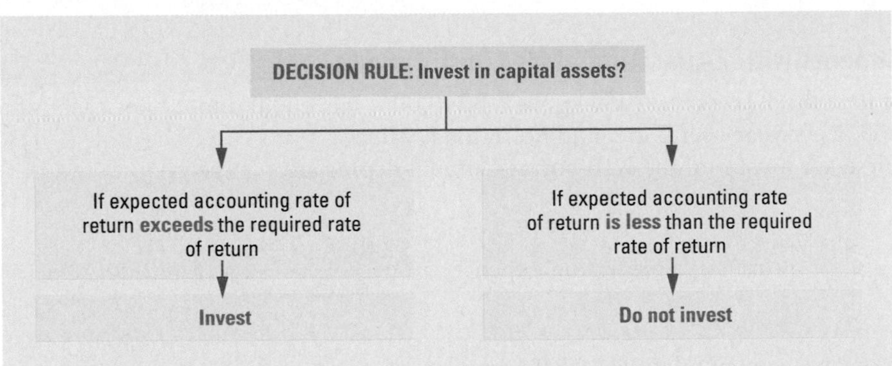


In summary, the payback period focuses on the time it takes for the company to recoup its cash investment but ignores all cash flows occurring after the payback period. Because it ignores any additional cash flows (including any residual value), the method does not consider the profitability of the project.

The ARR, however, measures the profitability of the asset over its entire life using accrual accounting figures. It is the only method that uses accrual accounting rather than net cash inflows in its computations. As discussed in Chapter 11, company divisions are often evaluated based on accounting income. Therefore, the investment's ARR helps managers see how the investment will affect their division's profitability. The payback period and ARR methods are simple and quick to compute, so managers often use them to screen out undesirable investments and to gain a more complete picture of the investment's desirability. However, both methods ignore the time value of money.

## TRY IT!

The Bruce Company is considering investing in a wind turbine to generate its own power. Any unused power will be sold back to the local utility company. Between cost savings and new revenues, the company expects to generate $750,000 per year in net cash inflows from the turbine. The turbine would cost $4 million and is expected to have a 20-year useful life with no residual value. Calculate the accounting rate of return (ARR).

Please see page 772 for solution.

# DECISION GUIDELINES

## Capital Budgeting

Maplewood Equestrian Centre was started with the purchase of existing facilities. Improvements to the facilities were needed, some of which were major capital investments such as rejuvenating unused fields into sustainable pastures for grazing by the horses. This included tilling, seeding, and cultivating the appropriate plants and fencing the acreage for specific herd sizes and grazing needs. Why is this necessary? The health and welfare of the horses is of primary concern. Since horses can be quite sensitive to changes in food and feeding routines, the grazing areas need to be designed with specific equine behaviours in mind. Here are some of the guidelines that the Maplewood managers used as they made their capital budgeting decisions.

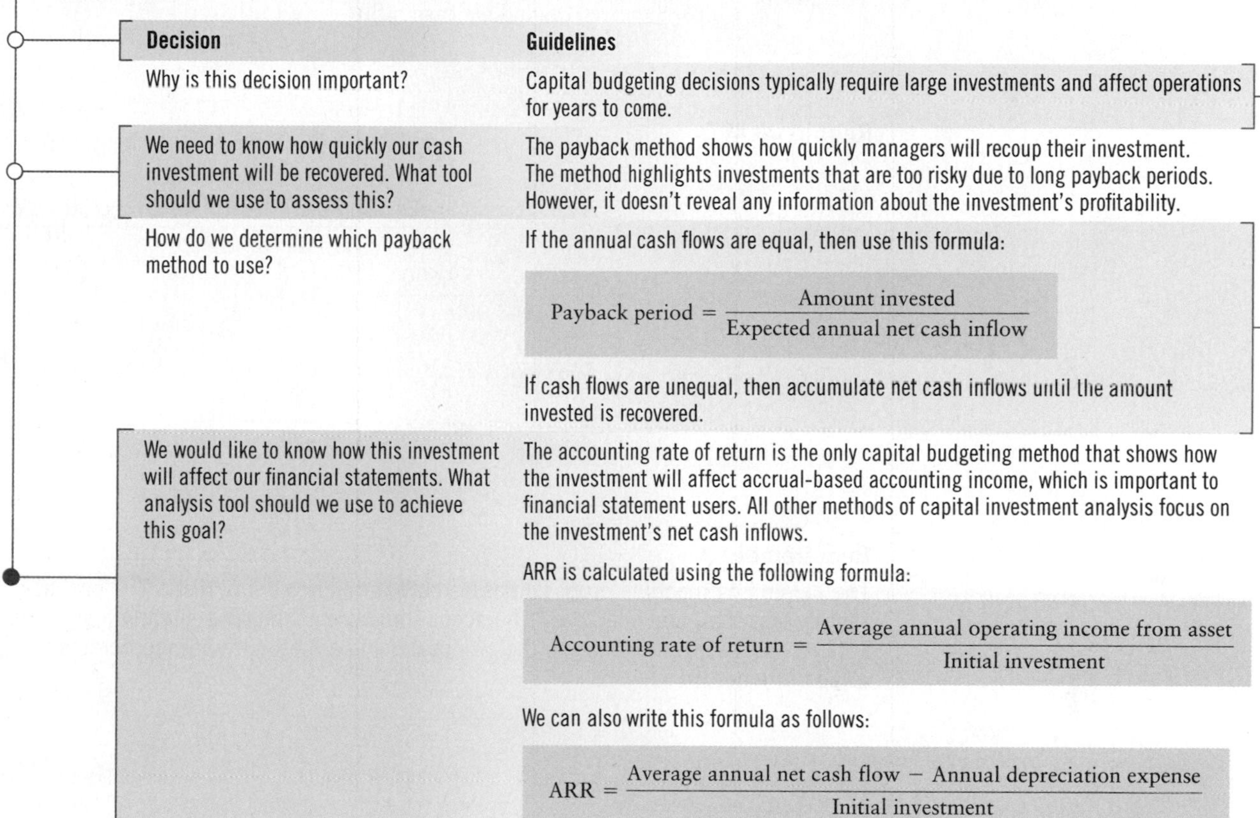

| Decision | Guidelines |
|---|---|
| Why is this decision important? | Capital budgeting decisions typically require large investments and affect operations for years to come. |
| We need to know how quickly our cash investment will be recovered. What tool should we use to assess this? | The payback method shows how quickly managers will recoup their investment. The method highlights investments that are too risky due to long payback periods. However, it doesn't reveal any information about the investment's profitability. |
| How do we determine which payback method to use? | If the annual cash flows are equal, then use this formula: $\text{Payback period} = \dfrac{\text{Amount invested}}{\text{Expected annual net cash inflow}}$ If cash flows are unequal, then accumulate net cash inflows until the amount invested is recovered. |
| We would like to know how this investment will affect our financial statements. What analysis tool should we use to achieve this goal? | The accounting rate of return is the only capital budgeting method that shows how the investment will affect accrual-based accounting income, which is important to financial statement users. All other methods of capital investment analysis focus on the investment's net cash inflows. ARR is calculated using the following formula: $\text{Accounting rate of return} = \dfrac{\text{Average annual operating income from asset}}{\text{Initial investment}}$ We can also write this formula as follows: $\text{ARR} = \dfrac{\text{Average annual net cash flow} - \text{Annual depreciation expense}}{\text{Initial investment}}$ |

# SUMMARY PROBLEM 1

Zetamax is considering buying a new bar-coding machine for its Sault Ste. Marie plant. The company screens its potential capital investments using the payback period and accounting rate of return methods. If a potential investment has a payback period of fewer than four years and a minimum 7% accounting rate of return, it will be considered further. The data for the machine follow:

| | |
|---|---|
| Cost of machine | \$48,000 |
| Estimated residual value | \$ 0 |
| Estimated annual net cash inflow (each year for five years) | \$13,000 |
| Estimated useful life | 5 years |

**Requirements**

1. Compute the bar-coding machine's payback period.
2. Compute the bar-coding machine's ARR.
3. Should Zetamax turn down this investment proposal or consider it further?

## ▪ SOLUTIONS

**Requirement 1**

$$\text{Payback period} = \frac{\text{Amount invested}}{\text{Expected annual net cash inflow}} = \frac{\$48{,}000}{\$13{,}000} = 3.7 \text{ years (rounded)}$$

**Requirement 2**

$$\text{Accounting rate of return} = \frac{\text{Average annual net cash inflow} - \text{Annual depreciation expense}}{\text{Initial investment}}$$

$$= \frac{\$13{,}000 - \$9{,}600^{*}}{\$48{,}000}$$

$$= \frac{\$3{,}400}{\$48{,}000}$$

$$= 7.08\%$$

*Depreciation expense = $48,000 ÷ 5 years = $9,600

**Requirement 3**

The bar-coding machine proposal passes both initial screening tests. The payback period is slightly less than four years, and the accounting rate of return is slightly higher than 7%. Zetamax should further analyze the proposal using a method that incorporates the time value of money.

# Computing the Time Value of Money

3 Use the time value of money to compute the present and future values of single lump sums and annuities.

A dollar received today is worth more than a dollar to be received in the future. This is based on the assumption that you can invest today's dollar and earn extra income. The fact that invested money earns income over time is called the time value of money, and this explains why we would prefer to receive cash sooner rather than later. The time value of money means that the timing of capital investments' net cash inflows is important. Two methods of capital investment analysis incorporate the time value of money: the net present value (NPV) and internal rate of return (IRR). This section reviews time value of money concepts to make sure you have a firm foundation for discussing these two methods.

## Factors Affecting the Time Value of Money

The time value of money depends on several key factors:

1. The principal amount *(p)*
2. The number of periods *(n)*
3. The interest rate *(i)*

The principal *(p)* refers to the amount of the investment or borrowing. We state the principal as either a single lump sum or an **annuity**. For example, if you want to save money for a new car, you may decide to invest a single lump sum of $10,000 in a certificate of deposit (CD). However, you may not currently have $10,000 to invest. Instead, you may invest funds as an annuity, depositing $2,000 at the end of each year in a bank savings account. An annuity is a stream of *equal instalments made at equal time intervals*. An *ordinary annuity* is an annuity in which the instalments occur at the *end* of each period. An *annuity due* is an annuity in which the instalments occur at the *beginning* of each period. Throughout this chapter we use ordinary annuities since they are better suited to capital budgeting cash flow assumptions.

The number of periods *(n)* is the length of time from the beginning of the investment until termination. All else being equal, the shorter the investment period, the lower the total amount of interest earned. If you withdraw your savings after four years rather than five years, you will earn less interest. If you begin to save for retirement at age 22 rather than age 45, you will earn more interest before you retire. In this chapter, the number of periods is stated in years.[11]

**Why is this important?**

The **time value of money** is a critical factor in many management **decisions**. In addition to its use in capital investment analysis, it's also used for **personal financial planning** (such as retirement planning), **business valuation** (for purchasing businesses), and financing decisions **(borrowing and lending)**.

The interest rate *(i)* is the annual percentage earned on the investment. **Simple interest** means that interest is calculated *only* on the principal amount. **Compound interest** means that interest is calculated on the principal *and* on all interest earned to date. *Compound interest assumes that all interest earned will remain invested at the same interest rate, not withdrawn and spent.* Exhibit 12-6 compares simple and compound interest on a five-year, $10,000 CD (rounded to the nearest dollar). As you can see, the amount of compound interest earned yearly grows as the base on which it is calculated (principal plus cumulative interest to date) grows. Over the life of this particular investment, the total amount of compound interest is about 13% more than the total amount of simple interest. Most investments yield compound interest, so we assume compound interest rather than simple interest for the rest of this chapter.

Fortunately, time value calculations involving compound interest do not have to be as tedious as shown in Exhibit 12-6. Formulas and tables (or business calculators programmed with these formulas) simplify the calculations. In the next sections, we will discuss how to use these tools to perform time value calculations.

**EXHIBIT 12-6** Simple versus Compound Interest for a Principal Amount of $10,000 at 6% over Five Years

| Year | Simple Interest Calculation | Simple Interest | Compound Interest Calculation | Compound Interest |
|---|---|---|---|---|
| 1 | $ 10,000 × 6% = | $ 600 | $10,000 × 6% = | $ 600 |
| 2 | $ 10,000 × 6% = | 600 | ($10,000 + 600) × 6% = | 636 |
| 3 | $ 10,000 × 6% = | 600 | ($10,000 + 600 + 636) × 6% = | 674 |
| 4 | $ 10,000 × 6% = | 600 | ($10,000 + 600 + 636 + 674) × 6% = | 715 |
| 5 | $ 10,000 × 6% = | 600 | ($10,000 + 600 + 636 + 674 + 715) × 6% = | 758 |
| | Total interest | $3,000 | Total interest | $3,383 |

## Future Values and Present Values: Points Along the Time Continuum

Consider the timeline in Exhibit 12-7. The future value or present value of an investment simply refers to the value of an investment at different points in time.

[11]The number of periods can also be stated in days, months, or quarters. If so, the interest rate needs to be adjusted to reflect the number of time periods in the year.

**EXHIBIT 12-7** Present Value and Future Value Along the Time Continuum

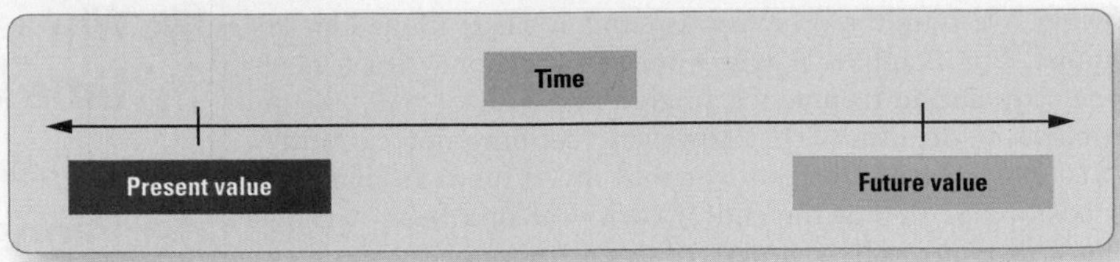


We can calculate the future value or the present value of any investment by knowing (or assuming) information about the three factors listed earlier: (1) the principal amount, (2) the period of time, and (3) the interest rate. For example, in Exhibit 12-6, we calculated the interest that would be earned on (1) a $10,000 principal (2) invested for five years (3) at 6% interest. The future value of the investment is its worth at the end of the five-year time frame—the original principal *plus* the interest earned. In our example, the future value of the investment is as follows:

$$\begin{aligned}\text{Future value} &= \text{Principal} + \text{Interest earned}\\ &= \$10{,}000 + \$3{,}383\\ &= \$13{,}383\end{aligned}$$

If we invest $10,000 today, its *present value* is simply the $10,000 principal amount. So, another way of stating the future valuc is as follows:

$$\text{Future value} = \text{Present value} + \text{Interest earned}$$

We can rearrange the equation as follows:

$$\begin{aligned}\text{Present value} &= \text{Future value} - \text{Interest earned}\\ \$10{,}000 &= \$13{,}383 - \$3{,}383\end{aligned}$$

The only difference between present value and future value is the amount of interest that is earned in the intervening time span.

## Future Value and Present Value Factors

Calculating each period's compound interest, as we did in Exhibit 12-6, and then adding it to the present value to figure the future value (or subtracting it from the future value to figure the present value) is tedious. Fortunately, mathematical formulas simplify future value and present value calculations. Mathematical formulas have been developed that specify future values and present values for unlimited combinations of interest rates *(i)* and time periods *(n)*. Separate formulas exist for single lump-sum investments and annuities.

The formulas are calculated using various interest rates and time periods and the results displayed in tables. The formulas and resulting tables are shown in Appendix 12A.

1. Present Value of $1 (Table A, p. 748)—*used for lump-sum amounts*
2. Present Value of Annuity of $1 (Table B, p. 749)—*used for annuities*
3. Future Value of $1 (Table C, p. 750)—*used for lump-sum amounts*
4. Future Value of Annuity of $1 (Table D, p. 751)—*used for annuities*

Take a moment to look at these tables because we are going to use them throughout the rest of the chapter. Note that the columns are interest rates *(i)*, and the rows are periods *(n)*.

The data in each table, known as future value factors (FV factors) and present value factors (PV factors), are for an investment (or loan) of $1. To find the future value of an amount other than $1, you simply multiply the FV factor found in the table by the principal amount. To find the present value of an amount other than $1, you multiply the PV factor found in the table by the principal amount.

## Calculating Future Values of Single Sums and Annuities Using FV Factors

Let's go back to our $10,000 lump-sum investment. If we want to know the future value of the investment five years from now at an interest rate of 6%, we determine the FV factor from Table C: Future Value of $1. We use this table for lump-sum amounts. We look down the 6% column and across the five periods row and find that the future value factor is 1.338. We finish our calculations as follows:

$$\begin{aligned}\text{Future value} &= \text{Principal amount} \times (\text{FV factor for } i = 6\%, n = 5)\\ &= \$10{,}000 \times (1.338)\\ &= \$13{,}380\end{aligned}$$

This figure agrees with our earlier calculation of the investment's future value ($13,383) in Exhibit 12-6. (The difference of $3 is due to two facts: (1) The tables round the FV and PV factors to three decimal places, and (2) we rounded our earlier yearly interest calculations in Exhibit 12-6 to the nearest dollar.)

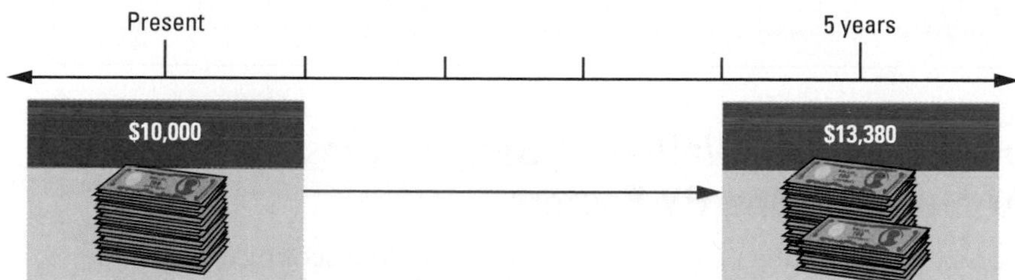


Let's also consider our alternative investment strategy: investing $2,000 at the end of each year for five years. The procedure for calculating the future value of an annuity is similar to that for calculating the future value of a lump-sum amount. This time, we use Table D: Future Value of Annuity of $1. Assuming 6% interest, we once again look down the 6% column. Because we will be making five annual instalments, we look across the row marked five periods. The annuity FV factor is 5.637. We finish the calculation as follows:

$$\begin{aligned}\text{Future value} &= \text{Amount of each cash installment} \times (\text{Annuity FV factor for } i = 6\%, n = 5)\\ &= \$2{,}000 \times (5.637)\\ &= \$11{,}274\end{aligned}$$

This is considerably less than the future value ($13,380) of the lump sum of $10,000 even though we invested $10,000 out of pocket either way.

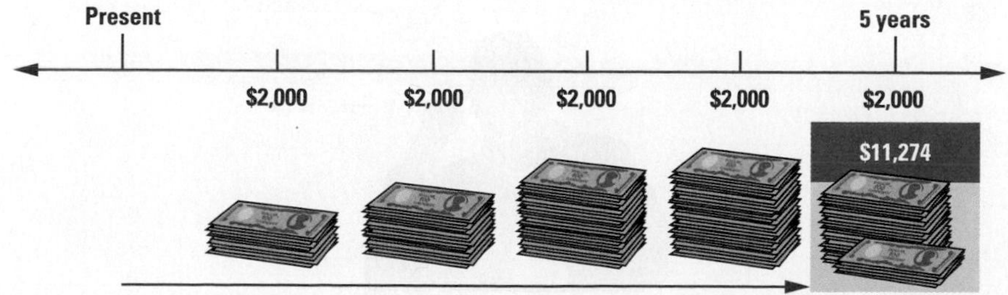

## STOP & THINK

Explain why the future value of the annuity ($11,274) is less than the future value of the lump sum ($13,380). Prove that the $11,274 future value is correct by calculating interest using the "longhand" method shown earlier.

**Answer:** Even though you invested $10,000 out of pocket under both investments, the timing of the investment significantly affects the amount of interest earned. The $10,000 lump sum invested immediately earns interest for the full five years. However, the annuity doesn't begin earning interest until Year 2 (because the first instalment isn't made until the end of Year 1). In addition, the amount invested begins at $2,000 and doesn't reach a full $10,000 until the end of Year 5. Therefore, the base on which the interest is earned is smaller than the lump-sum investment for the entire five-year period. As shown here, the $11,274 future value of a $2,000 annuity for five years is correct.

| Year | Interest Earned During Year (6%) (rounded) | Investment Installment (end of year) | Cumulative Balance at End of Year (investments plus interest earned to date)* |
|---|---|---|---|
| 1 | $ 0 | $2,000 | $ 2,000 |
| 2 | 120 | 2,000 | 4,120 |
| 3 | 247 | 2,000 | 6,367 |
| 4 | 382 | 2,000 | 8,749 |
| 5 | 525 | 2,000 | 11,274 |

*This is the base on which the interest is earned the next year.

## Calculating Present Values of Single Sums and Annuities Using PV Factors

The process for calculating present values—often called discounting cash flows—is similar to the process for calculating future values. The difference is the point in time at which you are assessing the investment's worth. Rather than determining its value at a future date, you are determining its value at an earlier point in time (today). For our example, let's assume that you've just won the lottery after purchasing one $5 lottery ticket. The lottery corporation offers you three payout options for your prize money:

| |
|---|
| Option #1: $1,000,000 now |
| Option #2: $150,000 at the end of each year for the next 10 years |
| Option #3: $2,000,000 10 years from now |

Which alternative should you take? You might be tempted to wait 10 years to "double" your winnings. You may be tempted to take the money now and spend it. However, let's assume that you plan to prudently invest all money received—no matter when you receive it—so that you have financial flexibility in the future (for example, for buying a house, retiring early, and taking vacations). How can you choose among the three payment alternatives when the *total amount* of each option varies ($1,000,000 versus $1,500,000 versus $2,000,000) and the *timing* of the cash flows varies (now versus some each year versus later)? Comparing these three options is like comparing apples to oranges—we just can't do it—unless we find some common basis for comparison. Our common basis for comparison will be the prize money's worth at a certain point in time—namely, today. In other words, if we convert each payment option to its present value, we can compare apples to apples.

We already know the principal amount and timing of each payment option, so the only assumption we have to make is the interest rate. The interest rate varies depending on the amount of risk you are willing to take with your investment. Riskier investments (such as stock investments) command higher interest rates; safer investments (such as Canada Deposit Insurance Corporation [CDIC]-insured bank deposits) yield lower interest rates. Let's assume that after investigating possible investment alternatives, you choose an investment contract with an 8% annual return.

We already know that the present value of Option #1 is $1,000,000. Let's convert the other two payment options to their present values so that we can compare them. We'll need to use Table B: Present Value of Annuity of $1 to convert payment Option #2 (since it's an annuity) and Table A: Present Value of $1 to convert payment Option #3 (since it's a single lump sum). To obtain the PV factors, we look down the 8% column and across the 10 period row. Then, we finish the calculations as follows:

<u>**Option #1**</u>

Present value = $1,000,000

<u>**Option #2**</u>

Present value = Amount of each cash installment × (Annuity PV factor for $i$ = 8%, $n$ = 10)
Present value = $150,000 × (6.710)
Present value = $1,006,500

<u>**Option #3**</u>

Present value = Principal amount × (PV factor for $i$ = 8%, $n$ = 10)
Present value = $2,000,000 × (0.463)
Present value = $926,000

Exhibit 12-8 shows that we have converted each payout option to a common basis—its worth today—so that we can make a valid comparison of the options. Based on this comparison, we should choose Option #2 because its worth, in today's dollars, is the highest of the three options.

Now that we have studied time value of money concepts, we will discuss the two capital budgeting methods that incorporate the time value of money: net present value (NPV) and internal rate of return (IRR).

**EXHIBIT 12-8** Comparing Present Values of Lottery Payout Options at $i = 8\%$

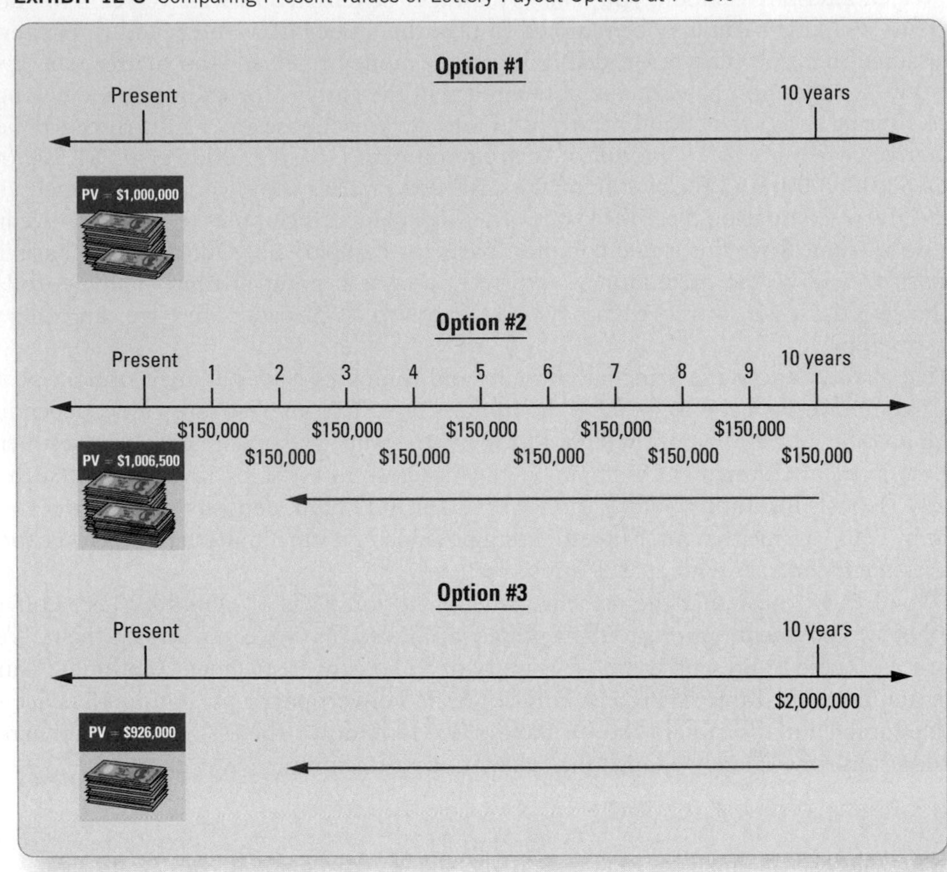


## STOP & THINK

Suppose you decide to invest your lottery winnings very conservatively in a risk-free investment that earns only 3%. Would you still choose payout Option #2? Explain your decision.

**Answer:** Using a 3% interest rate, the present values of the payout options are as follows:

| Payment Options | Present Value of Lottery Payout (Present value calculation, $i = 3\%$, $n = 10$) |
|---|---|
| Option #1 ........................................ | \$1,000,000 (already stated at its present value) |
| Option #2 ........................................ | \$1,279,500 (= \$150,000 × 8.530) |
| Option #3 ........................................ | \$1,488,000 (= \$2,000,000 × 0.744) |

When the lottery payout is invested at 3% rather than 8%, the present values change. Option #3 is now the best alternative because its present value is the highest. Present values and future values are extremely sensitive to changes in interest rate assumptions, especially when the investment period is relatively long.

## Calculating the Net Present Value and Internal Rate of Return

4 Use discounted cash flow models to make capital investment decisions.

PROFESSIONAL COMPETENCY

Neither the payback period nor the ARR incorporate the time value of money. Discounted cash flow models—the NPV and the IRR—overcome this weakness. These models incorporate compound interest by assuming that companies will reinvest future cash flows when they are received. The Government of Canada states that the discounted cash flow system is the most prevalent method for valuing firms for investment purposes because of its accuracy.

The NPV and IRR methods rely on present value calculations to compare the amount of the investment (the investment's initial cost) with its expected net cash inflows. Recall that an investment's *net cash inflows* include all *future* cash flows related to the investment, such as future increased sales and cost savings netted against the investment's future cash operating costs. Because the cash outflow for the investment occurs *now* but the net cash inflows from the investment occur in the *future*, companies can make valid apples-to-apples comparisons only when they convert the cash flows to the *same point in time*—namely, the present value. Companies use the present value rather than the future value to make the comparison because the investment's initial cost is already stated at its present value.[12] In a favourable investment, the present value of the investment's net cash inflows exceeds the initial cost of the investment.

**Why is this important?**
The **NPV method** lets managers make an **apples-to-apples comparison** between the **cash flows** they will receive in the **future** from the investment and the **price** they must **currently pay** to "purchase" those future cash flows (the cost of the **investment**).

### Net Present Value (NPV)

Allegra is considering producing Blu-ray players and digital video recorders (DVRs). The products require different specialized machines, each costing $1 million. Each machine has a five-year life and zero residual value. The two products have different patterns of predicted net cash inflows:

| | *Annual Net Cash Inflows* | |
|---|---|---|
| **Year** | **Blu-ray Players** | **DVRs** |
| 1 | $ 305,450 | $ 500,000 |
| 2 | 305,450 | 350,000 |
| 3 | 305,450 | 300,000 |
| 4 | 305,450 | 250,000 |
| 5 | 305,450 | 40,000 |
| Total | $1,527,250 | $1,440,000 |

The Blu-ray player project generates more net cash inflows, but the DVR project brings in cash sooner. To decide how attractive each investment is, we find its net present value (NPV). The NPV is the *difference* between the present value of the investment's net cash inflows and the investment's cost. We *discount* the net cash inflows to their present value—just as we did in the lottery example—using Allegra's minimum desired rate of return. This rate is called the **discount rate** because it is the interest rate used for the present value calculations. It's also called the **required rate of return**, or **hurdle rate**, because

[12]If the investment is to be purchased through lease payments rather than a current cash outlay, we still use the current cash price of the investment as its initial cost. If no current cash price is available, we discount the future lease payments back to their present value to estimate the investment's current cash price.

the investment must meet or exceed this rate to be acceptable. The discount rate depends on the riskiness of investments. The higher the risk, the higher the discount rate. Allegra's discount rate for these investments is 14%.

Compare the present value of the net cash inflows to the investment's initial cost to decide which projects meet or exceed management's minimum desired rate of return. Management must decide whether the $1 million is worth more (because the company would have to give it up now to invest in the project) or whether the project's future net cash inflows are worth more. Managers can make a valid comparison between the two sums of money only by comparing them at the *same* point in time—namely at their present value.

### NPV with Equal Annual Net Cash Inflows (Annuity)

Allegra expects the Blu-ray player project to generate $305,450 of net cash inflows each year for five years. Because these cash flows are equal in amount and occur every year, they are an annuity. Therefore, we use Table B: Present Value of Annuity of $1 to find the appropriate annuity PV factor for $i = 14\%$, $n = 5$.

The present value of the net cash inflows from Allegra's Blu-ray player project is as follows:

Present value = Amount of each cash inflow × (Annuity PV factor for $i = 14\%, n = 5$)
= $305,450 × (3.433)
= $1,048,610

Next, we subtract the investment's initial cost ($1 million) from the present value of the net cash inflows ($1,048,610). The difference of $48,610 is the net present value (NPV), as shown in Exhibit 12-9.

**EXHIBIT 12-9** NPV of Equal Net Cash Inflows—Blu-ray-Player Project

| | Annuity PV Factor ($i = 14\%, n = 5$) | | Net Cash Inflow | Present Value |
|---|---|---|---|---|
| Present value of annuity of equal annual net cash inflows for five years at 14% | 3.433* | × | $305,450 = | $ 1,048,610 |
| Investment | | | | (1,000,000) |
| Net present value of the Blu-ray player project | | | | $ 48,610 |

*Annuity PV factor is found in Appendix 12A, Table B.

A *positive* NPV means that the project earns more than the required rate of return. A *negative* NPV means that the project fails to earn the required rate of return. This leads to the following decision rule:

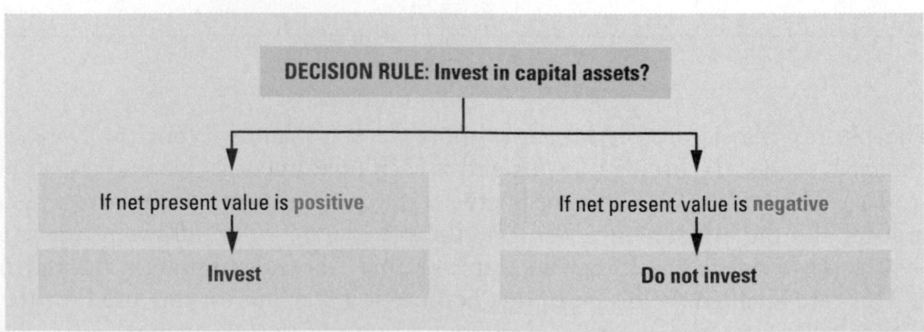


In Allegra's case, the Blu-ray player project is an attractive investment. The $48,610 positive NPV means that the Blu-ray player project earns more than Allegra's 14% target rate of return. In other words, management would prefer to give up $1 million today to

receive the Blu-ray player project's future net cash inflows. Why? Because those future net cash inflows are worth more than $1 million in today's dollars (they are worth $1,048,610).

Another way managers can use present value analysis is to start the capital budgeting process by computing the total present value of the net cash inflows from the project to determine the *maximum* the company can invest in the project and still earn the target rate of return. For Allegra, the present value of the net cash inflows is $1,048,610. This means that Allegra can invest a maximum of $1,048,610 and still earn the 14% target rate of return. Because Allegra's managers believe they can undertake the project for $1 million, the project is an attractive investment.

## NPV with Unequal Annual Net Cash Inflows

In contrast to the Blu-ray player project, the net cash inflows of the DVR project are unequal—$500,000 in Year 1, $350,000 in Year 2, and so forth. Because these amounts vary by year, Allegra's managers *cannot* use the annuity table to compute the present value of the DVR project. They must compute the present value of each individual year's net cash inflows separately (as separate lump sums received in different years) using Table A: Present Value of $1.

Exhibit 12-10 shows that the $500,000 net cash inflow received in Year 1 is discounted using a PV factor of $i = 14\%$, $n = 1$, while the $350,000 net cash inflow received in Year 2 is discounted using a PV factor of $i = 14\%$, $n = 2$, and so forth. After separately discounting each of the five year's net cash inflows, we find that the *total* present value of the DVR project's net cash inflows is $1,078,910. Finally, we subtract the investment's cost ($1 million) to arrive at the DVR project's NPV: $78,910.

Because the NPV is positive, Allegra expects the DVR project to earn more than the 14% target rate of return, making this an attractive investment.

**EXHIBIT 12-10** NPV with Unequal Net Cash Inflows—DVR Project

| | PV Factor ($i = 14\%$) | | Net Cash Inflow | | Present Value |
|---|---|---|---|---|---|
| Present value of each year's net cash inflows discounted at 14%: | | | | | |
| Year 1 ($n = 1$) | 0.877* | × | $ 500,000 | = | $ 438,500 |
| Year 2 ($n = 2$) | 0.769 | × | 350,000 | = | 269,150 |
| Year 3 ($n = 3$) | 0.675 | × | 300,000 | = | 202,500 |
| Year 4 ($n = 4$) | 0.592 | × | 250,000 | = | 148,000 |
| Year 5 ($n = 5$) | 0.519 | × | 40,000 | = | 20,760 |
| Total present value of net cash inflows | | | | | 1,078,910 |
| Investment | | | | | (1,000,000) |
| Net present value of the DVR project | | | | | $ 78,910 |

*PV factors are found in Appendix 12A, Table A.

## Capital Rationing and the Profitability Index

Exhibits 12-9 and 12-10 show that both the Blu-ray player and DVR projects have positive NPVs. Therefore, both are attractive investments. Because resources are limited, companies are not always able to invest in all capital assets that meet their investment criteria. For example, Allegra may not have the funds to invest in both the DVR and Blu-ray player projects at this time. In this case, Allegra should choose the DVR project because it yields a higher NPV. The DVR project should earn an additional $78,910 beyond the 14% required rate of return, while the Blu-ray player project returns an additional $48,610.

This example illustrates an important point. The Blu-ray player project promises more *total* net cash inflows. But the timing

> **Why is this important?**
> The **profitability index** allows managers to **compare** potential investments of **different sizes** so that they can choose the **most profitable** investment.

of the DVR cash flows—loaded near the beginning of the project—gives the DVR investment a higher NPV. The DVR project is more attractive because of the time value of money. Its dollars, which are received sooner, are worth more now than the more distant dollars of the Blu-ray player project.

If Allegra had to choose between the Blu-ray player and DVR project, it would choose the DVR project because that project yields a higher NPV ($78,910). However, comparing the NPV of the two projects is valid *only* because both projects require the same initial cost—$1 million. In contrast, Exhibit 12-11 summarizes three capital investment options that Raycor, a sporting goods manufacturer, faces. Each capital project requires a different initial investment. All three projects are attractive because each yields a positive NPV. Assuming that Raycor can invest in only one project at this time, which one should it choose? Project B yields the highest NPV, but it also requires a larger initial investment than the alternatives.

**EXHIBIT 12-11** Raycor's Capital Investment Options

| | Project A | Project B | Project C |
|---|---|---|---|
| Present value of net cash inflows | $150,000 | $238,000 | $182,000 |
| Investment | (125,000) | (200,000) | (150,000) |
| Net present value (NPV) | $ 25,000 | $ 38,000 | $ 32,000 |

To choose among the projects, Raycor computes the **profitability index** (also known as the **present value index**). The profitability index is computed as follows:

Profitability index = Present value of net cash inflows ÷ Investment

The profitability index computes the number of dollars returned for every dollar invested, *with all calculations performed in present value dollars*. It allows us to compare alternative investments in present value terms (like the NPV method) but also considers differences in the investments' initial cost. Let's compute the profitability index for all three alternatives.

| | Present value of net cash inflows | ÷ Investment | = | Profitability index |
|---|---|---|---|---|
| Project A: | $150,000 | ÷ $125,000 | = | 1.20 |
| Project B: | $238,000 | ÷ $200,000 | = | 1.19 |
| Project C: | $182,000 | ÷ $150,000 | = | 1.21 |

The profitability index shows that Project C is the best of the three alternatives because it returns $1.21 (in present value dollars) for every $1.00 invested. Projects A and B return slightly less.

Let's also compute the profitability index for Allegra's Blu-ray player and DVR projects:

| | Present value of net cash inflows | ÷ Investment | = | Profitability index |
|---|---|---|---|---|
| Blu-ray player: | $1,048,610 | ÷ $1,000,000 | = | 1.049 |
| DVR: | $1,078,910 | ÷ $1,000,000 | = | 1.079 |

The profitability index confirms our prior conclusion that the DVR project is more profitable than the Blu-ray player project. The DVR project returns $1.079 (in present value dollars) for every $1.00 invested. This return is beyond the 14% return already used to discount the cash flows. We did not need the profitability index to determine that the DVR project was preferable because both projects required the same investment ($1 million).

## NPV of a Project with Residual Value

Many assets yield cash inflows at the end of their useful lives because they have residual value. Companies discount an investment's residual value to its present value when determining the *total* present value of the project's net cash inflows. The residual value is discounted as a single lump sum—not an annuity—because it will be received only once, when the asset is sold.

Suppose Allegra expects the Blu-ray player project equipment to be worth $100,000 at the end of its five-year life. This represents an additional future cash inflow from the Blu-ray player project. To determine the Blu-ray player project's NPV, we discount the residual value ($100,000) using Table A: Present Value of $1. We then *add* its present value ($51,900) to the present value of the Blu-ray player project's other net cash inflows ($1,048,610) as shown in Exhibit 12-12:

**EXHIBIT 12-12** NPV of a Project with Residual Value

| | PV Factor ($i = 14\%, n = 5$) | | Net Cash Inflow | Present Value |
|---|---|---|---|---|
| Present value of annuity | 3.433 | × | $305,450 = | $ 1,048,610 |
| Present value of residual value (single lump sum) | 0.519 | × | 100,000 = | 51,900 |
| Total present value of net cash inflows | | | | $ 1,100,510 |
| Investment | | | | $(1,000,000) |
| Net present value (NPV) | | | | $ 100,510 |

Because of the expected residual value, the Blu-ray player project is now more attractive than the DVR project. If Allegra could pursue only the Blu-ray player or the DVR project, it would now choose the Blu-ray player project because its NPV ($100,510) is higher than the DVR project's ($78,910), and both projects require the same investment ($1 million).

## Sensitivity Analysis

Capital budgeting decisions affect cash flows far into the future. Allegra's managers might want to know whether their decision will be affected by any of their major assumptions. For example, consider the following:

- Changing the discount rate from 14% to 12% or to 16%
- Changing the net cash flows by 10%
- Changing an expected residual value

Managers can use spreadsheet software or programmed calculators to quickly perform sensitivity analysis.

### TRY IT!

The Bruce Company is considering investing a wind turbine to generate its own power. Any unused power will be sold back to the local utility company. Between cost saving and new revenues, the company expects to generate $750,000 per year in net cash inflows from the turbine. The turbine would cost $4 million and is expected to have 20-year useful life with no residual value. Calculate the NPV assuming the company uses a 12% hurdle rate.

Please see page 772 for solution.

## Internal Rate of Return (IRR)

The NPV method tells management only whether the investment exceeds the hurdle rate. Since both the Blu-ray player and DVR projects yield positive NPVs, we know they provide *more* than a 14% rate of return. But what exact rate of return would these investments provide? The IRR method answers that question.

The internal rate of return (IRR) is the rate of return, based on discounted cash flows, that a company can expect to earn by investing in the project. *It is the interest rate that makes the NPV of the investment equal to zero*:

$$\text{NPV} = 0$$

Let's look at this concept in another light by inserting the definition of NPV:

$$\text{Present value of the investment's net cash inflows} - \text{Investment's cost} = 0$$

Or if we rearrange the equation, we obtain the following:

$$\text{Investment's cost} = \text{Present value of the investment's net cash inflows}$$

In other words, the IRR is the *interest rate* that makes the cost of the investment equal to the present value of the investment's net cash inflows. The higher the IRR, the more desirable the project. Like the profitability index, the IRR can be used in the capital rationing process.

IRR computations are very easy to perform on programmed calculators. However, IRR computations are much more cumbersome to perform using the tables.

### IRR with Equal Annual Net Cash Inflows (Annuity)

When the investment is an annuity, we can develop a formula that will tell us the Annuity PV factor associated with the investment's IRR. We start with the equation given previously and then substitute in as follows:

Investment's cost = Present value of the investment's net cash inflows

Investment's cost = Amount of each equal net cash inflow annuity PV factor ($i$ = ?, $n$ = given)

Finally, we rearrange the equation to obtain the following formula:

$$\frac{\text{Investment's cost}}{\text{Amount of each equal net cash inflow}} = \text{Annuity PV factor } (i = ?, n = \text{given})$$

Let's use this formula to find the annuity PV factor associated with Allegra's Blu-ray player project. Recall that the project would cost $1 million and result in five equal yearly cash inflows of $305,450:

$$\frac{\$1{,}000{,}000}{\$305{,}450} = \text{Annuity PV factor } (i = ?, n = 5)$$

$$3.274 = \text{Annuity PV factor } (i = ?, n = 5)$$

Next, we find the interest rate that corresponds to this annuity PV factor. Turn to Table B: Present Value of Annuity of $1 and scan the row corresponding to the project's expected life—five years, in our example. Choose the column or columns with the number closest to the annuity PV factor you calculated using the formula. The 3.274 annuity factor is in the 16% column.

Therefore, the IRR of the Blu-ray player project is 16%.

Allegra expects the project to earn an internal rate of return of 16% over its life. Exhibit 12-13 confirms this result: Using a 16% discount rate, the project's NPV is zero. In other words, 16% is the discount rate that makes the investment cost equal to the present value of the investment's net cash inflows.

**EXHIBIT 12-13** IRR– Blu-ray Player Project

| | Annuity PV Factor ($i = 16\%, n = 5$) | | Net Cash Inflow | | Total Present Value |
|---|---|---|---|---|---|
| Present value of annuity of equal annual net cash inflows for five years at 16% | 3.274 | × | $305,450 | = | $ 1,000,000 † |
| Investment | | | | | (1,000,000) |
| Net present value of the Blu-ray player project | | | | | $ 0‡ |

†Slight rounding error.
‡The zero difference proves that the IRR is 16%.

To decide whether the project is acceptable, compare the IRR with the minimum desired rate of return. The decision rule is as follows:

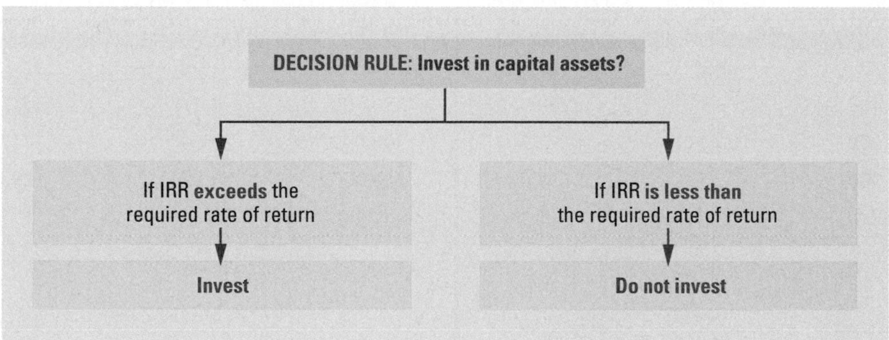


Recall that Allegra's hurdle rate is 14%. Because the Blu-ray player project's IRR (16%) is higher than the hurdle rate (14%), Allegra would invest in the project.

In the Blu-ray player project, the exact annuity PV factor (3.274) appears in Table B: Present Value of an Annuity of $1. Many times, the exact factor does not appear in the table. For example, let's find the IRR of Parlee Manufacturing's B2B Portal. Recall that the B2B portal had a six-year life with annual net cash inflows of $60,000. The investment cost $240,000. We find its annuity PV factor using the formula given previously:

$$\frac{\text{Investment's cost}}{\text{Amount of each equal net cash inflow}} = \text{Annuity PV factor } (i = ?, n = \text{given})$$

$$\frac{\$240{,}000}{\$60{,}000} = \text{Annuity PV factor } (i = ?, n = 6)$$

$$4.00 = \text{Annuity PV factor } (i = ?, n = 6)$$

Now, look in Table B: Present Value of Annuity of $1, in the row marked six periods. You will not see 4.00 under any column. The closest two factors are 3.889 (at 14%) and 4.111 (at 12%).

Thus, the B2B portal's IRR is somewhere between 12% and 14%.

If we used a calculator programmed with the IRR function, we would find that the exact IRR is 12.98%. If Parlee Manufacturing had a 14% hurdle rate, it would *not* invest in the B2B portal because the portal's IRR is less than 14%.

## IRR with Unequal Annual Net Cash Inflows

Because the DVR project has unequal cash inflows, Allegra cannot use Table B: Present Value of Annuity of $1 to find the asset's IRR. Rather, Allegra must use a trial-and-error procedure to determine the discount rate that makes the project's NPV equal to zero. Recall from Exhibit 12-10 that the DVR's NPV using a 14% discount rate is $78,910. Since the NPV is *positive*, the IRR must be *higher* than 14%. Allegra performs the trial-and-error process using higher discount rates until it finds the rate that brings the net present value of the DVR project to *zero*. Exhibit 12-14 shows that at 16%, the DVR has an NPV of $40,390; therefore, the IRR must be higher than 16%. At 18%, the NPV is $3,980, which is very close to zero. Thus, the IRR must be slightly higher than 18%. If we use a calculator programmed with the IRR function rather than the trial-and-error procedure, we would find that the IRR is 18.23%.

**EXHIBIT 12-14** Finding the DVR's IRR through Trial and Error

| | Net Cash Inflow | | PV Factor (for $i = 16\%$) | | Present Value at 16% | Net Cash Inflow | | PV Factor (for $i = 18\%$) | | Present Value at 18% |
|---|---|---|---|---|---|---|---|---|---|---|
| Year 1 ($n = 1$) | $500,000 | × | 0.862* | = | $ 431,000 | $500,000 | × | 0.847* | = | $ 423,500 |
| Year 2 ($n = 2$) | 350,000 | × | 0.743 | = | 260,050 | 350,000 | × | 0.718 | = | 251,300 |
| Year 3 ($n = 3$) | 300,000 | × | 0.641 | = | 192,300 | 300,000 | × | 0.609 | = | 182,700 |
| Year 4 ($n = 4$) | 250,000 | × | 0.552 | = | 138,000 | 250,000 | × | 0.516 | = | 129,000 |
| Year 5 ($n = 5$) | 40,000 | × | 0.476 | = | 19,040 | 40,000 | × | 0.437 | = | 17,480 |
| Total present value of net cash inflows | | | | | $ 1,040,390 | | | | | $ 1,003,980 |
| Investment | | | | | (1,000,000) | | | | | (1,000,000) |
| Net present value (NPV) | | | | | $ 40,390 | | | | | $ 3,980 |

*PV factors are found in Appendix 12A, Table A.

The DVR's internal rate of return is higher than Allegra's 14% hurdle rate, so the DVR project is attractive.

**TRY IT!**

The Bruce Company is considering investing in a wind turbine to generate its own power. Any unused power will be sold back to the local utility company. Between cost savings and new revenues, the company expects to generate $750,000 per year in net cash inflows from the turbine. The turbine would cost 4$ million and is expected to have a 20-year useful life with no residual value. Calculate the internal rate of return (IRR).

Please see page 772 for solution.

## Capital Budgeting Methods in Comparison

5 Compare and contrast the four capital budgeting methods.

PROFESSIONAL COMPETENCY

We have discussed four capital budgeting methods commonly used by companies to make capital investment decisions—two that ignore the time value of money (payback period and ARR) and two that incorporate the time value of money (NPV and IRR). Exhibit 12-15 summarizes the similarities and differences between the two methods that ignore the time value of money.

**EXHIBIT 12-15** Capital Budgeting Methods that *Ignore* the Time Value of Money

| Payback Period | ARR |
|---|---|
| • Simple to compute<br>• Focuses on the time it takes to recover the company's cash investment<br>• Ignores any cash flows occurring after the payback period, including any residual value<br>• Highlights risks of investments with longer cash recovery periods<br>• Ignores the time value of money | • The only method that uses accrual accounting figures<br>• Shows how the investment will affect operating income, which is important to financial statement users<br>• Measures the average profitability of the asset over its entire life<br>• Ignores the time value of money |

Exhibit 12-16 considers the similarities and differences between the two methods that incorporate the time value of money.

**EXHIBIT 12-16** Capital Budgeting Methods that *Incorporate* the Time Value of Money

| NPV | IRR |
|---|---|
| • Incorporates the time value of money and the asset's net cash flows over its entire life<br>• Indicates whether the asset will earn the company's minimum required rate of return<br>• Shows the excess or deficiency of the asset's present value of net cash inflows over its initial investment cost<br>• The profitability index should be computed for capital rationing decisions when the assets require different initial investments | • Incorporates the time value of money and the asset's net cash flows over its entire life<br>• Computes the project's unique rate of return<br>• No additional steps needed for capital rationing decisions |

Keep in mind that managers often use more than one method to gain different perspectives on the risks and returns of potential capital investments.

### STOP & THINK

A pharmaceutical company is considering two research projects that require the same initial investment. Project A has an NPV of $232,000 and a three-year payback period. Project B has an NPV of $237,000 and a payback period of 4.5 years. Which project would you choose?

**Answer:** Many managers would choose Project A even though it has a slightly lower NPV. Why? The NPV is only $5,000 lower, yet the payback period is significantly shorter. The uncertainty of receiving operating cash flows increases with each passing year. Managers often forego small differences in expected cash inflows to decrease the risk of investments.

# DECISION GUIDELINES

## Capital Budgeting

Here are more of the guidelines that Maplewood Equestrian Centre's managers used as they made the major capital budgeting decision to invest in pasture development for grazing.

| Decision | Guidelines |
|---|---|
| Which capital budgeting should we use for this decision? | No one method is best. Each method provides a different perspective on the investment decision. |
| Why do the NPV and IRR models calculate the present value of an investment's net cash flows? | All of the cash flows must be converted to a common point in time because an investment's cash inflows occur in the future, yet the cash outlay for the investment occurs now. These methods use the *present* value as the common point in time. |
| How do we know if investing in a barn for hay and shavings storage will be worthwhile? | Investment in a barn may be worthwhile if the NPV is positive or the IRR exceeds the required rate of return. |
| How do we compute the net present value (NPV) if the investment has equal annual cash inflows? | Compute the present value of the investment's net cash inflows using Table B: Present Value of an Annuity of $1, and then subtract the investment's cost. |
| How do we compute the net present value (NPV) if the investment has unequal annual cash inflows? | Compute the present value of each year's net cash inflows using Table A: Present Value of $1, sum the present value of the inflows, and then subtract the investment's cost. |
| How do we compute the internal rate of return (IRR) if the investment has equal annual cash inflows? | Find the interest rate that yields the following annuity PV factor: $\text{Annuity PV factor} = \dfrac{\text{Investment's cost}}{\text{Amount of each equal net cash inflow}}$ |
| How do we compute the internal rate of return (IRR) if the investment has unequal annual cash inflows? | Use trial and error, a business calculator, or spreadsheet software to find the IRR. |

## SUMMARY PROBLEM 2

Recall from Summary Problem 1 that Zetamax is considering buying a new bar-coding machine. The investment proposal passed the initial screening tests (payback period and accounting rate of return), so the company now wants to analyze the proposal using the discounted cash flow methods. Recall that the bar-coding machine costs $48,000, has a five-year life, and has no residual value. The estimated net cash inflows are $13,000 per year over its life. The company's hurdle rate is 16%.

### Requirements

1. Compute the bar-coding machine's NPV.
2. Find the bar-coding machine's IRR (exact percentage not required).
3. Should Zetamax buy the bar-coding machine? Why or why not?

## ▪ SOLUTIONS

### Requirement 1

| | |
|---|---|
| Present value of annuity of equal annual net cash inflows at 16% ($13,000 × 3.274*) | $ 42,562 |
| Investment | (48,000) |
| Net present value | $ (5,438) |

*Annuity PV factor ($i = 16\%$, $n = 5$).

### Requirement 2

$$\frac{\text{Investment's cost}}{\text{Amount of each equal net cash inflow}} = \text{Annuity PV factor } (i = ?, n = \text{given})$$

$$\frac{\$48{,}000}{\$13{,}000} = \text{Annuity PV factor } (i = ?, n = 5)$$

$$3.692 = \text{Annuity PV factor } (i = ?, n = 5)$$

Because the cash inflows occur for five years, we look for the PV factor 3.692 in the row marked $n = 5$ on Table B: Present Value of Annuity of $1. The PV factor is 3.605 at 12% and 3.791 at 10%. Therefore, the bar-coding machine has an IRR that falls between 10% and 12%. (*Optional.* Using a programmed calculator, we find an 11.038% internal rate of return.)

### Requirement 3

*Decision:* Do not buy the bar-coding machine. It has a negative NPV, and its IRR falls below the company's required rate of return. Both methods show that this investment does not meet management's minimum requirements for investments of this nature.

# APPENDIX 12A

## Present Value and Future Value Tables

### Table A: Present Value of $1

| Present Value of $1 | | | | | | | | | | | | | |
|---|---|---|---|---|---|---|---|---|---|---|---|---|---|
| Periods | 1% | 2% | 3% | 4% | 5% | 6% | 8% | 10% | 12% | 14% | 16% | 18% | 20% |
| 1 | 0.990 | 0.980 | 0.971 | 0.962 | 0.952 | 0.943 | 0.926 | 0.909 | 0.893 | 0.877 | 0.862 | 0.847 | 0.833 |
| 2 | 0.980 | 0.961 | 0.943 | 0.925 | 0.907 | 0.890 | 0.857 | 0.826 | 0.797 | 0.769 | 0.743 | 0.718 | 0.694 |
| 3 | 0.971 | 0.942 | 0.915 | 0.889 | 0.864 | 0.840 | 0.794 | 0.751 | 0.712 | 0.675 | 0.641 | 0.609 | 0.579 |
| 4 | 0.961 | 0.924 | 0.888 | 0.855 | 0.823 | 0.792 | 0.735 | 0.683 | 0.636 | 0.592 | 0.552 | 0.516 | 0.482 |
| 5 | 0.951 | 0.906 | 0.863 | 0.822 | 0.784 | 0.747 | 0.681 | 0.621 | 0.567 | 0.519 | 0.476 | 0.437 | 0.402 |
| 6 | 0.942 | 0.888 | 0.837 | 0.790 | 0.746 | 0.705 | 0.630 | 0.564 | 0.507 | 0.456 | 0.410 | 0.370 | 0.335 |
| 7 | 0.933 | 0.871 | 0.813 | 0.760 | 0.711 | 0.665 | 0.583 | 0.513 | 0.452 | 0.400 | 0.354 | 0.314 | 0.279 |
| 8 | 0.923 | 0.853 | 0.789 | 0.731 | 0.677 | 0.627 | 0.540 | 0.467 | 0.404 | 0.351 | 0.305 | 0.266 | 0.233 |
| 9 | 0.914 | 0.837 | 0.766 | 0.703 | 0.645 | 0.592 | 0.500 | 0.424 | 0.361 | 0.308 | 0.263 | 0.225 | 0.194 |
| 10 | 0.905 | 0.820 | 0.744 | 0.676 | 0.614 | 0.558 | 0.463 | 0.386 | 0.322 | 0.270 | 0.227 | 0.191 | 0.162 |
| 11 | 0.896 | 0.804 | 0.722 | 0.650 | 0.585 | 0.527 | 0.429 | 0.350 | 0.287 | 0.237 | 0.195 | 0.162 | 0.135 |
| 12 | 0.887 | 0.788 | 0.701 | 0.625 | 0.557 | 0.497 | 0.397 | 0.319 | 0.257 | 0.208 | 0.168 | 0.137 | 0.112 |
| 13 | 0.879 | 0.773 | 0.681 | 0.601 | 0.530 | 0.469 | 0.368 | 0.290 | 0.229 | 0.182 | 0.145 | 0.116 | 0.093 |
| 14 | 0.870 | 0.758 | 0.661 | 0.577 | 0.505 | 0.442 | 0.340 | 0.263 | 0.205 | 0.160 | 0.125 | 0.099 | 0.078 |
| 15 | 0.861 | 0.743 | 0.642 | 0.555 | 0.481 | 0.417 | 0.315 | 0.239 | 0.183 | 0.140 | 0.108 | 0.084 | 0.065 |
| 20 | 0.820 | 0.673 | 0.554 | 0.456 | 0.377 | 0.312 | 0.215 | 0.149 | 0.104 | 0.073 | 0.051 | 0.037 | 0.026 |
| 25 | 0.780 | 0.610 | 0.478 | 0.375 | 0.295 | 0.233 | 0.146 | 0.092 | 0.059 | 0.038 | 0.024 | 0.016 | 0.010 |
| 30 | 0.742 | 0.552 | 0.412 | 0.308 | 0.231 | 0.174 | 0.099 | 0.057 | 0.033 | 0.020 | 0.012 | 0.007 | 0.004 |
| 40 | 0.672 | 0.453 | 0.307 | 0.208 | 0.142 | 0.097 | 0.046 | 0.022 | 0.011 | 0.005 | 0.003 | 0.001 | 0.001 |

The factors in the table were generated using the following formula:

$$\text{Present Value of } \$1 = \frac{1}{(1 + i)^n}$$

where

$i$ = annual interest rate
$n$ = number of periods

## Table B: Present Value of Annuity of $1

| Present Value of Annuity of $1 | | | | | | | | | | | | | |
|---|---|---|---|---|---|---|---|---|---|---|---|---|---|
| Periods | 1% | 2% | 3% | 4% | 5% | 6% | 8% | 10% | 12% | 14% | 16% | 18% | 20% |
| 1 | 0.990 | 0.980 | 0.971 | 0.962 | 0.952 | 0.943 | 0.926 | 0.909 | 0.893 | 0.877 | 0.862 | 0.847 | 0.833 |
| 2 | 1.970 | 1.942 | 1.913 | 1.886 | 1.859 | 1.833 | 1.783 | 1.736 | 1.690 | 1.647 | 1.605 | 1.566 | 1.528 |
| 3 | 2.941 | 2.884 | 2.829 | 2.775 | 2.723 | 2.673 | 2.577 | 2.487 | 2.402 | 2.322 | 2.246 | 2.174 | 2.106 |
| 4 | 3.902 | 3.808 | 3.717 | 3.630 | 3.546 | 3.465 | 3.312 | 3.170 | 3.037 | 2.914 | 2.798 | 2.690 | 2.589 |
| 5 | 4.853 | 4.713 | 4.580 | 4.452 | 4.329 | 4.212 | 3.993 | 3.791 | 3.605 | 3.433 | 3.274 | 3.127 | 2.991 |
| 6 | 5.795 | 5.601 | 5.417 | 5.242 | 5.076 | 4.917 | 4.623 | 4.355 | 4.111 | 3.889 | 3.685 | 3.498 | 3.326 |
| 7 | 6.728 | 6.472 | 6.230 | 6.002 | 5.786 | 5.582 | 5.206 | 4.868 | 4.564 | 4.288 | 4.039 | 3.812 | 3.605 |
| 8 | 7.652 | 7.325 | 7.020 | 6.733 | 6.463 | 6.210 | 5.747 | 5.335 | 4.968 | 4.639 | 4.344 | 4.078 | 3.837 |
| 9 | 8.566 | 8.162 | 7.786 | 7.435 | 7.108 | 6.802 | 6.247 | 5.759 | 5.328 | 4.946 | 4.607 | 4.303 | 4.031 |
| 10 | 9.471 | 8.983 | 8.530 | 8.111 | 7.722 | 7.360 | 6.710 | 6.145 | 5.650 | 5.216 | 4.833 | 4.494 | 4.192 |
| 11 | 10.368 | 9.787 | 9.253 | 8.760 | 8.306 | 7.887 | 7.139 | 6.495 | 5.938 | 5.553 | 5.029 | 4.656 | 4.327 |
| 12 | 11.255 | 10.575 | 9.954 | 9.385 | 8.863 | 8.384 | 7.536 | 6.814 | 6.194 | 5.660 | 5.197 | 4.793 | 4.439 |
| 13 | 12.134 | 11.348 | 10.635 | 9.986 | 9.394 | 8.853 | 7.904 | 7.103 | 6.424 | 5.842 | 5.342 | 4.910 | 4.533 |
| 14 | 13.004 | 12.106 | 11.296 | 10.563 | 9.899 | 9.295 | 8.244 | 7.367 | 6.628 | 6.002 | 5.468 | 5.008 | 4.611 |
| 15 | 13.865 | 12.849 | 11.938 | 11.118 | 10.380 | 9.712 | 8.559 | 7.606 | 6.811 | 6.142 | 5.575 | 5.092 | 4.675 |
| 20 | 18.046 | 16.351 | 14.878 | 13.590 | 12.462 | 11.470 | 9.818 | 8.514 | 7.469 | 6.623 | 5.929 | 5.353 | 4.870 |
| 25 | 22.023 | 19.523 | 17.413 | 15.622 | 14.094 | 12.783 | 10.675 | 9.077 | 7.843 | 6.873 | 6.097 | 5.467 | 4.948 |
| 30 | 25.808 | 22.396 | 19.600 | 17.292 | 15.373 | 13.765 | 11.258 | 9.427 | 8.055 | 7.003 | 6.177 | 5.517 | 4.979 |
| 40 | 32.835 | 27.355 | 23.115 | 19.793 | 17.159 | 15.046 | 11.925 | 9.779 | 8.244 | 7.105 | 6.234 | 5.548 | 4.997 |

The factors in the table were generated using the following formula:

$$\text{Present value of annuity of } \$1 = \frac{1}{i}\left[1 - \frac{1}{(1+i)^n}\right]$$

where

$i$ = annual interest rate
$n$ = number of periods

# Table C: Future Value of $1

| Future Value of $1 | | | | | | | | | | | | | |
|---|---|---|---|---|---|---|---|---|---|---|---|---|---|
| Periods | 1% | 2% | 3% | 4% | 5% | 6% | 8% | 10% | 12% | 14% | 16% | 18% | 20% |
| 1 | 1.010 | 1.020 | 1.030 | 1.040 | 1.050 | 1.060 | 1.080 | 1.100 | 1.120 | 1.140 | 1.160 | 1.180 | 1.200 |
| 2 | 1.020 | 1.040 | 1.061 | 1.082 | 1.103 | 1.124 | 1.166 | 1.210 | 1.254 | 1.300 | 1.346 | 1.392 | 1.440 |
| 3 | 1.030 | 1.061 | 1.093 | 1.125 | 1.158 | 1.191 | 1.260 | 1.331 | 1.405 | 1.482 | 1.561 | 1.643 | 1.728 |
| 4 | 1.041 | 1.082 | 1.126 | 1.170 | 1.216 | 1.262 | 1.360 | 1.464 | 1.574 | 1.689 | 1.811 | 1.939 | 2.074 |
| 5 | 1.051 | 1.104 | 1.159 | 1.217 | 1.276 | 1.338 | 1.469 | 1.611 | 1.762 | 1.925 | 2.100 | 2.288 | 2.488 |
| 6 | 1.062 | 1.126 | 1.194 | 1.265 | 1.340 | 1.419 | 1.587 | 1.772 | 1.974 | 2.195 | 2.436 | 2.700 | 2.986 |
| 7 | 1.072 | 1.149 | 1.230 | 1.316 | 1.407 | 1.504 | 1.714 | 1.949 | 2.211 | 2.502 | 2.826 | 3.185 | 3.583 |
| 8 | 1.083 | 1.172 | 1.267 | 1.369 | 1.477 | 1.594 | 1.851 | 2.144 | 2.476 | 2.853 | 3.278 | 3.759 | 4.300 |
| 9 | 1.094 | 1.195 | 1.305 | 1.423 | 1.551 | 1.689 | 1.999 | 2.358 | 2.773 | 3.252 | 3.803 | 4.435 | 5.160 |
| 10 | 1.105 | 1.219 | 1.344 | 1.480 | 1.629 | 1.791 | 2.159 | 2.594 | 3.106 | 3.707 | 4.411 | 5.234 | 6.192 |
| 11 | 1.116 | 1.243 | 1.384 | 1.539 | 1.710 | 1.898 | 2.332 | 2.853 | 3.479 | 4.226 | 5.117 | 6.176 | 7.430 |
| 12 | 1.127 | 1.268 | 1.426 | 1.601 | 1.796 | 2.012 | 2.518 | 3.138 | 3.896 | 4.818 | 5.936 | 7.288 | 8.916 |
| 13 | 1.138 | 1.294 | 1.469 | 1.665 | 1.886 | 2.133 | 2.720 | 3.452 | 4.363 | 5.492 | 6.886 | 8.599 | 10.669 |
| 14 | 1.149 | 1.319 | 1.513 | 1.732 | 1.980 | 2.261 | 2.937 | 3.798 | 4.887 | 6.261 | 7.988 | 10.147 | 12.839 |
| 15 | 1.161 | 1.346 | 1.558 | 1.801 | 2.079 | 2.397 | 3.172 | 4.177 | 5.474 | 7.138 | 9.266 | 11.974 | 15.407 |
| 20 | 1.220 | 1.486 | 1.806 | 2.191 | 2.653 | 3.207 | 4.661 | 6.728 | 9.646 | 13.743 | 19.461 | 27.393 | 38.338 |
| 25 | 1.282 | 1.641 | 2.094 | 2.666 | 3.386 | 4.292 | 6.848 | 10.835 | 17.000 | 26.462 | 40.874 | 62.669 | 95.396 |
| 30 | 1.348 | 1.811 | 2.427 | 3.243 | 4.322 | 5.743 | 10.063 | 17.449 | 29.960 | 50.950 | 85.850 | 143.371 | 237.376 |
| 40 | 1.489 | 2.208 | 3.262 | 4.801 | 7.040 | 10.286 | 21.725 | 45.259 | 93.051 | 188.884 | 378.721 | 750.378 | 1,469.772 |

The factors in the table were generated using the following formula:

$$\text{Future Value of } \$1 = (1 + i)^n$$

where

$i$ = annual interest rate
$n$ = number of periods

## Table D: Future Value of Annuity of $1

| Future Value of Annuity of $1 | | | | | | | | | | | | | |
|---|---|---|---|---|---|---|---|---|---|---|---|---|---|
| Periods | 1% | 2% | 3% | 4% | 5% | 6% | 8% | 10% | 12% | 14% | 16% | 18% | 20% |
| 1 | 1.000 | 1.000 | 1.000 | 1.000 | 1.000 | 1.000 | 1.000 | 1.000 | 1.000 | 1.000 | 1.000 | 1.000 | 1.000 |
| 2 | 2.010 | 2.020 | 2.030 | 2.040 | 2.050 | 2.060 | 2.080 | 2.100 | 2.120 | 2.140 | 2.160 | 2.180 | 2.200 |
| 3 | 3.030 | 3.060 | 3.091 | 3.122 | 3.153 | 3.184 | 3.246 | 3.310 | 3.374 | 3.440 | 3.506 | 3.572 | 3.640 |
| 4 | 4.060 | 4.122 | 4.184 | 4.246 | 4.310 | 4.375 | 4.506 | 4.641 | 4.779 | 4.921 | 5.066 | 5.215 | 5.368 |
| 5 | 5.101 | 5.204 | 5.309 | 5.416 | 5.526 | 5.637 | 5.867 | 6.105 | 6.353 | 6.610 | 6.877 | 7.154 | 7.442 |
| 6 | 6.152 | 6.308 | 6.468 | 6.633 | 6.802 | 6.975 | 7.336 | 7.716 | 8.115 | 8.536 | 8.977 | 9.442 | 9.930 |
| 7 | 7.214 | 7.434 | 7.662 | 7.898 | 8.142 | 8.394 | 8.923 | 9.487 | 10.089 | 10.730 | 11.414 | 12.142 | 12.916 |
| 8 | 8.286 | 8.583 | 8.892 | 9.214 | 9.549 | 9.897 | 10.637 | 11.436 | 12.300 | 13.233 | 14.240 | 15.327 | 16.499 |
| 9 | 9.369 | 9.755 | 10.159 | 10.583 | 11.027 | 11.491 | 12.488 | 13.579 | 14.776 | 16.085 | 17.519 | 19.086 | 20.799 |
| 10 | 10.462 | 10.950 | 11.464 | 12.006 | 12.578 | 13.181 | 14.487 | 15.937 | 17.549 | 19.337 | 21.321 | 23.521 | 25.959 |
| 11 | 11.567 | 12.169 | 12.808 | 13.486 | 14.207 | 14.972 | 16.645 | 18.531 | 20.655 | 23.045 | 25.733 | 28.755 | 32.150 |
| 12 | 12.683 | 13.412 | 14.192 | 15.026 | 15.917 | 16.870 | 18.977 | 21.384 | 24.133 | 27.271 | 30.850 | 34.931 | 39.581 |
| 13 | 13.809 | 14.680 | 15.618 | 16.627 | 17.713 | 18.882 | 21.495 | 24.523 | 28.029 | 32.089 | 36.786 | 42.219 | 48.497 |
| 14 | 14.947 | 15.974 | 17.086 | 18.292 | 19.599 | 21.015 | 24.215 | 27.975 | 32.393 | 37.581 | 43.672 | 50.818 | 59.196 |
| 15 | 16.097 | 17.293 | 18.599 | 20.024 | 21.579 | 23.276 | 27.152 | 31.772 | 37.280 | 43.842 | 51.660 | 60.965 | 72.035 |
| 20 | 22.019 | 24.297 | 26.870 | 29.778 | 33.066 | 36.786 | 45.762 | 57.275 | 72.052 | 91.025 | 115.380 | 146.630 | 186.690 |
| 25 | 28.243 | 32.030 | 36.459 | 41.646 | 47.727 | 54.865 | 73.106 | 98.347 | 133.330 | 181.870 | 249.210 | 342.600 | 471.980 |
| 30 | 34.785 | 40.568 | 47.575 | 56.085 | 66.439 | 79.058 | 113.280 | 164.490 | 241.330 | 356.790 | 530.310 | 790.950 | 1,181.900 |
| 40 | 48.886 | 60.402 | 75.401 | 95.026 | 120.800 | 154.760 | 259.060 | 442.590 | 767.090 | 1,342.000 | 2,360.800 | 4,163.200 | 7,343.900 |

The factors in the table were generated using the following formula:

$$\text{Future Value of Annuity of } \$1 = \frac{(1 + i)^n - 1}{i}$$

where

$i$ = annual interest rate

$n$ = number of periods

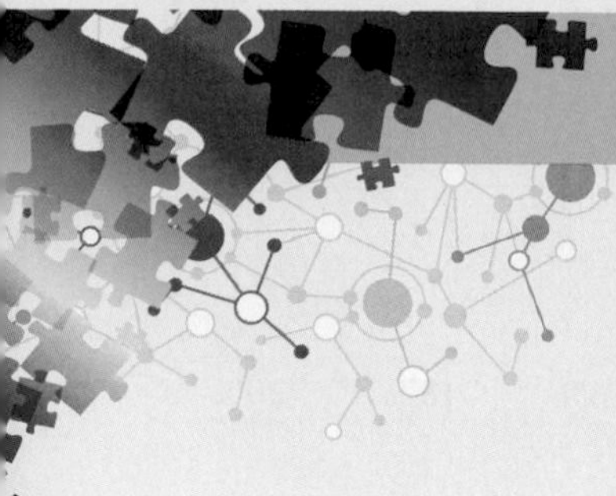

# END OF CHAPTER

## LEARNING OBJECTIVES

1 Describe the importance of capital investments and the capital budgeting process.

2 Use the payback and accounting rate of return methods to make capital investment decisions.

3 Use the time value of money to compute the present and future values of single lump sums and annuities.

4 Use discounted cash flow models to make capital investment decisions.

5 Compare and contrast the four capital budgeting methods.

## ACCOUNTING VOCABULARY

**Accounting Rate of Return (p. 720)** A measure of profitability computed by dividing the average annual operating income from an asset by the initial investment in the asset.

**Annuity (p. 731)** A stream of equal instalments made at equal time intervals.

**Capital Budgeting (p. 720)** The process of making capital investment decisions. Companies make capital investments when they acquire capital assets—assets used for a long period of time.

**Capital Rationing (p. 722)** Choosing among alternative capital investments due to limited funds.

**Compound Interest (p. 731)** Interest computed on the principal and all interest earned to date.

**Discount Rate (p. 737)** Management's minimum desired rate of return on an investment; also called the hurdle rate and required rate of return.

**Hurdle Rate (p. 737)** Management's minimum desired rate of return on an investment; also called the discount rate and required rate of return.

**Internal Rate of Return (IRR) (p. 721)** The rate of return (based on discounted cash flows) that a company can expect to earn by investing in a capital asset. The interest rate that makes the NPV of the investment equal to zero.

**Net Present Value (NPV) (p. 721)** The difference between the present value of the investment's net cash inflows and the investment's cost.

**Payback (p. 720)** The length of time it takes to recover, in net cash inflows, the cost of a capital outlay.

**Post-Audits (p. 723)** Comparing a capital investment's actual net cash inflows to its projected net cash inflows.

**Present Value Index (p. 740)** An index that computes the number of dollars returned for every dollar invested, with all calculations performed in present value dollars. It is computed as present value of net cash inflows divided by investment; also called profitability index.

**Profitability Index (p. 740)** An index that computes the number of dollars returned for every dollar invested, with all calculations performed in present value dollars. It is computed as present value of net cash inflows divided by investment; also called present value index.

**Required Rate of Return (p. 737)** Management's minimum desired rate of return on an investment; also called the discount rate and hurdle rate.

**Simple Interest (p. 731)** Interest computed only on the principal amount.

**Time Value of Money (p. 721)** The fact that money can be invested to earn income over time.

# QUICK CHECK

1. (Learning Objective 1) Examples of capital budgeting investments could include all of the following *except*
   a. building a new store.
   b. installing a new computer system.
   c. paying bonuses to the sales force.
   d. developing a new Website.

2. (Learning Objective 2) Suppose Canadian Tire is considering investing in warehouse-management software that costs $500,000, has $50,000 residual value, and should lead to cost savings of $120,000 per year for its five-year life. In calculating the ARR, which of the following figures should be used as the equation's denominator?
   a. $225,000
   b. $500,000
   c. $450,000
   d. $275,000

3. (Learning Objective 2) Using the information from Question 2, which of the following figures should be used in the equation's numerator (average annual operating income)?
   a. $120,000
   b. $20,000
   c. $30,000
   d. $10,000

4. (Learning Objective 3) Which of the following affects the present value of an investment?
   a. The interest rate
   b. The number of time periods (length of the investment)
   c. The type of investment (annuity versus single lump sum)
   d. All of the above

5. (Learning Objective 5) When making capital rationing decisions, the size of the initial investment required may differ between alternative investments. The profitability index can be used in conjunction with which of the following methods to help managers choose between alternatives?
   a. IRR
   b. ARR
   c. Payback Period
   d. NPV

6. (Learning Objectives 3 & 5) The IRR is
   a. the same as the ARR.
   b. the firm's hurdle rate.
   c. the interest rate at which the NPV of the investment is zero.
   d. none of the above.

7. (Learning Objectives 2 & 5) Which of the following methods uses accrual accounting rather than net cash flows as a basis for calculations?
   a. Payback
   b. ARR
   c. NPV
   d. IRR

8. (Learning Objectives 2 & 5) Which of the following methods does *not* consider the investment's profitability?
   a. Payback
   b. ARR
   c. NPV
   d. IRR

9. (Learning Objectives 1 & 5) Which of the following is *true* regarding capital rationing decisions?
   a. Companies should always choose the investment with the shortest payback period.
   b. Companies should always choose the investment with the highest NPV.
   c. Companies should always choose the investment with the highest ARR.
   d. None of the above.

10. (Learning Objectives 1 & 5) Which of the following is the most reliable method for making capital budgeting decisions?
   a. NPV method
   b. ARR method
   c. Payback method
   d. Post-audit method



**Quick Check Answers**

1. *c* 2. *b* 3. *c* 4. *d* 5. *d* 6. *c* 7. *b* 8. *a* 9. *d* 10. *a*

# SHORT EXERCISES

**S12-1 Order the capital budgeting process** *(Learning Objective 1)*

Place the following activities in sequence to illustrate the capital budgeting process:

a. Budget capital investments.
b. Project investments' cash flows.
c. Perform post-audits.
d. Make investments.
e. Use feedback to reassess investments already made.
f. Identify potential capital investments.
g. Screen/analyze investments using one or more of the methods discussed.

**Allegra Data Set used for S12-2 through S12-5:**

Allegra is considering producing Blu-ray players and digital video recorders (DVRs). The products require different specialized machines, each costing $1 million. Each machine has a five-year life and zero residual value. The two products have different patterns of predicted net cash inflows:

| | *Annual Net Cash Inflows* | |
|---|---|---|
| **Year** | **Blu-ray Players** | **DVRs** |
| 1 | $ 312,500 | $ 500,000 |
| 2 | 312,500 | 350,000 |
| 3 | 312,500 | 300,000 |
| 4 | 312,500 | 250,000 |
| 5 | 312,500 | 40,000 |
| Total | $1,562,500 | $1,440,000 |

Allegra will consider making capital investments only if the payback period of the project is less than 3.5 years and the ARR exceeds 8%.

**S12-2 Compute payback period—equal cash inflows** *(Learning Objective 2)*

Refer to the Allegra data set. Calculate the Blu-ray player project's payback period. If the Blu-ray player project had a residual value of $100,000, would the payback period change? Explain and recalculate if necessary. Does this investment pass Allegra's payback period screening rule?

**S12-3 Compute payback period—unequal cash inflows** *(Learning Objective 2)*

Refer to the Allegra data set. Calculate the DVR project's payback period. If the DVR project had a residual value of $100,000, would the payback period change? Explain and recalculate if necessary. Does this investment pass Allegra's payback period screening rule?

**S12-4 Compute ARR—equal cash inflows** *(Learning Objective 2)*

Refer to the Allegra data set. Calculate the Blu-ray player project's ARR. If the Blu-ray player project had a residual value of $100,000, would the ARR change? Explain and recalculate if necessary. Does this investment pass Allegra's ARR screening rule?

**S12-5 Compute ARR—unequal cash inflows** *(Learning Objective 2)*

Refer to the Allegra data set. Calculate the DVR project's ARR. If the DVR project had a residual value of $100,000, would the ARR change? Explain and recalculate if necessary. Does this investment pass Allegra's ARR screening rule?

**S12-6 Compute annual cash savings** *(Learning Objective 2)*

Suppose Allegra is deciding whether to invest in a DVD-HD project. The payback period for the $5 million investment is four years, and the project's expected life is seven years. What equal annual net cash inflows are expected from this project?

**S12-7 Find the present values of future cash flows** *(Learning Objective 3)*

Your grandfather would like to share some of his fortune with you. He offers to give you money under one of the following scenarios (you get to choose):

1. $10,000 a year at the end of each of the next eight years
2. $50,000 (lump sum) now
3. $100,000 (lump sum) eight years from now

Calculate the present value of each scenario using a 6% interest rate. Which scenario yields the highest present value? Would your preference change if you used a 12% interest rate?

**S12-8 Show how timing affects future values** *(Learning Objective 3)*

Assume that you make the following investments:

a. You invest a lump sum of $5,000 for four years at 12% interest. What is the investment's value at the end of four years?
b. In a different account earning 12% interest, you invest $1,250 at the end of each year for four years. What is the investment's value at the end of four years?
c. What general rule of thumb explains the difference in the investments' future values?

**S12-9 Compare payout options at their future values** *(Learning Objective 3)*

Refer to the lottery payout options on page 734. Rather than comparing the payout options at their present values (as is done in the chapter), compare the payout options at their future value 10 years from now.

a. Using an 8% interest rate, what is the future value of each payout option?
b. Rank your preference of payout options.
c. Does computing the future value rather than the present value of the options change your preference of payout options? Explain.

**S12-10 Find the relationship between the PV tables** *(Learning Objective 3)*

Use Table A: Present Value of $1 to determine the present value of $1 received one year from now. Assume a 14% interest rate. Use the same table to find the present value of $1 received two years from now. Continue this process for a total of five years.

a. What is the *total* present value of the cash flows received over the five-year period?
b. Could you characterize this stream of cash flows as an annuity? Why or why not?
c. Use Table B: Present Value of Annuity of $1 to determine the present value of the same stream of cash flows. Compare your results to your answer in (a).
d. Explain your findings.

**S12-11 Compute NPV—equal net cash inflows** *(Learning Objective 4)*

Skyline Music is considering investing $600,000 in private lesson studios that will have no residual value. The studios are expected to result in annual net cash inflows of $100,000 for the next 10 years. Assuming that Skyline Music uses an 8% hurdle rate, what is the net present value (NPV) of the studio investment? Is this a favourable investment?

**S12-12 Compute IRR—equal net cash inflows** *(Learning Objective 4)*

Refer to Skyline Music in S12-11. What is the approximate internal rate of return (IRR) of the studio investment?

**S12-13 Compute NPV—unequal net cash inflows** *(Learning Objective 4)*

The local Giant Tiger department store is considering investing in self-checkout kiosks for its customers. The self-check-out kiosks will cost $45,000 and have no residual value. Management expects the equipment to result in net cash savings over three years as customers grow accustomed to using the new technology: $14,000 the first year; $19,000 the second year; $24,000 the third year. Assuming a 10% discount rate, what is the NPV of the kiosk investment? Is this a favourable investment? Why or why not?

**S12-14 Compute IRR—unequal net cash inflows** *(Learning Objective 4)*

Refer to Giant Tiger in S12-13. What is the approximate internal rate of return (IRR) of the kiosk investment?

**S12-15 Compare the capital budgeting methods** *(Learning Objective 5)*

Fill in each statement with the appropriate capital budgeting method: payback period, ARR, NPV, or IRR.

a. _____ and _____ incorporate the time value of money.
b. _____ focuses on time, not profitability.
c. _____ uses accrual accounting income.
d. _____ finds the discount rate that brings the investment's NPV to zero.
e. In capital rationing decisions, the profitability index must be computed to compare investments requiring different initial investments when the _____ method is used.
f. _____ ignores salvage value.
g. _____ uses discounted cash flows to determine the asset's unique rate of return.
h. _____ highlights risky investments.
i. _____ measures profitability but ignores the time value of money.

# EXERCISES Group A

**E12-16A Identify capital investments** *(Learning Objective 1)*

Which of the following purchases would be considered capital investments?

a. Land for the new administrative offices will cost $250,000.
b. Salary costs for the upcoming year are projected to be $2,000,000.
c. The cost of electricity and other utilities for the manufacturing facility is approximately $575,000 per year.
d. The construction and installation of special-use machinery to produce a new model of washer is projected to cost $450,000.
e. The new advertising campaign for the first quarter of the upcoming year will cost $175,000.
f. Twelve new cars are purchased for a total of $300,000 to expand the fleet of cars used by the salespeople.
g. New self-scan registers are purchased for all store locations at a total cost of $700,000.
h. A new network system throughout corporate headquarters will be installed for a cost of $200,000.
i. The cost of paper and toner for the company printers is projected to be $150,000 for the upcoming year.
j. The purchase cost plus installation for a second extrusion machine in a plastics recycling firm will be $500,000.



**E12-17A Compute payback period—equal cash inflows** *(Learning Objective 2)*

Check sum: Payback period is 3.75 years.

Quiksilver is considering acquiring a manufacturing plant. The purchase price is $1,236,100. The owners believe the plant will generate net cash inflows of $309,025 annually. It will have to be replaced in eight years. To be profitable, the investment payback must occur before the investment's replacement date. Use the payback method to determine whether Quiksilver should purchase this plant.

**E12-18A Compute payback period—unequal cash inflows** *(Learning Objective 2)*

Check sum: Payback period is 5.75 years.

Sikes Hardware is adding a new product line that will require an investment of $1,500,000. Managers estimate that this investment will have a 10-year life and generate net cash inflows of $315,000 the first year, $285,000 the second year, and $240,000 each year thereafter for eight years. The investment has no residual value. Compute the payback period.

**E12-19A Compute ARR—unequal cash inflows** *(Learning Objective 2)*

Check sum: ARR is 6.80%.

Refer to the Sikes Hardware information in E12-18. Compute the ARR for the investment.

### E12-20A Compute and compare ARR *(Learning Objective 2)*

Engineered Products is shopping for new equipment. Managers are considering two investments. Equipment manufactured by Atlas costs $1,000,000 and will last five years and have no residual value. The Atlas equipment will generate annual operating income of $160,000. Equipment manufactured by Veras costs $1,200,000 and will remain useful for six years. It promises annual operating income of $238,800, and its expected residual value is $100,000.

Check sum: ARR on Veras is 19.8%.

Which equipment offers the higher ARR?

### E12-21A Compare retirement savings plans *(Learning Objective 3)*

Assume that you want to retire early at age 52. You plan to save using one of the following two strategies: (1) Save $3,000 a year in an RRSP beginning when you are 22 and ending when you are 52 (30 years), or (2) wait until you are 40 to start saving and then save $7,500 per year for the next 12 years. Assume that you will earn the historic stock market average of 10% per year.

Check sum: Req. 1 Cost is $90,000 either way.

#### Requirements

1. How much out-of-pocket cash will you invest under each of the two options?
2. How much savings will you have accumulated at age 52 under each of the two options?
3. Explain the results.
4. Assume you let the savings continue to grow for 10 more years (with no further out-of-pocket investments). Under each scenario, what will the investment be worth when you are age 62?

### E12-22A Show the effect of interest rate on future values *(Learning Objective 3)*

Your best friend just received a gift of $5,000 from his favourite aunt. He wants to save the money to use as starter money after school. He can (1) invest it risk-free at 3%, (2) take on moderate risk at 8%, or (3) take on high risk at 16%. Help your friend project the investment's worth at the end of four years under each investment strategy, and explain the results to him.

Check sum: Future value at 3% is $5,630.

### E12-23A Calculate the payback and NPV for a sustainable energy project *(Learning Objectives 2 and 3)*

Maplewood Equestrian Centre is evaluating investing in solar panels to provide some of the electrical needs of its stables. The solar panel project would cost $540,000 and would provide cost savings in its utility bills of $60,000 per year. It is anticipated that the solar panels would have a life of 20 years and would have no residual value.

Check sum: Payback is nine years.

#### Requirements

1. Calculate the payback period of the solar project in years.
2. If the company uses a discount rate of 10%, what is the net present value of this project?
3. If the company has a rule that no projects will be undertaken that have a payback period of more than five years, would this investment be accepted? If not, what arguments could the energy manager make to try to obtain approval for the solar panel project?
4. What would you do if you were in charge of approving capital investment proposals?



### E12-24A Fund future cash flows *(Learning Objective 3)*

Janet wants to take the next five years off work to travel around the world. She estimates her annual cash needs at $30,000 (if she needs more, she'll work odd jobs). Janet believes she can invest her savings at 8% until she depletes her funds.

Check sum: Req. 1 Present Value is $119,790.

#### Requirements

1. How much money does Janet need now to fund her travels?
2. After speaking with a couple of banks, Janet learns she'll only be able to invest her funds at 6%. How much does she need now to fund her travels?

### E12-25A Choosing a lottery payout option *(Learning Objective 3)*

Congratulations! You've won a major lottery, which offers you the following payout options:

Check sum: Option 1 PV is $8,172,000.

| |
|---|
| Option #1: $12,000,000 five years from now |
| Option #2: $2,250,000 at the end of each year for the next five years |
| Option #3: $10,000,000 three years from now |

**Requirement**

1. Assuming that you can earn 8% on your funds, which option would you prefer?

### E12-26A Solve various scenarios involving the time value of money *(Learning Objective 3)*

**Requirements**

Check sum: Option 1 future value is $5,487.50.

1. Suppose you invest a sum of $2,500 in an account bearing interest at the rate of 14% per year. What will the investment be worth six years from now?
2. How much would you need to invest now to be able to withdraw $5,000 at the end of every year for the next 20 years? Assume a 12% interest rate.
3. Assume that you want to have $150,000 saved seven years from now. If you can invest your funds at a 6% interest rate, how much do you currently need to invest?
4. Your aunt plans to give you $1,000 at the end of every year for the next 10 years. If you invest each of her yearly gifts at a 12% interest rate, how much will they be worth at the end of the 10-year period?
5. Suppose you want to buy a small cabin in the mountains four years from now. You estimate that the property will cost $52,500 at that time. How much money do you need to invest each year in an account that bears interest at the rate of 6% per year to accumulate the $52,500 purchase price?

### E12-27A Calculate NPV—equal annual cash inflows *(Learning Objective 4)*

Check sum: Project B maximum acceptable price is $372,960.

Use the NPV method to determine whether Salon Products should invest in the following projects:

- *Project A* costs $272,000 and offers eight annual net cash inflows of $60,000. Salon Products requires an annual return of 14% on projects such as this one.
- *Project B* costs $380,000 and offers nine annual net cash inflows of $70,000. Salon Products demands an annual return of 12% on investments of this nature.



**Requirement**

1. What is the NPV of each project? What is the maximum acceptable price to pay for each project?

### E12-28A Calculate IRR—equal cash inflows *(Learning Objective 4)*

Check sum: IRR is 14.69%.

Refer to Salon Products in E12-27A. Compute the IRR of each project and use this information to identify the better investment.

### E12-29A Calculate NPV—unequal cash flows *(Learning Objective 4)*

Check sum: NPV is $19,935.

Bevil Industries is deciding whether to automate one phase of its production process. The manufacturing equipment has a six-year life and will cost $900,000. Projected net cash inflows are as follows:

| | |
|---|---|
| Year 1 | $260,000 |
| Year 2 | $250,000 |
| Year 3 | $225,000 |
| Year 4 | $210,000 |
| Year 5 | $200,000 |
| Year 6 | $175,000 |

### Requirements

1. Compute this project's NPV using Bevil Industries' 14% hurdle rate. Should Bevil Industries invest in the equipment? Why or why not?
2. Bevil Industries could refurbish the equipment at the end of six years for $100,000. The refurbished equipment could be used one more year, providing $75,000 of net cash inflows in Year 7. In addition, the refurbished equipment would have a $50,000 residual value at the end of Year 7. Should Bevil Industries invest in the equipment and refurbish it after six years? Why or why not? (*Hint*: In addition to your answer to Requirement 1, discount the additional cash outflow and inflows back to the present value.)

## E12-30A Compute IRR—unequal cash flows *(Learning Objective 4)*

Ritter Razors is considering an equipment investment that will cost $950,000. Projected net cash inflows over the equipment's three year life are as follows: Year 1: $500,000; Year 2: $400,000; and Year 3: $300,000. Ritter wants to know the equipment's IRR.

Check sum: IRR is 13.92%.

### Requirement

1. Use trial and error to find the IRR within a 2% range. (*Hint:* Use Ritter's hurdle rate of 10% to begin the trial-and-error process.)

*Optional*: Use a business calculator to compute the exact IRR.

## E12-31A Make a decision regarding capital rationing *(Learning Objective 4)*

Sheffield Manufacturing is considering three capital investment proposals. At this time, Sheffield Manufacturing has funds available to pursue only one of the three investments.

Check sum: Profitability index shows that Equipment A returns 1.1.3.

| | Equipment A | Equipment B | Equipment C |
|---|---|---|---|
| Present value of net cash inflows | $1,695,000 | $1,960,000 | $2,200,000 |
| Investment | ($1,500,000) | ($1,750,000) | ($2,000,000) |
| NPV | $ 195,000 | $ 210,000 | $ 200,000 |

### Requirement

1. Which investment should Sheffield Manufacturing pursue at this time? Why?

**Flint Valley Expansion Data Set used for E12-32A through E12-35A:**

Assume that Flint Valley's managers developed the following estimates concerning a potential Snow Park Lodge ski resort expansion project (all numbers assumed):

| | |
|---|---|
| Number of additional skiers per day | 125 |
| Average number of days per year that weather conditions allow skiing at Flint Valley | 160 |
| Useful life of expansion (in years) | 8 |
| Average cash spent by each skier per day | $ 240 |
| Average variable cost of serving each skier per day | $ 140 |
| Cost of expansion | $8,000,000 |
| Discount rate | 12% |

Assume that Flint Valley uses the straight-line depreciation method and expects the lodge expansion to have a residual value of $960,000 at the end of its eight-year life.

## E12-32A Compute payback and ARR with residual value *(Learning Objective 2)*

Consider how Flint Valley, a popular ski resort could use capital budgeting to decide whether the $8 million Snow Park Lodge expansion would be a good investment.

Check sum: Average annual cash flow is $2,000,000.

**Requirements**

1. Compute the average annual net cash inflow from the expansion.
2. Compute the average annual operating income from the expansion.
3. Compute the payback period.
4. Compute the ARR.

### E12-33A Continuation of E12-32A: Compute payback and ARR with no residual value *(Learning Objective 2)*

Check sum: ARR is 12.5%.

Refer to the Flint Valley expansion data set. Assume that the expansion has zero residual value.

**Requirements**

1. Will the payback period change? Explain and recalculate if necessary.
2. Will the project's ARR change? Explain and recalculate if necessary.
3. Assume that Flint Valley screens its potential capital investments using a five-year minimum payback period and a 10% minimum ARR. Will Flint Valley consider this project further or reject it?

### E12-34A Calculate NPV with and without residual value *(Learning Objective 4)*

Check sum: The Year-8 cash flow is $2,960,000.

Refer to the Flint Valley expansion data set.

**Requirements**

1. What is the project's NPV? Is the investment attractive? Why or why not?
2. Assume that the expansion has no residual value. What is the project's NPV? Is the investment still attractive? Why or why not?

### E12-35A Calculate IRR with no residual value *(Learning Objective 4)*

Check sum: IRR is 18.62%.

Refer to the Flint Valley expansion data set. Assume that the expansion has no residual value. What is the project's IRR? Is the investment attractive? Why or why not?

### E12-36A Comparing capital budgeting methods *(Learning Objective 5)*

The following table contains information about four projects in which Elsmaili Corporation has the opportunity to invest. This information is based on estimates that different managers have prepared about their potential project.

| Project | Investment Required | Net Present Value | Life of Project | Internal Rate of Return | Profitability Index | Payback Period in Years | Accounting Rate of Return |
|---|---|---|---|---|---|---|---|
| A....... | $ 200,000 | $ 52,350 | 5 | 22% | 1.26 | 2.86 | 18% |
| B ...... | $ 400,000 | $ 72,230 | 6 | 25% | 1.18 | 2.96 | 15% |
| C....... | $1,000,000 | $224,075 | 3 | 20% | 1.22 | 2.11 | 11% |
| D ...... | $1,500,000 | $ 85,000 | 4 | 13% | 1.06 | 3.00 | 22% |

**Requirements**

1. Rank the four projects in order of preference by using the following:
   a. Net present value
   b. Project profitability index
   c. Internal rate of return
   d. Payback period
   e. Accounting rate of return
2. Which method or methods do you think are best for evaluating capital investment projects in general? Why?

# EXERCISES Group B

## E12-37B Identify capital investments *(Learning Objective 1)*

Which of the following purchases would be considered capital investments?

a. The plant manager wants to purchase 12 new forklifts for use in materials management for a total of $660,000.

b. The company purchases $368,000 of a raw material to be used in the construction of its most popular product.

c. A company purchased a parcel of land for $550,000; the company's new manufacturing facility will be built on this land next year.

d. The company has $125,000 in a money market account.

e. The payroll for the administrative and sales staff is projected to be $580,000 for the upcoming year.

f. Salespeople for the company are provided with new cars for business use; the cost of these new vehicles is $512,000.

g. New clothing racks and display shelves are installed in four of the company's retail locations; the total cost of these new displays and their installation is $325,000.

h. A clothing retailer purchases clothing merchandise for $8,200,000 to be resold in its 20 retail locations.

i. The company's utility costs for the year are projected to be $800,000.

j. A merchandiser adds 80,000 square feet of floor space to its flagship store for a total cost of $3,300,000.

## E12-38B Compute payback period—equal cash inflows *(Learning Objective 2)*

Safieh Corp. is considering acquiring a manufacturing plant. The purchase price is $2,480,000. The owners believe the plant will generate net cash inflows of $310,000 annually. It will have to be replaced in five years. To be profitable, the investment payback must occur before the investment's replacement date. Use the payback method to determine whether Safieh should purchase this plant.

Check sum: Payback period is eight years.

## E12-39B Compute payback period—unequal cash inflows *(Learning Objective 2)*

Walken Hardware is adding a new product line that will require an investment of $1,418,000. Managers estimate that this investment will have a 10-year life and generate net cash inflows of $300,000 the first year, $280,000 the second year, and $250,000 each year thereafter for eight years. The investment has no residual value. Compute the payback period.

Check sum: Payback period is 5.352 years.

## E12-40B Compute ARR with unequal cash inflows *(Learning Objective 2)*

Refer to the Walken Hardware information in E12-39B. Compute the ARR for the investment.

Check sum: ARR is 8.19%.



## E12-41B Compute and compare ARR *(Learning Objective 2)*

Zoom Products is shopping for new equipment. Managers are considering two investments. Equipment manufactured by Miron costs $800,000 and will last for four years with no residual value. The Miron equipment will generate annual operating income of $156,000. Equipment manufactured by Root costs $1,100,000 and will remain useful for five years. It promises annual operating income of $236,500, and its expected residual value is $105,000. Which equipment offers the higher ARR?

Check sum: Miron ARR is 19.5%.

## E12-42B Compare retirement savings plans *(Learning Objective 3)*

Assume you want to retire early at age 54. You plan to save using one of the following two strategies: (1) Save $3,300 a year in an RRSP beginning when you are 24 and ending when you are 54 (30 years), or (2) wait until you are 42 to start saving and then save $8,250 per year for the next 12 years. Assume you will earn the historic stock market average of 14% per year.

Check sum: FV is $1,177,407.

### Requirements

1. How much out-of-pocket cash will you invest under the two options?
2. How much savings will you have accumulated at age 54 under the two options?
3. Explain the results.
4. Assume you let the savings continue to grow for eight more years (with no further out-of-pocket investments). Under each scenario, what will the investments be worth when you are age 62?

## E12-43B Show the effect of interest rate on future values *(Learning Objective 3)*

Check sum: Future value at 10% is $6.655.

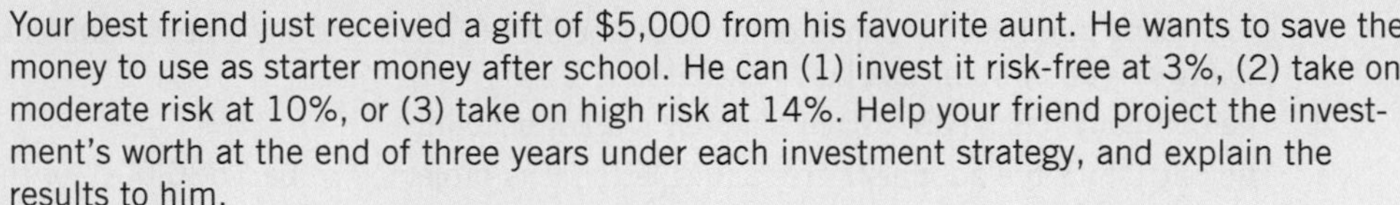

Your best friend just received a gift of $5,000 from his favourite aunt. He wants to save the money to use as starter money after school. He can (1) invest it risk-free at 3%, (2) take on moderate risk at 10%, or (3) take on high risk at 14%. Help your friend project the investment's worth at the end of three years under each investment strategy, and explain the results to him.

## E12-44B Calculate the payback and NPV for a sustainable energy project *(Learning Objectives 2 & 3)*

Check sum: Req. 1 Payback is eight years.

Maplewood Equestrian Centre is evaluating investing in solar panels to provide some of the electrical needs of the stables. The solar panel project would cost $540,000 and would provide cost savings in its utility bills of $67,500 per year. It is anticipated that the solar panels would have a life of 20 years and would have no residual value.

### Requirements

1. Calculate the payback period of the solar project in years.
2. If the company uses a discount rate of 8%, what is the net present value of this project?
3. If the company has a rule that no projects will be undertaken that would have a pay-back period of more than five years, would this investment be accepted? If not, what arguments could the energy manager make to try to obtain approval for the solar panel project?
4. What would you do if you were in charge of approving capital investment proposals?

## E12-45B Fund future cash flows *(Learning Objective 3)*

Check sum: PV is $161,805.

Minh wants to take the next six years off work to travel around the world. She estimates her annual cash needs at $35,000 (if she needs more, she'll work odd jobs). Minh believes she can invest her savings at 8% until she depletes her funds.

### Requirements

1. How much money does Minh need now to fund her travels?
2. After speaking with a few banks, Minh learns she'll be able to invest her funds at 10%. How much does she need now to fund her travels?

## E12-46B Choosing a lottery payout option *(Learning Objective 3)*

Congratulations! You've won a major lottery, which offers you the following payout options:

Check sum: Option 1 PV is $9,220,500.

| Options |
| --- |
| Option #1: $13,500,000 four years from now |
| Option #2: $2,050,000 at the end of each year for the next six years |
| Option #3: $12,500,000 three years from now |

### Requirement

1. Assuming that you can earn 10% on your funds, which option would you prefer?

## E12-47B Solve various time value of money scenarios *(Learning Objective 3)*

Solve these time value of money scenarios.

### Requirements

1. Suppose you invest a sum of $5,000 in an account that bears interest at the rate of 10% per year. What will the investment be worth six years from now?
2. How much would you need to invest now to be able to withdraw $9,000 at the end of every year for the next 20 years? Assume a 12% interest rate.
3. Assume that you want to have $145,000 saved seven years from now. If you can invest your funds at an 8% interest rate, how much do you currently need to invest?
4. Your aunt plans to give you $3,000 at the end of every year for the next 10 years. If you invest each of her yearly gifts at a 12% interest rate, how much will they be worth at the end of the 10-year period?
5. Suppose you would like to buy a small cabin in the mountains four years from now. You estimate that the property will cost $51,500 at that time. How much money would you need to invest each year in an account bearing interest at the rate of 6% per year in order to accumulate the $51,500 purchase price?

Check sum: Question 1 FV is $8,860.

## E12-48B Calculate NPV—equal annual cash inflows *(Learning Objective 4)*

Use the NPV method to determine whether Vargas Products should invest in the following projects:

Check sum: NPV of Project B is $64,730.

- *Project A* costs $285,000 and offers eight annual net cash inflows of $64,000. Vargas Products requires an annual return of 12% on projects such as this.
- *Project B* costs $390,000 and offers 10 annual net cash inflows of $74,000. Vargas Products demands an annual return of 10% on investments of this nature.

### Requirement

1. What is the NPV of each project? What is the maximum acceptable price to pay for each project?

## E12-49B Calculate IRR—equal cash inflows *(Learning Objective 4)*

Refer to Vargas Products in E12-48B. Compute the IRR of each project and use this information to identify the better investment.

Check sum: IRR for project A is 15.23%.

## E12-50B Calculate NPV—unequal cash flows *(Learning Objective 4)*

Fielding Industries is deciding whether to automate one phase of its production process. The manufacturing equipment has a six-year life and will cost $910,000.

| Projected net cash inflows are as follows: | |
|---|---|
| Year 1 | $264,000 |
| Year 2 | $254,000 |
| Year 3 | $222,000 |
| Year 4 | $210,000 |
| Year 5 | $204,000 |
| Year 6 | $178,000 |

### Requirements

Check sum: The positive refurbishment NPV is $3,678.

1. Compute this project's NPV using Fielding Industries' 16% hurdle rate. Should Fielding Industries invest in the equipment? Why or why not?
2. Fielding Industries could refurbish the equipment at the end of six years for $105,000. The refurbished equipment could be used for one more year, providing $77,000 of net cash inflows in Year 7. Additionally, the refurbished equipment would have a $55,000 residual value at the end of Year 7. Should Fielding Industries invest in the equipment and refurbish it after six years? Why or why not? (*Hint:* In addition to your answer to Requirement 1, discount the additional cash outflows and inflows back to the present value.)

### E12-51B Compute IRR—unequal cash flows *(Learning Objective 4)*

Check sum: IRR is 10.76%.

Tiptop Tables is considering an equipment investment that will cost $965,000. Projected net cash inflows over the equipment's three-year life are as follows: Year 1: $494,000; Year 2: $382,000; and Year 3: $282,000. Tiptop wants to know the equipment's IRR.

**Requirement**

1. Use trial and error to find the IRR within a 2% range. (*Hint*: Use Tiptop's hurdle rate of 8% to begin the trial-and-error process.)

### E12-52B Capital rationing decision *(Learning Objective 4)*

Check sum: Equipment A profitability index is 1.04.

Bradfield Manufacturing is considering three capital investment proposals. At this time, Bradfield Manufacturing has funds available to pursue only one of the three investments.

| | Equipment A | Equipment B | Equipment C |
|---|---|---|---|
| Present value of net cash inflows | $1,690,000 | $1,955,000 | $2,190,000 |
| Investment | ($1,625,000) | ($1,700,000) | ($1,825,000) |
| NPV | $ 65,000 | $ 255,000 | $ 365,000 |

**Requirement**

1. Which investment should Bradfield Manufacturing pursue at this time? Why?

**Cherry Valley Data Set used for E12-53B–E12-56B.**

Assume that Cherry Valley's managers developed the following estimates concerning a potential Brook Park Lodge ski resort expansion project (all numbers assumed):

| | |
|---|---|
| Number of additional skiers per day | 122 |
| Average number of days per year that weather conditions allow skiing at Cherry Valley | 162 |
| Useful life of expansion (in years) | 9 |
| Average cash spent by each skier per day | $ 245 |
| Average variable cost of serving each skier per day | $ 135 |
| Cost of expansion | $10,000,000 |
| Discount rate | 10% |

### E12-53B Compute payback and ARR with residual value *(Learning Objective 2)*

Check sum: Payback period is 4.6 years.

Refer to the Cherry Valley data set and assume the expansion has a residual value of $950,000 at the end of nine years. Consider how Cherry Valley, a popular ski resort, could use capital budgeting to decide whether the $10-million Brook Park Lodge expansion would be a good investment.

**Requirements**

1. Compute the average annual net cash inflow from the expansion.
2. Compute the average annual operating income from the expansion.
3. Compute the payback period.
4. Compute the ARR.

### E12-54B Continuation of E12-53B: Compute payback and ARR with no residual value *(Learning Objective 2)*

Check sum: ARR is 0.63%.

Refer to the Cherry Valley data set. Now assume the expansion has zero residual value.

**Requirements**

1. Will the payback period change? Explain and recalculate if necessary.
2. Will the project's ARR change? Explain and recalculate if necessary.

3. Assume Cherry Valley screens its potential capital investments using the following decision criteria: maximum payback period of six years, minimum accounting rate of return of 8%. Will Cherry Valley consider this project further or reject it?

### E12-55B Calculate NPV with and without residual value *(Learning Objective 4)*

Refer to the Cherry Valley data set. Assume that Cherry Valley uses the straight-line depreciation method and expects the lodge expansion to have a residual value of $950,000 at the end of its nine-year life. It has already calculated the average annual net cash inflow per year to be $2,174,040.

Check sum: Net present value of expansion is $ 2,520,296.

**Requirements**

1. What is the project's NPV? Is the investment attractive? Why or why not?
2. Assume the expansion has no residual value. What is the project's NPV? Is the investment still attractive? Why or why not?

### E12-56B Calculate IRR with no residual value *(Learning Objective 4)*

Refer to the Cherry Valley data set. Assume that Cherry Valley uses the straight-line depreciation method and expects the lodge expansion to have no residual value at the end of its nine-year life. The company has already calculated the average annual net cash inflow per year to be $2,174,040 and the NPV of the expansion to be $2,923,096. What is the project's IRR? Is the investment attractive? Why?

Check sum: The IRR is slightly over 16%.

### E12-57B Compare capital budgeting methods *(Learning Objective 5)*

The following table contains information about four projects in which Rostis Corporation has the opportunity to invest. This information is based on estimates that different managers have prepared about the company's potential project.

| Project | Investment Required | Net Present Value | Life of Project | Internal Rate of Return | Profitability Index | Payback Period in Years | Accounting Rate of Return |
|---|---|---|---|---|---|---|---|
| A....... | $ 215,000 | $ 42,475 | 5 | 22% | 1.20 | 2.87 | 20% |
| B ...... | $ 410,000 | $ 72,724 | 6 | 25% | 1.18 | 2.97 | 15% |
| C....... | $1,020,000 | $163,812 | 3 | 19% | 1.16 | 2.14 | 13% |
| D ...... | $1,515,000 | $ 85,850 | 4 | 13% | 1.06 | 3.00 | 21% |

**Requirements**

1. Rank the four projects in order of preference by using the following:
    a. Net present value
    b. Project profitability index
    c. Internal rate of return
    d. Payback period
    e. Accounting rate of return
6. Which method or methods do you think are best for evaluating capital investment projects in general? Why?

# PROBLEMS Group A

### P12-58A Solve various time value of money scenarios *(Learning Objectives 3 & 4)*

1. Merridee just hit the jackpot in Las Vegas and won $25,000! If she invests it now at a 12% interest rate, how much will it be worth in 20 years?
2. Walid would like to have $2,000,000 saved by the time he retires in 40 years. How much does he need to invest now at a 10% interest rate to fund his retirement goal?
3. Assume that Stephanie accumulates savings of $1 million by the time she retires. If she invests these savings at 8%, how much money will she be able to withdraw at the end of each year for 20 years?

4. Shu-Fan plans to invest $2,000 at the end of each year for the next seven years. Assuming a 14% interest rate, what will the investment be worth seven years from now?
5. Assuming a 6% interest rate, how much would Euna have to invest now to be able to withdraw $10,000 at the end of each year for the next nine years?
6. Devin is considering a capital investment that costs $485,000 and will provide the net cash inflows listed below. Using a hurdle rate of 12%, find the NPV of the investment.

| Year | Net Cash Inflow |
|---|---|
| 1 | $300,000 |
| 2 | 200,000 |
| 3 | 100,000 |

7. What is the IRR of the capital investment described in Question 6?

## P12-59A Plan for retirement in two stages *(Learning Objective 3)*

You are planning for a very early retirement. You would like to retire at age 40 and have enough money saved to be able to draw $225,000 per year for the next 40 years. (Based on family history, you think you'll live to age 80.) You plan to save for retirement by making 15 equal annual instalments (from age 25 to age 40) into a fairly risky investment fund that you expect will earn 12% per year. You will leave the money in this fund until it is completely depleted when you are 80 years old. To make your plan work, answer the following:

1. How much money must you accumulate by retirement? (*Hint:* Find the present value of the $225,000 withdrawals. You may want to draw a time line showing the savings period and the retirement period.)
2. How does this amount compare to the total amount you will draw out of the investment during retirement? How can these numbers be so different?
3. How much must you pay into the investment each year for the first 15 years? (*Hint:* Your answer from Requirement 1 becomes the future value of this annuity.)
4. How do the total out-of-pocket savings compare to the investment's value at the end of the 15-year savings period and the withdrawals you will make during retirement?

## P12-60A Evaluate an investment using all four methods *(Learning Objectives 2 & 4)*

Water World is considering purchasing a water park in British Columbia for $1,850,000. The new facility will generate annual net cash inflows of $520,000 for eight years. Engineers estimate that the facility will remain useful for eight years and have no residual value. The company uses straight-line depreciation. Its owners want payback in less than five years and an ARR of 10% or more. Management uses a 12% hurdle rate on investments of this nature.

### Requirements

1. Compute the payback period, the ARR, the NPV, and the approximate IRR of this investment. (If you use the tables to compute the IRR, answer with the closest interest rate shown in the tables.)
2. Recommend whether the company should invest in this project.

## P12-61A Compare investments with different cash flows and residual values *(Learning Objectives 2 & 4)*

Locos operates a chain of sandwich shops. The company is considering two possible expansion plans. Plan A would open eight smaller shops at a cost of $8,450,000. Expected annual net cash inflows are $1,690,000 with zero residual value at the end of 10 years. Under Plan B, Locos would open three larger shops at a cost of $8,400,000. This plan is expected to generate net cash inflows of $1,120,000 per year for 10 years, the estimated life of the properties. Estimated residual value is $980,000. Locos uses straight-line depreciation and requires an annual return of 8%.

**Requirements**

1. Compute the payback period, the ARR, and the NPV of these two plans. What are the strengths and weaknesses of these capital budgeting models?
2. Which expansion plan should Locos choose? Why?
3. Estimate Plan A's IRR. How does the IRR compare with the company's required rate of return?

# PROBLEMS Group B

## P12-62B Solve various time value of money scenarios *(Learning Objectives 3 & 4)*

1. Fahim just hit the jackpot in Las Vegas and won $45,000! If he invests it now at a 14% interest rate, how much will it be worth 20 years from now?
2. Marc would like to have $2,500,000 saved by the time he retires 40 years from now. How much does he need to invest now at a 14% interest rate to fund his retirement goal?
3. Assume that Magda accumulates savings of $1.5 million by the time she retires. If she invests these savings at 12%, how much money will she be able to withdraw at the end of each year for 15 years?
4. Hannah plans to invest $2,500 at the end of each year for the next eight years. Assuming a 14% interest rate, what will her investment be worth eight years from now?
5. Assuming a 12% interest rate, how much would Xuzhi have to invest now to be able to withdraw $13,000 at the end of every year for the next nine years?
6. Stefan is considering a capital investment that costs $505,000 and will provide the net cash inflows listed below. Using a hurdle rate of 10%, find the NPV of the investment.

| Year | Net Cash Inflow |
|---|---|
| 1 | $298,000 |
| 2 | 205,000 |
| 3 | 96,000 |

7. What is the IRR of the capital investment described in Question 6?

## P12-63B Plan for retirement in two stages *(Learning Objective 3)*

You are planning for an early retirement. You would like to retire at age 40 and have enough money saved to be able to draw $205,000 per year for the next 35 years. (Based on family history, you think you'll live to age 75.) You plan to save by making 10 equal annual installments (from age 30 to age 40) into a fairly risky investment fund that you expect will earn 14% per year. You will leave the money in this fund until it is completely depleted when you are 75 years old. To make your plan work, answer the following:

1. How much money must you accumulate by retirement? (*Hint*: Find the present value of the $205,000 withdrawals. You may want to draw a time line showing the savings period and the retirement period.)
2. How does this amount compare to the total amount you will draw out of the investment during retirement? How can these numbers be so different?
3. How much must you pay into the investment each year for the first 10 years? (*Hint*: Your answer from Requirement 1 becomes the future value of this annuity.)
4. How do the total out-of-pocket savings compare to the investment's value at the end of the 10-year savings period and the withdrawals you will make during retirement?

## P12-64B Evaluate an investment using all four methods *(Learning Objectives 2 & 4)*

River Wild is considering purchasing a water park in Niagara Falls for $2,000,000. The new facility will generate annual net cash inflows of $510,000 for nine years. Engineers estimate that the facility will remain useful for nine years and have no residual value.

The company uses straight-line depreciation. Its owners want payback in less than five years and an ARR of 12% or more. Management uses a 10% hurdle rate on investments of this nature.

**Requirements**

1. Compute the payback period, the ARR, the NPV, and the approximate IRR of this investment.
2. Recommend whether the company should invest in this project.

## P12-65B Compare investments with different cash flows and residual values

*(Learning Objectives 2 & 4)*

Sub Hut operates a chain of sub shops. The company is considering two possible expansion plans. Plan A would open eight smaller shops at a cost of $8,840,000. Expected annual net cash inflows are $1,600,000, with zero residual value at the end of nine years. Under Plan B, Sub Hut would open three larger shops at a cost of $8,240,000. This plan is expected to generate net cash inflows of $1,250,000 per year for nine years, the estimated life of the properties. Estimated residual value for Plan B is $1,125,000. Sub Hut uses straight-line depreciation and requires an annual return of 8%.

**Requirements**

1. Compute the payback period, the ARR, and the NPV of these two plans. What are the strengths and weaknesses of these capital budgeting models?
2. Which expansion plan should Sub Hut choose? Why?
3. Estimate Plan A's IRR. How does the IRR compare with the company's required rate of return?

# CAPSTONE APPLICATION PROBLEMS

## APPLICATION QUESTION

### A12-66 Apply time value of money to a personal decision *(Learning Objective 3)*

Samer Almasri, a second-year business student at the University of Ottawa, will graduate in two years with an accounting major and a Spanish minor. Almasri is trying to decide where to work this summer. He has two choices: work full-time for a bottling plant or work part-time in the accounting department of a meat-packing plant. He probably will work at the same place next summer as well. He is able to work 12 weeks during the summer.

The bottling plant would pay Almasri $600 per week this year and 7% more next summer. At the meat-packing plant, he would work 20 hours per week at $10.00 per hour. By working only part-time, he would take two accounting courses this summer. Tuition is $225 per hour for each of the four-hour courses. Almasri believes that the experience he gains this summer will qualify him for a full-time accounting position with the meat-packing plant next summer. That position will pay $750 per week.

Almasri sees two additional benefits of working part-time this summer. First, he could reduce his studying workload during the fall and spring semesters by one course each term. Second, he would have the time to work as a grader in the university's accounting department during the 15-week fall term. Grading pays $50 per week.

#### Requirements

1. Suppose that Almasri ignores the time value of money in decisions that cover this time period because it is so short. Suppose also that his sole goal is to make as much money as possible between now and the end of next summer. What should he do? What non-quantitative factors might Almasri consider? What would you do if you were faced with these alternatives?
2. Now, suppose that Almasri considers the time value of money for all cash flows that he expects to receive one year or more in the future. Which alternative does this consideration favour? Why?

## CASE ASSIGNMENT

*Source:* duckeesue/Shutterstock

### C12-67 Bean There Done That Coffee Company

Bean There Done That Coffee Company is a fair-trade coffee shop with three locations in Halifax. The locations are picked specifically to be near the universities and colleges in order to draw on the student crowds. Its cafés are designed so that there is plenty of comfortable seating, and free Wi-Fi is offered to customers. Study clubs, book clubs, and artists all find a space to be creative, relax, and enjoy the specialty coffees and pastries. The company is proud of its eco-friendly focus and free-trade initiative. And the community has responded well. The shop draws good crowds most days and evenings from the academic and surrounding communities and has made enough profit in three years to put aside $100,000 for improvements. The owners, Abeer and Walid, have asked for input from customers, friends, and family on what they could invest in for the business, and the choices that they have now are almost too overwhelming.

A number of people mentioned the furniture. The current furniture will probably last only one more year. When they opened the café, Abeer and Walid purchased some used furniture, picked up some from garage sales and recycling centres, and purchased only a few new pieces to fill the space. Recommendations from the survey cards included re-covering the furniture to give it a more cohesive look, and a number of people mentioned replacing all of the furniture with new pieces. Abeer looked into these options. Having a company re-cover all of the furniture would be somewhat complicated because the furniture can't be in the café while it is being re-covered, a limitation that would affect the available seating. The reupholstery company has stated that it can take two pieces at a time and transport them to its shop, do the re-covering, and then bring them back and pick up the next two pieces in order to minimize the inconvenience to customers. This will increase the cost of the re-covering, though, so the cost of re-covering the furniture will be $35,000 in total. The furniture is anticipated to last six years with no residual value. New furniture is also expected to last for six years, but it will cost $25,000 and have a residual value of $2,000. Re-covering of the furniture is anticipated to generate additional cash flows of $10,000 per year for six years, while the new furniture is anticipated to generate $8,000 per year for six years in cash flow.

Walid wanted to look into new equipment. New coffee machines would cost $17,000, last eight years, and have a residual value of $3,000 while providing additional cash flows of $5,000 per year for the life of the machines. A new computerized system to integrate all of the financial, point-of-sale, and inventory systems of all three stores would cost $48,000, have a life of five years and no residual value, but the cost savings are expected to increase cash flows by $14,000 per year for the five years.

Two major projects suggested were the creation of a patio at each location and to enlarge the busiest café near Saint Mary's University. Creating the three patios would cost $78,000, have a life of 14 years, have a residual value of $5,000, and generate additional cash flows of $90,000 per year for the life of the patio, but the investment would need to be made up front and it would take a year before the patios are ready to be used. Enlarging the one location would cost $22,000, last 10 years, and have a residual value of $10,000. This should generate an additional $30,000 in cash flows for 10 years, but similar to the patio constructions, the investment is made up front and it takes one year before the new construction can be used.

The employees asked about a benefits package. In order to set up a self-funding benefits package, Bean There Done That would need to put aside $100,000. It is estimated that with the interest generated, this fund should be able to provide some basic benefits to the café's staff for 25 years. Another employee asked about having the café sponsor her children's soccer team for $6,000. This money would buy the children new jerseys and equipment, and it would also help provide transportation to some of the big tournaments.

Abeer and Walid gathered all of this information, grabbed fresh cups of coffee, and sat down to discuss their options and come up with a plan.

# DISCUSSION & ANALYSIS

1. Describe the capital budgeting process in your own words.
2. Define capital investment. List at least three examples of capital investments other than the examples provided in the chapter.
3. "As the required rate of return increases, the net present value of a project also increases." Explain why you agree or disagree with this statement.
4. Summarize the net present value method for evaluating a capital investment opportunity. Describe the circumstances that create a positive net present value. Describe the circumstances that may cause the net present value of a project to be negative. Describe the advantages and disadvantages of the net present value method.

5. Net cash inflows and net cash outflows are used in the net present value method and in the internal rate of return method. Explain why accounting net income is not used instead of cash flows.
6. Suppose you are a manager and you have three potential capital investment projects from which to choose. Funds are limited, so you can choose only one of the three projects. Describe at least three methods you can use to select the best project in which to invest.
7. The net present value method assumes that future cash inflows are immediately reinvested at the required rate of return, while the internal rate of return method assumes that future cash inflows are immediately invested at the internal rate of return rate. Which assumption is better? Explain your answer.
8. The decision rule for NPV analysis states that the project with the highest NPV should be selected. Describe at least two situations in which the project with the highest NPV may not necessarily be the best project to select.
9. List and describe the advantages and disadvantages of the internal rate of return method.
10. List and describe the advantages and disadvantages of the payback method.

# APPLICATION & ANALYSIS

## 12-1 Evaluating the Purchase of an Asset with Various Capital Budgeting Methods

In this activity, you will be evaluating whether you should purchase a hybrid car or its gasoline-engine counterpart. Select two car models that are similar, with one being the hybrid model and one being the non-hybrid model. (For example, the Honda Civic is available as a hybrid or a gasoline-engine model.) Assume that you plan on keeping your car for 10 years and that at the end of the 10 years the resale value of both models will be negligible.

## Discussion Questions

1. Research the cost of each model (include taxes and title costs). Also, obtain an estimate of the fuel efficiency (L/100 km) of each model.
2. Estimate the number of kilometres you drive each year. Also estimate the cost of a litre of fuel.
3. Using your estimates from 1 and 2, estimate the total cost of driving the hybrid model for one year. Also estimate the total cost of driving the non-hybrid model for one year. Calculate the savings offered by the hybrid model over the non-hybrid model.
4. Calculate the NPV of the hybrid model, using the annual fuel savings as the annual cash inflow for the 10 years you would own the car.
5. Compare the NPV of the hybrid model with the cost of the gasoline-engine model. Which model has the lowest cost (the lowest NPV)? From a purely financial standpoint, does the hybrid model make sense?
6. Now look at the payback period of the hybrid model. Use the difference between the cost of the hybrid model and the gasoline-engine model as the investment. Use the annual fuel savings as the expected annual net cash inflow. Ignoring the time value of money, how long does it take for the additional cost of the hybrid model to pay for itself through fuel savings?
7. What qualitative factors might affect your decision about which model to purchase?

## Classroom Applications

**Web:** Post the discussion questions on an electronic discussion board. Have small groups of students choose a hybrid model of car and its gasoline-engine counterpart for the groups to analyze. Students should collaborate to perform the analysis as outlined in the discussion questions.

**Classroom:** Have students form groups of three or four students. Each group should choose a hybrid model of car and its gasoline-engine counterpart to analyze. Group members should collaborate to perform the analysis as outlined in the discussion questions and then prepare a five-minute presentation that covers the group's responses to the discussion questions.

**Independent:** Research answers to each of the questions. Turn in a two- or three-page typed paper (12-point font, double-spaced with 2.5 cm margins). Include references, including the URLs for sites containing the cost information used in your analysis.

# TRY IT SOLUTIONS

**page 726:**

Since the net cash inflows are expected to be equal each year, payback is calculated as follows:

$$\text{Payback period} = \frac{\text{Initial investment}}{\text{Expected annual net cash inflow}} = \frac{\$4{,}000{,}000}{\$750{,}000} = 5.33 \text{ years}$$

**page 728:**

ARR is calculated as follows:

$$\text{ARR} = \frac{\text{Average annual net cash inflow} - \text{Annual depreciation expense}}{\text{Initial investment}}$$

The ARR focuses on the operating income generated from the investment, not the net cash inflow from the investment. Thus to use this formula, we need to find the annual depreciation expense, which will be used to reconcile net cash inflows back to operating income:

$$\text{Annual depreciation} = \frac{\$4 \text{ million}}{20 \text{ years}} = \$200{,}000$$

Now we calculate ARR as follows:

$$\text{ARR} = \frac{\$750{,}000 - \$200{,}000}{\$4{,}000{,}000} = 13.75\%$$

**page 741:**

The NPV is the difference between the present value of the wind turbine's future net cash flows ($750,000 per year for 20 years) and the cost of the initial investment ($4 million). It can be found using the Annuity PV factor for $i = 12\%$, $n = 20$, as follows:

| | A | B | C | D | E | F |
|---|---|---|---|---|---|---|
| 1 | **NPV Calculation for *Equal* Annual Net Cash Inflows** | **Annuity PV Factor ($i$ = 12%)** | | **Annual Net Cash Inflow** | | **Present Value** |
| 2 | Present value of annuity, $n$ = 20 | 7.469 | × | $ 750,000 | = | $ 5,601,750 |
| 3 | Less: Initial investment | | | | | 4,000,000 |
| 4 | Net present value (NPV) | | | | | $ 1,601,750 |
| 5 | | | | | | |

Alternatively, one can use the NPV function in Excel to arrive at an NPV of $1,602,083. The positive NPV indicates that the wind turbine will earn more than the company's 12% hurdle rate. Therefore, it is a favorable investment.

**page 744:**

The easiest way to calculate the IRR is by using the IRR function in Excel, which results in an IRR of 18.07%.

Alternatively, one can look for the Annuity PV factor for $n = 20$ that is closest to the following:

$$\frac{\text{Initial investment}}{\text{Amount of each equal net cash inflow}} = \frac{\$4{,}000{,}000}{\$750{,}000} = 5.33$$

The Annuity PV factor at $n = 20$ that is closest to 5.33 occurs when $i = 18\%$. At 18%, the Annuity PV factor is 5.353. Thus, the IRR of the wind turbine is close to 18%.

# COMPANY INDEX

## W



## X



## Y



## Z

# SUBJECT INDEX

Key terms and their page numbers appear in bold type.

# D

## J



## K



## L



## M



## N

## O



## P



## Q



## R



## S

# Prepare, Apply, and Confirm

- **Auto-Graded Excel Projects**—Using proven, field-tested technology, MyAccountingLab's new auto-graded Excel Projects allow instructors to seamlessly integrate Excel content into their course without having to manually grade spreadsheets. Students have the opportunity to practice important Accounting skills in Microsoft Excel, helping them to master key concepts and gain proficiency in Excel. Students simply download a spreadsheet, work live on an accounting problem in Excel, and then upload that file back into MyAccountingLab, where they receive reports on their work that provide personalized, detailed feedback to pinpoint where they went wrong on any step of the problem.

- **Enhanced eText**—The Pearson eText gives students access to their textbook anytime, anywhere. In addition to note-taking, highlighting, and bookmarking, the Pearson eText offers interactive and sharing features. Instructors can share their comments or highlights, and students can add their own, creating a tight community of learners within the class.

- Keep students engaged in learning on their own time, while helping them achieve greater conceptual understanding of course material through author-created solutions videos, multimedia interactives, animations, and opportunities to Try It!

- **Accounting Cycle Tutorial**—Accessed by computer, smartphone, or tablet, the ACT provides students with brief explanations of each concept in the Accounting Cycle through engaging, interactive activities.